1974

# A HISTORY OF
# MODERN
# EUROPEAN
# PHILOSOPHY

*By* JAMES COLLINS

PROFESSOR OF PHILOSOPHY
SAINT LOUIS UNIVERSITY

THE BRUCE PUBLISHING COMPANY
MILWAUKEE

# PREFACE

THIS textbook is designed primarily for students who have some acquaintance with Scholastic philosophy and who seek an introduction to the vast field of modern thought. During the past quarter century, great forward strides have been taken in recovering the genuine doctrine of the major medieval thinkers, especially St. Thomas Aquinas. Similar progress must now be made in the work of establishing fruitful intellectual communication between Scholastic teachings and the representative modern systems. Sound critical appreciation of the modern currents in philosophy can be obtained only on the basis of a painstaking historical study of the sources. The purpose of the present history is to aid in some measure the efforts of students to understand and weigh the leading postmedieval philosophies.

To make the introductory course in modern philosophy a more rewarding experience, several new methods of presentation have been tried in recent histories. One approach is to marshal the materials around six or seven outstanding problems, rather than to follow the individual systems in chronological order. Another treatment is to select key statements from the chief philosophers for linguistic dissection, in accord with the techniques developed by the school of logical analysis. Still a third way places emphasis upon the social background of each system, pointing out its cultural roots and its consequences for the general history of ideas. Each of these methods has its peculiar advantages and drawbacks. The stress upon doctrinal problems and linguistic analysis sharpens the student's wit but often at the expense of weakening his historical sense and his willingness to face the issue of truth and systematic consequences. The history-of-ideas approach enables him to correlate the history of modern philosophy with his other college studies and thus encourages an integration of the several disciplines. Yet it runs the risk

of becoming sidetracked on a literary description of remote influences and analogies, without bringing the reader to grips with
the properly philosophical questions themselves. Especially at the
introductory level, then, these methods are valuable only when they
are kept in an auxiliary position. It is indispensable to be grounded
primarily in a study of the doctrinal systems of the individual
thinkers.

Nevertheless, the distinction must be preserved between a textbook
and an encyclopedic work of reference. The present history makes no
attempt to mention every school and author in the modern era.
Instead, it confines itself, rigorously, to some twenty major figures in
the modern European philosophical tradition. In each chapter, the
aim is to give some brief biographical indications, explain the method
and guiding principles of the man's thought, and describe his
position in regard to some of the chief philosophical problems.
Preference is given to the following issues: the nature of method,
the possibility of metaphysics, the object of the human intellect,
the relation between God and the world, the nature of the human
composite, and the foundation of morality. Other doctrines are introduced, however, as dictated by the achievements and emphasis
of the individual philosopher under examination.

An attempt is made to sift and test the main assumptions and
method operative in each system. A critical appraisal is also made,
from the Thomistic standpoint, of some of the particular arguments
advanced by the philosopher in question. But by no means every
questionable point in a man's system is challenged. Ample opportunity
is given to the instructor to develop his own line of criticism, on
the basis of the explanations provided in the text. Furthermore, the
instructor may want to recast in more formal Scholastic fashion the
critical suggestions I have made. My plan has been to express the
evaluations in the manner and temper of modern philosophy itself,
so that the student may become aware of the direct relevance of his
own systematic principles to the discussions occupying the great
modern thinkers. Finally, instructors who follow some non-Thomistic
form of realism and theism will be able to reformulate the criticisms
within the context of their own school.

The requirements of a one-semester, upper-division course, taking
three semester hours, have been kept in mind. This does not mean
that all nineteen chapters must be covered in that time. There is
sufficient leeway, on a year-to-year basis, to permit the instructor

to introduce some variety in his presentation of the modern philosophical development. It is my conviction, however, that the most
profitable introduction to the modern period is made through a
careful study of the seventeenth- and eighteenth-century philosophers.
The typically modern procedures and problems can be studied here
in all their powerful freshness, and yet also in historical relation
with their medieval antecedents. Consequently, the chapters devoted
to these two centuries are more detailed than those dealing with the
nineteenth century. Hegel is the significant exception to this rule, since
(despite his continued unpopularity in twentieth-century America)
he is a thinker of major stature and wide influence upon present
tendencies in philosophy.

Several special aids to instruction are provided. The bibliographies
are intended to guide the student toward the best editions of the
primary sources, the most competent English translations, and a few
outstanding secondary books. As a slight compensation for omitting
chapters on lesser thinkers, like Malebranche, Vico, and Rousseau,
some bibliographical information is supplied concerning introductory
works on a few minor philosophers. The threefold purpose of the
footnotes is to identify the quotations used in the main text, to indicate
the precise passages in the sources where a doctrine under discussion
can be found, and to suggest worth-while articles on the same topic.
In this way, the student is encouraged to consult the primary sources
themselves and to make acquaintance with the best in twentieth-
century scholarship. Reading assignments can be based upon footnote
citations and selected chapters in the books mentioned in the
bibliographies. The foreign titles, unavoidably included in the bibliographies and footnotes, will at least indicate the breadth of scholarship abroad and invite some students to make use of their language
tools in the field of philosophy. The tables and diagrams serve to
clarify some difficult matters. But such devices remain only rough
approximations and points of departure for the instructor's further
explanations.

Despite the care taken to achieve accuracy and fairness, it is inevitable that some mistakes and defects should remain undetected.
I will be grateful for any suggestions sent to me for the improvement
of the work.

My prime debt in preparing this book is owed to St. Louis University and particularly to Father William L. Wade, S.J., director of
the philosophy department, for lightening my academic work during

several semesters, for bearing the expense of typewriting the good copy of the manuscript, and for providing considerable library assistance. I have also profited by the discerning criticism of Professor Thomas P. McTighe of Georgetown University. Several other friends have helped me in various ways. Discussions with the undergraduate and graduate students in my modern philosophy classes at St. Louis University contributed definitely to the shape of the work. Finally, I wish to record my lasting gratitude to my own teachers in the area of modern philosophy: Monsignors John K. Ryan and John J. Rolbiecki, both of The Catholic University of America, and Professor Rudolf Allers, now of Georgetown University.

JAMES COLLINS

St. Louis University
January 10, 1953

# CONTENTS

PREFACE . . . . . . . . . . . . iii

*1.* THE HISTORICAL STUDY OF MODERN
PHILOSOPHY . . . . . . . . . . 3
Summary. Bibliographical Note.

2. THE RENAISSANCE BACKGROUND . . . 13
1. The Humanist Indictment of Scholasticism. 2. Man as the
Central Problem. 3. Niccolò Machiavelli. 4. Giordano Bruno.
5. Skepticism and Stoicism. Summary. Bibliographical Note.

*3.* SCIENTIFIC OUTLOOKS AND METHODS:
BACON, GALILEO, AND NEWTON . . . 51
A. FRANCIS BACON
1. Expurgation of the Mind. 2. The Great Instauration. The
Division of the Sciences. 3. The New Organon.

B. GALILEO GALILEI

C. ISAAC NEWTON
Summary. Bibliographical Note.

*4.* HOBBES . . . . . . . . . . . . 101
1. Life and Writings. 2. The Nature and Method of Philosophy.
3. First Philosophy and Materialistic Mechanism. 4. Human
Knowledge. 5. The Passions and the Will. 6. Man in the State
of Nature. 7. The Social Contract and the Commonwealth.
8. Sovereign and Subjects. Summary. Bibliographical Note.

*5.* DESCARTES . . . . . . . . . . . 138
1. Life and Writings. 2. The Nature and Divisions of Philosophy. 3. The Method for the Discovery and Demonstration of

Truth. 4. Universal Doubt and the Cogito. 5. The Existence
and Nature of God. 6. Metaphysical Principles of the Material
World. 7. Mind and the Human Composite. 8. Toward the
Moral Life. Summary. Bibliographical Note.

6. SPINOZA . . . . . . . . . . 199

1. Life and Writings. 2. The Method of Healing the Understanding. 3. Divine Substance and Its Attributes. 4. The Emanation of the Modal World. 5. Human Nature. 6. Determinism
and Its Affects. 7. Man's Liberation and Beatitude: The Power
of Reason. Summary. Bibliographical Note.

7. LEIBNIZ . . . . . . . . . 252

1. Life and Writings. 2. A Universal Science and Universal
Harmony. 3. First Principles and Individual Substance. 4. From
Essence to Existence. 5. A World of Monads. 6. God and Pre-
established Harmony. 7. Human Knowledge. 8. Freedom,
Evil, and Optimism. Summary. Bibliographical Note.

8. LOCKE . . . . . . . . . 311

1. Life and Writings. 2. The Standpoint of the "Essay." 3. The
Discrediting of Innatism. 4. The Anatomy of Ideas. 5. Problems
Concerning Ideas. 6. Abstraction of General Ideas. 7. The Structure of Knowledge. 8. Practical Philosophy. Summary. Bibliographical Note.

9. BERKELEY . . . . . . . . 366

1. Life and Writings. 2. Abstraction and the Sensible Thing.
3. The Polemic Against Matter. 4. The Reality of the Sensible
World. 5. The Realm of Minds. 6. Mind and Nature. Summary.
Bibliographical Note.

10. HUME . . . . . . . . . 404

1. Life and Writings. 2. The True Skeptic and the Science
of Human Nature. 3. The Elements of Human Cognition.
4. Imagination and the Association of Ideas. 5. Relations and
Reasoning. 6. The Analysis of Cause. 7. External Bodies and
the Personal Self. 8. God and Religion. 9. Passions and Moral
Principles. Summary. Bibliographical Note.

*11.* KANT ON KNOWLEDGE AND METAPHYSICS 455

1. Life and Writings. 2. From Dogmatism to Criticism: The Pre-Critical Period. 3. The Structure of the "Critique of Pure Reason." 4. Space, Time, and Sensuous Intuition. 5. Deduction of the Categories. 6. The Paralogisms and Antinomy of Pure Reason. 7. God as the Transcendent Ideal of Pure Reason. Summary. Bibliographical Note.

*12.* KANT'S ETHICAL AND ESTHETIC DOCTRINE 515

1. The Good Will and the Moral Law. 2. The Categorical Imperative. 3. The Postulates of Practical Reason. 4. Judgment: Esthetic and Teleological. Summary. Bibliographical Note.

*13.* FICHTE AND SCHELLING . . . . . 544

A. Fichte

1. Life and Writings. 2. Systematic Unity and the Method of the Theory of Science. 3. The Fundamental Principles and the Constructions of Consciousness. 4. Morality and Right. 5. Rational Faith and the Absolute.

B. Schelling

1. Life and Writings. 2. Beyond Dogmatism and Criticism. 3. Philosophy of Nature and Transcendental Philosophy. 4. God, Freedom, and Evil. 5. Negative and Positive Philosophy. Summary. Bibliographical Note.

*14.* HEGEL . . . . . . . . . . 600

1. Life and Writings. 2. Hegel and His German Predecessors. 3. The Absolute as Spirit. 4. Experience as the Pathway to Spirit. 5. The Dialectical Method. 6. Speculative Logic. 7. Philosophy of Nature and the Doctrine on Subjective Spirit. 8. The Ethical Order and History. 9. Art, Religion, and Philosophy. Summary. Bibliographical Note.

*15.* SCHOPENHAUER . . . . . . . 662

1. Life and Writings. 2. The Principle of Sufficient Reason. 3. The World as Presentation. 4. From Phenomenon to Noumenon: The Defense of Metaphysics. 5. Cosmic Will and Metaphysical Pessimism. 6. Release Through Esthetic Contemplation. 7. Moral Liberation Through Sympathy and Ascetic Denial. Summary. Bibliographical Note.

*16.* COMTE . . . . . . . . . . 701
    1. Life and Writings. 2. Positivism and the Law of the Three
    States. 3. The Hierarchical Classification of the Basic Sciences.
    4. Social Order and Progress. 5. The Religion of Humanity.
    Summary. Bibliographical Note.

*17.* JOHN STUART MILL . . . . . . . 738
    1. Life and Writings. 2. Psychological Analysis of Consciousness.
    3. Principles of Scientific Method. 4. The Logic of the Moral
    Sciences. 5. Utilitarian Ethics and Liberalism. 6. God and
    Religion. Summary. Bibliographical Note.

*18.* NIETZSCHE . . . . . . . . . 774
    1. Life and Writings. 2. Critique of Nineteenth-Century Culture.
    3. The Rejection of God and Absolute Truth. 4. Revaluation of
    Moral Values. 5. The Will to Power: Superman and Eternal
    Recurrence. Summary. Bibliographical Note.

*19.* BERGSON . . . . . . . . . 809
    1. Life and Writings. 2. Intuition as the Method of a Meta-
    physics of Real Duration. 3. Three Metaphysical Problems.
    4. Creative Evolution. 5. Morality and Religion. Summary.
    Bibliographical Note.

INDEX . . . . . . . . . . . 849

# A HISTORY OF
# MODERN EUROPEAN PHILOSOPHY

# Chapter 1. THE HISTORICAL STUDY OF MODERN PHILOSOPHY

OUR approach to modern philosophy is determined by certain principles that hold good for any sort of historical study in philosophy. We may begin with a comparison between the *systematic* and the *historical* courses of instruction in philosophy. Some obvious differences appear, as soon as we pass from a systematic to a historical treatment. For one thing, the *content* of the discussion is enormously broadened and diversified. In metaphysics or ethics, the object of the science determines the content, confining it to but one part of philosophy. But in a general historical survey of some period, many philosophers are consulted and attention is paid to what each one has to say in all the major branches of philosophy. Again, where philosophy is taken as the pursuit of wisdom, understood as a scientific knowledge of the supreme principles and causes in various orders of being, a systematic course will seek *demonstration* of the universal truths in its area of philosophy. Now, the first task in the history of philosophy is to gain an accurate and sympathetic understanding of the methods, general standpoints, and special doctrines of the great thinkers in a given age. Nothing can replace a careful, enlightened study of the sources, with the purpose of sharing in the outlook of these men through an act of historical insight. The historical data themselves are contingent and not open to demonstration, even though intelligible necessities may subsequently be discerned in materials that are first accepted in an inductive way. The first step in historical studies is to submit the mind to the contingent evidence and thus to accompany the individual philosophers over their own terrain, relying upon *precise description* rather than demonstrative methods.

But if this docile submission to the given materials is indispensable, it is nevertheless neither the whole aim nor the main one in the history of philosophy. The *historicist* school despairs of ever attaining to universally valid truths. Hence it reduces philosophizing to historical "fact-gathering" and concludes that philosophical conclusions are purely contingent and relative to a particular historical setting. Historicism has a grasp on a partial truth: man is a temporal, reasoning being, all of whose discoveries are made in some particular historical situation. But it does not follow that all the truths discovered *in* some particular time are relevant and valid only *for* that period: the problem of the origin of a view is not coterminous with that of its validity. The entire trend of philosophical thinking is toward the uncovering of truths that dominate the temporal flow and hence that hold good also for other ages than the one in which they are found. This does not exclude the factor of progress from one historical period to another, since intellectual progress supposes that some gains are permanently made and can be used as a basis for further inquiries. Historicism overlooks the peculiar kind of facts under scrutiny in the history of philosophy.[1] The data in question are the efforts of human minds to reach some permanent truths, even though the reports may concentrate upon the limitations and feebleness of our knowing powers. Fidelity to facts of this sort places upon us the responsibility of evaluating the various historical solutions, of measuring them by the evidence as we ourselves can view it. In this way, the historical study of philosophy integrates itself with philosophy proper and serves the ends of the search for wisdom.

Historicists also point out that some *principle of selection* must be used in gathering the data for the history of philosophy. This is a common requirement in every type of history, since it is neither possible nor desirable to take as our historical ideal an indiscriminate lumping together of every recorded deed and saying. To organize the materials in an intelligible way inevitably means to employ a principle of selection, which will determine the relevance and worth of the data for one's project. In the historical study of philosophy, however, the governing rules for choosing and weighing are open to rational examination and justification. This justification is carried out only indirectly in the historical study itself, but even an indirect defense of one's general standpoint is valuable. Every historically orientated

---

[1] Cf. F. H. Heinemann, "Reply to Historicism," *Philosophy*, XXI (1946), 245–57; W. H. Walsh, *An Introduction to Philosophy of History* (London, Hutchinson, 1951), 94–118; L. B. Geiger, O.P., "Métaphysique et relativité historique," *Revue de Métaphysique et de Morale*, LVII (1952), 381–414. Geiger shows that the threefold resolution of knowledge (to sensation, to being as existent, and to the principle of contradiction) is compatible with genuine historical progress in philosophical truth.

philosophy must give an actual exhibition of its ability to take account of the various systems of thought formulated throughout intellectual history. Thomistic philosophy is under a special obligation to manifest its relevance to every period of speculation and its power of assimilating truths, wherever found.

The historical approach performs, then, a dual service for the student of philosophy. First, it removes a dilemma that often stultifies philosophical research. If one accepts Thomistic realism, one must maintain the infrangible bond between intellect and being, as well as a precise relationship between the essential and existential principles of being. And yet many philosophical systems have been built upon a denial of this basic realism. The *dilemma* presents itself either of ignoring these other philosophies and thus of committing oneself to sterile isolationism or of accepting their premises and thus entailing the conclusions that necessarily flow from them. In such a predicament, one may turn to history for aid. The historical attitude as such is one of understanding and correlating what has actually been thought by men. The record of philosophical speculation can be studied in itself, without compromising one's own position. As Etienne Gilson has put it, the philosopher finds in the history of philosophy the equivalent of the scientist's laboratory. Initially at least, the various systems of thought can be regarded as so many *laboratory specimens.* They can be analyzed in a descriptive way, without requiring the student to embrace their special starting points and premises. Second, the findings of the history of philosophy supply the philosopher with precious materials for his own critical reflection. The philosopher can perform various experiments, which will exhibit the *necessary connections* obtaining between certain principles and doctrinal conclusions, despite the contingency of their historical origin. Thus, if Thomistic philosophy seeks to determine the relation between thought and being, it can do so not only by examining the direct evidence but also by asking "history what that relation has been in order to ascertain what it should be."[2] In these two ways, the history of philosophy enables us to overcome intellectual parochialism, without endangering either the realistic foundations of philosophy or its ordination toward necessary structures.

The remark was once made by Joseph Maréchal, S.J., that the best

[2] E. Gilson, *Being and Some Philosophers,* x. (NOTE: *Full bibliographical information is not supplied in the footnotes for those items which are also listed in the bibliographies.*)

preparation for studying modern philosophy is to gain a deep familiarity with the thought of St. Thomas Aquinas, since this thought gives one the requisite doctrinal equilibrium and tempered mind.[3] In taking Aquinas as our companion in this book, we should pay close attention to his directions concerning historical studies in general. His suggestions may be summarized under four headings. (a) The study of philosophy is directed not to a knowledge of *what men think* but to how the *truth of things* stands. This does not mean that the opinions of men are to be ignored in favor of a purely abstract, nonhistorical treatment. This latter is an illusory aim. If one seeks to gain a genuine understanding of any philosophy, including that of St. Thomas himself, one must engage in a historical examination of the text and the concrete intellectual situation surrounding it. But one should never lose sight of the ultimate purpose of historical investigations, which is to facilitate one's access to integral truth. (b) In seeking to determine the truth adequately, however, we should not take a hostile attitude toward those whose statements are being weighed but should resemble judges and *investigators of both sides*. Carping criticism, a closed mind, and blind prejudice exclude one effectively from making fruitful contact with the sound insights that course through the channels of history. Only a scrupulous examination of all the available evidence can render service to a living philosophy. (c) The opinions of past thinkers must be weighed on the important issues in philosophy, both in order to *gain help* for ourselves from their good points and to learn to *avoid* their *errors*. The story of philosophical development is not a black-and-white record, with unmitigated error on one side and exclusively possessed truth on the other. The seeds of truth have been sown widely in the minds of great philosophers of all ages and doctrinal standpoints: we should gladly be debtors to them all, in accord with our own ability to deal with the problems. This does not entail a spineless eclecticism, which compromises principles and thus deprives itself of any basis for judging the opinions of men. Rather, our aim in historical work is to discern the healthy deliverances of human intelligence in even

---

[3] See *Mélanges Joseph Maréchal* (2 vols., Paris, Desclée, 1950), I, 12–13. Maréchal studied modern philosophy with the conviction that "it is impossible that everything in a philosophical system be falsehood" (*ibid.*, I, 6). The Thomistic statements on the history of philosophy, paraphrased in this paragraph, will be found in the stimulating article by J. I. Conway, S.J., "Reflections on the Function of the History of Philosophy in a Liberal Education," *The New Scholasticism*, XXI (1947), 419–37.

the most unfavorable contexts, to extract these truths from their distorting setting, and to incorporate them into the living body of perennial truths. Even a close analysis of erroneous doctrines is profitable, since it provides a test of our own resources and offers an indispensable lesson in the alternatives confronting the human mind. In tracing back particular errors to their root sources, we gain an understanding of the fundamental options open to philosophers and of the implications necessarily entailed by a set of premises. (*d*) Finally, St. Thomas remarks that, under God's providence, the discovery of truth is a *co-operative task* of the human race. One man's positive contribution may be quite small, when viewed in isolation, but it can be integrated with the findings of others. The total expression of truth is great and leads to a wonderful increase. This is the long-range view of the operations of a realistic philosophy, as it dominates all periods of the history of philosophy and aggregates to itself all the valuable discoveries of the human intellect concerning ultimate questions. Thus a balance is to be sought between permanent principles, healthy criticism of accepted views, and increment of fresh insights.

These Thomistic principles of historical orientation can be applied confidently to the study of *modern European philosophy*. At the outset, we require only an extrinsic description of the subject matter. In *chronological* terms, this period of philosophy extends from about 1600 to 1900 or from Bacon and Descartes to Nietzsche and Bergson. By confining our survey to these three centuries, we give only brief consideration to Renaissance philosophy and do not follow the development of thought into the contemporary, twentieth-century world. There is something arbitrary about any designation of the boundaries of modern philosophy, especially when it is correlated with the conventional division of the history of philosophy into *three periods:* ancient, medieval, and modern. This division is sometimes employed in a polemical way, as though "modern" and "philosophically sound" were synonymous. Actually, the history of philosophy presents the same continuity and overlapping of phases that marks the development of the other components in our culture. Ancient and medieval philosophy are not reduced to objects of mere archaeological interest, simply because of their anterior temporal position in respect to the modern period. As Gilson has once more observed, "the history of philosophy cannot be a graveyard for dead philosophers, because in philosophy there are no dead. Owing to history, all great philosophers are still alive,"[4] and modernity is no self-evident criterion of the philosophical relevance and vitality of a doctrine. Vitality comes from the recognition and appropriation of a truth by a living mind, regardless of when the truth was first expressed in the past. *Geographically* speaking, we are limiting ourselves to major European philosophers of modern times, thus excluding any formal consideration of the Oriental and American philosophies contemporaneous with the European development.

One internal principle of division in modern philosophy is the perennial tension between *reason* and *experience*. During the classical period of modern thought, extending from Descartes to Kant (roughly, from 1630 to 1790), the two main schools were rationalism and empiricism. The *rationalists* (Descartes, Spinoza, Leibniz) stressed the predominant role of reason in the construction of a system of knowledge. The *empiricists* (Locke, Berkeley, Hume) emphasized experience and the empirical origin of all ideas. But this distinction is one of stress rather than a rigid, exclusive contrast, since the two schools shared many common features. The rationalists admitted the need for experience, although in a subordinate position; the empiricists allowed for the operations of reason, but subject to empirical limitations. *Kant's* great project was to combine the best features of rationalism and empiricism in a system which would reconcile reason with experience. But his synthesis was an explosive and short-lived one. The development of philosophy after 1790 led to a revival of the old oppositions under the new forms of idealism and positivism. The *idealists* (Fichte, Schelling, Hegel) supported the extreme claims made for reason and systematic thinking. The *positivists* (Comte, Mill) appealed once more to our experience of facts and the limits of knowledge. Finally, efforts were made during the nineteenth century to reunite these philosophical currents by means of the central synthetic notions of "will" and "life." This *philosophy-of-life* movement (Schopenhauer, Nietzsche, Bergson) achieved only a temporary success. New developments in physical science, mathematical logic, and phenomenology have suggested to the twentieth century some

[4] E. Gilson, *History of Philosophy and Philosophical Education* (Milwaukee, Marquette University Press, 1948), 42. In this Aquinas Lecture, Gilson discusses the relations between Thomistic philosophy and the historical approach. On the importance to Thomists of a study of modern philosophy, see D. C. O'Grady, "The Value of Modern Non-Thomistic Philosophy," *Proceedings of the American Catholic Philosophical Association*, XVII (1941), 150–56; J. Collins, "The Absolute and the Relative as a Problem in Modern Philosophy," *ibid.*, XXII (1947), 80–94.

fresh problems and solutions, which constitute the field of *contemporary* philosophy.

The *individual* philosopher may be approached at three levels: his life, his own system, and the relation of his system with other representative ones. No single aspect can be totally separated from the rest, although each can be considered by itself for the sake of convenience. The *biographical* study often illuminates a man's speculation, since it calls attention to the living individual, his education, temperament, moral character, and aims in life. Although it is dangerous and illusory to reduce a philosophy to the psychological traits of its author, some acquaintance with the person behind the intellectual edifice is indispensable. Both exposition and criticism rest upon a detailed study of the philosopher's *own system*. It is well to pay attention to the general intellectual background of his thought, the peculiar way in which he envisages philosophical inquiry, and the "central intuition" (as Bergson calls it) that may inspire all his speculation. In addition to these general features, there are the problems of his distinctive terminology, his theory of method, and the basic options he makes concerning being and knowing. At this level, criticism can operate as a testing for internal consistency between the various parts of his system, as well as a weighing of the cogency of his individual arguments.

Finally, the particular systems in modern philosophy should be viewed synoptically in their broad *mutual relations*. Since this comparison is quite intricate, due to the number of factors involved, it may be facilitated by concentrating upon some *major problems* that run through the modern systems. This problematic approach enables us to grasp the continuity within modern thought, since the leading questions cut across our conventional divisions into special schools. There is an internal dialogue transpiring among the modern philosophers. Its accents must be caught, in order to appreciate why problems are formulated in certain ways and why certain areas of evidence are employed and others ignored. This domestic discussion among the modern minds involves a good deal of mutual criticism, which needs to be grasped and underlined. What makes it almost impossible to speak about "the" modern outlook is this fact of serious conflicts, which reach down to the most fundamental issues. Often the back-and-forth play of discussion involves a delayed reaction and hence demands patience on the student's part. An instance is the reply that Bergson gave to Hume's analysis of freedom and the foreseeability of human acts, a reply that had to wait for a century and a half.

It is noteworthy that the central problems of modern philosophy are also those of ancient and medieval philosophy. A common woof runs through the whole history of philosophy. The great representatives of *all periods* are concerned with the problems of the one and the many, the nature and possibility of metaphysics, the starting point and structure of knowledge, the world's relation to God, man's freedom and destiny. Once these basic concerns are identified, history of philosophy rejoins philosophy proper in virtue of its own dynamism. For, the common situation of man in the world prevails for questing intelligence in every age. The recurrence, in analogically similar ways, of the same fundamental problems and the same few generic solutions, manifests the response of the philosophical mind to some intelligible necessities both in being and in the human intellect This is the historical induction which a study of modern philosophy can contribute to philosophical realism. In its light, some relevant evaluations of the modern systems can also be undertaken.

## SUMMARY OF CHAPTER 1

The historical approach aims at a precise understanding of what philosophers have thought on the major philosophical problems. History of philosophy is not thereby cut off from the search after truth, since it studies the attempts of great minds to ascertain the nature of the real, whether in the world about us or in human nature. These efforts invite us to weigh the various historical answers in the light of our own acquaintance with man and the world. Our own view of the real helps to determine the principle of selection for choosing and organizing the historical facts. St. Thomas suggests that our study of the historical record be scrupulously honest, open to instruction from all quarters, and yet directed toward a determination of the truth about being and not merely toward the truth about human opinions concerning being. In modern philosophy, the classical period extends from Descartes to Kant, with rationalism and empiricism as the leading schools. Kant made an imposing but temporary synthesis of reason and experience, but in the nineteenth century the idealists and positivists perpetuated the old division under new forms. The individual philosopher can be studied and evaluated in terms of his personal formation, his systematic aims, and his interrelations with other philosophies. The great problems of philosophy run throughout its history, and so do the governing principles of the philosophy of being.

## BIBLIOGRAPHICAL NOTE

Part Three of Louis De Raeymaeker's *Introduction to Philosophy*, tr. by Harry McNeill (New York, Wagner, 1948), is entitled: "Initiation to the Life of Philosophy." Along with general directions concerning intellectual works and schools, it provides a useful section of bibliographical information, listing the various encyclopedias, dictionaries, histories of philosophy, philosophical journals, and current bibliographies, which are indispensable tools. Among over-all interpretations, three are specially noteworthy: J. H. Randall, Jr., *The Making of the Modern Mind* (revised ed., Boston, Houghton Mifflin, 1940); J. Royce, *The Spirit of Modern Philosophy* (Boston, Houghton Mifflin, 1892); E. Gilson, *The Unity of Philosophical Experience* (New York, Scribner, 1937). Randall gives a general cultural account of the modern development, from a naturalistic standpoint; Royce's lectures are a persuasive argument for an idealistic interpretation; Gilson places the entire modern experiment within the dual perspective of its medieval roots and the inherent necessities of metaphysical positions. Frank Thilly's *A History of Philosophy* is a well-balanced and objective survey, thoroughly revised and brought up to date by Ledger Wood (third ed., New York, Holt, 1957), Part III, on modern philosophy. Another reliable general survey is B. A. G. Fuller's *A History of Philosophy,* third edition revised by S. M. McMurrin (New York, Holt, 1955); the part dealing with modern philosophy is extensively rewritten and obtainable as a separate volume. W. T. Jone's *A History of Western Philosophy*, Vol. 2: *The Modern Mind* (New York, Harcourt, Brace, 1952) is noteworthy for its extensive readings in the primary sources and for its adaptation of the "laboratory manual" technique to the discussion of philosophical problems. Generous selections from the sources are also found in N. P. Stallknecht and R. S. Brumbaugh, *The Spirit of Western Philosophy* (New York, Longmans, Green, 1950), which maintains a critical, Aristotelian attitude toward the various systems. The simplest and clearest introductory work is W. K. Wright, *A History of Modern Philosophy* (New York, Macmillan, 1941); although superficial in content, Frederick Mayer, *A History of Modern Philosophy* (Cincinnati, American Book Company, 1951) is of supplementary value as a reference book, because of the wider range of thinkers and movements covered. *An Introduction to Modern Philosophy in Six Problems* (New York, Macmillan, 1943), by A. Castell, follows the problematic approach, organizing the materials around six main questions in the fields of natural theology, metaphysics, epistemology, ethics, politics, and philosophy of history. The bearing of scientific methods and discoveries upon the philosophical development is stressed in H. Miller's *An Historical Introduction to Modern Philosophy* (New York, Macmillan, 1947). Older histories, by men like J. E. Erdmann, R. Falckenberg, and W. Windelband, are permeated with the Hegelian view of the history of modern philosophy, which found its classical expression in K. Fischer's *Geschichte der neueren Philosophie* (Jubilee edition, 10 vols., Heidelberg, Winter, 1897–1904; later editions of some separate volumes, by other editors). Vol. II of J. Hirschberger's *The History of Philosophy,* tr. by A. N. Fuerst (2 vols., Milwaukee, Bruce Publishing Co., 1958–1959), is a reliable and sympathetic Catholic approach to modern philosophy, in terms of a vital "perennial philosophy." For bibliographical purposes, F. Ueberweg's *Grundriss der Geschichte der Philosophie* is still a basic point of departure, in its later editions (published by Mittler, in Berlin): v. 3, *Die Philosophie der Neuzeit bis zum Ende des 18. Jahrhunderts,* twelfth ed. by M. Frischeisen-Koehler and W. Moog (1924); v. 4, *Die Deutsche Philosophie des 19. Jahrhunderts und der Gegenwart,* twelfth ed. by T. K. Oesterreich (1923; the thirteenth ed., 1951, is a reprint of this); v. 5, *Die Philosophie des Auslandes des 19. Jahrhunderts bis auf die Gegenwart,* twelfth ed. by T. K. Oesterreich (1928). É. Bréhier's *Histoire de la philosophie* (2 vols., Paris, Alcan, 1926–1932; Vol. II on modern philosophy) is also worth consulting. Three useful collections of readings are: B. Rand, *Modern Classical Philosophers* (second, enlarged ed., Boston, Houghton Mifflin, 1936); D. S. Robinson, *An Anthology of Recent Philosophy* (New York, Crowell, 1929); T. V. Smith and M. Grene, *From Descartes to Kant* (Chicago, University of Chicago Press, 1940). For an introduction to bibliographical instruments in the field of philosophy, cf. I. M. Bocheński, O.P., and F. Monteleone, *Allgemeine philosophische Bibliographie*

(Bern, Francke, 1948; fascicle I of: *Bibliographische Einführungen in das Studium der Philosophie,* edited by I. M. Bocheński, O.P.). Current books and articles can be followed with the aid of the *Répertoire Bibliographique,* issued as a supplement to the *Revue Philosophique de Louvain* (1934 ff.). For the period, 1934–1945, consult G. A. De Brie, *Bibliographia Philosophica, 1934–1945* (2 vols., Utrecht and Antwerp, Spectrum, 1950–1953), on historical and doctrinal items. A concise bibliographical and doctrinal introduction to the pre-Kantian period in modern philosophy is provided by J. Maréchal, S.J., *Précis d'histoire de la philosophie moderne, de la Renaissance à Kant* (revised and enlarged edition, Paris, Declée de Brouwer, 1951). *Bibliography of Philosophy* (Paris, Vrin) has UNESCO support. A compact introductory bibliographical tool for the history of philosophy and the philosophical disciplines is the *Manuel de bibliographie philosophique,* by G. Varet (2 vols., Paris, Presses Universitaires, 1956). For names, dates, and titles, A. E. Avery, *Handbook in the History of Philosophy* (New York, Barnes & Noble, 1954), provides basic information, but not accurate doctrinal interpretation. Written by a pioneer in the history-of-ideas approach, George Boas' *Dominant Themes of Modern Philosophy* (New York, Ronald Press, 1957) highlights the minor movements and men forming the undersoil of modern philosophy. The following volumes belong in The Mentor Philosophers series (New York, New American Library, 1955–1956): G. de Santillana, *The Age of Adventure* (Renaissance); S. Hampshire, *The Age of Reason* (Seventeenth-Century Rationalism); I. Berlin: *The Age of Enlightenment* (Eighteenth-Century Empiricism and Enlightenment); H. D. Aiken, *The Age of Ideology* (Nineteenth Century); M. White, *The Age of Analysis* (Twentieth Century). The editors combine selections from the sources with continuing commentary, most successfully in the Hampshire and Aiken volumes.

Preliminary reference work in modern philosophers and their theories can be done with the aid of *The Concise Encyclopedia of Western Philosophy and Philosophers* (New York, Hawthorn, 1960), edited from an analytic standpoint by J. O. Urmson. For a much more thorough treatment in the light of Christian spiritual philosophy, we have the *Enciclopedia Filosofica,* edited by C. Giacon, S.J. (4 vols., Rome, Instituto per la Collaborazione Culturale, 1947–1948). Students will profit by consulting the reliable, extensive, and well-written treatment of the modern thinkers in the multivolume *A History of Philosophy* by F. J. Copleston, S.J. (Westminster, Md., The Newman Press): Vol. 3: *Ockham to Suarez* (1953), Vol. 4: *Descartes to Leibniz* (1959), Vol. 5: *Hobbes to Hume* (1959), and Vol. 6: *Wolff to Kant* (1960). An example of carrying a major problem through the modern philosophers is provided by James Collins, *God in Modern Philosophy* (Chicago, Henry Regnery, 1959). There are two comprehensive collections of readings in the Modern Library Series: *The European Philosophers from Descartes to Nietzsche,* edited by M. C. Beardsley, and *The English Philosophers from Bacon to Mill,* edited by E. A. Burtt. New publications can be followed through the prompt reviews in *Philosophical Books,* edited at Leicester University by P. H. Nowell-Smith (1960 ff.).

# Chapter 2. THE RENAISSANCE BACKGROUND

## I. THE HUMANIST INDICTMENT OF SCHOLASTICISM

EVER since the first appearance of Jacob Burckhardt's classical study on *The Civilization of the Renaissance in Italy* (1860), historians of culture have been trying to formulate a satisfactory *definition* of the *Renaissance*. Although many distinguishing notes have been suggested — such as respect for antiquity, emergence of individualism, cultivation of science, naturalistic quickening of arts and letters — none of these traits are peculiar to the period in question or enjoy a single, unequivocal meaning. Historians have warned against the exclusiveness of the term *"the* Renaissance," since there have been several cultural resurgences or "rebirths" in the Western and Eastern worlds. It is best to start out with a rough *chronological* indication of the field: the European cultural movement extending from about the middle of the fourteenth to the end of the sixteenth century. We can then proceed inductively to an examination of the major philosophical trends of this age, filling in the framework with some concrete characteristics of Renaissance speculation.[1] The philosophical harvest of the period is bountiful but multifarious and seldom elevated to the first rank. The philosophical minds point in many divergent directions, so that only a few samplings can be analyzed as a background for the strictly modern systems.

Except for some oblique references, the present chapter leaves out of consideration one of the major strands in Renaissance thought: the *scientific* movement. A study of the ripest philosophicoscientific

---

[1] For the conflict of opinion among historians on how to interpret the Renaissance, see the readings edited by K. H. Dannenfeldt, *The Renaissance: Medieval or Modern?* (Boston, Heath, 1959). Some pertinent advice on the philosophical issues, with ample bibliographical information, is given by P. O. Kristeller and J. H. Randall Jr., "The Study of the Philosophies of the Rennaissance," *ibid.,* II (1941), 449–96.

outlook, that of Galileo, is reserved for the following chapter. But many of the modern scientific presuppositions are clearly formulated by Nicholas Copernicus and Johannes Kepler, both of whom exerted profound influence upon Galileo. Something of the authentic spirit of Renaissance scientific thinking can be captured from the notebooks of that versatile genius, *Leonardo da Vinci* (1452–1519). He regarded nature itself as the offspring of the divine mind and hence as a rational structure of necessary causes. The order of nature proceeds from the natural cause itself to the experience produced by it in our mind. Human knowledge proceeds in the reverse order: starting with our *experience,* it works back to its efficacious source in the natural thing. Thus "all our knowledge originates in our sensibilities . . . [and] wisdom is the daughter of experience." But our perceptions are contingent and particular, whereas the mind wants to seize upon the necessary, rational order operative throughout nature. Thus *mathematics* is required in order to interpret experience and achieve wisdom or a genuinely scientific understanding of nature. "There is no certainty where one can neither apply any of the mathematical sciences nor any of those which are based upon the mathematical sciences. . . . Therefore, students, study mathematics and do not build without foundations."[2] The practical applications of the union between experience and mathematics are rich in human satisfactions, but most highly prized by the scientist is the certainty itself, the speculative vision of mathematically described, natural causes.

Especially among those *humanists* who were primarily men of letters rather than philosophers or scientists, there was a concerted attack upon the Aristotelians and Christian Scholastics of the day. Many of the subsequent complaints registered by a Bacon or a Descartes were anticipated in the satirical descriptions made by Petrarca and Erasmus. In his famous tract *On His Own Ignorance and That of Many Others* (1370), *Francesco Petrarca* (1304–1374) lashes out against the *secular* or *Averroistic Aristotelians* in the Italian universities and at Paris. He ridicules their blind worship of Aristotle's *ipse dixit,* even when there is no support in reason or experience for their master's position. The Aristotelians are completely lacking in clarity and literary elegance, and yet they persist

---

[2] The quotations are from *The Notebooks of Leonardo da Vinci* (MacCurdy translation, I, 73, 85, 634, 88; punctuation modified). Quoted with permission of Harcourt, Brace Company. See J. H. Randall, Jr., "The Place of Leonardo da Vinci in the Emergence of Modern Science," *Journal of the History of Ideas,* XIV (1953), 191–202.

in voicing opinions about everything at all times. More seriously, Petrarca charges them with diverting attention to logical problems and natural philosophy, at the expense of ethics and what is profitable for salvation. "Their god Aristotle" is an unsure guide in establishing the unicity of God, the temporal creation of the world, personal immortality, and the precise source of human happiness. Moreover, although Aristotle defines virtue and vice quite well, "his lesson lacks the words that sting and set afire and urge toward love of virtue and hatred of vice or, at any rate, does not have enough of such power."[3] The secular Aristotelians (due to Stoic influence) place the end of man in virtue itself, rather than in the possession of God through virtuous action. Hence in the name of Christian religious humanism, Petrarca bids us turn to Plato, Cicero, and Augustine. On all these points of conflict between the Aristotelians and Christianity, he surrenders the Thomistic hope of purifying and transforming Aristotle himself in a new synthesis. In setting up a total opposition between Christian and Aristotelian principles, Petrarca announces the conflict between the Christian Platonism of Ficino and the secular Aristotelianism of Pomponazzi (cf. Section 2, below).

The Praise of Folly (1511) by Desiderius Erasmus (1467–1536), the Dutch leader of humanism in northern Europe, strikes directly at the Christian Scholastics. Dedicated to his friend, St. Thomas More, the book is a classical declamation or "eulogy," pronounced by Folly herself before an audience of her faithful votaries. She praises her innumerable children, drawn from all ranks of society, from gamblers and merchants to kings, monks, and popes. The irony of the address becomes specially acute, however, when Folly turns to those who are usually regarded as wise men: grammarians, rhetoricians, lawyers, logicians, and, above all, natural philosophers and theologians. With acid satire, the follies of the wise men in the two latter categories are paraded for ridicule. The natural philosophers (who are half-Faustian magicians as well) pretend to uncover the secrets of nature, but the only result of their labors is an abstract pack of "ideas, universals, forms without matter, primary substances, quiddities, and ecceities — things so tenuous, I fear, that Lynceus himself could not

---

[3] Petrarca, On His Own Ignorance and That of Many Others, in The Renaissance Philosophy of Man (edited by E. Cassirer, P. O. Kristeller, and J. H. Randall, Jr., 103; hereafter, this volume is referred to simply as Renaissance).

see them."[4] One is bewildered by the numerous, conflicting parties among the Scholastics. Folly makes a roll call: Realists, Nominalists, Thomists, Albertists, Ockhamists, and Scotists — each school defending a different method and set of principles, annihilating its opponents, and claiming the whole truth for itself. A plain man stands no chance in the face of the Scholastic artillery of terms, distinctions, loopholes, subtle definitions, and counterappeals to authority.

Toward the end of her discourse, Folly almost forgets herself by presenting a serious antithesis between the *foolishness of the Cross* and the *wisdom of men*. "The Christian religion on the whole seems to have a kinship with some sort of folly, while it has no alliance whatever with wisdom,"[5] at least as the world understands this term. Although he regarded the Religious Revolt as fatal to humanistic values, Erasmus agreed with the Brethren of the Common Life (the religious community in the Lowlands to which Gerard Groote and Thomas à Kempis belonged and to which Erasmus owed his early education) that the Scholasticism in the universities was a hindrance to the spiritual vitality of the Catholic Church. His attitude of hostility toward Scholasticism, in the name of both sound reason and faith, makes more understandable the position of Descartes and some of his ecclesiastical supporters. The latter looked upon the Cartesian attack on traditional philosophy as a defense of God and a matter of religious vocation.

The humanist men of letters did lay bare many weak features of the Scholasticism of the age, but they also exaggerated their case and oversimplified the situation. The *oversimplification* appears, as soon as one studies the writings of men like Ficino, Pico, and Cusanus. These Renaissance philosophers incorporated large segments of Scholastic terminology, methods, and doctrines into their new doctrinal syntheses. Even such an exponent of pantheism as Bruno was obliged to take account of the Scholastic milieu, not only in a negative way but also for a constructive purpose. Among the philosophers of the Renaissance, there was no wholesale rejection of the medieval heritage but a serious attempt to assess it from other leading standpoints, some of them latent already in fourteenth-century Scholasticism and others due to the new influx of classical and scientific discoveries.

The *exaggeration* in the humanistic indictment of Scholasticism

---

[4] Erasmus, *The Praise of Folly* (Hudson translation, 77).
[5] *Ibid.* (Hudson, 118).

results from the policy of citing only the weaknesses and the worst examples. Despite the generally low estate of Scholastic thinking, the Renaissance years also witnessed a quickening in some Scholastic circles. During the period from Petrarca to Guillaume Du Vair, the following great representatives of later Scholastic thought flourished: Capreolus, Francis de Sylvestris of Ferrara, Cajetan, Vitoria, Suarez, and John of St. Thomas. Some of these men influenced, and were in turn influenced by, contemporary non-Scholastic currents in philosophy. Already, however, the disastrous separation between "Scholastics" and "moderns" had set in, so that full communication between the best Scholastic minds and the Renaissance leaders was rendered impossible. But the intricate history of the two-way relationships that did exist, remains to be written. Until this lacuna is filled, our knowledge of Renaissance philosophy will continue to be considerably out of focus.

## 2. MAN AS THE CENTRAL PROBLEM

Among the Italian humanistic philosophers of the early Renaissance, the main preoccupation was *man*. A study of God and nature was not excluded but was deemed important mainly for its contribution to a well-rounded appreciation of man's place in the universe. In trying to reach the meaning of human nature with the aid of previous philosophical traditions, however, the Renaissance thinkers fell heirs to the difficulties and disagreements of their predecessors. The way in which man was taken as a central problem is well illustrated by the conflict between the Platonic and Aristotelian schools in Italy. The center for the former school was the so-called Platonic Academy, founded by Cosimo de' Medici in Florence in 1462. Here, a predominantly Neo-Platonic outlook was blended with the Christian religion and with many Scholastic notions. The guiding spirit of Renaissance Platonism was *Marsilio Ficino* (1433–1499), whose *Platonic Theology* (1474) and *Letters* (1495) had as a major theme the defense of personal immortality. But this doctrine, together with the temporal creation of the world and human freedom, was placed under fire by the secular Aristotelians, as Petrarca already testified. The stronghold for these followers of Averroës and John of Jandun was the University of Padua, which stressed the logical doctrines of the Stagirite and problems in scientific method. Although they continued in the Paduan way, *Pietro Pomponazzi* (1462–1525) and *Giacomo Zabarella* (1532–1589) were not pure Averroists but were also responsive to the humanistic and Stoic views of man. Pomponazzi admitted the multiplicity of individual souls and intellects, even though he denied personal immortality. The clash between Pomponazzi, on the one side, and Christian Scholasticism and Ficino's Platonism, on the other, in regard to human immortality, shows how acute the problem of man became in Renaissance thought.

Ficino's *Five Questions concerning the Mind* (written in 1476 and printed among his *Letters*) has a medieval ring to it, as regards method, terminology, and some of its arguments. There is a definite predominance of principles drawn from his favorite Neo-Platonic sources. The five *questions* at hand concern: whether the mind's motion is directed toward a definite end; whether this end is motion or rest; whether this end is particular or universal; whether the mind is able to attain its end; and whether it can lose its end, having once attained it. Ficino's entire discussion supposes that the universe has received its order, harmony, and unity from the divine mind. God's providential reason and will direct various individuals and kinds to their special ends, and the whole universe to a common end. The human mind is no exception to this teleological ordination. Its end, moreover, is a vital kind of rest rather than a continuous movement. Here, Ficino adduces the kinship of the mind with the immutable, eternal reasons of things and its tendency to move away from the changing traits of matter. In proving that the intellect can grasp universal being, he exclaims: "Since the intellect, according to the Platonists, can devise the one and the good above being and below being, how much more will it be able to run discursively through the broad whole of being!"[6] Thus he makes a characteristic Neo-Platonic subordination of being to the one and the good. The intellect and will can never remain satisfied with particular modes of truth and goodness but must press on to infinite truth and goodness, as supplying the only ultimate goal of human desire. And unless the mind somehow possessed the excellence of infinity and eternity in itself, it could not incline toward an infinite end.

The proof of *immortality* may now be presented, with the aid of a paradoxical contrast. The rational soul is more perfect than sense and, consequently, man is more perfect than the brute animal. Ficino offers a dozen arguments to establish the superiority of intellect over sense and its distinction from every bodily function. Along

---

[6] Ficino, *Five Questions concerning the Mind* (*Renaissance*, 200).

with proofs based upon the reception of intelligible species, the ability to reflect, and free choice, he gave special emphasis to the contact and affinity of intellect with the highest perfection. Now, if the intellectual power is the most perfect and if the perfection of a thing consists in the possession of its proper end, then we might expect the rational soul to reach its end more easily than does sense. But, in fact, brute animals and the animal side of our nature are readily given satisfaction, whereas the natural desire of the rational soul is left unsatisfied in this life. During our earthly existence among finite things, this superior part of our being is restless and miserable, disturbing even our moments of sensory happiness with imaginings of further perfection.

Since reason

is nowhere at rest while thus affected, it certainly never gains possession of its desired end or permits sense to take possession of its proper end which is already present. Nothing indeed can be imagined more unreasonable than that man, who through reason is the most perfect of all animals, nay, of all things under heaven, most perfect, I say, with regard to that *formal* perfection which is bestowed upon us from the beginning, that man, also through his reason, should be the least perfect of all with regard to that *final* perfection for the sake of which the first perfection is given.[7]

This conflict between the formal perfection of reason and the lack of attainment on earth of the final perfection of infinite truth and goodness is the tragic source of our human misery. Were there not an afterlife, in which each one of us will receive his heart's desire to the full, our basic *natural desire* would be frustrated and hence the order and rationality of the universe would be destroyed. As a good Christian, Ficino adds that, once obtained through God's grace and our freedom, eternal happiness is unfailing and demands the reunion of the individual, immortal soul with its own body.

In his treatise *On the Immortality of the Soul* (1516), Pomponazzi does not have Ficino primarily in view, although some of his remarks do bear upon the above argument for immortality. His main adversary is St. Thomas Aquinas, who defended immortality with the aid of Aristotelian principles and Christian faith. Pomponazzi accepts the

[7] *Ibid.* (*Renaissance,* 208; italics mine). Consult P. O. Kristeller, "The Theory of Immortality in Marsilio Ficino," *Journal of the History of Ideas,* I (1940), 299–319; for Ficino's medieval antecedents, cf. P. O. Kristeller, "The Scholastic Background of Marsilio Ficino," *Traditio,* II (1945), 257–318.

Thomistic refutation of the Averroistic teaching on a single intellect in all men. He also agrees that the unity of man would be threatened, were the individual, intellective soul related to the body merely as mover to moved, or were there several substantial forms in the same individual. Yet he holds that the Thomistic explanation of the rational principle in man departs from Aristotle's meaning and relies upon revelation for its cogency. Pomponazzi does not call in question the revealed truth about the soul's immortality, but (at least in the present treatise) he declares the problem to be a "neutral one," which philosophical reason can neither prove nor disprove. In later writings, however, his position grows more radical: reason can prove positively that the human intellectual soul is divisible and mortal.

His main thesis is that the human soul "is essentially and truly mortal but relatively immortal."[8] From a *hierarchical* standpoint, this soul stands midway between the separate intelligences and the souls of brutes. Separate intelligences are entirely free from matter; hence their knowing act requires a body neither as subject nor as object. Brute souls are entirely immersed in matter; their cognition requires a body both as subject and as object. Occupying a median position, the human soul is *per se* material and *secundum quid* immaterial, insofar as some of its operations make contact with the immaterial order. The human soul does not need a bodily organ as the subject of its knowing but does need it as object. Because the soul is the first act of a body and always requires phantasms in its cognition, it remains *objectively* dependent upon an organic basis. Hence it is essentially a material form and a mortal one. Granted that it is the highest and most perfect material form studied in natural philosophy, still it owes its beginning to an act of natural generation (not to creation) and it ceases to exist, when the body ceases.

Two further aspects of this theory are important: the sense in which the soul is *secundum quid* immaterial and immortal, and the moral consequences of the psychological doctrine. At this critical juncture, Pomponazzi brings out his essential debt to Averroës and to a Neo-Platonic theory of participation. He distinguishes between the agent and the possible intellect: the former is a separated intelligence and constitutes no part of the soul. The possible intellect is the highest human knowing power. But its proper operation is demonstration, and it is called reason more properly than intellect.

---

[8] Pomponazzi, *On the Immortality of the Soul*, IX (*Renaissance*, 313).

It possesses the perfection of intellect and immateriality only in an equivocal way, in the sense that it can gain a weak and obscure knowledge of the universal and the immaterial. It is more proper to say that our possible intellect *participates* in immateriality, intellectuality, and immortality than that it *contains* them.

> For containing takes place by way of form, and being contained by way of matter. Whence the container is perfect and superexcellent, but what is contained is imperfect and exceeded. But the contrary holds of the participant and what is participated in. For what is participated in exists rather by way of cause and exceeding; the participant by way of effect and exceeded. . . . [Man] is properly said to participate in the immaterial, because he *lacks* much of immateriality.[9]

Participation is an operational contact with a superior mode of being, which the participant as such does *not* contain intrinsically and *per se*. Hence the human soul is not essentially immaterial and immortal, precisely because it participates in, but does not contain, these perfections.

As for the *moral* consequences, Pomponazzi touches upon Ficino's main argument when he observes that the end assigned for each thing is only what suits its nature and is proportioned to it. Revelation may tell us that man's determinate end is infinite truth and goodness, but philosophy says otherwise. The human race is like a single man, having one end in common and several special or functional ends for the various members. There are three intellects in man: the *speculative*, the *productive*, and the *practical*. We all share in a minimal degree in the operations of the first two intellects, since we are all in possession of some first principles and are all engaged in some productive enterprise. But Pomponazzi denies that the maximal perfection possible for the speculative and productive intellects is common to all men as a final end. The speculative and productive ends perfect man only in a qualified way, whereas man is rendered unqualifiedly good only through his practical intellect. Only the perfection of the practical intellect is available to all men and comprises the final end for the human race. This practical, moral perfection consists in cultivating virtue and avoiding vice. Pomponazzi invokes the Stoic ideal, as providing a sublime but thoroughly this-worldly end for man.

It is characteristic of the temperate man to be content with what

---

[9] *Ibid.*, XII, XIV (*Renaissance,* 339, 376; italics mine).

suits him and what he can have. . . . The essential reward of virtue is virtue itself, which makes man happy. For human nature can possess nothing greater than virtue itself, since it alone makes man secure and removed from every perturbation. . . . One who acts conscientiously, expecting no other reward than virtue, seems to act far more virtuously and purely than he who expects some reward beyond virtue. . . . Wherefore those who claim that the soul is mortal seem better to save the grounds of virtue than those who claim it to be immortal. For the hope of reward and the fear of punishment seem to suggest a certain servility, which is contrary to the grounds of virtue.[10]

This text might have been taken from some present-day defender of a naturalistic morality! The wise and good man will seek only *finite virtue,* which is completely attainable in this life. Hence immortality is required neither by natural teleology nor by morality. Only the agent intellect is essentially immortal, but it forms no part of human nature.

Although Pomponazzi was conversant with St. Thomas, he did not appreciate the force of the *Thomistic critique* of the secular philosophers at Paris and of the Platonic theory of participation. The materiality of the human soul is not demonstrated by appeal to the *hierarchy of forms,* since the latter can be formulated in another way. The intelligences have subsistent and separate forms, not substantially united with matter; the brutes have nonsubsistent forms actuating matter; the human substantial form agrees with the angels in being subsistent and with the brutes in being the first act of matter. Moreover, it receives the act of existing precisely with a view toward communicating it to the composite constituted by this substantial form and prime matter. The human intellect does know things objectively in the phantasm, and all intellectual cognition does bear some sort of reference to the phantasm. This establishes the sensory origin of our knowledge and the substantial union between the intellectual principle and matter. But the fact that the phantasm is used as an instrumental cause of intellectual knowledge does not make the intellectual operation or its substantial principle *intrinsically* dependent upon matter. The immateriality of the human intellect and of its substantial principle is manifested in the separative or negative judgment that being, the act of existing, unity, substance, and the like are *not* confined to matter. This judgment of separation or negation is constitutive of the metaphysical standpoint, but Pomponazzi treats of

---

[10] *Ibid.,* XIV (*Renaissance,* 358, 361, 375).

the human soul only within the limits of *natural philosophy,* thus methodologically cutting himself off from decisive evidence of its positive immateriality.[11] Like Averroës, he fails to show how an individual man can know being in a nonmaterial way and can know immaterial modes of being, no matter how imperfect and rare the knowledge.

Pomponazzi's references to a "shadow" or a "savoring" of intellectuality and immateriality in the human soul remain within the metaphorical, Platonic tradition of participation and contact. The relevant contrast is not between containing and participating but between *primary* and *secondary analogates* in the predication of participation. Sheer equivocation results, unless the participated perfections of intelligence and immateriality are found intrinsically and properly, although in a finite way, in the participant or secondary analogate. Either intellect is present in no way in the human soul (and then the individual man, having this soul, has no intellectual knowledge, even of an attenuated sort) or it is found analogically and yet properly in the soul. In the latter case, however, all men share radically and properly in the ordination of intellect as such to infinite being and of will to infinite good. Hence the human soul is immortal in a *per se* or essential way and not merely *secundum quid.* And it is

---

[11] Pomponazzi's objections against the Thomistic doctrine on the immaterial human soul are reducible to two main points. First, he does not see how the intellective soul can be both something subsistent in itself and also the act of matter whereby the composite subsists. Next, he argues that, because the human soul is the act of an organic body, it requires imagination and bodily organs in all its cognitive operations, and thus is a material form. The first objection rests upon the three following erroneous interpretations of the teaching of Aquinas: (*a*) that the Aristotelian definition of *soul* applies univocally to all first principles of life; (*b*) that the *esse* which the human subsistent form receives is different from the *esse* of the human composite and is unordained to this composite; (*c*) that the soul alone, and not the composite, is the subject of the sensory and vegetative powers and operations, and that therefore the soul becomes material, when it operates at these lower grades of life. His second objection supposes that our knowledge of immaterial being "in" the phantasm is completely exhausted in the act of apprehension of material essences, without reference to the judgment of *separatio* concerning being and *esse,* as judged *not* to be confined to the material mode. These shortcomings in his understanding of St. Thomas reflect upon the quality of the Thomism taught to Pomponazzi, who was a classmate of Cajetan and Contarini. For St. Thomas' own account of the judgment of negation or separation, cf. St. Thomas Aquinas, *The Division and Methods of the Sciences,* Questions V and VI of his Commentary on the *De Trinitate* of Boethius, translated with Introduction and Notes by A. Maurer, C.S.B. (Toronto, Pontifical Institute of Mediaeval Studies, 1953), 26–32. Commentaries are furnished by L. B. Geiger, O.P., "Abstraction et séparation d'après saint Thomas," *Revue des Sciences Philosophiques et Théologiques,* XXXI (1947), 3–40, and M. V. Leroy, O.P., "*Abstractio et separatio* d'après un texte controverse de saint Thomas," *Revue Thomiste,* XLVIII (1948), 328–39.

proper to every human being to seek possession of unbounded perfection and to direct virtuous action as a means to this transcendent end. It is not a question of bribing with a system of rewards and punishments but one of conforming scrupulously to the capacity of our higher powers and the ordination of our natural desire. However far apart Aquinas and Ficino are metaphysically, they agree that the man who orients his life toward the vision of God is not being intemperate but rather is displaying practical wisdom in its most characteristic form.

The differences between the Renaissance Platonists and Aristotelians did not prevent them from joining in celebration of the *dignity of man*. They reminted several medieval notions about man as the *nodus et vinculum universi* and particularly as the *microcosm* or smaller world, reflecting the macrocosm or larger world. The most famous development of this theme is found in the *Oration on the Dignity of Man* (composed, 1486; published, 1495-1496) by *Giovanni Pico della Mirandola* (1463-1494). Pico was a friend and follower of Ficino, a careful student of Scholasticism, and an intrepid explorer of the byways of the Jewish Cabala and theosophical thought. He begins his laudation with a recapitulation of the grounds adduced by the medievals for regarding man as wonderful and a great miracle. Man is the intermediary among all creatures; he stands on the horizon of time and eternity; he is the bond uniting all things together; he is the interpreter of one order of being to another, through his cognitive ability to become somehow all things. These are important reasons for exalting man but they might also apply to the angels. Hence Pico seeks a unique proof of man's special rank in the universe.

He bids us picture the universe as already framed by the Creator in all its special parts and grades of being. The intelligences are there; so are the animals, plants, and inorganic elements. But now God wishes that there were a created thing which could contemplate, love, and wonder at the entire cosmos, without being confined to any particular level of reality. Thus man is brought forth as a creature belonging to no special degree in the ladder of things but expressing in his composite nature all the principal degrees. Man's dignity resides in his *universality*, for he alone contains in his nature the reality of angel, brute, plant, and mineral. He recapitulates the entire universe not merely through knowing it but through incorporating each level physically in his own microcosmic nature. Having placed man at the ontological point of convergence, God addresses these words to him:

The nature of all other beings is limited and constrained within the bounds of laws prescribed by Us. Thou, constrained by no limits, in accordance with thine own free will, shalt ordain for thyself the limits of thy nature. . . . With freedom of choice and with honor, as though the maker and molder of thyself, thou mayest fashion thyself in whatever shape thou shalt prefer. Thou shalt have the power to degenerate into the lower forms of life, which are brutish. Thou shalt have the power, out of thy soul's judgment, to be reborn into the higher forms, which are divine.[12]

Man's dignity consists, then, not only in his physical universality and position outside the grades of being, but also in his *indeterminateness* or *freedom* to shape his life in accordance with a lower or a higher standard. Thus his self-transforming nature cannot be divorced from the test of the use of freedom for his own corruption or ennoblement. Many Renaissance thinkers give a purely Faustian, naturalistic interpretation to Pico's declaration that *"we can become what we will,"*[13] but Pico himself admits that our freedom is measured by the rule of divine providence. He locates our proper perfection in an inward, religious union with God at the summit of our own spirit.

Another vigorous development of religious humanism, gravitating around the microcosmic approach to man, was made by *Paracelsus* (Philippus Aureolus Theophrastus Bombastus von Hohenheim, 1493–1541). Born in Switzerland, he studied medicine and other sciences at Vienna, Ferrara, and many other universities. He had a stormy career as a physician and surgeon, in which field he did pioneer work both in psychosomatic medicine and surgery. He regarded the *physician* as nature's servant and distinguished three types: the natural-born healer, the university-trained physician, and the physician taught directly by God. The good physician should combine the gifts of nature with skilled technique and reliance upon God's help. God is the Highest Physician of the universe at large. Paracelsus (whose complex personality fascinated the poet, Robert Browning) also believed in "rational" alchemy and had the reputation of being a magician and charlatan.

His philosophical views on man were expressed in many works, including *On the Origin of Man* (c. 1520), *On the Highest Good and*

---

[12] Pico della Mirandola, *Oration on the Dignity of Man*, 3 (*Renaissance*, 225).
[13] *Ibid.*, 6 (*Renaissance*, 227; italics added). H. Jantz (following the lead of E. Cassirer) gives a Faustian interpretation of Pico's thought: *Goethe's Faust as a Renaissance Man* (Princeton, Princeton University Press, 1951), 41–45.

*the Eternal Good* (c. 1533), and *The Great Astronomy or the Whole Sagacious Philosophy of the Great and Small World* (1537-1538). There is a mutual bond of sympathy and influence flowing between *man,* the *microcosm,* and the *macrocosmic universe.* A study of the latter is helpful not only for the control of nature but also for the better understanding of human nature, since the same elements are present in both regions. This provides a basis for a humanistic orientation of natural sciences. Conversely, reflection on man illuminates the nature of the larger world and enables us to harness it for human purposes. Although man must become nature's servant in order to learn its secrets, his own wisdom and freedom are not subjugated to natural forces. Instead, he is placed in the cosmos to become its master.

Man's dignity derives ultimately from his being made in the *image of God* and being given the task of bringing all creation back to God.

> The center of all things is man, he is the middle point of heaven and earth. . . . The *compositio humana* is prodigious, and its oneness is formed of a very great diversity. . . . Man is born of the earth, therefore he also has in him the nature of the earth. But later, in his new birth, he is of God and in this form receives divine nature. . . . God is in His Heaven, i.e., in man. For He Himself says that He is in us, and that we are His temple.[14]

Our duty is to render explicit God's image and omnipresence in the macrocosm and to bring all the elements in our own microcosmic nature into a religious union with God. Integration of our personality is only achieved when we unify all our internal drives and aspirations in the love of God. Both Pico and Paracelsus bid us become "twice-born men," renovating our nature through the exercise of freedom, with the aid of God's grace and the interior light of the Holy Spirit.

## 3. NICCOLÒ MACHIAVELLI

The leading Renaissance anatomist of man in his social and political functions was Niccolò Machiavelli. Born in Florence in 1469, he passed his childhood in this Italian city-state under Lorenzo de' Medici, The Magnificent. After Savonarola's brief rule was ended with his death on the gibbet (1498), Machiavelli was appointed a

---

[14] *Paracelsus: Selected Writings* (edited by J. Jacobi, 112, 118, 119). The various conceptions of microcosm have been traced historically and classified by R. Allers, "Microcosmus from Anaximandros to Paracelsus," *Traditio,* II (1944), 319-407.

secretary of state to the Florentine republic. His duties gave him firsthand acquaintance with both the internal operations of government and foreign affairs. He was active in outfitting armies and assisting in diplomatic missions, the latter work bringing him into close contact with Cesare Borgia, Pope Julius II, Louis XII of France, and other personages. In 1512, the French allies of the Florentine republic suffered a reversal and the Medici were returned to political power. Machiavelli was dismissed from all public offices and spent the next twelve years as a private citizen, mostly in retirement at his country home outside Florence. There, he composed the two books upon which his reputation in political philosophy rests: *The Prince* (written, 1513; published, 1532) and *Discourses on the First Ten Books of Titus Livy* (written, 1513-1518; published, 1532). These two treatises supplement each other nicely, the former dealing with principalities (states ruled by a single man, the prince) from the standpoint of the prince's rule, the latter with republics and other forms of government from the standpoint of the citizens being ruled. The *Discourses* is a broader work, however, since it deals with many political principles and problems common to both principalities and republics. Machiavelli took as his model, the early Roman republic, as described by Livy. He re-entered public life in 1525 as a minor official but died shortly thereafter, in 1527.

Machiavelli was not a political philosopher and yet he placed political philosophy upon a new and distinctively modern footing. This he accomplished more through his concrete attitude toward political problems than through any abstract theory. He reported with unblinking honesty and cool cynicism the working principles behind high policy in his day, principles that still remain dominant in our time. He was not a co-conspirator with tyrants (as he was depicted in Elizabethan literature) but rather a *specialist* reporting on the phenomena in his field of study. He *isolated* the political sphere for separate analysis and, in so doing, removed its laws from the regulation of morality. This amoral way of regarding political processes foreshadowed the nationalistic and totalitarian conceptions of the absolute state. Machiavelli himself recognized the radical innovation of his "realistic" approach.

> I break away completely from the principles laid down by my predecessors. But since it is my purpose to write something useful to an attentive reader, I think it more effective to go back to the practical truth of the subject than to depend on my fancies about it. And many

have imagined republics and principalities that never have been seen or known to exist in reality. (For there is such a difference between the way men live and the way they ought to live,) that anybody who abandons what is for what ought to be will learn something that will ruin rather than preserve him, because anyone who determines to act in all circumstances the part of a good man must come to ruin among so many who are not good. Hence, if a prince wishes to maintain himself, he must learn how to be not good, and (to use that ability or not as is required.[15])

In the conflict between what is and what ought to be, political decisions must be regulated solely by practical consequences. Machiavelli would like to restrict moral considerations to the individual's private life, and to place the governance of the commonwealth upon a completely nonmoral, pragmatic basis. He looked upon the state as a self-contained organism, ruled exclusively by its own functional laws and rooted in human passions and desires, rather than in a divine foundation.

Yet this naturalistic view of the state did not lead Machiavelli into a purely descriptive empiricism, which finds no place for general political principles. Like the natural scientists of his day, he held that, although our political speculations must have an inductive basis in experience, the mind can formulate certain universally valid *laws* from the empirical materials. His basic approach in political thought supposed that human actions are regulated just as completely by causal laws as are the motions of bodies. Thus he anticipated Hobbes in appealing to the universal reign of natural causal laws as the ground for making political theory into a strict science. But, unlike Hobbes, he did not think that the special causal laws formulated by mechanistic physics can be transferred to the political sphere. He was not concerned with deducing causal sequences in political life from any higher principles but simply with observing and stating them precisely and emancipating them from moral control.

Particular causal sequences can be generalized into universal laws of political conduct, on the supposition that human nature is relatively

---

[15] Machiavelli, *The Prince*, XV (Gilbert translation, 141; punctuation modified). In *The Counter-Renaissance*, 662, H. Haydn points to an analogous passage in Shakespeare:

*Lady Macduff:*   I have done no harm. But I remember now
I am in this earthly world; where to do harm
Is often laudable, to do good sometime
Accounted dangerous folly. (*Macbeth*, IV, ii, 74–77.)

stable at all times and places. Because of the uniformity of human nature and conduct, *history* is a major aid in developing a political theory and determining practical policy. Machiavelli looks to Greek and Roman political and social history for guidance in making present decisions affecting the commonwealth. Ancient history reveals certain recurring connections between human passions and desires and their practical consequences. If these causal connections can be verified also in fairly recent history, then we are in possession of a stable pattern of human action that can be generalized as a *political law* or *rule*. With the aid of such a law, one can then determine how certain proposed courses of action will turn out or how certain desired effects can be obtained. Complete certainty can never be gained from political rules, however, since human actions occur under concrete circumstances, which are always shifting. Probability will always infect our political predictions. But we can render them more reliable by taking account of historically proven causal sequences of conduct and by adapting the general rules to the prevailing circumstances.

The dynamic tension between the causal pattern one would like to realize and the pressure of actual conditions constitutes the polarity between *freedom* and *necessity* or *fortune*. Machiavelli likens fortune to a rampant flood bearing down irresistibly upon our little villages. Yet there is nothing to prevent men from using foresight and diligently preparing dikes and channels to turn the next flood in a less destructive direction. The trend of fortune is to cut down our possible choices to but one. This leads to a hypothetical sort of necessity: if we would achieve a certain end, we cannot but take a certain path, already marked out by the drift of circumstances. But the work of historically informed intelligence is to open alternate routes to success, so that free choice can be exercised. Thus our life is about evenly divided between the rule of necessity and the use of freedom, between following the only means presently open to a desired goal and developing several possibilities for attaining the result.

Granted that history and personal experience lead to valid *generalizations of fact,* can such factual theorems be converted into *maxims* or normative precepts of conduct? Machiavelli would regard this question as irrelevant, if by norms are meant moral standards having a divine sanction. But he would answer in the affirmative, if norms mean procedures that must be followed in pursuit of a chosen end. His writings are stocked with what Kant calls *conditional* or *hypo-*

*thetical* (rather than categorical) imperatives: such-and-such must be done or avoided, on condition that you seek to obtain or avoid such-and-such a consequence. The famous precepts in *The Prince* concerning how a tyrant may consolidate his power are instances of such technical imperatives. Machiavelli is not recommending tyranny as a desirable end. But he is laying down the causal sequences to be followed, provided that a tyrant wishes to be successful. Political maxims dictate the means to be employed, but they do not assess the value of the ends of action. In the *Discourses,* however, Machiavelli shows a strong interest in the problem of political ends and declares himself in favor of a republican form of government and the increase of personal freedom. Republicanism and liberty thus provide him with a standard for evaluating political actions. But he fails to preserve a clear-cut distinction between technical norms, bearing solely upon the *means* to be employed, and a norm for the *end* of political existence. In the last analysis, he cannot maintain this distinction, since his ultimate grounds for preferring republicanism and freedom are themselves purely pragmatic and hence are just as hypothetical and concerned with means as are his technical maxims.

This same difficulty about specifying the end of political action from an exclusively political standpoint also hampers Machiavelli's treatment of *virtù,* or the ideal condition for political man. For the most part, he describes *virtù* solely in reference to the adaptation of appropriate means to whatever end one may choose. The man of *virtù* is marked by his efficiency or technical skill in choosing the proper means, by his resolute decision in putting the instrumentalities promptly to work, and by his strength of will in pursuing his goal, in the face of adversity. The "virtuous" man is thus the powerful and successful individual, whatever his goal in life. Nevertheless, Machiavelli finds that some qualifications must be placed upon this description, in order to conform with what the early Romans meant by the man of *virtus.* Such a man must be inspired by the hope of glory or fame and he must be public-spirited enough to put the common interest and security before his private profit. These additional notes compel Machiavelli to move into the realm of ends, in order to distinguish *virtù* from sheer ruthlessness. But the independence of political life from moral considerations prevents him from defending the values of fame and the common good in any other way than by appealing once more to the pragmatic consequences of actions performed in accord with these motives. They tend to increase the individual's own vigor and to encourage a similar increase in the native power of other men. Yet this reason would not be effective against those who would question the desirability of sharing power with others and who would define their own feeling of vigor in purely selfish terms.

The closest Machiavelli comes to extricating himself from this impasse is in his theory of republican government. The main reason for preferring republican to monarchical government is that *freedom* is better secured and more widely distributed, where political rule lies in the hands of the citizens. Hence freedom may serve as a measure for appraising governmental forms and as an end toward which *virtù* should incline the person. In order to sustain this view, however, Machiavelli would have to explain why freedom should be taken as an absolute value and why its general distribution is desirable. Instead of making any theoretical defense, which would oblige him to renounce the absoluteness of the political order, he gives some concrete descriptions of political freedom. These descriptions show that, in point of fact, Machiavelli regards freedom as a means and a condition, so that it does not contain an ultimate answer to the problem of political ends. Intelligent political self-determination, development of industry and arts, unhindered enjoyment of one's goods, and security in life and limb, are among the basic components of the free life. Moreover, these conditions must have a guarantee in public law. Machiavelli believes that princes are superior to the people in the first acts of legislation, whereas the people as a whole are superior in maintaining laws and institutions.

The history of human society is not a record of steady progress but of *oscillation* between social order and disorder, health and corruption. Politically speaking, it is difficult for men to be either wholly good or wholly bad. Yet looking at his own contemporaries, Machiavelli was convinced that the *corrupt* side of human nature was in the ascendancy. The people had lost the ability to rule themselves; both princes and people were more readily moved by envy, ambition, fear, and the lust for wealth than by fame and public interest. In such a situation, a republic on the Roman plan could not be instituted, so that some kind of monarchy or even tyranny became inevitable. "Where the material is so corrupt, laws do not suffice to keep it in hand; it is necessary to have, besides laws, a superior force, such as appertains to a monarch, who has such absolute and overwhelming power that he can restrain excesses due to ambition and the corrupt practices of the powerful."[16] This being the condition of the times, Machiavelli's maxims for princes desiring to gain or hold supreme power had a quite practical bearing.

The prince must always be ready to sacrifice moral precepts to expediency, if his power is threatened. He must be both a lion and a fox, knowing when to apply *force* and when to use *guile*. If his regime is a recently established one, he should ruthlessly exterminate all internal opposition. But he must do so at one blow, so that the memory will heal under the gentle balm of wise laws and benefits gradually meted out. The use of force is expensive, however, so that the prince should resort to *propaganda,* wherever possible. People are basically credulous: they believe things as they appear, more readily than things as they are. Hence the prince's prime concern must be to play upon the passions of the people and keep up certain appearances. There are five indispensable good qualities he should have or at least dissemble. The prince must "seem compassionate, trustworthy, humane, honest, and religious, and actually be so; but yet he should have his mind so trained that, when it is necessary not to practice these virtues, he can change to the opposite, and do it skilfully."[17] Foreign relations are based upon *fraud*. By "fraud," Machiavelli sometimes meant mere evasion but he also included bad faith and the breaking of treaties among the deliberate acts of successful policy. The international relations described by him are governed by power politics, ceaseless plans for expansion, and systematic deceit. His ambiguous notion of *virtù* and his political amorality prevented Machiavelli from understanding the common good in any higher terms than the *nation-state*. He foresaw that the dynamism of the nation-state would tend toward continual expansion and conquest, and this development he not only described but approved. How political life organized along these lines can be reconciled with universal freedom was one of the unanswered problems forming Machiavelli's heritage to the modern world.

Of the five basic traits enumerated above, that of seeming to be

---

[16] Machiavelli, *The Discourses,* I, 55 (Walker translation, I, 335). On the historical circumstances in Italy and the rest of Europe which, after 1494, favored the idea of overweening power as the only saving source of civic order, read E. Voegelin, "Machiavelli's *Prince:* Background and Formation," *The Review of Politics,* XIII (1951), 142–68.

[17] *The Prince,* XVIII (Gilbert, 149). On the divorce in modern life between ethics and absolutized politics, cf. J. Maritain, *The Range of Reason* (New York, Scribner, 1952), Chapter XI, "The End of Machiavellianism," 134–64.

religious is the most important for the prince to cultivate. Machiavelli had a thoroughly pagan attitude toward *religion*. He venerated
the old Roman religion only because of its civic usefulness. It taught
the Roman citizens devotion to the common good, respect for laws
and oaths, and obedience to military commanders. But Machiavelli
blamed Christianity for the present corrupted state of humanity.

> The old religion did not beatify men until they were replete with
> worldly glory: army commanders, for instance, and rulers of republics.
> Our religion has glorified humble and contemplative men, rather than
> men of action. It has assigned as man's highest good humility, abnega-
> tion, and contempt for mundane things, whereas the other identifies it
> with magnanimity, bodily strength, and everything else that tends to
> make men very bold. . . . The generality of men, with paradise for
> their goal, consider how best to bear, rather than how best to avenge,
> their injuries.[18]

This exaltation of "boldness" at the expense of Christian love found
an echo, later on, in Nietzsche's repudiation of the Christian virtues.
Both thinkers used the same tactics of blaming present woes upon a
Christian education, instead of recognizing in domestic and international corruption the unavoidable consequences of rejecting belief
in God and the rule of morality. Machiavelli's real quarrel with
Christianity concerned its claim to have a supernatural origin, apart
from the state, and its defense of a natural moral law by which political life itself must be governed. Machiavelli would not countenance
the regulation of political decisions by reference to the unqualified
good for man which Christianity placed in God and the supernatural
life. Since he eliminated this positive aspect of Christian morality,
the latter appeared to him to be merely repressive and antivital. In
this respect, Machiavelli heralded the modern tendency to accept
religion only on condition that it remain subservient to the state and
national policy.

#### 4. GIORDANO BRUNO

Cardinal *Nicholas Cusanus* (1401-1464) has sometimes been regarded as the forerunner of modern science and the true father of
modern philosophy. In cosmology, he denied any essential difference
between celestial and terrestrial matter, upheld uniform laws of motion for all bodies, rejected the notion of an absolute center of the

---

[18] *The Discourses*, II, 2 (Walker, I, 364).

material universe, abandoned the geocentric theory (without arriving at the heliocentric), and concluded that the world must have a wobbly kind of motion. In these respects, however, he was the continuator of the late medieval scientific tradition, especially that professed by the Oxford school, rather than an independent pioneer. Philosophically, his emphasis upon mathematical knowledge, the method of limits, the mutual relation between the individual and the universe, the restricted scope of reason and its antithetic character, and the doctrine that the universe is the "contraction" and "explication" of God, pointed ahead to the major systems of the modern era. But here again, he was prolonging an indigenous medieval philosophical tradition, in which Neo-Platonism, mathematicism, and mysticism predominated.[19] Although his writings were known slightly to Descartes and Leibniz, his influence upon modern philosophy has been mainly of an indirect sort. Cusanus entered the main stream of modern thought only through the pantheistic adaptations which Giordano Bruno made of some of his doctrines.

A native of Nola in Italy, *Giordano Bruno* (1548-1600) had a restless and unhappy career. At the age of seventeen, he entered the Dominican Order at Naples, was ordained priest, and continued to lead the religious life until 1576. During this time, however, he began to question some articles of faith and to imbibe new philosophical views. Rather than face the charges prepared against him by the convent at Naples, he fled the religious life and wandered about in France, Switzerland, England, and the German cities. Excommunicated by the Catholic Church, he was too irascible and independent to please the Calvinists and Lutherans. In Elizabethan London, Bruno was befriended by Sir Philip Sidney. There, in two crowded years (1583-1585), he poured forth his thoughts in six short works, written in Italian. Three of these books were cosmological writings (*The Ash-Wednesday Supper; Concerning the Cause, Principle and One; On the Infinite Universe and Worlds*), whereas the remaining three were ethical treatises (*The Expulsion of the Triumphant Beast; Cabal of the Cheval Pegasus; On Heroic Frenzies*). In 1585, he returned to the continent, drew up 120 theses at Paris against

---

[19] On the continuity of Cusanus' scientific thought with late medieval speculations, see W. H. Hay, "Nicolaus Cusanus: The Structure of His Philosophy," *The Philosophical Review*, LXI (1952), 14-25. His use of traditional doctrines and anticipation of modern philosophical currents are discussed by J. Ritter, "Die Stellung des Nicolaus von Cues in der Philosophiegeschichte," *Blätter für Deutsche Philosophie*, XIII (1939-1940), 111-55.

Aristotelian philosophy, and expounded his own views in some Latin works, including *On the Monad, Number and Form* and *On the Innumerables, the Immense, the Formless* (both issued in 1591). He then took the fatal step of returning to Venice, where he was committed to the Inquisition and eventually sent to Rome. The Roman Inquisitors (including St. Robert Bellarmine) were concerned primarily with his admitted Arianism, his view on transubstantiation and other theological matters, rather than with his scientific opinions. He was declared an impenitent heretic and burned at the stake on February 19, 1600. This harsh penalty did not remove the need, however, for a careful study and criticism of his philosophical position.

Bruno sets out to show that the universe consists of but *one indivisible substance,* which is infinite, eternal, immutable, and divine. He lays down the *rationalistic postulate* that there is one and the same scale by which nature or God's causal power descends to the production of things and by which the human intellect ascends in its knowledge of things. This enables him to argue from the operations of our mind to the constitution of things. "When the intellect wishes to comprehend the essence of a thing, it simplifies as much as possible. . . . The intellect in this openly shows that the substance of things consists in unity,"[20] i.e., that there is a unique substance comprising the reality of the universe. This conclusion admittedly runs contrary to the immediate testimony of the senses and even to rational arguments based on sensory evidence. Hence Bruno combines his rationalistic postulate about the order of thought and being with a *critique of our knowing powers.* We must elevate ourselves above sense and sense-bound reason to the plane of understanding and mind in general, in order to grasp the universe as a single divine whole. Bruno agrees with Cusanus in setting up an antithesis between sense-bound reason and understanding, as well as in awarding the deeper vision to the latter power.

The senses are not intrinsically untrustworthy but they do fail to give a complete account of their objects, and to this extent they can be deceptive. Bruno makes philosophical capital out of the conflict between the Ptolemaic and Copernican cosmologies, since the older view failed to make allowance for the *relativity of all sense perception.* If one were an observer located upon the moon, the moon would seem to be stationary and the earth to be in motion. From this, it follows

---

[20] Bruno, *Concerning the Cause, Principle and One,* V (translated as an Appendix in S. Greenberg's *The Infinite in Giordano Bruno,* 167).

that all motion is relative to the observer's position. Each of the fixed stars is in motion, relative to some frame of reference. Each one of these stars is a sun like our own, with planets moving around it. Copernican astronomy shows that there is no absolute place, motion, or center of the universe. Once these absolutes are removed, all the Aristotelian arguments in favor of a finite universe fall to the ground. Bruno views the universe as being infinite in space, time, and matter. It contains an infinite number of worlds, each of which is finite in itself. Taken together, however, these worlds constitute the *one infinite universe,* any position within which can be regarded now as a center and now as a point on the circumference, from some limited perspective.

To have recognized that sense and sense-bound reason operate within a relative and finite framework, is already to have transcended their limitations and to have reached the standpoint of *understanding* and *infinite mind.* From this eminence, it can be seen that there is but one substance and that its substantial principles are constitutive of the entire universe. Bruno's pantheism rests upon an attempt to combine the Aristotelian doctrine about matter and form with the doctrine of Cusanus about God and the world. What Aristotle says about matter and form can be transformed into a theory of divine attributes, within which the universe is comprised.

### BRUNO'S METAPHYSICAL PRINCIPLES

1. Universal prime matter.
2. Universal form.
   a) As world-soul, it animates all matter.
   b) As universal intellect, it activates all the particular forms in matter through efficient, formal, and final causality.
3. God as the absolute identity or infinite indifference of matter and form. God as the immanent principle and transcendent cause of the universe.

*Prime matter* is the one, ingenerable, passive potency and subject of all modes of being. But Aristotle and the Schoolmen need to be corrected with the aid of Avicebron and David of Dinant. Bruno agrees with Avicebron that matter is present everywhere in the universe and is not confined to corporeal things. And he rehabilitates the theory of David of Dinant that infinite matter (without any dimensions) is an attribute of God. In the Brunonian system, prime or absolute matter is something excellent and divine; it is not *prope nihil* but is perfect and intelligible in itself; it does not receive particular forms from without but contains them indifferently within itself and sends them forth from its bosom to constitute particular things. Bruno's revolutionary proposal is to establish a total correlation between prime matter and substantial form (comprising formal, efficient, and final causes), and then to determine the nature of God in function of the matter-form theory of the universe. "There is one matter out of which everything is produced and formed . . . there is one soul and formal principle that becomes and informs everything."[21] Just as prime matter is a divine attribute, so the universal or absolute form is another aspect of the one divine substance of the universe. Spinoza's attribution of thought and extension to God runs parallel to (although it is not historically dependent upon) this hylemorphic natural theology elaborated by Bruno.

The *universal, absolute form* is also really one, ingenerable, eternal, and infinite. It has the dual function of animating matter and activating its forms. As the universal animating principle, absolute form is the *world-soul;* as the activating agent, it is the *universal intellect.* Both the animating and the activating functions of the universal form entail special consequences for Bruno's view of the universe. Because the world-soul combines with matter in the constitution of all things, ours is a *panpsychistic* universe of living things. "Spirit, mind, life is found in all things,"[22] even though they do not all exhibit life at the level of animals. The particular forms determinative of the grades of living things are drawn forth from universal matter by the universal form, considered as an activating cause or universal intellect. Bruno calls this intellect the principal faculty of the world-soul. That is why not only life but also spirit and mind are present as formal principles in all things. The universal intellect (which includes will) is the single dynamic principle in the universe. It expresses itself variously as the efficient, formal, and final cause of things in the universe.

The rest of Bruno's philosophy is woven out of his attempt to answer two outstanding questions: What is the relation between matter, form, and God? What is man's moral vocation in a pantheistic universe? In dealing with the first problem, he uses some of Cusanus' notions for his own purpose. The key to the knowledge of God and

---

[21] *Ibid.*, III (Greenberg, 134).
[22] *Ibid.*, II (Greenberg, 119).

the world is the doctrine of the *coincidentia et coexistentia oppositorum,* the reconciliation of all opposites in God. In the infinite One, all the contrary qualities found in our experience are amalgamated and rendered indifferently identical with each other. Hence the distinctions and oppositions of our finite experience are due to the limited perspective of the senses and sense-bound reason. From the superior viewpoint of understanding and universal mind, these *distinctions* are seen to be merely *provisional* and *logical,* not permanent and real. Both prime matter and substantial form are identified with each other in God, since in the divine abyss potency and act are indifferently the same. God *is* matter and form, insofar as they are indistinguishably one in infinity; He is *not* matter and form, insofar as they are viewed finitely as distinct correlatives, limiting each other.

This method of identity or the coincidence of opposites is imposed upon Bruno, as being the only way in which he can derive knowledge of God from a study of matter and form. Nevertheless, he tries to make a compromise between the divine *identity* with the universe and some trace of divine *transcendence.* This he does in terms of the distinction between a principle and a cause: a *principle* is intrinsic to the composite, whereas a *cause* is extrinsic to it. Now, God can be viewed either as the formal principle of all things and the universal material subject or as the universe's efficient cause. In the first way, God is identical with the universe, but in the second way He is its distinct, efficient cause. On Bruno's own principle of the identity of opposites, however, there is only a relative distinction between universal form and universal intellect, between God as formal principle and God as efficient cause of the world. Therefore, the distinction of God from the universe is a provisional and logical one, which the understanding learns to overcome. Bruno does not succeed in establishing God's real transcendence. The outcome is a thoroughgoing *pantheistic monism:* the divine substance is the total being of nature. "Substance is essentially without number and without measure and, therefore, one and indivisible in all particular things."[23] There can be many particular *things* but only one *substance:* God or infinite nature.

Bruno tries in another way to save some kind of divine transcendence, with the aid of Cusanus' distinction between God as *omnia complicans* and as *omnia explicans.* God may be viewed either as

---

[23] *Ibid.,* V (Greenberg, 168).

containing the reality of the universe within Himself in a concentrated and unified way or as expressing this reality in the universe in an unfolded and diversified way. The divine production of the universe is a *necessary* act; moreover, God cannot but produce an *infinite* universe or infinite image of Himself. "If infinite power actuates corporeal and dimensional being, this being must necessarily be infinite; otherwise there would be derogation from the nature and dignity both of creator and of creation. . . . Efficient infinity would be utterly incomplete without the [infinite] effect thereof."[24] Some distinction remains, however, between the *comprehensive* or *intensive infinity* of God (God as *natura naturans*) and the *total* or *extensive infinity* of the universe (God as *natura naturata*).

> I say that the universe is entirely [i.e., totally] infinite because it has neither edge, limit, nor surfaces. But I say that the universe is not all-comprehensive infinity because each of the parts thereof that we can examine is finite and each of the innumerable worlds contained therein is finite. I declare God to be completely infinite because he can be associated with no boundary and his every attribute is one and infinite.[25]

Hence the basic difference between God and the universe is that there is no finite aspect whatsoever in God or *natura naturans,* whereas the various parts and individuals in the universe are finite, even though the universe as a whole or *natura naturata* is infinite. But once again, these distinctions depend upon one's relative viewpoint rather than upon a comprehensive grasp of all reality. Seen from the eminence of infinite mind, the opposition between comprehensive and total infinity sinks into the indifference of identity between contraries.

Just as Pomponazzi tried to determine the question of the immortality of the human soul solely within the sphere of philosophy of nature, so Bruno tried to determine the relation between God and the universe solely within the same context. That is why he had to transform the universal principles of explanation of material being — matter and form — into unconditionally universal principles of all being and hence into attributes of God. The standpoint of understanding and infinite mind is none other than that of an *absolutized philosophy of nature.* Bruno was driven into this position by his lack of any doctrine on the analogical predication of being and hence by his

---

24 Bruno, *On the Infinite Universe and Worlds,* Introductory Epistle (translated as an appendix in D. W. Singer's *Giordano Bruno, His Life and Thought,* 233, 234; spelling in this dialogue modernized).

25 *Ibid.,* I (Singer, 261).

fear that no certainty about God could be obtained, except by projecting into the divine nature the material and formal principles that are proportionate to our intellect. The metaphysical consequence could be calculated in advance: the integrity of both God and natural things was placed in jeopardy. Bruno set himself the hopeless task of explaining the *infinite* reality of God by means of material and formal principles, which are precisely the principles of *finitude* in the order of composite essence. This led him to fluctuate between equivocity and univocity of predication of perfections between God and the universe. The doctrine on the coincidence of opposites expressed this fluctuation in quasi-mystical language, enabling him to speak now about the identity of substance and now about the distinction between God and the universe. There was also an epistemological motive behind his requirement that God must produce the universe necessarily and as an infinite effect. The necessity of the production guaranteed the necessity of the dialectical ascent of intellect up the ladder of being to God, whereas the infinite character of the effect was the only surety of making contact with an infinite reality.

Not only the infinite being of God but also the finite being of natural things is compromised in Bruno's system. *Particular finite things* are not substances or beings: they are only *modes* of the unique divine substance or being. "All that we see of diversity and difference are nothing but diverse and different aspects of the same Substance."[26] Particular things are expressions or manifestations of God but they have no subsistent being of their own. Bruno was unable to reconcile finitude with *per se* being, since he gave to *per se* being a single, univocal meaning: infinite self-founded reality. Thus an insensible transition was made from the subsistent character of substance to the aseity of the infinite substance. Only on these grounds could Bruno maintain that "finite substance" is a contradiction in terms. His identification of *per se* being with the causally independent, infinite substance reduced finite things to the status of modes of this unique substance: the *substance-pantheism* doctrine is the outcome.

Bruno was also compelled to deny the reality of *substantial changes,* once granted that matter and form are ingenerable and that substance is unique. Just as the manyness of finite things is that of a diversity of appearances of the same substantial being, so the changes

---

[26] *Concerning the Cause, Principle and One,* Introductory Epistle (Greenberg, 86).

transpiring among finite things are only *alterations* within the self-same substance. Bruno accepted Lucretius' conception of atoms or primal minima of the universe but preferred to regard them spiritually as *monads*. The change in the universe consists of a ceaseless process of cosmic aggregation and disaggregation of the monadic units. Complex finite things come to be and pass away in accord with this "cosmic metabolism," which is a process of alteration rather than of substantial change. But neither monads nor their combinations constitute subsistent beings, since they are only ways of explicating and viewing the divine substance. Whatever the differences and changes present in the universe, the "contrary and diverse mobile parts converge to constitute a single continuous motionless body, wherein contraries converge to the constitution of a single whole."[27] If all being constitutes a single whole, there is no room for autonomous persons in the world of particular appearances. Human minds are conscious monads, but their ontological status is that of particularizations of the universal intellect, contractions of its power at particular points.

Bruno's moral attitude of "heroic frenzy" had its speculative roots in his struggle to preserve some shadow of integral, personal existence within this purely modal conception of finite things. He realized that the moral and religious life required a polarity between the human soul and God, and yet his theory of being involved a collapse of both poles into an indifferent identity. Because it is the image of God's absolute infinity, the universe has a natural tendency to perfect the divine likeness within itself. In man, this appetite for the divine takes the form of a desire to enter into cognitive and affective union with the infinite substance. The negative condition for this union is the expulsion of the vices or "beasts" from the soul. In their stead, there must grow a clear understanding of infinite nature, an understanding which transforms itself into *love of God* and complete acceptance of our fate, i.e., the necessity with which we are produced and guided by God. Our real *freedom* lies in the *recognition of necessity,* since from the divine standpoint, the contraries of necessity and freedom are merged in one. Like Spinoza, Bruno locates our highest perfection in the intellectual love of God and the acceptance of necessity. Some kind of *immortality* is thus assured for the intellectual principle in man. What remains eternal and incorruptible,

---

[27] *On the Infinite Universe and Worlds,* II (Singer, 287–88).

however, is the infinite intellect itself or universal form. The heroic
frenzy and ecstasy, with which this fate is freely embraced, do not
relieve Bruno of the metaphysical necessity of transforming an abiding personal union between the infinite God and finite persons into
an identification between substance and its own particularized
attributes.

## 5. SKEPTICISM AND STOICISM

The Renaissance did not reach France until comparatively late. As
far as philosophy is concerned, the new trends did not become noticeable until the last third of the sixteenth century. By that time, a good
deal of the original exuberance of humanism had been spent. The
influx of Italian thought into France was due largely to the *freethinkers,* who stressed the difficulties latent in the earlier Renaissance views
on man, God, and the universe. Doubt was cast upon the mind's
ability to demonstrate personal immortality, freedom, and even the
existence of God. New translations of Sextus Empiricus and other
classical sources of skepticism added to the intellectual confusion.
Futhermore, during the latter part of the sixteenth century, France
was rent by civil wars, followed by the victory of the religiously
cynical Henry of Navarre and the Edict of Nantes (1598). Religious
truth seemed to be settled by the strongest army and reasons of state
alone.

These conditions favored the development of an attitude blending
skepticism in speculative matters, Stoicism in the practical order, and
fideism in regard to religious truth. This synthesis of intellectual
despair and moral fortitude is found most characteristically in *Michel
de Montaigne* (1533–1592) and *Pierre Charron* (1541–1603). Montaigne, as a courtier and country gentleman, and Charron, as a Catholic priest and court chaplain at Paris, were conversant with all the
new problems and doubts. They mocked at the earlier humanistic
eulogies on the theme *De Dignitate Hominis,* at least as far as man's
intellectual power is concerned. They advised faith to cease looking
for rational support, and morality to cast itself loose from questionable metaphysics. Thus they prepared the spiritual and intellectual
atmosphere which Descartes and Pascal were soon to breathe and
which gave a direct impetus to the modern attempts at reconstruction in philosophy.

Montaigne repeats the arguments of classical, Pyrrhonian skepticism and adds a few considerations of his own to show the lowness

and weakness of man. In his *Essays* (first edition, 1580; important additions in the 1588 and 1595 editions), he points to the *conflicting opinions* among philosophers concerning the nature of God, the heavenly bodies, and the human soul, as proof that philosophy cannot attain speculative certainty but is a sophisticated brand of poetry. The extravagant and contradictory teachings of philosophers result from two traits of human nature: the defectiveness of our understanding and the weakness of our senses. Our judgments are constantly shifting, since the *understanding* is subject to the alterations of the body, the flow of passing moods, and the urgency of the passions. But the fundamental ground for mistrusting reason lies in its dependence upon the *senses*. "Now all knowledge makes its way into us through the senses: they are our masters . . . [Man] cannot escape the fact that the senses are the sovereign masters of his knowledge; but they are uncertain and deceivable in all circumstances."[28] Montaigne recalls the familiar illusions caused by jaundice and other subjective conditions, as well as the differences in perception resulting from the age, position, and previous training of the observers. He muses that perhaps the fable-writers were right in ascribing more intelligence and prudence to animals than to men, seeing that many animals surpass us in respect to the senses we share in common. In case of conflicting testimony among the senses or at the rational level, there is no way of settling the issue without becoming involved in an infinite regress of principles of verification. Montaigne concludes that we ought to rely solely upon experience, custom, and social order as the guides of life.

Charron sharpens these skeptical arguments, converting Montaigne's unsettling question: "What do I know?" into his own positive motto: "I know nothing." In his treatise *Of Wisdom* (1601), he declares that the office of true religion is "to subdue and beat him [man] down, as a lost worthless wretch; and when this is once done, then to furnish him with helps and means of raising himself up again."[29] Once the utter incapacity of natural reason to establish God's existence and the soul's immortality is established, the truths of revealed religion can be inculcated in all their purity. This is the position of *fideistic skepticism*, which rejects the orthodox Catholic confidence in both reason and faith. But the freethinkers and libertines flourishing in Paris around 1600 dismissed Charron's articles of faith (the three

---

[28] Montaigne, *Essays*, II, 12 (Frame translation, 443, 447). See E. H. Henderson, "Montaigne and Modern Philosophy," *The Personalist*, XXXIV (1953), 278–89.

[26] Charron, *Of Wisdom*, II, v, 16 (Stanhope translation, II, 766).

basic truths of God, Christianity, and Catholicism) as mere expediency. They argued consistently that, once our ability to know the truth in a natural way is called in question, there is no longer any rational ground for accepting revelation. Futhermore, they converted Charron's Stoic advice to follow nature into an excuse for moral libertinage. Charron's moral counsel rested upon an identification of "nature" with "that universal reason and equity, which is given for a light to my mind," and ultimately with "the God of nature and the dictates of eternal reason."[30] But the proponents of *freethinking skepticism* pointed out Charron's inconsistency in attacking human reason and then requiring submission of the will to a universal and eternal reason, the existence of which cannot be proved by our minds.

There was also a tendency toward a nonskeptical version of *Christian Stoicism,* as the basis of morality. The leading representatives of this school were *Justus Lipsius* and *Guillaume Du Vair.* Lipsius (1547–1606), who wavered between Catholicism and Protestantism and who ended his stormy career as a Louvain professor, sketched the Stoic moral ideal in two major works: *Of Constancy* (1584) and *Introduction to the Stoic Philosophy* (1604). He was anxious to correct the Stoics in regard to destiny, the necessary sequence of causes, chance, and freedom. He defined *destiny* as an eternal decree of God's providence. Hence it is subordinate to providence and God's free decrees. God is a personal agent, subject to no impersonal destiny or linkage of natural causes, and sovereignly transcendent of the world. His decrees are immovable, but they respect the contingency of things, the freedom of man, and the possibility of miracles.

Given these basic adjustments, however, Christians can profit by appropriating the noble Stoic attitude of constancy. In troublesome times, we acquire peace of mind not by traveling around or otherwise distracting ourselves but only by an inward change, which gives steadfastness and serenity of spirit. *Constancy* is *"a right and immoveable strength of the mind, neither lifted up, nor pressed down with external or casual accidents."*[31] The constant mind is rooted in *patience,* which is a voluntary acceptance of all things that can happen to man. Patience and constancy are the twin fruits of regulating our mind according to the rule of *right reason,* i.e., of *"a true sense and*

---

[30] *Ibid.,* II, iii, 7, 16 (Stanhope, II, 677, 696).

[31] Justus Lipsius, *Tvvo Bookes of Constancie,* I, 4 (Kirk edition, 79; spelling modernized in Lipsius and Du Vair).

*judgment of things human and divine.*"[32] These prime virtues flow from inward meditation on the truth that whatever happens to man occurs in accordance with God's decree. Hence we should bear with the necessary evils of life, remembering that they are subject to divine providence and are intended for our improvement. In his innermost self or mind, the constant and patient man is undisturbed by external happenings, whether of good fortune or ill. Grounded in his conformity with right reason and God, he comes as close as any creature can to the supreme attribute of God: His immutability.

In his three main books — *The Holy Philosophy* (1584?), *The Moral Philosophy of the Stoics* (1585?), and *Constancy* (1594) — Guillaume Du Vair (1556-1621) continued the work of harmonizing Stoicism with the Christian conception of a personal, free God, who is the source of fortune and destiny. Stoic virtues can bring us strength and consolation in times of trial (such as the years of the French civil wars). But Du Vair is careful to observe that his purpose is not to ask Christians to abandon

> the clear and sacred fountain of God's word, from whence all holy and wholesome precepts of manners and discipline must be drawn: but only to let you understand, that they [the Stoic moralists] have been and will be a reproach unto us Christians, who being born and bred in the true light of the Gospel, shall see and perceive how many there be that have been lovers and earnest embracers of virtue even amidst the times of darkness and ignorance.[33]

Above all, the Stoic writings can enkindle once more in our hearts a respect and love for *practical wisdom*, which is the mother of all virtues.

> For causing us to have an exact and true knowledge of the condition and quality of things which come into our considerations and views, she [wisdom] teaches and tells us what is according to nature, and what not, and likewise what is to be desired and followed, or shunned and avoided. She removes all false opinions out of our heads. . . . We must go to school to philosophy, to know the right use of wisdom.[34]

It was probably with Du Vair's description of the functions of wis-

---

[32] *Loc. cit.*

[33] Guillaume Du Vair, *The Moral Philosophie of the Stoicks* (Kirk edition, 50).

[34] *Ibid.* (Kirk, 61, 62). An annotated edition of Du Vair's *De la Sainte Philosophie* and *Philosophie morale des Stoïques* (Paris, Vrin, 1945), by G. Michaut, provides scholarly help. For a useful survey of French Neo-Stoicism, cf. J.-E. D'Angers, O.F.M. Cap., "Le stoïcisme en France, dans la première moitié du XVIIe siècle," *Études Franciscaines*, N.S., II (1951), 287-97, 389-410; III (1952), 5-19, 133-57.

dom before him, that the great seventeenth-century master of French prose, Jean-Louis Guez de Balzac, once hailed Descartes as the modern reincarnation of the sage or Stoic wise man. Descartes did accept the Stoic moral philosophy, but for its own positive qualities rather than as a refuge from skepticism (as Charron had done).

By the middle years of the seventeenth century, however, theologians were asking where sin, repentance, and grace fitted into the Christian Stoic pattern. The Stoic sage, in his self-containment and rational power for attaining peace of mind, would seem to stand in no need of supernatural redemption. The Jansenistic stress upon man's weakness and corruption was an extreme reaction — not far removed from fideistic skepticism — against the Stoic's appeal to man's native strength and natural ability to conform with eternal reason. With Jansenism, the Renaissance problem of man was rephrased in theological terms as the question of grace and freedom.

# SUMMARY OF CHAPTER 2

The humanist men of letters attacked the secular Aristotelians for relying too slavishly upon Aristotle and for siding with Averroës rather than the Christian faith on disputed points. But they also criticized the Christian Scholastics for their excessive use of distinctions, their proliferation of methods, and their failure to make a fresh inspection of man and nature. Renaissance Platonists and Aristotelians concentrated mainly upon the problem of man and his relations with the world and God. The contrasting views of Ficino and Pomponazzi on human immortality show how extensively indebted the Renaissance philosophers were to previous philosophical traditions and how deeply the cleavages concerning human nature ran. In Pico and Paracelsus, the key notion of man as microcosm guaranteed the metaphysical unity and order of nature, as well as its accessibility to human understanding and control. But this cosmic harmony scarcely seemed to be reflected in human social relations, at least as reported "realistically" by Machiavelli. He converted the methodological convenience of separate study of social processes into an unqualified declaration of the independence of political life from moral regulation. One last Renaissance attempt to see man wholly and steadily was made by Bruno. He sought to obtain certitude in knowledge and unity in being by breaking down the ultimate distinction between God and the universe. Within the confines of a monistic pantheism, he tried to make room for some sort of divine transcendence and human personal existence. The knell of Renaissance humanism was sounded by Montaigne and Charron, with their radical distrust of our cognitive powers. Once the speculative order was undermined, there seemed to be no other support for man than moral fortitude and a strong faith. The Christian Stoicism of Lipsius and Du Vair provided consolation and strength in a period of social and intellectual disorder.

## BIBLIOGRAPHICAL NOTE

1. *Humanist Indictment of Scholasticism.* The breakup of the medieval synthesis and the transition to the Renaissance are discussed by M. De Wulf, *Histoire de la philosophie médiévale,* Vol. 3: *Après le treizième siècle* (sixth ed., entirely recast, Paris, Vrin, 1947; English translation being prepared by E. C. Messenger, in the fourth or definitive English edition, to be published by Nelson of London); E Gilson, *History of Christian Philosophy in the Middle Ages* (New York, Random House, 1955), Part XI, including pp. 534–540 on Cusanus; G. de Lagarde, *La naissance de l'esprit laïque au déclin du moyen âge* (second ed., 6 vols., Paris, Presses Universitaires, 1948). Detailed accounts of the Renaissance Scholastic movement, especially in Spain, will be found in: C. Giacon, *La seconda scolastica* (3 vols., Milan, Bocca, 1944–1950), and M. Solana, *Historia de la filosofía Española, época del Renacimiento (S. XVI)* (3 vols., Madrid, Asociación Española para el progreso de las ciencias, 1940–1941). Along with J. Burckhardt's famous *The Civilization of the Renaissance in Italy,* translated by S. G. Middlemore (New York, Boni, 1935; from fifteenth German ed.), should be read W. K. Ferguson's *The Renaissance in Historical Thought: Five Centuries of Interpretation* (Boston, Houghton Mifflin, 1948), which states Burckhardt's thesis and charts the various reactions to it by historians since 1860. A reliable general history is H. S. Lucas, *The Renaissance and the Reformation* (New York, Harper, 1934). The cultural and philosophical trends of Italian Humanism and Renaissance, along with their continuity with the medieval past, are given masterful synthesis in Msgr. F. Olgiati, *L'anima del' Umanesimo e del Rinascimento* (Milan, Vita e Pensiero, 1924), and C. Carbonara, *Il secolo XV* (Milan, Bocca, 1943). An easy way to make a first acquaintance with the vast number of Renaissance thinkers is to read the brief entries in: *A Catalogue of Renaissance Philosophers (1350–1650),* edited by J. O. Riedl (Milwaukee, Marquette University Press, 1940). Leonardo da Vinci may be studied in the following collections: *The Notebooks of Leonardo da Vinci,* arranged and translated by E. MacCurdy (2 vols., New York, Reynal and Hitchcock, 1938); *The Literary Works of Leonardo da Vinci,* edited and translated by J. P. and I. A. Richter (second edition, New York, Oxford University Press, 1939). E. MacCurdy's *The Mind of Leonardo da Vinci* (New York, Dodd, Mead, 1928) explores the many interests and achievements of this genius. *The Renaissance Philosophy of Man,* edited by E. Cassirer, P. O. Kristeller, and J. H. Randall, Jr. (Chicago, University of Chicago Press, 1948), contains a translation of Petrarca's *On His Own Ignorance and That of Many Others,* together with some of his shorter pieces. H. H. Hudson has issued a useful translation of Erasmus' *The Praise of Folly* (Princeton, Princeton University Press, 1941), which also includes an outline of the rhetorical moments in this declamation. See M. Phillips, *Erasmus and the Northern Renaissance* (London, Hoddes and Stoughton, 1949); P. S. Allen, *The Age of Erasmus* (New York, Oxford University Press, 1914); J. Huizinga, *Erasmus of Rotterdam* (reprint edition with new translation of selected letters, New York, Phaidon Press, 1952). In *The*

*Counter-Renaissance* (New York, Scribner, 1950), H. Haydn distinguishes provocatively between the classical Renaissance or Humanism (which was continuous with the medieval period and stressed the power of reason and moral preoccupations), and the Counter-Renaissance (which made a definite break with the past in the sixteenth century, becoming skeptical about reason and the soundness of human nature, so that Calvin and Machiavelli, Luther and Montaigne, showed definite affinities).

2. *Man as the Central Problem.* The question of a Christian humanism may be approached at various levels. G. Vann, O.P., *On Being Human* (New York, Sheed and Ward, 1934), evokes a philosophical dialogue between St. Thomas and Aldous Huxley on the meanings of humanism; G. Walsh, S.J., *Medieval Humanism* (New York, Macmillan, 1942), outlines the medieval pattern; F. Hermans, *Histoire doctrinale de l'humanisme chrétien* (4 vols., Tournai, Casterman, 1948), provides comparative materials from the various historical realizations of the Christian humanistic ideal. A representative sourcebook for the Italian Renaissance philosophers is *The Renaissance Philosophy of Man* (mentioned above), which, in addition to Petrarca, contains translations of: Lorenzo Valla's *Dialogue on Free Will,* Ficino's *Five Questions concerning the Mind,* Pico's *Oration on the Dignity of Man,* Pomponazzi's *On the Immortality of the Soul,* and Juan Vives' *A Fable about Man.* V. M. Hamm has made a translation of Pico's *Of Being and Unity* (Milwaukee, Marquette University Press, 1943). The Christian and Scholastic aspects of Pico are emphasized by E. Garin, *Giovanni Pico della Mirandola* (Florence, Le Monnier, 1937), and A. Dulles, S.J., *Princeps Concordiae: Pico della Mirandola and the Scholastic Tradition* (Cambridge, Mass., Harvard University Press, 1941). See also the general studies by A. H. Douglas, *The Philosophy and Psychology of Pietro Pomponazzi* (Cambridge, University Press, 1910), and P. O. Kristeller, *The Philosophy of Marsilio Ficino,* translated by V. Conant (New York, Columbia University Press, 1943). From an idealistic standpoint, E. Cassirer has focused attention upon the microcosm idea, in his *Individuum und Kosmos in der Philosophie der Renaissance* (Berlin, Teubner, 1927). The philosophy of Paracelsus may be sampled in *Paracelsus: Selected Writings,* edited by J. Jacobi, and translated by N. Guterman (New York, Pantheon, 1951). See H. M. Pachter, *Magic into Science: The Story of Paracelsus* (New York, Schuman, 1951), and W. Pagel, *Paracelsus: An Introduction to Philosophical Medicine in the Era of the Renaissance* (New York, Karger, 1958).

3. *Machiavelli.* A. H. Gilbert translation of *The Prince and Other Works* (New York, Farrar and Straus, 1941), with a fact-laden introduction by the translator; L. J. Walker, S.J., translation of *The Discourses* (2 vols., London, Routledge and Kegan Paul, 1950), with a valuable introduction in Volume I and copious notes in Volume II. The background of the period is provided in D. E. Muir, *Machiavelli and His Times* (New York, Dutton, 1936); a sympathetic exposition of Machiavelli's works and viewpoint is given by J. H. Whitfield, *Machiavelli* (Oxford, Blackwell, 1947); his policy is assessed by H. Butterfield, *The Statecraft of Machiavelli* (London, Bell, 1940). For a better understanding of the literary genre

into which *The Prince* fits, see A. H. Gilbert, *Machiavelli's Prince and its Forerunners* (Durham, N. C., Duke University Press, 1938). For Machiavelli's place in the general development of political philosophy, consult G. H. Sabine, *A History of Political Theory* (revised ed., New York, Holt, 1950); Sabine also provides an accurate résumé of the political theories of Hobbes, Locke, Hegel, and other modern thinkers. The best, advanced philosophical study of Machiavelli is given by P. Mesnard, *L'essor de la philosophie politique au XVIe siècle* (second ed., Paris, Vrin, 1951), 17–85, who also analyzes the political theories of Erasmus, More, Calvin, Bodin, Mariana, Suarez, and others. A convenient collection of source materials is: *Masters of Political Thought* (general editor, E. McC. Sait), Vol. II: *Machiavelli to Bentham,* edited by W. T. Jones (Boston, Houghton Mifflin, 1947).

4. *Cusanus and Bruno.* The *Of Learned Ignorance,* by Cusanus, is translated by G. Heron, O.F.M. (New Haven, Yale University Press, 1954). There are helpful studies by H. Bett, *Nicholas of Cusa* (London, Methuen, 1922); M. Gandillac, *Le philosophie de Nicolas de Cues* (Paris, Aubier, 1941); K. H. Volkmann-Schluck, *Nicolaus Cusanus* (Frankfurt a M., Klostermann, 1957). For a Scholastic critique of the mathematicism of Cusanus, see V. Martin, O.P., "The Dialectical Process in the Philosophy of Nicholas of Cusa," *Laval Théologique et Philosophique,* V (1949), 213–68. Complete and accurate translations of Bruno's two main treatises are available: *On the Infinite Universe and Worlds* is appended to D. W. Singer's *Giordano Bruno: His Life and Thought* (New York, Schuman, 1950); *Concerning the Cause, Principle and One* is appended to S. Greenberg's *The Infinite in Giordano Bruno* (New York, King's Crown Press, 1940). Singer's biography is specially well informed about Bruno's English years, during which he composed his main works. Greenberg's book contains a close analysis of Bruno's central conception of the infinite, and should be compared with the best general study: L. Cicuttini's *Giordano Bruno* (Milan, Vita e Pensiero, 1950), which concludes that Bruno's philosophy is an immanentistic, naturalistic monism. On his ethics, see his poem *The Heroic Enthusiasts,* translated by L. Williams (London, Redway, 1887); J. C. Nelson, *Renaissance Theory of Love* (New York, Columbia University Press, 1958). For his trial, attention must be paid to the documents published by A. Mercati, *Il sommario del processo di Giordano Bruno* (Vatican City, Bibliotheca Apostolica Vaticana, 1942), as well as to the careful account given by L. Firpo, *Il processo di Giordano Bruno* (Naples, Edizioni scientifiche Italiane, 1949). It is abundantly clear from these sources that Bruno was not punished as a "martyr to science." For a portrait of another important Italian philosopher, Campanella, cf. G. Di Napoli, *Tommaso Campanella: Filosofo della restaurazione cattolica* (Padua, Cedam, 1947), which underlines the Christian and Platonic motifs in his thought.

5. *Skepticism and Stoicism.* For the skeptical and libertine background, see H. Busson, *La pensée religieuse française de Charron à Pascal* (Paris, Vrin, 1933); F. Strowski, *Pascal et son temps* (3 vols., Paris, Plon, 1907–1913); R. Pintard, *Le libertinage érudit dans la première moitié du XVIIe siècle* (Paris, Boivin, 1943). A useful modern translation of Montaigne

is by J. Zeitlin: *The Essays of Michel de Montaigne* (3 vols., New York, Knopf, 1934–1936). F. Strowski's *Montaigne* (second ed., revised and corrected, Paris, Alcan, 1931) is still the most balanced general study. J. V. Mauzey's *Montaigne's Philosophy of Human Nature* (Annandale-on-Hudson, N. Y., St. Stephan's College, 1933) explains his basic philosophical anthropology. Scholars are not agreed upon whether or not to include Montaigne among the *fideistic* skeptics, in a class with Charron and Francis Sanchez; the debate is well summarized in M. Dréano, *La pensée religieuse de Montaigne* (Paris, Beauchesne, 1936), and H. Friedrich, *Montaigne* (Bern, Francke, 1949). G. Stanhope issued an early translation of Charron's *Of Wisdom* (third ed., corrected, 3 vols., London, Walthoe, 1729). The two classical Renaissance Stoic sources are: *Tvvo Bookes of Constancie written in Latine by Iustus Lipsius. Englished by Sir John Stradling,* edited with introduction by R. Kirk, and notes by C. M. Hall (New Brunswick, Rutgers University Press, 1939); *The Moral Philosophie of the Stoicks, written in French by Guillaume Du Vair. Englished by Thomas James,* edited with introduction and notes by R. Kirk (New Brunswick, Rutgers University Press, 1951). The fundamental study of Renaissance Stoicism continues to be L. Zanta's *La renaissance du stoïcisme au XVIe siècle* (Paris, Champion, 1914). The only full-length study on Lipsius is by J. L. Saunders: *Justus Lipsius: The Philosophy of Renaissance Stoicism* (New York, Liberal Arts Press, 1955). The whole question of Renaissance skepticism has been reopened by D. M. Frame, *Montaigne's Discovery of Man* (New York, Columbia University Press, 1955), in which the possibility of a sincere attitude of skeptical fideism is rightly recognized, within the Renaissance perspective. A similar view of Charron is taken by J. B. Sabrié, *De l'humanisme au rationalisme: Pierre Charron* (Paris, Alcan, 1913). D. M. Frame has also translated *The Complete Works of Montaigne* (Stanford, Stanford University Press, 1957).

That Renaissance humanism centers in an educational and literary core, remaining open to Christian tradition and relatively neutral in philosophy, is suggested by P. O. Kristeller, *The Classics and Renaissance Thought* (Cambridge, Mass., Harvard University Press, 1955). George Sarton's *Six Wings: Men of Science in the Renaissance* (Bloomington, Indiana University Press, 1957), describes the scientific activities of the Renaissance, adding a new factor to the humanist strain. The complexity of the Renaissance mind is brought out in P. O. Kristeller's *Renaissance Thought: The Classic, Scholastic, and Humanistic Strains* (New York, Harper Torchbooks, 1961). Two major ideas are traced through by E. F. Rice, Jr., *The Renaissance Idea of Wisdom* (Cambridge, Harvard University Press, 1958), and by N. W. Gilbert, *Renaissance Concepts of Method* (New York, Columbia University Press, 1960). The methods of Pomponazzi and Ramus respectively are analyzed by J. H. Randall, Jr., *The School of Padua and the Emergence of Modern Science* (Padua, Antenore, 1959), and W. J. Ong, S.J., *Ramus, Method, and the Decay of Dialogue* (Cambridge, Harvard University Press, 1958). L. Strauss offers his *Thoughts on Machiavelli* (Glencoe, Ill., Free Press, 1958).

# Chapter 3. SCIENTIFIC OUTLOOKS AND METHODS: BACON, GALILEO, AND NEWTON

AT THE very outset of modern philosophy, a close alliance was established between philosophy and the new developments in scientific method. Three of the major contributors toward the modern approach in science were Francis Bacon, Galileo Galilei, and Isaac Newton. Bacon was himself an amateur scientist, whereas Galileo and Newton were the great founders of modern classical physics. All three men were reflectively interested, moreover, in the general nature of scientific thinking and its bearing upon the larger philosophical problems of man and the universe. Through their influence, the scientific outlook and method made a decisive impact upon the course of philosophical speculation itself, thus helping to characterize and unify the modern era in philosophy.

## A. *Francis Bacon*

Francis Bacon (born in London, 1561) had a background of high station, being a son of Sir Nicholas Bacon, Lord Keeper of the Great Seal under Queen Elizabeth, and a relative of the Cecils. His stay in Trinity College, Cambridge, lasted from early in 1573 until Christmas, 1575. There, he acquired a permanent dislike for the Aristotelianism of the Universities, because of its contentiousness and practical sterility. He enrolled for the study of law at Gray's Inn (1576) but spent some time in the retinue of the English ambassador to France. After his father's death in 1579, Bacon studied the law seriously, became a member of Parliament (1584), and began his steady search after advancement at Court. Although befriended by the Queen's favorite, the Earl of Essex, he did not advance very far under Elizabeth. With the accession of James I in 1603, however, Bacon's fortunes took an upward turn. He was knighted and, between 1607 and 1618, held the following high offices of state: Solicitor General, Attorney General, Lord Keeper of the Great Seal, and Lord Chancellor (1618). These promotions were matched by his being created Baron Verulam (1618) and Viscount St. Albans (1621). A few days after receiving the latter title, he was accused of accepting bribes, found guilty, and stripped of all offices and access to the Court. Bacon admitted having received gifts from parties whose cases were before him, but pointed out that this was the common custom and maintained that the favors did not sway his judgment. He went into retirement, devoting himself mainly to his writings and experiments. Death came in April of 1626.

Bacon often contrasted the two sides of his personality: the man of political affairs and the man of wit and learning. Although he intended to use power and wealth for the sake of his studies, the former pursuit interfered seriously with his learned projects, most of which remained in fragmentary form. Nevertheless, he managed to write a number of influential works. His *Essays* first appeared in 1597 and was frequently issued in revised editions. The one philosophical book written in English was *Of the Proficience and Advancement of Learning* (1605), which made important proposals for the division and betterment of the sciences. His new inductive method was described in the *Novum Organum* (1620), which was followed by a revised Latin version of the *Advancement of Learning* entitled *De Dignitate et Augmentis Scientiarum* ("On the Dignity and Advancement of the Sciences," 1623). He also prepared a number of special "histories" or collections of scientific facts. After his death, his scheme for a utopia and new center of scientific learning, the *New Atlantis,* was published (1627).

## I. EXPURGATION OF THE MIND

Bacon sounded a typically modern note when he expressed to James I of England his dissatisfaction not only with the older Scholastic systems but also with the humanist ideal that had replaced them in many quarters. Surveying the state of learning at the beginning of the seventeenth century, he complained that it suffered from three major *distempers:* contentions, affectation, and fantasy.[1] The first disease was rampant at the Universities, where a corrupted sort of Scholasticism still held sway, with the customary results. However

---

[1] *Of the Proficience and Advancement of Learning,* I (all page references in Bacon are to J. M. Robertson's edition of *The Philosophical Works of Francis Bacon;* cf. 53–60).

sharp their wits and active their minds, the Schoolmen were handicapped by a dearth of materials upon which to excogitate. They turned their minds from the inexhaustible riches of nature to a barren and *contentious* picking-over of traditional texts. Their concern was rather to overcome an adversary through subtlety of argument than to make a direct study of the universe. The Reformers and humanists hated the Scholastic method and returned to ancient authors. But instead of testing the soundness of their classical sources, they became entranced with them for their own sakes. Humanistic learning was beset by *affectations,* since it paid more heed to the choice of fine words than to the matter expressed, more to classical authority than to present truth. Finally, Bacon decried the *fantastical* quality of many contemporary "scientific" minds — their loose way of receiving and giving testimony about natural happenings. Alchemy and foolish magic were warmly pursued; old wives' tales were accepted as natural history; the Greek philosophers of nature were worshiped like statues, which had survived without development down the ages.

Half measures would be ineffective in dealing with this parlous situation. Bacon argued that minor remedies only prolonged the disease, since they shared the maladies which they were supposed to cure. The famous "Protestant Logic" of Peter Ramus was only a variation on Aristotle, and the scientific researches of William Gilbert were one-sided and unenlightened. Nothing less than a *radical reconstruction* of all our convictions was called for, and this could be undertaken only with the aid of a *new method.* On these points, Bacon voiced an attitude that was fast becoming a commonplace in his century. Moreover, he offered powerful reasons why a thorough sifting of opinions and revision of procedures were needed. To continue to regard the human mind as a totally blank tablet, upon which experience may freshly inscribe its message, was to ignore the steady pressure exerted from the outset of a man's life by the traditions and prevailing outlook of his day.

Hence a preliminary process of criticizing and uprooting some fixed habits of mind is the indispensable prelude to any renovation of learning. The mind must be made a purged and well-scrubbed tablet, washed clean of abstruse speculation, bookishness, and fantasy. Bacon proposes a *threefold "refutation,"* as a way of purging the mind. He intends to criticize natural human reason, the prevailing philosophical systems, and the logic of demonstration. These refutations are made in conjunction with the *doctrine on the idols,* which gives a systematic and colorful form to his strictures.[2] By "idols" or *eidola,* he means not perverted objects of religious worship but the phantoms and false notions that people our minds. (This is reminiscent of Plato's warning against the practices of the sophists, who fashion *eidola* after their own nature and limitations, rather than *eikona* modeled after real paradigms.) A contrast is evident between the divine ideas, i.e., those notions which give a true and exact model of nature's actual being, and the idols or baseless figments constructed by ourselves. These false opinions are divided into *four genera:* the idols of the tribe, the cave, the market place, and the theater. A refutation of these deep-seated fallacies is the equivalent, in natural philosophy, of the logical doctrine on the sophisms. The first three idols are "natural" fallacies, whereas the fourth kind is "artificial." Hence Bacon does not claim entirely to uproot the first three classes of idols, since they are innate in our nature, or at least in its conditions and instruments. But by calling attention to their baleful influence, he hopes to counterbalance them and thus loosen their hold on the mind. And he is quite confident that, in any event, he can completely eradicate the idols of the theater, which are human products and capable of being dispelled by sound logic.

## BACON'S "REFUTATION" OF THE MIND

1. Objects of criticism.
   a) Natural human reason.
   b) Philosophical systems.
   c) Practical science and the traditional logic of demonstration.

2. Idols of the mind.
   a) Natural prejudices that cannot be extirpated but that can be counteracted: idols of the tribe, the cave, and the market place.
   b) Artificial prejudices and fallacies that can be completely removed (with the aid of the proper method): idols of the theater.
      1) Theologism.
      2) Empiricism.
      3) Rationalism.

The *idols of the tribe* signify those superstitious and erroneous beliefs to which human nature as such inclines us. Up to a point, Bacon agrees with the skeptics in casting doubt upon our knowing powers. He never tires of contrasting the depth and subtlety of inanimate nature with the impotence and shallowness of our minds.

[2] *Novum Organum,* I, 38–67 (Robertson, 263–74).

The defects of the senses, which are the fountainhead of our knowledge, receive special attention. The senses can fail us both by giving no information and by giving false information. The former weakness is due to the fact that many natural events are too slow or swift for detection, too familiar or too minute for mention. On the other hand, sensation can be a source of error as well as ignorance, for it always bears a pragmatic reference to man's welfare rather than to the objective structure of things. Whereas the skeptics conclude from the debility of our knowing power to our incapacity for gaining truth, Bacon infers that we cannot get very far in knowledge without some special methodic aids. If our minds and senses are weak and empty in themselves, then the moral is to turn from sterile introspection to experience of nature and from unguided to guided investigations.

Various particular idols of the tribe result from the defects of our native powers. Sense and intellect tend to take their measure from our own will and emotions rather than from nature itself. We read into nature an order and regularity that it does not have; we spring from finite occurrences to first movers and, above all, to final causes that seem to minister to our wishes; we support our opinions exclusively with positive, confirming evidence and close our eyes to contrary data and negative instances. What strikes the senses most forcibly is regarded as most significant. We are prone to rely upon chance associations among items of our experience that happen to affect our imagination. Instead of laboriously searching out nature's secrets, our intellect retreats to its own abstractions, where it enjoys an illusory mastery and lucidity. Purely potential matter, separated forms, and axioms about act and potency beguile us into believing that the universe itself must conform in advance with our abstract notions.

The *idols of the cave* are, as Plato's myth suggests, those idiosyncrasies arising from our individual histories. Each man carries within himself his own cave or private image of the world. His personal temperament, education, associations, inclinations, and talents give his mind a special bent and perspective. Unfortunately, he often confuses his individual outlook with the objective conditions of things. Aristotle's specialty was logic, and to it he subordinated his whole philosophy. Democritus was so fascinated by viewing things in disintegration that he lost sight of their wholeness; other men found the holistic approach so congenial that they failed to investigate the particles of matter. Each of us mistakes his own garden for the entire universe. And when we enter into social intercourse, we succumb to the *idols of the market place:* the tyranny of words. Men fondly think that they are masters over their words but the latter, like the Tartar's bow, rebound to entangle their users in error. Words are made the substitute for things we do not understand, or are used to name nonexistent figments of our mind. Then we become disputatious over the consequences of names, instead of looking to their true originals, the individual instances in nature. Words can weave a self-sealing web around our minds, making it impossible to break through the circle of phantoms to an understanding of real things. Bacon's counsel is not to repudiate individual viewpoints and verbal communication but rather to submit both instruments to the discipline of a steady inquisition of the actual world.

Having criticized the natural condition of our mind in terms of the first three idols, Bacon then offers a refutation of philosophies and logical methods under the fourth heading: the *idols of the theater.* The prevalent philosophical systems belong to the theatrical sphere, since they are like stage plays that unroll before the mind plots of our own devising. The *three main schools* of philosophy are: the superstitious, the empirical, and the rational or sophistical. *Superstitious* or *theologistic* thinkers intermingle imaginative notions or theological considerations with philosophy, in order to form a fantastic doctrine. Appeal to transcendent entities, separated forms, final causes, and first movers, as grounds of explanation in natural philosophy, is characteristic of the thinking of Plato and the Schoolmen. Another variety is exemplified in men like Paracelsus and Robert Fludd, who base philosophy upon wild interpretations of Scripture. Bacon is convinced that the influence of theology and revealed religion is always disastrous for philosophy. The first condition of philosophical reform is a sharp separation of philosophy from any sort of theological reasoning. It is imprudent to hand over to faith not only what is faith's but also what is natural reason's. This becomes an accepted canon in modern philosophy.

The *empiricists* propound a second kind of philosophical system, whose main failure is to provide a due place for reason. This school is so anxious to gain immediate practical results through *fruit-bearing experiments* (practical research formally directed to particular, useful consequences) that it slights *light-bearing experiments* (the long-range speculative investigations of pure science), which carry in their train a whole troop of useful effects, rather than just a few. Bacon insists on the importance of the latter type of inquiry as a counterbalance to the narrow view of experience taken by the practicing scientists. Some "empirics" think that it is sufficient to plunge into wave after wave of experiment, but they only lose their bearings and never arrive at truly fruitful generalizations. Others plow a deep but narrow furrow in one special field and then extend its principles to all philosophical issues. A scientist like Gilbert is too ready to jump from a narrow sampling of facts about magnetism to the broadest speculations about cosmic spaces, interstellar vacuums, and a universal, magnetic force. Finally, the scientists usually remain at the level of appearances and fail to reach the determinative essence behind them. Hence Bacon remains neutral in the astronomical dispute between the Ptolemaics and the Copernicans, contending that both sides are able to explain the heavenly phenomena and that neither offers a decisive solution. He fails, however, to assess the Copernican claim to provide a mathematically simpler and more elegant account, since he does not acknowledge the mathematical standard of scientific explanation.

Aristotle and the Schoolmen embody the common fallacies of the *sophistical* or *rationalistic* school. This type of mind fails to dwell long enough on the level terrain of experience. It is impatient to make abstraction from particulars and form the most general concepts and axioms. The rationalists fail to see that our understanding needs the weights of a cautious study of individual facts rather than the wings of a priori reasoning. They use logical categories not to clarify experience but to force it into preconceived molds. Deductive reasoning predominates, while the experimental study of nature is kept at a minimum. The mind is held captive by metaphysical abstractions, centered around act and potency, matter and form. Bacon's criticism is directed mainly to the School philosophers at the English Universities who did not follow Aristotle in the cultivation of original scientific research. Bacon shows no awareness of a philosophical approach to nature which would be formally distinct from that of the experimental sciences and which would nevertheless not render the latter superfluous. Since he can make no sense out of an unformed matter and a potential principle as instruments in laboratory experiments, he ridicules their role in the Aristotelian interpretation of nature.

Bacon's refutation of the accepted *modes of demonstration* is continuous with his attack on the idol of the theater and also marks the transition from the destructive to the constructive part of his philosophy. He criticizes four traits of the traditional method of demonstration: its purpose, starting point, order, and form.[3] It is defective in *purpose,* since it is more concerned with winning dialectical victories over opponents by means of probable arguments than with achieving scientific certitude and practical control over nature. Because of its uncritical acceptance of the conventional stock of primary notions and the report of the untrained senses, Aristotelian logic relies upon imperfect premises or *starting points* for inference. The *order* with which it proceeds is also faulty. Ordinary logic begins with experience but it abandons the empirical terrain too hastily, without making a careful study of particular facts. Furthermore, it moves by a single bound from a few particulars to the most general principles and axioms, which it then employs in a deductive way to construct the middle axioms or those of lesser generality (the working laws of the sciences). By contrast, Bacon is suggesting that the ascent from particulars to general principles must be made in a gradual and uninterrupted fashion, so that the middle axioms will be derived inductively from an empirical basis, rather than deduced from purely abstract general principles. Hence the *form* of reasoning must be transformed from a primarily deductive one to an inductive one. However, Bacon criticizes the Aristotelians for relying too heavily upon induction by simple enumeration of instances and for paying exclusive attention to affirmative instances, to the neglect of negative ones and the process of rejection. He does not examine Aristotle's own strictures on enumerative induction or his use of other types of induction, especially that employed in the establishment of first principles of being. Nevertheless, Bacon acknowledges that Plato's method of definition by dichotomy is an adumbration of his own theory.

## 2. THE GREAT INSTAURATION. THE DIVISION OF THE SCIENCES

Bacon had a keen sense of his unique philosophical vocation, not only as the destroyer of ancient idols but also as the founder of a new order of things, practical as well as theoretical. He referred to himself as a true priest of the sense, as one whose mind bears a special affinity with the truth about nature. At the same time, he felt that the reform of knowledge inaugurated by himself was some-

---

[3] *The Great Instauration: The Plan of the Work* (Robertson, 248–50); *Novum Organum,* I, 69 (Robertson, 274).

thing inevitable, a birth of time and happy accident rather than of genius alone. Yet it would be a masculine birth of time, one that would fertilize the minds and institutions of men for generations to come. He named his project the *Great Instauration of Human Control in the Universe.* Its stated objective was to seek "whether that commerce between the mind of man and the nature of things, which is more precious than anything on earth, or at least than anything that is of the earth, might by any means be restored to its perfect and original condition."[4] Although finality was excluded from the scheme, Bacon's enthusiastic conviction rested upon a belief that mind and nature are mutually ordained and that the idols of the mind result from a violation of this teleology. The proper object of human inquiry and endeavor is nature; the latter is fitted to be known by us and used for our ends; any disturbance of this order is a perversion of the native tendencies of both mind and nature.

There are to be six phases in the Great Instauration: (1) The Division of the Sciences, (2) The New Organon or Logic, (3) The Phenomena of the Universe, (4) The Ladder of the Intellect, (5) The Forerunners or Anticipations of the New Philosophy, and (6) The New Philosophy or Active Science. Of this grandiose program, Bacon was able to complete only the first part and to make some contributions toward the second and third. Of the last three parts, he provided only the headings and brief hints of their content. By the *Ladder of the Intellect* is meant a collection of tables that would supply some models of the discoveries already made with the aid of the new method. These examples would be furnished, by way of encouragement along the road, to investigators using the method in their research. The *Forerunners* would comprise a description of genuine discoveries made through the ordinary exercise of reason, acting concretely without benefit of the new organon and its axiomatic knowledge. Bacon confessed that most of his own experimental findings were "anticipations" or "learned experience" of this unmethodic sort, rather than strict "interpretations" of nature carried out with the help of the new logic. Thus natural truths can be discovered independently of the new method but cannot be acquired surely and economically or organized into a body of scientific knowledge. Bacon did not even hope to write the *New Philosophy* itself,

---

[4] *The Great Instauration: Prooemium* (Robertson, 241). For the sixfold division of the *Instauratio Magna,* see *The Great Instauration: The Plan of the Work* (Robertson, 248–54).

for this is the task of subsequent thinkers. His role was that of a trumpeter, summoning others to give battle for the truth. Nevertheless, he was confident that his inductive logic supplied the indispensable instrument for successful completion of the *philosophia secunda*. In fact, he augured that this might be achieved in the space of a few years, provided that the inductive method and the directions for gathering the empirical data were followed.

These latter directions, together with the actual collections of facts, are the work of the third part of the Great Instauration. The inductive method cannot operate in a vacuum. It is essentially a procedure for evaluating empirical materials, and the purpose of the *Phenomena of the Universe* is to gather these materials in the form of natural histories. Bacon laid down numerous precepts for such compilations of natural phenomena. The descriptions are to be in a plain, unadorned style, such as that of aphorisms. Superstitions and unverified tales are to be excluded. Nature is to be described carefully and even with mathematical exactitude, where that is possible. The scope of natural history is wide enough to include nature's usual happenings, the exceptional events, and the results achieved through human arts that "vex" or experimentally control nature. But even very familiar and shameful things should be given notice, lest vital information be overlooked. Bacon's own collections of facts did not always adhere to these admirable canons. He made heroic but hasty efforts to fill in the outlines of a number of proposed histories, only to realize that the task as a whole lay beyond the ability of any one man to accomplish. The gathering of facts and the making of experiments and technical advances should be a "royal work," a collective enterprise receiving the support of the civil powers. The relations between science and society provided a favorite theme of Bacon's Utopian ruminations, culminating in his picture of the House of Solomon (described in the *New Atlantis*), a sort of subsidized university and technological institute.

The one section of his project that Bacon completed to his own satisfaction is the *Classification of the Sciences*. Like the encyclopedists and positivists of a later period, he recognized that this theme is no mere perfunctory task but rather the first major step in the reconstitution of knowledge. His remarks on classification had both a polemical edge and a bearing upon the problem of scientific method. He suggested that a *subjective* difference among the chief faculties of the mind (memory, imagination, and reason) provides the broadest principle of division for the fields of human learning. The basic disciplines are: *history* (in which memory predominates), *poetry* (in which imagination predominates), and *philosophy* (in which reason plays the leading role). History studies individuals, "the impressions whereof are the first and most ancient guests of the human mind, and are as the primary material of knowledge."[5] History may be natural or civil, depending upon whether it recalls the works of nature or human deeds. Natural history collects natural facts either for the sake of amassing factual information or as an aid to induction. The difference between poetic imagination and reason is one between a lawless faculty, that can compose and divide individual impressions according to the mind's good pleasure, and a faculty that must respect the actual structure of natural things. Reason combines and divides the facts in order to form general notions, but these general notions bear a relation to objective patterns in nature. Once the mind is purged through the doctrine of the idols, Bacon raised no questions about the direct reception of impressions from

### BACON'S DIVISION OF THE SCIENCES

1. History — memory.
2. Poetry — imagination.
3. Philosophy — reason.
   a) Philosophy of God, Natural Theology.
   b) Philosophy of Man.
      1) Man as an individual.
         (a) The undivided composite of body and mind.
         (b) The divided state of man (body and mind considered separately).
      2) Man in society: communication, business, government.
   c) Philosophy of Nature.
      1) Speculative Philosophy of Nature.
         (a) Physics: mutable (material and efficient) causes.
         (b) Metaphysics: immutable (formal and final) causes.
      2) Practical or Operative Philosophy of Nature.
         (a) Mechanical arts.
         (b) Natural magic.
4. Other sciences: Sacred Theology, *Philosophia Prima*, Mathematics.

---

[5] *A Description of the Intellectual Globe,* I (Robertson, 677); Chapters I and III of this work set forth the divisions of human learning, with stress on the varieties of history. For the divisions of philosophy, see *Of the Proficience and Advancement of Learning,* II (Robertson, 89–101); translation of *De Dignitate et Augmentis Scientiarum,* III–IV (Robertson, 453–98).

individual entities or about reason's ability to conform with an independent order of reality. His realism was relatively untroubled by epistemological doubts, so confident was he of the directive power of his method.

*Philosophy* is predominantly a work of natural reason, and only here is the ideal of scientific knowledge fully realized. As a natural discipline, it excludes any data of revelation and any influence of sacred theology. Under the latter heading, Bacon includes not only what Christian theologians called strictly supernatural truths (such as the Trinity and Incarnation) but also all references to God's nature considered in itself, the argument to an infinite first mover, and any speculation concerning the origin, nature, and destiny of man's rational soul. Thus he eliminates from philosophical discussion numerous issues which were the central concern of Scholastic metaphysics and philosophy of man and nature.

In the natural order, the human mind operates with the aid of a threefold illumination. Its direct light is focused upon nature, its reflected light upon man himself, and its refracted light upon God. These three objects constitute the *three branches* of philosophical science: the philosophies of nature, man, and God. By the philosophy of God is meant natural rather than sacred theology. But since so much of what traditionally fell under the natural, philosophic study of God is relegated by Bacon to sacred theology, his conception of *natural theology* leads to an extremely constricted and impoverished discipline. It depends upon a weak illumination refracted from nature in our minds. Nature does not contain God's true image but only certain faint traces of His presence. Hence philosophy can tell us absolutely nothing about the divine essence in itself or about the intrinsic will and decree of God. It is even impossible to argue causally to His existence, since He produces every causal series and yet remains completely above all causes and effects. Nevertheless, it can be gathered somehow that God does exist and that He is all-powerful and provident. This is enough, remarks Bacon, to refute atheism and yet not enough to establish the claims of any particular religion. Although this is an effective way to forestall the *odium theologicum,* it leaves us without any specific way of proving God's existence, since inferences to a first cause and infinite being have been declared out of bounds, by definition. It was left for Hobbes to underline the agnostic implications of Bacon's deliberately vague teaching on the scope of natural theology.

In his *philosophy of man,* Bacon is less polemical and less original. It has two major subdivisions, dealing with man the individual and man in society. The former part treats of the individual man either as an undivided composite of mind and body or in his divided state, wherein mind and body are given separate consideration. Social man is studied in the light of the three occupations involving the group: communication, business, and government. The most important statement dealing with man concerns the separate treatment of the human mind. Bacon holds that man possesses a twofold soul, rational and sensible. The rational soul differs in kind from that of the brute. However, since Scripture says that God breathes the rational soul directly into us, its origin, nature, and destiny lie beyond the competence of philosophy and can only be settled by sacred theology. Once more, the traditional scope of philosophy is being narrowed down to exclude nonmaterial modes of being. Philosophy of man studies only the sensible soul, which is similar in man and brutes and can, therefore, be subjected to empirical analysis. Without explaining the assertion, Bacon nevertheless maintains that at least the rational powers of understanding and will do come within the ken of philosophy, thus providing a basis for the study of grammar, rhetoric, and ethics. He remains quite unconcerned, however, about any epistemological or metaphysical problems that might be raised concerning a theory of two souls and of two sets of powers in man.

Philosophical speculation is gradually concentrated upon a *philosophy of nature* from which all questions about a first mover, last end, and immaterial soul have been eliminated. The direct light of our mind beams upon material nature as its proper and exclusive object. To this reality we are proportioned, and in a study of it we are most at home. A working division is set up between speculative and practical or operative philosophy of nature, but it is abundantly evident that this is made only for the sake of clear exposition. There is but a single philosophy of nature, of which the speculative and practical divisions are phases or moments. In general, philosophy of nature is concerned with the real causes of things. The *speculative* moment in this discipline studies the natural causes for the sake of the knowledge itself; the *practical* aspect has regard primarily for the use to which this causal knowledge can be put in establishing control over nature, for human purposes. Apart from a reliable basis in the speculative knowledge of causes, there can be no adequate control over nature, but conversely, our knowledge of nature is not perfected until it is formally directed toward practical operations or use. Like Galileo and Newton, Bacon tries to synthesize the speculative and technical aspects in a single philosophy of nature, which is both a contemplation of natural order and an art of manipulating this order for utilitarian ends.[6]

The *speculative* side of Baconian philosophy of nature centers around the investigation of the four causes, which are divided into the *mutable* causes (the material and the efficient) and the *immutable* causes (the formal and the final). This provides a principle of division for the two main parts of the speculative philosophy of nature: physics (in the narrower sense) and metaphysics. *Physics* studies the mutable causes, whereas *metaphysics* seeks after the immutable ones. Bacon retains the traditional terminology of the four causes, as a matter of policy, but he empties the causal doctrine entirely of its metaphysical content. An exclusively physicalistic interpretation is given to the four causes. The material cause is always identified with some actual, particular stuff; the efficient cause is confined to the technique for producing local motion and some qualitative changes; the formal cause is never examined apart from its material embodiments. As for the final cause, Bacon terms it a sterile virgin in philosophy. In physical investigations, it is quite barren of results and has no proper use. Bacon is more interested in banishing it from natural philosophy than in assigning it any positive role. After its original enumeration among the immutable causes, it disappears from sight, as far as Baconian metaphysics is concerned. Finality is carefully restricted to the sphere of human actions or morality.

A kind of *first philosophy* is also recognized, in contradistinction to both metaphysics and natural theology. Its only content would be provided by certain axioms common to several sciences (e.g., "things that are equal to the same are equal to each other" is an axiom of mathematics that is also used in logic) and by certain relative but extrinsic or nonformal essences (such as indefinite quantity, likeness, diversity, and possibility). *Mathematics* is also given a place, but only as a subordinate instrument of natural philosophy. It aids in the exact physical determination of "how much," and to that extent is useful in making experiments more precise and in cataloguing the results.

---

[6] For emphasis upon the latter aspect, consult the section entitled "Empiriological Physics is Primarily Art, Not Science," in V. E. Smith, *Philosophical Physics* (New York, Harper, 1950), 162–69; also, 172–77.

But Bacon thoroughly distrusted any primarily mathematical interpretation of nature and hence never appreciated the leading role of mathematical hypotheses in the systems of Copernicus and Galileo.[7] He commended mathematical reasoning rather for its precision and psychological value, as a sharpener of our wits, than for giving us access to the structure of things.

Philosophy of nature is consummated in its *practical* or *operative* phase, where application is made of the causal knowledge gathered precisely with a view to operation. There are two divisions of practical philosophy of nature: *mechanics* as a continuation of physics in the narrower sense, and *natural magic* as the operative continuation of metaphysics. Just as physics and metaphysics are related as a less and a more general study of natural causes, so mechanics and natural magic are related as a less and a more general set of practical rules. He who can mechanically manipulate nature in terms of its material and efficient causes, can produce a limited range of effects; but he who can "magically" manipulate it in terms of its formal causes, is able to achieve the more universal effects. Bacon derides the ordinary view of magic, since it has no basis in a metaphysical study of forms. But he agrees with Telesio (the Italian philosopher of nature) that an understanding of the universal desires and affections of matter, as expressed in the form, is the cornerstone of human control over the whole of nature. Bacon stands midway between the Renaissance and the strictly modern attitude toward nature.

### 3. THE NEW ORGANON

#### *a*) THE INDUCTION OF FORMS

Bacon hailed his new logic as the ground of reconciliation between the empiricists, who exalt nature and experience, and the rationalists, who make reason and universal concepts supreme. If the bond between nature and mind is to be restored, it must issue from "a true and lawful marriage in perpetuity between the empirical and the rational faculty."[8] We may liken the empiricists to *ants:* they store away their

---

[7] Mathematics ought to remain the handmaid of physics and "only to give definiteness to natural philosophy, not to generate or give it birth." *Novum Organum,* I, 96 (Robertson, 288). A sympathetic explanation of Bacon's distrust of mathematically inspired theories of nature, as being nonempirical constructs, is given by J. Storck, "Francis Bacon and Contemporary Philosophical Difficulties," *The Journal of Philosophy,* XXVIII (1931), 169–86.

[8] *The Great Instauration: Author's Preface* (Robertson, 246); the simile of the ants, spiders, and bees is used in *Novum Organum,* I, 95 (Robertson, 288).

particular impressions, just as they are received, and then live off their capital, without ever having risen above particular causes and notions to a generalized view. The rationalists resemble *spiders,* since they spin out fine systems from their own entrails, with results that are cleverly wrought but lacking in any real foundation in nature. The happy marriage of the two attitudes is symbolized in the activities of *bees,* which rely upon materials from the outside and yet transform them through their own internal power. The new method aims to combine fidelity to experience with rational analysis, leading to well-founded general notions and forms. This goal of combining reason with experience, generality with concrete particularity, has served as a lodestone for a good many modern philosophers, howsoever strongly they may disagree with Bacon's personal solution.

Bacon assures us that we may safely take *plus ultra* as our motto in our voyage of discovery around the intellectual globe. We may be confident of reuniting mind and nature, once we have fitted mind with an adequate instrument. Just as the ruler and compass enable the hand to achieve results it could scarcely attain by itself, so the new logical *method* is the *mind's machine* for securing undreamed-of victories over nature. Bacon takes a mechanical view of the new logic, promising that its effect will be to level minds to the same plane and compensate for the lack of native genius. Everyone who heeds its precepts will be master of nature's secrets. The method itself is thus destined to become one of mankind's common goods, just as its purpose is to improve mankind's common estate and magnify the glory of God.

*Induction* is the only method that can realize these aims.[9] It allows for both an experiential and a rational moment in the genesis of knowledge. It does not proceed exclusively from one set of experiments to another, and neither does it consist only in a deduction from principles. Rather, the inductive process includes both an *ascent* from experience to principles and a *descent* from principles to new practical consequences. The ascent is a gradual and uninterrupted one, for it avoids bounding at once from a few particular data to universal axioms and seeks to make an unbroken, continuous approach to generality of statement. The middle axioms or statements of intermediate generality are not deduced from primary principles

---

[9] There is a general description of the inductive process in *Novum Organum,* I, 98–107 (Robertson, 289–91).

but are reached through a mounting expansion of less general meanings. Only at the end of the inductive ascent do we finally arrive at the most general axioms. These basic propositions are perfectly general without being hasty generalizations; they are abstracted from experience without being mere abstractions, generated by imagination. After the road upward to the highest axioms is successfully traveled, the downward process can begin. Here, there is opportunity for making deductions and, above all, for applying our knowledge to immediate practical projects for man's benefit.

Use and action provide the pragmatic criteria of scientific knowledge. The fruits of knowledge manifest its truth as well as its profitableness. Bacon does not assert that because axioms are practically profitable they must be true, but that those axioms which remain sterile are certainly untrue. His famous sentence that "human *knowledge* and human *power* meet in one,"[10] rests on the view that induction eventually leads to a knowledge of forms, and that forms are the only true causes of natural events. On this supposition, a purported principle that had no practical import would be suspect, even in the theoretical order. For there would be a presumption that the so-called principle did not express a formal cause and hence was not a general source of knowledge at all. What is *causal knowledge* from the speculative standpoint is a *rule of action* from the practical standpoint. Because these two aspects are continuous phases in the same inductive process, truth and utility are bound to coincide. Man must obey nature before he can command it: unless he submits to the given facts, he can never acquire an understanding of the formal causes at work in nature and hence can never regulate the principles of production of natural effects. Man is the interpreter of nature, so that he may exploit its laws; he is the servant of nature, so that he may establish his dominion therein. These thoughts underlie Bacon's efforts to break down the distinction between speculative and practical philosophy, science, and art. Knowledge is power, because it is pre-eminently a true grasp of the forms that control natural processes.

For detailed justification of his conception of induction, Bacon relies upon the theory of natures and forms. The axioms or scientific propositions that guide practical action are composed of terms, which themselves express well-founded notions in the mind. In turn, these

---

[10] *Novum Organum*, I, 3 (Robertson, 259; italics mine); cf. *ibid.*, I, 124 (Robertson, 298).

notions are arrived at inductively and are true models of the world. When a material object strikes our senses, it produces in us a number of impressions. These mental impressions are founded upon the objective *natures* or appearances that comprise the thing itself, insofar as it is referred to the human knower. The natures are the traits which the thing manifests to our mind. These natures are either *simple* (the various qualities, considered separately) or *complex* (the totality of qualities, considered as constituting the body or material substance). Gold, for instance, is a complex unity of appearances, composed of such simple natures as yellowness, heaviness, ductility, and solidity of a certain sort. An inductive study of natures is carried out by physics, both concrete and abstract or philosophical. *Concrete physics* describes the given bodies or complex natures in their concrete and individual character. Induction requires these concrete descriptions of the complex wholes met with in experience, but it cannot remain satisfied with an account of particular traits in their infinite variety. Some generalization and classification must be made, with the aid of *abstract* or *philosophical physics*. Its interests are mainly centered upon the simple natures, considered by themselves and in their general structure. Bacon assumes that the number of basic simple natures is finite and that, from their composition, an infinite number of particular bodies can be constituted. Philosophical physics constructs its empirically grounded, abstract and general notions on the basis of the simple natures, drawn from experience. The process of inductive generalization and legitimate abstraction gradually becomes more and more comprehensive, until at last it attains to the truly "radical and formative natures,"[11] the forms themselves. But the apprehension of the forms is reserved for metaphysics, operating on the foundation of the generalized simple natures provided by physics.

Bacon strives, without complete success, to clarify what he means by *form*. His difficulty lies in the fact that he employs many Scholastic terms to state a doctrine that is, from a Scholastic viewpoint, a physical rather than a metaphysical one. In respect to forms, he would like to retain the advantages of a Scholastic theory of knowledge, without accepting the liability of a Scholastic theory of being.

---

[11] *Valerius Terminus,* XI (Robertson, 199); an inductive approach to the form of whiteness is discussed in this chapter. On the natures and forms, read *Novum Organum,* II, 2–5 (Robertson, 302–05); *Of the Proficience and Advancement of Learning,* II (Robertson, 94–96); translation of *De Dignitate et Augmentis Scientiarum,* III, 4 (Robertson, 460–71).

Negatively, he insists that there are no subsistent, universal forms or essences, a position which he considers to be the common Scholastic one. The form is inseparable from its material base and, in the natural order, only individual bodies exist. But the natures constituting bodies do act and change according to fixed laws. Philosophy of nature studies these laws in themselves and in their general import for various embodiments of the natures in question. The form, then, is identical with the *fixed law of action* governing the changes in bodily appearances. Since it regulates the particular appearances that constitute the body for us, form can also be called the thing itself in its innermost constitution or *essential nature*. And because the differences between one body and another are due ultimately to the different laws determining their various properties, the form also has the right to be designated as the *specific difference* of the body.

The relation between the form and the given natures is stated sometimes causally and sometimes logically (but never mathematically, as a precise, quantitative function). In *causal* terms, the form is referred to as the *natura naturans* or *fons emanationis,* from which the sensible natures flow. It would be thus a sort of formal cause, having the collection of sensible appearances as a consequence. To grasp the form is, therefore, to grasp an unfailing set of operational directions for producing certain effects in nature. The totality of forms constitutes an immutable and *eternal order,* that determines the ordinary course of nature and that can be perceived and utilized only by reason, fortified by the proper method. Elsewhere, Bacon underlines the *logical* significance of form. It enables the mind to connect the particular data with a more general nature, present in several individual natures and intrinsically more intelligible than the individual instances. Induction seeks to define a given nature in respect to another nature (the form itself) which, in turn, is seen to be a specific limitation of a yet more general nature or genus. The particulars find their specific difference in the form, whereas the form points to a more inclusive genus, of which it is the specifying determinant. When heat is defined as expansive and restrictive motion, the simple nature of heat is thus referred to the genus motion by means of the form or specific difference, which is motion of this expansive and restrictive sort. This does not mean that motion generates heat but that heat in its essence *is* nothing other than motion existing under these specifying and limiting conditions. The form is our access to the essence of heat, taken as the actual appearance of a certain type of motion. There is thus a fluctuation in Bacon's mind between a logical and a causal view of form as the defining principle. This would fit in with his theory of speculative and practical phases of induction, if it could be shown that knowledge of form as a specific determinant of a genus places in our hands directions about the causal power governing bodily appearances. Bacon, however, assumes rather than establishes this point.

The relation between *metaphysics* and *physics* can now be restated in terms of forms and natures. Physics seeks to determine the more restricted kinds of simple natures, comprised of the schematisms of matter and the varieties of simple motion. The *schematisms* are types of material qualities (such as dense and rare, hot and cold, volatile and fixed) that are widespread in things and that affect their production. The simple *types of motion* (including resistance, congregation, and excitation) are combined to yield the moving forces, regulative of all material changes. By discovering both the type of material schematism and the motion involved, the physicist arrives at the simple natures combining to make a body. This knowledge places him in a position to produce substances similar in appearance to those in nature, which is as good as being able to produce the original things themselves. Indeed, the products of human art and of nature differ only in respect to their efficient cause: man in the one case, and God in the other.

All "light-bearing" experiments seek to enhance our knowledge of simple natures. Now, there are various degrees of comprehensiveness among simple natures. Physics deals with those that are relatively restricted in scope and variable in operation. But there is an ascending series of natures, culminating in a few most general natures or forms. The latter constitute the alphabet of the elements of the world, the fundamental and universal principles by the combination of which all material bodies are constituted and all changes effected. Metaphysics brings the inductive process to a climax by attaining to these *alphabetic forms*. This metaphysical comprehension of forms assures philosophy of its three distinctive traits: unity, certainty, and liberty. A knowledge of the universal forms gives *unity,* since the forms are the highest syntheses of natural elements; *certainty,* since the forms provide effective and unfailing directions for producing things; *liberty,* since the forms are universal and confined within no particular material schematism or process. Natural magic or the operative face of metaphysics manifests the truth of the induction of forms by actually securing man's empire over nature.

## *b*) Aids to Induction

Human knowledge may be likened to a pyramid. Its broad base is supplied by the facts gathered in the several natural histories. Physics rests upon this empirical foundation and constitutes the middle portion of the pyramid, the middle axioms reaching from particular experiences to more general natures. The apex of the pyramid is the locus of metaphysics, since knowledge culminates in the apprehension of the forms. Whether the very pinnacle can be reached through a summary law of all phenomena is a troublesome question for Bacon. The major obstacles are furnished by the infinity of particular facts and the obscurity of experience. To overcome these difficulties, Bacon proposes a number of aids to the senses, memory, and understanding. Scientific instruments and the rules for compilation of natural history enable the *senses* to master the mass of facts to be described. *Memory* is served by the precept of writing down our findings and arranging them in tables for constant review. Induction itself is the tool of *reason* in its quest of forms. Some of the more particular means of furthering induction are listed by Bacon in considerable detail. Among these, the three tables of induction are most important as assuring an orderly arrangement of instances for the understanding. The use of these tables is illustrated by a sample definition of heat which is offered as a first vintage or hypothesis supplied by the true method of interpreting nature.

The *tables of induction* enable the mind to sift out the relevant facts bearing on a specific inquiry.[12] They perform this function in virtue of the relation already established between the form and the simple nature it controls. This relation suggests that when a given nature is present, its proper form will also be present; that when the nature is absent, its form will be absent; that variations in the nature will correspond to variations in the form. Thus there are three tables of induction: the table of *essence* or *presence,* the table of *deviation* or *absence,* and the table of *comparison* or *degrees.* With their help, the mind can reduce facts to a manageable condition and order. In seeking the form or essence of *heat,* for instance, the investigation begins with a listing of those natures which are present along with heat in our ordinary experience of appearances. These include the rays of the sun, ignited substances, boiling liquids, and the bodies of animals. Then, it is necessary to note down cases of proximate

---

12 *Novum Organum,* II, 10–19 (Robertson, 307–23).

relevance in which there is no heat. Thus the moon's rays, cold flames, unheated liquids, and cold-blooded animals would provide significant data of a negative sort. Finally, account is to be taken of proportional changes of heat along with such phenomena as increased friction or increased muscular exertion.

On this basis, one can then eliminate from the list of possible forms of heat those natures which are absent when heat is present, or present when heat is absent, or which remain unaffected under conditions of increase or decrease of heat. These exclusions are distinguishing marks of the new inductive technique, preserving the mind from the fallacy of drawing conclusions solely from affirmative cases and immediate experience. "Then indeed after the rejection and exclusion have been duly made, there will remain at the bottom, all light opinions vanishing into smoke, a form affirmative, solid and true and well-defined. This is quickly said; but the way to come at it is winding and intricate."[13] In the case of heat, we are left with the form of motion, differentiated by being an expansive movement in an upward direction, in which the smaller parts of the body are agitated and yet restrained. This first vintage of a definition was the only specific application Bacon was able to make of his method, apart from passing references to the nature of whiteness. Its scientific value was negligible and its theoretical status within his thought was left undetermined. It indicated the direction of his search for small particles or atomic constituents of matter, but its precise degree of approach to an ultimate resolution of matter was not measured.

Bacon's tables of induction and other aids to the understanding anticipate in a rough way the canons of scientific inquiry later proposed by Mill. No precise comparison is possible, however, since Bacon's view of induction is bound up with a metaphysics of form-and-nature which is entirely foreign to Mill and the scientific practices he had in mind. Bacon still believed that the mind can attain to some domain of necessary essences, to an eternal, immutable, and rational order of natural causes, from which generalizations can be made. Because these claims were of no use in scientific investigations, they were discarded by later scientists and philosophers. They found no way to test Bacon's assumptions that the basic forms are few in number and that there is a causal, as well as logical, connection between immutable forms and the sensible natures given in experience. His

---

[13] *Ibid.*, II, 16 (Robertson, 320); the hypothesis about heat is presented in *Novum Organum*, II, 20 (Robertson, 323–27).

general plea for the inductive and experimental approach met with warm response, however, even after its theoretical underpinnings were rejected. This combined enthusiasm for Bacon's empirical attitude and disregard for his detailed theories is reflected in William Harvey's famous gibe that Bacon wrote science like a lord chancellor, rather than like a practicing scientist. Hume voiced the common criticism made by subsequent thinkers, when he observed that we must turn from Bacon to Galileo and Newton in order to appreciate the pre-dominance of mathematical reasoning and hypotheses in modern science. Bacon did not entirely ignore these procedures, but he failed to give mathematics a central role and to formulate an unequivocal theory about the nature of scientific hypotheses, especially mathe-matically controlled hypotheses.

Perhaps the most far-reaching of Bacon's particular achievements was the restriction of philosophy to the study of nature, taken as the proper and adequate object of our intelligence. Another hint that slowly germinated among naturalistic thinkers was his convic-tion that the same method elaborated for the physical and meta-physical interpretation of material nature can also be extended, in principle, to the domain of human psychology and ethics. Finally, his definition of body or material substance as a collection of simple natures or appearances opened the way for a thoroughly phenome-nalistic conception of material things as the sum of their sensible traits. Whatever the metaphysical claims made for the Baconian form, it is only a prolongation of the simple natures attained by abstract, philosophical physics. Since Bacon regarded metaphysics as nothing more than the culminating moment in philosophy of nature itself, he set the stage for describing the essence and existential unity of things in terms of their sensible appearances alone.

## B. *Galileo Galilei*

Galileo Galilei (born 1564) entered the university of his native Pisa in 1581, with the intention of becoming a physician. But a chance encounter with the mathematical sciences determined him in the latter direction. His advance in mathematical and physical studies was very rapid. During his professorship at the University of Pisa (1589-1591), he made many fundamental discoveries in dynamics. He became intimately acquainted with the advanced Aristotelian physics and scientific methodology being taught at the University of Padua, where he himself served as professor of mathematics from

1592 until 1610. The year 1610 was important in his development, for several reasons. The previous year, he had learned about the invention of the telescope in the Netherlands and immediately succeeded in constructing a much more powerful type. With its help, he was able to observe the craters on the surface of the moon, as well as Jupiter's moons. He now began to profess the Copernican view openly, whereas previously he had continued to teach the older astronomy, out of fear of ridicule. He reported his empirical findings in *The Sidereal Message* (1610), which suggested that all the heavenly bodies are constituted of the same sort of matter as the earth. In the same year, he transferred to the University of Florence and thus came much closer to the power of the Roman Inquisition. During a visit to Rome (1615–1616), Galileo was informed by Cardinal Bellarmine, in the name of the Holy Office, that he could neither hold nor defend as demonstrated truths the central position of the sun, its immobility, and the motion of the earth. These views might be entertained as hypotheses and a demonstration for them sought, but Galileo was asked to promise not to teach and disseminate the new theory in any way. Having given his promise, he returned to his work at Florence. In 1623, he wrote a treatise on the comets, *The Assayer,* in which he attacked the views of the conservative astronomers. Finally, in 1632, he published the *Dialogue on the Two Main Systems of the World*. In this dialogue, the representative of the Ptolemaic theory is made to appear ridiculous and all the evidence is shown to lodge with the exponent of Copernicanism (although Galileo's actual demonstrations were faulty ones). The following year, Galileo was summoned to Rome for breaking his previous promise. He recanted before the Holy Office (1633), was condemned and imprisoned, under comfortable circumstances, first in the Duke of Tuscany's villa at Roma, then with his friend, the Archbishop of Siena, and finally at his own villa in Arcetri and house in Florence. Among other distinguished visitors, he received Thomas Hobbes and John Milton. Galileo continued to make investigations in the field of mechanics, completing his basic treatise on dynamics: *Discourses and Mathematical Demonstrations* (or, more briefly, *Dialogues*) concerning *Two New Sciences* (1638). By this time, Galileo was totally blind but he continued to work, with the aid of assistants, until his death in 1642.

When someone once reminded Galileo of the Grecian oracle's reply that Socrates alone was wise, because he alone was aware of his ignorance, Galileo observed that the truth about the human mind lay in avoiding any extreme position. Our mind is certainly not omniscient and yet neither is it totally incapable of attaining truth. By comparison with the divine mind, we know nothing, and nevertheless the few things we do know about nature are genuine truths. This response characterizes Galileo's sturdy confidence in the human intellect, together with his recognition that it is measured by its object in nature as well as by its divine source and exemplar. Although he never wrote a formal philosophical treatise, he was tremendously interested in the problem of the nature and grounds of knowledge, as exemplified in his own scientific discoveries.[14] His reflections on the scientific method were eagerly read by philosophers of his century as constituting a specially authoritative witness to the ways of scientific research. He himself related these methodological ideas to a metaphysics, upon which they seemed ultimately to rest.

The scientific mind is *realistic* in a twofold way, according to Galileo.[15] It accepts the independent existence of the natural world and also affirms our ability to know this world in some degree. Galileo liked to repeat the apothegm that nature comes first, our names and attributes for things second. We should not pretend that God first created the human intellect and then made the world in conformity with it. Quite the reverse: God first brought forth the world and then gave us an intellect fitted to conform with the world. Consequently, the true philosopher is he who opens his eyes enough to read the great book of nature, rather than he who looks only at the books of previous philosophers. In his correspondence with Kepler and others, Galileo often made fun of the timid Aristotelians, who were steeped in their master's text but afraid to confront Aristotle's own master — nature itself. He reported the case of one Peripatetic who was present at an anatomical exhibition, at which the nerves were traced experimentally to their source in the brain, and who yet refused to believe the evidence because it con-

---

14 For convenience, Galileo's philosophical views are cited mainly from *Discoveries and Opinions of Galileo,* edited by S. Drake, and cited hereafter as: Drake, *Discoveries.* Consult also the texts given in E. A. Burtt's *The Metaphysical Foundations of Modern Physical Science,* 61-95. Two good introductory studies on Galileo are contained in *The Philosophical Review,* LII (1943): A. Koyré, "Galileo and the Scientific Revolution of the Seventeenth Century," 333-48; L. Olschki, "Galileo's Philosophy of Science," 349-65.

15 For his mathematical realism or objectivism, see Drake, *Discoveries,* 92, 237-238.

tradicted the written opinion of Aristotle. Galileo himself was repeatedly unsuccessful in persuading the Peripatetic professor of philosophy at the University of Padua to look through a telescope, the gentleman either fearing to find some contrary data about the moon and planets or deeming the use of such instruments to be unnecessary for his system. Indeed, the Aristotelians considered themselves to be the real empiricists and looked askance at Galileo's use of mathematical calculations and specialized instruments to demonstrate natural conclusions.

The main difference between the old and the new philosophy of nature lay not in particular discoveries but in conflicting notions about *demonstration* and *method*. The current Peripatetic textbooks in natural philosophy had relaxed considerably Aristotle's own rigorous standards of demonstration. They abounded in merely dialectical or probable arguments, appeals to authority, unverified stories, conjectures, and loose comparisons. Galileo contended that these features were out of place in a strictly demonstrative science. If a science aims at truth, then it should conform with the conditions prevailing in nature. Now in nature, nothing is ambiguously or probably existent: either it exists in a determinate way or does not exist at all. Similarly, there is no room in a rigorous philosophy of nature for mere conjecture, probability, or the other customary techniques. Either there is genuine demonstration of the necessity of objects or there is only paralogistic reasoning. Philosophical demonstration must take as its motto *aut Caesar aut nihil*: it must either succeed in uncovering the necessary connections among things or fail entirely to be demonstration. The elimination of *probability* from philosophical reasoning about nature is a fundamental Galilean proposal that is accepted by modern classical physics. It goes hand in hand with a philosophical rejection of the Aristotelian notion of prime matter and a description of bodies exclusively in function of extension and local motion.

Aristotelian logic is an excellent tool for analyzing the forms of thought and giving consistent proofs of truths already discovered, but it cannot advance the original finding of truths about nature. It is exclusively a logic of *exposition,* whereas what is most needed is a logic of *discovery.* Men will find the latter not in the logic textbooks but in the mathematical ones, which alone give increase to our knowledge of nature. Whereas Bacon made of mathematics an appendix of physics rather than its source, Galileo hailed mathematics as the fruitful principle of all scientific progress. He could appeal to his own development of mechanics as proof of the advances made through the application of mathematics to natural phenomena. The free fall of bodies and the motion of projectiles, for instance, can be given a scientific demonstration as soon as they are analyzed, respectively, with the aid of the mathematical formula for uniform acceleration and the theory of parabolic curves. Moreover, mathematical demonstrations concerning further implications of these physical events can be made even in advance of observation of the actual facts. Observations and experiments provide a marvelous verification of mathematical predictions about the motions of bodies.

There are two indispensable preliminaries to the scientific method: sensation and doubt. The *senses* reveal the *(an sit,)* the fact of the existence of some natural phenomenon. Initially, there is only this uncriticized experience, this factual registering of the physical presence of an event. But our mind is never satisfied with the bare statement *that* something is: it tends to raise the further question of the *(quomodo sit,)* the *how* a thing is. The Aristotelians were interested mainly in making a passage from the *that* to the *what* and *wherefore* of a thing's nature. Galileo, on the other hand, restricts scientific inquiry to the *how,* since this is equivalent to a mathematical description of the object's movement in space and time. The office of *doubt* is to urge the intellect onward to more adequate formulations of this mechanistic description. ("In philosophy, doubt is father of invention, making way for the discovery of the truth."[16]) All appeals to occult, qualitative forces or to teleological reasons for motion are to be placed under doubt and excluded from scientific consideration, since they cannot be given mathematical demonstration. Doubt prepares for the quantitative explanation given by reason and keeps the mind resolute, even when this rational explanation seems to do violence to the evidences of the senses, as in the case of the Copernican theory of the earth's motion.

## GALILEO'S SCIENTIFIC METHODOLOGY

1. Sensation: an *sit?*
2. Doubt: quomodo sit?
3. Resolution, reduction, analysis.
4. Composition, deduction, synthesis.
5. Experimental verification.

---

16 Text given in V. De Ruvo, *Il problema della verità,* 86. On his method, cf. the unpublished master's thesis by T. P. McTighe, *The Nature of Method and Its Place in the System of Galileo* (St. Louis University, 1952).

There are three steps in the scientific approach to a problem: resolution, composition, and experiment. In outlining these phases, Galileo skillfully interwove elements drawn from the modified Aristotelian logic developed by Zabarella and others at Padua with the mathematical procedures of contemporary astronomy and mechanics.[17] The first stage is called the *method of resolution* or *reduction*.  Its function is to liberate the object under investigation from any impediments of concrete matter. The object is stripped of its qualitative traits and resolved into its mathematically definable quantitative components. Sense experience and practical experiments serve to guide the resolutive method, whenever there are alternate ways of defining the object. Thus several analyses could possibly be made of the projectile's motion in terms of the various types of curves known to pure mathematics. The testimony of the senses tells us that the projectile actually describes the path of a parabola and not another type of curve. Reason formulates the definition of the projectile's motion, but does so in the light of what is perceived actually to occur in nature. The resolutive process terminates in an intuitively grasped truth: either in a self-evident mathematical proposition about the behavior of the body or in some principle that bears on the issue and has been proved elsewhere. Only then can the second phase or the *method of composition* begin to operate. Here the deductive power of mathematics holds full sway. The structure of the object is recomposed in a necessary way out of its mathematical elements, and its further consequences are explicated. Once the definitions have been established resolutively from sense experience, the scientist may confidently make inferences that obtain for the physical world, as well as for an abstract mathematical system. This compositive or deductive reasoning provides natural philosophy with strict demonstrations.

The twofold process of resolution and composition can be restated in more traditional terms. Natural philosophy begins with sense perception of the effects and works back to a knowledge of the causes. Our empirical acquaintance with the effects is initially confused and

---

[17] For the Paduan background and Galileo's connection with one medieval tradition in dynamics, cf. J. H. Randall, Jr., "The Development of Scientific Method in the School of Padua," *Journal of the History of Ideas*, I (1940), 177–206; E. A. Moody, "Galileo and Avempace," *ibid.*, XII (1951), 163–93, 375–422. Moody also summarizes the researches on the Oxford and Paris schools made by the German scholar, Annaliese Maier.

inadequate, so that from the effects we can acquire only an indistinct knowledge of their causes — such knowledge as artisans and other "men of experience" have. *Reductive analysis* on the part of the mind is needed to give a clear conception of the causes of the given physical events. Once the causes or quantitative elements are known with mathematical clarity, then the mind may return to the effects by a *compositive synthesis*. Knowing the causes, we may now know in a distinct and precise way the nature of the effects as that which must follow, once such quantitative principles are posited. This causal knowledge of effects is a mathematical description of their local motion (of which all other sorts of motion are variants) and hence is a reliable demonstration.

If the type of prediction attained through compositive reasoning is strictly demonstrative, the third step in scientific method — *the experimental verification* — is apparently superfluous. Galileo approaches this difficulty from two angles. First of all, it is correct that no further recourse to experience is strictly needed in order to establish the truth of the scientific inference. Considered *in itself,* the inference is not a mere hypothesis or probable argument, for it partakes of the necessity of nature itself. Second, one may regard the compositive or synthetic method not in itself and its intrinsic cogency but *in its persuasive effect* upon various minds. Many men are unable to follow mathematical demonstrations; others can follow particular demonstrations but have no notion of the mathematical character of all natural processes; still others are convinced that all premises and definitions are arbitrarily formed and that this quality infects even the most consistent conclusions. For such people, the method of composition or synthesis appears to be only a hypothetical deduction. Instead of disabusing them directly, Galileo prefers to show in a convincing perceptible way the agreement between mathematical reasoning and the ways of nature. He therefore devises experiments to show this correspondence and to verify — for such people — the predictions made about bodily behavior.

Far from treating the observational and experimental moment with condescension, however, Galileo is grateful for being compelled to *devise experiments* that give visible manifestation to the mathematical orderliness of nature. The fact that 45 degrees is the angle of elevation best suited for obtaining the maximum range for projectiles, was well known to experienced gunners. The reason for this fact was supplied by Galileo's analysis of parabolic paths. The further inference was drawn from this mathematical analysis that, of the other angles for shots, those that exceed or fall short of 45 degrees by equal amounts have an equal range — a prediction easy to verify through convincing artillery performances. On the other hand, considerable ingenuity was required to provide experimental verification of the corollary, drawn from the definition of uniformly accelerated motion, that the distances traversed by a falling body are to each other as the squares of the times. Galileo had to cut a channel in a piece of wooden molding, polish the groove, and line it with smooth parchment, in order to reduce friction to a minimum. Then he rolled down the channel a smooth, hard, bronze ball, observing the time required for the descent. The experiment was repeated several times to achieve accuracy in the time measurement, which was done both with the natural pulse beat and with a specially devised chronometer. Then the ball was rolled for various fractions of the full distance and at various angles of elevation of the channel, thus establishing the ratio of times and distances which Galileo "had predicted and demonstrated for them."[18] After many repetitions and variations, Galileo was satisfied that there was no appreciable discrepancy between his calculations and the experimental results and that his laws would hold true in all other cases.

In this latter example, we find clearly illustrated all the features of the *scientific method,* as conceived by Galileo. There must be sensory acquaintance with actually falling bodies, reduction of the fall to a mathematical formula, and prediction of further results for other cases. Then must follow verification of the prediction through carefully constructed experimental situations and with the aid of special instruments and materials, variation of conditions, correlation of data of measurement (especially in regard to time), recognition of slight discrepancies, and generalization of the results to cover all cases of falling bodies and thus confirm the general theoretical statement. Galileo differs from Descartes, however, in regarding the experimental results not as an indispensable way of deciding between two equally possible mathematical deductions but only as a way of

---

[18] *Dialogues concerning Two New Sciences,* III (Crew and de Salvio translation 179); most of the philosophically relevant texts from the *Dialogues* are collected in *From Descartes to Kant,* edited by T. V. Smith and M. Grene, 25–30. For a thorough analysis of the background and content of Galileo's other great book, together with its ultimate failure to demonstrate the thesis of Copernicus, see A. C. Crombie, "Galileo's 'Dialogues concerning the Two Principal Systems of the World,'" *Dominican Studies,* III (1950), 105–38.

giving sensible form to absolutely certain deductions. For him, the choice between possible mathematical statements is decided in the earlier, resolutive phase, where the basic definitions are formulated with the aid of sense experience. Thereafter, the mathematical physicist is sure that his inferences also express the exigencies of natural laws.[19]

Experimental verification of quantitative calculations led Galileo to inquire into the reason why there is an exact *conformity between nature and mathematics.* The answer cannot be given in purely methodological terms but depends upon a metaphysics of nature, belonging in the Platonic tradition of the geometrization of nature and natural science.[20] The great *book of nature* is written in the *language of mathematics,* its characters being numbers, circles, triangles, and other mathematical elements. That is why mathematics, rather than traditional logic, is the only instrument for the discovery of truth in natural philosophy: it alone can decipher the very language in which natural phenomena are written. But the book of nature *is* written in this language only because mathematics is the native tongue of nature's author. Galileo combines a mathematical realism with a mathematical theism, in order to supply a ground for scientific method.

The author of nature is a *geometrizing God.* His mode of understanding is the exemplar of all mathematical thinking, and His mode of creation follows this manner of thinking. When God produces the world, He produces a thoroughly mathematical structure that obeys the laws of number, geometrical figure, and quantitative function. Nature is an *embodied mathematical system.* To say, then, that our minds must conform to nature, is also to affirm the sovereignty of a mathematical analysis of nature. And to make this approach is to imitate and, indeed, share in the divine knowledge of nature. Every time we uncover a mathematical constancy governing a physical event, we are increasing our share in God's own vision of the world, retracing the course of His own creative understanding of things.

Galileo distinguishes two aspects of our knowledge: its extension or range and its intension or truth-character. *Extensively,* we fall far short

---

[19] Compare the saying of Leonardo da Vinci: "Understand the cause and you will have no need of the experiment." *The Notebooks of Leonardo da Vinci* (E. MacCurdy translation, I, 70).

[20] Cf. A. Koyré, "Galileo and Plato," *Journal of the History of Ideas,* IV (1943), 400-28.

of the divine knowledge, since God knows an infinite multitude of things, whereas we can know only an ever increasing but finite multitude. *Intensively,* however, the human mind can acquire the same sort of knowledge as God enjoys, since it can attain the same objective *certainty.* Both God and man know by means of pure mathematics, which reveals the necessity resident in natural objects. Since there can be no greater surety than that provided by the necessary laws controlling things, both the divine and the human understanding have the same absolute certainty. As conceived in God's mind, the order of nature is a unique, immutable, and necessary one. Granted the divine decision to create, the universe can realize only one, unchanging, mathematical plan. This is the ultimate basis of Galileo's confidence in mathematical deduction. Grounded in the original sense experience and reductive analysis, our compositive reasoning simply expresses the single, inexorable order that is nature itself. Physical events cannot occur otherwise than our well-founded inferences determine, since these inferences are specified by the same necessity that prevails for the phenomena of nature. By sharing in God's mathematical wisdom, we can demonstrate with complete assurance the motion of bodies through space and time.

Along with this exalted estimate of the mathematical interpretation of nature, Galileo reveals a vivid sense of the *limitations* of our actual knowledge. Our manner of understanding is contradistinguished from the divine not only by its narrower extension but also by its *temporal* character. Whereas God grasps all the infinite implications of mathematical principles in a single, eternal intuition, we must gradually acquire the basic notions and their implications through a long process of reasoning and experimentation. Galileo agrees with Bacon that time is the father of truth, and our mind its mother. Furthermore, the mathematical perspective demands that philosophy forego three claims that are usually made for it. First, there can be no philosophical investigation of *final causes,* since they cannot be submitted to mathematical analysis. As far as scientific method is concerned, nature must be interpreted as a great machine determined solely by its formal, structural necessity. In the second place, no pretense can be made to penetrate to "the true and internal *essence of natural substances.*"[21] Galileo discovers in himself no special faculty for discerning this favorite object of previous speculation. He confesses his ignorance of the substantial elements of either the earth

[21] Drake, *Discoveries,* 123.

or the moon. Every attempt to furnish a substantialist explanation must end, if honestly conducted, in similar ignorance. Clouds may be explained in terms of humid vapors, the latter in terms of water attenuated by heat, and water by reference to fluid bodies. But at the end, we are none the better off, as far as the essence of clouds is concerned, by making this reduction to fluid bodies. The latter are closer to our senses but are not more manifest, in their essential nature, to our intellect. The only advantage of studying things near at hand is that their particular sensible features, but not their essences, are more readily grasped. "To determine precisely all the particulars is the true understanding of things."[22] The ideal of a mathematical description of the affections of things must replace that of an insight into their substantial essence. Without denying that such essences are real and are actually known by God, Galileo discourages the human intelligence from seeking them. We can only hope to know them in the Beatific Vision, when we will see natural things exhaustively in God, the font and light of truth.

A third limitation placed upon philosophical inquiry concerns the *affezioni* of things. The distinction — soon to be adopted by most  modern philosophers — between *primary* and *secondary qualities* or affections of bodies stems mainly from Galileo.[23] It should not be confused with the Scholastic distinction between *proper* and *common sensibles,* which was based on whether the sensible aspect is grasped, respectively, by one sense alone or by several senses working in conjunction. The Scholastics did not imply that the common sensibles alone were really present in things. But Galileo's distinction is based squarely upon the mathematical touchstone of objective reality. The primary qualities (number, motion, rest, figure, position, size, physical touch or contact) are those that can be given a precise quantitative formulation. They are called the *true* and *real* accidents of bodies. The secondary qualities (tastes, odors, colors, heat, sounds) are those  affections that elude mathematical analysis in quantitative terms. They have no real existence on the side of objective bodies but have only a *subjective* reality in the sensing subject. Although they have real causes among the primary affections, the secondary ones would be nothing but names, on the supposition that the percipient organism were removed. The material world that furnishes the proper object

[22] Text in De Ruvo, *Il problema,* 97; cf. Drake, *Discoveries,* 123–124.
[23] Consult the texts in Drake, *Discoveries,* 273–278.

of natural philosophy is thus bereft of its qualitative aspects and retains only the quantitative features susceptible of mathematical treatment.

Although Galileo thereby assured the truth and certitude of a mathematical philosophy of nature, his solution raised numerous *problems* for his successors. The net effect of his restriction of demonstration to the primary affections of bodies was to lend weight to the phenomenalistic assertion that bodies contain no real substantial essence, existing somewhere "behind" the ascertainable properties. If the rationalists wished to preserve the reality of substance, they were then obliged to criticize Galileo's conception of mathematical reasoning, so that its scope might be enlarged to include the substantial essence. Even within Galileo's own framework, there are difficulties that cannot be entirely removed by appeal to God as a geometrizing mind. If we may expect an increase of knowledge in the Beatific Vision, it means not only that there is more to be known in nature than can be grasped mathematically but also that the divine knowledge is something more than a geometrical vision. Galileo never makes it clear whether his occasional remarks on substantial essence and the *extramathematical knowledge* gained of it in the Beatific Vision are only concessions to the prevailing outlook or genuine admissions. If they are the latter, then they introduce a disturbing factor into his mathematical realism, since both nature and the divine knowledge contain intensive as well as extensive aspects that transcend the domain of mathematical demonstration.

Problems of the *divine freedom* are also raised that are not resolvable on any grounds furnished by Galileo. God could conceive of several possible mathematical systems that might be realized in nature. That He adopts the prevailing system is due to His respect for the simpler means and, in this sense, Galileo says that nature prefers *unity* and *simplicity*. These criteria are aids to a mathematical study of nature, since they transfer to nature the ideals of our mathematical reasoning. But Galileo does not show how God's freedom is preserved in respect to these same criteria. For Malebranche and Leibniz, the pressing question arose of whether there is any real possibility of an alternate universe. The assertion that the actual mathematical structure of nature is Copernican cannot be established solely by historical comparison with the Ptolemaic explanation, since the simplicity of the Copernican system is a relative one that can be superseded by an even more comprehensive and economical synthesis. But to make the claims for a particular mathematical explanation rest on absolute grounds of a standard of simplicity, to which God must adhere, is to endanger the divine freedom.

Galileo criticized the Pythagoreans and their Renaissance counterparts for failing to observe the distinction between geometrical figures and numerical functions in their *abstract purity* and in their *concrete embodiment* in matter. There must be *some* modifications, when mathematical laws are realized under material conditions. That is why matter introduces certain "impediments" which resolution seeks to remove, and also why there are very slight "discrepancies" encountered in experimental work. This implies, however, that concrete nature is not equivalent, in every respect, to the formal object studied by natural philosophy, as mathematically constituted. The necessity and immutability of mathematical deduction are thus restricted to the formal aspect of nature and do not account for its entire material reality. For Newton, this consideration led to the query whether mathematical demonstration has any independent validity in dealing with natural bodies. Newton was more keenly aware than Galileo of the profound distinction between the *physical object* itself and the *object of mathematico-physics*. The latter is by no means exhaustive of the real being of natural things.

From the human standpoint, there is a similar limitation placed upon the successful application of the scientific method. If philosophy has nature as its object and mathematics as its organon, then *man* either falls outside philosophical investigations or is included in them only in his common quantitative features, not in what is distinctively human. Galileo admits that the secondary qualities are real, even though they are not objectively existent. His method cannot deal with nonquantitative aspects of the human percipient, such as the secondary affections and freedom. Hence scientific description in terms of Galileo's method is admittedly incomplete, even in respect to quite relevant portions of human experience. This leads him to affirm the need for the *studi umani,* such as law and history, alongside of philosophy and science proper. But he is forbidden to apply the attributes of truth or falsehood to these humane disciplines, since they do not employ mathematical demonstrations and therefore cannot attain to mathematical certainty. The upshot is that Galileo recognizes the presence of a region of reality which urgently requires some explanation and yet which falls outside of mathematically inexorable nature, as he has described it. Confronted with this problem, Descartes,

Locke, Leibniz, and others were compelled to discover ways in which the distinctively human side of reality might be made the proper subject of philosophical analysis. This extension of scientific knowledge became possible, however, only by resorting to a radical dualism of mind and body or by submitting the mathematical ideal in philosophy to a searching criticism. Like Bacon, Galileo raised the issue, for later philosophers, of whether a single method can be devised to embrace both man and the rest of nature within a common perspective.

## C. *Isaac Newton*

Born in the manor house at Woolsthorpe, near Grantham, in 1642, Isaac Newton attended grammar school at Grantham and entered Trinity College, Cambridge, in 1661. He received his first introduction to higher mathematics at Trinity, where he obtained the bachelor's degree in 1665. Due to a plague raging at Cambridge, Newton was forced to remain at Woolsthorpe during 1665–1667. During this brief period, he discovered the method of fluxions or the calculus, the law of the composition of light, and the law of gravitation. He became a Fellow of Trinity (1667), Lucasian Professor of Mathematics (1669), and a Fellow of the Royal Society (1672). Under constant prodding from the astronomer, Halley, and other members of the Royal Society, Newton finally concentrated upon the problems leading to his general explanation of the universe according to mechanical laws. *Mathematical Principles of Natural Philosophy* was composed in less than two years and published in 1687. Newton was always extremely diffident about his mathematical work, which he rated lower than his investigations in the fields of alchemy, ancient chronology, theology, and scriptural criticism. These latter interests consumed increasingly more of his time after the *Principles* was issued. And after having had a taste of London life, during his term as a member of Parliament (1689–1690), Newton desired a permanent role in the world of affairs. Through an influential friend, Charles Montague, he was appointed Warden of the Mint (1696) and carried through the reform of coinage so vigorously that he was made Master of the Mint in 1699. He resigned his fellowship and professorship at Cambridge (1701) and removed to London for his remaining years. In 1703, he was elected president of the Royal Society and re-elected annually for the rest of his life. His *Opticks* (1704) contained his views on light and (in its later editions) further precisions about the method of experimental philosophy, whereas the second edition of the *Principles* (edited by Roger Cotes, 1713) included a *General Scholium*, outlining Newton's notions on God's nature. The last twenty years of Newton's life were clouded by controversies with Flamsteed, the Astronomer Royal, over the use and printing of the latter's observations, and with Leibniz over priority in the discovery of the calculus. Newton died in 1727, after overexerting himself in connection with a meeting of the Royal Society.

In the preface to his masterwork, Newton gives a clear account of his philosophical standpoint, beginning with an explanation of the title: *The Mathematical Principles of Natural Philosophy*. He is examining natural things with the aid of the science of mechanics. Mathematics is to be used only insofar as it bears upon the motion of natural things. Its function in natural philosophy is to furnish accurate measurements of quantities and the means of demonstration, leading to a universal science of motions. But the demonstrations must start from mechanical principles, derived from the actual phenomena of motion, as observed in nature. This preliminary statement indicates the balance Newton intends to strike between the empirical and rational aspects of natural philosophy. Mathematics is the mind's sovereign tool of universal demonstration, but it must be adapted to the conditions of a dynamics that is regulated at every stage by the sensory evidence of motions. Both Galileo and Bacon are contributors to Newton's definitive formulation of the method of classical modern physics.

The aim of inquiry in natural philosophy is:

> From the phenomena of motions to investigate the forces of nature, and then from these forces to demonstrate other phenomena. . . . As in mathematics, so in natural philosophy, the investigation of difficult things by the method of analysis, ought ever to precede the method of composition. This analysis consists in making experiments and observations, and in drawing general conclusions from them by induction. . . . And the synthesis [or composition] consists in assuming the causes discovered, and established as principles, and by them explaining the phenomena proceeding from them.[24]

---

[24] *The Mathematical Principles of Natural Philosophy*, Preface to the first edition (Motte-Cajori translation, xvii–xviii); *Opticks*, III, i, query 31 (reprint edition of 1952, 404–05; the text of this work is modernized). The basic philosophical texts of Newton are given in the H. S. Thayer anthology. See the introductory study by H. R. Burke, "Sir Isaac Newton's Formal Conception of Scientific Method," *The New Scholasticism*, X (1936), 93–115.

Hence the *method* consists in an *analytic induction* from experience and a *synthetic* or *compositive demonstration* of further consequences, with constant recourse to precisely measured sense data. Since a beginning is made with sensible phenomena, natural philosophy is neither a pure mathematical science nor an abstract application of mathematical principles. Its sources are both physical and mathematical, and only so much mathematical demonstration can be given as is warranted by sense testimony about the physical order. Nevertheless, even in the initial gathering of phenomenal instances and the making of experiments, bodies are considered only insofar as they describe mathematically determinable motions. This is a considerable restriction of the method, since it involves a rigid selection of relevant evidence. By comparing and varying the relevant mechanical phenomena, we can make exact quantitative measurements, which constitute a *deduction* about the properties of bodies in motion. Deduction is not contrasted with induction but is an early stage in the inductive process, that phase of induction in which mathematical proportions of lesser generality are discovered.

Aided by the use of fluxions or the calculus, the mind can now set out to make the general *analytic induction* of scientific laws. Newtonian induction is a search after the widest quantitative proportions and functions, terminating ultimately in a few universal principles of motion and mechanical properties. These broadest rules of measure are the culmination of the analytic movement of thought, corresponding to the results of Galileo's method of resolution.[25] We reason from composite bodies to the simple factors constituting them, from effects to causes, from particular to more general causes and, finally, to the most general causes of motion. In every stage of induction, however, the business of natural philosophy is to explain the causes of actually perceived sensible effects. In stating the universal mathematico-physical laws of motion, any observed exceptions should be explicitly mentioned as qualifications placed upon these laws. Consequently, Newton does not regard induction as an absolutely certain demonstration: he recommends it as the best way men have of dealing with sensible phenomena of motion. It is all the more cogent, the more general it becomes, but induction never reaches the point where it can exclude, in principle, experimental corrections of its

---

[25] E. W. Strong, in "Newton's 'Mathematical Way,'" *Journal of the History of Ideas*, XII (1951), 90–110, stresses the role of mathematics in providing rules of measure that can be formulated in a general way, as physical laws.

results or even the possibility of a truer method of studying nature. There is a fundamental doctrinal, as well as personal, humility about Newton that resists the extravagant claims made for his method by his followers and exploiters.

### NEWTON ON THE METHOD OF EXPERIMENTAL PHILOSOPHY

1. Induction from experience by analysis.
   a) Sense testimony.
   b) Mathematical "deduction."
   c) General induction of laws, especially the most general laws of motion.
   1) Mechanical laws or causes.
   2) Hypothetical, physical causes.
   3) The efficient, metaphysical cause: God.
2. Demonstration of further phenomena by synthesis.
3. Rules of reasoning: parsimony, uniformity, universality, empirical caution-and-confidence.

Newton distinguishes sharply between three meanings of the term "cause": (1) *Mechanical causes* or laws of motion, (2) *physical causes* or hypothetical physical agents, and (3) the *metaphysical, efficient cause:* God. He believes that natural philosophy can make a demonstrative inference from the universe of motion to God, considered as the metaphysical, efficient cause of bodily movements and harmonious order in nature. But he does not regard his laws of motion as genuine efficient causes. They do not exercise any real efficient causation but are mathematical rules of measure and mechanical laws, stating a functional correlation. Hence he reserves the term "mechanical causes" for these descriptive laws of dynamics, in order to underline their status as mathematical measures and correlations. He places a wider gap between the descriptive, mathematical laws of motion and the actual physical agents, operative in nature, than Galileo would allow. The physical causes are agents postulated to account for phenomena that resist reduction to mechanical laws and to explain the conformity of actual motions to the mechanical laws themselves. Such physical causes are entertained only hypothetically in natural philosophy, however, since its main purpose is to establish the mechanical causes or laws in a nonhypothetical way. Thus the *law of gravity* states that every body tends to attract every other body with a force directly proportional to the product of their masses and inversely proportional to the square of the distance between them.

The gravitational "force" is a mechanical rather than a physical cause, a quantitative function of the mass and distance of bodies. Certain physical agents and entities may be supposed, to account for the universal prevalence of this law in the actual world, but these physical causes remain hypothetical suppositions.

Similarly, the inertial character of mass is expressed in the *laws of motion*. Since they are mechanical causes, the problem of efficient causality is not involved when Newton states that *"every body continues in its state of rest, or of uniform motion in a straight line, unless it is compelled to change that state by forces impressed upon it"* (Law I), and that *"to every action there is always opposed an equal reaction"* (Law III).[26] From neither the Newtonian nor the Thomistic standpoint do these laws of motion affect the question of efficient cause or the real principle of change in nature. Since the mechanical cause is not the origin of being or becoming in the effect, there is a total equivalence of motion throughout the mechanical system, so that the nature and principle of real, natural change do not come within the purview of an explanation in terms of the laws of motion.

Induction can establish the two or three most general mechanical causes of motion, but this is not the same as ascertaining the physical agents and conditions that determine the appearances, in accordance with these laws, and that supplement the laws in the case of erratic phenomena. Newton is sure that the universal science of mechanics is empirically founded in the observed phenomena, as brought under a general theorem, even though the physical causes at work should remain forever hidden. Inductive analysis and deduction can deal with the quantitative functions and properties of *gravity*, for instance, without ever inquiring into the intrinsic nature and qualities operative in the physical bodies. Newton expressly denies having any strict knowledge of the physical essence and causes that might be correlated with the law of gravity. Gravity is not an "occult force," as the Leibnizians charged, since it is formulated on the basis of

---

[26] *The Mathematical Principles of Natural Philosophy*, Axioms, or Laws of Motion (Motte-Cajori, 13). On the problems posed by these laws (and other modern scientific concepts) for natural theology, see V. E. Smith, "Scientism and the Five Ways of St. Thomas," *Journal of Arts and Letters*, III (1951), 35–47. A comparison between the mechanical and metaphysical approaches to universal attraction is made by R. Garrigou-Lagrange, O.P., "L'attraction universelle: Saint Thomas et Newton," *Philosophia Perennis*, edited by F. J. von Rintelen (2 vols., Regensburg, Habbel, 1930), II, 845–53.

the manifest behavior of bodies in motion. But the real, physical causes governing these bodies are "occult," in the sense of remaining beyond the power of induction to establish with certainty.

As far as the second major phase in scientific method — the *synthetic* or *compositive demonstration of further phenomena* — is concerned, a knowledge of the real physical causes is again unnecessary. Natural philosophy may ignore this latter question and yet regard the principles of motion as already established from the phenomena themselves. These principles now become the premises for a synthetic process, in which the mechanical properties of still further sets of appearances are demonstrated. This corresponds to the compositive and deductive phase of Galileo's method, although Newton's explanations are hedged in by qualifications that are foreign to Galileo. The same natural laws that hold for earthly bodies are applied deductively to heavenly bodies. Since these laws are quite general in principle, Newton is confident of their application to all natural phenomena whatsoever. Nevertheless, any specific synthetic demonstration must submit to the test of empirical verification. Since Newton does not make the assumption that nature is a unique mathematical system, he relies much more heavily than Galileo upon observational confirmation of mathematical deductions. He is ready, at any moment, to modify or even scrap the most magnificent synthetic extension of his principles, should the empirical evidence require it. Merely to entertain the possibility of such a revision shows how much deeper the experiential requirement goes in Newton. The moment of sense verification is intrinsic, rather than extrinsic, to the synthetic inferences in Newton's natural philosophy.

As a guidepost to the use of the method of analysis and synthesis, Newton offers four *rules of reasoning in natural philosophy*.[27] Subsequent philosophers, especially Hume and Kant, took these precepts as basic requirements of scientific knowledge and based their own philosophical examination of knowledge largely upon these rules. By way of identification, we may refer to them, respectively, as the rules of: parsimony, uniformity, universality, and empirical caution-and-confidence.

The first rule counsels *parsimony* or *economy of causal explanation,* provided that the explanation is both true (founded upon mathematically analyzed phenomena) and sufficient (inclusive of all known,

---

[27] The four rules are quoted from *The Mathematical Principles of Natural Philosophy,* III, Rules of Reasoning in Philosophy (Motte-Cajori, 398–400).

relevant phenomena). If we *"admit no more causes of natural things than such as are both true and sufficient to explain their appearances,"* we are following the ways of nature itself. Newton concurs with Kepler and Galileo in the view that nature tends toward simplicity and economy of means. He also agrees with them that the ultimate reason for these standards is to be found in God's own decision to shape nature in this way. But in Newton, there is no implication that God is a geometrizer or that our scientific inferences are true because they participate in the divine mode of simple reasoning. The second rule states that *"to the same natural effects we must, as far as possible, assign the same causes."* This rests on a belief in the *uniformity of nature* and, ultimately, in the self-consistency of nature's divine maker. The light of our household fire and that of the sun are traceable to the same cause, making any distinction in kind between terrestrial and celestial matter quite untenable.

On the basis of the first two rules, Newton is able to formulate the procedure for making *universal propositions about natural properties.* The third rule reads: *"The qualities of bodies, which admit neither intensification nor remission of degrees, and which are found to belong to all bodies within the reach of our experiments, are to be esteemed the universal qualities of all bodies whatsoever."* Newton accepts the Galilean distinction between primary or objective qualities and secondary or subjective qualities. His own experimental work in optics convinced him, for instance, that colors do not reside in the rays of light but are sensations produced in our minds through the operation of various objective powers and dispositions of light. On the other hand, he opposed the twofold Cartesian tendency to make pure understanding the faculty of grasping primary qualities and to reduce these qualities to their mathematical minimum. The senses are indispensable for distinguishing the *actual* qualities of things from merely *possible* qualities. Moreover, if the senses inform us separately about different qualities, the latter need not be reduced to each other, merely out of regard for mathematical economy of explanation. Hence in addition to figure, extension, and mobility, Newton lists as primary qualities: hardness, impenetrability, and the inertial powers. The senses remind us that bodies are *masses,* as well as geometrical entities. The primary qualities may be attributed not only to the bodies we can sense but also to those bodies that lie beyond our sensory range. Given the preference of nature for simplicity and consistency, along with the fact that certain constant traits or primary qualities are found without diminution in all the bodies of our acquaintance, we have sufficient theoretical grounds for ascribing such properties to all bodies in nature. Gravity is also universal, but it cannot be called a primary quality or essential force, since it is subject to variation in proportion to distance. Finally, Newton offered a fourth rule, both as an *encouragement* and a *warning* to natural reasoning:

> *In experimental philosophy we are to look upon propositions inferred by general induction from phenomena as accurately or very nearly true, notwithstanding any contrary hypotheses that may be imagined, till such time as other phenomena occur, by which they may either be made more accurate, or liable to exceptions.* This rule we must follow, that the argument of induction may not be evaded by hypotheses.

The first part of this precept was aimed against the English Cartesian physicists, who employed mere abstract possibilities (such as the theory of cosmic vortexes and subtle spirits) to raise vain doubts concerning Newton's physical theories, which were based upon observation and mathematical analysis of actual motions. Experimental philosophy cannot be distracted and shaken by the demand that every proposed alternative that is internally consistent be examined, before one assents to the results of careful induction. Such delaying tactics provoked Newton's well-known maxim: "I frame no hypotheses."[28] A suggested explanation that advances no empirical evidence in its favor is stranger to a science based upon the phenomena of nature. Consequently, no one may use such speculations either to withhold assent from inductive propositions or to hinder positive studies, by wrangling over what might be. Yet there is another meaning of hypothesis that is fully compatible with Newton's practice as well as his methodology. No progress is possible without attending to hypotheses suggested by the observed facts and experiments: these are leads provided by nature itself and hence susceptible of empirical testing. Such *empirically framed hypotheses* may be admitted into natural philosophy, but only on condition of being unmistakably marked as "queries," rather than inductive principles.

In the case of the physical entities or causes responsible for the

---

[28] *Ibid.*, General Scholium (Motte-Cajori, 547); cf. *Opticks*, III, i, query 28 (reprint edition, 369). The question of Newton's attitude toward hypotheses is carefully examined by R. M. Blake, "Sir Isaac Newton's Theory of Scientific Method," *The Philosophical Review*, XLII (1933), 543–86; see also Cajori's note to his edition of the *Principles*, 671–76.

phenomena expressed in mechanical laws, there is rich opportunity for making cautious hypotheses. Newton himself opines that gravitation may be due to variations in density of the ether, and that light may be due either to corpuscular emissions or to waves in the same ether. Within Newton's total outlook, such hypotheses or "queries" about the physical causes stand midway between the mechanical principles of motion and the metaphysical view of God as the first, efficient cause of motion. Actual scientific practice thus vindicates the rightful role of probable arguments, which Galilean-Cartesian rationalism had sought to eliminate.

In the latter portion of the fourth rule, Newton tries to temper the extreme claims made for mathematical demonstrations about physical phenomena. Unlike Galileo, he does not consider nature a unique, inexorable, mathematical machine. Mathematics illuminates the operations of nature with astounding success, but this is no proof that these operations are exclusively mathematical or that a more adequate method cannot be found for understanding them. By producing atomic particles of another size, figure, density, and force than those that actually constitute material bodies, God could vary the laws of nature and produce several different worlds, in different parts of the universe. Hence mathematics, as an instrument of experimental philosophy, must accept the guidance of experience not only at the outset but during every phase of reasoning. Something of Bacon's sampling of sensible instances remains firmly implanted within the mathematical context of Newton's method. Since the inductive principles never become independent of their reference to

sense phenomena, synthetic demonstrations never achieve the autonomous and definitive character of pure mathematical deductions. They remain forever open to the possibility of revision and even replacement, provided only that an empirical source can be cited for the modification. The essential corrigibility of scientific propositions is the counterpart of the repudiation of purely abstract hypotheses.

The second edition of the *Principles* (1713) contains the famous "General Scholium," which Newton appended in reply to Leibniz' charge that the Newtonian world machine dispenses with God or at least degrades Him to the level of absolute space. On the contrary, Newton conceived it to be the proper office of experimental philosophy not only to establish mechanical laws but also to mount up to the first efficient cause of nature. This primary cause is not itself mechanical and yet is compatible with the mechanical system of nature.[29] Newton lent the weight of his great authority to the argument for God's existence drawn from design, an argument that was popular among the rationalistic divines of his age and that became a major theme in Hume's discussion of natural religion and Kant's discussion of the proofs of God's existence. Only a personal, intelligent, all-powerful being — a nonmechanical, truly efficient first cause — can account for the present order in nature, as described in the universal mechanics.

To pave the way for an explanation of God's relation to the world, Newton appeals to the analogous case of the human mind's relation to its own body and thus to the rest of the material world. Accepting the current dualistic view of man, Newton pictures the human soul as a small substance, lodged in a part of the brain to which the ingoing motions are brought and whence the outgoing ones arise. This *control box* or *sensorium* is the depository for the images which the various organs of sense convey to the mind. Our knowing power has no direct knowledge of external things but  only of their images. Through this means, however, the mind learns something about the nature of things. Moreover, our will can move the human body and thus affect other bodies through the impulses it emits from its seat, the sensorium. Newton is quite oblivious to the metaphysical and epistemological difficulties raised by this naïve dualism of mind and body. Its main purpose is to provide a limping analogy with God's manner of presence to the entire world.

*Absolute space* and *time* provide a *divine sensorium* for God, the omniscient and omnipotent agent.[30] Through this sensorium, God's mind can perceive all things by their immediate presence in space to Him. This control box also enables God to move all bodies by

---

[29] Commentators disagree about the precise relationship between Newton's mechanics and his natural theology. For opposing statements, see E. A. Burtt, "Method and Metaphysics in Sir Isaac Newton," *Philosophy of Science*, X (1943), 57–66, and E. W. Strong, "Newton and God," *Journal of the History of Ideas*, XIII (1952), 147–67.

[30] "Does it not appear from phenomena that there is a Being incorporeal, living, intelligent, omnipresent, who in infinite space, as it were in his sensory, sees the things themselves intimately, and thoroughly perceives them, and comprehends them wholly by their immediate presence to himself? . . . [God,] being in all places, is more able by his will to move the bodies within his boundless uniform sensorium, and thereby to form and reform the parts of the universe, than we are by our will to move the parts of our own bodies." *Opticks*, III, i, queries 28, 31 (reprint edition, 370, 403).

His will and to sustain all natural agencies and laws. Thus the spatiotemporal sensorium is the instrument of both the divine knowledge of the world and the divine exercise of power over it. Because absolute space and time are properties of the divine sensorium, they may be taken as properties of God, at least in respect to the world. Nevertheless, Newton rejects a pantheistic view of God and the world. The world is not related to God as His body and, strictly speaking, He has no need of organs. He is not dependent upon the cosmic sensorium in the way that our mind is completely dependent upon its "little sensorium," since somehow God remains the transcendent and independent creator of all things. He constitutes absolute space and absolute time, simply by existing everywhere and always. Newton contrasts absolute, true, mathematical space and time with the relative, apparent, common space and time of particular bodies. His theory of absolute space and time serves both to make God's knowledge and dominion over the world more intelligible to us and also, as a rational postulate, to explain absolute motion.

The God of the Newtonians not only created the system of the world but also prevented it from going out of gear. When Laplace explained the mechanical motions of the world without having any recourse to a divine mechanic, many people thought that the main argument for God's existence had also been discredited. The Encyclopedists popularized the view of the world as a *self-sustaining mechanism,* acting according to the universal and autonomous causal force of gravity alone. Newton's careful explanation of the meaning of "mechanical cause," as applied to gravitation, was ignored and his theology discarded. The historical fate of his "General Scholium" would seem to justify the ferocity with which Bishop Berkeley attacked the Newtonian claim that natural philosophy can ascertain a truly active, efficient, metaphysical cause, as well as a set of mechanical laws or causes. Berkeley rightly feared that those who did not share Newton's religious belief would see no cogency in his speculations about God's existence and agency, and would be led into atheism. Hence the Anglo-Irish bishop denied outright the competence of Newton's natural philosophy to deal with efficient causes and to determine philosophic methodology.

## SUMMARY OF CHAPTER 3

Bacon was a transitional figure between Renaissance and modern philosophy. His doctrine on the idols of the mind or typical sorts of error sought to clear out the prejudices of the past or at least to put us on guard against their sources in human nature, individual training, and social communication. He criticized the theologizers, the mere empiricists, and the abstract rationalists. The net effect of his new division of the parts of philosophy was to reduce effective philosophical research to the philosophy of nature. Within this domain, his main objective was to discover the forms or natural laws of action of bodies, with the aid of an empirical study of the sense appearances or simple natures. The Baconian tables of induction were intended to determine the connection between simple natures and forms, so that man could obtain the mastery over nature for his own benefit. But the real practical consequences of scientific knowledge have come from the use of mathematically controlled hypotheses, the method employed by Galileo and Newton. Galileo was confident about the use of mathematics in natural philosophy, since he regarded nature itself as having a mathematical structure. The senses are needed to ascertain the factual existence of objects, but thereafter the scientist need rely only on the mathematical method of resolution and composition. Experimental verification is possible and useful but not strictly required, since God works mathematically in nature and thus provides the guarantee of our quantitative predictions. Galileo's metaphysical assumptions about the mathematical character of divine action and the inner constitution of nature did not seem self-evident to Newton. He was more cautious about the scope of scientific laws and predictions, and stressed the indispensable role of experience in all natural philosophy. His four rules of reasoning counseled economy, uniformity, universality, and empirical balance in the formulation of scientific propositions. Newton accepted Galileo's distinction between primary and secondary qualities, as well as the subjective nature of the latter. He associated his theory of absolute time and space with a theological explanation of God's connection with the world, by means of the "divine sensorium."

## BIBLIOGRAPHICAL NOTE

1. *Development of Science.* Among the best general histories of scientific ideas are: W. C. Dampier, *A History of Science and Its Relations with Philosophy and Religion* (fourth ed., revised and enlarged, Cambridge, University Press, 1949), and W. P. D. Wightman, *The Growth of Scientific Ideas* (New Haven, Yale University Press, 1951). For the medieval period and its importance as the root of modern conceptions of science, two books by A. C. Crombie are of first importance, both historically and theoretically. *Medieval and Early Modern Science* (revised second ed., 2 vols., New York, Doubleday Anchor, 1959) surveys medieval and Renaissance science; *Robert Grosseteste and the Origins of Experimental Science, 1100–1700* (Oxford, Clarendon Press, 1953), is a more specialized study, showing how Grosseteste anticipated the basic aspects of modern science. The broad historical outlines of the transition are sketched by H. Butterfield, *The Origins of Modern Science, 1300–1800* (London, Bell, 1950); for a more detailed account, see L. Thorndike, *A History of Magic*

*and Experimental Sciences* (8 vols., New York, Macmillan, and Columbia University Press, 1923–1958); A. R. Hall, *The Scientific Revolution, 1500–1800* (Boston, Beacon Press, 1956); both have bibliographies. From the philosophical side, A. Maier has made pioneer studies in the physical theory and mechanics taught at Paris and Oxford in the late medieval period; see especially *Die Vorläufer Galileis im 14. Jahrhundert: Studien zur Naturphilosophie der Spätscholastik* (Rome, Storia e Letteratura, 1949) and *Die Mechanisierung des Weltbildes im 17. Jahrhundert* (Leipzig, Meiner, 1938). Although weak in philosophical analysis, there is a wealth of factual data in A. Wolf's *A History of Science, Technology and Philosophy in the Sixteenth and Seventeenth Centuries* (second ed., revised by D. McKie, London, Allen and Unwin, 1950) and his *A History of Science, Technology and Philosophy in the Eighteenth Century,* revised by D. McKie (second ed., London, Allen and Unwin, 1952). The most informative study of the philosophical aspects of classical modern physics is E. A. Burtt's *The Metaphysical Foundations of Modern Physical Science* (revised ed., London, Routledge and Kegan Paul, 1932). Burtt's basic metaphysical orientation has been sharply challenged by E. W. Strong, *Procedures and Metaphysics: A Study in the Philosophy of Mathematical Physical Science in the Sixteenth and Seventeenth Centuries* (Berkeley, University of California Press, 1936), who offers a procedural and naturalistic interpretation. The impetus for recent philosophical analyses of modern science came from E. Cassirer's fundamental researches, *Das Erkenntnisproblem in der Philosophie und Wissenschaft der neueren Zeit* (3 vols., Berlin, B. Cassirer, 1906–1920; Vol. I, third ed., 1922; Vol. II, third ed., 1922; Vol. III, second ed., 1923). Vol. I covers the Renaissance, Galileo, and Descartes; Vol. II is on the empiricists, rationalists, and Kant; Vol. III studies the post-Kantian idealists. Cassirer brought his survey to a close with a fourth volume, which first appeared in English translation: *The Problem of Knowledge: Philosophy, Science and History since Hegel,* translated by W. H. Woglom and C. W. Hendel (New Haven, Yale University Press, 1950). Cassirer high-lighted the epistemological problem, because of his Neo-Kantian preoccupations; for a brief, realistic study of the same materials, cf. F. Amerio, *Epistemologia* (Brescia, Morcelliana, 1949).

2. *Bacon.* Collected edition: *The Works of Francis Bacon,* edited by J. Spedding, R. L. Ellis, and D. D. Heath (14 vols., London, Longmans, 1858–1872). It contains Rawley's early *Life of Bacon,* a valuable General Preface by Ellis, Prefaces and Notes by Ellis and Spedding, and translations of Latin works. It was reprinted by Houghton Mifflin (15 vols., Boston, c. 1900), and by other publishers. J. M. Robertson's edition of *The Philosophical Works of Francis Bacon* (London, Routledge, 1905) is the most complete, single-volume selection, based upon the Spedding-Ellis-Heath edition. For a biographical account, pointing up Bacon's import for a technological age, see B. Farrington, *Francis Bacon, Philosopher of Industrial Science* (New York, Schuman, 1949). A comprehensive philosophical analysis is given by F. H. Anderson, *The Philosophy of Francis*

*Bacon* (Chicago, University of Chicago Press, 1948); a succinct and pointed statement of his inductive theory is supplied by C. J. Ducasse: "Francis Bacon's Philosophy of Science," in *Structure, Method and Meaning: Essays in Honor of Henry M. Sheffer*, edited by P. Henle, H. M. Kallen, and S. K. Langer (New York, Liberal Arts Press, 1951), 115-44. The value of W. Frost's *Bacon und die Naturphilosophie* (Munich, Reinhardt, 1927) lies in its synoptic view of Bacon, along with Copernicus, Kepler, Galileo, Gassendi, Huyghens, and Newton. For Bacon's place in English philosophy, see W. R. Sorley, *A History of English Philosophy* (Cambridge, University Press, 1920).

3. *Galileo.* The critical edition is the *Edizione Nazionale* of *Le Opere di Galileo Galilei,* edited by A. Favaro and I. del Lungo (20 vols., Florence, Barbera, 1890-1909). A handy collection of philosophical texts is made by V. De Ruvo, *Il problema della verità* (Bari, Laterza, 1946). English versions: *Discoveries and Opinions of Galileo,* translated by S. Drake (New York, Doubleday, 1957); *Dialogue concerning the Two Chief World Systems,* translated by S. Drake (Berkeley, University of California Press, 1953); *Dialogues concerning Two New Sciences,* translated by H. Crew and A. de Salvio (Evanston and Chicago, Northwestern University Press, 1939). For a comprehensive study of Galileo's scientific, philosophical, and religious ideas, see A. Aliotta and C. Carbonara, *Galilei* (Milan, Bocca, 1949), as well as the centenary volume, *Nel terzo centenario della morte di Galileo Galilei,* edited by the Faculty of Philosophy in the University of the Sacred Heart in Milan (Milan, Vita e Pensiero, 1942). The latter contains chapters on Galileo's views about: science and faith, mechanics, physics, astronomy, metaphysics, theodicy, theory of knowledge, empiricism, and decadent Scholasticism, together with an analysis of the two trials and a bibliography. There is also a brief study in English by F. S. Taylor, *Galileo and the Freedom of Thought* (London, Watts, 1938). For Galileo's debt to his medieval predecessors, as well as his own original work in science, see the following chapters from the two books by A. C. Crombie mentioned above, Section 1: *Augustine to Galileo,* Chapter VI, "The Revolution in Scientific Thought in the 16th and 17th Centuries," 274-403; *Robert Grosseteste and the Origins of Experimental Science,* Chapter XI, "The Historical Foundations of the Modern Theory of Experimental Science," 290-319 (with references also to Bacon, Descartes, and Newton).

4. *Newton.* The *Opera quae existant omnia* was edited by S. Horsley (5 vols., London, Nichols, 1779-1785). The A. Motte translation of *Mathematical Principles of Natural Philosophy and System of the World* was revised and superbly annotated by F. Cajori (Berkeley, University of California Press, 1934). There is a reprint of the fourth or 1730 edition of the *Opticks* (New York, Dover Publications, 1952). A good sampling of Newton's theological writings is given in *Sir Isaac Newton: Theological Manuscripts,* selected and edited by H. McLachlan (Boston, Beacon Press, 1950). For an outstanding account of his life and works, see L. T. More, *Isaac Newton, A Biography (1642-1727)* (New York, Scribner, 1934).

The impact of Newtonian science upon society is investigated by G. N. Clarke, *Science and Social Welfare in the Age of Newton* (second ed., Oxford, Clarendon, 1949). On the significance of Newton's "Mathematical Experimentalism" for philosophy, see J. H. Randall, Jr., "Newton's Natural Philosophy: Its Problems and Consequences," *Philosophical Essays in Honor of Edgar Arthur Singer, Jr.*, edited by F. P. Clark and M. C. Nahm (Philadelphia, University of Pennsylvania Press, 1942), 335–57. For Newton's Unitarian religious views, as well as those of Milton and Locke, see H. McLachlan, *The Religious Opinions of Milton, Locke and Newton* (Manchester, Manchester University Press, 1941). For the philosophy student, source materials are H. S. Thayer, *Newton's Philosophy of Nature* (New York, Hafner, 1953), and I. B. Cohen, *Isaac Newton's Papers and Letters on Natural Philosophy* (Cambridge, Mass., Harvard University Press, 1958). *Franklin and Newton*, also by I. B. Cohen (Philadelphia, American Philosophical Society, 1956), traces Newton's influence on the Enlightenment. A beginning has been made in editing the important materials in *The Correspondence of Isaac Newton*, ed. by H. W. Turnbull (Vol. I, Cambridge, the University Press, 1959).

5. *Further Studies.* The background in medieval science is presented textually in M. Clagett, *The Science of Mechanics in the Middle Ages* (Madison, University of Wisconsin Press, 1959), and descriptively in J. A. Weisheipl, O.P., *The Development of Physical Theory in the Middle Ages* (New York, Sheed and Ward, 1960). The first phase in modern science is explained briefly by I. B. Cohen, *The Birth of a New Physics* (New York, Doubleday Anchor, 1960), more analytically by T. S. Kuhn, *The Copernican Revolution* (New York, Modern Library, 1959), with a philosophical emphasis by A. Koyré, *From the Closed World to the Infinite Universe* (Baltimore, John Hopkins Press, 1957), and with dramatic focus on the fate of one individual in G. De Santillana's *The Crime of Galileo* (Chicago, University of Chicago Press, 1955). A. G. Van Melsen's *From Atomos to Atom* (New York, Jarper Torchbooks, 1960) stresses the particulate theories of matter, whereas C. C. Gillispie's *The Edge of Objectivity* (Princeton, Princeton University Press, 1960) regards the objectifying methods of modern science as a decisively new approach to nature. The interplay of science, philosophy, and religion in early modern England is described in two books: P. H. Kocher, *Science and Religion in Elizabethan England* (San Marino, Calif., Huntington Library, 1953), and R. S. Westfall, *Science and Religion in Seventeenth-Century England* (New Haven, Yale University Press, 1958). Readings are collected in *Roots of Scientific Thought*, ed. by P. Wiener and A. Noland (New York, Basic Books, 1957).

# Chapter 4. HOBBES

## I. LIFE AND WRITINGS

BECAUSE he was born prematurely at the coastal town of Westport in Malmesbury, on the eve of the projected invasion of England by the Spanish Armada (1588), Thomas Hobbes reported that his mother conceived him and fear as twins. His life spanned one of the most troubled eras in English history, extending from the reign of Elizabeth to the Restoration of Charles II. Hobbes did not even enjoy domestic tranquillity and security, since his father was a quarrelsome parson, who often neglected his ecclesiastical duties and was forced to flee from his parish and his family. Fortunately, the son was given a good classical secondary education and was enabled by his uncle to attend Oxford for five years, 1603–1608. Hobbes formed a low estimate of the philosophy taught there, since it concentrated upon mechanical rules for reducing the figures of the syllogism and featured the corrupt Scholastic doctrine of traveling forms or species, that supposedly went from the perceived thing to the perceiver's eye. After leaving Oxford, Hobbes entered the service of the Cavendish family, serving as tutor to the son of the first earl of Devonshire. With his charge, he made the grand tour of France and Italy in 1610, learning foreign languages, observing new customs, and discovering (to his great satisfaction) that the brand of philosophy taught at Magdalen was held in disdain upon the continent. During the next eighteen years, Hobbes lived in a quiet, scholarly way at the Cavendish house, Chatsworth, where he read the classics and many romances, as well as completed a translation of *Thucydides*. After the death of the second earl of Devonshire (1628), he served as tutor for another lad and made a second European tour. It was during this stay upon the continent that two incidents occurred which turned his interests in a philosophical direction. Picking up Euclid at the forty-seventh proposition of the first book, Hobbes is said to have exclaimed: "By God, this is impossible!" Being forced back gradually to the very first proposition, he became convinced of the entire deduction and henceforth took mathematical reasoning as his model. At another time, Hobbes observed a learned gathering grow silent, when the question of the nature of sensation was propounded. This set him thinking about the nature of bodies and motion, with special reference to their effect upon the senses. Hobbes began to suspect that light, sound, and other secondary qualities are only phantasms in the mind.

In 1631, he returned to the service of the Cavendish family, with whom he resided during his remaining years. His last European tour (1634–1637) brought him into contact with Galileo near Florence and, above all, with Mersenne in Paris. Father Marin Mersenne, of the Order of Minims, was the clearinghouse for philosophical and scientific correspondence among leading minds of the day. Through his mediation, Descartes invited Hobbes to read a manuscript copy of the *Meditations* and to submit objections, which Descartes printed together with his own replies. Hobbes was now ready to present his own system, the outlines of which he set forth in *The Elements of Law, Natural and Politic*. Although composed in 1640, this work was not published until 1650, in two parts: *Human Nature* and *On the Body Politic*. Because he held that sovereignty entails the power to raise funds and make war, Hobbes thought it prudent to leave England, then being governed by the Long Parliament. He fled to France in 1640 and stayed there for eleven years, serving as a mathematics tutor to the future Charles II. While in Paris, he began work on a trilogy entitled *Elements of Philosophy*, the three parts of which were to deal, respectively, with body in general, human nature, and the social polity (man, the citizen of the commonwealth). He published the third part of this system — *On the Citizen* — in 1642, revising the doctrine contained in *On the Body Politic*. During his Parisian stay, he also wrote his main work in political philosophy, *Leviathan* (1651). Hobbes' return to England was hastened by opposition raised among Catholics and Presbyterians abroad to some violent sections on religion in *Leviathan*, which was circulated in manuscript form. Early in 1652, Hobbes made his peace with the Commonwealth and took up residence again in England. But after the Restoration, Charles II bore him no resentment and even paid him a pension, referring to Hobbes indulgently as the bear whom everyone liked to bait.

Hobbes finally completed his trilogy with the publication of its first two parts: *On Body* (1655) and *On Man* (1658). Thereafter, the old man spent his energies in numerous, futile polemics. He fought Bishop Bramhall over human freedom and tried his best to convince the learned world (in opposition to the mathematician, John Wallis) that he had discovered how to square the circle and duplicate the cube. His opponents used the term "Hobbist" as synonymous with "atheist" and, in the fashion of the day, warned readers against "the monster of Malmesbury." Even in his eighties, he was able to turn out a complete translation of Homer. Hobbes died at the age of ninety-one, in 1679.

## 2. THE NATURE AND METHOD OF PHILOSOPHY

Hobbes shared the confidence of his age that a new era was opening for the advancement of science. It was his conviction that past ages had produced but a single science or body of demonstrated truths: geometry. Largely by following the procedure of the geometricians, astronomy had been constituted a genuine science by Copernicus, and mechanics by Galileo. Even the human body had been studied scientifically by the great English scientist, Thomas Harvey. The only unknown land lay within man himself, insofar as he is a being capable of knowledge, passions, and social life. In principle, Hobbes saw no reason preventing the application of the scientific method to this last frontier. His proud boast was that political philosophy, as a scientific discipline, was no older than his own first publication, *On the Citizen*. His supreme confidence in dealing with man's social nature sprang from a general doctrine of what makes a philosophical investigation truly scientific. Hobbes cultivated a narrow acre but did so with the utmost thoroughness and consistency. Once he had determined the method of philosophy in general, he was sure that its application to man was bound to yield scientific knowledge.

He likens philosophical reason to Noah's dove, whose flights established vital commerce between man and the surrounding world. Philosophy springs from the co-operation between the material world, producing sense images in man, and the activity of reason, working out the order and causal relations of the data of experience. The essential features of philosophy can be gathered from its *definition:* *"Such knowledge of effects or appearances, as we acquire by true ratiocination from the knowledge we have first of their causes or*  *generation; and again, of such causes or generations as may be from knowing first their effects.*"[1] Hobbes offers a detailed explanation of the parts of this definition, since it provides the basis for his entire argument.

We may regard the *remote subject matter* of philosophy as being *effects* OR *appearances,* since the only effects with which we are indubitably acquainted, at the outset, are those produced in our sentient awareness by the action of external bodies. All experience begins with sense appearances, the objective origin of which Hobbes neither doubts nor justifies. They are matter for absolute knowledge, in that we are naturally constrained to accept sense and its deliverances. Philosophy, however, is not naturally given knowledge but artificial or acquired knowledge. Hence it is not the same as sensation and imagination, and even goes beyond experience, considered Aristotelianwise as the direct outcome of our memory of many sense images and sequences. There is a *universal* factor in philosophy, showing that it is in the scientific order, which builds upon experience with the help of reason and names.

The *differentia* in the above definition of philosophy are: ratiocination and causal knowledge. What makes philosophy an acquired, scientific perfection is *reasoning* about causes and effects; at the same time, this is what sets off man from the other animals, so that only he is a philosophizing animal. Hobbes admits that, in both animals and man, there is a concrete sort of reasoning about particular causal sequences of events, insofar as expectations are always raised by past experiences of the organism. But the distinctive feature of the human understanding is its ability to form *general names* and, with their aid, to frame the general propositions and syllogisms which comprise scientific reasoning. Hobbes is a complete *nominalist,* in that he denies not only the independent existence of universal entities but also the mental existence of universal ideas. The name alone is universal, and only in the sense that it stands for a number of particular images taken severally, without signifying any distinct, common nature. The universal name "man" is a mark applying to Peter, John, and the rest, but not to anything like mankind or human nature as such. Why this name applies only to certain of our images or particular conceptions, and not to others, is explained

---

[1] *Concerning Body,* I, i, 2 (Molesworth edition of *The English Works of Thomas Hobbes,* I, 3). Chapter I of *Concerning Body* is Hobbes' clearest statement of his general view of philosophy. In footnotes, works are cited according to the title given by the editor or translator of the work in question.

rather hazily as being due to the likeness among such particulars. Hobbes does not examine any further the nature of this similarity or "suchness," which permits one common name to signify but one definite group of images.

Reasoning or ratiocination is defined as *computation,* a process of addition and subtraction of the consequences of general names. Addition and subtraction are not confined to arithmetic but are only most clearly illustrated there. All other functions of the mind can be reduced to these two ways of manipulating the names or counters wherewith we reason. As a crude but traditional illustration of additive reasoning, Hobbes instances the case of a man standing on a hill and perceiving an object approaching him through a fog. Beginning with the designation "body," what is perceived is progressively called "animate" and "rational," in the degree that the conditions of perception improve and give rise to the images answering to these names. Finally, the observer formally adverts to the fact that all these names belong to the same object and hence can be summed up in the single name "man." The opposite operation of subtraction would be carried out as the man recedes again in the distance. Sometimes, Hobbes speaks as though the computation of reason concerns only the names, without any direct reliance on the images and things. This hesitation is traceable to his incomplete analysis of the universal element in thought. If the universal as such is restricted to the nominal order, then reasoning concerns only the relations among names. But this leaves out of account the *controlling influence* of objects of perception and mental conceptions upon the use of words. In the adduced example, the motive for adding "rational" rather than "nonrational" to "animal" is not purely nominal but is founded on an intellectual grasp of the implications of the manifested traits of the approaching thing. In practice, Hobbes readily grants the influence of actual perceptions, but his nominalism compels him to underplay the relation between such perceptions and reason in its scientific function.

It is noteworthy that rational computation is directed toward the *consequences* of general names. Experiential knowledge is of mere matter of fact, whereas scientific knowledge is of the consequences of fact. This underlines the second differential note of philosophy: its *causal nature.* Hobbes agrees with Scholastic tradition that scientific knowledge is causal and that philosophy studies the most comprehensive causes. His originality consists in limiting the meaning of cause to its current scientific acception. Since only "efficient" and "material" causes of motion are required in mechanics, these are the only proper objects of philosophical inquiry. Hence the definition of philosophy limits causal explanation to generative processes. Only bodies subject to generation, through some variation of motion, can be accounted for in scientific terms of cause and effect.

The direct consequence is a radical restriction of the *immediate subject matter* of philosophy. As stated by Hobbes, philosophy treats of "every body of which we can conceive any generation, and which we may, by any consideration thereof compare with other bodies, or which is capable of composition and resolution; that is to say, every body of whose generation or properties we can have any knowledge."[2] Whatever is not of a *bodily nature and capable of generation through motion* falls outside the realm of philosophical demonstration. This automatically excludes any study of God, angel, and an immaterial soul. Hobbes does not deny their existence outright but subjects them to a dilemma: either they are totally irrelevant for philosophy or come within its scope at the price of being regarded as bodies or properties of bodies. Philosophy is also forbidden to discourse about the nature of the eternal, the ingenerable and the uncaused, since these objects cannot be regarded as consequences of facts, within an order of generable causes and effects. Hobbes continues Bacon's work of narrowing down the field of philosophy by also declaring the infinite out of bounds. Whatever we imagine is finite, and our thoughts cannot transcend the images of finite bodies and their properties. At least within a philosophical context, Hobbes equates the *real* and *conceivable* with the *finite* and *imaginable*. God Himself is not only incomprehensible but also completely inconceivable by our minds. Philosophy uses the names "God" and "infinite power" not to designate the infinite being itself but only to characterize the defects of our knowledge and certain human attitudes of reverence.

The *method* of philosophy is implied in the description of its subject matter and leads to a similar elimination of anything incorporeal, whether infinite or finite. Philosophy enters the scene only where reasoning is possible, viz., only where there is computation of more and less, through the dual process of the resolution and composition of bodies and their properties. In philosophy, "incorporeal" and "spiritual" are meaningless words, taken by themselves, and lead to absurdity when used in such combinations as "incorporeal sub-

---

[2] *Ibid.*, II, i, 8 (Molesworth, I, 10).

stance" or "spiritual infusion." By method is meant the most expedite way of finding out effects from known causes or causes from known effects. Philosophical reasoning proceeds in both directions, but Hobbes prefers to use the Galilean terms "composition and resolution" rather than the Baconian terms "deduction and induction" to describe them. The *resolutive* or *analytical method* begins with a given complex whole or effect and breaks it down into its elements. The latter are then rendered general by connecting them with the common traits of material things and with the universal causes of these traits. The *compositive* or *synthetical method* begins with the general causes and component factors, in order to construct the effect with their aid. In no case can these methods apply to modes of being which, by supposition, do not have bodily parts and causes which could affect us in ways subject to resolution and composition. The exclusion of immaterial things is a strict consequence of Hobbes' decision to make Galileo's procedure the sole appropriate one in all departments of philosophy.

Hobbes usually made a *threefold division* of philosophy into the study of body, man, and state. Under the heading of a *study of body* are included: the principles of geometry, the mechanical laws of motion, some common philosophical definitions, and the general properties of bodies. The *treatise on man* covers the special affections of the individual human body: the cognitive operations and the passions that move the individual. Finally, *civil philosophy* studies man as subject to rights and duties and as comprising the artificial body or body politic, the commonwealth. Sometimes, Hobbes mentioned another triple division into natural philosophy or physics (geometrical and mechanical principles, sensible qualities, human sentiency or cognition), moral philosophy (the individual's passions and their causes), and civil philosophy. The only advantage of this second classification is to accentuate the continuity of man with the rest of nature, through the reduction of his knowledge to the laws governing physics. Hobbes always found man the individual a most troublesome object to classify, because of the danger that his cognition would seem too *distinctive* to be given a mechanical cause, and his passions too *private* to issue in society. On the whole, he preferred to take the risk implied in the first classification, namely, that the occurrence of certain effects of bodily motion (sensible qualities and images, as well as passions) required the presence of a peculiar type of body called the sentient subject. In both classifications, however, Hobbes called for *univocity of method* and *continuity of analysis*. The philosopher must base his knowledge of politics upon a knowledge of the passional motions of the mind, the latter upon a study of the motions of sense, and this in turn upon a general study of geometrical and mechanical principles of bodily motion. Philosophy is a scientific body of truths only on condition that the mind proceed in order from body in general to man the individual and then to social man.

In applying the philosophical method to the content of philosophy, Hobbes distinguishes between the order of discovery and the order of teaching or demonstration to others. The movement of *invention* or *discovery* begins with resolutive analysis. An analysis of our notions must first be made in order to reach the most universal traits of our knowledge of things. The task of formulating our primary definitions is purely analytical and requires a clarification of our names for causes. With the aid of the universal knowledge of principles thus gained, the synthetic method can be employed, in order to make demonstrative discoveries. Hobbes places great reliance upon the movement of compositive synthesis from known cause to effect, from known elements to the compound whole. Indeed, as far as the *teaching* or *exposition* of philosophy is concerned, it must be carried on exclusively in terms of synthesis and composition. Demonstration to others begins from premises that cannot be demonstrated or validated by synthesis itself. The universal definitions are to be posited, and then the process of combining the universal elements of things can follow the laws of motion, as formulated by Galileo. Hobbes' own writings are cast in this *synthetico-demonstrative* mold, preventing us from following in detail the way in which he analytically discovers and justifies the universal definitions that control all his reasoning.

Since philosophy is a study of the causes and forces that can produce effects in the world, its end is to put this productive knowledge to use. In a Baconian spirit, Hobbes declares that the mere "inward glory and triumph of mind,"[3] resulting from the possession of speculative knowledge, is not worth the pains of philosophical investigation. *Knowledge* is acquired *for the sake of power,* for the performance of action or the production of a thing. Philosophy thus remains in the line of mechanics as a practical discipline.

---

[3] *Concerning Body,* I, i, 6 (Molesworth, I, 7).

Hobbes does not claim that philosophy apprehends the *actual* causes at work in nature, but it does determine the causes that *might* necessarily produce natural effects. Hobbes' doctrine on sense images as the mind's proper object, and on universal reasoning as a calculation with names and given elements of definition, prevents him from ever removing the *hypothetical* and *phenomenalistic* character of the demonstrations in his philosophy. Yet in the practical order, the presence of philosophy is what distinguishes a civilized country, fundamentally, from an uncivilized one and what gives solid hope of ridding social life of the scourge of war. The greatest achievement of philosophy is to develop reliable knowledge of social and political institutions, such that stable peace may come within our power to realize. Whereas Bacon takes "power" to mean primarily a technical control over nature, Hobbes understands it primarily as social control within the political community.

### 3. FIRST PHILOSOPHY AND MATERIALISTIC MECHANISM

Invariably, Hobbes attributes the defects of previous philosophies to their failure to follow geometry in its careful formulation of basic definitions and universal principles. To construct these premises of demonstration is the task of *philosophia prima,* but instead of placing it after natural philosophy, he makes it the initial phase in philosophy. The doctrine of the *first grounds of philosophy* explores the immediate consequences of primary definitions.[4] The definitions themselves are precise statements of the basic general postulates and causal principles, discovered by rational analysis of general terms. For instance, the resolutive method may begin with a given singular thing that is square in shape. The object is then resolved into certain universal characteristics: line, plane, terminated, angle, etc. Next, the causes of these characteristics and of their combination in this shape are sought. In the case of the most universal causes, no method is needed. They are self-evident or known "to nature," i.e., manifest to our reason rather than to sense. Although they do not require or permit of demonstration, our names expressing the highest causes need to be refined and explicated in primary definitions, which provide the principles for scientific demonstration.

Under the heading of *self-evident, universal, causal principles,*

---

[4] Part II of *Concerning Body* is devoted to an exposition of the "first grounds of philosophy." See also Section I of "A Short Tract on First Principles," printed as Appendix I in *The Elements of Law* (edited by F. Tönnies, 152–55).

Hobbes included the *fundamental theses of Galilean mechanics,* in a universalized form.[5] The basic kind and prototype of all motion is local motion or the relinquishing of one place and gaining of another; the universal cause of both geometrical and perceptible objects is mechanical motion; motion has no other cause than motion, mechanistically conceived; every sort of mutation consists in motion of bodily parts. Descartes and Scholastic readers protested against this easy way of labeling one's favorite theses as self-evident principles, beyond all need of a critical foundation, and against the unqualified generalization made of the laws of mechanics, now elevated to the rank of first principles of philosophy. Whereas Descartes wanted to restrict mechanistic explanation to *extended* substance, Hobbes boldly proclaimed it to be the ground of *all* philosophical demonstration. Because the axioms he formulated held true of the conditions for sensation, he extended them to all possible objects of demonstrative knowledge.

Methodologically, Hobbes was committed not only to mechanism but also to *materialism.* Without saying that bodies are the only reality, he held them to be the only philosophically ascertainable realities. Hence he equated substance and body, stigmatizing "bodiless or immaterial substance" as a contradiction in terms. The universe is an aggregate of bodies, and there is no real part of it that is not also a body. Every *substance* or thing subsisting in itself is a bodily being, extended and independently existent. The aggregate of accidents or appearances constitutes the thing's knowable nature, without being identical with the thing itself. This is implied in the definition of an *accident* as the faculty of the body whereby it produces a conception in us or, still more subjectively, as the manner of our conception of body. The only way in which accidents exist in the extramental thing is after the manner of motion and rest, figure and extension. All the accidents — with the exception of figure and extension — may continually perish, without affecting the perceived substance itself. Only figure and extension are present in the perceived body in such fashion that, for them to perish, is for the body itself to perish. Thus Hobbes agrees with Galileo and Descartes on

---

[5] Taking Hobbes as the typical modern mechanist in philosophy, H. F. Tiblier, S.J., points out, in "The Foundations of Mechanism," *The Modern Schoolman,* XXI (1943–1944), 90–100, 162–69, that Hobbes combined scientific mechanism with an Eleatic monism of matter, thus making the study of real motion and change doubly impossible, within the limits of his philosophy.

the subjectivity of all accidents, save those primary qualities that belong to the mathematico-mechanical explanation of bodily motion.

Another important definition laid down in first philosophy is that of *cause*. In the strict sense, philosophy asks about the entire generation of an event rather than about any single cause. Not one particular causal factor but the entire causal scheme or principle of generation is the object of inquiry. Hence Hobbes defines cause as such as the *entire cause, "the sum or aggregate of all such accidents, both in the agents and the patient, as concur to the producing of the effect propounded; all which existing together, it cannot be understood but that the effect exists with them."*[6] The body which generates motion in another body is the agent, and the body in which the motion is generated is the patient. The aggregate of accidents in the agent is the *efficient* cause, whereas the aggregate in the patient is the *material* cause. Together, they constitute the entire cause or generation. Formal and final causes are only aspects of efficiency. *Formal* cause is reduced to the producing of knowledge in us by the definition of the essence; *final* cause is found only in beings with sense and will, and is equivalent to the way efficient cause operates, with deliberation, in man. Since philosophy seeks only the generation or material-and-efficient cause of things, it can be developed exclusively within the mechanistic framework. That causal power is always accidental and always conditioned by spatial contiguity and variations of local motion, is a postulate read into the very definition of cause, thus forestalling any discussion of creative causation or immaterial activity.

There is an aspect of Hobbes' doctrine on cause that is apt to be overlooked. The use of the term "accident" in the definition of cause is a warning that his causal theory is bound up with his theory of knowledge. Accidents concern motions of bodies precisely insofar as they affect the sentient subject. Hence Hobbes' entire approach to the axioms of motion and the nature of cause is infected by a deep-seated *subjectivism* and *skepticism,* that often go unacknowledged and that definitively set him off from Galileo. There is always a reference of the causal or generative process to the human mind and the names it employs in reasoning. Hence philosophical knowledge of consequence of fact or cause-and-effect is always conditional or *hypothetical*. What we know through the senses are only the causal conditions leading to sensation. What we know through reason

---

[6] *Concerning Body*, I, vi, 10 (Molesworth, I, **77**).

are the relations connecting certain of our names. We can legitimately affirm only that, *if* the causal process were of such-and-such a nature, then it *might* with necessity be generated through such-and-such elements. Hobbes' hesitation about the objectivity of causal demonstrations, together with his insistence on the necessity of the cause, gave Hume considerable food for thought.

Although Hobbes is not sure that causal sequences among things agree with the connections among our names, he is certain that we cannot pretend to know causal relations, scientifically, except as *necessary* ones. The entire or sufficient cause is such that, being present, the effect is produced instantaneously and necessarily. As far as philosophical understanding is concerned, the effect cannot but be conceived as following with necessity from its entire cause. All effects have a necessary cause and can eventually be traced to antecedents from which they must flow. This is required in principle by the definition of cause. If it cannot always be verified in fact, then we should look for the contingency rather in our ignorance of all the factors than in the causal principles themselves. Like Spinoza, Hobbes maintains a rigid *determinism* among all finite causes and effects. This rules out ordinary human freedom. And since Hobbes differs from Spinoza in not applying the causal doctrine to God and hence in not invoking any extraordinary meaning for freedom, his mechanistic determinism is an unrelieved outlook.

## 4. HUMAN KNOWLEDGE

Hobbes' deepest-running criticism of Descartes is that he fails to trace our knowledge back to its real source in sensation. There is no intellectual "I think" that is not dependent upon, and constructed from, an original "I sense." The one conviction withstanding all doubt is that *our mind has sensory representations* of the qualities of things, which exist outside of us. Hobbes refers to the representations indifferently as ideas, images, conceptions, or thoughts, thus furthering the breakdown of a difference in kind between sense and intellect. He treats our representations, first *singly,* and then as they are associated in some sort of *train* or *sequence.* His purpose is to determine the elementary constituents of experience, on the basis of which he can establish the nature and limits of experiential knowledge as such. Last, he seeks to establish the distinction between *man* and *brute,* without fracturing the continuity among our cognitions or their ultimate resolution in sense.

## HOBBES ON MAN THE INDIVIDUAL

1. Cognition: endeavor outward.
   a) Representations taken singly.
      1) Motion received from extramental, extended body.
      2) Sensation or original fancy.
      3) Imagination or decaying sense:
         (a) Memory.
         (b) Experience.
         (c) Understanding.
   b) Representations taken in a train or sequence of thoughts.
      1) Unguided mental discourse.
      2) Guided or regulated mental discourse: causal inference.
2. The Passions: endeavor inward.
   a) Pleasure, desire, good.
   b) Pain, aversion, evil.
   c) Deliberation, will, determinism.

Our *single* conceptions proceed originally from the actions of the extramental thing. The endeavor of the thing exerts itself upon the sentient subject, arousing motion in the latter through its contiguity and pressure upon the external sense organs. The motion continues in an inward direction, until it reaches the organic sense-center in the brain and heart. Here again, the laws of mechanics may be invoked to explain the reaction of the organic center, for this reaction is but an endeavor opposite to the original endeavor from the external body. Since the original direction of motion was *inward* from the external body to the organ, the reaction constituting sense or sensation proper is an *endeavor outward* or an objective reference. The sensation has a certain duration in the knowing subject. It may be called a *seeming*, an apparition, or an original fancy, since the results of the motion *in* the sentient subject appear or seem to belong to the *external* world, in conformity with the outward reference of the reaction. All this may be summed up in the definition of *sensation* as *"a phantasm [or image], made by the reaction and endeavour outwards in the organ of sense, caused by an endeavour inwards from the object, remaining for some time more or less."*[7]

The various kinds of sensations are due to the variety of motions

[7] *Ibid.*, IV, xxv, 2 (Molesworth, I, 391). For Hobbes' theory of knowledge, read *The Elements of Law*, I, 1-6 (Tönnies edition, 1-21); *Concerning Body*, IV, xxv, 1-10 (Molesworth, I, 387-405); *Leviathan*, I, 1-5 (Oakeshott edition, 7-30); W. A. Gerhard, "The Epistemology of Thomas Hobbes," *The Thomist*, XIX (1946), 573-87.

among external bodies and to the various sense organs for receiving and propagating the motions in the sensory subject. But the color, sound, odor, taste, and heat are nothing objectively real, over and above these mechanical motions and reactions. The *secondary sensible qualities* inhere in the knower rather than in the object. They are called fancies or seemings, since the outward endeavor of the sense makes them appear to belong to the moving body outside us and hence endows them with objective reference. This explanation of *why* we believe that secondary qualities are objectively real marks an advance over Galileo's simple distinction among kinds of qualities. Its success, however, depends upon an accommodated use of the terms "motion" and "reaction" that removes them considerably from the basic definition of motion as a gaining and relinquishing of place. Hobbes fails to specify any determinate sense in which the objective, *intentional reference of meaning* can be construed as being a variety of *outward-going motion*. His mechanistic description of organic reactions deals only with the conditions accompanying cognition, not with cognition itself. But the main factor he fails to explain mechanistically is the distinctive nature of that sort of body called a *sentient subject*. He simply accepts the fact that philosophy of man is distinguished from physics precisely in virtue of the constitution of one of the bodies in the universe: sensation results only when other bodies interact with the sentient organism. But Hobbes does not inquire into the real ground for the distinctive nature of the human subject. He is content with a description of the consequences of the difference, without attempting a causal explanation. For, such an explanation would lead beyond the boundaries marked for mechanistic philosophy.

Classical mechanics does provide a ready analogy to the duration of the sense representation or phantasm. Motion will continue within the knowing subject, until it is counteracted by other and opposite forces. Like Aristotle, Hobbes locates the difference between sense and *imagination* in whether or not the object causing the original motion is actually present. When the external object is removed, the image still retained in the perceiver is a function of imagination. But as imagination, the representation is obscured and weakened by the present sensations that continue to pour in upon sense. Just as sense is original fancy, so imagination is decaying sense. Imagination and *memory* are only logically distinct, the former adverting to the content itself of the fading image, and the latter referring to the fading or decaying condition of the image, by contrast with its original vitality as a sensation. Hobbes adds that *experience* is "much memory, or memory of many things,"[8] and that *understanding* is nothing more than that type of imagination which can be aroused in man or other animals by means of words or other voluntary signs. Human understanding is distinctive, only in being able to discover in such signs not only the commands of will but also the significance of thoughts. Hobbes has no room for a noncorporeal intellectual power, so that *reason* (the reckoning of the consequences of general names) is wider in function than, but not different in kind from, imagination.

Subsequent empirical philosophers, particularly Hume, have paid special attention to Hobbes' remarks on the *consequence* or *train of thoughts*. Mental discourse or the discursive train of thoughts is any succession of our images, one upon the other. The fundamental principle is that the coherence and consequence of thoughts in imagination follow from the original coherence and consequence in sensations. What is sensed in a certain sequence, tends to be called up by imagination and memory in a similar sequence or mental transition. But *probability* rather than certainty governs natural mental discourse, since in nature the same perceived thing may be followed now by one consequent and now by another. This qualification affects not only our unguided or inconstant trains of thought but also those that are regulated, including remembrance, experience, prudence, and conjecture. The major epistemological problem centers around regulated mental discourse and its fruits.

A mental transition is *guided* rather than unguided, when it springs from some passionate thought, some organizing design based upon desire. Appetite sets a goal, and this leads to a searching of our thoughts for an appropriate sequence of means to that end. The search may go from an imagined effect to the causes that produce it (a process common to man and beast), or it may go from an imagined cause to all the possible effects it can have (a synthetic process proper to man alone). Remembrance is an aid in ferreting out these sequences. An "experiment" is a remembrance of some particular consequence of thought, containing antecedents and consequents, whereas "experience" is nothing more than one's having had many experiments or remembrances of sequences. In linking experience with memory of causal sequences, Hobbes is led to maintain that our *natural, regulated discourse about cause and effect* never rises above strong probability. The *experiential* knowledge of causation, whether it be presumption of the past or conjecture of the future, cannot achieve the necessity and universality required for *scientific causal knowledge.* The prudent man is one who takes his thoughts as signs, antecedent or consequent, of other thoughts with which they may confidently be joined, in determining what is likely to come to pass or to have already occurred. But this assurance is always approximate rather than absolute, so that the prudent man is wary in his use of signs of causal sequence. He who has the most experience in guessing by signs proceeds with the most certainty in his causal inference, but (Hobbes comments) "not with certainty enough."[9]

From a reading of this analysis of cause, it is not difficult to anticipate the doubts that actually took shape in Hume's mind. For, if we can never have complete assurance in our experiential connection of antecedents and consequents, then of what value is the axiom that from like causes like effects must follow? This is a universal and necessary statement that experience never fully warrants. If Hobbes replies that the situation is different in the scientific determination of causal sequences, then Hume's problem will be whether a nominalistic sort of science has any right to make causal pronouncements about consequences of matters of fact. Do the names and definitions used in scientific reasoning apply at all to real sequences in nature? Hobbes has left this application in a hypothetical state, but Hume will want to know whether the discrepancy is not due to the mathematical orientation of Hobbes' conception of science and demonstration. If this be the case, then the Hobbesian theory of a single method in philosophy does not succeed in overcoming the dualism between experience and science, the inferences of the prudent man and those of the philosopher, the existential import of causality and the necessity of its connections. And if these cleavages remain unhealed in regard to basic speculative issues, a sound foundation has not been provided for the practical study of the passions and social life.

In addition to sense, the thoughts in imagination and the train of conceptions, Hobbes admits no other *natural* cognitive equipment in man. The differences between *man* and *brute* rest not upon these

---

[9] *Ibid.,* I, 3 (Oakeshott, 16).

natural motions but upon the *artificial* motions that man's understanding can generate with the aid of speech and method.[10] Hobbes
sets a pattern for later empiricism by describing these differences in
terms of the instruments specially forged and employed by man,
but without raising the question of the ground in actuality for
man's unique ability to fashion and use speech and scientific method.
His aversion to the Cartesian notions of an immaterial substance
and an immaterial knowing power led him to suppress inquiries
into the human substantial principle and to merge the powers of
man with their operations and instruments.

Man can fix his thoughts by means of marks, especially words or
names. When words are connected together, they constitute speech,
which is the means whereby the train of mental discourse can be
transformed into communicable, verbal discourse. *Speech* is an aid
both to memory and to communication with others. It enables man
to become reflectively conscious of his thoughts, since reflection is
the same as the use of words with deliberate and precise meaning.
*Truth* and *absurdity* belong only to speech and, indeed, are identical
with true and absurd propositions. (Strictly speaking, *error* is found
only in natural experience, when our conjectures about antecedents
and consequents are not borne out by events.) Man alone can acquire
true knowledge, since he alone can grasp the function of speech
to signify thoughts. But just as truth is man's privilege, because of
his ability to use words, so is absurdity — and for the same reason.
Philosophical absurdities are traceable to the misuse of words and
the want of a sound method. Reason and science are nourished upon
the correct and methodical use of universal names, so that the
consequences of facts may be determined. Just as the man of much
experience is prudent, so the man of much science is wise. Brutes
can be prudent, but only man can be wise or foolish. Certainty
is found unqualifiedly only in science and its culmination, philosophical wisdom. The welfare of mankind is mainly furthered by
the efforts of the wise man or philosopher.

---

[10] R. Polin, in "La nature humaine selon Hobbes," *Revue Philosophique de la France
et de l'Étranger,* CXLII (1952), 31–52, notes that the entire Hobbesian anthropology
rests upon the view that the only distinctive feature about man is his ability to construct his own reality, with the aid of words. Cf. John Dewey, *Logic: The Theory of
Inquiry* (New York, Holt, 1938), 44–56, where the highly significant human power
of forming symbols and language is also taken as the ultimate explanation of man's
difference from the brute. Both philosophers substitute a *descriptively ultimate trait*
for a *causally ultimate principle.*

## 5. THE PASSIONS AND THE WILL

Hobbes distinguishes the *passions* or the *motive power of the mind* from both the mind's cognitive power and the motive power of the body. He paves the way for a mechanistic psychology of the passions and ethics by describing these distinctions in terms of local motion. The motive power of the body is that by which it moves other bodies, whereas the motive or active power of the mind is that whereby the mind gives motion to its own body. And whereas our cognitive acts result from a movement outward from the sense center toward the perceived object, there is also an inward direction of the same motion which was first caused by the external body. This inward movement or passion passes from the brain to the depths of the heart, with a consequent quickening or slackening of our vital motion. *Pleasure* is nothing more than such inward motion as helps this vital motion, whereas *pain* is inward motion that hinders the movement of the heart. Just as conceptions are only agitations within the brain, so the passions of pleasure and pain are only agitations within the heart. To reach this conclusion, Hobbes blurs the distinction between an isolation of the purely mechanistic factors for our convenience of description and a definitive assertion that these factors are the sole causal agencies involved in thought and the passions. His purpose is to show that all our passional and moral attitudes are derived from pleasure and pain. Pleasure carries over into *appetite* or *desire* for whatever causes such motion; pain leads to *aversion* from the objects at its base. Thus we love and pursue the pleasurable, hate and avoid the painful. Human life is a sort of vector resolution of these hedonistic lines of force.

Good and evil are not absolute but are, in every respect, relative to man's passions or acts of desire and aversion. Through repeated reactions to objects, we become accustomed to regard the object of desire or love as *good,* and the object of aversion or hate as *evil.* This pleasure-pain theory of good and evil is based, like Spinoza's, upon a primitive urge, endeavor, or *conatus* toward self-preservation. What each isolated individual regards as good, is relative entirely to his own constitution, needs, and history. In society, good and evil are determined by a spokesman for the social group. If there be any constant good or commonly desirable object among men, it is the *pursuit of felicity through increase of power;* if any supreme evil, it is *death,* especially sudden and violent death. The life of man is depicted by Hobbes as a competitive race, about which the wisdom of the passions can be given in two maxims:

Continually to out-go the next before, is felicity.
And to forsake the course, is to die.[11]

The concrete content of basic motives is provided, at least in the state of nature, by the individual's own appraisal of what is to his benefit or harm.

The calculation of one's benefits and harms is the work of *deliberation*. Deliberation is required to the extent that appetite and aversion are concerned with a future situation, rather than with present pleasure and pain. Consideration of a proposed course of action entails an imagining of its good and bad consequences, as well as of what in the present situation has the power to produce or avoid them. At this juncture, the moral aspect of what Hobbes had previously called guided discourse or passionate thought is evident. Imagination operates in the service of the passions by searching out the probable consequences of our hopes and fears and by giving an experienced judgment about the proper causal sequences to follow. The alternation of the passions of desire and aversion is terminated when the action is either done or declared impossible. The final act, in the deliberative series of appetites and aversions, which immediately adheres to the action or omits it, is the *will*.

There is no separate power of will: the universal name signifies only that act which is the last desire in the deliberative series.[12] There is no real distinction between other acts of appetition and the final appetitive act of will, except that appetite may sometimes function without deliberation, whereas will is always deliberative appetite. Deliberation, however, is not a peculiarly human operation. Since it consists in an interplay between acts of passion and of imagination, it can be performed by brutes as well as men. Therefore,

---

[11] *The Elements of Law*, I, 9 (Tönnies, 37). On the passions and moral distinctions, see *ibid.*, I, 7–9 (Tönnies, 21–37); *Concerning Body*, IV, xxv, 12 (Molesworth, I, 406–08); *Leviathan*, I, 6 (Oakeshott, 31–39). The connection between the passions and the man-centered scale of subjective moral values is pointed out by R. Polin, "Le bien et le mal dans la philosophie de Hobbes," *Revue Philosophique de la France et de l'Étranger*, CXXXVI (1946), 289–321.

[12] On will and freedom, compare *The Elements of Law*, I, 12 (Tönnies, 47–49); *Concerning Body*, IV, xxv, 13 (Molesworth, I, 408–09); *Leviathan*, I, 6 (Oakeshott, 37–38). Among Hobbes' numerous minor tracts on this question is *Of Liberty and Necessity* (Molesworth, IV, 231–78).

will can also be present in brutes, when deliberation occurs. Because will is not a separate power and not confined to man, there is no reason for according man the privilege of free will, except in the sense of absence of external impediments to bodily motion — but this may also be said of water that is "freely" descending a hill. The *denial of freedom* is clinched by application of the general doctrine of the entire cause of motion. The voluntary action proceeding from will could not be performed unless there were present a sufficient cause of that action. Every sufficient cause is the entire cause of the action, and from the entire cause the action follows necessarily. As the last appetite, immediately issuing in the voluntary action, the will has its entire and sufficient cause, determining its action with necessity. It would be contradictory to affirm that the will is both a sufficient cause and a nonnecessitated one. Every effect actually produced is produced with necessity: this law applies without modification to the effect of volition.

Hobbes reaches this conclusion partly on the strength of the assumption that all causes act in the same way, in producing motion, and partly on the ground that reason is no different in kind from imagination. He sees that, once the final practical judgment is pronounced, the will is bound to choose. But he does not recognize any distinctive cognitive power that can surpass the particular, imaginative visualization of concrete courses of action, in order to compare the proposed end with the good in general. The repudiation of an immaterial intellectual power leads to a denial of our ability to conceive of the good in general, distinct from particular goods. From the standpoint of the causality of the will, the issue is already decided, once the general definition of cause and effect is identified with the scientific notion of necessary entailment. The only freedom left for man in the Hobbesian system is *to do* what he wishes: but he has no power of determining freely his own *wishes* or *acts of choice*. Jonathan Edwards, the American Calvinist proponent of divine predeterminism, will allow man so much freedom, and no more.

## 6. MAN IN THE STATE OF NATURE

Having explained the motion of natural bodies, including man the individual, Hobbes next proceeded to a study of the compound motion resulting in artificial bodies or human societies. He felt that the mechanical approach to individual human actions had made their nature just as evident as geometrical figures and that, with the aid of such knowledge, all erroneous opinions about right and wrong in the social sphere could easily be exposed. The fruitage of this inquiry would be an all but total elimination of the causes of war and an establishment of perpetual peace. The object of civil philosophy is the body politic, the commonwealth. Following his general method, Hobbes undertook to show the material and efficient causes of the generation and corruption of the body politic. Since men are the material causes or constituent members of the social artifact and the human will its efficient cause, there is close continuity between the analysis of man's natural equipment — his strength of body, senses, reason, and passions — and that of his social and political relations.

When the resolutive method is applied according to the analogy of mechanics, it must be terminated at some indivisible, unitary body. Whereas in natural philosophy this leads usually to some form of physical atomism, in civil philosophy it leads Hobbes to a form of *social atomism*. The bedrock of social analysis is the isolated, solitary, self-enclosed *individual man*. The main problem is to discover how a number of such atomic units can be led to form a commonwealth. Hobbes denies that man is by nature a political animal, even though he needs some meeting ground with others of his kind. The individual never ceases to concentrate upon seeking his own good and satisfying his own irreducible, unassimilable endeavor. Hobbes tries to retain this notion of the individual as an end in himself and yet show that the individual's natural dynamism leads to the erection of an absolute political power. This combination of apolitical individualism and political absolutism announces one of the major polar tensions around which modern political thinking is organized.

The lone individual pursues his own felicity, striving constantly to increase his power and ward off the supreme evil, death. He is sometimes deluded by pride into thinking that his own unaided power is sufficient, by itself, to secure his proper good. But the individual's predicament — the brute fact conditioning his existence and deriving from no anterior premise — is that he must live along with other individuals. His *fellow men* constitute his fate, his ill condition. The self-endeavoring individual finds himself striving after his own satisfactions along with other similarly motivated, self-centered subjects. What the others do, ineluctably affects his own projects and limits his actual ability to attain what he regards as his own good. The individual's power is qualified in its concrete exercise by his relations with other men, and about this qualifying relationship he can be either honest or misled by vainglory.

Hobbes' account of the *state of nature* is a description of the relations existing among individuals in the absence of any overawing social power.[13] It is essentially an analytical rather than a historical conception. For, the traits of the state of nature are ascertained not by appeal to historical documents but by reference to the passions and their social consequences. Hobbes does mention conditions obtaining in seventeenth-century America but the major empirical confirmation of his analysis of the passions is found in our everyday life, even within the present political community. We bar our doors and windows at night, rely upon police and courts, and spend a good portion of tax money for a standing army. The implication is that political order always builds upon a seething volcano of conflicting individual forces, wherein we can discern the features of man's natural, apolitical condition. Times of natural disaster and civil war give us a stark glimpse into the manner of human behavior in a situation where sovereign political power is absent.

Two conditions concur to make the state of nature one of universal and perpetual warfare: the fact of *equality* and the *competitive tendency* of the passions. Men are equals who can do equal things against each other. Hobbes bases the claim to equality not upon our common nature and origin but upon the physical ability of even the weakest man to bring the *summum malum* of death to another and upon the equality of our experience, in that no man's prudential judgments achieve certainty. Although some men are moderate enough to acknowledge their equality with others in these respects, the fact is unpalatable to the great majority. Most men are led by vainglory to overrate their own capacities and then to consolidate the illusion by invidious comparisons and competition. They engage in social intercourse more for personal gain and glory than for the sake of the commonweal. The passions are not intrinsically perverse but, under the lash of such vainglory, they have a chaotic and immoderate effect upon each man's will, prompting him to hurt and outdo his fellow men at all costs.

The equality among individuals is further displayed by the absolute necessity imposed upon every man to seek what appears good to him and to avoid the evils of death and suffering. Since it is not

[13] *The Elements of Law*, I, 14 (Tönnies, 53–57); *De Cive or The Citizen*, I, 1 (edited by Lamprecht, 21–30); *Leviathan*, I, 13 (Oakeshott, 80–84).

against reason to carry out what our nature impels us to do, Hobbes calls this *absolute liberty to use our natural power for self-preservation* the *basic natural right*. This right is expanded into the further rights of employing all means necessary for self-defense and of being one's own judge about what is necessary and good for oneself. These rights do not inhere in a fictitious "human nature" but in each individual man, who is impelled to seek his own good. It follows that every man has a natural right to all things, i.e., to do whatever he wishes to others and to use whatever he wishes as leading to his own satisfaction. If nature gives all things to all men in this sense, then *right* and *profit* coincide for the individual. But in a world of limited material goods, several men are bound to desire the same thing, without the possibility of dividing or enjoying it in common. Men thus become enemies, making counterclaims and counterjudgments, backed up by the use of force. The result is a state of war, brought on by the conflicting individual lines of desire and power.

The natural condition of man is that of *perpetual war of all against all*. What one man defends as his own, is precisely what another man claims for himself. The state of war consists not so much in actual combat as in the declared will of contesting by force and gaining one's desire by force. The stronger man will retain what many others can only desire, and only the sword will decide who is actually the strongest. In this state of unrestrained warfare, effective right reaches no further than one's might. Except for the "law of nature," i.e., the irresistible tendency of one's own being toward self-preservation, there exists *no law:* to have all and to do all are "lawful" for all. Since Hobbes gives a purely legal definition of right and wrong, he concludes that in the state of nature, where there is no law, there is also no objective right and wrong, justice and injustice, social good and evil. Combat decides everything, elevating force and fraud into the "cardinal virtues," without which a man is considered weak and fit prey for the stronger. When such conditions prevail, there are "no arts; no letters; no society; and which is worst of all, continual fear, and danger of violent death; and the life of man, solitary, poor, nasty, brutish, and short."[14] Only such abuses of oneself as drunkenness and pointless cruelty run sufficiently against oneself to make the individual's natural impulses toward

---

[14] *Leviathan*, I, 13 (Oakeshott, 82).

self-preservation and felicity rebel and seek to call a halt.

By painting an extreme and unrelieved picture of man's natural predicament, Hobbes seeks to generate the *countermotion* that will drive men into civil society. Being a good mechanist, he must make the one force (natural warfare) sufficiently powerful to call forth, by way of reaction, the great power that is embodied in the commonwealth. He looks for salvation in two factors that are present even in the state of nature: the *passions* themselves and *reason*. Although natural man has the disposition to treat his fellow man as a wolf would a wolf, he is also moved by passions other than ravenous pride and superiority. He has a deep-seated fear of death, which is translated into mutual fear among men, who are the main causes of death to each other. Not mutual good will or a benevolent general will but *mutual fear* is the motive force urging men into political society.[15] They discover that association with others provides some safeguard against injury, sudden death, and loss of possessions. Furthermore, their very desire for the commodities of life and their hope of obtaining them by industry are mighty passions, which are thwarted in a state of nature that allows for no development of material and cultural goods. It is a contradiction in terms to desire what is good for oneself and also to adhere voluntarily to the natural state of warfare and unlimited liberty to do and take whatever one wants. Hence the nisus of the passions both creates the state of nature and leads us to transcend it, by seeking peace and social order. In this movement to rid ourselves of total anarchy, reason is a help. It can formulate certain theorems or articles of peace that may guide man in devising social means for taming the passions and cultivating the fruits of civil life.

## 7. THE SOCIAL CONTRACT AND THE COMMONWEALTH

The only right recognized in the state of nature is that of every man to seek his own good without hindrance. Reason can reflect upon this natural right, the consequences of its exercise in the natural state, and the resultant conflict between the pursuit of happiness and the misery and danger of natural existence. It recognizes that one's

---

[15] L. Strauss, in "On the Spirit of Hobbes' Political Philosophy," *Revue Internationale de Philosophie*, IV (1950), 405-31, shows that the political hedonism of Hobbes relies upon the fear of death, as the strongest natural motive, and that the content of virtue is reduced to political virtue, especially to peaceableness, cultivated for its own sake.

self-preservation depends upon securing the minimal conditions of peace. Hence reason supplies some general rules for reaching this objective. The sum of moral philosophy is contained in the *dictates of reason* concerning things to be done or omitted, so that individual appetites may be satisfied. These dictates may be called the laws of nature, but this is using the term "law" improperly, since law requires a declaration by him who has authority to command, and as yet there is no such person. The dictates of reason, in the natural state, are not strict laws and carry no obligation. They are given the force of obligation only when they are commanded by the will of God or the political sovereign. (Hobbes subscribes unhesitatingly to the voluntaristic view of law, as being constituted formally by the sovereign's command.) But unless we do follow reason, our self-endeavor is in vain.

The precepts of reason for the development of man's passions are summed up in a negative version of the Golden Rule: Do not that to another, which you would not have done to yourself. By imagination, the individual should try to put himself in the position of another and hence to refrain from willing anything that would hinder the other's primary endeavor toward self-preservation. *Mutual non-interference under the rule of an absolute power* is the ultimate intent of reason's counsel. Of the twenty or so particular *laws of nature* or *articles of peace* enumerated by Hobbes, three are fundamental to the formation of civil society. The first states that every man ought to strive for peace as far as possible and, for the rest, seek all means of war in self-defense. The second one declares that — when and insofar as others are also willing — a man should be willing to lay down his right to all things for the sake of peace and self-defense. The third theorem is a corollary of the second: men should keep their covenants. Otherwise, they would both desire peace and render it impossible, by failing to live up to the promises upon which it is built.

Hobbes makes a rigorously legalistic deduction of the *contract* by which the commonwealth is constituted, but his argument is always enlivened by observations about human passions. In the second major dictate of reason is conveniently found a means of extricating men from their miserable condition of perpetual warfare. For, the basic meaning of laying down one's right is that one should divest oneself of *the* natural right, the liberty of man to do all and take all. Although one individual cannot give to another anything to which the other man does not also have an equal right, he can agree not to stand in the other's way. The conveyance of rights dictated by reason is thus a foregoing of the right to resist, at pleasure, another's basic liberty to seek his own felicity. This right of interference is laid aside not by being renounced but by a definite *transfer to a beneficiary,* which is not itself a contracting party. Moreover, there is mutual transfer of rights and hence a genuine contract, one with a view to reciprocal benefit. This contract involves a covenant or promise of performing what is to be done.

What is to be done is not a particular deed or the transference of particular goods but rather a determination of the will to make perpetual transference of absolute liberty to the beneficiary and to refrain from interfering with the beneficiary's exercise of power over oneself. Someone is designated to whom I transfer my absolute liberty, without resistance, on condition that others do likewise. But a covenant of this sort runs counter to all the powerful emotions that lead to the natural state of war; hence its performance is constantly threatened by the solicitations of these same passions. By itself alone, a covenant is not effective to the point of securing peace and preventing attack upon one's person and goods. As long as fear cannot quell inclinations to revoke one's transfer of rights, the articles of peace are binding only internally, requiring one only to have the readiness of will to make the transfer. Actual transference can be made only when the contract is such as to institute a social authority, with coercive power enough to overawe men and prevent them from assailing one another. A *common power* is needed to *terrify* men to the point where they will cease to be their own judges of when they will and will not exercise absolute liberty of interference with others. Consent among a considerable multitude is a necessary condition, and this consent must be backed up by the sword of justice (compelling them to keep the peace within the community) and the sword of war (compelling men to join strength against outside enemies). Only through this common power can men be reduced, in fact, to the unity of the body politic or civil society.

The specific nature of the social contract can be gathered from the definition of the commonwealth, which is its outcome. The *commonwealth* is *"one person, of whose acts a great multitude, by mutual*  *covenants one with another, have made themselves every one the author, to the end he may use the strength and means of them all,*

*as he shall think expedient, for their peace and common defence."*[16]
This formula accords both with Hobbes' general canons of definition
and with the aims of his political philosophy. It declares that a
multitude of individual men comprise the material cause of the
generation of a commonwealth, their covenanting wills its efficient
cause, and mutual peace and defense its unifying final cause (which
is reducible to the tendency of human appetite, i.e., to the efficient
cause). The multitude must be comparatively great: a relative and
safe majority in the area. It cannot consist merely of two or three
men or even of a larger number, whose security might easily be
threatened by the addition of a few men to some opposing faction.
The multitude must not merely come together but must also consent
or concur in will, for the attainment of security and peace.

Hobbes agrees neither with the divine-right theory of sovereignty
nor with that which traces it ultimately to the people as a whole.
Political power and authority come originally from men but not
from men united as a people, since the unity of a people is a consequence rather than a cause of sovereignty. The efficient causes
of the commonwealth are, in the first instance, the individual wills,
contracting singly with each other and made one only as a result
of their contract and the erection of a common power, which alone
is the "people." Hence the pivotal importance of the words *one
person,* in the definition of the commonwealth. In general, a person
is one whose words or actions are considered either as his own (a
natural person) or as representing the words or actions of another
(an artificial person). Now, it would be no relief from our natural
condition to transfer our right of absolute liberty to a natural person
as such, for this would mean unreserved slavery and insecurity. But
an *artificial person* or *sovereign* can be authorized as the representative of a multitude of natural persons or individuals, for the sake
of their mutual security. Each individual gives up his right of
unconditioned self-government to the man or assembly of men who
will hold political power and whose actions will, without hindrance,
represent one's own. The artificial or representative person will act
with authority, since it will have the right to act in the name of
the multitude.

The only way the multitude is reduced to one is through the *unity*

---

[16] *Leviathan,* II, 17 (Oakeshott, 112). This chapter is entitled "Of the Causes,
Generation and Definition of a Commonwealth."

*of the political office:* not the represented but the representer provides the basic political unity. The multitude also confers its entire
strength upon the man or group in whom the artificial person is
embodied. Thus, out of many natural wills, *one representative* (*not
common*) *will* is formed, whose actions everyone authorizes and fears
to resist. The union of civil society is not only moral but real, in
virtue of the very real, effective, and absolute power that is transferred. Since men have assigned unrestricted coercive power to the
commonwealth, Hobbes is ready to hail the latter as "that great
LEVIATHAN, or rather, to speak more reverently . . . that *mortal
god,* to which we owe under the *immortal God,* our peace and
defence."[17] It has the power to marshal individual wills for domestic
peace and protection against foreign attack, and these are the
greatest terrestrial goods within man's reach.

Hobbes' account of the origin of civil society reveals the limitations as well as the strength of a universal mechanistic philosophy.
Its strength lies in its effort to achieve great rigor and logical
consequence in drawing out the social implications of the passions.
But in order to make the mechanistic genesis of the state seem
plausible, Hobbes must insert many elements that represent fresh
drafts upon experience and the tradition of political thinking. Thus,
reason is now enabled to make generalizations about the conditions
of peace that are much more than nominal analyses, since they
express the actual, common conditions for securing our welfare.
Again, a number of other-regarding impulses and powers crop up
in the egoistic individual, disposing him toward a mutual giving-
over of rights. He is found to be not quite so egoistic that he cannot
and will not imagine himself in another's predicament and open
his heart to the appeal which fellow feeling makes against placing
obstacles in the other man's path. Although he is not strictly obli-
gated by the dictates of reason, at least an inner zone of responsibility
for the ready state of his will-to-transfer-rights is now carved out.
Even man's absolute determinism is somewhat relaxed, to permit
him to condition his action upon reason's calculation of the appropriate time for giving mutual consent. Finally, the individualistic
self-seeking drive is tempered, first by the common situation of
men (which is the real foundation for reason's political generalizations) and, next, by an appeal to their common peace and defense

---

[17] *Loc. cit.*

(which moves them to mutual agreement, because it conveys a meaning that is not negative or merely distributive in its generality). The attraction of the common peace, as a genuine final cause, is covertly substituted for respect for a negative Golden Rule, in order to furnish adequate motive power for an actual decision, on the part of many men, to enter into social covenant.

## 8. SOVEREIGN AND SUBJECTS

Civil society unites a multitude of *subjects,* by their compact, under the *sovereign* or holder of the common, absolute power. Through the covenant of their natural wills, the contracting individuals create an artificial will, to which they make absolute transfer of their natural liberty. What each could do in the state of nature now becomes the prerogative of the sovereign alone. He does everything with impunity, for he cannot injure those who have authorized his every deed and promised not to hinder him. The sovereign is not subject to the law, since he is its source. Hobbes' voluntarism is exhibited in his definition of *law as a command of will* rather than ✓ an ordinance of reason. The sovereign is the soul of the commonwealth rather than its head, for what is proper to him is the power of will and not reason. He cannot violate the law, in the sense of infringing upon an independent standard. The so-called "natural law" or the dictates of reason become truly legal and obligatory only upon the command and declaration of the sovereign. He may be brought to task only for those laws which he allows to stand and which he nevertheless could abrogate. Since the power of prescribing rules or civil laws determines *propriety,* it is to the sovereign's will that we must trace all distinction of property rights, as well as what is lawful and unlawful, socially good and evil, just and unjust.

The following *rights of absolute sovereignty* are also earmarks whereby we can tell whether a man or assembly holds sovereign power.[18] It can, at pleasure, make or abrogate laws, adjudge and administer laws, use unlimited coercive power, decide upon war and peace, and appoint the required officials. Sovereignty is not only absolute but also indivisible and inalienable. Hobbes will hear nothing in favor of limited sovereignty. He argues that this conception rests upon an impossible compromise between the state of nature and

---

[18] *The Elements of Law,* II, 1, No. 19 (Tönnies, 91–92); *De Cive or The Citizen,* II, 6 (Lamprecht, 70–86); *Leviathan,* II, 18 (Oakeshott, 113–20).

civil society and, furthermore, that it supposes the possibility of civil
laws existing even before the civil body is constituted. Nor is there
any room for mixed forms of government, in which various aspects
of sovereignty would be distributed among several authorities. There
are only the *three traditional forms of government*, depending upon
the nature of the person to whom supreme power is committed. It
is committed to one man in a monarchy, to some few men in an
aristocracy, and to an assembly of all in a democracy. These forms
of government differ in no way, in respect to the absolute and
indivisible character of sovereign power. Only on the basis of their
aptitude to achieve the ends of political life, can they be assessed.
Hobbes advises that, whatever the state of subjection in civil society,
it is always preferable to the brutal and unfruitful liberty of the
state of nature. He himself prefers a monarchy to the other kinds
of commonwealth, although he admits that, in any particular situation, prudence must be the judge of which type of government best
fits the circumstances.

*Subjects* cannot release themselves from the social covenant, since
they have irrevocably conveyed to the sovereign all their liberty
of private judgment concerning the commonwealth. They cannot
pretend that any action of his is in violation of a contract between
him and the people, for the contract is made among the individuals
*qua* individuals and not between a people and a sovereign. Before
the commonwealth is instituted, the multitude has no unity, and
at the dissolution of the commonwealth the individuals revert to
the disaggregated state of nature rather than to a popular unity.
*Release from obedience* to the sovereign never comes about, rightfully, through the initiative of the subjects. Hobbes allows such
release only upon the following occasions: loss of the sovereign's *de
facto* power by defeat abroad, voluntary relinquishment of authority
by the sovereign, banishment or capture of a subject by the enemy,
and a subject's ignorance about the rightful successor to office.
As a general rule, the obligation of subjects remains as long as
the sovereign's effective power to protect them and rule strongly
also lasts.

Hobbes' political philosophy culminates not in the doctrine of the
sovereign's absolute power but in the attempt to reconcile this doctrine with a certain *liberty on the part of the subjects*.[19] Such liberty

---

[19] On the freedom of the subjects and the duty of the sovereign to secure the
*salus populi*, cf. *The Elements of Law*, II, 9 (Tönnies, 142–46); *De Cive or The*

is, admittedly, a sorely circumscribed one, at the very most. Meta-physically, it was shown that freedom means only the absence of external impediments of bodily motion. In man's case, this means the absence of physical hindrances to do what one has a will to do — it being understood that the willing itself is fully determined, as the last deliberative act of appetite. In the state of nature, every man has the right to do whatever he wills, whereas he foregoes this liberty upon entrance (explicit or implicit) into the social contract. In civil society, men are no longer free to break the covenant and release themselves from subjection to the sovereign. Nevertheless, Hobbes maintains that, just as freedom is compatible with intrinsic necessity and fear, so is it compatible with political subjection to absolute power and civil laws.

A freeman is one who is not hindered from doing things which he can do and has a will to do. If freedom be taken in its most proper sense as a corporal liberty, then anyone in the commonwealth who is not hampered by chains or prison bars is free. If freedom be understood as exemption from law, then citizens are in utter subjection in regard to civil laws. The commands of the sovereign are authoritative, carry obligation with them, and are re-enforced by adequate power. But the covenanting act is the measure both of our obligation and of our liberty, since *some portion of our liberty cannot be transferred* to a sovereign. Our remaining liberty is measured by the purpose of the social contract and by the nature of civil law. Since sovereignty is instituted by covenant for the sake of peace and security, subjects are not obliged to obey the com-mands of the sovereign in matters that would intrinsically defeat this purpose. Our natural liberty cannot be transferred by the covenant in regard to the following commands: that a man abstain from self-defense, testify against himself, maim or kill himself or his parents, or risk his life in war, when he can provide a substitute. Furthermore, laws are general in intent and do not regulate all our actions. Where the law is silent, men are left at liberty to follow their own deliberation in the particular issues of life.

Hobbes is clearly trying to find a place for the dearly won English

---

*Citizen*, II, 13 (Lamprecht, 141–54); *Leviathan*, II, 21, 30 (Oakeshott, 136–45, 219–32). S. P. Lamprecht, "Hobbes and Hobbism," *The American Political Science Review*, XXXIV (1940), 31–53, and A. E. Taylor, "The Ethical Doctrine of Hobbes," *Philosophy*, XIII (1938), 406–24, appeal to such texts in order to explode the myth that Hobbes had no regard for the liberty of citizens or the duties of rulers.

civil liberties, at least those that directly bear upon preservation of one's own life. His resolution of the problem of freedom and authority depends upon his conception of atomic individuals, congregated into civil society. What is given up to the sovereign is matter of *utter subjection* to his will. Hobbes allows no freedom gained through rational obedience to the law, since he does not admit freedom as a rational and moral perfection or law as a guide to freedom. A man is not free within the sphere of law but only where law falls short. *Man's natural will* is neither incorporated within society nor intrinsically affected by it. Hence this will provides a refuge for freedom, because of its exclusion of society. Hobbes has provided not a theory of political liberty but rather a theory of *residual apolitical liberty,* insofar as a portion of the individual escapes from the body politic. Not the perfection of law but its shortcomings provide a guarantee. A man is never free as a citizen but only as a partial rebel against assuming the burden of citizenry.

Nevertheless, Hobbes also holds that unreserved submission of subjects to the person of the commonwealth does not lead to tyranny. Granted that the sovereign is not subject to civil law and hence has no strict *obligations,* he does have *duties.* They derive from the fact that he who holds the supreme office is also a natural, individual man, whose dominion is related to the tendencies of his nature. He is still bound by the dictates of reason, in the interests of peace and a reasonable use of power. But on Hobbes' own principles, these dictates do not obligate the sovereign as real laws, unless they can be demonstrated to derive from the commands of God. In principle, such demonstration is banished from the Hobbesian philosophy. Hence the sole safeguard against tyranny resolves itself into a mere counsel of reason, lacking any aspect of command or force of law.

Within this framework, however, Hobbes specifies a number of *rights* that are also *duties of the sovereign,* in seeking the well-being of his subjects. Hobbes regards the relations between states as a return to natural warfare, this time among artificial persons, who are restrained by no fear of any sovereign international power. Hence the national sovereign must keep the commonwealth in a state of readiness for war, as an armed camp. Domestic peace requires him to keep careful watch over the opinions of the citizens, to make proportionate distribution of burdens and benefits, to establish and maintain proprietary rights, and to assure the due execution of justice by the magistrates. The sovereign must try to be a good lawmaker. Here, it is a question of the issuing of *good* laws and not merely just ones. By his very commands, the sovereign always makes *just* laws, and no laws are unjust. Good laws, however, are such as are necessary rather than meddlesome, aimed at the good of the people, and perspicuous or accompanied by clearly stated reasons. The best way of eliminating dangerous opinions is by explaining the motives for the rules of the commonwealth, both in the laws themselves and through rigid control of the means of communication and public opinion, including the universities.

Two of the opinions designated by Hobbes as politically dangerous are specially noteworthy. One seditious claim is that of *"the liberty of disputing against absolute power,* by pretenders to political prudence."[20] Hobbes does not encourage any tradition of loyal dissent but identifies all critics of the regime with treasonous agents. He is skeptical about all reasoning on political matters. Within the framework of the *Leviathan,* it is difficult to discover any ground upon which citizens could disagree with the sovereign about policy, without becoming threats to public order. One could make no ultimate appeal to the principle that the ruler is subject to civil law, since this is only the case when the ruler gives it his consent and hence the force of law. Nor could critics appeal to every man's conscience about good and evil. For good and evil are either a matter of individual appetite and aversion, such as in the state of nature, or a matter of civil law, as determined by the sovereign himself. "Conscience" either concerns purely apolitical issues or is one with the sovereign's commands. For, in the social covenant we transfer to the sovereign our equal power of making prudential judgments about our common welfare. Once more, *the natural man* and *the citizen* are held apart by Hobbes, so that within the commonwealth the dire choice exists of either making unquestioning submission to sovereign power or placing oneself in rebellion. There is no rational standard of natural justice by which civil law can be measured, within its own sphere. Hobbes' references to the duties of the sovereign and to natural law do not resolve the question of political liberty of subjects, should the sovereign choose to challenge it.

---

[20] *Leviathan,* II, 29 (Oakeshott, 218; italics added); see *The Elements of Law,* II, 6–7 (Tönnies, 113–32), and *De Cive or The Citizen,* II, 12 (Lamprecht, 128–40), for a further discussion of subversive beliefs and practices, as they appear from Hobbes' perspective. The last two parts of *Leviathan* treat of the Christian commonwealth and the powers of darkness (superstition and popery).

The second dangerous belief, worthy of extirpation, is that which distinguishes between *temporal* and *spiritual sovereignty*. This would lead to a situation where there would be two souls in one commonwealth or two rival kingdoms, each claiming supremacy and absolute obedience to its laws. But a man can serve only one master. Hobbes frames the dilemma that either the temporal order is subordinate in all things to the spiritual or the spiritual is completely subordinate to the temporal power. Unless the sole authority be that of the temporal sovereign, there is constant danger of civil war. St. Thomas à Becket and other defenders of the liberty of the Church are accused of dividing the supreme power, which by right should remain undivided. Those dissenters who appeal to religious conscience are stigmatized as wild visionaries and dangerous fanatics, all on a level with the Anabaptists, who seized civil power in Münster. Religious liberty, like the other liberties, must retreat to the inner sanctuary of the individual and must surrender public life to the temporal sovereign and his commands.

Although religion is in no way autonomous, it is indispensable for both individual and social existence.[21] Its justification lies in the emotional rather than the cognitive order. Hobbes admits that those who pursue the causes of natural events to their furthest extreme are led to posit a first cause of bodily motion. But this inference to God has no standing in philosophy and hence cannot be adjudged in terms of truth or absurdity. What God's nature may be, remains an unfathomable mystery to us. The divine attributes, mentioned in treatises on natural theology, signify only our human, emotional responses in the face of what we take to be an unknown reality. *Religion* is the reverent attitude of men toward that which seems to surpass the scope of reason and prudence, and which is nevertheless feared as a center of power. For both Hobbes and Hume, fear of an  unknown power, which cannot be reckoned with in rational terms, is the source of religion. Since both reason and experience are limited in their foresight, in political as well as private life, religion will have a function in the state as well as in the individual's heart.

---

21 For an explanation of how Hobbes could advocate politically controlled religion and yet be entirely lacking in personal belief in God, cf. S. Holm, "L'attitude de Hobbes à l'égard de la religion," *Archives de Philosophie*, XII (1936), 227-48. In *The Political Philosophy of Hobbes*, 59-78, L. Strauss shows that, in his historical development, Hobbes first reduced natural theology to sacred theology, and then showed that a positive religion, based upon the claim to revelation and relying upon sacred theology, must be measured solely by its usefulness to the state.

In order to preserve the indivisible and absolute nature of sovereignty, however, Hobbes allows no basic difference between *state* and *church* in the Christian commonwealth. It is the right and duty of the Christian sovereign to determine what doctrines are to be professed about God's nature. As for a revelation, every individual must transfer to the sovereign the right to interpret Scripture, just as he must transfer the right of making prudential political judgments. Whatever God may command, in sacred as well as secular matters, He commands through the sovereign. To the latter we owe obedience in all things, spiritual as well as temporal. There is a basic identity between the content of natural law and revelation: the articles of both are determined and given the status of binding law by the sovereign's command. Thus Hobbes indicates the political advantage that can be drawn from a Deistic reduction of the supernatural to a natural revelation. It is also the sovereign's office to set the manner of public worship, which must be uniform throughout the commonwealth. Although the sovereign does not deal with internal belief, he has the right to impose uniform religious profession and worship upon his subjects. Religious dissenters are on a par with political dissenters: in outward actions, they must either obey unquestioningly the ordained rules of religion or accept martyrdom. There is no reconciliation of the private and public aspects of human nature, no common agreement of minds and wills on a pluralistic and rational basis, in respect to the common good, temporal or spiritual. Hobbes retains both authority and freedom at the price of widening the gap between the natural individual and the citizen, thus nullifying the work of the social contract, which is supposed to effect the transition between them.

## SUMMARY OF CHAPTER 4

Hobbes wanted to discover how far a rigorous application of the principles of Galilean dynamics would carry him in the solution of philosophical problems. He contracted the scope of philosophy within the boundaries of material bodies, interacting mechanically upon each other. This quantitative and deterministic approach eliminated on methodological grounds the immaterial order, a qualitative world, teleological action, and human freedom. Hobbes had to use "motion" and "reaction" in an accommodated sense, however, in order to extend his principles into the domain of organic processes, cognition, and appetition. He reduced the various sense functions and understanding to so many outward-tending responses of the organism to stimulations received from the environment. Although he noted that our causal statements never attain more than a high probability, he left for Hume the full-dress treatment of the causal problem. His hedonistic reduction of good and evil to pleasure and pain accorded with his mechanistic premise and his aim of treating social life as an interplay of calculable forces. His doctrine on man in the state of nature provided a transition between psychology and political philosophy, since the natural condition of man is so wretched that a reaction generated by the laws of dynamics drives men into civil society. But in the political order itself, Hobbes posited a conflict between the atomistic individual and that mortal god, the commonwealth. In the social contract, individuals transfer their right to all things to the sovereign, who therefore wields absolute power over his subjects. His commands as such are just laws, and he himself is subject to no civil laws. But still, there is a core of individuality which men cannot surrender and which does not come within the sovereign's jurisdiction. Hobbes never fully incorporated the individual within Leviathan, even though he gave to the latter an overawing power and curtailed religious freedom and freedom of political dissent.

## BIBLIOGRAPHICAL NOTE

1. *Sources.* W. Molesworth edited the two following collections of Hobbes' writings: *Opera philosophica quae latine scripsit* (5 vols., London, Bohn, and Longman, 1839–1845), and *The English Works of Thomas Hobbes* (11 vols., London, Bohn, and Longman, 1839–1845). Using manuscript sources, F. Tönnies provided a critical edition of *The Elements of Law, Natural and Politic* (new ed., Cambridge, University Press, 1928), with excerpts from *A Short Tract on First Principles* and *Tractatus Opticus.* A convenient separate edition of *De Cive or The Citizen* is edited by S. P. Lamprecht (New York, Appleton-Century-Crofts, 1949). M. Oakeshott's edition of *Leviathan* (Oxford, Blackwell, 1946) is enhanced by an acute Introduction on Hobbes' thought.

2. *Studies.* G. C. Robertson's *Hobbes* (Edinburgh, Blackwood, 1886) is a general introduction, still worth reading; a vigorous, more recent presentation is J. Laird's *Hobbes* (London, Benn, 1934); German interest in Hobbes is evidenced by F. Tönnies' exacting manuscript researches and his *Thomas Hobbes: Leben und Lehre* (third ed., Stuttgart, Frommann, 1925). Among more specialized works, see F. Brandt, *Thomas Hobbes' Mechanical Conception of Nature* (London, Hachette, 1928); L. Strauss, *The Political Philosophy of Hobbes,* translated from the German manuscript by E. M. Sinclair (Oxford, Clarendon, 1936); R. Polin, *Politique et philosophie chez Thomas Hobbes* (Paris, Presses Universitaires, 1953). The lively, contemporary English political discussions aroused by Hobbes' theories are recalled in J. Bowle's *Hobbes and His Critics: A Study of Seventeenth-Century Constitutionalism* (London, Cape, 1951). For orientation in the history of the social-contract theory, see J. W. Gough, *The Social Contract: A Critical Study of its Development* (New York, Oxford, 1936). A critical evaluation of Hobbes' determinism is made by J. Rickaby, S.J., *Free Will*

*and Four English Philosophers* (London, Burns, Oates, 1906), the other three thinkers being Locke, Hume, and Mill. B. Willey's *The Seventeenth Century Background* (London, Chatto and Windus, 1934) presents Hobbes, Descartes, Locke, and other representatives of "the century of genius" in terms of the general intellectual and cultural climate; for a detailed description of all phases of civilization in that age, cf. G. N. Clark, *The Seventeenth Century* (second ed., New York, Oxford, 1950). In his *Hobbes* (Baltimore, Penguin Books, 1956), Richard Peters gives an exposition and criticism of him with the aid of recent techniques in linguistic analysis.

There is a reprint of Sir Leslie Stephen's study on *Hobbes* (Ann Arbor, University of Michigan Ann Arbor Paperbacks, 1961). H. Warrender's *The Political Philosophy of Hobbes* (Oxford, Clarendon Press, 1957) seeks to show that there is some sort of moral obligation in the state of nature, but its condition still requires a sovereign arbitrator in civil society.

# Chapter 5. DESCARTES

## I. LIFE AND WRITINGS

THE son of a provincial gentleman, René Descartes was born at
La Haye in Touraine, in 1596. He received his basic education at
the newly founded Jesuit college of Henry IV at La Flèche, where he
studied from 1606 until about 1614. There, he took the regular curriculum in the humanities (grammar, history, poetry, and rhetoric)
and then in philosophy (logic, philosophy of nature, metaphysics,
and ethics) and mathematics. The philosophy professors based their
lectures mainly upon Aristotelian manuals. He continued his studies at
the University of Poitiers, where he received the degrees of bachelor
and licentiate in law (1616) and also took instruction in medicine.
There followed a period in which he turned from the academic life
to the great book of the world, joined the army of Maurice of Nassau
in the Netherlands, and broadened his knowledge of men and
customs. His friendship with Isaac Beeckman led him to investigate
several problems in mechanics, mathematics, and music. In 1619,
he went to Denmark and the Germanies, joined the army of the
Duke of Bavaria for a while, and witnessed the coronation of the
Emperor Ferdinand at Frankfort. He spent that winter near the
town of Ulm, meditating upon the project of solving all geometrical
problems by a single method. Gradually, he conceived the plan of
dealing with all philosophical problems by means of a single, mathematically orientated method and (thus of achieving a perfect unity
among the sciences.) Descartes' famous dreams occurred on the night
of November 10-11, 1619. They confirmed his resolve to bring all
the sciences into a single body of wisdom and led him to regard this
task as a heaven-sent mission. The "private thoughts" which he jotted
down in notebooks during the next few years have been lost, except
for some fragments copied out by his first biographer, Abbé Baillet,
and by Leibniz.

By 1627-1628, the main features of his system were fairly well established in Descartes' mind. He had sufficient confidence to enter into a public discussion at Paris, in the presence of the papal nuncio, Cardinal Bérulle and Father Marin Mersenne. Descartes so impressed Bérulle with his claims for a clearer and surer method of thinking that the cardinal urged it, as his duty, to publish his doctrine against the skeptics and atheists. Descartes' thoughts on methodology were set down in the *Rules for the Direction of the Mind* (written about 1628; circulated in manuscript, posthumously, among philosophers; published in 1701). At the same time, he made a rough draft of his metaphysical position in a set of notes, later expanded into the *Meditations on First Philosophy.* He settled permanently in the Netherlands in 1628, a move dictated mainly by reasons of health and the desire for greater privacy in study. But throughout the years, Descartes kept up a vast correspondence, which provides precious biographical and doctrinal information about him.

He was working on his conception of the physical universe, *The World* or *Treatise on Light,* which advocated the motion of the earth, when he received news of Galileo's condemnation by the Holy Office (1633). Descartes refused to take the risk of publication of this book during his lifetime; editions of the surviving first part were issued posthumously in 1664 and 1667. In order to prepare a more favorable reception for his physical doctrines, he issued in 1637 three specimens of his scientific work (*Dioptrics, Meteors,* and *Geometry*), along with an introductory essay on the spirit of his method and philosophy, the *Discourse on Method.* This was followed by the *Meditations on First Philosophy* (1641), his metaphysical masterpiece, to which were appended the criticisms offered by several eminent philosophers and Descartes' detailed replies. In the vain hope of having his system adopted as a Jesuit textbook, he next cast his thoughts into Scholastic form in *Principles of Philosophy* (1644). During his closing years, Descartes' interests turned more definitely toward moral philosophy, although he continued his dissections of bodies and other scientific activities. His letters to the exiled Princess Elizabeth of Bohemia and his treatise on *The Passions of the Soul* (1649), which he first submitted to the Princess for criticism, contained a sketch of his psychologico-moral views. In 1649, he went to Sweden to give philosophical instructions to Queen Christina. Her custom of discussing philosophy with him at five o'clock in the morning undermined Descartes' congenitally weak constitution and he died in February, 1650.

## 2. THE NATURE AND DIVISIONS OF PHILOSOPHY

Despite his dissatisfaction with the theories taught him by teachers and books, Descartes was not discouraged about the prospects for philosophy. He felt that it was his mission to achieve a singlehanded reconstruction of philosophy, with the aid of new principles. The revolution was to begin with the very notion of philosophy itself. Starting in the traditional way with the meaning of the word itself, he defined philosophy as the study of wisdom. But he pointed out, at once, certain traits of wisdom which had been overlooked or obscured by his predecessors of the Middle Ages and Renaissance.

In opposition to Renaissance humanists like Montaigne, Descartes sought to close the gap between *science* and *wisdom*.[1] Instead of retaining the contrast between the two, he affirmed that wisdom is an affair of scientific reason rather than of erudition. Its resources are drawn not from memory, history, and literature (as the humanists believed), but from the same rational power that operates in mathematics. Yet even the mathematicians had failed to recognize this truth, since they were reluctant to apply their procedures to the most lofty questions of metaphysics and morals. For his part, Descartes affirmed that nothing was more sorely needed than precisely this extension of mathematical reason into wider fields. At the same time, he wished to preserve two characteristics of the humanistic view of wisdom: its purely (*natural* basis) and its concern for (*practical moral*) issues. He told his interlocutor, Burman, that he wrote his philosophy so that it could be accepted everywhere, even among the Turks. Philosophical wisdom is grounded in the natural use of reason, without seeking reliance upon, or guidance from, revelation and theology. It is the work of man as man, and studies man himself *prout in naturalibus,* rather than as the recipient of supernatural revelation. Philosophical wisdom (is also orientated toward man's welfare and permanent happiness.) The ancient Stoic regard for human conduct joins company, in Descartes' mind, with the modern scientific concern for the control of nature and the betterment of human living conditions.

---

[1] On the wisdom, principles, and divisions proper to philosophy, see both Descartes' "Letter to the Translator" of the French edition of *The Principles of Philosophy,* and his "Dedication" of the same work (in *The Philosophical Works of Descartes* [translated by Haldane and Ross], I, 203–18). Cf. J. Segond, *La sagesse cartésienne et la doctrine de la science* (Paris, Vrin, 1932).

Descartes was not unmindful of the Scholastic distinction between speculative and practical wisdom, nor of the Scholastic teaching that the latter should build upon the former. For this reason, he observed that the practical wisdom in which philosophy comes to full flower is something more than shrewdness in managing one's affairs. It springs from *a perfect knowledge of all that is needful* for human life. In this plenary sense of a complete knowledge of the truth, only God is truly wise; but men can share more or less in wisdom, to the extent that they acquire an understanding of at least the major truths. Philosophy's task is to supply the principles of knowledge and thus bring the mind to the highest peak of humanly attainable wisdom.

Although this conception recalls the Aristotelian definition of philosophy as a study of all things in their highest principles and causes, Descartes interprets "principles" in a distinctive way. They mean principles of knowledge, even more than of being. The two requirements for *philosophical principles* are that they be absolutely *indubitable* in themselves, due to their clarity and evidence, and completely *independent* of other truths in such a way that the latter can be known only through these principles, without involving any reciprocal dependence of the principles upon the subsequent truths. Both these criteria bear the mark of Descartes' distinctive approach. He explains that his principles alone achieve perfect clarity and evidence, since they are established only *after* an attempt is made to reject everything that is in the least way doubtful. Thus the theory of first principles has a solidarity with the method of universal doubt. The absolutely first principle of philosophy is the indubitable knowledge of the existence of the thinking self. The traditional principle of contradiction and other general principles are themselves true, only by reason of their implication in this unconditionally first concrete truth and principle.

Moreover, Cartesian principles have the independence belonging to the very first steps in a deductive process. They must be such that from them all other truths can be derived by necessary inference. Once Descartes has deduced God and extended matter from the thinking self, he is equipped with the basic principles for demonstrating the truth of all other things in a systematic fashion. This claim is only possible in virtue of his conception of the *unity of all the sciences*. They are so connected and interdependent that they constitute a single body of truth. Explicitly repudiating the Scholastic differentiation of sciences on the basis of formal differences in their objects,

Descartes stresses the *subjective unity of the mind,* in which the sciences reside, and of the *act of scientific knowing,* whereby they are apprehended. Human knowledge remains one and the same process: the methodic combining of self-evident truths. In place of the older doctrine of an interconnection among the moral virtues, Descartes substitutes an interconnection and mutual dependence of the speculative sciences. Philosophical first principles are generative of a chain of truths, each link of which is arrived at by the same sort of scientific act and attains the same scientific certitude. This homogeneity of scientific knowledge assures the unity of philosophy, the fruitfulness of its principles, and the rigor of its demonstrations.

Distinctions within the body of philosophy arise only in terms of the mind's manner of application to the study of principles and their consequences. Descartes employs the metaphor of the tree of wisdom, in order to convey the organic unity and order existing among the *parts of philosophy.* Metaphysics comprises the roots of the tree; physics its trunk; medicine, mechanics, and ethics its branches. *Metaphysics* or first philosophy treats of the first principles of all knowledge: the finite thinking self, the infinitely powerful and veracious God, the criterion of truth, the common notions of the mind, the existence of an external world. To this extent, Descartes agrees with St. Augustine that God and the soul are the most proper objects of philosophical contemplation. But at the same time, metaphysics provides the basis for a philosophical account of the physical universe. Only insofar as it is founded upon metaphysical principles, does *physics* acquire a strictly scientific standing. There may be many discoveries in physics previous to its incorporation into philosophical wisdom, but as a rigorous body of indubitable truths, it awaits the principles of deduction and other guarantees of knowledge supplied only by metaphysics.

The *practical parts* of philosophy, in their turn, depend upon the completion of philosophical physics and its prolongation in philosophical anthropology. Although the practical disciplines occupy a subsequent position in the movement of philosophical thought, they also provide the (goal) of all philosophy. For, they enable man to become the master of nature, the possessor of bodily health, and the subject of moral perfections and blessings. *Wisdom* in the unqualified sense embraces all these sciences, speculative and practical, as a totality. Only in the sense that all branches of philosophy serve to nourish and develop the single tree of wisdom, is it true that metaphysics is for the sake of physics, and physics for the sake of the practical sciences. The ultimate aim of the philosopher is to attain the happiness which ensues upon a synoptic understanding and controlled use of the entire order and concatenation of scientifically established truths. The happy life is the life of wisdom, as it enlightens the mind and fortifies the practical judgment in the face of life's contingencies. Here lies man's sovereign good in the natural order.

Descartes does not regard this ideal as impossible of attainment. Although it belongs only to the gifted few to *discover* the proper method and philosophical truths, yet all men are natively equipped with the rational power of discerning the true from the false, and hence all men can *recognize* these truths, once discovered. It is because all men have *reason* or *good sense* in at least a minimal way, that there is solid assurance of their attaining the fullness of good sense, which is nothing other than philosophical wisdom. Descartes regards his principles as sufficiently clear to be grasped by all men, and his conclusions as sufficiently evident in their demonstration to be accepted by all men. But, like Bacon, he warns that the mind can apprehend philosophical truths only after it frees itself from prejudice and accepts some reliable guide. The guide is furnished by the new method, which is nothing else than the way in which the mind must proceed in order to acquire wisdom.

### 3. THE METHOD FOR THE DISCOVERY AND DEMONSTRATION OF TRUTH

*Three fountainheads* contributed to Descartes' theory of method: his own natural habits of thinking, the precepts of Scholastic logic, and the procedures of mathematics. The first two sources gave him some general guidance, whereas the more specific techniques were supplied by his study of Greek analysis and modern algebra. The synthesis of these three sources was achieved in function of his notion of a universal mathematics, which provided the organizing principle of his entire methodology.

Through reflection upon his own common-sense habits of mind and the testimony of ordinary men, Descartes found that unspoiled *natural intelligence* has an active tendency to grasp certain great, simple truths and to reason in the right way concerning more complex problems. He referred to this native ability of the mind as the seedbed of our knowledge, as a sort of divine principle containing the germs of true science, somewhat as a flint stone contains its sparks.[2] Although basic truths are not present in any ready-made fashion, they are innate in the understanding, insofar as this power is stirred from within to come to an explicit apprehension of them, with the aid of experience and reasoning. No one has to wait for learned definitions, before finding out what it means to exist, to feel, to think, or to doubt. Through his natural inclination and perspicacity, even the untutored individual seizes, at once, upon the meaning of these terms. Moreover, he learns to deal with more complicated issues by meditating upon the simple, primary truths, to which his own mind impels him, in order to discover some connection between these starting points and the more remote and subtle problems. As Descartes viewed it, the gradual approach of common sense to theoretical difficulties displays the same sort of orderliness found in the operations of a weaver. Starting from a few simple but basic movements of the mind, the ordinary man can gradually develop a grand pattern of thought, embracing the most universal truths about his life. Surely, there is something here for the philosopher to attend to and imitate.

Furthermore, Descartes found that the maxims of informal thinking agreed, in large measure, with the practical directions about correct thinking provided in his logic course at La Flèche. *Scholastic logic* teaches the student to proceed from simple to complex cognitions, from the easier to the more difficult, and from what one understands better to what is more intelligible in itself. This logic advises one to remove nonessentials in the statement of a problem or definition and to reduce complicated questions to their basic parts. In the case of induction, it also recommends as complete a survey of the parts of the problem and the classes of instances as is feasible. Comparing these precepts with those of his own informal studies, Descartes became convinced of their soundness and practical value. They were to be incorporated into the definitive method as permanent acquisitions of mankind, reflecting upon its own mental operations.

But there was one teaching in Scholastic logic that troubled Descartes, because it set a high goal without also supplying the

---

[2] *Rules for the Direction of the Mind,* IV, VIII (Haldane-Ross, I, 10, 12, 25–26). This work presents the Cartesian methodology in a highly technical way, whereas the *Discourse on Method* offers a more popular and personal presentation. The *Discourse* begins with the programmatic statement that "good sense [*le bon sens*] is mankind's most equitably divided endowment." *Discourse on Method,* I (Lafleur translation, 1). Everyone's mind has a native impulsion toward truth to which Descartes constantly appeals, over the heads of academic thinkers.

means of its attainment. Knowledge in the strict sense of *scientific knowledge* was traditionally defined as true, certain, and evident cognition, based on the proper causes of the thing. Yet it did not require the diatribes of Galileo and Bacon to convince Descartes that a major part of the actual curriculum in philosophy was being devoted to speculations that never attained more than a high degree of probability and that failed to remove the original obscurity of the question. The widespread use of dialectical arguments supplied no adequate answer to the skeptical contention that strict knowledge is beyond our ability to attain. In searching for an answer to this charge of the skeptics, Descartes turned to mathematics for assurance and guidance concerning our possession of scientific knowledge.

Even the mathematics books used at La Flèche regarded *mathematics* as the key and primary science, since it not only excludes the false and merely probable but also proves its own conclusions by the most certain and universally accepted demonstrations.[3] These sources did not add, however, that all knowledge constitutes a single body of science, based solely on the mathematical type of reasoning. This radical step was reserved for Descartes to take. He resolved to accept as scientific truth only those propositions which contain the same sort of evidence and certitude as is found in mathematics. He did not mean that philosophical reasoning must embody all the features of mathematical inference but that it must employ the *same kind* of method and cognition as in mathematics. The basic Cartesian assumption here is that the *ingenium mathematicum* is nothing other than the reasoning power and method proper to "man as thinking." This led him to take a univocal view of the common instrument of speculation and of the standards for philosophical knowledge.

Descartes' own discoveries in analytic geometry convinced him of the possibility of generalizing mathematical procedures. He found that the heretofore unyielding distinction between continuous and discontinuous quantity could be overcome through his *analytic geometry,* in which geometrical figures, laid out upon co-ordinates, are expressed by algebraic equations. Conversely, he was able to express numerical quantities and algebraic functions in terms of lines and figures. The mind's intrinsic power was also strengthened, when it learned to take advantage of both the brevity of algebraic nota-

[3] The opinion of the Jesuit mathematician Clavius (whose writings were probably known to Descartes at La Flèche) is quoted at length by E. Gilson, *René Descartes: Discours de la méthode, texte et commentaire,* 128.

tion and the pictorial clarity of geometrical figures. Thus two broad regions of mathematics were brought together, through the discovery of an underlying unity. This unification on a relatively small scale suggested to Descartes that a new science might be founded, which would resolve all problems concerning every sort of quantity, continuous as well as discrete. It was only a step from this ambitious scheme to an even more daring and comprehensive project: the foundation of a *completely universal science* or *mathesis universalis,* which could resolve all philosophical problems, even those lying entirely beyond the realm of quantity, with the aid of the mathematical method.[4]

## THE CARTESIAN METHOD OF PROOF

1. Formal object of universal mathematics: order and measure.
2. Instruments of proof.
   a) Resolutive analysis, the logic of discovery and intuition.
      1) Objects of intuition: simple natures (material, spiritual, and their links and axioms).
      2) Necessary condition for the systematic employment of the findings of intuition: universal methodic doubt, leading to indubitable knowledge of an existential basis for ideas and a point of departure for the philosophical system.
   b) Compositive synthesis, the logic of demonstrative deduction.
      1) Immediate deduction.
      2) Mediate deduction (aided by induction, analogy, and experience).
3. Criterion of truth: clarity and distinctness of ideas.
4. Order of proof: from the first indubitably known existent thing, as the first principle in the order of knowing, to its noetic consequences in the chain of existential truths.
   a) The finite, thinking self.
   b) The infinitely powerful and veracious God.
   c) The extended, material world.

In determining the *formal object* of his new universal mathematics, Descartes followed a clue provided by ordinary mathematics. All the branches of mathematics, both pure and applied, are concerned with a study of quantitative order and measure. Descartes saw no intrinsic reason why these relations should be confined to the quantitative sphere. Hence he proposed as the formal object of

---

[4] *Rules for the Direction of the Mind,* IV (Haldane-Ross, I, 11–13); *Discourse on Method,* II (Lafleur, 12–13).

universal science: *the general study of order and measure,* insofar
as they are implicated in our knowledge of all sorts of beings, regardless of particular subject matter. This would enable all the sciences
to share in a common pattern of inquiry: a comparison among objects
in virtue of some shared trait, which establishes an order among them
and a certain proportion that can be measured. The Cartesian claim
for the unity of the sciences and the homogeneity of philosophical
wisdom rested upon this determination of a common formal procedure in scientific investigation. But, in fact, the issue cannot be
resolved solely in methodological terms, apart from all reference to
subject matter or the actual modes of being in which order and
measure are realized. Where the method in question is that of
*philosophical knowledge of real existents,* there can be no purely
formal methodological study, in which the relation of objects to our
understanding is divorced from the manner in which they exercise
their own act of being. As far as the philosophical sciences are
concerned, a general study of our way of ascertaining order and
measure among objects can be carried through, only within the
context of a metaphysical doctrine on the ways of real order and
measure. Descartes himself eventually recognized the inadequacy of
a purely formal methodology. But he failed to see that, in providing
an existential foundation, one must either revise drastically the theory
of the homogeneity of the sciences or else adopt a pantheistic metaphysical basis of method, as Spinoza suggested.

In specifying the *instruments of proof* for his universal science,
Descartes was guided by the examples of both the pure mathematicians
and Galileo. *Analysis* or *the method of resolution* and *synthesis* or
*the method of composition* are the main tools of scientific reasoning.[5]
In Euclidean geometry, for instance, one starts with certain definitions,

---

[5] The contrast between analysis and synthesis is brought out in *Replies to Objections,*
II (Haldane-Ross, II, 48–50). This should be compared with the Thomistic doctrine
on *resolutio* and *compositio,* as explained by L. M. Régis, O.P., "Analyze et synthèse
dans l'oeuvre de saint Thomas," *Studia Mediaevalia in honorem . . . Raymundi Josephi
Martin, O.P.* (Bruges, De Tempel, c. 1948), 303–30. St. Thomas emphasizes the
nonmathematical, properly metaphysical analysis or resolution of knowledge to the
senses, to being and its first principles, and to the judgment of separation. This type
of resolution includes both the *experiential* and the *intellectual* principles of knowledge,
and hence transcends the modern controversy between the empiricist and the rationalist
types of resolution or analysis. The intermediate developments, leading from Cusanus,
Zabarella, Copernicus, and other Renaissance thinkers to Descartes, are discussed by
R. I. Markus, "Method and Metaphysics: Origins of Some Cartesian Presuppositions in
the Philosophy of the Renaissance," *Dominican Studies,* II (1949), 356–84.

postulates, and axioms. With their aid, the synthetic approach demonstrates the conclusions of the science so rigorously, that a denial of any particular step also entails a denial of all the previous ones. Yet however coercive this synthetic method may be, it has the serious drawback of failing to justify its foundations by showing how the original set of definitions, postulates, and axioms was reached. Hence the priority must be given to the analytic method, which does show the *how* and the *why* of the premises themselves. Analysis is preeminently a *logic of discovery*, a justification of the basic truths upon which all subsequent inferences depend. It works back from given complex wholes to their constituent elements, from given problems to the underlying principles of solution. Hence the analytic method must be used, in order to discover the first principles of philosophical knowledge, the metaphysical truths upon which the entire edifice of wisdom rests. Only after these principles have been ascertained in analytic or resolutive fashion, can the work of synthetic demonstration or deduction begin. Unlike Hobbes (who held that the synthetic method alone should be used in exposition of one's system), Descartes felt that the philosopher had the prime obligation of showing the genesis of his first principles and definitions. Hence he wrote the *Meditations on First Philosophy* in the analytic manner, showing precisely how he arrived at his basic truths; subsequently, he presented his system synthetically in the *Principles of Philosophy*.

Descartes' main contribution here is to establish a firm correlation between analysis and synthesis, on the one hand, and intuition and deduction, on the other. Analysis is the mental operation that clears a path for intellectual intuition, whereas the synthetic composition of principles is a scientific process, only if it results in a demonstrative deduction. Hence there are only two methodic ways of arriving at the truth of things: *intuition* and *deduction*.

> By a method I mean certain and simple rules, such that, if a man observe them accurately, he shall never assume what is false as true, and will never spend his mental efforts to no purpose, but will always gradually increase his knowledge and so arrive at a true understanding of all that does not surpass his powers. . . . But if our method rightly explains how our mental vision [*mentis intuitu*] should be used, so as not to fall into the contrary error, and how deduction should be discovered in order that we may arrive at the knowledge of all things, I do not see what else is needed to make it complete.[6]

---

[6] *Rules for the Direction of the Mind*, IV (Haldane-Ross, I, 9).

Descartes is sure that his method is not only useful but definitive, because his rules rest upon the requirements of the only two operations whereby the systematic body of truths can be discovered and organized.

He affirms that *intuition* (*intuitus:* inspection, insight, or view) is "the undoubting conception of an unclouded and attentive mind, and springs from the light of reason alone."[7] It is the proper operation  of the natural light of the understanding and hence is the primary means for bringing the truth in evidence before our minds. The fact that this act springs from reason or the pure intellectual power alone is important to note, since this means that the intuitional view is possible only when the mind has been freed from dependence on the senses. It is a *purely intellectual* operation and is not integrated with sense perception. Furthermore, the mind must learn to *discipline its attention* upon the object of intuition in its intelligible structure, so that the mind will not be distracted by opinions derived from some sensory source. Because insight or intuition is conditioned upon this purgation and disciplining of the mind, it is by no means a facilely acquired perfection. The painful work of analytic resolution of complex data into their simple elements is also required, before the mind can gain a vision of the simple truths.

Reflection upon the undoubting quality of intuition provides Descartes with his *criterion* of philosophical truth: *clarity and distinctness* of our intellectual perception. "I term that *clear* which is present and apparent to an attentive mind . . . but *the distinct* is that which is so precise and different from all other objects that it contains within itself nothing but what is clear."[8] The object is inspected or seen in its evident truth, when it is given to the mind in an act of intuition. This involves an immediate self-presence of the object, in the idea, under conditions of clarity and distinctness. The clarity of the idea means the actual presentation of an intelligible structure to a mind that is undividedly attentive. Clarity supposes not only that what belongs to the nature of the object is present but also that the mind  itself is attentive and responsive, in a purely intellectual way, to this

---

[7] *Ibid.*, III (Haldane-Ross, I, 7).

[8] *The Principles of Philosophy*, I, 45 (Haldane-Ross, I, 237). Since the *Principles* was written in textbook fashion, it contains concise definitions of many terms which Descartes elsewhere left undefined. A. Gewirth, in "Clearness and Distinctness in Descartes," *Philosophy*, XVIII (1943), 17–36, shows that this criterion has a logical and objective import for Descartes, not merely a psychological and subjective one, since it is integrated with his metaphysics.

presented structure. Hence it rests on the same conditions as does the act of intuitional insight, which is the mind's proper response to the object thus furnished. An idea is distinct when *only* that which clearly belongs to the nature of the object is placed before the mind, and all else is excluded. A distinct idea is clear to the point of excluding all obscurity, even though it may not be comprehensive of the entire reality of the object. When the mind acquires a direct mental vision of the object in this clear and distinct perception, it is in possession of the evident truth in an undoubting way. Intuition eliminates both doubt and falsity about the object known.

The objects about which the mind is directly concerned are its own ideas. These ideal objects are either simple or composite natures. Composite natures are capable of being analyzed into simpler and more distinctly known parts. Analysis terminates in the *simple natures,* which are analytically irreducible elements of intelligibility.[9] Intuition is directed primarily toward these simple natures, which can be known immediately and *per se,* without engaging any judgment about their significance for the order of existent things. Descartes distinguishes between three classes of simple natures: purely *spiritual* natures or those which the mind knows through reflection upon its own intellectual light (knowing, doubting, willing); purely *material* ones or those grasped only insofar as the mind turns its attention to bodies (extension, figure, motion); those that are *common to both* spiritual and corporeal things (existence, unity, duration). In the latter class are also included the common notions and axioms (such as the principle of causality), which are links connecting the other simple natures together and thus permitting deductions to be made.

Although these simple natures loom large in Descartes' *Rules for the Direction of the Mind,* they do not hold as important a place in his later systematic work as might be expected. They raise a number of difficult questions, which Descartes never satisfactorily answered. If the simple natures are to fulfill any systematic function, they must be able to serve the purposes of deductive demonstration. To do so, they must satisfy the three following conditions: (1) the

---

[9] Cf. *Rules for the Direction of the Mind,* VI, VIII, XII (Haldane-Ross, I, 15–17, 27, 41–47). Cartesian scholars are divided over whether the simple natures are ontological principles, as well as logical ultimates in the order of mental analysis. For this debate, consult S. V. Keeling, "Le réalisme de Descartes et le rôle des natures simples," *Revue de Métaphysique et de Morale,* XLIV (1937), 63–99, and J. Hartland-Swann, "Descartes' 'Simple Natures,'" *Philosophy,* XXII (1947), 139–52.

number of unconditionally absolute, simple natures must be finite;
(2) the simple natures must have intrinsic relations with each other;
(3) they must be connected in a serial arrangement, according to
a natural order. Although the Cartesian conception of the unity of
scientific knowledge hinged upon these conditions, Descartes was
unable to show that they are satisfied by the simple natures. The
Baconian and Cartesian assumption of a finite number of simple
natures was eventually abandoned by Leibniz, who saw that, on
purely methodological grounds, there is no way of setting a limit to
the points at which analysis may terminate in some irreducible
intelligibility. The second difficulty revealed one of the dangerous
tensions in Cartesian methodology. The emphasis placed upon clear
and distinct objects of intuition offered a threat to deductive inference, since the *distinctness* was apt to *isolate* one idea completely
from another. As a remedy, Descartes suggested that the meaning
of any one simple nature includes its reference to other natures,
as well as its own intrinsic constitution. He posited that the simple
natures are bound up with each other by various links in a natural
order, establishing both contingent and necessary relations among
the ideas. Once more, however, the criticism of Spinoza has to be
faced: either these connections are an *ad hoc* device to counteract
the atomizing effect of analytic intuition and the standard of distinctness or else they rest upon an implicit metaphysical foundation
in a doctrine on the monism of being. When Descartes invoked a
"natural order" of truths in serial arrangement, he was overpassing
the boundaries of methodology and supposing some special metaphysical conception. Spinoza's monism and Leibniz' calculus of
essences were historical efforts to provide a more adequate metaphysical
basis for scientific demonstration of a rationalistic sort.

Toward the resolution of a fourth difficulty connected with the
doctrine on intuition and simple natures, Descartes marshaled all the
resources of his philosophy. Even granted the connections and order
among simple natures, they remain in the *ideal* order. A deductive
system built upon them would have no guarantee that its connections
have any bearing upon the relations among real things or that its
conclusions demonstrate anything about the structure of actual beings.
This consideration led Descartes to seek for some *existential foundation,* in which the basic simple natures could be seen to be implicated.
Such an existential basis would both show the ontological relevance
of the simple natures and provide a real point of departure for the

philosophical system. But even here, the general condition of intuition — that it be an undoubting conception of the pure understanding — would have to be fulfilled. There was no other way open for Descartes to show that his existential foundation was indeed indubitable than by subjecting all his beliefs about existing beings and our ways of knowing them to a *methodic doubt*. The primary existential certitude was found to be the thinking self, in which the simple natures were given metaphysical significance for the system of philosophy. Thus the problem of methodic doubt and the thinking self (examined more at length in the following section) had its roots in the relationship between the theory of method and metaphysics.

*Deduction* or *compositive synthesis* supposes that the intuitive basis of the elements and principles of knowledge has already been secured. Descartes defines deduction, briefly, as "all necessary inference from other facts that are known with certainty."[10] Deduction can be either *immediate* or *mediate,* depending upon whether the link among objects can be established through a simple comparison or whether a complicated process of reasoning is required. When a direct comparison can be made between A and B, and again between B and C, the deduction concerning A and C is an immediate one. Where the issues are complex, however, a long series of inferences may be required, before another link in the chain of indubitable truths can be forged. Under the heading of "mediate deduction," Descartes includes such auxiliary processes as induction or enumeration, hypothesis, analogy, conjecture, and the appeal to experience. Their aid is needed to gather together all the relevant evidence. The question is to be divided into its basic parts, and no more truth may be sought than can be drawn from these component data, considered in relation with the general chain of inferences already established. Further simplification of the issue can be achieved by distinguishing between the known and the unknown factors and by determining the precise points of contact between the two groups. A mediate deduction can then be made from what is already demonstrated to a newly discovered truth.

But deduction is always less simple and, therefore, less certain than intuition. Each stage in the deductive process must itself be grasped by an intuitive act. And the ultimate purpose of science is to reduce the entire series of deductions as closely as possible to

---

[10] *Rules for the Direction of the Mind*, III (Haldane-Ross, I, 8).

*a single intuitive comprehension* of the whole body of truth. For this purpose, constant reviews and enumerations are helpful. They assure us that no necessary step has been overlooked, and they dispose the mind to seize the concatenation of inferences in a quasi-intuitive vision, in which philosophical wisdom consists.

The *order of Cartesian proof* rests upon a fundamental distinction between the order of knowing and the order of being. Whereas Spinoza held that these two orders should be made to coincide, Descartes insisted upon their distinction. In this respect, he remained in contact with the tradition of theistic realism, which denies that the human mind can begin its inferential activity with God. But while St. Thomas recognized sense apprehension of the material world as constituting a true principle of philosophical knowledge, Descartes subjected the senses to doubt and looked rather for a starting point that would be appropriate to the act of a purely intellectual intuition or mental vision. This he found in the *finite thinking self.* Its finite character set his point of departure off from Spinoza's, whereas its purely immaterial nature distinguished it from the Thomistic beginning of knowledge. Since he had called the senses into question, Descartes was unable to proceed directly from the existence of the finite thinking self to that of the material world. His second step was to prove the existence of an *infinitely powerful and yet veracious God.* Since this demonstration was made through an analysis of certain implications in the finite thinking self, the latter manifested itself as the first noetic principle or principle in the order of knowing. But Descartes could prove the existence of the *extended, material world,* only with the aid of God, who is the first principle in the order of being and the guarantor of the trustworthiness of our cognitive power. After this third existential truth was established, Descartes was in possession of all the principles needed for a methodic reconstruction of the physical world and the world of human power and conduct.

In the *Discourse on Method,* Descartes summed up his general views on methodic doubt in four well-known rules:

> The first rule was never to accept anything as true unless I recognized it to be evidently such: that is, carefully to avoid precipitation and prejudgment, and to include nothing in my conclusions unless it presented itself so clearly and distinctly to my mind that I had no occasion to doubt it.
> The second was to divide each of the difficulties which I encountered

into as many parts as possible, and as might be required for an easier solution.

The third was to think in an orderly fashion, beginning with the things which were simplest and easiest to understand, and gradually and by degrees reaching toward more complex knowledge, even treating as though ordered materials which were not necessarily so.

The last was always to make enumerations so complete and reviews so general, that I was certain that nothing was omitted.[11]

This text is a masterpiece of philosophical diplomacy. It could be read with some understanding and profit by readers trained in the traditional logic manuals. Each of these four precepts had its counterpart in the ordinary directions given for definition and reasoning by the Scholastic logicians. These authors suggested that we avoid prejudice, strive after clear and distinct knowledge, divide a problem into its parts, proceed from the better known to the more difficult, and assure the completeness of a complex inference through a review of the subordinate steps. But on each of these points, Descartes offered a distinctive interpretation, in conformity with his own methodology. His safeguard against prejudgment and haste was universal, methodic doubt; his standard of clarity and distinctness was correlated with the technique of doubt and with an attempt to argue from the ideal to the real order; division into parts became, in his hands, a definite method of resolutive analysis; Cartesian simple things are simple natures, intuitively grasped; the gradual order of inferences must respect the requirements of a chain of truths and the necessity of proceeding existentially from self to God and the world; the reviews are made with a view toward securing the homogeneous body of wisdom, through a single intuitive habit of mind. And throughout these four rules can be noticed the unobtrusive but dominating presence of the first personal pronoun — an indication that all methodic thinking is referred ultimately to the Cogito, the thinking self, which alone has withstood the initial test of doubt. In this respect, these four precepts bear the indelible mark of Descartes' unique venture in philosophizing.

## 4. UNIVERSAL DOUBT AND THE COGITO

Descartes came to realize that his methodology was not self-validating but required a metaphysical foundation. Not only the problem of the simple natures but also certain features about

---

[11] *Discourse on Method*, II (Lafleur, 12).

mathematical thinking itself convinced him of this need. Mathematics has two shortcomings, as far as philosophical knowledge is concerned: it is a *nonexistential* discipline and it is *not resistant to the ultimate doubt* that the human mind may be intrinsically framed so as to deceive itself about even the clearest and simplest mathematical propositions. Now, without an existential content, known to be proof against any extreme of doubt, philosophy can only build upon shifting sands, which are incapable of supporting the edifice of the sciences. Hence Descartes was led to seek a sound basis for his thought in the *existing,* thinking self or Cogito ("I am thinking"), which withstands and triumphantly survives the test of a *universal doubt.* Cartesian metaphysics is more than an application of method: it is the ultimate validation and existential grounding of method.

The first rule of method, requesting us to avoid precipitation and prejudgment, entails the condition that a properly conducted metaphysical inquiry must begin with a methodic doubt. For at any given moment, the mind is laden down with many uncritically accepted opinions and prejudices. The only way to make sure that none of these unfounded convictions remain to infect our philosophical system is to subject all our presently held beliefs to a radical doubt. Obviously, each individual conviction cannot be treated separately, for then the process of doubting would go on indefinitely, without ever leading to the reconstruction of philosophy. Hence Descartes proposes to concentrate his doubt upon the *foundations* of accepted knowledge, with the consequence that everything based upon these foundations will topple along with them, leading to a general over-throw — *eversio generalis* — of all previous opinions.[12] To carry out this project of sapping the foundations of customary belief, Descartes must cast doubt upon the *principles* of these opinions, i.e., upon the several knowing powers and areas of objects supposedly known. He questions our external senses, our powers of imagination and memory, and even our purely intellectual power. Judgments about the external world, one's own body, the constructions of the physical and mathematical sciences, and the existence of God, are all submitted to doubt and found to be wanting, in the present condition of philosophy. Finally, Descartes arrives at the finite thinking self

---

[12] In *The Meditations concerning First Philosophy,* I (Lafleur translation, 15–20), Descartes shows us the methodic doubt in actual operation; in *The Principles of Philosophy,* I, 1–7 (Haldane-Ross, I, 219–21), he gives a systematic analysis of the entire process.

as an indubitable existent and, by a careful analysis of its implications, proceeds to give a scientific basis to our convictions about God, the material world, and the various sciences.

In executing this ambitious plan, Descartes relies upon two maxims that are explicitly directed against any variety of moderate realism. The first is that one should treat *the probable* as though it were entirely *false;* the second is that one should make the *senses* the special target of doubt and should therefore detach the understanding from reliance upon the senses and belief in the material world.

> Since reason already convinces me that I should abstain from the belief in things which are not entirely certain and indubitable no less carefully than from the belief in those which appear to me to be manifestly false, it will be enough to make me reject them all if I can find in each some ground for doubt. . . . Everything which I have thus far accepted as entirely true [and assured] has been acquired from the senses or by means of the senses. But I have learned by experience that these senses sometimes mislead me, and it is prudent never to trust wholly those things which have once deceived us.[13]

It is fortunate that Descartes himself has high-lighted these two points, since they do express the basic grounds of his quarrel with realism. The issue does not simply concern the use of a universal doubt but also the use of precisely this sort of doubt, in which the probable is methodically merged with the false and in which the existential judgment based upon sense perception of the material world is revoked, as a genuine principle of knowledge.

Descartes regards the first maxim as the natural teaching of reason, because he is disposed to erect a psychological experience into a methodological principle. The experience is the fact that sometimes we give to mere opinions or probabilities the unqualified assent due only to evidently certain truths. As a curative against this excessive practice, he proposes that we refrain entirely (at the outset of metaphysics) from giving assent to the probable. In effect, this counterbalancing policy places the probable on an equal footing with the false, since we seek to withhold assent entirely from both. Cartesian doubt is a sort of secular, ascetic technique for detachment from the probable. Now, in some instances, this may be a *psychologically* helpful rule; but no justification is given for transforming it into a *universal, methodological* principle. Even Descartes admits a place (further on in philosophical inquiry) for hypothesis, conjecture,

---

[13] *The Meditations concerning First Philosophy,* I (Lafleur, 15–16).

and probable reasoning, functioning in the service of mediate deduction. The aim of methodic thinking is to give to a proposition the sort of assent that its evidence warrants. Even at the outset of metaphysical investigations, one can proceed cautiously on the rule of giving to a proposition only the kind of assent *proportioned* to the evidence at hand. Here, the systematic aim is to treat the probable as probable, without either mistaking it for apodictically certain truth or classifying it strategically with the false.

Furthermore, some definite indications must be provided concerning the "entirely certain and indubitable" standard, in respect to which some particular proposition is to be adjudged merely probable. Descartes cannot yet define it as that which passes the test of universal doubt, since this would be a circular argument. Nor can he appeal here to the mathematical kind of evidence, since he has not established precisely what sort of modifications are needed before this sort of evidence can be accepted as prototypal for existential matters, from which mathematics as such prescinds. Hence, in dealing with the senses, he merely appeals to the advice of prudence that we should not place complete confidence in anything that has once deceived us. Two critical comments can be made upon this advice.

1. A distinction is required between a morally malicious counteragent, such as a deceiving human being, and an occasion for speculative deception on the part of one's own knowing powers, as in the present instance. Since the senses are not malicious counteragents, the same sort of avoidance need not be demanded in both cases. We need not shun the senses entirely, in order to avoid cognitive deception, but should maintain a cautious watch over the conditions of sense perception. Furthermore, the probable state of a body of evidence is not deceptive by itself. It becomes the occasion of deception, when the investigator follows the policy of accepting the probable as demonstrated or when the polemist presents dialectical arguments as though they were strict demonstrations. But these are *intellectual decisions about how to use the probable:* they are not generated by the probable character of the evidence itself, and they are not decisions made by the senses. Hence we can effectively oppose such unwarranted uses of probable evidence, without going to the opposite extreme of regarding the probable as false and the senses as untrustworthy. Methodic, universal doubt is not a necessary and indispensable means to the attainment of certain and indubitable knowledge.

2. If the deception concerns the senses as a supposed source of truth, then the principle of deception must be traced to the *judging power,* rather than to the senses. Descartes agrees that the senses can be only "materially false," insofar as they may dispose the mind toward false judgments. But it does not follow that intellect and will must be methodically severed from reliance upon sense data. Such a severance would remove the human way of access to existential reality. In this instance, ordinary good sense or prudence distinguishes between not trusting a source *in every instance* and not trusting it *at all as a basic principle* of knowledge. Sensory occasions of deception oblige us to be watchful over the senses in particular instances but not to reject their constant testimony to sensible existence. Descartes wanted to meet Montaigne and other skeptics on their own grounds. He accepted their arguments against the senses, as sources of speculative truth. But he sought to undercut the entire skeptical conclusion by showing that the basic metaphysical truths are founded in no way upon the senses and hence are in no way affected by the unreliability of the senses. To carry out this strategy against skepticism, however, he also had to deny the realistic grounding of all existential demonstration in sense perception. Were it not for his polemical intent, Descartes could have understood the advice of prudence to mean that one should exercise vigilance in every instance where sense perception makes a report that can become philosophically significant. This program of dealing *distributively* or one-by-one with cases of sense perception cannot be incorporated within a rationalistic method, that seeks to doubt *collectively* about an entire cognitive source, on the basis of particular occasions of deception. But it does have the merit of drawing no more from the particular instances than is warranted, and hence of permitting each deliverance of the senses to be appraised on its own weight and in view of its own set of attendant circumstances.

Descartes observes that not only the external senses but also *imagination* and *memory* often deceive us. In line with his general principles of doubt, then, they must also be regarded as being infected with falsity. This application of doubt is intended to tell heavily against mathematics and mathematical physics, which rely upon imaginative constructions and upon complicated reasonings, in which memory must be used. Yet even in the case of an immediate mathematical proposition, such as that 2 plus 2 equal 4, there is no absolute certainty. God might have so constructed our minds that we could not but assent to such propositions, even though they were untrue. In this event, even the atheist would be subject to an ironical delusion by the very Being whom he so confidently denies. As for our awareness of *our own existence,* it may well be, as Calderón puts it, that "life is a dream." There seems to be no definite criterion for distinguishing between a waking and a sleeping state. No conviction, personal or scientific, is left untouched by this general overthrow of human knowledge.

The full power of this doubt is concentrated and personified in the hypothesis of a *spiritus malignus, a demon as powerful as it is evil,* one whose will it is to deceive man even in his clearest and most distinct ideas. This extreme supposition is intended to fulfill the final condition of testing the bases of knowledge to the utmost. If any conviction can withstand the assault of this supposed demonic mind, then certainty comes automatically within our grasp and the fear of intrinsic self-deception is removed. Descartes' doubt culminates in the appeal to an evil genius, precisely because of his high standard for philosophical truth.[14] The only route to an unassailable first truth and a real criterion of knowledge lies through the purgatory of entertaining such a suspicion.

This positive purpose of doubt distinguishes the Cartesian position from the skeptical one. The skeptics regard doubt as a permanent state of soul, whereas for Descartes it is a means or method of attaining  reliable knowledge. Descartes is not the *victim* of doubt but the *technician* of the method of doubt. His doubt is theoretical, hyperbolical, and metaphysical.[15] It is *theoretical,* in that it concerns the

---

[14] Read H. G. Wolz, "The Universal Doubt in the Light of Descartes's Conception of Truth," *The Modern Schoolman,* XXVII (1949–1950), 253–79. Descartes' own three reasons for employing the doubt are the following: "Although it is not immediately apparent that so general a doubt can be useful, it is in fact very much so, since it delivers us from all sorts of *prejudices* and makes available to us an easy method of accustoming our minds to become independent of the *senses.* Finally, it is useful in making it subsequently *impossible to doubt* those things which we discover to be true after we have taken doubt into consideration." *The Meditations concerning First Philosophy,* Synopsis (Lafleur, 11; italics added).

[15] *Replies to Objections,* VII (Haldane-Ross, II, 266, 277). Descartes recommends his methodic doubt to Mersenne, on the ground that, "although many have already maintained that, in order to understand the facts of metaphysics, the mind must be abstracted from the senses, no one hitherto, so far as I know, has shown how this is to be done." *Ibid.,* II (Haldane-Ross, II, 31–32). The Thomistic judgment of separation and the Cartesian methodic doubt are conflicting ways of making a metaphysical removal from sense experience and sensible modes of being. The former affirms at once the existential trustworthiness and the limited character of the sense report; the

order of speculative truths rather than the practical conduct of life; hence it fails to paralyze one's activities, customs, and beliefs. It is *hyperbolical,* in the sense of advancing the extreme possibility of a deceiving demon and of rejecting as false whatever has the least suspicion of doubt attached to it. This strategy is Descartes' special way of counteracting our proneness to accept mere opinion as truth. Its outcome is to be a critical balance of mind that is neither credulous nor unreasonably skeptical. Cartesian doubt is also hyperbolical (but not fictitious) insofar as it arises from an act of will, that must be deliberately and methodically elicited, rather than from a natural attitude or a facile pose of mind. Methodical doubt is an instrument of human freedom in its cautious search after truth. This illuminates the *metaphysical* aspect of doubt, since it is a device for inquiring "once in a lifetime" whether there is any bedrock, existential truth. Since he lacks the separative judgment grounding metaphysics in both sense and intellect, Descartes must use the purely rationalist means of a universal doubt to achieve some metaphysical abstraction and certainty.

Under the impact of the hypothesis of an evil and all-powerful spirit, the self is led to suspect its various cognitive powers, its scientific accomplishments and, at last, its very existence.

I have just convinced myself that nothing whatsoever existed in the world, that there was no sky, no earth, no minds, and no bodies; have I not thereby convinced myself that I did not exist? Not at all; without doubt I existed if I was convinced [or even if I thought anything]. Even though there may be a deceiver of some sort, very powerful and very tricky, who bends all his efforts to keep me perpetually deceived, there can be no slightest doubt that I exist, since he deceives me; and let him deceive me as much as he will, he can never make me be nothing as long as I think that I am something. Thus, after having thought well on this matter, and after examining all things with care, I must finally conclude and maintain that this proposition: *I am, I exist,* is necessarily true every time that I pronounce it or conceive it in my mind.[16]

latter regards the senses as initially untrustworthy for purposes of existential knowledge, and requires a subsequent deductive validation of sensation, as a practical tool and index of sensible existents.

[16] *The Meditations concerning First Philosophy,* II (Lafleur, 21–22); cf. *Discourse on Method,* IV (Lafleur, 20–21). Descartes' contemporaries, Mersenne and Arnauld, called his attention to the similarities between the Cartesian and Augustinian ways of quieting skepticism, through a concrete inspection of situations of thinking and being deceived. For a brief report on the likenesses and differences between St. Augustine and Descartes, cf. E. Gilson, *The Unity of Philosophical Experience,* 155–58.

The formula *Cogito ergo sum* (I am thinking, therefore I am) expresses the one existential judgment that can never fall victim to radical doubt, since its evidence is brought home irresistibly in the very act of calling it into question through the extreme supposition of an evil genius. The existing, thinking thing, which is the human self, is the unconditionally first noetic principle of Descartes' philosophy, because it is the first indubitable, existential truth.

Despite its incontrovertible appeal to Descartes' own mind, this first step in his metaphysics became at once a storm center among his contemporaries. The three recurrent objections were: (1) that the Cogito supposes some unproved premises; (2) that it smuggles in the substantial self, without proof; (3) that it leads to a vicious circle, since its full certitude depends upon the demonstration of God's existence — a demonstration that depends, in turn, upon the criterion of truth and the causal principle established along with the Cogito. Since these criticisms are still the outstanding ones, it is worth listening to Descartes' defense of his own position.[17]

1. The use of the word "therefore" contributes to the impression that *Cogito ergo sum* is the conclusion of a syllogism, whose major premise states that "whatever thinks, must exist." But Descartes maintains that the formula is not based on a syllogistic inference but expresses the *most simple intuition* of the human mind, one wherein it sees at a single glance the mutual implication between the simple natures of "actual thinking" and "actual existing." His opponents proceed on the assumption that general, abstract principles must first be posited, in order that concrete, particular truths can be derived. But Cartesian logic takes the concrete, particular, and immaterial existent as a starting point. General principles are discovered to be latent in the particular object and hence are *concomitant* with, rather than *antecedent* to, the judgment about the individual instance. Along with perceiving the truth of the Cogito, the mind also formulates a general proposition about the relation between thought and existence. The emphatic necessity of the connection between the

---

[17] *Replies to Objections*, II, IV (Haldane-Ross, II, 38–43, 114–15). For a survey of the main charges and a historical defense of Descartes, see E. G. Salmon, "The Cartesian Circle," *The New Scholasticism*, XII (1938), 378–91. For a critical comparison between Descartes and St. Thomas, see Peter Hoenen, S.J., *Reality and Judgment according to St. Thomas* (Chicago, Regnery, 1952), Chap. XII: "The *Cogito ergo sum* of St. Thomas" (274–86). But Hoenen does not emphasize sufficiently the capital difference between Descartes and St. Thomas, in respect to sensation as a primary, speculatively valid principle of knowledge and index of existence.

thinking and the existing is conveyed by the use of the word "therefore," but it implies no inference from anything prior. In addition, the mind discovers, by implication, the truth of three common axioms, which serve as bonds among simple natures and things. The principles of *contradiction, substantiality,* and *causality* are seen to be immediate general implications of the Cogito-situation. Descartes is all too ready to concede their validity and to shelter them under the wing of the first truth. Whereas he assigns these three principles among the common truths to which the natural light of the mind bears immediate witness, they become moot points of discussion among his successors. The latter regard his systematic use of substance and cause as only an uncriticized survival of an earlier dogmatism.

2. Coming to the second objection, Descartes does not challenge the observation that, in order to understand the import of *Cogito ergo sum,* one must already possess some notion of the meaning of thinking and existing and doubting. He classifies these objects among the simple natures, which can be known by intuition. Insofar as they are merely apprehended natures or ideal objects, entailing no existential judgment, they do not fall within the scope of methodic doubt and hence are present throughout the inquiry. Doubt attacks none of these notions in their purely *ideal* and *essential* character. The metaphysical orientation of methodic doubt means precisely that it applies to judgments about *really existing* things. Although in some respects this is an effective reply, it has two drawbacks that Descartes does not consider. First, it makes of existence an essential notion or simple nature, that is first grasped in a nonexistential, nonjudgmental act of apprehension. The problem then arises whether existence, as so understood, is the same as what is expressed in a judgment of existence. Second, Descartes assumes that we all have a fairly clear and distinct notion of what it means to think, to doubt, and to exist. Here, the difficulty is to find any definite content remaining for these facts, after the vagueness and obscurity have been removed — and, at least, methodic doubt must remove these obstructing factors.

In any case, once these simple natures are found to be present in an indubitable existential situation, the mind attends at once to the fact that they are being conceived by it precisely *as modifications of some subject.* Instead of covertly interpolating a substantial self, Descartes maintains that this latter affirmation is a necessary implication of the inhering function of thinking and doubting. These operations are ascertained along with a reference to their subject. What reveals itself to my introspection is nothing other than myself thinking, myself existing. To expand the basic formula a bit: it is the *I who am thinking* that is also known as the *I who am existing*. Descartes remains close to the Scholastics, in the degree that it is natural for him to think of being primarily in terms of substantial things and their affections. Whether the naturalness of positing a subject for acts of thinking is due to the natural light of the understanding or only to the inclination of training and habitual association, is the question raised by Malebranche and carried to its skeptical conclusion by Hume.

3. At least at this point in the study, the truth of the Cogito is known only as often as I actually pronounce the proposition. It is true *here and now,* since the perception is borne in upon me with utmost clarity and distinctness. The *criterion of truth* is itself implicated in the Cogito, because the conditions of this perception irresistibly draw the will to assent to its truth. What is more reasonable than to suppose that every clearly and distinctly perceived idea is true and informative about reality? This question may be answered by a universal affirmative, Descartes replies, on condition that there is no ground for suspecting that, in the future, clear and distinct ideas may turn out to be false. The truth of the Cogito is not sufficient to remove this suspicion *about the future,* and hence its truth is limited to present perception in pronouncing the judgment. But unless the suspicion can be removed somehow, the suggested universal criterion can never function at all times and hence can never aid in the construction of a philosophical system. This exigency led Descartes, next, to prove the existence of God.

Contemporary readers urged that Descartes was guilty of circular reasoning, when he accepted the Cogito as indubitable and later on declared that no truth is absolutely certain, until the existence of a veracious God is established. His reply to this criticism was based on a distinction between present, actual perception and remembrance of a former perception. A divine guarantee is needed for *memory* and *reasoning* about past apprehensions of truth but not for *present perception* of clear and distinct ideas. Once having ascertained the existence of a nondeceiving God, Descartes gains retroactive assurance that the situation of the Cogito can be extended to other instances of clear and distinct perception of the connections among ideas. The temporal proviso attached to the criterion of evidence may then be confidently removed. A good God would not permit us to take the false for the true, whether in immediate perception or in memory and reasoning, for otherwise we would be irresistibly drawn to make the judgment and yet would have no means of rectifying the error. Viewed in conjunction with what we come to know about God's nature, the criterion of truth cannot reasonably be doubted and hence can be made a universal rule of reasoning.

## 5. THE EXISTENCE AND NATURE OF GOD

In reply to a satirical comment that the actual results of his philosophy are surprisingly meager, in comparison with the great energy expended in developing it, Descartes made a distinction between two sorts of innovators. Some thinkers strive at all costs to be original in respect to the *conclusions* of their philosophy, whereas others bestow their care mainly upon the *reasoning* which supports the conclusions. Descartes ridiculed Bruno and Campanella for advancing farfetched innovations for their own sakes. He himself regarded the existence of an immaterial soul, a transcendent God, and an extended universe as the sum of philosophical principles, and did not consider himself original in this respect. His personal contribution lay rather in suggesting new ways of proving these traditional truths. Yet in offering new proofs, he was obliged to change the content of the conclusions much more than he cared to admit. This is clearly seen in his treatment of natural theology, especially his three proofs of God's existence.

1. True to his method, Descartes seeks to prove God's existence solely from truths already established. Hence his point of departure can only be the ideas present in himself as a thinking thing. These he classifies, first of all, according to their descriptive origin. Ideas seem to fall into three classes: (*adventitious*)(coming from without), (*factitious*)(coming from the mind's constructive power), and (*innate*) (coming from the inborn dynamism of the mind). Our idea of God can be tested by this threefold classification. Although the imagination is undoubtedly capable of fashioning its images freely, the *idea of God* does not have a factitious origin. Whenever Descartes thinks of God, he is constrained to think of "an infinite substance, eternal, immutable, independent, omniscient, omnipotent."[18] He cannot think

---

[18] *The Meditations concerning First Philosophy*, III (Lafleur, 40). For the various statements of the proofs for God's existence, compare *ibid.*, III, V (Lafleur, 32–47, 58–61); *Discourse on Method*, IV (Lafleur, 22–23); *The Principles of Philosophy*,

of God otherwise than in these terms, and hence this idea does not have a factitious origin. Nor does it come to him suddenly from without. Indeed, the external origin of *any* idea is doubtful, at this stage of his meditations. Material things, including the self's own body, are not yet known to exist. Our spontaneous impulse to believe that some ideas are adventitious may well be erroneous, since it may be due to some unknown power unconsciously at work in the mind. By elimination, it follows that the idea of God is innate or native to the mind.

Yet the bare fact that the idea of God has an innate origin is not decisive for the problem of God's existence. For, as Suarez taught, any idea can be regarded in two ways: either *formally* (in its own mental mode of being) or *objectively* (as representing various objects). From the formal standpoint, all ideas are on the same level and are adequately accounted for by the human mind, in which they reside. Representatively or objectively, however, they differ vastly and can be arranged in an ascending order, insofar as they refer to different grades of being. Now, Descartes is sure that, even from the standpoint of their representative reality, all ideas (except that of the infinite being) might be accounted for by himself as a thinking being. The crucial question is whether he is also the adequate source of the representative reality of the idea of a purely infinite being.

To answer this question, Descartes appeals to the *principle of efficient causality,* the certainty of which has already been guaranteed in the Cogito. This principle states, in its Cartesian formulation, that there must be at least as much reality in the efficient and total cause as in the effect. Descartes also takes as immediately evident the following propositions: that a thing cannot give what it does not have; that something cannot come from nothing; that the more perfect cannot come from the less perfect. He regards them as inborn truths, taught us by the natural light of the mind. And, following another hint from Suarez, he adds that a sufficient cause is required to explain the *objective* or *representative reality* of the idea, as well as for the formal reality of the idea, taken as a mental mode. From the above principles, it is clear that a finite, thinking self is insufficient to account for the objective reality of the idea of a purely infinite being. This reality comes neither from nothing nor from a being

I, 14–21 (Haldane-Ross, I, 224–28); *Replies to Objections,* II (Haldane-Ross, II, 57–58; these demonstrations are in geometrical form).

that is of less reality than the infinite being. Hence it must have been implanted in the human mind by a being which possesses as much reality in a formal, actual way as the idea possesses in a representative way. The conclusion is that the infinitely perfect being, God, must exist as the adequate efficient cause of my idea of God.

2. As a second proof, Descartes shifts his perspective slightly, so as to consider the implications of *the self which possesses this idea* of a being, infinite in perfection. There is no complete distinction between the two proofs, since the self is inspected precisely insofar as it is the subject of the idea of God. But the second one is advanced by Descartes as being more accommodated to a Scholastic audience, which might see in it a proof cognate to the familiar ones from contingency and efficiency. The thinking self is *not independent* or the author of its own being, since in that case it would confer upon itself, in the formal order, whatever reality it can conceive representatively through its ideas. Were it self-caused, the human self would confer infinite perfection upon itself, in correspondence with its idea of God. That I am *not infinite,* however, is evident from my being subject to change of thought, from my capacity both for error-and-doubt and for increase of knowledge, and from my desire for an infinite good existing beyond my own nature. The Cogito participates in the perfection of the simple natures of existence and thought, but it is not their unconditioned actualization. Similarly, the successive moments of my duration are discrete and externally related, so that even if I always existed, I would be everlastingly dependent upon the same cause that produced my first moment of existence. God is the creating and conserving cause of the very being of the thinking self, not merely of its first act of coming-to-be. He provides the only principle of unity among the discrete, atomic moments of the self's duration. The limited and dependent thing which contains the idea of an infinitely perfect being could neither exist nor endure, except as being caused and conserved in being by the infinite being. The idea of God is innate in the thinking self, in the sense that it is, as it were, the seal placed upon His product by the divine artisan. In creating a human self, God also communicates to it the ability to conceive or cause an idea having the infinitely perfect actuality as its object.

3. In order to clear the way for his final proof of God's existence, Descartes has to attack the *problem of error.*[19] In principle, it follows

---

[19] Descartes devotes the fourth section of *The Meditations concerning First Philosophy*

from the infinite perfection of God that He is veracious and cannot
be a deceiver, i.e., cannot have the malicious intent of deceiving us.
Hence God may not be charged with being the cause of error, and
man may not be described as the innocent and impotent victim of
error. Descartes' approach to error is quite similar to the approach
of St. Thomas to *evil,* an analogy that is not surprising, in view of the
fact that Descartes considers the *act of assent or judgment to be an
act of the will.* Error is not a positive reality but a privation, a lack
of knowledge which ought to be present. The possibility of having
this privation rests on the self's condition as a finite being, a creature
drawn from nothing. The senses give a confused and indistinct
report and hence can be a material source of error, in that the state
of sense evidence may lead to a false judgment. But it is in the
judgment itself that error formally resides. The judgment is an act ✓
of the will rather than of the understanding, since it requires an
assent, over and above the cognitive perception of objects. Understanding and will, taken by themselves as faculties given by God,
are veracious powers. But in point of fact, they act conjointly in
the knowing act, which is a synthesis of *intellectual perception* and
*voluntary assent.* By nature, understanding has only a finite range of
operation, whereas the range of will is unlimited. Descartes agrees
with Mersenne and St. Bernard that man most closely resembles
God in respect to will. The uncircumscribed quality of will is both
man's glory and his Achilles' heel. For the will often outraces the
evidence presented by the understanding and gives a firm assent in
matters that are not clearly and distinctly presented. To take the
false for the true is thus a misuse of the will's freedom of indifference, ✓
and is traceable to a refusal to keep modestly within the bounds set
by our cognitive power. Whatever is positive and sound in the act
of judgment comes from God, but man himself is the principal
cause of the privation or misuse of the will's assent, in which error
formally consists.

From this exposition, it follows both that God is not responsible
for error and that He has not left us without *remedy* against it. At
least, we have the minimal power of recognizing the source of error
within us and of refraining from judgment on occasions when the
conditions of clarity and distinctness are absent from our ideas.

---

(Lafleur, 47–66) to this subject; other passages are collated and criticized by L. W.
Keeler, S.J., *The Problem of Error from Plato to Kant* (Rome, Gregorian University
Press, 1934), 141–77.

Training in method is nothing more than cultivation of the habitual attention required for observance of this rule of refrainment. Both the avoidance of error and the attainment of truth require the mind's disciplined attention to the canons of evidence. The methodically directed mind need have no fear of deceit, when it is in the presence of clear and distinct perceptions. It can reason with confidence from the order of knowing to that of being: *a nosse ad esse valet consequentia.*[20] The mind's *clear* and *distinct ideas,* which alone are direct objects of perception, are nevertheless adequate grounds for drawing conclusions about *existent things.*

Descartes immediately exploits this fully guaranteed criterion in the interests of a third proof of God's existence: that drawn from the perceived connection between *essence and existence in the idea of God.* Just as the first two proofs tend to merge together, so the third proof tends to assimilate the two prior ones. Descartes sometimes confesses that God's existence can *only* be proved from the idea of God, with God taken as efficient rather than final cause.[21] Such proof is either a posteriori (from the representative reality of the idea of God, and from the self which has this idea) or a priori (from the content itself of this idea). Although the a priori or so-called ontological argument cannot be advanced before the objective validity of our ideas has been established, it represents the deepest point of penetration of Cartesian analysis into the significance of human thought. The ultimate meaning of the Cogito is that the finite thinking self shares to some degree in the *divine dynamism* itself, in the *self-affirmation* that is God's distinctive way of being. One becomes aware of this affinity in reflecting upon the import of the clearest and most distinct idea in the mind: the idea of an infinitely perfect being. This essence contains existence as a property, just as necessarily as the notion of triangle contains the properties demonstrable of it. The notion of actual and eternal existence is a positive perfection, clearly and distinctly known as belonging to the infinitely perfect essence, and hence it can be affirmed as true of this essence

20 "The argument from knowledge to existence is quite valid, because it is impossible to know anything, unless it really is as we know it." *Replies to Objections,* VII (Haldane-Ross, II, 313).
21 That the contrast between St. Thomas and Descartes in natural theology is fundamentally that between a point of departure taken in the sensible existent and one taken in the idea of God, is established by P. Mesnard, "Les preuves cartésiennes de l'existence de Dieu dans les *Méditations métaphysiques,*" in *Cartesio nel terzo centenario del 'Discorso del Metodo,'* 599–614.

*in the actual order.* Once existence is seen to be a perfection, I cannot truly think of God or the perfect being otherwise than as actually existing. For the necessity and self-affirmation of His real existence are imposed upon (or rather, determine from within) the structure of my idea of God. I am constrained by necessity of thought, i.e., by the perfect, self-imposing evidence of the connection between a perfect essence and existence, to conceive of the object of that idea as necessarily existing. Since the constraint comes from the most clearly and distinctly perceived connection, the truth of God's own actual and necessary existence follows from the truth of the necessity of including existence in one's idea of God's essence.

Descartes' arguments were placed under fire at once. His atheistic opponents objected against the sudden appeal to the principle of efficient causality, whose validity was not established by a distinct, formal argument. Indirectly, however, Descartes had provided the materials for a defense of this principle. The various modes of the thinking thing not only inhere in it but are also causally determined by it. That is why Descartes held that the finite thinking self could adequately account for the formal being of all ideas and for the representative reality of all ideas, save that of the infinite being. The Cogito is presented immediately to consciousness as an agent, *as the efficient cause* of its own states of thought. Moreover, training in method is a process of learning to use the mind's power of attention, in maintaining its free control over the act of judgment. The ability to give assent or refrain from giving it was, in Descartes' eyes, a supreme instance of human freedom and of finite, efficient causality. Hence he regarded the reality of causation as being adequately founded in such inward facts. But unfortunately, he did not work out any detailed explanation of the principle of causality and left sufficient loopholes for Malebranche to deny created causality, while still speculating *en bon cartésien.*

The argument from the idea of the infinite was attacked by contemporary theologians on the ground that the *idea of an infinite being* need not be an *infinite idea.* They held that the so-called objective or representative reality of ideas does not demand any special causal explanation.[22] Meaning can be adequately accounted for by the mind's

---

[22] The theologians, Caterus and Arnauld, presented some serious objections to the Cartesian proofs for God's existence: *Objections,* I, IV (Haldane-Ross, II, 1–8, 86–93); cf. Descartes' *Replies to Objections,* I, IV (Haldane-Ross, II, 9–22, 104–15), for his rejoinders. See H. G. Wolz, "The Function of the Will in Descartes' Proofs for the Existence of God," *The New Scholasticism,* XX (1946), 295–322.

ability to abstract intentional likenesses, and by the contribution of experienced things to our notions. Must an exception be made in the case of the idea of God? Descartes maintained that this idea is a *positive* one, even though it is not *comprehensive* of God's infinite perfection. It is a clear and distinct idea, and hence can be used somewhat like the distinct ideas in mathematics which are applied to the infinite limit. Just as geometry deals with the properties of the circle by superposition of a rectilinear polyhedron, having an indefinite number of sides, so our idea of infinite perfection can be used to know, but never to comprehend, the infinite God. This answer did not really meet the Scholastic objection, since the point at issue would then be whether our mind has the power to frame this idea, with the aid of its knowledge of finite things and its ability to negate imperfections. Furthermore, the comparison was not a happy one, since the mathematical type of analogy is reducible to univocal predication. Both terms of the mathematical relation (the circle and the polyhedron) belong to the class of geometrical figures, whereas Descartes' own theism would prevent him from placing God and any finite entity in the same class. His predicament was that he had to use the mathematical example, if he wanted to evade the alternative of either discarding innatism in favor of an *abstraction-*theory of the origin of the idea of God or else claiming to have a fully *comprehensive* idea of infinite perfection.

It was pointed out to Descartes, moreover, that the traditional view of the idea of God's infinite perfection is not that of a mere negation of finitude but also an eminent affirmation of all pure perfections. The human mind is able to conceive these perfections and to affirm them of God, apart from the finite modes in which they are embodied in our experience and thought. This activity of *predication by way of eminence and analogical affirmation,* along with a denial of limitation, would account for the idea of God, without having recourse to innatism. In the face of this explanation, Descartes was obliged to make an important concession. He allowed that, in the order of our *explicit* notions, the idea of finite perfections comes first. But he still awarded an *implicit* priority to the notion of the infinite, on the ground that otherwise we could never have a standard of comparison in the light of which finite things are seen to be finite. To this distinction, his Thomistic critics replied that the transcendental notions of being and actual perfection are sufficient to account for our recognition of the finite character of the objects of experience.

Descartes' final remark was in the form of a question about the source of the mind's power of *amplifying* perfections somehow, so that they may signify the infinite. This reference to the mind's power of amplification marks Descartes' failure to release himself from a purely mathematical approach to the infinite and his substitution of a question about the causal origin of a mental power for the more pertinent one about the range of that power's knowledge.

When the theologian Caterus remarked that the second proof resembles the Thomistic proof from efficient causality, Descartes approved of the general comparison but added a list of four significant differences. (1) Descartes never argued from an order of efficient causes operating in the sensible world. He had to start from immaterial entities, since the existence of sensible things was still under doubt. (2) Moreover, he thought (incorrectly) that the Thomistic proof from efficient cause was based on the impossibility of an infinite series of accidentally subordinated agents. He did not appreciate the import of the Thomistic conception of divine efficient, *per se* causality of the entire *esse* of presently existing things. Descartes pointed out two further points of difference. (3) His starting point was the self only as a thinking thing and, indeed, only as a thing having the idea of the infinite. (4) Finally, he disagreed with the remark of Thomas that nothing can be its own efficient cause. Descartes juggled a good deal with the terms "efficient cause" and "cause of itself." At times, he reduced God's self-causation to the fact that the divine essence is its own positive principle of intelligibility, comparable to the formal cause of His nature. Yet at other times, he called God a *causa sui* in the sense of having a positive self-origination of His being, in virtue of the affirmation of His infinite efficient power. This obscure notion of the divine being, as standing somehow in relation to itself as an efficient cause to its effect, stems from Descartes' metaphysical view that the divine essence is basically infinite power, and that existence (divine or otherwise) is a terminal perfection in the line of essence itself.

When reminded about St. Thomas' criticism of the argument of St. Anselm, Descartes granted that the Thomistic strictures told against a proof based on the meaning of the *word* "God." But he regarded his own third proof as dealing with the true and immutable *nature* of God, as objectively contained in a clear and distinct idea. Descartes did not join issue with Aquinas over whether the divine essence can be known directly in this way by our minds, so as to permit an a priori proof. For him, it was enough to have a distinct and certain idea, in order to draw an existential conclusion. One reason why Descartes characterized God as *causa sui* was to lend force to the a priori truth of the proposition "God exists," as it follows from our idea of God.[23] The immensity and infinite power of God are such that, needing no cause outside itself, the divine essence nevertheless bestows being upon itself after the manner of an efficient cause. Because God cannot be prior to, or distinct from, His own being, the creaturely meaning of efficient causality is not fully realized in Him, and to this extent God produces His being more after the manner of a formal cause. Still, the active power of the infinite principle is exercised in supplying its own being, as well as in the creation of finite things. The divine existence flows somehow as a property of God's infinite essence. In this sense, Descartes wants to reduce all proofs of God's existence to one grand proof, taken from the idea of God as an efficient cause. His self-causality is mirrored in the necessity with which our mind is led to affirm His existence, on the basis of our clear and distinct idea of His essence. To this idea, the divine workman imparts all its representative vigor of affirming existence. It is not merely the idea of existence that is seen to be entailed by that of the divine essence, but the *true* or *existentially relevant idea* of necessary existence.

Descartes follows the voluntaristic strain in later Scholasticism in his explanation of the *divine attributes:* infinity, incomprehensibility, omnipotence, independence, and immutability. Each of these attributes is made to perform a distinctive function in the Cartesian synthesis. The divine *infinity* and *incomprehensibility* are used to eliminate *final cause* as an explanatory principle of the visible universe. It is true that God Himself does set an end for the universe and hence does exercise final causality in its respect. But the infinite depths of the divine purpose are inscrutable and incomprehensible to us, preventing any appeal to this purpose in our physical investigations.

---

[23] Another reason was that the principle of causality is metaphysically useful, only if it applies in some manner to God, as well as to finite things. The Cogito assures the existential relevance of this principle, only because it reveals that this principle expresses an ontological exigency of *every* being to have a cause. Unless God is *esse a se tanquam a causa*, the ultimate existential and systematic ground for regarding everything else as *esse a causa* is lacking, in accord with the Cartesian method of tracing the dependence of eternal truths upon the divine will and its self-affirmation of existence. Cf. H. Gouhier, "Les exigences de l'existence dans la métaphysique de Descartes," *Revue Internationale de Philosophie,* IV (1950), 123–52.

A mechanistic explanation of the world can be given, without recourse to the ends for which God intends the various motions. Descartes limits the meaning of the term "finality," however, to this universal extrinsic purpose. He readily admits that the human mind can discover the intrinsic adaptation of parts to the whole, in particular things, but he assigns such adaptation to the efficient cause alone. One of Leibniz' points of dispute with Descartes concerned whether the purely mechanistic interpretation of living things is adequate and, indeed, is a truly philosophical approach. Leibniz held that a thorough metaphysical interpretation of living things requires an appeal to final cause, and that the philosopher can make use of final causality, without pretending to have sounded the depths of the divine infinity or to be privy to God's secret designs.

Descartes uses the divine *omnipotence* and *independence* to resolve the question of the *eternal truths,* including immutable mathematical propositions.[24] He wants to steer a middle course between what he regards as the ordinary Scholastic position and that of the atheistic freethinkers. He interprets Suarez as holding that the eternal truths have an independent, objective presence in the divine understanding, in such a way that the divine will must conform with an independent set of essential necessities. And it is the atheistic contention that eternal truths can be adequately understood and founded, apart from any reference to God, with the consequence that God is superfluous for a true system of philosophy. The Cartesian doctrine on the eternal truths is completely determined by a resolve to avoid these extremes. There is no indication that Descartes ever weighed the Thomistic position that the eternal truths are founded in the divine creative essence, considered as identical with the divine act of existing and as being the primary object of the divine intellect. He cannot allow the atheistic view that our knowledge of the eternal truths may dispense with a divine foundation, for then it would be exempt from his universal doubt and hence could not be shown to have any existential reference. And he cannot grant that these truths constitute a quasi-autonomous region in the divine mind, for then God would be subjected to a mythological sort of Fate. Consequently, the

---

[24] Descartes' most forthright declarations about the dependence of eternal truths on the divine will and about the divine power to make these truths untrue, are contained in a series of letters to Mersenne, written during April and May, 1630 (*Correspondance,* edited by Adam and Milhaud, I, 135-36, 139-42), and in *Replies to Objections,* V, VI (Haldane-Ross, II, 226, 248, 250-51).

eternal truths must have their foundation in the divine will, in such a way that the infinite power and independence of God's action are not compromised.

Descartes asks us to consider that a truth is a form of being, and that a being is either independent or dependent on the divine will. Now since the eternal truths can be *comprehended* by us, they are finite and hence utterly *dependent* upon God. In God, to know and to will are the same. Hence divine knowledge of the eternal truths is also a free, divine determination of them, through an act of will. God's will produces them, just as completely as it creates individual, contingent things: but in producing the eternal truths, He specifically determines them to an immutable mode of being. God could have decreed that it should be untrue that twice four equals eight, even though we cannot comprehend how He could have done so. No limits can be set upon the divine power by our understanding. Even though God *can* do everything which we can comprehend, we have no right to conclude that He *cannot* do that which we cannot comprehend, such as a counterdecree concerning the eternal truths. Divine power is bounded only by its spontaneous ordination to the infinite, divine perfection. Thus the structure of the eternal truths depends upon God's eternal will and affirmation of His own existence.

By using this method of safeguarding the divine omnipotence and independence, however, Descartes imperils the *rational foundations of science.* If the basic truths are contingent upon an exercise of God's power, then they are wholly arbitrary and subject to imminent change. This outcome would also be self-defeating for Descartes' own project of establishing a universal body of certain and reliable truths. Hence he is obliged, finally, to enlist the special aid of the divine attribute of *immutability.* Although God is autonomous and indifferently free in respect to the eternal truths, He does not leave the essential natures and laws of things in utter chaos. Within the context of his unlimited power over all essences, He institutes *a stable order of nature* and gives continuity of duration to the atomic moments of things having temporal existence. Scientific knowledge is based upon this order of nature, which shares in the immutability of the divine essence itself. Philosophical truths are measured ultimately by the divinely established, immutable order of ideas and things. This solution rests upon the qualifying phrase: "within the context of God's unlimited power." The question of the eternal truths remained a lively one for post-Cartesian rationalists, precisely because they suspected that this qualification nullified the effectiveness of Descartes' appeal to the divine immutability. Hence Spinoza suggested that the power and immutability of God should be merged, with the consequence that God cannot but produce precisely this determined world and its laws. Since this solution endangered the divine freedom in creation, Leibniz turned to the view that the world of ideal essences has its own inviolable structure, but that the actual world of existents is freely chosen by God, in accordance with His decree to produce the maximum of perfection. Between fate and chaos, it is difficult to find a middle ground for either the eternal truths or the act of creation, when the problem is formulated in such a way that the relation between the divine ideas and the divine existing essence is given no controlling role.

## 6. METAPHYSICAL PRINCIPLES OF THE MATERIAL WORLD

Descartes once informed Mersenne that he would never have discovered the principles of his physics, had he not first meditated upon the metaphysical themes of God and self. This does not mean that Cartesian metaphysics is merely a prelude to a philosophy of nature. But it does underline the fact that, despite his early successes in mathematical physics, Descartes was unable to organize his views on the material world in a systematic and demonstrative way, until he settled the main lines of his metaphysics. Only then did he possess the principles which would permit *an a priori explanation of material phenomena through their distinctly perceived causes.* Descartes had tried to reduce physics directly to mechanics and thus to mathematicize the entire study of nature, without having recourse to metaphysical truths. This project had not met with success. Even in pure mathematics, he had encountered types of curves which he despaired of expressing in mathematical equations (yet which, as the later history of mathematics shows, he was overhasty in declaring to be irreducible to equational form). As for the physical phenomena, he found them to be even more multifarious and intractable before exact mathematical analysis and deduction from general notions.

These obstacles forced him to refine his conception of geometrical demonstration and to seek out the metaphysical principles that could confer scientific status upon his physical views. He remarked on the great difference between *abstract* and *concrete geometry,* a distinction which his followers tended to ignore and which Newton had to bring again to the fore. Abstract geometry limits itself to problems that exercise the mind in the realm of pure constructive imagination, which operates without disturbance from actual sense experience. But in *applying* mathematical findings to the actual, concrete universe, grave difficulties are encountered. Even after they agree to regard only the quantitative aspects of things, mathematical physicists are exposed to the insecurities and obscurities of the sensible world and hence must remain satisfied with something less than absolute mathematical certainty. Physical investigations must begin with commonly known facts, together with suppositions or hypotheses about these facts. If the hypotheses lead to further deductions of a predictive sort, which are borne out by the actual phenomena, then there is a *mutual confirmation* between hypothesis and fact.[25] The hypothesis renders intelligible a wider range of phenomena, whereas the facts furnish experimental proof of the predictions. Once verified in this way, the tested hypotheses can be regarded as reliable physical theories.

But even such reliable theories do not satisfy the strict standards of an a priori development of scientific knowledge. Hence Descartes argued for the need to supply *metaphysical principles* for physical science. Metaphysics is at least as certain as geometry, and enjoys the additional advantage of not being confined by the limits of imagination. Pure understanding is the proper metaphysical instrument in dealing with the natural world, since only this power enables one to grasp the true nature of material substance and differentiate it properly from the mind or immaterial substance.

The first contribution of metaphysics to physical theory is its *critique of the senses* and its consequent elimination of the *Scholastic philosophy of nature*. Descartes' famous *analysis of a piece of wax* has no other purpose than to illustrate this contribution. Fresh from the hive, the wax has a definite white color, a lingering odor and taste of honey, a certain figure and size. It is hard and cold; it emits a sound, when struck with the finger. But upon being brought close to the fire, some of these qualities disappear and others are modified. It loses its qualities of taste and smell; its hue is altered, as are its figure and size. The wax becomes a liquid, hot to the touch, soundless; yet it is still recognized as being this piece of wax. The wax has no necessary connection with the forms of its previous appearance, and hence its real nature is to be sought elsewhere. Having stripped

---

[25] *Discourse on Method*, VI (Lafleur, 49). Cf. R. M. Blake, "The Role of Experience in Descartes' Theory of Method," *The Philosophical Review*, XXXVIII (1929), 125–43, 201–18, for the empirical moment in Cartesian thought.

off the various modes that are not essential to it, "certainly nothing is left but something extended, flexible, and movable."[26] This perception is not an act of the senses, since it provides a correction of the sense conviction that all the appearances constitute the wax's nature. Neither is it an act of imagination, since I can clearly conceive that the wax may assume an infinite variety of shapes and modifications in extension, even beyond those that I can imagine. The true nature of this wax or of any other material thing is accessible only to a *purely intellectual* insight. Only pure understanding can judge that a *material substance* or *body* is nothing else than an *extended thing, having figure and motion.* Only the understanding, operating at its own level, can discern the subjective character of the remaining qualities. This correlation of the doctrine of primary and secondary qualities with a theory of pure understanding is the distinctive mark of Descartes' approach to this question.

The senses have only a *utilitarian* value in ministering to our bodily needs. They are not instruments of reliable cognition: those who rely upon them are bound to mistake subjective need for objective fact. Descartes accuses the Scholastics of systematizing the everyday illusion that the material thing resembles, in every respect, the perceptions we have of it. He takes no account of the persistent criticism of precisely this thesis by St. Thomas, in his discussion of universals and Platonic forms.

In his polemic against *hylemorphism,* Descartes avoids the metaphysical issue entirely, by outlawing the theory of actual and potential coprinciples and by concentrating upon a psychological critique. In the Cartesian vision of the real order, there is room only for actual, substantial *things* and their *affections.* Substantial principles of being that are not the same as substantial things are inconceivable to him, since their status in being evades precise mathematical determination. Matter is an extended, actual thing, since potency is only a confused notion of sense. And there is no cogent metaphysical reason why substantial form should be admitted. If the form is substantial, then it must be capable of subsisting by itself and hence must be a thing or complete substance. Now, in addition to the matter, which is a

---

[26] *The Meditations concerning First Philosophy,* II (Lafleur, 27). For the psychological criticism of the senses, secondary qualities, and hylemorphism, see *ibid.,* VI (Lafleur, 73–74); *The Principles of Philosophy,* I, 66, 71, and II, 3 (Haldane-Ross, I, 247, 249–50, 255); *Replies to Objections,* VI (Haldane-Ross, II, 254–55); also, the *Letter to Regius,* cited below in note 31.

complete, actual thing or substance, there is no need to suppose another substantial thing, the form. It is superfluous and can be eliminated. Since the full force of the Thomistic distinction between a *thing* and a *principle of being* eludes him, Descartes is obliged to invoke a purely subjective reason why the Thomists defend substantial form. They do so, only because they expect to find in material things the same generic sort of independent substance as the human mind, in respect to its body. Similarly, he explains real secondary qualities and powers of bodies as entities that have been read into material things by analogy with the human soul and its powers. This psychological line of criticism never comes to grips, however, with the metaphysical doctrine on the principles of act and potency, as applied to moving, material things of various kinds.

In Descartes' own metaphysical outlook, a radical distinction is drawn between *mind* or thinking thing (*res cogitans*) and *body* or extended thing (*res extensa*). Each is regarded as a complete thing or finite substance, derived from the infinite substance, God. Minds are immaterial substances, having *thought* (*cogitatio*) as their principal or special attribute, and the various acts of thought (knowing, opining, willing, perceiving, feeling, doubting) as their modes. Bodies are reducible to one corporeal substance, having *extension* as its principal or special attribute, and the varieties of figure and motion as its modes. This explanation rests upon a doctrine on the nature of substance and its affections, along with a special theory of distinctions.

## DESCARTES' METAPHYSICAL SCHEMA
### (The Order of Being)

| | | |
|---|---|---|
| 1. Absolute substance. | God | |
| 2. Relative substances. | Minds | Body |
| 3. Attributes. | Thought | Extension |
| 4. Modes. | Knowing, Willing | Figure, Movement |

A substance is a thing or singular being. Descartes defines *substance* as "a thing which so exists that it needs no other thing in order to exist."[27] This meaning departs from the traditional minimal

[27] *The Principles of Philosophy*, I, 51 (Haldane-Ross, I, 239); the second definition, given at the end of the paragraph, is from *Replies to Objections*, II (Haldane-Ross, II, 53).

requirement of "that by which the being exists in itself," and hence Descartes admits that it applies in the strict sense only to God. He is the only *absolute* substance, in that He alone has a completely independent manner of existing. All other things stand in need of God's creative and conserving power. Finite minds and body are substances only in a *relative* sense, and Descartes even speaks of them as being quasi-modes of God. Without explaining the meaning of nonunivocal predication in his system, he nevertheless denies that "substance" applies univocally to the one absolute substance and to the relative substances. Yet he advances two reasons why created things may be regarded as substances. Although extended thing and thinking thing depend on God, they do not depend on, or inhere in, *each other* for existence. Furthermore, created things do serve as the *support* of their various affections, and thus satisfy one meaning for "substance." As far as finite things are concerned, then, substance may also be defined as "everything in which there resides immediately, as in a subject, or by means of which there exists anything we perceive, i.e., any property, quality, or attribute, of which we have a real idea."

This second definition casts some retrospective light upon why Descartes affirms unhesitatingly that the thinking self is a *substantial* self. Since I have a real idea of the property of thought, I am assured of the real presence of a mental substance or subject of this property. Similarly, my idea of extension and its modes is sufficient ground for affirming the presence of a material substance or subject of these properties. Substance cannot be apprehended in a completely bare condition, however, but must be grasped along with at least one privileged affection, the *attribute*. Descartes refers, in a loose way, to all the qualities and perfections of a thing as its attributes. But in a more special sense, this term is reserved for "one principal property of substance which constitutes its nature and essence, and on which all the others depend."[28] Thought is the *special* attribute of mind, and extension the *special* attribute of bodily substance. There are also certain *general* attributes (e.g., existence *per se*, unity, duration) which are found commonly among all kinds of substances. The remaining properties and qualities are classified as *modes* of substance, since the substance may be regarded as being "modified" in these different ways.

Although Descartes follows some Scholastics in holding that sub-

---

[28] *The Principles of Philosophy*, I, 53 (Haldane-Ross, I, 344).

stance is known only through its properties, still he goes much farther in maintaining that the special attribute gives an *adequate, essential knowledge* of the substance which surpasses our knowledge of its various affections. In apprehending the attribute, I thereby directly apprehend the substantial essence itself, since there is only a logical distinction between the two. The attribute is nothing other than the substance itself, insofar as it stands open to our direct vision. The philosopher of nature need not worry about hidden forms and qualities since, in grasping the attribute of extension, he gains sufficient insight into the substantial nature of bodily things to dispense with any occult powers.

The Cartesian theory of distinctions confirms this view of substance and its affections. Descartes uses for his own purpose the terms that were common among his Scholastic contemporaries. Distinctions are of three sorts: real, modal, and logical.[29] A *real distinction* obtains between two substances, whether they belong to the same class or to different classes. Two things are known to be really distinct when the one can be clearly and distinctly conceived without the other, not by reason of an act of abstraction but because of a positive understanding of its nature. This means that the one can be seen in its own essence to be at least capable of separate existence. *Modal distinctions* hold either between a mode and the substance of which it is properly a mode or between two modes of the same substance. In the former case, the substance can be conceived distinctly without the mode, but conversely, the mode cannot be conceived distinctly apart from reference to its subject of inherence. Where two modes of the same substance are concerned, one can be understood without the other, but neither can be properly understood without reference to the common substance supporting them. As for the distinction between modes belonging to *different* substances or between a mode and the substance to which it does not *properly* belong, Descartes assigns this to the class of real distinctions, in view of the real distinction between the different substances that are ultimately implicated. Finally, the *logical distinction* or distinction actively drawn by reason is made between a substance and its attributes (both special and general) or between two attributes of a substance. Without the

---

[29] *Ibid.*, I, 60–62 (Haldane-Ross, I, 243–45); for the Scholastic background, cf. E. Gilson, *Index scolastico-cartésien*, 86–90 (quotations from Suarez and Eustace of St. Paul).

attribute, the substance cannot be known clearly and distinctly; if there be two attributes, the one cannot be known clearly without reference to the other.

This discussion of distinctions is tailored to achieve two ends: to guarantee an adequate, essential understanding of the nature of mind and matter through their respective attributes, and to secure a real distinction between these widest classes of created substance. Descartes is careful to describe each type of distinction in terms of the mind's manner of knowing its objects. Thus the classification is a thorough-going application of the criterion of clear and distinct knowledge. This is manifest in the test case of the *real distinction between mind and body* in man. Introspection reveals a sharp contrast between the clear and distinct idea of self as a *thinking* and *unextended* thing, and the clear and distinct idea of body as an *extended* and *unthinking* thing. It can be safely concluded that the thinking thing is really distinct from the body and can exist without it. Because the thinking self can be conceived clearly and distinctly apart from the body, it is not only really distinct from the latter but can be made by God to exist apart from bodily substance. Hence mind and body are really distinct substances. In knowing the attributes of thought and extension in an adequate way, we know mind and body "completely," i.e., we know each as a complete substance, capable of separate existence. No confusion is possible between the two substances; their respective properties should therefore be kept strictly apart.

This real distinction between thinking and extended things can be established, even before the real existence of a material world and our own body has been proved. The mind is known to exist as a complete substance, even before any material things are known to exist. Even the Cartesian proof of the *existence of material objects* outside the mind is based on an analysis of the contents and acts of the mind.[30] I recognize in myself a *passive* power of perception which is capable of entertaining the images of sensible things. This power could not function, unless there were a corresponding *active* power, whether in myself or in some other being, for arousing these images in me. Such an active power is not resident in myself as a pure thinking thing, since some impressions come about without my deliberate intention or even (as in the case of a painful experience

---

[30] See the sixth section of *The Meditations concerning First Philosophy* (Lafleur, 64-80) and, more schematically, *The Principles of Philosophy*, II, 1 (Haldane-Ross, I, 255).

of heat) against my own desire. Hence the excitation or active arousal of sense perceptions in me is due to *some other substance,* which contains either formally or eminently all the reality found objectively in the sense ideas themselves. The sense arousal of my mind may come either from God or from another immaterial agent or from a material body. Descartes eliminates the possibility that sense perceptions are excited in us by God alone or by some other immaterial agent alone, and that existing sensible things contribute in no way to the arousal of such ideas. Were this so, a conflict would arise between God's *veracity* and the incorrigible, *natural belief* that these ideas somehow come directly from existing corporeal things. We cannot help but think that our mind has sense perceptions because it is somehow aroused by sensibly existent things, i.e., by beings that possess the objective reality of sensible ideas in a formal but noneminent way, and hence at the material level of existence. God is the author of this natural belief. Hence if He is not to violate His own truthfulness, a world of material substance, having concrete geometrical attributes of extension, must really exist. My own body and the world of extended nature enjoy an extramental reality of their own. Thus Descartes bridges the gap between real mind and real matter not directly but by an appeal to the divine veracity and to an incorrigible fact of natural belief. He does not anticipate the attempt of Berkeley to show that this belief in the reality of matter is indeed corrigible and that, therefore, the *non*existence of matter is perfectly reconcilable with God's truthfulness.

A final service rendered by metaphysics to philosophical physics is to supply the most general principles of physical deduction, along with the guarantee of *memory* as a God-given and, therefore, trustworthy power needed in all reasoning. Demonstration in physical matters rests upon the assurance of God's *immutability* (His fixed resolve to act in the same way in the production of the same sort of effect) and His constant *conserving* action from moment to moment of temporal duration. On this metaphysical foundation, Descartes formulates the three laws of motion which govern all change, specification, and duration of extended bodies. These explanatory laws of mechanics are so universal that they express the basic way in which *any* world would be framed by an efficient cause of local motion, acting without regard for substantial forms or qualitative change. The very infinity of the divine power and the generality of the primary physical laws prevent, however, any rigorous a priori derivation of *this* particular world of ours. Only by appeal to the deliverances of sense can one settle the question about which of several equally possible worlds has been *actually* produced by the cosmic maker. There is need of the empirical touchstone of *sensible experience,* as an indispensable principle of verification of the actual structure of material things.  Descartes feels that he can appeal to the senses as a test of hypotheses about the real world, now that he has proved God's existence, His veracity, and hence the trustworthiness of the God-given senses in cases where reason is constrained to appeal to them, in order to anchor its deduction about our world. Cartesian rationalism admits this saving grace of an empirical residue of nondeducible experience, which provides a certain measure for deductive reasoning, whenever the latter claims to draw conclusions about the actual constitution of this world. But the senses hold a posterior and auxiliary position and are never permitted by Descartes to contribute toward the principles of knowledge.

## 7. MIND AND THE HUMAN COMPOSITE

There is a double gain for Descartes in the theory of mind and body as radically different substances, based upon mutually exclusive attributes of thought and extension. This dualism justifies at once a *mechanistic* philosophy of nature and a *spiritualistic* philosophy of mind. The *immateriality* of the mind is an immediate corollary from its nonextended character. It is sufficient to know that thinking is an attribute of mind, in order to conclude that extension and materiality have no foothold in the self. Does the *immortality* of the human mind flow from its immateriality? After some hesitation, Descartes declined to furnish a demonstration of immortality, a refusal shared in common with the nominalistic Scholastic thinkers. He contended that his critique of the senses and his proof of a substantial and immaterial (or spiritual) self supply the requisite principles for at least a strong belief in the mind's survival. Since it is nonmaterial and substantial, it *can* continue to exist after the body's dissolution. But in order to transform this possibility into an uncontrovertible fact, the disposition of divine providence must be consulted, and this consultation lies beyond our power. Descartes refrained from making any final pronouncement about the issue, lest he be accused by freethinkers of pretending to have special access to the actual designs of God's providence.

The steep price Descartes had to pay for achieving this sharp dualism between the mechanism of matter and the spiritualism of mind was to place in jeopardy the *composite nature of man*. This is a capital instance where his methodic approach compelled him to become an innovator not only in regard to the mode of proof but also the content itself. His problem was to explain how two complete, substantial things, each essentially unordained to the other, could nevertheless form a composite whole of a substantial sort. When his onetime disciple Regius declared that the doctrine of two complete substances leads merely to a *per accidens* unity in man, Descartes replied with acerbity that, according to his intention, the unity is a *per se* one, a true substantial union or "commingling" of mind and body.[31] From the standpoint of an act-potency theory of the nature of a *per se,* substantial union, Regius was right in drawing such an inference. What Descartes had to do, then, was to redefine the meaning of a "per se unity," in order to bring it in line with his dualism. This task he carried out in two steps: first, by explaining a composite entity in terms of his theory of distinctions, and, second, by explaining a substantial union in terms of his doctrine on nature.

1.   A *composite entity* is a subject in which are found two or more special attributes, each of which can be understood distinctly without reference to the rest.[32] If two special attributes are present in the same subject, and yet each can be understood distinctly without reference to the other, in that subject there are two really distinct substances, which are not united together by any necessary bond. The only kind of union possible between these two substances is a *contingent* one, that is, one which is not required essentially by the natures in question and hence not capable of an a priori, scientific deduction. Only a sheer fact of *experience* can assure us of the actual presence of a composite entity. Now this is precisely the case with man. He is subject to such states of confused awareness as sensations and feelings of pain and hunger, which seem to invade the thinking thing from without and yet which belong intimately to it. We could describe the pure thinking thing, apart from such disturbing states, but we could never describe the actual man of our experience, without pointing out that these confused states — where thinking and being

---

[31] *Letter to Regius,* January, 1642 (*Correspondance,* Adam-Milhaud, V, 112–14, 134–35).
[32] *Notes Directed against a Certain Programme* (Haldane-Ross, I, 437); for the application to man, cf. *The Meditations concerning First Philosophy,* VI (Lafleur, 72).

extended are intermingled — belong to his make-up. The actual fact of the union of thought and extension in a common subject cannot be deduced from the essence of either a thinking thing or an extended thing: it can be grasped only in an empirical way. The composite nature of man is an unexpected melange, a disconcerting datum that remains irremediably obscure and confused within the Cartesian perspective of mental and bodily substances.

2. Given the undeniable fact of the human composite entity, however, can it at least be explained in such a way that the union of the two substances is more than an accidental one and yet not modeled after the Thomistic account of a matter-form union? Descartes attempts to satisfy these conditions with the aid of his doctrine on *nature*. The term "nature" has four distinct, real meanings.[33] It signifies: (*a*) God Himself, insofar as He is the author of the system of the world and its all-powerful conserver; (*b*) the total order and system of finite things themselves, as dependent upon God; (*c*) the arrangement or assemblage of all that God has disposed for the thinking self alone or for the bodily world alone; (*d*) the arrangement of things bearing reference to the human composite entity, taken precisely as a union of mind and body.

The significance of the third and fourth senses of "nature" is that there is a difference in nature between the self and the man.[34] *The self* is the mind alone, the thinking substance, completely independent from, and unreferred to, matter. *The man*, however, is the human composite entity, a contingent whole, made up of the two substances: thinking thing and extended thing. The self and the man agree, insofar as each is a substantial unity in itself. But they are different kinds of substantial unity, since they are different kinds of natures. Descartes usually reserves the term *substantial unity of essence or nature* to characterize the essential undividedness of the self, with its single, special attribute of thought. He calls the human composite entity or the man a *substantial unity of composition*, i.e., of nature in the fourth sense. The man does not enjoy a strict unity of essence, since there is no essential and necessary ordination of the thinking thing and the extended thing to each other, or of their respective attributes to each other. They are present together in the same human

---

[33] *Loc. cit.* (Lafleur, 72–73); later on (p. 76), Descartes mentions a purely conceptual meaning of "nature," as when we say that something has a faulty nature.

[34] On the problem of the human composite, cf. *Replies to Objections*, IV, VI (Haldane-Ross, II, 97–99, 102, 242–43, 256).

subject or unity of composition but they do not constitute a unity of essence or of nature in the third and stricter sense. The unity of composition between two complete things or substances is a fact, manifested to us by our own experience of sensations and feelings, but its nature remains *incomprehensible* to us. All that we can say is that God produces such composite things for the sake of securing the order and unity of nature as a whole (in the second sense of "nature"). But since this involves God's final purpose for the universe, Descartes restrains philosophical inquiry at this point and rests content with the given but confused fact of the composite human entity, the man.

In working out this theory, Descartes accomplished a philosophical revolution. With respect to previous philosophy, he changed the meaning of the very problem of a substantial union. For the medievals, this problem was primarily one of *how* substantial principles could be joined in a composite whole. Descartes relegated this question entirely to the realm of the incomprehensible, since the previous solutions depended upon the theory of actual and potential coprinciples, which he had rejected. Instead, he restricted the problem of a substantial union to a description of the *fact* or *outcome* of the composition of two complete substances. The fact is known, since the special attributes of thought and extension indicate that the constituents in the composition are not merely logically distinct or related in a modal way: they are complete, substantial things. How the union can occur and what its structure is, are questions deliberately placed beyond human explanation and left for the infinite power and purpose of God. To say that mind and body are joined in a *per se* unity, then, does not specify anything positive about the manner of their union but only adverts to a given fact. The real distinction and independence of each constituent substance remain uncompromised by the union of composition, since the mind is still conceived as being an unextended and thinking thing.

For Descartes, *the self* remains intrinsically and essentially unaffected by its incorporation into *the man*. This is the conclusion he wishes to draw from his doctrine on the unity of the human composite, since it seems to provide an incontrovertible answer to the skeptical arguments against the immateriality and immortality of the soul. There is no intrinsic difficulty against survival of the self, since its contingent union with the body leaves its independence intact. The most that Descartes will concede to the experience of human unity is the following highly qualified admission:

> Nature also teaches me by these feelings of pain, hunger, thirst, and so on that I am not only residing in my body, as a pilot in his ship, but furthermore, that I am intimately connected with it, and that [the mixture is] so blended (as it were) that [something like] a single whole is produced.[35]

The "I" or the self is connected and "blended" with the body, but also retains its sovereign independence and essential lack of reference to the body and to the composite whole, which the soul and body together constitute. The union is a substantial one, only in the sense that the composite as such can exist, but this specifies nothing about the way in which the components are united. In the final analysis, Descartes admits that the union of mind and body can be looked at in two ways: from the standpoint of the self and from the standpoint of the man. In reference to *the man,* the union constitutes an *ens per se,* insofar as the human composite would not be an actual fact of unity of composition, unless the two substances were somehow joined together. But from the standpoint of the parts, especially *the self,* the union is *somehow accidental,* since it disturbs in no way the essential independence and self-subsistence of the substances involved. To counteract the freethinkers, Descartes is ready to sacrifice the substantial unity of the human composite to the immateriality of the thinking self.

This sinuous argument proved unsatisfactory both to Descartes' Thomistic opponents and to his rationalistic successors. The former regarded it as an ignoring of the main issue, which concerns the unity of the essence. Descartes did not establish the unity *of* a composite, substantial essence, actuated by a *single act of existing,* but rather a composition *among* substances, each of which retains its own act of existing. In the Thomistic meaning of the term, then, he did not secure the *per se* unity in the human essence. He transformed the problem from that of a union between proper act and potency to that between two substantial acts. Spinoza regarded this as an impossibility, unless there were a reduction of the supposed extended and thinking substances to the ontological status of modes of the one divine substance. Leibniz recoiled from this pantheistic solution but saw more

---

[35] *The Meditations concerning First Philosophy,* VI (Lafleur, 72).

clearly than did Descartes that (however one may choose to name it) the only possible sort of union between two or more substances, each of which retains its own existential act, is an operational one. But he contended that this operational union between act and act could rest upon essential relations among the united substances, even though each maintains its intrinsic autonomy. Among the empiricists, there developed the tendency simply to bypass any metaphysical explanation of the mind-body problem by declaring the investigation of substances to be out of bounds for the human mind. Whereas Descartes wanted to draw the line of inquiry at an explanation of the fact of a substantial union, the empiricists questioned even whether we can have any knowledge of a fact in the substantial order.

Another obstacle against securing a *per se* unity in man was Descartes' *mechanistic explanation of life.* In eliminating substantial forms in general, he also eliminated the soul, taken in the strict Aristotelian sense of the first informing principle of life. Hence he usually formulated the problem of man as one concerning *mind and body,* rather than *soul and matter.* Life is found only in mind and at the level of mind. Hence Descartes regarded animals as being only more complicated and subtle automata, the movements of which can be explained just as mechanically as the operations of cleverly constructed clocks or the fountains in the royal gardens. The human body is itself a machine, although one that gives ample evidence of being in intimate union with a higher substance. But that union cannot be patterned after the substantial union between a rational soul and its matter. Descartes had to explain it mechanistically, in terms of an *interactionist theory* of mind and body.[36] There is reciprocal influence of mind and body, each acting upon the other through efficient causality. The mind or soul (in a loose, non-hylemorphic sense) is joined to the whole body, but exercises its controlling functions through its special association with the pineal gland. This gland, which is the main seat of the soul, is a small and undivided mass in the brain. When an external object impinges upon the corporeal organs, it arouses an impulse that is carried by the nerves to the animal spirits (minute parts of the blood), bathing the cavity in which the pineal gland is situated. By this mechanism, different objects agitate the pineal in different ways. Since the mind

---

[36] Cf. *The Passions of the Soul,* I, 30–39 (Haldane-Ross, I, 345–49). See S. V. Keeling's expository and critical essay, "Cartesian Mechanism," *Philosophy,* IX (1934), 51–66.

is naturally attuned to the movements of the pineal, the various agitations in that gland incite the mind to entertain perceptions corresponding to these movements and to their sources in the external world. Conversely, the pineal is so responsive to the commands of the mind, that it communicates the decisions of the human will to the animal spirits and thence to the nerves and muscles. In this way, the mind is affected by the body and can, in its turn, direct the body according to its own will.

Thus Descartes shifted the problem of the human composite from the metaphysical to the physiological plane. But the change of venue did not alleviate his difficulties, as his contemporaries were quick to point out. For one thing, the smallness of the pineal gland and the fact that it is not composed of two halves, do not dematerialize it or endow it with spiritual simplicity. It remains completely on the side of extended substance, leaving the chasm still unbridged between extended thing and thinking thing. Descartes begged the question of the mutual attunement of the mind and the pineal, as well as their ability to act directly upon one another. Having eliminated any intrinsic, act-potency causality between material and formal principles, Descartes was restricted to a mechanistic, efficient causality between mind and body. But his previous analysis of the antithesis between the special attributes of thought and extension militated against the ability of two mutually exclusive and independent kinds of substance to join together and act upon each other. A signal indication of the failure of interactionism to explain the unity of being and operation in man was the strictly *equivocal* way in which Descartes had to treat sensation, the presumed outcome of the interaction. Since he did not have a composite substantial essence, constituted by the substantial union of actual and potential principles, he could not regard sensation and feeling as *distinctive acts of the composite*. He was obliged to posit a *double set of sensations*. The sense powers and operations were viewed now as bodily states, and now as aspects of the mind, insofar as it attends to the body. This did not bridge the gap between corresponding modes belonging to really different and even opposed substances.

A similar stalemate is reached in regard to the *origin of ideas*. Descartes cannot allow the provisional description of their origin (as being adventitious, factitious, and innate) to stand unmodified. The measure of a successful theory of the human composite is its ability to explain ideas that seem to be adventitious or external in origin.

Descartes does not dismiss the note of externality as an illusion; yet his dualism of mind and body does not permit him to grant a genuine derivation of ideas from material existents. His compromise lies within the ambit of the Plotinian-Augustinian *active theory of sensation.*[37] Although mind as such is purely intellectual, it counts sense, imagination, and memory among its modes. These modes signify the mind's attention or reference to corporeal objects in certain of its cognitive acts. Adventitious ideas are said to come from bodies, insofar as the presence of certain bodily states determines the particular time of appearance, the complexity, and the obscure condition of certain ideas. The mind cannot really receive any corporeal likeness, but the presence of such a likeness as a bodily state is required so that the understanding may exercise the functions of sense, imagination, and sense memory. Even under these latter modes, the understanding neither *receives* the corporeal likeness nor *abstracts* from it an intentional or cognitive likeness, after the manner of the Aristotelian agent intellect. Rather, the mind *actively attends* to the bodily image and, in virtue of its own attending action, draws forth the "adventitious" ideas from itself.

Descartes feels himself warranted in calling the bodily motions the (occasion) of such ideas, since they furnish the external, bodily circumstances that stimulate the mind to act at a certain time and to refer its ideas to a certain external object. The mind itself is the principal cause, but, in its imaginative and sensitive functions, it requires an excitation from material things and images. In effect, this reduces *adventitious* to *innate ideas,* since the effect of the occasional cause is only to arouse the mind to produce ideas *by itself* and out of its own capacities. This satisfies the definition of innate ideas and, at the same time, re-enforces the doctrine of the self-enclosure of minds, which Descartes describes (in anticipation of Leibniz) as existing with closed windows. The manner in which bodily images can arouse or

---

[37] For the historical background of this theory, consult V. J. Bourke, *Augustine's Quest of Wisdom* (Milwaukee, Bruce, 1945), 111–12, and the unpublished doctoral dissertation of Sister Mary Ann Ida Gannon, B.V.M., *The Active Theory of Sensation in Plotinus and Saint Augustine* (St. Louis University, 1952). Bourke notes that this view of sensation suffers from an essential subjectivity and requires an appeal to God as the guarantor of the veracity of human knowledge. For the Cartesian position on sensation, imagination, and innate ideas, cf. *The Principles of Philosophy,* IV, 189–90 (Haldane-Ross, I, 289–91); *The Passions of the Soul,* I, 20–23 (Haldane-Ross, I, 341–42); *The Meditations concerning First Philosophy,* II, VI (Lafleur, 24–25, 64–66); *Replies to Objections,* V (Haldane-Ross, II, 217, 227–28, 231); *Notes Directed against a Certain Programme* (Haldane-Ross, I, 442–44).

stimulate the mind is rendered no more intelligible, however, than the hypothesis of the pineal gland will permit.

## 8. TOWARD THE MORAL LIFE

Since Descartes never completed his work in the other parts of philosophy, he was never in the methodologically warranted position of developing a systematic ethics. But there is a moral purposiveness to all his speculations. Just as method begins with an appeal to every man's *bon sens* or good sense, so it culminates in the cultivation of *bona mens* or the capacity for acquiring moral wisdom. It is the same good sense and sound judgment which Descartes counts on, in us all, to develop from the universal doubt, through the various speculative parts of philosophy, to the plenitude of moral perfection, which crowns the search for philosophical wisdom.

The distinction between the *contemplation of truth* and the *conduct of life* means that methodic doubt, whose aim is the contemplation of truth, does not apply immediately to the moral convictions. For, unlike the order of pure thought, practical life consists of situations where a man must make forced options on probable grounds. He must choose some definite line of conduct, and hence he cannot and ought not wait for scientific certitude before making his decisions. Hence Descartes offers a *provisional code of morality,* intended to govern the active sphere during the period of doubt and critical inspection of all speculative truths. There are three basic precepts in this interim morality of temporal happiness, as set forth in the *Discourse on Method.* (1) Obey the prevailing laws and customs, adhere to the traditional religion, and follow the more moderate opinions; (2) be firm in resolutions and act on doubtful decisions just as firmly as on certain ones; (3) conquer oneself rather than fortune, be concerned about controlling one's own ideas, and be indifferent to whatever remains in external matters, after having done one's best.[38] These counsels reflect the popular Stoic moral attitude of the late Renaissance, especially as presented in the Lowlands by Justus Lipsius and in France by Guillaume Du Vair. Lest the program degenerate into sheer conformism and opportunism, Descartes specifically integrates it with his continued search after truth. The views of others are temporarily acceptable, only because

[38] *Discourse on Method,* III (Lafleur, 15–18). See H. Gouhier, "Descartes et la vie morale," *Revue de Métaphysique et de Morale,* XLIV (1937), 165–97.

one is prepared eventually to *follow his own judgment,* when it becomes enlightened, and is presently doing all in his power to sift his convictions and discover better ones, if possible. Practical decisions are made with a view to their eventual revision, in the light of tested knowledge.

In a letter to the Princess Elizabeth, Descartes gave a succinct statement of the *definitive morality* toward which he was aiming.[39] Significantly, its three major precepts parallel those of the *Discourse,* thus giving a sample of the transformation to which moral convictions must submit. The chief difference is that, at the end of its quest, the trained mind is now equipped with a sound conception of reason, its fundamental truths and its central habitus, especially the power of critical attention. (1) The well-disposed individual will use his mind as best he can in discovering what should be done; (2) he will have a firm and constant resolution to do all that his reason counsels; (3) doing all that he can, in accord with reason's dictates, he will regard the rest as lying beyond his power and will accustom himself not to desire it. In a word, the moral life depends upon a virtuous will, but the latter is one that is formed according to the truths perceived by right reason.

Man, however, is vulnerable to the exaggerated valuations induced by the passions, which sometimes displace the right estimates of reason. Descartes defines the *passions* as "the perceptions, feelings, or emotions of the soul which we relate specially to it, and which are caused, maintained, and fortified by some movement of the [animal] spirits."[40] He explains their genesis in the soul with the aid of the pineal gland, which is ordained "by nature" to make the mind sensitive to certain states of body and thus to arouse passions within it. The passions dispose us to desire the things that are of use to the maintenance and perfection of the body. They do not absolutely compel the will, and they can be indirectly controlled, by calling to mind images of the things which are usually united with the passions we desire to have. Descartes discards the Scholastic principle of division of the passions into the concupiscible and irascible, on the ground that it involves a distinction of parts in the soul. In its place, he substitutes an enumeration of *six primitive passions:* wonder, love, hatred, desire, pleasurable joy, and painful sadness. They are the

---

[39] *Letter to Princess Elizabeth,* August 4, 1645 (*Oeuvres de Descartes,* edited by Adam and Tannery, IV, 265–66).
[40] *The Passions of the Soul,* I, 27 (Haldane-Ross, I, 240).

components, by the combination of which all our passional states are formed. The discipline of the moral life consists in *mastering the passions*, by training the mind to judge deeds not merely by their immediate satisfaction but according to their real nature. Reason's estimate must then be adhered to, throughout a particular course of action and throughout a lifetime's search after happiness.

Two metaphysical truths are especially helpful in gaining self-control. Once God is known to exist and exercise a *loving providence*, a man can bear the ills of fortune with the assurance that they must eventually work to his true welfare. In the Cartesian blend of Stoicism and Christianity, "to follow nature" means to adhere to God's will and benevolent governance of all events. Similarly, the knowledge of the *soul's immateriality* and the belief in its *immortality* help the mind to overcome bodily dangers, especially the fear of death, and to establish a proper scale of values in which the primacy is given to the goods of the mind. All men aim at pleasure, but not all men are philosophically prepared to distinguish between pleasures of imagination and those of pure intelligence. The highest pleasure is *contentment of mind*. It springs from a stable will and an informed reason, from the inner assurance of making a virtuous use of free will or right judgment in practical affairs. The aim of the virtuous man's actions is the sovereign good, and his beatitude consists in the possession of this good. *God* is the objective sovereign good. If philosophy cannot put us in possession of Him, it can at least endow us with the degree of wisdom and self-control proportionate to our nature.[41]

The philosophical beatitude of a mind that is content within itself, and safe from fortune's slings and darts, is only surpassed on this earth by the certitude of faith. Descartes includes religion among the areas not touched provisionally by doubt, since religion is primarily a matter of salvation rather than of speculation, and stands on the side of the practical goods of life. Although he seeks to divorce

---

[41] In "The Moral Philosophy of Descartes and the Catholic Doctrine of Grace," *Dominican Studies*, I (1948), 149–67, M. Versfeld suggests that Cartesian morality finds its true center of gravity not in the objective good, God, but in a Neo-Stoic independence of mind, which comes close to Pelagianism (although Descartes formally denied this consequence). In the chain of the sciences, morality depends upon the progress made in the natural sciences. Since scientific progress is indefinite, we are never definitely sure of our concrete, objective moral good, and hence must rely inwardly upon mental contentment and outwardly upon the commands of civil authority.

philosophy from *theology,* Descartes claims that his philosophy is better able to defend the truths of *faith* than is Scholastic theology. He depreciates the intellectualist tendency in theology and views religion and faith as belonging in the practical domain of the will. Faith has a foundation in reason but is formally an *act of will.* After completing his inspection of the nature of reason, Descartes draws an analogy between the natural light of reason and the light of grace. Both can move the will infallibly and freely in its act of judgment. The supernatural authority of God makes the *light* of grace more evident and certain than that of natural evidence. But the *matter* or *content* of faith remains obscure in this life, whereas the content of philosophy and reason is clear and distinct. The point of contact between faith and philosophy is, as Pascal also surmised, *the idea of the infinite.* For all his tremendous urge to bring the knowable within the range of mathematical lucidity, Descartes allows the presence of the mystery of the infinite, as confronting our natural intelligence, and permits the hope of a further beatitude in eternal life. He avoids theological entanglements whenever he can, but he cannot finally seal off the movement of good sense toward a wisdom that is more than the wisdom of his philosophy.

## SUMMARY OF CHAPTER 5

Descartes' aim was to give philosophy a rigorous, scientific method that could demonstrate the new world of physics and also some metaphysical truths about God and the soul. He broadened the meaning of the mathematical method to include every precise determination of order and measure, whether in the quantitative or the immaterial sphere. In order to have demonstration, he supposed that the number of simple natures is finite and that these natures are joined by an objective set of connections, observable by the mind. By "mind," moreover, he meant the purely intellectual power, operating apart from the senses in the formation of clear and distinct ideas. He accepted the Renaissance skeptical distrust of the senses, but added triumphantly that pure intelligence does not depend upon the senses for its proper data. His use of methodic doubt was aimed at providing philosophy with a starting point at once existential and independent of the testimony of the senses. Having obtained a purely intellectual grasp of the Cogito, however, he found himself faced with a new set of difficulties. He had to prove God's existence solely from himself, existing as equipped with the idea of God. This provided a wholly spiritual and inward demonstration, leading to an infinitely powerful essence, which brings forth its own existence and an idea of itself in the finite mind. From the twofold premise of self and God, Descartes then had to derive the knowledge of his own bodily existence and that of the physical world. The divine attributes of veracity and immutability were exploited, respectively, in the existential demonstration of the body and the world and in that of the laws of physical motion. Because of the complete distinction between the idea of a thinking thing and that of an extended thing, Descartes concluded that there are two different and complete substances in man. The self or thinking thing is immaterial and hence intrinsically independent of the body. This provides philosophical ground enough for belief in the immortality of man's spiritual principle. But then Descartes was faced with the problem of the human composite or the man, in which these two substances are somehow united in a substantial way. His appeal to the pineal gland extended the mechanistic view of man as far as possible, whereas his affirmation of the mind's ability to influence bodily states fitted in with his theory of the passions and his Stoic conception of moral self-control.

## BIBLIOGRAPHICAL NOTE

1. *Sources.* The critical edition of the *Oeuvres de Descartes* was edited by C. Adam and P. Tannery (12 vols., Paris, Cerf, 1897–1910, with a Supplement and General Index issued as Volume 13 in 1913). C. Adam and G. Milhaud are issuing a new edition of the *Correspondance de Descartes* (Paris, Presses Universitaires, 1936 ff.; 6 vols. to date, letters up to 1645), which features modernized spelling and punctuation, as well as a French translation of Latin letters and brief biographical notes about Descartes' correspondents. Until recently, the standard translation of Descartes was that of E. S. Haldane and G. R. T. Ross: *The Philosophical Works of Descartes* (2 vols., reprinted with corrections, Cambridge, University Press, 1931). A new translation, improved in many ways, is now being made by L. Lafleur; the two works issued to date are: *Discourse on Method* (New York, Liberal Arts Press, 1950) and *The Meditations concerning First Philosophy* (New York, Liberal Arts Press, 1951).

2. *Studies.* E. S. Haldane's excellent biography, *Descartes, His Life and Times* (London, Murray, 1905), is based upon a thorough study of the Adam-Tannery edition. The twelfth volume of this same edition contains Charles Adam's *Vie et Oeuvres de Descartes,* which has become authoritative; Adam has also summarized his findings in a shorter book, *Descartes, sa vie et son oeuvre* (Paris, Boivin, 1937). A more recent synthesis is C. Serrurier's *Descartes, l'homme et le penseur* (Paris, Presses Universitaires, 1951). In English there are two unusually informative introductions to Descartes' philosophy: S. V. Keeling, *Descartes* (London, Benn, 1934), and A. B. Gibson, *The Philosophy of Descartes* (London, Metheun, 1932), the latter being somewhat more advanced and detailed. L. J. Beck, *The Method of Descartes* (Oxford, Clarendon, 1952), examines Cartesian methodology in detail, from the standpoint of the *Rules for the Direction of the Mind.* In *La méthode de Descartes et son application à la métaphysique* (Paris, Alcan, 1933), C. Serrus outlines the general method and makes a vigorous plea for the primacy of method over metaphysics in the Cartesian system; the methodological question is also decisive in L. Roth's

*Descartes' Discourse on Method* (Oxford, Clarendon, 1937), which is both a commentary on the *Discourse* and an evaluation of the entire philosophy of Descartes from the perspective of method. A vindication of the originality and force of Cartesian metaphysics, as set forth in the *Meditations,* is made by M. Versfeld, *An Essay on the Metaphysics of Descartes* (London, Metheun, 1940). That the Cartesian method and metaphysics contain empirical as well as rational strains is the thesis of J. Laporte's *Le rationalisme de Descartes* (second ed., Paris, Presses Universitaires, 1950). For lucid accounts of Descartes' moral and religious positions, see P. Mesnard, *Essai sur la morale de Descartes* (Paris, Boivin, 1936), and H. Gouhier, *La pensée religieuse de Descartes* (Paris, Vrin, 1924). A place apart must be given to the publications of E. Gilson in the Cartesian field: his *Index scolastico-cartésien* (Paris, Alcan, 1912) lists key terms in Descartes, provides the references in the Adam-Tannery edition, and then gives apposite quotations, under each term, from Scholastic sources probably known to Descartes; *La liberté chez Descartes et la théologie* (Paris, Alcan, 1913) still casts considerable illumination upon Descartes' relations with the Oratorians, even though some of its findings are no longer acceptable to Gilson himself; *Études sur le rôle de la pensée médiévale dans la formation du système cartésien* (which is the second part of *Études de philosophie médiévale,* revised and considerably augmented, Paris, Vrin, 1930) discusses the Scholastic background of many Cartesian arguments; *René Descartes: Discours de la méthode, texte et commentaire* (second ed., Paris, Vrin, 1939) reprints the Adam-Tannery text of the *Discourse* and makes an exhaustive commentary, doctrinal and historical, which has ramifications throughout the entire Cartesian system; the second part of *The Unity of Philosophical Experience* is on "The Cartesian Experiment." Among Thomistic criticisms of Descartes, the following are noteworthy: J. Maritain, *Three Reformers: Luther, Descartes, Rousseau* (London, Sheed and Ward, 1928); J. Maritain, *The Dream of Descartes,* translated by M. L. Andison (New York, Philosophical Library, 1944); F. Olgiati, *La filosofia di Descartes* (Milan, Vita e Pensiero, 1937); P. Garin, *Thèses cartésiennes et thèses thomistes* (Paris, Desclée, 1933), which concentrates upon the eternal verities and problems about God; J. De Finance, S.J., *Cogito cartésien et réflexion thomiste* (Paris, Beauchesne, 1946). The Faculty of Philosophy in the Catholic University of the Sacred Heart in Milan edited a commemorative volume of essays on Descartes by leading European and American scholars: *Cartesio, nel terzo centenario del 'Discorso del metodo'* (Milan, Vita e Pensiero, 1937). In the comparative field, A. G. A. Balz, *Descartes and the Modern Mind* (New Haven, Yale University Press, 1952), views Descartes' modernity as a decisive secularization of the Thomistic conception of the relation between faith and reason, theology and philosophy. L. Lévy-Bruhl's *History of Modern Philosophy in France* (Chicago, Open Court, 1899) begins with chapters on Descartes and Cartesianism, and is still valuable for the French development between Descartes and Comte. In his *Studies in the Cartesian Philosophy* (London, Macmillan, 1902), N. K. Smith traces the influence of Descartes upon

Spinoza, Leibniz, and Locke, and discusses the criticism of Cartesianism made by Hume and Kant. For the role of mathematics in modern philosophy from Descartes to Comte, see E. A. Maziarz, C.PP.S., *The Philosophy of Mathematics* (New York, Philosophical Library, 1950), Part I, Chapters 4-6; in the remainder of the book, a Thomistic theory of mathematical knowledge is proposed.

3. *Other Philosophers.* A start in the study of Descartes' contemporaries, Gassendi and Mersenne, can be made with the aid of G. S. Brett's *The Philosophy of Gassendi* (New York, Macmillan, 1908), and R. Lenoble's *Mersenne, ou la naissance du mechanisme* (Paris, Vrin, 1943). Lenoble suggests that Mersenne's mechanism is a reaction, not so much against Scholasticism as against Renaissance naturalism, with its pantheistic doctrine on secret forces in nature, the animated macrocosm, and psychic projections into natural processes. The tangled history of the Cartesian school was sketched by F. Bouillier, *Histoire de la philosophie cartésienne* (third ed., 2 vols., Paris, Delagrave, 1868). A. G. A. Balz's *Cartesian Studies* (New York, Columbia University Press, 1951) gives a detailed analysis of the difficulties encountered by the followers of Descartes, in respect to the mind-body problem, but Balz's final chapters on the Thomistic view of the human composite are unreliable. Malebranche's *Dialogues on Metaphysics and on Religion* has been translated by M. Ginsberg (London, Allen and Unwin, 1923); two good secondary studies on him are: R. W. Church, *A Study in the Philosophy of Malebranche* (London, Allen and Unwin, 1931), and H. Gouhier, *La philosophie de Malebranche et son expérience religieuse* (second ed., Paris, Vrin, 1948). H. F. Stewart edited a French-English edition of Pascal's *Pensées* (London, Routledge and Kegan Paul, 1950); see also, the *Great Shorter Works of Pascal*, translated by E. Cailliet and J. C. Blankenagel (Philadelphia, Westminster, 1948). M. Bishop's *Pascal, the Life of Genius* (New York, Reynal and Hitchcock, 1936) is a lively biography, while J. Mesnard's *Pascal, His Life and Works* (New York, Philosophical Library, 1952) is an enthusiastic and informative study of his personality and thought, with a good report on recent Pascalian studies. F. Strowski, *Pascal et son temps* (cf. the Bibliographical Note to Chapter II, 5), is still a standard reference for the seventeenth-century French climate; J. Russier, *La foi selon Pascal* (2 vols., Paris, Presses Universitaires, 1949), examines the central problem of Pascal's conception of faith. The materials are now available in English for rehabilitating the philosophy of Vico: *The Autobiography of Giambattista Vico,* translated by M. H. Fisch and T. G. Bergin (Ithaca, Cornell University Press, 1944); *The New Science of Giambattista Vico,* translated by T. G. Bergin and M. H. Fisch (Ithaca, Cornell University Press, 1948). Along with Fisch's Introduction to Vico's *Autobiography,* cf. R. Flint, *Vico* (Edinburgh, Blackwood, 1884), and H. P. Adams, *The Life and Writings of Giambattista Vico* (London, Allen and Unwin, 1935). Since most recent English writings on Vico are colored by the idealistic interpretation proposed by Croce, Gentile, and Nicolini, one should also consult F. Amerio, *Introduzione allo studio di G. B. Vico* (Turin, Società

Editrice Internazionale, 1947), which brings out the following points: Vico's critique of Descartes, his fundamental realism, his Christian Platonism, and his stress upon divine providence in the state and history (in opposition to Bayle). Vico's notion of history is analyzed by R. Caponigri, *Time and Idea: The Theory of History in Giambattista Vico* (Chicago, Regnery, 1953). The later history of Italian philosophy, from Vico to the rise of Neo-Hegelianism in the mid-nineteenth century, is traced by M. F. Sciacca, *La filosofia nell'età del Risorgimento* (Milan, Vallardi, 1948), with rich bibliographical suggestions for further study in the Italian area.

4. *Further Publications.* Descartes is available in two more translations: *Descartes' Philosophical Writings,* tr. by N. K. Smith (New York, Modern Library, 1958), and Descartes, *Philosophical Writings,* tr. by E. Anscombe and P. Geach (New York, Nelson, 1954). Stress is laid on his physical theories in N. K. Smith's *New Studies in the Philosophy of Descartes* (London, Macmillan, 1952), and on his new methodic ideas in H. H. Joachim's *Descartes's Rules for the Direction of the Mind* (London, Allen and Unwin, 1957). The "anti-Renaissance" attitude of the early Descartes in opposing science to erudition and history is analyzed by H. Gouhier, *Les premières pensées de Descartes* (Paris, Vrin, 1958). Two general interpretations note the importance of his ordering of thoughts and his new scientific-religious humanism: M. Guéroult, *Descartes selon l'ordre des raisons* (2 vols., Paris, Aubier, 1953); R. Lefevre, *L'humanisme de Descartes* (Paris, Presses Universitaires, 1957).

The importance of mathematics, immortality, and wisdom in the Cartesian system is brought out in: J. Vuillemin, *Mathematiques et métaphysique chez Descartes* (Paris, Presses Universitaires, 1960); J. Russier, *Sagesse cartésienne et religion* (Paris, Presses Universitaires, 1958); and J. Combès, *Le Dessein de la sagesse cartésienne* (Lyon-Paris, Vitte, 1960). The breadth of Descartes' scientific achievement is conveyed in J. F. Scott's *The Scientific Work of René Descartes* (London, Taylor and Francis, 1952). Pascal's personality and his *Pensées* are closely studied in E. Mortimer's *Blaise Pascal: The Life and Work of a Realist* (New York, Harper, 1959) and in *Pascal's Unfinished Apology* (New Haven, Yale University Press, 1952), by Sister Marie Louise Hubert, O.P. Under the general editorship of A. Robinet, a 20-volume *Oeuvres complètes de Malebranche* is now being published (Paris, Vrin, 1958 ff.). Perhaps the most thorough modern philosophical analysis of his thought is made by M. Guéroult: *Malebranche* (3 vols., Paris, Aubier, 1955-1959), stressing the vision in God, occasionalism, and the relation of nature and grace. On the complex relationship of both Descartes and Spinoza to the Dutch Calvinist Scholastic milieu, there are two excellent studies: E. J. Dijksterhuis, *et al., Descartes et le cartésianisme hollandais* (Paris, Presses Universitaires, 1950), and P. Dibon, *La Philosophie néerlandaise au siècle d'or* (Vol. I, Amsterdam, Elsevier, 1954).

# Chapter 6. SPINOZA

## I. LIFE AND WRITINGS

IN 1593, a band of refugee Spanish and Portuguese Jews sought asylum in Amsterdam, thus forming the core of a Jewish community which soon had its own religious, educational, legal, and economic system. Baruch or Benedict Spinoza was born into this community in 1632. He received a thorough training in Hebrew literature, becoming well versed in the Bible, the Talmud, and the Cabala. Nevertheless his dissatisfaction with the anthropomorphic conceptions of God in the Talmud and the phantasmagoria in the Cabala led him to consult Maimonides, Gersonides, Crescas, and other great Jewish medieval thinkers for rational statements about God and the world. From these latter sources (as well as from certain passages in the Cabala), Spinoza obtained suggestions for his own position concerning the power of reason, the oneness of God and infinite nature, the attribution of infinite, indivisible extension to God, panpsychism, and a deterministic emanation of the world from God. Between 1651 and 1654, his interests broadened to include non-Jewish thought. His mastery of Latin was perfected under an ex-Jesuit, Francis van den Enden, who also probably introduced him to Cartesianism. Besides doing work in physics and mathematics, Spinoza read some of the Renaissance versions of Neo-Platonism and Stoicism and even consulted some Dutch Protestant Scholastic manuals. He ceased to observe Jewish regulations and was tricked into disclosing his belief that extension is present in God, that angels are imaginary beings, and that the Bible does not teach the immortality of the soul. He was examined by a board of Jewish theologians and was solemnly excommunicated from the Jewish community (1656).

After his expulsion, Spinoza supported himself by grinding lenses, the income from which was supplemented by a pension reluctantly accepted from the estate of one of his students who had died prematurely. Spinoza gave private philosophical instruction to several students and engaged in wide correspondence with learned men and amateurs alike. His first book, *Parts I and II of René Descartes' Principles of Philosophy* (with an appendix, *Metaphysical Thoughts;* issued, 1663), was the only one published under his own name during his lifetime. It explained the first two parts of Descartes' *Principles* and made some veiled criticisms. Yet it refrained from making an explicit attack on Descartes, in the hope of interesting Cartesian readers in a formal presentation of Spinoza's own philosophy. He began this positive exposition in the *Short Treatise on God, Man, and His Well-Being* (written, 1658–1660; Latin original lost, but two Dutch translations found and published, 1862 and 1869). The main lines of his pantheism were now fixed but he was still searching for the proper order and form of exposition. After 1660, Spinoza began to recast his thought in the *Treatise on the Healing of the Understanding,* where a general introduction to his philosophy and a theory of method may be found. But the work was never completed and was published only posthumously (1677) in fragmentary form. Its interruption was probably due to the fact that Spinoza had already settled upon the geometrical order of reasoning and had started to develop his definitive philosophy in *Ethics Demonstrated According to the Geometrical Order.* By 1665, he completed a first draft of the *Ethics,* in three parts, but interrupted the project in order to help his friend, Jan De Witt, the Grand Pensionary of Holland.

De Witt's efforts to disestablish the Reformed Church in the Netherlands had met with stiff opposition from the Calvinist clergy. In his *Theologico-Political Treatise* (published anonymously, 1670), Spinoza argued that the Church as such has no sovereignty, either within or alongside of the state. He also undermined the authority of the clergy by giving a rationalistic interpretation of revelation and miracles. When the De Witt brothers were murdered in 1672, Spinoza was outraged. In 1673, he politely refused the offer of the chair of philosophy at Heidelberg University, lest his freedom of thought be restricted by the condition that he should say nothing to disturb the established religion. During the years 1670–1675, he revised his *Ethics* and expanded it to its present five parts. But so great was the public furore at the news of its imminent publication that, in 1675, Spinoza was forced to withdraw it from the printer. He died in February, 1677, the victim of tuberculosis, aggravated by the dust breathed in from the lenses he ground. In November of the same year, his *Ethics* appeared, along with the *Treatise on the*

*Healing of the Understanding* and the unfinished *Political Treatise* (started in 1675).

## 2. THE METHOD OF HEALING THE UNDERSTANDING

*Descartes' influence* upon Spinoza was great but not overpowering. Sometimes the Cartesian contribution is exaggerated to the point where Spinoza is regarded merely as drawing out the latent pantheistic consequences of his predecessor's thought. However, this view overlooks two crucial facts: Spinoza's claim to have made radical innovations, and the origin of the principles wherewith he criticized Descartes. A man who could be accused by the Jewish community of holding that God is somehow a body, that there are no pure spirits or angels, and that the soul is one with the body's life, was already in firm possession of a nucleus of views that were at variance with those of Descartes, even before he became acquainted with the latter's works.[1] Spinoza's early speculation on the nature of God, man, and the material world furnished him with a basic *set of standards* for appraising the Cartesian philosophy and appropriating precisely those elements which proved to be congenial.

Nothing is gained, of course, by going to the other extreme of claiming that Descartes' part in the formation of Spinoza's mind was negligible. His contact with Cartesian philosophy was of decisive importance to his development, saving him from being a minor heterodox thinker, like Uriel da Costa, and installing him at the very center of seventeenth-century speculation. Descartes communicated to Spinoza that confidence in the scientific spirit and the mathematical way of reasoning that marks the difference between inarticulate protest against tradition and a powerfully constructed effort in philosophy. Whereas Maimonides encouraged Spinoza to make independent use of his reason, it was Descartes who introduced him to the *specific procedures, terminology,* and *problems* that made Spinoza's arguments relevant to his own age.

Spinoza surpassed Descartes both in recognizing the importance of forging a sound method and in refusing to cultivate methodology for its own sake. Methodological inquiries are to be integrated with those of philosophy as a whole and are to respect the metaphysical and moral ordination of philosophizing. The purpose of method is not only to promote the theoretical explanation of reality

---

[1] Cf. *The Oldest Biography of Spinoza* (A. Wolf edition, 45–46).

but also to advance the soul in its search after lasting happiness. Both the Cartesian and the Spinozistic doctrines on wisdom have a primarily *practical* and *moral import*. Even to inquire in a speculative spirit about whether there is an infinite and eternal good, and whether it is worth striving for, involves a change of pace and a redirection of one's practical life and energies. Spinoza makes the moral context of his methodology unmistakably clear. We must inquire about the kinds of knowledge and the way to attain the highest sort, because such knowledge is necessary *for pursuing the highest good* and for discovering the extent to which other things are good or evil, i.e., lead us toward or away from the supreme source of happiness.

This underlying moral purpose is brought out in the very title of his book on method: *On the Healing of the Understanding (De Intellectus Emendatione)*. The word *emendatio* means something stronger than an "improvement": it connotes a "correction" or, better still, a "healing" of the mind. The implication is that the understanding, in straying away from the truth, has injured itself and deprived itself of due perfection. To apprehend things truly and without fear of error belongs to the birthright of the understanding, considered in its own nature. *Not* to have the truth is a *privation* that affects one's happiness. In restoring the capacity to judge things correctly, philosophy is simultaneously restoring one's moral power and capacity for lasting happiness. Methodology provides the first step in the right direction, since it makes us aware that there are various grades of knowledge and provides a guide for acquiring the highest.

Spinoza distinguishes *four degrees of perception:* (1) that arising from hearsay and conventional signs, (2) that based upon undisciplined experience, (3) that based on scientific inference from effect to cause or from general definition to a property or particular application, and (4) that issuing from a direct sight of the essential nature, either in itself or in its proximate cause. There is no difficulty about evaluating these sources of information, once the *goal of knowledge* is made clear. Spinoza's theory of method is an instrument for leading people to the summit of wisdom: "the knowledge of the union existing between the mind and the whole of nature."[2]

---

[2] *On the Improvement of the Understanding* (Elwes translation, as reprinted in *Spinoza Selections,* edited by J. Wild, 5). The four degrees of perception are described in *ibid.* (Wild, 7); cf. *Ethics,* II, 40, Scholium 2 (White translation, as reprinted in

There is an entire metaphysics packed behind this simple observation, a metaphysics that is also the core of man's moral rehabilitation. One of the difficulties about examining Spinoza's theory of method is that it is regulated throughout by this *basic postulate* about the goal of human knowledge, which postulate in turn is then defended in terms of the new method. From his own standpoint, this circular procedure is justified by the overruling conviction that a way must be found for conveying the truth about the union of mind and nature to intellects that are crippled and led astray by temporal appearances.

Which of the above modes of perception is *best suited* to yield man a knowledge of himself and nature? The first two varieties are obviously inadequate, since they never attain the essence of the thing and hence never give definite, reliable knowledge. The scientific understanding of the essence begins only at the third level, that of the physical and mathematical sciences. They furnish the genuine idea or essence of the thing and therewith a reliable basis for further inference. But they are far from providing the highest sort of knowledge and the perfection that stems from it. The peak is reached only with the fourth type of perception. For, it is not as satisfactory to infer the cause a posteriori, from the effect, as it is to see the cause directly in its own nature; similarly, a thing is not known as precisely and exhaustively through a general definition as through a priori knowledge of its proximate cause. Hence Spinoza concludes that the proper method in philosophy is the one adapted to the *fourth* or *highest conceivable* sort of knowledge.

He chooses to model his method upon the pattern of the fourth mode of perception because, considered in itself, it would yield the most perfect sort of knowledge. He is impatient of the objection that the highest conceivable degree of knowledge might not be *within the reach of man,* in his actual condition, and hence might not provide a suitable pattern for philosophical method. Spinoza's philosophy is a tremendous plea that the highest knowledge does come within our power. The theory of man's nature must be modified so as to substantiate the claim that a human philosophy can lead to an intuition of the whole of reality. This is the ambitious *emendatio* attempted by Spinoza: it is both a *purging* of human limits and

---

*Spinoza Selections,* edited by J. Wild, 186–87). For an epitome of Spinoza's methodology, cf. *Letter XXXVII* (*The Correspondence of Spinoza,* translated by A. Wolf, 227–28). Quotations from *Spinoza Selections* are made with the permission of Charles Scribner's Sons.

an *elevation* to the divine standpoint. Yet, in practice, Spinoza cannot leave behind the three inferior modes of perception. Not only in making contact with other minds but also in building up his own position, he must often conform with the residue of limitations, still remaining upon human intelligence.

Through his doctrine on the *true idea*, Spinoza hopes to show the feasibility of his plan of obtaining intuitive insight into the entire order of nature.[3] A true idea differs from its *ideatum* or referent in the real order. Employing Cartesian terminology, Spinoza distinguishes between the *formal essence* or actual nature of the thing known and its *objective* or *representative essence,* which is nothing other than the true idea of the thing in the mind of the knower. The mind can possess the objective essence of things and thus have truth and certainty about the things in their formal essence. In order to show that there is a complete identity between the objective essence, the true idea and objective certainty about the physical thing, Spinoza explains the meaning of *reflection.* Since the true idea is itself an essence or mode of being, the mind can regard this essence in two ways: either in its objective, representative capacity (as *informing about* the essential nature of another real thing) or in its own formal reality (precisely as *having* an essential structure of its own, albeit one in the ideal order only). Viewing the idea from the latter perspective, the mind can then form an idea of this idea, by a reflective act. Now, in order to know, it is not necessary to know *that I know*. Quite the contrary, in order to know *that I know* (i.e., in order to have reflective knowledge), I must first of all directly know something. Knowledge is grounded ultimately in a direct apprehension of the formal essence of the physical thing, through its objective essence. Possession of this objective essence constitutes truth and certainty in the primary sense. Reflection is possible only within the context of a *given* true idea or objective essence of a thing. Otherwise, there would be an infinite regress and no foothold for the least item of actual knowledge.

This discussion of the true idea is relevant for a *criticism of the*

---

3 *On the Improvement of the Understanding* (Wild, 11-13); that we do, in fact, possess a true idea as the natural equipment or inborn tool of the mind, is the underlying presupposition. On this theory of truth, see L. Terrasse, "La doctrine spinoziste de la verité d'après le *Traité de la Réforme de l'Entendement,*" *Chronicon Spinozanum,* III (1923), 204-31. The *Chronicon Spinozanum* was a specialized journal, devoted to studies on Spinoza's philosophy written by the leading Spinozistic scholars.

*Cartesian method.* For an idea is *true by its own nature* and not by reason of any added traits. Instead of occupying himself with the signs or criteria of true ideas, Spinoza declares that it is enough to have the ideas themselves. They carry their own guarantee, through the intrinsic weight of their representative function. To be certain about them, there is no need to go outside of them or to subject them to any technique of doubt. Furthermore, Spinoza's rigorous dualism of mind and body will not permit him to compromise, even in language or loose expression, concerning the origin of true ideas. They are brought forth by the native power of the understanding and are in no way derived from things. True ideas do, indeed, *conform with* the order of reality and inform us about it, but they are *not drawn from* the things they represent. Hence the existential status of the finite thing is not decisive for human knowledge.

Not only do individual, true ideas conform with individual things: they also display the same order, connection, and *ratio* as the order, connection, and *ratio* of things.[4] This is the extreme *rationalistic principle* which enables Spinoza to assert that the highest conceivable sort of knowledge can come within our human reach. He censures Descartes for stressing the limits and weakness of the human mind, since to this extent Descartes withdraws from the ultimate consequences of rationalism and refuses to grant a perfect, mirrorlike knowledge to the human mind. Spinoza uses his principle of the correspondence between true ideas and things to settle the important question of the *proper starting point* of methodic thinking. In general, method is the same as reflective knowledge: it is an idea of an idea. Everything depends, therefore, upon the character of the original idea, of which the method is a reflective articulation. A true method will be based on a true idea, and the best method on the best or most perfect idea. As Descartes taught, ideas are graded according to their objective reality or what they represent. If the order of our thoughts should correspond in all ways to that of things, then the best methodic reflection should begin with *the idea of the most perfect being, God,* the origin of all things. Spinoza glides from saying that our thought should *recapture* as much as possible of the order of

---

[4] "The *ratio* existing between two ideas is the same as the *ratio* between the formal essences corresponding to those ideas." *On the Improvement of the Understanding* (Wild, 14; translation modified and italics added). "*The order and connection of ideas is the same as the order and connection of things.*" *Ethics,* II, 7 (Wild, 149).

things, to saying that, to be true in the highest, attainable way, human thought must *follow* the same path as the order of things. He lays down an identity between the order of being and the best order of human knowing, between the order of discovery and that of exposition. Hence he criticizes Descartes for starting with the human Cogito. In the real order — which our reflective thought should exactly reproduce — it is from God, and not from the human self, that things emerge to comprise an existing, orderly universe. The right method begins with the idea of God, since in the realm of thought, the idea of God has the same creative vigor as the power of God enjoys in respect to real things.

There is another reason why Spinoza had to deny a proper distinction between the order of knowing and the order of being, at the level of the highest kind of knowledge within human reach. For, he felt that Descartes had provided no adequate ground, epistemological or ontological, for the *process of scientific inference.* In Spinoza's estimation, Descartes was so thoroughly committed to the criterion of distinctness among ideas, that he ultimately cut off one idea from another. His system provided no means of justifying the passage of thought from one true idea to another, except by begging the issue and assuming that all ideas, as well as things, have a participated or interconnected nature. A *discrete* logic of distinct ideas could never develop a system, where *continuity* of inference should reign. Both the empiricists and Spinoza pressed home this difficulty. Hume sought a solution in the psychological laws of association, but Spinoza relegated these laws to the side of the individual organism. They could not serve as the foundation of a meaning open to all men. Hence his solution had to be a metaphysical one.

The continuity of philosophical deduction is only the obverse face of the continuity of things. Even in his treatise on method, Spinoza is obliged to postulate that all things are *connected and rendered continuous by and in God.* He establishes a correlation between a monism of modal things and a methodological precept that reflection should begin with the idea of God. Only by starting reflection with the principle from which things proceed in continuous gradation, can one also achieve continuity in thought. Philosophy becomes an interconnected system of true ideas, by reproducing the concatenation and dynamic unity of things or modes in God. Once in reflective possession of the primal, productive idea of God, the human mind will be nourished by its fertile power and will deduce, in proper order and continuity, the entire series of natural things. If Spinoza had not become a pantheistic monist in virtue of his early religious difficulties, his criticism of Descartes' atomistic logic would have led him to his view, as providing the best guarantee of systematic deduction.

All this supposes, however, that in fact we have a true idea, that we can gain a true idea of God, and that we can explain error and widespread ignorance about having the true idea. The last point represents a serious objection, as Spinoza admits. Skeptics may argue that an infinite regress is unavoidable, since method must start with a given true idea and yet must also prove that any given idea is a true one. Spinoza's reply uncovers another facet of the nature of method. He shows no tolerance toward those cautious, skeptical people, who refuse to take the risk of using their minds in one forthright act, which may well be one of real knowledge. They are rendered speculatively dumb and, in practical affairs, are automata, subject to the necessities of life. Above all, they remain unconscious of their own nature, since they are unwilling to observe it in actual operation. Method, as Spinoza conceives it, is *a practice in inward meditation, a growth in self-consciousness, a coming into reflective awareness of what we really are.*[5] The outstanding hindrances to self-understanding are: current misconceptions of the nature of the human mind (especially the philosophies of Descartes and Bacon), the obscurity of mind caused by the changing temporal order (which convinces us that the mind is not governed by eternal laws), and the lack of disciplined attention and discernment.

Spinoza's metaphysics will show that the human mind is a thinking thing, whose nature is precisely *to give birth to a true idea.* There is no need to pass the test of Cartesian doubt, for this procedure is a sign of the mind's weakness, not of its strength. He who grasps the essence of an idea also perceives its truth: he cannot honestly frame fictions about it, regard it as false, or call it into doubt. Method must begin with the recognition of the presence of a true idea within oneself. More precisely still, Spinoza plans to show that the human mind *is* a true idea, *is* a finite modal expression of the divine substance itself, under the attribute of thought. This is the hidden

---

[5] Men who fail to use the proper method "are not conscious of themselves. . . . [Method] will be absolutely perfect when the mind gains a knowledge of the absolutely perfect being or becomes conscious thereof." *On the Improvement of the Understanding* (Wild, 14, 17).

suggestion toward which the treatise *On the Healing of the Under-standing* is directed. Spinoza implies that a sufficiently penetrative self-awareness will reveal that the understanding, in its own nature, is nothing other than a true idea, correlated with a mode of extension, both of them expressing an aspect of the divine being. To look for the true idea is to look for the nature of one's own mind. To seek the idea of God is to seek to know oneself in the most radical way, as an expression of the divine thought: the human mind not only *has* but *is* an idea of God.

Nevertheless, the fact of error presents a stumbling block to this entire project of methodic thinking. Under ideal conditions, there would be no need to expend great mental energies in order to attain the grand metaphysical truths about God, mind, and nature. They would be the natural, undisputed points of departure for all specula-tion. Spinoza maintains that these truths still have the right to this primary position, and yet he must explain why error can and does arise. He rejects Descartes' explanation, based on the infinite freedom and range of the will. Such a conception of the boundless power of will is highly repugnant to a mind that is seeking an order of rational necessities, to which both our intellect and our will must submit. Instead, Spinoza advances *four causes of human error* that will not embarrass his general outlook.[6] (1) The basic condition, making error possible, is the partial nature of our minds: they are only parts of the divine thinking substance and often give only (fragmentary expression) to its ideas. (2) The imagination is affected by particular physical objects and external causes, thus subjecting the mind to ideas in a complex, confused state. (3) Our reasoning is often carried on in too abstract and general a fashion. (4) We fail to follow the due order of investigation, which should begin with the primary elements of thought.

The remedy for these defects is, in every case, the same: *make a return to the idea of God* immanent within one's nature. (1) The more the mind feeds on the idea of the most perfect being, the more perfect the mind itself becomes and the less subject to the partial, finite condition of our nature. The power of self-affirmation that Descartes claimed for the idea of God, in proving God's existence, is now extended by Spinoza to include its generative power for producing an entire system of philosophical truths. (2) This growth

---

[6] *Ibid.* (Wild, 28–30). For an idealistic criticism of Spinoza's theory of error, see H. H. Joachim, *Spinoza's Tractatus De Intellectus Emendatione*, 151–81.

in the power of the understanding enables it to rely upon its inward resources and thus to distinguish between its own clear and distinct ideas and the inadequate ones of imagination. Especially, the idea of God cannot be confused with ideas representing mutable things in an indistinct way. (3) Moreover, this idea of God is not a mere abstraction or general principle. It is the supreme concrete and individual idea, required as the principle of metaphysical deduction. (4) Finally, the primary elements from which thought should proceed are not the atomistic results of Cartesian reductive analysis, doubt, and introspection. We must begin with the simple nature and power of God. In the idea of God is found both the sovereign specific against error-and-doubt and the *primum* of methodic thinking about the real. Right order in philosophy consists in permitting the idea of the cause of all things to be itself the cause of our other ideas, so that the concatenation of our ideas will exactly reproduce the eternal order and law of things, as originally produced by God.

Yet even this elaborate treatment of error describes its conditions rather than renders intelligible *why* and *how* such conditions could arise in a universe comprised of but the one divine substance. The first two reasons for error, given above, amount to saying that error arises because we are finite, composite beings. They do not explain how we could have become so *forgetful* of our partial nature or so *reliant* upon, and vulnerable to, imagination and outside influences. Another question they raise is how there can arise, in a monism of substantial power, disruptive and deceiving lines of causal influence. Similarly, the last two reasons for error leave unanswered the question of why most people must find their way to the knowledge of God by starting with something more immediately within their experience and ability to comprehend. The *factual discrepancy* between the order of reasoning and the order of being, within a strictly determined universe, means that there is some unexpected gap between what is, and what should and (by right) must be, the order of our thinking. At least, the answer cannot be given in purely methodological terms.

Spinoza raises the hope that, whatever the difficulties of explaining the causes of error, at least they can be overcome by allying ourselves with the *eternally necessary laws* operative in the mind as well as in the external world. He bases this hope upon an analysis of the properties of the understanding, even risking a return to the third mode of perception, in which a thing's nature is inferred from its properties. He seeks to transcend a mere a posteriori inference by noting that, if we reflect sufficiently upon the mind's properties and thus come to know them and the mind *adequately,* then by the definition of adequate knowledge the mind will have manifested itself and provided the essential a priori grounds for grasping its own properties. This is typical of Spinoza's approach to the modes of perception. He is obliged, in human fashion, to work back to a nature from its properties. But, having reached the nature itself, he then takes a *de jure* view of the properties, as flowing from the nature, and maintains that this essential knowledge belongs to the fourth mode and overcomes its a posteriori origin. In point of fact, however, Spinoza reaches his highest mode of perception only by transforming the *way of discovery* into the *way of demonstrative exposition.* This methodological shift does not actually cancel out the inherent difference between the order of being and that of knowing, as far as *men* are concerned.

If we examine our own ideas from the standpoint of their objective or representative perfection, we see that those which express the *affirmative,* the *absolute,* the *eternal,* and the *infinite,* are more perfect than those which signify the negative, the relative, the temporal, and the finite. Hence the former set of traits furnishes Spinoza with a clue about the properties of the understanding and its essential nature. It is essentially fitted to grasp the idea of that being in which alone are realized the perfections by which knowledge is measured. If the mind be a thinking thing, which gives birth to a true idea, then the primary true idea, to which it is naturally ordained, is that of the affirmative, absolute, eternal, and infinite being of God. Method calls attention to the nature of the mind as the faculty of the divine, and asks philosophy to begin there. That is precisely where the *Ethics* does begin.

### 3. DIVINE SUBSTANCE AND ITS ATTRIBUTES

The *Ethics* is composed *ordine geometrico,* a phrase that can be interpreted in two ways. In its most obvious sense, it refers to the *literary mold* in which the matter is cast. Like Euclid, Spinoza begins his masterpiece by laying down certain definitions and axioms, and then proceeds to offer demonstration of a series of interdependent propositions, flanked by numerous corollaries, scholia, and lemmata. This machinery is intended to supply for the weakness of our mind, by fixing concepts clearly and distinctly, by spelling out the precise inferences, and by giving memory an easy path to retread. It also has the incidental advantage of presenting an impersonal philosophy impersonally and unsentimentally, so that the reader will be convinced that he is witnessing the fertile power of the idea of God working out its own articulations, through Spinoza's pen. A philosophy presented in the geometrical form also had, for Spinoza's century, an airtight appearance of absolute rigor and consistency. In actual practice, of course, Spinoza uses his frequent scholia and appendixes to break through the confines of the geometrical pattern. These asides contain a budget of unscheduled observations, polemical attacks, and psychological notes, which will not bear confinement.

The deeper meaning of the phrase *ordine geometrico* is that the *Ethics* has been thought out in Spinoza's mind in accord with the *geometrical spirit of philosophizing,* made familiar by Descartes. There is a passage from known premises to previously unknown conclusions, through demonstrative reasoning. Whereas Descartes had mainly employed the analytic method, as more appropriate to the discovery of first truths imbedded in our experience, Spinoza deemed the time to be ripe for using the *synthetic method* of starting at once from primary truths and demonstrating their consequences. The synthetic approach begins from that which is most intelligible in itself, God, and proceeds to the things of our experience. Hence the *Ethics* supposes that the methodological recall of man to meditation upon the idea of God within himself, has been successful. Thereupon, it begins at once with the first real being and advances synthetically to the things that proceed from God. What had been the proper theological order in the medieval *Summa* now becomes the only proper philosophical order in the modern system, constructed in the full mathematical spirit. Moreover, whereas Descartes banished final cause only from philosophy of nature, Spinoza removed finality and freedom from all philosophical investigations. He agreed with Hobbes that, in a thoroughly mathematical philosophy, they have no legitimate place, any more than does the Cartesian appeal to God as an *asylum ignorantiae* or inscrutable center of arbitrary power.

The first book of the *Ethics* begins with the following definitions, which determine the whole course of the argument.

I. By cause of itself, I understand that, whose essence involves existence; or that, whose nature cannot be conceived unless existing.

II. That thing is called finite-in-its-own-kind which can be limited by another thing of the same nature. . . .

III. By substance, I understand that which is in itself and is conceived through itself; in other words, that, the conception of which does not need the conception of another thing from which it must be formed.

IV. By attribute, I understand that which the intellect perceives of substance, as if constituting its essence.

V. By mode, I understand the affections of substance, or that which is in another thing, through which also it is conceived.

VI. By God, I understand Being absolutely infinite, that is to say, substance consisting of infinite attributes, each one of which expresses eternal and infinite essence. . . .

VII. That thing is called free which exists from the necessity of its own nature alone, and is determined to action by itself alone. That thing, on the other hand, is called necessary, or rather compelled, which by another is determined to existence and action in a fixed and prescribed way.

VIII. By eternity, I understand existence itself, so far as it is conceived necessarily to follow from the definition alone of the eternal thing.[7]

However arbitrary the assigned meanings may be, these propositions are in strict formal accord with the conditions, laid down in Spinoza's methodological treatise, for *definitions of uncreated and created things* (taking "creation" in the loose sense of any production from a first cause).[8] In the case of an *uncreated,* self-existent being or *causa sui,* four rules must be observed. (1) It must be defined solely through its own essence and not through another being as its cause — hence philosophy is not adequately defined by Descartes and others as a search after causes. (2) The definition must be such as to leave no room for doubt about the existence of the thing defined — it is to be specified as an eternal existent. (3) The definition must not be abstract but must express a particular affirmative essence. (4) Wherever possible, the definition should be generative of all the properties of the thing defined. A *created* thing, i.e., one that is not self-existent but dependent upon a cause, must be defined through its proximate cause. From the definition, one should be able to deduce all the properties of the thing, considered only in itself.

These canons of definition are followed scrupulously in the initial set of Spinoza's metaphysical definitions. Thus (1) it is clear that God as *causa sui* cannot be explained through anything else. He is

---

[7] *Ethics,* I, Definitions (Wild, 94–95).

[8] *On the Improvement of the Understanding* (Wild, 37–38). On the connection between the geometric method and Spinozistic metaphysics, cf. R. McKeon, "Causation and the Geometric Method in the Philosophy of Spinoza," *The Philosophical Review,* XXXIX (1930), 178–89, 275–96.

substance, which can only be conceived through itself. (2) As cause of Himself, God is also an essence which necessarily involves its own existence. He cannot be conceived except as self-existent, so that doubt cannot touch this connection. God is the eternal essence, whose existence must be regarded as flowing from its own essence. The latter retains its primacy in Spinozism, since existence is a consequence of essence. (3) It must not be supposed that these definitions are concerned with abstract, general categories and transcendental relations. Cause-of-itself, substance, freedom, and eternity are defined precisely as characterizing the particular affirmative essence of God. No passage is made from substance in general to the divine substance. It is already anticipated that substance, as so defined, refers to a unique, particular, yet infinitely powerful, existent. The affirmative essence of substance has, as its primary and most radical affirmation, its own eternal, particular existence. Whatever other things may exist, they cannot (by definition) exist as substantial entities. (4) The last requirement of the definition of an uncreated being cannot be satisfied by the human mind, under present conditions. Whereas the attributes of God are infinite in number, we can only define His nature in such a way that we perceive to follow from it the two attributes (thought and extension), whose modes constitute our own nature. This is one mark of our finiteness and dependence upon the given universe which Spinoza does not claim to erase by elevation to the divine standpoint. Finally, to place these propositions at the beginning of a philosophical inquiry, harmonizes with the spontaneous tendency of the human mind to know first of all the affirmative, infinite, eternal, and absolute. *De jure,* philosophy unfolds from the fountainhead of being; Spinoza's intellectual ascesis is undergone to insure that the *de facto* order of thought will conform with the *de jure* one.

By including definitions of the finite and the modal within a set of propositions devoted mainly to God, Spinoza is continuing his fundamental division of definitions into those for uncreated, and those for created, beings. The contrast is between that which is conceived through itself (uncreated being) and that which is conceived through its proximate cause (created beings). Spinoza is suggesting that, because only the particular substantial essence of God is conceived through itself, therefore other things are *not substances but modes of the one divine substance.* Spinoza identifies substantial existence *in oneself* with existence entirely *from one's own power of being,* and consequently he has no difficulty in concluding that no finite thing can satisfy the definition of substance. Already, a metaphysical dilemma is proposed implicitly in these definitions: a thing must be either *absolutely independent* in being or else *modally dependent* upon another as its cause. It is stipulated that to be caused by another is equivalent to being dependent upon that other, after the relation of mode to substance. Like Bruno, Spinoza regards "dependent substance" as a contradiction in terms. Under these conditions, there is place for caused, dependent, finite entities only as modes of the unique, uncaused substance of God. The verdict is sealed in the very definitions, before the case is tried.

Spinoza shows himself to be both the *heir and the critic of Descartes.* He exploits the latter's definition of substance, since even Descartes admitted that, in the strict sense, God alone exists in such a way as to need no other for His existence. As for Descartes' qualification that mind and body are at least relative substances, Spinoza replies that there is no middle ground between the absolute self-sufficiency of substance and modal dependence upon substance. Our ability to conceive of mind and body separately only indicates that they belong to different series of modes. Spinoza bolsters his monism of substance with the aid of three further hints in Descartes: the remark that the dependence of creatures upon God makes them abstract and, in a way, modes of God; the doctrine that, while there is a plurality of mental substances, there is but one material substance in the world of extension; the identification between God and the first of the meanings assigned to the term "nature." Although on all three counts Descartes offers a theistic explanation, Spinoza rejects the explanation in favor of one that disposes the mind toward his own pantheistic monism.

Spinoza consulted the current Protestant Scholastic manuals in regard to his definitions, but made significant alterations to fit his purpose. The addition of *conceived through itself* and *conceived through another* to the definitions, respectively, of substance and mode marks the decisive difference.[9] These added words indicate the

---

[9] The best Thomistic criticism of the Spinozistic definitions of substance and mode is made by S. Vanni Rovighi, "La teoria spinoziana della sostanza e la metafisica tomistica," in *Spinoza nel terzo centenario della sua nascita,* edited by the Faculty of Philosophy in the Catholic University of the Sacred Heart (Milan, Vita e Pensiero, 1934), 7–20 (also as a supplementary volume to *Rivista di filosofia neoscolastica,* XXV [1933]). The author shows that Spinoza and Aquinas part company over the

epistemological and methodological orientation of the new definitions. Substance and mode are designated *by our ways of knowing them,* even more than by their manner of being. This enables Spinoza to argue that, because knowledge of dependent entities involves a reference to a cause, their own being is that of a reference to, or mode of, their causal source. It also bolsters his contention that our knowledge of the primal being must itself be a primal principle, held independently of our knowledge of anything else. There is negative significance in the two facts that substance is not called the *subject* of the modes and that the latter are not referred to as *accidents.* The modes are not described as inhering in substance as a subject, lest something static, imperfect, and potential be imported into the divine substance. Spinoza agrees with the Scholastic arguments against applying accidents to God, because of the intrinsic imperfection of a subject requiring accidents. The modes are His *affections,* but they are not His accidents, and He is not their subject. It is easier for Spinoza to state what the relation is *not,* than to give an intelligible, positive account of how modes are "in" substance, without having substance as their subject. His problem is to ground the modes in the only available substance and yet to avoid destroying the infinite perfection of the latter. This is difficult to do, without covertly reinstating the equivalent of dependent but substantial created things.

Spinoza identifies a priori reasoning from cause to effect with reasoning from substance to its mode and makes this procedure the standard for philosophical inference. Because of the sameness between the order of things and the order of true ideas, there can be no strict a posteriori knowledge about God from the things that flow from Him. If our knowledge of the divine substance were dependent upon something else and yet pretended to be truly philosophical knowledge, it would compromise the independence of the divine substance. Hence Spinoza bases his *proofs of God's existence* ultimately on a clear and distinct *a priori idea* of His essence.[10] The a posteriori

question of whether the perfect, intuitive knowledge implied by these definitions is available to human minds, i.e., they disagree about whether or not these proposed definitions can function as principles within a *human* philosophy. The Cartesian methodic doubt and the Spinozistic theory of the degrees of perception and the nature of definition are jointly opposed to the Thomistic emphasis upon the existential limitations placed by the senses upon human intelligence.

10 *Short Treatise on God, Man, and His Well-Being,* I, 1 (A. Wolf translation, as reprinted in *Spinoza Selections,* edited by J. Wild, 45–49); *Ethics,* I, 11 (Wild, 103–06). In the *Short Treatise,* the a posteriori argument seeks the formal reality which causes

proofs he does offer of God's existence are meant as concessions to the weakness of ordinary minds and, upon closer inspection, turn out to be dependent for their probative force upon the a priori idea of a necessarily existing and infinite essence, a substance having the power of self-existing. That a substance must be conceived through itself means, not only that *it must be asserted* to have its being in and from itself, but also that the *human knower must base his assertion* ultimately upon the idea of this substance and upon nothing else. Only the a priori proof rigorously satisfies this condition.

It follows also that a *plurality of substances* would either be totally irrelevant to each other and undeducible from each other, or else would share perfections with each other. Spinoza recognizes only one way in which substances could share perfections: univocally and by a mutually real relation *(commune cum se invicem)*, and such sharing would automatically cancel their claim to be substances. Hence he concludes that there is but one substance, and it is infinite. What Spinoza proves is not the uniqueness of substance but the impossibility of conceiving many substances coherently, in a system which requires that the individual, existing substance be known a priori. The one Spinozistic substance must enter into all other things not merely as a cause present to its effects but also as a substance to its modes, a genus to its species, and a whole to its parts. The requirements of scientific deduction, after the manner of the highest degree of perception, dictate such a relationship and hence are incompatible with a multiplicity of created substances. A monism of substance is the only way in which the highest conceivable knowledge could also be regarded as the natural human way of knowing.

A distinction is made between the *properties* and attributes of God. The former are general characteristics, describing either the necessary existence of substance, by way of extrinsic denomination, or its essence considered as a source of actions. Properties are required in order that God may be what He is, but they do not reveal His essential nature in itself. Spinoza demonstrates that the divine sub-

---

the idea of God in the human mind; the a priori proofs examine the implications of the identity between the divine existence and the immutable, eternal essence of God. In the *Ethics,* the a posteriori proof states that, if finite beings exist, then surely the infinite being is not lacking in the power to exist; the a priori proof rests on the definition of substance as cause of itself and therefore as existing through itself, unhindered by any counterpower in the substantial order.

stance is infinite, unproduced, immutable, and enjoying identity between essence and existence. These properties establish the distinctive sort of existence belonging to the divine being. Other properties, based on His actions, concern the way in which God is a determining cause of things; they can best be discussed in the following section, on the modes produced by God.

Whereas the properties only define God by comparison with the finite, contingent, temporal universe of produced things, the *attributes* give direct access to what God is in His own nature. If they were not constitutive of the divine essence, we could gain no intimate knowledge about God. Later commentators have remained divided about whether Spinoza intends the attributes to have any reality apart from their function of enabling the intellect to grasp the divine substance.[11] The *subjective* interpretation states that the attributes express the divine substance only for intellect, either infinite or finite, and that their sole reality is that of being aids to intellectual perception of God's substantial nature. The more *objective* view is that the attributes are both auxiliaries to knowledge and real, objective constituents of the divine substance, from which the real world of modes takes its rise. Spinoza gives occasion to both interpretations, by stressing now their constitutive presence in substance and now their presence there precisely as the intellect's means of access to the substantial essence.

Spinoza's hesitation on this issue is connected with the problem of the *simplicity* of the divine substance. It is simple and indivisible in itself, since it is infinite and could not be divided, without leading to the contradiction of several infinite substances or several finite parts of one infinite substance. Yet because the divine essence is infinite, it must express itself in an infinite number of attributes, each of which is infinite in its kind. If the objective interpretation of the attributes is accepted, the plurality of real attributes destroys the simplicity and paves the way for some sort of divisibility in God.

[11] See, for instance, the subjective interpretation proposed by H. A. Wolfson, *The Philosophy of Spinoza*, I, 146–57, and the objective reading suggested by P. Siwek, S.J., *Spinoza et le panthéisme religieux*, 247–53. Since the discussion between Wolfson and Siwek turns about whether or not Spinoza's reference to the attributes as "expressing" the divine substance commits him to a subjective, purely logical view of the attributes, one may profitably read F. Kaufmann's essay, "Spinoza's System as Theory of Expression," *Philosophy and Phenomenological Research*, I (1940–1941), 83–97, which shows that the power of nature or substance is primarily an ontological expression, in the real order. This supports an objective approach to the attributes.

Spinoza admits that the attributes are independent of each other, at least to the extent that each is knowable by itself, without reference to the others, and that each gives rise to a distinct series of modes. If the objective reality of the several attributes is weakened, however, their function of leading to knowledge of the divine essence is correspondingly weakened. But at least the subjective reading makes it easier to reconcile manyness of attributes with simplicity of substance. The attributes would be really identical with the divine substance and each other, but distinguished rationally as an aid to the intellect's knowledge of God.

In any case, Spinoza states definitely that only two of the infinite number of divine attributes are known by us: *thought* and *extension*. His denial of secondary substances leaves him with no other recourse than to attribute to God these two most general characteristics, in which the Cartesian analysis of finite being terminated. If the world of experience discloses these ultimate traits, they must be traced back to God and acknowledged as His attributes. Since our minds operate only within the given universe, constituted by God under the attributes of thought and extension, our knowledge of the divine essence is limited to these two notes. There seems to be no intrinsic obstacle from the standpoint of eternity, however, against associating the modes of thought with the nonextensional modes that flow from the innumerable other divine attributes. But such knowledge is not within reach of human nature, constituted as it is precisely by the correlation between modes of thought and extension alone. Because of the definitive character of the Cartesian description of the world, Spinoza does not regard further attributive knowledge of God as being even conceivable for human philosophy.

The main difficulty concerns the attribution of *extension* to God.[12] Spinoza is well aware that this is repugnant to most religious and philosophical traditions. But he remarks that, just as his predecessors were mistaken in ascribing modes of intellect and will to God under the guise of attributes, so they were mistaken in failing to ascribe a genuine attribute, like extension, to Him. Like the medieval Jewish philosopher, Crescas, Spinoza is then compelled to reinterpret extension, so that it may become compatible with God's unlimited perfection. Characteristically, he settles the metaphysical issue by an appeal to his theory of knowledge rather than by a direct analysis

---

[12] *Ethics*, I, 14–15 (Wild, 107–13); *Letter XII* (A. Wolf translation, as reprinted in *Spinoza Selections*, edited by J. Wild, 412–13).

of the humanly available evidence. A distinction is drawn between extension as apprehended by *imagination* and as apprehended by *intellect*. The former power cannot grasp extension in its own nature but only in its modal expression, where it is perceived as being finite, composed of parts, and divisible. But imagination operates at the lowest level of perception and is the main source of error; its defect at this point is to confuse the finite manifestations of extension with its essential nature. By transcending the sphere of imagination, an unfettered intellectual view can be obtained of extension as something infinite, without parts, and indivisible in itself. It is this pure perfection of extension that constitutes an attribute of the divine essence.

A twofold price is paid for establishing this conclusion. First, the divine attribute is rendered completely *equivocal* in respect to the extended objects of our temporal experience. The only common bond between imagined and intellected extension, apart from the name, is the logical stipulation that the very widest properties of finite things must be grounded in corresponding divine attributes. What Spinoza proves to be present in God is not extension, in any settled and identifiable meaning with which we are acquainted, but some perfection sufficient to permit God to be the first cause of extended modes of being. To establish that extension is indivisible, for instance, he shows that *whatever* constitutes the divine substance must be indivisible. *If* extension were to belong to the divine being as an attribute, it would be free from imperfections like divisibility — this is the only conclusion reached. Such an inference does not demonstrate that God's nature is extended but only reiterates that whatever perfection is attributed to God, must be indivisibly present in Him. In the second place, Spinoza contrasts *imagined* matter or *unreal,* finite extension with extension as it *really* is, for the *intellect.* The purely finite aspects of extension are strangers to the domain of real things, as they actually are in the sight of eternity. Despite his best efforts to avoid it, Spinoza is thus obliged to erect a dichotomy between *illusion* and *reality,* in order to attribute extension to God. Although he does not deny the reality of the finite, modal world, he holds that it is unreal from any but the standpoint of his own eternal perspective. Since the traits of finitude, contingency, and temporal duration are implicated in the ordinary or "imaginative" view of extension, the shift to a purely intellectual and eternal treatment of these traits endangers their empirically grasped nature.

The dialectic of illusion and reality may formally posit eternal equivalents for them, but it is a question whether they themselves can survive the sea-change.

## 4. THE EMANATION OF THE MODAL WORLD

Regardless of whether the attributes are taken subjectively or objectively, Spinoza defends the thesis that, outside the intellect, there is nothing but substance and its modes or affections. The latter have their being somehow in God, and can neither be nor be conceived properly apart from Him. Hence a doctrine on the modal world must be the consequence of a doctrine on God as cause, and of modes as His effects and affections. It is important for Spinoza to establish the *fact* and *manner of divine causality* by means of a carefully chosen mathematical comparison.[13] God not only *is* a cause, as can be seen from the factual presence of effects, but *must* be a cause, just as an essence cannot but generate its own properties. It is this comparison between God and an essential definition that establishes the nature of divine causality. Just as an informed intellect sees that properties must flow from any defined essence, so it sees that from an infinite essence an infinite number of effects must flow. By the sheer fact of being infinite affirmative essence, God must give rise to effects. The existing things of the world are in exactly the same relation to God as are the properties of triangle to the notion of triangle: in both cases, the essential perfection of the nature cannot but entail consequences. For Spinozistic rationalism, there is a complete equivalence between the relation of *logical ground* and *consequence* and that of *real cause* and *effect*. This is made possible, because Spinoza conceives *causation* to be fundamentally an expansion or *explication of essence* as such. For the divine substance to be an affirmative essence, means that it is cause of itself and cause of modal effects.

This purely essentialist notion of divine causality has weighty consequences for the problem of God and the world. Essence and

---

13 "From the supreme power of God, or from His infinite nature, infinite things in infinite ways, that is to say, all things, have necessarily flowed, or continually follow by the same necessity, in the same way, as it follows from the nature of a triangle, from eternity and to eternity, that its three angles are equal to two right angles." *Ethics,* I, 17, Scholium (Wild, 115). Cf. *ibid.,* I, 16–18 (Wild, 113–18), on the various aspects of divine causality. For an exposition of the Spinozistic doctrine on the procession of things from God as *causa sui,* and their causal return to God by intellectual love, see T. M. Forsyth, "Spinoza's Doctrine of God in Relation to his Conception of Causality," *Philosophy,* XXIII (1948), 291–301.

existence are identical in God, not by reason of any distinctive perfection in the properly existential order but because the divine essence is infinitely active power. Consequently, God is *causa sui,* because His essence exists through its own active power and necessity. Essence, existence, and duration are distinct from each other in all finite, modal things, since their essence comes from another as a cause. Up to this point, Descartes would concur with this reasoning, but he would recoil from admitting the consequence that Spinoza next draws. God produces the world in the same way in which He is cause of Himself, namely, *by the necessity and power of His own nature.* He cannot *not* act in the production of modes, any more than He can cease to be His own essence or to affirm His own existence. All things flow from the divine nature with the rigid necessity of a mathematical demonstration. Even if the factor of knowledge be added, Spinoza draws a parallel between God's necessary knowledge of Himself and His necessary production of things.

Open issue is taken with the Thomistic doctrine that God creates the world not from the necessity of His nature but *through intellect and will.* Spinoza's reply reveals that, for him, the theory of the divine attributes is a storm center of the new outlook rather than a repetition of a commonplace. For him, intellect and will are not divine *attributes* at all, but are *modes* produced by the divine nature, under the attribute of thought. Hence they are not involved at all in the first production of things. Since he also denies a real distinction between intellect and will from the human standpoint, Spinoza has none of the requisites for grasping the conception of a nonnecessitated creation by God. Spinoza does allow that, if intellect and will were taken as absolutely identical with the divine essence and its infinitely actual power, then they could be said to be present in God. But in that case, they would be predicated of God and creature just as equivocally as "dog" is predicated of the dog-star and of Fido. In proof, he cites the Platonic-Plotinian axiom that "an effect differs from its cause precisely in that which it has from its cause."[14] A divine intellect and will that would be identical with God's essence,

---

[14] *Ethics,* I, 17 (Wild, 117); the correct interpretation of this text is made by A. Koyré, "Le chien, constellation céleste, et le chien, animal aboyant," *Revue de Métaphysique et de Morale,* LV (1950), 50–59. For a Thomistic appraisal of Spinoza's general doctrine on predication between God and finite things, cf. J. F. Anderson, *The Bond of Being* (St. Louis, Herder, 1949), Chap. V: "The 'Univocist' World of Spinoza" (70–76). Anderson's book sets forth the Thomistic doctrine on analogy.

would have only the name in common with our intellect and will, regarded either essentially or existentially. Lacking a doctrine of analogical predication, Spinoza is forced to move between a univocal and an equivocal view of God's causal activity. *Univocity* is present in the comparison between divine causality and the emanation of properties from a definition, since this favors a theory of divine determinism. *Equivocity* is invoked in the face of the Thomistic attempt to attribute intellect and will to God, and hence to establish that He does not produce the world from the necessity of His nature.

Although the world emanates from the necessity of God's nature, Spinoza does not therefore conclude that God lacks freedom. Instead, he revises the definition of *freedom,* so that it excludes coercion or external force but coincides with an internal necessity of action. The divine power wells over into a spontaneous emanation, which is free because it is not compelled from without (there being no other substance, outside of God, to compel Him). God is not only free: He is the only free cause. This follows, since He is the only being that is not produced by another. The divine freedom is that of self-necessitation in existence; the being and operation of all other things are compelled or necessitated from without and hence are not free. God is also the *per se* and *first* cause, since He acts through His own primordial nature. His causality is only in the *efficient* order, efficient causality being equated here with the logical movement involved in a mathematical demonstration. God produces both the essence and the existence of finite things, and yet does so with all the necessity and purposelessness of a geometrical line of proof. In virtue of the attribute of thought, God is conscious of His own essence and its entailments in reality, but it is as though a mathematical essence were aware of its properties. Far from regarding this mathematicizing of divine causality as a derogation of God's perfection, Spinoza deems it the only proper way to conceive God's properties as first efficient cause.

God is the efficient cause but not the final cause of the modal world. The mathematical view of causation prescinds entirely from final cause, and even from any sort of efficient cause that is not reducible to the formal, logical entailment of properties from a definition.[15] Spinoza interprets *finality* exclusively as an acting for

---

[15] See P. Siwek, S.J., "Final Causes in the System of Spinoza," *The Modern Schoolman*, XIII (1936), 37–39, and (more at length) in Siwek's book, *Au coeur du spinozisme* (Paris, Desclée, 1952), 49–83.

the sake of a good to be gained, and a perfection to be acquired, by the agent. Most theistic philosophers agree that it would be a derogation from divine perfection to regard God as *this sort* of final cause. But Spinoza fails to apply to final cause the technique of determining the meaning of the "pure perfection" involved, as he did in the attribution of extension to God. This is an indication that the conditions of mathematical explanation, rather than the analogical requirements of being, regulate the Spinozistic doctrine on divine causality.

Last, Spinoza teaches that God is an *immanent* rather than a transitive cause. By this proposition, he excludes the crude notion of a first cause placed spatially "outside" the world. He also directs it against the Cartesian view that, as an immaterial cause, God is substantially other than the world of material substance. The only kind of *transcendence* open to the first cause is that of the natural primacy belonging to absolute substance over relative modes or the primacy of a constitutive whole over its parts. God is a *remote* cause only in a relative way, insofar as some of His effects proceed more immediately than others from substance. Absolutely speaking, God as immanent principle is also the *proximate* cause of all His effects, and that is why the proper definition of any mode includes a reference to divine substance.

The divine immanence is re-enforced by Spinoza's conception of "God or Nature," *Deus sive Natura.* Whereas Descartes had referred to God as nature and had nevertheless maintained the substantial distinction between Him and finite substances, Spinoza employed the phrase *Deus sive Natura* to express the substantial oneness of all reality, and the relation of substance and modes obtaining between God and the finite things of the world. Like Bruno, he revived the medieval terms *natura naturans* and *natura naturata* to advance this doctrine, but his position is more complex and technically articulated than that of Bruno.[16] *Natura naturans* includes the divine substance and attributes, considered as the dynamic source and free cause of all else; *natura naturata* embraces the entire world of infinite and finite modes. The universe of modes is determined by *natura naturans* and hence is subject to a necessitating compulsion, without any room

---

[16] *Short Treatise on God, Man, and His Well-Being*, I, 8–9 (Wild, 80–82); *Ethics*, I, 29, Scholium (Wild, 126). On the medieval background of the terms, cf. H. A. Lucks, "*Natura Naturans — Natura Naturata,*" *The New Scholasticism*, IX (1935), 1–24.

for freedom. God or the totality of nature includes both *natura naturans* and *natura naturata,* as seen in their proper order, connection and causal relations. Spinoza qualifies his pantheistic conception of nature to the extent that, although substance is constitutive of the essence of modes, still the modes do not belong to the essence of substance. Some distinction is maintained within the unity of nature between the first cause and its effects, but it is only that sort of distinction permitted by the uniqueness of the divine substance and the purely modal character of all other things. Within these limits, *Deus sive Natura* is a concise formula for Spinoza's pantheistic monism.

## SPINOZA'S METAPHYSICAL FRAMEWORK

| | | | |
|---|---|---|---|
| 1. One substance (with a distinctive set of properties and an infinite number of attributes). | God | | Natura Naturans |
| 2. Two known attributes, infinite and eternal. | Thought | Extension | |
| 3. General modes, infinite and eternal. | | | Natura Naturata |
| a) Immediate infinite modes. | Infinite Intellect | Motion-and-Rest | |
| b) Mediate infinite mode. | Pattern of the Entire Universe | | |
| 4. Particular finite modes. | Minds (ideas of bodies) | Bodies | |

A complicated scheme of modes is elaborated in an attempt to explain the familiar world, without compromising the key doctrine of substance and modes. The two known attributes, thought and extension, are eternal and infinite in their kind and partake of the productive power of the divine essence. Hence each gives rise to an infinite series of modes, but does so according to a certain order. The broadest division of modes is into general and particular. *General modes* resemble the attributes in being themselves infinite and eternal. Among general modes, a further distinction is made between *immediate infinite modes* and a mediate infinite mode. The immediate infinite mode under the attribute of extension is *motion-*

*and-rest in general;* that under the attribute of thought is *infinite intellect* (from which will is not really distinct), having as its object the idea of God, in which all the properties and attributes of the divine essence are reflected. Spinoza mentions only one *mediate infinite mode,* calling it the *facies totius universae,* the face or pattern of the entire universe.[17] He does not indicate whether it belongs under only one attribute or both, but it is more likely that it comes under both attributes and proceeds from both immediate infinite modes. Perhaps by the "fashion or make of the entire universe" is meant the most universal pattern of the modal universe, considered not precisely as coming forth from *natura naturans* but as constituting a *natura naturata,* in which there is strict correspondence between modes of thought and modes of extension. This joint pattern remains the same in its general features and laws, even though it embraces an infinite number of particular, changing events and things.

From general or infinite modes flows the series of *particular* or *finite modes.* This is the domain of the particular things (minds and bodies) which we experience. Spinoza speaks of finite modes as *things,* without implying that they are *substances.* His main problem is to explain the origin and characteristics of finite reality. He agrees with the medieval emanationists that, from the infinite first cause, only an *infinite* effect can *immediately* proceed (although he adds that this effect can be a mode of extension as well as one of thought, since extension is also a divine attribute). This is consistent with his anti-creationist and nonexistential theory of God's efficient causality. The eternal and infinite attributes give rise to the immediate infinite modes, from which in turn the mediate infinite mode follows. It is from the mediate infinite mode that the finite modes proceed. Any given particular thing is determined by some previous particular mode of being, so that the finite modes proceed in an infinite series from the mediate infinite mode.

What Spinoza does not explain is how any sort of *finite* reality can proceed by necessary emanation from an *infinite* reality, regardless of whether the infinite reality is immediate or mediate, and regardless of whether there is an infinite number of finite modes. Although

---

[17]*Letter LXIV* (Wild, 463). The translation "fashion or make of the entire universe" was proposed by H. F. Hallett, in "On a Reputed Equivoque in the Philosophy of Spinoza," *The Review of Metaphysics,* III (1949–1950), 207, who suggested that this system of universal nature stands related to the finite individual mode as the macrocosm to the microcosm, as the complement to the self.

it is clear that any given particular thing follows from another, insofar as the prior thing is a finite, determinate mode, the transition from general to particular, infinite to finite, is never established. Even the *mediacy* of the mediate infinite mode is only a relative one, since the first cause remains a proximate cause, immanent to all its effects and modes. Spinoza has not escaped from the emanationist difficulty of rendering intelligible the advent of the many from the one, the finite from the infinite, within a conception of God as producing out of the necessity of his own nature.

Finite particular things are mutable, contingent, and temporal. These notes only render the emanation-problem more acute for Spinoza, due to the immutable, necessary, eternal nature of infinite substance and the everlastingness of the infinite modes. Yet, despite Hegel's charge that Spinoza's substance occupies a lion's den, where all the footprints of finite things point inward and none point outward again, Spinoza does strive to avoid an outright acosmism or denial of the reality of the universe of particular things. He distinguishes between two ways of viewing finite things: through *imagination* and through *reason,* thus using the same epistemological contrast that helped to explain error and extension. He never doubts the real existence of finite modes, but he underlines the inadequate and illusory character of the ordinary way of describing them.

Individual things are finite modes, having a determinate existence. Their *existence* can be approached from two perspectives: that of *eternity* or a necessary entailment from the divine attributes, and that of *duration* or indefinite and contingent continuation in being.[18] The eternal view of modal existence is that taken by reason; the durational view of modal existence is that taken by imagination. These two standpoints are open to us, since the essence of derived, finite things is not identical with its existence. Men ordinarily consider the essence of individual things in an isolated way, as being cut off from divine substance and the necessary causal order of nature. This is the work of imagination, which studies modal entities only in themselves and their factual, contingent connections. Imagination is not intrinsically erroneous, but it suffers from the twofold disability of being affected by the chain of external agents and of

---

[18] *Ethics,* II, Definitions 5, 7, and Propositions 8 (Corollary), 44–45 (Wild, 144, 151, 190–93); *ibid.,* V, 29 (Wild, 387–88). On contingency, as based upon a deficiency in our knowledge of the eternal order of causes, cf. *ibid.,* I, 33, Schol. 1, and IV, Definition 3 (Wild, 130, 287).

never rising beyond the domain of finite being as such. Hence it usually leads to error by encouraging the common-sense description of the *common order of nature,* in which things are not recognized as modes of the divine being or as necessarily determined by it, but are regarded as contingent, temporal substances. Because imagination can discover no intrinsic reason in the finite essence for its existence, people usually conclude that the individual thing is *contingent.* And because imagination cannot locate the proper cause in the order of nature, it is concluded that the individual thing is *merely possible* in itself or due to *chance* determinations. But contingency and corruptibility are only names for our lack of knowledge of the essence, taken in all its relations. Similarly, imagination treats the finite thing's continuation of existence in an abstract way, as duration. *Time* is a handy tool of imagination for measuring *abstract duration* by means of determinate units.

The contingent view of durational existence is due to the deficiency of our knowledge at the level of imagination. The only way to remedy this inadequate description of finite things in terms of contingency, chance, and duration, is to elevate the mind to the standpoint of reason. Only reason, brought to perfection in the intuition of God, can view the finite essence in intrinsic relation to God and the *eternal order of nature* (in contradistinction to the merely temporal, common order of nature, described by imagination), including the laws governing the infinite modes. From this adequate perspective, the finite essence is seen to be necessarily determined to existence through its first cause, even though it is not necessarily existent from any power in its own nature. Contingency is thus transmuted into the necessity proper to a particular entity existing within *natura naturata.* Actual existence is now known to be determined within the modal world and not to be due to chance or a mere external agency. Reason's function, at the highest level, is to know finite things as they are in themselves. Paradoxically, their true and real being *in themselves* is precisely their modal being *in another,* in the divine substance. Their continuance in existence is tracked back to God's necessary determination of their existence: hence it is no longer an indefinite, abstract, contingent duration but a determinate mode of eternal being. Temporal duration is thereby caught up in eternity or, rather, is replaced by eternity. For, to understand finite things according to their real and true essence, is to understand them from the standpoint of the eternity described in Spinoza's theory of substance, attributes, and modes. *Sub specie aeterni*, their existence is seen to flow from the causal necessity of God's nature and hence to be a shared eternity rather than a temporal duration.

It is for this reason that the question was posed, at the end of the previous section, whether the antithesis between imagination and reason, the abstract and the concrete, the erroneous and the true view of reality, can ultimately salvage the empirical content of our notion of finite things. It is not a question about the *fact* of their reality but about our *description* of that fact, on the basis of what is given through the senses. Spinoza teaches that the real and true being of finite things is not properly expressed in terms of contingency, duration, and temporality. This is a lower or interim viewpoint that becomes positively erroneous, unless it is overcome by his own interpretation of the emanation of the modal world. True, finite existence is necessitated *rather than* contingent, is a participated eternity *rather than* a temporal duration. This contrast is something more than a refinement of our experience of finite existents. It is a criticism and replacement of that experience to the extent that none of the original traits remain and an opposite meaning is installed in the philosophically formed mind. If the genuine reality of finite things is only their reality as modes affecting the divine substance, then Spinoza's view of existence maintains no continuity of meaning with the conviction that the finite existents are irreducibly contingent and durational entities. At least as irreducible characters of finite things, contingency and temporal duration are sacrificed to the exigencies of a metaphysical deduction. As traits due to the deficiency of imagination, they must give way before the systematic demands of Spinozistic pure reason or intellect. Spinoza is both the heir to Descartes' suspicion of sensuous cognition and the herald of Hegel's difficulty about explaining how any recognizable traits survive from "abstract" experience, once it has been "overcome" by the requirements of a pantheistic monism.

## 5. HUMAN NATURE

Spinoza's philosophical anthropology is not only in conformity with his epistemological and metaphysical principles but is also a strict inference from them. His doctrine in this field tells what human nature *ought to be* within the designated framework, rather than what it *discloses itself as being* in our actual experience. This a priori approach is indicated at once in the definitions of *mind* and *body*.[19] They are defined as modes that express in a determinate, finite way the essence of God considered, respectively, as a thinking thing and as an extended thing. Hence the main task of the philosophical study of man's mind and body is to show how they can be explained as finite, modal consequences of God's attributes of thought and extension, and of the infinite modes of intellect and motion-and-rest. The human composite is treated as a phase in the joint emanation of the finite modes from the divine nature. Our experience of human nature is rectified and reconstructed from this overruling standpoint.

Spinoza first proposes a *general theory of mind and body* and then makes a specific application to the human mind and body. The methodological postulate about the close agreement between the order and connection of ideas and that of things may now be stated in a more metaphysical way. God's active essence gives rise to an infinite series of finite things, that may be considered now under the attribute of thought and now under that of extension. Because of the oneness of the divine substance, it is *one and the same thing* that is being expressed *under the different modes* of extension and thought. That which is expressed in a corporeal way, as following from the divine nature under the attribute of extension, is given a mental expression under the attribute of thought. The content of the mode of thought is specified by its proportionate mode of extension.

Sometimes, Spinoza stresses the *sameness of the modal thing,* expressed under the two attributes, while at other times he stresses the *one-to-one correspondence* established between the co-ordinate series of the modes of thought and the modes of extension. Within the finite world, the extended modes constitute bodies, whereas the mental modes, regarded in their own formal nature, constitute minds. Every body has its proper idea or correlated mental expression, under the attribute of thought. Taken in its own formal being, the idea of a body is the same as the *mind* or *soul* of that body. All bodies are animated or besouled in this sense, but Spinoza differs from the panpsychism of many Renaissance Neo-Platonists and of Leibniz, in that the presence of a mind or soul need not entail some vague feel-

---

[19] *Ethics*, II, Definition 1 and Proposition 11 (Wild, 143, 155-56). For a sustained comparison between Spinoza's theory about man and the deliverances of human experience, consult H. Barker, "Notes on the Second Part of Spinoza's *Ethics*," *Mind*, N. S., XLVII (1938), 159-79, 281-302, 417-39.

ing or perception in every body. In its minimal and most widely exemplified meaning, a mind or soul is merely the ideal correlate of a body, the manner in which the bodily thing proceeds from God under the attribute of thought. There is *no causal interaction* between mind and body, however, since they are referred to different attributes of God.

Spinoza's doctrine on mind is worked out largely by reference to the nature of body, to which the mind or idea of the body is proportioned.[20] He admits a hierarchy among minds, because of an evident gradation among bodies. The *grades of being* are not accounted for by graded actual and potential principles, however, since, for Spinoza, potency is due only to our inadequate knowledge of the actual fullness of the total system of beings. It is a true fact, however, that the infinite intellect conceives of an infinite number of finite, modal consequences of the divine essence, and that these are necessarily brought forth by the divine power. In the region of extended things, there is a continuous gradation from the simplest bodies or ultimate modal units up to material nature as a whole. *Individuality* is an extremely supple characteristic of things, being based upon the establishment of a proportion of motion and rest among the ultimate constituent parts. Spinoza gives a purely functional account of the individual. The dynamic harmony among several bodies, acting together as one agent in the production of effects, is sufficient to constitute them as one individual thing, since their joint action achieves some fixed proportion. Increasingly more comprehensive operational unities result in ever more comprehensive individual natures. Finally, Spinoza takes the whole of material nature as a single, inclusive individual, because all particular variations occur within the fixed pattern of motion-and-rest set by the laws of nature. This perspectival notion of corporeal individuality leads to a similar view of the individual nature of minds, since the ideas of bodies enter into similar relations of unity and subordination to a more inclusive whole.

There is something *distinctive* about both the human body and the human mind. The former is composed of many kinds of subor-

---

[20] After showing in *Ethics,* II, 13, that the object of the human mind is an actually existing body, Spinoza then adds a special series of axioms and lemmata about bodies in general, and six postulates about the human body in particular (Wild, 157–64). Unlike Descartes, he is able to construct a theory of mind on the basis of a mechanistic conception of bodies, due to his doctrine on the exact correlation between mental and extended modes.

dinate bodily individuals, each of which is composed in turn of the most simple bodies. The *human body* is thus a very complex sort of dynamic unity. It is sympathetically responsive to modifications from the various quarters of the material universe and, for its part, can act upon a broad field of things. These multiple contacts established between the human body and its environment are important for the human mind, since it can know other things only through their effects upon the human body. Both Spinoza and Leibniz agree that only through this medium are other material things brought to focus for the human mind. The human mind is of a higher nature than other types of minds or ideas of bodies, because it can become conscious of its own body. Alone among all the varieties of minds, this one is an *intellect* or *spiritual automaton.*[21] The human mind or soul is nothing other than the formal reality of the idea of the human body. As such, it is posited in being by the actual presence of the existing human body. It is axiomatic with Spinoza that we do have perceptions of our own body, by which conscious acts the human mind is rendered actual and distinctively intellectual.

Man's mind and body are not, as Descartes supposed, distinct finite substances. Rather, they are distinct modal aspects of one and the same thing, which is expressive of the one divine substance. The entire Cartesian discussion of the *per se* unity between two substances is undercut and dismissed by Spinoza's arguments that there is only one substance present in man; that it is the infinite substance of God and not a finite, human substance; and that the human composite is only a *modal unity,* under the divine attributes of thought and extension. Whereas Descartes' difficulty lay in the fact that these attributes are mutually exclusive and seem to require mutually exclusive substances in man, Spinoza makes them attributes of the same divine substance, issuing in one thing that can be regarded under two modally different series. There is, however, a strict correspondence and mutual implication between the modes of extension and of thought, and hence between body and mind. The mind is the idea of *this* body, whereas the body is expressed mentally by *this* idea, which is its mind and soul. Spinoza does not try to *solve* Descartes' problem of uniting two substances: he *substitutes* for it the more manageable problem of correlating an idea and its ideatum. In making this

---

[21] "Quasi aliquod automa spirituale." *On the Healing of the Understanding (Spinoza Opera,* edited by C. Gebhardt, II, 32).

substitution, however, he has to rely upon his doctrine about the unicity of substance, in order to make it inevitable that mind and body can be nothing more than mental and extended modes of one divine substance. This is the sense in which his theory of man is deductively constructed from his theory of method and of being.

Cognition is the fundamental activity of the human mind. This operation is not carried on by means of any faculty of knowledge. Spinoza rejected the *faculty theory* (as gathered from the Dutch Scholastic manuals), on the ground that it hypostasizes individual cognitive acts and thus creates metaphysical fictions.[22] In the Spinozistic view of the universe as *a plenum of mathematically determinate actual things,* it would be difficult to make room for *powers* that both perfect a thing and are ordained to further act. At most, he is willing to speak about the powers of the mind in the sense of class names for various kinds of individual activities. The mind is, by its very nature, a dynamic source of cognitive acts. Each one of these acts is determined by other such acts, in the infinite series of finite modes of thought, without the special intervention of any faculty for performing the operations. A consequence may now be drawn from the fact that man is not an ultimate, substantial supposit and that his mind — as a finite mode — is only a part of the divine intellect or infinite mode of thought. Spinoza says that when the *human mind has* an idea and knows an object, it is *God who has* that idea and knows the object. But God has this knowledge, not according to His infinite nature, but insofar as He causally forms the essence of the human mind (under the attribute of thought) and thus manifests Himself through the human mind. But it is a doleful fact that the "sensual man" has no awareness of God's implication in his cognitive activity or its ultimate attribution to God. Our consideration of this truth is achieved only by reflecting methodically upon the acts of thinking, in the light of Spinoza's own doctrine on substance and modes, which provides the higher viewpoint of eternity.

What the mind knows directly are the *ideas of the affections of its own body.* The bodily affections themselves do not enter the mind, but the mind is affected by ideas exactly representing the nature and state of the bodily affections. Spinoza thus provides a metaphysical anticipation of the nineteenth-century psychological hypothesis of

---

[22] *Ethics,* II, 48, Scholium (Wild, 195–96).

*psychophysical parallelism.*[23] The reciprocal relation of mind and body as a whole extends to that between the particular mental and physical acts. An event which is expressed formally or physically as a mode of extension, an affection of the body, receives its representative or psychic expression as a mode of thought, an affection of the mind. There is *no causal communication* between modes considered under different attributes, but there is a *strict correlation* between the individual acts of mind and those of the body. Yet Spinoza is not an occasionalist, like Malebranche, who denied all secondary causality. Spinoza allows a determined causation *within* the same modal series or among the modes which belong under the same attribute. Sometimes, he does refer to God as the sole efficient cause. This is intended to stress the unique origin and determination of all causal power, as well as God's causal presence in all modal activities, rather than to deny causal efficacy to modal agents, within the same series. God is the immanent cause of both the *esse* and the *fieri* of all modes, whereas finite modes of the same kind can contribute to the *fieri* or ordered becoming of things in *natura naturata,* in virtue of the original impulse received from *natura naturans.* Because there is no causal interaction between modes of body and modes of mind, the ideas are not derived from a bodily source. But since other bodies in the material universe leave their traces upon the states of our body, the ideas of our own bodily states tell us something about bodies other than our own. Mainly, however, the ideas of one's bodily affections inform the mind about these affections in themselves.

Yet it is a far cry from preoccupation with the affections of one's own body to loving contemplation of the divine essence. The distance between them measures the task Spinoza now faces, of elevating the mind from the lowest to the highest kind of knowledge. He feels that the work is made all the more difficult by reason of the *false starting points of philosophizing,* as proposed by the Scholastics and Descartes. The former begin with the sensible world, the latter with the thinking self. Spinoza minimizes the knowledge of these objects that can be gained by beginning philosophical investigations with them. When the mind is dependent upon the ideas of affections of the body, it is operating at the lowest levels. Apart from what we can

---

[23] For an exhaustive critical study of this question, cf. P. Siwek, S.J., *L'âme et le corps d'après Spinoza* (Paris, Alcan, 1930).

know in general about the most simple bodies, the common notions or traits of all bodies, and some immediate deductions therefrom, our ideas of the sensible world remain confused and limited in scope. Taking a starting point in sensation, we can learn little about the specific constitution of external bodies or even our own body. Furthermore, there is no direct insight into the nature of the mind, taken merely as a thinking self. It is known only imperfectly by Cartesian introspection, since it is being viewed only as the correlate of the body and its affections. All is darkness, until it dawns upon a man that his mind is indeed a portion of an infinite intellect, that this intellect has for its necessary and proper object the idea of God, and that therefore this idea is the true gravamen of all human thinking. To make this light shine upon the mind is a major step toward wisdom and the happiness we all seek. Insofar as there are obstacles to its ready propagation in the human mind, the problem of man becomes a moral problem.

## 6. DETERMINISM AND THE AFFECTS

There are two features in the Spinozistic philosophy of man that seem to militate against any effective search for happiness: the denial of freedom and the emphasis on the grip of the passions upon us. The position on *freedom* is dictated by metaphysical considerations. Because of man's location within the modal world of *natura naturata*, he is, by definition, subject to a rigorous determinism in all his actions. The divine causality imposes compulsion or necessity-from-another upon all the modes, mental as well as bodily, thus preventing any modal entity from conforming with the definition of freedom. It does no good to distinguish mind from body: mind is not only modally determined in itself but is correlated, in all its acts, with the determined series of physical events. One finite mode of thought causes another in an infinite series of necessitated mental actions, each of which has its physical counterpart in the similarly compelled series of modes of extension. Even the last refuge of libertarian doctrine — free will — is scuttled by Spinoza. For if by *free will* is meant a *faculty,* it falls beneath the general criticism of faculties of the mind. And if it means an *act* of free choice, there is no special class of acts to sustain the general name. There is no real distinction between acts of knowing and willing. To will is nothing more than to affirm or deny that which is true or false in our ideas. This is a cognitive function and offers no ground of distinction for another class of powers or acts. Descartes had defended freedom by making judgment an act of will. Spinoza reduces the will to the cognitive function of judgment, making it subject to the same determinism governing all our cognitive operations.

Nevertheless, men do recognize themselves as beings of desire and striving. Hence Spinoza's next step is to study the appetitive aspect of our nature. His purpose is to acknowledge the power of the passions and then to suggest the means for becoming their master rather than their slave. This program he seeks to carry out, without reinstating the doctrine of free choice. His solution is *to convert ethics into a metaphysics of the degrees of knowledge,* a course that is prepared for by the suppression of any real distinction between the cognitive and appetitive orders. Hence Spinoza can echo Hobbes' boast of treating human actions and passions just as one would treat of lines, planes, and solids. The univocity of his philosophical method permits him to make this radical reduction of our affective and moral life to a geometrical determinism, which nevertheless leads eventually to happiness.

Cartesian ethics had hinged upon the passions of the soul and their control by free will and reason. Since he denied both free will and interaction between body and mind, Spinoza had to reject the Cartesian theory of the passions. For it, he substituted his own doctrine of the affects, which can be either passions or actions and which are not radically distinct from the virtues. *Affects* are defined as "the affections of the body, by which the power of acting of the body itself is increased, diminished, helped or hindered, together with the ideas of these affections."[24] They include, then, both the bodily affections and the ideas of these affections in the mind. In its broad meaning, an *affection* includes any modification that enters into the constitution of the human essence, whether under the attribute of thought or of extension, or under both attributes. The affections under consideration are precisely those that bear upon the power of acting, whether of the body or of the mind. An affection of the body helps to determine its modal nature; this affection entails a corresponding idea, which is, in turn, an affection of the mind. From the combination of a bodily affection and its idea is constituted an affect of human nature. An affect is essentially *dynamic* in nature, since

---

[24] *Ethics,* III, Definition 3 (Wild, 207); cf. *ibid.,* III, *ad fin.:* General Definition of the Affects (Wild, 281).

it determines in some way the body's power of acting and the corresponding mental power of acting.

Spinoza does not allow any purely passive affective state, even in
the case of the passions. The distinction between passion and action
is not that between merely receiving and producing motion but
rather between different ways and degrees of causing affections. The
difference turns upon whether a man is an inadequate cause or an
adequate cause in the production of affections of the body. In the
former case, the affect is a *passion;* in the latter case, an *action.* The
criterion of whether or not a man is the adequate cause of his affections is found in the condition of his knowledge, thus inserting a
*cognitive* determinant and standard at the very core of *affective* life.
An *inadequate cause* is one "whose effect cannot be understood by
means of the cause alone," but which requires a reference to some
external agent. This is due to the fact that the cause — the human
mind, in this case — has only an inadequate or confused knowledge
of its own nature and power, and hence regards itself as being only
a partial cause. An *adequate cause,* on the other hand, is one "whose
effect can be clearly and distinctly perceived by means of the cause,"
without an extrinsic reference.[25] Although there is causation of affections in both cases, Spinoza reserves the term "action" for what we
do as an adequate cause, and "passion" for what we do as an inadequate or partial cause of the affection.

The human condition is a mixed one, a synthesis of actions and
passions in various proportions. Man is never entirely the slave of
passions and never entirely free from them, even though he begins
perilously close to the former state and may strain eagerly toward the
latter. Spinoza offers three instructive, metaphysical reasons for the
*composite character of our emotional life.*[26] (1) Just as the human
body is composed of many subordinate individual bodies, so the mind
is composed of many subordinate ideas. Some of our ideas are confused, whereas others are clear and distinct. Hence some of the
things we do proceed from adequate ideas and issue in actions.
whereas others proceed from inadequate ideas and lead to passions.
(2) Again, it is a metaphysical principle that every determination of
being involves a negation. The divine substance is purely undetermined being, in that it is an infinite and affirmative nature, deter-

---

[25] The definitions of inadequate and adequate cause are combined in *Ethics,* III,
Definition 1 (Wild, 206).

[26] *Ibid.,* III, 1, 3, 61 (Wild, 207–08, 214, 259–60).

mining others and itself remaining undetermined. All the modes
of *natura naturata* are determined by the first cause and hence have
some negation, along with their modal reality. (This negation, entailed by determination of being, is Spinoza's substitute for the
Thomistic composition of actual and potential principles in finite beings, and will become a mainspring in the Hegelian dialectic.) All
finite, individual things may be regarded as determined partial causes,
and to this extent man must have passions. But since we may also
regard ourselves not merely in a confused way, as parts of the common order of nature, but also, clearly and distinctly, as one with the
eternal order of nature, we are also capable of being the source of
actions. (3) Finally, the melange of passion and action is similar to
that of imagination and reason. We are subject to the passions insofar
as we imagine, for to imagine is to know in a confused way and as
being affected by our own body and some external cause. Reason, on
the contrary, frees us from this extrinsic reference and hence permits
our emotions to be evaluated as being actions that proceed from the
mind's own nature.

Spinoza reduces Descartes' sixfold enumeration of the *basic passions* to three primitive ones: desire, pleasurable joy, and painful
sadness.[27] They are already implicated in the definition of an affect.
Increase or decrease of the body's power of acting supposes a standard
by which to gauge the consequences of an affection. This standard is
provided by the *conatus,* the drive, endeavor, or effort that is intrinsic
to every body and mind, impelling it to persevere in its own being.
Spinoza agrees with Hobbes in stating that the body's power of acting
is increased or decreased in the degree that an affection furthers or
hinders the drive toward self-preservation. But he leaves Hobbes behind with his further assertion that this endeavor is the permanent
impress of God's power upon all modal entities, since He produces
both the beginning and the continuance of their existence. No special
act is needed for this *conatus:* it is one with the being's actual, existing essence or its natural appetite and love. The active essence of
the body is to persevere in its own proper proportion of motion-

---

[27] *Ethics,* III, 11, Scholium (Wild, 218): *cupiditas, laetitia, tristitia.* I have translated
the Cartesian-Spinozistic terms *laetitia* and *tristitia,* respectively, as "pleasurable joy" and
"painful sadness." This somewhat redundant rendering brings out the pleasure-pain
contrast and the co-ordination between mental and bodily states, in the passions. H. A.
Wolfson, *The Philosophy of Spinoza,* II, 206-07, translates these terms primarily as
"pleasure" (*hedone*) and "pain" (*lupe*), secondarily as "joy" and "sorrow." On the
*conatus,* read *Ethics,* III, 6-11 (Wild, 215-19).

and-rest, just as the mind's active essence is to persevere indefinitely in the life of intellect, whether through confused or distinct ideas. There is an exact co-ordination between the inclination of the body toward its self-preservation and the so-called decree of the mind for its well-being.

Will, appetite, and desire are only various ways of designating the *conatus*. The only legitimate moral meaning of *will* is not as a special appetitive power but as the *conatus* itself, considered as related to the mind alone. When the same endeavor is related to both mind and body, it is termed *appetite*. Since the essence of any individual thing is precisely a modal correlation between mind and body, appetite expresses the effort of the individual's essence or composite nature to persevere in its being. Appetite is found in all modal things, but man alone is conscious of his appetite. *Desire* is nothing more than the conscious appetite present in man, who can become aware of the endeavor of his essence. Desire is the fundament and measure of all the other affects. The primary drive of the mind is to affirm the body's existence, since the mind is the affirmative idea of the body.

Along with desire, Spinoza lists pleasurable joy and painful sadness as the other primitive passions of man. They are dynamic developments of desire, and are required because our nature is subject to great changes. Insofar as our nature varies, so the desire varies. It differs from one individual to another, and undergoes increase or decrease within the same man, i.e., it expresses itself in him either as pleasurable joy or as painful sadness. *Pleasurable joy* is the passion whereby the mind increases its endeavor and passes from a lesser to a greater perfection. *Painful sadness* is the passion whereby the mind diminishes its endeavor and passes from a greater to a lesser perfection. All other passional affects are either compounded out of the three primitive ones or are derived from them, in respect to various objects by which we may be affected. Thus *love* and *hatred* are nothing other than pleasurable joy and painful sadness, respectively, along with an accompanying idea of an external cause.

Painful sadness cannot be an action, as well as a passion, since it always involves a lessening of the mind's power of acting. But there are *actions of desire and pleasurable joy,* as well as passions of the same. Man's endeavor or desire operates with either inadequate or adequate ideas, and hence desire can be either a passion or an action. Moreover, when the mind acquires adequate ideas, it takes pleasurable joy in conceiving them and contemplating, with their aid, its own true nature and power of acting. Hence, insofar as man thinks or employs the power of reason, instead of relying upon imagination, he has the active affects of desire and pleasurable joy. All other actions spring from some combination or relation of these basic components.

## 7. MAN'S LIBERATION AND BEATITUDE: THE POWER OF REASON

The main ethical problem for Spinoza is to render possible the passage from passion to action. In order to clear the ground for his own solution, he first examines the view of the Stoics and Descartes that the passions are to be controlled by virtue and a knowledge of good and evil. This teaching is acceptable to him only on condition that it be thoroughly transformed, in conformity with his own leading principles. Spinoza's procedure consists, first, in giving a realistic account of man's actual condition and, then, in asking in what sense virtue and a knowledge of good and evil can improve the prevailing situation for man.

The first step is to emphasize the extent of our *bondage to the passions.* "A man is necessarily always subject to passions, and . . . he follows and obeys the common order of nature [as distinguished from the true, eternal order], accommodating himself to it as far as the nature of things requires."[28] This subjection to the passions is a necessary and permanent part of our human lot, since the individual man is a part of nature and must be conceived as being affected by the other parts. The effort or endeavor whereby a man perseveres in being is the power of God or nature, taken not infinitely but *finitely,* insofar as it is manifested in an actual, limited essence. Hence the *conatus* is limited in the individual, suffers changes, is subject to the passions, and is infinitely surpassed by the power of external causes. The individual man is a battleground for conflicting affects and causes, the stronger ones replacing or restraining the others. His limited endeavor is overwhelmed by the passions and alien influences, which exert their power upon him both from without and from within. He is impotent to control them or, at least, to retain his control for very long. Such is the somber picture Spinoza paints of the state of human bondage, which is to be the point of departure for the effort toward moral elevation and happiness. This is an analogue, in the order of

---

[28] *Ethics,* IV, 4, Corollary (Wild, 292).

the passions, to Hobbes' description of man in the state of nature. Of what use is a knowledge of good and evil to such a fragile and battered center of endeavor as man? Spinoza calls good and evil *entia imaginationis*, products of the mind insofar as it is subject to imagination and the rule of external causes.[29] They are completely relative notions, without any absolute standard. Their origin is traceable to the model of human perfection which we invariably set before ourselves. Anything aiding our approach to this paragon is called *good*, and anything hindering our approach is called *evil*. Good and evil, then, are nothing more than the useful and the harmful to us. Use and harm can be calculated by the standard of the individual's *conatus*. That is called useful or good which aids one's drive to persevere in being, whereas that is called harmful or evil which presents an obstacle to this drive. This also means that good and evil are the factors tending to increase or diminish our power of acting. Consequently, knowledge of good and evil is the consciousness of pleasurable joy and painful sadness: the idea of these states that necessarily follows from the affects themselves.

By itself alone, ordinary knowledge could not remove a passion. The latter is rooted in the influence of an external cause upon us, whereas the lower sort of knowledge does not rise above this "eccentric" viewpoint. At this level, the only remedy would be to call upon a stronger passion, one that is based upon a more powerful, but still external, cause. Only when *imaginative knowledge of good and evil is converted into a philosophical understanding of our affects of pleasurable joy and painful sadness*, does it acquire the intrinsic power to modify or remove the passions. Similarly, no fiat of a special power of will could overcome them. For if will has any meaning in an ethical context, it is as a name for the *conatus*, considered in relation to the mind alone. Since this endeavor is not an absolute and separate force but only the individual's actual nature, it partakes of his limits and plight as a partial, conditioned entity. No easy way to salvation is to be found in an appeal to will, taken as a special source of energy.

---

[29] For Spinoza's treatment of evil, see *Short Treatise on God, Man, and His Well-Being*, I, 10 (Wild, 82–83); *Ethics*, I, Appendix; III, 39, Scholium; IV, Preface (Wild, 140–43, 243, 285–86). In his article, "Spinoza's Doctrine of Privation," *Philosophy*, VIII (1933), 155–66, R. Demos discusses the antithesis between ordinary ethical motives and Spinoza's reduction of good and evil to a purely relative status, within a world governed by natural necessity.

The notion of *virtue* is also critically redefined by Spinoza in terms of philosophical knowledge. He begins with the etymological equivalence between "virtue" and "power." Human virtue is the same thing as the essence of man, regarded as having the power to perform deeds that can be understood through the laws of his nature alone. The *conatus* is the basic and sole foundation of virtue. What one's endeavor impels one to do, is also the supreme rule of virtue: "Every one is bound to seek his own profit."[30] To be virtuous is to follow our nature, which bids us desire what we deem to be good or profitable to us and avoid what is deemed evil or harmful to our endeavor. This explanation of virtue enables Spinoza to endow with his own distinctive meaning the old Stoic counsel: follow nature in our actions. We can *act* virtuously only when we have clear and distinct ideas, that enable us to be adequate causes and to follow the laws of our own nature. Hence the precept of *seeking one's own profit* means, basically, *seeking to heal and improve one's understanding*. The true significance of acting virtuously, of acting according to nature or according to reason, now becomes clear. No appeal is being made either to external forces or to an act of free will. We are asked, instead, to recognize that the necessary laws of our own inner nature are the laws of reason as well. The human endeavor is a prompting to increase the understanding's power by discovering a more definite criterion of the good and the useful than Stoic-Cartesian ethics can supply.

There is now a rapid convergence, in Spinoza's reasoning, between *goodness, virtue,* and *power.* Their synthesis is achieved in the *act of knowing God.* For this act is at once the highest good of the mind, its highest virtue, and its supreme source of inward power. Our true profit lies in the increase of our power of understanding, following upon its direction toward the infinitely actual being of God. Spinozistic methodology, metaphysics, and ethics concur in this conclusion. Since the useful and the good coincide, our knowledge of the good is most helpful when it springs from a contemplation of the divine essence. In this knowledge the supreme virtue or development of the mind's power of acting consists. The human *conatus,* strengthened by effective knowledge of the good and the discipline of virtue, is rendered most active, steadfast, and powerful when the mind shares in the vision of God. An analysis of this contemplative act will show

---

[30] *Ethics,* IV, 18, Scholium (Wild, 303); cf. *ibid.,* IV, Definition 8, and Proposition 22; V, 41 (Wild, 288, 305, 397).

how it comprises man's final happiness and the eternity of his mind. The crux of Spinoza's ethical philosophy lies in the assertion that man *can* attain to the contemplation of God and that therefore he *can* pass from passion to action, from bondage to liberty and blessedness. He makes this assertion in a qualified way. Although in the present life we cannot completely transcend the passions, we can master them with at least the *major part* of our mind. The human mind may hope to obtain an unshakable foundation and a share of blessedness under present, temporal conditions. Spinoza re-examines the same three reasons previously adduced to show that the affective life of man is a mixed one, in order to demonstrate now that he can increase the scope of the active affects, through the power of reason.[31]

1. The fact that a man has *some* clear and distinct ideas is a pledge of his ability to develop still more such ideas, with the aid of philosophical method. Methodic intellectual progress is made by transforming our given confused ideas into adequate ones, after the pattern set by the *distinct ideas* already in our possession. The passage from confused to distinct ideas involves a *detachment* from reference to external causes and an *attachment* of the understanding to the eternal laws of its own nature. For Spinoza, this process of "inward conversion" is the foundation for a transformation of passions into actions, since what was previously done by the mind as an inadequate cause, is now performed by it as an adequate cause.

2. If it is true that every determination of finite being involves a negation, it is equally true that determinate finite things embody a positive expression of the divine power. The *self-affirmation* at the heart of our being is the *conatus,* which shares in the affirmative power of God's own self-affirmation. Like the Hobbesian individual in relation to the state, this endeavor can never be fully quenched or imprisoned by the passions. Under all circumstances, it retains its nisus of perseveration in being and acting. Although desire may display itself through confused ideas and the passional affects, it does not do so to its own satisfaction. Spinoza must now reinstate a kind of *intrinsic finality,* as a guarantee of the survival and orientation of the endeavor in man. Appetite or desire takes its own increase in perfection as the end, for the sake of which everything is done. The effort toward what supplies the maximum profit, viz., toward active

---

[31] *Ibid.,* V, 20, Scholium (Wild, 381–83).

understanding and adequate ideas, is a finite manifestation of the divine power itself. No matter how many external forces may over-awe and overwhelm the individual man, this internal impulse stubbornly continues to assert itself and seek progressive control over the passions and external deeds.

3. As crowning assurance, Spinoza recalls a major theme in his theory of knowledge: the doctrine of *the degrees of perception*.[32] This doctrine was never confined to the speculative domain: its secret ordination was always toward the ethical relief of man's estate. Its present application was skillfully prepared for through Spinoza's thoroughly intellectualized account of will, virtue, and the affects, especially the key remark that the prime difference between passive and active affects lies in one's state of knowledge. The four grades of perception enumerated in the treatise on method are reduced to three in the *Ethics:* opinion, reason, and intuitive knowledge. But under opinion, Spinoza includes the first two modes of perception listed in the previous classification, v.g., hearsay and what we gather through vague, uncriticized experience, memory, and imagination.

From an ethical standpoint, the defect of *opinionative* or *imaginative perception* lies in its partial view of man. It never rises above the common order of nature, the outlook dominated by contingency, chance, and determination by external causes. The passional affects are attitudes of mind and body proportioned to this fragmentary and even illusory conception of human nature and its operations. *Scientific reason,* the second grade of knowledge, subjects the opinions of sense and imagination to the mind's sifting process and hence begins to assert the proper activity of man. It reveals the common traits and necessary patterns present throughout the universe, thus proving that all modal entities are governed by the necessary, intrinsic laws of their own nature. This knowledge is true and adequate to the task of detaching the affects from the idea of an external cause. Reason, operating at this second level, can form clear and distinct ideas of the affects, taken in themselves, and hence can acquire greater power over them. The more we know their intrinsic nature and origin, the more we can control them and transform them from a passional to an active condition.

Scientific reason, however, still remains dependent upon external sources for its original data. With its aid, we might be able to frame

---

[32] *Ethics,* II, 40, Scholium 2 (Wild, 186–87; cf. above, note 2).

practical maxims for use in emergencies, but we could never achieve the maximal control over the passions that is open to us in this life. The latter is the gift of the third grade of knowledge, based wholly upon the mind itself and the intuitive exercise of reason. The *scientia intuitiva* grasps the divine attributes in themselves and proceeds to an a priori understanding of the essence of modal realities, including one's own affects. This accords with the requirements for the best way of defining uncreated and created things: to know God and the modal world by means of intuitive knowledge is to view reality *sub specie aeternitatis*. Insofar as our knowledge is of this sort, it contains the supremely clear and distinct ideas that make us the adequate causes of what we do. Since this is the condition for controlling the passions and developing the active affects, man is liberated by *scientia intuitiva* as much as he can be, within temporal existence, from servitude to the passions and the sway of fortune. Retrospectively, it can be seen that, unless such knowledge *were* within his grasp, Spinozistic man would be deprived, in this life, of the measure of stability and power upon which his *peace of mind* rests. This is the urgent practical motive behind Spinoza's earlier insistence that we have an adequate idea of God and can achieve an a priori and geometrically certain knowledge of Him.

This highest, intuitive knowledge gives birth to a *love directed toward God,* considered as an immutable and eternal object.[33] This love is not a passion but an active affect, since it springs from a perfect sort of knowledge of oneself in relation to the eternal order of nature. The mind is able to form an adequately clear and distinct idea of itself and its body, by viewing them intuitively and a priori in their eternal essence, as constituted by the eternal power and attributes of God. The mind rejoices in this perfect knowledge and refers the joy to God as its cause. Thus the definition of love is fulfilled at an eminent level, where the senses do not intervene and where the mind is serene in the face of the vicissitudes of temporal life. Hence the intuitive degree of knowledge is consummated in an intellectual love of God, *amor Dei intellectualis.* This love is just as eternal as the knowledge from which it springs. It furnishes the mind with an impregnable seat for controlling the passions, increasing the scope of the active affects, and thus achieving stable happiness in this life. Through our intellectual love of God, we become par-

---

[33] The doctrine on love of God is set forth in *Ethics,* V, 15-20 (Wild, 379-81).

takers in God's own love for Himself, insofar as He expresses Himself through the eternal essence of the human mind. But Spinoza's God loves men only in the sense that He loves Himself and makes *our* intellectual love for Him *a part of His* infinite love for His own nature, in all its aspects. There can be no distinctive love of God for us, since (on the definition of the active affects) this would involve an increase of perfection on God's part. Once more, the cleft of equivocal predication opens up between love as a human affect and God's love for Himself. Spinoza cannot accept St. John's sentence that God is caritative love, since he has no way of attributing such love to God without derogating from His infinite perfection.

Spinoza's entire methodology and metaphysics are ordered toward the outcropping of an eternal and intellectual love of God in time. This love is the most striking proof of the power of sovereign reason, operating according to its own laws, amid the passions, painful sadness, and misfortune of temporal existence. Fortified by his reflection upon the power of eternal substance, Spinoza brings the *Ethics* to a conclusion with this triumphant confession of faith: "Our salvation, or blessedness, or liberty consists in a constant and eternal love toward God, or in the love of God toward men."[34] Our intellectual love of God constitutes for us: salvation, blessedness, liberty, and eternity. Each of these notes deserves special analysis.

Spinoza's philosophy is for him a doctrine of *salvation*. It is a religious rationalism, bringing all the emotional power of the religious search to bear upon philosophical issues and, at the same time, transferring to philosophy the functions previously associated with religion. Our increase in knowledge, along with the corresponding moral ascesis or liberation from the passions, is a process of transforming our entire manner of being. Basically, it is a growth in understanding and the power of mind. Salvation comes from our moral advance, and the latter is acquired through a meditative, philosophical clarification of our ideas. Morality and philosophical reason thus appropriate the content of religion, insofar as it makes a truth-claim and seeks to save men. All that is left for *religion* — as distinct from the cultivation of reason and the active affects — is the practical work of encouraging us to seek personal perfection and social amity. Miracles,

[34] *Ibid.*, V, 35, Scholium (Wild, 392–93). R. McCall, "The Teleological Approach to Spinoza," *The New Scholasticism*, XVII (1943), 134–55, advises that an adequate evaluation of Spinoza must take account of his struggle to accommodate the idea of natural necessity to an ethicoreligious search after rebirth and social communion in God.

prophecy, revelation, and the supernatural are eliminated from an outlook that regards the universe as a rigidly determined and exhaustively expressive manifestation of God's power. Faith has nothing to do with the apprehension of *truth* but is confined to the inculcation of *piety* and *obedience*. Spinoza's *fides catholica* is a set of natural maxims about the existence and unity of God and our own duty of obedience.[35] It is recommended solely as a means of providing a minimal basis of practical agreement among all men. The Deists approved of this minimal code but made it the substance of their philosophy. For Spinoza, however, faith and philosophy are completely separate, the quest of truth being reserved for philosophy and natural reason.

At the outset of his treatise on method, Spinoza had stated that all men seek happiness or the possession of the highest good. He had also suggested that happiness would only be found in a knowledge of the union existing between mind and nature. Now, at the end of his investigation, he reaffirms this conviction in his statement that our *beatitude* comes from the love of God, insofar as it issues from the intuitive knowledge of God's attributes and their consequences in the modal world of *natura naturata*. Blessedness is not a reward for being virtuous but is, as the Stoics claimed, virtue itself. When we become aware that our endeavor is to persevere in our being as an eternal mode of God, power and virtue are perfected within us and comprise our beatitude. Blessedness is the peace of soul belonging to the wise man: it is indistinguishable from his hardwon wisdom.

Spinoza also revises the meaning of *liberty,* so that it can apply to man as well as God. Although he cannot accept the Stoic ideal of the free man in its original formulation, he does seek to reconcile it somehow with his own determinism. Insofar as man *acts,* in the pregnant sense of being an adequate cause, he is liberated from the passions and thus enjoys a negative freedom from external bondage. But he owes this liberation precisely to his unblinking recognition that, as a modal being, he is determined by God and hence is necessitated by another. The sole freedom available to us is just this lucid

consciousness of being inwardly determined by God and of doing
what He determines us to do. Whereas God has the *spontaneous
freedom* of the primitive power affirming its own substantial being
and all other things, the enlightened mind may acquire the *acquiescent
freedom* of being clearly aware of its inwardly necessitated mode of
being. Since this is an adequate knowledge, the mind comes to view
the necessary emanation of modes from God's eternal standpoint.
This insight into the wellspring of all determined being is an act
of love and our only true liberty.

Nevertheless, if freedom means no more than this, many aspects
of Spinoza's argument become unintelligible. A number of covert
admissions of another sort of freedom must be made, in order to
explain the return of man to God. This is evident in the mind's
turning away from imagination and its adherence to reason, as well
as in its deliberate replacement of inadequate ideas by clear and
distinct ones. Similarly, a positive measure of finite freedom is needed
to detach our affects from the idea of an external cause and to
concentrate attention upon our own nature. Spinoza gives a *retrospective* interpretation of these decisive conversions of soul, in accord
with his metaphysical principles. But in their own nature and
*original act,* they manifest a responsible and deliberate dominion
that surpasses the conduct of even a spiritual automaton, however
inwardly aware of its determination by an infinitely powerful cause.

Although Spinoza sometimes speaks in a popular way about the
*immortality of the soul,* his characteristic doctrine concerns the
*eternity of the mind.*[36] His position is not articulated with all desirable
clarity, and commentators are divided about its precise import. The
account in the *Ethics* is doubly complicated by the fact that Spinoza
wants to adjust his solution to his total system and also take a
critical stand toward the popular interest in personal survival. Significantly, he bases his argument for the eternity of the human mind
upon an analysis of the human body. The body can be regarded

[36] *Short Treatise on God, Man, and His Well-Being,* II, Preface, Chap. 22, and
Appendix 2 (Wild, 84–85 n., 86–93); *ibid.,* II, 23, 26 (A. Wolf's separate edition, 136–
37, 147); *Ethics,* V, 22–23, 40, Scholium (Wild, 384–85, 397). In the *Short Treatise,*
the soul is represented as being capable of looking either in the direction of the
perishing body (in which respect, the soul itself disappears at death) or of turning by
an act of love to the eternal, divine substance (in which respect, the soul undergoes a
spiritual rebirth or regeneration in eternal life). In the *Ethics,* an attempt is made to
demonstrate the mind's eternity, from the standpoint of the eternal essence of the
body itself. For a personalist criticism, cf. R. A. Tsanoff, "Pantheism and Personal Immortality," *The Rice Institute Pamphlet,* XL (1953), 1–23.

in two ways: either as a durationally existent, contingent arrangement of figure and motion or as the realization of an eternal, essential structure. Considered in the first way, the body has a limited duration and is perishable. Insofar as the human mind is the idea of this temporally existing, corporeal configuration, it is also perishable. Viewed in the second way or from the standpoint of eternity, however, the essence of the body is seen to flow with eternal necessity from God's essence. Correlatively, the idea expressive of the essence of the human body is an eternal mode of thought and appertains necessarily to the essence of the human mind. Hence there is an eternal aspect of the human mind which is not subject to temporal duration and dissolution. Spinoza concludes that "this something" (*hoc aliquid*) must have an eternal existence precisely as an eternal mode of thinking and an integral part of the infinite intellect or mode of God's attribute of thought.

In the Spinozistic system, there is no "personal survival," as this term is commonly understood. Spinoza eliminates the question of survival entirely, in the sense of a prolongation of the conditions of durational or temporal existence. For, his point is that our eternity (like our blessedness) belongs to us here and now, as soon as we cease to rely upon imagination and its standpoint of existence-as-duration. The mind is eternalized in the degree that it attains the *scientia intuitiva* and thus learns to view its own nature as an eternal expression of the divine attribute of thought, within the modal totality of the infinite intellect. Since the philosophically instructed mind can make the transition even now from *existence-as-duration* to *existence-as-eternity*, it is even now capable of gaining its eternity. In the process of eternalization, the contingent and temporal features of the mind are reduced to the status of deficiencies in the imaginative outlook. Hence after death, there will remain none of the empirical memories and durational experiences of our contingent life. Some individual, modal traits may share in the rebirth to eternity, but the integral personal self of our temporal experience is exchanged for a *hoc aliquid*, which is a subsumed part of the infinite intellect.

The doctrine on the eternity of the mind shows that Spinoza overcomes the Cartesian *horizontal* dualism of two co-ordinated sub-substances in man, only to fall victim to a *vertical* dualism of imagination and reason, durational and eternal existence. "Eternity cannot be defined by time or have any relationship to it. Nevertheless we feel and know by experience that we are eternal."[37] The nature of this quasi-mystical, experiential feeling does not become a direct subject of analysis for Spinoza. It cannot be identified with the lowest degree of perception but is rather a way of expressing the burning faith in the power and reality of eternal substance which permeates all his philosophy. The doctrine on the attributes and modes is an attempt to state geometrically how something other than this unique substance can exist. At the end of the systematic explanation, however, Spinoza admits that the approach of his a priori rationalism to the problem of the one and the many leaves us with no analogical mode of predication between the eternal one and the temporal many. Mind may eternalize itself and gain a new life in this system, but it does so at the cost of denying a relationship between time and eternity, considered as distinct and real ways of existing on the part of finite persons and the infinite person.

## SUMMARY OF CHAPTER 6

How can the human mind gain the highest conceivable union with God? Spinoza begins his philosophical quest after happiness with this leading question. It supposes both that we are now deprived of this union and that it lies within our power to achieve it. The union with God is absent, insofar as we view ourselves and the world through the eyes of imagination and the common order of nature. Methodic, intellectual discipline is needed, therefore, in order to detach ourselves from inadequate cognitions (which stand for our temporal duration, contingency, and finite freedom) and attach ourselves to a superior kind of knowledge (which reveals the eternal and necessary power of God as constitutive of our own being). True philosophy must make the order and connection of ideas mirror exactly the order and connection of things. Hence Spinoza opens his metaphysics with the self-affirmation of the divine substance as cause of itself. His entire explanation of the attributes of God and the procession of the modal world is a bold essay at capturing in philosophical thought the creative power and causal order of the unique, divine substance itself. Human nature must be remade in conformity with this standpoint of eternity, which treats man as a finite union of mind and body, i.e., as a correspondence between two finite modes of the infinite attributes of thought and extension. This view of man is intended not only to eliminate the Cartesian dualism of substances but also to facilitate the moral return to God. The more the mind meditates upon the eternal order of necessary causes, the more is it enabled to transform its passions into active affects and thus increase its power and virtue. Following its proper *conatus*, the

---

[37] *Ethics,* V, 23, Scholium (Wild, 385).

mind feeds upon the intuitive vision of God and gives expression to an intellectual love of God. Thereby, it undergoes a rebirth to the eternity of its own essential nature as a part of the infinite intellect.

## BIBLIOGRAPHICAL NOTE

1. *Sources.* The critical edition of Spinoza's *Opera* was prepared by C. Gebhardt (4 vols., Heidelberg, Winter, 1925). English translations: *The Principles of Descartes' Philosophy,* translated by H. H. Britan (Chicago, Open Court, 1905) — also includes *Metaphysical Thoughts; Short Treatise on God, Man, and His Well-Being,* translated by A. Wolf (London, Black, 1910) (also includes Wolf's *Life of Spinoza*); *The Chief Works of Benedict De Spinoza,* translated by R. H. M. Elwes (originally published in 2 vols., London, Bell, 1883; the two volumes are bound together in a reprint edition, New York, Dover, 1951) — contains: *Theologico-Political Treatise, A Political Treatise, On the Improvement of the Understanding, Ethics,* and *Selected Correspondence; The Correspondence of Spinoza,* translated by A. Wolf (New York, Dial Press, 1928). In his edition of *Spinoza Selections* (New York, Scribner, 1930), J. Wild used the best existing translations (Elwes translation of *On the Improvement of the Understanding,* selections from the Wolf translations of the *Short Treatise* and *Correspondence,* and the W. H. White version of the *Ethics*), but a new translation of the entire corpus is long overdue.

2. *Studies.* Along with Wolf's *Life of Spinoza* (in his edition of the *Short Treatise*), one may consult *The Oldest Biography of Spinoza,* edited and translated by A. Wolf (London, Allen and Unwin, 1927), which contains the French text and English translation of the *Life* probably written by J. M. Lucas in 1678 and first published in 1719. Important biographical and philosophical findings were made by S. von Dunin-Borkowski, S.J.: *Der junge De Spinoza* (Münster, Aschendorff, 1910), and *Aus den Tagen Spinozas* (4 vols., Münster, Aschendorff, 1933–1936). His researches are summarized in the first part of P. Siwek, S.J., *Spinoza et le panthéisme religieux* (new ed., Paris, Desclée, 1950), which is an excellent general account and Thomistic critique. Other reliable introductions are: R. McKeon, *The Philosophy of Spinoza* (New York, Longmans, Green, 1928); L. Roth, *Spinoza* (London, Benn, 1929); S. Hampshire, *Spinoza* (Baltimore, Penguin Books, 1952). H. Wolfson's *The Philosophy of Spinoza* (2 vols., Cambridge, Mass., Harvard University Press, 1934; one-volume ed., 1948) is invaluable for the medieval Jewish background but the references to Aristotle and Aquinas are to be used with caution; D. Bidney's *The Psychology and Ethics of Spinoza* (New Haven, Yale University Press, 1940) makes some acute dialectical observations but lacks historical scholarship. Concerning Spinoza's *On the Healing of the Understanding,* see H. H. Joachim, *Spinoza's Tractatus De Intellectus Emendatione, A Commentary* (Oxford, Clarendon, 1940), and A. Darbon, *Études Spinozistes* (Paris, Presses Universitaires, 1946). Joachim's approach is philological, analytic, and idealistic, tending to reduce Spinoza to the

rank of a forerunner of Hegel; Darbon shows a keen appreciation of the problem of method and the theory of the eternal mind of man. The latter theme is the point of departure for H. F. Hallet's *Aeternitas, A Spinozistic Study* (Oxford, Clarendon, 1930), which, as the author remarks, is not a strict exposition of Spinoza but an essay inspired largely by Spinozistic notions. For a general analysis of the *Ethics,* consult H. H. Joachim, *A Study of the Ethics of Spinoza* (Oxford, Clarendon, 1901). R. L. Saw, *The Vindication of Metaphysics: A Study in the Philosophy of Spinoza* (London, Macmillan, 1951), restates his metaphysics in terms of modern linguistic analysis and defends it on practical grounds. J. Ratner's *Spinoza on God* (New York, Holt, 1930) explains the role of God in the Spinozistic system, whereas P. Lachièze-Rey's *Les origines cartésiennes du Dieu de Spinoza* (Paris, Alcan, 1932) explores the delicate problem of the relation between Descartes and Spinoza on this point. Further comparisons are made by L. Roth in his brief essay, *Spinoza, Descartes and Maimonides* (Oxford, Clarendon, 1924); the references to Maimonides, Crescas, and other medieval Jewish sources can be better understood with the aid of I. Husik, *A History of Mediaeval Jewish Philosophy* (Philadelphia, Jewish Publication Society, 1941). R. A. Duff, *Spinoza's Ethical and Political Philosophy* (Glasgow, Maclehose, 1903), shows the continuity between the metaphysical and practical portions of Spinoza's thought. The *Spinoza Dictionary,* edited by D. D. Runes (New York, Philosophical Library, 1951), contains excerpts from the Elwes translation and Wolf's edition of the *Short Treatise;* it is useful for making a first acquaintance with Spinoza's use of terms. A radical criticism of Spinoza through the epistemological crevice is made by G. H. R. Parkinson, *Spinoza's Theory of Knowledge* (Oxford, Clarendon Press, 1954).

3. *Further Publications.* A. G. Wernham has edited Spinoza, *The Political Works* (Oxford, Clarendon Press, 1958), consisting of the full text and translation of the *Tractatus Politicus,* a part of the text of the *Tractatus Theologico-Politicus* and its translation, and a highly informative analysis of Spinoza's political position. H. F. Hallett underlines the basis in experience for Spinoza's general outlook in *Benedict De Spinoza: The Elements of His Philosophy* (Fair Lawn, N. J., Essential Books, 1957), whereas C. J. Sullivan points out a deep split between Spinoza's eternal and naturalistic views of man in *Critical and Historical Reflections on Spinoza's "Ethics"* (Berkeley and Los Angeles, University of California Press, 1958).

# Chapter 7. LEIBNIZ

## I. LIFE AND WRITINGS

BORN at Leipzig in 1646, Gottfried Wilhelm Leibniz had the advantages of comfortable circumstances and an intellectual environment. Although his father (who was a professor of moral philosophy at the University of Leipzig) died when his son was only six years old, the child had full access to the excellent family library. Teaching himself Latin, Leibniz read omnivorously in classical history, literature, and philosophy. He familiarized himself with Plato, Aristotle, and several of the later Scholastics. All his days, Leibniz remained basically a self-taught mind, even though he underwent a complete academic education. He entered the University of Leipzig in 1661 and prepared a remarkable *Metaphysical Disputation on the Principle of the Individual* (1663) for his bachelor's degree. This essay manifested his wide acquaintance with Suarez and other Scholastics, as well as his early preoccupation with a central problem in his later philosophy: the nature of the individual. After taking the master's degree at Leipzig, Leibniz continued his legal studies and presented himself for the doctorate in law. Since Leipzig refused to grant him this degree, because of his youth, he went to the University of Altorf. There, he was not only awarded the doctor's degree for a brilliant dissertation, *On Perplexing Cases in Law* (1666), but was also invited to take a professorship. His refusal of this position indicated his desire to participate in practical matters and affairs of state rather than to devote himself professionally to the teaching of philosophy and jurisprudence. He did publish a *Dissertation on the Art of Combination* (1666), which set forth his project for a universal set of symbols, by the combination of which all philosophical problems could be solved with mathematical exactitude. This plan reflected his enthusiasm after spending a semester at Jena in mathematical studies. But he balanced this work with a treatise on jurisprudence, which won the attention of the influential Baron Johan von Boineburg, a councilor of the Elector of Mainz. With the Baron's aid, Leibniz secured a post with the Elector. He soon aided his employer's political cause with a demonstration *ordine geometrico* that the Elector's candidate, and no other, was fitted to be chosen King of Poland!

In 1672, Leibniz was sent on a diplomatic mission to Paris. His task was to distract Louis XIV from an attack on Holland and the Germanies by dangling before him the alternative of a glorious conquest of Egypt. The interview with the French king was never obtained but Leibniz profited in an intellectual way by his visit. He took a side trip to England, in order to establish scientific contacts. Back in Paris, he agreed with Malebranche and Arnauld that the Cartesian mathematical method was valuable, and yet added that Descartes' mechanistic physics stultified scientific research. Leibniz received expert guidance on mathematical problems from the great physicist, Christian Huyghens, and by 1676 he had worked out the calculus. Although he reached his conclusions quite independently of Newton, there was an unfortunate controversy, twenty years later, over the question of priority between Newton and Leibniz. While still in Paris, Leibniz transferred his services to the Duke of Brunswick-Lüneburg. On his way to the ducal court at Hanover, he paid a visit (1676) to Spinoza and copied some notes from the manuscript of the *Ethics*. Leibniz always respected Spinoza's metaphysical vision but sought to provide metaphysics with a more rigorous method of demonstration and to defend the freedom of God and the personal immortality of the human soul.

At Hanover, Leibniz served as librarian and historian of the House of Brunswick. He was indefatigable in tracing down genealogical lines, ransacking archives in several countries for the early history of the House, and defending its claims on historical and legal grounds. Yet he also found time to engage in correspondence with Bossuet and Arnauld concerning the reunion of Catholic and Protestant Churches, to invent a calculating machine for extracting root numbers, and to encourage the foundation of learned societies in the European capitols. He himself founded and was the first lifetime president of the Prussian Academy of Sciences at Berlin; he also founded the first learned journal in the Germanies: *Acta Eruditorum* (1682). His philosophical writings were somehow fitted into this busy schedule, although most of them were short notes, incidental papers, and outlines sent to correspondents. The *Discourse on Metaphysics* (1686) probably originated as part of the preface to a projected work aiming at the reunion of the churches. In the *New Essays concerning the Human Understanding* (completed in 1704 but laid aside at Locke's death; published, 1765), Leibniz made a careful analysis of Locke's empiricism and pointed to the active role of the understanding and its native ideas. In reply to Bayle's challenge that the goodness and power of God cannot be reconciled rationally, in view of evil, Leibniz composed his *Essays on Theodicy* (1710). He summarized his philosophy for a princely correspondent in *Principles of Nature and Grace* (1714) and especially in *The Monadology* (German translation published, 1720; French original published, 1840), which restated his fundamental views in terms of monads. Leibniz was engaged in a polemical correspondence with the English Newtonian, Samuel Clarke, concerning Newton's doctrine on space and time, when death put a halt to his work (1716). He had not been permitted to come to England in 1714 for the coronation of George I, of the House of Brunswick, because of his controversies with English scholars. His death went uncommemorated at home but a suitable eulogy was pronounced by Fontenelle before the French Academy.

## 2. A UNIVERSAL SCIENCE AND UNIVERSAL HARMONY

Leibniz' philosophical interests are so far-flung and his influence upon later developments so varied that it is difficult to hold his thought in proper focus. He has been hailed as a forerunner of symbolic logic, as a metaphysical genius, and as a religious apologist. These facets, and many more, are essential to the understanding of his mind. In order to obtain a principle of orderly interpretation of his work, we may pay heed to his own compendious statement that happiness depends upon knowledge of the nature of God and the soul, whereas this knowledge depends in turn upon the ability to demonstrate by means of a method of certainty. Leibniz was convinced of the solidarity between the *love of God,* the *promotion of human welfare,* and the *perfecting of reason.* These goals were the main ones that enlisted his energies, and he felt that if they could not all be promoted together, there would be a relapse of Western culture into barbarism. Philosophy has an ultimately religious and moral orientation in that it directs the mind to contemplation and love of God, along with a well-ordered relationship with one's fellow men. But there is no conflict between this exalted end and a conscientious regard for temporal problems, both practical and theoretical. The reconciliation of piety and reason is a basic premise of the efforts of Leibniz. Reason is able to offer strict demonstration of the basic metaphysical truths, but it can do so only with the help of a sound method. Mathematics provides the tools for over-hauling our logical techniques and assures a uniform rigor in all our inquiries. These are familiar themes in the seventeenth century, but they are given a vigorous and subtle development by Leibniz.

Beginning with his early writings and persisting to the end of his career, there is a dual leitmotiv that provides the organizing principle of his speculations: the foundation of a *universal science* (*scientia generalis*) and the elucidation and defense of the *universal harmony of being*. Leibniz' mathematical and logical studies are polarized around the former purpose, his metaphysical and ethico-religious studies around the latter. The relation between these two basic themes is one of mutual support and confirmation, rather than of conflict. The universal science is to provide the logical groundwork, without which all discussion about universal harmony would be mere loose dreaming, whereas the theory of universal harmony is to insure the relevance of consistent thinking for the real world. Together, these twin guideposts are to lead to a philosophy that is both rigorously constructed and fruitfully engaged in searching out the meaning of actual entities.

Even as a schoolboy, Leibniz was fascinated by Aristotle's teaching on the categories. For here was a classification that claimed to account for all our concepts and simple terms. Leibniz wanted to enlarge the boundaries of categorization, by working out the funda-mental classification of all judgments as well as concepts, so that all our thoughts could be derived from a few basic elements. Further-more, he sought to place the categorization of thoughts upon a sound, mathematical footing. Descartes had entertained a similar plan but — in Leibniz' estimation — had abandoned it, in the course of his actual attempts at physical and metaphysical analysis. Leibniz agreed with Descartes on two main points: that the human mind can elaborate a *common scientific method,* in abstraction from the content of the particular sciences, and that *analysis* and *synthesis* must be employed in constructing this common logic of the sciences. But he claimed originality on three further scores. (1) Analysis is to be brought to bear, not merely upon the ideas resident in the individual, introspective mind, but also upon the actual findings of the sciences. Hence Leibniz emphasized the need to make a *complete inventory* of our reliable knowledge, in order to provide the best materials for analysis. (2) Descartes had left in obscurity the type of order obtaining among the elements or simple natures, in which his analysis terminated. Leibniz agreed that it would be desirable to be able to arrange the analytic elements according to a natural order, but at least we can treat them as *components in a calculus or system of combination.* (3) The work of combining the elementary units of thought, in order to recompose the totality of our thoughts and discover new truths, is to be facilitated by assigning to every elementary object its *characteristic symbol* or number. From a combination or synthesis of these symbols, complex truths can be derived. "If we could find characters or signs appropriate for expressing all our thoughts as definitely and exactly as arithmetic expresses numbers or geometric analysis expresses lines, we could in all subjects *in so far as they are amenable to reasoning* accomplish what is done in Arithmetic and Geometry."[1] Leibniz was specially enthusiastic about the prospects for this universal language or *characteristica universalis.*

Once the content of human knowledge is gathered together in a Baconian sort of encyclopedia of truths, the operation of *analysis* or resolution can begin. Its aim is to reduce complex judgments and concepts to simpler ones, until at last the mind arrives at a "catalogue of simple thoughts . . . a kind of alphabet of human thoughts."[2] These analytically irreducible elements constitute a set of *primitive terms* and *universal principles,* which provide the groundwork of all scientific knowledge. These few primitive terms and principles are certain, and not merely hypothetical; they do not depend on any prior noetic conditions, but are known *per se.* Since they have been drawn from orderly bodies of knowledge, we can treat them as components in a system of combinations. This enables us to employ

[1] *Preface to the General Science* (*Leibniz Selections,* edited by P. Wiener, 15); cf. *Towards a Universal Characteristic* (Wiener, 17–25). The mathematical realism of this method is brought out in *Dialogue on the Connection between Things and Words* (Wiener, 6–11). Quotations from *Leibniz Selections* are made with the permission of Charles Scribner's Sons.

[2] *On Wisdom* (Wiener, 80); *Towards a Universal Characteristic* (Wiener, 20). The analytic discovery of basic terms and principles is outlined in two essays: *Precepts for advancing the Sciences and Arts* and *The Art of Discovery* (Wiener, 29–46, 50–58). In connection with Leibniz' criticism of Raymond Lull (*ibid.,* 53), see the description of the combinatory projects of Lull and other medieval thinkers given by E. W. Platzeck, O.F.M., "Die Lullsche Kombinatorik," *Franziskanische Studien,* XXXIV (1953), 32–60,

the methods of mathematical calculus, in working out the universal science or general logic of the sciences.

The *synthetic* or combinational aspect of the new method is greatly aided by the substitution of universally accepted signs or characteristics for the basic categories of thought. Once the alphabet of thoughts is fixed in a set of symbols, Leibniz augured that the work of synthesis will become just as infallible as the combining of letters into words, and of words into phrases and sentences. At least in his early writings, he gave special preference to numerical symbols. Number is a sort of basic metaphysical form, because everything (including our concepts and judgments) can be subsumed under it. Later on, as his logical studies developed, he broadened his conception of the symbolic notations to be employed in the combinational calculus. But whatever the symbols, their use is advantageous. They fix the meaning of a term in a definite way, aid the memory, relieve the mind of excessive dependence upon its visualizing power, and reduce the incidence of controversies. Disputes can be settled by suggesting: "Gentlemen, let us calculate." Submission of issues to the impersonal and unequivocal test of symbolic calculation not only achieves a settlement, but also reveals errors of reasoning just as visibly and easily in metaphysical, as in mathematical, questions. Similar claims have been made by some exponents of symbolic logic, in our day.

Leibniz was interested, not only in constructing a universal logical method, but also in employing it for the discovery of philosophical truths. Hence he was concerned about the relation between the results of a combination of characteristics and the real world. He did not claim that the *isolated* symbols have any representative function or that they are natural signs of things. But he did hold that the symbolical notations are not arbitrary in their *relation of combination* with one another.[3] In their mutual connections, they are regulated by the order of our ideas and, ultimately, by the natural order of the things expressed in ideas. Because of this objective reference of the order among formal symbols, it is easy to explain, for instance, how it is possible in mathematics to reach the same conclusion through the use of different systems of notations. A common result can be obtained, because of a common relation of the several sets of signs to the order and connection of concepts and things. *Truth* is based

<hr>

[3] *Dialogue on the Connection between Things and Words* (Wiener, 10-11).

upon the relationship that a system of characters bears toward things in their interconnectedness. Symbolical combinations express natural relations among our basic categorial concepts and among the things to which those concepts ultimately refer, in the real world. Hence Leibniz regarded his *scientia generalis* as a system of the fundamental concepts common to all the sciences, and not merely as a formal calculus of terms and propositions.

A distinction must be made, however, between the use of the common logical method in the more speculative fields and its use in the more practical fields of study. In *speculative* sciences, it is enough to have the primitive terms and principles, together with the new art of combination and discovery, in order to guide experimental work and arrive at remote conclusions. Even in matters which require some basis in experience, theory can anticipate practice, provided only that the experimental findings can be given some kind of rational explanation. The role of observation and experiment can never be completely eliminated from speculative studies, and it is given special prominence in the *practical* disciplines. In matters of personal and public policy, Leibniz bids us look with suspicion upon bare rational inference, unsupported by experimental findings. The same standard of certainty cannot be required in ethical and political problems as in mathematics or metaphysics, since we must make practical decisions on the basis of the more likely opinion. But the use of a scientific method can guide our determination of what is, in fact, the more likely opinion. Leibniz suggests that a theory of ethical and legal probability can be made just as reliable and objective as the statistical approach to games of chance and insurance risks, with the aid of a suitable symbolical language. Moral certitude can be obtained, not only from the testimony of human witnesses, but also from the logically calculated likelihood of events and consequences of practical decisions.

In attempting to realize this ideal of a universal science, Leibniz was soon confronted with three serious difficulties. (1) Like Bacon, he found that it lies beyond the power of an individual man to make an *adequate collection* of the materials of knowledge. Since Leibniz himself did not have the encyclopedia of knowledge at hand, he could not supply a sufficiently broad basis for the analytic phase of the logical method. His constant interest in the welfare of learned societies and journals indicated his hope that co-operative labor might eventually supply the materials for a comprehensive analysis. (2) But even granted the success of an encyclopedic project, analysis itself supposes the presence of a determinate set of elementary terms and real definitions, so that the analytic process can be terminated. Leibniz began by sharing the assumption of Bacon and Descartes that the number of simple terms is *finite*. His scientific studies and his metaphysical account of real substances soon convinced him, however, that their number is *infinite*. Since the number of primitive indefinable ideas and real definitions is infinite, the resolutive analysis can never be completed by our minds. It follows that the primitive terms reached by Leibniz' new art of discovery are not primary in an absolute way, but only in relation to the finite mind. (3) Finally, analysis can never completely *isolate* the basic terms and definitions. This is not due to any purely logical obstacle but to the interrelatedness of the beings in the universe to which our thoughts and categorial terms ultimately refer. Because an unconditionally primitive set of terms cannot be reached and given in isolation, the conditions are not present for a perfectly comprehensive process of synthesis or combination.

These considerations forced Leibniz to modify his claims for the universal logical method. But he never abandoned the ideal of a common logic of the sciences. From the inability of logical analysis to secure its own foundations with complete satisfaction, it does not follow that the search for a general logic of the sciences is futile. The only legitimate inference is that the human mind cannot make a purely *logical* founding of knowledge. Hence Leibniz set about integrating his methodological requirements with a general *metaphysical* outlook, so that the universal science might be as well founded as is humanly possible.

Leibniz sought this foundation in God and the principle of harmony. The only way we can have a priori assurance that the interconnected ideas (upon which our basic terms rest) are themselves in conformity with the interconnected universe of things is by reference to God. He is the *common creator* both of things and of our ideas of things. In creating the real order, He had regard for their conformity with the ideas to be communicated to our minds, whereas in furnishing our minds with the primitive set of ideas, He also had regard for their conformity with real things. Hence the process of logical analysis terminates properly in the primitive ideas, considered precisely as having their foundation in the divine intellect.[4] Even though the number of primitive indefinables be infinite, we can be sure that those which terminate our analytic resolution, do express the real relations obtaining among things. Furthermore, since God has *respect for the ideal of universal harmony* in his production of both the real things and their signs in our minds, we may achieve some systematic comprehensiveness and rigor, by regulating our finite set of terms and definitions according to the exigencies of this same ideal. In this way, at least a reliable approach can be made to the establishment of the universal method or common logic of all the sciences.

Leibniz did not have to cut the metaphysics of harmony hurriedly out of whole cloth. Already in his earliest writings, he evinced great sympathy toward the references of Platonic writers to the *principle of universal harmony*. He defined it tersely as "unity-in-variety," and added that "the greater the unity-in-variety, the greater is the harmony."[5] Harmony provided an answer to the *problem of the one and the many,* which Leibniz posed at all levels of his philosophy. The human individual is aware of his own abiding identity and also of the ceaseless succession of his perceptions: this is the psychological way of viewing the tension between the one and the many, being and becoming. The individual's perception reaches out to the bodies in the universe which are many and yet bound together, both by their inclusion in the same cosmos and by their common presence in the individual's consciousness. Moreover, if the universe is produced by God, the difficulty arises of reconciling the infinite simplicity of the first cause and the infinite multitude of its effects. In the moral order, we are asked to acquire the stability of virtue and a unified character, so that we will not become confused and disintegrated in the face of the bewildering number of situations and evils of life. Even the logical enterprise is an attempt to bring to the several sciences the unity of method and a common formal structure. Confronted with these various aspects of the problem of the one and the many, Leibniz felt that the notion of harmony alone could provide an adequate synthesis, capable of

---

[4] *What is an Idea?* (Wiener, 282–83); cf. P. Wiener, "Notes on Leibniz' Conception of Logic and its Historical Context," *The Philosophical Review,* XLVIII (1939), 567–86.

[5] *The Elements of True Piety* (G. W. Leibniz, *Textes inédits,* edited by G. Grua, I, 12); cf. *The Monadology,* 58–59 (Wiener, 544–45).

avoiding the extremes of Spinoza's monism and Gassendi's unbridled pluralism.

Harmony is impossible, if everything is reduced to the one or dispersed in the many. For it is nothing other than a *unity of order and relation among many factors*, a *diversity tempered by a certain identity*. Mathematics supplied a hint of the fertile power of harmony through the method of universals, employed successfully by Descartes and Pascal. They discovered certain harmonies or proportional similarities among figures hitherto regarded as quite unrelated, and in this way established a general idea for solving problems in several fields. The same technique could be used in physical questions, since the closer one studies nature, the more one sees it to be geometrical. But Leibniz did not accept a purely mathematical interpretation of nature, since he saw that mathematical principles cannot be *applied* to nature without first having recourse to a metaphysical explanation. He agreed with Galileo that the extension of mathematics to nature can be made with assurance only because *God* is "a perfect Geometer,"[6] the creator who produces things in accordance with the standards of harmony. Thus God supplies the fundamental link between harmony and the view that real, natural being is intelligible in a mathematical way. The project of a universal characteristic is fundamentally possible, because God has made all things according to number and harmony. The Leibnizian art of discovery receives its guarantee of objective validity for existential propositions, through its connection with the metaphysics of harmony.

Taken in the most general way, the idea of harmony is the *seminal source of the major doctrines* that control Leibniz' speculation. The close relation between harmony and intelligibility is a preparation for connecting harmony and essence. In seeking out the harmonies of the universe, philosophy is also bringing to light the essences or reasons of things. Confidence in the ultimate intelligibility of things and their availability to the a priori art of discovery supposes that every being has its *raison d'être*, or sufficient reason, grounded in its own essence. But there is nothing static about the Leibnizian conception of essence. Each essence is a center of striving after existence in its own right. In this respect, the role of harmony is to secure the existence of the greatest amount of essence that is possible. The principle of perfection or plenitude states that our universe

---

[6] *On a General Principle, Useful for the Explanation of Laws and Nature* (Wiener, 66).

contains the greatest possible amount of essential perfection. But this maximum is reached only because the claims to existence on the part of a certain number of essences have been reconciled in a harmonious system of compossible being. That the world is made in accordance with the ideal of harmony means, therefore, that it secures as great a variety of essential natures as is compatible with the greatest possible order. The endeavor of an essence for a foothold in the existential world is carried to fruition, only when a harmonious composition can be made between this endeavor and the possibilities of other striving essences. That is why, for Leibniz, *to exist* means *to be integrated harmoniously with other things* in a relation of mutual fitness and essential fullness or perfection. Existence signifies the effective entrance of an essence into the conditions of harmony governing the world.

Nevertheless, Leibniz does not want to erect harmony into an autonomous, impersonal, cosmic principle. It is basically an expression of God's own understanding and (in respect to the existing order) of His will. The essential intelligibility and the plenitude of the actual world are due to the fact that God creates things freely, in the light of His own wisdom or standard of harmony. Hence God is the radical seat of harmony, the *ultimate principle of reconciliation* of life's antagonisms. For this reason, Leibniz is confident about a final synthesis of the great dualisms that enliven his thought. Nature can be interpreted both mechanistically and teleologically; the order of phenomena is well founded in the order of being; mind and body are discrete and yet compose in a unity; the microcosm and the macrocosm are mutually proportioned; the kingdom of nature and the kingdom of grace enclose each other. These eirenic theses, so characteristic of Leibniz' approach to theoretical and practical problems alike, derive their logical force and coherence from his metaphysical conviction that the universe is conspiring toward a harmonious totality of being, under the dynamic governance of divine wisdom and will.

## 3. FIRST PRINCIPLES AND INDIVIDUAL SUBSTANCE

Of all the great seventeenth-century rationalists, Leibniz was the most concerned about establishing the foundations of knowledge in a formal way. He saw that the ideal of constructing a comprehensive and yet ontologically relevant system cannot be executed, until the basic principles have been secured beyond doubt. His studies in this fundamental area were marshaled around three universal *principles governing all essences and existences* (the principles of sufficient reason, contradiction, and contingency or perfection), and two *principles regulative of the actual universe* (the principles of the identity of indiscernibles and continuity). From these primary truths, most of the leading conceptions in his philosophy can be derived. And since the import of his principles is real as well as ideal, their examination also involves a study of *individual substance,* which supplies their point of insertion in the actual world.

## Leibniz' Basic Principles

1. Sufficient reason: the ground of all true propositions and of the intelligibility of things.

2. Contradiction and identity: the laws determining all true propositions which express necessary truths, through a finite, terminative analysis.

3. Contingency or perfection: the law determining all true propositions which express contingent truths, through an infinite, nonterminative analysis.

(Note: These first principles govern true propositions about all possible worlds and our actual world. The actual universe is a plenum of individual substances, the best possible world, conforming to the following principles.)

4. Identity of indiscernibles: a world of many qualitatively different individual substances, arranged in a graduated scale or hierarchy.

5. Continuity: there are no gaps or interruptions in this hierarchy of actual beings.

Every aspect of thought and reality is governed by the *principle of sufficient reason. Nihil est sine ratione:* nothing is without a sufficient reason — Leibniz hails this as the grandest axiom of his entire system. In its most general logical form, this principle states that the predicate is contained analytically in the subject of every true proposition. "The content of the subject must always include that of the predicate in such a way that if one understands perfectly the concept of the subject, he will know that the predicate appertains to it also."[7] At least in principle, every true proposition is analytic in its logical foundation, so that the predicate can be shown to be

---

[7] *Discourse on Metaphysics,* VIII (Wiener, 300); cf. the texts gathered under the heading: *The Principle of Sufficient Reason* (Wiener, 93–96).

contained analytically in the concept of the subject. This is the foundation of our conviction in the radical intelligibility of the universe and of our solid hope that systematic explanation of things is possible, through a universal characteristic. Leibniz sometimes refers to it as the principle that a reason must be furnished (*principium rationis reddendae*), since a reason is supplied by manifesting the analytic connection between the concepts of predicate and subject.

Although the principle of sufficient reason regulates all true propositions, it does not furnish specific directions for determining which propositions are, in fact, true. Leibniz noticed that, in its actual operation, human reason employs two different ways of establishing the truth or analytic character of propositions, depending upon what is being expressed in the propositions.[8] Some propositions express *necessary truths* or *truths of essence,* the contradictory opposite of which is absolutely impossible. In determining that propositions belong to this class of truths, the mind can employ a finite sort of analysis. Every *finite analysis* is *terminative.* Demonstration of the truth is made through a limited number of steps, reducing complex propositions to simpler ones and eventually terminating in some primitive, irreducible principles and ideas. The connection among the primitive ideas, to which the complex proposition has been reduced, is immediately seen either to involve a contradiction or to be self-coherent. Hence the process of finite or terminative analysis is regulated by the *principle of contradiction,* with which Leibniz regularly associates what he calls the *principle of identity.* Every finitely or terminatively analytic proposition is known to be true, according to the principle of contradiction. For any proposition seen to involve a contradiction is known to be false, and whatever is opposed to the false is true. The primary principles themselves are identical propositions, in which the analytic inclusion of the predicate in the concept of the subject is immediately evident.

But another process of analytic reduction is needed, in the case of propositions expressive of *contingent truths* or *truths of fact and existence.* For here, the contradictory opposite of the proposition is not absolutely impossible, in the sense of involving a logical con-

---

[8] *Discourse on Metaphysics,* XIII (Wiener, 305–09); *The Monadology,* 31–38 (Wiener, 539–40). For a discussion of the views of Couturat, Russell, and other logicians on Leibniz' first principles, together with a defense of the independence of the principle of contingency or perfection, read N. Rescher, "Contingence in the Philosophy of Leibniz," *The Philosophical Review,* LXI (1952), 26–39.

tradiction. The truth of such propositions can never be established by a finite analysis, relying solely upon the principle of contradiction, since they concern the sphere of contingent, existential facts, where the number of states or details is infinite. Two questions faced Leibniz, in regard to propositions containing truths of fact: (1) how are such propositions shown to be true; (2) can they express a contingent truth and still agree with the analytic requirements laid down by the principle of sufficient reason for all true propositions? He found an answer to both questions in the *principle of contingency or perfection,* which he also called the *principle of existence* and the *principle of the best.* This principle governs the mind, when it is forced to make an *infinite* or *nonterminative analysis* of a proposition containing matters of fact or existence. Some truths can be ascertained in this latter domain, by adverting to the law that God creates things according to His standard of choosing the maximum amount of perfection or the best possible world. Although the finite mind cannot reduce existential propositions to the point where their relation of compatibility or incompatibility with the principle of contradiction is evident, it can at least make an indirect demonstration of the analytic inclusion of the predicate in the concept of the subject. For, it can show that the contradictory opposite of such a proposition would, indeed, involve a violation of God's standard of promoting the most perfection or what is best. In a positive way, the truth of a proposition about contingent matters is established by determining that the perfection of the world or the maximum quantity of essence is promoted more by the inclusion of this particular predicate in its subject than by any other one.

Such an analytic process is infinite or nonterminative, from the human standpoint. Although the divine mind can see the direct inclusion of the predicate of an existential proposition in the concept of its subject, we can only see their *convergence.* We approach analytic insight as a mathematical limit, by appealing to the principle of contingency or perfection, as regulative of God's choice of the actual facts and existential conditions prevailing in the world. Thus we can know indirectly *that* the analytic inclusion of predicate in subject does obtain, even though the connection itself escapes our direct gaze. This is sufficient to satisfy the principle of sufficient reason and hence to establish the *truth* of the proposition in question. At the same time, the *contingency* of the existential fact is respected, since the nonterminative analysis does point to infinity. It is important to notice that what Leibniz really establishes here is the contingency of *our knowledge,* rather than the contingency of the *existential order.* This distinction will play a considerable role in evaluating his defense of the divine freedom in creation.

As the next section will show, the principle of contingency or perfection is operative in the sphere of pure essences themselves, insofar as they strive with each other for the opportunity to enter the world of actual existents. Hence Leibniz is sure that there is a rational ground accounting for the existence of all actual things, and this ground is the cause. "Nothing exists but that some reason can be given (at least by an omniscient mind) why it should be rather than not be, and why it should be thus rather than otherwise. . . . Nothing happens without a cause."[9] Hence, although the finite mind is not omniscient and not intuitively aware of analytic inclusions concerning matters of fact, it can explain contingent events with the aid of the *principle of causality.* Causal explanation or furnishing of reasons is made with the aid of both the mechanical, *efficient* cause and the *final* cause. Physics employs the efficient cause to give a mechanistic account of the universe: this approach is accurate but is not a definitive explanation. Hence metaphysics makes distinctive use of the final cause, especially by inquiring about what tends toward achieving the maximum perfection in the actual universe. Philosophical demonstration of essential truths can attain *metaphysical necessity,* since the opposite of the true proposition in the essential order entails a contradiction. But the philosophical investigation of existential affairs can attain at least a *moral necessity.* A proposition is morally necessary, when its opposite would violate the principle of perfection or contingency, especially as specified in terms of final cause. Because of its extension into the existing order, in function of efficient and final cause, the principle of contingency or perfection gives sufficient rational determinateness to existential propositions to assure metaphysics a wide field of scientific research, over and above the truths it ascertains about purely essential relations.

The entire Leibnizian discussion of the first three principles rests upon an analysis of the characteristics of *true* propositions and of our ways of establishing their *truth.* The truth-value of propositions rests ultimately upon the actual existence of real beings, in which the analytic connections are realized. When Leibniz speaks about the

---

[9] *The Elements of True Piety* (Grua, I, 13); untitled fragment (Wiener, 94).

concept of the subject, he means primarily an essence or intelligible form that is eventually embodied as a real, subsistent thing. Propositions concerning the inherence of predicates in the concept of a logical subject are true, in final analysis, because this concept is grounded in a real subject of inherence or a *substance,* containing the qualities or events expressed in these predicates. It is because the truth of propositions is founded ultimately upon real beings, that Leibniz is confident about using a logical argument in favor of the reality of substance.[10] He defines substance as the ultimate term of predication in which the various predicates inhere, and which is not itself predicated of anything else. The logical relation of *in-esse* between the predicates and their ultimate or absolute subject is true, only because it is a reflection of the real relation of *in-esse* between attributes or modes and a substantial subject, existing in the real world. The subsequent rationalistic textbooks in Germany used this subject-predicate argument, without making clear its connection with the theory of truth. Hence it became a favorite target for later empirical critics, who could only discover a grammatical argument, divorced from metaphysical considerations.

Leibniz himself, however, furnished an a posteriori, existential proof for the reality of individual substances. In addition to the three basic principles of sufficient reason, contradiction and contingency or perfection, there are also two irreducible, primitive truths of a wholly existential sort. These latter are given through experience: the *fact of thinking* and the *fact of thinking a variety of thoughts.* The former truth implies the existence of at least my own individual, substantial, thinking self, which is the real source of my cognitive operations. So far, Leibniz agreed with Descartes. But he added that the fact of my having a variety of thoughts is just as distinct, irreducible, and indubitable as the fact of thinking. Now the only sufficient reason of this variety is that I, an individual substance, am not alone in existence but am one member of a universe of many individual, existent substances. My perceptions are representative of what *is,* i.e., of a universe composed of many perceiving substances. Leibniz did not deem himself obliged to argue his way out of solipsism, since he regarded the existence of other individual substances as being given in a truth, just as primitive as that upon which

---

[10] *Discourse on Metaphysics,* VIII (Wiener, 299–300); *Further Discussion of Vis Viva* (Wiener, 181). For the a posteriori proof, cf. *New Essays concerning Human Understanding,* IV, ii, 1 (Langley translation, 404–05).

the assurance of my own substantial existence rests. For Leibniz' empirical successors, this proof presented the challenge of explaining the facts of mental life sufficiently, without supposing the inherence of thoughts in a real subject.

Within the Leibnizian universe, only the *individual substance* is fully real and qualifies as a complete being. It is the ground and reason of all the predicates attributable truly to the thing. The individual substance is no mere static subject of inhesion but a *center of force,* an active source from which the various operations and modifications dynamically emerge. By definition, a *"substance* is a being capable of action."[11] Hence from the concept or essence of the individual substance can be gained, at least in principle, an a priori knowledge not only of the substance itself but also of all the operations and relations that belong to it in its temporal course. Although the human mind cannot complete this analysis of the predicates dynamically enfolded in the individual substance's concept, it can conduct its investigations with the assurance of a rational origination and radication of all contingent, temporal happenings. For the individual substance is precisely the *regulative law* and *active tendency* governing the development of the orderly series of perceptions or phenomena, by which a thing lives its effective existence in the actual universe. In Leibniz' system, the view of individual substance as the *nature,* or active law of its series of perceptual operations, is much more important than the role of substance as the *subject* of inherence. His emphasis upon substance as a regulative law or active tendency prepared the way for Kant's phenomenalistic interpretation of the category of substance, as signifying a permanent ratio or pattern among phenomenal events themselves. The Kantian position on substance as a category represented a compromise between Leibniz' ontological meaning of individual substance and the empiricist criticism.

By integrating his three first principles with the reality of individual substances, Leibniz hoped to counter the assertion of Hobbes that all our definitions and demonstrations are purely nominal. Since his first principles explain the reality of existing substances, Leibniz claimed for them a *real,* and not merely a nominal, significance. Hence he was confident about their extension to the entire actual universe.

---

[11] *The Principles of Nature and of Grace,* i (Wiener, 522).

Their application to the existing universe is facilitated by the two principles of the identity of indiscernibles and continuity.[12]

The *principle of the identity of indiscernibles* states that no two substances in the actual world are completely similar. Substances cannot differ merely in respect to their spatial location and configuration, as atomistic philosophy contends. Spatial and configurational differences are relatively superficial: they are consequences of more deep-seated differences, which reach down to the very substances or seats of activity themselves. Things do not differ merely in number or because they are quantitatively two, but in virtue of some more profound qualitative and operational differences. This qualitative basis of differences among individual substances is required by the principle of contingency or perfection. For if two substances were completely similar, there would be no sufficient reason why God should choose them both for inclusion in the best possible world. Since the addition of the second would not contribute significantly toward the maximal possible perfection of the universe, God would have no adequate ground for bringing it into existence. Things or states that are completely indiscernible from each other are really identical and not distinguished in the real order. Leibniz admitted, however, that the differences among existing things often remain hidden from our mind and especially from our imagination, so that they seem to be distinguished only by position and shape. His principle of the identity of indiscernibles provided research workers with the rule that they may expect to find that the differences among objects of investigation are basically of a qualitative nature, stemming from differences in structure and function. He pointed to the microscopic findings of a Leeuwenhoek as evidence of radical structural differences even among drops of water or snow.

Underlying all other types of differences among individual substances are those based upon *perception,* which is the native activity of substances. Leibniz sought to balance two affirmations: that all finite substances are basically *homogeneous,* and that they are *qualitatively differentiated* one from another. Their likeness is founded upon their sharing in a common kind of activity: perception. Their qualitative differences spring from their different capacities for perceptual

---

[12] *Letters to Samuel Clarke,* IV, 5–6, and V, 26 (Wiener, 228–29, 245); *New Essays concerning Human Understanding,* Preface (Langley, 50); *Letters to De Volder* (Wiener, 157–58); *On the Principle of Continuity* (Wiener, 184–88).

operation. To say that no two substances are exactly alike, is to say that no two substances have the same degree of perception. There is an infinitely graduated scale of perceptual operations and of perceiving substances. But no matter how infinitesimal the differences among substances, they concern the ability to perceive and hence are genuinely qualitative in nature. Leibniz recalled with approval the dictum of St. Thomas that, among the angels, every individual is a distinct species. He added that this "is true of all substances, provided that the specific difference is understood as Geometers understand it in the case of figures."[13] Each new degree of perception is an index of a new degree of substantial perfection. Thus there is a hierarchy among the individual substances in the world, each one occupying a distinctive station in the scale of things.

This great chain of beings is so closely intermeshed, that there are no gaps or hiatuses between the several links. The *principle of continuity* is a further extension of the principle of perfection or contingency. Since the actual world is the best possible world, there can be no empty spaces in the gradation of beings. There is an uninterrupted transition from one degree of perceptual and substantial perfection to the next, such that our world is a true plenum of individual substances. Leibniz also appeals to the infinitesimal calculus to support his contention that nature does not tolerate sudden breaks among existing things. He argues that the harmony and unity of scientific knowledge would be violated, unless the principle of continuity were to hold just as rigorously in natural philosophy and metaphysics as in the calculus. Because the mind trained in the method of the calculus finds discontinuities repugnant, Leibniz concludes that discontinuities must also be ruled out of nature itself. This latter argument is an example of his tendency to *ontologize the requirements of mathematics* and to reduce the intelligibility of being to the standard of mathematical intelligibility.

Leibniz expressed the principle of continuity in the famous axiom: *nature never acts by a leap (natura non facit saltum)*.[14] This provides scientific workers with a valuable procedural rule, especially in the physical and biological fields. The dispute about the presence of a vacuum in nature can be settled in the negative, since this would imply some gap in the field of compatible essences constituting the

13 *Discourse on Metaphysics*, IX (Wiener, 301); cf. *Identity in Individuals and True Propositions* (Wiener, 96).
14 *On Some Philosophical Axioms and Mathematical Fictions* (Wiener, 71).

best possible world. As far as biology is concerned, there is unbroken continuity from one living species to another. Hence biologists should work on the assumption that organisms that approximate each other in some one essential trait are also closely related in their other basic structures and functions. Thus, there are bound to be borderline cases, such as the zoophytes or plant-animals, which provide empirical evidence of the continuity among living things. Leibniz' stress upon the continuity of nature made a powerful contribution toward the general *evolutionary mentality* of the modern era, although he did not anticipate the Darwinian theory of the transformism of species. Instead, he accepted the current *preformationist hypothesis,* according to which the organized living body is already precontained in another organism of the same kind, and needs only to increase in size, in order to carry on its independent organic functions. He also applied the principle of continuity to the temporal aspect of nature, remarking that the present is laden with the past and pregnant with the future. There is an unbroken temporal process, consisting of the activities and events flowing forth from the individual substances.

Whereas the principle of the identity of indiscernibles defends the irreducible differences among things, the principle of continuity provides a guarantee that things also hold together in an intimate unity. Taken together, therefore, these two principles are Leibniz' assurance that the ideal of harmony is being realized, to the fullest possible degree, in the actual universe. If all existing natures are qualitatively different and yet in closest continuity with each other, in a plenitude of perceiving substances, then the greatest possible *unity-in-variety* or harmony is being achieved. Leibniz' next problem is to approach this same issue from the standpoint of the essential natures themselves and the Creator of the actual universe. His task is to show why his first principles must be the graven law for all essences which enter into the existential order.

## 4. FROM ESSENCE TO EXISTENCE

Pure essences are in the order of eternal things. Taken by them-selves, they are subject to an absolute or metaphysical necessity, since their contradictory opposite is impossible. Pure essences, and the eternal verities in which they are expressed, contain the measure of the possibilities of things. They are immutably determined and cannot become other than what they necessarily are. And yet ours is a universe of change and contingency. Hence a question arises about *the passage from essential necessity to existential contingency.* First, Leibniz attempts a solution based solely upon essences and first principles themselves, and then he shows the need to base this reasoning upon a reference to God as the ultimate ground of existential and essential being.

We may start from the given fact of contingent existence. A sufficient reason must then be sought in the essences themselves, why they exist rather than do not exist, since they are under no absolute necessity of existing. This reason can only be that actual being is better than possible being. If there were no such reason, nothing could ever become an actual existent, for lack of a sufficient ground for making the existential determination. Essences are not indifferent to existence but have an intrinsic inclination toward it. Every essence has a *conatus for existence.*[15] Yet although all essences agree in possessing such a drive toward existence, each one expresses its drive according to its own distinctive *degree of perfection* or *quantity of essence.*

It is a further fact that not all possibles are actualized, not all essential exigencies for existence are carried out. There is, as it were, a *strife among the essences* for the privilege of coming into existence. Certain essences, possible in themselves, are yet incompatible with each other: if one essence or series of essences exists, another essence or series is prevented from having simultaneous existence. Since there may be an infinite number of combinations of essences and their series, the only basis for a decision between competing essences and combinations lies in the principle of contingency, perfection, or the best, which states that, in the actual world, the quantity of essence or perfection must be as great as possible. The wider the range of any system of compatible essences, the stronger is its claim to be given actual existence. That combination of possibilities must ultimately prevail which assures the entrance into existence of the greatest amount of essence or the richest system of compatible natures.

Leibniz is compelled on logical grounds to posit this *principle of plenitude* and its optimistic consequence that *our world is the best possible one.* He is not moved by any silly sentimentality, after the manner of Voltaire's *Candide,* but by the unavoidable consequences of his premises. The only reason why *our* world exists and exists in *this* particular way (rather than another world or another course of

---

[15] *The Exigency to Exist in Essences: The Principle of Plenitude* (Wiener, 91–93).

things) is the relative perfection of our system. It affords more opportunity than any other arrangement for the realization of a harmonious totality of graded, continuous essences. This position is dictated neither by an empirical weighing of evidence nor by apologetic aims, although Leibniz is confident of its agreement with both. He admits the presence of imperfections and even dire disorders in the several parts of the universe, but he has the a priori weight of his principles to assure him that things as a whole attain to the greatest possible perfection and essential plenitude, achieved at a minimum expenditure or with perfect economy of means.

Leibniz recoiled from the suggestion that this "divine mathematics or metaphysical mechanics" might explain the production of the world in a quite autonomous and impersonal way, without recourse to God's creative act.[16] Yet he represented essences as full-bodied things, jostling with each other and securing their own hold on existence, in virtue of an internal dialectic of relative fullness and harmony of meaning. Given two mutually incompatible essences, that one can gain a real hold on existence which is compatible with a wider range of other essences, systematically correlated. "Moreover, it is my principle that whatever can exist, and is compatible with others, does exist."[17] There is nothing more distinctive about the existential act than being the outcome and resolution of a conflict among essential structures, concerning their systematic compatibilities. Instead of making a radical criticism of this view of essence and existence, however, Leibniz tried to combine it with a theory of free, divine creation. The result was a compromise, that held together only in virtue of alternating concessions on the part of the doctrine on God and that on essence and existence.

Leibniz was now placed in a delicate position between Descartes and Spinoza. He sided with Spinoza in removing *essences* and eternal verities from the free decrees of the divine will: God cannot

---

[16] *On the Ultimate Origin of Things* (Wiener, 348). In the third section of his Aquinas Lecture on *Saint Thomas and the Greeks* (Milwaukee, Marquette University Press, 1939), 50–57, A. C. Pegis observes that there can be no such thing as a best possible world, if the world is genuinely created by God, through freedom of choice and not through necessity of nature; cf. P. Siwek, S.J., "Optimism in Philosophy," *The New Scholasticism*, XXII (1948), 417–39. St. Thomas explains (*Summa Theologiae*, I, 25–6) that the actual universe could not be made in a better way, i.e., made from greater wisdom, order, and goodness. But God could make a better universe, i.e., He could make other things or give further perfections to the things already made.

[17] Untitled fragment (*Opuscules et fragments inédits de Leibniz*, edited by L. Couturat, 530); cf. *On the Analysis of Notions and Truths* (*op. cit.*, 360).

make and unmake the eternal possibilities of things, at will. Yet he did not care to follow Spinoza in affirming that the world emanates from God by absolute necessity. Although essences do not depend upon God's will, all *existential* perfections do proceed from the will, as well as the understanding, of God. There are two characteristics of the divine creative act: it proceeds from *choice* (in accord with God's adherence to His own decree to choose the best), and it has only a hypothetical or *moral necessity* (the actual product is a contingent existent, whose contradictory opposite is not impossible but would be a violation of the resolve to choose the best universe). An act that proceeds from choice and moral necessity fulfills the Leibnizian definition of a free act.[18] *Creation is a free act* not because it proceeds from God's indifference to the outcome, as Descartes held, but because it issues from His regard for considerations of His own wisdom and goodness. The more a will is determined by these motives, the more sovereignly free it is. Spinoza had also maintained a sort of divine freedom, but one that is identical with an absolute necessity of the divine nature to produce its effects. Leibniz proposes his notion of a hypothetical or moral necessity as a median position between the Spinozistic and Cartesian versions of divine freedom in creation.

In saving the divine freedom, however, this explanation makes it an *active acquiescence* in the results of the *calculus of essences.*[19] Once the maximum of compossible perfection is presented to the divine understanding, God cannot fail to will to create the prevailing combination, expressive of what is best. Leibniz qualifies this consequence as much as he can, without giving in to the Cartesian notion of divine liberty. He repeats Plato's remark that reason is an inclining or persuasive force, rather than an absolutely necessitating one, in respect to the creative decision. Regarded absolutely or in an isolated way, the divine power could either refrain from creating or could create things otherwise than in the best possible combination. But God's power must, in fact, be considered along with the divine

---

[18] See *Theodicy*, I, 37, and II, 132 (translated by E. M. Huggard, 144, 203); *Letters to Clarke*, V, 4–10, 76 (Wiener, 238–40, 264); *On the Ultimate Origin of Things* (Wiener, 346). In this last opuscule, Leibniz refers to moral necessity as an inclining, rather than a necessitating, reason; for the comparison with Plato, cf. P. Schrecker, "Leibniz and the *Timaeus*," *The Review of Metaphysics*, IV (1950–1951), 495–505.

[19] For a criticism of the sufficient-reasons-in-themselves, which determine the choice of Leibniz' Deity, cf. A.-D. Sertillanges, O.P., *Le problème du mal*, Tome I: *L'histoire* (Paris, Aubier, 1949), 234–37.

understanding (the region of the possibles and eternal truths) and the divine will (which freely chooses to create the best possible world). Under these conditions, God's power is *morally bound,* by hypothetical necessity, to create only that system which emerges from the ideal conflict among essences, in His understanding, as being the most perfect possible series of things. Otherwise, a sufficient reason for producing this particular combination of things would be lacking — in which case, the divine creative act would have no intelligible ground. Existence may now be taken to mean entrance into the universal harmony, precisely in virtue of *God's ratification* both of the entire system and of any particular component's consequent right for inclusion in actual existence. If an essence is compossible with the prevailing system, its existence is assured and God's creative act in its regard will not be withheld.

Leibniz adds that the essences are the *objects* but not the *products* of the divine understanding. His final problem is to retain this bulwark against Descartes and yet to establish as close a dependence of essence, as well as of existence, upon God as is compatible with this view. Although existence can never be conceived properly without reference to God, there is a way of viewing essences without such reference. They are *possible in their own right,* insofar as they have an intrinsic, intelligible nature of their own. But when essences are considered in isolation from God, they are *irreal* and *ineffective,* as far as their bond with a possible existing order is concerned. Only through their relation with God's understanding are they "realized," to the point of having real essential being or an exigency for existence. The acquiescence of the divine will and power are required, however, to settle which system of competing exigencies-for-existence will actually be brought forth. God, in whom alone essence and existence are identical, is the cause not only of the actual existence of finite essences but also of their *real striving* toward existence. Consequently, all other essences are contingent in respect to their existential *conatus,* as well as their actual existence. So far forth, these essences are implicated from eternity in God's understanding and, conversely, the divine essence cannot be conceived perfectly except as being inclusive of all other essences, as objects of its understanding. Hence Leibniz concludes that God is the source of all essences, as well as of all existences.

Leibniz cannot achieve a closer synthesis of the several strands of his solution. His difficulty is the fundamental metaphysical one of trying to avoid both arbitrary chaos and a necessitarian world, without benefit of a thoroughgoing doctrine on the relation between the *divine exemplar ideas* and the *divine essence*. He is prevented from settling this relationship, because he is the heir of the Cartesian and Spinozistic tendencies to conceive of the divine essence primarily in terms of self-affirming power, rather than as the subsistent act of existing. Leibniz is reluctant to ground the essential possibilities of things entirely and unequivocally in the divine essence, lest the intelligible structures become compromised by the bottomless force of the divine power. Hence he reserves an inviolable zone for the essences, considered just in themselves and their intrinsic meaning. They constitute a shadowy kingdom of their own, as a safeguard against any incursions by an arbitrary divine power. They have an "irreal being" of pure, essential meaning, anterior to their endeavor toward existence. But this attempt to consider essences in themselves and apart from an intrinsic reference to the act of existing, leads to serious difficulties. For the inherent relations of compossibility among essences constitutes a *prior* law and an *autonomous* standard, to which God must submit, thus endangering His freedom and creative primacy. The kind of "irreal being" belonging to the essences is not explained, since the distinction between logical constructions and real principles is wiped out, when essences are given a structure that has no intrinsic reference to existence. Essential relations and the principle of sufficient reason enjoy an independent, obscure being of their own and succeed in imposing themselves upon the divine geometer.

The situation is not improved when a real tendency toward existence is invoked, by bringing the possibilities into relation with the divine understanding. For the *conatus* toward finite existence, which God now gives to the essences, is an overflow from the self-affirming power of His own essence. Leibniz does not successfully answer Spinoza's argument that God affirms the *conatus* and existence of other things with the same necessity wherewith He affirms His own existence. The Leibnizian answer is that God is not under any absolute necessity to choose the world He actually does choose, but does so only in conformity with His own freely accepted standard of the best. Everything depends upon whether it can be established that God's adherence to the principle of perfection, contingency, or the best is a free one. What Leibniz actually proves is not the freedom of the divine choice of this standard but the inability of our minds to see the connection between God's power, goodness, and adherence to the best. He shows that, in dealing with this question, we must employ an infinite analysis rather than a finite one. This establishes the contingent character of *our proposition* about the creative act but not the freedom of the *creative act* itself. The fact that our analysis is unterminated and directed toward infinity rescues our knowledge from Spinozistic determinism, but it does not save God's creation from determinism. Whether existence be conceived as the outcome of the strife among the essences or as the result of the ratification of this strife by God, it remains only a consequence in the line of essence itself. God's choice of this world as actual, is a recognition of the finite terminus for the maximum assertion of essential quanta of power. Our world is guaranteed as the best possible one, but it also ceases to be the handiwork of creative freedom.

## 5. A WORLD OF MONADS

The various strands of Leibniz' speculation are woven together in his monadology. In this doctrine, he comes closest to realizing the systematic ideal toward which his logical and metaphysical findings were directed.

1. *The Existence and Nature of Monads.* Leibniz begins his treatise, *The Monadology,* with these two keynoting propositions:

> 1. The *monad* of which we shall here speak is merely a simple substance, which enters into composites; *simple,* that is to say, without parts.
> 2. And there must be simple substances, since there are composites; for the composite is only a collection or *aggregatum* of simple substances.[20]

The second proposition suggests that the theory of monads has a basis in facts of our experience. Given the existence of composite things, Leibniz infers the existence of their irreducible, composing elements. These elementary components cannot be found on the side of matter, however, since matter is indefinitely divisible and hence cannot account for the substantial unity of experienced composites. The principle of substantial unity must be sought in some formal, "metaphysical atoms" or *immaterial* monads. Through the composition of several simple, monadic substances, the complex things of our experience are formed. Because each individual monad is simple, it is also *indivisible* and *free from parts of extension.* Its simple character prevents the individual, monadic substance from being subject to

---

[20] *The Monadology,* 1–2 (Wiener, 533).

alteration by external, finite agents and from undergoing the process of generation and corruption. Monads can only come into existence through creation by God; thereafter, they are subject only to an increase and diminution of their native power and effective combination with each other. Monads "have no windows through which anything can enter or depart."[21] Each is a world by itself, a "little divinity" sealed off from any direct interaction with the other finite monads, inhabiting the teeming pond of the universe. Direct, causal contact is maintained only between the individual monad and God, upon whom every monad depends for its being.

Although they are simple and unextended, the primary substances have some intrinsic modifications and multiplicity, in addition to their substantial nature. Without some further modifications or affections, the monads could not be differentiated from each other and hence could not exist as distinct entities. At this point, Leibniz brings his previous doctrine on individual substance to bear upon his general theory of monads. Each individual substance or monad is a primitive, unified center of force, which is the source and regulative law of all its activities. There is a composition of powers plus activities, even though there is no composition within the substance. These activities are of an immaterial nature, considered in themselves, since the monads are unextended, unitary beings. Flowing from the simple substance are two main kinds of activities: *perceptions* and *desires*. The monad is essentially a thing capable of perception, in the widest sense of giving rise to a living representation or expression of the universe. Desire or appetition is nothing other than the tendency of the monad to make a transition from one perception to another, for the sake of securing the maximum clarity and distinctness among its perceptual states. These activities introduce the factors of *transiency* and *multiplicity* into the life of the monad. The multiplicity does not militate against the unextended nature of the monadic individual, since it is a manyness of perceptual and appetitive acts and relations, rather than of extended parts. The transient and multiple character of these immaterial activities is an indication of the *finitude* of the individual monads. The drive of their desire or natural appetite is toward ever more adequate perceptions of the universe and hence toward constant increase of perfection.

Since all monads exercise the operations of perception and appetition

---

[21] *Ibid.*, 7 (Wiener, 534); cf. *Discourse on Metaphysics*, XXVI (Wiener, 327-28).

— in which *life* itself consists — ours is a world of living things. Leibniz makes no fantastic claim that all monads enjoy conscious life, but he does clash with Locke over whether *unconscious perception* is a contradiction in terms. Although some perceptions are able to cross the threshold of consciousness, there is an entire lower order of perceptual activity which remains below this conscious level. In order to show the reasonableness of his theory of unconscious perceptions, Leibniz gives a metaphysical interpretation of *perception*.[22]  He defines it, in the most general way, as any expression of, or structured correspondence to, the universe. Now the individual, monadic substance is created by God in such fashion that its being and activity are adapted and proportioned to the structure of the rest of the universe. There is a one-to-one correspondence between the traits of the microcosm and those of the macrocosm, such that the activities of the former are expressive of the structure of the latter. Hence the activities of every monad are expressions in conformity with the universe, and fulfill the general definition of perception or representation. There is no need to confine the meaning of perception to a conscious expression of objects.

Leibniz makes a distinct advance over Paracelsus and Bruno, when he provides a metaphysical foundation for the venerable *microcosm-macrocosm* doctrine. He regards it as a logical consequence of his teaching that an individual essence can acquire existence, only by proving its harmony or *compossibility* with the rest of the given universe. This relation of compossibility means that the essential structure of this particular essence is intrinsically related and proportioned to the other essences. The compatibility is a *dynamic adaptation,* that reaches down to every activity stemming from the essence, considered as an individual substance. Hence it is the very nature of a monad *to be representative* of the entire universe. Perception is only the operational development of this intrinsic correspondence between the individual monad and other beings, with which it is harmonized to constitute our universe. In creating the individual substance, God ordains its operations to be expressions of

[22] *Letters to De Volder* (Wiener, 161); *New System of Nature and of the Communication of Substances,* 14–15 (Wiener, 114–16); *The Monadology,* 14, 60–62 (Wiener, 535, 545–46). J. Jalabert, "La psychologie de Leibniz," *Revue Philosophique de la France et de l'Étranger,* CXXXVI (1946), 453–72, shows that the profoundly tendential and dynamic quality of Leibniz' psychology stems from this view of perception, as an expression of inner spontaneity and conformity with the world.

the universe. These perceptual expressions can transpire either unconsciously or at the level of consciousness.

Leibniz supports his metaphysical doctrine with an empirical theory of *unconscious* or *minute perceptions,* backed up by the demands of his principle of continuity.[23] Since a monad cannot exist without its activities, the latter must be constantly present, even apart from conscious states. From internal experience, it is evident that there is a gradation among our perceptions, some being relatively obscure and others attaining considerable clarity. The clear and distinct perceptions are those which have been brought successfully to conscious awareness. But the principle of continuity is warrant that there are no sudden gaps in our perceptual life: perceptual activity is not cut off abruptly at the point where the clarity of consciousness ceases, but continues down into the depths of the unconscious. There is an uninterrupted series of perceptual activities reaching from states of reflection down to those that are unconscious, yet genuinely expressive of the universe. The continuity of psychic life amid sleep, dreams, and other interruptions of consciousness, indicates that conscious perception rests upon a vast substrate of unconscious perceptual activities. There is a constant increment of "minute perceptions," operating beneath the surface of consciousness. A person living beside a waterfall is constantly perceiving the sound of the water, but habit deadens his conscious attention, during most of the time. Similarly, a person walking along the seashore pays no conscious attention to individual waves. But sometimes, he does advert to the roar of the surf, at some point where a combination of smaller sounds is strong enough to engage his notice. Our conscious knowledge is made possible through the unnoticed contributions of innumerable unconscious, minute perceptions. Thus Leibniz laid the philosophical cornerstone for the modern psychological conviction that a great part of our mental life transpires in the dark pool of the unconscious. He also stressed the great importance of the *petites perceptions* in shaping our attitudes, moral decisions, and general outlook.

2. *The Hierarchy of Monads.* All monads agree in the *general*

---

[23] The classical development of this teaching is in *New Essays concerning Human Understanding,* Preface, and II, i, 10–15 (Langley, 47–52, 111–17). The constant bombardment of the mind by unconscious perceptions belies the *tabula rasa* theory of the mind, assures the individual mind's objective connection with the rest of the universe, and provides the unnoticed determining factors inclining our will to choose in one definite direction. For the Cartesian background of this issue, cf. G. Lewis, *Le problème de l'inconscient et le cartésianisme* (Paris, Presses Universitaires, 1950).

*object of perception,* since they all express the universe in its infinite variety. But they differ profoundly among themselves in respect to the *act of perceiving,* i.e., in their subjective ability to achieve distinct perceptions of the things in the universe. A scale of perfection exists among the various types of perceptions. At the lowest level, there is bare perception or expression of the universe, unaccompanied by any glimmering of consciousness. This is the field occupied by the insensible or *unconscious* perceptions. A new plane is reached, when perception is accompanied by memory and thus gives rise to *consciousness* and automatically connected experience. Finally, the summit of the grades of perception is occupied by *reflective knowledge* or *apperception,* in which there is awareness of the very act of perceiving and of the substantial self, from which the act proceeds. Like Spinoza, Leibniz is interested in the problem of the degrees of perception mainly for metaphysical, rather than strictly psychological, reasons. For, the degrees of perception provide him with a standard for arranging simple monads in the hierarchy of being and, at the same time, enable him to give a systematic explanation of the actual objects of perception: the composite things peopling our universe.

What we perceive directly are not simple substances but composite things or aggregates of simple substances. Although there is no composition *within* the substance of the individual monad, there can be composition *among* several simple monads to constitute a *composite thing.* The sufficient reason for this aggregation is to be sought in the fact that a given finite monad requires the proximate co-operation of several associated monads, so that it may bring its perceptions to a condition of maximum clarity and distinctness. Hence the composite thing is an operational unity between the particular monad, attempting to clarify its perceptual states, and those other monads that contribute proximately and directly to this process of clarification. The self-clarifying monad in question is called the *entelechy;* the associated monads are called the *body* of this entelechy. Thus in any composite thing, that monad whose own states are being perfected as a consequence of the composition is the entelechy-monad, whereas those monads contributing proximately to the improvement of this other monad's perceptions are body-monads. Thus a special relation of domination and subordination is set up, resembling the relation between the queen bee and the workers in the beehive. The entelechy-monad assumes a dominating role, and the body-monads are subordinated teleologically to the needs of the entelechy. Leibniz' functional view of the composite thing resembles Spinoza's functional theory of the individual.

Although he borrows the term "entelechy" from Aristotle, in order to signify the organizing principle, setting the end or measure of perfection for the entire composite, Leibniz does not accept the Aristotelian theory of act and potency. Instead, he regards the composite as an *operational union between a principal act and subordinate acts.* Since each of the subordinate acts or bodily monads remains a simple substance, Leibniz discovers no obstacle against regarding it, in turn, as an entelechy in respect to a new set of inferiors. Every bodily monad retains a nisus toward perfecting its own perceptual activities, as well as those of another. Hence it can also operate as an entelechy-monad, by subordinating and organizing some other monads around its own purpose. This functional relationship of entelechy-to-body goes on to infinity, reaching far below the range of our distinct, conscious perception of the divisions among composite things.

## LEIBNIZ' HIERARCHY OF MONADS

1. God as infinite, prime monad and principle of pre-established harmony among created monads.

2. Finite, created monads.

| a) Entelechy or dominant monad. | b) Body or subordinate monads. | c) Living composite of entelechy and body, regulated by pre-established harmony. |
|---|---|---|
| 1) Bare entelechy. | 1) Lower body. | 1) Inferior living matter, having only unconscious perceptions. |
| 2) Soul. | 2) Animal body. | 2) Animal, having conscious perceptions. |
| 3) Spirit or mind (rational soul). | 3) Human body. | 3) Man, the higher animal, having reflective consciousness and knowledge of eternal truths. |

The variety and specific gradation of composites are due to the presence of entelechies of different degrees of perfection. The hierarchy among entelechies is determined according to the increasing perfection of the power of perception. Entelechies or dominating monads belong to three main classes: bare entelechies or perceptive principles, souls, and minds. The higher orders include the perfections found at a lower level. "As therefore mind is rational soul, so soul is sentient life, and life is perceptive principle."[24] The *bare entelechies* or *mere perceptive principles* have some perceptual and appetitive activities, and hence they are true principles of life. But their perceptions resemble a dreamless sleep or a permanent swoon, since they remain forever in a confused and unconscious state. Consciousness appears at the higher level occupied by *souls*. In the soul-monads, perception is accompanied by memory, attention, and feeling. Souls can have some sort of connected experience but are incapable of reflecting upon their operations. Reflection or apperception is characteristic of the highest class of dominant monads: the *minds* or *rational souls* or *spirits*. They can reflect upon their conscious acts, become aware of their own selfhood, and thus achieve freedom and moral character. Minds are also able to apprehend simple innate ideas, eternal truths, and first principles of philosophy. Hence rational knowledge can rise from empirical truths of fact to essential truths of reason. Leibniz states the contrast between bare entelechies and souls, on the one hand, and minds, on the other, in a decisive way: the former are images of the universe alone, whereas the latter are images both of the universe and of God, the creator of the universe.

The grades of composite things are constituted by the union between bodily monads and entelechies of these three sorts. *Lower living things* are composed of a bare entelechy and its bodily aggregate of monads. *Animals* are constituted through the union of a soul with an appropriate bodily group of monads. *Men* or rational animals are composite things, made up of a mind or rational soul and the body proportioned to the highest level of perceptual activity. No finite entelechy, of whatever sort, can exist without its proper set of bodily monads. To be a finite monad means to require the proximate aid of other simple substances in the work of perfecting one's perceptions, and hence to require a body. Only the infinite monad, God, is entirely free from union with a body.

---

[24] *On the Active Force of Body, on the Soul of Brutes,* 3 (Wiener, 505). Cf. *Discourse on Metaphysics,* XXXIV–XXXV (Wiener, 339–42); *The Principles of Nature and of Grace,* 4–5 (Wiener, 524–26); *The Monadology,* 18–30, 63–70 (Wiener, 536–39, 546–47). In Leibniz' explanation of the monadic hierarchy, the tensions latent in his previous compromise between the homogeneity and differentiation among individual substances are made explicit. In order to defend his view of the basic homogeneity of all monadic substances from the charge of agreement with Spinozistic monism, he is obliged to emphasize the sharp differences between rational and nonrational monads, thus opening the door once more to a Cartesian dualism. Cf. G. Lewis, "La critique leibnizienne du dualisme cartésien," *Revue Philosophique de la France et de l'Étranger,* CXXXVI (1946), 473–85.

3. *A Monadological Description of the Physical World.* With the aid of his theory of monads, Leibniz tried to describe the familiar world. This was a difficult task, since he had to show how the universe of material, extended things can be constructed out of immaterial, unextended substances. The only route open for him was to reinterpret body, extension, space, and time in purely perceptual terms. This did not explain the material world, but rather gave a description of what this world *would be like,* were it composed of simple substances, having only perceptual and appetitive activities.

Within such a context, the *body* and bodily organs can only mean a subordinate group of monads, providing functional aids to the clarification of one's perceptions.[25] Leibniz' main concern was to show that there is a sufficient reason why every entelechic monad must have a body, as so defined. This reason can be seen from a comparison between finite monads and God. God alone is without a body, since He alone has an infinite understanding of the world and needs the aid of nothing else. Hence his knowledge of the universe is infinite or confined to no special viewpoint. But every finite understanding does operate within a special viewpoint, and this is supplied by the monad's body. Although the monad's knowledge is not *derived* from the body, it is *proportioned* to the states of the bodily monads. Thus the body is a principle of individuation for the finite monad, providing it with a *distinctive perspective* in time and action. The entelechy-monad knows the entire universe, but it knows the world through knowing its own body. The rays from the rest of the monadic cosmos are concentrated in a distinctive focus, and that focus is called the body. The body is the *point of insertion* of the individual substance in the harmonious system of the existing world. Were the body eliminated, the bodiless monads would become "like deserters from the general order" of things.[26] In Leibniz' system, the body is the proximate means for securing the connectedness among individual monads and thus for guaranteeing the harmony in the existent universe.

Leibniz' treatment of *extension* is complicated by a double polemical aim. He wants to explain extension in such a way that he can fit

---

[25] The body is described as "the organized mass in which the point of view of the soul lies." *New System of Nature and of the Communication of Substances,* 14 (Wiener, 115). Cf. *Discourse on Metaphysics,* XXXIII (Wiener, 338–39), and *The Monadology,* 60–62 (Wiener, 545–46).

[26] *Considerations on the Principles of Life, and on Plastic Natures* (Wiener, 199).

it into his system and, at the same time, provide a refutation of the Cartesian and Spinozistic views of material substance.[27] He draws a distinction between *extension* (which he sometimes calls "prime matter") and *the extended thing* (sometimes called "second matter"). Extension is an abstraction made by our mind, whereas the extended thing is what really exists and serves as a basis for the abstraction. The extended thing is the physical mass, constituted by a plurality of monads, coexisting and continuous with each other. The coexisting and continuous mass of monads constitutes a functional unity, and this *common field of activity* is the extended thing. The human mind can gain a confused and indistinct perception of the mass, by making an indefinite repetition. At this level, it abstracts from the substantial differences among the coexisting substances and regards them as one indiscernible whole of extension. In this way the notion of homogeneous extension is acquired.

Leibniz employed this theory of *dynamism* to defend his philosophy against both Descartes and Spinoza. Against the former, he noted that, if extension does not exist but is a mental abstraction, it cannot serve as the special *real attribute* defining material substance. Furthermore, if the real ground of extension in "the extended thing" is reducible to the plurality, coexistence and continuity of several simple and unextended substances, then an extended thing is not a *substance* at all. It is only an operational effect flowing from the conjoint activity of several real substances. The Cartesian *res extensa* must therefore be reduced to the Leibnizian *res agens:* the simple substance, considered as a primitive center of force. This does not provide any solace, however, for Spinoza. For the real foundation of the extended thing or mass is a *plurality of finite substances,* rather than the one divine substance. A bodily mass is an aggregate of substances. Because of the confused perceptions in the aggregated substances, as well as in the perceiving mind, we may regard the extended world as an indefinitely repeatable region of homogeneity. But more careful analysis shows, with the aid of the principle of the identity of indiscernibles, that the manyness of extended things is due ultimately to the manyness of finite substances. Leibniz refuses to define substance in such a way that it can apply only to God. He points out that the powers and operations of things really do belong to them and are exercised by them, precisely because they are finite centers of

---

[27] *Letters to De Volder* (Wiener, 163–75); *Refutation of Spinoza* (Wiener, 485–97).

force or finite substances. The minimal definition of a substance as "a being capable of action," permits the perfection of substance to be applied to finite things, as well as to the infinite being.

This doctrine is more successful as a polemical device than as a positive analysis of extension. Its net effect is to explain away extension. This is done, not so much by making extension a consequence of active forces, as by ascribing its origin to the confused condition of perception. Matter and extension are possible only through the conjunction of two sets of confused perceptions: on the part of the extended thing or mass of bodily monads, and on the part of the perceiver, who abstracts the notion of extension. The indefinite repetition could not be made *by* the perceiver, and *in respect to* the mass, if it were not for this dual confusion, which encourages an imaginative view of a homogeneous, extended world. Leibniz claims to "demonstrate that the ideas of size, figure, and motion [the so-called primary qualities] are not so distinctive as is imagined, and that they stand for something imaginary relative to our perceptions, as do, although to a greater extent, the ideas of color, heat, and the other similar qualities in regard to which we may doubt whether they are actually to be found in the nature of the things outside of us."[28] Although he gives to extension a real foundation in the extended thing, he removes primary qualities just as completely as secondary ones from the extended thing. Extension is "a well-founded phenomenon," but it has a foundation in existent substances, only insofar as they are subject to conditions of imagination or confused perception —conditions which their native tendency seeks to overcome.

A similar result follows from Leibniz' account of space and time.[29] Things are said to be near at hand or far distant, of recent or remote occurrence, depending upon whether our perception of them is clear or not, and whether a lesser or a greater number of mental steps is required to grasp their mutual order. *Space* is the order of *coexisting*

---

[28] *Discourse on Metaphysics*, XII (Wiener, 304-05). Leibniz' obscure views on the nature of matter are examined by J. A. Irving, "Leibniz' Theory of Matter," *Philosophy of Science*, III (1936), 208-14, and by S. Russo, "The Concept of Matter in Leibniz," *The Philosophical Review*, XLVII (1938), 275-92.

[29] *Metaphysical Foundations of Mathematics* (Wiener, 201-12); *Letters to Clarke*, III, 4-6; IV, 41; V, 47 (Wiener, 223-24, 235, 251-54). For an analysis of the Leibniz-Clarke correspondence, read E. Cassirer, "Newton and Leibniz," *The Philosophical Review*, LII (1943), 366-91. Leibniz' arguments on the nature of space are carefully analyzed by O. Pohley, S.J., "Des Leibniz Lehre von Raum," *Gregorianum*, XV (1934), 325-48, and F. S. C. Northrop, "Leibniz's Theory of Space," *Journal of the History of Ideas*, VII (1946), 385-498.

things, and *time* the order of *successive* things. Space and time are real but they are also relative and phenomenal. Newton was wrong in treating them as substantial entities, since they depend upon our perception and ability to grasp a universal order of coexistence and succession. Space and time are *well-founded phenomena,* however, since there are real coexisting things and real successive actions, upon the perception of which the universalized notions of space and time rest. Since we cannot acquire God's perfect knowledge of the order of coexistence and succession among monads, our spatial and temporal notions are always deficient. Nevertheless, they help us to organize our knowledge of the world and to place our practical plans on a sound footing.

Leibniz is justifiably critical of the Newtonian conception of absolute space and time, since he shows the considerable part played by the *mind* in the elaboration of our notions of space and time. His suggestion that these notions are really founded upon the coexistence and change of existing things, is also sound. But his efforts to give a detailed account of the real foundation meet with systematic frustration. For, in explaining the relations of coexistence and succession, as they obtain among several simple and unextended substances, he must bear in mind both his doctrine on the isolation of the individual monads and his explanation of the extended thing as a secondary feature. Since the monads constituting the real foundation are related to each other only in an "ideal" or nonphysical way, through the mutual reference of *their perceptions,* he does not secure a foundation for space and time beyond the order of perceptions. Hence it is customary for Leibniz to shift attention from the monadic foundation in the world to the conditions of perception found in the perceiver himself. He observes that the mind's own acts of perceiving display the traits of psychological quantity, togetherness and succession. This involves a substitution, once more, of the *conditions of perceiving* for the *objects of perception.* The latter collapse into the former, thus rendering doubtful the establishment of the foundation for the phenomena of space and time.

## 6. GOD AND PRE-ESTABLISHED HARMONY

To cope with some special problems concerning the relation between minds and bodies, Leibniz had to bring to the fore the role of God in his monadology. He formulated several proofs of God's existence, recasting some of his predecessors' arguments in function of his own system.[30] In its usual Cartesian form, the *ontological argument* has only a moral force, since it assumes the possibility of the idea or essence of God, considered as the all-perfect being. Leibniz set out to remedy this defect. To do so, he returned to the given fact that some things exist. Since they do exist, their essences enjoy a real possibility, not merely a logical one. These essences are real and not merely logical or imaginary, because they are founded in God, who is the region of all ideas, essences, and eternal truths. If God were not unconditionally and *really possible in Himself,* the essences of existing things would not have real claim upon existence and would not be really embodied in existents. Finite essences are really possible, only by reference to the self-founded, real possibility of the divine essence.

This proof of the real possibility of God's essence is, simultaneously, a proof of His existence and infinite perfection. For God's essence is intrinsically possible, precisely as being the foundation of the claim of real finite essences to their perfection or degree of essence, which is the principle of existence. Hence their reality must be grounded in a metaphysically necessary essence or subject, which draws its actual existence from itself alone. If God is really and unconditionally possible, in this sense, then He must exist. For, His possibility is that of the all-powerful source of the reality of essences or their *conatus* toward existence. Other things are really possible and eventually existent, only in virtue of their harmonious relation with the *actually existing, divine essence.* That this essence is infinitely perfect, follows from the consideration that it draws its whole reality from within itself and through its own power. Since there is nothing within His own existing essence (or outside it) to thwart the absolute affirmation of His absolute quantity of essence or perfection, God exists as the *infinitely perfect being.* Thus Leibniz renovates the ontological argument, by drawing upon his own theory of the conditions under which alone essences can enter into the zone of existence.

It is imperative for him to prove the possibility of God, since otherwise the essence of God would not be established. Because Leibniz accords to essence a sort of pre-existential reality of its own, the divine

---

[30] *New Essays concerning Human Understanding,* IV, x (Langley, 499–511); *On the Ultimate Origin of Things* (Wiener, 345–50); *The Principles of Nature and of Grace,* 7–8 (Wiener, 527–28); *The Monadology,* 36–38, 43–45 (Wiener, 540–42); *New System of Nature and of the Communication of Substances,* 16 (Wiener, 116); *Theodicy,* I, 7 (Huggard, 127–28). See also the extracts entitled *On the Cartesian Demonstration of the Existence of God,* in *The Philosophical Works of Leibniz,* translated by G. M. Duncan (New Haven, Tuttle, Morehouse, and Taylor, 1890), 132–38.

essence must first be demonstrated as possible. Then, existence can be established as a necessary consequence of this essence. Whereas the meaning of existence in other things consists in the relations of compatibility of their essences within the prevailing system, the meaning of the necessary being's existence is drawn entirely from its own unbounded essence or affirmation of power. Criticism of Leibniz' argument has focused upon the view that existence is contained within essence, regarded as an underlying principle or "power." Kant objects that an unconditioned essence can never be given more than the standing of a *possible concept* in our minds, so that we cannot know it as a *real subject*. Thomistic realists agree with Kant in denying that existence is a predicate or result, flowing from essence. They also point out that the precise problem is not that of determining the meaning of existence but of demonstrating the truth of the proposition *God exists*. The task of an existential proof is to ascertain not *what God's essence affirms* but *what we can affirm demonstratively about His existence*. Otherwise, one becomes involved in equivocation concerning the different meanings of "power" and what we can validly assert about it.

The monadology also affords Leibniz an opportunity to give a distinctive turn to the usual *a posteriori arguments*. On the basis of the dual axiom that existence can be explained only by existence and the contingent only by the necessary, he traces back all contingent existents to God, viewed as the necessary existent and cause of the existing universe. The *contingency of finite monads* is seen from their subjection to continuous change of perception and appetition. They lack a sufficient reason within themselves for their existence. And since the condition of transient perceptions is a universal one, the entire world of existing monads demands a sufficient reason in a being existing outside itself. Hence God exists and gives being to all finite monads.

That the transcendent cause of the monadic universe is an intelligent being — *intelligentia supramundana* — is the conclusion of what Leibniz calls his new proof from the *harmony among all monads*. The marvelous mutual correspondence between individual monads, as well as between groups of monads (such as mind and body or several interrelated bodies), is not the outcome of any direct, causal influence from one to the other. Each monad is a sealed-off empire of its own, and yet it is an empire *within* the larger empire of the harmonious universe of monads. The delicate adaptation and ordering of things obtain in the actual world, only because all the monads stand under the effective guidance of a single intelligent cause, itself existing above the world and yet working powerfully and meaningfully within it. Only a being at once transcendent and intelligent can provide the sufficient reason for the harmony of the existent world. This is Leibniz' version of the argument from order and design.

Leibniz sometimes refers to God as the *prime monad,* since He possesses, in an eminent way, some of the characteristics of monads. He is an active substance, although one that admits neither of a reactive-passive aspect nor of any reference to another as its cause. Corresponding to the substantial subject, perceptual and appetitive powers in finite monads are, respectively, the divine power, knowledge, and will. They are one in the simplicity of the divine substance, which escapes all internal change, accidental composition, and determination by correspondence with other things. God is unique, absolutely perfect, and self-sufficient. He is limited by no particular, perspectival views of the universe but embraces them all in His infinite vision of all aspects of all things. In Him, the meaning of mind, spirit, and person finds its highest fulfillment.

Imagery redolent of Neo-Platonic and Spinozistic emanationism is often used by Leibniz to describe the *genesis of things* from God, whose name is *ens existificans.* Created or derived monads proceed from the underived monad "by continual fulgurations [outflashings] of the Divinity, from moment to moment."[31] These words connote the unquenchable welling-over of the divine power, in its drive to realize the maximum of perfection in the universe. Recognizing that this sort of description compromises the transcendence and freedom of a creator-God, Leibniz seeks some compensating safeguards. Created things derive their *perfections* from God, but their *imperfections* and limitations come from their own natures. Hence they are both dependent upon God and really distinct from Him. The distance is that between infinite and finite substances. Leibniz' *principle of limitation* is not a distinct constituent of finite essences but the relative systematic requirement that *mutual concessions* and *accommodations* must be made by a plurality of essences, in order to constitute one, harmonious world. The fact that every derived monad possesses a body is an index of its submission to the condition of finitude and co-existence in a system of essences. The principle of

---

[31] *The Monadology,* 47 (Wiener, 542).

limitation retains the same sort of *tenuous independence* of God as do the essential meanings, considered in themselves, since it is nothing more than the requirement of mutual compatibility and adjustment among these meanings.

Once he has established the freedom of the creative act, in the sense of its moral but not absolute necessity, Leibniz allows the requirements of the best possible world to hold sway over God's creative action. God is constantly viewing the various aspects or perspectives of the world He has chosen. *Each aspect viewed by God* is eventually given existence as *a monad* or *collection of monads.*[32] God thoroughly comprehends each monadic essence, both as an individual entity and as an integral component of the world, both in its intrinsic possibility and its *com*possibility with the rest. And the monad is brought into existence by God, just as it is comprehended by His divine understanding: it is actualized as a complete thing, adapted to the conditions of coexistence with other monads in the best possible world. This is the metaphysical foundation for the doctrine of pre-established harmony.

The reason why Leibniz was compelled to advance the doctrine of *pre-established harmony* can be appreciated by recalling his conception of the individual substance. By definition, a complete, individual substance is a being whose nature affords a concept so complete that from it can be deduced all the predicates of which it may ever be the subject, throughout the course of its temporal career. Whatever happens to the monadic substance is a strict consequence of its own nature, considered as the regulative tendency to give rise to such happenings or representations. One implication of this teaching is that there can be *no direct, physical influence* of one finite substance upon another. Each individual monad is a world apart, cut off from causal influxes from other finite monads, and incapable of producing any causal influx in them. Given these monadic, sealed fortresses, how can the evident harmony and apparent interaction among the components in the universe be explained? This is the question that led Leibniz to formulate his theory of pre-established harmony.

The harmony among things must be *pre*-established, since it cannot be the achievement of genuine causal relationships among the empirically existing substances. There are two stages in the anterior harmonization of things, and Leibniz does not always respect the

---

[32] *Ibid.*, 57, 60 (Wiener, 544, 545); *The Principles of Nature and of Grace*, 12–13 (Wiener, 529–30).

distinction between them.[33] The *immediate* ground of harmony is found in God. For although the finite monads are isolated horizontally from each other (as far as causal communication is concerned), they are all vertically open to the causal influence of God, upon whom they depend for actual existence. It is the *regulative influence of God* that prevents the monadic world from disintegrating into chaos. Although one simple substance does not act upon another, God regulates them all in such fashion that what happens within one substance is co-ordinated with what happens in all the others. In creating each individual substance, God bears in mind the requirements of the whole universe, and in creating the universe He bears in mind the needs of each individual. In this way, there is perfect harmony and mutual adaptation among the activities of all monads. Monads can influence each other, *indirectly* and *ideally,* through God. Leibniz explains the apparent system of actions and passions among things, in terms of God's "regarding" or intellectual consideration of the needs of each and all. Without entering into causal transactions with each other, things may be said to be related by bonds of action and passion, since the activities of each individual promote, and in turn are promoted by, the welfare of the entire cosmos.

But there is a *more ultimate* ground of the anterior harmonization of things. There must be a sufficient reason why God chooses to create precisely this universe, instead of the other possible combinations. This sufficient reason is found in the superior fitness of our universe, its ability to contain a greater amount of essence, and hence of perfection, than any other combination of essences. Now any particular essence has a right to inclusion in our universe, only if it can establish such connections with the entire system as will achieve a greater unity-in-variety or harmony. The connectedness of the component essences in our universe means that there is a *relationship of mutual adaptation* among them, viewed merely in their own essential structures. Considered in their "irreal being," anterior to their reception of a *conatus* toward existence, the essences contain relations of mutual inclusion and adaptation, in order to form a systematic whole. God's "regarding" of the needs of each and all, which is the proximate basis for the harmonious actions and

---

[33] *The Monadology,* 49–61 (Wiener, 542–45); on action and passion, see also: *Discourse on Metaphysics,* XXXIII (Wiener, 338), and *Refutation of Spinoza* (Wiener, 494–95).

passions of things, is a recognition and ratification of the *inherent, essential connectedness* among the component members of that system which contains the greatest amount of essence or harmony. The ultimate reason for the harmony of our universe lies in the relations of mutual fitness and proportion, among the essences comprising the system. Once again, the divine geometer must submit to the independent relations holding good among the essences, as well as to the principle of sufficient reason.

The most striking instance of such harmony is the relationship between *mind* and *body*. Leibniz agrees with Malebranche and Spinoza in ruling out any *causal interaction* between them, but he adduces his own reason. Mind and body are not modes under utterly different attributes, as Spinoza taught; mind is a substance in its own right, and body is an operational unity of several subordinate monads. Malebranche was also in error, when he held that finite substances have no real, causal efficacy. Leibniz admits that the individual monad controls its own perceptions in a causal way. His denial of causal interaction between mind and body is simply an application of the general doctrine, denying causal influence between *any* finite substances or collections of substances. Nevertheless, there is a marvelous correspondence between the activities of mind and those of body. They are perfectly harmonized through a system of noncausal actions and passions, having a one-to-one correspondence. Leibniz compares mind and body to *two clocks,* which have been perfectly synchronized by God, at the outset. Although the two series of activities merely run parallel, within any causal interchange, everything happens "as if each influenced the other."[34]

This "as if" is as far as Leibniz can go, since neither at the finite level of existence nor at the level of purely essential meanings is there any mutual causal influence. He divorces action and passion from the causal relationship and, indeed, from any framework of act and potency, so that they become only *ways of regarding the order*

---

[34] *The Monadology*, 81 (Wiener, 550). For the example of the synchronized clocks, compare *Second Explanation of the System of the Communication of Substances* (Wiener, 118–19); *Considerations on the Principles of Life, and of Plastic Natures* (Wiener, 192). Here, as well as in *New System of Nature and of the Communication of Substances* (Wiener, 113–16), Leibniz denies that pre-established harmony is a *deus ex machina* or extrinsic tinkering with the machinery of the universe. But his real task is to show that his description of the causal necessities governing the creation of the cosmic machinery itself, is not a mere contrivance for saving the unity of the universe, in the face of his analytic doctrine on individual substances.

among essential structures, belonging to the same system of harmonious perfection. Although Leibniz thinks that this "as if" explanation of mind and body covers the appearances and saves the divine veracity, it raises a special problem concerning the widespread belief that there *is* some causal relationship between mind and body. This question left Hume wondering whether the *causal belief* may not always be reducible to an "as if" situation, which has a purely psychological explanation, without foundation in really interacting principles.

Leibniz accepted, integrally, the mechanistic explanation of the physical world in terms of *efficient causes*. For, the harmonious correspondences within the physical plenum constitute a visible image of the correspondences among essential structures. In neither case is there any causal operation of one being upon another, although there is a detailed adaptation of activities, in function of the pre-established harmony. Leibniz also sought to rehabilitate *final cause* as a way of supplementing the mechanistic description of nature. Souls and minds act according to the laws of final cause, rather than of efficient cause. Since their activities suppose the presence of consciousness, we must take account of the influence of conscious desires, chosen ends, and the known relation between ends and means. These considerations belong in the domain of final cause. Pre-established harmony operates to achieve a correspondence between the realms of mechanism and teleology, so that, within the context of the world of *nature* and efficient causes, a moral world of *grace* and final causes can grow. The latter world is the joint product of the activities of spirits or minds. They are images expressive not only of the universe but also of the eternal God Himself. Hence spirits can enter into reflective relationships of knowledge and love, both with God and, through and in Him, with each other. The social communion of spiritual monads in God constitutes the *City of God,* which is a teleological order that comes to birth within the framework of a world of natural, efficient motions.

## 7.  HUMAN KNOWLEDGE

The theory of monads obliges Leibniz to take a definite position concerning certain epistemological issues. In the debate between Descartes and Locke over the *origin of ideas,* he sides with the former. Since monads are basically independent of each other, there can be no abstraction of knowledge, in the sense of an abstractive derivation of ideas from the outside world. Their only possible source is from the monad itself and, ultimately, from the creator of the monadic nature. The simplicity of the finite monad is a dynamic, fecund one, spontaneously giving birth to all the ideas and actions constituting its temporal experience. This conclusion is confirmed by the logical doctrine on the complete individual substance. Since the notion of the individual contains within itself all the predicates belonging to the thing, the real substance must be equipped, from the outset, with the active tendency to bring forth the ideal content of its various states of consciousness. By "innate idea," Leibniz means not only the *meaning-content* but also the intellectual *power and impulse to express* this content and thus to know the object of perception.[35] Innate ideas, in this plenary sense, are in the mind by the very fact that the mind is a dynamic inclination to bring forth the essential content of thought, in an orderly and appropriate way.

Leibniz repeats the Scholastic axiom that there is nothing in the intellect which was not first in the sense — but he adds the significant qualification that the intellect itself does not have a sensory origin.[36] Under the term *intellect,* he includes not only the power of understanding but also the primary ideas (such as substance, being, possibility, cause, perception, and identity) and the first principles, based upon these primary ideas. Hence the intellect is not, as Locke maintains, an unmarked tablet that must wait upon sense experience for its first traces. It is already *preformed with dispositions* and aptitudes, both active and passive. Ideas and principles are inbornly present in the understanding, in at least a virtual way. Whereas Locke limits the presence of ideas to those that are actually being experienced or that are memories of past experiences, Leibniz widens

---

[35] "Our soul has the power of representing to itself any form or nature whenever the occasion comes for thinking about it, and I think that this activity of our soul is, so far as it expresses some nature, form or essence, properly the idea of the thing. This is in us, and is always in us, whether we are thinking of it or no." *Discourse on Metaphysics,* XXVI (Wiener, 327); cf. *What is an Idea?* (Wiener, 281–83). Against Malebranche, Leibniz insists that the idea is *in the soul* and not in God; but against Locke, he insists that the idea is in the soul *at all times* and not merely during conscious perception. Cf. L. E. Loemker, "Leibniz's Doctrine of Ideas," *The Philosophical Review,* LV (1946), 229–48.

[36] *"Nihil est in intellectu, quod non fuerit in sensu, excipe: nisi ipse intellectus."* *New Essays concerning Human Understanding,* II, i, 2 (Langley, 111). The first book of Leibniz' *New Essays,* like the first book of Locke's own *Essay,* is entirely devoted to the problem of innatism and is the major source for this aspect of Leibniz' doctrine.

the meaning of the mental presence of ideas to include the active capacity to bring them forth from the mind, through the native vigor of its immaterial dynamism. The acquisition of knowledge means the passage of ideas and principles from a *virtual* to an *actual* state of being known.

Since "intellect" is such an important exception to the sense origin of knowledge, Leibniz must specify the way in which *any* knowledge is due to the senses. Here, the distinction between truths of reason and truths of fact can be given a new significance. Necessary *truths of reason* are known by the mind, operating in an independent and purely intellectual way. It can summon forth the ideas and principles constituting these truths, without invoking outside aid and in sole reliance upon its own natural light. *Truths of fact,* however, do require sense experience in order to be distinctly apprehended. Sensation is a necessary, but not a sufficient, condition for grasping truths of fact. It provides the *occasion* for this knowledge but does not serve as its strict *cause.* The ideas comprising a truth of fact are drawn from the mind, on the occasion of a sense experience. The function of the latter is only to arouse the mind's attention concerning some particular connection of ideas, and thus to urge the mind to bring its own ideas to a state of distinct awareness.[37] It is not the *truth* or *meaning-content* itself but only our mental *act of thinking about* the truth which requires a sensory occasion. The actual, empirical perceiving of the meaning-content may be excited through some external expression of a connection which arouses the understanding to advert to a similar (but, until now, unattended) connection among its own ideas. But although our thoughts about truths of fact require sense experience, the truths themselves are of innate origin. They fulfill the definition of an innate truth, namely, one whose entire causal source lies in the understanding.

Three questions immediately come to mind, with respect to this innatist view of knowledge. Why does Leibniz want to reduce the scope of sensation so drastically; what meaning can be given to sensation in a monadic context; what guarantees the objectivity of knowledge, since sensation plays no genuinely causal role?

1. In discussing the hierarchy among monads, Leibniz has already stated that minds or rational souls are distinguished by their ability

---

[37] *Discourse on Metaphysics,* XXVII (Wiener, 329). On the anti-Lockean distinction between the content of truth and the actual considering of that content by the mind, cf. *Specimen of Thoughts upon the First Book of the Essay on Human Understanding* (Langley, 21).

to apprehend necessary truths of essence or eternal verities. This is the mark of the distinctively spiritual level of monadic life, where the human self is found. Hence Leibniz does not want to compromise, in any way, the characteristically human ability to have distinct knowledge of truths of reason, upon which the sciences themselves depend. Since he is fortified by no realistic conviction that our minds can reach things directly and can make abstraction of their necessary and essential structures, he has no confidence in an experiential origin of knowledge, in which the senses make a real contribution. His historical referent, in this instance, is Locke. Since Locke's empirical explanation for the universal and necessary aspects of knowledge fails to satisfy him, Leibniz despairs entirely of finding a source in sense experience for them. Hence his historical position, as well as his general metaphysics of substance, forces him to depreciate the senses and to rule out any abstractive origin of first principles and necessary truths.

2. But in reducing sensation to the position of a mere occasion of knowledge, Leibniz nevertheless does not eliminate it entirely, especially with respect to existential truths of contingent fact. Indeed, it is one of his basic theses that the *finite mind must have a certain area of confused perception* and hence a certain measure of knowledge affected by sensation.[38] Since the substantial being of every mind is structurally proportioned to the rest of the universe, the proper object of perception is the universe in its infinite variety. But the finite nature of our mind prevents it from reducing this object to a perfect unity of rational order. Our limited attention is directed now toward one sector of the universe and now toward another, bringing some particular objects of perception to clear and distinct knowledge, but leaving a wide area of peripheral objects in the condition of confused perception or sensation. Sensation and intellection do not differ in kind but they do differ in degree of clarity and distinctness. With respect to purely intellectual knowledge, the mind is relatively active and autonomous, whereas in sensation it is passive and dependent upon occasions furnished by other monads, especially bodily monads. Although knowledge of contingent truths is not derived from the outside world, the indispensable function of the latter is to direct the attention of the mind upon hitherto unseen mental relations. Sensation, then, signifies the mind's condition of passion and confused perception, which compels it to have regard

---

[38] *Discourse on Metaphysics,* XXXIII (Wiener, 338–39).

for the determinate state of the body and the rest of the universe. This is a large concession to empiricism and the given character of our knowledge of matters of fact. Yet Leibniz never concedes any authentic reception of the content of knowledge from the world. Both his metaphysical analysis of action and passion, and his assumption that a cognitive operation is not truly intellectual, if it has any potential and receptive phase, stand in the way of recognizing the full extent of the dependence of the human intellect upon the actual world revealed by sense.

3. Leibniz is supremely confident that his innatism and reduction of sense experience to the status of an occasion will not lead to *subjectivism*. The ground of his confidence is not an empirical study of cognition but an a priori, metaphysical certainty.

> God has from the first created the soul or any other real unity in such a way that everything arises in it from its own internal nature through a perfect *spontaneity* relatively to itself, and yet with a perfect *conformity* to external things. . . . And this nature of the soul being representative of the universe in a very exact though more or less distinctive manner, the series of representations produced in the soul will correspond naturally to the series of changes in the Universe itself.[39]

This teaching on the natural conformity of our representations with the world is merely an epistemological consequence of the pre-established harmony among substances. For the cognitive operations share in the substance's correspondence-to-the-universe, which is the condition under which alone any essence is realized, both in its substance and its activities. Our ideas arise spontaneously or innately from within ourselves, but the requirements of universal harmony guarantee that they are in natural conformity with the being of the objects perceived. Hence every monad is a reliable, *living mirror* of the world.[40] Leibniz' answer to the Lockean query about how we can ever be sure that our ideas — which both thinkers admit to be the immediate objects of perception — conform with real things, is that the question can never be settled at the finite and empirical level. We must turn to the harmonizing Deity and to the even more fundamental metaphysics of essential systems of perfection, for complete assurance that the spontaneity and real conformity of our ideas are the graven laws of mental life.

---

[39] *New System of Nature and of the Communication of Substances*, 14, 15 (Wiener, 114–15).
[40] *Letters to Clarke*, V, 87 (Wiener, 267); *The Monadology*, 56 (Wiener, 544).

Berkeley will accept this way of settling the epistemological problem, but it will prove unsatisfactory to both Hume and Kant. Hume's difficulty is that the use of God as a guarantor of the conformity of our ideas with things is invalid, since the arguments for God's existence already suppose the objective conformity of our ideas. Furthermore, the distinction between necessary truths of reason and contingent truths of fact runs deeper than Leibniz suspects. Empirically viewed, the mind requires the senses to provide literal data — *given contents* — and not merely occasions for intellectual reminiscence or introspection. The fact that necessary truths concern the essential order, whereas contingent truths concern matters of existence, is also indicative of a wider cleavage than Leibniz is willing to admit. Once Hume realizes the *distinctiveness of the existential order* and its resistance to reduction to the status of a mere culmination of an essential dialectic, he can point out that the existence of God is not established through an analysis of essential requirements and that the metaphysics of harmonizing essences may not be relevant for questions about existential matter of fact. Consequently, he can reject the two pillars underlying Leibniz' confidence in the natural conformity between his ideas and the actual world. The stage will then be prepared for Kant's tremendous effort to synthesize the Leibnizian world of necessary, universal truths of essence and the Humean world of contingent, existential facts, without making appeal to God and a metaphysic of essences.

Finally, Leibniz bases his theory of the *personal self* upon his doctrine of perception. The natural desire or tendency of every monad is to introduce the greatest amount of clarity and distinctness into its perceptions. This movement toward maximum perfection accounts for the upward-tending, continuous effort of perceptual states, from unconsciousness to animal consciousness and finally to human self-awareness. The apex is reached in *reflection* or spiritual apperception, which deliberately relates our ideas to first principles and the divine source of all ideas. Complete clarity and distinctness of thought can never be reached during our temporal existence. Nevertheless, we may approximate unceasingly to this ideal, by reflecting upon our own nature and seeing it to be an image of God as well as of the world. Personal perfection is attained in proportion to one's reflective approach to God.

Leibniz distinguishes between the *physical,* real identity of every monad with itself and the *moral identity* or selfsameness of spiritual monads or minds. His view of personality is similar to Locke's but has a definitely religious coloration. The *person* is a moral identity or reflective affirmation of the selfhood of a rational soul or mind. It consists in a *conscienciosité* or heightened self-awareness, which is the immanent goal of mental life. This goal must be harmonized with the transcendent one of making approach to God. Their reconciliation is found in the consideration that a human spirit becomes fully aware of its own nature, and hence attains the full stature of personal self-possession, only in the act of recognizing itself as a son of God. This clarity about one's personal being is man's true *immortality*.[41] In this sense, Spinoza is right in saying that we have our immortality in this life. But, for Leibniz, immortality entails personal survival. No individual monad ever goes out of existence, and even the composite only increases or diminishes its range of perceptibility. But it is the distinguishing mark of the continuance-in-existence of spiritual monads that they persist as moral identities — individual, substantial subjects which are also personal selves — retaining all their happenings and moral responsibility for their temporal choices and orientation. His personalist metaphysics of spiritual monads kept Leibniz from accepting the Spinozistic solution to the problem of immortality.

## 8.  FREEDOM, EVIL, AND OPTIMISM

Human freedom raises some special difficulties, when it is brought into relation with the doctrine of pre-established harmony. Leibniz gives a secular version of the theological dispute about divine predestination and man's freedom. The notion of the individual substance contains all that will happen to it, thus enabling God to have an a priori, analytically certain knowledge of the individual's entire life and actions. The entire content of the individual's temporal career unrolls from the constitution of its essence, from the moment of its entrance into the existent world. How can freedom be reconciled with God's foreknowledge and causation, as well as with the essential

---

[41] Since every simple, finite monad is imperishable and forever attached to a body, death (in the strict sense of substantial corruption) cannot transpire. Monads come into existence by divine creation and can go out of existence only through annihilation by God. Nevertheless, Leibniz distinguishes between the mere *incessibility* of nonrational monads and the *immortality* of rational persons. Cf. *The Monadology*, 73–77 (Wiener, 548–49); *On the Active Force of Body, on the Soul and on the Soul of Brutes* (Wiener, 505–08); *New Essays concerning Human Understanding*, II, xxvii, 9 (Langley, 245–47).

determination of all predicates belonging to the individual?

In searching for light on the relationship between divine fore-knowledge and human freedom, Leibniz read widely in the current theological controversy about the assistance of divine grace. He tried to reconcile God's mediate knowledge with His predeterminism.[42] The *foreknowledge* of God has nothing to do with determining the truth of contingent futurities (events which will freely happen or which would happen, under certain circumstances). These truths are already determinate, and foreknowledge adds nothing to their truth or specific content. Yet they are foreseen by God, precisely as being what they are: truths about free contingencies. Hence the divine mediate knowledge (*scientia media*) preserves the freedom of our actions. Nevertheless, God's *foreordinances* or decrees do con-tribute toward the determination of contingent futurities and hence toward the foundation of God's certain knowledge of these truths. In the case of what *would* happen under certain circumstances, the free contingencies are not arbitrarily specified but depend on the harmonious combinations possible within a given collection of essences. God can assign as a determinate reason for possible happenings, that which would promote the best within a given system of essences. As for what *will* actually occur in our free acts, God does pre-determine the will, insofar as He decrees the existence of the best possible world and its essential requirements, but He does not pre-determine it with absolute or metaphysical necessity. For the achieve-ment of the best possible world, God decrees that men will always do that which appears best to them, and will do it in a rational or free way. This decree inclines their will certainly and efficaciously, through a moral necessity, and yet it does not *coerce* the will. Hence Leibniz holds both that the divine foreknowledge is infallibly true (since it is based upon certain, determinate truths) and that our choices remain free. The worth of this argument depends upon the relation between essential combinations and divine decrees, as well as upon the implied doctrine about human choice.

On the human side, freedom is the *spontaneity of an intelligent being.*[43] It is grounded neither in indifferent equilibrium nor in

[42] *Theodicy*, I, 36–48 (Huggard, 143–50); *Letters to Clarke*, V, 5–8 (Wiener, 238–39).
[43] *Theodicy*, I, 51–52, and III, 288–311 (Huggard, 151, 303–14); *Letters to Clarke,* V, 11–17 (Wiener, 240–42); *New Essays concerning Human Understanding*, II, xxi (Langley, 179–221).

abstention of judgment. For, indifference is not a sufficient reason for a free action, whereas abstention is itself a prior act that has a prior reason. Our wills are laden with the spontaneous dispositions of our rational nature, including the influence of the unconscious, "minute perceptions." Moreover, intelligent agents can grasp the nature of the good and, within our universe, will *always choose what appears to be the best.* This provides the only sufficient reason for their action. A free act is always rationally motivated and is the more perfectly free, the more it is determined by what seems best, i.e., by the strongest motive. Leibniz argues here in much the same way as in his explanation of divine creative freedom. Human choice is not a blind impulse but proceeds from a reflective deliberation upon our motives and desires. Although whatever seems best will be the prevailing motive, this reason inclines or persuades the will efficaciously rather than coerces it. We act not under an absolute necessity but under a *moral necessity,* which is the condition of freedom. Nevertheless, we always do that which seems to be best and which therefore provides the strongest motive or reason of choice.

Leibniz' theory of human freedom encounters the same difficulties as his doctrine on divine creation, since in both cases he regards the sufficient reason of an action as imposing itself independently upon the agent. The difference between absolute and hypothetical necessity becomes nugatory in a theory that identifies freedom with rational spontaneity. Although intellectual apprehension of the grounds of choice prevents it from being a *blind* impulse, the choice is nevertheless *determined* by the total spontaneous striving of one's nature and not by the agent's uncoerced judgment. Leibniz shows that human choice is internally motivated but not that it is freely made. He confuses a merely passive and motiveless indifference with the intellect's dominating power to judge a particular good in the light of the good in general, and thus to control its own final practical judgment.[44] If a man is bound to follow the most strongly inclining apparent good, it is difficult (as Locke observed) to see how his

---

[44] In his *Traité du libre arbitre* (Liège, Sciences et Lettres, 1951), 105–10, Y. Simon remarks that the real question in free choice is not about which is the greater or lesser good, but about the condition under which a particular good becomes unconditionally desirable here-and-now for a rational appetite, so that it will actually choose this concrete good. Whether the multitude of insensible perceptions and sentiments inclines us to regard an object as a greater or a lesser good, there is still need for a last practical judgment, declaring this object to be a good absolutely desirable, to the point of being here-and-now chosen in a concrete way.

choice could ever be determined freely by himself. Leibniz recognizes that an objection can be drawn from the fact that men often choose deliberately a *lesser good* or even a *known evil*. His reply does not salvage his position. He states that no action is possible unless it be determined by the strongest motive, which alone gives a sufficient reason for this particular choice. The strength of the motive is determined not merely by rational appraisal of the proposed action but also by all the habits, dispositions, and passions that make up our character. This notion of freedom is little different from Spinoza's outright necessitation by another, the "other," in Leibniz' case, being the total bent of one's nature and character. Whatever one does, would then bear the stamp of spontaneity and hence of freedom, leaving no distinction between the acts merely done by man and the distinctively free or human acts that are morally significant. For both Spinoza and Leibniz, the human mind is best characterized as a spiritual automaton, whose law of spontaneous, rational necessity is its only freedom.

The presence of evils in the best possible world compels Leibniz to compose a *theodicy* or justification of God's ways in the world. He borrows from the Scholastic discussions of the problem of evil, but reformulates the issues in accord with his own philosophy. On God's side, a fundamental distinction must be drawn between the antecedent and the consequent divine will. In his *antecedent* or *previous will*, God simply wills the production of every good, considered as such and separately, and the prevention of every evil, also considered as such and by itself. The antecedent will is directed toward essences, each taken individually and without reference to the conditions of existence. But for the production of any actual world, the several goods and evils must be considered together, in order to determine the essential, systematic relations of compatibility and incompatibility, which constitute the conditions of existence. God's "consequent will, final and decisive, results from the conflict of all the antecedent wills, of those which tend toward good, even as of those which repel evil; and from the concurrence of all these particular wills comes the total will."[45] Whereas God's antecedent will tends toward *the good*,

---

[45] *Theodicy*, I, 22 (Huggard, 137). Leibniz' argument in the *Theodicy* is labyrinthine and repetitious, reminding one of the discussions engaged in by the more subtle minds among the ranks of Milton's fallen angels:

"Others apart sat on a Hill retir'd,
In thoughts more elevate, and reason'd high

His *consequent* or *decretory will* (from which the act of creation emerges) decrees the actual existence of *the best possible world*. Through His consequent will, God wills physical evil, not absolutely but as a means to greater good or as a penalty for sin. But even His consequent will never wills moral evil. The conditions of the best possible world require Him to *exclude* some goods that are incompatible with the prevailing system of essences, and to *permit* moral evil, but His infinite goodness prevents God from ever *willing* moral evil, even as a means to a good. The mixture of goods and evils is a concomitant result of the consequent will to make the best possible world exist.

Leibniz' explanation of the divine consequent will is solidary with his stand on the divine freedom and the relation between God and the world of pure essences. This consequent will is a rational acquiescence to the mechanical, vector resolution of the countertendencies among various essences, striving objectively among themselves. At the pre-existential level, even evil has an essence of some sort and exerts its weight upon the possible combinations of essences. The transition from the antecedent will of the good to the consequent will of the best possible world is left obscure by Leibniz. It is here that he regards God as adopting the standard of perfection or the contingent existence of the best possible combination of essence. Once this standard is taken as the rule of creative production, God freely chooses the maximum system of essential perfection, one which must contain a mixture of goods and evils, in accord with the relations among essences. Leibniz' theodicy amounts to a moral justification of the ways of essences among themselves and as the ultimate determinants of the structure of our world.

*Evil* as such is a privation, and its cause is a deficient one.[46] This thesis is advanced by Leibniz, once evil is considered in respect to the actual world. It does not lead him, however, to underplay the strength and bitterness of evil or the imminence of a barbaric submergence of all civilized values. Hence he does not claim any more

---

Of Providence, Foreknowledge, Will and Fate —
Fixed Fate, free will, foreknowledge absolute —
And found no end, in wandring mazes lost."
                              *Paradise Lost,* II, 557–61.

[46] *Theodicy,* I, 10–12, 21–25; II, 119 (Huggard, 129–30, 136–38, 189–90); *Summary of the Controversy* (Huggard, 383); *On the Ultimate Origin of Things* (Wiener, 351–55).

than that ours is the best *possible* (or "least defective") world. An imaginative selection can certainly be made of all the most desirable features of existence, omitting the undesirable ones. But this is an idle exercise, since it ignores the question of compatibility among the various elements selected for inclusion in an absolutely perfect universe. Leibniz only contends that, among the compossible combinations, ours is the best. Taken as a whole, it could not be improved. There cannot but be defects and deformities in the particular parts, considered in isolation. Evil is of three sorts: metaphysical, physical, and moral. These varieties correspond to the three kinds of privation or lack to which we are subject: finitude or lack of unlimited essential perfection (*metaphysical* evil); suffering or lack of bodily well-being and integrity (*physical* evil); sin or lack of adequate judgment and rectitude of choice (*moral* evil). The possibility of any sort of lack or evil stems from our finite nature, so that metaphysical evil is the ultimate reason for the other kinds. It is an evil in a very loose and general sense, however, since there could not be any sort of harmonious universe composed of many entities, without the composing members being finite. With regard to the special evils, physical and moral, Leibniz asks us to consider them within the larger context of the world order.

There would seem to be no opportunity for moral evil in a universe in which man's actions are directed to what is best. In dealing with this problem, Leibniz scrutinizes the fact of human finitude, in order to find a reason why men are prone to sin. From the very fact that they are limited beings, men cannot avoid having some of their ideas, and hence some of their motives of action, in a relatively confused state. Because their knowledge is not perfectly clear and distinct in all respects, men can be mistaken and hence can sin. They can, in effect, *act upon confused perceptions and mistaken judgments.* This explanation of moral evil has the drawback, however, of reducing good conduct to distinct knowledge, sin to ignorance and error. It fails to recognize a man's definite moral responsibility for the state of what *seems* best to him and for acting in the absence of adequate knowledge. Malice has no meaning in this perspective, and vice is reduced to the hindrance placed upon the power of acting, by reason of imperfect perceptions. Moral evil is thereby transformed into the disorderly consequences of acting upon certain of one's unclarified motives. Here, as well as in Leibniz' analysis of freedom, attention is deflected from the will-act of *election itself* to some of the *conditions* surrounding it and *effects* flowing from it. The logic of sufficient reason hides freedom and sin from view, in the very process of explaining their possibility in perceptual terms.

In discussing the actual presence of physical and moral evils, Leibniz follows the lead of pagan and Christian apologists in making a comparison with our evaluation of a great painting or symphony. If we confine ourselves to one section of the picture, it may appear to be only a confused mass of colors and jagged figures, grotesquely incomplete and jumbled together. But if we view this fragment as integrated with the rest of the painting, its harmonious function in the total pattern becomes clear. Again, a composer mingles discords with harmonies in order to achieve a satisfactory, total effect. The sweet is pointed up by the bitter, the secure by the dangerous. Without labor, no crown of satisfaction; without temptation, no triumph of loyalty; without sin, no repentance and conversion of heart. These laws of finite being warn us to suspend judgment about the physical and moral universe, until we can comprehend the total harmony of being in the light of eternity. God, the supreme artist, uses physical evils to place the goodness of things in sharper relief. God, the omnipotent provider, can draw good out of even the evil of sin, and can reconcile individual interests with cosmic harmony. Leibniz reminds us that the Holy Week liturgy refers to Adam's sin as *felix culpa,* in respect to the Redemption it brought. Our world is not only a vale of tears but also (as Keats phrased it) a vale of soul-making. We should come to love the place where the maximum of moral, as well as physical, perfection is realized, within the limits of finiteness.

The main reason why Leibniz bids men love the world, wherein they suffer, is that the dominion of God is bound to work not only to the universal good but also to the particular good of men. This optimism is not a pious wish but the consequence of the logic of the best universe. The achievement of the maximum reality of essence means the realization of the most perfection. Now the physical perfection of man is itself in the moral order, since it involves the actualizing of a spiritual nature. Hence the perfecting of the universe requires a *distinctive perfecting of man in his moral and spiritual being.* Good and bad actions are given their proper reward with mechanical efficiency, since the mechanism of nature promotes the ends of spiritual beings. The ultimate reconciling of the physical and moral realms of being is the work of divine omnipotence. The same God is both the architect of the world's mechanism and the monarch of the kingdom of spiritual beings.

Whereas God brings all monads to their proper measure of perfection, He confers a distinctive *personal happiness* upon minds or spiritual monads. Their reflective and loving participation in eternal life is the same as their eternal happiness. This participation supposes the immortality of the rational soul, not only in its substantial nature but also in its entire personality, including memory and acquired knowledge. This is the moral-religious face of the teaching on personal immortality. Minds are called to a special union of knowledge and love with God, considered as Lord and Father. This common vocation of all men should find outward expression in the religious organization of the earth, through a single, universal, or Catholic faith. Leibniz' work for the reunion of the Christian Churches was intended as a first step in this direction.[47] And men can win citizenship in the City of God only by performing the free and reflective act of giving glory to God, from whom the harmony of being comes and to whom it returns through the office of men.

## SUMMARY OF CHAPTER 7

A logical and a metaphysical vision of the universe are combined in Leibniz' philosophy. If all things have their characteristic numbers and if the elementary concepts are both finite and ordered, then there can be a universal science, based on the interconnection among the logical characteristics. Such calculation need not be confined to mathematical objects but may extend to all fields, including moral judgments. Even after he saw that the number of primitive elements is infinite, Leibniz did not abandon his logical ideal of a priori demonstration. Instead, he synthesized it more closely with his metaphysics of the harmony of the universe: the underlying unity amid the variety of individuals and aspects of experience. His analysis of the basic first principles and the nature of individual substance supplied the foundation for a universe in which the greatest number of compossible essences are realized. Leibniz' metaphysical center of gravity was the intelligible essence, which jostles with its neighbor for the privilege of entering into the existing order and thus of contributing to the perfection of this best possible universe. The great problem was how to reconcile this logico-metaphysical position, required as the basis of scientific certainty, with the traditionally accepted divine attributes

---

[47] Cf. J. H. Crehan, S.J., "Leibniz and the Polemics of Reunion," *Thought*, X (1935–1936), 16–29. For a historical study of the ideal of the City of God, see E. Gilson, *Les métamorphoses de la cité de Dieu* (Louvain, E. Nauwelaerts, 1953; 228–47, on Leibniz).

of freedom and omnipotence. Leibniz made the essences of things existentially dependent upon the divine will, while at the same time he reserved for them a certain quasi-independence in respect to their content of meaning. Hence the divine creative will operates as a ratification of the outcome of the strife among the essences, granted God's free decree of choosing the best. The actual outcome is a world of monadic substances, each of which microcosmically mirrors the entire universe from its own finite, bodily viewpoint. Leibniz called upon God and the order among essences to pre-establish the harmony among monads, in view of achieving the best possible world. Although there is no direct causal interaction among finite monads, they conspire together to constitute a harmonious and unified system of activities. Spiritual monads can rise above animal consciousness to a knowledge of first principles and the infinite being of God. Persons or spiritual monads enjoy a special, intimate communion in the City of God.

# BIBLIOGRAPHICAL NOTE

1. *Sources.* Great masses of unpublished Leibniz manuscripts remain at the Hanover library. The Prussian Academy of Sciences began a complete, critical edition of his writings, but the project has proceeded at a disappointingly slow pace. This edition of the *Sämtliche Schriften und Briefe* (1923 ff.) is to contain forty volumes, divided into the following seven series: (1) general, political, and historical correspondence, 11 vols.; (2) philosophical correspondence, 6 vols.; (3) mathematical, scientific, and technical correspondence, 5 vols.; (4) political writings, 4 vols.; (5) historical writings, 4 vols.; (6) philosophical writings (also theological and juristic writings), 6 vols.; (7) mathematical, scientific, and technical writings, 4 vols. To date, four volumes in the political and historical fields have appeared, together with the following: (1) the first volume in the second series, *Philosophischer Briefwechsel* (Darmstadt, Reichl, 1926); (2) the first volume in the sixth series, *Philosophische Schriften* (Darmstadt, Reichl, 1930), containing the early works of Leibniz from the Leipzig-Altorf period (1663-1666) and the Frankfort-Mainz period (1667-1672). For practical purposes, one must still rely upon the two following collections made by C. I. Gerhardt: *Die mathematischen Schriften von G. W. Leibniz* (7 vols., Berlin, Asher, 1849-1863), and *Die philosophischen Schriften von G. W. Leibniz* (7 vols., Berlin, Weidmann, 1875-1890). Further additions will be found in L. Couturat, *Opuscules et fragments inédits de Leibniz* (Paris, Alcan, 1903); G. Grua, *G. W. Leibniz, Textes inédits* (2 vols., Paris, Presses Universitaires, 1948). Grua observes, encouragingly, that all of his recently published manuscripts agree with what we already know in general about Leibniz' personality and philosophical positions, so that it is unlikely that radical revisions will have to be made in the light of the documents still to be published. Microfilms of his unpublished papers are available at the University

of Pennsylvania Library. The best translations are by P. Wiener, *Leibniz Selections* (New York, Scribner, 1951), and by L. E. Loemker, *Leibniz: Philosophical Papers and Letters* (2 vols., Chicago, University of Chicago, 1956). For the important correspondence with Arnauld, in connection with the *Discourse on Metaphysics,* consult *Leibniz's Discourse on Metaphysics, Correspondence with Arnauld, and Monadology,* translated by G. R. Montgomery (Chicago, Open Court, 1902). H. W. Carr's translation of *The Monadology* (Los Angeles, University of Southern California Press, 1930) is enriched by a useful commentary and supplementary essays. See also: *New Essays concerning Human Understanding,* translated by A. G. Langley (third ed., Lasalle, Ill., Open Court, 1949); *Theodicy,* translated by E. M. Huggard, with an informative Introduction by A. Farrer (New Haven, Yale University Press, 1952).

2. *Studies.* The biographical materials contained in G. E. Guhrauer's German work were condensed in English by J. M. Mackie, *Life of Godfrey William von Leibnitz* (Boston, Gould, Kendall and Lincoln, 1845). The wide range of approaches toward Leibniz' fundamental doctrines can be seen from the better introductory studies: B. Russell, *A Critical Exposition of the Philosophy of Leibniz* (second ed., London, Allen and Unwin, 1937); H. W. Carr, *Leibniz* (London, Benn, 1929); H. W. B. Joseph, *Lectures on the Philosophy of Leibniz* (Oxford, Clarendon, 1949); G. Stammler, *Leibniz* (Munich, Reinhardt, 1930); K. Huber, *Leibniz* (Munich, Oldenbourg, 1951); K. Hildebrandt, *Leibniz und das Reich der Gnade* (The Hague, Nijhoff, 1953). Russell and Joseph are highly analytical and stress the logical foundations; Carr brings out the metaphysical element, but colors it with his own Crocean idealism; a good balance between logical and metaphysical themes is achieved by Stammler, Huber, and Hildebrandt. The two latter authors summarize the findings of recent biographical research, while Russell adds a long Appendix of extracts from Leibniz' writings. The genesis of Leibniz' logico-metaphysical views is studied by W. Kabitz, *Die Philosophie des jungen Leibniz* (Heidelberg, Winter, 1909); the logical problems are discussed circumstantially by L. Couturat, *La logique de Leibniz* (Paris, Alcan, 1901). For more particular metaphysical issues, see M. Guéroult, *Dynamique et métaphysique leibniziennes* (Paris, Les Belles Lettres, 1934); J. Iwanicki, *Leibniz et les démonstrations mathématiques de l'existence de Dieu* (Paris, Vrin, 1934); J. Jalabert, *La théorie leibnizienne de la substance* (Paris, Presses Universitaires, 1947); A. O. Lovejoy, *The Great Chain of Being* (Cambridge, Mass., Harvard University Press, 1936), Lecture 5, "Plenitude and Sufficient Reason in Leibniz and Spinoza" (144–82). A more extended comparison between Leibniz and Spinoza is made by G. Friedmann, *Leibniz et Spinoza* (fourth ed., Paris, Gallimard, 1946). Leibniz' impact upon cultural change is brought out by R. W. Meyer, *Leibnitz and the Seventeenth-Century Revolution,* translated by J. P. Stern (Chicago, Regnery, 1952); see, also, P. Hazard, *The European Mind (1680–1715),* translated

by J. L. May (London, Hollis and Carter, 1953). M. Wundt's *Die deutsche Schulmetaphysik des 17. Jahrhunderts* (Tübingen, Mohr, 1939) describes the textbook philosophy which was taught in the German universities during Leibniz' age and which considerably influenced both his mode of expression and his doctrine. In G. Grua's *Jurisprudence universelle et theodicée selon Leibniz* (Paris, Presses Universitaires, 1953), will be found a well-documented study of the rationalistic basis of his theodicy and a concise Thomistic critique. G. Grua's further work *La justice humaine selon Leibniz* (Paris, Presses Universitaires, 1956), applies the general theory of jurisprudence to the special case of human justice. H. G. Alexander's edition of *The Leibniz-Clarke Correspondence* (New York, Philosophical Library, 1956), fully documents and explains the famous quarrel between Leibniz and the English Newtonian, Samuel Clarke. One of Leibniz' important but condensed works, the *Discourse on Metaphysics,* is carefully explained in P. Burgelin's *Commentaire du Discours de Métaphysique de Leibniz* (Paris, Presses Universitaires, 1959). Jalabert takes up his concept of God in *Le Dieu de Leibniz* (Paris, Presses Universitaires, 1960).

# Chapter 8. LOCKE

## I. LIFE AND WRITINGS

LOCKE was born in the small town of Wrington, near Bristol, in 1632. Both from his father and from Westminster School in London, he received a strict, Puritan upbringing. He entered Christ Church, Oxford, in 1652, received the bachelor's and master's degrees there, and held the senior studentship at that college until 1684. While at Oxford, his religious sympathies turned toward the Church of England, since it provided a broader basis for national unity. In later life, Locke agreed with the latitudinarian party that belief in Christ should be the only test of religious fellowship. He regarded his undergraduate training in philosophy as unintelligible, although his own speculation always bore traces of this early "Scholastic" formation. During graduate studies, he received his first introduction to Descartes' writings, an experience that gave him a relish for things philosophical and reassured him that clear and rational thinking was just as possible in philosophy as in the empirical sciences. Most of Locke's active years at Oxford, however, were spent in scientific investigations. During Robert Boyle's stay at Oxford (1654–1668), Locke became the great chemist's close associate and aided him in numerous experiments. Locke himself studied medical subjects but never had more than an informal practice.

In 1667, he joined the household of Lord Ashley, later the first Earl of Shaftesbury. Employed at first as a medical aide, Locke's great practical abilities were soon recognized. He then served as advisor and friend to Shaftesbury, who was moving toward the peak of his political career. When Shaftesbury was made Lord Chancellor (1672), Locke was appointed secretary for the Presentation of Benefices, a post that gave him practical acquaintance with ecclesiastical politics. In the following year, he became secretary to the important Council of Trade and Plantations, acquiring further knowledge of economic matters. But the press of work impaired his health, forcing him to retire to France for a long period (1675–1679), in order to regain his strength. Fortunately, this enforced leisure enabled Locke to develop his own philosophical views. In 1671, a group of five or six friends had gathered with him to discuss the problem of the foundations of revealed religion and morality. They were unable to settle the issue because, as Locke remarked to them, they failed to treat the preliminary question of the scope and objects of our understanding. Locke agreed to submit a paper on the nature of the understanding and knowledge, and thus launched out into the inquiry that led eventually to *An Essay concerning Human Understanding.* Two early drafts were completed in 1671; further expansions were made during his years in France; he continued to work on it after his return to England and during his exile in Holland. Finally, the first edition was published in 1690. Locke continued to revise and add to the *Essay,* in the four editions appearing during his lifetime.

Locke's return from France to England (1679) was not for long. His patron, Shaftesbury, headed the Protestant opposition to James II and was forced to flee to Holland, where he died in 1683. That same year, Locke also exiled himself to Holland, where he kept his movements secret for a while, since his name appeared on the list of eighty-five Englishmen wanted by the government, in connection with Monmouth's unsuccessful rebellion. His health improved in Holland, where he enjoyed the company of the Protestant theologian, Philip van Limborch, and of Jean Le Clerc, who edited the literary journal *Bibliothèque Universelle.* In this journal (1688), Locke published an abstract of his *Essay.* The same year marked the "Glorious Revolution," which drove out James II and installed William and Mary on the British throne, under Whig sponsorship. Locke came back to England early in 1689. He published immediately his controversial *Letter concerning Toleration* (1689), which was followed by two other letters on the same subject (1690 and 1693) and a fragment of a fourth letter. In 1690 appeared not only *An Essay concerning Human Understanding* but also the *Two Treatises of Government,* in which Locke opposed the divine-right theory of sovereignty and offered a defense of the Whig settlement. He also published *Some Thoughts concerning Education* (1693) and *The Reasonableness of Christianity* (1695), books that reflected his lifelong interest in educational and religious matters. This latter preoccupation involved him in a controversy with Bishop Stillingfleet, who traced the Unitarian tendencies of the day to the Lockean "way of ideas." Although broken in health, Locke continued his career of public service, as a member of the new Board of Trade and Plantations (1696–1700). But from 1691 onward, he spent most of his leisure time at Oates, the estate of his friends, the Mashams. Lady Masham was the daughter of the Cambridge Platonist, Ralph Cudworth, and was herself a woman of intelligence and sympathy. Locke retired permanently from public service in 1700, received Newton and other friends at Oates, and died peacefully (1704), while Lady Masham was reading the Psalms to him.

## 2. THE STANDPOINT OF THE "ESSAY"

With disarming frankness, Locke admits that his "discontinued way of writing" *An Essay concerning Human Understanding* leads to certain defects.[1] His treatment lacks the order, coherence, and structural tightness of a work conceived and executed according to a more systematic plan. His use of common language and customary turns of thought makes an appeal to the reader and yet exposes the argument to the vagueness and ambiguity that surround ordinary usage. The *common-sense* tone of the discussion often enables Locke to take advantage of realistic convictions about the mind and the world that do not follow rigorously from his own principles. Nevertheless, the book also has the strength of its weaknesses: it triumphs over all its defects and becomes the landmark of the movement known as British empiricism. The other leaders in this tradition return to Locke's *Essay,* as the common point of departure for their own speculations. For it is successful in formulating the problems and the method that are characteristic of the *empiricist approach* in philosophy.

Instead of discoursing, at once, about sublime issues concerning the inner nature of God, the fine points of moral doctrine and the precise content of revelation, Locke proposes first to inquire into the nature of the knowing faculty which must be used in such investigations. To bypass the problem of the nature of the understanding is to begin at the wrong end of philosophical inquiry. Locke is a

---

[1] *An Essay concerning Human Understanding,* The Epistle to the Reader (Fraser edition, I, 10). For a succinct and informative introduction to Locke, read R. I. Aaron, "Great Thinkers: (X) John Locke," *Philosophy,* XII (1937), 19–32; the series of essays on "Great Thinkers" in *Philosophy* is worth examining, since it includes authoritative essays on most of the great modern philosophers.

strong advocate of the *primacy of theory of knowledge* over the metaphysical, ethical, and cosmological branches of philosophy. For, unless the structure and scope of the mind are determined with some precision at the outset, it becomes impossible to eliminate sterile controversies and confine our study to questions where there is some solid hope of gaining certainty, or at least high probability. The modern Ockham's razor is found in this concern to relieve the mind of fruitless issues and direct it only toward matters where it has some competence.

The *purpose* of the *Essay* is stated concisely in the Introduction: "To inquire into the original, certainty, and extent of *human knowledge,* together with the grounds and degrees of *belief, opinion* and *assent.*"[2] This program is reflected in the organization of Locke's materials. In Book I, a negative answer is given to the problem of the origin of knowledge, by showing that innatism is an inadequate explanation. Book II discusses the positive origin of knowledge by means of an analysis of the different kinds of ideas, their relation to experience, and their combination according to the various intellectual operations. A long detour is made in the third book, for the purpose of examining the nature and use of words, with special reference to general terms as signs of essences. Finally, the fourth book applies the previous findings to the main issue: the nature and scope of human knowledge, together with the distinction between knowledge, probability, and belief.

In order to carry out this ambitious project, Locke makes two crucial decisions in the methodological order. The first is to employ only the "historical, plain method"; the second is to take ideas as the primary objects of analysis. (1) The *historical, plain method* is a thoroughly empirical approach to the understanding, considering it precisely in its actual operations and treating its objects precisely as they appear in actual consciousness.[3] When a man observes the conscious workings of the cognitive process, as it goes on within himself, he is following the dictates of this method. Its aim is to copy nature and provide an exact description of the functions of the mind-as-engaged-in-thinking, somewhat as "the incomparable Mr. Newton" made a descriptive study of the actual movements of observed bodies. Just as one cannot see the physical world through another man's pair of eyes, so one cannot know the nature of the

---

[2] *An Essay concerning Human Understanding,* Introduction, 2 (Fraser, I, 26).

[3] *Loc. cit.* (Fraser, I, 27).

understanding merely by examining the written reports of others. As the American radical empiricist, William James, was later to say, one must catch experience on the wing, like a bird in its flight. This requires an introspective attention to our own internal acts.

Metaphysical and physicophysiological considerations are not supposed to come within the purview of the historical, plain method, but Locke finds it hard to respect this restriction. This is evident, for instance, in his reply to Stillingfleet, who had cast suspicion upon Locke's reasonings, because of their novelty and their failure to consult the systematic accounts of other thinkers. In defense of his procedure, Locke calls it *a new history of an old thing,* an explanation of the *common* functions of understanding which nevertheless rests upon one's *own* testimony. Personal exploration of one's own consciousness is needed, both because of the privacy of individual consciousness and the differences among individual minds. This would seem, however, to threaten the validity of generalizations made from findings about one's own cognitive history. Hence Locke adds that the intellectual power and operations are *alike* in most men, that most men are of his own mental size and structure. This is a metaphysical belief, resting upon an appeal to common-sense convictions. Locke also desires to be excused from giving any physiological description of perception and from making metaphysical pronouncements about the essence of mind and the dependence of ideas upon a material basis. But in practice, he must assume that really existing, material things emit imperceptible particles or corpuscles, which strike the organs and brain, agitate the animal spirits or nerves, and thereby produce ideas in the mind. Similarly, he makes at least negative pronouncements about the essence of mind, and probable statements about the relation of cognition to the body. These concessions indicate how difficult it is to elaborate a pure theory of knowledge, apart from commitments about the real world, which gives our cognitions their first impulse and content.

(2) The second major feature of Locke's methodology is to begin with an analysis of the *idea,* defined as "whatsoever is the *object* of the understanding when a man thinks . . . whatever is meant by *phantasm, notion, species,* or *whatever it is which the mind can be employed about in thinking.*"[4] In starting with ideas as the atomic

---

[4] *An Essay concerning Human Understanding,* Introduction, 8 (Fraser, I, 32). J. Buchler, "Act and Object in Locke," *The Philosophical Review,* XLVI (1937), 528–35, notes that there is a fundamental ambiguity running through Locke's thought, as to

elements of knowledge, Locke accepts the analytic approach of Descartes and most scientifically inclined thinkers. The two main assumptions of *elementarism* are: (*a*) that the elements into which knowledge can be analytically resolved, are more authentic and reliable starting points than the complex wholes themselves, and (*b*) that the elements remain basically unchanged, whether taken in isolation or in composition. The elementarist viewpoint underplays the uniqueness of complex, cognitive wholes, and overlooks the profound modifications undergone by analytic units, upon their reintegration in the total context. But this method gives Locke assurance that he can determine the limits of knowledge "from the right end," i.e., from a prior examination of the knowing power and its mental building blocks, the ideas. Whereas Bacon and Spinoza advise us to test our abilities by first trying them on definite realities, Locke seeks to ascertain *beforehand* which of the imputed realities fall within the mind's range. By resolving judgments into ideas, in order to gain a starting point, he proposes a way to settle in principle the capacity of human intelligence. From this angle, the aim of empiricism is a highly ambitious and rationalistic one.

The Cartesian influence is prominent in Locke's definition of an idea. Both philosophers agree in making "idea" a capacious enough term to cover the mental objects of sensation and imagination, as well as intellection. They also regard the idea as the direct and proper object of the understanding: what is known directly is the idea itself. Locke adds that the idea should also be treated as a sign or representation of existent things. But it remains that sort of sign which is known first of all in and as itself (instrumental sign), before it conveys information about an independent world. The method of starting with ideas, rather than judgments, encourages the treatment of the idea *primarily as an object,* and only *later on as a sign* representing something else. Locke himself was not unaware of the vexatious problems attaching to the representationist hypothesis. He asked Malebranche how one could ever know whether the idea or picture in the mind is like what it is supposed to represent, when the understanding is barred, by definition, from making any independent acquaintance with the thing, in order to make the com-

---

whether "idea" means an object-of-mind distinct from the act of perceiving or an object-of-mind identical with the perceiving act itself. This may be compared with the dual meaning of "experience" mentioned below, Section 4.

parison.[5] He found this question easier to propound than to answer, unless he were to make a metaphysical surmise about the relation of similarity between the extramental thing, as a cause, and the idea, as its effect in the mind. From a strictly phenomenalistic standpoint, however, he could not make any statements about a "background" class of independent things and hence could not directly test the reliability of ideas as signs. Considerations of this sort had forced Leibniz to transfer the whole question to a nonempirical, metaphysical terrain of essential laws.

For Locke himself, two circumstances tended to soften the impact of his radical limitation of method. For one thing, he viewed his function as that of a humble underlaborer rather than a Cartesian master builder. He expressed the empiricist suspicion of constructing elaborate systems through the pure understanding. His work was to clear out the rubble of overgrown prejudice, so that the philosophical edifice might be erected upon firm, well-prepared ground in experience. Philosophy is nothing but the true knowledge of things. Since "things" include natural entities, human actions, and the signs of natural entities and human actions, Locke accepted the Platonic-Stoic, threefold *division of philosophy* into: physics or natural philosophy, ethics or practical philosophy, and semiotic or logic.[6] Since his own *Essay* deals with ideas and words as signs, Locke assigned it to logic or semiotic, which provides the foundation for any knowledge in the other two fields. Hence he often remarked that his inquiries bore upon our ideas of beings rather than upon beings. The main problem, however, was to provide guidance for *making the passage* from a logic, or theory of knowledge and signs, to a study of the actual physical and moral worlds. Berkeley and Hume concentrated upon the weaknesses in Locke's account of this transition, thus encouraging a detachment of his epistemological views from the rest of his philosophical outlook.

The second qualification placed upon his investigations in the *Essay* contains at the same time Locke's protest against such separate consideration of his theory of knowledge. For the *Essay* has a *practical orientation,* in keeping with the circumstances leading to its com-

---

[5] *An Examination of P. Malebranche's Opinion of Seeing All Things in God,* 52 (*The Philosophical Works of John Locke,* edited by J. A. St. John, II, 454). Locke maintained that his own analysis of ideas for purposes of knowledge was at least more defensible than Malebranche's, since Locke held the empirical origin of ideas in things, rather than in God (as Malebranche taught).

[6] *An Essay concerning Human Understanding,* IV, xxi, 2-4 (Fraser, II, 461-62).

position. If the analysis often leads to the replacement of a claim to certitude by one to probability, Locke is not perturbed by the outcome. For, men must learn to be content with but a narrow sphere of certitude and, for the rest, agree to hold their views as matters of probability and belief. Echoing the words of the Cambridge Platonists about reason as the candle of the Lord, Locke affirms that "the Candle that is set up in us shines bright enough for all our purposes."[7] These purposes are mainly practical ones, aiming at the technical and moral ordering of the present life and the preparation for life eternal. *Probability* is a sufficient guide for attaining these ends, provided that it builds around the hard core of a few demonstrative truths. Having renounced the Cartesian pretense to universal demonstrative knowledge as the philosophical ideal, Locke begins the process of opening up more and more room for probability and secular faith as regulative principles of practical intelligence. That this was also a tendency of the Cartesian tradition itself, can be seen from Descartes' defense of valid conjecture and Leibniz' accommodation of the technique of mathematical probabilities to problems in ethics and legal philosophy.

## 3. THE DISCREDITING OF INNATISM

To clear the path for his main thesis on the experiential origin of all knowledge, Locke must first contend with the counterthesis that at least some of our knowledge is due to innate ideas and principles. He takes in a wide arc of opponents: the school philosophy taught at Oxford and in Holland, the speculative doctrine of Descartes, the dogmatism of the Cambridge Platonists, and the moral innatism advanced by Herbert of Cherbury. These thinkers present by no means a united front of common doctrine, so that Locke's criticism is broadly phrased and does not always tell against the particular arguments employed by one or another innatist. Although his reasoning seems flat and obtuse to us today, its historical importance is considerable. The theory of innate knowledge never recovered its full strength, after his vigorous blows were delivered. It is noteworthy that, in his formal discussion of innatism, Locke directs his attack primarily against innate first *principles,* which may be either speculative or practical. But the remainder of his philosophy may be regarded as an indirect but

---

[7] *Ibid.,* Introduction, 5 (Fraser, I, 30).

sustained criticism of the innatist hypothesis. For, in tracing out the actual origin of *ideas* in experience, he implies that, if these components have a purely empirical origin, the principles composed out of ideas must share a similar origin.

Among *speculative principles,* Locke singles out the principles of identity and contradiction as test cases.[8] He does not deny their truth but only the necessity of explaining our knowledge of them by recourse to innatism. Their widespread acceptance can be adequately accounted for on the ground of our having an intuitive grasp of their import. Once the significance of the terms of the propositions is explained, the truth of these propositions is perceived immediately by the normal, mature mind. Assent is given to them because of their *self-evidence,* rendering any appeal to innate equipment otiose. Taking the offensive, Locke declares that the innatist theory suffers from an impenetrable obscurity concerning how such principles can be in the mind in any innate way. For a truth can be "in the mind" only *through actual perception* or *memory.* An innate idea or principle which is said to be present only virtually in the mind, has never been actually perceived and hence has never been there, in any understandable way. If it is present there by the memory, then it can be revived without the aid of outside impressions and, in being recalled, is remembered or perceived as being not entirely new. But our experience shows no case in which a first principle is rendered originally present to the mind through its innate resources, apart from any previous perception or the aid of sense experience.

This argument, based on the meaning of "being in the mind," was the provocation for Leibniz' distinction between the innate truth itself and our thinking or perceiving it.[9] Leibniz declared that universal assent is not advanced as a basis of proof but only as a convincing suasion about the innate origin of first principles. He added that Locke failed to distinguish sufficiently between necessary truths of reason and contingent truths of fact. In the case of the latter propositions, Leibniz was willing to allow the need for sense experience: not, however, to supply the ideas and connections that

---

[8] *Ibid.,* I, i, 4-28; IV, vii, 12-20 (Fraser, I, 39-63; II, 285-91). That the dogmatic use of innate ideas by the Cambridge Platonists was the main target of Locke's attack, was brought out by S. P. Lamprecht, "Locke's Attack upon Innate Ideas," *The Philosophical Review,* XXXVI (1927), 145-65.

[9] See above, Chapter VII, note 37.

constitute the truth itself, but only to arouse the mind to a definite perceiving of these ideas in the required connections. It is obvious that our *act* of perceiving or thinking about any truth cannot be present in the mind otherwise than by an actual perception or remembrance. But this does not settle the origin of the *active tendency* of the mind to grasp the *meaning-content* of the ideas, which content is distinct from the conscious acts of perceiving or remembering. The content of the principles may be present virtually in the mind, without requiring such conscious acts, somewhat in the way in which the mind contains the suppressed steps in an enthymeme. Locke granted that truths are implicitly present, in the sense that the understanding itself belongs to human nature from the outset, but Leibniz added that the understanding is present precisely as a dynamic aptitude for drawing its principles from its own active dispositions. In the case of truly first principles or truths of reason, moreover, he contended that sense experience was not needed even for the act of thinking about the truths. For his proof, however, Leibniz had to summon the aid of his entire metaphysics. Keeping to the safe but narrow rule of his historical, plain method, Locke would outlaw any complicated metaphysical demonstration and hence would conclude that innatism has no empirical evidence in its favor.

In his zeal to secure the experiential origin of the principles of identity and contradiction, however, Locke went to the opposite extreme from innatism, by calling into question their *universal acceptance* and *scientific value*. He doubted their presence in the minds of children, the illiterate, savages, and idiots; he also added that they serve no useful purpose in scientific investigations. To this extent, they are trifling and not fundamental for all knowledge. One need not become a defender of innatism in order to question this line of criticism. Locke employs three main criteria: that first principles are only present in the mind when they are formally and explicitly stated, in textbook fashion; that they are useless, unless they can serve as the proximate premises for scientific deductions or hypotheses; that they are not genuine principles, unless they may be applied without any guidance from experience. The first rule is a somewhat satirical corrective for the extravagant claims being made by the Cambridge Platonists about the universal presence of first principles, and it is questionable how seriously it is meant by Locke. All that one may conclude from interrogating a child about the principle of contradiction, for instance, is that his apprehension of it is concrete and bound up with particular instances of distinguishing between mustard and sugar, his mother and a stranger. The second criterion is much more significant, since it reveals a conflict between the Cartesian conception of the role of first principles and their actual function in a realistic philosophy and natural science. Descartes assigned a *deductive* function for his first principles, whereas the principle of contradiction serves a *resolutive* function in Thomistic realism and in Newtonian natural science. The dependence of specific propositions upon this principle is by way of a resolution, rather than a deductive derivation. Moreover, the physicist as such need not always complete the reduction of a proposition to the point of establishing its direct relationship with the principle of contradiction. Locke decides nothing about the fruitfulness of this principle, by showing that it does not bear fruit in the way specified by Descartes for first principles. Finally, Locke's remarks about the role of experience are pertinent only for an innatist conception of first principles. In a realistic outlook, our experience of the existent world is required for both the genesis and the application of principles.

Locke deals with *practical first principles* in a somewhat different way. He shows that, although they are no less true than speculative ones, they rest upon some reasoning process, which disqualifies them from being innate. Whether it be the Golden Rule or the precept of keeping contracts or any other moral rule, the proposition is not self-evident and requires a certain amount of inference, in order to be seen as true. Locke does not examine the very widest principle in the moral order — that good should be done and evil avoided — but confines himself to the Golden Rule and other less general precepts. His aim is not to relativize morality but only to show that it supposes the right use of our reasoning power, rather than draws upon an innate reservoir. He suggests that education, custom, and pragmatic needs often lead us to regard as naturally given a moral principle which has, in point of fact, been communicated in a social way and with the aid of implicit reasoning.

Finally, he brings the case down to *innate ideas* as such, by considering those of identity and God. This choice is a shrewd one, since Locke regards the idea of identity as necessary for first speculative principles, and the idea of God as essential for first moral principles (duty implying law, and law a lawgiver). But his arguments are hurried and inconclusive. He attacks the innateness of the idea of identity, by urging his special difficulties about personal identity. How can we be sure that there might not be some sort of sameness between "Socrates and the present mayor of Queenborough,"[10] such that the latter would be the reincarnated soul or consciousness of the former? In regard to the idea of God, Locke recites travelers' reports (which so fascinated the seventeenth century) about conflicting notions of God and even alleged cases where no such notion could be found. But this evidence was insufficient, by itself, to unseat Descartes, however effective it may have been against the English Platonists. Descartes had already forestalled the objection based on differing views of God or even on the absence or denial of the idea of God, by observing that the effect of sense and prejudice is profound enough to distort the idea of God and even to hide the reasons for admitting His existence. Innate ideas can be warped and covered over, without destroying their claim to be innate. It is this latter statement by Descartes which Locke should have subjected to closer analysis.

Locke goes as far as he can, consonant with his empiricism, in meeting the claims of innatism. He grants that human nature has certain inborn powers, not given by experience. He even admits that the *appetitive* powers are endowed with some innate principles of tendency or action, which incline us toward desire, from the outset of life. But he remains firm in his rejection of any innate *cognitive* principles. The understanding may, indeed, acquire prenatally certain particular sense ideas of hunger, warmth, and pain, based upon the conditions of uterine life. But these ideas are drawn from sense experience and are neither determinate nor universal enough to give rise, of themselves, to first principles. The real purpose of the Lockean polemic against innatism comes out in the remark that we ought not to invoke *special innate sanctions* for our principles of philosophy but should gather our knowledge of universal truths from "the being of things themselves, when duly considered."[11] The doctrine of innate ideas and principles was being used, popularly, to cover all sorts of dogmatic assertions, which one could deny only at the cost of also

---

[10] Locke uses this amusing comparison later on in the *Essay,* II, xxvii, 19 (Fraser, I, 460); cf. I, iii, 3-18 (Fraser, I, 93-107). On the innateness of the idea of God, consult the *Second Set of Objections,* sent to Descartes by Mersenne, who cites missionary tales about the absence of the idea of God among the Huron Indians (*The Philosophical Works of Descartes,* translated by Haldane and Ross, II, 26); Descartes' answer is given in advance, in *The Meditations concerning First Philosophy,* V (Lafleur translation, 61).

[11] *An Essay concerning Human Understanding,* I, iii, 25 (Fraser, I, 117).

denying truths said to be implanted in our minds by God or nature. Locke wants to eliminate this nonempirical way of settling issues. Therefore he suggests that we make a patient study of our ideas, which are undoubted objects of our understanding, and thus discover what means we do have for reaching a well-founded conclusion.

## 4. THE ANATOMY OF IDEAS

If there are no innate ideas or principles, they must all be drawn from a single source: *experience*. This is Locke's basic positive thesis. But (to employ John Dewey's phrase) "experience" is one of those weasel-words which are capable of many twistings and turnings. Locke takes "experience" sometimes to mean the *operations of experiencing* and sometimes the *objects experienced*. He is using it in the former sense, when he states that the two sources of experience are *sensation* and *reflection*.[12] They are the operations of experiencing, whereby all knowledge is gained. The objects immediately experienced are ideas and, on the basis of the origin of ideas, there is a distinction drawn between sensation and reflection. Sensation receives ideas from the external world of sensible things, whereas reflection draws its materials from the internal operations of the mind. These operations of experience are the twin inlets or sluices, through which all the components of knowledge flow into the mind.

Locke accords a definite *priority* to sensation. It supplies the mind with its unconditionally first ideas, and apart from this source there could be no mental life. In its natal condition, the mind is comparable to an empty cabinet, a blank paper, or a dark room. The ideas of sensation provide, as it were, the mind's initial furniture, its primary stampings, its first dawn of light. Thereafter, the understanding can perform distinctive operations of its own, the observation of which issues in the ideas of reflection. Our own thinking and desiring, action and passion, provide a distinctive fund of ideas which enrich and extend our experience. Human knowledge has a purely *empirical* origin, in that it is constructed with the aid of the operations of sensation and reflection, which provide the mind with the ideas of sensation and reflection.

The filiation of our ideas with the dual source in experience is more direct and apparent in some cases than in others. Hence there

---

[12] *Ibid.*, II, i, 2–5 (Fraser, II, 121–25).

## Locke's Treatment of Ideas

1. Ideas of sensation and reflection from experience (not from innate source).
2. Simple and complex ideas.
3. Kinds of simple ideas.
    a) From one sense only.
    b) From several senses.
    c) From reflection only.
    d) From sensation and reflection.
4. Kinds of complex ideas (formed by combining, comparing, separating).
    a) Modes (simple and mixed).
    b) Substances (single and collective).
    c) Relations (e.g., cause and effect, identity and diversity, moral rules).
5. Primary, secondary, and tertiary qualities.
6. Abstraction of general ideas.
7. Ideas as determinants of the nature, degrees, extent, and reality of knowledge.

is a fundamental division of ideas into *simple* and *complex* ones.[13] The distinction is made partly in terms of objective content and partly in terms of cognitive operations. From the standpoint of *content,* a simple idea is defined as a single, unmixed appearance, whereas a complex one involves the compounding of several simple ideas, whether of the same kind or of different kinds. From the *operational* standpoint, there is a striking difference in the mind's role, in each case. It is relatively passive in the reception of simple ideas, whereas it is predominantly active in the forming of complex ideas. Despite these clear-cut distinctions, adjustments are necessary in the treatment of particular cases.

Locke fluctuates between calling the understanding "merely passive" and "for the most part, only passive" in respect to simple ideas.[14] He stresses the *passivity* of the mind, when he wishes to demonstrate the noninnate origin of simple ideas and the objective reliability of their content. But in order to avoid the Hobbesian, mechanistic view of the understanding, he seeks to retain the distinctive nature of *cognitive activity,* even in the first reception of simple ideas of

[13] *Ibid.,* II, ii, 1–2 (Fraser, I, 144–46). See W. C. Swabey, "Locke's Theory of Ideas," *The Philosophical Review,* XLII (1933), 573–93.
[14] Cf. *An Essay concerning Human Understanding,* II, i, 25; ix, 1 (Fraser, I, 142, 183).

sense and reflection. The mind is passive, insofar as it must be initially receptive of simple ideas from the sensible world or its own internal domain. These ideas cannot be invented, and without them the mind would be totally ignorant of what transpires within itself and in the outer world. Simple ideas seem to force an entrance and can neither be blotted out nor altered in their main lines. Still, cognitive experience is an activity of man, even though it requires a receptive aspect. Perception, the basic act of the understanding, cannot occur without at least a *minimal conscious attention,* on the part of the knower. The contents of sense and reflection cannot be "given" to the understanding in experience, without some observation, conscious attending, or taking notice of the data. Locke comes much closer to Descartes than to Hobbes in his notion of experience, to the extent that he stresses the factor of mental attention over that of a mere mechanistic reaction to external stimuli.

Sensation and reflection provide a principle of division among simple ideas. Simple ideas belong to four classes, depending upon whether they are received through: one sense only, several senses, reflection only, or both sense and reflection.[15] (a) In the first class are included ideas of particular sounds, colors, tastes, smells, and tangible traits (especially solidity). There is a special adaptation of the *individual sense power* to the reception of ideas from the corresponding aspect of the thing. (b) Through the co-operation of *several senses* — notably, sight and touch — the mind acquires the following ideas: extension, figure, rest, and motion. (c) From *reflection* upon its own operations, the mind acquires a special group of ideas, all of which can be classified as ideas of perception or ideas of volition. Under perception or thinking are included ideas of the acts of discerning, remembering, judging, knowing, believing, etc. The different passions and modes of willing give rise to ideas of volition. (d) The final division consists of the ideas of pleasure and pain, existence and unity, power and succession, all of which are derived from both *sense* and *reflection.* All other ideas result from various combinations of these primary ones, and all knowledge is framed with their help.

The active power of the mind comes much more to the fore in the formation of new complex ideas, out of the original stock of simple ones. Among the relevant acts of the mind, Locke emphasizes: *combining, comparing,* and *separating.* It is difficult to keep an air-

---

[15] *Ibid.,* II, iii, 1 (Fraser, I, 148).

tight distinction between these fundamental operations. All complex ideas result from a certain combining and comparing, and at least all general complex ideas also involve some separating or abstraction. However, there is a distinction between combining ideas in such a way as to form a compound unit, and comparing ideas so that they may be viewed together in their relations, without resulting in a compound unit. Separation of a certain trait is, again, a distinct sort of operation, resulting in the formation of abstract, general ideas.

With the aid of these three cognitive operations, Locke tackles the huge task of classifying all our complex ideas. He suggests that they come under three headings: *modes, substances,* and *relations.* Just as the operations cannot be kept entirely separate, so there is a good deal of overlapping in this division of ideas, despite Locke's best efforts. The distinctive character of ideas of substances is particularly difficult to maintain; moreover, the boundary between certain ideas of relation and simple modes, like power, is often crossed. Locke's initial definitions provide the basis for his own more detailed examinations, as well as for the investigations made by subsequent empiricists.

> *Modes* I call such complex ideas which, however compounded, contain not in them the supposition of subsisting by themselves, but are considered as dependences on, or affections of substances. . . . The ideas of *substances* are such combinations of simple ideas as are taken to represent distinct *particular* things subsisting by themselves; in which the supposed or confused idea of substance, such as it is, is always the first and chief. . . . The last sort of complex ideas is that which we call *relation,* which consists in the consideration and comparing one idea with another.[16]

Two common features of these definitions are worth pointing out, at once. First, in keeping with the standpoint of the *Essay,* they are concerned with objects precisely as ideas. They state the definitions of *our ideas* of modes, substances, and relations, rather than the realities as they exist apart from the mind. Second, the definitions high-light the *active role of the mind* in the formation of complex ideas, which result from a "consideration" or a "taking" by the understanding. The reader is thereby prepared to expect a thorough revision of accepted opinions concerning the realistic import of these ideas.

Each of the major kinds of complex ideas contains, in turn, a number of subdivisions. Modes are either *simple* or *mixed,* depending

---

[16] *Ibid.,* II, xii, 4, 6, 7 (Fraser, I, 215–16).

upon whether the mind combines several simple ideas of the same kind or unites together several different kinds of simple ideas. Space, duration, number, and infinity are examples of simple modes; theft, wrestling, hypocrisy, and beauty illustrate the mixed modes. In making simple modes, the mind either follows combinations already existing in nature or else joins the ideas together according to its own intent. Mixed modes, however, are usually put together without any reference to actually existing combinations in nature, and hence are sometimes given the special name *notions,* to signify that they are the outcome of the mind's own synthesizing operation. Locke does admit that, at least in the first instance, the mind may use *observed complex unities* as a pattern for its complex modal ideas. Hypocritical actions and a wrestling game may have guided the first formation of the ideas of hypocrisy and wrestling. But Locke insists that, thereafter, men usually derive such ideas at secondhand: from custom, education, and dictionary explanations. In his later treatment of mixed modes, Locke unfortunately depreciates the original derivation from observation and emphasizes almost exclusively the roles of inventiveness, education, and linguistic convention. This leads him to state that these ideas have *no* other reality and reference than a purely mental one and that, therefore, their truth does not depend upon *any* correspondence with natural existents. This is an extreme conclusion, since it suppresses his own initial recognition that at least some mixed modes are originally constituted with the aid of observation and practical testing. There is no good reason for denying that the tests of observation and use may also serve as ultimate criteria, even for people who were originally given the mixed modes in a purely conventional way.

Ideas of substances are also of two sorts: single and collective. *Single* substances, like a man or a sheep, are such as are conceived to exist separately. *Collective* substances also constitute a single complex idea, by uniting the ideas of several individual substances into that of a single entity: an army of men or a flock of sheep. For purposes of later criticism, Locke draws a sharp contrast between these particular ideas of substances, single and collective, and the general idea of substance as such. He lists several varieties of relations or references of comparison among the various kinds of ideas. The main ones studied in the *Essay* are: cause and effect, identity and diversity, and the moral relations. This choice of examples is a deliberate one, since it enables Locke to bring his analysis to bear upon the crucial problems of causal relation, personal identity, and moral inference.

## 5. PROBLEMS CONCERNING IDEAS

Locke is at his best in the analysis of particular ideas. He sets a pattern for the empirical way of approaching a problem, even though his own solutions have not been adopted always by his successors. A selection is made here of his treatment of four major questions: the distinction between primary and secondary qualities, the ideas of substances, the relation of cause and effect, and the nature of the self. The distinctive views of Berkeley and Hume on these four issues cannot be appreciated, without some previous understanding of how they were originally formulated in Locke's mind.

1. *Primary and Secondary Qualities*. Locke admits that almost insuperable difficulties attend his attempt to discuss qualities, in a precise but informal way, within his own epistemological framework. His common-sense approach alternates disconcertingly between references to "qualities" and to "ideas of qualities." Often, what he says about qualities can only be said about mental objects or ideas; conversely, he speaks occasionally about the ideas of qualities as though they were present in extramental things. These difficulties stem, in part, from Locke's loose handling of the problem of secondary qualities. But another source is the conflict, in his mind, between his definition of idea as the direct object of the understanding and the common-sense conviction that what we know directly are real things, and that sense percepts are primarily instruments for achieving such knowledge and only secondarily formal objects of knowledge in their own right.

A *quality* is a power in a real thing to produce ideas of qualities in the mind.[17] Qualities are either primary, secondary, or tertiary. A *primary quality* is a power inseparable from a body, under whatsoever conditions it may be placed and observed by us. It is such a quality as is observed to produce a simple idea in us, an idea that not only corresponds with the real quality but also resembles it. In the full sense, a primary quality is really present in a body and supplies a likeness of itself to the mind. Whether or not the mind

---

[17] *Ibid.*, II, viii, 8–26 (Fraser, I, 169–82). For a clarifying discussion of this somewhat obscure portion of Locke's philosophy, cf. R. Jackson, "Locke's Distinction between Primary and Secondary Qualities," *Mind*, N. S., XXXVIII (1929), 56–76.

actually perceives the quality, it is really present in the thing. As for a *secondary quality,* it is nothing real in the thing, except a "bare power" to produce an idea in the percipient subject. This power can operate only by means of the primary qualities of insensible parts of bodies, and is sometimes described by Locke as being nothing more than a certain combination, proportion, or texture found among the primary powers. Although there is a *conformity of causal origin* between the bare secondary power or quality and its idea, there is no relation of *pattern* and *likeness* between them. What people usually take to be the real secondary quality is, in fact, only the idea of it present in the mind. This idea bears no resemblance to the real power in the thing and ceases to exist, once the perception itself ceases.

Locke states the contrast between primary and secondary qualities as that between *real, original* qualities and *imputed, sensible* ones. This way of expressing the difference is apt to be misleading, since by "imputed, sensible qualities," he means the *ideas* of secondary qualities which most people take to be the secondary qualities themselves. Locke does not deny the reality of secondary qualities, in his own meaning of the term. Bare powers do exist outside the sentient subject and do cause a set of its ideas, even though these ideas have no likeness to their causal sources. But he wants to emphasize that the heat, color, taste, and sound, which are ordinarily deemed to be "real qualities, existing right out there," are only the mental effects of bare powers, and that the powers themselves depend on the disposition and operation of the primary qualities. Since the ideas of secondary qualities have their entire formal reality in the percipient, they should not be attributed to the external thing. Locke also mentions a class of *tertiary qualities,* which are also bare powers in the thing resulting from the make-up of its primary qualities. Through its tertiary qualities, one body has the power so to change the texture of another body, that the latter will produce a new idea of a secondary quality in the observer's mind. Thus the sun has the power to affect wax in such a way that it takes on a different appearance, i.e., produces the idea of a different color in the person observing the change. Since tertiary qualities are also bare powers in bodies, they merely repeat, at one remove, the epistemological situation of the secondary qualities.

Significantly enough, Locke does not fully correlate his previous distinction between simple ideas of one sense and those of several senses with the present distinction between secondary and primary qualities. It is true that the simple ideas of one sense are — with but the single exception of the idea of solidity — ideas of bare powers or secondary qualities. But this single exception is of decisive importance. Although the *solidity* of bodies is revealed through the single sense of touch, it must be included as a primary quality, along with extension, figure, number, rest, and motion. The latter traits are all grasped through the co-operation of several senses, but they admit solidity to equal standing as a primary, original quality of real bodies. On this issue, Locke sides with Newton, against the Cartesians. His inclusion of solidity in the list of primary qualities achieves a double purpose. First, it challenges the view of Hobbes and Descartes that primary qualities are objectively real only because they are reducible to extension and hence to exact mathematical description. Although Locke admires the demonstrative power of mathematical reasoning, he never seeks to measure either reality or the demonstrative process by an exclusively mathematical standard. Solidity is irreducible to extension and its modes, and yet is a primary aspect of bodies. Second, the fact that solidity is a real quality of bodies and yet is not reducible to extension and its modes is an argument against the Cartesian doctrine that extension is the special attribute of body and expresses its essence. Locke notes that solidity is just as indispensable as extension for bodily things. He displays a Newtonian reluctance to accept *res extensa* and *res cogitans* as truly essential definitions of body and mind.

Locke offers variations on the familiar Cartesian arguments in favor of the subjectivity of what men ordinarily take to be real, secondary qualities. He observes that water may seem hot to one hand and cold to the other, that the taste and color of an almond change upon its being pounded, that the color of a jewel changes with but a slight modification of the lighting conditions or the observer's perspective. He also stresses the connection between sensations of pain and pleasure and those of secondary qualities. The same bright fire produces comfortable warmth at a safe distance and intense pain at a closer distance. There is no stronger reason for locating the brightness and warmth in the fire itself than there is for locating the pain there. Berkeley's critique of primary qualities will take its start in these Lockean analyses. In Berkeley's estimation, his predecessor's theory is vulnerable on several scores. Locke passes unwarrantedly from saying that the ideas of qualities are caused in us, to saying that we know them to be caused in us precisely by distinct, subsistent, material things. Furthermore, he fails to clarify the sense in which the ideas of primary qualities are "like" the existing primary qualities, since he regards them as having another mode of being. Again, the close association between the bare powers or secondary qualities and the real primary qualities casts suspicion upon the knowability and objectivity of the latter. Finally, the subjective character of even the primary qualities is suggested by the fact that the primary quality of solidity is given through the same sense of touch which, admittedly, centers mainly upon the states of the perceiver. Berkeley readily exploits these openings in favor of his own immaterialism.

2. *Ideas of Substances.* These ideas are naturally aroused in the mind, because of two traits observable in our perception of particular modes of sensation or reflection. (*a*) The various modes are usually perceived as *belonging together* in different groups. To the qualities so united in a complex idea, we give the name of a single thing and then proceed to forget about its origin as a complex idea. (*b*) Moreover, the qualities so associated are regarded precisely *as modes,* since we cannot imagine them as having that ability to subsist of themselves which is characteristic of things. Consequently, the mind demands a principle sufficient to account for the coexistence of the modes as one thing, and to assure the thing's subsistent existence, as the support of the modes. The mind thus accustoms itself to suppose a unifying source and support of the complexus of modes. The complex idea of a particular substance is nothing more than this *customary supposition* of a substrate or unifying subject for a certain combination of simple ideas. The red color, sweet taste, peculiar texture, and shape of a cherry are modal ideas, united as one thing, and not themselves capable of independent existence. They carry with them the note of inherence or being supported, and hence they generate the idea of a subject or support. Since the relation of being supported cannot be founded in nothing, the mind conceives the vague but proportionate idea of a "something," which upholds these qualities and unites them in one thing.

If the mind tries to abstract from the ideas of particular substances a *general idea of substance* as such, it is left with "only an uncertain supposition of we know not what" support for the powers which produce simple ideas in us.[18] Sensation and reflection show a need

---

[18] *An Essay concerning Human Understanding,* I, iii, 19 (Fraser, I, 107). Despite this tenuous definition of substance in general, Locke remained a firm believer in the

for particular, material and spiritual substances to exist, but these experiential sources tell nothing about the nature of substance as such. Our minds reach only as far as the qualities and powers which produce our ideas of qualities; any real, underlying support of these qualities and powers remains supposed but unknown. The idea of substance as such resolves itself into a vague, obscure, and indistinct notion of a *something,* which bears the *relation of a support* to powers and is not itself upheld by anything else. The notion of a something or being is too general and indeterminate to give specific knowledge about substantial essence; the relational note suggests that our idea of substance is not of what it *is,* but only of what it *does.* Hence it is futile to search after the general nature of substantial essence: philosophy must restrict itself to modal ideas of particular substances. Locke comes upon no Cartesian special attribute that would give the mind any insight into the nature of either material or spiritual substance as such.

The line followed by Locke's empirical successors is adumbrated by his own analysis. Berkeley and Hume will agree that he is not being cautious enough even in restricting our knowledge to the ideas of particular substances, material and immaterial. Berkeley will challenge the need to make any transition from ideas of qualities to supposed real qualities, existing outside the mind and *in* some material subject. His contention will be that all the qualities *are* ideas and that, therefore, the only substrate we are forced to suppose is the mind itself or *immaterial* substance. As for Hume, he will inquire further into what it means to be *forced by custom to suppose* a substrate or substantial support. If the individual ideas of modes are distinct mental entities, the only ground for such compulsory supposition is a mental one, arising from habitual association. In that case, an empirical explanation can be given of our ideas of both immaterial and material substances, without having recourse to *any* real substantial beings, material or immaterial.

3. *Cause and Effect.* The lineaments of Hume's radical critique

---

existence of real particular substances. It was this belief that prevented him from taking a radically relational and phenomenalistic view of knowledge, to which his emphasis upon perceiving the relations among ideas might otherwise have led him. The role of substance, in keeping Locke halfway between a substantialist realism and radical phenomenalism, is described by J. Dewey, "Substance, Power and Quality in Locke," *Freedom and Experience,* edited by S. Hook and M. R. Convitz (Ithaca, Cornell University Press, 1947), 205–20.

of causality are also discernible in the Lockean handling of the ideas of cause and effect. Locke himself holds in check the implications of his phenomenalistic treatment of these ideas, because of his strong realistic conviction about actual causal transactions. The whole fabric of his philosophy supposes the reality of causal operations, without which the real existence of qualities, finite substances, and God cannot be proved.

Locke concentrates attention upon efficient cause, since this is the only one obtainable through a direct analysis of ideas. The empirical origin is found in the experience of *alteration among ideas,* such that there is a beginning of new ideas. Change of ideas of modes and substances is observable by both sense and reflection. An idea of a sense quality comes to be, whereas before it was not present in the mind; collections of modes are seen to be altered by some beginning; a new thought or act of volition makes its appearance. Such beginnings among ideas point to operations going on, and operations point to the ideas of active and passive powers. When applied in act, the active power is a *cause;* the motion received in the passive power, through operation, is an *effect.* Hence operations and powers supply the middle term between observed beginnings and the relation of cause and effect. The *causal principle* states that "everything that has a beginning must have a cause."[19] The cause is that which operates to produce any simple or complex idea, whereas the effect is that idea which is produced. The cause makes another thing begin to be; that which does have its being from the application of an operating power of another thing, is the effect. Cause may even be extended to include the substance, in which the active power is supposed to reside, although we can gain no knowledge of how the substance exerts causal action.

Although Locke's analysis rests upon observed cases of change, these instances belong entirely to the *field of ideas.* He does not begin with real changes transpiring in the sensible world, and hence he does not employ the Aristotelian distinction of act and potency, in the elucidation of the causal relation. His active and passive

---

[19] *First Letter to Stillingfleet,* quoted in Fraser, I, 433, n. 1. Another formulation, given in conjunction with the proof of God's existence, reads: "Nonentity cannot produce any real being . . . and what had a beginning must be produced by something else." *An Essay concerning Human Understanding,* IV, x, 3 (Fraser, II, 308). For Locke's formal analysis of power and cause, see *ibid.,* II, xxi, 1–5; xxvi, 1 (Fraser, I, 308–14, 433–34).

powers, in the first instance, bear reference to actual states of ideas. Since the change under description involves the displacement of one already-constituted idea or mental state by another, there is no opportunity for interpreting the change as the actualization of a real, natural potency. Nevertheless, Locke is not content to let the analysis remain only within the realm of ideas. His examination of alteration among ideas is intended to lead to the affirmation of real causal agents and operations.

The inference from operation upon perceivable ideas to real causal powers is conditioned, however, by the limits of experience. Locke has no doubt that observable change leads the mind to real effects and, in most instances, to a *passive power,* or stable capacity to receive similar changes in the future. But he encounters difficulty in respect to the real *active power* or cause. Undeniably, the mind is under compulsion to look for the cause, in each case of observed change. But whence comes the idea of an active power? There are two main classes of action: *motion* (communication of local change by bodily impulse) and *thinking. Bodies* cannot inform us about an active power involved in either sort of action. The behavior of bodies tells us nothing about the thinking process. Nor can bodies inform us about the formal beginning of motion, i.e., about the putting of oneself into action by one's own power. A body at rest conveys no such information, surely, whereas a body in motion tells us only about the passion or reception of communicated motion, not about the action or communicating of motion as such. Sense perception reaches only to the *transfer* of motion (as in the case of colliding billiard balls), not to its *production* by an active power. Sensation reveals only sequences of change and results of action, rather than the beginning of action or application of active power. For obtaining the latter idea, *reflection* is the sole empirical source. Even here, thought is a passive power, insofar as it is operating under the influence of outside sources. Only in acts of remembering, combining, and relating ideas, as well as in voluntary decisions to move one's bodily members, are the beginnings of action genuinely given in experience. Reflection upon these actions gives rise to the idea of cause or active causal power.

The upshot of Locke's investigation is that the idea of cause is grounded solely in reflection, and gets only an obscure and implicit support from sensation. This raises the question of whether cause and effect can ever be applied validly to the material world or to any other context than the production of ideas and voluntary states. The transition from ideal to real causation is not adequately made by Locke. Hume will want to know what sort of an anomaly is presented by the idea of an active power, which is founded in reflection and which cannot be traced back, with any determinate evidence, to sensation. Either reflection is an *independent source* of objectively valid ideas (and then sensation loses its primacy among the sources of experience) or else the idea of cause is traceable solely to *mental conditions* and does not apply to real things, as far as empirical knowledge is concerned. Unwittingly, Locke has prepared the way for Hume's own position on substance and cause, by giving a reason why our mind is unable to imagine a mode without a substance or a beginning of change without a cause. He notes that chance and the force of habit often alter our judgments, without our notice. Such ideas as mode and support, beginning of change and active power, are often joined together inadvertently and yet indissolubly, under the pressure of *fancy* or *the imaginative association of ideas*. Locke, to be sure, does not make a universal principle of explanation out of this observation. He even regards the association of ideas apart from the natural order of connection, as a kind of madness: it is the generative source of insanity, fanaticism, and bad reasoning. It is left for Hume to maintain that the association of ideas is the same as the natural order of connection (as far as empirical knowledge goes), and that the associative bonds are the source of whatever sanity, moderation, and good reasoning the human race possesses. Whereas Locke regards the compulsions of imagination as something of an aberration. Hume hails them as the very principles of stability and intelligibility in our view of the world of fact.

4. *Personal Identity*. Locke begins this inquiry by defining identity in a special way and by distinguishing various types of identity.[20] Following his "way of ideas," he settles the manner in which a being may be compared with itself, by giving a description of how the *idea of identity* arises. This idea applies to all things (whether substances or modes) which have their existence in place and time. The *principle of individuation* is existence itself, since it is in virtue of its existence that a being enjoys undisturbed its own time and place, to the exclusion of other beings of the same kind. A thing is known to be its own selfsame being by reason of our knowing it

[20] *Ibid.*, II, xxvii (Fraser, 439-70).

*to exist somewhere at some time.* The understanding can then compare its ideas about the thing, as presently existing, with ideas concerning its former existence. If these ideas are seen *not* to vary, the thing is known as identical with itself. The idea of identity is not used univocally but is applied to different kinds of things, according to their different ways of existing. Thus an inorganic thing is the same only as long as the same mass of atoms or body is present. But a living thing is self-identical in virtue of a continuous organization of parts, permitting participation in the same life, even though the particles of matter may be completely changed. Like the ideas about other animals, the idea about a man remains selfsame by reference to the same organized body and continued life, not merely in virtue of the idea about the same soul or thinking being.

Descartes had distinguished between the man and the self, regarding the former as the composite of mind and body and the latter as the thinking thing alone. Locke also is careful to distinguish between the man and the self, but in neither case does his meaning coincide with the Cartesian one. Since he does not recognize special attributes telling us about the nature of substances, he does not infer the necessary presence of two substances in man from the admitted presence of both thought and extension in him. Although it is quite likely that both material and spiritual substances are found in man, this opinion is only probable. It involves no contradiction to suppose that God might endow material substance with the power of thinking. Hence Locke's cautious conclusion about the idea of *the man* is that it must include ideas of a bodily substance and a thinking principle, the latter being *probably* a distinct, immaterial substance, rather than a function of the material substance. In any case, the sameness of an organized bodily life is indispensable for establishing the identity of the man.

Locke denies the Cartesian assumption that the problem of the identity of *the self* must be solved in terms of substance. The unity of material substance does not explain how plants and animals retain their identity, nor does the unity of a thinking spiritual substance explain the abiding identity of a man. A thinking being is a self, in virtue of the *consciousness* that always accompanies the thinking operation. It is a self to itself here and now, because of its consciousness of its present thoughts and actions. This provides a ground for the comparison of identity between the consciousness of past thoughts and actions and the consciousness of present thoughts and actions. There is an abiding personal identity, only insofar as this comparison can be made. Where conscious comparison trails off, there the personal identity also ends.

This psychological approach to personal identity remains independent of the question whether several substances share the same consciousness or whether the same substance enjoys several distinct consciousnesses. Locke thinks it more probable that a single, conscious self accompanies a single, spiritual substance, but he does not rule out the other possibilities. He could welcome later psychological findings about multiple and alternating personalities. It is largely through Locke that the problem of personal selfhood became divorced from that of the substantial nature of man. This development is an indication of the bankruptcy of the Cartesian theory of substance. But in cutting off his notion of personal identity from any ontological basis and making it solely an affair of comparative acts of consciousness, Locke is left with *three separate sorts of identity:* that of the substance, that of the man, and that of the person or self. He does not explain how the identity of the self can be that of *one human person,* smacking always of "a tang of the cask."[21] The three identities disrupt the unity and selfsameness of the single human person of our experience.

## 6. ABSTRACTION OF GENERAL IDEAS

Instead of proceeding directly from the study of various kinds of ideas to the problem of knowledge proper, Locke first examines how ideas are abstracted and rendered universal. If men limited themselves to particular ideas and names, the process of discovery and communication would be rendered endless and uselessly complicated. Actually, we are able to form general ideas and words, which are of incalculable advantage for the advancement of knowledge. *Words* as such are the sensible marks or signs of ideas. Their proper and immediate signification is only of the *ideas in one's own mind,* and it is a perversion to obscure this basic reference. Nevertheless, the mind naturally tends to regard words also as standing for real things and for the common meanings of ideas in other minds. Especially in the use of general words, we often forget the primary reference of words to our own ideas and hence relate them immediately to things. As a counterbalance, Locke sometimes says that

---

[21] *An Essay concerning Human Understanding,* II, i, 17 (Fraser, I, 136).

words refer to *nothing but* one's own ideas. He does strive, however, to establish an ultimate reference to the real order of things and common meanings.

Against Hobbes' nominalism, Locke maintains the distinction between ideas and words or sounds. The latter are only the signs of the former. Since all existent things are particular beings, our original ideas are particular ones, having particular names. But we are led to generalize our ideas under the pressure of various considerations: the limits of memory, the infinite number of particular existents, and the requirements of research and social intercourse. Locke gives both a psychological and a logical account of the *process of generalization of ideas,* whence general names result.[22]

*Psychologically* considered, the child's first ideas and words are the particular ones which refer to the most important individuals in his narrow sphere of life. Gradually, his experience widens to the point where he notices certain resemblances between, say, his father or mother and other individuals. All these individuals agree in shape and some other qualities, which agreement persists, despite obvious differences on other points. The common aspects are used to frame the general idea, which carries the name "man." What has been done is to leave out of account the peculiarities involved in the complex idea of one's father, and retain only the traits which observation shows to be shared by many other individuals. Nothing new has been added to the particular complex ideas of various individual men, but a new complex idea has been formed by combining only the *jointly shared* notes. The fresh idea is a general one, to which is given (or accepted from conventional usage) a distinctive, general name. This abstracted, general idea, along with its name, is then laid up in memory precisely as containing the essence of a sort or *species* of thing. It is presumed that all knowledge gained about this species is rightfully applicable to all individuals in the class.

A *logical* justification is demanded, however, for the presumption that the abstract idea expresses a universal species and is predicable of a certain group of individuals. With what right does the understanding bind its particular ideas together in bundles and rank them in classes? In reply, Locke appeals to two relevant operations of the mind: separating and relating. The process of *separating* or *abstracting*

[22] *Ibid.,* III, iii, 6–11 (Fraser, II, 16–22); cf. II, xi, 9; IV, iii, 31; vii, 9 (Fraser, I, 206–07; II, 224–25, 274).

isolates an idea from its experiential context and from the other ideas
originally accompanying it. Since existence under the conditions of
place and time constitutes the principle of individuation, abstraction
is primarily a removal from the concrete conditions of existence.
A certain idea is separated from the particular setting of place and
time, and is regarded as a bare appearance or isolated unit of
meaning. So abstracted, the idea becomes capable of representing more
than one individual. It is now a general representative, constituting
a genus or species, and its name becomes applicable to all those
individual existents which *show a conformity* with this idea. Their
conformity gives them the right to be classified under this genus or
species, and to receive its name. General ideas are thus erected into
standards, by reference to which the various individuals can be
arranged and analyzed for practical and scientific purposes.

Nevertheless, an explanation in terms of separating or abstracting
cannot yield the full solution of the problem of universal ideas. For,
since nothing is added to the particular complex idea in forming
the universal, it follows that the abstracted idea also remains *particular*. After omissions are made, the remainder is still a particular
idea or complexus of ideas, in which a number of individuals are
found to agree. This leads Locke to inquire how one particular idea
or set of ideas, even taken in separation from other circumstances,
can stand for a number of singular existents. He is obliged to
specify more definitely the manner in which the general idea is
"framed and set up," precisely *as a representative*. Taking advantage
of the Cartesian distinction between the formal and objective reality
of ideas, he distinguishes between the *formal existence* of the abstracted
idea and its *objective signification*. The former aspect remains particular, whereas the latter becomes general. The meaning of an idea
is rendered general by means of the second relevant operation of
the mind: *relating*. The general meaning of ideas is "nothing but
the capacity they are put into, by the understanding, of signifying
or representing many particulars. For the signification they have is
nothing but a relation that, by the mind of man, is added to them."[23]

To the extent that they are general in meaning or signification,
ideas are *products of the understanding*, considered as a relating
function. Locke emphasizes that the relation of signifying many
particulars is added by the mind, so that he can overcome the tendency

[23] *Ibid.*, III, iii, 11 (Fraser, II, 22).

to attribute real existence to genera and species. Only individual things are really existent; general meanings are the workmanship of the mind and have their being only in the mind. Still, Locke is not entirely satisfied with this conceptualistic position, since he observes that the mental function of relating and generalizing is guided by certain deliverances of experience. He expresses his belief that "nature" has made things *alike* in certain respects. Hence the mind puts into a certain idea the capacity of signifying many particulars, only because of the testimony of sense to the presence of a likeness or similar set of sensible qualities, in a number of individual existents. This perceived likeness is the ultimate regulator of the abstraction of certain notes, the generalization of their signification, and their application to rightful members of the species.

Locke's precarious balance between the contribution of sense perception and the mental operations of separating-and-relating tends to get upset, however, as soon as he considers particular instances of general ideas. The difficulties crop up when he inspects mathematical ideas and the species of natural substances.

> For, when we nicely reflect upon them, we shall find that *general ideas* are fictions and contrivances of the mind, that carry difficulty with them, and do not so easily offer themselves as we are apt to imagine. For example, does it not require some pains and skill to form the general idea of a triangle (which is yet none of the most abstract, comprehensive, and difficult) for it must be neither oblique nor rectangle, neither equilateral, equicrural, nor scalenon; but all and none of these at once. In effect, it is something imperfect, that cannot exist; an idea wherein some parts of several different and inconsistent ideas are put together.[24]

As for the species of natural substances, Locke is guided by the requirements of his method and doctrine on the knowledge of substances, on the one side, and certain experimental procedures, on the other. The chemist continues to call a substance sulphur or vitriol, even though it displays quite different sets of properties, under different experimental conditions. Locke reasons that, if the definition of the chemical species involved the real substantial essence, then there could not be such a shift of sensible appearances from one experimental situation to another. Hence the specific definition of things does not express the real substantial essence in any way, but is solely concerned with the nominal essence. This *nominal essence* is

---

[24] *Ibid.*, IV, vii, 9 (Fraser, II, 274).

an artificial construction of the logical genus and species, based upon the sensible qualities alone. It is not governed by the inner, substantial constitution of the thing or its *real essence*. This accords with Locke's methodological limitation to a description in terms of ideas, as well as with his general denial that the human mind can know the nature of real substances. The effect of such particular analyses is to stress the "fictitious" and "contrived" character of general ideas, and to render their real foundation in experience extremely insecure.

There are several tangled skeins of reasoning in Locke's doctrine on general ideas. (1) He opposes Hobbesian nominalism by distinguishing between ideas and names, and by admitting the existence of general ideas, of which general names are only the signs. (2) He also opposes any extreme view that would accord real existence to our generic and specific notions. Locke firmly respects the realistic theses that only individual things can exist and that the mind itself contributes the formal universality of signification. (3) But Locke's historical, plain method falters in the explanation of the foundation of generality of meaning. The two operations of separating and relating are not radical enough principles to save the real ground of reference for general meanings. The process of separation or abstraction can work, only when the mind is in possession of some selective basis for determining *which* ideas are capable of isolation and also capable of combination with each other in a complex general idea. Similarly, the relating process can establish generality of meaning, only on condition that the mind has some guidance about *which* things can find in a certain idea their common representative. In a word, the operations of abstracting and relating, as described by Locke, *presuppose* the apprehension of similarities as such. But such an apprehension does issue in a distinctively general idea, that is not reducible to an isolated segment of our particular images. For, the abstractive process is not just a separating and bundling of particulars, but a penetration to the essential structure.

(4) Locke himself hints at the real foundation for general meanings, when he remarks that "nature" makes things to be alike and that things display an intrinsic conformity with the general idea. These observations are only a hair's breadth removed from granting that there is an intellectual apprehension of the real, substantial essence. But the admission is never made. This failure is due, in part, to Locke's ingrained suspicion of any distinctively intellectual apprehension. For, he has in mind the Cartesian and Cambridge Platonist

claims to a "purely intellectual act," which operates apart from, and often in opposition to, sensory perception. Another reason for Locke's reluctance to push the analysis any deeper, is that his "way of ideas" prevents him from passing from supposition of the factual existence of substances to knowledge of their essential nature. As a consequence of this methodological limitation, however, he can speak only metaphorically about "nature's way" of making things alike. He is defenseless before Hume's emendation, which maintains that by "nature" is meant only the customary drift of our thoughts, rather than a real participation of things in a similarity of essence. Locke's opportunity to escape this Humean consequence comes with his recognition of an intrinsic conformity of things with their general idea, giving them the right to be classified in one determinate species. But his phenomenalism requires him to interpret this conformity entirely in terms of the sensible qualities themselves. Instead of *manifesting* something about the real substantial essence, the determinate combination of sense qualities *constitutes* the nominal essence or definition by means of genus and specific difference. Hence the likeness among many individuals and the determinate structure of conformity, within the sensible thing, are never connected with the real, substantial essence, in howsoever indirect a way.

(5) Locke's particular analyses of the idea of a triangle and that of a physical substance, like sulphur, are specially illuminating. Locke admits a difference between mathematical and physical abstraction, but it is one of degree and not of kind. His difficulty in respect to the object of mathematical abstraction arises from his failure to distinguish between the composite image of a sort of common-denominator triangle and the concept of triangle. The particularity of his "general idea of *a* triangle," which must be "all and none" of the several types of triangles at once, leads to a noetic monstrosity. One can sympathize with Berkeley's despair of making any sense out of abstract ideas of this sort. Perhaps more significant for the general direction of modern thought, however, are Locke's animadversions concerning real essences and their relationship with scientific research. On two scores, his approach is typical of the subsequent handling of this issue by empiricists. (*a*) He makes no distinction between the meaning of "species" in metaphysics and in the natural sciences. Because the scientific conception of a species is often only a tool for classification and nominal definition, he concludes that the human mind is *always* confined to the nominal essence. (*b*) He identifies all

philosophical views of the real, substantial essence with that of Cartesian rationalism. Since the extravagant claims of rationalism to have an adequate understanding of the essence of material substance and to use that as a guiding principle in scientific demonstration cannot be confirmed by the actual condition of our knowledge, Locke rules out *any* grasp of the real essence. He is right in stressing the fragmentary and superficial state of so much of our knowledge, as well as the presence of contingent events and monstrosities in nature. But this evidence is decisive only against an extreme claim to essential insight and against a natural philosophy that rules out the distinctively material or potential principle in natural things. Somewhere between these extremes of rationalism and phenomenalism, there is room for the realistic claim that the human mind can gain a minimal, essential knowledge of at least the nature of man and the broad division between the living and the nonliving. The limitations of human intelligence and the relative opacity of material things prevent us from having a perfect vision of the structures of material things, and recommend the cultivation of the various scientific techniques of descriptive analysis. As Locke formulates it, the problem of species is a misleading one, since it consolidates a number of issues that should be kept distinct.

## 7. THE STRUCTURE OF KNOWLEDGE

There are two major areas of tension in Locke's theory of knowledge which urgently call for some sort of resolution. The first polarity is between the *analytic* and *synthetic* tendencies in his thought. His chosen method is basically an analytic, elementaristic one, laying stress upon the atomic units of our mental life. But there is an equally strong need to reunite the analyzed elements in a unified knowledge, achieved through intellectual *perception* or the mental act of grasping the bonds among ideas. Locke reinterprets the traditional maxim about knowledge being found in the judgment to mean that it is found most properly in *judging as an act* reducible to mental perception. However, *judgment as a special faculty* does not yield knowledge but probable assent. Perception or the act of judging is the proper locus of knowledge, and the analysis of ideas is only preliminary to it. Once innatism is eliminated, Locke allows the mind's teleology for unified knowledge. The second tension concerns Locke's previous teaching that the idea is the mind's immediate object. Now he must admit that the mind is also oriented mediately toward an apprehension of real being. A way must be found, then, to reconcile the *immediate* and the *mediate* objects of our understanding. The fourth book of the *Essay* seeks to bind these various contrasts together in a coherent doctrine about the nature, degrees, extent, and reality of human knowledge.

1. The point of departure is the definition of the *nature* of knowledge as:

> *The perception of the connexion and agreement, or disagreement and repugnancy of any of our ideas.* In this alone it consists. Where this perception is, there is knowledge, and where it is not, there, though we may fancy, guess, or believe, yet we always come short of knowledge.[25]

This definition conforms with the basic premise that the understanding is concerned directly with its own ideas and their various bonds. The various types of judgment depend upon the various relations of agreement or disagreement among ideas. Locke reduces these to four kinds: identity and diversity, relation, coexistence and necessary connection, and real existence. The perception of *identity* and *diversity* is called the first act of the mind in the order of knowing, since it is concomitant with the mental possession of any idea. In having any idea, the understanding grasps it precisely as being what it is (identity) and as distinct from every other idea (diversity). Relation and coexistence are both instances of relation, in the broader sense. But Locke establishes a sharp epistemological distinction between abstract, purely mental connections and concrete ones, grounded in a real subject (a distinction which Hume reformulated as the pivotal one between ideal relations and relations among matters of fact). Hence he restricts *relation,* in the stricter sense, to perception of agreement or disagreement among ideas only, whereas *coexistence* bears upon the mutual presence of qualities in the same real subject. Finally, there is a distinct sort of agreement whereby the mind gains knowledge of *real existence,* from an examination of certain ideas.

2. The *degrees* of knowledge are: intuition, demonstration, and sensation. Locke describes the first two degrees mainly in the Cartesian

---

[25] *Ibid.,* IV, i, 2 (Fraser, II, 167–68). In his critical study, "Some Points in the Philosophy of Locke," *Philosophy,* XII (1937), 33–46, A. C. Ewing observes that, in terms of this definition, the object of knowledge is shifted from *ideas* to the *relations among ideas.* In order to accommodate knowledge of real existents, however, Locke is forced subsequently to expand the meaning of knowledge still further, from a grasp of relations solely among ideas to include a grasp of relations between our *ideas* and *real existents.*

spirit. *Intuition* consists in an immediate perception of the agreement or disagreement among ideas, which are seen together at first sight and without the intervention of any other ideas. The difference between a circle and a triangle is at once evident, requiring no intermediate connections and inferences. *"It is on this intuition that depends all the certainty and evidence of all our knowledge. . . .* A man cannot conceive himself capable of a greater certainty than to know that any idea in his mind is such as he perceives it to be; and that two ideas, wherein he perceives a difference, are different and not precisely the same."[26] *Demonstration* or reasoning is a process of supplying the intervening links required in order to join together two ideas, which originally stood in no immediate connection. In demonstrative knowledge, the agreement or disagreement is perceived through the mediation of other ideas.

Like Descartes, Locke requires that every stage in the demonstration be itself secured by an intuitive perception, and that these intermediate intuitions be kept in mind throughout the inference. Both thinkers also agree in emphasizing the difficulties of reasoning, which requires considerable attention, memory, and perseverance, in order to carry out all the required steps. These conditions tend to weaken the clarity and force of the connection, especially by comparison with a simple intuition. Locke departs from Descartes, however, on several particulars. *Doubt* functions only as a prelude to demonstration and does not touch the immediate intuitions, mathematical or otherwise. And although he demands an intuition at each step in demonstration, as well as a memory of previous intuitions, Locke does not aim at a quasi-intuition of the entire course of the demonstration. Locke does not provide *memory* with any divine guarantee but appeals to our ability to form abstract, general ideas and to demonstrate general truths. It may be safely presumed that general connections, once demonstrated, will remain self-identical and true, forever. Finally, the Cartesian predilection for mathematical demonstration is criticized. What makes *mathematical reasoning* demonstrative is no special feature associated with extension, figure, and number, but only a ready perception of the agreement or disagreement among such ideas. Numbers and

[26] *An Essay concerning Human Understanding,* IV, ii, 1 (Fraser, II, 177–78). For a documented report on Locke's close knowledge of Descartes and the Cartesians, see C. S. Ware, "The Influence of Descartes on John Locke. A Bibliographical Study," *Revue Internationale de Philosophie,* IV (1950), 210–30; this article is based upon papers in the Lovelace Collection (mentioned in the bibliography to this chapter).

geometrical figures are precise and steady symbols, which therefore aid discourse and memory. But there is no intrinsic reason for making a prototype out of mathematical procedures, since nonmathematical ideas (especially moral ones) also have determinate relations of agreement and disagreement which can, in principle, be discovered by a proper method. The essential factor in demonstration is *not the nature of the formal object* but the *evidence of the connection* among ideas. Locke does admit that the demonstrative rigor of even moral philosophy would be increased through the use of mathematical symbols and method. Unlike Leibniz, however, he makes no definite attempt to treat moral problems mathematically.

Locke's own account of knowledge, as a perception of ideal connections, would seem to limit the kinds of knowledge to intuition and demonstration about *ideas*. But the empirical fact is that I am certain of the existence of this *thing,* here and now affecting my senses. To accommodate this fact, a distinction is made between the degrees of *general knowledge* (intuition and demonstration, as described) and sensation as a *particular knowledge* of individual, finite existents. This particular, existential knowledge holds an anomalous position, somewhere midway between mere probability and the full certainty of intuition and demonstration.[27] *Sensation,* as knowledge, consists in an awareness of the actual entrance of ideas from sensible existents. Locke speaks loosely about perceiving the existence of particular things, through this means. More accurately, he can only claim that one perceives certain ideas, precisely as being received here and now from an actually operating, causal source. To grasp the existential act of another thing, in an existential judgment, would sap the foundations of the Lockean method of ideas. But he allows that there can be practical assurance of the existing reality of the particular source of some ideas, especially those that are accompanied by pleasure or pain. It is this pragmatic conviction which Locke locates between probability and certainty, so that there may be guidance enough in the practical conduct of life.

3. It is now possible to determine the exact *extent* of human knowledge.[28] It can extend no farther than we have ideas and, indeed, no farther than we can perceive *connections* among our ideas. There are various ways of gauging the extent of knowledge,

---

[27] *An Essay concerning Human Understanding,* IV, ii, 14 (Fraser, II, 185–88).
[28] *Ibid.,* IV, iii (Fraser, II, 190–225).

one of which is provided by the theory of the degrees of knowledge. From the mind's need to employ reasoning, it is evident that we do not have intuitive knowledge of all the agreements and disagreements among ideas. Furthermore, it is not always possible to find the middle terms linking ideas together, so that demonstrative knowledge can be acquired. Finally, sensitive knowledge is circumscribed even more severely than intuition and demonstration, since it is confined to particular, sensible things, existing here and now. Locke draws the modest conclusion that our knowledge not only falls short of the great expanse of real being which exists beyond the limits of "this little canton," our solar system, but is also of lesser extent than our ideas. Although clear and distinct ideas are requisite for knowledge, they are not — as Descartes held — sufficient criteria for acquiring knowledge of objects beyond their own self-identity and mutual diversity.

Another way of determining the scope of knowledge is provided by the various kinds of agreement and disagreement. We can know intuitively that every idea in the mind is one with its own content and distinct from every other idea. Hence there is intuitive knowledge of the self-identity and diversity of all our ideas. But it is difficult to determine beforehand the extent of our knowledge of *abstract* relations, since the mind is self-reliant in determining purely ideal connections. Locke sets no a priori limit to our ability to construct and relate purely ideal entities. He contents himself with observing that demonstration is just as cogent in the field of moral relations as in that of quantitative ones.

In regard to the *concrete relations of coexistence,* however, Locke does venture to draw some rigid lines of demarcation for our knowledge of coexisting qualities. Relying heavily upon the attitude of Boyle, Newton, and the British scientific school, he specifies certain limits beyond which the mind cannot go, in principle, in the investigation of nature. Although we can have sensitive knowledge of the actual copresence of certain sense qualities that give content to our ideas of particular substances, we cannot convert this *contingent* kind of information into a general principle of *demonstration.* Hence we must abandon the Cartesian pretension to a rigorous science of bodies, based on essential knowledge and necessary connections. Locke is rationalist enough, however, to admit that a philosophy of nature *should* realize this Cartesian ideal of determining beforehand, and without trial, what further properties and operations of bodies may be expected. But in fact, the necessary connections and negative inferences that can be drawn from an analysis of the ideas of qualities, are too contingent and restricted to provide a foundation for an a priori science of nature.

Locke cites three major hindrances to the development of a Cartesian-like *natural philosophy,* in which reason would anticipate and transcend the findings of sense observation. First, our ideas of qualities do not convey a knowledge of the real essence of substances. Hence we remain ignorant of the supposed *root* from which the properties and operations flow. Second, our certitudinal knowledge of primary qualities is of a very general sort. We know that every body must have *some* degree of extension, solidity, figure, and other traits, but we have no purely rational way of determining the *precise* size, figure, and texture of the parts of any particular body. And Locke is pessimistic about the prospect of ever acquiring circumstantial knowledge of the "insensible parts" or minute, submicroscopic particles, upon the determination of which, nevertheless, our whole knowledge of bodies is ultimately dependent. Finally, he is able to discover in experience *no connection between primary and secondary qualities.* Hence no demonstration is possible in regard to the sensible qualities of bodies. This does not put an end to the advance of the sciences, but it does force them to rely heavily upon the intrinsically less perfect, but humanly more proportionate, means of *observation* and *experiment.* Our knowledge of immaterial substances is even more meager than that of material ones, since it is based solely upon an analogy with what we experience in our own internal operations of thinking and willing.

4. Because of its philosophical importance for later British empiricism, the *extent* of our knowledge of agreements and disagreements of *real existence* deserves separate consideration. Abstract ideas and general propositions inform us only about essences and ideal connections, not about factual existence. Nevertheless, the mind can have intuitive knowledge of its own existence, demonstrative knowledge of God's existence, and sensitive knowledge of the existence of other things.[29]

Locke does not follow Descartes in according a privileged, systematic place to the *intuition of the existing self.* He merely ranges this one existential intuition alongside of the various essential intuitions we have of ideal identities, diversities, and relations. Having given a

[29] *Ibid.,* IV, iii, 2; ix, 2–3; x, 1–11; xi, 1–10 (Fraser, II, 212, 304–16, 325–36).

psychological definition of personal self-identity, Locke is aware of no special problems in this area. No proof is needed, and little critical explanation is given, for the evident, internal perception that we are existent. If anyone doubts his own existence, in the face of his experience of thinking, willing, or feeling pain, Locke makes the Cartesian retort that doubting itself is an incontrovertible and immediate evidence of the self's existence. The self is presented, by concomitant awareness, in all our conscious entertainment of ideas. Locke gives no satisfactory account, however, of how the general theory of intuition, as an immediate perception of connections *among ideas,* is to be adapted to this situation, in which the perceived connection is between an *idea* and an *existent.* An explanation may perhaps be sought in the twofold way of looking at an idea: either as a content of meaning or as a particular, existing perfection. But then the problem is only pushed back a step, namely, to how the mind can pass from the idea regarded as a self-identical meaning to the idea regarded precisely as an existential perfection.

There is one sense, however, in which the intuition of the existing self does fill a special role in Locke's philosophy. *Demonstration of God's existence* must start from an intuitive and existential basis, which is provided only by the apprehension of one's own existence. I know intuitively that I actually exist and that my real being cannot be produced by nothing. It is demonstratively certain, from the fact of my real being and the force of the principle of causality, that something must have existed from eternity. This eternal being is either myself or, if I give evidence of having a beginning, some other being that is itself eternal and the cause of my coming to be. The changes and limits in my way of being indicate that I did have a beginning. This was due to the causal activity of a being, in whom there is at least as much perfection as is contained in myself and the rest of the world of things subject to a beginning. This eternal being is the first cause or God. He is an all-powerful, intelligent being, wholly immaterial, and the providential source of the unity and perfections in the visible world.

Locke considers this proof to be just as cogent as any mathematical demonstration, and more certain than knowledge of anything else existing outside oneself. Yet he makes no attempt to overhaul the *principle of causality,* so that it may be used in this instance. Since the principle itself is an abstract, general proposition, it may perhaps be confined to the ideal order of demonstration. And since the idea of an active, causal power has been traced to an empirical source only in reflection, some justification is needed to apply it to a transcendent and nonempirical reality. A more elaborate discussion of the logical foundation of the proof of God's existence is required. This is especially urgent, since Locke bases his rejection of the Cartesian, a priori argument on the double ground that the idea of the infinite has an empirical origin and that existential demonstration cannot be made from a purely ideal meaning. Locke should show in more detail that he has secured an existential and empirical starting point in the intuited self, and that the principle of causality can be used to infer (from this starting point) the existence of a supraempirical being. This line of criticism suggested itself naturally to Hume, upon examination of Locke's demonstration of God's existence.

The weakest sort of existential knowledge is that of things other than the self and God. There is neither intuition nor demonstration, but only *sensitive knowledge,* in the case of the *real existence of material things.* This knowledge is limited to individual cases, and obtains only while the existent source of ideas of sensation is here and now operative, in respect to my sense powers. Knowledge of past existence is only as strong as the memory of past reception of ideas. About the future reality of a material thing and its future influence on consciousness, only probable opinions can be advanced. The existence of other spiritual beings is matter for natural belief. But within this narrow compass, sensitive knowledge is adequate to the practical needs of life.

In defense of our conviction about a *real external world,* Locke makes several observations that have become common patrimony for most subsequent realists. That our senses do receive their ideas from a nonsubjective origin is suggested by the fact that, whenever one sense organ is lacking, the corresponding proper ideas are also lacking. Moreover, there are some ideas which we cannot avoid receiving, even though we might prefer to escape from them or declare them nonexistent. This is especially true in the case of perceptions accompanied by pain. We do not have them at our disposal, in the way in which we can control or dismiss our own mental creations. Empirically considered, there is also a notable difference between receiving a painful perception and recalling that experience in the tranquillity of memory. Finally, Locke observes that the various senses tend to corroborate each other's report, thus providing us with reliable, convergent testimony that our certainty about existing things is no product of our own consciousness or fancy. To this extent, Locke maintains that we do perceive our ideas of sensation precisely as being received from an extramental causal source.

5. Briefly, the problem of the *reality* of knowledge is that of the agreement between ideas and things.[30] The entire tendency of the previous examination of aspects of knowledge has been to widen the definition of knowledge to include some kind of assurance about the connection between ideas and real things, as well as between one idea and another. With this revision in mind, Locke now makes a review of the various kinds of ideas. *Simple* ideas are naturally produced by existent things, operating upon the mind, in accordance with God's ordination. The ideas of primary and secondary qualities *conform with* the things from which they derive, even though the ideas of secondary qualities do not *bear a likeness to* their objective foundation in bare powers. *Complex* ideas (with the exception of substance) are not intended to be copies of independent things but are of our own making. Hence they are their own archetypes and need only be combined and related in consistent ways, in order to have reality and truth of a nonexistential sort. The *ideas of substances* are of an intermediate nature. Like other complex ideas, they are formed by the mind itself. Yet like simple ideas, they claim to conform with independent archetypes, existing outside the mind. Because of this existential reference, combined with the absence of any perceivable necessary connection among the ideas of primary and secondary qualities, the mere *mutual compatibility* among the various qualitative ideas, making up an idea of a substance, is not a sufficient criterion for determining that this is an idea of any really existing substance. Many ideal combinations among qualitative ideas can be made by the mind, but there is no a priori way of settling which combination refers to a really existing thing. Only that grouping of complex ideas which has *actually been drawn* from the existent thing, constitutes a real idea of a substance, expressing a conformity with an existing archetype. How the connection can be traced from ideas, as instrumental signs, to the existent things signified by ideas, remains fundamentally unclarified by Locke.

This doctrine on the reality of knowledge contains an implicit rebuke of attempts to measure the real world by the scope of our

---

[30] *Ibid.*, IV, iv (Fraser, II, 226–43).

knowledge. The conditions of an ideal science cannot be imposed upon real things. Neither can these conditions be imposed upon the human mind, making it discard all cognitions that do not meet the strict requirements for knowledge. There is plenty of room for probable views, especially in the fields of practical improvement and religion. Locke himself tried to advance the economic welfare of his country in quite empirical ways, through currency reforms and tedious economic studies. The practical effect of his religious outlook was *deistic,* since he made reason the final arbiter in religious matters. Although Locke restricted the competence of reason in natural philosophy, he tried to reduce Christian belief to its "reasonable" elements.[31] The foundations of religion are the purely natural demonstrations of God's existence and the moral law. For the rest, practically orientated, probable views must regulate religious, moral, and political life.

## 8. PRACTICAL PHILOSOPHY

Since Locke originally devised his method for the resolution of practical problems, he transferred to this sphere his characteristic blending of confident rationalism and cautious empiricism. In principle, he claimed that moral science can be demonstrated just as stringently as mathematics. For, moral reasonings concern abstract relations among ideas, and hence fall within the domain where demonstrative certainty is obtainable. But Locke's own samples of ethical demonstrations were tautologous and trifling, so that for the most part he offered a compromise way of thinking, in moral as well as natural philosophy. He recognized that, in any practical elaboration of an ethical doctrine, difficulties are presented by the complex and mixed character of ethical ideas, the vagueness of ethical language, and the special distractions of interest and the passions. Moreover, ethics would be a singularly ineffective and unreal science, if it were severed from all connection with existential grounds. Hence Locke related the content of morality to God on the one side, and to the actual operations of the self on the other.

---

[31] C. J. O'Neil gives an affirmative answer to his question: "Is Locke's State the Secular State?" *The New Scholasticism,* XXVI (1952), 424–40, in view of the fact that faith is reduced to reason, and charity to natural duty. For an appraisal of the influence of his religious position on the rest of Locke's philosophy, see J. T. Noonan, "The Protestant Philosophy of John Locke," *Philosophical Studies in Honor of The Very Reverend Ignatius Smith, O.P.,* edited by J. K. Ryan (Westminster, Md., The Newman Press, 1952), 92–126.

Morality rests upon the *relation of human actions to law,* whether it be the law of God, of the civil community, or of private convention.[32] The demonstration of God's existence provides morality with an ultimate foundation. The true ground of morality is in the *will* and *law of God.* The will of God is the basis of moral law, but God's decrees are those of a reasonable agent. As a providential creator, God sets an eternal law for men to find and follow. This law is embodied in the nature of things and is discoverable by the unaided *natural light,* i.e., by sense and reason working together to grasp the practical import of particular facts and the permanent relations among general ideas. Finite beings are dependent upon God and owe Him their obedience and free service. Moral ideas of good and evil concern the *obligatory conformity* of our voluntary actions to rules, especially the natural law of the divine lawmaker.

From the standpoint of the human agent, however, *good* and *evil* can be defined in terms of the *pleasure* and *pain* produced by actions.[33] Locke tries to reconcile a natural-law and a hedonistic theory of morality. The great end of human action is the possession of happiness, a motive that can be made to serve the purposes of moral law. Morally good and evil deeds entail the consequences of pleasure and pain, attached by the lawmaker. God associates certain rewards or punishments with actions that stand, respectively, in conformity or disconformity with the moral law. Men are moved more forcefully by hedonistic considerations than by reflection upon rational relations and obligation, but both routes provide a natural guide to right action. Under optimum conditions, reason should regulate self-interest, and the latter should assure the practical application of general precepts to the individual and social search after happiness. The morally good man will recognize his obligation to conform with the moral law, as well as the advantages accruing from such virtuous conduct.

In underlining the role of God's *will* as the determinant of the eternal law, Locke reflected the voluntarist influence upon moral philosophy. Descartes had combined this emphasis with a confidence in the ability of reason to furnish practical guidance and to elaborate

---

[32] *Draft A of An Essay concerning Human Understanding,* 26 (edited by R. I. Aaron and J. Gibb, 39); *Excerpts from Journals for April 3 and June 26, 1681* (Aaron and Gibb, 114-16); *An Essay concerning Human Understanding,* II, xxviii, 7-14 (Fraser, I, 475-80); *The Second Treatise of Civil Government,* II, 6, 8 (*Two Treatises of Government,* edited by T. I. Cook, 123, 124).

[33] *An Essay concerning Human Understanding,* II, xx, 2-3; xxi, 63; xxviii, 5 (Fraser, I, 303-56, 474).

a moral philosophy. But Locke's appeal to the natural light of reason, as a means for discovering the law of God, did not have the same force as the similarly worded appeal made by Descartes and the Cambridge Platonists. For, he rejected their metaphysical explanations of the relation between God and the human mind, without providing a specific theory of his own. Hence his conception of "reason," as a guide in moral life, was a quite pliable standard. In respect to problems of individual and social morality, it tended to mean the prevailing views of his own age and social group.

In what sense is the individual free to act for or against moral ends? Locke declared the question of the *freedom* of *the will* to be strictly nonsensical, since freedom is one power and will another.[34] The one power cannot be predicated of the other, but both belong to the man or concrete subject exercising these powers. Will is an ability to determine our thought and preference in regard to a course of action, whereas liberty is an ability to do an action which we have chosen or willed. Hence the only authentic question concerns whether *the man* is free. He is certainly free to do what he wills (and so much, Hobbes admits), but it is not so clear that he is also free in respect to willing itself. At first, Locke followed the opinion that the will is always determined by the greater positive good. But further analysis disclosed that, although good and evil do work upon the agent, what immediately determines the will is some uneasiness or desire for an absent good. Not until desire is aroused and uneasiness excited, does the greater good determine the will. For, only through the mediation of desire, does a good object pass from a purely theoretical to a practical, appetitive relation with the mind. More precisely stated, then, the will is determined, for the most part, by the most urgent, *present uneasiness* or particular manifestation of our general desire for happiness.

For the most part, but not always. Man is no mere plaything of the dialectic of conflicting desires: both materialistic and rationalistic determinism misread his mode of choice. Experience shows that a man can suspend his desires sufficiently, so that they do not determine his will, until he can subject their objects to due examination. This *suspension of the effective operation of desires,* in order to insure a

---

[34] *Ibid.,* II, xxi, 7–57 (Fraser, I, 315–53). Cf. A. Messer, "Die Behandlung des Freiheitsproblems bei John Locke," *Archiv für Geschichte der Philosophie,* XI (1898), 133–49, 404–32, which highlights the Scholastic distinctions employed by Locke's Dutch friend, Philip van Limborch, with whom he discussed freedom.

fair inquiry into the good and evil of proposed actions, is the source of man's liberty. The very necessity of our pursuit of happiness in general permits us to be free from any absolute determination by desire for particular goods. We can suspend our pursuit of a particular good long enough to ask whether it will really contribute toward our total happiness, and effectively enough to preserve our freedom of choice. In this way, men can determine for themselves what is to be taken as a necessary, particular component of their happiness and hence as the most pressing and important uneasiness in the present situation.

To this extent, man has some freedom for morally responsible *action*. Freedom is not cultivated indifference or self-centeredness: it has an end and a use. It enables us to attain a good of our own choosing. The agent desires, wills, and acts in conformity with a deliberate appraisal of the object. A man's will is determined by his own judgment about what is worth seeking. Actions, determined ultimately by one's own mature judgment, are the mark and fruit of freedom. In this argumentation, Locke has made his own empirical adaptation of the discussions of freedom presented in the Scholastic textbooks, which his Dutch friends summarized.

Locke's deepest influence upon practical thinking was felt in *social* and *political philosophy*. In reflecting upon the political situation in the England of James II and William III, he sought to discover some general and permanent conditions of political life. As the immediate target of his criticism, he chose Sir Robert Filmer's *Patriarcha or The Natural Power of Kings* (1680). In this and other writings, Filmer had defended the theory of the divine right of kings, the paternal or patriarchal nature of royal power, and the absolute monarchy. It was against this last contention that Locke's most serious arguments were directed. He was no opponent of the monarchial form of government, but he supported the Whig Settlement, involving a constitutional rather than an absolute monarchy. It was no mere coincidence that his political theories should agree in the main with Whig policies. Locke provided the "Glorious Revolution" with an apologia and a platform, supplying the backbone of political thinking and institutions in the English-speaking countries for several generations. He gave clear and unified expression to a number of current social and political concepts, that were ripe for such a synthesis. He provided a way of using the notions of the state of nature, personal liberty, the social contract, and the rule of the majority, in the service of a constitutional monarchy.

In the *Second Treatise of Civil Government,* Locke transfers to the social plane his basic practical tension between a definitive knowledge of the *natural law* and the working criterion of *personal preservation* and happiness. He reaffirms, in a more informal and popular way, his view that the natural law is a declaration of the will of God. But this eternal rule is addressed to human agents and must be promulgated through the workings of man's own mature reason. Considered concretely and historically, however, men are often ignorant of God as the author and sanction of the natural law, so that for them this law is not formally and effectively accepted as the law of their lives. But they do respond vigorously to the actual promptings of the fundamental law of nature: the self-preservation of mankind. They recognize their natural right to life itself, to the power of appropriating goods, and to the pursuit of happiness. Although Locke is confident that human reason can ground these rights ultimately in the natural law, taken in its plenary meaning, he undertakes to construct his social and political philosophy upon the immediate conviction of the individual in his right to self-preservation.

For one thing, this tendency is common to all men, binding them together into what Locke refers to as the universal society or great natural community of mankind. As Hobbes had observed, men must live together in a common world, even before they join in civil society. The original condition is that of the *state of nature,* which Locke understands to be the condition of living together under the guidance of our natural reason, but without any settled superior power.[35] He differentiates between his own state of nature and that outlined by Hobbes, since the Hobbesian state of nature is essentially a state of war of all against all. Although Locke grants that in practice his view of the state of nature also leads to perpetual conflict, he does not define it essentially as a declared intent of applying force, without right, upon another person. The state of nature is not anarchical, since men are always endowed with the law of nature or reason. But under unsettled social conditions, men do not reflect sufficiently and hence deprive this law of its proper promulgation. Only through the consequences of trying to pursue their self-interest,

[35] Chapter Two of *The Second Treatise of Civil Government* is entitled: "Of the State of Nature" (Cook, 122–28).

can men be convinced of the need to establish and follow rules of conduct.

The state of nature is one in which men are all free and equal. Natural *freedom* is not an unbounded right to do as one pleases. The right of self-preservation assures each man of a twofold freedom: to do all in his power for the preservation of his life, liberty, and possessions, and to judge and punish those who damage him in these respects. These rights are not absolute in their exercise, however, since the individual must pursue his welfare with a view to the peace and improvement of all mankind. He should also temper his punishment of a wrongdoer by the rational intent of securing reparation and the reintroduction of the offender into the community of mankind. Similarly, the *equality* of men does not wipe out differences of age, birth, capacity, and virtue. Their basic equality resides precisely in the sphere of dominion: every man is absolute lord over himself, and no man is rightfully subject to the will or authority of another. Men in the natural state are independent of one another, as far as any rightful submission of one individual to another is concerned. Each has an equal share in freedom, the preservation and cultivation of which is the main end of the law of nature.

Yet *want* is not absent from the state of nature, since bodily needs are present, urgent, and slackless. This natural fact provides Locke's theory with the dynamism required to generate both property and the body politic. Locke appropriates the medieval commonplace that, in the beginning, God gave all material goods to men in common. But He also constituted men of such a frame that they need to consume these goods, and can do so only with the help of their own labor. A man's fundamental *propriety* or *dominion* is over his own person, activity, and labor. His radical, social freedom lies in his power to dispose his own being and labor as he will, within the general framework of the natural law. Since he cannot gather or develop material goods without mixing therein something of his own labor and personality, he cannot satisfy his natural wants without appropriating things to himself. The earth and its riches cannot be used in a human way, without establishing individual dominion over them. This is the foundation for the right to *private property.*[36]

The will of God and the promptings of his own nature incline a man to labor: to use this power is, unavoidably, to appropriate goods

---

[36] On property, see *ibid.,* V (Cook, 133–46).

to himself or make them his own property. Marx's labor theory of value is anticipated by Locke's remarks that, in the state of nature, property rests on *labor* (the active extension of self-dominion to embrace the things to which a man donates something of himself), and that ninety-nine hundreths of the value of goods derives from the labor expended in developing them. But labor remains, for Locke, an *individual* rather than a *social* act and, similarly, property value is created by the private individual and not by civil society. Like other natural rights, that to property must respect certain conditions placed upon its exercise. The amount of privately owned goods is limited, in the state of nature, by the individual's ability to appropriate them by his labor, as well as by his ability to consume them, without letting them spoil. This simple limitation gives way, eventually, to the complicated opportunities for acquisition permitted by the introduction of money as a medium of value and commercial exchange. Where money and commerce prevail, Locke maintains that there is a tacit social consent to the accumulation of many more times the amount of goods or value than the individual can gain by his personal labor or than he needs for personal consumption, and that he now has the right to such widened property gains. The transition from the state of nature to the settled framework of civil society means a transition from an economy of scarcity to one of plenty. Civil laws regulate the exercise of the property right, in view of the ends for which men have banded together in the political community. This social regulation of property is intended, however, to secure each man in his right to accumulate goods, since this tends to increase the general good of society.

Material possessions constitute a major, although not the sole, occasion for the passage from the state of nature to civil society. If Locke's state of nature is not amoral, it is nevertheless subject to the same *intolerable conditions* that plagued the Hobbesian state of nature. Men are prone to overreach their neighbors in search of an unreasonable amount of power, honor, and property. Appeal to the natural law is insufficient to restrain them or secure harmony. For the natural law is unwritten: its dictates remain obscure to the indolent, and tempt the passionate or selfish to pervert them in practice. The state of nature lacks three *essential elements of a stable society:* a clearly known and publicly accepted law, an impartial judge of disputes, and an adequate power to execute sentences by force, used in the service of right.[37] Instead, every man is his own judge and executioner. His judgments are apt to be passed in his own favor, whereas his ability to carry them out is often lacking. In the state of nature, then, the preservation of life, liberty, and estate is an extremely precarious undertaking. The insecurity and inconvenience of this condition impel men to unite in political society.

Locke refers to the motive behind this transition, variously, as a *voluntary inclination,* a *need,* and a *compulsion.* Apparently, the more definite arrangement of life in civil society is in accord with the promptings of human nature, as constituted by God. But Locke touches only lightly on this natural inclination and love of men for a regulated social life, since his polemical aim requires him to lay stress upon the independence and equality of men in their natural state. Man is a political animal not so much by nature as by reason of the deficiencies of his natural condition. Hence, Locke often follows Hobbes in explaining how the insecurities of natural, non-political existence "drive" men into civil society, forcing them to "take sanctuary" in government and to accept the bonds of law.[38] Several times, he makes a contrast between what is natural and what is social or political. Locke's natural man is not completely asocial, since he is organized along with others, under the natural law. But he is lacking in the main ingredient of any terrestrial society: submission to recognized public authority, having the right to legislate and the power to exact penalties.

Earthly civil society is fully constituted only with the erection of the political power, which men are driven to establish, because of the inconveniences accompanying its absence. Each independent individual agrees to forego two of his natural powers: that of doing whatsoever he sees fit (within the bounds of the law of reason or nature) to secure the preservation of himself and others, and that of acting as his own judge and punisher of crime. The latter power is surrendered completely to the community and replaced by public authority, whereas the former is foregone in the degree that the

---

[37] *Ibid.,* IX, 124–26 (Cook, 184–85).

[38] *The Second Treatise of Civil Government,* IX, 127 (Cook, 185). Formal reference is made, however, to "necessity, convenience, and inclination," in *ibid.,* VII, 77 (Cook, 159), as joint motives provided by God for impelling men to join in civil society. The comparison with Hobbes is developed by H. Johnston, "Locke's Leviathan," *The Modern Schoolman,* XXVI (1948–1949), 201–10.

welfare of men is promoted by civil laws. The transfer of individual powers to the community is made through the *social contract* or compact, which rests on the freely given consent of the individuals involved.[39] Only when men agree to make this transfer and thus institute the public authority of the community, can they be said to belong to political society.

Locke construes the social contract in such fashion that neither Filmer's absolute monarchy nor Hobbes' Leviathan will result. Political power and authority reside in the people or community as a whole, and not in the person of an absolute monarch. Moreover, the effective aims of the community are determined by the will of the majority, which is directed toward the common good of the whole people. Government is established only as a definite way of carrying out the will of the majority and thus securing the common good of the community. Laws enacted by the legislature must conform with the long-range end of civil society: *the better preservation of property* — understood in the inclusive sense of the integrity of life, liberty, and possessions. Public authority will revert to the people as a whole, either at the expiration of the term of a government (if some temporal limit has been specified for it) or through forfeiture on the part of a government that misuses political power and perverts the ends of legislation. Government is by the consent of the governed and for the sake of an increase of freedom among the citizens. When life, liberty, and possessions are endangered through the use of political authority by a particular government, the existing laws are unjust and the government tyrannous. Under such circumstances, revolution against the oppressive regime is permitted, in order to reorientate the political community toward its proper goal.

Three points in this social theory have come under frequent criticism, ever since Locke's own day: the concept of the state of nature, the meaning of the common good, and the right of property.

1. Just as Locke analytically reduces the richness of cognitive experience to its two inlets and its ideal elements, so he analytically reduces the social life of men to the atomic individuals, from which it might be supposed to originate. He never makes it quite clear whether the state of nature is intended *historically* or as a rational concept and *analytical* limit. He often refers to an actual state of

---

[39] *The Second Treatise of Civil Government,* VIII, 95–99, 116–22 (Cook, 168–70, 180–83).

affairs, when "in the beginning all the world was America,"[40] and along this historical line he mentions various institutional developments and travelers' reports. But his main procedure is to prove the state of nature by rational analysis. Taking as a definition of the state of nature, the absence of any freely and rationally accepted earthly law and judge, Locke exemplifies it by the relations among heads of nations (agreeing with Hobbes' description of the "natural" condition of continuous conflict in international life), the status of children, and the master-slave relationship. He does not extend his reasoning about the inconveniences of natural existence to the inference that a world political community should be placed over the national, sovereign states. The example of children is illuminating, since on Locke's premises, they are not members of the political community, for lack of giving free, express consent. On this reasoning, it makes no difference whether one has been raised in a long-established society or brought up in the wilds: he is in the state of nature and is not a member of the civil community. Locke does allow that enjoyment of property entails a tacit consent to abide by the laws of the land. But this tacit consent is not enough to make a man a member of that civil society, since such incorporation rests on an actual and explicit agreement. In this respect, Locke is more radically individualistic than Hobbes, who maintains that tacit consent is sufficient to incorporate men into a given political community.

2. Perhaps the most elusive notion in Locke's political philosophy is that of the common good. Neither in the state of nature nor in civil society is the individual permitted to seek his own welfare at the expense of others or to their total neglect. Locke acknowledges the natural-law basis for the general welfare of mankind in almost every context where he defends the individual's concern for his own liberty and happiness. He declares that government and law are ordained to the general good of those under the law. But he never firmly establishes the meaning of a distinctive *common good of society,* which cannot be resolved simply into the *aggregate sum of individual goods* or into the *interests of the majority.* All of the social criteria proposed by Locke are affected by the powerful tendency of his philosophical method toward analytic reduction of the common

---

[40] *Ibid.,* V, 49 (Cook, 145). To those who objected that there is no historical evidence about men living in the state of pure nature and then coming together for a social contract in "the mighty leviathan," Locke replied that the state of nature is not conducive to the writing of history and that government antecedes written records.

good to that of many individuals, having natural rights. This introduces a certain ambivalence into Locke's view of the relation between the government and the public good. He speaks in traditional language of the dedication of political power and legislation to the betterment of the whole people, and yet he also refers to the state as an umpire, settling disputes among individuals. In last analysis, the state is an instrument of the people, and yet the welfare of the people is determined by the self-interests of the majority. Locke's trust in the rectitude of the will of the majority, as invariably promoting the well-being of the whole community, rests in part upon the contingent circumstances surrounding the Whig Settlement in England, and in part upon his general conviction that practical life must be regulated by readily ascertained probabilities. This theory of government counteracts any idolatry of the state, but it does not meet the need for well-determined safeguards against a tyrannous majority, with whom the political power ultimately lies. This problem became acute by the time of John Stuart Mill, in the nineteenth century, and is even more urgent in our day, due to the threats and fascinations of totalitarianism.

3. Locke's ambiguous treatment of the common good benefited the growing *capitalist* conception of property. The majority he had in mind were the leaders in commerce and banking, who were coming to wield effective social power. Despite his generous conception of "property," as including the happiness and liberty of individuals, Locke's dictum that "government has no other end but the preservation of property,"[41] worked historically as a bulwark of individualistic and laissez-faire policies. Locke wanted to regulate the accumulation of property by the requirements of the community as a whole, but the common good in turn resolved itself into the search of the majority of individuals for their own prosperity. Hence, in practice, the "preservation" of property meant the provision of stable conditions for a dynamic increase in the rate of individual accumulation.

Locke did not succeed in reintegrating the impulse toward self-preservation with the natural law, as a declaration of God's will. This was reflected in his shift from *duties* to *rights,* which are extensions of the individual's urge toward self-preservation.[42] Locke's moral volun-

---

[41] *Ibid.,* VII, 94 (Cook, 168); cf. VII, 87 (Cook, 163), on government acting as an umpire.

[42] Read L. Strauss' penetrating study, "On Locke's Doctrine of Natural Right," *The Philosophical Review,* LXI (1952), 475–502.

tarism encouraged the emphasis upon rights, regarded as moral powers resident in persons. This subjective view of rights was not integrated firmly with any objective foundation of rights in the relations among persons and their joint relation with the common good. Hence the property right was not grounded in a relation of objective justice among men and between men and the community, in respect to external goods. With this definite measure and control of the personal disposition of property eliminated, it was easy for proponents of economic individualism to dispense entirely with the common good or social purpose, as a relevant standard for regulating the use of property.

## SUMMARY OF CHAPTER 8

Locke observed that we cannot undertake high metaphysical investiga-tions without first discovering the capacity and limits of the human under-standing. He approached this latter task with the aid of the historical plain method, which studies the mind in its actual operation, apart from physiological and metaphysical inquiries about the whence and whither of cognition. But the understanding cannot be divorced from ideas, which are the objects about which it is concerned. After eliminating innate princi-ples and ideas, Locke was left with the mind as a clean tablet, and with experience as the only certified stylus. Taking sensation and reflection as the twin sources of experience, he set about classifying ideas according to the mental powers and operations by which they are received and then correlated. He made a vigorous case for the classical modern doctrine on the subjectivity of what men usually regard as real, secondary qualities, but he did not elucidate how the ideas of primary qualities can be both other than, and similar to, the primary qualities themselves. The Lockean way of ideas yielded a psychological explanation of efficient causality and human personality, although it did not open up any road to a philosophical knowl-edge of the real essence of substances, spiritual or material. Locke pro-posed a doctrine of abstraction based upon the mental operations of separating and relating. General meaning is due to the mind's ability to relate an idea to several particulars, which it is then able to represent. Since Locke defined knowledge as a perception of agreement or disagree-ment among ideas, he felt confident about specifying beforehand the limits of strict knowledge. He distinguished between intuitive knowledge of oneself, demonstrative knowledge of God, and sensitive knowledge of the external world. Although intuition and demonstration are the supreme modes of general knowledge, Locke sought to locate sense knowledge of the world a little below genuine demonstration and yet a little above probability. In practical philosophy, he defended man's freedom, proposed a doctrine on the state of nature and the subjective right to property, and gave a version of the social contract permitting constitutional control of the ruler by the people.

## BIBLIOGRAPHICAL NOTE

1. *Sources.* Collected edition: *The Works of John Locke* (tenth ed., 10 vols., London, Johnson, 1801). A convenient philosophical collection is: J. A. St. John, editor, *The Philosophical Works of John Locke* (2 vols., London, Bohn, 1854) — it contains: *On the Conduct of the Understanding, An Essay concerning Human Understanding,* Controversy with Bishop Stillingfleet, *An Examination of P. Malebranche's Opinion, Elements of Natural Philosophy,* and *Some Thoughts concerning Reading.* The best separate edition of the *Essay* is that of A. C. Fraser: *An Essay concerning Human Understanding* (reprint, 2 vols., New York, Dover Press, 1959), prefaced by elaborate Prolegomena, annotated, and well indexed; Fraser's views, however, have not always been sustained by later investigators. A number of Locke's papers, forming the Lovelace Collection, were for many generations reserved by the Lovelace family. The collection has now been bought by the Bodleian Library and is being catalogued and prepared for publication by Prof. W. von Leyden of Durham University. Meanwhile, from the Lovelace Collection have come two early drafts of the *Essay: An Early Draft of Locke's Essay, together with Excerpts from His Journals,* edited by R. I. Aaron and J. Gibb (Oxford, Clarendon, 1936); *An Essay concerning the Understanding, Knowledge, Opinion and Assent,* edited by B. Rand (Cambridge, Mass., Harvard University Press, 1931). The Aaron-Gibb text is earlier than the Rand text and is better edited. Professor von Leyden states, however, that the Lovelace Collection contains an unpublished 15,000-word Latin treatise, which is anterior to both the Aaron-Gibb and the Rand drafts; it also contains unpublished correspondence, notebooks, and journals covering the years 1675–1704 (cf. *The Philosophical Quarterly,* 2 [1952], 63–69). T. I. Cook has edited Locke's *Two Treatises of Government* (New York, Hafner, 1947), which facilitates comparison by also including the full text of Sir Robert Filmer's *Patriarcha. The Correspondence of John Locke and Edward Clarke,* edited by B. Rand (Cambridge, Mass., Harvard University Press, 1927), shows Locke as a man of affairs, especially in dealing with current problems in economics, education, and politics.

2. *Studies.* In preparing his biography, *The Life of John Locke* (new ed., 2 vols., London, Colburn and Bentley, 1830), Lord King had access to the Lovelace papers, from which he made long extracts; H. R. Fox Bourne had to rely upon King's report in the preparation of his own *The Life of John Locke* (2 vols., New York, Harper, 1876). There are two excellent general introductions to Locke's philosophy: *John Locke,* by R. I. Aaron (New York, Oxford University Press, 1937), and *John Locke,* by D. J. O'Connor (Baltimore, Penguin, 1952). Aaron's approach is mainly historical, whereas O'Connor evaluates Locke in terms of modern analytic philosophy. J. Gibson, *Locke's Theory of Knowledge and Its Historical Relations* (Cambridge, University Press, 1917) gives an accurate account of his epistemology but the historical comparisons suffer from lack of sufficient data. Despite the work of É Krakowski, *Les sources médiévales de la philosophie de Locke* (Paris, Jouve, 1915), and A. Tell-

kamp, *Das Verhältnis John Lockes zur Scholastik* (Münster, Aschendorff, 1927), Locke's Scholastic background has not yet been precisely determined; publication of his integral notebooks and journals may aid this study. Among more specialized accounts are: J. G. Clapp, *Locke's Conception of the Mind* (Columbia University dissertation, 1937), which studies mind as power, substance, and knower; A. Petzäll, *Ethics and Epistemology in John Locke's Essay concerning Human Understanding* (Göteborg, Wettergren and Kerber, 1937); S. P. Lamprecht, *The Moral and Political Philosophy of John Locke* (New York, Columbia University Press, 1918); J. W. Gough, *Locke's Political Philosophy* (New York, Oxford University Press, 1950), which makes somewhat debatable use of Locke's private papers; C. J. Cjaikowski, *The Theory of Private Property in John Locke's Political Philosophy* (University of Notre Dame dissertation, 1941); S. G. Hefelbower, *The Relation of John Locke to English Deism* (Chicago, University of Chicago Press, 1918). E. T. Campagnac's *The Cambridge Platonists* (Oxford, Clarendon, 1901) is a book of source readings in a school that deeply influenced Locke. See the two well-informed studies on this movement by G. P. Pawson, *The Cambridge Platonists and their Place in Religious Thought* (London, Society for Promoting Christian Knowledge, 1930), and W. C. de Pauley, *The Candle of the Lord: Studies in the Cambridge Platonists* (New York, Macmillan, 1937). E. Cassirer's *The Platonic Renaissance in England,* translated by J. P. Pettegrove (Austin, University of Texas Press, 1953), contains valuable comparative material on the Cambridge School; special attention is paid to the leader of this school in J. A. Passmore's *Ralph Cudworth: An Interpretation* (Cambridge, University Press, 1951). For Locke's relations with his empirical successors, cf. C. R. Morris, *Locke, Berkeley, Hume* (New York, Oxford, 1931).

3. *Further Lockean Publications.* From the Lovelace materials have come *Locke's Travels in France, 1675–1679,* edited by J. Lough (Cambridge, the University Press, 1953), and John Locke, *Essays on the Law of Nature,* edited by W. von Leyden (Oxford, Clarendon Press, 1954), a series of early moral essays. The new sources provide rich biographical data for Maurice Cranston, *John Locke* (New York, Macmillan, 1957), and permit an evaluation of the French influence by Gabriel Bonno, *Les relations intellectuelles de Locke avec la France* (Berkeley, University of California Press, 1955). Locke's impact upon contemporary religious discussion is more closely measured by J. W. Yolton, *John Locke and the Ways of Ideas* (New York, Oxford University Press, 1956). Locke's *Two Treatises of Government* is now critically edited by P. Laslett (Cambridge, the University Press, 1960), whose Introduction stresses Locke's preoccupation with Filmer and the probable composition of much of the *Two Treatises* in the years 1679–1683, with some additions on the Whig Revolution written in 1689. C. A. Viano's *John Locke, Dal razionalismo all' illuminismo* (Turin, Einaudi, 1960), is a remarkable general study working from Locke's political, social, religious, and scientific interests to his philosophy. His political views are examined by R. Polin, *La Politique morale de John Locke* (Paris, Presses Universitaires, 1960), and R. H. Cox, *Locke on War and Peace* (New York, Oxford University Press, 1960).

# Chapter 9. BERKELEY

## I. LIFE AND WRITINGS

GEORGE BERKELEY, an Irishman of English ancestry, was born in Kilkenny in 1685. He matriculated at Trinity College, Dublin, in 1700, receiving the degrees of bachelor and master of arts and, later on, bachelor and doctor of divinity. Appointed a fellow of Trinity in 1707, he served as tutor and lecturer there for two periods: 1707-1713 and 1721-1724. During the first period of service, his philosophical genius matured rapidly and his basic works were written. At Trinity, Locke and Descartes were staple fare, while considerable attention was also paid to Malebranche, Newton, and Clarke. The views of Hobbes and later freethinkers were critically discussed, but Berkeley was soon convinced that the issues could not be settled as long as both sides accepted the reality of matter. His first approach to the immaterialist hypothesis was made in two notebooks, written in 1707-1708, the so-called *Philosophical Commentaries* (discovered and published in a defective edition, 1871; accurate edition, 1944). Berkeley ventured to publish part of his findings, bearing on the sense of sight, in *An Essay Towards a New Theory of Vision* (1709). There, he established the mental nature of the actual object of sight, although he accorded extramental reality to the object of touch. His thoroughgoing immaterialism was explained and defended in *A Treatise concerning the Principles of Human Knowledge* (1710). Since some of his friends regarded the theory as oversubtle and mad, Berkeley recast his thought in popular form and stressed its accord with common sense, in *Three Dialogues between Hylas and Philonous* (1713). Thus, before his thirtieth year, Berkeley had set forth his entire system of philosophy and carefully weighed the objections commonly raised against it.

In order to broaden his experience, he went to London in 1713 and became the companion of such wits as Swift, Steele, Addison,

Gay, Pope, Prior, and Arbuthnot. A series of anonymous articles against freethinking was contributed by Berkeley to Steele's *Guardian*. He was a member of the party accompanying Lord Peterborough to the coronation of the King of Sicily and, during this trip (1713–1714), he may have had a philosophical interview with Malebranche. There followed a four-year tour of France and Italy (1716–1720), during which Berkeley acted as tutor to a friend's son, began a treatise on psychology and ethics (lost in an accident), and wrote a short work *On Motion* (1721), in which the relations between immaterialism and the mechanical sciences were discussed. After his return to London, Berkeley was impressed by the corruption and frivolity of society, as exemplified by the panic upon the bursting of the South Sea Bubble, a fabulous financial scheme. He resumed his lecturing at Trinity College but was convinced (as the famous line from his own poem reads) that "westward the course of empire takes its way." Berkeley resigned his Trinity fellowship upon being appointed Dean of Derry (1724). He then made elaborate plans for the founding of St. Paul's College in Bermuda, having as its purpose the education of sons of English planters and native Indians both for the ministry and for useful work in agriculture and trade. A charter was obtained in 1725, some subscription monies were raised, and both the King and Parliament agreed to a grant of 20,000 pounds. On the strength of this assurance, Berkeley took his newly wedded wife to Newport, Rhode Island, in 1729 and built a house called Whitehall. (The edifice is still in good condition.) He wanted to develop the Newport farm into a continental base for his proposed college and also to survey the American situation at firsthand. While in America, he corresponded with the American idealistic philosopher, Samuel Johnson, and wrote a sustained critique of freethinking: *Alciphron or the Minute Philosopher* (1732). The British prime minister, Robert Walpole, was finally persuaded not to pay the grant to the college, so that in 1731 the disappointed Berkeley returned to England. As a parting gift to America, he left his books to Yale and Harvard libraries and deeded his house and estate at Newport to Yale University for the support of three scholars.

As recognition of his faithful service in the Church of Ireland, Berkeley was appointed Bishop of Cloyne (1734). He labored for twenty years for the spiritual and material welfare of his flock, instituting economic self-help programs and offering his famous remedy of tar water as a cure for dysentery and other diseases afflicting the people. His last important work was *Siris, a Chain of Philosophical Reflexions and Inquiries Concerning the Virtues of Tar-Water* (1744), which (as Coleridge put it) begins with tar water and ends with the Holy Trinity, the *omne scibile* forming the interspace. In 1752, Berkeley went to Oxford to see his son, George, safely settled in his studies. He died peacefully in January of the following year, while his wife was reading the passage in St. Paul's first letter to the Corinthians on Christ's victory over death.

## 2. ABSTRACTION AND THE SENSIBLE THING

From his study of Descartes and Malebranche, Locke and Newton, Berkeley familiarized himself thoroughly with the main trends in seventeenth-century philosophy. His own position grew out of an attempt to describe experience from the accepted starting point in the mind, having its own ideas as its direct objects. The main question raised by his predecessors concerned how the human mind can bridge the chasm between its own ideas and the surrounding world, so that we can have some objective certainty about real things. The answers given to this question were quite divergent and not very convincing to Berkeley, who viewed them in the light of the rising tide of popular, eighteenth-century skepticism. The skeptical currents of thought would not be so strong, he reasoned, if there were not a fundamental weakness about all the previous constructive answers. Berkeley did not challenge the accepted *mentalistic starting point* of philosophical inquiry. But he did bring criticism to bear upon the way in which the main philosophical *question* itself had been posed. For, to ask how a passage can be made from mind to things, is to suppose that sensible things are really different from our ideas or mental objects. Berkeley's entire philosophical effort stems from a removal of this supposition. He reformulated the major philosophical problem, to read: how can a coherent account of the world be given, if the idea or mental object and the real sensible thing are one and the same? If a successful explanation of sensible reality can be furnished, under this condition, then the skeptics will forever be quieted. For, there will be no further need to search behind our ideas for another world, to which our ideas must be shown to conform.

Berkeley stated this fresh hypothesis in what he termed his New Principle. In one of his early philosophical commentaries, he gave a succinct and comprehensive formulation of the *New Principle:* "Existence is *percipi* or *percipere* or *velle,* i.e., *agere.*"[1] This statement shows that, for Berkeley, the crucial issue in philosophy concerns the meaning of existence. His answer was that "existence" has two distinct and even opposed meanings. It signifies either the state of being perceived or the act of perceiving, which is basically the same as willing and acting. *To-be-perceived* is the kind of existence belonging to the *sensible thing:* its entire to-be consists in its to-be-perceived. Hence there is no real distinction between the real sensible thing and the mental object, called the idea of the sensible thing. But there is a real distinction between the sensible existent or mental object and the perceiver. *To-perceive* is the sort of existence proper to the *mind:* its to-be is that of an active, perceiving, and willing principle. Hence sensible things and minds are the sole existents — and sensible things are identical with the ideas of sense possessed by minds.

In order to clear the path for acceptance of his New Principle, Berkeley had to perform a negative and a positive task. (1) The negative step was taken in his *critique of abstraction.* This move was dictated by the obvious retort that any Lockean thinker would give to Berkeley's theory of sensible existence. The Lockean reply would be a distinction between the thing's mental presence and its real existence, as a movable, extended substance, outside the mind. Since the force of this distinction depends upon our ability to abstract sensible existence, motion, and extension from the condition of being perceived, Berkeley was obliged to criticize Locke's theory of abstraction and abstract, general ideas. (2) The positive move was to offer a new *definition of the sensible thing,* in line with the requirements of the New Principle. Since Berkeley agreed with Descartes and Locke that the idea is the formal and direct object of the mind, his strategy was to show that a starting point in ideas must lead to such a definition of the sensible thing as would confirm his theory of sensible existence. Once these two steps were taken, there was nothing to prevent Berkeley from indicating the metaphysical consequences of his New Principle. It issues in an *empirical immaterialism,* in which material substance is eliminated and the totality of human experience is explained in function of the infinite mind, finite minds, ideas, and notions.

---

[1] *Philosophical Commentaries,* 429–429a. All references in Berkeley are to the Luce-Jessop edition of *The Works of George Berkeley, Bishop of Cloyne;* cf. I, 53 (italics and punctuation added). This edition is referred to hereafter as *Works.*

1. *The Critique of Abstraction.* Although Berkeley decries the learned dust raised by "the Schoolmen, those great masters of abstraction,"[2] his real target of criticism is Locke. As representative of what is commonly meant by an abstract, general idea, he quotes the passage (see above, p. 340) in which Locke describes the idea of a triangle. Berkeley gives practically a word-for-word commentary on this text, which was so familiar to his contemporaries.

First, he bids us notice how Locke stresses the *difficulty* of forming these abstract ideas. It follows that abstraction is not an easy process, one to be performed unthinkingly by children. But does there *ever* come a time, even in our mature years, when we deliberately set about to frame these ideas? And even if we should decide to do so, can we *actually form* such an idea as Locke's triangle? As a good empiricist, Berkeley invites us to try to picture to ourselves the general idea of a triangle that is "neither equilateral, equicrural, nor scalenon; but all and none of these at once." He challenges us to try to visualize the general, abstract idea of color, which is neither white nor black, nor any other particular shade, but something abstracted from all of these. Little wonder that Locke should confess that the abstract, general idea contains inconsistent elements. For his own part, Berkeley reports that he always has in mind some particular shape or color, and never entertains a bare, abstract idea of shape as such or color as such.

Berkeley was unable, however, to press this psychological argument very far. For it rested on the assumption that an idea is only a percept or image, and that abstraction is a process of picturing or *concrete visualization* of the object. If this assumption is admitted, it is obvious that some concrete image must always be kept in mind. But the Cartesians would reply that, at the philosophical level of clear and distinct ideas, abstraction is an act of purely intellectual apprehension, which cannot be confined to the conditions of sense imagery. Furthermore, the psychological argument may prove too much, if it implies a denial of universal meaning. For then, philosophical inference is rendered impossible, and even a system of empirical immaterialism is ruled out.

These considerations forced Berkeley to introduce a capital dis-

---

[2] *The Principles of Human Knowledge,* Introduction, 17 (*Works,* II, 35). This Introduction to the *Principles* (*Works,* II, 25–40) is the *locus classicus* for Berkeley's attack on abstraction. See also *An Essay towards a New Theory of Vision,* 122–31 (*Works,* I, 220–24).

tinction between the *abstractness* and the *generality* of ideas. He sought a way to reject the former trait and yet retain the latter. The abstract character of ideas is founded on two pretended operations of the mind: (*a*) the claim to be able to frame an "absolute, positive nature or conception of any thing,"³ such as the idea of motion as such, apart from any particular kind of motion, and yet corresponding to them all; (*b*) the claim to be able to separate mentally those traits or qualities that cannot possibly exist separately, such as the idea of motion as such, apart from the body that moves. These two operations constitute what Berkeley termed *abstraction proper*. He remained unalterably opposed to abstraction proper and to the abstract ideas, which are its supposed outcome. For, each of these abstracting operations would provide an entering wedge against the validity of his New Principle. Thus, the Cartesians would separate extension and motion as such from their particular modes, and would then give a clear and distinct definition of extended substance and thereby prove its extramental reality. And the Lockeans would separate sensible existence as such from the conditions of perception, and would then attribute it to the extramental material substance. Both of these procedures illustrate what Berkeley regarded as a vicious sort of abstraction, since they disintegrate the concrete unity of the sensible existent. (*a*) If the New Principle holds good, then to grasp the absolute nature of an isolated quality as an object of perception is equivalent to attributing to it a real, sensible existence. The real existence of motion or extension, as general natures, is in violation of the commonly accepted principle that only the concrete individual can exist. (*b*) According to the New Principle, it is impossible to separate or abstract the *esse* from the *percipi* of a sensible thing. Hence it is only verbally possible to treat of a sensible existent independently of the condition of its being perceived by the mind. Berkeley regarded abstraction proper as a psychological impossibility, only because it is basically a metaphysical and epistemological impossibility, granted the truth of his New Principle.

Nevertheless, he agreed with Locke that generality of meaning is required for scientific knowledge and demonstration. Having eliminated the abstractness of our ideas, he now attempted to defend their general signification. Of the two operations invoked by Locke in

---

³ *The Principles of Human Knowledge,* Introduction, 15 (*Works,* II, 33–34); the Scholastic manuals familiar to Locke sometimes called this the direct universal. On the two distinctive acts of abstraction proper, cf. *loc. cit.,* 7–10 (*Works,* II, 27–30).

explanation of general ideas — separating and relating — Berkeley rejected the first, insofar as it is a process of abstraction proper. Still, he admitted a legitimate kind of *mental separating* or *considering,* "as when I consider some particular parts or qualities separated from others, with which though they are united in some object, yet, it is possible they may really exist without them."[4] Thus the eye or the nose can be considered apart from the rest of the human body, since they may also exist in some other animal. Berkeley was quite willing to call this sort of separating or considering an abstraction, but in an *improper* sense. It never terminates in *abstract, general ideas* but only in *nonabstract, general ideas.* He made this concession, since it did not involve the crucial separation of an absolute nature from particular things, or of sensible existence from the condition of being perceived.

In further explanation of the general significance of ideas, Berkeley developed Locke's doctrine on the relating of particular ideas. Berkeley called this process a *considering* by the mind. Although the mind can never frame an abstract idea of an absolute nature, it does have the power to confine its attention to only certain aspects of the concrete, particular idea. In thinking about an isosceles triangle, for instance, the mind can focus its consideration upon this figure, precisely so far forth as it is triangular, without paying special attention to the equality of the angles or sides. The idea remains particular in its own formal nature, but it becomes *general in its signification,* since it indifferently connotes other particulars of the same sort. It can now be taken as a sign for all other particular triangular figures, toward which it stands in the functional relation of representative sign to represented objects. Similarly, although the mind never attains the abstract, general idea of man, as an absolute nature, it can consider Peter precisely insofar as he is a man. Although his particular traits are not evacuated, attention is directed toward those aspects in him which hold equally true of any other particular men. The universality of meaning does not reside in an abstracted common nature but in the function of considering certain particular traits as a sign, applicable to several other individual objects.

Berkeley's explanation of general ideas modifies Locke, in two important respects. First, he bypasses the abstract, common nature, so

---

[4] *Ibid.,* Introduction, 10 (*Works,* II, 29–30). For Berkeley's behind-the-scenes development of the distinction between abstraction and considering, cf. *Philosophical Commentaries,* 254, 318, 440 (*Works,* I, 32, 39, 54).

that there is generality of meaning, without abstractness of an ideal nature. Locke had already remarked that the abstract, general idea is imperfect and cannot exist. But Berkeley's New Principle now assures him that the inability of this presumed absolute nature to *exist* is sure proof that it cannot be *perceived* at all by the mind, since to exist and to be perceived are correlative in the sensible order. Locke was led astray by the peculiarities of *language* into supposing that an abstract general, mental entity corresponds to an abstract, general name. It is only in a verbal way that one can infer the existence of abstract, general ideas, because there are abstract, general names. Berkeley holds that words stand for particular operations, attitudes, and ideas of the mind, rather than for abstract, general ideas. In the second place, Berkeley amends the nature of the real particular things, to which any general idea is related by signification. The other particular ideas to which a general idea relates, are themselves the sensible existents, and bear *no further reference* beyond themselves, as far as sensible things are concerned. Such a reference is impossible to think about, and hence impossible to reach through abstraction, since the only to-be proper to sensible things is their to-be-perceived. On both these counts, Berkeley's corrections are dependent upon the validity of the New Principle itself.

Even after this emendation of Locke, however, Berkeley does not escape from his predecessor's basic difficulties. Lockean abstraction is not a realistic process, since it involves a manipulation of ideas, rather than a penetration of the intelligible structure of the real. Berkeley's remedy is to identify the percept with the sensible existent. He formally raises the question of how we can know that a meaning holds true for several particular ideas, considered now as particular sensible existents. His answer, however, consists in a repetition of his description of the operations of considering and signifying, whereas the question requires an explanation of *how and why* these operations can validly be performed. How can the mind determine which other particulars are, in fact, "ideas of the same sort," so that it can be sure that a certain set of traits "indifferently denotes . . . [and] holds equally true of them all"?[5] To reply that the mind attends only to those features which can be found in all other particular men, triangles, or motions, merely restates the question of how we know that other particulars can be signified together, as being human, triangular,

---

[5] *The Principles of Human Knowledge*, Introduction, 11, 12 (*Works*, II, 31, 32).

or mobile. On what grounds is the mind justified in attending to a certain group of traits and in making no mention of others? What guides the operation of considering, so that it views Peter precisely so far forth as he is a man, and carefully distinguishes these factors from the ones peculiar to himself?

The latter questions must remain unanswered in the Berkeleyan system, since a definite answer would involve a *dilemma*. Either Locke's absolute nature must be reinstated (with the consequence, for Berkeley, that this object of perception also has sensible existence) or else the barrier of mentalism must be broken through, and the admission made that the mind grasps certain similar traits in the essential natures of things, whose mode of real existence is distinct from the intentional being of the idea (with a resultant undermining of the New Principle). Since neither alternative is acceptable to Berkeley, he prefers simply to point to the fact of general meaning, without trying to supply the adequate metaphysical and epistemological bases for the fact. His removal of Lockean abstraction still leaves the problem of the relation between general meanings and particular existents fundamentally unresolved.

2. *The Definition of the Sensible Thing.* Underlying the entire discussion of abstraction is a definite theory about the sensible thing. Berkeley appeals both to common sense and to Locke's premises, in order to establish a doctrine on the nature of the sensible thing which will be in conformity with his New Principle. He asks himself, first, what is ordinarily meant by saying that there is a sound or an odor, that my desk exists, or that my horse is in the barn.[6] To assert the existence of these objects is the same as to assert that they are *perceived by some mind* — and nothing more. The common-sense meaning of sensible existence is that the sound is being heard, the odor smelled, the desk perhaps seen and felt, the horse perceived in some similar way. At the very minimum, the affirmation of the real existence of a body or sensible thing involves either recalling a past sense perception or stipulating that, if I were to place myself in the proper circumstances, I would receive the specified perceptual experience. Thus, if I were to walk out to the stable, I would see the horse to be there. And even when I am not actually perceiving the horse's existence, it is the object of actual perception perhaps for other finite minds and

---

[6] For this interrogation of common sense, see *ibid.*, I, 3-4, 23 (*Works*, II, 42, 50-51); *Three Dialogues between Hylas and Philonous*, I (*Works*, II, 195; on the tulip one "really" sees).

certainly for the infinite mind of God. No more is meant by affirming the existence of bodies or bodily qualities than their being perceived or their capacity for being perceived by the finite mind, together with their always being perceived by the divine mind.

On Locke's premises, an idea is the immediate object of thought, that about which I am thinking. But, Berkeley asks, is there any difference between the common-sense conviction that the mind is immediately concerned with the sensible thing and the Lockean doctrine that the mind is directed immediately toward the idea or mental object? That in which the cognitive operation immediately terminates is the *idea* or *sensible thing,* which are one and the same.

The Lockean mind will admit the following definition: "*Sensible things are those only which are immediately perceived by sense. . . .* Sensible things therefore are nothing else but so many sensible qualities, or combinations of sensible qualities.*"[7] But the same mind will balk at the inference that, since what is being immediately perceived is nothing other than an idea, therefore the entire reality of the sensible thing consists in its being perceived by the mind. The follower of Locke will interject that sensible things enjoy "a real absolute being, distinct from, and without any relation to their being perceived." Berkeley's reply is that such an existence would be quite irrelevant to what has been defined as the sensible thing, since an absolute existence would be divorced from the condition of being immediately perceived by the mind. Furthermore, an absolute or mind-independent existence could never be known by our mind, which has ideas as its immediate objects. For, *"an idea can be like nothing but an idea."*[8] Hence if the immediately known object refers to anything else, the latter must also be of an ideal nature. The only significant distinction between idea and ideatum is one that lies wholly within the sphere of mental objects. Berkeley does allow a difference between *ideas of sense* and *ideas of imagination.* The former are immediate, irreducible presentations, simply given to the mind, whereas the latter are copies and involve a mental operation. Berkeley identifies his ideas of sense with Locke's real things or archetypes of the reality of existential knowledge. Hence he interprets the distinction between real things and ideas to mean nothing more than the distinction between ideas of sense and those of imagination. Although the latter may be said to reflect the former,

[7] *Loc. cit.* (*Works,* II, 175); the next quotation is from the same page.
[8] *The Principles of Human Knowledge,* I, 8 (*Works,* II, 44; italics added).

both terms in the representative relation are located squarely within the realm of ideas or mental objects. Hence the existence of sensible things is not "absolute" but is the same as their state of being perceived by the mind.

Berkeley's favorite way of defending his New Principle consists in a description of the situation of the perceiving subject. Seated at my desk, I may look out the window and see the houses, the trees, the river, and the mountains. I cannot mention these things at all, except by bringing them into the relation of objects of perception for my mind. It is impossible for me to "conceive them existing unconceived or unthought of, which is a manifest repugnancy. . . . What is conceived, is surely in the mind."[9] When we try to consider the trees by themselves, apart from any perceiving mind, we are simply forgetting or methodically refraining from mentioning the fact that they are still objects of perception for our mind and hence have only the existence of being perceived.

In America, the strongest challenge of this analysis came from R. B. Perry, following some suggestions made by his master, William James.[10] James had observed that there is a considerable difference between saying that we cannot think of a thing without actually thinking *of* it, and saying that we cannot think of a thing without thinking it *to be* an idea or mode of thought. Berkeley's description of the cognitive situation emphasizes the former statement, which is a truism, but it adduces nothing to show that every object *of* perception is nothing but an object *in* perception. As an extension of this criticism, Perry taxed Berkeley with two fallacies: that of definition by initial predication and that of the egocentric predicament. The fallacy of *definition by initial predication* consists in defining a thing's essential nature exclusively in terms of some early or familiar trait, which it displays to us. The reference of a thing to our perception shows only that it is a perceivable nature, not that its intrinsic reality consists solely in being actually perceived or having a reference to the perceiver's mind. Merely to ascertain that a thing bears a relation to consciousness, is to show the intelligibility of its nature: it does

---

[9] *Ibid.*, I, 23 (*Works*, II, 50).

[10] R. B. Perry, *Present Philosophical Tendencies* (New York, Longmans, 1912), 126–32. James and Perry continued the criticism of the Scottish philosopher, Thomas Reid, that we can distinguish between the sensation or feeling itself and the qualitative nature which we know; cf. S. C. Rome, "The Scottish Refutation of Berkeley's Immaterialism," *Philosophy and Phenomenological Research*, III (1943), 313–25.

not show that this nature has no other existential act than that of being actually perceived by and in consciousness. Berkeley has failed to complete the analysis of the cognitive relation. If it can be shown that this relation is an extrinsic or nonmutual one, then the fact that the thing is logically related to the mind does not determine the intrinsic nature and natural mode of existing, proper to the thing. The fallacy of the *egocentric predicament* means an attempt to infer more than is warranted from the fact that, in thinking about something, we cannot avoid referring it to our own mind. It is redundant to state that, in order to know a thing, one must know it, i.e., one must bring it into cognitive relation with one's perception. This is an inescapable condition of knowledge, regardless of the nature of the thing to be known. From this condition, nothing can be inferred about the nature of the thing, which is brought into relation with the mind. Whether that thing has a distinct physical existence of its own or has no other existence than that of being perceived, the condition remains the same and remains equally incapable of settling the issue. No metaphysical conclusion whatever can be reached by restating the common requirement of all cognition, since this requirement remains the same, no matter what the nature of the thing to be known.

Two related difficulties in Berkeley's argument are significant for realists. The first concerns his axiom that ideas can only be like other ideas. This is another truism, if the idea is taken only in its own physical being, as a mental mode. As such, it has its similitudes in other mental modes or objects in the mind. But if the idea is considered in its signifying function, it is begging the question to state that it can represent nothing else than other ideas. The point at issue concerns precisely whether the *intentional* or *signifying relation* of a concept reaches beyond its own physical condition, as a mental mode of being. Berkeley's negative answer rests on the dual assumption that the mode of being of the sign must be the same as that of the thing signified, and that an idea is always an instrumental sign.[11] Once the distinction between the intentional and physical modes of being is drawn, however, a concept can be shown to be the *intentional* likeness and *formal* sign of a thing, whose real, *physical* act of exist-

---

[11] *Three Dialogues between Hylas and Philonous*, I (*Works*, II, 203–06). For a realistic criticism, cf. J. Wild, "Berkeley's Theories of Perception," *Revue Internationale de Philosophie*, VII (1953), 134–51. Wild overemphasizes, however, the later preoccupation of Berkeley with objectivity and rationality, since such a preoccupation is evident even in the *Philosophical Commentaries*.

ing is distinct from the condition of being perceived. But this distinction would also tell against the New Principle, which is relevant only for the physical being of the concept or object-in-cognition, not for the act of existing of the thing that is cognized. The second point of interest concerns the manner in which Berkeley describes an "absolute" or extramental manner of existing. He specifies that it must be not only distinct from, but also entirely unrelated and unrelatable to, the mind. Yet defense of the real distinction between the physical *esse* of the existing thing and its *percipi* does not entail a denial of any possible relation between the mind and the existing thing. Since the same mode of being need not be present in both terms of the cognitive relation, there is no repugnance in maintaining both the distinction between the real to-be and the to-be-perceived, and also the intelligibility of the real act of existing and its actually being known in the existential judgment. Indeed, the act of existing can be rendered present in the knower, only on condition that the existential judgment affirm, at least implicitly, the real otherness between the act of judging and the act of being.

## 3. THE POLEMIC AGAINST MATTER

In the subtitle to his *Principles of Human Knowledge,* Berkeley proposed to inquire into "the chief causes of error and difficulty in the sciences, with the grounds of scepticism, atheism, and irreligion." This program characterized his entire approach to philosophical problems, since his constant concern was for the fate of common-sense beliefs and religious truths, in an age when skepticism, atheism, and irreligion were coming into the intellectual ascendancy. He believed that they could all be refuted together, and that the key to their common refutation lay in the *rejection of matter,* as a real entity.[12] Bayle's *Dictionary* had spread the attitude of Pyrrhonian *skepticism*

---

[12] *The Principles of Human Knowledge,* I, 86–96 (*Works,* II, 78–82). By way of clarification of the lines of battle, Berkeley adds: "The question between the materialists and me is not, whether things have a real existence out of the mind of this or that person, but whether they have an absolute existence, distinct from being perceived by God, and exterior to all minds." *Three Dialogues between Hylas and Philonous,* III (*Works,* II, 235). By posing the problem of the existence of material substance in this way, however, he precluded the possibility that this substance can be at once totally dependent upon God, completely known by Him, and also endowed by Him with an act of existing that is distinct from the act of being known by either God or finite minds. For Berkeley's central preoccupation with finding a refutation for skepticism, cf. R. H. Popkin, "Berkeley and Pyrrhonism," *The Review of Metaphysics,* V (1950–1951), 223–46.

by claiming that, if we can know only our own ideas directly, there is no certain way of coming to know a world distinct from these ideas and lying behind them. But if it can be shown that there is no material substance lying in the dark, then to know our own ideas is to have a perfectly evident and sure grasp upon the only real world: that of sensible things or ideas of sense. Again, *atheism* rests upon the view that the material universe is self-existent and hence requires no support from a God. But if the true situation is that matter is completely nonexistent and that the world of sensible bodies is a world of mind-dependent ideas, based ultimately upon the infinite spirit, then the grounds of atheism are removed. Finally, *irreligious materialism* will be unable to identify the first principle of the world with matter, if it is made manifest that all sensible existents are ideas and, as such, require the existence of a divine mind or immaterial substance. Hence, in his criticism of matter, Berkeley found a way of removing the greatest errors of his age, and of doing so in terms of the world view that most appealed to him. This double advantage sharpened the edge of his logical tools, when he applied them to the concept of matter.

The attempt of Locke and Malebranche to refute the above errors by means of their doctrine on matter is, in Berkeley's eyes, a total failure. In their philosophy, *matter* is:

> an inert, senseless substance, in which extension, figure, and motion, do actually subsist. . . . The matter philosophers contend for, is an incomprehensible somewhat which has none of those particular qualities, whereby the bodies falling under our senses are distinguished one from another. . . . It neither acts, nor perceives, nor is perceived.[13]

It is against this notion of matter that all of Berkeley's arguments are directed, and no alternative view is considered. If the direct objects of perception are ideas, we can know only ourselves as having this or that sensation or idea. Granted that ideas can only be like other ideas, the following dilemma develops: either matter must be reduced to the status of an idea, in order to be known, or else it must be placed entirely beyond our knowledge. In respect to sensible things, we cannot go beyond our ideas and hence cannot attain to a material sub-

---

[13] *The Principles of Human Knowledge*, I, 9, 47, 68 (*Works*, II, 44–45, 60, 70; spelling modernized). Although Malebranche did not deny the existence of matter, he held it on faith, rather than on reason, and explained matter in such a way as to prepare for Berkeley's outright denial; cf. A. D. Fritz, "Malebranche and the Immaterialism of Berkeley," *The Review of Metaphysics*, III (1949–1950), 59–80.

stance which, by definition, lies beyond the relation between the perceiver and his ideas. If material substance is banished beyond knowledge, there is no rational ground for supposing its existence.

The burden of proof is thus laid upon those who make some positive affirmation about matter. They may answer that, although material substance is unknowable in itself, it can be known in its *relation with the qualities.* To meet the argument that matter is required at least as the support of qualities, Berkeley reviews the nature of these supposed modes of matter. He exploits the received distinction between primary and secondary qualities, since it already grants one half of his thesis. To hold that ordinary secondary qualities have only a subjective reality, is to concede the point that they exist only as ideas or objects of perception. All that remains for Berkeley to show is that there is *no essential epistemological difference between primary and secondary qualities.*[14] Hence the former must be considered just as mind-dependent as the latter. *All* qualities have their reality only as ideas related objectively to the percipient mind.

Extension, figure, motion, and solidity are reckoned by Locke among the primary qualities. But Berkeley appeals to the testimony of experience, that these aspects are never presented *in isolation* from the other properties of bodies. What is actually perceived, is not extension alone or motion alone but rather this extended, moving, colored, tangible thing. We are confronted with a *sensible whole:* if one group of its components are ideas in and for the perceiver, the same sort of being must be assigned to the remaining components. The argument about the relativity of ordinary secondary qualities to the perceiver can be extended to the primary qualities. Just as the color and taste of a thing vary with the subjective condition of the perceiver, so do the texture and shape and velocity. To the same person at different times or to several simultaneous observers, placed at different perspectives, the same object may appear now as small, smooth, and round; now as large, uneven, and angular. Solidity is easily reducible to a datum of touch and hence to an idea of sense.

The only recourse left for Berkeley's opponents is to distinguish between *particular,* variable instances of extension, figure, and motion and the *absolute,* general nature of these properties "considered in themselves." As a countermove, Berkeley recalls his attack upon

---

[14] For this dialectic, read *The Principles of Human Knowledge,* I, 9–15 (*Works,* II, 44–47); *Three Dialogues between Hylas and Philonous,* I (*Works,* II, 175–92); *Alciphron,* IV, 8–10 (*Works,* III, 150–54).

abstract, general ideas. The separation of extension as such from particular instances of extended bodies is an instance of vicious abstraction. Similarly, the uncoupling of primary from secondary qualities is due to an invalid abstraction from the integrity of concrete experience. Apart from particular sensible ideas, there are no existent qualities.

As a consequence, material substance is left literally existing *no-where* and supporting *no-thing*. The sensible thing or bodily complexus of qualities is not self-existent. But since its entire reality is that of a group of ideas, it finds its entire support *in the perceiving mind*. The mind has the qualities, in the only way in which they can be "had": as objects in and for the perceiver. On the other hand, "for an idea [i.e., a sensible quality] to exist in an unperceiving thing, is a manifest contradiction; for to have an idea is all one as to perceive: that therefore wherein colour, figure, and the like qualities exist, must perceive them; hence it is clear there can be no unthinking substance or *substratum* of those ideas."[15] Robbed of its supporting function and relation to the qualities, material substance shrivels up to a completely vacuous concept. Since it would be distinct from extension, it could not even conform to the vulgar view of material substance, as something spread out under the qualities or as an under-girding for them. Apart from these images, however, a material *substrate* is meaningless.

The remaining avenues of escape from complete immaterialism are easily blocked off. One of these would be the argument that, despite the impotence of the senses in regard to substance, it can nevertheless be apprehended by pure intelligence or reason. Berkeley's retort is that, if this be so, matter can have nothing in common with the bodies of our experience, since the latter are nothing more than *sensible* things or objects of sense imagination. As Locke admits, the purely rational view of substance-as-such resolves itself into the concept of *being* in general plus the function of *supporting* modes or accidents. In the case of material substance, the supporting function has been eliminated, in view of the subjective nature of all sensible qualities. As for being or something in general, Berkeley terms it

---

[15] *The Principles of Human Knowledge*, I, 7 (*Works*, II, 44). If one gives a "soft" meaning to matter, however, and identifies it with Berkeley's definition of the sensible thing, then he will not quibble about words but will admit it into his immaterialism; cf. *Three Dialogues between Hylas and Philonous*, III (*Works*, II, 261–62).

"the most abstract and incomprehensible of all" ideas,[16] since it evacuates all particular modes and instances of things. This comment on the concept of being as such is a clear indication that Berkeley's purview extends only to the Lockean version of abstraction as a total evacuation. Berkeley thinks that being is abstracted in the same way as the universal concepts, and merely carries the total abstraction to its limits. He fails to consider whether the metaphysical notion of being may not have a distinctive origin that cannot be reduced to the abstractive process, whether vicious or legitimate.

If matter does not vanish in a cloud of empty words, it is the locus of a flagrant set of contradictions. Material substance is supposed to be *inert,* and yet to be the *cause* of ideas in us. How matter could affect mind (especially within the Cartesian and Malebranchean dualism of substances) is just as inconceivable as how an idea could be compared with a nonmental kind of being. Matter is supposed to be *unperceiving* and yet to possess qualities, i.e., ideas, whose mode of existence is *to be perceived* by mind. On Locke's own reckoning, material substance has no necessary connection with its qualities, and nevertheless the latter are said to give some information about matter, at least enough to conclude that such a substance exists and has a certain function, as an underpinning. To sum up in one statement this congeries of contradictory predicates: matter is said to have *absolute existence apart from the mind.*[17] But the whole burden of Berkeley's reflections is that only minds and their idea-objects exist, and that it is illegitimate to separate sensible existence from the condition of being perceived by mind.

The success of Berkeley's argument depends, however, upon the soundness of the commonly held seventeenth-century thesis concerning the subjectivity of the secondary qualities. The Galilean doctrine on secondary and primary qualities was *methodologically* useful for securing the mathematical interpretation of the material world, but the progressive empiricist criticism revealed its inadequacy as a general philosophical tool. After Berkeley's critique, the problem of secondary and primary qualities became a peripheral one, since nonmathematical principles of interpretation came to the fore.

Berkeley consigns matter to the lumber room of useless philosophical concepts. This is an overhasty dismissal. The only certain conclusion

---

[16] *The Principles of Human Knowledge,* I, 17 (*Works,* II, 48); cf. *Three Dialogues between Hylas and Philonous,* III (*Works,* II, 237).

[17] *The Principles of Human Knowledge,* I, 24 (*Works,* II, 51).

that follows from his dialectical analysis is that there is a serious conflict between Locke's notion of matter and Locke's doctrine on ideas and the proper philosophical method. Largely for the sake of securing an advantage over skepticism, atheism, and irreligious materialism, Berkeley sacrifices matter and yet retains the more basic Lockean conception of philosophical method and its object, the idea. Accepting this residue of empiricism, he has no other choice than to pose the problem of matter exclusively as a *problem concerning perception*. When the question is formulated solely in terms of the conditions of perception, it is not surprising that the answer should also be one in which sensible existence is reduced to the condition of being perceived by and in the mind. Now, this way of framing the issue excludes, beforehand, any doctrine of matter as a real principle of being. Hence Berkeley proves, not that the idea is the only sensible existent, but that a starting point in the analysis of ideas can tell nothing about the act of existing, exercised by material things. Either the analysis of ideas must be accepted integrally, and the elimination of real principles of being carried through even more radically than in the Berkeleyan polemic against matter, or else the empirical method and starting point must be subjected to a fundamental criticism. Hume accepts the first horn of this dilemma, whereas Kant explores one aspect of the second.

## 4. THE REALITY OF THE SENSIBLE WORLD

Seventy years after the publication of the *Principles of Human Knowledge,* Kant (with an eye to the critics of his own theory of space and time) gave classic expression to the charge that Berkeley's immaterialism destroys the objective world. According to Kant, Berkeley reduces natural things to subjective states and eventually to sheer illusion. This criticism was anticipated and most vigorously rejected by Berkeley himself, some of whose contemporaries likewise charged him with professing a doctrine of illusionism. Berkeley's rejoinder is that, quite on the contrary, his doctrine alone leaves intact and even re-enforces the common-sense view of the world. His arguments are intended only to expel the sophisticated philosophical doctrine of *matter:* they vindicate the ordinary man's conceptions about *real bodies* or *sensible things*.[18] The latter remain exactly what

---

[18] *Ibid.,* I, 35 (*Works,* II, 55); *Three Dialogues between Hylas and Philonous,* III (*Works,* II, 262). For Kant's opinion of Berkeley, cf. *Prolegomena to Any Future*

they are, but the mind is enabled now to slough off the false speculations of philosophers about a hidden material substance. The ordinary man believes that the objects of his immediate perception are the real things. Berkeley heartily agrees with this conviction — but he adds that the real things immediately perceived are ideas, and that there is no material existent, apart from our mental objects. In this way, the "vulgar" and the "philosophical" views of sensible reality are reconciled. But his agreement with, and defense of, common-sense realism is of a quite critical and, in its own way, sophisticated sort. The real world of common sense stays intact, within the Berkeleyan vision of things, only on condition that "reality" is brought in line with the New Principle. For Berkeley as well as Leibniz, there must be a transformation of the common-sense outlook, rather than a simple acceptance of it.

Berkeley offers a systematic reinterpretation of three notes that are usually attached to the sensible order of being: its reality, its distinctness from the perceiver, and its permanent existence.

1. The only available criterion of *reality* is found within the order of ideas themselves or, rather, in their various relations to the mind.[19] The distinction between ideas of sense and ideas of imagination is again invoked by Berkeley. The human mind is receptive in respect to *ideas of sense,* whereas it is the originative source of *ideas of imagination.* The understanding can frame images at will, but it must simply accept sensory ideas as they are given. This fundamental difference of relation between the mind and these two classes of ideas cannot be erased. It is confirmed by an analysis of the ideas themselves. By comparison with sense perceptions, ideas of imagination are weak, faint, unsteady, and incoherent. On the contrary, there is a characteristic strength, liveliness, distinctness, and order about ideas of sense. This contrast may be used as a criterion of the reality of sensible things or ideas of sense. As effects impressed upon our mind directly by God, they have a special claim to more reality than the ideas derived from our invention and combination. Ideas of sense constitute the real order, the *rerum natura,* whereas ideas of imagination are either likenesses of this given reality or chimeras of our own framing. Although dependent upon the divine will, ideas of sense

---

*Metaphysics,* 13, Remark, and the Appendix (L. W. Beck's revision of the Carus translation, 41, 123–25).

[19] *The Principles of Human Knowledge,* I, 29, 30, 33–36, 90–91 (*Works,* II, 53–56, 80–81); *Three Dialogues between Hylas and Philonous,* II (*Works,* II, 215).

are not products of our human will, and cannot be called mere chimeras or free constructions of our mind. This accounts for the common distinction between the real and the imaginary.

2. The skeptical retort would be that both real and imaginary objects agree in being ideas, and hence in being mere subjective modifications of the mind. Berkeley accepted their ideal nature but not the inference that they are mere subjective modifications. The more he read in contemporary philosophy, the more he became convinced that the customary pairing of substance and mode would have to be abandoned, especially if any answer were to be made to skepticism and the materialism of Hobbes (with whom he associated Spinoza, for attributing extension to God). In addition to the refutation of material substance, it became necessary for Berkeley to eliminate the view that ideas are *modes* of the mind, whether divine or human. Ideas are *objects* of the mind's perceiving operation and in this sense alone are they in the mind. "Those qualities are in the mind only as they are perceived by it, that is, not by way of *mode* or *attribute,* but only by way of *idea.*"[20] This nonmodal sort of mental presence of ideas of sense guarantees the *objectivity* of sensible things. Hence they cannot be regarded as mere subjective modifications. The sensible world is also *really distinct* from the perceiver, in the sense that there is a real distinction between the mind and the objects of the mind, between perceiving and being perceived. Furthermore, the dependence of sensible things or ideas upon the human understanding is accidental, rather than essential. We cannot specify, at will, the structure of ideas of sense. They are essentially dependent only upon the divine mind and will. The sensible world is neither a mode nor a product of the human mind, and hence there is a basis in immaterialism for the common-sense belief in the objectivity and distinctness of the world. Berkeley even allowed that the sensible world is *external,* insofar as sensible things or ideas may exist apart from my individual mind, even though their existence is confined to the minds of other finite perceivers or God.

3. Berkeley foresaw the Humean objection that, if the existence of ideas is one with their being perceived, then (at least, for all we can know) the sensible world ceases to exist, whenever the acts of perception themselves cease. This would lead to the doctrine of intermittent existence and a consequent denial of the *permanence* of sense

---

[20] *The Principles of Human Knowledge,* I, 49 (*Works,* II, 61); cf. *Three Dialogues between Hylas and Philonous,* III (*Works,* II, 237).

things. Berkeley struggled with this objection from several angles.[21] He assumed a position closer to Leibniz than to Locke, concerning whether the mind ever ceases to perceive. If the nature of the mind is nothing other than to be an active center of willing and perceiving, then it continues to will and perceive in some degree, as long as it exists. Its own existence is a temporal process, one that supposes a continuous flow of volitions and ideas, and hence continuous acts of willing and perceiving. Although Berkeley did not develop a detailed theory, corresponding to Leibniz' doctrine on the minute, unconscious perceptions, he did give distinctive emphasis to the volitional or appetitive side of the life of the mind.

An objection can be made that, however continuous the perceiving operation, it does not always have *these* particular sensible things as its objects, and hence that uninterrupted perception of some sort does not guarantee the continuance in existence of *these* particular sensible things. This criticism forced Berkeley to appeal to the distinction between God's mind and our own (and thus to make the problem of our knowledge of God a central problem for Hume, even in regard to an analysis of the sensible world). Sensible things depend essentially upon the divine mind, which always actually wills and perceives them. When they are not being perceived by one individual finite mind, they *may* be perceived by some other human mind and *must* be perceived and willed by the divine intelligence. The sense world does not alternately come to be and cease to be, in rhythm with individual human perceptions, since the unconditional ground of its existence is its permanent status as an object of *God's unfailing actual perception* and *volition*.

Within the human perspective, however, a distinction does obtain

---

[21] *The Principles of Human Knowledge*, I, 45, 48, 98 (*Works*, II, 59, 61, 83–84). The genesis of this doctrine can be traced in the following entries in *Philosophical Commentaries*: 41, 52, 282, 472–73, 478, 791, 802, 812 (*Works*, I, 11, 13, 35, 59, 60, 95, 96, 97). When he remains at the finite plane of analysis, Berkeley comes close to making the existence of sense things depend solely upon our power to perceive and will them, or even upon our power to imagine them. In order to establish a firm distinction between the real and the imaginary, he must understand the New Principle strictly in terms of actual perception and must ground this actual perception in the divine mind. In "The Place of God in Berkeley's Philosophy," *Philosophy*, VI (1931), 18–29, J. D. Mabbott brings out the indispensable role of God, but he sets up a needless conflict between God as perceiver and God as willer. Berkeley retains both functions in God, although his view that there is a passive aspect in perception raised a special problem, for him, of how to attribute cognition to God.

between *the perceived* and *the perceivable*. Berkeley exploits it in a skillful way, to meet the objection about intermittent existence. For, that which is only perceivable to one man may be actually perceived by another man, and must be perceived and willed by God. It may be inquired, however, whether this distinction does not make a breach in the system of immaterialism. Since a sensible thing may nevertheless be actually existing, even on the extreme hypothesis of its being the object of no human perception whatsoever, there would seem to be a clear case of a real distinction between *esse* and *percipi*. Berkeley's response to this difficulty is not entirely satisfactory. He remarks that this distinction does not obtain in every respect. When the object is only potentially perceived by human observers, its claim to real existence is founded upon its actual perception by God. In the extreme instance, then, the gap between existing and being actually perceived is closed, only on the supposition of God's actual, ceaseless perception and volition of the thing. Whatever the legitimacy of an *eventual* appeal to the divine knowledge, however, it cannot serve as a proper defense of the New Principle, considered precisely as the *first* principle in the immaterialist philosophy.[22] For, Berkeley's proof of God's existence and nature depends, in turn, upon the implications that can be drawn from this principle, once its truth is established. Hence, if circular reasoning is to be avoided, the principle itself cannot be defended in terms of one of its consequences. For this reason, Berkeley's usual practice is to establish his principle in respect to actual perception of sensible things, and to give special treatment to the question of perceivability only as an answer to the difficulty about intermittent existence. But this procedure conceals the extent of the circular dependence of his theory of knowledge upon an implicit theory of the divine mind.

## 5. THE REALM OF MINDS

Despite his defense of the reality of the sensible world and the

---

[22] In a helpful survey and criticism of the various arguments adduced by Berkeley in defense of his immaterialism, J. P. de C. Day ("George Berkeley, 1685–1753," *The Review of Metaphysics*, VI [1952–1953], 83–113, 265–86, 447–69, 583–96), shows that the distinction between the perceivable and the perceived is ultimately of no avail to Berkeley as an epistemological foundation, since he wishes to preserve his system from illusionism. Hence he must invoke God's actual perception of objects. In doing so, however, he makes the divine perception both the ground and the consequent of his New Principle.

basic reliability of the common-sense outlook, Berkeley often refers to the objects of perception as *ideas,* rather than as *things.*[23] He offers two main reasons for this usage. First, although ideas of sense are the things comprising the sensible world, nevertheless in the popular mind "thing" conveys the meaning of an entity *existing absolutely* or without relation of dependence on any mind. By speaking primarily about sense ideas, Berkeley removes the presumption in favor of a self-contained material world, as well as Locke's anxiety about how to compare sensory likenesses with independently existing things. Another reason for preferring "idea" to "thing" is that "thing" is a wider term. The domain of things contains two broad classes: *ideas* and *minds.* Ideas are sensible things, but there are other things, viz., minds, that are something more than objects of perception. Since minds are not the same as ideas, it would be misleading to use "thing" exclusively as a synonym for "idea."

Berkeley's doctrine on *mind* is constructed mainly by way of contrast with ideas or objects of perception. The three natures to which human knowledge attains are: ideas of sense, ideas of imagination, and minds (the latter being grasped by attending to our internal operations).[24] If the *esse* of ideas is *percipi,* the *esse* of mind is *percipere.* Whereas ideas as such are passive and inert, minds are essentially active and causal. Ideas are fleeting, dependent, and perishable; minds are enduring, subsisting, and incorruptible. In the sensible order, there is no substance; the only substances are immaterial ones, i.e., minds or spirits. None of the reasons that tell against material substance can be transferred to a critique of *immaterial substance.* There are no intrinsic contradictions in the latter conception. For, a spirit is neither an inert cause nor an unperceiving bearer of ideas nor an unperceivable, bodily thing.

---

[23] *The Principles of Human Knowledge,* I, 38–39 (*Works,* II, 56–57); *Three Dialogues between Hylas and Philonous,* III (*Works,* II, 235–36). Berkeley substitutes "things" for "ideas" in certain contexts, so that it will seem less "harsh and ridiculous" that we should eat and drink *ideas.* For the sake of ordinary sensibilities, one should say: we eat and drink the *things* immediately perceived by our senses. This is an instance where Berkeley follows the maxim that "we ought to *think with the learned, and speak with the vulgar." The Principles of Human Knowledge,* I, 51 (*Works,* II, 62; the editor of this volume traces the quotation to a sixteenth-century Italian, Augustinus Niphus, and notes that Bacon also used it).

[24] This interpretation of *ibid.,* I, 1 (*Works,* II, 41) follows the reading suggested by A. A. Luce, *Berkeley's Immaterialism,* 39–40.

## BERKELEY'S IMMATERIALIST UNIVERSE

1. God, the infinite mind or spirit (unlimited, immaterial substance or personal self, whose to-be is to-perceive and to-will: pure creative activity).

2. Men, finite minds or spirits (limited, immaterial substances or personal selves, whose to-be is to-perceive and to-will, but with reception of their being, power to act, and ideas from God).

3. Contents of finite minds.

   a) Ideas of sense: the nonmaterial, nonsubstantial world of real sensible things, communicated to finite minds by God, according to orderly, settled patterns (the natural laws of the sensible world).

   b) Ideas of imagination: produced by the wills of finite minds.

   c) Notions: the cognitive means for knowing minds, activities, and relations.

To establish the existence of spiritual substances, Berkeley appeals to familiar experience. We refer meaningfully to ourselves as perceiving agents, by way of contrast with our percepts. That which does the perceiving, willing, and imagining, enjoys a mode of being distinct from the things perceived, willed, and imagined. Hence "by the word *spirit* [or *mind*] we mean only that which thinks, wills, and perceives."[25] It is to this immaterial substance that the ideas are said to belong, and in which they are said to be present as objects. In regarding the *mind* or *self* as a *substance*, Berkeley rejects the Lockean phenomenalistic view of the self and provides, in advance, an answer to Hume's contention that the self is a floating system of ideas. "I know that I, one and the same self, perceive both colours and sounds: that a colour cannot perceive a sound, nor a sound a colour: that I am therefore one individual principle, distinct from colour and sound; and, for the same reason, from all other sensible things and inert ideas."[26] Berkeley traces the purely phenomenalistic view of the

---

[25] *The Principles of Human Knowledge*, I, 138 (*Works*, II, 104); cf. *ibid.*, I, 27, 135–39 (*Works*, II, 52–53, 103–05), on the nature of mind or spirit. The characteristic activity of minds is discussed by A. Leroy, "Remarques sur l'activité des esprits dans la philosophie berkeleyenne," *Revue Philosophique de la France et de l'Étranger*, CXXXV (1945), 256–72.

[26] *Three Dialogues between Hylas and Philonous*, III (*Works*, II, 233–34). A series of entries, often cited from *Philosophical Commentaries* (*Works*, I, 72–73) as proof of Berkeley's own early phenomenalism of self, should rather be taken as a dialogue between Berkeley and a Lockean, who assumes that all words have corresponding ideas and that only ideas are the direct objects of our knowledge.

self to the twin assumptions that there are no words without corresponding ideas, and that we can know only that of which we can have ideas. On the contrary, to the word "self," there corresponds a spiritual substance, rather than an idea. And, in order to locate the mind in the substantial order, he is now forced to deny that we have any *idea* of the mind or substantial self. On the principle that an idea can be the likeness only of another idea, it follows that there can be no idea of the mind, which is defined by contrast with the characteristics of ideas.

In one sense, then, the mind is unknowable: it cannot be known through ideas. But its existence is nevertheless a primary deliverance of consciousness. This forces Berkeley to posit a new means of knowledge, essentially different from the idea. This is the reason for his fundamental distinction between *idea* and *notion*.[27] The latter is the instrument for grasping those things that lie beyond the domain of ideas: one's own self, other minds, actions, and relations. Moreover, since one's mind is not a sensible thing, the manner of apprehending it must also differ from that of apprehending sensible things. It can be seized by oneself only intuitively, in the very act of willing and perceiving. Berkeley employs the language of Malebranche, in referring to this immediate apprehension of the substantial self as an *inward feeling* or *reflection*. Yet he makes no detailed analysis of this cardinal operation, simply continuing the tradition of Descartes that we do have an intuitive understanding of our own substantial self. Both "notion" and "inward feeling" are regarded by Berkeley as imperfect ways of transcribing an undeniable experience of knowing an immaterial, substantial, personal self. But in Hume's view, they are *ad hoc* inventions, made in order to avoid his own doctrine on the self. Berkeley contributes to this judgment, insofar as he devotes nowhere near the amount of circumstantial analysis to the knowledge of the self, as he does to the knowledge of the qualities.

The mind or personal self is an active reality, containing *understanding* and *will*.[28] The relation of these latter perfections to the spiritual substance became a troublesome issue for Berkeley. His two

---

[27] On notion and inward feeling or reflection, cf. *The Principles of Human Knowledge*, I, 140, 142 (*Works*, II, 105, 106); *Three Dialogues between Hylas and Philonous*, III (*Works*, II, 231–34). On the Cartesian background of the purely intellectual reflection or intuition, cf. T. A. Kantonen, "The Influence of Descartes on Berkeley," *The Philosophical Review*, XLIII (1934), 483–500.

[28] *Philosophical Commentaries*, 643, 645, 674, 713, 841, 848 (*Works*, I, 79, 82, 87, 100, 101); *The Principles of Human Knowledge*, I, 27, 143 (*Works*, II, 52–53, 106–07).

chief difficulties concerned the active nature of the understanding and the general theory of mental powers. On the first problem, his early speculations were considerably influenced by the views of Descartes and Locke concerning the passive character of the understanding. Hence, he tended to erect a sharp contrast between understanding and will, taken respectively as the passive and active sides of the mind. But there was a twofold inconvenience about considering the understanding as a purely passive power: to do so, would be to break down the difference between the active mind and its passive ideas, and also to wipe out the basis for a difference between the operations of willing and perceiving. Hence Berkeley finally concluded that, although the finite understanding has a *passive* aspect (insofar as it receives ideas from God), it is not entirely inert but also has an *active* aspect (insofar as it actually perceives the ideas it does receive). As for the theory of mental powers, Berkeley suspected that it rests upon a vicious abstraction. Since Locke treated understanding and will as abstract ideas, Berkeley concluded that the power theory always results in the hypostasization of the various faculties of the mind and thus destroys the indivisible unity of mental life. Consequently, he preferred to regard understanding and will as *functional aspects* of the mind, rather than as *powers,* in the Lockean sense. The understanding is nothing other than the mind, considered as perceiving given ideas of sense; the will is nothing other than the mind, now considered as forming new ideas of imagination or as ordering something in respect to our ideas. Since these two functions are mutually ordained and convergent in nature, the mind or spirit is the actual concretion of perception and volition.

Despite his restricted historical appreciation of the meaning of a mental power, Berkeley does show a keen awareness of the concrete unity of mental life and the interpenetration of knowing and willing. Yet he is prevented from resolving the issues he raises, both because he confines his analysis to the Lockean view of powers and because his own New Principle is better fitted for dealing with *things* (in Berkeley's system: minds and ideas) than with *principles of being.* That is why the results of Berkeleyan analysis fall just short of being metaphysical explanations of finite reality. In the case of powers of the mind, he is confronted with anomalies, which can be reduced neither to mind-thing nor to idea-thing. He is right in refusing to reify the powers, but not in refusing them any metaphysical status. He cannot account for powers of the mind, because of the limitations of his New Principle, which does not recognize that these powers are *principles whereby* the concrete substance itself achieves its operational perfection. Thus, the opportunity is lost to provide a solid metaphysical basis for his conviction about the dynamic unity of mental life and the need for a subordinate principle of unity, integrating the personal substance and its operations. The metaphysical theory of powers performs this function, but it does so, only by regarding the powers, operations, and substance of man in terms of act and potency. The thing-bound New Principle of Berkeley is essentially unfitted to perform an analysis of powers as operative principles, within the unity of human nature.

The only strictly immediate knowledge is that of one's own mind and perceptual contents. Berkeley tries his best to avoid the *solipsistic* implications of this description of the cognitive situation. He bases his escape from solipsism mainly upon the demonstration of *God's existence.*[29] He announces that immaterialism provides the only definitive answer to atheism, since it alone offers a proof of God's existence which is both intelligible to the average man and yet strictly demonstrative. Once more, Berkeley makes use of the distinction between ideas of sense and ideas of imagination. The latter can be produced by the finite mind, employing its own active power of will. But our mind is passive, in respect to the content of the ideas of sense. Perceiving is an operation of the mind, but *what* we perceive lies beyond our control. Some other active principle must be invoked, in order to account for the actual presentation of sensory contents to our mind, since we cannot voluntarily determine this content. Now, the sole source of the ideas of sense is some voluntary, spiritual principle. These ideas cannot come from material substance, the existence of which has been disproven. Nor can sensible things (as defined by Berkeley) be responsible for these ideas. For, there is no real distinction between ideas of sense and sensible things; consequently, sensible things partake of the inert, causally inefficacious character of all ideas. The active source of the ideas of sense is some spiritual substance. It is not a finite, spiritual substance, since the active principle must be powerful enough to convey to the finite mind the entire order of nature, which is nothing more than the regulated

---

[29] For the demonstration, see *ibid.*, I, 146–49 (*Works*, II, 107–09); *Three Dialogues between Hylas and Philonous*, II (*Works*, II, 211–15); *Alciphron*, IV, 2–5 (*Works*, III, 142–48). For the problem of solipsism, consult D. Grey, "The Solipsism of Bishop Berkeley," *The Philosophical Quarterly*, II (1951–1952), 338–49.

series of ideas of sense. The order and variety of these ideas manifest the existence of an infinite, spiritual substance or mind, having intelligence and will. The ideas of sense must have their primary being as objects in an infinite mind, and must be communicated to us through a deliberate, intelligent act of volition, on the part of the first principle. The *personal* nature of God is an immediate consequence of the presence of infinite will and understanding, as aspects of His spiritual being.

The question of the relationship between the New Principle and the existence of God has already been raised, in connection with the problem of intermittent existence. Berkeley relies implicitly upon the existence of God, as an infinite and actual perceiver, in order to secure the identification between sensible *esse* and *percipi*. Unless the constant, actual, divine perception is presupposed, Berkeley cannot avoid the Humean consequence of foregoing any assurance about the permanence or continuity-in-existence of sensible things. The capital distinction between what is strictly perceivable and what is only imaginable by us, is secured only by measuring the *humanly perceivable* by the implicit standard of what *God actually perceives*. But this means that the New Principle itself both serves as the basis for the proof of God's existence and stands in need of His existence for its own foundation. Furthermore, as Hume and Kant later pointed out, Berkeley's appeal to the totality of nature, as proof of the infinity of the active source of our ideas of sense, leads only to a very powerful orderer, not necessarily to an infinite mind. Berkeley's principles of inference are not sufficiently founded in the finite act of existing to enable him to reach the infinite act of existing.

In considering how a finite mind can gain some knowledge of God's infinite nature, Berkeley consulted many traditional treatises on the divine names. He mentioned the views of Dionysius the Pseudo-Areopagite, Aquinas, Cajetan, and Suarez. He applauded Cajetan's distinction between metaphorical and proper analogy, for our knowledge of God is more than a genial guess or metaphor. Although he agreed with Cajetan that our knowledge of God is according to the *analogy of proper proportionality*, Berkeley was prevented by his own method and starting point from appropriating the content of this doctrine on analogical predication. The fundamental metaphysical obstacle was his view that, although "*thing* or *being* is the most general name of all, it comprehends under it two kinds entirely distinct and heterogeneous, and which have nothing common but the name, to wit, *spirits* and *ideas*."[30] This theory did not permit sufficient analogical unity to provide a basis for analogy of proper proportionality. But Berkeley did offer a concrete description of the human mind's operation, in reasoning about God's nature. The finite mind removes the imperfections present in itself, and then heightens its own perfections, thus following the ways of negation and eminence. It uses its own intuited nature as a sort of image or mirror, in which to spy something about the nature of an infinitely perfect spiritual substance, having understanding and will. Only a far-off glimpse of the infinite spirit is gained in this way, but of his existence and personal providence we have complete assurance.

Berkeley does not display the same confidence about proving the existence of *other finite minds*.[31] He never doubts the fact of their existence, but neither does he claim that we can come to know this fact with the same certainty that marks our knowledge of God. Sufficiently cogent grounds for the belief in other minds are found, however, to warrant calling the argument a demonstration. I seem to receive certain ideas as a result of bodily motions, apparently originating from another agent, at my own finite level of being. When the mouth I see before me moves, and words are spoken and heard, ideas are then aroused in my mind that correspond to the very ideas I would intend to evoke, through the use of similar bodily gestures and words. I can conclude, with high likelihood, that these received ideas are communicated to me, in view of the intentions of another finite spirit. I may take such ideas as signs of the presence of other finite minds, who are constituted like myself.

Although he calls this argument a demonstration, Berkeley admits that the evidence does not permit of a strict causal proof. The

---

[30] *The Principles of Human Knowledge*, I, 89 (*Works*, II, 79); cf. *ibid.*, I, 142 (*Works*, II, 106). This sharp contrast between spirits and ideas is an attempt to stress (against Malebranche) both the objectivity of ideas and their objective presence in and for finite minds, which exercise causal operations of perceiving and willing, in respect to their own ideas. We do not see all things in God, as Malebranche claimed, but see the ideas in our own minds, and then reason to the existence and nature of God. For these historical differences, cf. T. E. Jessop, "Malebranche and Berkeley," *Revue Internationale de Philosophie*, I (1938–1939), 121–42. On our analogical way of knowing God, see *Three Dialogues between Hylas and Philonous*, III (*Works*, II, 230–32); *Alciphron*, IV, 19–21 (*Works*, III, 166–70).

[31] *The Principles of Human Knowledge*, I, 140, 145, 147–48 (*Works*, II, 105, 107, 108–09); *Three Dialogues between Hylas and Philonous*, III (*Works*, II, 231–33, 239–40); *Alciphron*, IV, 5 (*Works*, III, 146–47). Berkeley does not treat this problem separately but interweaves it with his discussion of our knowledge of God.

bodily gestures, apparently existing in an independent entity, cannot be shown to be more than ideas belonging solely to my own mind. Furthermore, it is God alone who "maintains that intercourse between spirits, whereby they are able to perceive the existence of each other."[32] I can command the motions of my own bodily limbs and organs, but this only means that I can control the ideas of motion, as signs of my purpose. Like all other ideas, the *ideas of motion* are inert and causally inefficacious. God is required to produce in another mind the appropriate ideas, corresponding to what I intend by my bodily motions. The causal inference returns once more to God, the primary active principle, considered this time as the causal bridge between finite minds. To address another person means to have the intention to communicate with him, but to do so solely through God's communication of appropriate ideas of sense to that other person. Berkeley's interpretation of interpersonal communication is a strained one, and yet is required by his principles. Because he has defined spiritual substance mainly by contrast with sensible things and has reduced the latter to inert ideas, he has deprived incarnate human persons of any direct, causal means of establishing relations and achieving mutual understanding.

Once the existence of several finite minds is established, the problem of *intersubjective knowledge* arises. The American philosopher, Samuel Johnson, posed the difficulty to Berkeley of how several men may be said to see the *same tree* or to agree upon any common piece of knowledge, since each individual mind has *different ideas* or *perceived objects*.[33] Berkeley distinguished between the vulgar and the philosophical meaning of identity, as applied to the question of identity of knowledge. He himself sided with the vulgar view that identity means absence of any perceptible difference. Thus there might be individual differences between the ideas in various minds, but as long as these differences remained unperceivable, the knowledge would be practically the same for all observers. Berkeley is hampered by lack of a doctrine on intentional likeness, from establishing any stricter unity of agreement among the judgments pronounced by several minds, concerning the same existing thing. He appeals again to the divine mind, to furnish a safeguard for immaterialism against

[32] *The Principles of Human Knowledge*, I, 147 (*Works*, II, 108).

[33] For Johnson's question, cf. *Philosophical Correspondence between Berkeley and Samuel Johnson* (*Works*, II, 285–86); Berkeley's positive position is stated in *Three Dialogues between Hylas and Philonous*, III (*Works*, II, 247–48).

utter *relativism*. For although there is no independent, material referent for our individual ideas, the same function is fulfilled by the divine idea. The divine idea is the *archetypal pattern* and *essential measure* of all ideas in individual, finite minds. Hence it provides the basic sameness of meaning, that enables several minds to perceive the same thing and share the same knowledge. Because of this divine archetype for both our immediate perceptions and our reasoning, there can be objective truth and a science of nature, commonly known by many minds.

## 6. MIND AND NATURE

Throughout his writings, Berkeley was interested not only in refuting skepticism, atheism, and irreligious materialism but also in establishing the foundation and limits of the sciences. For, one major reason leading to the three former errors was a lack of precision concerning the proper province of mathematical and physical reasoning. Contemporary skepticism, for instance, flourished on the mathematical paradoxes concerning infinite divisibility. Berkeley challenged the assumption that the difficulties met with in mathematics are relevant grounds for casting suspicion upon the mind's ability to resolve philosophical issues.

Especially in his earlier years, he had an unbounded admiration for the demonstrative power of pure mathematics. But the more he became practiced in the empirical study of ideas and minds, the more clearly he saw that *mathematical* and *philosophical* demonstrations are of a different nature.[34] The former are purely analytic and (at least in reference to problems about spiritual and sensible existence) fall within the Lockean classification of trifling propositions. Philosophical reasoning is primarily concerned with the concrete, nonanalytic truths of coexistence, which are not susceptible of mathematical treatment and which also resist any philosophical treatment based on material substance. Berkeley stressed the nonexistential and basically practical orientation of mathematical thinking. The purpose of this emphasis is to ward off the inference that the mathematical paradoxes about extension and motion have any independent bearing upon the real nature of sensible things. These paradoxes do not show

---

[34] Berkeley's writings on mathematics are collected in Volume IV of the *Works*. He summarizes his position in *The Principles of Human Knowledge*, I, 118–32 (*Works*, II, 94–102).

that bodies are infinitely divisible, for in respect to the existing order the conditions of perception must be respected. There is no quantitative reality beyond the range of perception, and hence we must suppose that finite *minima sensibilia* are present, in the objects of our senses. To the extent that Bayle and his skeptical followers ignore the limitations of sense perception, they are dealing with purely abstract, general ideas, and come to conclusions that have only verbal significance. Such conclusions should not shake our confidence in the mind's ability to reach truths about real, existential objects.

At the other extreme from abstract mathematics would be a purely *concrete physics,* which might attempt to study the world, without the use of mathematical techniques. Such a project would never make progress, since it would be confined to a simple registration of sense data and would never achieve scientific generalization. Genuine advances in the understanding of nature have been made by mechanics, which applies mathematical reasoning to the field of sense objects. Berkeley greatly admired Newton's combination of reason and observation, in the development of a *natural philosophy.* But he opposed the pretentious claims being made by the Newtonians for this natural or experimental philosophy, whether the claims were made in the interest of religion or of irreligion.[35] For, the arguments rested upon

[35] For Berkeley's views on Newton and the Newtonians, cf. *ibid.,* 101–17 (*Works,* II, 85–94); *Three Dialogues between Hylas and Philonous,* III (*Works,* II, 257–58); the entire opusculum, *De Motu* (*Works,* IV, 11–30); *Siris* 285–93 (*Works,* V, 133–36). Berkeley gives pithy expression to his limitation of natural philosophy, in a reply to the American Samuel Johnson: "The true use and end of Natural Philosophy is to explain the *phenomena of nature;* which is done by discovering the laws of nature, and reducing particular appearances to them. This is Sir Isaac Newton's method; and such method or design is not in the least inconsistent with the principles I lay down. This mechanical philosophy does not assign or support any one *natural efficient cause* in the strict and proper sense; nor is it, as to its use, concerned about *matter;* nor is matter connected therewith; nor does it infer the being of matter." *Letter of November 25, 1729,* in *Philosophical Correspondence between Berkeley and Samuel Johnson* (*Works,* II, 279; italics added and spelling modernized). When these qualifications are respected, Berkeley sees no conflict between his immaterialism and Newtonian natural philosophy. For a logical positivist approach to Berkeley's theory of science, cf. G. Hinrichs, "The Logical Positivism of Berkeley's *De Motu,*" *The Review of Metaphysics,* III (1949–1950), 491–505. Both Kant and Berkeley contrast the philosophical method with the analytic procedure in mathematics. But, whereas Kant models philosophy after Newton's natural philosophy, Berkeley refuses to pattern philosophical thinking after the noncausal, nonexistential method of physics. See T. E. Jessop, "Berkeley and the Contemporary Physics," *Revue Internationale de Philosophie,* VII (1953), 87–100. For Berkeley's anticipation of Ernst Mach's famous criticism of Newtonian mechanics, cf. the two articles by K. R. Popper and G. J. Whitrow, in *The British Journal for the Philosophy of Science,* IV (1953), 26–45.

an inadequate conception of the scope and limits of the Newtonian method, as well as upon careless references to natural powers, forces, and absolute entities. Although he did not propose to eliminate these latter references entirely from the study of nature, Berkeley did suggest a severe restriction of their meaning. They are useful in elaborating mathematical hypotheses, but they should not be mistaken for real efficient causes or things in nature. At most, the mathematical description of bodies provides a compendious way of computing, making practical plans, and teaching others. But the convenience of mechanical formulas is no indication that they express the real qualities and agencies of nature.

Only from the vantage point of immaterialism, can the restricted scope of mathematical physics be assessed. It studies *ideas* or *sensible phenomena* in themselves and their mathematically determinable connections. But natural science is prevented, in principle, from reaching the *true causes of physical events,* since it does not study the only causal agents at work in nature: minds or spiritual things. It is misleading to refer to mathematical equations and correlations as causal powers (as the incautious Newtonians did) or to describe bodies in terms of vital entelechies and spiritual forces (as Leibniz did). The world of bodies is an inert world of effects, containing no intrinsic, causal power. *Natural laws* are neither *causal* nor *necessary.*[36] They are not causal, since their content is restricted to "corporeal motions," i.e., to the ideas of motions. But even ideas of motions must submit to the general law that all ideas are inert, inactive objects of perception. One idea may follow regularly upon another, so that in an accommodated sense one may speak of the sequence as being one of natural cause and effect. But philosophically regarded, this sequence of ideas expresses only the relation between *sign* and *thing signified.* Hence there is no intrinsic, necessary connection between prior and subsequent things, in the series of natural events.

Berkeley was willing to concede to Malebranche that the sign or prior event may be called an "occasional cause," but it receives this name, only because it determines *our mental expectation* of the event that regularly follows it. Because our practical expectations depend upon the sequence of ideas of sense, God communicates these ideas to our minds according to a settled pattern, called the *order of nature.*

---

[36] *The Principles of Human Knowledge,* I, 30–32, 62–66, 150 (*Works,* II, 53–54, 67–70, 109); *Three Dialogues between Hylas and Philonous,* III (*Works,* II, 230–31); *Siris,* 254 (*Works,* V, 120–21).

Having deprived the Newtonian world of its autonomy and causal efficacy, Berkeley was now ready to defend its regularity. The stability of the order of nature consists entirely in the regular way God follows, in giving ideas to finite minds. The only kind of necessity attributable to natural laws is this derived necessity, imparted by God's customary action. And since the order of nature is intended as an aid to our practical planning, scientific laws have a *utilitarian* import for Berkeley: they are sufficiently probable to serve the purposes of human foresight and conduct. Berkeley followed Malebranche in making this appraisal of natural science, but he did not limit causal power to God. Having made no critical examination of cause as such or of its transcendental application to God, he was untroubled about the causal power of finite minds over their own ideas or about the stability of the natural order. But Berkeley's principles cut much deeper than he realized. For, they led him to strip sensible things of all real causal power and to reduce our conviction in natural causation to a subjective, probable expectation, aroused by custom and practical needs. These consequences led Hume to remark that, from Berkeley, one may glean "the best lessons of scepticism. . . . That all his arguments, though otherwise intended, are, in reality, merely sceptical, appears from this, *that they admit of no answer and produce no conviction.*"[37] Although there is some elegant satire behind this comment, it does convey accurately the actual effect which a reading of Berkeley's account of the order of nature and natural causation had upon the young Hume.

Berkeley's own intention, in making this reinterpretation of nature, was to arouse quite the contrary of a skeptical response in his readers. The Newtonian search after an absolute space, lurking behind perceptible, relative space; the indiscriminate application of the term "infinite" to large or small bodies, or even to abstract terms; the quest of causes, supposed to exist at the sensible level — these were among the tendencies in natural science of which he disapproved. He felt that their psychological effect was to turn the human mind away from contemplation of God and toward an exclusive study of finite, sensible things. As a countermeasure, his own immaterialism presented another way of looking at nature, a way that did not stand in obscurantist opposition to the sciences but that opened up further

---

[37] David Hume, *An Enquiry concerning Human Understanding,* XII, 2 (Selby-Bigge edition, 155, n. 1).

religious prospects for our intelligence. Even in his early treatise, *A New Theory of Vision*, he had suggested that the objects of vision are not only ideas *for* the human mind but also messages *from* the divine mind. This view of sensible things deepened with Berkeley's detailed development of the theses on immaterialism. The theocentric interpretation of *nature as the language of God* marked the culmination of the religious tendency animating all his philosophical speculations.[38]

Berkeley agrees with Locke and Leibniz in rejecting the Malebranchean doctrine about seeing all things *in God*. The immediate objects of our perception remain the ideas *in our own mind,* together with our own mental operations. Nevertheless, we can habituate ourselves to see more in the objects of perception than the ideas themselves. Meditation upon the truth that the things of nature are nothing more than ideas directly communicated to us by God, enables us to develop an almost immediate awareness or "seeing" of God's presence in nature. Instead of seeing all things in God, we come to see *God's creative and conserving presence* in all the sensible things of our perception. The ideas imparted to us constitute a rational discourse, testifying to the intelligence, power, and benevolence of the infinite spirit. The world of bodily phenomena can be viewed in two ways: by sense and by intellect.[39] *By sense* and the scientific disciplines, nature is considered immanently, for its own sake. With the aid of the pure *intellect,* however, philosophy considers nature precisely as God's effect, proposed to man's mind. From this perspective, the world of sensible things is a region of fleeting shadows, adumbrating the intelligible world of spirits. Only mind, in its intellectual function, can grasp the sensible and intelligible orders together, as aspects of a single, interrelated universe. Just as notions are required in order to know the reality of minds and their operations, so notions are the proper means for apprehending the *relations* that bind different natures — things of sense and persons — together in the unity of existence.

One of Berkeley's earliest annotations was that "nothing properly but persons, i.e., conscious things, do exist: all other things are not so much existences as manners [*in the later works:* objects] of the

---

[38] On nature as God's language, cf. *An Essay towards a New Theory of Vision*, 147, 152 (*Works*, I, 231, 233); *The Principles of Human Knowledge*, I, 44, 108 (*Works*, II, 59, 88: *ad lin.* 25); *Alciphron*, IV, 6–7, 11–15 (*Works*, III, 148–49, 155–62).

[39] The dualism of sense and intellect is quite pronounced in *Siris*, 293–95, 348–49 (*Works*, V, 136–37, 157).

existence of persons."[40] This intensely *personalistic* view of the universe of beings underlies his entire doctrine on minds and their objects; in the *Siris,* it is combined with a theory of *participation in being.* One of the abiding difficulties in Berkeley's system is the metaphysical status of finite minds. They are described as *active* beings, in contradistinction to ideas. Yet they are equally effects of the infinite power, and therefore have a *receptive* side. They obtain their substantial reality and their ideas of sense from God. Berkeley never effects a complete reconciliation of the active and receptive aspects, but a step toward a solution is taken in his notion of participation, which he derived from his readings in Plotinus, Proclus, and other Neo-Platonists. Like his American counterpart, Jonathan Edwards, he underlines the participated character of all finite minds. A finite person exists, not only by perceiving ideas, but primarily by receiving these ideas precisely as gifts, coming from the unity of the infinite person. The personal self stands in just as much need of its ideas or objects of perception as the latter stand in need of the self. But the mind attains a fully personal grasp upon itself, only when it realizes that its *need for ideas* is only a phase in its *greater need for the divine source* of all ideas and minds. Hence the receptivity of the human mind is not an utterly passive and inert condition, such as that of the ideas. The human mind can reflectively recognize the source of its ideas, and so can elevate itself, by a free response of gratitude and worship, to the wholly active being of God.

Human persons are neither wholly passive, like ideas, nor wholly active, like God. They stand in a midway position, and can share in both extremes. Personal reality is constituted precisely by the mind, inasmuch as it participates intelligently and willingly in the unity and being of the divine mind. This sharing of personal reality, in and through God, leads to a communion of individual human spirits. Leibniz and Berkeley come by diverse routes to much the same final view of the *City of God,* as a unity of uncreated spirit and created spirits, in which God Himself is the bond of personal being among them.

## SUMMARY OF CHAPTER 9

Berkeley's ultimate purpose of moral and religious reform motivated his denial of matter, i.e., of a substance supposed to be unknowable and

---

[40] *Philosophical Commentaries,* 24 (*Works,* I, 10; spelling and punctuation modernized); cf. *Siris,* 346–47 (*Works,* V, 156–57).

yet to exist independently of any mind, divine or human. Matter can be removed, without making any difference in either the scientific or the common-sense outlooks, and hence without leading to general skepticism. The general meaning of ideas can be explained satisfactorily in terms of particular ideas and their relations, without recourse to abstraction proper or to abstract general ideas. Above all, a coherent immaterialist exegesis of common-sense convictions can be made. Berkeley did not turn to untutored common sense but rather to Locke's description of the understanding. What more does the Lockean individual mean by a sensible thing, Berkeley inquired, than that which is perceived, precisely *qua* perceived? Now, that which is perceived as such is only an idea. An idea cannot be present in an unperceiving substance, such as matter. Nor can anything resembling an idea be present in an unperceiving, material subject, since an idea can be like only another idea. There are only two general modes of existence: perceiving and being perceived, minds and sensible things or ideas. Neither solipsism nor chaotic subjectivism need follow from this immaterialist New Principle, according to Berkeley's explanation. He used the passive character of ideas of sense to prove the existence of God as their first cause and the cause of one's own spiritual being, as a mind. There are also positive signs indicating the presence of other finite minds, although Berkeley was unable to offer more than probable arguments for their existence. God communicates ideas or sensible things to our minds in a stable, predictable way, thus providing a basis for scientific laws (which are, however, noncausal in character). Like Leibniz, Berkeley looked to God as the common bond among minds or spirits. Finite persons can participate in the spiritual perfections of God, and thus join together in a community of perceiving and willing operations.

## BIBLIOGRAPHICAL NOTE

1. *Sources.* We now have an excellent critical edition of Berkeley to which scholars make their references: *The Works of George Berkeley, Bishop of Cloyne,* edited by A. A. Luce and T. E. Jessop (9 vols., London, Nelson, 1948–1957). This includes his correspondence and some important letters written to Berkeley. It is noteworthy that the *Philosophical Commentaries,* edited by Luce (in Vol. I of the Luce-Jessop edition), definitively replaces the editions of the "Commonplace Book" offered by Fraser (Vol. I of his edition, Oxford, Clarenden, 1901), and by G. A. Johnston, *Berkeley's Commonplace Book* (London, Faber and Faber, 1930). A convenient reprint of most of Berkeley's philosophical writings is edited by M. W. Calkins, *Berkeley: Essay, Principles, Dialogues, with Selections from Other Writings* (New York, Scribner, 1929).

2. *Studies.* A. A. Luce, himself an enthusiastic Berkeleyan, has written the definitive biography, *The Life of George Berkeley, Bishop of Cloyne* (London, Nelson, 1949). An interesting biographical sidelight on Berkeley's career is supplied by B. Rand, *Berkeley's American Sojourn* (Cambridge,

Mass., Harvard University Press, 1932). G. D. Hicks's *Berkeley* (London, Benn, 1932) is a good introductory account; it can be supplemented by A. A. Luce, *Berkeley's Immaterialism: A Commentary on his "Treatise concerning the Principles of Human Knowledge"* (London, Nelson, 1945), which uses the framework of the *Principles* to explain Berkeley's basic immaterialism and his replies to objections. The genesis of Berkeley's thought and the question of internal development in his system are moot points. Whereas Luce regards the *Principles* as definitive, considerable attention has been paid to the problem of earlier and later phases of Berkeley's philosophy by G. A. Johnston, *The Development of Berkeley's Philosophy* (New York, Macmillan, 1923), and by J. Wild, *George Berkeley: A Study of His Life and Philosophy* (Cambridge, Mass., Harvard University Press, 1936). F. Bender, *George Berkeley's Philosophy Re-Examined* (Amsterdam, H. Paris, 1946), agrees with Wild about the appearance of a new factor in Berkeley's last work, *Siris,* but identifies it as a tendency toward rational idealism. I. Hedenius, *Sensationalism and Theology in Berkeley's Philosophy* (Uppsala, Almqvist and Wiksell, 1936), calls attention to the theological orientation of Berkeley's analysis of sensation; see also, N. Baladi, *La pensée religieuse de Berkeley et l'unité de sa philosophie* (Paris, Vrin, 1945). Thomistic criticisms are offered by J. J. Laky, *A Study of George Berkeley's Philosophy, in the Light of the Philosophy of St. Thomas Aquinas* (Washington, Catholic University of America Press, 1950), and by F. Olgiati, *L'idealismo di Giorgio Berkeley ed il suo significato storico* (Milan, Vita e Pensiero, 1926). A. A. Luce's *Berkeley and Malebranche: A Study in the Origins of Berkeley's Thought* (New York, Oxford, 1934) is significant, not only for the genesis of Berkeley's immaterialism, but also as a reminder of the major role of Malebranche in the entire development of British empiricism. On the American philosophers, Samuel Johnson and Jonathan Edwards, cf. H. G. Townsend, *Philosophical Ideas in the United States* (Cincinnati, American Book Company, 1934), 25–32, 35–62. Berkeley's theism is reconsidered by M. Guéroult, *Berkeley: Quatre études sur la perception et sur Dieu* (Paris, Aubier, 1956), and by E. A. Sillem, *George Berkeley and the Proofs for the Existence of God* (London, Longmans, Green, 1957), with a Thomistic evaluation.

3. *Further Studies.* A.-L. Leroy's *George Berkeley* (Paris, Presses Universitaires, 1959) is a competent general analysis which uses recent scholarship and compares Berkeley with British and French thinkers. The bicentenary essays in *George Berkeley (University of California Publications in Philosophy,* Vol. 29, 1957) bring out his continued relevance for epistemology, metaphysics, and philosophy of science.

# Chapter 10. HUME

## I. LIFE AND WRITINGS

DAVID HUME (born, 1711, in Edinburgh) was the younger son of the laird of Ninewells, who died when David was a baby. He was educated at Ninewells by his mother and then at Edinburgh College (c. 1721-1725). The Arts course consisted of Greek, logic, metaphysics, and Newtonian natural philosophy, with options in ethics and history. Although he tried to study law and then to enter commerce, his heart was fixed upon religious and philosophical problems. Finally, he resolved to retire to France (1734), where he did private studies at Reims and then at La Flèche. Hume was certainly conversant with the writings of Locke, Berkeley, Hutcheson, Malebranche, and Bayle, but his reticence about his readings makes it difficult to trace his sources. Before coming to London in 1737, he had already finished his major work, *A Treatise of Human Nature*. The first two volumes were published in 1739 and the third in 1740. Although Hume reported that this anonymously issued book "fell dead-born from the press," it did receive a long but not very enlightened review. But through the offices of Francis Hutcheson, who held the chair of moral philosophy at Glasgow, the *Treatise* was brought to the attention of Adam Smith, then a student at Glasgow. Hume's friendship with Smith was lifelong. In order to gain the wide audience he desired, Hume next sent to the printer the more popular *Essays Moral and Political* (1741-1742), which sold very well. The success of this book convinced Hume that he should revise the *Treatise* in more polished style, making the argument more concise and orderly, and thus emphasizing its central themes. In the meanwhile, however, he made an unsuccessful bid (1745) for the chair of "ethics and pneumatic philosophy," at the University of Edinburgh. His reputation as a skeptic and atheist stood in the way of this appointment. Hume quickly compensated for this setback by obtaining a post as secretary to General St Clair, accompanying him first on an ill-fated expedition against the French and then on a diplomatic mission to Vienna and Turin.

While he was on the diplomatic mission, Hume's revision of the first part of the *Treatise* appeared as *Philosophical Essays concerning Human Understanding* (1748). This book, later known as *An Enquiry concerning Human Understanding,* high-lighted the problems of causality and skepticism and added two chapters on miracles, providence, and immortality. Returning to Ninewells in 1749, Hume spent three years upon an intensive writing project. His *An Enquiry concerning the Principles of Morals* (1751) went over the same ground as Part Three of the *Treatise;* his *Political Discourses* (1752) dealt with subjects of common interest and increased his renown both at home and abroad; his *Dialogues concerning Natural Religion* (withheld from publication until 1779) set forth his mind upon the problem of God's existence and the nature of religion. When his brother married (1751), Hume and his sister moved permanently to Edinburgh, where at last he received an official appointment as Keeper of the Advocates' Library (1752; resigned, 1757). Since this office gave him access to a vast collection of books, Hume undertook to write the history of England. The four volumes which he completed (1754-1761) became a focal point of contemporary controversy between Whigs and Tories. He also found time to edit *Four Dissertations* (1757), which dealt with the passions (his restatement of Part Two of the *Treatise*), tragedy, taste, and the natural history of religion. In the process of winnowing his materials, Hume destroyed an essay on geometry, at the advice of a mathematician, and left for posthumous publication his *Two Essays on Suicide and Immortality* (1777), which his friends deemed too outspoken for safety. Thereafter, Hume wrote nothing of great consequence.

But his fame had increased considerably and, at its height, he was invited to serve as acting secretary to the British embassy in Paris (1763). At the latter capitol, "le bon David" was lionized by the ladies and eagerly sought after by intellectuals like Helvétius, D'Alembert, Buffon, Turgot, Holbach, and Diderot. Hume thoroughly enjoyed the green fields of amusement but did not allow the adulation to turn his head. In 1766, he returned to London with Rousseau, in order to provide the latter with a quiet and secure abode. Rousseau's habitual egoism and suspicion led to the inevitable break and public quarrel. Hume stayed in London for a while as Undersecretary of

State (in charge of ecclesiastical patronage in Scotland!) and retired at last to Edinburgh in 1769, with an adequate income. He built a town house on St. David Street, entertained his friends at dinner, and shocked the troubled Boswell, when the latter questioned him about a future life. Hume summed up his character in a brief autobiographical sketch and died in 1776, after insuring in his will the publication of his *Dialogues concerning Natural Religion.*

## 2. THE TRUE SKEPTIC AND THE SCIENCE OF HUMAN NATURE

Like everyone else, Hume had his moments of dogmatic certainty and also his moments of skeptical doubt. Both his temperament and his philosophy were compounded of these two moods. He oscillated between belief and doubt, looking always for a means of synthesizing them and often playing the one against the other. In the privacy of his chamber, his intense speculation would tear down the fabric of certainty and common conviction. Then, he would surrender himself to the amenities of social life, playing at backgammon and meeting practical situations as they arose. In retrospect, his speculative doubts would seem to be artificial and overstated; yet honesty and an inquiring spirit would invariably send him back to the same meditations. From such experiences, he learned that the only balance open to him was to maintain an *equal diffidence* before both his philosophical doubts and his practical convictions. His motto was: "Be a philosopher; but, amidst all your philosophy, be still a man."[1] This rule enabled him to carry his speculations to the extreme, without losing the facility to enjoy the natural reliefs of social intercourse, business, and downright self-forgetfulness.

A distinction must be drawn, however, between two sorts of *dogmatism,* only one of which Hume was ready to defend. There is need for steady working beliefs, as a support to *practical* decisions. But it is the common error of most minds to confuse this exigency, at the pragmatic level, with a host of uncritical convictions of a *speculative* sort. Against this "metaphysical" dogmatism of both

---

[1] *An Enquiry concerning Human Understanding,* I (edited by Selby-Bigge, 9); cf. *ibid.,* Section XII: "Of the Academical or Sceptical Philosophy" (Selby-Bigge, 149–65). On the nature of Hume's skepticism, cf. P. Stanley, "The Scepticisms of David Hume," *The Journal of Philosophy,* XXXII (1935), 421–31, and R. H. Popkin, "David Hume: His Pyrrhonism and his Critique of Pyrrhonism," *The Philosophical Quarterly,* I (1950–1951), 385–407.

ordinary people and his philosophical predecessors, Hume found the skeptical attitude a useful antidote. He distinguished, however, between antecedent and consequent skepticism. *Antecedent skepticism* is represented by the Cartesian methodic doubt. Hume did not think that any man could sincerely embrace this outlook, in all its force. Even if it could be done, its only value would be the negative one of clearing out old prejudices and misconceptions. Methodic doubt is not a constructive method in philosophy, since it rests on the false assumption that some privileged principle can resist doubt. The net effect of the British empiricist movement and Malebranche's philosophy was, in Hume's eyes, to discredit forever the Cartesian conception of the substantial, thinking self, as the starting point in philosophy. And it is impossible to take a single forward step, unless one is prepared to use the very faculties which methodic doubt is supposed to call in question.

There remains the *consequent* type of *skepticism,* which does not start with a general doubt but which is the outcome of detailed inquiries into the actual exercise of our mind. Hume knew and employed the familiar arguments of Sextus Empiricus, as brought up to date in Bayle's *Dictionary.* But he did not think that the skeptical arguments against the *senses,* based on sensory illusions and deceptions, went deeply enough. They only proved that the senses, by themselves, are insufficient for gaining truth. They still left open the possibility that certainty lies within our grasp, provided that *reason* be invoked and that one make allowance for the condition of the medium and organs of sensation. Far more radical were the implications of Berkeley's empirical criticism of primary qualities and an independent material world. For, this criticism bore upon the natural tendency of the mind to believe the testimony of the senses, even under optimum conditions. Furthermore, Berkeley's animadversions on abstract ideas, space, time, and mathematics brought reason itself within the pale of doubt. The outcome could well be complete Pyrrhonism, which is the suicide of all our knowing powers.

It might be necessary, Hume observed, to pass through the purgatory of *absolute, Pyrrhonian skepticism,* but one need not take up permanent residence there. For absolute skepticism renders one unfit for action as well as for speculation, so that it gives birth to no positive, durable good. Hume was moving toward a more moderate sort of consequent skepticism, which would continue the empiricist attack upon pure, abstract reason and yet find a basis for conduct.

He referred to his position as a *mitigated* or *true skepticism*. Its two outstanding features are a concentration of analysis upon the problems of man and an adaptation of the Newtonian method to achieve this purpose.

This dual aspect of Hume's program is well stated in the subtitle of *A Treatise of Human Nature*: "An Attempt to Introduce the Experimental Method of Reasoning into Moral Subjects." This is a vindication of Hobbes for stressing the investigation of human nature, and of Bacon for holding that the same method used in natural philosophy should also be applied to man. The proper perspective in philosophy is only acquired when the *study of human nature* is recognized as being central. The other sciences are somehow tributary to this study, and "instead of taking now and then a castle or village on the frontier, [the philosopher ought] to march directly to the capital or center of these sciences, to human nature itself."[2] This dependence is apparent in the more humane disciplines: logic, morals, esthetics, and politics. But it is present also in mathematics, natural philosophy, and natural religion (disciplines which deal with some object other than man), since their objects must be brought within the range of our minds and must be judged by our knowing powers. Hume uses the term *moral subjects* in a broad way, to include all philosophical investigations into the nature and limits of our understanding, passions, and sentiments, as well as the principles of belief in matters of fact and the principles of conduct.

Just as the other sciences depend upon the cardinal science of man, so the latter is constituted by an application of Newton's experimental philosophy to moral subjects. *Newton's rules of reasoning and method* find their psychological and ethical equivalents in statements made by Hume. The true skeptic must avoid any appeal to occult powers in nature or in the mind. He must avoid purely abstract and rationalistic hypotheses about the constitution of material and spiritual substances or about our reasoning ability. He should draw his evidence from experience and observation, refer all his proposition to their sensory origin, be parsimonious in his causal explanations, and proceed gradually to a few general principles governing all mental phenomena. Hume transfers from natural to humane philosophy the scientific proscription against claims to have knowledge of the essences

---

[2] *A Treatise of Human Nature*, Introduction (Selby-Bigge, xx).

of things.[3] Minds, no less than bodies, remain completely unknow-able territory for the true skeptic, who seeks to develop an experi-mental philosophy of man. This *restriction of knowledge to the appearances* is taken by Hume as the distinguishing feature of the only "true metaphysics": the *phenomenalistic* study of human nature. This is significant, since Hume is thereby enabled, at the outset, to define experience in purely phenomenalistic terms and to rule out, as "going beyond experience," any efforts to ascertain substantial essences or ultimate principles of being. His decision to introduce the Newtonian method into philosophical anthropology is not a purely methodological one but is laden down with epistemological and metaphysical consequences for the interpretation of experience.

The limitation of our understanding to appearances is no more a reason for discouragement in the science of man than in the other sciences. Once we become reconciled to foregoing any ultimate onto-logical principles, we are free to observe the uniformities within our experience, identify and demarcate the powers at work, and render our principles of explanation as general as possible within empirical bounds. Yet Hume sees an important difference between experimental procedures in natural and in moral philosophy. The natural sciences can make deliberate experiments with bodies, without affecting the results in any way. (This assertion was legitimate in classical modern physics, where the problem of the influence of our measuring opera-tions upon the data was not acute.) But in moral philosophy, the reflective deliberation with which we collect the evidence, is apt to disturb the natural operation of our mental principles. The science

---

[3] "To me it seems evident, that the essence of the mind being equally unknowable to us with that of external bodies, it must be equally impossible to form any notion of its qualities and powers otherwise than from careful and exact experiments, and the observation of those particular effects, which result from its different circum-stances and situations. And though we must endeavour to render all our principles as uniform as possible, by tracing up our experiments to the utmost, and explaining all effects from the simplest and fewest causes, it is still certain we cannot go beyond experience; and any hypothesis that pretends to discover the ultimate original qualities of human nature, ought at first [i.e., at once] to be rejected as presumptuous and chimerical. . . . As long as we confine our speculations to *the appearances* of objects to our sense, without entering into disquisitions concerning their real nature and opera-tions, we are safe from all difficulties." *Ibid.,* Introduction and Appendix (Selby-Bigge, xxi, 638; spelling modernized here and throughout this chapter). Thus from first to last, the *Treatise* assumes that the methodological and epistemological limitations of Newtonian mechanics and Pyrrhonian skepticism must be imposed upon philosophy as a whole.

of man is the one discipline where the *investigator* also becomes an *object* of study; it is the one science where *introspection* may operate to gather direct evidence about the questions at issue. Although aware of this new situation, Hume does not appreciate the far-reaching methodological changes that are entailed by these basic contrasts between the study of man and the study of the rest of nature. It was left for Kant to remark that, however much we would like a strict parallel to obtain between physical and mental operations, the Newtonian method is transferred to man only by way of a certain "analogy" and on the strength of faith in that "analogy." In any case, the comparison is too loose to sustain the inference that philosophy of man must confine itself to a description of appearances.

### 3. THE ELEMENTS OF HUMAN COGNITION

True to his chosen method, Hume begins with an analytic reduction of our cognitive operations. He subscribes unquestioningly to the elementaristic view of Locke and Berkeley: that our knowledge and belief are best understood, when they are broken down into their elements, evaluated in terms of these constituents, and reconstructed from the analytic units. In the most general sense, the contents of experience are *perceptions*.[4] Hume proposes "perceptions" rather than Locke's "ideas," as the broadest descriptive term for mental contents, since he wants to stress the derived and referential nature of our ideas. The fundamental division of perceptions is into *impressions* and *ideas*. The former strike our mind with great force and vivacity, whereas the latter are relatively weak and languid. The impressions include all our sensations, passions, and emotions, considered precisely in their first, lively appearance to the mind. There is no difference in kind between impressions and ideas, since the greater or lesser force of perceptions concerns only the manner and degree in which they strike the mind. The ideas are derived from the impressions. Hume assumes that because ideas are *derivatives,* they must also be *copies* or faint images of the impressions. But Locke had maintained that the ideas of secondary qualities are derived from bare objective powers or qualities and yet do not resemble these powers.

---

[4] *Ibid.,* I, i, 1 (Selby-Bigge, 1–7); *An Enquiry concerning Human Understanding,* II (Selby-Bigge, 18–22).

## HUME ON THE ELEMENTS OF COGNITION

Perceptions
- Impressions
  - of sensation
  - of reflection
- Ideas
  - of memory
  - of imagination

Simple and complex

Hume encounters some difficulty in defending the *distinction* between impressions and ideas. First of all, he appeals to our common-sense recognition of the difference between seeing something (having an impression) and thinking about what one has seen (having an idea). This corresponds roughly to Berkeley's distinction between having ideas of sense and having ideas of imagination. But Hume is more willing than Berkeley to admit that the distinction breaks down in some particular instances, whereas so many metaphysical implications flow from Berkeley's contrast that he rigidly retains it in all cases. The criterion of force and liveliness fails, for instance, to cover situations in which our impressions are so low in intensity that they cannot be distinguished from "weak images." And in sleep, fever, or madness, ideas may be entertained with a degree of conviction and vividness that surpasses the force of most impressions. Under normal conditions, however, at least the *derived* and *referential* character of ideas sets them off from impressions. In some way, ideas come from impressions and point back to them. On the contrary, there is a self-contained quality about impressions which makes them the original perceptions of the mind.

Hume warns against basing a verbal argument upon the word "impressions." This term does not signify the manner of *production* of our original perceptions, but only the manner of their *entertainment* by the mind, and hence the inference cannot be made that they are imprinted on the mind by some external cause. Despite this protest, however, Hume's own usage often suggests such an inference. For he refers to the senses as inlets of perception, as well as to the secret, unknowable causes in nature that affect our organic states. Like Locke and Berkeley, he maintains and profits by an undeclared relationship between phenomenalism and common-sense realism.

In order to throw further light on the relations among perceptions, Hume makes a division between simple and complex impressions, and between simple and complex ideas. *Simple* perceptions, whether impressions or ideas, admit of no further separation into parts: they are the terminations of analysis in their own order. *Complex* perceptions, whether impressions or ideas, do permit further analysis and decomposition into constituent parts. This distinction helps to correct the preliminary view that there is a perfect correspondence between all impressions and all ideas. Clearly enough, there may be a complex idea, such as "The New Jerusalem," for which there is no corresponding complex impression. Conversely, to the complex impression a man on a parapet gains of the city of Paris, there is no complex idea that adequately reproduces its original in every detail. Despite the rough resemblance of our complex ideas to our complex impressions, the former are not always exact and exhaustive copies of the latter.

Nevertheless, Hume ventures the general proposition that at least "every simple idea has a simple impression, which resembles it; and every simple impression a correspondent idea."[5] This minimal position must be maintained at all costs. Otherwise, metaphysical statements cannot be criticized, by appeal to the *empirical criterion* of tracing back ideas to their corresponding impressions or empirical sources. The Humean conception of experience cannot be made the measure of all knowledge and belief, unless this *relation of origin* obtains, along with the implication that correspondence entails an exact *resemblance* between simple impressions and ideas. Despite the burden placed upon the proposition, Hume admits at least one exception, which Descartes and others had already pointed out. When the mind considers a series of colors arranged in a graduated scale, it is able to interpolate the idea or image of a shade not previously encountered in experience. Hume regards this phenomenon as too restricted in nature to merit closer examination or to require any drastic revision of his theory about simple impressions and ideas. Nevertheless, this exception does weaken the universality of the empirical criterion and opens up the possibility that other simple ideas (not necessarily limited to color qualities) may have an independent origin, due to the mind's constructive activity, and yet may also be valid for experience.

Our impressions, whether simple or complex, can be subdivided into those of sensation and those of reflection.[6] *Impressions of sensation* are due to unknown causes and must simply be accepted as original

[5] *A Treatise of Human Nature,* I, i, 1 (Selby-Bigge, 3). For an analysis of Hume's difficulties in respect to this proposition, read C. Maund, "Hume's Treatment of Simples," *Proceedings of the Aristotelian Society,* N.S., XXXV (1934–1935), 209–28.

[6] *A Treatise of Human Nature,* I, i, 2 (Selby-Bigge, 7–8).

factors of perception. The empiricist limitation of the mind to its own perceptions erects a barrier against any philosophical study of these causes. Like Locke, Hume leaves such investigations to the physicists and anatomists, without inquiring too closely into the scientific status of their findings. He is chiefly interested in the *impressions of reflection,* which include desires, passions, and emotions, along with certain determinations of the mind that are relevant to the question of belief and causal judgments. This second type of impression does not derive from unknown causes but can definitely be traced to our ideas. After the sensation of some pleasure or pain, for instance, there remains an idea of this pleasure or pain. When the idea is recalled by memory or imagination, it will produce a new impression of desire or aversion: this new emotional state is an impression of reflection.

This explanation obliges Hume to admit that *temporal priority* and *underived originality* do not absolutely differentiate all impressions from all ideas. Impressions of reflection are subsequent to, and derived from, certain ideas. In view of the admitted exceptions to Hume's proposed criteria of liveliness, force, temporal priority, and underived originality, the only unyielding mark definitively setting off impressions from ideas is the nonreferential nature of impressions, as contrasted with the representative nature of ideas. However, this mark is a matter of *stipulated definition* with Hume, for otherwise the empiricist criterion would have no firm basis. This definition is an extra-empirical factor at the heart of Hume's method.

Hume concludes his survey of the elements of cognition with a distinction between ideas (simple or complex) of *memory* and *imagination.* He gives a descriptive account of the "faculties" of memory and imagination, without making any metaphysical commitment in their favor. He offers two ways of distinguishing between their operation. Once present in the mind, impressions may reappear as ideas, which have either retained some of their original vivacity or have lost it. An idea of memory is one that enjoys a vivacity intermediate between the impression itself and a mere idea of imagination. The latter is faint and unsteady, having lost the original force and liveliness. Yet Hume himself points out the defect in this first manner of distinction, since memories may often be weaker than images of a vivid imagination. Hence, as a second basis of distinction, he suggests that memory is tied down by the order and form of the original impressions, whereas imagination is free in these respects. But even the office of memory, reproducing the order and position of the original impressions, does not give it a privileged epistemological status, since its operations can never be checked against an independent record — which would itself be an instance of memory. The prospects for an empirical theory of knowledge and belief depend, perforce, upon the successful establishment of a connection between imagination and reality.

#### 4. IMAGINATION AND THE ASSOCIATION OF IDEAS

The gravamen of Hume's mitigated skepticism is located in his theory of the imagination, which seems to be at once the most chaotic and the most harmonious power of the mind. Imagination not only reproduces the mere ideas or pale images but is also able to transpose and fuse them in an untrammeled way. Hume's originality lies, not in repeating this venerable distinction between reproductive and productive imagination, but in combining it with his *main logical doctrine*. That doctrine is stated as follows:

> Whatever is distinct, is distinguishable; and whatever is distinguishable, is separable by the thought or imagination. All perceptions are distinct. They are, therefore, distinguishable, and separable, and may be conceived as separately existent, and may exist separately, without any contradiction or absurdity.[7]

Imagination could not compose winged steeds and other fancies, were it not able to decompose complex ideas into their simple components and to detach one simple idea from another. Because ideas are copies of impressions, they must submit to the conditions imposed by impressions. All simple impressions are distinct, self-contained, atomic units, which are separable from each other. Therefore, all simple ideas are likewise distinct and separable, imagination being the keen-edged sword that cleaves one simple idea from another and assigns it freely to another partner. Taken objectively by themselves, our simple ideas are *loose* and *unconnected,* providing imagination with plastic materials for its own synthetic operations.

---

[7] *Ibid.,* Appendix (Selby-Bigge, 634). This principle is the ground for Hume's view that the objects of experience are loose and unconnected, and that therefore the source of the causal belief must be a subjective one. M. C. Beardsley, "A Dilemma for Hume," *The Philosophical Review,* LII (1943), 28–46, suggests that the doctrine of the looseness of the factors in experience holds true only of "objects" or the analytic elements, isolated for purposes of intrinsic description alone. But it does not give an accurate account of the actual "events," which furnish the materials and basis for analysis, since our experience of actual "events" manifests irreducible connections and references of a contextual sort, which Hume's logical principle fails to respect.

It is not unexpected to find Hume affirming also that what imagination conceives separately, may also be conceived as existing separately and may, indeed, exist separately. This is the rationalistic side of empiricism, carried through to the extreme point where the *possibilities of imagination* are also the *possibilities of existence*. Since the only realities attainable in experience are perceptual objects (i.e., perceptions *as* objects), every idea that is separately imaginable has at least a *logically* irrefutable claim to existence. Hume can discover no character of existence over and above the determinate content of the object or idea itself. *Existence* is not an additional predicate but is simply the *idea grasped as a perception or distinct object.* "Whatever we conceive, we conceive to be existent."[8] As far as logically necessary grounds of argument are concerned, there is no reason against supposing that whatever can be conceived separately by imagination, can also exist as a distinct entity.

But were this all that could be said, ours would be a nightmare world of arbitrary constructions of imagination. Since this is not actually the case, Hume concludes that our familiar experience cannot be explained satisfactorily by an analysis that concentrates exclusively upon the ideas as isolated objects or meaning-contents. There are *real, coherent wholes* of experience that never become confused with products of our free fancy. Instead of looking beyond imagination, to an *intellectual* power that could grasp the unity and existential act of things, however, Hume prefers to account for our coherent grasp of realities in terms of *imagination* itself — the very power which seems to reduce everything to arbitrary combinations. This is a bold stroke. But in order to invoke imagination in this new role, he must strengthen it with the operations of the so-called laws of association.

As Hobbes and Malebranche had already noted, the imagination is not a completely erratic and lawless power. It exhibits some well-defined constants, that lead it to combine ideas in definite ways. But it does not make its combinations *in virtue of necessary, objective connections* discovered among the ideas themselves. For, from the objective standpoint of the ideas, everything is loose and *un*connected: the bonds established by imagination are not based on the logical implications or internal relations among ideas. Hume turns to "nature," i.e., to the forces secretly at work on the *subjective* side

---

[8] *A Treatise of Human Nature*, I, ii, 6 (Selby-Bigge, 67).

of the mind. The *gentle force of association* inclines the imagination to make connections which, although not strictly inseparable, are often uniform and enduring, so that one idea naturally tends to introduce another in the mind. What the precise nature of this mental principle may be, Hume professes to remain ignorant. It is a kind of universal attraction, doing for the mental world what Newton's force of gravity does for the physical world. Just as Newton was able to calculate the effects of gravity, without ever perceiving its essence, so Hume is content to chart the course and consequences of the associative force, without inquiring into its ultimate foundation. In his philosophy, it remains an *unanalyzed given factor,* whose origin and structure are shrouded in the mystery of what he himself calls, in another context, "that vague undeterminate word *nature.*"[9]

Hume speaks enthusiastically about the *three principles of association:* resemblance, contiguity in time or place, and cause-and-effect. He hails them both as constituting the "universal principle, which had an equal influence on all mankind" and as supplying *"to us* the cement of the universe."[10] It must be assumed that they are found uniformly among all men, for otherwise no inference could be made from their operation in one individual's experience to the common conditions of human nature. Furthermore, they are needed as cement, in the sense of saving empiricism from the atomistic consequences of the analysis of ideas and existence. Whereas Locke appeals to judgment, and Berkeley to God's continuous providence, Hume looks to imagination and the principles of association for a counter-agent to the analytic emphasis upon ideas as elements. If ideas are naturally attracted together by a certain force operating upon imagination, then experience will consist of a connected series of images, joined in coherent wholes, rather than of an antic dance of detached fancies.

On one capital point, however, Hume admits that the forces of mental attraction differ from those of physical attraction. The principles of mental association are the only *general* ones to provide connections among ideas, but they are neither the *infallible* nor the

[9] *Dialogues concerning Natural Religion,* VII (edited by Smith, 178; italics mine); cf. *An Enquiry concerning the Principles of Morals,* Appendix III (Selby-Bigge, 307).

[10] *An Enquiry concerning Human Understanding,* III (Selby-Bigge, 23); *An Abstract of a Treatise of Human Nature* (edited by J. M. Keynes and P. Sraffa, 32). See also, *A Treatise of Human Nature,* I, i, 4 (Selby-Bigge, 10–13). J. K. Ryan has worked out the comparison with St. Thomas: "Aquinas and Hume on the Laws of Association," *The New Scholasticism,* XII (1938), 366–77.

*sole* causes of such connections. They act as a persuasive force upon imagination. Yet, unlike physical agents, imagination retains its intrinsic freedom and may be moved by other considerations to join ideas in unexpected ways. In addition, Hume follows the Newtonian popularizers, rather than Newton himself, in attributing *real, causal efficacy* to the universal force of attraction. These serious differences render questionable his arguments based on a comparison of mental association with gravity, and indicate clearly the obstacles against using the Newtonian method to construct a philosophy of human nature.

Three applications of Hume's doctrine of association are noteworthy. They concern: general ideas, the belief in reality, and causal connections.

In dealing with *abstract, general ideas,* Hume professes to be following Berkeley but, in fact, he comes closer to Hobbes' position. An abstract idea is one that is particular in its own nature, but general in its representation.[11] It acquires generality not from containing a universal *meaning* but from its connection with a general *term*. A term is called general in virtue of a twofold association that is built up in the mind *by usage:* first, between the term and the habit of the mind that evokes a particular idea; second, between the evoked idea and the other particular ideas with which customary bonds have been established. Upon presentation of the term, imagination not only calls forth the particular idea, associated with the term, but also places itself in a state of readiness to recall the remaining ideas in the associative group. The generality of abstract ideas resides in this readiness for associative recall of images.

A second application of association is in explaining our *belief in reality*.[12] Taken in isolation from the associative force, imagination can never arouse a belief in the reality of its objects. For, taken in this way, it is merely exercising the privilege of separating and recombining, at will, perceptions that are intrinsically distinct and unconnected. We

---

[11] *A Treatise of Human Nature,* I, i, 7 (Selby-Bigge, 17–24). An extensive study of this question is made by R. I. Aaron, "Hume's Theory of Universals," *Proceedings of the Aristotelian Society,* N.S., XLII (1941–1942), 117–40, and (much more critically) by K. B. Price, "Hume's Analysis of Generality," *The Philosophical Review,* LIX (1950), 58–76. Price notes that Hume fails to provide any empirical objection against objectively repeatable qualities and relations, which could serve as the basis for universals, apart from the associative mechanism.

[12] On "reality" as a coherent system of beliefs, cf. *A Treatise of Human Nature,* I, iii, 9, and Appendix (Selby-Bigge, 108, 629).

accept the workings of imagination as real and existentially credible, only when they are guided systematically by the principles of association. It is only then that these operations approximate, in constancy and coherence, to the impressions of sensation. Apart from its bare beginnings in the impressions of sensation, the major portion of what Hume regards as belief in the real world is *a system of constant and coherent images,* knitted together by imagination, acting under the gentle promptings of the power of association. Berkeley's rigid criterion for determining real, sensible things is thus dissolved, giving Hume a thoroughly phenomenalistic meaning for "the real world."

Finally, Hume makes an innovation by including *cause-and-effect* among the aspects from which the association of ideas springs. In so doing, he is gradually formulating the problem of causality in a special way. For, the principles of association are brought to bear upon objects or ideas that do *not* have any intrinsic linkage, based on their own nature or operation. To reckon the bond of cause-and-effect among these principles is to suggest, at long range, that the objects themselves are somehow loose and unconnected, and that their causal union is due solely to a mental force generated by custom. This remote predetermination of the nature of the causal connection is advanced another step with Hume's discussion of relations, making his own solution of the causal problem a foregone conclusion.

## 5. RELATIONS AND REASONING

The association of ideas gives rise to the three Lockean classes of complex ideas: substances, modes, and relations. Hume makes short work of the general ideas of substance and mode. All of Berkeley's arguments against material substance tell against *substance as such.* Hume finds that the idea of substance can be traced to no distinctive impression, either of sense or of reflection. It owes its origin to a collection of simple ideas, united by imagination and given a common thing-name, which facilitates the recall of this particular collection. In the case of *mode,* the associative force is also needed to account for the unity of the complex idea. Hume proposes to extricate empiricism from the dead-end reached in previous analyses of substances and modes, by making a fresh start in the neglected area of relations. With him, the problem of relation comes to the forefront of empiricism, just as with Leibniz' discussion of harmony, it became centrally important for the rationalist school.

## HUME'S THEORY OF RELATIONS

1. Natural relations.
   a) Resemblance.
   b) Contiguity in time or place. } Principles of association.
   c) Cause-and-effect.

2. Philosophical relations.
   a) Resemblance.
   b) Degrees of quality. } Intuition. } Invariable relations, relations of ideas, scientific knowledge and certainty.
   c) Contrariety.
   d) Quantity or number. Mathematical demonstration, demonstrative reasoning.

   e) Identity.
   f) Space and time. } Immediate perception of present existence within experience. } Variable relations, matters of fact or existence, probability and belief.

   g) Cause-and-effect. Moral reasoning to existence beyond experience.

(N.B. Compare: 1, a, b, c, with 2, a, f, g.)

A distinction is drawn between two main types of relation: natural and philosophical.[13] In *natural relations,* ideas are connected through the force of association, so that one introduces the other "naturally" or by customary reference. Hume regards this as the ordinary kind of relation meant when people say that certain things are related by a connecting principle. People mean that they experience a certain mental compulsion to turn their minds from one idea to the other. The natural relations are precisely those involved in association: resemblance, contiguity in time or place, and cause-and-effect. On the other hand, *philosophical relation* is simply any matter of comparison among objects, without implying any connecting principle or associative bond. Certain qualities of objects make them fit for mental comparison, so that we may make an *arbitrary* union of such objects

---

[13] *Ibid.,* I, i, 5; iii, 1-2 (Selby-Bigge, 13-15, 69-74).

or ideas (i.e., a union where there is no *natural* force, subjectively compelling the mind to refer from one term to the other). There are seven types of philosophical relation: resemblance, identity, space and time, quantity or number, degrees of quality, contrariety, cause-and-effect. It is noteworthy that resemblance, contiguity in space or time, and cause-and-effect may be viewed both as natural and as philosophical relations. But Hume wants to call in question whether, as a philosophical relation, cause-and-effect rests on any real, distinctive trait that permits inferences to be drawn.

All relations are founded upon some *common quality,* distributed among the objects to be related. Without this identical quality, there could be no resemblance, and without a resemblance no ground of comparison or relating. Hence, *resemblance* is the basis for philosophical relations. But the resemblance is not something over and above the distributed quality itself: it *is* this quality, regarded precisely as matter for comparison. Resemblance-as-such is only an abstract, general term, which does not go beyond the identical qualities given widely in experience. Resemblances implicated in natural relations require not only the distributed quality but also the force of association, leading the mind from one qualitative embodiment to another. Hume gives no definite indication, however, of how we know that there is an *identical* quality that is only numerically multiplied.

Philosophical relations fall into the two wide subdivisions of invariable and variable relations. The *invariable relations* depend exclusively on the ideas under comparison: as long as the ideas remain the same, the relations also remain invariably the same. In conformity with the Cartesian and Lockean views of science, Hume states that only the invariable relations can provide *strict knowledge,* because of their *purely ideal* character. In this class, he includes the relations of resemblance, contrariety, degrees of quality, and proportions of quantity or number. The first three of these invariable or constant relations are discoverable at first sight, and hence belong to intuition rather than to demonstration. But the relations of quantity and number provide the matter for *mathematics,* which is therefore the only science constituted by strictly *demonstrative reasoning.* In the *Treatise,* Hume concedes perfect exactness and certainty only to arithmetic and algebra. Geometry does not attain perfect precision of measurement, since it concerns the general appearances of sense objects and is therefore limited by the variations and complexities of natural being. In the first *Enquiry,* however, he allows that pure geometry is also a demonstrative science, although he still rejects (along with Berkeley) an infinite divisibility of quantity, since this idea is at bottom particular and finitely determinate. Since Hume's main interest centers about metaphysical and moral problems, he does not provide any satisfactory, empirical account of the foundations of mathematics.

The *variable relations* are those of identity, time and place, and cause-and-effect. These relations may be changed, without entailing any change either in the objects so related or in their ideas. For instance, the relation of distance between two bodies may vary without variation in the objects (the complex impressions) or their corresponding ideas. Since these relations are not exclusively ideal, their establishment by the mind depends upon *experience* and *observation.* This involves a kind of reasoning or comparison of the objects entering into the relation. But Hume observes a difference between the comparisons that establish the inconstant relations of identity and of time and place, and the comparison at the basis of cause-and-effect.  The former are not genuine reasonings at all but rather are *immediate perceptions,* since both the relata and the relation itself are presented to the senses for comparison. However, in trying to establish the causal relation, the mind must reason from a given object or impression to a cause or effect that is not given in experience. This inference is *sui generis.* It does not deal mathematically with ideal connections alone, for it concerns a variable rather than an invariable relation and seeks a bond among existents. Yet it does not find the relation given intuitively along with both terms of the relation, for it is a reasoning from what is given in experience to what is not so given.

The distinction between demonstrative and moral reasoning helps to demarcate the sphere of the causal inference. All reasoning consists in a discovery of the relations that objects bear to each other. These relations may be either *relations of ideas* or *matters of fact* (as Locke had already noted).[14] Hence there is a corresponding distinction between two kinds of reasoning: demonstrative and moral. *Demonstrative reasoning* investigates the relations between ideas. Here, the mind is concerned solely with its own defining operations and ideas, regardless of questions about actual existence. The proper objects of this abstract demonstration are relations of quantity and number.

---

[14] *An Enquiry concerning Human Understanding,* IV, 1 (Selby-Bigge, 25–26).

Hence only the mathematical sciences yield demonstrative knowledge, which Hume defines rationalistically as that sort of reasoning, a denial of whose conclusions entails a contradiction. Any attempt to extend the scope of demonstration beyond mathematical relations is bound to end in illusion. Matters of fact and existence can be investigated only by *moral reasoning*. The only *certitude* about existential affairs is gained, when sensation or memory immediately presents the objects in their relation. But memory never attains full certitude, because of the difficulties surrounding its verification.

Moral reasoning proper attempts to go beyond what is presented in sense perception and memory, in order to discover something about the existence or action of objects that lie beyond experience. The only relation upon which such reasoning can be founded is *cause-and-effect*. All "metaphysical" (in the pejorative sense of supraempirical) reasoning relies upon the appeal to causal relations. By this route, conclusions are reached concerning the existence of the external, substantial world, the human soul, and God. But such inferences concern matters of fact and must submit to the limitations placed upon moral reasoning. In the existential order, we can never hope to reach demonstrative knowledge. For a denial of an existential conclusion does not lead to any contradiction. In the realm of matters of fact, whatever *is,* may also *not be.* "The contrary of every matter of fact is still possible; because it can never imply a contradiction, and is conceived by the mind with the same facility and distinctness, as if ever so conformable to reality. . . . *Nothing we imagine is absolutely impossible.*"[15] Thus Hume invokes the Cartesian ideal of a demonstrative science and a criterion of clear and distinct ideas, which he identifies with vivid, sharp images. By comparison with this standard, one may never expect to gain more than probability through causal inference. Moral reasoning in general can never yield more than a high degree of *probability* or *moral certitude,* and causal reasoning can never surpass this intrinsic limitation.

Hume is now ready to explain the significance of regarding cause-and-effect now as a philosophical, and now as a natural, relation.[16] A *comparison of ideas* can be made with the aid of the philosophical relation of cause-and-effect, but an *actual connection among objects* can be made only by cause-and-effect considered as a natural relation.

---

[15] *Loc. cit.* (Selby-Bigge, 25); *A Treatise of Human Nature,* I, ii, 2 (Selby-Bigge, 32).
[16] *Ibid.,* I, iii, 6, 14 (Selby-Bigge, 92–94, 170).

As a philosophical relation, it depends upon resemblance. But it has been shown that philosophical resemblance is nothing more than the distribution of an identical quality among several *given* objects. This resemblance does not embrace the existence or qualities of objects not given in experience, so that there is no objective basis for extending the causal inference beyond experience. As a *philosophical* relation, in fact, cause-and-effect enjoys no independent status and makes no distinctive union of ideas. It is reducible to some variation of spatial or temporal relation, such as contiguity, succession of before-and-after, and constant togetherness. The philosophical relation of cause-and-effect supplies no foundation for metaphysical inferences about realities existing outside experience. In order to provide this basis, cause-and-effect must be taken as a *natural* relation. But in consequence, everything applies to it that has been established about imagination, operating under the influence of association. The natural relation whereby we can make causal inferences beyond experience is due to a union, established by regulated imagination, among ideas that are unconnected in their own nature.

The findings of Sections 4 and 5, above, may be summarized in one phrase: *the loosening of ideas.* Ideas are loosened by showing the power of imagination over distinct, separable ideas and by reducing the philosophical relation of cause-and-effect to impotence. Detached ideas permit of no inference whatever, since they are perfectly uninformative concerning objects lying beyond sense experience. The only way to rehabilitate causal inference is to overcome the loosening of ideas. This can be done by recognizing the stabilizing effect of custom upon imagination and, consequently, by appealing to the natural associative powers operating in the mind itself to build up natural relations. The result is, however, that causal inference is a form of moral reasoning and can achieve only moral certitude or probability. All this is established by Hume even before he begins his formal examination of cause. He has succeeded in framing the question in such a way that his own answer is inevitable, within the given framework.

## 6. THE ANALYSIS OF CAUSE

In his discussion of the idea of cause and our belief in it, Hume drew generously upon the criticisms offered by the skeptics, Hobbes, Malebranche, and Berkeley. But although he often echoed his predecessors, even in the choice of words, he produced a unified and powerful critique of his own, which affected the principle of causality as such and did not stop short at some particular instance of causation. He began by asking whether the idea of cause is derived from some qualities in the objects themselves (the original sense impressions) or from some relation among the objects. The former alternative is excluded without much consideration. Whatever *intrinsic quality* one may choose as characterizing cause, one may also find an object that lacks this quality and yet figures in a causal connection. Hence the search turns toward the various *relations* among objects. Among the philosophical relations that bear upon matters of fact, there are three that seem to enter into the notion of cause-and-effect: *contiguity, temporal priority,* and *necessary connection.* The objects related as cause-and-effect are in some contact; the object designated as cause enjoys a temporal priority over the effect; there is a necessary link between the two terms. Hume did not give a serious hearing to causal theories in which contiguity and temporal priority do not belong to the essential conditions of the causal relation. But he did grant that, although these notes are components in the causal relation, they are not its sole and sufficient constituents. There are cases where objects are contiguous and related according to a temporal series, and yet where the relation of cause-and-effect is absent.

Hence the main investigation concerns the origin of the idea of a necessary connection. There are two ways of tracing it to its source. The first is a *logical* examination of its role in the general principle of causality; the second is a *psychological* description of how it arises in the mind, in the case of particular causal inferences. Hume's analysis will be given according to these two stages, logical and psychological, reserving criticism of his argument for a third division.

1. The previous *logical* defenses of causality made by Hobbes, Clarke, and Locke provide Hume with a set of easy targets. The common objection he makes is that his predecessors suppose the need for a cause, in the very proofs they advance to establish this need. He takes as a generally received statement of the causal principle Locke's dictum: *Whatever begins to exist, must have a cause of existence.*[17] Locke's justification of this proposition rests upon his analysis of the idea of power, which alone provides the transition from observed beginnings to the relation of cause-and-effect. From Hume's

---

[17] *Ibid.*, I, iii, 3 (Selby-Bigge, 78; cf. 79–82, 157, for Hume's criticism). See above, Chap. 8, note 19.

standpoint, there are two insuperable objections to Locke's argument. First, Locke jumps directly from experiences of beginnings to the rational inference that powers must be present. But this implies that the idea of power is *original to reason*. This contradicts the empirical principle that ideas derive not directly from reason but from some impression given in experience. Since Locke does not identify the original impression, Hume concludes that the idea of causal power either has no empirical origin or has a source in a direction where Locke fails to look. Hume himself accepts the second alternative, but postpones examination of it until the psychological study of particular instances of causal belief.

His second criticism of Locke is directly damaging against the accepted formulation of the causal principle. He contends that *"reason, as distinguished from experience,* can never make us conclude, that a cause or productive quality is absolutely requisite to every beginning of existence."[18] Italics have been added, in making this quotation, so that Hume's position will not be misunderstood. His purpose is to show, not that the relation of cause-and-effect is groundless, but rather that it cannot be validated by *abstract reason,* acting apart from experience. Since reason acts in this way only when it is making mathematical or ideal demonstrations, Hume has already ruled out the abstract use of reason as a method to be employed in determining causal matters of fact. Hence the point of his second objection is that no *demonstrative* proof can be made of the principle of causality. This follows because demonstration is limited to the relations among ideas, whereas no reasoning from mere ideas can establish the need of a real cause and the necessary, existential connection between cause and effect.

Demonstrative proof is such that a denial of the conclusion entails a contradiction. All of Hume's critical remarks on the causal principle are intended to show that it can be denied, without leading to a logical contradiction. In his main logical doctrine on separability and existence, he has already set the stage for proving this thesis. The *ideas* of cause and effect are distinct and separable from each other — otherwise we beg the issue and label them correlative notions. Hence it is entirely possible for imagination to divorce the idea of a cause from that of a beginning of existence. It is then "easy for us to conceive any object to be non-existent this moment, and existent the next,

---

[18] *A Treatise of Human Nature,* I, iii, 14 (Selby-Bigge, 157).

without conjoining to it the distinct idea of a cause."[19] Since a causeless beginning of existence is conceivable by imagination, without involving a contradiction, the opposite of the causal principle is possible, as far as the *objective, logical content of ideas* is concerned. This eliminates any strict demonstration of the principle, since a demonstration concludes to that, the opposite of which cannot be consistently conceived. We must look elsewhere than to demonstrative reasoning about ideas for the source of the idea of a necessary connection.

Rather indignantly, Hume once told one of his correspondents that he never maintained the absurd proposition that anything might arise without a cause, but only held that the certainty of the falsehood of such a causeless beginning cannot be obtained by intuition or demonstration.[20] From his own standpoint, his protest is justified in two ways. First, the word *things* is equivocal, since it may refer either to beings as they exist outside of our perceptions or to the immediate objects of our experience: the impressions and ideas. Hume's discussion is confined to "things" in the second sense, as objects-in-cognition, whereas his opponents were referring to the extramental existents. He does refer sometimes to the secret causes operating in nature, but such references have no strict empirical standing and can only lead to the Kantian problem of how we can affirm the reality of unknowable things. In the second place, Hume does not champion causeless beginnings, even among things or objects taken in his sense of the word. He is only concerned with showing the *nondemonstrative, extralogical* nature of our rejection of the idea of a causeless beginning. In regard to matters of fact, abstract reasoning about mere ideas is the same as the play of imagination in separating distinct ideas. The case for causality would be hopeless, were demonstrative certainty the only alternative to complete skepticism. But the moderate or true

---

[19] *Ibid.*, I, iii, 3 (Selby-Bigge, 79). In "Professor Stace and the Principle of Causality," *The New Scholasticism*, XXIV (1950), 398–416, F. X. Meehan criticizes Hume and his contemporary exponent, W. T. Stace, for inferring from one's ability to *imagine* an object without *imagining* its cause, that therefore one can *conceive* of an object as *coming to be* without *any* cause. The cause may be unimaginable, and nevertheless be conceivable and known to be necessary for the actual production of the thing.

[20] *Letter of February, 1754,* in *The Letters of David Hume* (edited by J. Y. Greig, I, 187). Hume deals with "things" or "facts," only in the sense of the contents of our statements about the occurrence or regularities of our perceptions. Since these statements can succeed each other without any ontological dependence among themselves, he finds no objective basis in his "facts" for the causal inference. The first task of realism is to distinguish unequivocally between the Humean fact and the act of being, on the part of the existent thing.

skeptic, finding the justification of his causal belief blocked off in the direction of demonstrative reason and the intrinsic nature of ideas, may still turn to the area of disciplined imagination, moral reasoning, and probable assurance. The constructive side of Hume's argument is manifested when he shifts to a psychological discussion of particular instances of causal inference. His purpose is not to deny their existence but to explain them on other than demonstrative grounds.

2. From the *psychological* standpoint, a cause may be defined as *"an object followed by another, and whose appearance always conveys the thought to that other."*[21] What is the source of the inference that leads the mind from this cause to this effect, say, from flame to heat? What is given in a particular encounter is a flame conjoined with heat: each is a distinct object or perception. But we notice that, after this experience is repeated several times, it is no longer necessary to furnish both objects. Upon the presentation of but one of them by sense or memory, the understanding will recall the other. It will do so in conformity with the past experience, and will relate the objects in necessary connection, as cause and effect. On the side of the objects themselves, there has been perceived only a contiguity and temporal succession. The source of the necessary connection must be sought on the side of the mental operations: in the *repetition* of the experience of contiguity and temporal sequence. We affirm a necessary connection between the two objects, joined in the natural relation of cause-and-effect, because we have experienced them in constant — or rather, in *frequent — conjunction*. The leap from factual conjunction to necessary-connection-in-virtue-of-a-causal-power is made by the mind, acting involuntarily under the force of habitual association. Imagination or the understanding makes a *customary union* between the ideas of flame and heat. Hence it can make a confident inference even in regard to what heat will do in the future, although the particular case has not yet been experienced.

The causal inference rests not upon a *connection perceived in the*

---

[21] *An Enquiry concerning Human Understanding*, VII, 2 (Selby-Bigge, 77). One of Hume's major psychological arguments against Locke is that we do not even experience real causation on the part of our own will. This assertion was challenged by the French philosopher, Maine de Biran, who declared that we must approach the facts of interior life with a specially proportioned attitude (the *sens intime*), and not measure them exclusively in terms of external events (through the *sens externe*). For Biran's criticism, see P. P. Hallie, "Maine de Biran and the Empiricist Tradition," *The Philosophical Quarterly*, I (1950–1951), 152–64.

*objects* but upon one *instituted by the mind,* operating in accordance with the principles of association. Repetition of given conjunctions "causes or produces" (at least, Hume allows that this one instance of real causation is given!) a definite set or mental determination. The mind acquires a feeling of being constrained to pass from the one idea to the other, and to link them necessarily through a causal power. This *determination of mind or feeling of a necessity* to make the causal inference constitutes the causal belief and is the source of the idea of a necessary connection. Although this idea does not arise from any impression of sensation, it does have an empirical origin in an *impression of reflection:* in the felt necessity to pass from the one idea to the other.[22] The only necessity lies in the mind so constrained, not in the objects. Thus an empirical but nonobjective explanation is given of the genesis of our idea of cause and the causal belief.

Repetition of the experience of conjunction does not *increase insight* into any relation among the objects but only *generates a habit* of mind to link them together. The connecting principle remains unintelligible, since it operates "naturally" only to produce the custom of associating the ideas, rather than to reveal dependencies in being. The only difference lies in the manner in which the conjoined ideas eventually come to strike the mind. Under the impetus of custom, the conjunction addresses itself more forcefully and vivaciously to the mind, thus approximating to the strength of an original impression of sense. The impression of reflection or feeling of constraint is (to use the language of Malebranche) a *je-ne-sais-quoi,* that makes the mind believe in the causal connection. Hence the causal inference becomes a *settled belief,* that may be integrated with the rest of the system of reality, developed by imagination and the force of association. It never attains the absolute certainty of scientific knowledge, but it is more than a reckless conjecture. It gives sufficient assurance to shape our practical life with sagacity. Yet Hume admits that his explanation cannot still the doubts of a skeptical mind, whose goal is strict knowledge or nothing at all. Whatever the strength of probability behind any causal belief, the fact remains that *"even after the observation of the frequent or constant conjunction of objects, we have no reason to draw any inference concerning any object beyond those of which we have had experience."*[23] Not an abstract reason

---

[22] *A Treatise of Human Nature,* I, iii, 14 (Selby-Bigge, 155–56); *An Enquiry concerning Human Understanding,* VII, 2 (Selby-Bigge, 74–75).

[23] *A Treatise of Human Nature,* I, iii, 12 (Selby-Bigge, 139). Malebranche's influence

but a customary inclination is the basis for making the causal inference. Belief in the presumed likeness between what we have experienced and have not experienced is a practical necessity; we cannot demonstrate it and yet we cannot live without accepting and acting upon it.

3. A critical appraisal of this theory may point out, first, that its greatest service is to have brought out into the open an *inherent conflict* between rational and empirical motives that had been troubling British philosophy for a century. Hume illustrated this conflict in the central instance of causality, upon which so many fundamental doctrines rest. His analysis could only be made within a philosophical tradition nourished by two major disjunctions: between reason and experience, and between ideal demonstration and existential belief. Hume's skepticism was a vigilant refusal to confuse the members of these disjunctions or to water down the basic oppositions. His skeptical attitude was a "mitigated" one, only insofar as he made provision for coherent experience and reliable action even within the context of these antitheses.

The opposition between *reason* and *experience* dominates Hume's treatment of cause-and-effect. Of the former power, he offers a caricature that even an enthusiastic Cartesian would find difficult to recognize. In its metaphysical employment, reason is supposed to  operate in a purely abstract and a priori way, entirely apart from the guidance of sense observation. Its insights are attained effortlessly and penetrate at once into the very essences of things, laying bare, in a definitive and unalterable way, the entire causal order of the universe. Hume finds it easy to puncture these inflated claims, but he has no right to ask that a valid conception of empirical understanding be governed solely by opposition to *this view* of reason. Reason may be regarded in a moderate way, as working in closest dependence upon the deliverances of sense, as relying upon patient observation of the natural world, and as recognizing that its findings are never exhaustive of the nature of things. Between reason, so understood, and experience a breach need never occur, since reason is then a major component in shaping a humane sort of experience. In point of fact, Hume never succeeds in realizing his own ideal of "experimental reasoning," since he is unable to integrate reason with sense and imagination, without depriving reason of its distinctive function

upon Hume's causal theory has been assessed by R. W. Church, "Malebranche and Hume," *Revue Internationale de Philosophie*, I (1938–1939), 143–61.

within the whole and thus reducing it to the status of a captive, habit-dominated imagination.

In respect to the causal problem, the key assertion is that *"causes and effects are discoverable, not by reason but by experience."*[24] This statement contains an amphibology, since it can mean either that experience *rather than* reason discovers causal relations or that reason *apart from* experience *cannot* discover them. The latter meaning is perfectly compatible with the realistic view that reason must draw from an experimental source its original data about causation and the causal principle. Hume's intent, however, is to assign causal belief to a type of experience from which reason is barred. He has in mind the operations of what he likes to call "abstract reason, derived from inquiries *a priori*."[25] And it must be granted that this nonexperiential sort of reason does not discover causal relations. This was a commonplace with Malebranche and other Cartesians, who pointed out that, if material substance is a passive, extended thing, then no amount of rational analysis of this inert object can show real causation among created things. But to affirm that a supposedly autonomous Cartesian reason cannot discover causal relations, is still to leave unaffected the rational power, as it actually functions in human experience. For, the rational principle in experience co-operates with the sensory powers, so that it may discover — with their aid and yet in a distinctively intellectual way — causal relations furnished by the beings of our experience. Hume is systematically prevented from recognizing this aspect, since he restricts the valid function of reason to abstract, mathematical calculation. In causal inference, he can make room for the understanding only by reducing it to the imagination, as stabilized by associative bonds.

---

[24] *An Enquiry concerning Human Understanding*, IV, 1 (Selby-Bigge, 28). For a sustained Aristotelian-Thomistic criticism, read Marie-de-Lourdes, R. J.-M., "Essai de commentaire critique sur l'*Enquiry concerning Human Understanding* de David Hume," *Laval Théologique et Philosophique*, II (1946), 1–78.

[25] *Dialogues concerning Natural Religion*, IV (Smith, 160); compare J. Dewey's similar remarks about speculative reason, in *Logic: The Theory of Inquiry*, 87. Hume is correct in rejecting the rationalistic, Leibnizian employment of sufficient reason and causality as purely a priori and deductive principles. Relying solely upon the formal necessity of these principles, we can make no analytically certain deductions about finite existents. This does not lead, however, to Hume's postulatory phenomenalism, since the intellect can grasp being and the experientially warranted necessities imposed by actually existing finite beings. We can base the causal inference upon the exigencies of finite existents, thus avoiding both rationalism and phenomenalism. Consult E. Gilson, "Les principes et les causes," *Revue Thomiste*, LII (1952), 39–63.

The second general contrast — between *ideal demonstration* and *existential belief* — springs from the first. It follows from the doctrine that the immediate object of experience is the mental percept and that a strict rational science is based on purely ideal connections. On Hume's part, there is no critical revision of this common patrimony of Descartes and Locke, but only an attempt to work out its radical implications. On this rationalistic basis, he legitimates reason only as a mathematical, *non*metaphysical function and, by the same token, disqualifies it from making any existential and causal inquiries. He is following a sound lead, when he distinguishes between mathematical and causal investigations, and when he regards the latter as existential or bearing on matter of fact. It is also true that many problems, concerning matters of fact and particular causal connections, cannot be settled with more than probable assurance. But it is something else to hold that the causal principle itself has *no* demonstrative foundation and that causal inferences *never* give more than probable assurance.

The Humean notion of *demonstration* would rule out every attempt to make a demonstrative causal inference. But the view that a demonstration is excluded, as long as the contrary of a matter of fact is conceivable, suffers from two defects: one, *historical,* and the other, *theoretical.* Newton (whose method Hume adopts) had faced the contention that, since the Cartesian vortexes are conceivable, they present a serious alternative explanation of the world and detract from the certainty of his own conclusions. His rule against using abstract hypotheses in natural philosophy was intended to undermine arguments based merely upon what is conceivable, according to scientific imagination. In regard to matters of fact, demonstrations are not disturbed merely by pointing out logically possible alternatives. Conclusions in natural philosophy are always open to further revision, not because of the abstract possibility of thinking given facts as nonexistent but only because research is always revealing further existential facts, bearing on the issue.

From the *theoretical* standpoint, it is difficult to determine whether Hume is referring to the contrary or the contradictory opposite. In either case, he argues as though the contingent matter of fact were the *conclusion* rather than the *point of departure* for causal reasoning, or as though it were a point of departure *only as a member of a temporal series.* It is true that any contingent existent can cease to be, but under the supposition of its actual existence it cannot be regarded as nonexistent, here and now. What has to be explained is its actual existence as a given fact: this is the beginning rather than the end of the inference. Although the thing could either be or not be, the given situation is that it actually does exist, in a contingent way. It is this determinate matter of fact that requires explanation through a present, actual, *per se* cause of its being. Viewed in this way, a demonstration can be made from a contingent matter of fact to a cause it must have, whatever we may imagine about its temporal antecedents or consequents.

Hume is distracted from the proper question by his notion that causal reasoning always concerns a *prediction* about future consequences or a *recapture* of temporal antecedents. He takes this temporalistic view of causal inference, since he has in mind the Lockean arrangement of ideas and Newtonian scientific reasoning in which the locating of an event in a temporal series is of prime importance. Now, within this context, the ability of imagination to isolate an event from its temporal connections would render the Lockean formulation of the causal principle meaningless. It would also block the operation of the associative process, as described by Hume. But it would leave intact the need for a cause to explain the actual existence of whatever being is *presently given*. This latter exigency is independent of the question of prediction and retrospection. The only conclusion Hume might legitimately draw from the isolating power of imagination is that it reveals the inadequacy of Locke's statement of causality and also the discrepancy between Hume's scientific relation of cause-and-effect and the actual causal inference about existent things.

Hume admits that the ability of imagination to conceive of distinct objects as separately coming into existence, without invoking the idea of a cause, does not bear upon real conditions. It is only the obverse side of the inability of abstract reason to find intrinsic causal connections among objects of perception. But the Humean matter of fact or existence refers back no farther than to the original impressions and their ideas. The only reason why imagination is free to conceive of a causeless entrance into existence, is that the *new existent* is no more than a *percept-object*. To save our sanity about belief in the reality of such percept-objects, Hume turns to the natural, subjective forces working coherently through imagination. But he does not come to close grips with the problem presented by an existential judgment about things, insofar as they exercise a *contingent act of being*, apart from our perceptions. Hume has no distinctive existential judgment and hence no *rational* ground in experience for cause-and-effect, as bearing upon the need for an influx of being in actual things.

Consequently, there are two sharply divergent ways of interpreting Hume's dictum that causal reasoning goes "beyond the evidence of our memory and senses."[26] On a realistic view, this would mean that sense and memory convey more data than they themselves are formally able to appreciate. Reason would then be said to grasp the significance of sensory deliverances for the question of the being of things, and thus to attain its own distinctive aspect of the object, through and in the empirical materials. Working along with sense, the human intellect would apprehend the given, contingent matter of fact, precisely in respect to its *dependence for being.* This would constitute a foundation for the causal inference — a foundation provided by the sensorily grasped fact and discerned by reason, from the distinctive standpoint of the participated existence or act of being that requires causal explanation. In Hume's reading of the situation, however, the understanding is simply *outrunning the objective evidence,* instead of seizing upon given connections and implications. Sense and memory tell us only about perceptual objects that can be rendered loose and unconnected, as far as their objective content is concerned. It is in spite of the atomistic reduction of sense evidence, that the Humean understanding can establish causal connections and make inferences from the natural relation of cause-and-effect. The conflict, in Hume's mind, between skeptical analysis and causal belief is brought into sharp relief in connection with the major types of causal inference in metaphysics.

## 7. EXTERNAL BODIES AND THE PERSONAL SELF

Hume regards *metaphysics* as an effort to prove the existence of  three supraempirical objects: the world of external bodies, the personal self, and God. One purpose of his elaborate discussion of causality is to provide the principles of criticism for evaluating these three claims of metaphysics. He declares that his critique of metaphysics does not tell against the *reality* of external bodies, the personal self,  and God, but only against philosophical assertions of having *knowl-*

<sup></sup>26 *An Enquiry concerning Human Understanding,* IV, 1 (Selby-Bigge, 26). For a realistic defense of the co-operation of sense and reason, in the apprehension of causation, cf. D. J. Hawkins, *Causality and Implication* (London, Sheed and Ward, 1937), Chap. IV: "Direct Apprehension of Implication and Causation" (65–88, with special reference to Hume and Kant).

*edge* about their existence. His argument is aimed at showing that our conviction about them is a matter of probability and natural belief, rather than of scientific demonstration. The tomes of metaphysics can safely be consigned to the flames, without loss, since they contain neither mathematical demonstrations about quantity and number nor an empirical analysis of the natural grounds of belief (v.g., imagination and association). Metaphysics can acquire no foothold in a system that reduces our knowledge of existence to an awareness of the percept as an object being perceived.

1. *Bodies in the External World.* Hume acknowledges that everyone begins by believing, blindly and instinctively, that material things exist apart from ourselves and would continue to exist, even if our percipient organism were removed. But this naïve conviction was challenged by Locke, who posited a *double* sort of existence: first, of the ideas as immediate objects of perception and, then, of the extramental things in the world. This theory of a double existence was challenged, in its turn, by Berkeley's criticism of primary qualities and material substance. Hume now seeks to eliminate Berkeley's own position, by furnishing a completely empirical account of belief in the external world, in which the intervention of God, as the supplier of stable ideas of sense, is rendered superfluous. He analyzes this belief into two related affirmations: that bodies enjoy a *continued* existence, and that they enjoy a *distinct* existence.[27] The problem is to discover whether belief in the continued and distinct existence of bodies is due to sense, reason, or imagination. In principle, the issue has already been decided, through Hume's attitude toward existence and existential inference.

By giving a special definition of *continued* existence, he has no difficulty in showing that it is never perceived by the *senses.* Continued existence cannot become the object of sense perception, since the kind of continuance meant here is a persistence that would remain, even after the senses cease to perceive it. Here, Hume is adopting the same type of argument that led Berkeley to the fallacy of the egocentric predicament. He defines continued existence (just as Berkeley defined extramental existence) as that which would persist, after every perception of it ceased — and then concludes that the senses could not have a perception of such a state. His argument

---

[27] *A Treatise of Human Nature,* I, iv, 2 (187–99). Cf. A. Leroy, "Statut de l'objet extérieur dans la philosophie de Hume," *Revue Internationale de Philosophie,* VI (1952), 199–212.

justifies no conclusion about existential continuation in being or even about our judgment on such continuance, except on the assumption that sensation can inform us only about "internal and perishing" impressions. It is this same phenomenalistic premise which enables Hume also to maintain that the senses give no information about a *distinct* and independent existence. If the original impressions of sense are single and nonrepresentative (nonintentional forms), they do not point beyond themselves and do not give rise to the idea of a double existence. *Reason* is also barred from making the inference upon which such an idea would rest. If reason identifies the perception and the object, it is meaningless to speak about an inference from the one to the other. If it distinguishes between them, it can never move from the existence of the perception to that of an independent object. For, this would depend upon a causal relation. It has already been shown that this relation is confined to the conjunctions among several perceptions, so that reason would have no basis for extending it to a conjunction between perceptions and nonperceptual, external objects.

We are left with *imagination* as the only source of belief in independent bodies. Our conviction about a continued bodily existence is based on a natural, habit-generated inference of imagination. Imagination or concrete understanding passes insensibly from awareness of the coherence and constancy of certain impressions to an affirmation of the coherence and constancy — and, therefore, the *continued* existence — of their supposed bodily counterparts. Imagination suggests, irresistibly, that bodies enjoy a continued existence. Any interruptions can then be assigned solely to my perceptions, whereas the continuity and identity belong to independent objects. Continuance of existence on the part of bodies, regardless of my perception, implies their *distinctness* from me and thus their independent reality in an external universe.

Having dissected this belief in the external world, Hume reminds himself of his leading principles. Impressions remain "internal and perishing"; perceptions, however much alike, are distinct and separable; there is no perceivable connection between perceptions and an independent bodily existence; hence there is no ground for the causal inference to bodies, except the coherence and constancy of the perceptions themselves. The whole edifice of our conviction about an independent material world rests on the supposition and lively belief of imagination, aroused by the resemblances among perceptions

and by nothing more. In a skeptical mood, Hume confesses that
at present:

> [I] am more inclined to repose no faith at all in my senses, or rather
> imagination, than to place in it such an implicit confidence. I cannot
> conceive how such trivial qualities of the fancy, conducted by such false
> suppositions, can ever lead to any solid and rational system. . . . Care-
> lessness and in-attention alone can afford us any remedy. For this reason
> I rely entirely upon them; and take it for granted, whatever may be the
> reader's opinion at this present moment, that an hour hence he will be
> persuaded there is both an external and internal world.[28]

The wry humor of the last remark illustrates Hume's attitude of
mitigated skepticism, which admits that nature provides relief against
its most unpalatable findings. But the text also reveals the vast
disproportion between Hume's epistemological principles and the
convictions which they are supposed to illuminate and explain. These
principles go as far as one can go, on the assumption that the mind's
direct and primitive objects are "single," autonomous impressions,
rather than sensible existents themselves. Hume himself detects the
implausibility of the resultant attempt to explain ordinary views about
the material world. For, it depicts that everyday realistic outlook as
being based entirely on a shaky supposition about perceptions,
rather than on the implications of the original existential judgment
about the sensible thing, grasped precisely as another act of existing.

2. *The Personal Self.* Hume agrees with his British predecessors
that a theory of self must be constructed in conformity with one's
theory of mind, but he takes a more radically phenomenalistic view of
mind than they do. *Mind* may be defined as "nothing but a heap or
collection of different perceptions, united together by certain relations,
and supposed, though falsely, to be endowed with a perfect simplicity
and identity. . . . [It is] that connected mass of perceptions, which

---

28 *A Treatise of Human Nature,* I, iv, 2 (Selby-Bigge, 217–18). In this passage,
Hume sounds a pragmatic note, testing even his own theories by their consequences
for life. Hume began with the traditional empiricist view that the worth of ideas
is determined by their *origin* in experience; but he came to see that, although all beliefs have some sort of empirical origin, they do not all have the same *consequences*
for experience. This shift from what William James called retrospective empiricism to a
prospective, pragmatic, or radical empiricism was never completed by Hume, who
remained skeptical in the face of the breakdown of the familiar empiricist principle, in
crucial cases. On the two empiricist strains in Hume's thought, see J. H. Randall, Jr.,
"David Hume: Radical Empiricist and Pragmatist," *Freedom and Experience* (edited
by S. Hook and M. R. Convitz), 289–312.

constitute a thinking being."[29] The *substantiality* of the mind is conspicuous by its absence from this definition. If by substance is meant something which may exist by itself, then (at least, as far as the free play of imagination is concerned) every distinct perception, being capable of separation and separate existence, is a genuine substance. But if substance is said to be something entirely different from a perception, then we can have no idea of its nature and cannot raise questions about the immateriality and substantiality of the soul. Contrary to Locke's and Berkeley's contention, Hume states that perceptions are grasped *as distinct objects,* and hence never convey to the mind any evidence about their manner of inherence in a subject or even about their need for such inherence. Hence causal inference is not justified in arguing from a requirement that is lacking in empirical meaning. In this clash of opinion among the empiricists, Hume is relying once more upon a strictly phenomenalistic approach to perceptions and upon his logical doctrine about distinct perceptions. Perceptions are distinct not only from each other but also from any subject and, indeed, from any reference to a subject of inherence. This *reification of perceptions* is the extreme consequence of the analytic method and the notion of a percept-object.

From the same standpoint, we are barred from attributing *simplicity* and *identity* to the mind. The idea of identity would have to rest upon some impression that remains invariant throughout a lifetime; the idea of simplicity would suppose that some impression reveals an indivisible center of union for the moments of experience. Neither of these conditions can be satisfied in terms of the Humean theory of knowledge. When I enter intimately into what I call *myself,* Hume says, I always stumble upon some particular perception. I never catch myself without some perception, and neither do I come upon myself as anything but a bundle or collection of different perceptions, each succeeding the other with inconceivable rapidity. In face of this situation, only one set of conclusions is possible for the Humean logic, based on the loosening of ideas. Since each perception is a distinct existent, no substance is needed; since the perceptions are all different and successive, there is no identity or invariant sameness of being; since the perceptions comprising the self are many, the self is not a simple thing.

---

[29] *A Treatise of Human Nature, loc. cit.* (Selby-Bigge, 207).

As usual, Hume employs this failure on the part of abstract reason as a recommendation that we seek a binding principle on the side of the "natural" forces, operating through imagination. Thought is under some kind of constraint to pass from one given perception to the next, and thus to generate the self through this continuous transition. The *personal self* arises when, in reflecting upon a past series of perceptions, we feel that one perception naturally introduces the next. Personal identity is a powerful fiction, aroused by the circumstance that imagination is able to pass smoothly from one perceptual object to the next, and hence comes to regard the series as invariable and uninterrupted. The similarity in the mind's *act of apprehending* the different perceptions instigates imagination to affirm a continuous identity of the self, on the side of the *objects perceived*. The easy transition is made under the associative force of resemblance and the natural relation of cause-and-effect. Thus the self is "a system of different perceptions or different existences, which are linked together by the relation of cause and effect, and mutually produce, destroy, influence, and modify each other."[30] *Memory* is the source of personal identity, insofar as it summons up images resembling past perceptions and grasps the causal succession of our perceptions, in the direction of the past. *Passion* and concern extend the same frame of causal reference forward as well as backward, strengthening the easy passage of thought and the reflective feeling that the perceptions belong to an identical, personal self.

For once, however, this counterprocess of binding together what empirical analysis has loosened, fails to achieve the kind of unity to which our experience bears testimony. Hume observes that he cannot find a satisfactory explanation of the feeling of *belongingness,* on the basis of which imagination declares that all our perceptions belong to the same personal self.

> In short there are two principles, which I cannot render consistent; nor is it in my power to renounce either of them, viz., *that all our distinct perceptions are distinct existences,* and *that the mind never perceives any real connexion among distinct existences.* Did our perceptions either inhere in something simple and individual, or did the mind perceive some real connexion among them, there would be no difficulty in the case. For my part, I must plead the privilege of a skeptic, and confess, that this difficulty is too hard for my understanding.[31]

---

30 *Ibid.,* I, iv, 6 (Selby-Bigge, 261).
31 *Ibid.,* Appendix (Selby-Bigge, 636).

This is a disarmingly frank passage. Hume concedes that an adequate synthesis of empirical findings about the personal self requires a knowledge of substance and objective causal connections, in respect to man. But his own first principle about distinct perceptions, leading as it does to a divorce of abstract reason from experience, prevents him from admitting the reality of *substance* in man. His second principle about real connections leads to his skeptical theory of relations and rules out any objectively given *causal principle,* operative in mental life. Nevertheless, he cannot avoid using substantial and causal terms, when he describes the self as a bundle and as a self-perpetuating series of perceptions. Although he warns against the imagery, he finds it convenient to compare the mind both to a *theater,* upon whose (substantial) stage various appearances are presented, and to a *republic* that perpetuates itself (causally) through the successive generations of its members.

The perceptions belonging to "our" mind are not an indiscriminate heap but constitute an ordered system. On the side of the cognitive acts themselves, these perceptions are already ordered by reference to "ourselves" and "our" imagination, even before Hume can apply his theory of how imagination produces the personal unity of the self. In order to give a plausible account of the association of perceptual objects, he covertly *presupposes some personal center of reference or intimate belongingness* for the perceiving operations. His empirical explanation of the self implies the effective presence of certain sub-stantial and causal factors, but his theory of knowledge prevents him from ever reconciling their reality with his own first principles.

Hume's passing remarks on immortality and freedom are consistent with his general view of knowledge and causality. No demonstration of *immortality* is possible, both because there is no clear idea of an immaterial, simple substance and because such demonstration would suppose that the causal principle can extend to a state that is, by definition, beyond present human experience. Hume admits that reason places man above the brutes but not that it guarantees his survival beyond this life. It is likely that man, like other animals, will lose consciousness and succumb to the universal frailty and dissolution of things. Neither immortality nor freedom has a bearing upon moral conduct, even if they could be established.

The only acceptable meaning of *freedom* is that of a power of acting or not acting, according to the determination of the will.[32]

[32] See *An Enquiry concerning Human Understanding,* Section VIII: "Of Liberty and

Hume defines the will — somewhat inconsistently, in view of his causal doctrine — as a cause or power giving rise to action. Hence it must conform with the general definition of a cause: it must have a *necessary* connection with its effect, the voluntary action. Since in his own system, the only ascertainable necessary connection is one established by imagination or habituated understanding, Hume stresses the necessity involved in *our knowledge* of human actions. Human history and practical wisdom reveal large uniformities in human conduct, based on a constant conjunction between certain motives and certain voluntary actions. Hence we customarily draw an inference from motives and circumstances to character and action. As for the subjective sense of freedom, Hume traces it to a feeling of looseness among ideas which sometimes steals over us, either when we reflect upon the past or when we are performing actions. The agent who feels his actions to be subject only to his will, and his will to be subject to no necessity, is simply overlooking his own motives, especially that of displaying freedom.

The curious turn of Hume's speculations on freedom indicates the straits in which he is placed, whenever he attempts to apply his general principles to any particular areas of our experience. He argues from a determination in the *spectator's knowledge* to a determinism of the *agent's conduct*. There are several reasons, however, why this inference cannot rule out freedom of choice. In the first place, Hume's causal doctrine maintains that the necessity of the connection involved in a causal inference has a *subjective* source, in the habits of mind generated in the observer through repetition of frequent conjunctions. Such repetition does not render any more intelligible or any more determined the nature of the objective relation between the things conjoined in a causal judgment. Hence a constantly observed conjunction between human motives and actions can generate a necessity on the observer's part, but this determination provides no ground for attributing any necessary connection between the action and the motives or circumstances affecting the agent himself. Second, the causal inference concerns matter of fact. Consequently, on Hume's own principles, the only type of necessity that is involved in historical and statistical inferences is a moral one. If such a moral necessity could be transferred from the associative habits of

---

Necessity" (Selby-Bigge, 80–103). That the foreseeability of some free acts does not destroy their freedom, is shown by Y. Simon, "On the Foreseeability of Free Acts," *The New Scholasticism*, XXII (1948), 357–70.

the spectator to the elections of the agent, it would not eliminate the free nature of the choice. Moral necessity has no more than a probable weight, and this *probability* is compatible with human freedom. Third, free choice is not eliminated by noting that human actions always have motives and that men often act in similar ways, in view of similar motives and circumstances. This observation is incompatible only with a position that identifies freedom with passive indifference and motiveless action. The point at issue is not the *presence* and influence of motives, but the precise *way* in which motives do influence the elective act. Finally, the remark that one's conviction of being free is explainable by the desire for a conspicuous display of freedom, raises the question of how the desire to display a nonexistent freedom can mysteriously arise in human experience. The personal conviction about freedom is not due to a vague feeling of looseness among ideas or a self-deceiving desire. It arises through reflection upon the actual exercise of reason's positive domination over its practical judgment, concerning motives and circumstances of action.

## 8. GOD AND RELIGION

Hume's *Dialogues concerning Natural Religion* deals mostly with the current proofs for God's existence. Clarke's statement of the proofs (*Discourse concerning the Being and Attributes of God,* 1705) is taken as the standard argument, and no attempt is made to examine more rigorous demonstrations. Clarke furnishes an a priori and an a posteriori proof. The so-called a priori one is a conflation of a number of current arguments. It states that every effect must have a cause, that we must come eventually to an uncaused cause of the whole series, and that this first cause must necessarily exist (since it contains within itself its own reason of being). The a posteriori argument is one from design (not the older teleological argument), in which the order, beauty, and harmony of the universe are cited as proof of the existence of an intelligent and benevolent Author of nature. As for their probative force, Clarke maintains that the first argument is as cogent and certain as the simplest mathematical proposition, and that the second is so obvious that no man can be excused from giving assent to it.

As usual, Hume concentrates upon the claim to *knowledge* of God's existence. He shows very easily the inaptness of the comparison between mathematical reasoning and the a priori proof, because of the *nonexistential* character of the mathematical type of inference.[33] Furthermore, he challenges the possibility of making any demonstration concerning such a matter of fact as God's existence. He declares that, for man, the words "necessary existence" are without consistent meaning and cannot signify the outcome of any demonstrative process. Nor can any a priori argument settle an existential question, which involves a bond among ideas that cannot be derived from mere analysis of their objective content. In short, the entire Humean doctrine on reasoning and causality prevents him from accepting Clarke's first argument.

The a posteriori *argument from design* elicits from him, however, a much more elaborate analysis. Since there can be no existential demonstration, probability is all that can be expected from this proof. It is a *proof from analogy,* using the general principle: like effects, like causes. The degree of probability depends upon the closeness of similarity between the effects. In this instance, the constitution of nature is regarded as being analogous to a work of human art, with the inference that there exists a divine maker somehow similar to the human artisan.

Hume follows several lines of attack upon this contention, perhaps the most serious of which is that even *analogical reasoning* is out of place.[34] For it employs the relation of cause-and-effect which, to serve as a basis of inference, must be established through repeated observation of the conjunction between the objects. Every causal inference deals with *species* of objects, where the objects may be observed several times in conjunction. But in the argument from design, the world as a whole is a *unique* effect, which we do not observe to be repeated elsewhere. Furthermore we have no experience of the origin of worlds, similar to our repeated experience of the origin of works of art. The universe is an unparalleled effect and, being without parallel, does not permit an inference based on the analogy between similar effects. Hume adds that the order observed in the world may well be due to some immanent principle of life or world

[33] *Dialogues concerning Natural Religion,* IX (Smith, 188–92).

[34] *Ibid.,* II (Smith, 149–50); on the probable character of "analogical reasoning," cf. *A Treatise of Human Nature,* I, iii, 12 (Selby-Bigge, 142). In the *Dialogues,* Hume had in mind not only Clarke but also Anglican Bishop Joseph Butler, author of the popular *Analogy of Religion* (1736). Hume reduced the import of analogical reasoning almost to the vanishing point, where it became indistinguishable from his own philosophical skepticism.

soul, rather than to a cosmic mechanic. Perhaps nature should be conceived as an animated whole, a great organism, rather than as a huge machine of the Newtonian type.

Nevertheless, Hume admits that, upon observation of nature as a whole, and especially of parts like the eye, we are carried along by the feeling that there is some vague likeness between the cause of the universe and human intelligence. Hume sides neither with dogmatic atheists, in their outright *denial* of God's existence, nor with Deistic and orthodox rationalists, in their claim to have strictly *rational demonstrations*. It is "nature" or *inward feeling* upon which we rely, when the idea of an intelligent, divine contriver strikes us with the strength of a sensation. On the basis of the operation of unknown, customary, practical forces in human nature, Hume admits that he is inclined to accept this proposition: *"The cause or causes of order in the universe probably bear some remote analogy to human intelligence."*[35] But he hedges in his acceptance with a number of provisos. First, this proposition is incapable of demonstration and attains only a degree of *probability,* under pressure of the feeling of its fitness. Next, although we can affirm the existence of the intelligent cause of the world, we can never penetrate to its essential nature. Its inner being will always remain mysterious and closed off from inspection, so that the analogy from experience cannot be rendered less remote and indefinite. Analogical inference never leads to knowledge of the moral qualities of the universal, ordering mind: only the *natural* attribute of intelligence is established. God's *moral* attributes of justice, benevolence, mercy, and rectitude may be compatible with the being of an infinite mind, but the world of our experience provides no ground for affirming them. The disorder and evil in the universe do not encourage the feeling that the cosmic mind is a moral agent.

This leads to the third and most important qualification attached to the above proposition, viz., that it can sustain no inference bearing

---

[35] *Dialogues concerning Natural Religion,* XII (Smith, 227). Because of its dialogue form, this book does not reveal Hume's position in unequivocal fashion. The principle of interpretation used here is that, whereas the orthodox Demea of the *Dialogues* in no way reflects Hume's own mind, the author's attitude is expressed mainly by the moderate skeptic, Philo, and by Cleanthes, in the degree that the latter champions the promptings of nature. For other interpretations, see N. K. Smith's Introduction to his edition of the *Dialogues,* E. C. Mossner's "The Enigma of Hume," *Mind,* N.S., XLV (1936), 334-49, and B. M. Laing's "Hume's *Dialogues concerning Natural Religion,*" *Philosophy* XII (1937), 175-90.

on human life and specific plans of action or forbearance. Only a "plain, philosophical assent," *purely theoretical in import,* can be given to the statement about God's existence. This is of the greatest moment for Hume, since it enables him at one stroke to define true religion, criticize existing religions, and keep religion entirely apart from morality. Belief in the existence of a supreme, intelligent mind may be called the religious hypothesis, but no new fact can ever be inferred from this hypothesis and no practical decision affected by it. In this sense, Hume speaks of *true religion* as being a species of philosophy: it is a cognitive assent to God's existence (under the above conditions), and nothing more. Philosophical religion admits no revelation, no rites, no miracles, no special merit or demerit, no distinctively religious duties or feelings. It consists entirely and exclusively in the empirical, speculative assent to theism, without entailing any repercussions upon human conduct.

Obviously, this rarefied attitude will always be confined to the few and is a far cry from what is usually called religion. In his *Natural History of Religion,* Hume attempted to trace back the popular conception of religion to its sources in human nature, as he has described it. *Religion* is not universal and uniform enough to be a primary instinct of man, but it is founded upon such primary passions as his fear of natural disaster and his hope for betterment. These passions are not themselves specifically religious, but become so when they are directed toward a certain object: an *invisible, intelligent power.* Religious feelings develop from the responses of hope-and-fear to belief in this object. Hume thought that religions were originally polytheistic and that they only gradually hit upon the notion of one, infinite power. Religious monotheism happens to coincide with the best philosophical view of God. But Hume's early training was such that he could never think about actual religions in an objective and balanced spirit. He constantly warned against their "superstition and fanaticism," refusing to tolerate any alliance between organized religion and philosophy.

Hume's theory of God and religion has a sharply limited theoretical range and yet has exercised great historical influence. As a criticism of the theistic arguments popular in Newtonian circles, it exposes their lack of logical rigor and their failure to secure any metaphysical foundations. Clarke offers no adequate defense of causality and no theory of existential demonstration. He fails to present a thoroughgoing a posteriori demonstration, based upon causation, contingency, and finality. Hume, in turn, gives such arguments no attention, on the ground that they are ruled out, in principle, by his previous treatment of demonstration, existence, and causality. Any fundamental criticism of his position must make a similar return to these underlying epistemological and metaphysical issues, especially to the nature of existential demonstration and the application of the causal principle to beings in their own reality (and not merely to our percepts). Furthermore, the distinction must be underlined between the Thomistic metaphysical doctrine on the analogical predication of being and the meaning of analogy found in Butler, Clarke, and Hume. The latter thinkers regard analogical reasoning as a manner of making loose comparisons, based on a fairly wide sampling of instances. As so defined, it could never be employed in strict demonstration but must be reserved for probable reasoning. Hume's suggestion that even analogical reasoning to God's existence is illegitimate, because of its application of the relation of cause-and-effect to the unique act of creation, is illuminating. For it is a reminder that Hume's "natural relation" of cause-and-effect rests upon the mechanism of repetition and habit, rather than upon intellectual apprehension of the essential dependence-for-being of one existent thing upon another. Clearly, the major problem lies in Hume's general conception of cause rather than  in his particular application of it to inference about God's existence.

Hume's notion of religion marks a turning point from Deism to  some of the later naturalistic tendencies in the philosophy of religion. He completed the process of reducing religion to its natural, philosophical content. At the same time, he disagreed with the Deists about the exact nature of that content. Belief in God rests on feeling,  imagination, and custom, rather than on abstract reason. To this extent, Hume prepared the way for the nineteenth-century stress upon the *emotional bases* of the religious attitude. But he refused to allow any practical influence to be exerted by the religious hypothesis. It is a belief generated by feeling and yet restricted to the speculative order, like so many other convictions that have a similar origin in the natural forces of the mind. By refusing to permit belief in an infinite mind to serve as a legitimate, animating principle of human conduct, Hume gave new impetus to two historical trends. He contributed toward the gradual *severance* of religious motives from the  central concerns of a secular, Western civilization, and he prepared for a *naturalistic morality* entirely divorced from religious considerations. Although he realized that this quarantine of religion can never be made complete, Hume did his best to reduce the area of religion's effectiveness, by suggesting that the affairs of life can be organized without reference to God, whose existence is likely but whose moral nature remains completely enigmatic to men. Conversely, any effective restoration of theistic and religious influences in our present world depends, in some measure, upon showing that human knowledge is not confined within the limits set by Hume's empiricist premises.

## 9. PASSIONS AND MORAL PRINCIPLES

Although later philosophers have given the lion's share of their attention to Hume's theory of the understanding, he himself regarded his theory of the passions and morals as the goal and completion of his philosophy of human nature. In a way, his moral doctrine is the answer to a dare, formulated in the speculative portions of his thought: Granted that we cannot base our actions upon an afterlife, freedom, or God — nevertheless show that human life can be conducted wisely and well. Hume accepts this challenge by rounding out his chain of reasoning and system of the sciences with a theory of passions and morals.

Hume is confident that the Newtonian method of experimental reasoning can be extended into the region of the *passions*.[36] He supposes them to be governed by a regular mechanism, which permits one to explain them by means of a few, general principles. The passions are taken to be natural states, in the sense of being fairly constant and uniform, not only within one individual's experience but also among all men. The distinction between primary impressions of sensation and secondary impressions of reflection may now be put to a new use. For among the *primary impressions* are included not only sensory data but also bodily *pleasures* and *pains,* due directly to the operation of physical causes in the world. And the *secondary impressions* (derived either from primary ones or from their ideas) consist not only in the dispositions bearing on causal inference but also in the *passions.* Although derivative in nature, the passions are also original impressions, insofar as they are complete and nonrepresentative states. They may be divided into the *direct* and the *indirect passions,* depending upon whether they arise from

---

[36] Through application of the few, simple laws of association to the passions, Hume hoped to effect a Copernican revolution in moral philosophy; cf. *A Treatise of Human Nature,* II, i, 3–4 (Selby-Bigge, 282–84).

feelings of pleasure and pain or require the aid of some other qualities.

In treating of the *direct passions,* Hume speaks very briefly of some few that "arise from a natural impulse or instinct, which is perfectly unaccountable."[37] Our desire for an enemy's punishment or a friend's happiness is a primitive passion that precedes any particular experience of pleasure or pain, and that is, indeed, productive of such feelings. We have to exercise basic impulses of this sort in order to discover, through experience, what things satisfy or thwart them. For the most part, however, the direct passions do follow, naturally and with comparatively little preparation, from the pleasure and pain (i.e., good and evil), which we undergo or consider. Desire and aversion, grief and joy, hope and fear, are passions of this sort, moving a man by a direct and original instinct. Despite their importance as components of our passional life, Hume does not analyze them in much detail. His general principles of association and sympathy are better displayed in the growth of the indirect passions, upon which he bestows his main attention.

To treat of the *indirect passions* and their attendant qualities, Hume makes use of his phenomenalistic notions of self and cause. For, he finds that passions always have an object and a cause. There is an unmistakable difference between the *cause* or idea that arouses a passion, and the *object* toward which the passion, so excited, is directed. From the standpoint of their object, the indirect passions are divided into *self-regarding* and *other-regarding* ones. The object of the indirect passions of pride and humility is the self, i.e., "that succession of related ideas and impressions, of which we have an intimate memory and consciousness."[38] In the case of the indirect passions of love and hatred, the object is some person other than the self. The direction of these various passions to their respective objects is not only a *natural* (steady and universal) property but also an *original* one, a primary ordination that Hume does not care to resolve into anything more simple. Although all the causes of the passions are natural, they are not all original. We can think of a thousand causes — many of them produced by human art or good fortune — that lead us to feel pride and the other passions. But all the causes of passions share in common two general traits: the production of pleasure or pain, and a reference to ourselves or others. Now it happens that the passions themselves have two corresponding properties: their very

---

[37] *Ibid.,* II, iii, 9 (Selby-Bigge, 439).
[38] *Ibid.,* II, i, 2 (Selby-Bigge, 277).

essence is to be *a pleasant or painful sensation* and their orientation is *toward oneself or others.*

Hume does not attempt further analysis of this happy correspondence between the properties of the causes of passions and the properties of passions themselves. He accepts it as a descriptively ultimate fact, so that he may apply to it his *principles of association* and thus construct a *system* of the passions. There is a correlation between a double set of ideas and impressions, permitting an easy transition and blending to be made, on the basis of the resemblances within the two sequences. The cause of the passion is directed to the very same idea or object to which the passion itself is naturally ordained: the self or some other person. Similarly, the impression or sensation produced independently by the cause of the passion is a pleasure or pain, which therefore resembles the passion itself. Through a mutual reinforcement of the two associative bonds among ideas and passions, the mind is given a *double impulse.* This accounts for the passional strength of anything that both conveys pleasure or pain and also bears a reference to oneself or another. There is an easy transition from one idea to the next (the ideas acquiring vivacity from association with the impressions), and from one passion to the next. Once a passion is aroused, it is likely to call forth a whole train of similar ones, especially under the influence of the mind's consideration of various aspects and relations of the causes and objects involved.

Another major factor, along with the association of resembling ideas and passions, is the operation of *sympathy,* taken not only in the restricted sense of benevolence but also as a general ability to appreciate the similar feelings transpiring within other selves.[39] The individual is not constitutionally egoistic — on this point, Hume agrees with the criticism of Hobbes made by Hutcheson and the Moral Sense School. The individual has an ardent desire for society and a capacity to imagine how others are feeling. There is a sort of psychic contagion, by which a sentiment may run from one man to another. From the appearances of another, I can gain an idea of what he seems to be feeling. By bringing this idea into relation with my own self, it acquires the liveliness of an impression. Thus it arouses similar passions within myself, although always sympathetically, with regard to the other person and his passional state. Although admitting that

---

[39] *A Treatise of Human Nature,* II, i, 11; III, iii, 1 (Selby-Bigge, 316–24, 575–78); *An Enquiry concerning the Principles of Morals,* II (Selby-Bigge, 176–82).

his system of basic self-regarding and other-regarding passions requires many qualifications, Hume believed that its principles can account for the most subtle complexities of our emotional attitudes.

One consequence of this theory is that the rationalistic view of the pre-eminence of *reason over passion* must be abandoned. Like Hutcheson, Hume has in view an abstract sort of reason, modeled along mathematical lines and reliant solely upon general definitions and eternal verities, in dealing with practical problems. Clearly, such a reason is proximately unfitted for making practical decisions. By itself, this purely speculative reason can never provide a sufficiently powerful motive for will and cannot oppose passion. Hume admits that reason (taken in a more concrete and practical way) can exert an oblique or mediate influence upon the passions. But it does so only by directing the passions toward other causal relations and objects or by opening up new possibilities, rather than by producing original, practical impulses of its own. Only a contrary impulse can oppose a passion: hence it is meaningless to speak of the conflict between reason and passion. Even at its most effective, *"reason is, and ought only to be, the slave of the passions,* and can never pretend to any other office than to serve and obey them."[40] It may be an enlightened and privileged servitor, working along with the passions in an advisory and guiding capacity. But of itself, reason cannot be an original passional power, such that to think of a proper course of action is to execute it in fact.

Despite his extreme language, Hume is moving here toward a moderate position that recognizes the guiding function of practical reason, the distinctive contribution of the appetitive powers, and the need for the mutual impenetration of reason and the appetitive powers in human conduct. But he is hindered from achieving a balance among these factors, because of his denial of free choice, his preoccupation with the rationalistic view of reason, and his own difficulties about the relation between reason and experience. Hence he tends to give a watered-down conception of reason in its moral function, coalescing it with the relatively mild and moderate passions. The practical reduction of reason to the mild passions corresponds to the speculative reduction of reason to imagination. In neither case does Hume preserve the distinctive role of reason in human experience.

---

[40] *A Treatise of Human Nature*, II, iii, 3 (Selby-Bigge, 415; italics added).

Hume repudiated the view of Locke, Clarke, and Wollaston that ethical and mathematical reasoning are basically the same. Ethics has an *existential* bearing and, therefore, is nonmathematical and non-demonstrative. Like Hutcheson again, Hume emphasized the *empirical* and *probable* character of moral science (as the study of practical matters of fact), as well as the need to base moral judgments on another basis than abstract reason. Moral distinctions are not grounded primarily upon an eternal fitness of things but upon a *moral sense,* with which reason must co-operate.[41] In pronouncing an action virtuous or vicious, we rely upon the constitution of our own nature, which supplies the sentiment of approval or disapproval, satisfaction or uneasiness. Fortunately, this moral sense has been uniformly distributed among men, so that *universal* valuation, and not mere individual preference, is expressed in its judgments. Moreover, although the moral approval or disapproval is a matter of pleasure or pain, it is also a sentiment that considers the action or character of others for their own sake and apart from our individual interest. Thus a certain *impartiality* is achieved, along with the universality. By making these suppositions about the moral sense, Hume sought to avoid the moral subjectivism toward which the theory leads.

We give our moral approval either to what is immediately agreeable to ourselves or others, or else to what is useful to ourselves or others. Actions or characters that give us *pleasure* by their mere sight may be termed *virtuous* or morally good. But since moral approbation is based on agreement of an action with human sentiment, *utility* can also be used as a criterion of virtue.[42] In judging what is useful, reason is helpful, since it provides information about the various means at hand and takes account of the long-range bent of our passions. Sympathy, for instance, works hand-in-hand with self-interest. We have a native sense of humanity or fellow-feeling, which sympathy cultivates to the point of approving not only what is personally useful but also what is of public utility. The whole *system of justice,* contracts, property, and the state, arises artificially from human self-interest. But when we see that these arrangements affect the happiness of humanity at large, we are moved to an immediate, sympathetic response of pleasure or misery, approbation or disapprobation.

---

[41] *Ibid.,* III, i, 2 (Selby-Bigge, 470–76); *An Enquiry concerning the Principles of Morals,* I, and Appendix I (Selby-Bigge, 170–75, 285–94).

[42] *A Treatise of Human Nature,* III, iii, 1 (Selby-Bigge, 578–91); *An Enquiry concerning the Principles of Morals,* V (Selby-Bigge, 212–32).

In this way, social arrangements are estimated as being virtuous or vicious. Despite the *conventional* origin of our several obligations in justice, they are a continuation of natural tendencies and win approval at once, within a settled society. Guided by reason, sympathy educates and strengthens the other-regarding impulses, so that the moral sense may include general approval of the interests of others on a social scale. The actions of men in society come to have moral significance through this immediate response of pleasure or displeasure, aroused by a contemplation of them.

Hume's ethics was transitional between the moral sense theories and the full-blown utilitarianism of Bentham and Mill. His adaptation of Hutcheson's view of moral sense enabled him to break with an ethics of abstract rules and eternal definitions, and to look for moral qualities in what affects our passions and impulses. But he did not think that there is a special sense, having as its object a special "moral" quality of things. Rather, he located moral distinctions in the impact of actions and characters upon our basic concerns, as expressed in a sentiment of agreeableness or disagreeableness. Utilitarianism looms on the horizon as an explanation of the good in terms of maximum happiness for the individual and society. But for Hume, utility and happiness are not sufficient measures of the moral good, unless they are integrated with a certain *contemplation* and *approval* of the springs of action leading to happiness, private and social. Kant's dissatisfaction with the Humean solution of the moral problem arose precisely at this juncture. For he was unable to see how approval of the agreeable can serve as a properly moral criterion, especially in situations where there is a conflict between agreeableness and obligation. Kant acknowledged that the feeling of approbation is a companion of moral judgment and action. But he pointed out that this accompanying circumstance does not establish the objectively valid principles upon which moral distinctions are based and in the light of which a man can choose a model or moral exemplar. The opposition between the Kantian ethic of duty and the utilitarian ethic of maximal happiness stems from their diverse estimations of Hume's account of moral judgments.

## SUMMARY OF CHAPTER 10

Hume wanted to take the castle of human nature by storm, with the aid of the Newtonian method. He agreed with his empiricist predecessors that the immediate objects of the mind are its own contents or perceptions.

But he added the qualification, taken from Newton, that scientific method cannot presume to give any knowledge about spiritual or material substances or any extramental order of essential causes. For a radical phenomenalism, our perceptions and their subjective connections are all that we can hope to know. Yet just as Newton was able to formulate uniform laws for all physical appearances, so Hume proposed the mechanical laws of association as regulative of all mental appearances. He distinguished between philosophical and natural relations, since some comparisons among ideas involve no connecting principle, whereas others rest upon a connecting bond. The philosophical relation of cause-and-effect has no independent status; its constitutive ideas are perfectly loose and provide no basis for metaphysical inferences beyond experience. Causal inferences are based upon the natural relation of cause-and-effect, in which the connecting bond must be traced back to custom or the influence of the laws of association on the imagination. Since the ideas of cause and effect are joined together only on the subjective basis of customary association, the inference has only subjective validity. Hume applied this conclusion rigorously to our inferences about external bodies and the personal self. Nevertheless, he was dissatisfied with his own atomistic view of the self as a congeries of perceptions, since his experience seemed to imply a knowledge of the substantial unity and causal power of the self, which his principles would not allow. He admitted a loose inference to the existence of a supreme intelligence but restricted religion to a purely speculative recognition of this intelligence, having no practical import. His theory of the passions extended mechanism into the affective order and assigned a subordinate role to reason. Hume sought associative ways of cultivating our other-regarding impulses, so that the social system itself might have a basis in the stable, customary laws of human nature.

# BIBLIOGRAPHICAL NOTE

1. *Sources.* There is no collected edition of Hume's works. A collection of his philosophical writings was edited by T. H. Green and T. H. Grose, *The Philosophical Works of David Hume* (4 vols., London, Longmans, Green, 1874–1875); this edition was reprinted in two series: Vols. I and II appeared as *A Treatise on Human Nature and Dialogues concerning Natural Religion* (2 vols., New York, Longmans, Green, 1909), whereas Vols. III and IV were issued separately as *Essays Moral, Political and Literary* (2 vols., New York, Longmans, Green, 1898). The Green-Grose edition is accompanied by Preliminary Dissertations and Notes, written from the standpoint of idealism, which triumphed over empiricism in England, during the latter part of the nineteenth century. Apart from this interest, it is customary today to refer to the two following editions, prepared by L. A. Selby-Bigge: *A Treatise of Human Nature* (Oxford, Clarendon, 1888); *Enquiries concerning the Human Understanding and concerning the Principles of Morals* (second ed., Oxford, Clarendon, 1902). These Selby-Bigge editions are distinguished by fulsome analytic indexes. For

Hume's own summary of the *Treatise*, see *An Abstract of a Treatise of Human Nature, 1740,* edited by J. M. Keynes and P. Sraffa (Cambridge, University Press, 1938). N. K. Smith's edition of *Dialogues concerning Natural Religion* (second ed., New York, Nelson, 1947) includes Hume's autobiography, *My Own Life,* and the editor's helpful analysis of his philosophy of religion. See also the J. Y. T. Greig edition of *The Letters of David Hume* (2 vols., Oxford, Clarendon, 1932), the R. Klibansky and E. C. Mossner edition of *New Letters of David Hume* (Oxford, Clarendon, 1954), and E. C. Mossner, "Hume's Early Memoranda, 1729–40: The Complete Text," *Journal of the History of Ideas,* IX (1948), 492–518.

2. *Studies.* The best biography is E. C. Mossner, *The Life of David Hume* (Austin, University of Texas Press, 1954); still useful is J. Y. Greig, *David Hume* (New York, Oxford University Press, 1931). Three introductory studies, in the order of their increasing difficulty, are: D. G. MacNabb, *David Hume: His Theory of Knowledge and Morality* (London, Hutchinson, 1951); B. M. Laing, *David Hume* (London, Benn, 1932); J. Laird, *Hume's Philosophy of Human Nature* (London, Metheun, 1932). To these may be added N. K. Smith's *The Philosophy of David Hume: A Critical Study of its Origins and Central Doctrines* (London, Macmillan, 1941), which stresses Hume's moral preoccupations and dependence upon the Scottish ethician, Francis Hutcheson; see also, R. Metz, *David Hume, Leben und Philosophie* (Stuttgart, Frommann, 1929), an unusually complete, synthetic study. Among the best accounts of Hume's epistemology are: R. W. Church, *Hume's Theory of the Understanding* (Ithaca, Cornell University Press, 1935); C. Maund, *Hume's Theory of Knowledge* (New York, Macmillan, 1937); H. H. Price, *Hume's Theory of the External World* (Oxford, Clarendon, 1940). In compensation for an earlier tendency to divorce Hume's theory of knowledge from the rest of his system, several scholars have concentrated upon the close relation between the theoretical and practical sides of his mind. N. K. Smith, *The Philosophy of David Hume,* contends that moral issues govern Hume's position in theory of knowledge; J. A. Passmore, *Hume's Intentions* (Cambridge, University Press, 1952), views his work mainly as a defense of the validity of the moral sciences of man. See also, R. M. Kydd, *Reason and Conduct in Hume's Treatise* (New York, Oxford, 1946), and A. B. Glathe, *Hume's Theory of the Passions and of Morals* (Berkeley, University of California Press, 1950); Glathe sharply challenges the thesis of N. K. Smith concerning the primacy of moral philosophy in determining the Humean epistemology. On Hume's religious position, see C. W. Hendel, *Studies in the Philosophy of David Hume* (Princeton, Princeton University Press, 1925), and A. Leroy, *La critique et la religion chez David Hume* (Paris, Alcan, 1930). Both authors stress the continuity between his general doctrine on cognition and the passions and his stand on religion. The contemporary currents of thought contributing to Hume's outlook are described by M. S. Kuypers, *Studies in the Eighteenth-Century Background of Hume's Empiricism* (Minneapolis, University of Minnesota Press, 1930),

and (more generally) by B. Willey, *The Eighteenth Century Background* (New York, Columbia University Press, 1941). Willey investigates the contemporary meanings of that mysterious Humean term "nature." In *Nicolaus of Autrecourt, A Study in 14th Century Thought* (Princeton, Princeton University Press, 1948), J. R. Weinberg portrays the medieval nominalist, Nicholas of Autrecourt, as a forerunner of Hume.

3. *British Moralists and Scottish Realists.* A comprehensive anthology of British moral philosophy was prepared by L. A. Selby-Bigge: *British Moralists* (2 vols., Oxford, Clarendon, 1897), which includes long extracts from Shaftesbury, Hutcheson, Butler, Adam Smith, Bentham, Clarke, Richard Price, and Balguy. See J. Bonar, *Moral Sense* (New York, Macmillan, 1930), and D. D. Raphael, *The Moral Sense* (Oxford, Clarendon, 1947). There are three recent, competent studies on Bishop Butler: E. C. Mossner, *Bishop Butler and the Age of Reason* (New York, Macmillan, 1936); W. J. Norton, *Bishop Butler: Moralist and Divine* (New Brunswick, Rutgers University Press, 1940); A. Duncan-Jones, *Butler's Moral Philosophy* (Baltimore, Penguin Books, 1952). On Hume's Scottish friend, Hutcheson, see W. R. Scott, *Francis Hutcheson* (Cambridge, University Press, 1900). Convenient source materials on the Scottish School can be found in *Selections from the Scottish Philosophy of Common Sense* (Chicago, Open Court, 1915). One of the last representatives in America of the Scottish School, James McCosh, has outlined the doctrines of the main representatives: *The Scottish Philosophy* (London, Macmillan, 1875); on the leading mind in this movement, Thomas Reid, see A. C. Fraser, *Thomas Reid* (New York, Scribner, 1898). For a suggestive comparison between the Thomistic and Scottish meanings of "common sense," see P. J. Jacoby, *"Common Sense" in Epistemology* (University of Notre Dame dissertation, 1942); also, D. J. B. Hawkins, *The Criticism of Experience* (New York, Sheed and Ward, 1945). The main teachings of this school are restated in analytic terms in S. A. Grave, *The Scottish Philosophy of Common Sense* (Oxford, Clarendon Press, 1960).

4. *Further Studies.* A.-L. Leroy's *David Hume* (Paris, Presses Universitaires, 1953) shows the centrality of Hume's theory of human nature as the basis for a tentative empiricism of actual human beliefs and actions, a standpoint whose influence is described by F. Zabeeh, *Hume, Precursor of Modern Empiricism* (Hague, Nijhoff, 1961).

# Chapter 11. KANT ON KNOWLEDGE AND METAPHYSICS

## I. LIFE AND WRITINGS

IMMANUEL KANT was born at Königsberg in 1724 and never traveled beyond his native East Prussia. His father was a humble saddler and the family lived in straitened circumstances. But Kant received an upright home training in Pietism, a religious movement stressing personal fervor, moral responsibility, and endeavor. At the local high school (*Collegium Fridericianum*), which he attended from 1732 until 1740, Kant was given further instruction in Pietism, of a strict and formalized sort, and in the classical languages. Upon his entrance to the University of Königsberg (1740), he came under the influence of Martin Knutzen, professor of logic and metaphysics, whose lectures covered the whole field of philosophy, the natural sciences, and mathematics. Kant was given the run of Knutzen's library, which was well stocked with the latest scientific treatises, especially works of the Newtonian school. Although Pietism and Wolffian philosophy were the ruling viewpoints at the university, Kant's scientific readings enabled him to cultivate independence of thought, in the spirit of the Enlightenment. For several years after leaving the university, he served as tutor in various East Prussian homes and continued his philosophic and scientific studies. His *Thoughts on the True Estimation of Living Forces* (1747) and *General Natural History and Theory of the Heavens* (1755) showed his ability to deal respectively with the calculation of the force of a body in motion and with the natural genesis of our universe. (Kant advanced an independent, speculative version of the nebular hypothesis.) In 1755, Kant received the equivalent of the doctorate for a scientific treatise on fire, and was recognized as a *Privatdozent* or lecturer at the University of Königsberg, after submitting an essay entitled *A New Exposition of the First Principles of Metaphysical Knowledge*. Although written from the rationalistic standpoint, this essay criticized Leibniz and Wolff on some crucial points, concerning the principle of sufficient reason and intellectual knowledge. Kant's readings in Newton and Christian Crusius (an anti-Wolffian theologian at Leipzig) convinced him that philosophy must pattern itself after the model of physics rather than pure mathematics. This thesis was vigorously defended in his prize essay, *An Inquiry into the Distinctness of the Fundamental Principles of Natural Theology and Morals* (1764); its skeptical consequences for metaphysics were tentatively explored in *Dreams of a Spirit-Seer Illustrated by the Dreams of Metaphysics* (1766), a *jeu d'esprit* penned against the pretensions of Swedenborg to give detailed knowledge about the afterlife and against the equally ungrounded pretensions of the rationalistic metaphysicians.

The Kant of the 1760's was not an academic recluse but a quite sociable man, eagerly sought after for dinner parties, because of his witty conversation. He liked the company of merchants, seamen, and booksellers, who opened out his frontiers in the way that the grand tour had served to broaden the outlook of a Hobbes. And from the testimony of Herder, who was his student during this period, it is clear that Kant's lectures were well prepared, stimulative of independent thinking, and not lacking in literary grace, classical quotation, and topical reference. As a *Privatdozent,* he lectured on a wide range of subjects, extending from his central courses on logic, metaphysics, and ethics to physical geography, anthropology, mathematics, physics, and mechanics. The courses in geography and anthropology were intended not only for cultured people and officers stationed at Königsberg but also for philosophical students, so that they might gain a proper respect for the factual basis of speculation. Adhering to Prussian educational requirements, Kant always used Wolffian textbooks: Meier in logic, and Baumgarten in metaphysics and ethics. But they served more as the point of departure for his discussion than as a norm for his judgments. The British moralists (particularly Shaftesbury, Hutcheson, and Hume) showed him that morality is a matter of sentiment and inclination, as well as of rational inference. Upon their publication, he hailed Rousseau's *Julie or the New Heloïse* and *Émile* as revelations of the true dignity of the individual and the presence of the moral law in human nature. When Leibniz' *New Essays* finally appeared in 1765, it strengthened Kant's interest in the problem of the a priori factor in knowledge, just as the sections on Plato in Brucker's *Critical History of Philosophy* focused his attention upon the problem of the intelligible world. Thus the 1760's marked a decade of intense intellectual ferment for Kant, culminating in the "great light" received around 1769. This illumination enabled him to see that the antinomies in which the metaphysical mind becomes involved can be removed, once the distinction between the sensible and intelligible world, the phenomenal and noumenal orders, is acknowledged.

This basic distinction, together with the consequent doctrine of the ideal nature of the forms of space and time and their restriction to phenomena, formed the core of Kant's *Dissertation on the Form and Principles of the Sensible and Intelligible World,* issued in 1770, upon the occasion of his long-delayed appointment as professor of logic and metaphysics at Königsberg. The next decade was a time of silent gestation, during which Kant painfully thought out the critical problem and its implications. About 1772, the remembrance of what he had read earlier in Hume aroused him from a "dogmatic slumber," i.e., it dawned upon him that if Hume's analysis of the causal connection were correct, it could be generalized in such fashion as to undermine not only metaphysics but also mathematical and physical sciences. Kant did not feel that he had the solution to the critical problem, until he could both justify the latter sciences and yet give good reasons for jettisoning a speculative, transcendent metaphysics. This he did in the *Critique of Pure Reason* (first edition or edition A, 1781; second edition or edition B, 1787). Because of some misunderstandings about his relation to idealism and other points connected with the first *Critique,* Kant published the *Prolegomena to Any Future Metaphysics* (1783), as an introduction to the critical standpoint for teachers of philosophy. A sketch of his moral position was provided in *Foundations of the Metaphysics of Morals* (1785), which was followed by his major ethical work, the *Critique of Practical Reason* (1788). The critical trilogy was rounded out with the *Critique of Judgment* (1790), a study of esthetic factors and purposiveness in nature.

Kant's *Religion within the Limits of Reason Alone* (1793) was the only book that brought him into conflict with the civil authorities. Frederick the Great's successor, Frederick William II, criticized Kant's unorthdox religious views and obtained from him a promise (1794) to remain silent on theological matters, even though Kant pointed out that his doctrines were intended only for mature scholars. After the king's death, Kant felt himself released from this personal promise

and took up the theological question again in a work on "the conflict of the faculties" in German universities. Another product of his
later years was the political essay on *Perpetual Peace* (1795), in which
he affirmed the need for republican government and international law,
as counterprinciples to war. In 1796, Kant retired from active teaching. He was working away intrepidly at a complete restatement of
his philosophy, in view of recent developments made by Fichte and
the young idealistic movement, when death interrupted his labors
(1804). These last notes, which betrayed the struggle between his
mind and old age, were later published as the *Opus Postumum*
(1920, 1938).

## 2. FROM DOGMATISM TO CRITICISM: THE
## PRE-CRITICAL PERIOD

Kant often reduced philosophical development to *three stages*:
dogmatism, skepticism, and criticism.[1] He saw these three phases
exemplified not only in the general history of philosophy but also
in his own mental evolution. He began with the rationalism of Leibniz
and Wolff, called this doctrine in question with the aid of empirical
currents of thought, and gradually arrived at a distinctively critical
position. There never was a time when he was wholly satisfied with
dogmatic rationalism, nor was there a time when he succumbed
entirely to the skeptical mood or the empirical viewpoint. The two
motives of *rationalism* and *empiricism* interplayed constantly in his
mind during the *pre-critical* period: the formative years preceding the
appearance of the basic *Inaugural Dissertation* of 1770. He came
to formulate the basic philosophical problems in such a way as to
synthesize both the rational and the empirical aspects of his mind.
Yet his critical philosophy was not a mere blending, but a radical
reconstitution, of the elements provided by the previous century of
modern speculation.

One major problem was to determine the extent of the contribution
of *sense experience* to knowledge. There were several indications in
Leibniz and Wolff that this contribution is a considerable, if not
altogether fundamental, one. Leibniz' distinction between necessary
truths of essence and contingent truths of fact was an admission of

---

1 *Critique of Pure Reason*, A 761: B 789 (Smith translation, 607). It is customary
to cite the *Critique of Pure Reason* according to the original pagination of the first
edition ("A" 1781) and the second edition ("B" 1787).

some considerable difference between knowledge based on purely intellectual grounds and that which requires some sort of collaboration of the senses. Similarly, Wolff popularized the division of philosophical sciences into their empirical and rational branches. He even recognized that the starting point of reasoning about grounds and principles is found in experiential knowledge of facts. But these concessions were not permitted to disturb the claim that, in principle, reason can overcome its empirical dependencies. The rationalists sought to uncover a necessary factor at the core of sensation itself, and thus to prepare for an a priori understanding of real things through their ultimate sufficient reasons. In effect, this would nullify the role of sense experience, by reducing its deliverances to a confused manner of presenting the same truths that reason itself can establish in a clear and distinct way.

One way to test the rationalistic claim to subsume experience within necessary principles was to examine its position in *natural philosophy*. In this procedure, Kant followed the lead of Christian Crusius, who had contrasted the success of Newton's experimental philosophy with the questionable results of Cartesian-Leibnizian physics. As Kant saw it, the most significant feature of this contrast lay not so much in the failure of rationalism to explain particular phenomena of weight, force, and movement, as in its underlying methodological mistake. He traced the weaknesses in rationalistic physics to its excessive reliance upon mathematical and deductive methods, whereas the success of Newtonian dynamics stemmed from its appeal to observation and experiment, as the indispensable means of verifying and controlling mathematical inferences.

This led Kant to give a detailed account of the differences in procedure between pure mathematics and philosophy of nature.[2] The former is a synthetic discipline, whereas the latter is an analytic science. The *mathematical* method of *synthesis* starts with clear definitions, expressing a rule or set of directions. By following the operational definition, an adequate concept is formed. The concept is expressed in a sign, the precise meaning of which is unambiguously determined by the definition itself. Since the objects of pure mathe-

---

[2] See *An Inquiry into the Distinctness of the Principles of Natural Theology and Morals*, I (Beck translation, in *Critique of Practical Reason and Other Writings in Moral Philosophy*, 262–68); *Critique of Pure Reason*, A 712–36: B 740–64 (Smith, 576–91). For a study of these diverse methods (based upon the texts in the first *Critique*), cf. C. D. Broad, "Kant's Theory of Mathematical and Philosophical Reasoning," *Proceedings of the Aristotelian Society*, N.S., XLII (1941–1942), 1–24.

matics are ideal ones, the mind can construct them in a synthetic way. It can also make a complete substitution of mathematical signs for the objects. The mind can reason directly with the concrete symbols, and intuitively discern the universal relations, as expressed in the signs. Newtonian physics or *natural philosophy* follows the opposite path of *analysis*. Its basic concepts are given in sense experience, rather than generated by a defined rule. Hence the starting points in experimental philosophy are confused and indistinct notions, which stand in need of clarification. Definitions are attained only at the terminus of the inferential process in natural philosophy, instead of at the beginning. Moreover, the natural philosopher employs language or merely verbal signs, which do not give a concrete picture of the elements and relations in the definition. He can never perceive his conclusions in the signs themselves; hence he must deal abstractly with universal notions and keep the real things of sense always in view. There is no concrete intuition of the universal available for him in the verbal marks.

From this comparison, Kant concluded that *philosophy as a whole must follow the method of physics rather than that of mathematics.* For, everywhere in philosophy, the initial concepts are many, confused, and difficult to grasp, rather than few, distinctly understood, and unambiguous. Hence Kant challenged Wolff's repeated assertion that philosophy can be rendered scientific only by entering on the path of mathematics. A test case was presented by the problem of the proper *object* and *method* of *metaphysics*. If there be such a science, Kant declared, it must deal with real existents in nature and not merely with possibles or ideal objects. In this existential bearing, it resembles Newtonian physics, rather than pure mathematics. This affinity between physics and metaphysics so impressed Kant that he sought to pattern metaphysical thinking after the standard of physics. If there is ever to be a genuine metaphysics, it must be reconstructed according to the *analytic method* and, to this extent, must make a radical departure from the systems of rationalism. Kant was sufficiently under rationalistic influence during the pre-critical period, however, to leave room for the hope that, at some later date, metaphysical speculation might rightfully proceed in a synthetic way. But he envisaged his own immediate task as that of submitting metaphysical propositions to the test of the analytic method, used with so much success in Newton's natural philosophy.

Two characteristic features of metaphysics recommended this

course: its search after causes and its concern with existence. Kant was indebted to both Crusius and Hume for focusing his attention upon the *causal problem,* as a means of undermining the rationalistic conception of metaphysics. Wolff himself had distinguished between the logical ground or reason of a thing and its cause, but in practice he assimilated the latter to the former, just as he assimilated the principle of sufficient reason to that of identity. Kant pointed out the deep chasm separating the *logical* from the *real* ground, the *ratio veritatis* of a thing from its *ratio existentiae vel actualitatis.*[3] The latter is the cause of the thing in the real order, whereas the former supplies only an explanation (whether prior or consequent to the fact) of the thing's ideal structure or essence. Explanation by means of the logical sufficient reason ultimately supposes an identity between the thing and its ground. But this shows the striking difference between the relation of ground-and-consequent and that of cause-and-effect, since the cause remains really other than its effect. Analysis can reveal the consequent to be an integral element in the logical ground, but no amount of inspection of concepts or appeal to identity can explain why one thing actually gives rise to another, really different thing. Kant concluded that either the causal relation is an arbitrary connection, made by the mind, or else it is drawn from experience. In the latter case, it belongs among those irreducible and yet confused concepts with which every nonmathematical science begins.

A similar result followed from Kant's examination of the second distinctive mark of metaphysical inquiry: its *existential orientation.*[4] He saw how important it was to avoid a confusion between the analytic method and the analytic judgment. Existential sciences, like physics and metaphysics, must follow the *analytic method* of starting with some irreducible concepts, given in experience, but their foundations do not rest upon the *analytic judgment,* in which the predicate is found by analysis of the concept of the logical subject. For, existence itself is neither a *component of the essential nature,* expressed in

---

[3] *A New Exposition of the First Principles of Metaphysical Knowledge,* II, viii, Scholium, and ix (translated as an Appendix in *Kant's Conception of God,* by F. E. England, 226, 228).

[4] *The Only Possible Basis of Proof for a Demonstration of God's Existence,* I, i (Prussian Academy edition of Kant's *Gesammelte Schriften,* II, 70–77). In this First Reflection, on existence in general, Kant establishes three points: existence is not a predicate or any sort of determination of a thing; existence requires an absolute positing, rather than the relative positing of a predicate of a thing; there is "more" in actual existence than in mere possibility.

the subject of a proposition, nor a *predicate of any sort*. Hence examination of the concept of the logical subject cannot furnish a predicate about actual existence, such that one might determine the existential propositions of physics and metaphysics by means of analytic judgments. From the standpoint of the essence and the logical subject, there is no difference ascertainable between the idea of Peter and the existing Peter, between the idea of the hundred dollars and the actual hundred dollars in one's pocket. Common sense, of course, does recognize the importance of the distinction between conceptual being and actual existence. But this capital distinction is ultimately irrelevant for a metaphysics constructed with the aid of analytic judgments alone. The distinction cannot be explained by Wolff's theory that existence is a mere modal determination, complement, or expansion of the possibility of the essence. As Kant put it, Wolff had confused the *relative* positing of a thing as an intelligible structure, in respect to its *logical* ground, and its *absolute* positing as an existent thing, in respect to its *real, causal* ground. Real existence adds to the essential nature something unique (neither an essential part nor a property), which cannot be reduced to a mere "complement" of the possibility of the essence. Precisely what the "more" of real existence over the order of possible essence might be, Kant did not venture to specify during his pre-critical period. But he did maintain that experience alone enables the mind to make the passage from the possible essence to the actual existent, from merely thinking about Peter's essence to knowing that Peter exists.

Kant's own problem now was to ascertain whether existential knowledge can be accommodated in any kind of metaphysical system. The more he emphasized the difference between ground and cause, possible essence and real existence, the more the cleft between thought and being seemed to grow. The very possibility of metaphysics was threatened by every argument Kant advanced to show that rationalism had misconceived its object. Fundamentally, the difficulty lay in Kant's retention of many other rationalistic tenets, which were incompatible with his discoveries about cause and existence. Although he had distinguished the analytic method from the analytic judgment, he still held that *philosophical* judgments must always be analytic. Since the import of his early findings was that such metaphysically important objects as cause and existence could not be obtained through analytic judgments, it seemed that these objects were placed beyond the scope of metaphysics, as a philosophical study of the real. The causal and existential aspects of reality were anomalies, defying incorporation into a philosophical system. Kant was led to question *the philosophical possibility of metaphysics,* not only in its rationalistic conception but even as an empirical inquiry into reality. It occurred to him that metaphysics may not be a science of *real being* at all. Perhaps it finds its legitimate office only in determining the *limits of human reason,* considered not as a power (in which respect it is limitless) but rather as a principle of strict knowledge (and hence as restricted by the scope of sense experience).[5] This suggestion meant the reduction of metaphysics to the theory of knowledge, so that its only genuine function would be that of self-criticism of the limits of knowledge.

Kant sought from physics the clue to a way out of this impasse. Nevertheless, he was dissatisfied with both reigning theories of natural science. The more empirical, Newtonian view respected experience but led to numerous irreducible concepts, for which no adequate criterion was provided. This would make the foundations of physical knowledge inexplicable and beyond rational control. Yet the a priori Wolffian view of science was anchorless and aimless: it knew neither the origin of physical principles nor the goal of reasoning concerning nature. On the crucial question of the *nature of space,* Kant was content, for a while, to make a compromise between the absolute space of Newton and the relative space of Leibniz.[6] He agreed with the former concerning the universality and objective reality of space, and with the latter concerning its necessity and reference to an order among actual bodies. But certain experimental facts — notably, the relation between incongruous counterparts, such as our hands, and the way in which we make primitive distinctions of regions in space — led Kant to develop a distinctive view, which was critical toward both previous doctrines. Our spatial perception of "up and down," "near and far," "left and right," depends primarily not upon the relation of parts to one another but upon their relation to ourselves and,

---

[5] "Metaphysics is the science of the boundaries of human reason." *Dreams of a Spirit-Seer Illustrated by the Dreams of Metaphysics,* II, ii (Goerwitz translation, 113). In the concluding chapter of this book, Kant suggests that moral faith will supplant rational metaphysics in dealing with immaterial things; cf. *ibid.,* II, iii (Goerwitz, 121).

[6] *On the First Grounds of the Distinction of Regions in Space* (Handyside translation, in *Kant's Inaugural Dissertation and Early Writings on Space,* 19–29). On Kant's early relations with Newton and Leibniz concerning space and time, compare J. T. Baker, "Some Pre-Critical Developments of Kant's Theory of Space and Time," *The Philosophical Review,* XLIV (1935), 267–82.

ultimately, to an absolute spatial frame of reference, which is the *universal ground* for the location of all bodies in space. To this extent, Newton was correct. Still, absolute space is not itself an object apprehensible by our outer senses: it is rather a *pure intuition* and *necessary structure of consciousness,* making possible all spatial perception. And in this respect, Kant sided with Leibniz.

In the *Dissertation* of 1770, Kant worked out the implications of his new conception of space. Acting on a suggestion from the mathematician, J. H. Lambert, he revived the old hylemorphic doctrine, as an explanation not of the essential constitution of extramental bodies but of human cognition. All cognition involves the union of a *form* and a *matter,* an organizing principle and a formless content.[7] The formal principle resides on the side of the cognitive subject, whereas the materials for knowledge come from without. In the case of sense cognition, *space and time are forms of the mind;* they have no absolute existence, apart from our knowing power. Their function is to organize sensory materials into the familiar world of natural events. They mold the matter furnished by sensation, so that we may grasp the appearances of things in their spatial and temporal aspects. Kant made a sharp distinction between the forms of space and time, which are intuitions or *singular* concepts at the level of *sense,* and the *universal* concepts of the *understanding.* There is an irreducible difference between the sensuous and intellectual factors in human knowledge. Kant stood opposed to both the materialistic reduction of intellectual to sense factors and the rationalistic reduction of sensation to intellection. Hence he assigned a distinctive status to the forms of space and time, so that they would not be confused with the universal concepts of the understanding.

Having drawn this distinction, Kant was then faced with the problem of explaining the joint contribution of sensory and intellectual elements to our knowledge. In the *Dissertation,* he enumerated two functions of understanding (*intellectus,* a neutral term that does not clearly set off understanding from reason): a *logical use* and a *real use.*[8] The former function is one of logical organization of

---

[7] *Dissertation on the Form and Principles of the Sensible and Intelligible World,* III, 13–15 (Handyside translation, 52–66).

[8] On the distinction between the real and logical, the critical and dogmatic, functions of concepts, cf. *ibid.,* II, 5–6, 9 (Handyside, 45–47, 49–50). Kant establishes the following relationship between these various employments of the understanding and its concepts:

1. Logical use of the understanding (*usus logicus*).

materials, drawn from either an intellectual or a sensuous source, whereas the latter is a means of furnishing concepts in a purely intellectual way from the understanding itself. This distinction enabled Kant to notice one striking difference between physics and metaphysics. Physics employs the understanding *primarily in its logical* function: it brings systematic order and gradation to the deliverances of sense intuition, without transforming their fundamentally sensuous character. The universal concepts of physics do come from the understanding (in its real use), but are employed precisely in organizing sensuous materials. Metaphysics, on the other hand, makes *only a real* use of understanding, to provide itself with *nonempirical concepts,* which enter into no essential liaison with sense materials. These pure concepts are, in turn, used in two ways: critically and dogmatically. Kant was confident of the legitimacy of the *critical aim* of pure concepts of the understanding, since its end is to prevent any misapplication of sensuous predicates to the whole realm of being. Many so-called antinomies (such as the principle of Crusius that "whatever exists, is somewhere") vanish, as soon as it is noted that a sensuous predicate drawn from our manner of knowing (such as "somewhere") need not signify a universal condition of reality in itself.

But Kant was not ready to concede that metaphysics can use its pure concepts *dogmatically,* to ascertain the intelligible nature of things as they are. The distinction between things as they *are,* in their intelligible or noumenal reality, and as they *appear* under the forms of space and time, helped him to evaluate the dogmatic aim of pure concepts. It is certain that we know the spatial and temporal appearances of things, since the forms of space and time have intuitive content, of a sensuous sort. But the pure concepts of the understanding are *bereft of any intellectual intuition,* which might provide real content for grasping things in their own nature.[9] Hence in their dog-

---

2. Real use of the understanding (*usus realis*).

   *a*) Critical aim of purely intellectual concepts (*finis elenchticus*).

   *b*) Dogmatic aim of purely intellectual concepts (*finis dogmaticus*).

  [9] On the way in which the important *Inaugural Dissertation* treats the problem of intellectual intuition and metaphysical knowledge, read C. B. Garnett, Jr., "Kant's Theory of *Intuitus Intellectualis* in the *Inaugural Dissertation* of 1770," *The Philosophical Review*, XLVI (1937), 424–32; H. Eibl, "Kants Metaphysik in der *Dissertation von 1770,*" *Blätter für Deutsche Philosophie,* XI (1937–1938), 152–76. Garnett shows that Kant's attribution of a symbolical "knowledge" to metaphysics is inconsistent with his denial to metaphysics of any intuitive content. Whatever his criticism of metaphysics, Kant never ceased to ask metaphysical questions and to posit some sort of acquaintance with the nonsensuous aspects of things.

matic aim, these concepts can only give *symbolic indications* of this order of intelligible or noumenal being. Lacking any intuitive grounding, the concepts brought forth by the understanding, in its *usus realis,* are open to error and incapable of giving strict knowledge of the noumenal realities toward which they point. Metaphysics might still be possible as self-criticism, i.e., as making a critical use of pure concepts. But its claims to any dogmatic determination of the intelligible nature of things as they are, stand open to question.

This discussion brought out, for Kant, another capital difference between physics and metaphysics. *Practice* can precede *method* in the former science, whereas in metaphysics it must wait upon the establishment of method. In physics valid discoveries can be made and particular problems settled, long before an adequate theory of physical method is formulated; indeed, the latter is usually the result of reflection upon the successful practice of working scientists. Independent, particular findings can be made, since the physicist relies upon concepts that have an intuitive foundation in sense. Since this condition does not obtain for the pure or nonempirical concepts of metaphysics, the possibility of a method of attaining to noumenal realities must first be established, before any particular metaphysical investigations can be made.

During the decade 1770–1781, Kant was ruminating upon the proper way to determine beforehand the scope of the understanding. This involved a test of the soundness of the claims for metaphysics as a dogmatic discipline, giving knowledge of things as they are in their intelligible nature. But, as Schopenhauer and Bergson later remarked, the one point which Kant never called in question was *the legitimacy of the Leibnizian description of what metaphysics ought to be.* He regarded metaphysics only as a science that draws its own concepts from the structure of the understanding, and that employs them in a purely nonempirical way, apart from an analysis of experience.[10]

---

10 "As concerns the sources of metaphysical knowledge, its very concept implies that they cannot be empirical. Its principles (including not only its maxims but its basic notions) must never be derived from experience. . . . It is therefore *a priori* knowledge, coming from pure understanding and pure reason. . . . Consequently it deals with concepts whose objective reality (namely, that they are not mere chimeras) and with assertions whose truth or falsity cannot be discovered or confirmed by any experience. . . . [This constitutes] the root and peculiarity of metaphysics, that is, the occupation of reason merely with itself and the supposed knowledge of objects arising immediately from this brooding over its own concepts, without requiring or indeed being able to reach that knowledge through, experience." *Prolegomena to Any Future Metaphysics,* 1 and 40 (Beck's revision of the Carus translation, 13, 75–76).

This does describe the rationalistic ideal of a metaphysics. But it is sharply antithetical to the realistic metaphysical tradition, which emphasizes the sensory origin of all concepts, the need for an intellectual abstraction of concepts from things, the separative judgment about existent sensible things, and the foundation of metaphysical inferences in the implications of experience. Kant assumed that metaphysics always relies on the *usus realis* of the understanding to furnish itself with a special type of concept, transcending the spatial and temporal appearances of things. What he challenged was not this description of metaphysics but only the claim that metaphysics, as so described, gives any knowledge of its objects. There is a vast historical shortsightedness about the entire Kantian treatment of the possibility of metaphysics, since it applies to only one conception of this science. But within its limited range, it makes a devastating attack upon the pretensions of rationalism.

For some time after 1770, Kant believed that he could set forth his views in a concise work on "The Limits of Sensibility and Reason."[11] It would have the two following divisions: (1) a theoretical part, treating of the phenomenology of knowledge and the nature and method of metaphysics; (2) a practical part on the principles of feeling, taste, and sense desires, as well as on moral principles. This project contained in germ the final trilogy that was eventually composed: the *Critique of Pure Reason,* the *Critique of Practical Reason,* and the *Critique of Judgment,* corresponding, respectively, to the current psychological distinction between the mental functions of thinking, willing, and feeling. What prevented Kant from encompassing his findings in a single brief treatise, was the unexpected difficulty he encountered in working out the first part, on the phenomenology of knowledge and metaphysics. He found that the critical problem required a more elaborate treatment than he had originally planned.

The *central critical problem* concerns the reference of all mental presentations (*Vorstellungen,* a neutral term that may be rendered variously as "presentations," "representations," "ideas," or "notions") to the objects of knowledge. In the case of sensuous presentations, resulting from the affections received in the knowing subject from the object, the objective reference may be traced back to the cause of the sensations. But intellectual presentations raise a serious problem. If

11 Kant outlined this project in a letter (dated February 21, 1772) to Marcus Herz, his former student; for a translation, cf. A. D. Lindsay, *Kant,* 32–36.

our understanding were creative, like the archetypal understanding of God, the objectivity of knowledge would be guaranteed by the fact that the mind is creative of its own objects. But, in Kant's view, our human understanding neither creates things through its concepts, nor abstracts the concepts from things, nor receives them through any affection from objects. The Kantian understanding (so similar to the medieval conception of the angelic mind) brings forth its pure intellectual concepts by reflection upon its own operations. How, then, do these pure concepts bear upon objects and even demand agreement from objects? Hume had raised this question about the notion of cause, and Kant extended it to all the universal notions constituting physical knowledge and supposed metaphysical knowledge. The critical problem inquires *how the understanding can determine a priori the concepts or principles for the possibility of objects* — principles with which objects must conform — when these principles are independent of sensation and in no way acquired by affection from objects.

## 3. THE STRUCTURE OF THE "CRITIQUE OF PURE REASON"

The structure of the first *Critique* can be studied in terms of its logical bases, its plan, and its method. The foundations laid here are carried over into the other two *Critiques,* so that there is a basic unity binding together the various sections in the critical enterprise, even though Kant's thought underwent continual development as it passed from speculative matters to a consideration of morals and esthetics.

1. The first *Critique* rests upon a *twofold logical basis:* a *new theory of conformity in truth* and a new theory of judgment. Kant sets out deliberately to make a revolution in our way of thinking about the relationship between mind and thing.[12] He believes that the entire drift of modern science requires him to repudiate the older realistic view that logical truth consists in that sort of conformity in which the thing is taken as the standard, and the mind is denominated "true," when it submits to this standard and expresses the independ-

---

[12] *Critique of Pure Reason,* Preface to Second Edition, B x-xviii (Smith, 18–23). Kant himself did not use the oft-quoted words, "a Copernican revolution," but he did mention an "intellectual revolution . . . a *revolution* brought about by the happy thought of a single man." *Loc. cit.,* B xi (Smith, 19). That this revolution in our way of thinking (due to the suggestion that we should seek in the spectator those factors previously supposed to lie only in the objects known) can appropriately be termed a Copernican revolution, is established by H. J. Paton, in his discussion with F. L. Cross, concerning "Kant's So-Called Copernican Revolution," *Mind,* N.S., XLVI (1937), 214–17, 365–71, 475–77.

ent nature of the thing. If logical truth is understood in this way, there can be no answer to the critical problem, as Kant formulates it. If the mind stands to the thing as the measured to the measure, it is impossible to determine a priori the conditions governing objectivity of knowledge. Moreover, the realistic conception of scientific truth requires that intellectual concepts, as well as sense perceptions, be derived somehow from the given existent. This runs counter to Kant's manner of saving the irreducible difference between sensation and intellection. He locates the difference not merely in the different cognitive *powers* at work but also in the *difference of origin* of sensuous and intellectual presentations. Kant fears that the realistic position will open the door to the skeptical and materialistic outcome of empiricism. Hence he sees no other way of saving a distinctive, intellectual element in knowledge than by attributing its origin exclusively to the intellectual power itself, considered as reflecting upon the laws of its own nature which are displayed in its operations. This compels him to reverse the relation between mind and thing, so that scientific truth may depend somehow upon the conformity of the thing with the mind.

It is not by chance that Kant invokes the examples of Copernicus and Galileo in support of his position, since he bases it upon an interpretation of the practice of mathematicians and physicists. Despite his previous contrast between the *method* of mathematics and that of physics and metaphysics, he now seeks to extend the *type of conformity* used in mathematics to all other legitimate sciences. He offers a special explanation of the procedure of mathematicians, so that there will not be even an indirect resolution of primary constructs in sense data. In geometry, progress has always been made, not by pretending to read off the properties inherent in independent geometrical figures, but by constructing the figures according to one's own rule or a priori concept. In this way, the geometrician can determine the properties of the figure with *a priori certainty* or independently of particular experiences, since he is only working out the implications of what he himself has prescribed in its construction. The rapid advance in modern physics is due to an application of the same *constructural* technique. It operates on the same assumption that "we can know a priori of things only what we ourselves put into them."[13] Kant interprets the physicist's procedure of asking questions about

---

[13] *Critique of Pure Reason*, loc. cit., B xviii (Smith, 23).

nature and devising experimental conditions, as a tacit recognition that nature provides answers only in terms of the factors that reason itself contributes.

Kant has brought out the unique role of mental constructs in modern physics, especially insofar as this science tends to be an art of practical control over nature, gained through mathematical hypotheses. But his view that the basic concepts and principles have an a priori origin is a residue of the Cartesian-Leibnizian theory of knowledge, rather than due to the testimony of the scientists themselves. In order to summon scientific practice as a witness for his doctrine on conformity, he is obliged to depreciate the realistic convictions of Galileo and Newton. Although these scientists did limit knowledge to appearances, they supposed that nature possesses its own intelligible structure, even in the order of appearances, and that the scientist's aim is to conform his mind with this structure as much as possible. They did not think that the intelligible, determinate pattern of sensible events is due, in final analysis, to a priori forms resident in the knowing subject. This is, rather, the properly philosophical position taken by Kant in resolution of the critical problem.

Having stated the procedure used in mathematics and physics, Kant now suggests that the same conditions of conformity must prevail for all concepts validly employed in philosophy. A Copernicus supposed that the real motion is found in the observer and his immediate frame of reference, rather than in the sun, which has only apparent motion. Similarly, the philosopher must trace back space, time, cause, and other traits of nature to ourselves, rather than to the intrinsic constitution of things. The consequence is that our reliable knowledge is restricted to things as they *appear, in conformity with our mental forms,* and does not reach to things as they *are in themselves.* Now, this proposition directly contradicts the pretensions of metaphysics to give knowledge about the reality of things in their own intelligible nature. Kant concludes that, therefore, the metaphysical search after such knowledge is illusory. But, bearing in mind his own earlier findings about the noncausal and nonexistential character of mathematical demonstrations, he might just as well have concluded that the mathematical sort of conformity is an inappropriate standard in metaphysical inquiries. His interpretation of scientific practice suggests that existential and causal investigations cannot be required to follow the constructural techniques proportioned to mathematical physics. Kant avoids this alternative suggestion, however, because of his prior commitment about the purely a priori source of metaphysical concepts in the *usus realis* of the understanding. This is a clear indication that his philosophical appeal to procedures in modern, classical physics is predetermined by what his special formulation of the critical problem requires him to conclude.

The second basic logical doctrine is the *theory of judgment*. Kant's pre-critical difficulties about how to reconcile analytic judgments with matters of fact and existence, led him eventually to revise the logical doctrine on judgment, in order to bring it more in line with scientific practice and his own epistemological principles. He based his new position upon a fresh study of empirical and a priori types of judgment, as well as of analytic and synthetic types. With regard to the first pair, he sided with the rationalists; with regard to the second pair, he reinstated the rights of empiricism.

Although the empiricists show that all our knowledge *begins with* sense experience, they fail to take account of the observation of the rationalists that not all elements in knowledge *take their origin from* sense experience. Even in a simple sensory act, there is a factor contributed by our knowing powers. Hence a distinction must be made between empirical or a posteriori knowledge and pure or a priori knowledge.[14] *Empirical judgments* express the particular, contingent features drawn from sense experience. *A priori judgments* express that "pure" portion of our knowledge which is independent of contingent sense experiences and which springs from the nature of the cognitive subject itself.

Kant's proof that we do possess a pure (nonempirical), a priori element of knowledge, consists in pointing to the *universal* and *necessary* character of admitted scientific propositions. This marks one of the major points of divergence between the Kantian and realistic theories of knowledge. The realistic thesis is that there is a *real foundation* in the natural things themselves for the traits of universality and necessity. These traits are based on the essential structure which the intellect, co-operating closely with the senses, abstracts from the real existents. But Kant's matter-form view of knowledge, as well as his theory of conformity, compels him to deny that the human mind penetrates by abstraction to the real essence of things. He attributes all the epistemologically warranted, formal and

---

14 *Ibid.*, Introduction, B 2–6 (Smith, 42–45); *Prolegomena to Any Future Metaphysics*, 18 (Beck, 45–46).

determinate factors in knowledge to the knowing subject itself. Hence it is axiomatic with him that necessity and universality can have no sort of empirical origin. They are due exclusively to our own human constitution, to the structure of *consciousness-in-general*. For Kant, knowing is a kind of *making*, a composing of material and formal elements. The material or empirical side of cognition is purely contingent and particular: it cannot supply the necessary and universal aspects of scientific knowledge. These aspects have their sole origin in the common structure of consciousness and hence come from a purely a priori source. Whereas realism admits the contingency and particularity of our sensory cognitive *acts*, it also holds that these acts supply the mind with an empirically grounded and yet sufficiently determinate *content* to give a real basis for some universal and necessary judgments. But Kant regards both the act and the content of sensation as too indeterminate to account in any way for the chief marks of scientific knowledge. Consequently, he appeals to these marks as proof of the a priori aspect of our knowledge.

Up to this point, the rationalists would concur with Kant. They would then draw the inference that the mind can determine truths about objects, without relying in any essential way upon sense experience. Because of its implications for metaphysics and its depreciation of scientific experimentation, Kant rejects this inference. Moreover, it does not square with the results of his study of judgments as analytic and synthetic.[15] *Analytic judgments* are those in which the predicate is found, by analysis, to belong at least implicitly to the concept of the subject. They serve an "explicative" function, in clarifying and rendering explicit the knowledge already in our possession. But however indispensable this function, it is incapable of insuring the steady advance of science through new discoveries. The actual increment of scientific knowledge comes from *synthetic judgments*, which alone are "ampliative" or inventive of

[15] *Critique of Pure Reason*, Introduction, A 6–10: B 10–18 (Smith, 48–55); *Prolegomena to Any Future Metaphysics*, 2–3 (Beck, 14–20). Recent logicians have followed B. Russell, in holding that propositions are either empirical and synthetic or a priori and analytic. C. I. Lewis is the major Kantian philosopher holding today that all analytic statements are knowable a priori. For criticisms of this position, cf. J. Wild and J. L. Coblitz, "On the Distinction between the Analytic and the Synthetic," *Philosophy and Phenomenological Research*, VIII (1948), 651–67; J. Collins, "Mr. Lewis and the A Priori," *The Journal of Philosophy*, XLV (1948), 561–72; M. G. White, "The Analytic and the Synthetic: An Untenable Dualism," in *John Dewey: Philosopher of Science and Freedom*, edited by S. Hook (New York, Dial Press, 1950), 316–30.

new truths. In the latter type of judgment, the predicate is not contained within the concept of the subject but is added thereto, by an act of synthesis. The mind must have recourse to what is given in sense experience, in order to gain new materials for the development of knowledge. The material factor in knowledge is indispensable, even though it cannot supply the necessary and universal aspects. This is the undeniable kernel of truth contained in the empiricist viewpoint.

Reviewing these divisions of judgment, Kant finds no difficulty with analytic judgments or with empirical synthetic ones. But his examination of scientific knowledge shows that all mathematical propositions are a priori synthetic, and that at least the principles of physics are of the same sort. Only judgments that are *both synthetic* and *a priori* satisfy the scientific ideal of a knowledge that is at once empirically founded and necessary-and-universal. The empirical and progressive traits of scientific knowledge are due to its synthetic aspect, whereas its universal and necessary features are due to the a priori character of scientific propositions. In the arithmetical proposition: "$7 + 5 = 12$," no amount of analysis of 7, 5, and their sum can disclose the concept of 12. A mental synthesis, aided by the pure intuition of number, is needed to make precisely the number 12 equivalent to the sum of 7 plus 5. Nevertheless, this proposition is true, necessarily and universally. Similar results are reached by Kant in the study of the geometrical proposition that "the straight line between two points is the shortest," and the physical principle that "in all changes of the material world the quantity of matter remains unchanged."

His test cases have been attacked by subsequent mathematicians and physicists.[16] Mathematicians have given analytical proof of arithmetical propositions, without having recourse to intuition, and have devised geometrical systems in which the Euclidean postulate is not accepted, whatever its natural and practical necessity. Similarly, physicists have offered fruitful alternatives to the closed mechanical model or system, described by universal and necessary laws. Seen in historical perspective, however, Kant was trying to develop a theory

---

[16] Cf. B. Bolzano, *Wissenschaftslehre*, 84, 305 (second edition [4 vols., Leipzig, Meiner, 1929–1931], I, 399–401; III, 178–99); L. Couturat, "La philosophie des mathématiques de Kant," *Revue de Métaphysique et de Morale*, XII (1904), 32–83; J. J. Toohey, S.J., "Kant on the Propositions of Pure Mathematics," *The New Scholasticism*, XI (1937), 140–57.

of scientific judgment that would both satisfy his new Copernican standpoint in philosophy and agree with the mathematical and physical conceptions of his own century.

2. Granted the presence of a priori synthetic propositions in the sciences, the general *problem* and *plan* of the first *Critique* are plainly seen to follow. For, this treatise provides a general answer to the question of how such a priori synthetic propositions are possible. In the case of the acknowledged sciences of mathematics and physics, Kant asks only *how* their propositions are possible. But in the case of the disputed discipline of metaphysics, he asks *whether* it can contain propositions of this sort. The two broadest divisions of the *Critique* are the theory of the *elements of knowledge* and the theory of *method*. The section on method concerns the manner in which pure reason can be brought to a complete system, an investigation that is important for understanding the later German idealists. The doctrine on the elements of knowledge contains, in turn, two major subdivisions: the Transcendental Esthetic and the Transcendental Logic (consisting of the Analytic and the Dialectic). The *Esthetic* studies the forms of our sensibility and shows how mathematics is possible, as a rigorous science. The *Analytic* examines the categorial concepts of the understanding and reveals the possibility of strictly scientific principles in physics. The purpose of the *Dialectic* is twofold: to show that reason has a natural disposition to construct a metaphysics, and to inquire into whether metaphysics is possible as a genuine science (and not merely as an inescapable inclination of reason).

There is a mounting tension in the argument. For, the aim of the Esthetic and Analytic is to establish the necessary conditions of *all* knowledge, through reflection upon the nature of mathematical and physical knowledge. Once these conditions are determined, Kant is at last equipped to answer the question that stimulated him to make the long, critical inquiry in the speculative order: can there be a proper science of metaphysics or transcendent knowledge of noumenal realities? The negative answer, presented in the Dialectic, has been anticipated by the previous discussion of the nature of sensibility and the limits of the understanding, as a knowing power. However much reason is inclined to go beyond the appearances, it cannot do so by way of any metaphysical knowledge but only by way of practical faith.

The division of the doctrine on the elements of knowledge into the Esthetic, Analytic, and Dialectic, corresponds to Kant's definitive division of the knowing powers into sensibility, understanding, and

## PLAN OF THE CRITIQUE OF PURE REASON
### (Doctrine on the Elements of Knowledge)

**UNITY OF APPERCEPTION**

| Transcendental Esthetic | Transcendental Logic | |
|---|---|---|
| | Analytic | Dialectic |
| 2 Forms of Sensibility — Outer, Inner | 12 Categories (corresponding to 12 types of logical judgments) | 3 Ideas |
| Space   Time | | God (Ideal) |
| | | World (Antinomy) |
| | | Soul (Paralogisms) |
| | SCHEMATA | |
| Sensibility | Understanding | Reason |
| Imagination | Judgments | Inferences |
| Sensuous Intuitions (matter and forms) | | Transcendent Illusions and Systematic Unification |
| | Knowledge of Appearances: Perception brought to Experience of Objects | |
| | TRANSCENDENTAL   CONSCIOUSNESS-IN-GENERAL | |

**Unknowable Thing-in-Itself**

**MATTER OF SENSATION**

476 .MODERN EUROPEAN PHILOSOPHY

reason.[17] The distinction between understanding and reason was one of Kant's crucial developments, since it finally enabled him to set off metaphysics (whose instrument is reason) from physics (whose instrument is the understanding, working along with sensibility). In a preliminary way, he states that objects are *given to us* through *sensibility* or sensuous intuition, and are *thought by us* through the *understanding* and its categories. Understanding co-operates with sensibility in achieving scientific knowledge of appearances. But *reason* has a tendency to abandon the zone of appearances and experience, in an effort to construct a metaphysical account of the intelligible reality of things-in-themselves. Yet Kant also seeks to unify man's cognitive powers in several ways. Both sensibility and understanding are needed to explain the possibility of experience, which is their joint product. Understanding and reason are also closely related, since they both are nonsensuous powers and deal with the nonsensuous presentations studied in the transcendental Logic. Although he does not want to soften the contrast between the sensible and intellectual powers, Kant also adds that sensibility and understanding may be regarded as two stems, rooted in a deeper, common source in the mind. It is mind or *Gemüt* which "has" and "employs" both these powers, in the determination of the objects of knowledge.

3. The *method* of the *Critique* is adapted to its stated purpose of uncovering the conditions for objective knowledge. This method is signified by the term *transcendental,* which is applied to both the Esthetic and the Logic. A transcendental study is one that concentrates upon those pure, general conditions in the knowing subject which make possible a knowledge of objects. A transcendental method may be either analytic or synthetic.[18] It is *analytic* or *regressive,* when it presupposes the truth of the a priori synthetic judgments, and then works back to the only conditions under which such judgments can be valid and true. It is *synthetic* or *progressive,* when it demonstrates the validity and truth of these judgments, by showing that their conditions constitute the very possibility of objective experience and knowledge of phenomenal objects. The movement of regressive investigation is from the conditioned to the conditions, whereas the

---

[17] *Critique of Pure Reason,* A 15: B 29, A 19: B 33, A 51: B 75, A 302: B 359 (Smith, 61, 65, 93, 303).

[18] *Ibid.,* A 782–83: B 810–11 (Smith, 621); *Prolegomena to Any Future Metaphysics,* Introduction, and Section 5 (Beck, 11, 23).

progressive movement is from the conditions to what they do condition. Although he does not make any rigid separation of these modes of the transcendental method, Kant employs the way of synthesis or progression mainly in the first *Critique,* and the way of analysis or regression in the *Prolegomena.*

In either case, the transcendental approach to the critical problem consists in an examination of the conditions of experience and the objectivity of knowledge. Kant regards as his greatest critical discovery the doctrine that *objects of experience are rendered possible by the same principles constituting the possibility of experience in general.*[19] The same general conditions whereby something can be a component in our experience are also the sole conditions under which that thing can become an object of our knowledge. A transcendental inquiry is one that studies the pure, a priori structures of consciousness-in-general, insofar as they determine objectivity and experience. This sets off Kant's standpoint from empirical psychology, which studies the contingent and empirical factors as given, and from traditional logic, which Kant regards as a purely formal discipline, unconcerned about the objectivity of knowledge and the material factor.

## 4. SPACE, TIME, AND SENSUOUS INTUITION

In the Transcendental Esthetic, Kant discusses the structure of sensibility and its relation to the object. He incorporates and elaborates upon the findings of the *Dissertation* on two important issues: sensuous intuition and the nature of space and time.

In general, *intuition* is the means whereby presentations or ideas are brought into immediate relation with individual objects.[20] It is the

---

[19] "The *a priori* conditions of a possible experience in general are at the same time conditions of the possibility of objects of experience." *Critique of Pure Reason,* A 111 (Smith, 138).

[20] *Dissertation on the Form and Principles of the Sensible and Intelligible World,* II, 10 (Handyside, 50–51); *Critique of Pure Reason,* A 19–22: B 33–36, B 72 (Smith, 65–67, 90); *Prolegomena to Any Future Metaphysics,* 7–9 (Beck, 28–30); *Critique of Judgment,* II, ii, No. 77 (Bernard translation, 320–24). The Kantian division of intuition is as follows:

1. Intellectual intuition (*intuitus originarius,* proper to *intellectus archetypus*).
2. Sensuous intuition (*intuitus derivatus,* proper to the sensibility of *intellectus ectypus*).
   *a*) Pure sensuous intuition.
   *b*) Empirical sensuous intuition.
   (N.B. Intuitions may be indeterminate or determinate. Like Locke's term "experience," Kant's use of "intuition" is ambiguous, since it may refer either to

way of establishing an immediate cognitive reference to the individual. Kant distinguishes between two main types of intuition: originary and derived. *Originary* or *creative* intuition is wholly active and is productive of the real existence of the thing known. By way of hypothesis, Kant reserves this kind of intuition for God, since only the divine being may be presumed to have an *archetypal* intellect, which would be the productive source of the very being of its objects. Although he pretends to no private insight about the divine mode of intuition, Kant makes strategic use of the notion. For he labels the divine intuition *intellectual,* thus setting the stage for determining the type of intuition proper to minds that are not divine. Finite minds have a derived kind of being and hence also a *derived* intuition. Finite minds are *ectypal,* in the sense that they must be affected somehow by extramental things, whose existence is supposed rather than created by such minds. The intuition proportionate to finite minds — which are both dependent in their own mode of being and noncreative of the existence of the things known — is a wholly receptive, nonspontaneous one. Since the divine, active intuition is intellectual, Kant calls the derived, receptive intuition of finite minds sensible or *sensuous.*

There is a broader and a narrower meaning of *sensuous intuition,* but unfortunately Kant does not always retain the distinction. In its widest Kantian meaning, intuition is called sensuous, because it supposes that the knower is *being affected by* the individual existent. We intuit only insofar as we are affected by things. As far as human beings are concerned, however, this affection occurs when the individual existent operates upon our senses. This circumstance provides the narrower meaning of sensuous intuition, viz., immediate apprehension *through sense affections.* Kant combines these two aspects of being-affected and being-affected-through-the-senses, so that by definition our affective aspect is the same as our sensibility. However, it is necessary to make a further distinction of sensuous intuition itself into empirical and pure sensuous intuition. *Empirical sensuous intuition* is founded in the contingent, a posteriori reception of the matter of sensation, through our sense powers. But the sense powers can function to produce empirical sensations only in virtue of the pure forms of sensibility, which are space and time. These pure, a priori forms are not only principles of intuition but also constitute

---

the act of intuiting or the object intuited. In the latter case, an intuition is a singular presentation of the mind, rather than a universal one.)

*pure sensuous intuitions,* in their own right. Kant must make this admission, as an explanation of how there can be a priori synthetic propositions in mathematics, which anticipates our particular perceptions and hence is not an empirical discipline. But he is always uneasy about pure sensuous intuition, since it would seem to supply its own matter and thus escape the limitation of knowledge on the empirical side, a possibility that did not escape Hegel's searching eye.

Although his positive treatment of intuition is brief, Kant employs its consequences as the *main refutation of the possibility of metaphysics,* as a transcendent science. In brief, man has only sensuous intuition. He has no intellectual intuition, and hence can give no real content to the concepts of reason that point to intelligible entities, beyond the realm of sense. Without an intellectual intuition, there can be no transcendent knowledge of things-in-themselves and hence no metaphysics.

Kant's argument rests upon three chief grounds, which may be tested at this point. First, he concludes from the contrast between the underived, divine mind and the derived, finite minds not only that finite intuition is *nondivine* but also that it is *nonintellectual.* This follows only on condition that there is a strict equation made between a creative and an intellectual way of intuiting. Second, Kant makes a sharp dichotomy between the *wholly active* intuition of the divine mind and the *wholly receptive* or passive intuition of finite minds. On other occasions, however, he is quite ready to admit the presence in man of operations that are not purely active, in the sense of being creative of their objects, and yet are not merely passive. The human condition is a mixed one. Our immanent operations suppose an initial, receptive phase, and yet this reception is itself a vital, operative response. The operations of intuition are not an exception to this situation, so that there is no need to accept the dilemma of an exclusively active, divine intuition versus an exclusively passive, sensuous intuition. Thomistic metaphysics recognizes the equivalent of a "finite, intellectual intuition" in the apprehension of being, which issues from the direct existential judgment about the concrete existent.[21] Although this experiential judgment depends closely upon sense perception of the existing thing, it is not itself a sensuous

---

[21] In "L'intuition de l'être et le premier principe," *Revue Thomiste,* XLVII (1947), 113–34, J.-H. Nicolas, O.P., appraises Kant's notion of an intellectual intuition, and suggests that the metaphysical requirements are met by the Thomistic doctrine of an immediate grasp of the concrete real by the mind, in the judgment of existence.

operation. And the resultant understanding of being does not create the reality of the existent, even though it is also not a mere passive reception but a living, conceptual expression of the meaning of being. Third, Kant takes *sensibility* in so broad and undifferentiated a way, that it includes every sort of *cognitive receptivity*. Outside of the Leibniz-Wolff tradition of a pure, intellectual spontaneity, however, there is no bar against an *intellectual nonsensuous receptivity,* due to the dependence of the intellect upon the actual existent and upon sense experience of this concrete thing. Receptivity or "affection" of this sort is not pure passivity, since the intellect receives precisely by becoming, in an intentional and actual way, the being of the thing known. Nor is this reception an operation of sense itself, since it involves a recognition of the thing in its essential nature and very act of being. Kant solidified his doctrine on the types of intuition too rapidly to take account of these other possibilities, which are nevertheless at the heart of the Thomistic claim to a valid metaphysical knowledge. What his arguments actually show is that an intellectual power, regarded in the rationalistic fashion as a pure spontaneity, must either be divine or else purely formal and nonintuitive. This entails the elimination of a rationalistically conceived metaphysics, but does not come to serious grips with a metaphysics constructed precisely along the lines of a basic repudiation of the notion that the human intellect is a purely active and nonempirical power.

Even sensuous intuition must submit to analysis in terms of the matter and form of cognition. From a strictly transcendental standpoint, which is concerned with the a priori conditions on the part of the knowing subject, Kant is forbidden to discuss the *origin* of the *matter of sensation.* The manifold of sensation itself falls within his scope, insofar as it is a constituent of the sensible appearances or objects of knowledge. But the origin of this matter of sensation may lie beyond the appearances or on the side of *things-in-themselves.* In that case, it is perfectly unknowable by the human mind.[22] Even

---

[22] "The true correlate of sensibility, the thing in itself, is not known, and cannot be known, through these representations; and in experience no question is ever asked in regard to it." *Critique of Pure Reason,* A 30: B 45 (Smith, 74). Nevertheless, Kant's private convictions and his practical interests led him constantly to pose questions about the thing-in-itself, even within the context of the critique of experience. The struggle between his private realism and critical phenomenalism is outlined by G. A. Schrader, "The Thing in Itself in Kantian Philosophy," *The Review of Metaphysics,* II (1949), 30–44. Attention must also be paid, however, to Kant's later attempts to explain the whole genesis of experience in terms of the self. For these idealistic trends in

to speak about the real nature of the cause of sensations is illegitimate, since "cause" and "reality" are categories, which apply properly only within the sphere of appearances themselves and have no valid application to things-in-themselves. Nevertheless, Kant insists that things-in-themselves, as the origin of the matter of sensation, cannot be denied. This conviction separates him from his successors, the absolute idealists. However circumscribed our mind is in regard to strict knowledge, we can at least *think* about the nonsensuous aspects of things and point toward them with the categories. In a problematic way, we may regard these unknowable aspects or things-in-themselves as the real correlates of our sensibility and of consciousness-in-general. They may be thought of as providing the real sources of the material content of sensuous intuition, as well as the ultimate explanation for the differences among experienced objects. Things-in-themselves do not constitute a separate realm of entities: they are only the nonsensuous, intelligible side of the world of appearances, which we do know. But we are brought none the closer to *knowledge* of the intelligible, nonphenomenal aspects. As far as strict knowledge of the matter of sensation is concerned, we can only ascertain that sensuous intuition contains a material content or manifold, irreducible either to concepts or to the formal factor of sensibility.

Critically viewed, the matter of sensation is indeterminate and formless. It needs to be organized by the *forms of sensibility,* in order to attain determination and structure. What the basic forms of sensibility are, may be ascertained by inquiring about the all-pervasive traits of our sense experience of the world. All objects of our experience must appear to us as temporal. Those which appear as being outside of, or other than, the knower, must be presented in a spatial as well as a temporal way. Hence *space* and *time* are the general forms of sensibility, its constitutive principles. Space is the form of outer sense, time the form of inner sense. Things, regarded in their externality or otherness from the self, are organized immediately under the conditions of Euclidean space, which can be known a priori in geometry. The self is known as a temporal succession of presentations. Hence time immediately qualifies one's self-knowledge and mediately qualifies things outside the self, insofar as they are referred to inner, temporal conditions.

his thought, see P. Lachièze-Rey, *L'idéalisme kantien* (second edition, Paris, Alcan, 1950).

Space and time are both *a priori* and *intuitive*.[23] They are the a priori principles which alone make possible the particular representations of objects, as spatial and temporal. The objective universality and necessity of geometry and the general laws of motion are guaranteed by the a priori nature of the forms of sensibility. For, there can be sense appearances and perceptual knowledge, only on condition that the matter of sensation submit to the requirements imposed by the structure of these forms. Hence geometrical propositions must hold good for the spatial world we perceive. The intuitive character of space and time differentiates them from the universal concepts of the understanding. For this reason, Kant usually refers to space and time as "forms" rather than as "concepts" or "ideas."

Kant defends both the empirical reality and the transcendental ideality of space and time.[24] By their *empirical reality* is meant their constitutive presence in all our empirical intuitions and hence their role in determining the objects of our experience. These forms do not manifest things as they are in themselves. But for us human beings, they do provide the constitutive principles of what we really experience: the *appearances*. These forms organize the sense manifold into definite structured patterns, which constitute the empirical objects or appearances. Kant repudiates the charge that this phenomenalism leads to subjective idealism and illusionism. Illusions (*Scheine*) are mere subjective impressions, whereas the appearances (*Erscheinungen*) are based upon the ways in which things appear to us and affect us: they constitute an objective world, that will sustain scientific propositions. Still, the *transcendental ideality* of space and time must also be upheld. We are affected by things according to *our own* structure of consciousness, our own capacity to be affected. Take away this subjective structure, and nothing remains of spatial and temporal

---

[23] *Critique of Pure Reason*, A 22–41: B 37–58 (Smith, 67–83); *Prolegomena to Any Future Metaphysics*, 10–13 (Beck, 30–41). Kant identifies the space of the Euclidean geometer with the outer form of sensibility. Although this enables him to ascribe a priori certainty to mathematics, it fuses mathematical and physical space. It also makes Euclidean space the absolutely necessary condition of experience and hence of the physical world. H. J. Paton (*Kant's Metaphysic of Experience*, I, 161–63) suggests that the Kantian doctrine could still be saved, in an age of non-Euclidean geometries, by abstracting a single form of space-time from the various geometries and physical systems in force. But this development would render the precise Kantian forms of sensibility contingent and historically conditioned, thus depriving them of the systematic necessity and universality required for a priori principles.

[24] Cf. G. A. Schrader, "The Transcendental Ideality and Empirical Reality of Kant's Space and Time," *The Review of Metaphysics*, IV (1950–1951), 507–36.

qualities. Apart from our peculiar manner of intuiting, space and time have no reality, for they are forms of human sensibility.

## 5. DEDUCTION OF THE CATEGORIES

In the Transcendental Analytic, Kant studies the nature of the understanding, insofar as it co-operates with sensibility in obtaining knowledge of objects of experience. His chief aim in this section is to show that the *categories or pure concepts of the understanding hold valid for these objects*. By the same token, he justifies the principles of physics or natural science, since they employ the categorial concepts. In principle, Hume's skeptical analysis of causal laws called in question the objective validity of all physical concepts and principles. Kant feels obliged, then, to show that cause, substance, and the rest are objectively, as well as subjectively, necessary categories.[25] He offers two deductions of the categories: a transcendental one to prove the need for categories in general, and a metaphysical one to establish the precise list of the categories.

1. The *transcendental deduction* begins with an experiential fact, and inquires about the conditions under which alone the experience is possible. The fact is one which the Esthetic has prepared us to recognize: an awareness of a manifold of presentations, organized in space and time. Now this manifold is not a sheer given contribution from the thing-in-itself. The sense data have already submitted to the forms of sensibility, so that they may become sensible appearances, belonging to the knowing subject. But the juncture of the matter of sensation and the forms of sensibility accounts only for the *diversity* within the presentation and not for its *unity*. There cannot be any adequate sensuous intuition, unless the sense manifold is brought to some sort of unity. The *unity of the sense manifold* is the result of a synthesis or combination produced by the understanding itself. Hence there could never be an object of experience, without such a unification. The application of the categories to sense intuition is required, so that a mere subjective impression may be given the unity

---

[25] Whether Kant did answer Hume effectively, is a disputed point among Humean and Kantian scholars. A good deal turns about Kant's distinction between pure and empirical physics. The objective necessity and universality of the categories are shown to hold for pure physics but not for the actual laws comprising empirical physics, with which Hume was primarily concerned. On this question, cf. W. H. Walsh, "Kant's Conception of Scientific Knowledge," *Mind*, N.S., XLIX (1940), 445–50, and B. M. Laing, "Kant and Natural Science," *Philosophy*, XIX (1944), 216–32.

needed for a genuine object of experience and knowledge. Kant defines an *object of knowledge* as "that in the concept of which the manifold of a given intuition is *united*."[26] To achieve objective standing, the sense impressions must be brought under unifying concepts supplied by the understanding. The concepts rendering the manifold unified and objective are the *categories* of the understanding.

It is well to emphasize that the categories, as a priori, belong to consciousness. Kant expresses this in the statement that all unification of sense presentations supposes a principle of unification, which is the unity of *consciousness-in-general*. The "I think" or *unity of apperception* is thus the most fundamental, a priori condition for constructing objects of knowledge. Kant's debt to Leibniz and (more remotely) to the Cartesian Cogito is evident in this doctrine. There is a radical reference to consciousness-in-general in every instance of knowledge, since the object is recognized as being an object *for* the thinking subject. The transcendental unity of apperception is the ultimate ground for synthesizing the sense manifold into a unity of meaning, under the categories or pure concepts of the understanding. A mere sensation becomes an object of knowledge, only when it is brought within the field of unifying consciousness, by means of its relation to the unity of apperception. Thereby, the subjective impression acquires the unity and necessity characteristic of an object, at least of an object of scientific knowledge (which is taken by Kant to be the only legitimate sort of objective status).

Having traced the synthesizing function back this far, Kant is now faced with the grave problem of uniting the two extreme poles in knowledge: the pure diversity of the matter of sensation and the pure unity of apperception. There are two stages in the process of bridging the gap between them. The first is, in effect, a further proof of the categories. In order to have *various types of unity* and hence various types of objects, the understanding must be provided with several pure concepts or categories. The categories help to bring the sense manifold under the unity of apperception, by producing various a priori syntheses, which determine the unity and necessity of *different kinds of objects* of experience. The framework of objectivity and experience in general is supplied by the transcendental unity of apperception. Within this framework, the understanding applies

<hr />

[26] *Critique of Pure Reason*, B 137 (Smith, 156).

its several categorial concepts, in order to secure the different types of unified objects.

But the categories alone are not able to close the chasm between understanding and sensibility. A second intermediate principle of unity is required, because of the pointed contrast between the particularity, contingency, and diversity of sensation and the generality, necessity, and unity of the understanding and apperceptive consciousness. Kant invokes the special aid of *imagination* to effect a still more intimate, mutual adaptation of the sense manifold and the categories. The manifold must be further synthesized, so that it can acquire an affinity for some particular category; the category must be schematized, so that it can be applied in a determinate way. Imagination, working together with the form of time or the inner sense, provides certain schematic patterns, that are at once concrete and general. The *schemata of imagination* enable the categories to become clothed under the concrete conditions of time and thus become adapted to the order of sense intuitions and images.[27] Simultaneously, these schemata or a priori rules of imagination group the sense presentations together, under certain concrete models or "monograms," which facilitate the application of the categories to definite sense contents.

Kant's groping speculation about the mediating function of imagination throws light on some of his epistemological problems. He is reluctant to reduce sensibility and understanding to each other. At the same time, the concepts of the understanding partake of all the characteristics of the understanding and, to this extent, are quite foreign to the realm of sensibility. Hence, unless the categories and the sense impressions can be rendered somehow proportionate to each other, they can never join in such a union as will yield objects of knowledge. Hence Kant enlists the aid of imagination, somewhat in the manner of the Thomistic *vis cogitativa* or "particular reason." Kant's use of imagination as a mediating principle is of special interest, since it high-lights his effort to establish a halfway house between realism and Hume. For St. Thomas, the inner senses receive sense data possessing an inherent structure of their own, a structure not entirely imposed by sensibility. This determinate sensible form guides the operation of the internal senses, as they bring the image

---

[27] *Ibid.*, A 137-47: B 178-87 (Smith, 180-87). For a thorough discussion of the role of the schemata, cf. R. Daval, *La métaphysique de Kant: Perspectives sur la métaphysique de Kant d'après la théorie du schématisme* (Paris, Presses Universitaires, 1951).

to the condition where it can provide an adequate basis for the act of intellectual abstraction of the intelligible structure. But the Kantian inner sense must provide its patterns entirely from its own constitution. Furthermore, there can be no derivation of the categories of the understanding from the sensible percept. The question is then raised of why imagination applies *certain* schematic forms only to *certain* sense presentations, and why it adapts *certain* categories to *certain* temporal and spatial configurations. Unless some determinate forms are received from the existent thing and manifest its own structure in some degree, the grouping of our percepts in definite classes will lead back eventually to the Humean explanation, in terms of habitual bonds of association. This psychological explanation would introduce a contingent and particular factor at the center of Kant's necessary and universal analysis of the elements of knowledge. Yet Kant cannot employ his conviction that the differences among perceptual objects come ultimately from the thing-in-itself, since this conviction is extrascientific, or beyond the limits of his phenomenalism.

One point emerges clearly from the transcendental deduction of the categories: "Without sensibility no object would be *given* to us, without understanding no object would be *thought*. Thoughts without content are empty, intuitions without concepts are blind."[28] Only from the marriage of the two powers can the object of knowledge spring forth, for its presence requires a thought that has received sense content, and an intuition that has been illuminated through concepts. Until they are unified under categorial rules, sense perceptions are mere subjective affections and cannot be counted as strict objects of experience. It follows that the categories:

> relate of necessity and *a priori* to objects of experience, for the reason that only by means of them can any object whatsoever of experience be thought. . . . Therefore objective validity and necessary universality (for everybody) are equivalent terms, and though we do not know the object in itself, yet when we consider a judgment as universal, and hence necessary, we thereby understand it to have objective validity.[29]

The "we" in this context refers primarily to the *scientific mind*, making the propositions that constitute the content of the physical sciences. Kant's theory of experience is an account of a scientific meaning for objectivity, but his transcendental technique is not

---

[28] *Critique of Pure Reason*, A 51: B 75 (Smith, 93; italics added).
[29] *Ibid.*, A 93: B 126 (Smith, 126); *Prolegomena to Any Future Metaphysics*, 19 (Beck, 46).

adapted to inquiring about the relationship between the scientific and the prescientific attitudes toward the experiential world. Kant can claim objectivity for his categories, insofar as they enter into the very constitution of objects, considered not as things-in-themselves but precisely as scientific constructions or objects-of-scientific-knowledge.

2. Kant's next task was to determine the individual categories by means of the *metaphysical deduction*. A totally a priori proof of any specific list would seem to be a hopeless undertaking. Kant's efforts were stalled, until he hit upon a "clue" to be followed in this matter: the correlation between the *kinds of logical judgment* and the *kinds of categories*. The only way to gain insight into the nature of the understanding is to observe it in its most characteristic operations, which are its acts of judgment or unification of sense presentations. No limit can be set upon the number of such *particular acts,* since the life of the understanding is expressed in its individual judgments. Nevertheless, there are only a few different *ways* in which the understanding can judge. These different ways have already been examined and catalogued by the logicians in their treatises on the types of judgment. But the logicians have not appreciated the full significance of their findings. They have accepted the twelve kinds of judgment as an irreducible and inexplicable fact, never inquiring about the reason behind that fact. This reason cannot even be sought after, until one has attained the standpoint of a transcendental investigation. From the critical viewpoint, it may be asked why the understanding can have these twelve kinds of judgmental unity and no others. The answer supplied by Kant is that these ways of judging are the only possible ones, because they are dictated by the very structure of the understanding. Hence the list of the kinds of logical judgment can be used to determine the list of the kinds of transcendental categories of the understanding. The categories are the a priori conditions determining the kinds of logical judgment. The analytic forms and functions of judgment are possible only in virtue of the prior unifying or synthetic function of the understanding, as expressed in its categorial concepts. From this standpoint, categories may be defined as "concepts of an object in general, by means of which the intuition of an object is regarded as determined in respect of one of the logical functions of judgment."[30] From the twelve types of logical functions

[30] *Critique of Pure Reason*, A 95: B 128 (Smith, 128). For the Kantian list of the categories, cf. *ibid.,* A 80: B 106 (Smith, 113); *Prolegomena to Any Future Metaphysics,* 21, 39 (Beck, 51, 69, 74).

of judgment can be determined with a priori certitude the twelve kinds of categories.

## KANT'S LIST OF JUDGMENTS AND CATEGORIES

1. Table of Judgments.

    a) *Quantity.*
       1) Universal.
       2) Particular.
       3) Singular.

    b) *Quality.*
       4) Affirmative.
       5) Negative.
       6) Infinite.

    c) *Relation.*
       7) Categorical.

       8) Hypothetical.

       9) Disjunctive.

    d) *Modality.*
       10) Problematic.
       11) Assertoric.
       12) Apodeictic.

2. Table of Categories.

    a) *Quantity.*
       1) Unity.
       2) Plurality.
       3) Totality.

    b) *Quality.*
       4) Reality.
       5) Negation.
       6) Limitation.

    c) *Relation.*
       7) Inherence and subsistence (substance and accident).
       8) Causality and dependence (cause and effect).
       9) Community (reciprocity between agent and patient).

    d) *Modality.*
       10) Possibility — impossibility.
       11) Existence — nonexistence.
       12) Necessity — contingency.

Kant's idealistic and positivistic successors were dissatisfied with the metaphysical deduction. The *idealists* sought either to lengthen or shorten the list, while yet retaining its a priori and necessary character. The *positivists* suggested that the entire a priori structure should be subjected to the historical process, with the likelihood of changes occurring among the present categories and the emergence of new ones, in the course of time. Kant could not accept the positivist suggestion of an evolutionary development of the mind, since it would require the transference of the categories from the understanding to sensibility, where the inner form of time prevails. Such a development would undermine the universal and necessary nature of the categories. As for the idealistic tamperings with the list, they would destroy Kant's claim to have made a rigorous deduction of these and only these categories. In point of fact, however, Kant's source for the list of the kinds of judgment was a historically conditioned one: the logic textbooks of his own century and country. Kant scanned and collated these textbooks, in order to arrive at a set of logical functions of judgment that would corroborate his own views on the nature of the categorial concepts of the understanding. Hence the metaphysical deduction of the categories must be kept subordinate to, and interpreted in the light of, the more fundamental, transcendental deduction of categories as such.

Any relevant realistic evaluation of this doctrine on the categories must pay close attention to its basis in the Kantian *theory of judgment,* as stated in the following texts.

> Since no representation, save when it is an intuition, is in immediate relation to an object, no concept is ever related to an object immediately, but to some other representation of it, be that other representation an intuition, or itself a concept. Judgment is therefore the mediate knowledge of an object, that is, the representation of a representation of it. . . . A judgment is nothing but the manner in which given modes of knowledge are brought to the objective unity of apperception. . . . Since we have to deal only with the manifold of our representations, and since that X (the object) which corresponds to them is nothing to us — being, as it is, something that has to be distinct from all our representations — the unity which the object makes necessary can be nothing else than the formal unity of consciousness in the synthesis of the manifold of representations.[31]

The Kantian understanding, being a completely nonabstractive and nonintuitive power, is always kept at one remove from any direct reference to things. It is not itself ordained to the being of existent things, and cannot reach this being, with the aid of sensuous intuitions. Hence there is no available way to express the essential nature and the act of existing, through acts of intellectual apprehension and judgment. In its own act of being, the thing remains an unknown X. Consequently, the judgmental acts are concerned with *unification of given perceptual knowledge,* rather than with the distinctively intelligible aspects of beings. The categories become purely logical functions or formal rules of unification. And they must look to the unity of the apperceiving subject, rather than to the act of being of the existent thing, for the general principle of unification of representations. The various Kantian categories express the generic ways in which consciousness-in-general combines the material of representation into

---

[31] *Critique of Pure Reason,* A 68: B 93, B 141, A 105 (Smith, 105, 159, 135). For a Thomistic treatment of the role of judgment in the foundation of metaphysics, read R. J. Henle, S.J., "Existentialism and the Judgment," *Proceedings of the American Catholic Philosophical Association,* XXI (1947), 40–53.

objects of knowledge, rather than the generic ways in which the being of things is realized in them. Kant criticized Wolff for making the principle of contradiction the sufficient criterion of all true judgments, synthetic as well as analytic. Kant himself restored the conditions of sense experience to their central role in the determination of experiential truths, but he did not carry his revision of Wolff far enough. For, he accepted the Wolffian view that the act of judging is essentially a formal combining of representative materials, instead of an intentional reaffirmation of the being of the other as other. Hence Kant located the determining motive of the true judgment about experiential objects only in the transcendental conditions of consciousness-in-general, especially the unity of apperception. This left the judgment totally inexpressive of the principles of being, within the existent thing.

In recapitulation of the sections on the Transcendental Esthetic and Transcendental Analytic, the following *components of objective experience and knowledge* are specified by Kant: the matter of sensation, the forms of sensibility, the schemata of imagination, the categories, and the transcendental unity of apperception.[32] Except for the first factor, these elements of knowledge are the a priori structural forms of consciousness-in-general (not merely empirical forms of this or that particular consciousness). Hence they are the a priori, transcendental conditions for the possibility of experience and objectivity as a whole. Without the co-operation of all these principles (including the matter of sensation), mere empirical judgments of perception cannot be transformed into scientifically valid judgments of experience. Similarly, without their integral presence, our pure concepts may generate thought and belief but can never yield strict knowledge (*Erkenntnis*) and experience (*Erfahrung*) of objects. The ground has now been prepared for dealing with the pretensions made by speculative reason in favor of its pure ideas.

## 6. THE PARALOGISMS AND ANTINOMY OF PURE REASON

The Transcendental Dialectic examines the claim of transcendent metaphysics to be a science. Kant distinguishes between the *inevitability* of metaphysics and its *scientific* character. Almost by definition,

32 For an authoritative summary, see H. J. Paton, "Kant's Analysis of Experience," *Proceedings of the Aristotelian Society*, N.S., XXXVI (1935–1937), 187–206.

he rejects the latter, since he describes metaphysics as an attempt to use pure concepts in a nonempirical way, in order to gain knowledge about things-in-themselves. The whole burden of the Esthetic and Analytic is to show the emptiness of pure concepts, taken apart from sensuous intuition, and the impossibility of knowing anything except the appearances. Nevertheless, Kant is not sanguine enough to hope that his critical findings will ever extirpate the tendency toward metaphysical thinking, since it is the native bent of our reason. His purpose is rather to make intelligible the persistence of this "natural and unavoidable dialectic of pure reason,"[33] so that our intelligence may be placed on its guard.

Its roots are traceable directly to the nature of the pure concepts of the understanding. The categories may be regarded in two ways: absolutely or in themselves, and relatively or in reference to sensuous intuitions. Taken in the latter way, the categories are schematized by the imagination and proportioned to a definite sense content. Only the *schematized categories* are able to give knowledge, since only in this respect do they receive the required intuitive filling or determinate content. But the categories may also be taken absolutely or as pure concepts. The *unschematized, pure categories* have an intrinsic meaning, a logical content, that remains even when they are not considered in relation to sensuous intuition. This meaning is not sufficiently determinate to provide knowledge; it is also wholly formal and deprived of an intuitive basis. Yet although the pure categories cannot *give knowledge* by themselves, they can be *thought of* by themselves. We can think the pure categorial meaning in itself, considered as a *logical* possibility, without reference to the empirical conditions required for the *real* possibility of objects.[34] Hence the categories have

---

[33] *Critique of Pure Reason*, A 298: B 354 (Smith, 300). Whether the dialectic described by Kant is natural to the human mind or only ingrained in the rationalist tradition in philosophy, is a major point at issue.

[34] Although Kant denies any determinate, objective meaning to the categories apart from the framework of space and time, he does allow an indeterminate and nonobjective meaning, yielding no strict knowledge; cf. *Critique of Pure Reason*, A 147: B 185; A 244–50: B 302–07 (Smith, 186–87, 262–68). This distinction is closely bound up with the Kantian doctrine on the kinds of possibility, as stated in *ibid.*, B xxvi, note (Smith, 27, note):

1. Logical possibility of the concept (what is thinkable).
2. Real possibility of the object.
   *a*) Theoretical real possibility (what is knowable).
   *b*) Practical real possibility (what is believable).

(N.B. What is a mere logical possibility in the speculative or theoretical order may become a real possibility in the practical order.)

a nonobjective significance, pointing in a vertical or transempirical direction. This residual meaning easily entices reason into the paths of metaphysical speculation, once reason blurs the distinction between logical and real possibility.

The open, unschematized categories provide the basis for concepts of things-in-themselves, as distinct from the world of appearances. This is the ground for the legitimate distinction between *phenomena* and *noumena*.[35] All our knowledge is phenomenal or confined to objects of appearance. Yet we can conceive in some measure how things-in-themselves might be, i.e., we can form noumenal concepts. Kant hedges in the significance of noumenal concepts by calling them indeterminate, negative, and problematic concepts. They convey some *indeterminate* meaning, to the extent that we can conceive of the logical possibility of the nature of things, as they would be in themselves, rather than in their appearance. But this meaning is not determinate enough to convert a logical possibility into a real one and thus to give any knowledge about things-in-themselves. Furthermore, these noumenal concepts have a *negative* rather than a positive meaning. They are *Grenzbegriffe,* limit-concepts, signifying that which would *not* be the object of a sensuous intuition. But they do not convey any information about a *non*sensuous or intellectual intuition of things-in-themselves. Finally, the concept of a noumenon is a *problematic* rather than an assertoric one. It contains no intrinsic contradiction, since we cannot affirm that sensuous intuition is the sole possible kind or that an intellectual intuition is impossible. To recall the distinction made in the *Dissertation* of 1770, the pure noumenal concepts have a critical but not a dogmatic aim. They prevent materialists and empiricists from maintaining that only sense appearances are real and that the conditions of the empirical world must obtain for all modes of being. But they do not contain any intuitive content that would give strict knowledge of the order of being that does lie beyond the appearances. Kant observes that it is difficult to retain these nice distinctions concerning the proper scope of noumenal concepts. The dialectical illusions of metaphysics ensue, once reason forgets these limits and seeks to gain positive knowledge of things-in-themselves through noumenal concepts.

The distinction between understanding and reason supplies the final

---

clarification needed to appreciate the Dialectic. The aim of *understanding* is a purely immanent one, directed toward objects that can be exhibited within our experience. The categories of the understanding supply the rules of unity for sensuous intuitions, so that there may result the objects of experience. *Reason* tends to go beyond the appearances and the limitations of sense intuition. Its concepts are the ideas, which develop out of the categories, as soon as the latter are viewed in their pure unschematized meaning. Whereas understanding unites the sense manifold under the unity of *categorial rules,* reason attempts to bring these rules themselves under the unconditioned unity of a few *ultimate principles or ideas.* Its goal is to ascertain the absolutely unconditioned principles of unity which determine all logical inferences, categorial functions of judgment, and objects of experience.

Reason is a sound power in itself and does not lead exclusively to illusion and error. There are two ways in which its ideas can go beyond the appearances: as regulative principles and as constitutive principles. In their *regulative* office, they serve the legitimate and even necessary purpose of urging on ("regulating") the understanding toward ever more consistent and comprehensive syntheses of phenomena. The ideas of pure reason hold up before the understanding a rational ideal of systematic explanation, a set of maxims of thought for the guidance and incitement of scientific inquiry. But reason inclines to mistake these maxims of mere thought (which bear direct reference only to the understanding, rather than to objects) for autonomous maxims of real knowledge. It pretends to gain knowledge through its ideas alone, using them in a *constitutive* way to ascertain ("constitute") real objects, rather than to guide the understanding. When the ideas of pure reason are used constitutively, they unavoidably lead to metaphysical illusion. It follows that reason can operate in two distinct ways: (*a*) as a *transcendental* power, it makes a legitimate, regulative use of its ideas; (*b*) as a *transcendent* power, it makes an invalid, constitutive use of its ideas.[36] In its transcendental employment, reason inquires into the systematic grounds of unity for the categorial rules of the understanding, so that the experiential knowledge already in our possession may be better organized and made more inclusive. But in its transcendent phase, reason claims to go

---

[36] On Kant's somewhat fluctuating use of this distinction, cf. N. K. Smith, *A Commentary to Kant's 'Critique of Pure Reason,'* 73–76.

beyond experience entirely and to gain positive knowledge about the intelligible principles of being or things-in-themselves. The latter usage generates a nest of dialectical illusions.

Kant makes an a priori deduction of the three general ideas of reason.[37] The forms of syllogistic reasoning (categorical, hypothetical, and disjunctive) correspond to the categories of relation (substance, cause, and community). Reason employs this correspondence as a guiding principle for bringing about complete unification among its operations. It seeks the unconditioned principle of categorical reasoning in a substance or thinking subject; that of hypothetical reasoning in the totality of the causal series of appearances; that of disjunctive reasoning (all objects reciprocally together) in the system of all perfections. This leads to the three ultimate synthetic principles or ideas of reason: *soul, world,* and *God.* These ideas are the organizing centers, respectively, for the sciences of psychology, cosmology, and natural theology, which together constitute the main divisions of Wolffian special metaphysics. The transcendent use of these three ideas involves reason deeply in a system of illusion and error. The faulty inferences concerning the soul constitute the *Paralogisms* of pure reason; those concerning the world lead to the *Antinomy* of pure reason; those about God generate the *Ideal* of pure reason. Under the three headings of the Paralogisms, Antinomy, and Ideal of pure reason, Kant concentrates his more particular criticisms of metaphysical reasoning, as exemplified in the textbooks written in the Wolffian tradition.

1. *The Paralogisms.* Rational psychology tries to infer from the given fact of a thinking "I," something about the soul's nature. It affirms that the soul is: a substance, simple, self-identical in a personal way, and related to a world that may be inferred to exist outside us, in space. From these four major traits of the soul are derived the remaining psychological theses about the soul's immateriality, spiritual-

---

[37] *Critique of Pure Reason,* A 333–35: B 390–92 (Smith, 322–24); *Prolegomena to Any Future Metaphysics,* 43 (Beck, 77–79). By means of this deduction from syllogistic functions, Kant hoped to substitute rigor for "mere rhapsody" in metaphysics, and to include all the parts of Wolffian special metaphysics: rational psychology (the soul), cosmology (the world), and natural theology (God). On Wolff's notion of philosophy as the science of possible things as such, and on his division of the philosophical sciences, cf. R. J. Blackwell, "The Structure of Wolffian Philosophy," *The Modern Schoolman,* XXXVII (1960–1961), 203–218. For Wolff's general metaphysics or ontology, which studied being in general as nonexistential possibility, Kant substituted his own critical study of the conditions of experience in general, which supplied the only context for knowable (but purely phenomenal) existence.

ity, incorruptibility, immortality, personality, and animation of a body. But none of these consequences can be any more firmly established than the four main pillars upon which they rest. Kant claims that the four basic principles are themselves vitiated by paralogisms or formal errors in reasoning, and that consequently the entire structure of rational psychology is built upon a crumbling foundation.

The typical case is the argument used to prove the *substantiality* of the soul. Kant throws it into the following syllogistic form, in order to reveal the fundamental fallacy of the ambiguous middle that underlies all psychological proofs.

> *That which cannot be thought otherwise than as subject does not exist otherwise than as subject, and is therefore substance.*
> *A thinking being, considered merely as such, cannot be thought otherwise than as subject.*
> *Therefore it exists also only as subject, that is, as substance.*[38]

The logical defect in the syllogism is that it contains four terms. In the major, "subject-that-is-thought" is an *objective* designation for an intuitively given, permanent substratum, to which the category of substance applies. In the minor, however, "subject-that-is-thought" means only the consciousness of the "I" that thinks. This is a non-intuitive awareness and, taken by itself, has only *subjective* weight. Even if it were capable of an objective meaning, there would be no reason for applying to the thinking subject the category of substance, since there is no observable element of permanence in mere consciousness of my thinking process. To this extent, Kant accepts Hume's account of the self. The other arguments in rational psychology make a similar shift from objective categories to merely formal, subjective notes.

Despite the assurance of this formal refutation, Kant found the problem of *self-knowledge* a very thorny one, and was never satisfied with his various solutions. His general position was clear-cut enough. The self cannot be an exception to the requirements of knowledge. Self-awareness is purely formal in itself. It must receive intuitive content from a sensuous source, and must accept this content as organized under the inner form of time. Hence self-knowledge attains only to the empirical self, the self as an *appearance* and not as a substantial *thing-in-itself*. But in his more detailed explanations, Kant

---

[38] *Critique of Pure Reason,* B 410-11 (Smith, 371). On the paralogisms, consult *ibid.,* A 341-405: B 399-432 (Smith, 328-83); *Prolegomena,* 46-49 (Beck, 81-86).

encountered a number of obscurities. In positing any mental state, the thinking subject also affects itself and *supplies itself with a certain manifold* or material content. Kant refused to allow that this manifold is sufficiently determinate to provide the matter of knowledge, for otherwise this would be a clear instance of an intellectual intuition. He called the original apperception of the thinking "I" a vague feeling, a mere existential awareness *that* some sort of thinking subject is present. Because this self-consciousness is excited only when some sense data are presented, Kant concluded that the intuition of the self must be a purely sensuous one. There is no knowledge of the determin*ing* subject or noumenal self but only of the determin*able* subject or phenomenal self.

Kant's conclusion on this question indicates that a theory of knowledge patterned after the standard of physics is limited, in principle, to what can appear as a physical object. Such a theory is not equipped for dealing with self-consciousness proper but only with the *limitations of the physicalist interpretation,* when applied to the subject's apprehension of itself precisely as an existing subject, rather than as a physical object. The fact that our self-awareness is conditioned by acts of sense perception does not warrant the conclusion that the reflective grasp of the self is confined to sensuous intuition and bereft of intellectual intuition. It shows only that our human sort of self-knowledge, although itself a properly intellectual act of self-possession, is actually acquired when our powers are engaged in knowing the material objects to which they are properly ordained. Reflection or intellectual self-awareness in man is *inseparable from* knowledge of sense things, even though it is *not reducible entirely to* the conditions of sense perception.

From another standpoint, Hegel has observed that Kant's argument proves only that the determining "I" cannot be known *as a physical object,* not that it cannot be known *at all in its own active nature.* The fact that it cannot be known through the schematized categories provides an occasion for questioning the restriction of knowledge to their domain, rather than a reason for foreswearing knowledge of anything other than the "empirical ego." Only Kant's physicalist definition of knowledge prevents him from recognizing in existential self-awareness a genuine instance of knowledge, albeit one that cannot be reduced to knowledge of physical objects, i.e., to the objects of physics.

2. *The Antinomy.* Kant saw that the "natural antithetic" of reason is more stubbornly deep-seated in its speculations about the world than

about the self, since, in the case of the world, reason can offer cogent arguments on both sides. It seeks to bring back the given appearances, constituting the world, to a complete synthesis of their conditions, subordinated to one another in a series. But the regression can be made — apparently with equal strength — along directly *contradictory* lines. Hence reason is held powerless between thesis and antithesis. Cosmological speculations lead either to a sterile *contretemps* or to outright skepticism at the paradoxical results.

There are four main antinomies, based on the four classes of categories (quantity, quality, relation, and modality).[39] In each instance, the thesis represents the standpoint of *rationalism* and practical, moral interest, whereas the antithesis expresses the viewpoint of *empiricism* and the standard of scientific rigor. In the first antinomy of *quantity,* it is argued with equal force that the world has a beginning in time and is limited in spatial extent, and that it has no such beginning and limits but is infinite, both temporally and spatially. In the second or *qualitative* antinomy, it is shown both that every composite substance in the world is made up of simple parts and every existent is either itself simple or composed of simple parts, and also that there is no composite made up of simple parts and no simple existent in nature. In respect to causal *relations,* the third antinomy states (in the thesis) that the predetermined causality among appearances in nature must be supplemented by a free sort of causality, and (in the antithesis) that freedom has no place in the world of appearances, which are determined exclusively by natural laws. The fourth antinomy, concerned with the *modality* of the series of appearances, announces both that an absolutely necessary being belongs to the world, either as a part or as its cause, and that this necessary being cannot exist either in the world or outside it, as a cause.

Kant uses the doctrine on the antinomies not only to display the futility of metaphysical reasoning but also to score a victory over previous philosophies. Rationalism and empiricism are locked in hopeless conflict, because neither can rise to the liberating standpoint of critical philosophy. The source of the antinomies lies, not in *experience* itself, but in the manner in which *reason* treats experience. Hence only a study of pure reason from the transcendental viewpoint can resolve the problem of the antinomies. Kant offers his solution in two stages: first, by exposing the general dialectic of the cosmological

[39] *Critique of Pure Reason,* A 420–61: B 448–90 (Smith, 393–421); *Prolegomena to Any Future Metaphysics,* 50–52b (Beck, 86–89).

antinomy and, second, by distinguishing between the first two and the last two particular antinomies.

1. In dealing with the world, reason operates on the principle that *"if the conditioned is given, the entire sum of conditions, and consequently the absolutely unconditioned* (through which alone the conditioned has been possible) *is also given."*[40] Since sensible appearances are given as conditioned objects, it is supposed that the absolute totality of subordinated conditions, including the unconditioned principle of the world, must likewise be given to inference. But the above principle fails to mention *how* the series of conditioned objects and conditions is given to our understanding. In point of fact, the human mind knows the conditioned objects *only as appearances,* grasped in a sensuous intuition and an empirical synthesis of time. These circumstances affect the way in which conditions themselves can be presented for valid inference. The limitations of time and a successive synthesis prevent any actual totality of conditions from being given. The unconditioned principle cannot be given in an essentially temporal and finite type of experience. All the mind can do, is to engage in an infinite regress in the temporal series, and from this regressive movement neither the thesis nor the antithesis can be established as an unconditioned truth. Rationalists err in applying directly to appearances the noumenal principle about a total series of conditions, whereas empiricists err in treating the world of appearances as though it were a world of things-in-themselves. Kant's remedy is to keep the noumenal and phenomenal orders strictly apart, limit our knowledge to appearances, and regard "the world" as a regulative rather than a constitutive idea.

2. The distinction between "world" and "nature" enables Kant to distinguish among the several antinomies. The *world* is the totality of appearances regarded as a homogeneous, quantitative aggregate, whereas *nature* signifies a dynamic, qualitative, causal view of the same totality. The first two antinomies are mathematical ones about the world, whereas the last two antinomies are dynamical ones in respect to nature.[41] The *mathematical* antinomies treat all the members of the series or world as having the same character, thus making the conditions always *homogeneous* with the conditioned objects of experience. Both thesis and antithesis are *false* in the first two antin-

40 *Critique of Pure Reason,* A 409: B 436 (Smith, 386).
41 *Ibid.,* A 583–90: B 611–18 (Smith, 495–99); *Prolegomena to Any Future Metaphysics,* 53 (Beck, 90).

omies, since all the conditions must be sensible appearances.)In such a situation, reason only confounds itself by treating noumenal realities in a phenomenal way and appearances in a noumenal way. On the other hand, the *dynamical* view of nature permits of some *heterogeneity* in the series of conditions and conditioned. For, there may be a difference in kind between cause and effect, as well as between the necessary and the contingent. Some of the conditions may possibly belong to the purely intelligible order (unknowable to us), rather than to the sensible order. Hence there is no necessary, intrinsic conflict between the assertions made in thesis and antithesis, in the case of the third and fourth antinomies. The thesis may refer to the *intelligible* order of things-in-themselves, whereas the antithesis certainly considers only the requirements within the order of *appearances.* Both contentions may be *true* in different respects, although we can never acquire strict knowledge of the truth of the thesis, concerning the things-in-themselves.

Thus a reconcilation is possible between *freedom* and *determinism* (the third antinomy). All events in nature — including those that constitute the empirical self — are predetermined by past events in the same series. But since appearances are not things-in-themselves, they may be conceived as having a basis that is not itself an appearance, and hence that is not regulated by the law of natural necessity. Universal empirical determinism is compatible with a noumenal cause, whose action is itself purely intelligible and free, even though its phenomenal effects are rigorously determined within the sensible world. Kant defines freedom as "the power of beginning a state *spontaneously.*"[42] Two kinds of causation may be at work in empirical objects: nontemporal and temporal, intelligible and sensible, spontaneously free and predetermined. There is room for at least the *problematic concept* of the existence of a first, free cause and of finite, free agents. Similarly, a reconciliation can be effected between the thorough contingency and temporality of nature and a necessary being (the fourth antinomy). Precisely because nature consists of a series of appearances, the contingent order may be conceived as being grounded in a necessary being, regarded as its intelligible or noumenal condition.

Kant does not pretend to prove the existence of freedom or the necessary being, from this resolution of the last two antinomies. It

---

[42] *Critique of Pure Reason,* A 533: B 561 (Smith, 464); cf. *Prolegomena,* 53, note 13 (Beck, 92).

only demonstrates that there is no intrinsic incompatibility between freedom and determinism, necessary and contingent being. Within the context of speculative philosophy and knowledge proper, this remains a mere *logical possibility*. It can never be converted into a *real, epistemic possibility*, such as would give knowledge of its object. But at least it is sufficient to refute the claims of antilibertarians and antitheists. And the Kantian resolution of the dynamical antinomies prepares the way for establishing the *real, practical possibility* of the theses about freedom and God, such that these realities may be believed in, as a matter of moral faith. This is the precise meaning of Kant's famous declaration: "I have therefore found it necessary to deny *knowledge*, in order to make room for *faith*."[43] What he actually denies is not our ability to know anything but our ability to bring all reality within the scope of our knowledge, in the strict sense. Whatever falls within the scope of knowledge is subject to the conditions of determinism and finitude. Were the claim to *know* freedom and God sustained, then their very nature would be destroyed: freedom would be a type of predeterminism within nature, and God would be a temporal, finite being. Kant does not deny knowledge so much as restrict it to appearances. He denies that it can extend to intelligible realities, like freedom and God. The minimum achieved by this restriction is to open up the logical possibility of their reality; the maximum is to allow faith or moral conviction to take up where knowledge fails us.

Yet despite the fact that the antinomy between nature and freedom involves the very ground of moral life, Kant's explanation leaves their mutual relationship unclarified. To save the freedom of noumenal actions, he places them entirely *beyond time,* the inner principle of the predetermination of appearances. There are some paradoxical consequences flowing from this extreme dualism. Kant teaches that an intelligible agent does not produce actions that either begin or cease, for then its causality would be subject to the form of time. Time makes no difference to its actions, even though it does make a difference to the relations among the effects of its actions. Nothing happens *to* the intelligible agent as such, and nothing transpires *in* it, although *of itself* it spontaneously produces free actions. Although the intelligible agent and its causality are free, the *effects* of this

---

[43] *Critique of Pure Reason,* Preface to Second Edition, B xxx (Smith, 29); cf. *ibid.,* A 745: B 773 (Smith, 597).

causality are not free, since they are occurrences in the determined, natural course of events. Hence the phenomenal event can be predicted with perfect certainty, even though its empirical causality is due to a free, nonempirical agent. This is Kant's answer to the Humean argument for determinism, based on our ability to make predictions about human events.

Kant is employing the category of causality in its pure, unschematized meaning, but it is difficult to ascertain whether his remarks retain even the minimum of logical conceivability. When the temporal character of moral decisions is emptied out, the resultant concept of freedom is too indeterminate to be related firmly to natural events. It leads to a sharp dualism of intelligible and empirical causality, which resists consistent formulation in language. In human experience, there is no way of testing even the logical possibility of a free, finite act that would have a definite effect without any happening occurring in the agent, or the possibility of a beginning of an effect that would not entail the temporal inception of the free action, at its finite source. Kant tries to make meaningful the statement that an event might be completely determined by natural antecedents, and yet issue from an original free act. To overcome the divorce of *act* and *effect,* he suggests that the empirical plane of causality is but the shadow of the intelligible region of moral character. This is a transcendent, metaphysical assumption, however, which Kant is not prepared to substantiate. Ultimately, an appeal is needed to God, as the author of nature and harmonizer of the intelligible and empirical causalities of finite agents. This view contains the seeds of Fichte's voluntaristic conception of nature and science.

## 7. GOD AS THE TRANSCENDENT IDEAL OF PURE REASON

The peak of unification among the ideas of reason is reached in the idea of the most perfect being (*ens realissimum*). This supreme idea is also the most notable instance of an *ideal* of pure reason, i.e., a concept of an individual thing, determined constitutively through the rational concept alone and used as an archetype. Reason tries to include all objects in general within one fundamental principle of all possibility, the idea of the most perfect being. Working under a natural tendency, reason hypostasizes this idea in the form of an individual idea, gives it the customary attributes of God, and affirms its real being. Kant's attack upon this procedure has two phases. First, he criticizes the general line of reasoning about the existence of an absolutely perfect being, and then he gives special consideration to the three types of proof offered in the German rationalistic textbooks on natural theology.

The *general procedure* of reason is to start with some given, contingent existent.[44] The latter supposes a being that exists according to an absolute necessity. Unconditioned necessity must, in turn, be fitted to some determinate concept, not incompatible with this character. Reason finds an appropriate concept in its own ideal of the most perfect being or completely real ground of possibility, *ens realissimum*. Kant does not deny that this is an appropriate choice, indeed, one to which we are compelled in the practical sphere. But he does question whether there is any theoretical coercion behind the identification between complete necessity and absolute perfection, even supposing the existence of an unconditionally necessary being. For, it cannot be shown that *only* an absolutely real or perfect being is a necessary one. There is no evident incompatibility between the concept of a limited being and that of unconditioned necessity.

Kant could find qualified support for this last statement among some defenders of metaphysical theism. Discussing Avicenna's notion of a necessary existent, for instance, St. Thomas remarks that a finite being (such as a pure, angelic form) could have a simple necessity of existence, if it were free from corruptible matter. Nevertheless, its finitude would be an indication that its necessity of existence is of a *derived* and consequent sort. Eventually, the cause of the necessary existence would have to be a being that exists necessarily, through its own nature or in an *underived* way. Here, proof is first made of an actual being, existing in a necessary way through its own nature, and then proof is given that a being having this underived necessity of existence must also be infinite. This is a typical theistic procedure, but it does not square with Kant's account. For, Kant does not distinguish satisfactorily between *conceiving* of unconditioned necessity and *proving* a being to exist in an underived and necessary way. Necessary existence remains for him a regulative idea, so that his hypothesis of signifying unconditioned necessity is not a hypothesis about proof of God, as exercising necessity in existence.

Kant is content with pointing out the distinction between the two

---

44 *Ibid.*, A 583–90: B 611–18 (Smith, 495–99).

*concepts* of "absolute perfection" and "unconditioned necessity," whereas the nub of the theistic argument concerns whether a *being proved to exist* in a necessary, yet finite, way is self-existent, and whether a *being proved to exist* with underived necessity is also infinite in perfection. The Thomistic demonstration goes from actual, contingent existents to an existent proved to be necessary and underived; the Kantian dialectic goes from the meaning of contingency to that of unconditioned necessity, and thence to the concept of complete perfection. Hence the Thomistic demonstration does not have to wait for the identification of unconditioned necessity and absolute perfection, before completing proof of God's existence. But the Kantian dialectic is never compelled to make this identification, simply because no being is ever supposed to be proved as a necessary existent. This discrepancy suggests that Kant's discussion of theistic arguments does not systematically dispose of all possible metaphysical proofs, as he claimed it to do.

Kant reduces all particular proofs of God's existence to three kinds: the *ontological* (starting a priori from the concept alone), the *cosmological* (starting from the broad, undifferentiated experience of objects), and the *physicotheological* (starting from the specific experience of causal order and purpose in the world). Reason is persuaded that it begins with the two latter proofs, based upon experience, whereas Kant detects the secret influence of the ideal of pure reason, as contained in the first proof. Hence he first exposes the fallacies in the ontological argument, and then shows how the cosmological proof covertly appeals to the ontological. Finally, he observes that, to obtain complete rigor, the physicotheological proof must fall back upon the cosmological, and so fall victim, in its turn, to the deficiencies in the underlying ontological argument. Although Kant referred to these three proofs as constituting the "natural course and the only possible proofs" of reason for God's existence, it is clear that he consulted only the current rationalistic arguments. His strictures are conditioned by the narrow historical scope of his study of the philosophical sources on this question.

1. *The Ontological Proof.* The usual a priori argument states that there is a necessary connection between existence and the concept of an absolutely perfect being. If a being is absolutely real or perfect, it must have existence among its attributes, for otherwise it would be lacking in the full complement of its unconditioned possibility. The Leibnizian-Wolffian notion of existence as the complement of

possibility is the kind of existence being concluded to, in this proof.

Kant concentrates his criticism upon two points: the necessity of the divine being and the attribution of existence. (*a*) There is insufficient content in our notion of an absolutely *necessary being*. Wolff defines it as that, the nonexistence of which is impossible. Kant points out that by "impossible," here, is meant "unthinkable to us." Rationalists cannot answer the simple argument that what may seem impossible from our limited standpoint may, in fact, be quite possible in itself. No purely formal criterion can decide whether the necessity under discussion bears upon the real order or merely expresses our mental limitations. When necessity is used in existential propositions, the difference must be respected between hypothetical and absolute necessity. If the existence of a triangle is given, the triangle must necessarily have three angles. But one can deny the existential supposition, and then the necessity of the thing or its predicates, taken by themselves, vanishes. In the present case, granted the existence of a necessary being, then the necessary connection between its reality and existence is seen. But this *hypothetical, conceptual* necessity cannot be transformed into an *absolute, existential* one, without appealing to some considerations outside the concept of a completely perfect being, in justification of supposing its actual existence. If no such reasons are forthcoming, then the real subject of the existential proposition is removed, and no contradiction results from denying actual existence to it.

(*b*) The proposition, "this thing exists," is either analytic or synthetic. If the former, then *existence* adds nothing to the thought of the thing. But it is clear to Kant, from his pre-critical researches, that existence does make some addition and hence that the proposition is synthetic. Hence a purely a priori proof of the existence of God, based on analysis of the concept of the most perfect being, is impossible. Kant now goes on to give his own positive view of the "more" or the *distinctive contribution of existence*. Existence belongs in the class of modal categories (possibility, existence, and necessity). The problem raised by the ontological argument is: how to distinguish the judgment of existence from that of possibility. This problem is equivalent to that of passing from an unschematized to a schematized use of the category expressing the subject of the existential proposition. If one remains, rationalistically, at the level of the pure or unschematized category, there is no way of distinguishing between the possibility and the real existence of the thing requiring existential proof.[45] This distinction can only be made when we submit the concept of the subject of the proposition to the determination of the schemata of imagination, and hence also to the conditions of time, sensibility, and human experience in general. This is the closest Kant gets to an explanation of the "more" added by existence to the conceptual order of essence. The index of real existence is *successful incorporation within the conditions and connections of our experience*. We are justified in making an existential pronouncement, only when we have shown that the thing in question is an integral component within the system of the world of appearances. Any other meaning of existence goes beyond knowledge and finds its foundation in faith.

The relevance of this conception of existence for evaluation of the ontological proof is clear. The concept of an *unconditionally* perfect being has complete conceptual determination but it cannot be exhibited, in any way, in sense experience. For, sense experience is completely conditioned in principle and reveals only *conditioned* modes of existence or components of experience. Hence experience provides no way of distinguishing between mere possibility and real existence, in the case of the concept of an unconditioned being. The judgment of existence is based solely upon knowledge of the connectedness of finite things, within the system of experience in general. Kant allows no knowledge of the existential act *as the ultimate act of being,* on the part of finite things, since their empirical connectedness reaches to them only *insofar as they are objective appearances.* Hence he denies not only that an unconditioned nature can be presented directly *in* experience but also that its existence can be inferred with rigor *from*

---

[45] "Through the concept the object is thought only as conforming to the *universal conditions* of possible empirical knowledge in general, whereas through its existence it is thought as belonging to the context of experience as a whole. . . . If we attempt to think existence through the pure category alone, we cannot specify a single mark distinguishing it from mere possibility." *Critique of Pure Reason,* A 600–01: B 628–29 (Smith, 506). Kant substitutes for the rationalistic conception of existence as a mere consequence in the line of essence, a *contextualistic* view of existence as insertion within the conditions of experience in general. This character of contextualistic existence does not attain, however, to existence as the ultimate act of being of the thing. The importance of Kant's conception of existence for his criticism of the ontological proof is signalized in the analytic study by S. Halldén: "Kants Kritik der ontologischen Gottesbeweises," *Theoria,* XVIII (1952), 1–31. For a comparison between Aquinas and Kant, on this argument, cf. O. Herrlin, *The Ontological Proof in Thomistic and Kantian Interpretation* (Uppsala, Lundequistska Bokhandeln, 1950).

what is given in experience. His criticism of the ontological argument goes far beyond this proof. For it is, implicitly, a rejection of every sort of speculative proof of God's existence. On the basis of his theory of the judgment of existence, there cannot even be an a posteriori proof of the existence of God as a nontemporal, nonfinite being, since this would transcend the limits of experience.

2. *The Cosmological and Physicotheological Proofs.* If a start is made with the contingent objects of experience, Kant holds that one can conclude, from the fact of contingency, that there must be an ideal ground of absolute necessity. But this notion of a necessary being is a purely indefinite one and requires some determination. If the determination is taken solely from the principle of contradiction, then no more than a logical meaning attaches to the existence of the necessary being. This compels reason to invoke the notion of *ens realissimum*, affirming that the being which must exist, is a perfect one. Although some conceptual determination is thereby given to the notion of unconditioned necessity, the cosmological argument is now dependent upon the ontological argument to show, in an a priori way, that the being which necessarily exists, has to be regarded as the unique, all-perfect being. For the a priori truth of the proposition: *every necessarily existent being is completely perfect,* rests upon its convertibility with the proposition: *every completely perfect being is necessarily existent.* Now the latter proposition is precisely the one upon which the ontological argument is built. Hence the deficiencies of the ontological proof are visited upon the cosmological one.

The critical comments made upon Kant's treatment of the general procedure of reason and the ontological argument, apply with renewed force here. Kant's formulation of the cosmological argument is colored by his own view that the only existence open to human knowledge is that of systematic integration with the general conditions of experience. These conditions determine the mind to phenomenal objects and concepts but not to things in their ultimate act of being. Hence the kind of cosmological argument analyzed by Kant neither *begins with* the existential act of contingent, finite beings nor *terminates in* the demonstrated existential act of God, as the being proved to exist in a necessary and underived way. That is why some determinate content must be sought outside the indefinite *concept* of unconditioned necessity. This concept must be determined in a purely ideal way by the further concept of complete perfection, so that it may gain definite meaning and existential standing. Kant puts it this way:

Experience may perhaps lead us to the concept of absolute necessity, but is unable to demonstrate this necessity as belonging to any determinate thing. For immediately we endeavour to do so, we must abandon all experience and search among pure concepts to discover whether any one of them contains the conditions of the possibility of an absolutely necessary being. If in this way we can determine the possibility of a necessary being, we likewise establish its existence.[46]

From this description it is clear that he is dealing only with the rationalistic version of the cosmological argument, which ultimately requires that existence be proved conceptually and a priori from a principle of absolute possibility. Such a procedure is inherently incapable of establishing the truth of the proposition: *God exists.* Whereas Kant criticizes the proof for relying upon the ontological argument, the realistic criticism is that it misconceives the nature of existential demonstration. It is not representative of the a posteriori manner of reasoning to God's existence. And unfortunately, Kant's theory of existence prevents him from extending existential demonstration beyond the immanent conditions of experience.

As an additional objection, Kant remarks that the cosmological proof supposes that the category of *cause* can be employed *transcendently,* to establish a causal relation between limited, contingent beings and an absolutely necessary being. Those who discover a way of presenting this proof without appealing to the notion of the most perfect being, are still obliged to apply causality beyond the conditioned order of experience to the unconditionally necessary being. For Kant, this involves the use of the unschematized concept of cause, and such a use can never lead to knowledge. It might lead to a vague, purely formal meaning, but this meaning would lack the determinateness and intuitive content required for genuine knowledge. Because the mind never grasps the being of contingent things in an unqualified way, Kant finds no ground for making causal inferences beyond the contingent objects of experience. This reasoning shows how misleading it is to maintain that Kant's criticism of the

---

[46] *Critique of Pure Reason*, A 607-08: B 635-36 (Smith, 510). E. J. Nelson, "Kant on the Cosmological Argument," *The Philosophical Review*, XLIV (1935), 283-87, shows that Kant does not establish the dependence of the cosmological argument upon the ontological. For the latter proof is not invoked, in order to show that there *is* a necessary existent. The equivalence of *ens realissimum* with the necessary existent is not indispensable to the proof of the latter's *existence*, but only of its *nature*, and hence the concept of *ens realissimum* is detached from its function in the ontological proof.

proofs for God's existence retains its force, even apart from his special theory of knowledge. On the contrary, his evaluation of the rationalistic proofs is a strict consequence of his doctrine on the categories and the structure of experience. Its probative force depends entirely upon his *epistemological* principles. If these principles are questioned, then the entire problem of how to prove God's existence can be reopened, without any obligation to restrict the discussion to the particular proofs which were familiar to Kant.

Men ordinarily arise to the conception of God from a contemplation of the order and purpose displayed in nature. Having rejected the argument for the ground of possibility (which had won his adherence, during the pre-critical period), Kant now reserved his highest praise for the third proof. He called the *physicotheological argument* "the oldest, the clearest, and the most accordant with the common reason of mankind."[47] It quiets skeptical doubts, makes us sensitive to the purposes at work in nature, and provides a transition to the realm of faith or practical reason. But from a strictly speculative and scientific standpoint, this line of reasoning reaches only to an ordering intelligence, a sort of Platonic demiurge, which fashions a given mass, rather than creates it from nothing. In order to demonstrate that the matter as well as the form of the world is contingent, and hence that there is an *infinite* creator, something more is needed than the analogy of the human craftsman. The argument from design must be subordinated to that based on contingency and the need for an unconditioned necessity and all-perfect reality. As a proof of a transcendent God, the physicotheological proof is reducible to the cosmological and, in this indirect way, to the ontological argument. The latter proof at once supports and vitiates all the other efforts of pure reason to prove God's existence.

We are inclined to ask Kant why reason continues to entertain its three main ideas, if they lead to such fallacious results. His reply is that they do serve a useful purpose, when they are used merely regulatively and transcendentally. The ideas of reason cannot increase the objective content of experience one whit, since they are not constitutive of objects. But, as regulative principles, they do stimulate the understanding to proceed as if it had achieved absolute unity. This assumption or metaphysical schema enables it to increase the comprehensiveness and consistency of the knowledge already in its pos-

---

47 *Critique of Pure Reason*, A 623: B 651 (Smith, 520).

session. The idea of God is specially valuable, even within the immanent sphere of experience. For, it encourages the speculative mind to
view nature *as if* it were produced by a divine intelligence and hence
were endowed with discoverable unity, intelligibility, and purpose. By
a sort of *"symbolical* anthropomorphism," we may conceive of the
relation which the transcendent being might bear toward the proper
objects of our experience. This is the nearest Kant comes to a doctrine
on *analogy*.[48] He seeks to distinguish this philosophical analogy from
mathematical analogy, on the ground that mathematical proportions
are constitutive of objects themselves, in the quantitative order,
whereas philosophical proportions are merely regulative of our ways
of thinking about qualitative relations, within experience. On this
reckoning, however, philosophical, analogical reasoning about God is
nonintuitive, nondemonstrative, and radically weaker, in every other
respect, than mathematical analogies. Just as in Hume's case, both
sorts of Kantian analogy are ultimately reducible to univocal
predication.

The regulative use of the idea of God does not attain to the being
of God. It reaches only to the *as-if* metaphysical schema of viewing
the experiential world under the hypothesis of its being the product
of an infinite intelligence and orderer. For Kant, knowledge remains
unredeemably univocal and immanent to experience, however much
it may strain symbolically toward the transcendent. Only moral faith
can pierce the vault of the transcendent order of being: but to do this,
the mind must abandon the terrain of strict knowledge.

We can now determine more precisely Kant's position concerning
the possibility of metaphysics in general. At the outset of the first
*Critique,* Kant had framed two questions concerning this discipline:
(1) Is metaphysics an unavoidable, natural tendency of the mind?
(2) Is metaphysics possible as a science? (1) An affirmative answer
must be given to the first question. By its very nature, reason brings
forth its ideas and attempts to use them to gain knowledge about the
intelligible transphenomenal aspects of things. The *usus realis* of
reason, for the dogmatic purpose of attaining to things-in-themselves, is

---

[48] *Ibid.,* A 179–80: B 222–23; A 643–45: B 671–73; A 670–74: B 699–702 (Smith,
210–11, 532–34, 550–52); *Prolegomena to Any Future Metaphysics,* 57–58 (Beck,
105–10); *Dissertation on the Form and Principles of the Sensible and Intelligible
World,* 10 (Handyside, 50). See above, note 9. The views of Kant and Hegel on
analogy are analyzed by E. K. Specht, *Der Analogiebegriff bei Kant und Hegel*
(Cologne, Kölner Universitätsverlag, 1952).

just as *ineradicable* a tendency of the human mind as are the first three idols of the mind in Francis Bacon's philosophy. And like Bacon, Kant did not pretend to be able to eliminate this metaphysical inclination of reason but only to put us critically on guard against its claims. (2) As a result of his critical investigations, however, Kant now saw that the second question can really be taken in two senses. (*a*) Is *transcendent metaphysics* possible as a science? Kant's negative answer was contained in the very meaning of the terms involved in the question. By a "transcendent metaphysics," he meant a discipline that derives its ideas in a wholly a priori way, apart from any sensory origin, and that also uses these ideas in a constitutive way, apart from any analysis of the implications of sense perception and experience. By "science," he meant the standard of knowledge found in mathematics and physics. Since, by definition, a transcendent metaphysics operates in a completely nonempirical way, it cannot stand in conformity with the conditions of experience and hence cannot yield knowledge but only dialectical illusions. On this reckoning, it would be a contradiction in terms to maintain that a transcendent metaphysics can be a science. (*b*) But there is a special Kantian sense in which metaphysics is possible, viz., as a *transcendental science,* which makes only a regulative use of the ideas of reason.[49] Kant distinguishes between a narrower and a wider meaning for this legitimate sort of metaphysics. In the restricted sense, it is confined to a study of the systematic connections and principles of unity, found in all purely a priori operations of mind (whether they give genuine knowledge or only dialectical illusions). In the wider sense, however, metaphysics is identified with the whole philosophy of pure reason, including the critique of a priori knowledge and the metaphysical foundations of natural science and morals. But such transcendental metaphysical inquiries never yield strict knowledge of things in their own transphenomenal being. They extend only to the a priori structure of reason itself and to a determination of the limits of knowledge, in the direction of natural science and morals.

From these precisions concerning the Kantian attitude toward meta-

---

[49] *Critique of Pure Reason,* A 841–47: B 869–75 (Smith, 659–63). Cf. W. H. Walsh, "Kant's Criticism of Metaphysics," *Philosophy,* XIV (1939), 313–25, 424–46; H. Heimsoeth, "Metaphysische Motive in der Ausbildung des kritischen Idealismus," *Kantstudien,* XXIX (1924), 121–59; the unpublished master's thesis of J. H. Heiser, "Kant's Notion of Metaphysics in the *Critique of Pure Reason* and in the *Prolegomena*" (St. Louis University, 1953).

physics, we can also understand the several directions taken by metaphysical inquiry during the post-Kantian period. The *German idealists* reopened the question of the possibility of a transcendent metaphysics, by defending the reality of a purely intellectual intuition. Such an intuition would provide actual content for the constitutive use of the ideas of pure reason, and hence would overcome Kant's objections against supraempirical knowledge. But in order to establish the presence of an intellectual intuition in man, the idealists treated human consciousness and freedom as phases in the activity of the absolute self. The *positivists* challenged this identification of human consciousness with the absolute, but in denying pantheism, they also tended to eliminate any absolute being. They accepted Kant's limitation of metaphysics to the status of a merely transcendental science. In the positivist tradition, metaphysics was reduced to a summation of the general conditions of scientific knowledge. Philosophy of science became the positivistic equivalent for Kant's transcendental metaphysics. The more recent efforts of *Thomistic realists* to rehabilitate metaphysics have been determined, in large measure, by this historical situation of modern philosophy. In regard to Kant, they have criticized both his description of metaphysics and his standard of scientific knowledge. Emphasis has been laid upon the perceptual judgment of existence, which is closely reliant upon sense perception of the existent. The way in which realistic metaphysics bases its transempirical inferences upon the implications of sense experience itself has been underlined. At the same time, the distinctive foundation of metaphysics in a grasp of the existential act and the intelligible, essential structure of being has been brought to the fore. This dual emphasis upon both the experiential basis and the distinctive object of metaphysics is also relevant for an appraisal of nineteenth-century idealism and positivism. In dealing with the former, the perceptual judgment of existence provides a corrective; in dealing with the latter, the grasp of being in its intelligible principles is significant. Thomistic metaphysics does not appropriate the idealistic identification between the finite and absolute selves or its reduction of sensation to a low grade of intellection. Hence the positivistic reaction against idealism is not the only viable way of defending the human manner of being and knowing. The positivistic rejection of God and intellectual knowledge is, in turn, a one-sided interpretation of human experience. Once a humane and realistic metaphysics has differentiated itself emphatically from Kant's description of transcendent metaphysics, it can determine its independent position in respect to the idealistic and positivistic currents of the nineteenth century.

## SUMMARY OF CHAPTER 11

Kant saw that the opposition between reason and experience could only have skeptical consequences. The only viable solution was to synthesize these two poles, in such a way that experience is impregnated with rationality and reason ordained to empirical data. This involved a correction of both rationalism and empiricism. Instead of accepting the rationalist ideal of a mathematical method in philosophy, Kant took as his model Newtonian physics, which emphasized the givenness of the materials of experience and the limitation of knowledge to the accidents or appearances. But Humean skepticism had to be overcome by vindicating the objectivity of scientific judgments, in their necessity and universality. By transferring the hylemorphic composition from the ontological to the noetic order, Kant found a way of saving both empirical givenness (the matter of sensation) and rational objectivity (the forms of sensibility and the categories of understanding). We are able to determine a priori the conditions for the possibility of objects, only because these conditions are the same as those holding for the possibility of experience in general. Because the structure of consciousness-in-general holds good for all individual minds, the judgments comprising scientific experience are universal and necessary. This is the only kind of objectivity open to human knowledge. All objects of experience require the application of sensibility and the categories to the matter of sensation, with the mediating aid of the schemata of imagination. In this way, the propositions in mathematics and physics are justified as holding good for all experience, since they are both synthetic or empirically grounded and a priori or universal and necessary. Yet knowledge is limited to the appearances and does not reach metaphysically to things-in-themselves. Kant found no way to regard transcendent metaphysical propositions about intelligible realities as a priori synthetic, since he accepted the rationalistic stipulation that transcendent metaphysics must be totally nonempirical. Whereas the categories of scientific understanding submit to schematization and adaptation to empirical conditions, the ideas self-produced by metaphysical reason are used in a nonschematic way or transcendently, without dependence upon empirical data and limitations. Kant then made a dialectical analysis of metaphysical reasoning about things-in-themselves. He exposed the paralogisms about the soul, the antinomy on the world, and the illegitimate arguments to God's existence. The speculative impotence of pure reason was thus established, although Kant was careful to refrain from declaring that reason is intrinsically corrupt.

## BIBLIOGRAPHICAL NOTE

1. *Sources.* The Prussian Academy of Sciences sponsored the critical edition of Kant's *Gesammelte Schriften* (23 vols., Berlin, W. de Gruyter, 1902–1955). Another useful edition is *Immanuel Kants Werke*, edited by E. Cassirer (11 vols., Berlin, B. Cassirer,

1912–1918), the last volume of which contains E. Cassirer's *Kants Leben und Lehre*. Among the English translations are: *Kant's Cosmogony*, translated by W. Hastie (Glasgow, Maclehose, 1900) — contains: *Essay on the Retardation of the Rotation of the Earth* and *Natural History and Theory of the Heavens; A New Exposition of the First Principles of Metaphysical Knowledge,* contained as an Appendix in F. E. England's book, *Kant's Conception of God* (London, Allen and Unwin, 1929); *An Inquiry into the Distinctness of the Principles of Natural Theology and Morals,* included in the L. W. Beck translation of *Immanuel Kant: Critique of Practical Reason and Other Writings in Moral Philosophy* (Chicago, University of Chicago Press, 1949); *Dreams of a Spirit-Seer Illustrated by the Dreams of Metaphysics,* translated by E. F. Goerwitz, and edited by F. Sewall (New York, Macmillan, 1900); the J. Handyside translation of *Inaugural Dissertation and Early Writings on Space* (Chicago, Open Court, 1929) — contains: *Dissertation on the Form and Principles of the Sensible and Intelligible World* [1770], *On the First Ground of the Distinction of Regions in Space,* and selections from *Thoughts on the True Estimation of Living Forces; Critique of Pure Reason,* translated by N. K. Smith (second impression, with corrections, London, Macmillan, 1933); L. W. Beck's revision of the P. Carus translation of *Prolegomena to Any Future Metaphysics* (New York, Liberal Arts Press, 1950).

2. *Studies.* The heart of the classical German biographies of Kant (by Borowski, Jachmann, and Wasianski) has been preserved in J. H. W. Stuckenberg's English biography, *The Life of Immanuel Kant* (London, Macmillan, 1882). In addition to Cassirer's *Kants Leben und Lehre* (mentioned above), the following introductions are recommended: F. Paulsen, *Immanuel Kant: His Life and Doctrine* (New York, Scribner, 1902); A. D. Lindsay, *Kant* (London, Benn, 1934); K. Vorländer, *Immanuel Kant, Der Mann und das Werk* (Leipzig, Meiner, 1924). A clear analytic introduction is provided by Stephan Körner, *Kant* (Baltimore, Pelican Books, 1955), who concentrates on the three *Critiques.* The essays, edited by G. T. Whitney and D. F. Bowers, *The Heritage of Kant* (Princeton, Princeton University Press, 1939), give in brief compass the results of recent scholarship concerning the various facets of Kant's philosophy. Kant's pre-critical development can be followed in H. J. de Vleeschauwer's *L'évolution de la pensée kantienne: L'histoire d'une doctrine* (Paris, Alcan, 1939), which is a masterful compression of Vleeschauwer's larger work: *La déduction transcendaniale dans l'oeuvre de Kant* (3 vols., Paris, Leroux, 1934–1937), devoted to the genesis of the doctrine on the categories. For a more schematic but thoroughly reliable account of the pre-critical development, cf. J. Maréchal, S.J., *Le point de départ de la métaphysique,* cahier III: *La critique de Kant* (third ed., Paris, Desclée, 1944), book i (17–83); the remaining books in this *cahier* provide a clear and acute exposition of the three *Critiques.* F. E. England, *Kant's Conception of God* (London, Allen and Unwin, 1929), and C. B. Garnett, Jr., *The Kantian Philosophy of Space* (New York, Columbia University Press, 1939), approach the pre-critical years in terms, respectively, of the problem of God and the nature of space. In English, we are fortunate in having some excellent guides to the *Critique of Pure Reason.* T. D. Weldon's *Introduction to Kant's Critique of Pure Reason* (Oxford, Clarendon, 1945) stresses Kant's background in the German, Wolffian tradition and the pivotal importance of the Analytic; A. C. Ewing's *A Short Commentary on Kant's Critique of Pure Reason* (London, Metheun, 1938) is the best brief exposition for the beginner; N. K. Smith's *A Commentary to Kant's 'Critique of Pure Reason'* (second ed., revised, London, Macmillan, 1930) is a detailed and critical analysis for advanced students; H. J. Paton's *Kant's Metaphysic of Experience: A Commentary on the First Half of the Kritik der reinen Vernunft* (2 vols., New York, Macmillan, 1936) reacts against the "patchwork theory" of how the *Critique* was composed, recognizes more consistency and sense in Kant's argument than the German commentators and N. K. Smith are willing to concede and, in sum, gives a most persuasive explanation of the Kantian solution of the problems of space, time, and

# 514 MODERN EUROPEAN PHILOSOPHY

the categories. Paton's study (and, along with it, most English Kantian scholarship) is confined, however, to the first two parts of the *Critique:* the Esthetic and the Analytic. Because the Dialectic has been relatively neglected, the metaphysical tendencies in Kant's thought have been nearly submerged beneath the dominant interest in his epistemology and ethics. The balance is righted by two books stressing metaphysical themes: G. Martin, *Kant's Metaphysics and Theory of Science* (Manchester, Manchester University Press, 1955); H. W. Cassirer, *Kant's First Critique* (New York, Macmillan, 1954), a full-scale commentary. This aspect of his mind cannot be understood properly without studying the Wolff-Baumgarten School-Philosophy, which reigned in the German universities during Kant's lifetime. Aid in this direction is provided by M. Campo, *Cristiano Wolff e il razionalismo precritico* (2 vols., Milan, Vita e Pensiero, 1939), and M. Wundt, *Die deutsche Schulmetaphysik im Zeitalter der Aufklärung* (Tübingen, Mohr, 1945). Because of the cardinal role of causality in the theoretical and practical orders, A. C. Ewing, *Kant's Treatment of Causality* (London, Kegan Paul, Trench, Trübner, 1924) is worth consulting. Thomistic appraisals include: E. Gilson, *Being and Some Philosophers* (Toronto, Pontifical Institute of Mediaeval Studies, 1949), 113-32, which stresses the metaphysical problem of existence in Wolff and Kant; C. Nink, S.J., *Kommentar zu Kants Kritik der reinen Vernunft* (Frankfurt, Carolus-drückerei, 1930), which makes some acute criticisms on detached issues; J. Maréchal, S.J., *Le point de départ de la métaphysique,* cahier V: *Le Thomisme devant la philosophie critique* (second ed., Paris, Desclée, 1949), the most thorough-going, contemporary Thomistic effort to appropriate and overcome Kant (see, also, the criticism of Maréchal in E. Gilson, *Réalisme thomiste et critique de la connaissance* [Paris, Vrin, 1939], Chap. 5); G. Ardley, *Aquinas and Kant* (New York, Longmans, Green, 1950), which divides the intellectual globe, overneatly, between the metaphysical realism of Thomism and the categorial constructions of Kant and modern science.

3. *Further Publications.* Kant's *Observations on the Feeling of the Beautiful and Sublime,* tr. by J. T. Goldthwait (Los Angeles and Berkeley, University of California Press, 1960), is a pre-critical esthetic with many empirical factors. The P. G. Lucas translation of *Prolegomena to Any Future Metaphysics* (New York, Barnes and Noble, 1953) has a helpful introduction and analysis. The influence of Enlightenment science on the pre-critical Kant is measured by G. Tonelli, *Elementi metodologici e metafisici in Kant dal 1745 al 1768,* vol. I (Turin, Edizioni di "Filosofia," 1959). The interwoven metaphysical and scientific themes in Kant's total position are considered by H. Heimsoeth, *Studien zur Philosophie Immanuel Kants* (Cologne, Universitätsverlag, 1956), and by J. Vuillemin, *Physique et métaphysique kantiennes* (Paris, Presses Universitaires, 1955). Wolff's deep impact on modern Scholastics is traced in J. E. Gurr, S.J., *The Principle of Sufficient Reason in Some Scholastic Systems, 1750–1900* (Milwaukee, Marquette University Press, 1959).

# Chapter 12. KANT'S ETHICAL AND ESTHETIC DOCTRINE

ONE of the deepest strains in Kant is his preoccupation with ethical issues. During his pre-critical period, he made an intensive study of the leading contemporary moralists, especially the British writers of the Moral Sense School and Rousseau. Shaftesbury, Hutcheson, and Hume showed him the folly of constructing a purely rationalistic, deductive system of ethics. Kant did not accept a distinctive moral sense, but he did learn from this group the importance of: psychological studies of moral attitudes, the emotional or material side of moral life, and the feeling for morality that accompanies our moral decisions. As for Rousseau, Kant placed him alongside of Newton: what the latter did for the physical world, the former did for the moral. Rousseau revealed the abiding presence of an orderly structure of human nature common to all men. He showed that there is no incompatibility between personal freedom and moral law. From Rousseau, as well as from his own Pietistic forebears, Kant derived his profound respect for the individual person and his sense of the moral solidarity within the human community.

What Kant missed in these sources, however, was a rational foundation of moral obligation and moral universality. The empiricists did not provide a distinctively moral basis for unconditioned duty, whereas Rousseau's basis in "the natural man" was an arbitrary and sentimental conception. Kant's problem was to transcend both descriptive morality and sentimentalism, without relapsing into the moral dogmatism of the rationalistic school. In the second *Critique,* he relied upon his own critical method, as a means for reconstructing ethical philosophy. He sought a *Grundlegung* or critical foundation of our ethical propositions that would be in harmony with his findings about the propositions underlying mathematics and natural science. However much the ethician may be interested in the content and particular laws of morality, his major concern must be directed toward the *universal, objective form* of the moral principle. Kant was a *formalist,* although not in the sense of overlooking the indispensable contribution of the material side of morality.[1] His moral philosophy emphasized the need for a basic discussion of the formal properties which distinguish moral propositions from other kinds, and which qualify an action or a character simply as moral. There are three main issues: the moral law, the categorical imperative, and the postulates of morality.

## KANT'S MORAL ARGUMENT

1. The moral law as the sole fact of practical reason: man under obligation.
2. The good will.
   a) An all-perfect, holy will.
   b) Will in man, as subject to duty.
3. Moral action motivated solely by conformity to law and duty. Moral feeling of reverence for the law.
4. The categorical imperative.
   a) Disinterestedness.
   b) Persons as ends-in-themselves.
   c) Persons as members of the kingdom of ends.
5. Autonomy versus heteronomy of will.
6. Postulates of pure practical reason.
   a) Freedom.
   b) Personal immortality.
   c) God.

## I. THE GOOD WILL AND THE MORAL LAW

Ethical inquiry begins with a given element, what Kant calls "the sole fact of pure reason" in the practical order.[2] This is the *fact of the moral law* itself. Different individuals may give different interpretations of the particular precepts of the moral law, but at least they all agree that man is subject to a moral obligation of some sort. In principle, our actions are regulated by some kind of *ought,* whether we agree upon its exact nature and obey it, or not. This fact of obliga-

---

[1] Kant's general attitude toward ethical inquiry is explained by O. C. Jensen, "Kant's Ethical Formalism," *Philosophy,* IX (1934), 195–208.

[2] *Critique of Practical Reason,* I, i, 1, No. 7 (Beck translation, in *Critique of Practical Reason and Other Writings in Moral Philosophy,* 143); cf No. 8 (Beck, 157). Kant fails to clarify the precise sense in which moral obligation is an indubitable "fact," comparable somehow to the factual starting points in the speculative order.

tion is acknowledged by the common man, whose judgments are just as important for moral philosophy as are those of the physical scientist for epistemology. In both cases, the work of critical philosophy is to uncover the principles constituting and making possible the given facts. The moral law presents itself to us as an unconditional command. Hence it contains a necessary and universal factor, which cannot be traced to an empirical source. According to his fundamental epistemological assumption, Kant must look for the origin of the universality and necessity of the moral law in a pure (nonempirical) and a priori principle. Hence this inquiry falls within the domain of *pure* reason, but of pure *practical* reason, since moral commands bear upon actions to be performed or omitted.

The transition from the theoretical to the practical aspect of reason is not explicable in terms of anything more ultimate. The fact is evident that men do engage in actions and that reason plays a determining role in many of these actions. Reason is called *practical*, when it influences or determines action. Kant usually treats practical reason and will as equivalents, defining *will* as the ability to determine oneself to action, in accordance with one's concept of certain laws or principles.[3] A man not only acts upon a particular practical judgment but can also regard the particular deed as an *instance* of a general principle of action. The principles are furnished by pure practical reason, the a priori structure of which is studied by critical philosophy.

Kant offers a challenging formulation of his central moral conviction, when he affirms that "nothing in the world — indeed nothing even beyond the world — can possibly be conceived which could be called good without qualification except a *good will*."[4] Although moral philosophy is mainly concerned with law-and-obligation, it has this orientation only because of the bond established, at the human level, between *the good* and law-and-obligation. How does the will stand in relation to unqualified goodness? Kant rejects the view that the will becomes good by acquiring certain perfections, producing

[3] "Only a rational being has the capacity of acting according to the conception of laws, i.e., according to principles. This capacity is will. Since reason is required for the derivation of actions from laws, will is nothing else than practical reason. . . . Will is a kind of causality of living beings so far as they are rational." *Foundations of the Metaphysics of Morals,* II, III (Beck translation, in *Critique of Practical Reason and Other Writings in Moral Philosophy,* 72, 101). Elsewhere (*ibid.,* I [Beck, 58]), practical reason is regarded as a cognitive power, exerting influence *on* will, which is a distinct causal agency.
[4] *Ibid.,* I (Beck, 55).

certain effects, or realizing certain ends, distinct from itself. This is the moral consequence of his Copernican revolution. Will or practical reason no more derives its goodness from conformity with an independent order of being than does theoretical reason acquire its truth from conformity with independent things. In both orders, there is a tendency toward autonomy in Kant, so that the universal and necessary traits can be saved. If will took its goodness from outside itself, it would become reliant upon empirical, contingent sources. Kant grants that the will is a purposive faculty, achieving results and states that are good in some respect. But the *unconditioned* moral goodness of the will cannot come from its *conditioned* results and its states of happiness. For, these consequences only share in moral goodness, by reason of some *intrinsic* quality of the will's own action, considered purely in itself. Kant makes will and moral law the determinants of the meaning of the good, rather than the converse.

As a rational power, practical reason is directed to no other primary end than the achievement of a will that is good in itself. This holds true of any rational being — in the world of appearances or beyond it — the only ultimate purpose of whose will is to act rationally or in harmony with itself and its own laws. Yet Kant notices a difference between an *all-perfect* or *holy will,* uninfluenced as it would be by passions and sensuous inclinations, and a *will that is imperfect,* to the extent of being subject to these sensuous influences.[5] A holy will would belong to a being that is wholly situated in the intelligible, noumenal world: it is attributable only to God. Such a will would spontaneously, necessarily, and exclusively will the unconditioned good, so that it would never feel inclined to will anything else than

---

[5] In view of the bearing of this distinction upon an appraisal of Kant's theory of moral autonomy, it is important at this juncture to notice the metaphysical basis of the distinction. The moral law "is thus not limited to human beings but extends to all *finite* beings having reason and will; indeed, it includes the *Infinite* Being as the supreme intelligence. In the former case, however, the law has the form of an imperative. For though we can suppose that men, as rational beings, have a *pure* will, since they are affected by wants and sensuous motives, we cannot suppose them to have a *holy* will, a will incapable of any maxims which conflict with the moral law. . . . In the *supremely self-sufficing* intelligence choice is correctly thought of as incapable of any maxim which could not at the same time be objectively a law, and the concept of *holiness,* which is applied to it for this reason, elevates it not indeed above all practical laws but above all practically restrictive laws, and thus above obligation and duty. This holiness of will is, however, a practical ideal which must necessarily serve as a model which all *finite* rational beings must strive toward even though they cannot reach it." *Critique of Practical Reason,* I, i, 1, No. 7 (Beck, 143–44; italics added).

its own goodness. But man is a member of two worlds: the intelligible and the sensible. Hence he *has* will, without *being* an exclusively rational nature. He feels the inborn tug of natural, sensuous inclinations and the lure of various kinds of happiness, quite as strongly as the tendency to realize the good will as such. St. Paul's description of the two laws at war within a man's breast, expresses correctly the moral situation of man.

The *dualism* in man gives a lead concerning the connection between the good and the duty to follow the moral law. Man's will is not totally absorbed in its direct adherence to unconditioned goodness: it must also *subordinate* relative goods to the supreme one, and *discipline* desires that may become wayward. Hence the general moral law of seeking the good will presents itself differently to an all-perfect, holy will and to the will of man. A holy will would seek to realize an absolutely good will, but it would not do so out of any sense of constraint or duty. There would be nothing in such a being to tame, command, or compel. In man's case, however, the moral law of seeking an unqualifiedly good will does present itself under the aspect of *obligation* and *duty*.[6] Kant's preoccupation with duty arises from his conviction that a *finite* will, belonging to a being that is native to both the intelligible and the sensible worlds, is related to the *absolute* good in terms of obligation. There is always the open possibility, for man, that the unconditioned good is to be willed in the face of contrary inclinations, and that the moral law is to be followed at a sacrifice and often only after a struggle. Because man is a finite and dualistic being, his moral problem is one of acting out of a rational, moral constraint to manifest a will that is good in every respect. Hence Kant determines the import of the moral law mainly in terms of the central notion of duty.

Kant distinguishes between a moral and a legal action. An action is morally good, when it proceeds *from* a motive of duty; it is a legal action, when it is performed merely *in accord with duty* and yet *from* some other motive. The other motives which Kant has chiefly in mind are: utility, sympathy, and happiness. He does not

---

[6] "The dependence of a will not absolutely good on the principle of autonomy (moral constraint) is *obligation*. . . . The objective necessity of an action from obligation is called *duty*." *Foundations of the Metaphysics of Morals*, II (Beck, 96); cf. *Critique of Practical Reason, loc. cit.* For an evaluation of this view of moral obligation, cf. T. J. Brosnahan, S.J., *Prolegomena to Ethics* (New York, Fordham University Press, 1941), Appendix A: "The Kantian Ought" (329-45).

require that the moral act be performed in complete isolation from these other motives, but only that they remain in an ancillary status and cease to determine the distinctively moral aspect of the act, as Hume and the British moralists had proposed. If an action is prompted solely by some form of *self-interest* and *usefulness,* there is no ground for regarding it as a moral action. In this action, the will is subordinating itself to some further end, and hence is not engaged in the unqualified manifestation of the good will, in which the moral property of actions resides. A more serious problem is presented, when an action conforms with the pattern of duty, and yet is done out of some immediate inclination or impulse. The ordinary man often confuses a deed motivated solely by *sympathy* and *kindness* with a morally good act. Kant admits that an impulsively benevolent deed is upright and praiseworthy; he also grants that an action may be motivated both by impulse and by a sense of duty.[7] But he refuses to amalgamate these motives in such a way that the moral worth of an act might be determined by something other than direct regard for one's duty. In the face of Rousseauvian sentimentality about the spontaneous goodness of the natural emotions, Kant stresses the need for a deliberate and steadfast aim at doing one's duty, regardless of whether or not the wellsprings of the heart dry up. This is the kind of *rigorism* upon which finite, rational beings must fall back, both in times of great crisis and in situations where obligation runs against the grain of impulsive desire.

It is every man's right, and often his indirect duty, to seek his own happiness, in harmony with the moral law, and to cultivate noble inclinations as aids to moral living. In his concrete condition, the

---

[7] Cf. *Critique of Practical Reason,* I, i, 3 (Beck, 189–90); *Religion within the Limits of Reason Alone,* I (Greene and Hudson translation, 19, note). For a discussion of the charges of excessive formalism and rigorism usually lodged against Kant, read H. H. Schroeder, "Some Common Misinterpretations of the Kantian Ethics," *The Philosophical Review,* XLIX (1940), 424–46. Kant was trying to reckon with the proper condition of the rational creature, whose sensuous desires have a nonmoral tendency and whose relation to the moral law is indefectibly one of obligation, under moral necessity. Such an agent cannot be asked to act morally out of sheer spontaneous inclination or to pretend that he is not bound in duty to do *certain* morally good actions, which he may also gladly undertake to perform. On the other hand, Kant did not show that the moral character of *every* morally good act derives from its being motivated solely by considerations of duty. Some morally good acts are not strict moral duties. Furthermore, the very strength of his case against moral sentimentality rested upon an assurance of man's creatureliness and finitude in being. But this conviction about a pure-but-finite will was not given due consideration, when Kant came to determine the nature of moral autonomy and self-legislation.

upright man usually needs these helps, in order to combat tendencies to depart from the path of obligation. Moral decisions need not, and usually are not, made entirely apart from accompanying motives of self interest, generous inclination, and the search for happiness. But their character as morally good derives solely and sufficiently from the motive of *being done solely for duty's sake*. This is the only morally decisive maxim under which to assume human actions. Kant is almost exclusively interested in this question: if it comes to an absolute *choice between* several motives, which one will qualify the will as being morally good? He formulates the basic moral problem as a *clash* between duty and the other considerations, rather than as an effort at *integration* and *hierarchy* of the several levels of morally good ends. Hence he defines virtue laconically as steadfastness or "moral disposition in conflict."[8] Kant locates the moral quality of the good will in its dutiful adherence to its own rationality, and not in its ordination to the unqualifiedly good end of man's nature as a whole. The autonomy of will, as well as the dualism between sensible and intelligible aspects in man, stands in the way of his acceptance of a teleological ethics.

Kant himself gave a warmhearted and deeply emotional response to the conception of acting solely out of regard for duty. This can be seen in his well-known *hymn to duty,* an apostrophe that breaks forth spontaneously (although with Rousseauvian overtones) in the second *Critique.*

> Duty! Thou sublime and mighty name that dost embrace nothing charming or insinuating but requirest submission and yet seekest not to move the will by threatening aught that would arouse natural aversion or terror but only holdest forth a law which of itself finds entrance into the mind and yet gains reluctant reverence (though not always obedience) — a law before which all inclinations are dumb even though they secretly work against it: what origin is there worthy of thee, and where is to be found the root of thy noble descent which proudly rejects all kinship with the inclinations and from which to be descended is the indispensable condition of the only worth which men can give themselves?

> It cannot be less than something which elevates man above himself as a part of the world of sense, something which connects him with an order of things which only the understanding can think and which has under it the entire world of sense, including the empirically determinable existence of man in time, and the whole system of all ends which is

---

[8] *Critique of Practical Reason,* I, i, 3 (Beck, 191).

alone suitable to such unconditional practical laws as the moral. It is nothing else than personality, i.e., the freedom and independence from the mechanism of nature regarded as a capacity of a being which is subject to special laws (pure practical laws given by its own reason), so that the person as belonging to the world of sense is subject to his own personality so far as he belongs to the intelligible world.[9]

From Kant's answer to his own question about the origin of duty, it is clear why he found it natural to pose the moral problem primarily as a conflict between duty and other motives. For, duty springs from the noumenal or intelligible aspect of the self, whereas the other motives are sensuous inclinations or self-regarding impulses, due to the phenomenal side of the self. The dualism of appearance and thing-in-itself in man is carried over into the moral realm as one between inclination and duty. Ultimately, there is no intrinsic contradiction between the intelligible world and the world of sense. But moral qualifications as such have their origin exclusively in the intelligible, free order, and must be conceived as exercising a *dominating* function in respect to the sensuous, temporal aspects of the self.

The subordination of the empirical to the intelligible personality is the source of the emotional factor that belongs properly to moral action. In action done solely from duty, the will is moved *objectively* by the practical moral law, and not by inclination or desire for advantage. *Subjectively,* however, the will is moved by the *emotion of pure reverence or respect for the moral law.*[10] Thus the moral law of acting solely for duty's sake provides an incentive or a priori, subjective determination of practical reason. This moral feeling arises necessarily and exclusively from reflection on the rational concept of law and duty: it is not a feeling caused by any external, sensible consideration. It is excited, when the agent reflects on the dual fact that the moral law imposes itself *unconditionally* upon his will, regardless of any self-regarding motives or motives of self-conceit, and that nevertheless the law is imposed *by himself,* by his own will, as a member of the intelligible world. Respect for the moral law is at the same time respect for human personality, in its intelligible aspect and dominating role.

Since the good will cannot be determined by any results of its action, it must be moved morally by the sole consideration of abiding

---

[9] *Loc. cit.* (Beck, 193).

[10] *Foundations of the Metaphysics of Morals,* I (Beck, 61–62); *Critique of Practical Reason,* I, i, 3 (Beck, 181–88).

by the law. The one formal condition, common to all morally good actions, is this *motive of conformity to universal law*. Not much is stated thereby: no particular laws and no concrete contents are specified, but only the intent of acting according to the principle of the law. Such an ideal presents itself to our human will in the form of a command or imperative. Whereas a holy will would simply say: *I will*, the human will says: *I ought*. Hence a study of imperatives is the only way to determine the further significance of the moral law, in the foundation of ethics.

## 2. THE CATEGORICAL IMPERATIVE

Kant distinguishes between various kinds of maxims and imperatives, in order to single out the imperative proper to morality.[11] A *maxim* is a general principle of volition. Kant is not interested so much in the material maxims, which state general rules for the content of particular actions, as in the formal maxims, which express only the formal condition of action. A formal maxim is a subjective one, if someone does act upon it, regardless of whether the action it informs is good or bad. An *objective, formal* maxim is a practical principle, upon which all rational agents would necessarily act, provided that reason had full control over the desires and passions. Such a principle is a *law,* and for men the law is conveyed in a *command*. A command is stated in an *imperative,* which imposes an objective principle of action in the form of an ought. Action which accords with an imperative is good action, since it is in conformity with some kind of law. But not all good actions, regulated by imperatives, are morally good. For there are two kinds of objective principles: hypothetical and categorical. *Hypothetical* principles declare an action necessary, only on condition that the agent decide to will a certain end, to which this action may serve as a means. *Categorical* principles state an unconditional, practical necessity of performing the action, even apart from willing any further end. Hypothetical imperatives, whether they be technical rules of skill and useful good or pragmatic counsels of prudence and happiness, do not provide the qualities of unconditional, a priori necessity and universality, that should mark a principle of moral action. Only the

---

[11] *Foundations of the Metaphysics of Morals*, II (Beck, 72–76). For some of the difficulties encountered in this passage, see R. Jackson, "Kant's Distinction between Categorical and Hypothetical Imperatives," *Proceedings of the Aristotelian Society*, N.S., XLIII (1942–1943), 131–66.

categorical imperative is the truly moral imperative, since it alone commands actions as being necessarily and universally good in themselves.

Kant observes that there is *only one categorical imperative*. It is the overarching principle of all our moral conduct. Every material maxim must be informed by the necessity of the categorical imperative, before it acquires the obligatory force of a moral principle. But there are various ways of stating this imperative, in order to bring out its several aspects.[12] (*a*) One formulation reads: "Act only according to that maxim by which you can at the same time will that it should become a universal law." The moral imperative is completely *a priori* and *formal*, so that it does not provide material content for moral choice or deduce particular moral laws. Rather, it suggests a test to which all proposed material maxims must submit, if they are to be acted upon in a moral way. The individual is to *look disinterestedly* upon his projected principle of action, and ask whether it could become binding upon all rational agents. The function of the categorical imperative is not to provide particular directives but only to lay upon the individual the obligation to measure his actions and material principles by the standard of universal law. Hence Kant's discussion of ethical principles from the standpoint of their critical foundation cannot be expected to yield a complete moral system. It does not provide *proximate guidance* concerning particular choices and the moral problems raised by shifting, contingent circumstances. Even in regard to maxims, Kant does not furnish sufficient criteria for determining *what* can be universalized as law for all men, and *what* cannot. In a general way, he suggests that moral maxims are those that promote agreement among rational wills, due to their expression of the general structure of self-coherent reason.

(*b*) Schopenhauer objected that Kant's moral doctrine is founded upon *egoism*, since the categorical imperative is based upon what the individual can will as a universal law. Kant has another expression of the categorical imperative that helps to correct this misinterpretation. "So act that the maxim of your will can always at the same time be

---

12 Of the four statements of the categorical imperative quoted here, the first, third, and fourth are taken from *Foundations of the Metaphysics of Morals*, II (Beck, 80, 87). The second formula is found in *Critique of Practical Reason*, I, i, 1, No. 7; the translation is that of H. J. Paton, *The Categorical Imperative*, 180 (rather than of Beck, 142). For Schopenhauer's attack, cf. R. A. Tsanoff, "Schopenhauer's Criticism of Kant's Theory of Ethics," *The Philosophical Review*, XIX (1910), 512–34.

valid as a principle making universal law." Once more, no specific directions are given about relating our action to God or to our fellow man, or about following a particular pattern of conduct. Instead, the moral imperative is expressive of a command concerning how every moral principle must be taken. The maxim is to be appropriated by the individual will but in such a way that its validity does not depend upon its acceptance by the individual. Whether or not he adopts it, he is obliged to recognize that the moral principle "*can* always be valid," i.e., that it is binding, in an *impartial* way, upon all wills. Nevertheless, Kant also maintains that the moral law is *self-imposed* by pure practical reason, considered as an autonomous, intelligible principle. The empirical individuals, who are subject impersonally to the law, must also recognize that *rational will as such is the source* of all obligation and law. Otherwise, there is no way open for Kant to save the universality and necessity of moral law, as well as its compatibility with freedom.

(*c*) Another facet of the categorical imperative is embodied in the formula: "Act so that you treat humanity, whether in your own person or in that of another, always as an end and never as a means only." Kant does not mean that men should never stand in useful relationships to each other and society, but that these relationships should not be the sole bonds or the morally decisive ones. Every rational agent, insofar as his maxims can have universal law-making force, is a *person* and an *end in himself*.[13] To reduce him to the status of a sheer means, would be to deny the unconditioned worth of the good will, within him. Self-respect and mutual respect among persons help to determine the moral standing of material maxims and particular courses of action.

(*d*) Kant adds that one should act as though one were, through his maxims, a lawmaking member of the *kingdom of ends*. The notion of a kingdom of ends helps to counterbalance the individualistic tone of the categorical imperative, in its other expressions. What we should respect is *humanity*, present in oneself and others. The dignity of

---

[13] For a Thomistic and an idealistic criticism, respectively, see G. Gračanin, *La personnalité morale d'après Kant. Son exposé, sa critique à la lumière du thomisme* (Paris, Mignard, 1935), and R. F. Hoernlé, "Kant's Concept of the 'Intrinsic Worth' of Every 'Rational Being,'" *The Personalist*, XXIV (1943), 130–46. Hoernlé inquires how Kant can show that the moral requirements for every rational-being-in-general obtain for empirical, human agents, in view of the cleft between the noumenal and phenomenal orders. The subordination of the latter to the former is a metaphysical assumption, that is not validated within Kantian dualism.

the person rests upon his capacity to formulate objective maxims that are valid as laws for all men, and that therefore tend to promote a unity of ends, as well as of principles. We should frame our moral principles with a view to the furtherance of harmony among enlightened wills, in the intelligible world or kingdom of ends. This becomes a practically efficacious ideal, when it is conceived after the analogy of a harmony of purposes in nature. (e) Hence the moral imperative also commands: "Act as though the maxim of your action were by your will to become a universal law of nature," i.e., such as could establish purposive harmony and rational coherence among moral agents. Kant examines the moral character of truth-telling, suicide, self-cultivation, and faithfulness to promises, on the basis of these formulations of the categorical imperative.

The transcendental method leads Kant to trace the universality and necessity of the moral law to the pure practical reason or pure will itself, since these traits must have a nonempirical but practical source. Hence the categorical imperative also entails the *autonomy of the will.*

Autonomy of the will is that property of it by which it is a law to itself independently of any property of objects of volition. Hence the principle of autonomy is: Never choose except in such a way that the maxims of the choice are comprehended in the same volition as a universal law.[14]

If the will regulates its choice by any other consideration than the fitness of its own maxims to serve as principles of universal law, then it is leaving its own pure autonomy and must discover a ground for its choice in some other object. But to do so, is to submit the will to the condition of *heteronomy* or determination by something else. Instead of giving a law to itself, the heteronomous will receives its law from an alien source, resident in the objects of will. Whether these objects be empirical considerations (such as happiness) or rational motives (such as perfection or the will of God), they provide only *conditional* reasons for choice and hence only hypothetical, nonmoral imperatives. Furthermore, Kant maintains that the heteronomous will loses its *freedom,* since it submits to a determining principle outside of itself. The will is free, negatively, when it

---

14 *Foundations of the Metaphysics of Morals,* II (Beck, 97); cf. *Critique of Practical Reason,* I, i, 1, No. 8 (Beck, 144–45). For a discussion of this principle, consult A. E. Gleason, S.J., "A Critique of Kantian Autonomy," *The New Scholasticism,* VIII (1934), 223–39.

escapes determination from without; positively, it is free when it legislates universally for itself. Only the will that is a law unto itself is also a free will. Yet moral freedom escapes anarchy, since "a free will and a will under [self-imposed] moral laws are identical."[15]

The strength and appeal of Kant's doctrine on moral autonomy lie in the defense of free self-determination and personal responsibility for one's plan of life. But in adjusting these sound convictions to his systematic requirements, he is led to set up an artificial antithesis between moral freedom and a theistic foundation of morality. In his previous, epistemological discussion of the antinomy between freedom and necessity, Kant had described freedom, negatively, as the absence of determination by a phenomenal series of causes. Now, in a moral context, he regards freedom as being the absence of decisive, moral influence by objects outside the will itself. He has a consistent reason for not accepting sensuous needs and inclinations as the ultimate determinants of morality, due to their subordinate position in respect to the entire man. But there is no similar reason for rejecting the reference of human actions to the eternal law of God, as the ultimate moral standard. Since the law of God is not phenomenal, submission to it does not involve a deordination in man. Nor does it lead to a submission of the human will to a series of phenomenally necessitated causes. The divine law is not "outside" the human will, in the sense of a spatially foreign object or causally alien counter-agent. Kant's quarrel with metaphysics deprives him of any speculative guidance concerning the immanence, as well as transcendence, of God and His causal interiority to human freedom.

As for the positive meaning of freedom — the giving of universal law to oneself — there are various ways in which this can be done. Here, Kant might have used his distinction between the infinite will and the finite will, not only to establish the relation of obligation for the latter, but also to determine the precise sense in which the finite will can be a law unto itself. There is a marked difference between a *pure-and-finite will* and a *pure-and-infinite will,* so that Kant's appeal to the requirements of pure will is not sufficiently determinate to support the burden of his doctrine on moral autonomy. Within his perspective, the will of the finite, rational agent is pure and unconditioned, insofar as it is not determined in its choices by some anterior event in the series of phenomenal causes. But it is not

---

15 *Foundations of the Metaphysics of Morals,* III (Beck, 102).

ontologically unconditioned in its own nature, since it remains the will of a finite, created nature.

Within the order of "pure wills," the will of man is not an all-holy will but a will under obligation. It is in the light of this capital Kantian distinction that the problem of autonomy must be posed, rather than in terms of the noumenon-phenomenon dichotomy. It is no derogation from the integrity of a pure-and-finite will, that its moral goodness should be a measured one, one that derives from its free conformity with the goodness and law of the pure-and-infinite will of God. The moral ideal for man is to manifest not simply "the good will" *in general,* but precisely that uprightness of will which is *appropriate to the human condition of being.*[16] The human will can give universal law to itself, but only in the way befitting a derived and finite being, not in the absolute manner of the un-derived and infinite being. What the finite person can do is to *appropriate* the divine law as his own, *interiorize* it, and *reaffirm* it as the animating principle of his moral life. He can take upon him-self the responsibility for working out the more particular precepts and applications of the divine law, for cultivating the moral virtues, and for making the prudential judgments and actual elections of concrete moral life. These are inalienable and free acts, resting upon the integrity and inviolability of human freedom, and yet they are incompatible with any claim to absolute self-legislation and uncon-ditioned autonomy.

The finite person gives himself the moral law in a rational, free and creaturely way, when he recognizes the ordination of his nature and will toward an infinite good, existing concretely in God. The bond

---

[16] See M. De Corte, "Le concept de bonne volonté dans la morale kantienne," *Revue de Philosophie,* N.S., II (1931), 190–221. Because Kant correlated his distinction be-tween nature and freedom with his underlying dualism between the sensible and intelligible orders, he was unable to integrate in a single doctrine the consideration of the will precisely as a natural tendency and as free. Since the phenomenon-noumenon dichotomy placed nature and freedom in opposition, he was led to treat moral freedom as an absolute autonomy of lawmaking reason, unregulated by whether or not the freedom was rooted in a will, whose natural tendency is toward an infinite good other than itself. When he did attempt to think nature and freedom together, Kant was unable to defend freedom coherently, in respect to will considered as nature. The problem of the Kantian opposition between freedom and nature is treated at length by J. Maritain, *Freedom in the Modern World* (New York, Scribner, 1936), 3–46; cf. the briefer notes by L. R. Ward, C.S.C., *Christian Ethics* (St. Louis, Herder, 1952), 116–27, and the essay by J. R. Rosenberg, "Freedom in the Philosophy of Kant," *Philosophical Studies in Honor of the Very Reverend Ignatius Smith, O.P.* (edited by J. K. Ryan), 257–69.

of finite beings to the infinite being, who is their creator and goal, is an unconditioned one and establishes a strict, moral obligation, rather than a hypothetical one. The relation of conformity with the law of God is not contingent upon our *choosing* to will a certain end: it is consequent upon our *being* rational creatures, with a natural ordination to the good. Similarly, actual union with the infinitely good God realizes our own perfection, without reducing God to the status of a means to that perfection, since the perfective union with God is achieved through a liberating love of Him for His own sake. A theistic ethics is an ethics of love as well as duty, since it respects the natural tendency in man to relate himself in a properly creaturely way to his creator. To seek the foundation of morality in this relationship of the finite will to God, is to undercut that Kantian alternative between autonomy and heteronomy.

It still remains to be determined more specifically, however, why Kant felt dissatisfied with the theistic foundation of morality, as he viewed it. His answer is given in a significant passage, where he holds that even the empty, rationalistic notion of the greatest possible perfection

is better than the theological concept, which derives morality from a most perfect divine will. It is better not merely because we cannot intuit its perfection [that of the divine will], having rather to derive it only from our own concepts of which morality is foremost, but also because if we do not so derive it (and to do so would involve a most flagrant circle in explanation), the only remaining concept of the divine will is made up of the attributes of desire for glory and dominion combined with the awful conceptions of might and vengeance, and any system of ethics based on them would be directly opposed to morality.[17]

These remarks reveal the twofold ground of Kant's opposition to a theistic ethics: a more proximate, ethical reason, and a more basic, epistemological reason. In direct, *ethical* terms, he thinks that a theistic ethics must identify the divine perfection exclusively with God's will, considered apart from His infinite wisdom and goodness. This would lead to an irresponsible, theological voluntarism, in which man's lust for domination would be exalted into the command of God's holy will. Although it is prudent to oppose such a theological voluntarism, Kant does not consider whether *every* doctrine of the eternal law rests upon an exclusive foundation in the divine will. His argument

---

[17] *Foundations of the Metaphysics of Morals,* II (Beck, 99). Both Kant and Hume advance humanistic reasons for their attempt to *de-theize* the basis of ethics.

from the dire ethical consequences fails to reckon with the non-voluntaristic doctrines on the eternal law and the will of God. Behind this immediate ethical appraisal, however, stands Kant's fundamental *epistemological* objection. According to his theory of knowledge, the human mind can have neither intuitive nor demonstrative knowledge of God and His infinite perfection. The only way to give real content to the concept of a perfect divine will, then, is to transfer it to the practical order of moral faith. But, at once, a vicious circle develops. For, the attempt is being made to secure the foundations of morality upon one's own moral notions (the content of moral faith), which themselves are said to stand in need of a foundation. Insensibly, the theistic ethician injects the drives of human power into the concept of the divine will, leading inevitably to an amoral, theological imperialism.

Manifestly, Kant's major difficulty with a theistic foundation of morality was epistemological: the inability of a nonintuitive intellect to gain strict knowledge of God's supersensuous perfection. Because he made no provision for a speculative demonstration of God's existence, Kant had no metaphysical basis for determining anything about His nature and perfections of intellect and will. Hence he could only regard the doctrine on the divine perfection, goodness, and will as employing *empty concepts,* which had to be *filled* either by begging the question of their determinate content or by extrapolating into the divine will an all-too-human content. His objections told against an ethics based on the speculatively empty concept of a perfect, divine will; they did not bear upon an ethics that secures a metaphysical basis in the speculative demonstration of God's existence and infinite, existential perfection of nature. Epistemological considerations were also decisive in rendering ineffective and irrelevant for the question of moral autonomy, Kant's private convictions about the infinite and the finite modes of being, the self-sufficient and the dependent intellects, the underived and the derived wills. Since these convictions were lacking in any metaphysical groundwork, they could not be employed significantly by Kant in determining the central issue of the relation of the human will to the moral law.

Given his attack upon transcendent metaphysics, Kant could conceive of no other theistic way of founding morality than one that would issue in the sort of irresponsible will-to-power which he rightly condemned. Conversely, however, a theistic critique of Kantian ethics should not permit itself to become sidetracked in a discussion of the limitations of ethical formalism — limitations of which Kant himself was well aware. Rather, it should focus steadily upon the root matter of Kant's despair over the competence of speculative reason, in dealing with existential problems about God.

## 3. THE POSTULATES OF PRACTICAL REASON

If Kant was reluctant to allow any influence of the ideas of pure a priori reason upon the *foundation* of morality, he was quite ready to accord them an important place among the *implications* of the moral law, which is founded upon autonomous and self-legislating practical reason or will. They do not serve as the proper *motives* or *incentives* of moral action, but they are required as *postulates,* rendering intelligible our obedience to the self-imposed categorical imperative. Three conditions are necessary, so that practical reason can conform with the command of the moral law. These conditions comprise the practical postulates of morality: *immortality, freedom,* and *God* (corresponding to the three speculative ideas of the soul, the world or antinomy between necessity and freedom, and God).[18] In postulating these ideas, we do not extend speculative knowledge about their objects, but we gain the moral conviction that these ideas do, indeed, have corresponding realities. Rational, moral faith provides us with a certainty that is beyond the power of knowledge to attain.

To arrive at the reality of *freedom,* we must begin, once more, with the moral law as the sole fact of practical reason. Although it is purely rational and internal, the moral law imposes itself upon our reason somewhat after the manner of a brute fact. Since this law proposes an unconditioned *ought* to us, it also presupposes a *can* on the part of the rational agents. The moral law informs us that, whatever the conditions prevailing within the determined series of appearances, we are unconditionally bound to conform our actions to the moral imperative. Hence the rational will must be presupposed to be free, if it is to be held responsible for acting in accordance with its own concept of the law.

The categorical imperative also commands us to bring our will into

---

[18] *Critique of Practical Reason,* I, ii 2 (Beck, 225-36); *Critique of Pure Reason,* A 337: B 295; A 634: B 662 (Smith translation, 325, 526, notes); *Critique of Judgment,* Appendix, No. 91 (Bernard translation, 411-14). These practical postulates are grasped by "moral faith," i.e., without any noetic insight into their own reality (hence "faith") and yet conceived as necessary implications of our moral life (hence "moral").

perfect conformity with the moral law, and such conformity constitutes our holiness. Although the will of a composite nature cannot simply *be* holy, it is nevertheless obliged to *become* holy. This can be done only by making an endless progress toward the condition of perfect adequation between the will and the moral law — a progress possible only on the postulation of man's endlessly enduring existence, as a rational agent. *Personal immortality* is thus another condition of plenary obedience to the moral law. Kant does not specify any closer the nature of this endless progress from level to level of moral perfection. It belongs to the intelligible order, where our temporal categories do not properly apply. Only *God* can gather up into one intuitive vision the various phases of moral striving, which constitutes the individual's approach to holiness or perfect conformity to the law. God's existence is demanded, if our endless, finite approximations to holiness are ever to be taken as the finite equivalent of an unconditionally holy will.

Another moral way of postulating God's existence depends on the distinction between the ground and the object of the moral will. Only the moral law itself can serve as the *determining ground* of the pure moral will, but the *object* of this will is the highest good (*summum bonum*). Kant observes that "the highest good" is an ambivalent term, since it may mean either "the supreme good" (*bonum supremum*) or "the whole and perfect good" (*bonum consummatum*).[19] The supreme good is the unconditioned condition of every good, and this can only be virtue itself, considered as the moral worth of a person and his worthiness-to-be-happy. The whole and perfect good includes virtue or the supreme good as its prime factor but also embraces happiness in exact proportion to one's virtue, moral worth, and worthiness-to-be-happy. Hence when Kant states that the object desired by the moral will is the highest good, he means it in the sense of the *bonum consummatum,* wherein virtue is wedded with happiness.

The entire and perfect good of a finite, rational being in the world embraces both moral worth, as its principal element, and happiness in exact proportion to this worth. Moral worth is not the same as happiness but it is a worthiness-to-be-happy. Now, basically, happiness means the harmony between nature, our wishes, and our rational will. Yet the moral agent is not the creative cause of nature and hence

---

[19] *Critique of Practical Reason*, I, ii, 2 (Beck, 213–15). Compare H. J. Paton, "Kant's Idea of the Good," *Proceedings of the Aristotelian Society*, N.S., XLV (1944–1945), i–xxv.

cannot assure himself of happiness in the world, let alone happiness proportionate to his moral worth. The ground of the necessary connection between virtue and happiness is not found in the moral law, and yet this law requires us to take the highest good as the object of action. This basic practical antinomy can only be solved by postulating, as the requisite link, the existence of "a cause of the whole of nature, itself distinct from nature, which contains the ground of the exact coincidence of happiness with morality."[20] Thus the exigencies of the moral life require belief in the existence of an *intelligent, moral God,* as the author of nature and the harmonizer of natural events, moral intentions, and the worthiness-to-be-happy.

God, the highest original or *underived* good, is the source of the highest *derived* good: the coincidence between morality and happiness. The highest good of the moral will is described adequately neither by Stoicism (virtue alone) nor Epicureanism (happiness alone) but only by the Christian moral conception of the *kingdom of God* (virtue or the worthiness-to-be-happy synthesized with a solid hope of everlasting happiness). The postulate of God gives more unity and consistency to Kant's moral doctrine than he acknowledges. It brings together the loose threads of morality, happiness, freedom, and continued existence, which had been kept rigidly apart in the discussion of the motive of morality. Kant keeps the metaphysical conception of uncreated and created being discreetly in the background, during his analysis of duty and the moral law, as the determining grounds of moral goodness. This leads to a number of practical dichotomies, which can be resolved only in function of the postulates of practical reason. Yet the distinction between underived and derived good is relevant for ascertaining not only the *object* of moral will but also its *motive* or determining ground, since it is the determining ground precisely of a will-in-search-of-a-derived-good that is under investigation. This is another indication that Kant is faced with more relevant data, concerning the problem of the autonomous moral will, than his critical standpoint permits him to acknowledge.

Kant's religious position, as outlined in *Religion Within the Limits of Reason Alone,* is that of *religious naturalism* and *rationalism.* Every sound feature of the religious outlook rests upon the three postu-

[20] *Critique of Practical Reason, loc. cit.* (Beck, 228). For a discussion of the moral arguments for immortality and God's existence, see C. D. Broad, *Five Types of Ethical Theory* (reprint edition with corrections, New York, Harcourt, Brace, 1934), 139-42. The fifth chapter in this book contains a lucid summary of Kant's ethical principles.

lates of practical reason, and these postulates in turn derive their force from independent belief in the moral law. Belief in God must be founded upon ethics (*moral* theology), but ethics cannot presuppose any independent conviction of God's existence (*theological* ethics). Kant shared the suspicion of the Enlightenment toward positive religion. Historical "revelation" is, at most, a means of communicating the deliverances of practical reason in popular symbolical fashion and with the sanction of external, social authority. The true church is not the external one but the internal one — and it is confined to the rational union of morally upright wills. In effect, this implies the reduction of religion to morality, the religious community to the ethical commonwealth. To be religious means to regard the duties of the moral law as direct divine commands.[21] In his last jottings (gathered together in the *Opus Postumum*), Kant reaffirmed the view that, although God can be approached only through analysis of the needs of practical reason, still he *can* be found along this route. The religious attitude stresses this positive aspect of our practical life, and hence treats conscience as though it were the intimate voice of God. What religion supplies is not an immediate divine revelation, but a way of treating the moral imperative *as if* it were such a revelation. The moral law and God are made *as one,* in the view of rational, moral religion. Fichte will simply remove these qualifications and make an outright identification of God with the immanent moral law.

## 4. JUDGMENT: ESTHETIC AND TELEOLOGICAL

The purpose of Kant's last *Critique* is not to add a third part to philosophy of nature and philosophy of morals, but to establish the transition, *in our mind,* from the one realm to the other.[22] It seeks

---

21 "An ethical commonwealth under divine moral legislation is a *church.* . . . Religion is (subjectively regarded) the recognition of all duties as divine commands. . . . The one true religion comprises nothing but laws, that is, those practical principles of whose unconditioned necessity we can become aware, and which we therefore recognize as revealed through pure reason (not empirically)." *Religion within the Limits of Reason Alone*, III, I, 4; IV, i and ii (Greene and Hudson, 92, 142, 156); cf. *Critique of Practical Reason*, I, ii, 2 (Beck, 232); *Critique of Judgment*, II, Appendix, No. 91 (Bernard, 423-24). For a critical assessment of this doctrine, cf. A. H. Dakin, "Kant and Religion," *The Heritage of Kant* (edited by G. T. Whitney and D. F. Bowers), 405-20. On Kant's final conception of God, cf. G. Schrader, "Kant's Presumed Repudiation of the 'Moral Argument' in the *Opus Postumum*," *Philosophy*, XXVI (1951), 228-41.

22 The relation between the three *Critiques* is discussed by A. Dorner, "Kants

to throw a bridge across the deep moat separating nature and morality, determinism and freedom, the sensible and the intelligible worlds. If a span cannot be found on the objective side, then at least it must be provided on the side of the mind, in order to assure the unity of consciousness. Kant looked for this connection in some relation between the power of *judgment* and *feeling*. In the first two *Critiques,* the act of judging had been presupposed in the formulation of both scientific and moral propositions. But a separate, critical investigation of judgment, as distinct from the other intellectual powers of understanding and reason, promised to bring about the necessary synthesis. Furthermore, the accepted division of mental functions into thinking, willing, and feeling suggested to Kant that the analyses of scientific thinking and willing should now be supplemented by a separate study of feeling. The distinctive act of feeling pleasure and displeasure contains both cognitive and appetitive aspects, making it a likely principle of connection between knowledge and moral faith. In the mind's act of regarding the *beauty* and *purposiveness of nature,* Kant found a way to relate judgment and the feeling of pleasure and displeasure. Hence the third *Critique* concerns judgment, as exercised in esthetic appreciation and teleological inquiry.

From the practical standpoint, we are sure that the gap between nature and morality can be closed, since the moral order is meant to *actualize itself within* our temporal, sensible world. We are under obligation to promote moral ends within the empirical order, "and consequently nature must be so thought that the conformity-to-law of its form, at least harmonizes with the possibility of the purposes to be effected in it according to laws of freedom."[23] We must, then, suppose some ground of unity, even though the supposition gives no knowledge of the underlying ground itself but only a rule for making the mental passage from the scientific to the moral conception of nature. There must be some a priori principle proper to judgment, as distinct from the understanding. Defining *judgment* in general to mean the power of thinking the particular under the universal, Kant distinguishes between two types of judgment: determinant and reflective. *Determinant* judgment begins with the universal as given, and seeks merely to subsume the particular instances under it. This is the

---

*Kritik der Urteilskraft* in ihrer Beziehung zu den beiden anderen Kritiken," *Kantstudien,* IV (1900), 248–85.

23 *Critique of Judgment,* Introduction, 2 (Bernard, 13). On determinant and reflective judgments, cf. *loc. cit.,* 4 (Bernard, 17–20).

procedure of the understanding, in applying the categories for the sake of gaining knowledge of objects. In the *reflective* judgment, however, only the particular instances are given, and a universal rule is sought for them. This is the proper function of the power of judgment, which does not determine nature as such but provides itself with a universal principle for reflecting upon the empirical instances presented by nature.

Even after scientific understanding constitutes objects of experience, through the categories, these objects present themselves in a bewildering variety and complexity. The understanding and the categories alone cannot tell why appearances take the form of precisely *this* causal sequence rather than another, or why we experience precisely *this* substantially permanent collection of qualities or *this* particular type of interrelation. The *empirical* laws, in which these more particular determinations are expressed, are contingent and subject to constant revision, at least from our limited standpoint. Yet all particular scientific inquiries rest upon certain very general *procedural* laws (such as the need for continuity of analysis and parsimony of explanatory principles), which state not only a *de facto* method but also the rules that we are logically bound to follow, in any situation. Whence the necessity and universality of these procedural laws, as well as the assumption about the intrinsic intelligibility of nature, in its specific modes? Their source is located in the a priori interpretative principle supplied by judgment: *the principle of the purposiveness of nature* or its reference to our cognitive faculties.[24] This is not an assertion of the effective presence of *ontological* ends, working in and for natural things, but only of the purposive suitability of objects for our *mind*. Nothing is prescribed by judgment for nature, but it enables our mind to proceed scientifically and practically, *as if* there were given, in nature, the universal principle for subsuming particulars and the unifying principle for connecting and subordinating all the specific types of objects. The principle of purposiveness means that we are to regard nature as though its laws were grounded in the unity of an extrahuman intelligence, disposing things for the sake of our own scientific investigations and practical plans. This principle develops out of the regulative use of the idea of God for the systematic study of nature.

Kant next indicates how the connection between judgment and

<hr>

[24] *Critique of Judgment,* Introduction, 5 (Bernard, 20–27).

feeling can be established, in an a priori way. The mind proceeds necessarily upon the assumption of purposiveness, even though it regards any particular, empirical laws as basically contingent and corrigible. Nevertheless, the happy chance that our a priori representation of the purposiveness of nature is actually borne out by the discovery of empirical connections, does cause us *pleasure*. This response is peculiar to the *power of judgment,* for no pleasure results from the necessary conformity of objects in general to theoretical understanding, and there is no question here of serving the practical ends of desire. The pleasure accompanying the empirical confirmation of purposiveness in nature is consequent upon the a priori principle of purposiveness, and hence is valid for *everyone*. It accompanies all our particular cognitions of specific and generic order, although habit dulls our awareness of its presence, in most cases. Some striking instances are needed to make us once more attentive to the harmony which we presume to exist between nature and the ends sought by our powers. Kant finds these stimulating experiences mainly in the appreciation of esthetic forms and the study of organic wholes.

Thus the third *Critique* examines esthetic and teleological judgments, concerned as they are, respectively, with a formal, subjective purposiveness and a real, objective purposiveness. *Esthetic judgment* rests on the special faculty of feeling pleasure or displeasure, as immediately attached to the representation of an object, whether in nature or in art.[25] It does not rest on the determinate, objective concept but on the *form* of the object, considered in relation to our *subjective* powers. When pleasure is felt in mere reflection on the form of the object, regardless of its universal concept or its function in knowledge, the judgment is an esthetic one. Its ground consists in the purposive conformity of the object with the powers of imagination and understanding, which are brought into harmonious and free play through the indeterminate representation. This *free play* or unimpeded exercise of the powers immediately arouses a feeling of pleasure, that is distinctively esthetic. Since the conjoining of the indeterminate repre-

---

[25] *Loc. cit.,* 7 (Bernard, 30–35). For background information on Kant's esthetic outlook, consult: K. E. Gilbert and H. Kuhn, *A History of Esthetics* (revised edition, Bloomington, Indiana, Indiana University Press, 1953), 289–370 (two chapters on "German Rationalism and the New Art Criticism" and "Classical German Esthetics: Kant, Goethe, Humboldt, Schiller"); *The Heritage of Kant* (edited by G. T. Whitney and D. F. Bowers), Part III, 323–402 — three essays on Kant and the problem of art. On the new meaning of "esthetic" in the third *Critique,* cf. H. N. Lee, "Kant's Theory of Aesthetics," *The Philosophical Review*, XL (1931), 537–48.

sentation with the pleasurable feeling is necessary a priori, the esthetic judgment based on this feeling can hold valid for all who will behold the object, under the proper circumstances.

Kant distinguishes between the strict judgment of taste, pronouncing an object beautiful, and an esthetic judgment about the sublime. He offers a formal analysis of *the beautiful,* in terms of the four classes of categories.[26] *Quantitatively,* the beautiful is an object of *universal* delight, in which all can share in principle, even though the judgment of taste is founded on a feeling, rather than on a universal concept. In respect to *quality,* delight in the beautiful is a *disinterested* pleasure taken in reflection upon the form alone, as ordained to the harmonious workings of imagination and understanding. This sets off esthetic pleasure from the interest which sense and practical reason take in the actual existence of the delightful thing, as a possible object of desire. From the standpoint of *relation,* an object is termed beautiful solely on the ground of the *form of purposiveness,* as contemplated by us. The beautiful object displays "purposiveness without purpose,"[27] a fitness for our powers, rather than an intrinsic striving toward an end in being. Beyond this purposive reference to our powers, the object grasped in esthetic experience reveals nothing of itself and its real principles. Last, the *modality* of the judgment of taste is that of *necessity.* It is not imposed as scientifically or morally necessary, but the judgment does assert, conditionally, that everyone ought to be in agreement about the delight or satisfaction necessarily obtainable from the object, provided that one actually contemplates it.

The judgment of taste concerns only the suitability of the form of the object for exciting the harmonious play of our cognitive powers, whereas the apprehension of *the sublime* betokens a finality on the part of the beholding subject itself. In the experience of the beautiful, there is restful contemplation of the object, whereas the feeling of the sublime arouses a characteristic *movement* on the part of the mind. In contrast with the definiteness of the form of the beautiful, the sublime object impresses one with its limitlessness and sometimes even its apparent formlessness. The sublime is that which is great beyond comparison. It both repels and attracts the mind, since it

---

26 *Critique of Judgment,* I, i, 1, No. 1–22 (Bernard, 45–96). For a comparative study, cf. A. W. Levi, "Scholasticism and the Kantian Aesthetic," *The New Scholasticism,* VIII (1934), 199–222.

27 *Critique of Judgment, loc. cit.,* No. 10 (Bernard, 68).

seems ill-adapted to the scope of imagination and yet supremely worthy of the feelings of admiration and awe.

On the basis of whether imagination refers the mental movement to the faculty of cognition or to that of desire, Kant distinguishes, respectively, between the *mathematically sublime* and the *dynamically sublime* object.[28] St. Peter's in Rome is an instance of mathematical sublimity, for in our cognitive effort to estimate its immensity, we are at first painfully bewildered, and eventually caught up in a delight of wonder, tempered with reverence. A dynamically sublime situation is found when an observer, himself placed in a safe position, views the mighty force of a storm at sea. He is both subdued by the tremendous power displayed in nature, and yet assured of the superiority of mind and consciousness-in-general, under whose structure the entire order of nature is organized. The very limitlessness of the sublime elicits an act of *recognition from reason,* since it sees in the sublime moments of nature a counterpart of its own ideas, which tend restlessly to break through the bounds set by the categories of the understanding. And moral freedom is encouraged to regard nature as the work of the supreme artisan, and hence to seek to realize in the world of appearances its own unconditioned imperatives. The experiences of beauty and sublimity are thus drawn from nature in such a way as to furnish *symbols of morality.* This is one way in which the spheres of nature and morality are brought closer together for men.

In his study of *teleological judgment,* Kant is seeking a means of overcoming the limitations of the purely mechanistic view of the world. Already in his solution of the third antinomy, he had suggested that "nature" is a way of regarding the totality of sensible appearances as purposive. Now, in his analysis of teleological judgment, he examines the basis for this purposive approach to nature. It finds justification in the excellent results obtained by scientific investigators, when they regard material things as though they were organized and directed by an objective, internal purposiveness. Reflective judgment is accountable for this teleological conception of natural processes. Judgment uses the concept of purposiveness in a *problematic* way, and does not pretend to determine anything about the actual causality present among things. For the purposes of research, however, teleology provides a leading principle for unifying appearances and explaining cases of order, among various kinds of natural

---

[28] *Ibid.,* I, i, 2, Nos. 24–29 (Bernard, 105–32).

phenomena. The analogy of human, artistic production is employed, with striking success, in the biological study of organisms. In this field, scientific advance is definitely favored by supposing that the parts of the *organism* are related reciprocally as ends and means, and that a concept of the integral whole governs the production and operation of the parts.[29] This purposive conception can be extended to all nature, viewing it as a vast system of natural ends, even in those parts which seem to be regulated by blind mechanism alone. This organic and teleological conception of nature is reminiscent of Hume's suggestion about the world as a great animal, and anticipative of the outlook on nature taken by the idealists and Goethe.

Kant denies, however, that theism or realism can make any capital out of the teleological principle. Nature may be treated as purposive, even though there be no genuine ends at work in nature. A procedural device should not be confused with a metaphysical commitment about the ways of things. To the last, Kant remains faithful to his epistemological doctrine on the limitation of knowledge to the appearances. No speculative proof of God's existence or our immortality can be based upon the purposive hypothesis about natural events and structures.[30] A divine, intuitive understanding might see the actual reconciliation of mechanism and teleology, but our understanding is not in possession of a universal, objective principle, under which to subsume the particular, contingent laws of the empirical world. This qualification, along with his recognition of a plurality of real things-in-themselves, keeps Kant from accepting the claims of Fichte about a completely a priori science of nature. We must remain content with treating purposiveness as a limit-concept and rule of reason alone, however much we may hope that the possibility of ends in nature is realized in fact. As far as intelligible realities are concerned, the significance of teleological judgment is practical and not theoretical. It aids the mind in passing from scientific understanding to moral faith, but it does not supplant the latter as our only human means of access to the intelligible world.

---

[29] "*An organized product of nature is one in which every part is reciprocally purpose, [end] and means.*" *Critique of Judgment*, II, i, No. 66 (Bernard, 280). Kant instances the mutual processes transpiring in a tree — cf. *loc. cit.*, No. 64 (Bernard, 274–75).

[30] *Ibid.*, II, Appendix, Nos. 85–88 (Bernard, 362–92).

## SUMMARY OF CHAPTER 12

What pure reason cannot achieve in the speculative order, it can bring to pass in the practical. Kant had to restrict knowledge in the strict sense to the field of appearances, so that practical faith could be exercised in regard to things-in-themselves. But critical philosophy still had the responsibility of adhering to its rigorous method of seeking an a priori foundation for given facts of experience. The central moral fact is the awareness that one is under obligation, that contingent choices are to be measured by a standard. This sense of duty would not be characteristic of practical reason or will, were the latter an all-holy and perfect will. But as found in man, will belongs to a being that has both a noumenal and a phenomenal aspect, and that therefore feels sensuous inclinations, as well as the law of pure will. Because he viewed the moral situation primarily as a conflict between sensuous inclinations and duty, Kant held that an action is rendered moral, only when it is performed solely out of conformity with the law or respect for duty itself. This preoccupation with the formal aspect of morality is manifested in the categorical imperative: "So act that the maxim of your will can always at the same time be valid as a principle making universal law." Disinterestedness and universal validity were, for him, the true marks of moral action, as rooted in an a priori foundation. He also showed how the reality of freedom, God, and immortality are implicated in the moral fact, as postulated conditions of its presence in man. Kant reduced the content of religion to morality. His third *Critique* examined the nature of beauty and esthetic appreciation, as well as the grounds for regarding nature in a teleological way.

## BIBLIOGRAPHICAL NOTE

1. *Translations.* The latest and best translation of Kant's moral writing is: *Immanuel Kant: Critique of Practical Reason and Other Writings in Moral Philosophy*, translated and edited by L. W. Beck (Chicago, University of Chicago Press, 1949). It contains (in addition to the *Inquiry* mentioned in the Bibliographical Note to Chapter 11, No. 1): *Foundations of the Metaphysics of Morals, Critique of Practical Reason, What is Enlightenment?, What is Orientation in Thinking?, Perpetual Peace: A Philosophical Sketch, On a Supposed Right to Lie from Altruistic Motives*, and selections from *The Metaphysics of Morals*. The older translation by T. K. Abbott: *Kant's Critique of Practical Reason and Other Works on the Theory of Ethics* (sixth ed., New York, Longmans, Green, 1909), includes most of the items in the Beck translation. *The Metaphysics of Ethics* was separately translated by J. W. Semple (third ed., Edinburgh, Clark, 1886). H. J. Paton has made an excellent, separate translation of *The Moral Law or Kant's Groundwork of the Metaphysic of Morals* (New York, Barnes and Noble, 1950), with a helpful introductory analysis of the entire argument. *Kant's Lectures on Ethics*, translated by L. Infield (London, Metheun, 1930), gives an interesting glimpse of Kant's classroom presentation of moral philosophy. There are two separate translations of the third *Critique*: J. C. Meredith's translation is in two parts: *Critique of Aesthetic Judgment* (Oxford, Clarendon, 1911), and *Critique of Teleological Judgment* (Oxford, Clarendon, 1928); the more adequate version is by J. H. Bernard: *Critique of Judgment* (second, revised ed., London, Macmillan, 1931). *Religion within*

*the Limits of Reason Alone* is translated by T. M. Greene and H. H. Hudson (revised ed., New York, Harper Torchbooks, 1960), with two informative essays on Kant's theory of religion by Greene and by J. R. Silber.

2. *Studies.* The best study of Kant's early ethical views is P. A. Schilpp, *Kant's Pre-Critical Ethics* (Evanston and Chicago, Northwestern University Press, 1938). Although written as a commentary on the *Foundation of the Metaphysic of Morals,* H. J. Paton's *The Categorical Imperative: A Study in Kant's Moral Philosophy* (Chicago, University of Chicago Press, 1948) explains and defends his basic ethics, as does R. Kroner, *Kant's Weltanschauung* (Chicago, University of Chicago Press, 1956). An able Aristotelian analysis is made by Sir David Ross, *Kant's Ethical Theory* (Oxford, Clarendon Press, 1954). *Morality and Freedom in the Philosophy of Immanuel Kant,* by W. T. Jones (New York, Oxford, 1940), goes to the heart of the Kantian moral philosophy, by analyzing the worth of the belief in the reality of freedom. H. W. Cassirer provides genuine aid to the student of the third *Critique* in his *A Commentary on Kant's Critique of Judgment* (London, Metheun, 1938). The first half of this *Critique* is also investigated by V. Basch, *Essai critique sur l'esthétique de Kant* (new, augmented ed., Paris, Vrin, 1927), and G. Denckmann, *Kants Philosophie des Aesthetischen* (Heidelberg, Winter, 1950). Basic not only to the last *Critique* but to the entire critical enterprise is the theory of reflective judgment, analyzed by M. Souriau, *Le jugement réfléchissant dans la philosophie critique de Kant* (Paris, Alcan, 1926). On Kant's religious views, consult C. C. J. Webb, *Kant's Philosophy of Religion* (Oxford, Clarendon, 1926), and the informed evaluation by B. Jansen, S.J., *Die Religionsphilosophie Kants* (Berlin and Bonn, Dümmler, 1929) — also available in a French translation and condensation, made by P. Chaillet: *La philosophie religieuse de Kant* (Paris, Vrin, 1934). There is also a full-scale commentary by J. Bohatec: *Die Religionsphilosophie Kants in der "Religion innerhalb den Grenzen der blossen Vernunft"* (Hamburg, Hoffmann and Campe, 1938).

3. *The Enlightenment and Rousseau.* Kant recognized in his own philosophy both the culmination and the catalytic dissolution of the Enlightenment. A witty, cultural description of the attitude of the *philosophes* is given in C. L. Becker, *The Heavenly City of the Eighteenth-Century Philosophers* (New Haven, Yale University Press, 1932). It is almost impossible to make valid generalizations about the sprawling movement of the Enlightenment, in its various national forms and cultural levels. E. Cassirer's *The Philosophy of the Enlightenment,* translated by F. C. A. Koelln and J. P. Pettegrove (Princeton, Princeton University Press, 1951), offers a working definition in the first chapter, and then proceeds to give synoptic statements of some typical achievements in the fields of physical science, psychology and epistemology, religion, history, law and the state, and esthetics. Other viewpoints may be found in: L. Stephen, *History of English Thought in the Eighteenth Century* (third ed., 2 vols., New York, Putnam, 1902); J. G. Hibben, *The Philosophy of the Enlightenment* (New York, Scribner, 1910); P. Hazard, *European Thought in the Eighteenth Century* (New Haven, Yale University Press, 1954); H. M. Wolff, *Die Weltanschauung der deutschen Aufklärung* (Bern, Francke, 1949). As specimens of the French phase of the movement, see: *Selections from Bayle's "Dictionary,"* edited by E. A. Beller and M. Du P. Lee (Princeton, Princeton University Press, 1952); Condillac, *Treatise on the Sensations,* translated by G. Carr (Los Angeles, University of Southern California Press, 1930); *Diderot: Interpreter of Nature. Selected Writings,* translated by J. Stewart and J. Kemp (New York, International Publishers, 1943). There are numerous editions of Rousseau's writings in English. Among the most helpful studies are: H. Höffding, *Jean-Jacques Rousseau and His Philosophy,* translated by W. Richards and L. E. Saidla (New Haven, Yale University Press, 1930); E. H. Wright, *The Meaning of Rousseau* (London, Oxford University Press, H. Milford, 1929); C. W. Hendel, *Jean-Jacques Rousseau, Moralist* (2 vols., New York, Oxford, 1934). P. Burgelin's *La philosophie de l'existence*

*de J.-J. Rousseau* (Paris, Presses Universitaires, 1952) is a systematic interpretation, influenced by contemporary existentialism. E. Cassirer's *Rousseau, Kant, Goethe,* translated by J. Gutmann, P. O. Kristeller, and J. H. Randall, Jr. (Princeton, Princeton University Press, 1945), traces the intellectual relations between these central men. A vigorous criticism of Rousseau is made by J. Maritain, *Three Reformers: Luther, Descartes, Rousseau* (see Bibliographical Note to Chapter 5, No. 2), Part III (93–164). An attempt to find a unified synthesis in Rousseau is made by E. Cassirer, *The Question of Jean-Jacques Rousseau,* translated by P. Gay (New York, Columbia University Press, 1954). For the relations of Herder to Kant, Rousseau, and the Enlightenment, consult R. T. Clark, Jr., *Herder: His Life and Thought* (Berkeley, University of California Press, 1955). F. C. Green's *Jean-Jacques Rousseau* (Cambridge, the University Press, 1955) examines Rousseau's personality and relates it to the other figures of the Enlightenment.

4. *Further Publications.* Kant's cultural and educational interests appear in his lectures on *Education,* tr. by A. Churton (Ann Arbor, University of Michigan Ann Arbor Paperbacks, 1960). The four centenary essays in *The Philosophy of Kant and Our Modern World,* edited by C. W. Hendel (New York, Liberal Arts Press, 1957), deal with his teaching on man, existence, esthetics, and the problem of democracy and peace. The L. W. Beck *Commentary on Kant's Critique of Practical Reason* (Chicago, University of Chicago Press, 1960) is a basic guide to the purpose, structure, and argument of the second *Critique.* The way in which Kant reconsiders all his major topics in his final writing is carefully described in V. Mathieu, *La Filosofia trascendentale e l' "Opus postumum" di Kant* (Turin, Edizioni di "Filosofia," 1958). We have a collection of readings and a general study of philosophical anthropology in the Enlightenment: *The Portable Age of Reason Reader,* edited by C. Brinton (New York, Viking, 1956), and L. G. Crocker's *An Age of Crisis: Man and World in Eighteenth Century French Thought* (Baltimore, Johns Hopkins Press, 1959). Rousseau's genetic and practical way of overcoming the split of spirit and sensuality in man is examined at length by M. Rang, *Rousseaus Lehre vom Menschem* (Göttingen, Vandenhoeck and Ruprecht, 1959).

# Chapter 13. FICHTE AND SCHELLING

## A. Fichte

### I. LIFE AND WRITINGS

JOHANN GOTTLIEB FICHTE was born in 1762, in the little Saxon town of Rammenau. His education was supervised by a Baron von Miltitz, to whom the young Fichte had ingratiated himself by repeating *verbatim* a sermon which the Baron had missed. After making his secondary studies at the Pforta school, Fichte went to the University of Jena (1780) and then to Leipzig for theological training. At this time, he was deeply influenced by the pantheistic determinism of Spinoza. He served as a tutor for a number of years in Leipzig and Zurich, but his overbearing temperament prevented him from maintaining cordial relations with his employers. At Zurich, he read Kant, Montesquieu, and Rousseau, and welcomed the French Revolution. After failing to retain a position as tutor in Warsaw, Fichte decided (1791) to visit his intellectual hero, Kant, in Königsberg. Since he was not received very warmly at first by the elderly Kant, Fichte retired to a room and in five weeks wrote an *Essay toward a Critique of All Revelation* (published, 1792), which applied, in a masterful way, the Kantian critical principles to the problem of the possibility and structure of revealed religion. Kant was impressed by this performance and saw to it that the manuscript was published. Somehow, the author's name and personal preface were omitted from the first edition of the book, so that many reviewers concluded that it was an anonymous treatise by Kant himself. Kant quickly corrected this error in public print and commended the young author. Fichte's reputation was made, and he soon commanded further public attention with two pamphlets, written in defense of the French Revolution and against autocratic government. Despite his growing reputation as a dangerous, "secret Jacobin," he was invited to teach at the University of Jena, at the insistence of Goethe.

Fichte's Jena period (1794-1799) was philosophically quite fruitful. Having reconciled Spinoza's metaphysical pantheism with Kant's practical doctrine on freedom, he was now ready to develop his own distinctive standpoint. In 1794, he published the fundamental statement of his idealism: *Basis of the Entire Theory of Science,* in which the transition from Kantian criticism to the new idealism was clearly marked. The essentially practical orientation of his thought was manifested in two other treatises: *Basis of Natural Right* (1796) and *System of Ethics* (1798), both of which were constructed "according to the principles of the theory of science." In 1799, however, Fichte's career at Jena came to a sudden halt. He had antagonized the students, through a program of reform of student societies, and had offended the religious leaders by scheduling some public lectures on Sunday mornings. Finally, the charge of atheism was circulated against him, because of an article published in the *Philosophical Journal,* of which he was the editor. Fichte threatened to resign and take a good portion of the faculty with him, if he were censured. With Goethe's concurrence, the government was pleased to accept this as a letter of actual resignation and dismissed the unruly philosopher, whose political views were even more frightening than his philosophical identification of God with the moral order of the universe.

Fichte came to Berlin in 1799 and, for a while, made common cause with the Romanticists, especially the Schlegels and Schleiermacher. The clash among these strong personalities forced them apart, however, especially after Fichte showed strong moral and religious convictions in *The Vocation of Man* (1800). His theory of a strictly regulated and autonomous economy was set forth in *The Closed Commercial State* (1800). But most of his Berlin publications were popular addresses, explaining his philosophy to the cultured public and applying it to contemporary issues. *On the Characteristics of the Present Age* was a series of lectures (delivered in Berlin in the winter of 1804-1805) attacking the Romanticists and locating his own era among the ages of world history; *The Nature of the Scholar* contained lectures on the scholarly life which Fichte gave at Erlangen University in 1805, during a brief professorship there; *The Way to the Blessed Life or Doctrine of Religion* explained his philosophy of religion to a Berlin audience, in the winter of 1805-1806. Shortly thereafter, Fichte fled from Berlin, at the news of Napoleon's invasion of Prussian territory. He taught for a while at the University of Königsberg, and returned to Berlin in time to deliver the famous *Addresses to the German Nation,* during the winter of 1807–1808. These lectures did not arouse much contemporary notice but were exploited by later nationalists. When the University of Berlin was founded (1810), Fichte was appointed professor of philosophy. He restated his theory of science, examined the facts of consciousness from an idealistic standpoint, and presented his later doctrine on law, ethics, and the state. He served briefly as rector of the university in 1811. When typhoid fever broke out among the Prussian soldiers engaged in the Wars of Liberation against Napoleon, Fichte's wife worked as a nurse among the victims. She caught the disease and was nursed back to health by her husband, who then was stricken down and died in January of 1814.

## 2. SYSTEMATIC UNITY AND THE METHOD OF THE THEORY OF SCIENCE

Fichte was the first major representative of the post-Kantian movement of metaphysical idealism, which dominated German philosophy during the first third of the nineteenth century. He called his own doctrine a *critical idealism,* thus differentiating it from both Kant's philosophy and dogmatism. By "dogmatism," he meant the various forms of realism, as well as some popular interpretations of Kant. He formulated the issue between idealism and dogmatism in a somewhat restricted way, taking the notion of the *thing-in-itself* as the dividing line. On this basis, there can be only two general, philosophical positions: dogmatism, which accepts the thing-in-itself, and idealism, which denies it. Insofar as he rejected the thing-in-itself and, at the same time, maintained the possibility of a positive metaphysics, Fichte was opposed to Kant, as well as to what he regarded as realistic dogmatism. But he admitted the need to retain Kant's critical or *transcendental method,* as a principle of scientific rigor. He sought to employ the Kantian method in the construction of a metaphysical idealism, without lapsing back into some form of dogmatism.

Fichte's initial description of the conflict between idealism and dogmatism is a persuasive one.[1] When we enter into ourselves and

---

[1] This conflict is described in Fichte's *First Introduction into the Science of Knowledge* (Rand translation, in his anthology, *Modern Classical Philosophers,* 486–96). For orientation in the post-Kantian world of Fichte-Schelling-Hegel, read R. Kroner,

attend to our presentations or contents of consciousness, we notice a striking difference among two broad classes. Some presentations seem to depend entirely upon the free determination of *our own will,* whereas others are referred to an *independent standard* of truth. The former states of mind are accompanied by a feeling of *freedom,* the latter states of mind by a feeling of *necessity.* Mental presentations accompanied by a feeling of necessity constitute *experience,* and the task of philosophy is to explain the ground of experience. This would seem to be a hopeless project, however, since the ground of experience lies somehow outside of experience or the totality of conditioned objects. Our minds are bound to experience, since there is a natural union between thing and intelligence, within experience.

But we also possess the power of abstraction or free separation of the constituent elements of experience. We are able to separate the concrete intelligence from the things it knows, and thus lift our consideration above the given unity of experience. If we abstract from the thing known, we reach the intelligence-in-itself or *ego-in-itself;* if we abstract from intelligence, we attain to the *thing-in-itself,* apart from its occurrence in experience. Idealism concentrates upon the former principle, whereas dogmatism focuses upon the latter. *Dogmatism* regards the thing-in-itself as the primary reality, which exists independently and causes our mental states. *Idealism* counters by affirming the complete independence of the intelligence or self and its causation of its own states of consciousness. (Fichte's *Ich* is rendered here, indifferently, as *ego* or *self,* meaning thereby the *I*-principle in consciousness.) There is no common ground between these two viewpoints. Each seems to have a strong case in its favor, but neither can directly refute the other. *Reason* has no way of settling the dispute, since the question concerns the first principle of knowledge and not some intermediate link.

Fichte appeals to the order of *interest* and *inclination* for resolution  of this issue, declaring that "what kind of a philosophy one chooses depends consequently upon what kind of a man one is."[2] A man must be prepared to sacrifice either the self to the thing (dogmatism) or the thing to the self (idealism). The choice of dogmatism is made by those, whose consciousness has not yet been developed fully, and who therefore regard the self as a mirror reflecting the reality of the

---

"The Year 1800 in the Development of German Idealism," *The Review of Metaphysics,* I (1947–1948), 1–31.

[2] *First Introduction into the Science of Knowledge* (Rand, 496).

external world. The dogmatist is bound to end in fatalism and materialism, regarding the conscious self as an epiphenomenal accident of the world. But the maturely developed consciousness will not tolerate this debasing view of the self. Rather, it will choose idealism, as providing the only safeguard of the independence of the self, its freedom, and its self-grounded nature. The idealistic position even holds a *theoretical* advantage over dogmatism. For the thing-in-itself can never be exhibited in experience, and therefore is a totally irrational concept, invented to explain the feeling of necessity. Idealism not only explains this feeling, in another way, but also takes as its first principle the I-in-itself or the freely acting intelligence, which can be *present in* consciousness or conditioned experience (even though it is not a conditioned *part of* experience).

Fichte's description of the basic choice confronting philosophers is, in fact, heavily weighted on the side of idealism. This is evident from his limitation of the primary conflict to the problem of the thing-in-itself, which is the basic issue only within the particular historical situation created by Kantian philosophy. Only within this context might the affirmation of independently existing things lead to epiphenomenalism, materialism, and a kind of Spinozistic determinism. The "mature consciousness" that poses the dilemma of sacrificing either the thing or the intelligent self, is proceeding upon two implicit premises. It supposes (*a*) that philosophy makes the movement of transcendence only by a complete separation and exaltation of one component of experience, and (*b*) that philosophy is a search after a single principle, from which everything else can and must be deduced. These two premises depend upon each other for support, since it is only where such an "abstraction" occurs, that there is need to reconstitute the experiential whole through an idealistic systematic deduction from some unique principle.

As Fichte defined it, the *systematic form* of any science means:

> The condition of the connection of the deduced propositions with the fundamental principle, and the ground which justifies us in drawing conclusions from this connection. . . . A science also can *not* have more than one fundamental principle, for else it would result in *many sciences*. The other propositions which a science may contain get certainty only through their connection with the fundamental principle.[3]

---

3 *The Science of Knowledge*, Introduction (Kroeger translation, 21, 15). An orderly survey of the main positions in Fichte's own system is given by X. Léon, "La philosophie de Fichte," *Revue de Métaphysique et de Morale*, X (1902), 26–68.

Fichte based this ideal of a tight, monolithic system upon Kant's remarks about the method and system of pure reason. But he felt that Kant himself had fallen short of his own standards. Kant had asked three questions: what can I know, what ought I to do, and what may I hope for? But his answers were left unsubordinated to a single primary response. He had established three absolutes: nature or the world of scientific knowledge, freedom or the world of moral duty, and the power of judgment as a mediating, "hopeful" principle of synthesis between nature and freedom. Fichte saw his own task to be that of reducing this multiplicity to systematic unity, in function of *one unconditionally absolute principle.*

Kant had been prevented from achieving this end, because of his distinction between the internal structure of reason and the world of objects. Reason can reach perfect, systematic unity in regard to its own nature and principles, since it can supply itself with all the requisite data. But in order to know objects of experience, more is required than the formal structure of consciousness: the matter of sensation must be received from without. Since this latter contribution is received and not deduced, complete systematic unity remained, for Kant, only an ideal limit, toward which he strived in his final speculations about the self-affection of the ego. Fichte placed the blame for failure to reach a completely deductive system squarely upon Kant's belief in the *reality of the thing-in-itself, as the source of the matter of sensation.*[4] This concept had to be removed, since it presented the outstanding obstacle to a deductive system. Only after its elimination could there be a successful *reduction of the Kantian dualisms* between: the matter and form of sensation, understanding and reason, theoretical and practical reason. These distinctions were relativized by Fichte and rendered subordinate to the unity of the ego, from which they were then deduced.

The functions of the defunct concept of the thing-in-itself nevertheless had to be accounted for, in terms of the subject or self. This accorded with Fichte's basic principle that *"nothing reaches the ego, except what it posits in itself."*[5] This cornerstone of his system was an unqualified generalization made from Kant's dictum that, in

---

[4] This center of dispute is discussed by B. Noll, *Kants und Fichtes Frage nach dem Ding* (Frankfurt a. M., Klostermann, 1936).

[5] *Outline of the Characteristic Feature of the Theory of Science,* I (*Sämmtliche Werke,* edited by I. H. Fichte, I, 333). The quotation from Kant is taken from *Critique of Pure Reason,* B xiv (Smith translation, 20).

studying nature, reason "must adopt as its guide . . . that which it has itself put into nature." Both philosophers recognized that they were risking the danger of transforming philosophy into arbitrary assertion and fancy; both appealed to the critical method as insurance against this consequence. Fichte's theory of science (*Wissenschafts-lehre*) rested upon a fundamental *construction of consciousness,* through a systematic deduction of all its elements. This construction was intended to have positive metaphysical significance, rather than to be merely another Kantian account of the limitations of reason.

In order to give metaphysical import to his method, Fichte had to undermine Kant's attack upon *intellectual intuition.* It was Fichte's claim that, if the spirit rather than the letter of Kant's doctrine is followed, there are good Kantian grounds for admitting this intuition. Three circumstances prevented Kant from recognizing this implication of his position. (*a*) He ruled out intellectual intuition of an already-constituted being or object. Fichte pointed out that, whatever the case with *phenomenal objects,* this still left open the possibility of an intellectual intuition of a *real act.* (*b*) Kant held that an intellectual intuition would have to be one that is cut off from sense intuition and feelings. Fichte replied that this is an unduly rational-istic assumption. It confuses the manner in which an intellectual intuition would *originally present itself* (along with sense intuition and feeling) and the manner in which it would be *isolated for subse-quent analysis* by philosophical reflection. (*c*) Kant posed the problem as a sharp contrast between a static, empty form and a blind matter. Yet in other instances, Kant allowed that *form* is present in human consciousness in a *dynamic* way, and that it contains some *matter of its own.* The nature of the form must be determined by its own structure and function in each distinct case, rather than by a general rule.

There were two positive hints in Kant which Fichte exploited in favor of an intellectual intuition: the theory of apperception and the doctrine on the categorical imperative, as a moral fact.[6] (*a*) Pure *apperception* is the unifying root and active source of all our powers, the formal principle determining all the structures of subjectivity and directing all the functions of consciousness. Here is a dynamic

---

[6] See *Second Introduction to the Theory of Science,* 5–6 (*Sämmtliche Werke,* I, 463–91). Fichte's relations with Kant are traced in W. Kabitz' essay, "Studien zur Entwicklungsgeschichte der Fichteschen Wissenschaftslehre aus der Kantischen Philo-sophie," *Kantstudien,* VI (1901), 129–205.

kind of form, one that is known immediately in reflection. Moreover, our intuitive grasp reaches not only to the empirical ego but also to the absolute principle of consciousness-in-general, the transcendental unity of apperception. (*b*) The fact of being under the moral law is another aspect of the intellectual intuition of the subject. It is brought home, with immediacy and direct insight, in the *categorical imperative*. Because the imperative is a categorical and unconditioned one, it conveys the reality of the *absolute self*, as well as of the finite, conditioned self. Since the absolute is attained intuitively in the categorical imperative, Fichte drew the following conclusions: the answer to the question *what ought I to do* is paramount and regulative of what I can know and hope for; the basic intuition concerns the *will* or *power of acting;* the absolute is revealed as *immanent* in self-legislating consciousness and as a *self-constituting principle.* Apperception is the last stage in the theoretical analysis, whereas the moral fact is the first stage in the practical analysis. Since there is an intellectual intuition of the same absolute principle in both apperception and the moral law, the theoretical and practical aspects of reason are synthesized in the single reality of the ego. Fichte was able to draw an intellectual intuition out of Kant's admissions, by suppressing any fully independent order of being and by rendering the absolute self totally immanent, as far as we are concerned.

Fichte sometimes calls the primary intellectual intuition "a fact of consciousness." But he also remarks that this phrase is misleading, insofar as it signifies a mere static result, presented to the mind. Only from the standpoint of the inquiring philosopher is this intuition an empirical fact, a *Tat-sache* or deed-already-done-in-accomplished-fact. From the perspective of the absolute self, which posits the intellectual intuition, it is a pure action, a *Tat-handlung* or deed-in-the-doing.[7] Taken in itself, it is a spontaneous and primitive dynamism, rather than a fixed product of some other operation. It manifests the pure activity of the absolute self, as positing itself in our consciousness. As the perfect identity between subject and object, this intuition of sheer action is the constitutive principle of self-consciousness and all conscious events. The primal acting is not given through anything else. Hence it cannot be apprehended originally through a concept or limiting form but only through an immediate intuition. It is the fundamental principle of all knowledge and deductive demonstration,

---

[7] *Second Introduction to the Theory of Science,* 5 (*Sämmtliche Werke,* I, 465).

so that it cannot be demonstrated or determined by anything else. If anything is known with certainty, this dynamic reality must be known. The intuition of the ego's pure activity provides the method with an intuitive basis and hence establishes the possibility of metaphysics. Since the intuition concerns activity, the central inspiration of Fichte's system is a moral one, an affirmation of the *Sollen,* the *ought* or duty, which animates all particular modes of becoming and forms of consciousness.

Nevertheless, the primary intuition and the Kantian transcendental method are not sufficient, by themselves, to construct the systematic theory of science. The Kantian method is better fitted to deal with objects than with the acting subject. And, taken by itself alone, the moral intuition is indeterminate and self-contained, so that no deductions can be made from it. In order to pass from the mere possibility of metaphysics to the actual construction of a metaphysical system, Fichte had to avail himself of another portion of Kant's doctrine: the theory of *antinomies.* Kant was never able to apply this theory to a positive metaphysical purpose, because of his denial of an intellectual intuition and his dualism between theoretical and practical reason. Once these hindrances are removed, it can be seen that thesis and antithesis are related contradictorily, only so that the mind may be led thereby to posit a reconciling synthesis. Thus Fichte based the hope for creative advance in philosophical thought upon the *thesis-antithesis-synthesis dialectic,* to which he subordinated the Kantian transcendental method. There is a *definite order and unity* among the antinomies uncovered by analysis, such that an orderly series of syntheses can be derived by systematic deduction from principles. This supposes that any particular, intermediate synthesis is *only partially successful.* It reconciles its own particular thesis and antithesis but, at the same time, brings to light some new and unresolved contradictions.

The mind is thus forced to construct a *systematically complete deduction* of all the elements of consciousness and hence of reality as well, insofar as it is significant for us. Not only the categories but also the forms of sensibility, the matter of sensation, and the various principles of practical life are to be rigorously deduced. Whatever occurs to the ego, is not only posited *in and by* the ego but is also posited *in such a way* as to permit a systematic derivation of the whole system of truths. In order to make the *I*-principle of consciousness his starting point, Fichte is required to make this supposition of a pre-established harmony between the original positings of the self and the requirements of systematic deduction. He does not demonstrate, directly, that the antinomies have any special mutual connection. Rather, he shows hypothetically that we must suppose them to have this order and unity, *if* they are to serve in a systematic deduction.

Fichte's methodology anticipated that of Hegel on several scores, especially the vindication of intellectual intuition, the use of the triadic scheme of thesis-antithesis-synthesis, and the use of incomplete syntheses as an incentive for developing a total system. But there were also some notable differences, which marked the distance from Fichte's critical idealism to the *absolute idealism of Hegel*.[8] Fichte was close enough to Kant to deny that an intellectual intuition of the absolute subject can be given through any concept, and hence he allied the intuition with feeling and the activity of the will. Hegel  claimed that this endangered the intellectual nature of the intuition, as well as the rational character of philosophy. He held that an intuition transcending the concept is too remote and inaccessible to serve as a dialectical principle in philosophy. Instead of separating intuition from conceptual knowledge, he suggested the need for a reform of the usual view of the *concept,* so that intuition and immediacy may be accommodated within the concrete universal concept. Along the same line, Hegel criticized Fichte's emphasis upon a moral first principle, and tried to reinstate the primacy of the *speculative* order. Furthermore, he sought to remove the hypothetical and deductive character of the ideal of a total system of truth, transforming it into a dialectical but apodeictic principle. A final difference concerned the Kantian distinction, which Fichte retained, between the absolute considered in-and-for-itself and considered for us or from the standpoint of consciousness. Hegel's whole aim was to make these two standpoints coincide perfectly, and to erect their coincidence into the motor principle of the dialectic itself. As long as any discrepancy was permitted, he held that the systematic construction would be lacking in demonstrative force and rigor. Hegel's absolute *is* the concrete universal concept and system of knowledge, whereas Fichte's absolute only *tends* to realize itself in reflective consciousness and the

[8] Cf. E. L. Schaub, "Hegel's Criticisms of Fichte's Subjectivism," *The Philosophical Review*, XXI (1912), 566–84; XXII (1913), 17–37. Hegel wanted to keep the distinction between the infinite and finite selves entirely within experience, considered as a single, rational whole.

scientific system, without ever becoming fully embodied in rational knowledge. On these points, Fichte remained at a halfway house between Kant and Hegel, never carrying his systematic monism to its ultimate, unequivocal conclusion.

### 3. THE FUNDAMENTAL PRINCIPLES AND THE CONSTRUCTIONS OF CONSCIOUSNESS

Fichte's *Wissenschaftslehre* supposes the presence of systematic bodies of knowledge. It inquires about the underlying principle of system as such, the nature of the connection among deduced propositions, and the ultimate ground to which every deduction must be attached. The theory of science determines the scientific character of *every* body of knowledge, by determining the fundamental principles which convert *any* set of presentations into genuine knowledge. All scientific certainty derives from a single principle that is unconditioned both in form and in matter. Along with it are ranged two other principles: one which is unconditioned only in its form, and the other unconditioned only in its matter. Together, these *three fundamental principles* supply the bases of knowledge, and are related to each other as thesis, antithesis, and synthesis.[9] Upon them rests the whole content of the theory of science and, ultimately, the scientific character of all bodies of knowledge. The synthesis of the first two principles in the third provides the deductive principle for the entire system of knowledge. Once the deduction has been carried through, the initial assumption about the presence of systematic knowledge is converted into a demonstrated truth.

The first two principles are disclosed, by analysis, to be involved in our most basic types of judgments. One general sort of judgment is expressed in the proposition: *A is A*. The reality of A-subject is not posited absolutely, but the claim is made hypothetically that, if A-subject is, then A-subject is the same as A-predicate. The proposition does affirm in an *absolute* way, however, the connection of identity between subject and predicate. This nexus of identity can be posited absolutely, only in and through the self, which contains both the terms and sees the kind and necessity of their connection, through its

---

[9] The doctrine of the three principles is found in *The Science of Knowledge*, I, 1–3 (Kroeger, 63–84; reprinted in Rand's anthology, *Modern Classical Philosophers*, 497–515). Kroeger's wording of the three underlined principles, given in the next three paragraphs below, is somewhat modified.

FICHTE'S DEDUCTION OF THE SYSTEM OF KNOWLEDGE

1. The principles of science.

a) Thesis or position: the ego simply posits in an original way its own being. Axiom of identity. Category of reality.

b) Antithesis or "op-position": A non-ego is simply "op-posited" to the ego. Axiom of difference. Category of negation.

c) Synthesis or "com-position": The ego "op-posits," within the [absolute] ego, a divisible [and finite] non-ego to the divisible [and finite] ego. Principle of sufficient reason. Category of limitation or determination.

2. The constructions of consciousness.

a) Theoretical deduction of the real series of acts and the categories of the world of scientific experience.

b) Practical deduction of the ideal series of acts (morality and right), and positing of the check or obstacle.

own identity. Hence propositions based upon identity presuppose the self-identical ego. At the root of the connection of identity and every judgment of identity lies the self-affirmed identity of the self: *I am I.* Therefore, the first and most fundamental principle of knowledge is this: *The ego simply posits in an original way its own being.* Since this principle states the absolutely primordial act of self-affirmation of the ego, it is unconditioned both in form and in content or matter. It provides the ground for the *axiom of identity* and the *category of reality.* For Fichte, "to posit itself and to be, are, applied to the ego, the same."[10] The whole reality of the self consists in its action of self-positing, an action which is given in the primary intellectual intuition. Since it *is,* simply insofar as it posits itself, the intuited self is the *absolute subject,* ungrounded in anything else. In this Fichtean context, being is not the same as the Kantian object of experience but means the sheer dynamic "agility" of the ego, as a self-positing process.

The second principle is manifested by analysis of propositions having the form: *non-A is not A.* This is not the equivalent of stating that *non-A is non-A,* for the latter proposition is merely a negative instance of the axiom of identity. Instead, the opposite of A is taken as the subject, and a denial is made that this non-A is the same as A. Underlying this logical process is the ontological act expressed in the second fundamental principle: *A non-ego is simply "op-posited" to the ego.* The matter of this principle is conditioned, since a negation

---

[10] *Ibid.,* I, 1 (Kroeger, 71; translation modified).

is made precisely of the ego as previously posited. But in form, it is completely unconditioned. For there is no way of deducing the form of *"op-positing"* from that of *positing*. Oppositing is an original form of action on the part of the absolute self. The second principle founds the *axiom of difference* and the *category of negation*. This negation is by no means a mere sterile protest. It is essentially the function of setting up a principle of otherness within the self, so that reflection and self-consciousness may occur. The absolute subject, in its original action of positing, is not acting in a conscious way. Opposition within the self is the means used by the absolute subject to acquire reflective awareness of its own nature, at least in a limited way. Hence the outcome of the act of negation is the *development of the non-ego, as an instrument for the realization of self-consciousness*. This is another suggestion adopted by Hegel, who nevertheless tried to establish a reason for the act of oppositing, within the original process of positing.

Next, Fichte takes stock of the situation produced by the joint affirmation of the first two principles, and concludes that they lead to a *contradiction*. For the self is not posited in the self, to the extent that the non-self is opposed there. And yet the non-self has no meaning apart from the self, of which it is the opposite and in which it is posited. Hence the self is both posited and not posited, insofar as the non-self is opposed in the self. There is danger that self and non-self will simply cancel each other out, destroying the identity of consciousness and, therewith, the absolute basis of knowledge. No solution can be derived from the first two principles, since they only generate the problem. Nor can the answer come from the analysis of another type of proposition, since what is needed is an integrating operation to retain both principles within the identity of consciousness. Hence Fichte has recourse to an *original act of synthesis,* on the part of intelligence. It must posit the new function of *mutual limitation,* since this is the only way to save both self and non-self, without destroying the unity of consciousness. Within the encompassing unity of the absolute subject, the self and non-self limit and cancel each other out, yet not completely but only in part. A factor of divisibility and quantification is thus introduced, in order to achieve this partial limitation of both principles. A third principle may now be formulated: *The ego "op-posits," within the [absolute] ego, a divisible [and finite] non-ego to the divisible [and finite] ego.* This is the source for the *axiom of the ground* or *sufficient reason* and for the

*category of limitation* or *determination*. The third principle is conditioned in form (since the relation of contradiction is determined by
the two prior principles) but is unconditioned in material content
(since it rests on an original synthesis or act of uniting thesis and
antithesis).

From the standpoint of absolute idealism, Hegel offers a brief but
incisive criticism of this derivation of first principles.[11] He advances
two main objections. First, the entire analysis remains within the
Kantian *dualism* between form and matter. It depends for its plaus-
ibility upon a manipulation of form and matter, as conditioned and
unconditioned. The result is an artificial schema. Second, no genuinely
*dialectical* explanation is given of the origin of the form of negation
(in the antithesis or second principle) and the act of mental synthesis
(in the synthesis or third principle). They are gratuitously invoked
to account for experiential facts and logical functions, rather than
drawn from the nature of the thesis. They do not constitute a dialectical
*anti*thesis and *syn*thesis, since they do not proceed, with any rational
necessity, from the thesis and the absolute ego. To call them "original"
activities of the ego is to confess that a systematic explanation of their
origin and function is wanting.

Fichte's way of establishing the fundamental principles of the theory
of science depends upon the assumption that ontological weight is
to be given to the highest conditions of logical functions. Fichte
reifies these conditions in terms of the absolute subject, the divisible
or finite ego, and the divisible or finite non-ego. This *ontologizing
of supreme logical conditions* is carried out, on the warrant presumably
supplied by the intellectual intuition of pure activity. But it requires
a separate decision, dictated by the needs of systematic construction,
to transform our *self*-awareness into an immediate awareness of the
*absolute ground of being* and real foundation of all logical truths.
Fichte's logical first principles become ontological first principles, only
if the experience of freedom is the same as an intellectual intuition of
the first being or primal active principle, in the absolute sense. He
overrules, rather than answers, Kant's objection that the immediate
data of moral consciousness are metaphysically neutral, even though
they may have practical implications bearing upon the ultimate
structure of being and activity. But these implications can be given
existentially valid, metaphysical import only in virtue of a prior,

---

[11] See below, Chap. 14, note 5.

speculative defense of our intellectual grasp upon being. Fichte rightly seeks an intuition of being as act, but he makes its cognitive significance depend upon a fiat of the will. This fiat is controlled, in the final reckoning, by the systematic requirement that the absolute reality must be given *as a first deductive principle,* rather than as the termination of a demonstration, based upon the implications of our experience. Hence Fichte's logical first principles are not only first principles of being in general but also denote first beings or acting realities.

Fichte regards his third or synthetic principle as the prototype for all subsequent syntheses in philosophy. All other synthetic resolutions of contradictories must be implicated in this germinal one. He makes two general deductions or constructions of consciousness, a theoretical and a practical one, based upon the distinction between the theoretical ego and the practical ego.[12] This distinction arises from the two ways of looking at the mutual limitation of ego and non-ego. The *theoretical* standpoint is one in which the ego is regarded as being determined objectively by the non-ego, whereas the *practical* standpoint is one in which the ego is seen to be the ultimate determinant of the non-ego, and hence the ultimate source of all determinations occurring in itself.

The first principle of the *theoretical construction of consciousness* is that the self posits itself as being limited by the non-self.[13] The theoretical self is directed toward the objects of experience and knowledge. It is engaged in a *real series of acts,* i.e., acts which are limited by the non-self and preoccupied with overcoming the limits set by the non-self. The main problem is to account for the various formal and material contributions from the absolute self to the situation of knowledge, where understanding is faced with a world of things. In this perspective, the mutual limitation of self and non-self becomes one of mutual activity and passivity, under the category of *reciprocity.* Fichte then deduces the further categories of cause, substance, quantity, and the mutual determination of act and passion. Finally, he posits the *productive imagination,* as the general means employed by the absolute subject in the construction of consciousness. Productive imagination is Fichte's tool for expounding the pragmatic history of the human mind, just as it was Kant's bond between understanding and sensibility. Fichte shows how the absolute self, in the face of self-made obstacles, brings forth matter, sensation, the forms of space and time, the categories and their objects. It posits not only imagination but also understanding, judgment, and reason or self-consciousness.

The theoretical deduction is not self-sufficient, however, since it cannot explain *why* the absolute self should posit limitations or obstacles to its activity. The final answer can come only from the *practical construction of consciousness.*[14] Here, the absolute self may be regarded as positing itself as the determining principle of the non-self. This is the same as positing the non-self as being limited by the self. The practical self is engaged in an *ideal series of acts* of self-realization, in which the emphasis is placed upon the ego's own activity, rather than upon the objects it encounters (as is the case with the real series, issuing from the theoretical self). In order to achieve reflective consciousness, the practical self must bring forth some *obstacle* or *check* (*Anstoss*) to its vital activity, an obstacle that will "shock" this infinite activity and make it recoil upon itself, in a definite way. This return to itself is carried out through *reflection,* which is the only way in which the absolute can become conscious of itself. Out of the primitive shock or obstacle, is gradually developed the entire world of the non-ego, a world that is autoproduced within the absolute self. Pure activity employs this practical device, so that its acts may be a genuine striving against resistant forces, and may acquire thereby the values of self-consciousness, if only in a limited way.

The practical self combines the independence and freedom of the original act of self-positing with the dependence of an intelligence, orientated toward real objects in the world of the non-self. Hence the theoretical self and the theoretical construction of consciousness are subordinate to, and dependent upon, the more fundamental operations of the practical self. The objectivity of theoretical knowledge

---

[14] *The Science of Knowledge,* III (Kroeger, 259–331). The basic aim of the practical constructions is to achieve the absolute autonomy of the ego. "But the *dependence* of the Ego, as intelligence, must be removed, and this is thinkable only on condition that *the Ego determine through itself that until-now-unknown Non-Ego,* to which the check [*Anstoss*] has been ascribed, which makes the Ego intelligence. In this way, the absolute Ego would determine the Non-Ego-entering-into-representation *immediately* and the representing Ego *mediately,* by means of that determination [of the Non-Ego]. The Ego would become solely self-dependent, that is, determined completely through itself." *The Science of Knowledge,* III (Kroeger, 261; translation modified).

rests upon the *feeling of necessity* and objective constraint, in the face of an experienced object. But the check or obstacle posited by the practical self accounts for this feeling and hence also for the speculative criterion of reality. This is the basic idealistic refutation of dogmatism in philosophy. Fichte not only reaffirms the Kantian primacy of the practical over the theoretical order but also lays the foundations of strict *knowledge* upon a *practical* basis. He unifies theoretical and practical reason, by grounding all certainty and reality in an act of pure practical reason or will. Fichte agrees with Goethe in maintaining that "in the beginning was the deed [or act]."

The Fichtean theory of the shock or obstacle set a pattern for metaphysical idealism. Where the Kantian method fell short, Fichte pressed ahead to deduce the matter of sensation and every determinant of consciousness. He did not deny the descriptive validity of the ordinary conviction about a real world, which is other than the self and which entails a firm distinction between the ideal and the real spheres. But he made this *real otherness* a *reducible,* rather than an *irreducible,* principle. In its reducible form, it can be accorded descriptive importance; yet it must be fitted into a context where the absolute ego is the single source of all principles of experience and knowledge. From the perspective of the *theoretical* self, the distinction between self and non-self will be solid and real. This is no deception, since theoretical consciousness is affected genuinely by the non-self. But the non-self, in turn, must be viewed comprehensively, as being the result of a positing act of the absolute self, in its *practical* nature. Moreover, the non-self is posited in and for the sake of the self, for the latter's advancement in the life of consciousness and thought. Idealism (or, as Fichte sometimes called it, "ideal-realism") alone considers the principle of otherness and the world of objects from the inclusive viewpoint of the absolute subject, which posits this entire realm of the non-ego within itself and permits itself to be determined by it.

Fichte's complete deduction of consciousness and objectivity rests upon a double ambiguity: in the meaning of the term *positing* (*Setzung*) and in the explanation of the relation between the divine absolute and the finite self. *Positing* is used sometimes to designate a merely *cognitive act of affirmation* or recognition, on the part of imagination or the other mental powers. But where the argument demands an ontological sense, it is also used to signify a *real bringing-forth* or production of the obstacle, of matter and the entire objective sphere of the non-ego. Fichte is able to glide from the one usage to the other on the strength of his ontological interpretation of the logical functions of thought. This ambiguity about the nature of the act of positing is encouraged, further, by the blurred relationship between the absolute and the finite self. When asked whether his system is a monism or a dualism, Fichte replied that it is a *dualism* from the standpoint of actual knowledge or the phenomenal human perspective, but a *monism* from the standpoint of the ideal and the absolute principle of pure activity.[15] Dualism prevails only within the given conditions of finite knowledge. In principle, it is replaced by a more adequate monism, when we attain to the infinite perspective of the absolute principle itself. Because of the ultimate subordination of our actual knowledge to the practical self-positing process of the absolute, the dualistic aspects of this critical idealism are less decisive than the monistic. The former are invoked in order to take account of the feeling of necessity and otherness, as well as to guarantee the earnestness of the moral struggle. But for the unqualified explanation of these facts of consciousness, Fichte's systematic deduction relies upon a basic monism of the absolute subject and its process of becoming. The relationship between the absolute and the finite self follows the course of this deliberate coalescence of principles and perspectives.

## 4. MORALITY AND RIGHT

Unlike Hegel, who encompasses morality and right within the single dialectical movement of ethical life, Fichte makes independent constructions of these two spheres of practical activity. *Morality* concerns the inner conscience of the self, whereas *right* bears upon the external relations among individuals and the problems of social institutions. Both doctrines have a common root, however, in the view that the practical self is an infinite striving.

Analysis of the structure of the practical self reveals a fruitful contradiction or *practical antinomy*.[16] Our practical consciousness shows the self to be both independent and dependent, both an unlimited assertion of freedom and an activity bounded by resistant objects. The limited aspect of human nature results from the law

---

[15] *Exposition of the Theory of Science* (1801), II, 32 (*Sämmtliche Werke*, II, 88–90). Here, Fichte compares his position with Spinoza's, and declares that he has been more successful than his predecessor in blending dualism with monism or "unitism" (the absolute as the "one-and-all").

[16] *The Science of Knowledge*, III (Kroeger, 265–78).

that the absolute itself can attain consciousness only through a struggle with obstacles and otherness. In principle, this process of becoming self-conscious is an endless one, so that the finite ego has the obligation of struggling continuously to overcome the resistance and dominate the non-ego. Because there is a core of unconditioned freedom or activity in the ego, its striving is *infinite* and ceaseless. But because this free activity is directed toward resistant obstacles, it is a genuine *striving* and not a mere play-acting. Hence the infinite striving is not only the principle of being, for the finite ego, but also an *ideal* that must be carried out in the world. The presence of this ideal means that pure freedom is found in man as a *Sollen,* a pure *ought* or duty, which constitutes the essence of the *moral law.* The practical self regards the world as a task, and sensible things as so many materials of duty or visible occasions for specifying the moral struggle and securing at least partial triumphs for consciousness. This moral purpose is the ultimate justification for positing the real world or sphere of the non-ego.

Fichte also expresses the practical antinomy as one between pleasure and freedom. The self-positing activity of the self may be looked at either objectively or subjectively. In its *objective* aspect, the practical self is implicated in a system of natural impulses, which become needs and desires, as soon as we become conscious of them and direct them toward definite objects in the world. Taken as a totality, these self-seeking impulses, needs, and desires direct man's will toward *pleasure,* which is their satisfaction. But this same power of will can be considered *subjectively,* as an impulse toward the self-positing of *freedom.* Hence the practical self is compounded of the natural impulse toward pleasure and the tendency toward unconditioned freedom. Their vector resolution is the infinite striving of the individual to do his duty, by realizing the moral law under temporal conditions. This duty is expressed in the categorical imperative: *"Always fulfill thy vocation . . . act according to thy conscience."*[17] Man's moral vocation is to harmonize his needs and wants with the free act of self-affirmation, so that the rational order of morality will be actualized in the sensible world, in constantly more effective ways and degrees.

Fichte believed passionately in the community of rational, finite selves. The individual's vocation is not confined to himself alone.

---

[17] *The Science of Ethics,* II, 12, 13 (Kroeger translation [modified], 159, 164).

He is a member of the moral order, the common actualization of which, in the life of all men, is the major goal of his strivings and duties. In his popular addresses, Fichte stressed this *social* aspect of one's vocation. He spoke eloquently of the special tasks assigned to great individuals, the heroes of history, in respect to the wider community of free agents. The dignity and responsibility of the calling of the *scholar* impressed him with extraordinary force. Fichte called the scholar: the priest of truth, the guide and teacher of the human race, an individual dedicated to the moral elevation of all men. His work is "to maintain among men the *knowledge* of the Divine Idea, to elevate it unceasingly to greater clearness and precision, and thus to transmit it from generation to generation, ever growing brighter in the freshness and glory of renewed youth."[18] In drawing this portrait of the scholar's vocation, Fichte had primarily in mind his own philosophical labors and their intended effect upon men. The philosopher comes closest to understanding and advancing the purpose of social existence: the mutual improvement of free individuals and, eventually, the moral perfection of the whole human race.

The *first principle of right* is "that each individual must restrict his freedom through the conception of the possibility of the freedom of others."[19] This principle is deduced, independently, from the concept of the rational, free individual, and is not derived from morality. It supposes, however, that the individual is already in contact with, or at least can come into contact with, other rational individuals. Right involves the positing of other centers of freedom, and hence is the principle regulative of social life. By *society,* Fichte means "the relation of reasonable beings to each other . . . *a free reciprocal activity founded on ideas.*"[20] Although this definition of society is framed in purely rational and ideal terms, the actual social relations among persons require the further positing of the material universe and the human body, which are regarded by Fichte as instruments of rational communication and purposive activity. Hence the social functioning of rights supposes a network of natural relations among persons, who communicate with each other not only

---

[18] *The Nature of the Scholar,* VII (Smith translation, in *The Popular Works of Johann Gottlieb Fichte,* I, 282).

[19] *The Science of Rights,* I, 4 (Kroeger translation, 78); cf. *ibid.,* Introduction (Kroeger, 17-19).

[20] *The Vocation of the Scholar,* II (Smith translation, in *The Popular Works of Johann Gottlieb Fichte,* I, 160, 163).

on the basis of rational ideals but also in respect to their conflicting natural needs and selfish desires.

There is no other way of securing the rights of personal freedom in society than for men to enter into a series of compacts, concerning property and mutual protection. Thus the *state* is summoned into being, in consequence of a series of mutual concessions and compacts.[21] Its purpose is to provide the restraining force of a common will, which endeavors to achieve the common welfare of all the rational individuals, joined in civil compact. Since the state's purpose is a rational one, individuals are bound to surrender their freedom to it. The state establishes *compulsion* or the social use of force as a rightful, legal relation among men. But Fichte does not exalt the state on essentially moral grounds. Whereas Hegel makes the state the culmination of ethical life and the divine idea in its objective form, Fichte (followed by Schopenhauer) regards it primarily as the groundwork of the nonethical network of rights and egoistic interests. It is not an end but a means, not part of the absolute purpose of human existence but a transitional moment. Eventually, the need for the state will cease and this institution, along with the whole system of rights, will disappear. But, Fichte prudently adds, governments will be rendered superfluous only in a distant, unforeseeable era. Like Marx, he is cautious about setting any definite historical time for the actual withering-away of the state.

Within our actual historical span, however, the state (along with the family and other social institutions) is both indispensable and also laden with moral responsibility. It is *indispensable,* since from the nonmoral, egoistic standpoint, individuals of a rational, free nature cannot satisfy their wants and desires, without mutual recognition and control. But the state is also the instrument of *moral* and *educational* life, since it can be used to instill in the citizens a sense of their moral vocation, and to establish the best social conditions for its realization. Fichte's theory of the isolated or *closed commercial state* is a utopian plan for raising the level of virtue very rapidly, within a single country.[22] The closed state is to aim at self-sufficiency,

[21] On the state, see Books I and II of Part Two of *The Science of Rights* (Kroeger, 205–85).

[22] See Fichte's work, *The Closed Commercial State* (*Sämmtliche Werke*, III, 389–513). For an account of how Fichte's ethical individualism led him to embrace economic and political socialism, as a protection against unregulated economic individualism, cf. H. Rickert, "Die philosophischen Grundlagen von Fichtes Sozialismus," *Logos*, XI (1922–1923), 149–80.

especially in the economic order, so that its citizens will not be contaminated by debasing contact with peoples of a different outlook. Free trade and international exchange must be suppressed. The internal affairs of the closed commercial state must also be subject to the strictest regulation. The community is to become a vast, supervised workshop. Everyone is to be assured of his material support and the opportunity to work, but property, work, and all social activities (with the exception of education, which provides the directive principle for governmental functions) are to be under complete political control.

This socialistic scheme for the total planning of social life dealt summarily with the pressing problem of how to combine *organization* with *freedom,* so that enlightened planning will not degenerate into stifling regimentation. Fichte held that, if his own philosophy were adopted as the regulative norm for social programs, political power *eo ipso* would be humanely exercised. For, by definition, it would then be respectful of individual freedom and solicitous for achieving the moral independence of men. Fichte anticipated the utopian socialists and Marx, by solving the question of freedom and power in terms of an abstract doctrine on the proper aims of human nature. In practice, however, this simplistic sort of solution often leads to a tyranny imposed by doctrinaire leaders.

The moral leadership that one nation should show other peoples was another theme that loomed large for Fichte, helping to counterbalance his stress upon the closed state. During his early years, he shared in the French revolutionary ideals and looked to France for the regeneration of other countries. But, like Hegel, he became disillusioned in Napoleon and turned to the German people as the prime agents of moral inspiration, in the modern era. His *Addresses to the German Nation* was delivered as a lecture course in Berlin, during the French occupation of 1807–1808. A nationalistic legend later sprang up, concerning the inflammatory effect of these speeches and their contribution to the German opposition to the Napoleonic armies. Actually, they made no stir whatever among Fichte's contemporaries. Nevertheless, they did contain useful materials which were exploited, subsequently in the nineteenth century, by German nationalists.

Fichte's *Addresses* contains an explosive intermingling of abstract doctrine and concrete political considerations, a mixture paralleling his theoretical synthesis between the infinite and the finite selves.[23] He appeals to the Germans as such, the bearers of *Germanness*, which is identical with the *essence of humanity*. Whatever their place of birth or language, individuals may be aggregated to this central ideal, provided that they are working for a free humanity, under the rational, moral law. Nevertheless, despite their present, wretched political and moral condition, the actual Germans of history are best suited, as a concrete group, to be the leaders of all mankind. The nation that gave birth to Luther, Pestalozzi, and Kant proves itself to contain the necessary resources for educating the rest of men. Most important of all, the German language is the native tongue of genuine philosophy, which means that the Germans are naturally fitted to grasp Fichte's own philosophy. This is a decisive reason in his eyes. Because they are able to understand and accept Fichte's ethical idealism, the Germans are the elect people, destined to lead other nations to the kingdom of God upon earth. Fichte's double vision of the Germans-as-such and the historical German nation was exploited for narrowly nationalistic and imperialistic ends after 1840, with the careful excision of his republican and cosmopolitan sympathies.

## 5. RATIONAL FAITH IN THE ABSOLUTE

Fichte installs the three postulates of Kantian morality completely within the immanence of practical consciousness. *Freedom* is not only the condition for obeying the moral imperative: it is seized upon in an intellectual intuition "from within" or in its own subjective nature. *Immortality* is not a projection into an endless future but a reality even now in the possession of the practical self, which recognizes its own nature as an infinite striving. And the Fichtean *God* actualizes Himself through nature and morality, and not merely reconciles them. He is not only revealed through the moral order but *is* that order. Fichte protested against the charges of atheism, preferred against him at Jena. He had an absolute, but it did not carry the traditional attributes of God. Although reflection cannot avoid substantializing and personalizing the *moral order,* the absolute in its own nature is not a given substance or personal individual. Consciousness and intelligence can be applied only negatively, to

---

[23] For an analysis of Fichte's attempted synthesis of nationalism and free humanity, read H. Kohn's article, "The Paradox of Fichte's Nationalism," *Journal of the History of Ideas*, X (1949), 319–43.

signify that the absolute is *not* a mere thing. At least for us, it is constantly engaged in the process of becoming aware of itself. Fichte sought to avoid the static consequences he conceived to follow from Spinoza's doctrine on God as substance. But he did not discover a principle of synthesis between God as *dynamic, free activity* and God as *transcendent perfection*. What stood in the way of such a reconciliation was the cleft separating the two halves of his notion of being. Fichte applied the term *being* equivocally to self-positing freedom and to the fixed objects of experience. He never succeeded in establishing a common, analogical meaning for being. In dealing with the absolute, therefore, he was severely handicapped. Fichte was able to attribute freedom to the absolute, only by making it a wholly immanent principle, identified with the inner dynamism of our conscious life. And he was reluctant to regard the absolute as a substantial reality, since in his estimation this signified the mere being of mindless things or objects of experience. This same fundamental hesitation about how to denominate the absolute, in view of the divergent meanings of being, is found in the other post-Kantian idealists.

In his later popular writings, especially *The Vocation of Man* and *The Way to the Blessed Life or Doctrine of Religion,* Fichte expounded his metaphysico-religious views on man's relationship with the absolute. This phase of his development did not mark a break with his previous theory of science, but it did shift the emphasis from the problem of knowledge to that of the conditions of action and being. Hence it underlined the *monistic* side of his thought, by interpreting human life from the vantage point of the absolute or divine order, as a moral reality.

The reflective self comes to see that its true vocation is not to know but to do. It is made for action and derives all its certainty from its own will or moral faith. Nevertheless (as Kant had already noted), the practical self is not pure will, since its existence is engaged in the world of nature. In the sensible world, value is placed upon the overt deed and its consequences, rather than upon the motives and free positing of the action. Man is thus a member of two worlds: the *sensible world of deeds,* determined by natural mechanisms, and the *eternal world of will and freedom.* He is responsible for *willing* to promote the moral law, within the sensible world, but he must be resigned about the *actual* results. His resolution to be loyal to duty is founded on *rational faith* in the supersensible world, as the true source of his life and worth.[24] Faith apprehends the moral order, not simply as an ideal but also as a present reality of freedom and rational action. Finite egos are joined to this realm through acts of will. They learn to treat their individual natures as so many modes of the divine being and nodules in the absolute, moral network of dutiful action.

Religion describes the adhesion of wills to the law of duty, as a dying to this world and a rebirth in eternal life and the kingdom of God. Through the agency of religious meditation, the moral order takes on the personal characteristics of a God, having intelligence, will, and providential power. Our infinite striving toward the absolute is now expressed more in terms of *love* than of duty, or rather, love is taken as the basis of duty. Religiously speaking, man is required to choose between love of the transient, phenomenal world and love of the eternal. Only the latter love is life-giving. *Love for the eternal* makes an infinite approximation toward the absolute: it constitutes both our duty and our blessedness. As Spinoza saw, blessedness is not reserved for another time but comes within our possession now, as soon as we freely identify ourselves with dynamic phases in the divine self-positing. "The true life and its blessedness consist in a union with the unchangeable and eternal: but the eternal can be apprehended only by thought, and is in no other way approachable by us. . . . Faith is the same thing which we have here named thought: the only true view of ourselves, and of the world, in the one unchangeable divine being."[25]

Fichte devotes an entire lecture to the proof that his religious doctrine is the same as that found in the Gospel according to St. John.[26] But he measures Christianity and all religious life according to the standard of his own philosophical idealism, which supplies the rational faith or "true view" by which to interpret religious imagery. Along with Kant and Hegel, Fichte *subordinates the religious standpoint to that of philosophy,* as far as its truth is concerned. Whereas the procession of multiplicity from the one, absolute principle is accepted by religion as a sheer, given fact, the manner and reason of the fact are explained by philosophical science. It alone can reduce the manyness of the non-ego to the absolute, and

---

[24] Book III of *The Vocation of Man* is an exposition of Fichte's conception of faith (Smith translation, in *The Popular Works of Johann Gottlieb Fichte,* I, 405–78).
[25] *The Way Towards the Blessed Life,* I (Smith translation, in *ibid.,* II, 306, 308).
[26] *Ibid.,* VI (Smith, II, 381–99).

then deduce the finite egos and objects from the absolute, considered as their genetic principle and ground. Fichte explains the procession of the many from the one as a *necessary emanation,* in harmony with his teaching that the absolute must posit the non-ego and the finite egos as means of attaining its own reflective consciousness. Similarly, the return of the many to the one is described as a recognition, on the part of individual selves, that their true nature is to be conscious *modes* and component *members* of the absolute subject. The absolute is never fully explicated in consciousness, so that its finite manifestations must continue to remain in process and engage in an infinite task. But these finite actualizations of the absolute know themselves for what they are, and become one with the divine life, through love. This explanation is a strict consequence of the view that the absolute posits finite egos both within itself and for the sake of its own infinite drive toward *self*-realization.

Fichte's answer to the problem of the one and the many is to reformulate it as the problem of the manyness within the one. This is the decisive sense in which the dualistic factors remain integral phases *within* his monism of the absolute. Hence he must explain away the Christian doctrine on free creation and the irreducible distinction between creatures and a God who is infinitely self-knowing and unchanging. In Fichte's system, *participation* in the divine nature becomes a wholly immanent relation between part and whole, rather than a relation between creature and transcendent creator. He thoroughly transforms Scripture and the data of religious consciousness, in conformity with the laws of his systematic deduction.

# B. *Schelling*

## I. LIFE AND WRITINGS

Since his father was a learned pastor and teacher, Friedrich Wilhelm Joseph Schelling (born, 1775, in Württemberg) received most of his secondary training at home. At the age of fifteen, he was sent to the Tübingen theological foundation, where he counted Hegel and Hölderlin as older classmates. Schelling's philosophical genius matured very rapidly. While still at Tübingen, he not only mastered Kant, Plato, and Leibniz, but also expounded Fichte's doctrine so thoroughly that he was known as "the second founder of the theory of science." He began to take an independent stand in his

*Philosophical Letters on Dogmatism and Criticism* (1795), which tried to reconcile Spinoza's determinism and dogmatic metaphysics with Fichte's strenuous affirmation of freedom and critical idealism. Schelling's characteristic preoccupation with nature and the objective side of idealism found expression in *Ideas toward a Philosophy of Nature* (1797) and *On the World Soul* (1798). Having won the approbation of Goethe and Fichte with these books, he was appointed professor of philosophy at the University of Jena (1798). His association with such leaders of Romanticism as the Schlegels and Novalis stemmed from this period. During his Jena professorship, Schelling coedited the *Critical Journal of Philosophy* with Hegel and developed his theory of art and objective idealism in *System of Transcendental Idealism* (1800). The identity of nature and spirit, within the indifference of the absolute, was proposed in two other writings: *Exposition of My System of Philosophy* (1801) and *Bruno or On the Divine and Natural Principle of Things* (1802). In 1803, Schelling married Caroline Schlegel and left Jena for Würzburg and Munich.

At about the time of his transfer from Jena to Würzburg, Schelling was introduced to the theosophical views of the early seventeenth-century German religious thinker, Jacob Boehme. He shared his enthusiasm for Boehme's utterances with the Romanticist philosopher, Franz von Baader, whom he met in Munich in 1806. According to Schelling, theosophy contained a speculative content but under a nonscientific form. He undertook to present in a distinct and rational way some of Boehme's insights concerning evil, freedom, and the dualism of forces in God and nature. This orientation of his thought was reflected in the last two major works published during his lifetime: *Philosophy and Religion* (1804) and *Philosophical Inquiries into the Nature of Human Freedom* (1809). By the time the latter work had appeared, however, criticism of Schelling's philosophy had started to mount. The greatest blow to him was Hegel's satirical account of his theory of intellectual intuition and absolute indifference. Even lesser critics, such as Jacobi and Eschenmayer, challenged his theory of God, on the ground that it led to pantheism and anthropomorphism. Such attacks convinced him that the time was not ripe for the publication of his doctrines, although this did not discourage him from presenting his philosophy in lectures. Indeed, throughout the period of Hegel's greatest popularity, Schelling kept lecturing away at Würzburg (1803–1806), Munich (1806–1820), and Erlangen

(1821–1826), providing an underground center of resistance against the reigning version of absolute idealism.

In 1827, he returned to Munich as professor of philosophy, and gradually began to exert considerable influence upon German intellectual life. He made a fundamental distinction between the negative and positive phases of philosophy. Hegel's system was classified as a negative philosophy, since it was concerned mainly with the analysis of conceptual principles and essential structures. In contradistinction, Schelling now presented his own position as the genuine positive philosophy, which alone can take account of existence, freedom, and concrete history. These themes had been foreshadowed in *The Ages of the World,* the first part of which was composed in 1811 but left unfinished. In 1841, Frederick William IV of Prussia invited Schelling to occupy the chair of philosophy at Berlin, for the express purpose of refuting Hegelianism through the presentation of his own positive system. Among his auditors in Berlin were Kierkegaard, Engels, and Bakunin. By this time, however, Schelling had lost most of his old fire, and his brief stay in Berlin was not successful. He retired to Munich, once more, and prepared his manuscripts for eventual publication. The two best statements of Schelling's later critique of Hegelianism and positive exposition of the unity of reason and existence are the posthumously published *Philosophy of Revelation* and *Introduction to the Philosophy of Mythology.* Schelling was revising the latter manuscript at the time of his death (1854).

## 2. BEYOND DOGMATISM AND CRITICISM

Unlike Fichte and Hegel, Schelling was never able to distill his essential position in a concise, yet representative, work. He regarded philosophizing as a constant exercise in freedom and reflection on creative action. Consequently, he was ever broaching new ideas and adding new dimensions to his thought. This has made it unusually difficult for historians of philosophy to settle upon a general statement of his position. Several periods of development are usually distinguished, although there is no unanimity even concerning their exact number and content. During his first years as a writer, Schelling was under Fichte's influence and helped to defend his general theory of science. Then came a second phase, during which he emphasized the reality of nature or the non-ego (in contradistinction to Fichte) and composed his transcendental philosophy. This was followed by a third stage, in which the example of Spinoza led Schelling to reduce the subject and object of knowledge to the unity and identity of the absolute. Eventually, this trend generated the problem of the origin of the world or the emergence of dualisms from the absolute identity. During his fourth period (and any later ones that may be specified), Schelling relied more heavily upon theosophical sources, especially the writings of Jacob Boehme, for an explanation of the world's "fall" from the divine nature. His closing years were occupied with the interpretation of myths and historical forms of religious belief, in an effort to show the presence of God and ideal powers operating in human consciousness.

Although this division into periods has the virtues of a rough map, it can also be misleading. For it conveys the impression that one system simply superseded another in Schelling's mind — with Romantic exuberance, indeed, but without regard for underlying continuity and consistency of thought. The fact is that his several shifts of vision were governed by a firm grasp on a dialectical principle and a set of problems arising from it. This principle is associated with the major question stimulating all of Schelling's speculations and  critical revisions: "Why is there anything at all? Why not nothing?"[27] His general principle is that the philosopher may not accept that-which-is unquestioningly, and must prove, rather than presume, its connection with a ground in being. The *search after a ground in being for the things that are,* led him to reflect, first, upon the current distinction between dogmatism and criticism, and then to develop his own views on nature, esthetic experience, freedom and evil, and the primacy of existence. These themes provide the divisions for the present exposition.

In treating of *dogmatism* and *criticism,* Schelling surveys the same ground covered by Fichte but from a new angle. These two positions are systematic formulations, respectively, of the outlooks of realism (belief in the reality of nature) and idealism. The typical dogmatic or realistic thinker is Spinoza (who was extraordinarily popular in Germany at the time, following a famous quarrel over him between Lessing, Jacobi, and Mendelssohn), whereas the representative of

---

27 *Philosophy of Revelation,* I, 1 (*Sämmtliche Werke,* edited by K. F. A. Schelling, II, iii, 7). A century later, this same question became the central preoccupation of the existential philosophy of Martin Heidegger. The debt of contemporary existentialists to Schelling and the other German idealists has been judiciously weighed by P. Tillich, "Existential Philosophy," *Journal of the History of Ideas,* V (1944), 44–70.

critical idealism is Fichte. For his part, Schelling proposes a distinction between *dogmaticism* and *dogmatism*. The former attitude consists in making uncritical claims to theoretical knowledge of God, whereas the latter foreswears the theoretical order and makes a practical approach to God. In eliminating dogmaticism, we do not *eo ipso* discredit dogmatism. Kant provides a support for both dogmatism and criticism, since he upholds both the reality of the thing-in-itself and the limitation of knowledge to phenomenal objects. There is no way of reaching a definitive decision about these two views, within a purely Kantian context. A fresh start must be made by inquiring about the *two conditions* required for making synthetic judgments.[28] These conditions are: (1) the synthetic operation must be preceded by an absolute unity, *from* which the multiple materials for synthesis originally proceed; (2) the synthesis itself must terminate eventually *in* some absolute thesis, as the goal of all synthetic operations. In a word, synthetic judgments are possible and meaningful only in relation to the absolute, regarded as both the principle and the end of the operations.

1. When the absolute is considered as the *source* of the world and the multiplicity of empirical materials, the problem of the *passage from the infinite to the finite* arises. Not only Spinoza, but every philosopher, must inquire how the absolute can come forth from itself and set a world over against itself. Critical idealism itself cannot side-step this issue, since it is the same as asking how there can be a domain of experience, within which a priori synthetic judgments are possible. This enigma of the world can be given a theoretical solution neither by dogmatism nor by criticism, since they merely juggle with ideas, in attempting to supply God with reasons for creating things. But if the direct passage from the infinite to the finite is blocked, still it may be possible to go *from the finite to the infinite* and thus to share indirectly in the viewpoint of the infinite. "Since there is no passage from the infinite to the finite, the tendency toward the infinite must be immanent in the finite itself."[29] Yet it does not follow, as Spinoza thought, that the finite self suppresses its own

---

[28] *Philosophical Letters on Dogmatism and Criticism*, III–IV (*Sämmtliche Werke*, I, i, 294–97). F. C. Copleston, S.J., "Pantheism in Spinoza and the German Idealists," *Philosophy*, XXI (1946), 42–56, traces the development of pantheistic tendencies among the German idealists, as a consequence of Spinoza's influence upon them.

[29] *Philosophical Letters on Dogmatism and Criticism*, VII (*Sämmtliche Werke*, I, i, 315).

reality in the face of the infinite. Schelling would rather say that the absolute "loses" or realizes itself in our self-consciousness. It is more precise to hold that, in the intuition of God, the absolute becomes identified with our selfhood than that we become identified with the absolute. God's viewpoint becomes ours, so that we may gain some notion of how the infinite gives rise to the finite.

Schelling agrees with Spinoza that the *ontological argument* is the only appropriate proof of God's existence, and hence the only passage from the finite to the infinite. This proof is not a strict demonstration, however, since God cannot be derived from anything prior or be determined by any external reason. God is given either through Himself alone or not at all. There must be a pure *intellectual intuition* at the base of all conviction about God's existence.[30] Schelling defends intellectual intuition (and the ontological proof) against Kant by defining intuition as *immediacy of experience,* rather than as passivity. The immediacy with which we are aware of an absolute principle in our consciousness is guarantee enough of the intuitive and nonsensible character of the awareness. Moreover, experience is not limited to the objects of scientific knowledge. Indeed, an intellectual intuition is present, only when the self is grasped precisely *as an acting principle* and not as an object. The self is seized in this way only in its practical aspects, in its use of freedom. Here, the producing of the act is one with the perceiving of it: the subject and object are identical. This is the essential requirement for an intellectual intuition and, in this identity, an *absolute* principle of consciousness or God is manifested. Schelling follows Fichte closely in regard to intellectual intuition and provides Hegel with a cue, by associating this intuition with the ontological proof of God's existence.

Because the intuition of self is an active, nonsensuous one, it fits Kant's definition of an intellectual, and therefore a divine, intuition.

---

[30] This intuition is discussed in *ibid.,* VIII (*Sämmtliche Werke,* I, i, 316–26), and in *System of Transcendental Idealism,* I, ii (Rand translation, in his anthology, *Modern Classical Philosophers,* 562–63). Schelling criticized Spinoza for objectifying the intellectual intuition, and forgetting that it is directed basically toward the ego, in its eternal being. In his later writings, Schelling held that the ontological proof is worthless, if it starts merely from the *idea* of God or any essential determination; it retains validity, only on condition of starting from the pure, dynamic *ground of existence* within God. Cf. *Philosophical Letters on Dogmatism and Criticism,* VI (*loc. cit.,* 308–09, note); *The Ages of the World* (Bolman translation, 125–26); *Philosophy of Revelation,* I, 8 (*Sämmtliche Werke,* II, iii, 156–60).

This *equation between intellectual and divine intuition* is one of the strongest motives impelling the post-Kantians toward *pantheism,* since their defense of metaphysics is bound up with a vindication of intellectual intuition. Schelling admits that this approach to the absolute through our active self-awareness leads to anthropomorphism, but he pleads that there is no other way of apprehending the absolute as the starting point of finite things.

2. When the absolute is treated as the *goal* of finite life and judgments, dogmatism and criticism are involved in a theoretically insoluble dilemma.[31] The synthesizing activity can be terminated only when the distinction between subject and object is overcome, through their identity in the absolute. This process may be conceived as a reduction either of the subject to the absolute object (dogmatism) or of the object to the absolute subject (criticism). In the former case, the knowing subject as such is suppressed; in the latter case, the object is canceled precisely as a knowable object for a subject. Both schools thereby endanger "my reality" as a finite self, engaged in experiencing a world of finite objects. Hence both schools shift their attention from a theoretical to a *practical approach to the absolute.* From this practical aspect, dogmatism and criticism differ not so much in the assigned goal of action as in their respective attitudes toward that goal. Spinoza's dogmatism regards union with the absolute as being actually realized, but this actual union crushes our personal freedom and activity. Fichte's critical doctrine, on the other hand, treats the goal as a realizable target of our endless striving, but never as an actually realized end. By describing the absolute as an ever-receding limit of our aspirations, criticism tries to preserve the integrity of human personality. To this extent, Schelling favors criticism as a practical attitude.

Weighing these two views in the balance, Schelling finds something valuable in each. The strong point of dogmatism is its defense of the objective reality of nature and of man's subordination to the eternal laws of nature. There is something sublime about Spinoza's serenity before natural necessity and his repose in the arms of the world. At the same time, he is handicapped by a mechanistic, Cartesian notion of the material universe. Fichte has a firm grasp on the truth that philosophy must be founded upon the self and an unconditioned principle, given in consciousness. But his view of nature is too

[31] *Philosophical Letters on Dogmatism and Criticism,* IX (*Sämmtliche Werke,* I, i, 326–35).

exclusively moral, for the material world is something more than a mere occasion for moral struggle.[32] Schelling seeks to combine Spinoza's affirmation of the reality of nature with Fichte's stress upon the self and freedom. His aim is to realize a synthesis between nature and spirit, objective law and subjective freedom, within the unity of the absolute.

### 3. PHILOSOPHY OF NATURE AND TRANSCENDENTAL PHILOSOPHY

In Schelling's own conception of philosophy, the study of nature is to be *co-ordinated* with the study of consciousness, rather than *subordinated* to it. That philosophy of nature and transcendental philosophy are coeval parts can be demonstrated both negatively and positively. If their equal footing is denied in favor of the primacy of consciousness, then idealism is left helpless before the simple empiricist objection that human consciousness is a late development in nature. Fichte's strenuously moral outlook on nature prevented him from correlating his general doctrine with the very specific findings of empirical science, concerning the *historical growth of consciousness* in man. On the other hand, empiricism cannot explain how nature is *knowable* by our minds, since it does not see that natural processes are basically the products of absolute mind. Schelling looked to an idealistic philosophy of nature that would account for both the empirical growth of mind and the intrinsic intelligibility of natural things.

More positively stated, knowledge is based on an agreement between an objective and a subjective factor, between nature and the ego or intelligence. To explain this agreement, philosophy must be able to start out indifferently from either pole: nature or intelligence.

> *Either the objective is made first, and the question arises how a subjective agreeing with it is superinduced. . . . Or the subjective is made first, and the problem is, how an objective is superinduced agreeing with it.*[33]

Philosophy of nature shows how natural phenomena become mental

---

[32] For the mutual criticism of Schelling and Fichte, after their break in 1801, cf. X. Léon, "Fichte contre Schelling," *Revue de Métaphysique et de Morale,* XII (1904), 949–76.

[33] *System of Transcendental Idealism,* Introduction, I (Rand, 536–37). For general introductions to Schelling's philosophy, based mainly on this work, cf. J. Lindsay, "The Philosophy of Schelling," *The Philosophical Review,* XIX (1910), 259–75, and A. S. Dewing, "The Significance of Schelling's Theory of Knowledge," *loc. cit.,* 154–67.

presentations, whereas transcendental philosophy shows how objective things take their origin in the intelligence. These two approaches are equally necessary and fundamental parts of total philosophy. Together, they constitute what Schelling calls his absolute idealism.

## SCHELLING'S SYSTEM OF IDEALISM

1. Philosophy of nature: from objective nature to the ego.
2. Transcendental philosophy: from the subjective ego to nature.
   a) Theoretical part: objective scientific experience.
   b) Practical part: free moral activity.
   c) Esthetic part or philosophy of art: synthesis of nature and ego (mind).
3. System of identity of opposites in the indifference-point of the absolute.

1. Schelling's *philosophy of nature* harmonized several contemporary views of the natural world. It made an *objective* idealistic approach to nature, in contradistinction to Fichte's subjective idealism, which treated nature merely as a phenomenal object and material for duty. The Romantic poets encouraged Schelling to respect nature in its own living reality, which is by no means exhausted by reference to our moral tasks. This is an *esthetic,* rather than an epistemologico-ethical, attitude toward nature. Nevertheless, as Spinoza and Goethe taught, the intrinsic significance of nature is found in the immanent evolution therein of the divine spirit and power. Nature is more than the field for our endless moral strivings, only because it is pre-eminently the field for the *strivings of the absolute spirit.* Kant had an intimation of this truth, when he tried to supplement mechanism with the teleological concept, as a guiding principle in the study of nature. But Kant failed to reach the independent activities of nature, over and above the interrelations among phenomenal objects of cognition. Schelling's intuition of the absolute self permitted him to retain purposiveness, not only as a regulative concept in our minds but also as a constitutive principle, operating in nature itself. Wherever empirical inquiry finds natural organisms to be organized in a teleological way, idealistic philosophy of nature also sees the real activity of mind, working at the unconscious level toward self-proposed goals.

The real presence of finality in nature is not an inductive conclusion for Schelling, however, but a strict deductive consequence of his doctrine on the absolute. The reality of the absolute consists in an act of eternal and *absolute knowledge,* i.e., knowledge in which there is pure identity between the subject and the object.[34] Our intellectual intuition of the self reveals that the absolute is this very identity between the ideal and the real. Recognition that *the ideal and the real are the same in the absolute* is the only way to obtain a principle for the reconciliation of mind and nature. For, the act of absolute knowledge not only constitutes the essence of the absolute being in itself but also specifies its eternal manner of productive activity. This activity has three main phases or moments.[35] (1) The infinite essence tends to take a definite, finite form and thus to become an objective reality. By this process, the absolute subject becomes completely *objective* in the world of nature. (2) Simultaneously, there is a countermovement, reflowing from finite form to infinite essence or substance. Nature or absolute objectivity tends to become reabsorbed in the ideal world of consciousness and *subjectivity.* (3) There is a mutual penetration and unification of the first two processes, insofar as their correlation reveals a distinctive essence of its own. Each of these three phases in the eternal activity of the absolute constitutes a particular unity: (1) *nature,* (2) the *ideal world,* and (3) their *apprehended interpenetration* and oneness. Schelling refers to these three unities as ideas, monads, or "absolutenesses." They are the modes of self-realization on the part of the absolute, considered as an eternal activity.

Nature may now be seen in its proper perspective. It is the *first moment or real side of the absolute's eternal activity,* the moment in which the absolute subject takes on finite form and objectivity. "Nature-in-itself or eternal nature is precisely spirit born into the objective order, the essence of God introduced into the [particular] form."[36] This is the eternal, inner reality of nature, taken in itself. What dogmatism refers to as the realm of things-in-themselves is precisely this ideal unity or mode of the absolute. There is a preponderance of the real or objective in nature, but also a nisus toward the ideal, as expressed in the finality of nature. The absolute takes an objective form, only so that it may recover its own essence or subjectivity in an ideal and conscious way. The bodily forms and

---

34 On absolute knowledge, consult *Ideas Toward a Philosophy of Nature,* Addition to the Introduction (*Sämmtliche Werke,* I, ii, 58–62).

35 *Loc. cit.,* (63–66); *The Ages of the World* (Bolman, 130–41).

36 *Ideas Toward a Philosophy of Nature,* Addition to the Introduction (*Sämmtliche Werke,* I, ii, 66).

temporal processes in nature are so many *preparations for the self-recovery of the absolute, through human knowledge.* Natural objects must gradually be transformed into the sensuous materials constituting the phenomenal objects of human knowledge. This is the answer to how the objective order of nature can enter our minds: the absolute is constantly working through material symbols, purifying them in order to bring the objective world back to the ideal world through the mediation of human consciousness.

Nature accomplishes this transformation in three grades of natural being, in accord with the three *potencies* (*Potenzen*) or ideal unities distinguishable within the natural order.[37] These three potencies are: the general structure of the world or series of bodies, the universal mechanism of light and dynamic laws of bodies, and the organic structures. The potencies of nature are relative ways of viewing the divine ideas, and hence are the teleological agencies for carrying out the aims of the absolute intelligence in nature.

Schelling anticipates Hegel, not only in the general conception that nature is an objective expression of the absolute spirit, but also in the special function assigned to organic structures in this process. The organism as such is the perfect potency, image, or symbolic realization of the absolute in nature. In particular, the *human organism* stands at the crossways of two universes: the objective and the subjective, nature and conscious spirit. The powers in nature are, fundamentally, ideal forces. As Fichte had suggested, they represent mind as operative at the unconscious level. The teleological direction of natural forces toward human consciousness is needed, so that the objective may return again to the subjective and so that man may grasp the interpenetration between the real and the ideal. The cosmic process, wherein the absolute realizes itself in nature and then idealizes nature in consciousness, is best symbolized by the relation between the human spirit and its organism. The human mind incarnates its purposes in the actions of the organism, and the organism succeeds in converting its states into the representative states of the human mind. This mutual working and its cosmic import are brought to rational expression in human consciousness, especially in the philosophical system of absolute idealism. Only from this standpoint, is it seen

---

[37] *Loc. cit.* (68). Cf. J. Schwarz, "Die Lehre von den Potenzen in Schellings Alters-philosophie," *Kantstudien*, XL (1935), 118–48, for a sympathetic explanation of how Schelling's theory of "potencies" or "powers" is continuous with his teaching on a dynamic ground of existence in God and living things.

that "nature must be visible spirit, and spirit invisible nature. It is here, therefore, in the absolute identity between spirit *in* us and nature *outside of* us, that the problem must be resolved of how a nature outside of us is possible."[38]

2. In his *transcendental philosophy,* Schelling makes the opposite deduction, beginning with the conscious existence of the human self and deriving the natural objects of knowledge. He divides this approach into three parts: *theoretical, practical,* and *esthetic* (or philosophy of art).[39] The first two divisions correspond to Fichte's treatment of the theoretical and practical ego, experience and moral action. In theoretical philosophy, a deduction is made of the reason why our mental presentations must agree with objects in the phenomenal order, and why these objects must be exactly the same as we represent them to be. Practical philosophy begins with our free, productive activity and inquires how the objective order is changeable and determinable by our freely conceived thoughts. There is an apparent contradiction, however, between these two standpoints. In the theoretical sphere, our thought is supposed to conform with necessary objects, whereas in the practical order it is supposed to exercise free domination over objects. These two types of conformity between mind and object suppose that there is an *underlying identity* between the actions that produce nature and those that produce our voluntary decisions.

Fichte's restriction of transcendental idealism to its theoretical and practical parts prevented him from demonstrating that "the same activity which is productive *with* consciousness in free action, is productive *without* consciousness in the production of the world."[40] Schelling's own philosophy of nature has established this identity from the side of objective nature. Now, his *esthetic philosophy* is to reach the same conclusion in terms of the subjective pole, the ego. Instead of subscribing to Fichte's moralistic orientation of idealism, Schelling proclaims that philosophy of art is "the universal organon of philosophy — the keystone of its entire arch."[41]

---

[38] *Ideas Toward a Philosophy of Nature,* Introduction (*Sämmtliche Werke,* I, ii, 56).

[39] *System of Transcendental Idealism,* Introduction, III (Rand, 541–44).

[40] *Loc. cit.* (Rand, 543).

[41] *System of Transcendental Idealism,* Introduction, III (Rand, 544). On the philosophy of art, see *ibid.,* Introduction, IV (Rand, 544–46); the German text of this work, Division VI: "Deduction of a Universal Organ of Philosophy, or Principles of the Philosophy of Art, according to the Basic Principles of Transcendental Idealism" (*Sämmtliche Werke,* I, iii, 612–29); *Philosophy of Art* (*ibid.,* I, v, 355–736). M.

Schelling not only defends the Romantic belief in the primacy of the esthetic factor in man and nature but also makes his philosophy of art serve an indispensable function within his transcendental philosophy. Art and philosophy agree in being constructive disciplines, since both rely heavily on *the esthetic act of productive imagination,* in the determination of their objects. Their differences come from the direction in which each focuses imaginative activity. Art directs it *outwardly,* so that it may obtain objectivity in sensuous works of art; philosophy directs it *inwardly,* so that it may reach objectivity within the order of mental life. The object of transcendental philosophy is the ego, which is constituted through the reflective identity between the subject and the object of mental activity. Since such identity is achieved through intellectual intuition, this intuition is the chief instrument of all transcendental philosophy. *Intellectual intuition* is the same as the *productive activity of imagination,* brought to a *reflective* state of awareness of its own operation, as self-initiated. But idealism is always plagued by the objection that the immediate experience in which intellectual intuition consists, has only *subjective* weight and ambiguous meaning. This intuition is also charged with being so *private,* that it cannot be communicated or defended in terms of public evidence.

This is where *philosophy of art* — the reflective bridge between art and philosophy — makes its distinctive contribution to the cause of idealism. For, it shows that one and the same intuition is used subjectively by philosophy and objectively by art. "Esthetic intuition is just intellectual intuition become objective."[42] The work of art achieves the *objectification,* in a universal and undeniable way, of the common structure of the basic intuition at the heart of philosophy. Furthermore, esthetic activity gives *public* expression to the purely non-objective, nonconscious, productive principle at the base of all in-

Honecker, "Die Wesenszüge der Deutschen Romantik," *Philosophisches Jahrbuch,* XLIX (1936), 199–222, gives an orderly exposition of the Romantic standpoint in: (*a*) *metaphysics* (the claim to grasp the ultimate grounds of all beings in an absolute way); (*b*) *theory of knowledge* (the ultimate grounds are apprehended through an intuition, which is diffused with feeling and esthetic sentiment); (*c*) *ethics* (the ideal of self-perfecting commands a central position and makes demands upon all our activities, including the artistic ones, in an effort to achieve union with God, regarded either theistically or pantheistically). See the two chapters on the Romantics, in A. O. Lovejoy, *The Great Chain of Being,* X–XI (288–326); also, the two chapters on German Romanticism and the esthetic doctrines of Absolute Idealism, in K. Gilbert and H. Kuhn, *A History of Esthetics,* XII, XIV (371–88, 428–55).

[42] *System of Transcendental Idealism,* VI (*Sämmtliche Werke,* I, iii, 625).

tuition and all philosophizing. In esthetic creation, there is an intermingling of unconscious and conscious factors. Philosophy of art points out the fundamental sameness between the unconscious principle in art and the unconscious principle in nature. By uncovering the identity between the active principle in nature and in esthetic creation, philosophy of art resolves the contradiction between the theoretical and practical parts of transcendental philosophy. For the *same agency* works entirely outside the context of consciousness to produce the natural world, and within the realm of human consciousness to mold natural materials, in accord with human designs. Hence the theoretical conformity of mind with necessary objects is reconciled with the practical conformity of objects with the free intent of mind.

In establishing a close association between esthetic and philosophical intuition, Schelling brought to a climax a trend found in Kant and Fichte. The liaison established by these latter thinkers between apperception, productive imagination, and intuition suggested to him a further significance of the work of art. It not only externalizes and expresses an internal state but objectifies precisely the same ground and act upon which philosophy rests. Furthermore, the unconscious strivings of esthetic creation may be regarded as analogous to those in nature. Unfortunately, Schelling did little more than hint at the evidence for these remarkable suggestions. In our own century, the importance of myth and symbol for philosophy has been recognized, along with their connection with the unconscious principle in human nature. But Schelling's special, idealistic interpretation placed a heavy burden upon esthetic activity. He identified artistic production or objectification with establishment of objective validity, but these are quite different operations. To give visible expression to an inner state of mind and feeling is to *reveal* that state, but not to *guarantee its truth*. It becomes manifest as a fact but not as a necessary and self-evident first principle, which is the requirement for Schelling's intellectual intuition.

Schelling completes the full circle of philosophical inquiry with his philosophy of art, since it not only consolidates his transcendental philosophy but also makes a junction with his philosophy of nature. For, both esthetic and natural philosophy view nature as an *unconscious poem* of the soul, a realization of the ideal under the limiting conditions of objective forms. Just as nature is the impregnation of finite form by an infinite content, so the work of art is a representation of the infinite in a finite way. Since this latter is also the definition of *beauty,* Schelling makes artistic activity synonymous with the production of the beautiful. Nature, however, need not be beautiful, since its production proceeds from a wholly unconscious principle, whereas in esthetic activity this principle is gradually breaking forth in consciously shaped forms. Hence Schelling locates beauty *essentially in the human work of art,* and only accidentally or *exceptionally in nature.* Nevertheless, he is readier than Kant to allow that the basic principle of beauty and the basic esthetic process are known to be inherently present in nature. While Schelling also stresses the harmonious workings of imagination in our perception of the beautiful, he gives this productive power more of an ontological significance than Kant would admit.

Anticipating Schopenhauer, Schelling also made neat philosophical use of the Romantic notion of *genius.*[43] The man of genius is one who reduces to unity certain contradictions which, apart from his work, would be irreconcilable. This power of embracing extremes to himself and expressing them in a new synthesis, belongs to him in virtue of his highly developed *imagination.* Now this same power of imagination is present in the philosopher as inner sense or capacity for *reflection* upon the life of consciousness. Hence the philosopher must also be one who is never satisfied with sharp antitheses but is always seeking ways to reconcile contradictory views.

In order to bring his own philosophy to complete systematic unity, Schelling subordinated his philosophy of nature and his transcendental philosophy to the *system of absolute identity.* Nature and mind must be brought together in the absolute, in which all antitheses tend to disappear. The absolute is the *point of indifference* for all the contrasting elements of our experience: subject and object, the ideal and the real, spirit and nature. It is all of these together in a condition of perfect identity, which removes the oppositions among the various poles. Schelling claimed that his system of absolute identity transcends the contrast between idealism and realism, since it is the single source from which both these limited viewpoints spring. Whereas Fichte sought to reconcile these extremes in terms of the *ego as all* (*subjective* idealism), Schelling emphasized both the reality of all things in *nature* and the oneness of the self and nature in *God as a living whole* (*objective* idealism). But since both Fichte and Schelling appeal to an immanent absolute mind, their reconciliations of idealism and

---

[43] *Loc. cit.* (*Sämmtliche Werke,* I, iii, 615–16).

realism are made in terms of some variety of idealism itself, and in the interest of its systematic deduction of the totality of experience.

## 4. GOD, FREEDOM, AND EVIL

Schelling's system of identity was attacked on all sides, especially by Hegel and other idealistic colleagues. The latter charged that his "holy abyss" of the absolute is such a morass of indifference that it can provide no dynamic principle for bringing forth the differentiated world of our experience. In order to meet this objection, Schelling was obliged to develop his views on God and the nature of creation, a theme closely linked with the meaning of freedom and evil. For historical guidance, he turned back both to the philosophies of Spinoza and Leibniz and to the theosophical writings of Jacob Boehme. Through this combination of sources, he hoped to overcome the abstractness of the rationalist philosophies and the obscurity of Boehme's theosophy. He accepted Spinoza's *pantheism* or theory of the immanence of all things in God, but only after introducing some important modifications. Schelling tried to divorce pantheism from fatalism and the denial of finite substances. For him, Spinoza's error lay not in placing the being of all things in God but in treating created beings, including the human spirit and will, as mere modal things. Against what he termed the lifeless mechanism of the Spinozistic view of nature, Schelling proposed a more dynamic kind of explanation, in which *becoming,* rather than immanence, provides the cardinal principle. In this respect, he availed himself of Leibniz' teaching on the sufficient reason of things, the vital union among spirits or personal beings, and the nature of freedom. But (on the advice of Franz von Baader) he injected into these rationalistic doctrines a strong dose of Boehme's irrationalism. Schelling regarded Boehme's theosophy as a "speculative mysticism," i.e., a body of genuine knowledge, cast in a nonscientific and incommunicable form. One of his major aims was to translate the content of this private wisdom into the clear and precise rational form of philosophical science. Boehme provided him with stimulating hints about how to reconcile the personal and the impersonal, perfection and development, good and evil.

Schelling's entire treatment of God is governed, first of all, by the *general idealistic premise,* and then by a set of five metaphysical principles. The general premise, already laid down by Fichte, is that philosophy must *begin with the unconditioned absolute,* which is met with in human consciousness. Schelling broadens out this thesis to include the *irrational* features of our inner experience, which he proceeds to attribute to God as well as to man. He subordinates a metaphysics of being to a metaphysics of freedom and its products: "Being, in this system, is only suspended freedom."[44] His point of departure in an intuition of absolute freedom enables Schelling to formulate his natural theology in such a way that all the factors required for a solution of the question of human freedom and evil, are introduced into the divine nature itself. He excuses this anthropomorphic procedure, once more, with the remark that there is no other way to treat of a personal God than by projecting into the absolute the conditions required for human, personal existence. In point of fact, however, this projection is made, not primarily to develop a natural theology for its own sake, but in order to supply himself with a basis for deducing certain propositions about human freedom and evil. Schelling finds anthropomorphism unavoidable, only because he requires God to serve this function within his systematic idealism.

The five metaphysical principles are formulated in such a way that they extend the conditions of finite being to God.[45]

1. "The profound logic of the ancients distinguished subject and predicate as the antecedent and the consequent (*antecedens et consequens*) and thus expressed the real meaning of the law of identity." The law of identity finds its full explanation in the relation between ground and consequent. This means not only that every relation between a ground and a consequent is ultimately a predication of *identity* (as pantheism requires) but also that the predication of identity always involves a *procession* of consequent from ground (as Boehme's emanationism requires). Application of this logical doctrine to the problem of God and creature leads to a *dynamic pantheism*. Finite beings are to be identified with the absolute precisely because

---

[44] *System of Transcendental Idealism*, I, 2 (Rand, 568).

[45] Of the five numbered quotations below, the first, second, fourth, and fifth are taken from *Of Human Freedom* (Gutmann translation, 14, 84, 79, 50). The third quotation, a composite one, is drawn from: *Memorandum on Jacobi's Work 'On Divine Things,'* 2 (*Sämmtliche Werke*, I, viii, 59), and *Of Human Freedom* (Gutmann, 32). The *Memorandum* was in reply to F. H. Jacobi's criticism of Schelling's book on freedom. These five principles are permeated with the notion of development or evolutionary becoming, as characteristic of nature and God; cf. K. Zöckler, "Der Entwicklungsgedanke in Schellings Naturphilosophie," *Archiv für Geschichte der Philosophie*, XXVIII (1915), 257–96.

they proceed from it, as consequents from the ground of their being. Lest the individual nature of finite beings be lost, Schelling adds that "identity" between God and creatures is not the same as undifferentiated "sameness," wherein the relation of ground and consequent would be entirely absent. But his compromise position leaves unanswered Kant's objection that the relation between creatures and God is based on the metaphysical principle of real cause and effect, which should *not* be confused with the logical principle of ground and consequent. What may hold true in the notional order concerning the rationalistic reduction of sufficient reason to identity, need not govern the real relation between infinite and finite being.

2. "All life has a destiny and is subject to suffering and development. . . . Being is only aware of itself in becoming." These two requirements of human existence are converted by Schelling (who is close to Hegel on this issue) into perfectly general metaphysical principles, applicable to God. If God is living and self-aware, then He must be subject to some *destiny* or inner determination and must undergo suffering and *development*. Like Hegel, Schelling presents his case in such a way that a denial of becoming in God would seem to entail a denial of life and self-consciousness in Him. This conjunction is made by the simple expedient of defining life and consciousness *as such*, according to the manner in which these perfections are realized *in man*.

3. "The ground of development is always necessarily *below* that which is developed; it raises *above* itself that which develops out of it. . . . As there is nothing before or outside of God he must contain within himself the ground of his existence." It is of crucial importance for Schelling to attribute a *ground of existence* to God. If propositions of identity apply to God and if He includes a process of becoming, then the existence of God has a ground that is distinct from, and even independent of, the existent God. Yet this ground is not outside of God but is from a deep abyss or irrational recess within Him. Hence it is not an external cause but an *intrinsic principle of His development*. If the principle of causality is invoked against the notion of the inferior serving as the unconditioned principle of the superior, Schelling will defend his metaphysical evolutionism by subordinating causal requirements to those of ground-and-consequent. And since the latter is coalesced with the principle of identity, the triumph of idealistic logic over being is rendered complete. The very basis of the *intelligibility of being* is shifted to the plane of the *logic of ground-*

*and-consequent,* so that Schelling may declare that only the self-developing is the perfect, and only the self-actualizing is the actual. Since his dialectical system is not as highly intricate as Hegel's, this conversion of a dynamic logic into an ontology of becoming may be observed more readily in Schelling than in Hegel.

4. "All existence must be conditioned in order that it may be actual, that is, personal, existence." It follows that if God has actual, personal existence, this existence is subject to a prior condition and is acquired through a process of self-differentiation and development. The divine personal existence stands under the condition of having an internal ground of being, an active essence from which it wells up into the clear light of self-consciousness. Leibniz' view of existence as the outcome of the *conatus* of essence is rigorously applied here to God, so that His personal existence is a consequence of a *prior, essential dynamism* in Him. Schelling succeeds in personalizing Spinoza's infinite substance, only at the cost of subjecting it to the condition of an independent, *impersonal* ground of being, within the divine nature.

5. Finally, "every nature can be revealed only in its opposite — love in hatred, unity in strife." The development in God is aimed at the clarification and actualization of His own nature or, in a word, at His *self-revelation.* This gives Schelling an opportunity for introducing into God's life the conditions of *strife* and *opposition,* which attend the development of finite natures. It is not surprising that the conclusion may then be drawn that the conflict between the principles of darkness and light, within our temporal world, is a mark of the world's divine origin and participation in the divine being. This enables Schelling to hope that the oppositions of temporal existence will lead eventually to the same reconciliation of extremes and self-actualization toward which the divine being is impelled, in its eternal nature. Philosophical anthropology and theodicy are merged together, with the latter occupying a subordinate position in the total schema.

With the aid of these principles and of Boehme's terminology, Schelling now makes a revision of his earlier system of absolute identity. A distinction must be drawn between three aspects of the absolute: the *primal ground* or *groundless abyss* (*Ur-grund* or *Un-grund*), the *ground of existence* (*Grund von Existenz*), and the *actual existence* or existing being (*Das Existierende*).[46] Both the ground of God's

---

[46] *Of Human Freedom* (Gutmann, 31-32, 87-90); *The Ages of the World* (Bolman, 96-97, 121-27).

existence and His actual existence arise from the groundless abyss of His being. This groundless abyss is the true *point of indifference,* the place where all antitheses break up and disappear. Schelling is still unable to provide a dialectical reason why this groundless abyss of indifference should issue in differentiations, both within God and in the world. He simply states that it is present precisely as giving rise to the two principles in the divine being: the obscure *will of the ground* and the clear *will of love.* The former is the irrational principle of darkness or particularity, and constitutes the ground of existence, the impersonal "nature in God" which is not the same as God. The will of love is the principle of light or universality, and constitutes the realm of God's personal existence, spiritual nature, and love. But this realm of personal existence arises only as a response to the stirrings of the will of the ground. The ground is neither personal nor conscious but yet is laden with a "yearning" for personal consciousness. The will of love meets this desire and actualizes God's proper existence, as a being of spirit and love.

Schelling now distinguishes between the *indifference* of all opposites, within the groundless abyss, and their *identity* in God's spiritual, personal being. In this personal reality, the divine essence is clarified and to it all the clashing opposites of experience are subordinated, through identity. But this explanation merely complicates the problem of manyness or differentiated being, since it leaves unspecified the manner in which the personal identity-of-differences itself can arise from the abyss of indifference.

A further separation of forces is made in the *creation* of the world. Creation is a *free act,* in the Spinozistic sense of being identical with absolute necessity. Schelling defines a result as being freely produced, when it proceeds from the necessity of the inner nature of the agent, acting according to the principle of identity. God's creative act is free, both because it is not compelled from without and because it is an expansion of the necessary law of His nature or ground.

The world is produced by a mysterious "leap" or "fall" from the divine nature. There is an intervention of will and free decision on the part of the personal God. But He acts according to a *moral necessity,* which in turn is governed by the absolute or *metaphysical necessity* of the primal ground of His being. Because this abyss is a drive toward self-revelation, it issues not only in the personal God or image of the absolute but also in finite beings, having some independence. This is the source of created freedom. Man is a kind of *derived abso-*

*lute* or independent selfhood, since he is drawn by the divine creative reason from the depths of the independent ground of existence or nature in God. In human nature are combined the principles of darkness and light, the will of the ground and the will of love, in their created form.

Although he criticizes the Kantian view of freedom as being too formalistic, Schelling himself locates *human freedom* ultimately in an *intelligible deed,* an eternal act transpiring outside of time. He observes that neither a man's particular actions nor his stable moral character comes to be, in a temporal way. They are determined by the same timeless act which determines the man to be *this particular individual,* rather than any other one. If there is anything like a moral revolution of character or a conversion of soul in this life, it is already contained, from eternity, in the definitive act whereby the individual is constituted this individual selfhood. Man's freedom, like God's, comes from the fact that his action is determined by the inner laws of his own intelligible nature, unrolling necessarily in accordance with the principle of identity. "The activity [of the intelligible nature of man] can follow from its inner nature only in accordance with the law of identity, and with absolute necessity which is also the only absolute freedom."[47] But since man's intelligible being is of a derived sort, human action is free only in virtue of its conformity with the divine idea of the individual nature. *"In the soul* [of the individual] *as such, there is no Freedom, for only the Divine is truly free, and the essence of the soul in so far as it is divine."*[48] Man does not act as a completely original agent, but lets the good principle or the evil principle act in him. His allowance of this action (*das In-sich-handeln-lassen*) is a rational act, however, and hence is included in the original, intelligible deed constituting his individual nature and spontaneous freedom.

Although he struggles manfully to save both the intelligibility and the freedom of human action, Schelling fails to accomplish either purpose. His basic difficulty is an inability to rise above his historical sources. He amalgamates Spinoza and Leibniz, Kant and Boehme,

---

[47] *Of Human Freedom* (Gutmann, 62). Cf. F. Maugé, "La liberté dans l'idéalisme transcendantal de Schelling," *Archiv für Geschichte der Philosophie*, XIV (1901), 261–83, 517–35.

[48] *System of General Philosophy and of Philosophy of Nature in Particular*, 305 (*Sämmtliche Werke*, I, vi, 541; the translation is from Gutmann's Introduction to *Of Human Freedom*, xxxix).

without achieving a genuine synthesis in defense of human freedom. His theory of the intelligible nature of the individual combines features from Leibniz and Spinoza, but without removing the inherent difficulties. The individual nature precontains all its actions and determines them from within, on the basis of its essential structure and the principle of identity. Like the Leibnizian individual substance, it enters upon a temporal course, in which all its actions are so many predicates flowing from the intelligible subject or essence. The Spinozistic factor is detected in the redefinition of freedom as inwardly determined necessity, a move that only secures the spontaneity of action, not its freedom. At the human level, this necessity is characterized as rational acquiescence in the operation of divinely determined principles within oneself. But the fact that this allowance is accompanied by knowledge does not rescue freedom of choice from a divine determinism. This predicament forces Schelling to take his main stand in the constitution of the intelligible deed itself. Here, he has recourse to both Kant and Boehme. Yet instead of clarifying and rendering more determinate Kant's notion of a purely intelligible and timeless act, that never strictly comes to be, he compounds the obscurity by associating this deed with the Boehmean doctrine on the various principles in God. Schelling's entire dialectic of freedom converges, finally, upon the respective roles of God and the human individual, in the determination of the intelligible deed and hence of the individual selfhood. Just as God's moral necessity and freedom are reducible to the metaphysical necessity springing from the primal abyss of His being, so that spontaneity with which God determines the ideal nature of the individual wells forth from the same primal necessity. Schelling's insistence upon the "irrational factor" in God and man does not permit him to escape from rationalistic determinism, since the irrational factors themselves operate according to the principle of identity, which is expanded into the creator-creature relation of ground and consequent.

Whereas Kant and Fichte characterized freedom primarily as the domination of will or practical reason over the sensuous impulses, Schelling defined it basically as the *possibility of good and evil*. Man is a central being, having a twofold freedom. He is free from the personal, existing God, insofar as he draws his individual being from the ground of existence in God; he is also free from the world, insofar as he receives illumination from the personal, existing God. His duty is to integrate the two principles within himself: particularity and universality, darkness and light. Man is free either to use his particularity and selfhood in the right way, as the basis and instrument of the universalizing power of reason, or to erect his own particularity into the supreme measure of his being. These alternatives represent, respectively, the path of goodness and the path of evil, opening out for his freedom to follow. Man is free, in the sense of having an equal impulse toward both good and evil.

Whence this dual impulse and dual possibility for freedom? In opposing the apologetic tendency to water down the *nature of evil,* Schelling insists upon its positive reality and strength.[49] It does not come from an evil principle outside of God, and it is not the same as the principle of finitude in created things. Evil is a *positive* principle of discord and disharmony, erected by human freedom. Although the ground of existence in God is not itself evil, it is the radical source of evil, to the extent that it is the source of man's freedom and even provides an incitement toward the evil exercise of freedom. The principles of particularity and universality are *indissoluble* only in God. If man is to be distinct from God, then these principles must be imparted to him *as dissoluble,* i.e., as entailing the possibility of their separation and evil synthesis. God may even be said to incite man to evil. The will of the ground constitutes man *as an intensified selfhood,* having the inclination to organize all his values around himself, in a selfish way. In this sense, every man is born with the evil principle within him. The actual espousal of evil on man's part is hidden, however, in the general obscurity overshadowing the original intelligible deed, formative of his character and conduct.

Having gone thus far in stressing the reality of evil and its divine origin, Schelling then makes a characteristic cancellation of his admissions, so that no guilt will attach to God and so that His self-actualization may be completed. Evil "is no being but a counterfeit of being, which is real only by contrast, not in itself."[50] It may be reduced to a state of potentiality or *relative non-being,* merging with the ground of existence in God and thus automatically ceasing to be in opposition to God's universal reason and love. Once its utter unreality is exposed, there can take place the subordination of all cosmic forces to the

---

[49] *Of Human Freedom* (Gutmann, 39–59). Schelling rejects Leibniz' identification of finitude with "metaphysical evil," since "evil is not derived from finitude in itself, but from finitude which has been exalted to independent being." *Ibid.* (Gutmann, 46, note 2).

[50] *Ibid.* (Gutmann, 90).

divine spirit, through love. All the predicates of our experience are thus to be identified with each other in the divine spirit. Schelling regards nature and history as tending infinitely toward a total actualization and manifestation of God's power and love, through the *reconciliation and identification of all opposites,* including good and evil.

With regard to both freedom and evil, Schelling reaches a solution only with the aid of some antithetical statements. Man acts freely and yet only allows the good or evil principle to act in him; evil is a positive reality and yet is revealed as an unreality. There are two ways in which these sets of propositions may be reconciled. The first way is through a return to the Kantian distinction between the intelligible and sensible orders; the second is through appeal to the requirements of a dialectical system. Schelling tries to straddle the fence, by availing himself of both methods. Hence he exposes himself to Hegel's dilemma: either invoke the noumenon-phenomenon distinction and thus cut off the possibility of a metaphysical system, or else give an adequate explanation of why a metaphysical system must be dialectical. Since such an explanation would require (from Hegel's standpoint) the subordination of the ground of existence to the divine reason or absolute concept itself, Schelling's entire view of the absolute would have to be radically transformed, in order to sustain his appeal to the different systematic facets reflected in his antithetical statements.

Schelling's predicament arises from his wish to save finite reality and nevertheless make consistent employment of his logical doctrine about the principles of identity and ground-and-consequent. There are some sound but groping tendencies in his thought. In dealing with freedom, for instance, he wishes to furnish a theory of divine exemplar ideas and divine concurrence, which will respect both God's primary causality and man's freedom. But his purely logical interpretation of causal action prevents him from achieving the desired synthesis. Similarly, his treatment of the reality of evil moves in the direction of a theory of evil as a *privation,* even though he himself formally rejects this doctrine. His reason for rejecting it is that it makes of evil a mere logical entity. This consequence need not follow from a theory of evil as privation, however, but only from a failure to retain the proper distinction between an abstract and a concrete approach to the nature of evil. Taken *abstractly* by itself, evil is a privation, but in the *concrete* it requires an actual subject. Schelling never succeeds in integrating these two aspects of the problem. When he recognizes the privative character of evil itself, he fears that the concrete reality of the evil thing is being endangered. And when he stresses the reality of this concrete subject, he fears that a positive nature is being attributed to the evil itself. He asks: "If that element in evil which has *being* is good, whence, then, comes that wherein it has its being, the *ground* which really constitutes the evil?"[51] By formulating the question as one about the good *element in* the evil, instead of the good *subject of* the evil, he misstates the issue and finds it impossible to save both the privative character of the evil and the good actuality of its subject. Consequently, Schelling wants to find the same answer to the question about the source of the concrete subject of an evil action or state, and that about the source of the privation of the perfection due to that subject. To find a common answer, he must have recourse to the theory about a dark ground or impersonal nature in God. If these two aspects are firmly distinguished, however, the need to import a ground of struggle and becoming into the divine nature vanishes.

### 5. NEGATIVE AND POSITIVE PHILOSOPHY

Schelling's philosophical evolution culminated in his doctrine on negative and positive philosophy, which is best explained in his final work: *Introduction to the Philosophy of Mythology*. Within philosophy as a whole, he distinguished two sciences: one treats of *what* a thing is, its *essence*, its being in the concept; the other establishes  *that* a thing is, and studies its *existence* or extraconceptual being. With the aid of this distinction, Schelling was able to offer his own criticism of Hegel. The latter's mistake was to have reduced the existential to the essential approach, and thus to have confused the thought of actual being with the actual exercise of being. If the primacy is given to thought over being, philosophy can attain nothing more than a conceptualized substitute for actual existence.

Instead of amalgamating these two aspects of philosophy, it is necessary to establish their distinct characters. The order of essence is reserved for *negative* philosophy, whereas the order of existence belongs to *positive* philosophy.[52] Negative or purely rational philoso-

---

[51] *Of Human Freedom* (Gutmann, 27; translation modified).

[52] On the distinction between essence and existence, negative and positive philosophy, reason and experience, cf. *Introduction to the Philosophy of Mythology*, II, 24 (*Sämmt-*

phy is best represented by Kant's criticism and the efforts of post-Kantian idealism, including Schelling's own previous theories. Kant showed that reason must unite all possible perfections in the idea of God. The idealists converted this idea into a real principle of metaphysical explanation for deducing the world and the ideal order. But although negative philosophy can deduce *what* actual existents must be, it cannot deduce their existential act as such. Negative philosophy culminates in the recognition that its entire systematic deduction is attached to a principle, which is confined within the domain of concepts and essences. It stands in need of a further principle, one that is *not* an idea or mere essence and *not* within the compass of reason.

The *transition* from negative to positive philosophy cannot be made by pure reason itself, since it involves a passage from what is pure act, only in the order of essence, to what is pure act in the very line of act or existence itself (*actu actus purus*). Kant was right in seeking for the bridge in the practical order, but he went astray in making God a postulate of practical reason. *Reason,* whether theoretical or practical, is confined to the sphere of the general essence, whereas it was Aristotle's peculiar glory to have observed that only the individual exists. The existent first principle of positive philosophy must be "absolutely individual" and in no way general or conceptual (a requirement which Hegel's "concrete universal" does not satisfy). Hence it cannot be attained by practical reason or consciousness-in-general but only by men acting as finite individual existents. Fichte grasped this truth, when he grounded metaphysics in a will-act of the ego. But, as Schelling came to see with greater clarity in his later years, idealism endangers the finite, dependent nature of the individual human existent. Hence he specified that the *will-act of the individual* is an *act of faith* or "ec-stasy," a willingness to make room for *God's own entrance,* as the principle of a human system of philosophy and a way of life.[53] The basic existential act is one of philosophical or *rational religion,* a restoration of the human self to vital union with the divine source of its existence.

In order to accept God as the efficient cause or commencement of the positive aspect of philosophy, Schelling had to overcome a serious

---

*liche Werke*, II, i, 562–65); *Philosophy of Revelation*, I, 4, and VIII (*Sämmtliche Werke*, II, iii, 57–62, 148–52). Bolman's Introduction to *The Ages of the World* (31–65) summarizes the main themes in Schelling's later philosophy.

[53] *Introduction to the Philosophy of Mythology*, II, 24 (*Sämmtliche Werke*, II, i, 565–69).

difficulty. The divine actuality is a completely *individual* being, transcendent of everything general, conceptual, and essential; it is even transcendent of the entire world of individual, contingent existents or beings-that-are. Since science is not of the individual but only of the *universal*, it would seem that the divine being cannot be the ground of a philosophical system. Somehow, God must be shown to be not only a *that* or pure existent but also a *what* or essential nature. Two connections must be established: (1) between God and the conceptual order of general essences; (2) between God and the actual order of things-that-are in nature and history.[54]

1. Schelling welds the first bond by incorporating some themes from his previous doctrine on God. The nature or ground of existence in God imposes an absolute necessity upon God: there must be a perfect identity in Him between being and thought. The existential being of God is thus a *true being,* and provides a basis for the *idea of God,* upon which the conceptual order depends. But the identity of being and thought in God is such that being enjoys the primacy. This follows from the fact that both the ground of existence and God's personal existence proceed from the groundless abyss of being. Hence the being of the absolute is the ultimate foundation of the idea of God, and provides the idealistic deduction with the requisite content of actuality and existence.

2. To prove that the purely actual being is also immanent in contingent existents, a dual procedure is followed. First, a deduction is made from the assumptions that God created things through a free act, that there was a prehistorical fall of creatures, and that there is still going on an effort of God to redeem created beings. This deduction, made with the aid of the various potencies in God and nature, is then verified by empirical study of the given facts of nature and history. Schelling carries out this second step or "metaphysical empiricism" through an *analysis of religious myths and revealed religion.* He interprets these data in the light of his own philosophical conception of religion. The empirically discovered agreement between the a priori deduction and the induction from empirical facts establishes the truth of the original supposition about the creative bond between God and the totality of individual existents. Once these two connections are secured, God is shown to be the *lord of all being,*

---

[54] *Loc. cit.* (570–71); *On the Source of the Eternal Truths* (*Sämmtliche Werke,* II, i, 586–89); *Philosophy of Revelation,* I, 8 (*ibid.,* II, iii, 160–69).

existential as well as ideal. This is the final word of positive philosophy and of philosophical science as a whole.

One of Schelling's auditors in Berlin, where he expounded his negative and positive philosophy, was Sören Kierkegaard, the Danish religious thinker. He reported how enthusiastically he received, at first, Schelling's remarks on existence and his criticism of Hegel. Kierkegaard was particularly impressed by Schelling's contention that a system, based primarily upon concepts and essences, is unsuited to deal either with the divine existence or with finite existents in human history. For history is the sphere of contingent freedom, rather than of necessary and eternal laws. But Kierkegaard eventually became disappointed with the positive side of Schelling's "break-through to actuality," which was never worked out in detail. The only extensive application made by Schelling was in the field of mythology and the history of religions, where his theosophical notions ranged unchecked. He never attempted to make a similar induction from the empirical facts of nature, where the findings of the natural sciences could provide an independent check.

Perhaps the fundamental reason why Kierkegaard and other auditors regarded the positive philosophy as impotent may be gathered from one of Schelling's remarks on the nature of philosophy. An integral philosophy must synthesize idealism and realism, but in such a way that *idealism* retains the primacy.[55] Realism can never provide the first principles of philosophy: it gives only the ground and the instrument, which are used by idealism to achieve its own systematic deduction. For all his keen awareness of the difference between the essential and the existential orders, Schelling ultimately wanted to use the latter only as a means of anchoring his metaphysical idealism. This subordination of the existential act to the exigencies of a deductive system is evident in his doctrine that God, as a personal existent, requires an irrational ground of existence. Behind existence lies the self-affirming power of the absolute, as Spinoza and Leibniz had maintained. The divine act of existing is referred back to a ground

---

[55] "Idealism is the soul of philosophy; realism is its body; only the two together constitute a living whole. Realism can never furnish the first principles but it must be the basis and the instrument by which idealism realizes itself and takes on flesh and blood." *Of Human Freedom* (Gutmann, 30). Cf. *The Ages of the World* (Bolman, 235–36), where realism is accorded that sort of temporal priority which belongs to an irrational ground of being, which the divine nature eventually masters for its own essentialist aims. On Kierkegaard's appraisal of Schelling, see J. Collins, *The Mind of Kierkegaard*, 107–09; for criticism of Hegel, 98–136.

of existence, so that the idealistic logic of ground-and-consequent can have a basis in God for its exegesis of development, particularity, and evil in the finite world.

## SUMMARY OF CHAPTER 13

If the self be taken as an absolute principle, Fichte argued, metaphysics can be rescued from Kant's attack. Metaphysical idealism removes the Kantian thing-in-itself, and then affirms the reality of intellectual intuition and the constructive outcome of the use of antinomies. Since the ego is the unconditioned absolute principle, its unity guarantees the systematic interconnection of the various antithetic principles of experience. Hence Fichte launched out confidently on a systematic deduction of the entire body of knowledge, starting with the three first principles posited by the self. His greatest triumph was the explanation of the origin of the non-self, which he regarded as an irreducible factor only from the standpoint of the theoretical ego. Ultimately, the non-ego is itself a product of the practical ego, which posits this zone of otherness, so that the resultant barrier will force the theoretical ego to turn back reflectively upon itself. Fichte also constructed the realms of morality and right, through a deduction from the infinite striving of the practical ego. With Schelling, however, there was a reaction against Fichtean moralism, which looked upon nature mainly as an arena for moral struggle and betterment. Schelling placed the study of nature and the study of consciousness on an equal footing. He made a dialectical deduction from nature to consciousness in his philosophy of nature, and a deduction from consciousness to nature in his transcendental philosophy. He signalized the importance of philosophy of art, since it demonstrates that the selfsame activity of the absolute is operative unconsciously in nature and consciously in the human mind. Having identified nature and consciousness within the absolute, Schelling was then compelled to describe the absolute in such a way that the world of nature and human freedom could be derived from it. He imported into God both becoming and a distinction between the groundless abyss, the ground of existence and actual existence. Freedom and evil were radicated in the divine activity in such a way that they could also be manifested in human activity. Schelling's later distinction between a negative philosophy of essence-and-generality and a positive philosophy of existence-and-individuality was an attempt to separate his absolute idealism from Hegel's brand, which he deemed to be inimical to the free, individual existent.

## BIBLIOGRAPHICAL NOTE

1. *Fichte.* Primary sources: *Johann Gottlieb Fichtes Sämmtliche Werke,* edited by his son, I. H. Fichte (8 vols., Berlin, Veit, 1845–1846); *Nachgelassene Werke,* edited by I. H. Fichte (3 vols., Bonn, Marcus, 1834–1835); *Werke,* edited by F. Medicus (6 vols., Leipzig, Meiner, 1911–1912) — an

improvement upon the I. H. Fichte edition, but not a critical edition; *Johann Gottlieb Fichtes Leben und literarischer Briefwechsel,* edited by I. H. Fichte (second, enlarged ed., 2 vols., Leipzig, Brockhaus, 1862); *Fichtes Briefwechsel,* edited by H. Schulz (2 vols., Leipzig, Haessel, 1925). Translations: *The Science of Knowledge,* translated by A. E. Kroeger (Philadelphia, Lippincott, 1868); *New Exposition of the Science of Knowledge,* translated by A. E. Kroeger (St. Louis, privately printed, 1869); *The Science of Ethics as based on the Science of Knowledge,* translated by A. E. Kroeger (new ed., London, Kegan Paul, Trench, Trübner, 1907); *The Science of Rights,* translated by A. E. Kroeger (new ed., London, Trübner, 1889). The Kroeger translations are extremely free and rearrange the divisions of the original work. See also: the W. Smith translation of *The Popular Works of Johann Gottlieb Fichte* (fourth ed., 2 vols., London, Trübner, 1889) — contains: *The Vocation of the Scholar, The Nature of the Scholar, The Vocation of Man, The Characteristics of the Present Age, The Way to the Blessed Life or Doctrine of Religion, Outlines of the Doctrine of Knowledge,* and a memoir on Fichte by W. Smith; *Addresses to the German Nation,* translated by R. F. Jones and G. H. Turnbull (Chicago, Open Court, 1922). Studies: R. Adamson, *Fichte* (Edinburgh, Blackwood, 1881), the best introduction in English; H. Heimsoeth, *Fichte* (Munich, Reinhardt, 1923), and M. Wundt, *Johann Gottlieb Fichte* (Stuttgart, Frommann, 1927), excellent German introductions; X. Léon's two basic studies: *La philosophie de Fichte* (Paris, Alcan, 1902), and *Fichte et son temps* (2 vols., in 3, Paris, Colin, 1922–1927), placing Fichte in his age; M. Gueroult, *L'évolution et la structure de la doctrine de la science chez Fichte* (2 vols., Paris, Les Belles Lettres, 1930), and J. Maréchal, S.J., *Le point de départ de la métaphysique,* cahier IV: *Le système idéaliste chez Kant et les postkantiens* (Paris, Desclée, 1947), Part II, Chap. 2 (335–449), careful analyses of the argument in the *Theory of Science;* R. W. Stine, *The Doctrine of God in the Philosophy of Fichte* (Philadelphia, University of Pennsylvania dissertation, 1945); H. C. Engelbrecht, *Johann Gottlieb Fichte: A Study of His Political Writings with Special Reference to His Nationalism* (New York, Columbia University Press, 1933). N. Hartmann, *Die Philosophie des deutschen Idealismus* (2 vols., Berlin and Leipzig, W. de Gruyter, 1923–1929), gives a unified conspectus of the classical German idealists: Fichte, Schelling, and the Romantics (Vol. 1), and Hegel (Vol. 2). The purpose of R. Kroner's brilliant investigation, *Von Kant bis Hegel* (2 vols., Tübingen, Mohr, 1921–1924), is to chart the course of the internal development of the idealistic movement. The books by Hartmann and Kroner should be consulted in regard to Kant and Hegel, as well as to Fichte and Schelling, since they describe in detail the continuity of thought and the intense domestic dialogue between the leading German idealists.

2. *Schelling.* Collected edition: *F. W. J. Schellings Sämmtliche Werke,* edited by his son, K. F. A. Schelling (14 vols., in two sections of 10 and 4 vols., Stuttgart and Augsburg, Cotta, 1856–1861). Translations: *Of*

*Human Freedom*, translated by J. Gutmann (Chicago, Open Court, 1936); *The Ages of the World*, translated by F. de W. Bolman, Jr. (New York, Columbia University Press, 1942). Studies: the Introductions by Gutmann and Bolman to their translations give good summaries of recent research; J. Watson, *Schelling's Transcendental Idealism* (second ed., Chicago, Griggs, 1892), a commentary on his earlier idealistic system. Two helpful general studies are H. Knittermeyer, *Schelling und die Romantische Schule* (Munich, Reinhardt, 1929), and S. Drago Del Boca, *La filosofia di Schelling* (Florence, Sansoni, 1943). R. Gray-Smith, *God in the Philosophy of Schelling* (Philadelphia, University of Pennsylvania dissertation, 1933), traces the successive views on God's nature and relation to the world; J. Gibelin, *L'esthétique de Schelling d'après la philosophie de l'art* (Paris, Vrin, 1934), on Schelling's conception of art and the esthetic order; V. Jankélévitch, *L'odysée de la conscience dans la dernière philosophie de Schelling* (Paris, Alcan, 1933) and H. Fuhrmans, *Schellings letzte Philosophie* (Berlin, Junker and Dünnhaupt, 1940), give detailed reports on the final phase of Schelling's thought. On German Romanticism, see R. E. Benz, *Die deutsche Romantik* (Leipzig, Reclam, 1937); for the contributions of Schlegel and Schiller, along with a cautionary statement about the various meanings of "Romanticism," see A. O. Lovejoy, *Essays in the History of Ideas* (Baltimore, Johns Hopkins Press, 1948), Essays X–XII. F. Von Schlegel's *The Philosophy of Life*, translated by A. J. Morrison (London, Bell and Daldy, 1872), is a representative pronouncement of the later German Romantic movement. Perhaps the most sensitive appreciation, in English, of Schelling's contribution to philosophy is found in J. Royce, *Lectures on Modern Idealism* (New Haven, Yale University Press, 1919), Lectures 4–5 (87–135). For Boehme's doctrines, see A. Koyré, *La philosophie de Jacob Boehme* (Paris, Vrin, 1929). For the Romantic contribution to literary criticism, cf. R. Wellek, *A History of Modern Criticism* (Vols. 1 and 2, New Haven, Yale University Press, 1955). Schelling's influence upon later German thought, including existentialism, is brought out by Karl Jaspers, *Schelling: Grösse und Verhängnis* (Munich, Piper, 1955), and by W. Schulz, *Die Vollendung des deutschen Idealismus in der Spätphilosophie Schellings* (Stuttgart, Kohlhammer, 1955). The similar structure of the romantic outlooks in German philosophy and English poetry provides the theme of E. D. Hirsch's *Wordsworth and Schelling* (New Haven, Yale University Press, 1960).

# Chapter 14. HEGEL

## I. LIFE AND WRITINGS

AFTER a thorough training in the *gymnasium* in his native Stuttgart, Georg Wilhelm Friedrich Hegel (born, 1770) was enrolled in the famous Tübingen *Stift* or theological foundation in 1788. Here, he had Schelling and the poet, Friedrich Hölderlin, as classmates. With them, he read Plato, Rousseau, and Kant. The young friends were enthusiastic about the Greek way of life and supported the French Revolution. After passing his theological examination (1793), Hegel worked as a tutor, first in Bern and then in Frankfort. His theological manuscripts of this period (1793-1801) were first collected and published in 1907, under the title: *Hegel's Early Theological Writings.* They included: a *Life of Jesus* (1795), in which Jesus was portrayed as a preacher of Kantian morality; *The Positivity of the Christian Religion* (Parts I-II, 1795-1796; Part III, 1798-1799), in which Hegel's Greek ideal of a "folk religion" and Kant's moral doctrine were blended together and contrasted favorably with Christianity; *The Spirit of Christianity and Its Fate* (1800), which recognized the constructive value of the Christian ideal of love; a number of fragments stressing the central notions of life and love, with a pantheistic view of the divine spirit among men. During these Bern and Frankfort years, Hegel was also engaged in a circumstantial study of historical, political, and economic questions. He wanted to elaborate his dialectic not in a cultural vacuum but on the basis of the closest familiarity with the empirical materials of human history and the present situation.

In 1801, Hegel accepted a position as *Privatdozent* in philosophy at the University of Jena. This university had been a vigorous philosophical center, with Reinhold and Fichte offering searching criticisms of the Kantian philosophy. When Hegel came there, he collaborated for two years (1802-1803) with Schelling in publishing the *Critical*

*Journal of Philosophy,* in which they made a common front against the intuitionism of Jacobi and Fichte's subjective idealism. Until Schelling's departure from Jena (1803), Hegel emphasized his measure of agreement with the former's theory of the unity of all opposites in the indifference of the absolute. But he also developed his own philosophy in his regular lectures. Published for the first time in 1923 and 1931–1932, this philosophy of the Jena period is seen to anticipate the doctrines of Hegel's mature years. His lectures constituted a system of speculative philosophy, dealing with logic and metaphysics, philosophy of nature, and philosophy of spirit (the latter being concerned mainly with the conflicts in economic life and the need for a rational state and laws to tame civil society). But the great achievement of this time was the *Phenomenology of Spirit,* which described the voyage of discovery by which the cultured mind is brought finally to the standpoint of the absolute spirit. Completed in 1807, at the time of Napoleon's invasion of Jena, this book marked Hegel's declaration of independence from Schelling. In the economic collapse ensuing upon the war, Hegel was forced to work as the editor of a newspaper in Bamberg (1807–1808), and then as rector and professor of philosophy at the *gymnasium* in Nuremberg (1808–1816). In this latter position, he gave forceful addresses on the function of the school and the value of classical studies. For his young students, he also drew up some "philosophical propaedeutics," covering the main parts of his system. At Nuremberg, Hegel composed his main work in systematic philosophy: *Science of Logic* (1812–1816), in which the traditional formal logic and Kantian logic were subordinated to the comprehensive, speculative logic of absolute spirit.

During a two-year stay as professor of philosophy in Heidelberg University (1816–1818), Hegel's reputation steadily increased. In the *Encyclopaedia of the Philosophical Sciences* (1817), he provided a conspectus of his entire system, in its three main divisions: logic, philosophy of nature, and philosophy of spirit. At Heidelberg, he also made a penetrating analysis of the constitutional reforms being undertaken in Württemberg, and gave a more balanced and positive evaluation of Jacobi's intuitive philosophy. Finally, he was invited to assume a professorship at Berlin, where he taught from 1818 until his death in 1831. This was the time of Hegel's greatest fame and public influence. He published his *Philosophy of Right* (1821), issued two new editions of the *Encyclopaedia,* and began to revise both the *Phenomenology* and the *Science of Logic.* He served as rector of the

University of Berlin in 1829–1830, and died the following year from cholera. After his death, devoted students published their notes of courses he had given in the philosophy of religion, history of philosophy, esthetics, and philosophy of history.

## 2.  HEGEL AND HIS GERMAN PREDECESSORS

Hegel gave the greatest impetus in modern times to a truly philosophical approach to the history of philosophy. Not only in his formal lectures on the subject, but in all his writings, he displayed a keen interest in the thoughts of earlier philosophers and a rare ability to seize upon the core of their outlook. Just as Aristotle made the early history of Greek speculation pay tribute to his own metaphysics, so Hegel regarded his system as the culmination of all previous philosophical traditions. He treated the views of his predecessors as so many preparatory views, exhibiting the workings of mind at various levels and in various antithetic relations. Out of the clash of many standpoints, he sought to show how human intelligence was gradually preparing for the advent of his own philosophy, which was to provide the crowning synthesis and reconciliation of the partial insights of the entire history of philosophy.[1]

Hegel was fascinated by the Greek mind, especially as expressed in Aristotle's speculations about the inner life of thought, proper to the prime mover. But he deemed his most urgent problems to be those presented by his immediate predecessors and contemporaries in Germany. In Kant, Fichte, and Schelling, he hailed the penultimate phase in the growth of philosophical consciousness, the moment in which the outlines of an adequate system were most firmly etched. His acknowledged debt to these three thinkers was a deep one, but Hegel also felt obliged to criticize them, in order to bring the immanent dialectic of philosophical development to completion. His own system was intended to be both the fulfillment and the overcoming of these cognate positions.

---

[1] For a summary statement, see *Encyclopaedia of the Philosophical Sciences*, Part I, *The Science of Logic*, 86 (Wallace translation: *The Logic of Hegel*, 159–60). Hereafter, this work is cited as *Encyclopaedia Logic*, in order to distinguish it from Hegel's larger book, *Science of Logic;* in his translation, Wallace prints in smaller type the Additions gathered from lecture notes of Hegel's students and inserted in the text by the editors of the first collected edition of his works. The fullest expression of Hegel's attitude toward the history of philosophy is found in the Heidelberg and Berlin introductory lectures, included in: *Lectures on the History of Philosophy. Introduction: System and*

1. *Kant.* While he was making his theological studies, Hegel became strongly attached to the *moral teachings* of Kant. His *Life of Jesus* portrays Jesus as a preacher of the Kantian doctrine of acting from a motive of duty and universal law alone. This enthusiasm for Kant's ethics was dampened, however, when Hegel observed that its scientific character was achieved at the price of deprecating the particular content in favor of the universal form. Hegel was certainly no enemy of the universal, formal element in thought and conduct, since it marks the organizing and dominating presence of reason. But he attributed to Kant precisely that sort of *formalism* which rests on the inability of thought to master its content. Kant never resolved the dualism between form and content, will and inclination, virtue and happiness. In Hegel's estimation, this was a sure sign that Kantian morality was not the absolute ethics for which he was seeking. Instead, Hegel appealed to the organizing concepts of *life* and *love*.[2] Life contains within itself both the particular motives and the universal maxims of conduct; it embraces both the individual and the kind; it provides a perpetually restless interpenetration of form and matter. An absolute ethics should be built around some such *unifying principle of synthesis,* rather than around a Kantian *dualism* of sensuous impulses and intelligible will.

Similar conclusions followed from Hegel's examination of the Kantian *theory of knowledge.* Kant was too ready to pronounce the dualism between the categories of understanding and the data of sense an insurmountable and ultimate one. It presents this aspect, only as long as one remains at the *finite* level of analysis and fails to detect certain implications, pointing toward another standpoint. The Kantian explanation of knowledge would be an exhaustive account, if man were confined within the finite scope of the *understanding.* This power is limited on both sides: from below, by the need to receive the matter of sensation *ab extra;* from above, by the unattainable ideal of an intuitive understanding. Kant drew the inescapable conclusion that pure thought is essentially finite and, taken in itself, merely formal and regulative. This entailed a denial of metaphysics as a science of supersensuous realities.

---

*History of Philosophy (Sämmtliche Werke, Kritische Ausgabe,* Vol. XVa, edited by J. Hoffmeister, 3-75).

[2] Hegel's early criticism of Kantian ethics is presented in *The Spirit of Christianity,* ii (Knox translation, in *Early Theological Writings,* 210-16). The positive themes of love and life are developed in *ibid.,* iii-iv, and in the fragment on *Love* (Knox translation, in *Early Theological Writings,* 224-81, 302-08).

Hegel sets out to challenge the major Kantian thesis about the understanding and the impossibility of a speculative metaphysics.[3] Viewed comprehensively, the understanding is not entirely bereft of intuition and knowledge-yielding content of its own. Kant's admissions about self-consciousness show that, in the act of reflection, the understanding comes to know itself *as something more than an empirical appearance*. One need not hesitate about calling this awareness an authentic instance of knowledge of being in its intelligible nature, unless one follows the circular procedure of first defining knowledge in terms of the empirical sciences, and then ruling out of the field of knowledge anything that surpasses the empirical standpoint. The understanding is restricted to the categorial, objective types of knowledge, only in its *finite* aspect. But since the mind has a clear awareness of the limits of the scientific understanding, it is superior to these limits and may regard them as being self-imposed. This consideration suggests the presence of an *unlimited* center of the understanding which Kant failed to notice.

Reason itself is that hidden principle at the heart of the understanding. In Kantian language, it is the understanding, considered insofar as it can become reflective or enjoy self-consciousness. The twofold limit placed by Kant upon the understanding does not obtain in every respect. For, in self-consciousness, the understanding furnishes its own epistemic content, and does not need to wait upon sensation and the schemata, in order to gain knowledge. To the extent that it transcends the conditions of objective knowledge, it reveals itself as an *infinite and intuitive reason*, which is no longer merely formal and regulative. Whereas Kant had referred obscurely to the thing-in-itself as the noumenal source of the given factor in knowledge, Hegel now assigns this function to reason itself. Reason supplies the content of its own intuition and knowledge, as well as its own forms. In this way, the Kantian dualism of cognitive matter and form, sensibility and understanding, is overcome. Their point of confluence is sovereign reason, which is the heir to Kant's unity of apperception. Since the limits of empirical knowledge are only relative and self-imposed

---

[3] A full-scale critical survey of Kant's philosophy is made in *Encyclopaedia Logic*, 40–60 (Wallace, 82–120); see also Hegel's article on Fichte and Schelling, mentioned below, note 5. The various strands of Hegel's criticism are knitted together by S. Vanni Rovighi, "Hegel critico di Kant," *Rivista di filosofia neoscolastica*, XLII (1950), 289–312. On the question of an intellectual intuition, cf. W. H. Walsh, "Hegel and Intellectual Intuition," *Mind*, N.S., LV (1946), 49–63.

by the activity of reason or thought, there is no basis for holding that thought is *essentially* finite, in respect to knowledge. Reason does have a finite *aspect* (viz., the understanding, as employed by the special sciences), but it also has the power to gain knowledge of its own unconditioned nature. Metaphysics may now be recalled from its banishment.

What Kant overlooked, is the fact that reason is a *self-dichotomizing process* and is itself responsible for the distinction between understanding and sensibility, subject and object, form and matter of knowledge. These dualisms are undeniably present and operative in our knowledge, but they do not pose insuperable antitheses for the philosopher who views them from the overarching perspective of reason. The rift between the sensible and intelligible aspects of the world need not be accepted as final, since it is subordinate to the unity achieved by self-reflective reason — a truth hinted at even by Kant, in his discussion of reflective judgment. To know reason is to know the *only noumenal being,* the only thing-in-itself. And to know reason's construction of the phenomenal world is, in final analysis, to know the development of actuality and not merely of appearance. Thought is not purely formal but is determinative of the real order, in its content as well as its formal structure, in its intelligible being as well as its sensible appearance.

The implication of this Hegelian criticism of Kant is that logic must take another step forward. Kant recognized the first two stages of logical development: *formal* and *transcendental* logic. He noted that his own transcendental logic advanced beyond a purely formal logic, by studying the matter of knowledge and its objective reference. But Hegel now seeks to complete the advance of logic, by adding the third and ultimate phase: *speculative* or *metaphysical logic.* This logic embraces the entire content of reality and hence is identical with metaphysics. Hegel brings to its culmination the process of ontologizing logic: "*Logic therefore coincides with Metaphysics, the science of things set and held in thoughts.*"[4] In his speculative logic,

---

[4] *Encyclopaedia Logic,* 24 (Wallace, 45). In *Science of Logic* (Johnston and Struthers translation, I, 74–75; because of its complicated subdivisions, this book is cited only according to the volume and page of the English translation), Hegel emphasizes that his logic is intended to supplant Wolffian metaphysics, regarded both as an ontology or science of being in general and as the special metaphysics of soul, world, and God. He usually prefers to speak of the three stages of logic as: the *abstract* logic of the understanding (formal logic), the *dialectical* logic of *negative* reason (Kant's transcendental logic), and the *speculative* logic of *positive* reason (Hegel's own logic,

the movements of thought are also interpreted as the pulsations of real being. The ultimate dualism between thought and being is the last Kantian idol to be overthrown. In reason's purview, they manifest a fundamental identity.

2. *Fichte and Schelling.* Although he agreed with Fichte's elimination of an extramental thing-in-itself, Hegel took him to task for not completing the transition from the finite to the infinite. He criticized the *residual empiricism,* which prevented Fichte from totally sublating the finite and given aspects of experience. In the Fichtean system, for instance, the finite ego can never gain knowledge about the infinite ego, in its own nature. Similarly, this philosophy retained the empirical datum as a kind of shock or priming-point, having a certain functional independence, even though Fichte ultimately reduced it to the absolute ego. Hegel regarded these features as a reversion to Kantian dualism. The only cure is to install philosophical speculation firmly on the central plateau occupied by reason, whence the origin of the data and limits of finite understanding can be properly explained.[5]

Fichte did give prominence to the moral striving toward infinity, as aroused by the practical *ought.* But Hegel brands this attitude a *bad infinity,* since it generates only an endless approximation to, rather than an actual attainment of, the infinite actuality. Furthermore, it supposes a lingering breach between theoretical and practical reason, which it is the business of a thoroughgoing philosophy of the absolute to heal. Hegel's speculative reason marks the meeting point of the *theoretical* and *practical* sides of reason. Reason is an intelligible structure and knowledge, but it is also a kind of activity and will. Speculative reason secures the unity between knowledge and will, speculation and praxis. At the same time, it transcends the Kantian contrast between faith and knowledge, since these are only special regions differentiated within the comprehensive domain of sovereign reason itself.[6]

---

identical with his metaphysics). Cf. *Encyclopaedia Logic,* 79 (Wallace, 143). J. Hyppolite, *Logique et existence: Essai sur la logique de Hegel,* 68–87, explains the transformation of metaphysics into speculative logic.

[5] Hegel's position with regard to Fichte and Kant (and, indirectly, Schelling) is outlined in his early essay, *The Difference between Fichte's and Schelling's Systems of Philosophy (Sämmtliche Werke, Kritische Ausgabe,* Vol. I, *Erste Druckschriften,* edited by G. Lasson, 3–113); cf. *The Phenomenology of Mind,* Preface (Baillie translation, 85).

[6] See the other early essay, *Faith and Knowledge* (in *Erste Druckschriften,* Lasson edition, 223–346), and the commentary by C. Michalson, "The Boundary between

Fichte's first law of self-identity does not express the unconditioned nature of the absolute. The latter can never be captured in a formal proposition, and can never be made the simple beginning of a deductive process. That is why the only ego which falls within Fichte's compass, remains a conditioned one. The standpoint of finite understanding is not transcended, and therefore the dualism of ego and non-ego, proportionate to the finite level of understanding, is never surmounted. The danger in Fichte's method is that the world is reduced to a mere foil for the ego, and yet is never given a completely rational genesis and justification. Fichte endangers the *actuality* of the world, without demonstrating its *ideality*.

Much of the above criticism of Kant and Fichte was inspired by Schelling's earlier philosophy. Hegel found extremely congenial the Schellingian search after a *focal point of identity* for the contrasting elements in experience, a center that is located in the absolute itself. Hegel's youthful Romantic-Christian conception of *love,* as a bond of cosmic reconciliation among the extremes of existence, led to a divine ground, similar to that proposed by Schelling. Moreover, Hegel liked the emphasis given by his Jena colleague to nature, the structured realm of the non-ego, and to esthetic intuition.

But here the agreement abruptly stopped. The more Schelling developed any one of his favorite theses, the more certain Hegel became that there was no inclusive principle of systematic unity at work in his mind and, consequently, that the result could only be another one-sided doctrine. The stress upon the underlying unity of opposites, for instance, led to the view that opposites sink out of sight into the indetermination of absolute being. Here, the self and the world lose all their distinctive features. Hegel referred satirically to this notion of the absolute as "the night in which, as we say, all cows are black."[7] There is a *suppression* rather than *synthesis* of differences, so that there is no rational way of recovering the contrasts of existence out of the bottomless pit of Schelling's indifferent absolute. Hegel mocked at Schelling's mysterious utterances about the "leap" or "fall" of

Faith and Reason: A Study of Hegel's *Glauben und Wissen,*" *Drew University Studies,* III (1951), 1–12. Also consult *Encyclopaedia Logic,* 61–66 (Wallace, 121–30).

[7] *The Phenomenology of Mind,* Preface, (Baillie, 79; cf. 77–79, 110). In *Encyclopaedia Logic,* 215, Hegel observes that Schelling's unity of thought and being is undialectical and hence "expresses an abstract and merely quiescent identity. . . . The infinite would thus seem to be merely *neutralised* by the finite, the subjective by the objective, thought by being" (Wallace, 357).

things from God's bosom, and the sudden appearance of various "potencies," to account for the grades and varieties of things in the world.

Despite his system of identity, Schelling failed to reconcile intuition and reflection, life and thought. Hence he failed to resolve the philosophical issues raised by Romanticism. His theory of an intellectual intuition of the absolute led only to a leap in the dark: it was powerless to explain either how our minds arrive at the absolute or how the latter gives birth to the world of ego and non-ego. Hegel concluded that Schelling's greatest deficiency was a lack of philosophical method. Fichte had at least attempted to make a rational and dialectical explanation of the procession of things from the absolute. Hegel himself sought to combine the good points in both thinkers, by impregnating Schelling's *intuition* with dialectical structure and endowing Fichte's dialectical *reflection* with intuitive richness of content. But the primacy must be awarded to *reason* itself, the principle accounting for every differentiation of intuition and reflection. Philosophy must remain a rational explanation, or else it ceases to be philosophy and succumbs to poetry and religion. Fichte was right in starting with rational consciousness rather than with nature, since the starting point of speculation is not a matter of indifference (as Schelling had contended).

## 3.  THE ABSOLUTE AS SPIRIT

Hegel's approach to the question of God's existence stands in marked contrast to that of Kant. The strategy of the former is to accept Kant's teaching that the cosmological and physicotheological (or teleological) proofs are reducible to the ontological, and then to offer a new defense of the ontological proof.[8] The arguments from

---

[8] *Lectures on the Proofs of the Existence of God* (Speirs and Sanderson translation, in *Lectures on the Philosophy of Religion*, III, 155-327); *Amplifications of the Teleological and Ontological Proofs* (Speirs and Sanderson translation, in *ibid.*, III, 328-67). The proofs for God's existence are valid only after the "untruth" and "taint" of the finite modes of being — the apparently irreducible otherness between the infinite and the finite, as well as between the mind and the world — have been eliminated. The amended Hegelian form of the proofs is: "The absolute *is*, just because the finite is self-contradictory opposition — just because it *is not*. . . . There are finite minds, but the finite has no truth, the truth of the finite spirit *is* the absolute Spirit. . . . The act whereby these higher thoughts [about the idea of God] are here reached *is* the act of the Spirit." *Science of Logic* (Johnston-Struthers, II, 70); *Amplifications of the Teleological and Ontological Proofs* (Speirs-Sanderson, III, 352-53) (italics mine, except for second set). The proofs of God's existence are also discussed in: *Science of*

contingency and cosmic order have some value, since they prepare
the mind for acceptance of the ontological argument. The *ontological
proof* can be directly revived, once it has been shown that there is an
intellectual intuition, founded upon the act of rational reflection. The
major purpose of our reflection is to discover the implications of the
fact that the understanding is subject to limitations. Finite consciousness gradually becomes aware that its finitude and the negative conditions of worldly existence are *self-imposed,* precisely because they can
be known reflectively as limits. In this act of recognition, there is an
overcoming of these limits and negations: they are seen to come from
the mind or spirit itself, considered in its *unconditioned actuality.* In
Hegel's estimation, this is no jejune repetition of the ontological argument of Descartes and Leibniz. For, Hegel is suggesting that the
"idea of God" is, quite literally, the form under which the absolute
spirit itself develops in human, reflective consciousness. The Hegelian
form of the ontological argument leads to the *monistic immanence
of the absolute spirit,* rather than to a transcendent God. Hegel is
ready to sacrifice the integrity of the finite, personal mind and the
finite world, so that their "truly actual being" may be revealed as the
absolute spirit itself.

In his doctrine on the absolute as spirit, Hegel forged a tool for
assimilating the findings of his predecessors to a philosophical position
distinctively his own. This doctrine constitutes his deepest personal
conviction, as well as the major premise of all his philosophizing.
"*The Absolute is Spirit*—this is the supreme definition of the
Absolute. To find this definition and to grasp its meaning and content
was, we may say, the ultimate purpose of all education and all philosophy."[9] The very term *Geist* enjoys a strategic ambivalence, since it
signifies what we mean by both "mind" and "spirit." As Hegel
employed the term, it is not so one-sidedly cognitive and contemplative in import as "mind," and not so exclusively associated with the
immaterial and religious spheres as "spirit." *Geist* includes will and
the passions, along with the knowing powers; it embraces the
structure of the material world and the whole range of man's

*Logic* (Johnston-Struthers, II, 69–70, 343–346); *Encyclopaedia Logic,* 36, 50–51, 193
(Wallace, 71–75, 102–09, 330–34); *Encyclopaedia of the Philosophical Sciences,* Part
III, *Philosophy of Mind,* 552 (Wallace translation, 281; hereafter cited as *Philosophy of
Mind*). These texts have been critically analyzed by H. A. Ogiermann, S.J., *Hegels
Gottesbeweise* (Rome, Gregorian University Press, 1948).
[9] *Philosophy of Mind,* 384 (Wallace, 164; translation modified).

secular interests, as well as his religious attitude and his direction toward immaterial goods. The term has the further advantage of applying to both the human mind and the divine spirit. It suggests both that the human mind is an aspect of the divine spirit and that the divine spirit is fully rational and self-conscious.

Spirit or mind is described by Hegel in several ways, with emphasis upon the pivotal contrast between substance and subject.[10] Hegel suggests that philosophical speculations on the absolute as *substance* culminated historically in the systems of Spinoza and Schelling, whereas Kant and Fichte did most toward developing the meaning of the absolute as *subject*. This historical evaluation is essential to Hegel's presentation, since it enables him to reduce all other views of substance and subject to these leading ones. He observes that people were shocked when Spinoza identified God with substance, because the latter notion popularly connotes an *inert, lifeless something*. Hegel gives a good deal of weight to this popular estimation, pointing to the difficulties encountered by Spinoza and Schelling in explaining the emergence of differentiated finite beings from absolute substance. He oversimplifies the historical picture, however, by ignoring what the Christian Fathers and Scholastics said about the sense in which God is substance, precisely because of His supreme possession of life, and the sense in which He is best denominated as a being above substance. Hegel does allow a legitimate meaning for the absolute spirit as substance, since spirit must be conceived as having real content, self-identity of being, and intuitive awareness of its own nature. But he is concerned chiefly to underline the inadequacy of the notion of substance, taken by itself, so that we will be driven to combine it with his view of subject.

The absolute spirit cannot be regarded merely as substance, merely as having identity and immediacy. This would be an abstract way of viewing the nature of spirit, since the latter would be reduced either to the immediacy of a *particular thing* or to the formal identity of an *empty universal concept*. Neither a mere particular thing nor a uni-

---

[10] The fundamental text is contained in the Preface to *The Phenomenology of Mind* (Baillie, 80–88), where he calls the identification of the absolute with *Geist* "the grandest conception of all, and one which is due to modern times and its religion. The spiritual alone is the actual." *Loc. cit.* (Baillie, 85–86; translation modified). Hegel means that Protestantism encouraged the growth of subjectivity and self-consciousness, to the point where philosophical formulation could be given to the view that spirit, actuality, and the absolute are the same. Read N. Rotenstreich, "Hegel's Concept of Mind," *Revue Internationale de Philosophie*, VI (1952), 27–34.

versal notion is an adequate transcription of the meaning of absolute spirit, since it includes the reality of both and yet escapes the one-sidedness or abstractness of each. Hegel appeals to our own internal experience, in order to convey an inkling of the proper way in which mind or spirit is substantial. This appeal is characteristic, since it prepares us to find in ourselves not only the *analogue* of the absolute but a *phase* in the development of the absolute itself. Our mind retains its self-identity, amid all the changing acts of thinking and willing. Indeed, the depth and strength of our substantial self-possession are proved, only when we retain possession of ourselves throughout the conflicts of human existence. This suggests that the absolute mind must be that sort of substance which is also a subject.

The absolute substance is *a subject, a true self*. As such, it has the identity of nature proper to a persistent and purposive mind, rather than to a stone or a generic concept. Hegel adds that, because it is both living and purposive, absolute spirit must undergo a *development,* in which it enriches rather than loses its selfsameness. If the absolute were divorced from change, it would be a mere static substance, a *caput mortuum,* rather than the vivifying principle of the universe. Hegel applauds Aristotle for attributing the life of pure thinking to the prime mover, but for Hegel this life is a *purposive self-becoming,* rather than an exemption from all process.[11] Once more, he summons the inward testimony of men to corroborate the view that mature selfhood is acquired only through painful changes and growth. A man develops his personality through knowing good and evil, without becoming corrupted or dissolved by the experience. He acquires his full stature through undergoing the trials of separation and conflict, and through tasting the sweet victory of self-recovery.

This evidence, drawn from the development of human personality, does show that, if the absolute is mind, it has a richer nature than that of inanimate things. But it does not establish that this superior reality is subject to the special conditions of human life. There is a double set of distinctions, relevant to this issue, which Hegel (follow-

---

[11] Hegel concludes his *Encyclopaedia of the Philosophical Sciences* with a summarizing quotation from Book Lambda of Aristotle's *Metaphysics* (1072 b18–30), the notable passage in which Aristotle declares that "life also belongs to God; for the actuality of thought is life, and God is that actuality; and God's self-dependent actuality is life, most good and eternal" — Ross translation, taken from *The Basic Works of Aristotle,* edited by R. McKeon (New York, Random House, 1941), 880. Hegel often quotes phrases from this Aristotelian text, but always with the purpose of introducing into the divine actuality a dialectical, temporal process.

ing the example of Schelling) finds it convenient to overlook. The first point concerns the difference between our way of getting to know life and the nature of life itself. Granted that the human mind *becomes acquainted with* life through a study of the manifestations of becoming, it does not follow that life must *consist in* the becoming process. This leads to a second reason for refusing to read the conditions of change into the essential meaning of life at every level. Analysis of finite living things requires us to distinguish between the *immanent operation* or perfect vital act itself and the attendant conditions of *becoming* and *conflict*. The former note characterizes the living thing precisely as living, whereas the latter conditions belong to it in virtue of its finite nature. The absolute mind cannot be conceived as being bereft of the immanent operations of knowing and willing. But it does not follow that the absolute mind would be degraded to the level of a nonliving thing, if it did not undergo the travails of becoming. Development follows from the *finite* character of some living things, rather than from the fact that they are *living,* conscious subjects. However difficult it is to gain any adequate notion of a manner of life and mental activity that would not entail development, this difficulty is no warrant for defining life essentially and univocally in terms of change and self-alienation. Rather, it is a sure indication that there are basic differences between the infinite and the finite ways of possessing the perfections of life.

Absolute mind is essentially a reflective process. *Reflection* provides Hegel with the clue to a reconciliation of immediacy and mediacy, intuition and dialectic, as exemplified historically in the opposition between Schelling and Fichte. Reflective thinking flourishes precisely upon the polar tension between these extremes. It guarantees to absolute mind both the content of immediacy or intuition and the vigor of a dialectical mediation of opposites. Although reflection need not always signify consciousness, it always means a return of being to itself. Hence mind, as a reflective process, contains the intuitive and dialectical elements within a *totality* or *systematic whole.* Hegel appropriates Kant's remarks about the completeness and systematic unity of reason, applying them to absolute mind. Yet he removes the Kantian qualifications concerning the purely formal and regulative nature of the ideas of reason. The rational whole encompassed by absolute spirit is one with the articulations of being itself: it constitutes an ontological totality, and not merely a logical one.

Finally, spirit may be identified with *systematic science* or *philoso-*

*phy* itself.[12] Absolute mind finds its perfect embodiment in philosophical science. The various particular sciences are approximations to the plenary meaning of science, which is found only in philosophy, more precisely, in the Hegelian philosophy, as the culmination of all philosophical development. But science or philosophy, in this inclusive sense, is also the same as the self-reflection of the absolute spirit. Hence the traits of the absolute mind must be present also in philosophy. The latter must combine intuition and dialectic, immediate substantial content and a dialectical sifting of the data, careful analysis and systematic synthesis. The total and organic nature of mind as such demands realization in a system of philosophy that is itself an organic whole: the actuality of absolute mind within consciousness. Only here is the ideal of system as such given its adequate formulation.

Two outstanding difficulties faced Hegel, as soon as he sought to construct a philosophy in accord with his doctrine on absolute *Geist*. First, how can this primary insight into the nature of spirit be communicated to others? Second, what is the most appropriate method for expounding the absolute system of philosophy? The two following sections are devoted to Hegel's answers to these questions.

### 4. EXPERIENCE AS THE PATHWAY TO SPIRIT

How to make an *introduction* to his philosophy is a special problem for Hegel. He admits that an ordinary sort of introduction is impossible. Absolute idealism cannot begin upon some common, neutral ground, develop one principle at a time, and thus lead the mind gradually to its own viewpoint. For Hegel, truth is resident only in the whole, only in the totality of the comprehensive system of philosophy. Hence any particular, true proposition already involves all the other propositions that must qualify its meaning, and behind any particular argument lies the basic conviction about the nature of absolute spirit. His thought is better represented by the image of a *closed circle* or a serpent of wisdom, grasping its own tail, than by the Cartesian metaphor of the great chain of truths, depending upon a primary but particular affirmation. Unless one is already sure of the constitutive presence of the absolute spirit, no particular proposi-

---

[12] *The Phenomenology of Mind*, Preface, and VIII (Baillie, 70–71, 111–15, 797–808); *Science of Logic* (Johnston-Struthers, II, 480–82); *Encyclopaedia Logic*, 14 (Wallace, 23–24).

tion can be correctly understood. And yet, to attain this insight, one must have seen the import of experience as a whole. Toward the solution of this delicate issue of making an appropriate introduction to his thought, Hegel devoted an entire work, the *Phenomenology of Spirit.*

Hegel acknowledges that a deep divide separates *common sense* and *philosophical science.* Each regards the other as being caught in a web of unreality and illusion. Naïve consciousness seeks to know objects as realities other than itself, and itself as distinct from the surrounding world. From the philosophical standpoint of absolute idealism, this attitude is literally a loss of mind, a failure to recognize the creative presence of mind in the world. Conversely, common sense detects an air of unreality about the idealistic explanation, since it seems to destroy our immediate certainties and yet offer nothing substantial in their place.

Hegel's usual procedure in the face of criticism is to admit it in its full strength, and then to incorporate the opponent's position, as being but one more phase in the *self*-criticism of his own philosophy. Hence this mutual charge of unreality must be accepted and converted into the starting point of philosophical science itself. The *Phenomenology* is the autobiography of the mind in its itinerary from naïve consciousness to absolute knowledge or reflective science. It provides the only effective *via inventionis,* capable of elevating the individual mind to the level of perfect self-consciousness or the absolute spirit. It does so, by examining the various forms taken by consciousness throughout human history. The general attitudes of mind have been embodied in representative cultural movements, institutions, revolutionary waves, religions, and philosophies. By grasping both the truth and the limitation of each of these outlooks, the individual man becomes educated in the history of the race and hence in the history of absolute spirit, operating at the human plane. Like Goethe's Wilhelm Meister, the attentive individual aggregates himself to humanity as such, through this *cultural* and *historical formation* of his consciousness. But humanity, considered as fully conscious of its tragedies and triumphs, is nothing other than absolute spirit come into reflective knowledge of its own actuality, as a realized process. Hence he who masters this educational effort, set forth in the *Phenomenology,* has formed his soul to the point of being able to philosophize in the proper way. He has been introduced to Hegel's absolute idealism and can now begin to view things according to the *via judicii* or in the light of the absolute spirit.

Consciousness is naïve in the degree that it is *empirical* and *realistic*. Hegel does not banish empirical realism but embraces it to himself, in such a way that it becomes transformed into a phase of absolute idealism itself. This is the sense in which there can be no neutral ground held in common between absolute idealism and realism. Men must be taken as they are, and they do manifest an almost ineradicable, realistic attitude. They think that the human mind is a thoroughly finite power and that it is directed toward finite objects, which are real precisely insofar as they are independent of our consciousness. This belief, in its various forms, serves as the main subject of critical analysis throughout the *Phenomenology*. Hegel ferrets out the realistic supposition in stage after stage of human experience. He constantly proclaims that finitude is only a category of the understanding, and hence that its value is only provisional. The conclusion is driven home, at every opportunity, that one cannot genuinely think about finite being, without seeing that it is caducal and essentially *a phase in absolute spirit's development*. Everything is directed toward the inevitable conclusion that *actuality and self-articulating reason are identical* and that, therefore, the finite is *unreal, when considered as irreducible to thought and spirit*. Having once admitted that the finite is actual, only insofar as it is a phase in the self-development of absolute spirit, the individual is saved from realism and is installed safely within the portals of absolute idealism.

Hegel widens the scope of the science of the experience of consciousness by analyzing not only Kant's scientific type of experience but also the cultural, moral, economic, political, artistic, and religious forms of human experience. *Experience* in general is the truth about an object and knowledge of that truth.[13] In studying each particular phase of experience, Hegel follows a common pattern. A description is first given of the spontaneous attitude of consciousness toward its proper object, at a given level of experience. Then, the question of how to unite consciousness with this object is raised. Inevitably, it turns out that the conscious subject has had a major role in the constitution of its object, indeed, that the object is an aspect of

[13] *The Phenomenology of Mind*, Introduction, and I (Baillie, 142–43, 158). By treating experience as a *consequence* of dialectical thinking, rather than as its origin, Hegel seeks to appropriate the positive side of empiricism and yet vindicate the self-sufficiency of his method and system.

consciousness, placed in a condition of alienation or otherness from the subject. Experience is precisely the dialectical process of destroying realistic convictions, by unbaring the mind's contribution to the being and otherness of its objects. Experience is not an immediate datum but the outcome of a progressive, skeptical disillusionment concerning the "hard realities," with which consciousness is seemingly confronted. Only when we view a thing as it is *in and for consciousness,* do we apprehend it in its proper nature. Only this *phenomenological* approach yields us the truth about it.

Thus, at the lowest level of conscious life, *sense certainty* believes that the self is placed in immediate contact with this and that independent, sensible thing, in an intuitive way and without the intervention of any universal factor of reason. But, Hegel asks, what is the *this* revealed by sense certainty? It is an object describable, perhaps, as this tree, present here and now before me. The *here* is the spot where the tree is rooted, and the *now* is noontime. But if the perceiver turns in another direction, a little later on, then the *here-before-me* is another plot of land, with a house resting on it, and the *now* is early in the afternoon. Hence the object of sense certainty is a complexus or intersection of *heres* and *nows.* The *here* as such includes: the spot where the tree is growing and where the house is not standing; the plot of land on which the house is built and where the tree is not growing; both regions indifferently and together. A similar analysis can be given of the *now* as such, in respect to noontime, early afternoon, and their mutual inclusion. In a word, the *here* and the *now* are universals, requiring the presence of reason and the constitutive activity of consciousness. Hegel concludes triumphantly that "the Universal is therefore in point of fact the truth of sense-certainty, the true content of sense-experience."[14]

This conclusion became a center of controversy among Hegel's immediate successors. It was attacked by the left-wing Hegelian, Ludwig Feuerbach, on the grounds that Hegel weights the case

---

[14] *Ibid.,* I (Baillie, 152); the dialectic of sense certainty is presented in *loc. cit.* (Baillie, 149–60). Special attention should be paid to two remarkable articles by J. Loewenberg: "The Exoteric Approach to Hegel's 'Phenomenology,' " *Mind,* N.S., XLIII (1934), 424–45; "The Comedy of Immediacy in Hegel's 'Phenomenology,' " *Mind,* N.S., XLIV (1935), 21–38. The first article explains how one should read the *Phenomenology;* the second one concentrates upon the dialectic of sense certainty. Loewenberg shows that, whereas Hegel sought to reveal a dialectical contradiction at the heart of sense certainty, the contradiction does not lie *in* sense certainty but only *between* it and Hegel's attempt to make it fit his scheme of discourse.

from the outset in favor of a universal, creative reason. As Feuerbach put it, Hegel begins "not with the reality-other-than-thought but with the *thought of the reality-other-than-thought*. Here, thought is naturally assured in advance of victory over its counterpart."[15] Sense consciousness and its object are described in such a way that they are already taken as phases in the dialectic of reason, even before the conclusion is reached. Furthermore, the argument does not prove any more than that sense and reason (as finite powers) co-operate in knowing the concrete thing. The existing thing is known, as having a certain intelligible structure or essence. When Hegel proposes his questions about comparative instances of the sensible thing, he is interrogating at the rational level: he is concerned, not with the thing in its own concrete and individual mode of being, but with the generalized notions constructed *by our reason,* on the basis of sense evidence of the individual thing. Hence the answer is also given in terms of the intelligible structures grasped by reason and rendered formally universal, under pressure of this questioning about comparative instances of place and time. To ask about *the here* and *the now* precisely *as such,* i.e., as reflectively elaborated by reason on the basis of sense experiences, is to ask about reflex or formally universal notions, founded upon individual things. But this does not establish that the existent things are themselves universal or that the observer is a universal subject, constituting their principles of being.

The senses support the realistic tendency of finite reason to hold fast by its existential judgment that the sensed thing is known precisely as exercising its own individual act of being, an act that is seen to be irreducible to an objectification or alienation of consciousness. The *categories* of *when* and *where,* together with the *concept* of finitude, are certainly universal. But the temporal, located, finitely existing things, upon which these concepts are founded, are manifested in the perceptual judgment of existence as being individual and other than the finite knower. Analysis of sense certainty does not support the view that finite mind and sensible thing are moments in the development of absolute mind, except by begging the issue.

Hegel appeals to the grand sweep of his entire argument, in

[15] Ludwig Feuerbach, *Toward the Critique of the Hegelian Philosophy (Sämmtliche Werke,* Vol. II: *Philosophische Kritiken und Grundsätze* [Leipzig, Wigand, 1846], 215). On Feuerbach's role as a critic of Hegel, cf. K. Löwith, "L. Feuerbach und der Ausgang der klassischen deutschen Philosophie," *Logos,* XVII (1928), 323–47; S. Hook, *From Hegel to Marx,* 220–71. See below, note 41.

which the same dialectical analysis is applied to all phases of experience. After each revelation of its own being in the object, consciousness hopes to come eventually upon a "truly objective" reality, which will resist incorporation within mind and thus vindicate its own autonomy. After each disclosure, *unhappy consciousness* moves restlessly onward to a new horizon, where perhaps it may find a nonmental other.[16] This hope of unhappy consciousness proves in vain, so that it comes to realize that the way of experience is also the way of doubt and despair. Consciousness continues to draw the veil from across its own features, revealing itself as a self-splintering, self-alienating process. Its very life is to divide itself off into the self and the other-than-self — and then to discover its own presence in the object thus posited. Gradually, reason comes sufficiently into knowledge of its own ways to discern a common pattern, operating throughout the history of consciousness. It perceives the presence of two points of view for estimating the deliverances of experience: that of *natural consciousness* and that of *philosophical consciousness*. At each stage of disillusionment about the objectivity of things, reason can reflect upon its previous naïve belief and thus subject the attitude of natural consciousness, along with its object, to the analysis of philosophical consciousness. The latter assumes more and more the position of a critical observer and judge of the natural flow of experience. Eventually, the whole gamut of human experience is evaluated critically as a series of conscious states and objects, which constitute so many moments or phases in the self-actualization of absolute spirit.

Thus the *Phenomenology* gradually achieves a juncture and perfect interpenetration between the natural, naïve attitude and the reflective, scientific attitude, between things as they *appear* in finite perspective and as they *are* in the absolute totality. The search for philosophy may now be transformed into philosophizing as such. The *de jure* exposition of philosophical themes can begin, now that empirical consciousness is lifted up to absolute spirit and acknowledges that its search after philosophical wisdom is the same as the absolute spirit's purposive drive toward reflective awareness of itself, in all its forms.

---

16 There is a special section on the Jewish, medieval Christian and pietistic outlooks, as instances of "the unhappy consciousness," in *The Phenomenology of Mind*, IV, B, 3 (Baillie, 250–67). But the entire work is permeated by the broader meaning of this term, signifying the restless, experiential search of mind after its own content and the truth about its objects (see J. Wahl's *Le malheur de la conscience dans la philosophie de Hegel*).

## 5. THE DIALECTICAL METHOD

There is a strict correlation between Hegel's *methodology* and *ontology*, between his theory of dialectic and his theory of absolute spirit. Although dialectical materialism has attempted to divorce the two, they are joined as one flesh in Hegel's own outlook, so that they stand or fall together. The one is proportioned to the other and receives its justification from the other, in circular fashion. Hegel criticized Kant precisely for trying to construct a critical method prior to metaphysics. Theory of knowledge and methodology have no autonomous standing, since they have more than a formal import. They concern the nature of being as well as formal thought, and hence must be adapted to the general theory of being. The Hegelian method is fitted to express his doctrine on absolute spirit and, in turn, receives its ultimate sanction from this doctrine. Hence Hegel can confidently affirm: "I know that it is the only true Method. This is already evident from the fact that the Method is no-ways different from its object and content — for it is the content in itself, *the Dialectic which it has in itself,* that moves it on."[17] And this dialectic is nothing else than the creative unrest of the absolute spirit itself.

In indicating the historical antecedents of his dialectical method, Hegel paid special tribute to Plato, Kant, Fichte, and Schelling. From Plato, he derived an appreciation of the dialogue as the tool of inquiry and of philosophizing as a search after the rational concept. The dialogue form is an open admission that all particular statements are one-sided and need supplementation by their opposite. Only in the *interplay* of partial insights does the truth emerge, as an expression of the whole of experience. Furthermore, Plato saw the importance of describing a thing in terms of what it is *not* and what is *unlike* it. Kant also valued the *negative factor* in thought, as well as the positive function of *antithetical reasoning.* But the antinomies are far more than Kant's four, since they permeate all our speculation. Reason not only gets entangled in antithetical thinking but deliberately involves itself in this tension between thesis and antithesis. Philosophical progress is made only when reason systematically engages itself in the dialectic, and conquers the truth in and through its own opposing affirmations. Whereas Kant's critical philosophy was in the

---

[17] *Science of Logic* (Johnston-Struthers, I, 65; cf. I, 36; II, 467–76). The general import of dialectical thinking is set forth in *Encyclopaedia Logic,* 81 (Wallace, 147–52).

position of an aloof umpire, Hegel's speculative philosophy embraced both contesting parties in the struggle for wisdom. He agreed with Fichte in locating the truth only in the synthetic outcome of the opposition between the self and the non-self.

Schelling and the Romantics anticipated Hegel in their celebration of the movement from one extreme of thought and mood to another. They found the most rewarding attitude to consist in remaining open to the "contradictions of life," the antithetic experiences available to the human soul. Hegel was strongly impressed by the Romantic conception but sought to correct it on two major scores. For one thing, the tensions of life must be given some *definite end,* or they will lead to self-depletion and sterility. Hegel sought to harness the oscillation between extremes, in the service of the absolute mind. Unless the polarity of thought leads to a progressive awareness of the laws of absolute spirit, it will perish from lack of orientation. A second qualification concerns the Romantic criticism of traditional logic and the *principle of contradiction.*[18] Hegel was unwilling to eliminate this principle entirely, since it serves as one basis for formal logic or the pattern of thought employed by finite understanding and the special sciences. It is even useful for organizing philosophies in the Cartesian, mathematical tradition, and for trimming the sentimental excesses from Romanticism itself. Still, Hegel agreed that the principle of contradiction is merely a law of formal thought, operating at the empirical level, rather than a law governing the entire order of being. It gives only negative guidance, and hence is valid only within the restricted sphere of *finite* understanding. It cannot serve as a fundamental principle in philosophy, which is the science of being in its totality and absolute significance. The ultimate law in philosophy must be *dialectical,* because it must reflect the antithetical and self-developing nature of absolute spirit. The reason why Hegel refused to acknowledge the ontological primacy of the principle of contradiction lies in his prior identification of being with absolute spirit, as described by himself.

<hr/>

18 *Science of Logic* (Johnston-Struthers, I, 42–47; II, 39–43, 66–69, 227–29); *Encyclopaedia Logic,* 115, 119 (Wallace, 213–15, 220–23). Hegel praises Aristotle for disengaging the forms of thought for separate study, and calls his own speculative logic a formal discipline. The capital difference is, however, that the Hegelian metaphysicologic is the science of the absolute form itself, which bears its own content and actuality within itself and hence expressed the basic dialectical laws of being. The "emptiness" of the principles of contradiction and excluded middle means that they do not rest on the premise that the absolute being undergoes dialectical development,

Hegel regards his theory of dialectic not merely as a doctrine on finite being or one on man's view of the infinite being, but primarily as an account of the method employed by the infinite mind to attain its own ends. The job of philosophy is still to explain being, but the explanation is now held to come *from within the absolute ground of being,* to which the finite mind is elevated. From this eminence, it is seen that the realistic distinction between thought and being, subject and object, holds true for the human mind only in its state of incomplete reflection on the truth of being. From the standpoint of the absolute spirit, however, the underlying identity amid these distinctions is brought to light and used as the primary principle for the dialectical method. Just because philosophy is the study of being, it may also be specified as the *science of reason,* as it becomes conscious of itself in and through *concept.* The native element of philosophical method is the concept, which is articulated in pure thought. This does not imply that philosophy and formal logic coincide. By *pure thought (das reine Denken)* is not meant an exclusively formal and cognitive process. Pure thought is the philosophical synthesis of all the operations of creative spirit, including intuition and feeling, categorial understanding and passion, willing and whatever dynamism is at work in material nature. Dialectical method is a reflection upon the structure of pure thought, and for this reason it is the universally adequate tool for philosophizing.

Until the term *Begriff* ("concept," not "notion"; a grasping-together of the factors in experience) is clarified, the nature of philosophical method cannot be understood.[19] Hegel's meaning can be summed up in the following three propositions. (1) The philosophical concept is not static and fixed but moving and fluid. (2) It is a concrete universal, rather than an abstract one. (3) It is not merely affirmative and immediate but also negative and mediated. An examination of these statements will permit a surer grip upon the Hegelian doctrine on dialectical method.

1. The Romantics (followed, later on, by Nietzsche, Bergson, and the philosophy-of-life current of thought) criticized rationalism for forcing our apprehension of life into perverting conceptual molds. They set up a contrast between reason and reality, *logic* and *life.*

---

[19] The third book of *Science of Logic* opens with an extensive section entitled "On the Notion in General" (Johnston-Struthers, II, 211–32). The third division of Hegelian logic (as presented in both *Science of Logic* and *Encyclopaedia Logic*) deals in detail with the doctrine on *Begriff.*

Hegel admitted both the justice of the Romantic strictures against rationalism and the impossibility of overcoming the antithesis between logic and life, at the customary plane of philosophical discussion. He offered his own absolute idealism as a way of elevating philosophical reflection to the position where the Romantic-Rationalist dispute can be transcended. Lacking in all previous investigations was any adequate theory of the concept, based upon the nature of absolute mind, rather than upon the conditions of finite, human intelligence. Hence the rationalists could not analyze the dynamic aspects of experience, without solidifying them and perverting their nature. The concept must be traced back to the absolute spirit, where alone it finds adequate expression. Now the absolute spirit is subject to a process of becoming and self-division, such that it constitutes both the realm of logic and that of life.[20] There is no possibility of reconciling the two realms from a purely finite standpoint: merely finite ideas are bound to do violence to vital aspects of being. But adequate philosophical concepts are framed from the standpoint of the absolute ("standpoint" is really a misnomer, since the absolute includes all standpoints and occupies no particular one). They express the movement or development of the absolute principle itself, as it constitutes life, differentiates life from logic, and reconstitutes the unity of life and logic once more, in philosophy as such. Hence such concepts are fitted, by nature, not only to seize the striving and flowing traits of life but also to unite them with the logical aspects of being, in the synthesis of the rational whole.

2. One of Hegel's major moves against realism is to redefine the nature of the *concrete*, in conformity with his criticism of sense experience. He recognizes that, if the meaning of the concrete is taken directly from our human experience of individual existents, there will be no opportunity to escape from the charge of vicious and hypostasizing abstraction. Like Spinoza, then, he revises its meaning in the light of his fundamental conviction about the absolute spirit, and then proceeds to criticize the "merely finite" significance of concrete being. Concreteness is found unqualifiedly only in the absolute spirit, since a thing is *concrete in proportion to its actuality*.[21] Positively, this

---

[20] *Encyclopaedia Logic*, 160–62 (Wallace, 287–91).

[21] *Ibid.*, 164 (Wallace, 294–95); *Philosophy of Mind*, 437–38 (Wallace, 204–05). The concept would be a mere abstraction, if one were to take the sensible, empirical thing as the standard of concreteness; but (in accord with his previous criticism of sense certainty and perception) Hegel regards this as an ultimately untenable position.

means that only the absolute or fully actual spirit is worthy of being called concrete, in an unconditioned way. Negatively, it follows that there is a proportionate lack of concreteness in every aspect of thought and being that falls short of the total perfection of absolute spirit. Hegel makes this metaphysical deduction by identifying the concrete with pure actuality and subsistent existence. This runs squarely contrary to the meaning based upon finite, existential acquaintance with things, which are called concrete insofar as they are composite and finite participants in the act of existing. In order to sustain his criticism of sense experience, Hegel has to supply a definition of the concrete that is at odds with the one based on the perceptual judgment of existence, and that can therefore be used to expose the "abstractness" of sense-based knowledge. This is the type of circular reasoning which Hegel regards as inevitable, *within* the organic totality. It is not coercive, however, when it is measured against a direct inspection of our human acquaintance with the concrete existent.

The first application of this doctrine is made in the sphere of finite thought, when it regards itself as being distinct from its objects in the real world. Concepts formed within this context are *abstract thoughts* or *concepts of the understanding,* rather than concrete concepts of philosophical reason. The abstract determinations of thought or the understanding (*Gedanken- oder Verstandes-Bestimmungen*) are best exemplified by the universals of Aristotle.[22] The ordinary universal, constituted by genus and specific difference, is intended to signify the essence common to many individuals. In order to form this concept, the mind leaves out the individual differences. What remains is a general essence, that does not itself exist but that is embodied in many individual existents. Hegel allows a place for such universals of the understanding, within the finite order and the special sciences. They become objectionable only when they are taken as the ultimate instruments of *philosophical*

Insofar as any particular concept is distinguished from its object, it does entail a certain abstractness, for Hegel. Yet this is a dialectical distinction, destined to be overcome at the highest level, where absolute reason (as the absolute idea) reveals the identity between the concept and the object, in the concrete universal.

[22] *Science of Logic* (Johnston-Struthers, II, 234–57); *Encyclopaedia Logic,* 80, 163 (Wallace, 143–46, 291–94). Hegel sees the inadequacy of ordinary universals for metaphysical speculation, but his remedy is to inject an absolute, dialectical content into the concept, rather than to found metaphysics upon the finite and sense-grounded judgment of existence.

thinking. In the latter usage, they encourage men to take the realistic and finitistic view of the world as the definitive one. Hence Hegel proposes a more adequate, concrete type of concept: the concept of reason.

The *concepts of reason* are *concrete universals* and are the proper components of the dialectical method. They include the individual differences explicitly and actually, along with the common features of things. They are formed not by evacuating the field of individuals but by assuming it into a rational unity. The concrete universal signifies what is found universally, and does so precisely insofar as this factor is embodied in the existing individuals of the kind. Hence the rational concept has intuitive content, as well as universal form and scope. In the concrete universal, there is a perfect interpenetration of form and content, such that the universal form has concrete content and the content itself enjoys a universal meaning. The concrete universal comes to life only by grasping the mutual relations among individuals. The concrete universal expresses the rationality of being, and hence signifies the *unity-in-difference* and the *connectedness* of actual beings. The more the togetherness of things is comprehended, the more adequate is the concrete universal. There are various grades of such concepts, based upon mounting degrees of concreteness and comprehensiveness. Ultimately, however, every concept, on this side of the absolute idea itself, bears a certain trace of abstractness or one-sidedness. There is only one unconditionally adequate, concrete universal: the *absolute or divine idea,* which is one with the absolute mind in the state of self-possession. To attain this fully concrete and self-determined concept, to bring it to rational formulation — this is the goal of all philosophy and of life's polar tensions.

A second application of the Hegelian teaching on concreteness is made in dealing with *empiricism.*[23] Locke and his followers traced back all universals to individual impressions and eventually to individual existents, causing these impressions in the mind. As Hegel sees it, this empiricist explanation of universals suffers from the

---

[23] *Encyclopaedia Logic,* 37–39 (Wallace, 76–82). Empiricism recognizes that truth must rest upon actually given existents, but it confines itself to individual and transient objects of sense and to the method of analysis. Hegel criticizes empiricism for failing to recognize its own reliance upon suprasensuous, metaphysical categories, as well as for refusing to rise above the abstract universals provided by the analytic method of the finite understanding.

abstractness of both perceptual impressions and finite existents. The finite individuality of these impressions and their external causes is an indication that they express the totality of actual being only in a partial and, therefore, abstract way. Hence even the so-called empirical, concrete individual is itself an abstraction, since it is not fully impregnated with universal mind. The concrete universal cannot be a mere *summation* of individual impressions and entities. It must *organize* these elements within the total, rational pattern of things, within the all-embracing concretion provided by absolute spirit. This is Hegel's solution to the perennial problem of the one-and-the-many. It guarantees the objects of philosophical knowledge, by making their divine and rational ground wholly immanent in the concrete order.

3. The contribution of *negativity* and *mediation* to the philosophical concept and method can now be weighed. These factors are required, if the vital and concrete traits of philosophy are to be respected. For if the concept is to be truly vital, it must respect the tendency of life to differentiate itself and to include that which is *other*. Similarly, the rule of concreteness requires that the concept correct the one-sidedness or abstractness of any particular nature, by making reference to what it is *not*. The philosophical concept cannot be confined to sheer immediacy or intuition, without thwarting the rational movement to locate a thing or a thought in terms of its relations or systematic connections with other points of reference. This demands reflection, comparison, and therefore mediation of the concept in a rational system.

The role of mediation and negativity is brought out by analysis of the *pattern of dialectical movement*.[24] Living, spiritual actuality develops from an implicit to an explicit state. Its possibilities are realized in and through this transition, which is rigidly governed by the end set for itself by absolute spirit. There is a common, rhythmic pattern displayed by all the varieties of passage from implicit to explicit, from potential to actual self-possession, on the part of the absolute spirit. The three phases or moments in this triadic development are: *thesis, antithesis,* and *synthesis.* Fichte referred to them as: position, op-position, and com-position. Hegel's technical designations

[24] Cf. *The Phenomenology of Mind,* Preface (Baillie, 80–88, 107–13); *Science of Logic* (Johnston-Struthers, I, 36, 65–68; II, 63–70, 468–80); *Encyclopaedia Logic,* 79–82, 214 (Wallace, 143–54, 356). Significantly, the dialectical movement is usually explained in conjunction with an exposition of the nature of the absolute as spirit, concept, and idea.

are: *An-sich-sein* (being-in-itself), *Ausser-sich-sein* or *Für-sich-sein* (being-external-to-itself or being-for-itself), and *An-und-für-sich-sein* (being-in-and-for-itself). The first moment of the dialectic is that of abstraction, the second that of dialectic (in a narrower sense), the third that of speculation. Hegel strives to prevent this analysis from degenerating into a mechanical formula, capable of automatic application. In practice, and especially in the study of nature, he allows many variations and exceptions. But in principle, this triadic schema governs all manifestations of thought and being, since it expresses the fundamental law according to which absolute spirit undergoes self-determination. The threefold dialectical principle, rather than the principle of contradiction, is the governing law of Hegel's philosophy.

### A PHASE IN THE DIALECTIC OF THE ABSOLUTE

| | Logical | Ontological | Phenomenological |
|---|---|---|---|
| 1. **Thesis** or moment of abstraction. | Position: in-itself. | Immediate determination: substance or being as implicit. | Untroubled immediacy: intuition. |
| 2. **Antithesis** or moment of dialectic. | Op-position or negation: external-to-itself, for-itself. | Alienation from immediacy, self-determination: subject or self as explicit. | Unhappy consciousness: reflection and self-estrangement. Mediation. |
| 3. **Synthesis** or speculative truth. | Com-position or negation of negation: in-and-for-itself. Sublation of contradictories in concrete universal concept. | Living, concrete actuality as synthesis of substance and subject, essence and existence. | Reintegration or reconciliation within the developed self: cultural maturity through unification of opposites. |

N.B. Any moment in the dialectic can be analyzed in logical, ontological, or phenomenological terms.

It is convenient to discuss thesis and antithesis together. No nature, posited in a finite way, can exist or be conceived without generating its opposite. For, the positing principle is on the track of a more adequate concrete universal. In determining itself as some particular content of thought or being (which appear as distinct, at the finite level), reason is thereby committing itself to something less than the totality possible at this stage. Hegel repeats Spinoza's dictum that *every determination includes a negation:* every thesis calls forth its own antithesis. No matter how empirically concrete the existent or the idea, it is only a partial actualization and hence is, to that extent, abstract. It is a one-sided position, eliciting its own opposition, in the form of a contrary or contradictory counterprinciple. One of the unsatisfactory features of the Hegelian dialectic is its consistent blurring of the difference between opposites related as *contraries* and opposites related as *contradictories.* Many cited instances of "creative contradiction" are only cases of relation among contraries, what Aristotelian philosophy would refer to (less dramatically) as the relation between a contingent act and its privation. But Hegel is obliged to sharpen the antagonisms, wherever possible, for only in this way will the dialectic seem to be an autonomous whole, driven ahead solely by its own internal combustive forces.

Hegel expresses this claim to dialectical self-propulsion in his doctrine on "the *portentous power of the negative,*"[25] or the creative function of the moment of antithesis. The second stage in the dialectic is intended to break through the narrowness of the original position. By bringing out what is other than the thesis, the state of being-external-to-itself helps to develop what is only latent and potential in the state of being-in-itself. The function of negation is not only negative but also, and primarily, positive: it renders explicit and determinate the germ of truth that was only implicit in the original thesis. This second moment underscores the truth of the converse of the Spinozistic axiom: *every negation also includes a determination.* The antithesis expresses a definite content, which supplements the given abstractness of the first moment. The immediately given condition of being-in-itself must submit to the law of life: unless a thing die, it cannot have life more abundantly. Its vital energy must pass out of this immediate state into the opposite state of being-external-to-itself, a state of fruitful negation or *mediation.* In establishing a certain distance from its immediately given condition, however, a being uncovers its own nature and thus returns upon itself through reflection. At the level of conscious life, this passage may be described as a transition from an unreflective to a reflective attitude, from an immediate preoccupation with other things to a condition of being-

---

[25] *The Phenomenology of Mind,* Preface (Baillie, 93; italics mine).

for-itself. The conscious subject must, as it were, place itself at arm's length, assume a critical attitude toward itself, in order to bring the original state of implicit self-awareness to explicit self-consciousness. The self passes from being merely a thing existing in itself, to being an object *reflectively for* itself.

Hegel refers to the negative or dialectical moment as one of *self-externality* and *self-estrangement* (self-alienation). Although these notions have gained new currency in contemporary psychiatric studies, Hegel employs them in a perfectly general metaphysical way, as applications of negativity at all levels of thought and being. Estrangement from the security of one's immediate possession of content is a universal requirement. This self-diremption is imposed by the finite, abstract character of all particular content, as well as by the law that genuine actuality is found only in the togetherness or integration of all the members of the system. Every posited thesis must absent itself from the felicity of its own immediate condition, so that it may open itself to the other factors in the whole of truth and actuality. It must pass out of itself, become stranger to itself, in order to generate the dialectical movement toward rational concreteness and universality, in accord with the overruling purposes of absolute spirit.

Where does the saving concretion lie: in the thesis or in the antithesis? Hegel answers that it lies in neither one, taken by itself. Each is a partial manifestation, embodying a positive factor and yet generating its opposite, because of its own abstractness. Because the Kantian antinomies are formulated within a purely formal and finite perspective, they have no positive metaphysical outcome. But Hegel regards his relation of thesis and antithesis as an instrument used by absolute spirit to achieve its own ends. Hence he has a priori assurance that the *coincidentia oppositorum* will bear fruit in a *concrete synthesis*. Indeed, thesis and antithesis are real only insofar as they express moments in a total dialectical movement, whose entire course is *finalized* by reference to the resultant synthesis. In retrospect, one can affirm that it is the rational concept as such that determines itself as an immediate position and then — always in its own interest of explicating an organic whole — passes over into opposition or externality to itself. Because the entire contradictory relationship is grounded in self-bifurcating spirit, the opposites can fertilize each other and give birth to a crowning synthesis. Because the synthesis marks a progressive phase in the self-manifestation of absolute spirit, this third dialectical stage is called the *speculative* moment. It has its guarantee and its principle of interpretation in the radical basis of all speculative philosophy: the doctrine on absolute spirit.

Dialectical materialists repudiate absolute spirit, but like to use the illustration of the seed (thesis), which must fall into the ground and die to itself (antithesis), so that the splendid tree and fruit may grow up (synthesis). *Biological metaphors* permeate Hegel's own discussion of the dialectical method. Life is a process of antagonism and reconciliation, differentiation and reintegration. Without the latter, the dialectical process would be a self-dissipating one, leading only to death. There must be a resolution of forces, a reaping of the harvest, a recuperation of both immediacy and otherness in a synthesis. The technical term for the final moment in the dialectical movement is *sublation* or *Aufhebung*. It means at once: to annul, to preserve, and to elevate.[26] All three senses of the word are required by Hegel's theory of dialectical synthesis.

First, there must be the *annulment* of the false claim, made by each particular thing or concept, to be complete and self-sufficient. The abstractness of both thesis and antithesis must be removed. Once this is done, the concern of dialectical reason is to *preserve* the kernel of positive truth, contained in both sides of the opposition. This involves the negation of negation itself, insofar as it is merely a negative protest against the exclusiveness of the thesis. By reference to each other, thesis and antithesis lose their exclusiveness and find their positive content preserved. Yet the special insights of the opposing members in the dialogue are not merely juxtaposed in their original form. They interpenetrate each other and thus become transformed in a new synthesis. This *elevation* to a higher plane of meaning is a qualitatively different expression of the rational concept, a new embodiment of concrete actuality. The *Aufhebung* makes return to the original thesis, but enriches the latter with the experience of otherness and alienation from oneself. There is a new sort of immediacy, one which is more mature and disciplined for having undergone the tension of negativity. The synthesis is a state of being-in-and-for-itself, a concrete universal. It is *in* itself, insofar as its elevated condition retains the values of substantial content and intuitive immediacy. But it affirms its self-identity across the vale of becoming and self-estrangement, so that the concretion is also

---

[26] *Science of Logic* (Johnston-Struthers, I, 119–20).

reflectively *for* itself. Just as the absolute spirit as such is both substance and subject, so any synthetic moment in the dialectical development of this absolute spirit shows forth this oneness of substance and subject, inner content and critical appraisal.

What has been analyzed so far is only a representative triadic *segment* of the entire dialectical process. Each synthesis must now be replaced within its *total setting*. Although in respect to its own thesis-and-antithesis it is a concrete universal, it is still finite, partial, and abstract, in relation to the organic totality of truth and actuality. From this standpoint, any particular synthesis becomes, in turn, a thesis for a new dialectical development. It generates its own antithesis and thus lays the ground for further qualitative progress toward the goal proposed by absolute spirit. This goal is the achievement of the full truth of the rational concept or concrete universal. *"The true is the whole."*[27] In this sense, Hegel's theory of truth is one of *coherence,* only because it is one of *organic totality.* The unqualified truth lies only in the complete articulation of all systematic connections, in a single dialectical vision. Hegel's criterion of coherence cannot stand alone. By itself, it assures only the logical agreement and relatedness of various elements of thought with each other, according to a dialectical principle of interconnection. This would be no more than a formal standard, were it not for Hegel's association of coherence with the unity of thought and being, in the absolute spirit. The only way in which he can assure the *truth,* as well as *formal consistency,* of dialectically derived propositions is by invoking the conception of a single organic whole of mind and actuality. This standard is determined by the doctrine of absolute spirit. The type of coherence and organic relation required by the Hegelian dialectic is precisely that which might be supposed, if the absolute spirit were undergoing self-development. This is the sense in which the dialectic and the doctrine on the absolute spirit are strict correlatives. The dialectic leads to philosophical truth, only where philosophizing and the self-actualization of the absolute idea are identified.

It is often objected that, on Hegel's principles, there is no intrinsic reason for the dialectic ever to reach its *consummation,* since the series of dialectical opposites is endlessly self-generative. From the standpoint of Hegelian methodology, this is not a fatal objection.

---

[27] *The Phenomenology of Mind,* Preface (Baillie, 81; italics added and translation modified).

For, what prods the dialectic onward to a new stage, is precisely the failure of the given synthesis to achieve the end set for the dialectical process by absolute reason. New antitheses will continue to crop out, as long as the synthesis is not the definitive concrete universal. But, by the same token, an ultimate consummation and rest are not only compatible with the dialectic but formally demanded by it. Once the absolute idea has been fully explicated or brought to rational expression in the concrete universal, there occurs a perfect, definitive over-coming and appropriation of the power of negativity. By definition, the *raison d'être* of dialectical movement is removed, so that there is no further function for negativity or the antithetic moment to fulfill.

Hegel's real problem lies in the contrary direction, in the attempt to give an intelligible account of how the dialectic is *already completed*. Like Aristotle's first mover, Hegel's absolute spirit is an unmoved mover. The movement of dialectical process and temporal development transpires somehow within the tranquillity of eternity. Poetically speaking, "the truth is thus the bacchanalian revel, where not a member is sober; and because every member no sooner becomes detached than it *eo ipso* collapses straightway, the revel is just as much a state of transparent unbroken calm."[28] The absolute already possesses its end in its beginning. It is at once *complete actuality* and a subject, purposively undergoing the process of dialectical *becoming* and *actualization*. Hegel lapses into poetry and paradox on this issue, in order to conceal the difficulties involved in his view of *philosophy*. Into the bosom of the absolute, he is forced to introduce the changes going on in the world and in the human mind, in order to back up the claims made for his philosophy. The dialectic can have ontological as well as logical import, and the synthetic moment is assured of its triumph as an expression of truth as well as of coherence, only on condition that the entire process transpire in and through the absolute mind. The truth and absoluteness of Hegelian philosophy have no other foundation than the identification of the dialectical process with the internal growth of infinite reason, which must already be in full possession of the goal, toward which it is dialectically progressing. This position endangers both temporal process and pure actuality, but Hegel is willing to pay this price, in order to give ontological weight to his philosophical analysis of the concepts of reason. He escapes the force of Kant's critique, only at the cost of proposing an

---

[28] *Loc. cit.* (Baillie, 105).

ineffable identity between real becoming, mental discursion, and divine actuality.

Hegel has revived, in the modern world, a major problem analogous to that which faced Plato in the ancient. Both thinkers are concerned about the relation between the one and the many, the universal concept and particulars. Hegel's criticism of Kantian formalism rests upon the fundamental objection that the Kantian forms of consciousness-in-general lead to a universal and necessary knowledge, in which particular things are insignificant. Hence Hegel seeks to refashion the

### HEGEL ON THE DEVELOPMENT OF THE ABSOLUTE CONCEPT

1. **Logic.**
   - a) **Being:**

     | 1) Quality. | 2) Quantity. | 3) Measure. |
     |---|---|---|

   - b) **Essence:**

     | 1) Essence as ground of existence. | 2) Appearance, existence. | 3) Actuality. |
     |---|---|---|

   - c) **Concept:**

     | 1) Subjective concept (concept as such, judgment, syllogism). | 2) Objective concept (mechanism, chemism, teleology). | 3) Idea (life, cognition, the absolute idea). |
     |---|---|---|

2. **Philosophy of Nature.**
   - a) **Mechanics:**

     | 1) Abstract mechanics (space and time). | 2) Finite mechanics (matter and motion). | 3) Absolute mechanics (gravitation, solar system, force). |
     |---|---|---|

   - b) **Physics:**

     | 1) Physics of individuality in general (the elements). | 2) Physics of particular individuality (specific gravitation, cohesion, sound, heat). | 3) Physics of total individuality. |
     |---|---|---|

   - c) **Organics:**

     | 1) Mineral nature. | 2) Vegetal nature. | 3) Animal organism. |
     |---|---|---|

3. *Philosophy of Concrete Spirit.*

a) Subjective spirit:

| 1) Anthropology: the soul. | 2) Phenomenology: consciousness (consciousness proper, self-consciousness, reason). | 3) Psychology: mind (theoretical, practical, and free mind). |
|---|---|---|

b) Objective spirit:

| 1) Right (property, contract, wrong). | 2) Morality (purpose, intention and welfare, the good and conscience). | 3) Ethical life (the family, civil society, the state . . . history). |
|---|---|---|

c) Absolute spirit:

| 1) Art. | 2) Religion. | 3) Philosophy, the completely developed concrete universal concept: absolute spirit in concrete actuality. |
|---|---|---|

forms of thought in such a way that, at least at the philosophical level of reason, they include particulars within the meaning of the universal. He sees that the type of abstraction used to obtain the concepts of the understanding, leaves out the individual traits and therefore cannot provide philosophical reason with its basis in a real world of individual things. Hence he has recourse to the dialectical method, as a remedy for the abstractness and emptiness of the ordinary universal. Precisely here, the parting of the ways occurs between Hegel and a realism of being. The latter would rely upon the completely finite and human operation of *judgment,* in order to supply metaphysically adequate concepts. It would base the metaphysically appropriate concept of being upon the existential judgment concerning singular, finite existents, together with the judgment denying that being and the act of existing are confined to the sensible manner of being. But Hegel seeks to reinstate particulars directly, *within the universal concept.* This he does by employing the principle of negativity, giving to nonbeing a power of its own, intrinsic to the concept. To guarantee that the particular determinations and negations do issue in a universal, rational whole, however, he must further maintain that their signification is real, as well as logical. This leads to the dialectical identification between the phases in his logical system and those in the absolute spirit's development. Like Plato's "participation," this "dialectical identification" specifies the universal principle of rational unity, but it does not establish its presence in finite things in such a way that the integral nature of the latter is preserved. Finite, temporal being and human history are engulfed in the atemporal immanence of the eternal spirit, thus justifying William James' remark that the doctrine of the absolute is "the great de-realizer of the only life we are at home in."[29]

The Hegelian dialectic of the rational concept is not only *about* the absolute: it *is* the absolute in its self-development. The course of dialectical progression is also the history of the coming-to-be of the absolute spirit. There are three broad phases in the absolute's self-actualization, constituting the three widest divisions of Hegelian philosophy. First, the divine idea is in the state of being-in-itself, which is studied by *logic*. Then, the divine idea "releases its content." It is alienated from itself and passes over into the condition of being-external-to-itself or nature, which is the content of *philosophy of nature*. Finally, the divine idea returns to itself as being-in-and-for-itself, a synthesis expressed in the *philosophy of concrete spirit*. Logic, philosophy of nature, and philosophy of concrete spirit thus comprise the all-inclusive triad of moments in the development of absolute idealism, since they articulate the three inclusive moments in the becoming of absolute spirit itself. Only in the total system of philosophy is truth realized as a systematic, organic whole, and only in the truth of this totality is the divine actuality fully present to itself in the rational concept or concrete universal.

## 6. SPECULATIVE LOGIC

The discussion on philosophical method has already verged upon the domain of logic, since the theory of method is a reflection upon the

[29] William James, *A Pluralistic Universe* (in the one-volume edition of *Essays in Radical Empiricism* and *A Pluralistic Universe* [New York, Longmans, Green, 1943]; separate pagination for each work), 49. Consult the second and third lectures, respectively, in *A Pluralistic Universe*, on "Monistic Idealism" and "Hegel and His Method," for James' empiricist criticism of absolute idealism. In his "Essai sur la logique de Hegel," *Revue Internationale de Philosophie*, VI (1952), 35–49, J. Hyppolite shows that the conflict in Hegel between absolutism and a humanism of time and history stems from his view that man does not make philosophy but that, through human thinking, philosophy or the absolute spirit makes itself and reconstitutes metaphysics as the equivalent of logic.

spontaneous movement undergone by the content of logic. There is a strict proportion between the *what* and the *how* of logic, between its content and its method. Furthermore, the method and content of speculative logic hold valid for the entire field of philosophy, since they are one with the self-unfolding of absolute spirit, according to its own all-pervasive pattern. It is this metaphysical interpretation of the findings of his logic that gives it so predominant a role in Hegel's philosophy.

Both traditional formal logic and Kantian transcendental logic are assimilated within the higher standpoint of the idealistic *speculative logic*. The value of formal logic is to have studied the structures of thought at the level of ordinary understanding. Its contribution is to insure accuracy and analytic distinctness in our inferences. But it fails to uncover the ultimate implications of finite thinking, especially the truth that all human thinking is a manifestation of the absolute mind. Hence the absolute, ontological validity of the forms of thought escapes the notice of formal logic. It also eludes the Kantian logic, which regards the categories as formal structures, empty of objective content. Kant holds that the *categories* would be without meaning for an intuitive, divine understanding, whereas Hegel views them as *self-determinations of absolute mind*, in its own thought and development. Hence he deems it misleading to speak depreciatingly of categories as "mere" forms of thought. Logic is "pure thought" and a "shadow-realm," indeed, but only in the sense of being intrinsically independent of sensuous sources and biased interests, not in the sense of being a pale and ineffective set of abstractions.[30] The structures of pure thought are eternal and necessary categories, that also function as the internal structure of the things of experience. Speculative logic studies logical forms not only as laws of reasoning but also as containing the objective, substantial essences and real laws of things. For "it is just Reason which is that substantial or real [principle], which holds together in itself all abstract determinations, and is their solid absolutely concrete unity."[31] Since the logical categories are also the self-determinations and self-definitions of absolute reason or spirit, they contain their own intuitive content and objectivity.

This permits Hegel to make the bold assertion that logic or the realm of pure thought is:

---

[30] *Science of Logic* (Johnston-Struthers, I, 60, 69–70).

[31] *Ibid.* (Johnston-Struthers, I, 58; cf. II, 227–30). See *Encyclopaedia Logic*, 160 (Wallace, 287–88).

*the Truth as it is, without husk in and for itself.* One may therefore express it thus: that this content *shows forth God as he is in his eternal essence before the creation of Nature and of a Finite Spirit.*[32]

Hegel's logic embodies the main moment of the *thesis,* in the over-all triad constituting philosophical science. It studies the rational concept or idea in its original condition as being-in-itself, "before" (without temporal connotation) the absolute spirit has passed over into its antithetic condition as nature, and "before" it has started to recover nature, through human consciousness. Logic gazes at the forms of pure thought from the speculative standpoint of absolute idealism; hence it apprehends the *truth* in its proper nature, without any husk or disguise of finitude. Although the laws and categories of pure thought are the same as those of nature and concrete spirit, the logician cannot facilely read off the traits of nature and concrete mind by an a priori deduction. The application of logical categories is always a *dialectical* process, that must conform with the conditions found in the other stages of development. When these conditions are respected, however, philosophy of nature and of concrete spirit can be considered as an applied logic, an exhibition of the categorial self-determinations of reason.

By healing the breach between form and content, speculative logic also binds together *truth,* as an objective state, and *certainty,* as a subjective conviction. Truth is not a conformity between thought and an independent thing but a correspondence of the rational concept with itself and, ultimately, with the totality of concepts. Hence systematic, rational thinking engenders not only subjective certainty but also objective truth, insofar as the nature of the concept is rendered explicit and exhibited as a rational whole. The distinctive task of speculative logic is to show that being itself has a conceptual principle at its basis, and that it is orientated toward the full expression of the concept. Hence the three divisions of Hegel's *Science of Logic* are: (*a*) thesis: *being;* (*b*) antithesis: *essence;* (*c*) synthesis: the *concept,* known precisely as concept.

The crucial problem in the thesis or *doctrine on being* is: *how to begin the dialectic,* since in a way this is also the absolute beginning of logic and philosophy as such. This problem corresponds to the previous one, met with in the *Phenomenology,* of how to introduce ordinary experience to the standpoint of absolute idealism. Hegel admits

---

[32] *Ibid.* (Johnston-Struthers, I, 60).

that this problem of a beginning can arise only for a *finite* mind, which has been elevated to the plane of the absolute and which must establish some sort of sequence among its thoughts about the totality of absolute truth. The difficulties he encounters in settling this issue, both in the *Phenomenology* and in the *Science of Logic,* are an indication that the finite traits of the human mind continue stubbornly to resist sublation into the absolute system.

In one sense, a beginning is made in logic, and in another sense a beginning is not made here. An unconditioned start is *not* made here, because finite consciousness must already have been educated phenomenologically, up to the point where natural and philosophical consciousness merge in an affirmation of the identity between thought and being. To this extent, the *Science of Logic* is dependent upon the *Phenomenology* for establishing the absolute oneness of thought and being (in the perspective of the absolute spirit), as the condition for all scientific thinking in philosophy, including logic. A beginning *is* made in logic, however, by deliberately disregarding the previous educative process, and resolving to expound philosophy *de jure* or according to its own proper order, regardless of any empirical prolegomena. A fresh start can be made only with what lies at hand for the mind that has been phenomenologically educated, viz., pure thought or absolute knowledge. But instead of treating this truth in all its richness, the logician makes a total evacuation of its content. Pure thought is accepted as a bare fact, of which one can only say that it *is*. This is equivalent to defining the absolute in the most abstract and indeterminate way, by calling it a *being*. "Being is here the beginning represented as arising from mediation, a mediation which transcends itself; it being assumed that pure knowledge is the result of finite knowledge, or consciousness."[33] By assuming that the standpoint of

---

[33] *Science of Logic* (Johnston-Struthers, I, 81). Part One of this work starts with a section inquiring: "With What must the Science begin?" (Johnston-Struthers, I, 79–90; cf. II, 222–23); the same question is treated in *Encyclopaedia Logic,* 17, 163, 236 (Wallace, 27–28, 293–94, 374). Hegel distinguishes between an *individual man's psychological* beginning of philosophical thought, and the true initiative taken by the onward-driving *concept* itself. In the latter sense, there is no absolute beginning of philosophy but a self-clarification of the concept, which returns to itself in a purely circular movement. O. Lee, "Method and System in Hegel," *The Philosophical Review,* XLVIII (1939), 355–80, points out that Hegel never resolved this question of whether philosophy has a genuine beginning or is a closed circle of self-sufficient speculation, because he never resolved the relationship between method and system. As a *methodic human* inquiry, philosophy involves a speculative (and not merely a psychological) beginning, and a course of discovery. As a self-contained *system of*

absolute knowledge is already won, the logician sublates the process of mediation or phenomenological education of the mind. This enables him to make a genuine, if bare, start with being.

Only in the light of the problem of the beginning of philosophizing, can one appreciate Hegel's initial logical doctrine on being. He organizes his materials around the well-known triad: *being, nothing, becoming*.[34] Being and nothing are related as thesis and antithesis, out of which issues becoming, as the synthesis. The concept of being, which serves here as the thesis, is by no means the same as the confused notion that accompanies our first existential judgments. Being, in this latter sense, has been sublated in the phenomenological elevation of the mind. Hegel does not start with the finite and sensuously presented real act of being, but rather with a concept of being that is nothing other than an utterly indeterminate way of regarding pure thought or absolute knowledge itself. The being of Hegel's primary thesis is the result of a total evacuation of determinate meaning, and the initial term of this "abstraction" is not the *existential act of finite being* but the *known identity between pure thought and actuality*. The Hegelian concept of being is a way of taking absolute reason or thought as an immediate fact, undifferentiated from any particular thing. Taken in this way, being is an empty abstraction, and Hegel is fully justified in declaring that it generates its own negation, which can only be nothing. Applying the dialectical principle, it also follows that being and nothing are one and the same, having the identity of inseparable opposites. The mind intends to keep them distinct, but at this wholly indeterminate stage of the rational concept, no further specification is permitted.

The Aristotelian principle of contradiction is not affected, however, by this dialectical explanation. As explained by Aristotle and Aquinas, this principle is not a purely formal principle of abstract thought. It is also, and primarily, a principle governing real being.

---

*absolute spirit*, it has no beginning but also ceases to be a human discipline. In terms of his writings, Hegel failed to synthesize the *Phenomenology* and the *Science of Logic*, since the former work called attention to features of human experience that did not conform with his dialectical definition of experience. For Sören Kierkegaard's comments on this problem, see *A Kierkegaard Anthology* (edited by R. Bretall), 197–201.

34 *Science of Logic* (Johnston-Struthers, 94–120); *Encyclopaedia Logic*, 86–88 (Wallace, 156–69). On this dialectic as the transition from experience (the *Phenomenology*) to rational thought (the *Science of Logic*), cf. E. Coreth, S.J., *Das dialektische Sein in Hegels Logik*, 118–35.

The meaning of the first principle of being is derived from an inspection of the significance of our existential and separative judgments about finite, sensibly existent things, rather than from a process of emptying-out the content of the notion of pure science or absolute knowledge. The real basis of the conflict between these metaphysical views of being and its first principles lies in the discussion of sense experience and existential judgment, rather than in the quite special construction of the dialectic between being and nothing. From the realistic standpoint, Hegel's initial concept of being, in the *Science of Logic,* must be appraised in the light of his previous argument for identifying pure thought and actuality, as presented in the *Phenomenology.* It cannot be evaluated solely in terms of his theory of dialectic, because of the circular relation between this theory and the logical doctrine as a whole.

Hegel has no difficulty in showing, dialectically, that the synthesis of being and nothing is *becoming.* For the indeterminate concepts of being and nothing are incessantly passing over into each other, after the manner of thesis and antithesis. This "passing over" or conceptual movement is the logical nature of becoming, and only this third moment is properly concrete. As befits thetic and antithetic concepts, being and nothing are abstract moments, which gain their hold upon the concrete only through their reference to the synthesis of becoming. Logic and philosophy as a whole begin with the recognition that *pure thought is a dialectical becoming,* and that only in and through this becoming is the concrete universal achieved.

The two remaining parts of the *Science of Logic* — the doctrine on essence and that on the concept known as such — record the story of the mind's restless search after the nature of pure thought, in the state of being-in-itself. This dialectical investigation is governed by the internal necessities contained in the rational concept, since it represents the self-explication of the concept. In the *doctrine on essence* (*Wesen,* "nature"), pure being begins to undergo determination, by passing over into the state of logical otherness or essence. The high point is reached in the theory of *actuality* (*Wirklichkeit,* which Hegel distinguishes from, and places higher than, mere empirical reality or *Realität*).[35] The actual springs from the dialectical union of the inward and outward aspects of being, the essential core and the existential

---

[35] *Science of Logic* (Johnston-Struthers, II, 160–205); *Encyclopaedia Logic,* 142–59 (Wallace, 257–86).

appearance. As it arises out of the possibilities of essence and existence, actuality reveals itself as their necessary law. But actuality is
that sort of necessity in which are plunged the roots of truly spiritual
freedom, as the later portions of the philosophy of concrete spirit are
intended to show.

The *doctrine on the concept* as such explains how being and
essence can be synthesized, once the mind discovers a conceptual
foundation for both. Hegel treats the concept as such in a triadic way:
subjectively, objectively, and as the absolute idea. The *subjective* aspect
of the concept incorporates most of the traditional, logical teaching
on judgment and syllogism. The *objective* categories of the concept
foreshadow the formal determinations of philosophy of nature, under
the three headings of mechanism, chemism, and teleology. Finally,
mind recognizes that its search after the developed actuality of the
concrete universal is satisfied only by taking the rational concept as
the *absolute idea,* the integration of both the good and the true in
absolute self-knowledge. This climax of speculative logic provides, at
the same time, the *leitmotiv* for subsequent discussions in the domain
of the concrete spirit.

## 7. PHILOSOPHY OF NATURE AND THE DOCTRINE
## ON SUBJECTIVE SPIRIT

Hegel's *philosophy of nature* is the least developed and least sure-
footed section of his system. The only extended exposition is the
second part of the *Encyclopaedia,* together with some accompanying
lecture notes, taken down by his students and added by the editor of
his collected works. This is one field where the dialectic grinds out
its triads remorselessly, mechanically, and sometimes with high disdain for the contemporary sciences. Because of methodic requirements, Hegel was led to criticize Newton intemperately in astronomy
and optics. Sometimes, he did recognize the inadequacy of his triadic
schemes for the study of nature. Nevertheless, he took this failure
as an occasion for explaining, dialectically, the intractability of empirical facts to his analysis, rather than for reforming the dialectic in the
light of its actual performance.

As Fichte and Schelling had already suggested, *nature* is the idea
in the state of otherness.[36] The rational concept now leaves the logical

---

[36] *Encyclopaedia of the Philosophical Sciences,* Part II, *Philosophy of Nature,* Introduction on the Concept of Nature, 245–51 (*Sämmtliche Werke, Kritische Ausgabe,*

sphere in order to become its own opposite, its own negation of pure thought and rationality. Nature is external to the idea, in the dialectical sense of constituting the moment of being-external-to-itself, which is one with the antithetic negation of the logical order of being-in-itself. The success with which reason carries out this "cunning" process of self-estrangement is testified by the conviction of common-sense realism and the special sciences that nature is completely extramental and independently existent. When philosophy is in its formative period, it shares this naïve view of common sense and the sciences. Only after it has attained to its full maturity, as the system of absolute idealism, does philosophy rest upon its own proper foundation in the rational concept and thus rescue itself from thralldom to the realistic outlook on nature.

From the basic dialectical premise that nature is the divine idea or spirit in the form of otherness, Hegel assures himself about three general features of nature: its contradictoriness, impotence, and hierarchy. The first two marks follow, at once, from its relation to the realm of logic. Far from being wholly nonmental, nature is nothing other than mind in alienation from itself, the idea in a fallen state. The rational concept, taken in the state of being-external-to-itself, does not fully express itself in, and assert its power over, its own outward manifestations. Nature's *contradictory* features stem from this incommensurability between the essential concept and the existential appearances, which results in a failure to achieve the synthesis of genuine actuality. Hence nature is a region of law and lawlessness, necessity and contingency, determination and indetermination. Nature is also basically *impotent*: it does not remain true to its categories, and does not shape all its events in a rationally conformable and orderly way. We detect the general traces of rational determination but they seem to peter out in individual instances, and to be flaunted in the case of anomalies and monsters.

Hegel's theory of the discrepancies between his own rational categories and the empirical evidence, available to common sense or uncovered by the sciences, explains too much. For, it can be used to justify *any* dialectical view of nature taken by Hegelian reason, oper-

---

Vol. V [edited by J. Hoffmeister], 202–08). A sympathetic exposition is given by E. E. Harris, "The Philosophy of Nature in Hegel's System," *The Review of Metaphysics*, III (1949–1950), 213–28; a critical evaluation, in terms of scientific method, is provided by É. Meyerson, *De l'explication dans les sciences* (Paris, Payot, 1921), 343–505.

ating solely in conformity with its own systematic necessities. Reason thereby "masters" the contingent facts and scientific laws, without being genuinely regulated or affected by them. Hegel's dialectic extends to the *idea of contingency* but not to *contingent modes of being*. The former can easily be accommodated under the rubric of reason's self-estrangement, but the latter suppose some potential and finite principle of being, which is irreducible to an ideal factor, considered in a state of otherness. The full scandal of contingent existents and anomalous events is covered up, rather than accounted for, by the a priori deduction from the nature of dialectic and by the metaphorical references to the idea in a fallen state of impotence. Neither ordinary experience nor scientific investigation is clarified by such remarks.

In his defense of the *hierarchy in nature*, Hegel hastens to affirm that nature's weakness is only the obverse side of the idea's indomitable strength. From the fact of graded modes of natural being, he concludes, not simply that there are various grades of essences and an intelligent author of nature, but that these essential grades represent so many stages in the development and self-recovery of the absolute spirit itself. He arranges his philosophy of nature according to the dialectical triad of the *mechanical, physical,* and *organic* stages of nature. The organism is the apex of nature's dialectical growth, as well as the culmination of nature's inherent contradictoriness. It is both organized from within and at the mercy of external circumstances. Yet there is one natural organism — man — which can deliberately face its own death, reflect upon it, and conquer death through this reflection. The appearance of *human consciousness* in the womb of nature reveals that the realm of nature is not so much *non*spiritual as *pre*spiritual. Nature is mind in a dreaming, self-forgetful phase. But in human consciousness, the rational mind — already at work in and as nature — begins to recover its own true nature.

Human consciousness thus marks the point of transition from the second great moment in philosophy to the third: it is the bridge between philosophy of nature and *philosophy of concrete spirit*. Through the agency of man, spirit completes its odyssey from being-in-itself and being-external-to-itself to its proper state of self-possession, as being-in-and-for-itself. The major moments in the dialectic of concrete spirit are: *subjective, objective,* and *absolute* spirit. Subjective spirit is subdivided, in turn, into the subordinate triad of anthropology, phenomenology, and psychology. Under the heading of *anthropology,*

Hegel treads the body-mind problem, sensation and feeling. The section on *phenomenology* condenses the development of mind from naïve consciousness to self-consciousness and reason, going over the materials of the *Phenomenology of Spirit,* but now from the standpoint of absolute philosophy.

The last phase in the doctrine of subjective spirit is devoted to a *psychological* account of spirit. Its importance comes from its specification of the subjective powers belonging to mind and its description of *der freie Geist,* the free human individual.[37] Mind or spirit includes both *theoretical* and *practical* elements. On the theoretical or cognitive side, it consists of: intuition, imagination, remembrance, and rational thinking. But spirit would be incomplete without the practical or appetitive factors of feeling, instincts, and will. These various powers do not exist side by side, but are ways of viewing reason itself in its far-flung relations and operations. Their synthesis in *the free individual* marks the perfection of subjective spirit. Only the will that unites the theoretical and practical aspects of spirit, is a free will or free intelligence. The rationally free will has content and a goal to achieve: to give existential embodiment to its own ideal essence in a free actuality. The proper zone of its activities is in human ethical institutions. In order to actualize the ideal of *rational freedom,* spirit cannot remain in the subjective sphere any longer but must pass over into the objective order of ethics and history.

## 8. THE ETHICAL ORDER AND HISTORY

Hegel's doctrine on *objective spirit* is perhaps the clearest and most persuasive section of his philosophy. It is certainly the one in which he has made best use of his wide observations of men and events. The free individual sets himself the task of molding nature into a world that embodies and subserves human purposes. The three moments of development of objective spirit, in pursuit of this aim, are: *right, morality,* and *ethical life.* Hegelian ethics is constructed through the dialectical contrast between right and morality, along with their synthesis in concrete ethical life. Right expresses the abstract thesis, concerning objective demands; morality expresses the equally abstract antithesis, concerning the subjective duty of the individual; the ethical life resolves these extremes in the state, as the supreme synthesis of objective spirit. Once the standpoint of the state

---

[37] *Philosophy of Mind,* 481–82 (Wallace, 237–39).

as an ethical institution is attained, it is also possible to gain insight into the nature and ends of history.

*Right* (*Recht, jus*) is the sphere in which freedom gives itself an immediate form in the outer world, according to the three submoments: property, contract, and wrong.[38] Hegel had read, with profit, the views of both the Roman jurists and modern economists (such as Say and Ricardo) on the basis of *property* and material value. The material things of nature have no "soul" and no end in themselves. They are there for appropriation by human will and hence for elevation to the human level, through the imprint of man's labor. Since the will in question is that of an individual person, it is a single and exclusive will. The right it claims over material goods is similarly exclusive, so that in actual fact property becomes *private* property. Despite his agreement with Locke on the personal basis of property, Hegel has a much firmer grasp on its social aspect. As the external embodiment of personality, property sets up a dual relationship: first, between the person and the whole world of things connected with his property, and second, between one person and another.

From the latter standpoint, the having of property depends upon recognition, by others, of one's right to it. This recognition is fundamentally a mutual respect for personality: it is a bond between human *will* and *will*, not merely between a will and a thing. *Contract* brings out this social and yet spiritual aspect of right, for here one enjoys the property right through the mediation of other personal wills, and not merely in virtue of exercising direct power over material things. The contracting parties are only related to each other in their immediate, singular existence, however, rather than through explicit reference to a universal principle of right. The latter is implicitly present in the contractual relation but is not formally integrated with the particular case. Hence there arises the possibility of discrepancy between the universal right and the private contractual terms. Conflict between the universal will of right and particular wills leads to a consideration of *wrong* or opposition to the principle of rightness. This is the penalty paid for the highly abstract and formal way in which right is first conceived by objective mind. As long as the bearer of right is a particular person in his immediate nature, wrong can exist.

---

[38] *Ibid.*, 488–502 (Wallace, 243–47); *Philosophy of Right*, 34–104 (Knox translation, 37–74). In his treatment of property, Hegel stresses ownership and possession, rather than use, although he states that the latter is more rational.

There is a gap between the capricious personal will and the universal will, underlying all mutual agreements about rights.

Reflection on the implications of wrong provides an impetus for the mind to pass from abstract, objective right to *morality* (*Moralität*). For, it becomes evident that wrong arises from an act of the particular will and that there is a failure to remove the contingency and immediacy of will. In order to fix moral responsibility, there must be a study of the person, not as the overlord of things or the nexus of objective rights, but precisely as an individual, moral subject. In sketching the standpoint of morality, Hegel draws largely upon Kant. The three phases of morality are: *purpose, intention and welfare, the good and conscience.*[39] Purpose and intention are both concerned with the conditions of moral responsibility. Action or the externalization of moral will belongs to the agent, only insofar as the action and its consequences are known to him and hence fall within his *purpose*. His accountability is proportionate to such purposive knowledge. *Intention* is only a deepening and broadening of moral purpose, so as to integrate the essential import of particular actions with their universal, systematic consequences. The mature moral subject perceives the wider context within which his deeds fit, and yet he views them mainly as satisfying his own *welfare* or needs-and-interests. His *conscience* is engaged profoundly with the problem of good and evil, precisely because of the clashes that inevitably arise among his various intentions and interests.

Moral consciousness tries to resolve the problem of *good and evil* in terms of *Kantian duty*. Hegel allows that the good resides in the universal will, but he adds that this Kantian formula is too abstract and indeterminate to be of much use in settling actual moral issues. Duties and goods are many and graded, so that they are often in collision and cannot be reconciled merely by appeal to the good will as such. Moral conflicts arise not only between duty and impulse but also among our several duties themselves. Kantian morality fails to specify an absolute end, in respect to which some kind of working subordination among duties and interests may be established. The dualisms between individual welfare and universal good, happiness and virtue, the empirical moral agent and the rational moral law, bring on a paralysis of all conduct attempting to base itself exclusively upon

---

[39] *Philosophy of Mind*, 503-12 (Wallace, 248-52); *Philosophy of Right*, 105-41 (Knox, 75-104).

Kant's precepts. Hegel sees that an *unconditioned end* is required for appraising actions that entail a conflict among duties and interests. His problem is to specify this end in such a way that the Kantian warning against heteronomous determination of freedom will also be respected. Hegel's own general doctrine on a self-developing absolute spirit is the only possible basis for combining absolute autonomy and the ordination of freedom to an unconditioned end. The only alternative, within a teleological ethics, would be to forego the claim to absolute autonomy and thus to retain the irreducible distinction between God and creatures.

Hegel's solution is to treat both objective right and morality as abstract moments, demanding sublation in the inclusive synthesis of *ethical life (Sittlichkeit)*.[40] This concrete ethical universality unites objective will and subjective freedom, legal personality and the intention of conscience. It does so by bringing out the *universal rational will,* as the explicit ruling principle of practical life. A passage is made from the *ought* of Kantian moral duty to the *is* of Hegel's rational totality of objective spirit. At the ethical plane, the particular agent comes to identify his own interests with those of the other individuals comprising the ethical totality, and all wills together are directed to the actualization of the universal good. The ethical concretion of objective spirit comes into being, only after the center of gravity for the will's efforts is transferred to the community as such. Rational freedom flowers in the *social whole,* within which particular persons have been integrated.

The three phases in the development of the ethical order are: the *family, civil society,* and the *state.*[41] Since these three moments are dialectically related, the state (as synthesis) must contain within it the sublated or *aufgehoben* forms of the family and civil society. Unlike the theorists of the totalitarian state, Hegel did not envisage

<hr/>

[40] The difficulties in this concept are discussed by E. F. Carritt, "Hegel's *Sittlichkeit,*" *Proceedings of the Aristotelian Society,* N.S., XXXVI (1935-1936), 223-36.

[41] *Philosophy of Mind,* 513-52 (Wallace, 253-90); *Philosophy of Right,* 142-360 (Knox, 105-223). See G. H. Sabine, "Hegel's Political Philosophy," *The Philosophical Review,* XLI (1932), 261-82; E. Weil, *Hegel et l'Etat* (Paris, Vrin, 1950), with an Appendix on "Marx and the *Philosophy of Right*" (105-16). The relations between Marx and Hegel are explained more at length by S. Hook, "Hegel and Marx," *Studies in the History of Ideas,* III (New York, Columbia University Press, 1935), 331-404. For a critical exposition of Hegel's thought, from the standpoint of its influence on Marx, cf. F. Grégoire, *Aux sources de la pensée de Marx: Hegel, Feuerbach* (Louvain, Editions de l'Institut Supérieur de Philosophie, 1947) — with a résumé of Feuerbach's system.

any bare relating of the individual to the state. It is as a member of the family and of some intermediate social groups that the individual is incorporated within the political whole. Hegel took a special interest in the writings of British and continental economists and social philosophers, concerning the divisive forces operating in modern society. Under the name of "civil society," he studied the clash of private and public interest in a laissez-faire economy, the role of social estates or classes in furthering social changes, and the specializations brought about by land, labor, machines, and bureaucracy. Karl Marx obtained his first hints about the critique of industrial capitalism from these pages in Hegel's *Philosophy of Right.* Hegel showed how even individualistic self-seekers are driven to make innumerable mutual adjustments, and thus to give rise to an interconnective system of services, laws, and corporative institutions. The individual is led to recognize that his own ends are both satisfied and transcended in the social organism. He acknowledges the need for a sovereign political power, to insure the harmonization of the various social and economic groups and to achieve the universal good of the community as such. The conception of political order is thus gradually evolved by men, living under social conditions.

Hegel regarded this development of social and political consciousness as another instance of the self-articulation of the rational concept, working this time through human minds and social relations. It is God's way with the world that there should be the state, as the synthesis of all the preceding moments in the development of objective spirit. *The state is the supreme actuality of the ethical idea* and hence the objective manifestation of the divine idea upon earth. It secures the objective organization of right and property and, simultaneously, enlists the intention of individual wills for the universal good of the community. In the state, men have borne home forcefully to them that they are free, personal subjects only within an encompassing whole, which is itself a self-conscious subject or social individual. The universal actuality, which began to display itself in family and civil society, is made manifest as the self-determining rational concept, in the state. Individuals and intermediate social groups are teleologically regulated by the concept of *rational freedom,* which is given its plenary incarnation in the state. Hence the state has absolute right over its component members, both as individuals and as groups, precisely in order to achieve maximal freedom.

Although Hegel stressed freedom and advanced numerous safeguards, he did give occasion to some of the leading notions behind the totalitarian views of the state. He saw a clear need for the political order, but his interpretation of the state is bound up with his metaphysical and dialectical preoccupations. His emphasis upon the divine character of the state, its organic and subsistent nature, its concreteness in respect to its components, and its absolute right over its members, helped to produce the *mystique* of the state as a superentity. Even when the further stages of his dialectic were rejected, his conception of the state was accepted by many totalitarian theorists, as providing the most effective way of combating individualism and an uncontrolled economy.

The relation between Hegel's political theorizing and the political conditions in the Prussia of his day is a disputed topic among Hegelian scholars. There is no solid basis for the charge that this great philosopher wrote his political doctrine as a paid lackey of the Prussian government. In discussing the types of *constitution* or rational self-organization of the state, it is true, he did express his preference for the hereditary monarchy. But this followed from his notion of the state as a sovereign self or individual subject, whose sovereign power is best embodied in the will of a single individual. However convenient his agreement with the Prussian political settlement (which, however, he also subjected to criticism), Hegel based his theory of the best constitution mainly upon his exaggerated doctrine of *sovereignty*. The latter, in turn, is only a corollary of his tendency to hypostasize the state, as a concrete, universal selfhood.

His famous saying that *"what is rational is actual and what is actual is rational,"*[42] has also aroused dispute, ever since its first appearance. As Heinrich Heine observed, the revolutionaries of the 1830's and 1840's stressed the first half of this pronouncement, whereas the conservatives seized upon the second half. Any given mode of existence, political or otherwise, can be criticized in the light of the absolute rational standard, to which the particular mode only approximates. This is Hegel's legacy to the radical socialists, who urged that

---

[42] *Philosophy of Right,* Preface (Knox, 10); cf. Hegel's own commentary on this text: *Encyclopaedia Logic* (later editions), 6 (Wallace, 9–12). Cf. T. M. Knox, "Hegel and Prussianism," *Philosophy,* XV (1940), 51–63, and the lively discussion on this theme between Knox and E. F. Carritt, in the same volume of *Philosophy,* 190–96, 313–17. On various pitfalls to be avoided in the interpretation of Hegel, see W. A. Kaufmann, "The Hegel Myth and Its Method," *The Philosophical Review,* LX (1951), 459–86. The procedures advocated by Kaufmann are applicable to the historical study of other modern philosophers as well.

any given social or political order must submit to change and replacement by a more adequate realization of the rational concept, in the social sphere. But Hegel adds that the discerning eye can also discover the rose of the rational concept, amid the cross of the present order of things: *"Here* is Rhodes, *here* is your jump." The conservatives understood this to mean a reconciliation of ideals and facts, that amounts to a compromise with the *status quo*. Careful Hegelian scholars have pointed out, however, that it is only the "actual" (*wirklich*) which is rational, not indiscriminately any aspect of the empirically "real." Only that political institution which embodies the essential concept of the state can achieve a genuine measure of actuality and can be called genuinely rational, in the political order. Since all given states fall short of the essential idea, the criterion of actuality also has a reformist consequence. Nevertheless, Hegel also wanted to point out a rational and necessary factor present in the given, "real" states: even under imperfect conditions, the yeast of the rational concept and of strict actuality is fermenting in political institutions.

Two consequences of Hegel's doctrine on the state as a sovereign individual self are noteworthy: his theory of interstate relations and his view on war.[43] Any particular state is only a finite and partial embodiment of the idea of *the* state. Hence it differentiates itself from other states and enters into relations with them. But Hegel's doctrine on sovereignty prevented him from admitting that particular states could become incorporated into a world political community. He did not share the vision of an international order of justice among states, such as was expressed in Kant's essay on *Eternal Peace*. For Hegel, international law holds between sovereignly autonomous states, and hence is always conditioned upon the wills of the parties involved. *Interstate relations* are always external, abstract, and pragmatic, so that international law rests on the shaky foundation of usage and what ought-to-be. There is no superstate to master the private interests of individual states, in the way in which the political order masters the conflicting interests within civil society. Although *war* is intended only as a temporary expedient, it is an ultimate exercise of a state's sovereignty. It is invoked, when the categorical imperatives among states are powerless to prevent a threat to the welfare of the political organism. In his earlier writings, Hegel took a somewhat lyrical,

<hr />

[43] *Philosophy of Right*, 321–40 (Knox, 208–16), and the Additions to Nos. 324–39 (Knox, 295–97). A brief analysis of these passages is made by H. G. ten Bruggencate, "Hegel's Views on War," *The Philosophical Quarterly*, I (1950–1951), 58–60.

romantic view of the great benefits wrought by war for the advance of civilization. His disillusionment with Napoleon and his closer acquaintance, in later life, with official machinery led him to temper his opinions. But he always regarded war as a test of the seriousness of one's belief in the ephemeral nature of all finite goods and temporal institutions, including this or that state.

As distinct from the rational concept of *the* state, this or that particular state is marked and doomed by temporality and finitude. Especially in their interstate relations, existing states display their one-sidedness and contingency, their vulnerability to the historical process of generation and decay. We gain access to the *meaning of history* from the perspective of ethical consciousness, as it culminates in the state. For, history is spiritual transition: it is the locus of the passage of the dialectic from objective to absolute spirit. History is both the perfect flowering of ethical life and the judgment passed by reason or providence upon every given ethical totality. Hegel's remark that the "history of the world . . . is the world's court of judgment,"[44] applies with special force to the destiny of states. A given state rests upon some unity of a nation or people. The nation provides it with concrete substance but also with limitations and the germ of decay. In the spirit of a people or *Volksgeist* is found one form of mind, and the glory of a state is to bring this form to rational, political unity. But since this spiritual form is a *particular* one, the nation is subject to the dialectical law governing all organisms. It has its time of growth, its high period, and its decline. (Hegel never specified the limits of this biological metaphor, which became so popular with later philosophers of history, including Spengler and Toynbee.)

The judgment of history is not passed externally upon this historical process: it is expressed *in* and *through* it. One facet of the *Weltgeist*

---

[44] *Philosophy of Right*, 340 (Knox, 216). On the general significance of history, confer *Encyclopaedia Logic*, 548–49 (Wallace, 275–79); *Philosophy of Right*, 341–60 (Knox, 216–23); *Reason in History*, Hartman translation in entirety. J. Hyppolite's *Introduction à la philosophie de l'histoire de Hegel* (Paris, Rivière, 1948), is specially valuable for its information about Hegel's earlier views of history, whereas Hegel's mature doctrine is explained by R. Kroner, "System und Geschichte bei Hegel," *Logos*, XX (1931), 243–58. Kroner notes that, for Hegel, there is history, because spirit has emptied itself in its passage from logic to nature, and must find its way back to itself. History is this rediscovery of absolute spirit through human consciousness and time. But every historical development also marks the heightened presence of the suprahistorical factor of absolute spirit and the victory of the eternal spirit over time. Human history thus becomes a means and a prelude to the eternal self-presence of absolute reason. See above, note 29.

or world-spirit is reflected in a particular state or concrete ethical whole. But the entire brilliance and vitality of the absolute spirit are bestowed upon no particular nation, state, culture, or epoch. In their particularity, they all fail to express the absolute actuality, and so they are all doomed to pass away. And yet the world-spirit or objective mind actualizes itself, dialectically, only by means of the historical interplay between these many particular embodiments and outlooks. History's verdict is the same as the moments in the rational concept's dialectical unfolding, on the plane of objective spirit. Only from the total procession of peoples and states, as contained in world history, can the full lesson be gathered.

History, as the temporal march of absolute spirit through the world, is the story of freedom's growth. Hegel took a somewhat parochial and linear view of world history, locating the focus of the world-mind in only one people or group, during any one historical epoch. He traced the historical progress of mind through the following forms: the Oriental, Greek, Roman, and Germanic-Christian. They correspond, respectively, to the *four ages* of human historical life: childhood, youth, manhood, and old age. Rational will is fixed in some objectively given order of things (Oriental despotism), embodied as an individual effort in beautiful objects (Greek esthetic morality), recognized abstractly in its formal grandeur and harshness (Roman state), and finally brought to fruition in the union of the subjective and objective aspects of freedom, belonging to every man as a member of the state (Germanic-Christian state). This generalization suffers from reliance upon the same uncontrolled biological metaphor, as well as from a lack of appreciation of non-European cultural developments, including those that run parallel with the more familiar Western ones. It gives a grand and bold perspective, but like other generalizations dictated by the dialectical outlook, it fails to hold up under a close, comparative scrutiny of historical evidence.

In its slow and painful conquest of its own meaning, the divine idea of freedom operates in history, by means of the will and activity of men. It is the *cunning of reason* to stir men's passions to seek personal, immediate gains and yet, in this same way, to bring about its own temporal actualization. Not only peoples and broad social movements but also *heroes,* "world-historical individuals," further the ends of the objective world-spirit. For, outstanding individuals display that union of *personal passion* and *consecration to an ideal,* out of which spring a new depth of freedom and a fresh draught of spiritual insight.

Historical reason is ruthless in using men and nations for its own ends. To avoid becoming mere tools of fate, individuals and states must become reflectively aware of the presence of reason itself, amid its various shapes and appearances. Dire necessity becomes the sweet yoke of rational freedom, once individual wills are joined with the universal will, in the state. "The rational, like the substantial, is necessary. We are free when we recognize it as law and follow it as the substance of our own being."[45] Like Spinoza, Hegel locates man's *freedom* in his *conscious recognition of rational necessity* as the law of actuality. And rational necessity is best embodied, as far as objective spirit is concerned, in the state.

Yet the state does not contain the supreme form of spiritual actuality, open to man. As the ultimate synthesis of the life of *objective* spirit, it points beyond itself to a new and final dialectical development on the part of concrete spirit. The two moments of subjective and objective spirit are ordained to the synthetic unity of *absolute spirit*. Hence the state has a purpose beyond itself: it must provide the rich soil for the cultivation of *art, religion,* and *philosophy,* which are the main phases of the life of absolute spirit. These highest manifestations of spiritual existence cannot have their full measure of being, apart from the state, and neither does the state realize all the implications of its rational concept, until it ministers to their growth. The goal of history is the advancement of artistic, religious, and philosophical freedom, within the context of the political order.

## 9. ART, RELIGION, AND PHILOSOPHY

Hegel's doctrine on absolute spirit marks the final synthesis, not only of concrete spirit, but of logic and nature as well. There is a return of nature without residue to mind, a complete reappropriation of otherness by the rational concept. This occurs through a dialectical ordering of art, religion, and philosophy, as the moments in the final triad of absolute spirit. Hegel expresses their principle of difference in one sentence: "The element in which the universal mind exists in art is intuition and imagery, in religion feeling and representative thinking, in philosophy pure freedom of thought."[46] The same ulti-

---

45 *Reason in History* (Hartman translation, 53).

46 *Philosophy of Right,* 341 (Knox, 216). On this final triad, see *The Phenomenology of Mind,* VII–VIII (Baillie, 685–808); *Philosophy of Mind,* 553–77 (291–316). Hegel's posthumously published lectures on esthetics and the philosophy of religion are further sources.

mate spiritual *content* is present under three different *modes* of apprehension. Art grasps the absolute spirit in concretely *sensuous intuitions,* at the imaginative level. Religion enjoys a direct feeling of union with the divine principle, and uses *symbolic representations* to express the nature of this principle. But the nature of the absolute is adequately articulated only by philosophy, in the *rational concept,* which alone apprehends absolute spirit according to its own proper actuality.

Empiricists often justify *art* by adverting to its pleasure-giving function and the auxiliary contributions it makes to moral sense and piety. Hegel reduces these aspects to a definitely secondary place; in its own essence, art has a noble purpose, subservient to no practical ends. It seeks to *render visible the divine,* presenting to our sensibility the form of God, if not God in His own spiritual being. In artistic creation, the spiritual meaning of the finite world is revealed, not in an abstract way but in some concrete medium. The successful work of art incarnates a spiritual content in sensuous form, thus providing the first absolute reconciliation between the transient external world and the realm of pure thought, between finite nature and infinite reason. But art remains only the first stage in the dialectic of absolute spirit, since it embodies its apprehension of the absolute in a sensuous way. In esthetic intuition, spirit is grasped through immediate images rather than through the concrete universal concept.

Taking *religion* in a broad, phenomenological way, as meaning the discernment of the absolute mind under the forms of finitude, Hegel distinguishes three types of religion: natural, artistic, and revealed. The Oriental religions perceive the divine, in an immediate and objective way, in *nature* itself. God is identified with light, vital forces, and certain sacred animals. Among the Greeks, *art* furnishes a religious outlet, not only in the formally religious hymns and cults of the gods, but also in poetic and dramatic expressions of man's struggle with the infinite. The Greeks prized the human body, as being the most fitting way of expressing the spiritual principle in sensuous form. But the perfect religious manifestation of absolute spirit must be given by itself, i.e., must come through *revealed religion.* Christianity is the sphere of religion proper, for it is no longer held captive by the immediacy and sensuousness of the less perfect religions of nature and art. As far as *content* goes, revealed religion specifies the absolute precisely as spiritual actuality, and hence attains the summit of truth. But from the standpoint of *form,* there is still a gap between the finite and the infinite, as religiously apprehended. For, religion employs a finite mode of representation, a sort of imaginative thinking, to express its absolute content of truth.[47] This imaginative form establishes a twofold separation, at the heart of the absolute. First, it creates the appearance of a distance between man and God, so that the latter is treated as a transcendent being; then, it splits up the dealings of the transcendent God with man into a temporal series of distinct phenomena, constituting sacred history.

Hegel finds the Christian religion wanting, in the degree that it supports the *irreducible distinction* between God and man, and gives unconditional worth to the *historical factor* in revelation. He looks to faith and religious feeling themselves for support, in sublating these two features of revealed religion. Simple faith affirms the indwelling presence of God as all in all, as well as the oneness of the believer with God. Religious feeling, for its part, concentrates the whole process of redemption in a single act of worship, in which the divine spirit returns to itself through human devotion. Hegel contends that these traits indicate the essential ordination of the religious outlook to the higher one of absolute, idealistic philosophy. His way of bringing the dialectical principle of interpretation to bear upon specific issues of this sort, reveals how arbitrary Hegel's handling of data must be, in order to wring out from the facts a conclusion in support of the doctrine of absolute spirit. Faith and religious feeling generate the attitude of *worship,* which supposes both creaturely distance from God as transcendent and the loving presence of God as immanent. The religious relationship is not a dialectical one between particular, abstract moments and their own concrete actuality. Rather, it obtains

[47] The Hegelian teaching that the God of religion must ultimately give way to the absolute of idealistic philosophy is clearly stated by the English Hegelian, F. H. Bradley, in *Appearance and Reality* (second, revised edition, New York, Macmillan, 1908): "Like morality, religion is not ultimate. It is a mere appearance, and is therefore inconsistent with itself. And it is hence liable on every side to shift beyond its own limits. . . . Hence, short of the Absolute, God cannot rest, and, having reached that goal, he is lost and religion with him" (444, 447). What divides Hegel from theism, on this issue, is a difference about whether man is destined ultimately for a *dialectical identification* or a *participative union* with the highest actuality. This anthropological conflict rests, in turn, upon the metaphysical conflict between a dialectical and an analogical view of being. For Thomistic statements, cf. B. Welte, "Hegels Begriff der Religion — sein Sinn und seine Grenze," *Scholastik,* XXVII (1952), 210–25, and E. Coreth, S.J., "Dialektik und Analogie des Seins. Zum Seinsproblem bei Hegel und der Scholastik," *Scholastik,* XXVI (1951), 57–86.

between men, who are irrevocably finite creatures in all that they are, and the living God, who is their creator and conserver in being. This religious bond is between the infinite personal being and *finite persons,* who are not destined to become sublated into a higher synthesis of being.

When Hegel appeals to the Christian doctrine on the indwelling of the Holy Spirit by grace in our souls, he overlooks the distinction between *becoming partakers* of the divine nature and *becoming the absolute,* by a dialectical ascension. The Hegelian philosophy of religion is scandalized by the religious person's retention of creatureliness and the Christian's respect for the unique events of sacred history. Yet these features are most strongly retained precisely by religious souls like St. Augustine and St. John of the Cross, in whom there is also the most intense awareness of man's participation in the divine life. They place man's ultimate perfection in this religious participation, which is destroyed by being transformed into a dialectical identification of being, as the philosophy of absolute spirit ultimately demands.

Art-as-thesis and religion-as-antithesis are destined for sublation in the last synthesis, the *philosophy of the absolute spirit.* As befits the circular nature of spiritual activity, Hegel terminates his discussion where it started: with the doctrine on absolute spirit. Humanly speaking, some progress has been made, in passing from a methodological view of spirit as dialectic to the philosophical doctrine on the various phases in spirit's development. What was implicit in methodology, becomes fully expressed in the philosophy of the absolute. Philosophy removes the last distracting shadow of finitude cast between content and form. They coincide perfectly in philosophical science, which is alone deserving of the name of *science,* in the sense of the unqualified truth about the totality of spirit. Philosophy expresses the absolute *content* of spirit through the absolutely proportionate *form* of the rational concept. Indeed, philosophy is the self-expression of absolute spirit, not under any of the lesser forms of manifestation but in the perfectly lucid medium of pure thought or the rational concept. In this last *Aufhebung,* all the travail of logic, nature, and concrete spirit is annulled, preserved, and elevated, within the organic unity and vision of absolute philosophical truth.

Two final questions may be posed concerning this awesome conception of philosophy. Is Hegel's doctrine pantheistic, and is it panlogistic? Hegel makes much of his denial of the charge of *pantheism*.[48] But he defines pantheism as a theory which teaches an *undialectical* identity between an indeterminate, substantial God and a substantial world. As so described, a pantheistic philosophy cannot make provision for a dialectical conception of identity, as being inclusive of antithetic differences, or for a notion of God as a self-differentiating subject. This amounts to a criticism of Schelling's special view of the relation between God and the world. Hegel's quarrel is not about the *fact* of absolute identity between God and the world, but about the *manner* in which it is to be conceived. His is a dialectical kind of pantheism or, better still, a *dialectical monism of the absolute spirit*, in which the absolute dichotomizes itself into all the contrasting finite modes of mind and nature, and then recovers its absolute unity in and through its diverse expressions. Hegel also objects to the term pan*theism*, since his is a philosophy of the absolute, rather than a philosophy of God. The distinction between God and the absolute is parallel to that between the religious and the philosophical views of the absolute *Geist*. Since Hegel sublates the religious God into the fully adequate philosophical doctrine on the absolute spirit, it might be better to call his position a doctrine of the *absolute-spirit-as-all* (a doctrine of *pneuma-panism*, to coin a clumsy neologism). This is *absolute monism*, provided that recognition be given to the teaching that the absolute differentiates itself into the myriad varieties of logical, natural, and spiritual modes of being. Hegel's absolute monism is hospitable to the manyness and finiteness of things, but only on condition that they all serve as moments in the self-growth of the unique, absolute spirit.

During the nineteenth century, it was customary to describe Hegel's philosophy as a *panlogism*, viz., a doctrine in which reason triumphs everywhere and reduces all to systematic intelligibility. But in our century, many Hegelian scholars prefer to stress rather the *alogical* and *irrational* traits in his thought.[49] They point out that logic, the doctrine on the *logos*, is only the first moment in the Hegelian dia-

---

[48] *Philosophy of Mind*, 573 (Wallace, 315).

[49] R. Kroner says that Hegel is *"without doubt the greatest irrationalist* known in the history of philosophy" (*Von Kant bis Hegel*, II, 271), in opposition to J. E. Erdmann's "panlogistic" view of him. H. Glockner characterizes Hegel's philosophy ultimately as a "pantragic outlook" (*Hegel*, II, 566); J. Hyppolite's *Introduction à la philosophie de l'histoire de Hegel* is a sustained analysis of this "pantragic" and "pantagonistic" motif. Cf. M. R. Cohen, "Hegel's Rationalism," *The Philosophical Review*, XLI (1932), 283–301.

lectic, and that this dialectic high-lights the tragic contradictions and self-estrangement undergone by reason. Hegel does not think that he is conceding too much to the irrational thereby, since he transfers the process of self-diremption to the bosom of the absolute. But his difficulty is, then, to give an intelligible account of such an absolute. His procedure is to appeal to the travail that marks human spiritual experience, but this only begs the question about the relation between the human mind and the absolute. His employment of the theosophical language of Jacob Boehme to describe the turbulent, inner life of the primal ground of being, involves him in the same predicament as Schelling, whom Hegel castigates for confusing philosophy with poetry and religion. The Hegelian dialectic rests upon the view of the absolute as synthesizing within itself both complete actuality and temporal process. Hegel does not succeed in reducing this synthesis to the intelligible state of the rational concept, since he is trying futilely to treat the Christian dogma of the Incarnation as though it were a philosophical concept, whose truth is self-evident to natural reason.[50] This discrepancy between a *human discourse about the absolute* and the *absolute's own knowledge of itself* is never overcome. Hegel wants philosophy to become the self-discovery of the absolute spirit, but it continues to be a purely human approach to the absolute. It could close the gap only by ceasing to use language and to respect the spatiotemporal conditions of discourse, but then it would also cease to be philosophy or anything humanly recognizable.

## SUMMARY OF CHAPTER 14

An access to Hegel's mind can be gained through his theory of absolute spirit. The absolute contains the actuality of substance and the values of immediate intuition and permanence. Yet, since the absolute is truly spirit and sovereign reason, it is also a subject and supreme life. In its vital nature, it must combine the permanence of substance with the flow of temporal becoming. And as a self-reflective subject, the absolute is through-and-through dialectical in nature, separating itself from itself and returning again to a more mature sort of unity. Hegel developed Fichte's hints into a rounded dialectic of thesis-antithesis-synthesis. Absolute spirit is essentially a self-purposive, dialectical, and systematically unified process of becoming, but a process somehow identical with eternal

---

[50] Cf. E. Przywara, "Thomas oder Hegel? Zum Sinn der 'Wende zum Objekt,' " *Logos*, XV (1926), 1–20; J. Möller, *Der Geist und das Absolute* (Paderborn, Schöningh, 1951).

and changeless actuality. Hegel was convinced that this view of the absolute could be made acceptable to others, through an analysis of experience. For, every phase in experience is an aspect in the reflective relation between mind and its object. Finite understanding seeks to maintain the complete otherness and finitude of its object, whereas philosophical reason reveals the dialectical identity between mind and object, within the unity of absolute mind. This synoptic comprehension of several particular factors within an absolute and universal unity was developed in Hegel's theory of the concept. The philosophical concept is a concrete universal, which affirms the unity of the universal essence precisely in and through the interconnections among individual things. The unconditionally concrete universal is the same as absolute spirit. This guarantees both the ontological significance of logic and the necessarily dialectical character of speculative logic. The Hegelian systematic philosophy traces the self-development of the absolute concept through the three grand dialectical phases of logic, philosophy of nature, and philosophy of the spirit. Special attention is paid to the ethical significance of the state and the dialectical development of freedom in history. The dialectical process does not culminate in religious worship, since the latter implies some residual distance between the finite mind and the absolute. The summit is only reached in philosophical speculation, which is also the self-actualization of all the dialectical potencies of absolute spirit and the full attainment of concrete-universal actuality, on the part of the philosophical concept.

## BIBLIOGRAPHICAL NOTE

1. *Sources.* The original edition of Hegel's *Werke* was edited by Marheineke, Michelet, and other followers of Hegel himself (19 vols., Berlin, Duncker and Humblot, 1832–1845 and 1887). This edition was reprinted in a new arrangement, in the jubilee edition of the *Werke,* edited by H. Glockner (26 vols., Stuttgart, Frommann, 1927–1939; Hegel's writings in Vols. 1–20; Glockner's *Hegel* in Vols. 21–22; Glockner's *Hegel-Lexikon* in Vols. 23–26). A critical edition was started by G. Lasson and is being continued by J. Hoffmeister: *Hegels Sämmtliche Werke, kritische Ausgabe* (Leipzig, Meiner, 1905 ff.; 17 of the projected 21 volumes published to date by Lasson and then by Hoffmeister); it includes several heretofore unpublished writings, and establishes the authentic text of the previously published works. (A new *Kritische Ausgabe,* also to be edited by J. Hoffmeister and published by F. Meiner, will contain 32 volumes.) Two other important publications, giving documents from Hegel's early years are: *Dokumente zu Hegels Entwicklung,* edited by J. Hoffmeister (Stuttgart, Frommann, 1936); *Hegels theologische Jugendschriften,* edited by H. Nohl (Tübingen, Mohr, 1907). Nohl's edition served as the basis for the T. M. Knox and R. Kroner translation of Hegel's *Early Theological Writings* (Chicago, University of Chicago Press, 1948) — contains: *The Positivity of the Christian Religion, The*

*Spirit of Christianty and Its Fate, Love, Fragment of a System,* and an
Appendix: *On Classical Studies.* Other translations: *Reason in History,*
translated by R. S. Hartman (New York, Liberal Arts Press, 1953);
*The Phenomenology of Mind,* translated by J. Baillie (second ed., re-
vised and corrected throughout, New York, Macmillan, 1931); *Science
of Logic,* translated by W. H. Johnston and L. G. Struthers (2 vols.,
New York, Macmillan, 1929); *The Logic of Hegel, translated from the
Encyclopaedia of the Philosophical Sciences,* translated by W. Wallace
(second ed., revised and augmented, Oxford, Clarendon, 1892); *Hegel's
Philosophy of Mind, translated from the Encyclopaedia of the Philosophical
Sciences,* translated by W. Wallace (Oxford, Clarendon, 1894); *Philosophy
of Right,* translated by T. M. Knox (Oxford, Clarendon, 1942); *Reason
in History,* translated by R. S. Hartman (New York, Liberal Arts Press,
1953); lecture series on *The Philosophy of Fine Art,* translated by F.
P. B. Osmaston (4 vols., London, Bell, 1920); *Lectures on the Philosophy of Religion, together with a Work on the Proofs of the Existence
of God,* translated by E. B. Speirs and J. B. Sanderson (3 vols., London,
Kegan Paul, Trench, Trübner, 1895); *Lectures on the History of Philosophy,* translated by E. S. Haldane and F. H. Simpson (3 vols., London,
Kegan Paul, Trench, Trübner, 1892–1896).

2. *Studies.* E. Caird's *Hegel* (Edinburgh, Blackwood, 1883) is a competent introduction by a convinced Hegelian; W. T. Stace's *The Philosophy of Hegel* (London, Macmillan, 1924), is a clear, systematic statement
of Hegel's position, objectively presented; G. R. G. Mure's *An Introduction
to Hegel* (Oxford, Clarendon, 1940), stresses the contribution of Aristotle
(or, at least, of what Hegel took to be Aristotle's doctrine) to Hegel's own
formation. Two of the most competent German introductions have already
been mentioned: Volume 2 of N. Hartmann's *Die Philosophie des deutschen Idealismus* (see Bibliographical Note to Chapter XIII, No. 1) is devoted to Hegel; H. Glockner's *Hegel* constitutes Vols. 21–22 of the
jubilee edition of Hegel's *Werke.* See also, W. Moog, *Hegel und die
Hegelschen Schule* (Munich, Reinhardt, 1930), which traces the development of the Right and Left wings of the Hegelian school, as well as
provides a careful analysis of Hegel's own writings. A good deal of research has been done on Hegel's early development. In addition to
Kroner's Introduction to the translation of Hegel's *Early Theological
Writings* and Kroner's more extended development in *Von Kant bis Hegel*
(see Bibliographical Note to Chapter XIII, No. 1), see P. Asveld, *La
pensée religieuse du jeune Hegel* (Louvain, Publications Universitaires,
1958); F. Grégoire, *Études hégéliennes* (Louvain, Publications Universitaires, 1958) is a systematic view. German researches are summed
up neatly in J. Schwarz, *Hegels philosophische Entwicklung* (Frankfurt a.M., Klostermann, 1938), which synthesizes the results of far-
flung, specialized investigations made by Dilthey, Nohl, Rosenzweig,
Lasson, Hoffmeister, Haering, and Steinbüchel. Also A. T. Peperzak, *Le
jeune Hegel et la vision morale du monde* (Hague, Nijhoff, 1960). On the

crucial question of the relation between method and doctrinal system, see B. Heimann, *System und Methode in Hegels Philosophie* (Leipzig, Meiner, 1927). What is lacking in the general studies by Stace and Mure is an appreciation of the role of the *Phenomenology of Spirit,* in determining Hegel's conception of method and the absolute. This shortcoming can be overcome by consulting the following: J. Baillie, *The Origin and Significance of Hegel's Logic* (New York, Macmillan, 1901); J. Royce, *Lectures on Modern Idealism* (see Bibliographical Note to Chapter XIII, No. 2), Lectures 6–8, 136–212; J. Wahl, *Le malheur de la conscience dans la philosophie de Hegel* (second ed., Paris, Presses Universitaires, 1951); J. Hyppolite, *Genèse et structure de la Phénoménologie de l'Esprit de Hegel* (Paris, Aubier, 1946), an exhaustive commentary and essay in internal criticism. Also J. Hyppolite, *Logique et existence: Essai sur la logique de Hegel* (Paris, Presses Universitaires, 1953), on the identification of thought and being. A brief but penetrating evaluation of the *Phenomenology,* in the light of Thomistic realism, is made by C. Nink, S.J., *Kommentar zu den grundlegenden Abschnitten von Hegels Phänomenologie des Geistes* (Regensburg, Habbel, 1931), with emphasis upon the Hegelian dialectic of consciousness and self-consciousness. A magistral presentation and defense of Hegelian logic are given in G. R. G. Mure's *A Study of Hegel's Logic* (Oxford, Clarendon, 1950). There is a significant convergence of realistic criticism of this logical system in the books by L. Pelloux, *La logica di Hegel* (Milan, Vita e Pensiero, 1938), H. Niel, S.J., *De la médiation dans la philosophie de Hegel* (Paris, Aubier, 1945), and E. Coreth, S.J., *Das dialektische Sein in Hegels Logik* (Vienna, Herder, 1952). Niel shows that the notion of mediation is the backbone of the Hegelian system and that it contains explosive factors, leading to the dissolution of the philosophy of the absolute; Pelloux notes that the Hegelian mediation stumbles over the problem of the given factor in experience; Coreth further specifies the problem as that of identifying the real becoming of things with the logical rhythm of dialectically ordered concepts. H. A. Reyburn, *The Ethical Theory of Hegel: A Study of the Philosophy of Right* (Oxford, Clarendon, 1921), displays expertly the continuity between the dialectical logic and the practical philosophy. For Hegel's political philosophy, see M. B. Foster, *The Political Philosophies of Plato and Hegel* (New York, Oxford, 1935); H. Cairns, *Legal Philosophy from Plato to Hegel* (Baltimore, Johns Hopkins University Press, 1949); F. Rosenzweig, *Hegel und der Staat* (2 vols., Munich and Berlin, Oldenbourg, 1920). Since Hegel's point of departure is his attitude toward Kant, J. Maier's *On Hegel's Critique of Kant* (New York, Columbia University Press, 1939) provides a valuable historical comparison.

3. *Marx and Kierkegaard.* A good deal of the contemporary European revival of interest in Hegel is due to the fact that both Marxism and Existentialism stem from reactions against Hegel which, nevertheless, were specified in large part by his massive system. A comprehensive Marx source book is edited in English by C. P. Dutt: *Karl Marx, Selected Works*

(2 vols., New York, International Publishers, 1936). The accepted biography is by F. Mehring, *Karl Marx: The Story of His Life,* translated by E. Fitzgerald (London, Allen and Unwin, 1936). His relations with the Hegelian movement are examined by H. P. Adams, *Karl Marx in His Earlier Writings* (London, Allen and Unwin, 1940), and by S. Hook, *From Hegel to Marx* (New York, Reynal and Hitchcock, 1936). Hook also gives a summary of the philosophy of Ludwig Feuerbach. Kierkegaard's standpoint can be gathered from *A Kierkegaard Anthology,* edited by R. Bretall (Princeton, Princeton University Press, 1946). W. Lowrie's *Kierkegaard* (New York, Oxford, 1938) is the standard biography in English. On his thought, see R. Jolivet, *Introduction to Kierkegaard,* translated by W. H. Barber (New York, Dutton, 1951), and J. Collins, *The Mind of Kierkegaard* (Chicago, Henry Regnery, 1953). Hegel's paramount influence upon Russian thinkers can be seen from V. V. Zenkovsky, *A History of Russian Philosophy* (2 vols., New York, Columbia University Press, 1953), where the Marxist impact is also analyzed. On Feuerbach, see W. B. Chamberlin, *Heaven Wasn't His Destination: The Philosophy of Ludwig Feuerbach* (London, Allen and Unwin, 1941). Also H. Arvon, *Ludwig Feuerbach ou la transformation du sacré* (Paris, Presses Universitaires, 1957), which contrasts his religious naturalism with the areligious naturalism of Marx. The latter's philosophical bases can be studied in L. S. Feuer, editor, *Marx and Engels: Basic Writings on Politics and Philosophy* (New York, Doubleday Anchor, 1959); the Soviet developments are analyzed by G. A. Wetter, S.J., *Dialectical Materialism* (New York, Praeger, 1958).

4. *Further Publications.* There is a complete translation of Hegel's *Encyclopedia of Philosophy* by G. E. Mueller (New York, Philosophical Library, 1959), including the part on philosophy of nature. C. J. Friedrich's selected readings, *The Philosophy of Hegel* (New York, Modern Library, 1953), contain some newly translated political writings and remarks on the history of philosophy. J. N. Findlay, *Hegel: A Re-Examination* (London, Macmillan, 1958), and the essays collected as *Studies in Hegel* (*Tulane Studies in Philosophy,* Vol. IX, 1960), reformulate Hegel in current terms intelligible to analytic and Whiteheadian philosophers.

# Chapter 15. SCHOPENHAUER

## I. LIFE AND WRITINGS

ARTHUR SCHOPENHAUER was born in 1788 in the free city of Danzig. His father was a wealthy and cosmopolitan merchant, who gave his son the advantages of education in France and England, as well as foreign travel, so that he might become acquainted with other languages and customs. The family moved from Danzig to the free city of Hamburg in 1793, when Prussia annexed the former city. There was a streak of mental instability in the family, since Schopenhauer's uncle was mentally deficient and his father probably committed suicide (1805). Out of respect for his father, Schopenhauer continued for two more years to work with a commercial firm, but in 1807 obtained permission from his mother to continue his higher education. He studied for a while in the *gymnasium* at Gotha and then at Weimar, where he pursued classical studies. From 1809 until 1813, Schopenhauer attended the Universities of Göttingen and Berlin, first studying medicine and then concentrating upon philosophy. At Berlin, he heard lectures by Fichte and Schleiermacher, and acquired his lifelong hatred and contempt for academic people, especially professors of philosophy. When the Prussians rose up to expel Napoleon in 1813, Schopenhauer prudently left Berlin for Rudolstadt, where he prepared his doctoral dissertation: *On the Fourfold Root of the Principle of Sufficient Reason* (accepted for the doctorate at Jena and published, 1813). The following year marked his definitive separation from his mother, Johanna, with whom he had always been at odds. She was a conceited woman, who had moved to Weimar, after her husband's death, in order to share in Goethe's circle and to advance her opportunities as a novelist. Schopenhauer's misanthropy was due in part to his strong egoism and in part to his unfortunate dealings with women. His mother was too lightheaded and satirical for him, whereas his acquaintance with other women was confined to an occasional liaison. Most of Schopenhauer's affection was spent upon animals, especially his own beloved poodles.

Being now a man of independent means, Schopenhauer was able to spend the next four years (1814–1818) in Dresden, studying Latin translations of Indian philosophy and composing his philosophical masterpiece, *The World as Will and Presentation* (1819). The book made no great stir, despite its excellent style and forceful arguments, since it ran against the popular Hegelian currents in philosophy. To further his cause, Schopenhauer received permission to teach as a *Privatdozent* at the University of Berlin, where he foolishly scheduled his lectures at the same time of day as those of the famous Hegel. His attempt to draw students to his philosophy was a complete failure, and he withdrew from academic life with the firm but mistaken conviction that Hegel (to whom he referred, thereafter, as a fool, windbag, and charlatan) had plotted his ruin. His later writings were marred by peevish outbursts against Fichte, Schelling, Hegel, and other professional philosophers, who continued to ignore his doctrine. From 1833 until his death, Schopenhauer lived in Frankfort, occupied with writing, attending the theater, looking for praise, and warding off imaginary assailants.

He kept constantly abreast of developments, both in the sciences and in daily life, that would tend to confirm his voluntaristic pessimism. In 1836, he published a collection of such evidence under the title *On the Will in Nature.* For the next few years, he occupied himself with answering two prize-essay questions (proposed by academies in Norway and Denmark), concerned, respectively, with free will and an intuitive foundation of morality. He won the prize for his reduction of free will to determinism, but (although his essay was the only entry in the Danish contest on the basis of morality) his explanation of sympathy as the ground of morality was deemed insufficient, as well as lacking in respect for the reigning idealistic philosophers. But he published both essays together as *The Two Fundamental Problems of Ethics* (1841). A second edition of *The World as Will and Presentation* was issued in 1844, containing a second volume of important commentaries on the original text. Schopenhauer was thoroughly frightened by the uprisings in 1848, since they seemed to threaten his own financial security. But the social revolutions helped to bring his own type of thought into fashion. His last book, *Parerga and Paralipomena* (1851), was a collection of essays on worldly prudence, noise, women, suicide, literary style, and other popular topics.

It soon won for him the fame he had always ardently desired. He died in 1860, after having enjoyed a decade of favorable reviews, personal adulation, and even some recognition from the universities.

## 2. THE PRINCIPLE OF SUFFICIENT REASON

Schopenhauer frequently advised those who wanted to grasp his mature philosophy, first to read his doctoral dissertation *On the Fourfold Root of the Principle of Sufficient Reason.* This work does, indeed, provide the required background for understanding his final standpoint. For, it enables one to gauge the extent of his dependence upon Kant, his attitude toward other philosophical predecessors, and the logical ground of his metaphysics.

As he reviewed the history of modern philosophy, Schopenhauer saw there a fundamental confusion between the *logical reason* and the *real cause.* He agreed with Kant that this confusion lies at the bottom of Descartes' ontological argument for God's existence, as well as Spinoza's identification of God and the world. Leibniz, too, failed to distinguish properly between reason and cause, but he did set forth the principle of sufficient reason clearly, as the main basis of human knowledge. Wolff gave the first hints about the different meanings to be assigned to this principle, but his overruling rationalism blinded him to the implications of his division. Kant's lasting contribution was to keep logical and real principles firmly apart. He also saw that Hume's criticism of the principle of causality made it forever impossible for us to regard the principle of sufficient reason as an independent truth (in the Leibnizian manner), to which both God Himself and our understanding must submit. Kant directed attention toward the transcendental principles of consciousness-in-general, principles which are determinative a priori of our experience and the world. He located the principles of knowledge squarely within the structure of consciousness. This position was accepted by Schopenhauer as a definitive conclusion, which stood in no need of critical revision, in its fundamental lines.

Schopenhauer presented his own standpoint as the heir to this entire historical development. Like Leibniz and Wolff, he treated sufficient reason as the integrating principle of all our knowledge. He accepted their working formulation of the principle: *Nothing is without a reason why it is, rather than is not.*[1] But he repudiated the

---

[1] *On the Fourfold Root of the Principle of Sufficient Reason,* I, 5; II, 19 (Hillebrand

rationalistic attempts to prove the principle, citing Aristotle's remark that the first principle of demonstration is itself indemonstrable. The very meaning of a proof is to offer demonstration of the reason for a judgment. Hence one would become involved in a vicious circle, in attempting to prove the need for a sufficient reason of logical truth.

Instead of a direct proof, Schopenhauer follows the Kantian transcendental procedure of analyzing the elements of objective knowledge, in order to establish sufficient reason as a synthetic a priori condition of that knowledge. Cognitive consciousness subdivides itself simultaneously into subject and object. To be a subject, is to be a knower and hence to have a mental presentation. A *mental presentation* (*Vorstellung*) is nothing other than an object-for-a-subject. Hence the conditions regulating the presentation are also those regulating objectivity. The most radical condition is the principle of sufficient reason itself.

> *All our presentations stand toward one another in a regulated connection, which may be determined a priori, and on account of which, nothing existing separately and independently, nothing single or detached, can become an Object for us.* It is this connection which is expressed by the principle of Sufficient Reason in its generality.[2]

Schopenhauer underlines Kant's view that the possibility of experience is the same as the possibility of connectedness among objects of knowledge, constituting a necessary, rational whole. Schopenhauer does not say, with Leibniz, that *everything* must have a sufficient reason, but only that everything that is to become an *object-of-knowledge-for-us* must have a sufficient reason. This is a notable amendment of the classical principle of modern rationalism. For, although it applies everywhere among the objects of experience, it applies *only* to those objects or to what Kant called the phenomenal

---

translation, 5, 20). The second chapter of this book offers a historical survey of previous teachings on sufficient reason. For Schopenhauer's relations with his predecessors, cf. P. Wapler, "Die geschichtlichen Grundlagen der Weltanschauung Schopenhauers," *Archiv für Geschichte der Philosophie,* XVIII (1905), 369–94.

2 *On the Fourfold Root of the Principle of Sufficient Reason,* III, 16 (Hillebrand, 30). Most English translations of Schopenhauer render his *Vorstellung* by "representation" or "idea." In the quotations used in the present chapter, the more neutral term "presentation" is usually substituted for the other renditions, so that a direct relation between the subject and the object will not be excluded, and so that the distinction between the "Platonic idea" and the forms of mental presentation may be preserved. For a genial introduction to the viewpoint of Schopenhauer, read B. A. G. Fuller, "Schopenhauer," *The Personalist,* XVI (1935), 227–40.

world. The restriction which Kant had placed upon the schematic and constitutive use of the categories is now extended to the principle of sufficient reason. Moreover, it enjoys no real anteriority to objects but is a condition of consciousness, generated simultaneously with the appearance of objects to a knowing subject. These qualifications prepare the remote ground for Schopenhauer's subsequent limitation of the field of rationality, order, and necessity to the phenomenal world.

Another advantage of associating sufficient reason with objects of knowledge is that it provides a principle of division for the several varieties of sufficient reason. Schopenhauer regards the rationalistic formula of *the* principle of sufficient reason as an abstraction, drawn from its several specific expressions. Since cognitive consciousness has different sorts of objects, there must be different kinds of objective connectedness in experience and hence different types of sufficient reason. There are four classes of objects of knowledge and therefore four types of relation of connectedness or sufficient reasons. Hence the principle of sufficient reason is traced by Schopenhauer to a corresponding *fourfold root*: the principles of *becoming, being, knowing*, and *acting* (*principia fiendi, essendi, cognoscendi, et agendi*). He borrows the first three terms from Wolff, and adds the fourth principle, in line with Wolff's remark that there must be a determining reason of the will. By blending these rationalistic principles with the Kantian theory of knowledge, Schopenhauer gives them a distinctive import for his own developing metaphysics.

## SCHOPENHAUER ON THE FOURFOLD ROOT OF THE PRINCIPLE OF SUFFICIENT REASON

1. Roots.
   a) Principle of being.
   b) Principle of becoming.
   c) Principle of acting.
   d) Principle of knowing.

2. Powers.
   a) Sensibility.
   b) Understanding.
   c) Inner sense or self-consciousness.
   d) Reason.

3. Knowledge.
   a) Pure formal intuitions of space and time.
   b) Intuitive, complete, empirical perceptions.
   c) Reflective intuition of the subject, as willing.
   d) Abstract concepts and inferences.

4. Sciences.
   a) Pure mathematics.
   b) Applied mathematics, physics, chemistry.
   c) Humane studies.
   d) Logic and the classifying sciences.

The principles of sufficient reason of becoming and knowing can be established together.[3] The first class of objects is that of intuitive, complete, *empirical perceptions*. They are intuitive, as opposed to abstract thought; complete, insofar as they include both the material and the formal constituents of appearances; empirical, both in having an origin in the stimulation of a sensory power and in being connected by space, time, and causality into what Kant called empirical reality. This sphere of objects-for-the-subject is governed by the principle of *sufficient reason of becoming (fiendi)*. This principle governs the conditions for the organization and succession of objects in time, according to the law of causality (which applies exclusively to temporal changes of material *states,* not to *things*). *Understanding* operates at this intuitive and empirical level, but *reason* tries to construct its own realm of objects, by means of *abstract concepts.* Schopenhauer views abstraction as the rational function of dropping out certain aspects of perceptual or empirical knowledge, retaining other aspects, and combining the latter into general presentations. Reason has no material content of its own but is dependent upon intuitive sources, outside itself. Its achievements are all in the purely formal order. Reason derives its universal concepts from intuitive, empirical presentations, and then combines them according to the rules of formal logic. The relations among concepts used in judgments are regulated by the principle of *sufficient reason of knowing (cognoscendi)*. The truth of a judgment rests upon a sufficient reason for the connection of concepts in the judgment. In grasping the reasons for making the judgment, reason apprehends the formal grounds of truth.

Certain other cases of objective knowledge convinced Schopenhauer, however, of the need to posit two more specific roots for the principle of sufficient reason.[4] For instance, if it be asked why the three sides of this triangle are equal, the answer is: because the three angles are equal. But the equality of the angles is neither a physical cause of becoming (since it produces no change of material state) nor a mere formal logical reason (since it determines directly the equality of the sides and only indirectly our knowledge about the sides). The inexorable and irreversible flow of time is another instance

---

[3] *On the Fourfold Root of the Principle of Sufficient Reason,* IV–V (Hillebrand, 31–152).

[4] *Ibid.,* VI–VII (Hillebrand, 153–76).

that can be explained neither by the physical conditions *within* time nor by a purely logical ground. Pure mathematics shows that our minds have another class of presentations, consisting solely of the formal elements or *pure perceptions,* implicated in empirical perceptions. These objects are the pure, a priori intuitions of space and time, which Schopenhauer described, in Kantian fashion, as the pure forms (respectively) of outer and inner sense. Knowledge in this area is specified by the principle of *sufficient reason of being* (*essendi*). It states the conditions for the a priori relations connecting objects in position and succession, as the respective foundations for geometry and arithmetic.

Lastly, Schopenhauer offers separate justification for the principle of *sufficient reason of acting* (*agendi*), which is constitutive for the objects of self-consciousness. Each individual has but one such object: *itself as the subject or will,* involved in knowledge. This is an inference from Schopenhauer's assumption that knowledge is impossible without a dichotomy between subject and object, knower and known. He never inquires phenomenologically about a cognitive situation prior to this distinction, such as the first awareness of being, or about a cognitive situation transcending this contrast, such as the divine self-knowledge. His sole concern is to draw out the implication contained in the Kantian dichotomy between subject and object. This distinction prevails even in self-knowledge, where the subject is known in inner experience or under the form of time alone. The object of reflective knowledge is not the subject, considered *as knowing* or representing, but the subject precisely *as willing,* as the subject in volition. The identity between the subject-as-willing and the subject-as-knowing is never grasped by knowledge: it must be accepted as an unavoidable postulate of cognition, indeed, as *"the* miracle, without qualification."[5] But at least, our knowledge of the self as a willer is the most direct and immediate knowledge we have. Sufficient reason, as the *ratio agendi,* gives insight into motivation or the action of motives, and thus reveals the "inner side" of the objective causal process. Schopenhauer's full-blown metaphysics of will supposes this special accessibility of the volitional subject and its intimate presence in causal events.

After this genetic presentation of the four forms of sufficient reason,

---

[5] *Ibid.,* VII, 42 (Hillebrand, 169; italics mine). Schopenhauer's foreign phrases are here translated.

Schopenhauer arranges them in *systematic order.*[6] He awards the primacy to the reason of being, since the form of time contains all that is essential to the other forms. This is followed by the principle of becoming or causation, and then by the principle of acting, which is only the special case of motivated causality. The last principle is that of knowing, which is derived mediately from the three immediate classes of presentations. These principles constitute the four main classes of objects and relations of objective connectedness. This enables Schopenhauer to infer the four *cognitive powers* of consciousness which grasp these objects in their relations. The powers are: *pure sensibility* (presenting the forms of space and time), *understanding* (presenting changing material states), *inner sense or self-consciousness* (presenting the subject of volition), and *reason* (presenting logical operations). Finally, this classification of principles serves as a guide to the *division of the sciences.* Pure mathematics follows the principle of being; applied mathematics, together with the physical and chemical sciences, relies on the principle of becoming; in history, psychology, and other humane studies, the principle of acting or motivation prevails; logic and the classifying sciences are organized around the principle of knowing.

There are two important implications of this investigation, as noted by Schopenhauer. In the first place, he declares that *to result from a given reason* and *to be necessary,* mean the same. *Necessity* signifies "the infallibility of the consequence when the reason is posited."[7] Once the ground or reason is present, the consequence follows with necessity. But since there are four kinds of reasons, there are also four kinds of necessity: mathematical, physical, moral, and logical (corresponding, respectively, to the principles of being, becoming, acting, and knowing). Every aspect of the phenomenal world is subject to necessity, under one or another of these four heads. In the second place, although every object of experience has its necessary reason, the principle of sufficient reason does not apply to the *world* itself, considered either as the totality of phenomenal presentations or as the noumenal thing-in-itself. The thing-in-itself (whatever be its nature) employs the principle of sufficient reason to organize the world of phenomenal objects. But

---

[6] *Ibid.,* VIII, 46 (Hillebrand, 177–78).

[7] *Ibid.,* VIII, 49 (Hillebrand, 181). For the second consequence and the argument for atheism, cf. *ibid.,* VIII, 52 (Hillebrand, 186–89).

this principle applies neither to its noumenal source nor to the total context of appearances, but only to the *objects within* the world of appearances.

From these twin consequences, Schopenhauer adduces an argument in favor of *atheism*. If all reasons are necessarily conditioned in turn by some prior ground, then it is a contradiction in terms to speak about an absolute or unconditioned reason or ground of reality. Furthermore, if the principle of sufficient reason does not apply to the world as a whole, then the basis of the cosmological argument for God's existence is destroyed. For, it then becomes senseless to inquire about a reason, outside the world, that will account for the existence of the world and everything in it. This criticism shows that Schopenhauer uncritically identifies the requirements of the *intelligibility of being* with his *principle of sufficient reason,* and then with the *Kantian requirements of experience.* Hence he allows to the principle of causality only an immanent use, preventing its application beyond particular objects within the world. But whereas Kant is ready to restore God's existence as a postulate of practical reason, Schopenhauer eliminates this sort of appeal to our practical exigencies. He advocates complete atheism, rather than the theoretical agnosticism of Kant. To understand why he rejects Kant's practical arguments for God, his main doctrine on the world and the will must be examined. Not content with reducing the rationalistic principles of explanation to their Kantian measure, he also wants to reform Kant's own view of reality, in such a way that the theistic postulates of practical reason are also eliminated.

## 3. THE WORLD AS PRESENTATION

Schopenhauer's major work, *The World as Will and Presentation,* opens with the keynoting declaration that "the world is my presentation."[8] The explanation of this statement rests upon a simplified version of Kant's theory of knowledge. The distinction between noumenon and phenomenon enables me to view the world or totality of experience in two ways: *phenomenally as my mental presentation, noumenally as the thing-in-itself or will.* The world is my mental presentation, in the sense that it is an object for me, the knowing subject. Schopenhauer cites the testimony of both the Vedanta and Berkeley in favor of the thesis that the existence of

---

[8] *The World as Will and Idea,* I, 1 (Haldane and Kemp translation, I, 3).

phenomenal objects is the same as their being perceived or being presented as objects of knowledge. However, he accepts neither Fichte's reduction of the object to the subject nor Schelling's reduction of the subject to the object. Both poles of the knowledge-situation must be maintained, for otherwise the empirical reality of the objects of experience would vanish.

Yet it is another Kantian thesis that the empirical reality of objects is itself founded upon their transcendental ideality or conformity to the conditions of perceptual knowledge. Schopenhauer distinguishes sharply between *perceptions* and *sensations,* since the latter provide only the subjective raw materials (cf. Kant's "matter of sensation") for perceptual knowledge of objects.[9] He takes the bodily organism as a given starting-point, which does not require further analysis, at least in an epistemological context. Our body is capable of receiving modifications, through the action of other material things: sensation is just our immediate consciousness of bodily changes going on. Sensations transpire within the organism and hence are purely subjective. The sense data of touch and sight supply the materials for the construction of the objective world, but there would be no such world without the contribution of the understanding. For, the materials of sensation assume *objective* significance as empirical perceptions, only in virtue of the *understanding's application of the forms of causality, space, and time.* The sole essential principle and law of the understanding is causality, which gives to sensations the status of effects and hence the value of objects of knowledge. These effects are traced back to causes existing in an external place, once

---

[9] For this distinction, consult *ibid.,* I, 4, 6 (Haldane-Kemp, I, 14–15, 23–25). Schopenhauer warns against confusing the relation between the perceiving subject and the perceived object with that between cause and effect. The principle of causality is applied *by* the understanding *to* the given sensations, in such fashion that the relation of cause and effect obtains only *between* the objects of perception themselves. Although he declares that this provides a way of bypassing the idealism-realism dispute about whether or not the outer world is caused by the perceiving subject, Schopenhauer also prides himself on drawing the radical conclusion from the entire movement of thought from Kant to Hegel. "Certainly from the most ancient times man had been called the *microcosm.* I have reversed the proposition and shown the world as the *macranthropos:* because will and presentation exhaust its nature as they do that of man." *The World as Will and Idea,* Supplements, I (Haldane-Kemp, III, 471; italics added). This completes the post-Renaissance tendency to empty the doctrine of microcosm of its realistic content. After reading a section in the main text of *The World as Will and Idea,* the student should consult the "Supplements" (which fill the second and third volumes of the English translation), to find out whether Schopenhauer added any commentary, in the second edition, on the section in question.

the understanding applies the pure form of space. The understanding can then grasp one's own body as a spatial object, interacting with the outside world, in which many kinds of bodies act upon one another. All these objective changes are viewed as temporal processes, when the understanding submits them to the pure form of time. The perceptual world owes its objective standing to the understanding, which constructs a phenomenal object or presentation for the knowing subject. The self, as an empirical reality in the world, is also phenomenal and needful of its correlative object.

Although this account adheres closely to Kant's doctrine, three significant modifications are introduced.[10] First, Schopenhauer identifies the *thing-in-itself* with the *will*. This shift is noticed only obliquely in the analysis of phenomenal knowledge, insofar as there is no mention of an unknown thing-in-itself as the extraempirical cause of the matter of sensation. Schopenhauer begins with the changes going on in one's organism; later on, he will explain the organism itself as the product and instrument of the will. To this extent, the will supplies its own matter of sensation. Second, the a priori forms of objective experience are reduced to three: *space, time,* and *causality.* Schopenhauer accepts the Kantian view of sensibility, as being constituted by the outer form of space and the inner form of time. But he reduces the categorial machinery of the understanding to the sole form of causality. This one category is favored by him, since it is easily correlated with will. Events are shaped phenomenally or on the outside by causality, and shaped noumenally or on the inside by will itself. Third, *understanding* is dissociated from *abstract* and *general conceptions.* As usually employed by Schopenhauer, the term "understanding" covers the total complexus of a priori conditions of objective perception, including the law of causality and the forms of sensibility. This usage breaks down the basic Kantian contrast between sensibility and understanding, so that Schopenhauer finds it natural to equate the understanding, sometimes, with the brain. The reduction of the forms of the understanding to causality greatly aids this assimilation of the understanding to the level of sensibility. Kant's other categories are included with the derivative concepts of

---

[10] Schopenhauer gives an extended account of his position toward Kant in *ibid.,* Appendix ("Criticism of the Kantian Philosophy"), and Supplements, I–IV (Haldane-Kemp, II, 3–227). For the import of Schopenhauer's phenomenal theory of causality, cf. M. Méry, *Essai sur la causalité phénoménale selon Schopenhauer* (Paris, Vrin, 1948).

*reason.* Reason and its abstractive operation belong to man alone, but understanding is shared by man and the other animals. As evidence of this common possession of understanding by all animals, Schopenhauer cites instances of animal behavior, in which a perception of cause is manifested. But he fails to distinguish between the brute's concrete apprehension of causal events, and man's ability to arrive at the causal principle as such, on the basis of these events.

Because of its coalition with sensibility, Schopenhauerian understanding has its own *intuitions,* instead of merely applying categorial forms to intuitions. Although its intuitions only refer to objects in the phenomenal world, the understanding provides all that is rich, original, and progressive in human cognition. The intuitive perceptions of the understanding constitute the primary knowledge of mankind, the only kind with a real, intuitive content of its own, capable of fertilizing the sciences. Perceptions provide either pure or empirical intuitions, depending upon whether they concern the pure forms of sensibility or also include the matter of sensation. Reason relies entirely upon the faculty of judgment, for supplying it with material content from the level of perception. Rational concepts are pale formalizations of what the understanding seizes in a vital, immediate way. *Understanding* (as inclusive of sensibility) gives the primary, "ir-rational" knowledge of perceptions; *reason* gives the derived knowledge of rational concepts.[11] *Perceptions* are intuitive, concrete, and particular; *rational concepts* are nonintuitive, abstract, and universal. It is not only the purely formal character of the concepts of reason (including most of Kant's categories), but also their abstract and universal nature, that places reason in a subordinate position. The ground is being broken for using Kant's empiricism and transcendental idealism in the service of a metaphysical irrationalism.

Schopenhauer anticipates Nietzsche and Bergson both in his criticism of reason and conceptual thinking and also in his emphasis upon the *practical motives* governing the use of concepts. Reason

---

[11] "The abstract concepts of the reason can only serve to take up the objective connections which are immediately known by the understanding, to make them permanent for thought, and to relate them to each other; but reason never gives us immediate knowledge. . . . A concept is an idea of an idea [*Vorstellung einer Vorstellung*], i.e., its whole nature consists in its relation to another idea," and ultimately to a totally different class of presentations, viz., the perceptions of the understanding which alone have real content. *The World as Will and Idea,* I, 6, 9 (Haldane-Kemp, I, 20, 53–54). On understanding and reason, cf. *ibid.,* I, 8–12; Supplements, V–VII (Haldane-Kemp, I, 45–75; II, 228–69).

fulfills the purely practical role of supplementing the shortcomings of perceptions, and serving the needs of the body. Although perceptions give us immediate access to empirical reality and serve immediate ends, their hold upon it is transient, particular, and incommunicable. The abstractive process, used by reason, removes some of these defects. Schopenhauer avoids giving a clear account of abstraction, since he does not want to admit that reason can discern any content that is not formally and explicitly known to sensibility or perceptual understanding. Like Hobbes and Locke, he concentrates upon *language,* the product of reason, without inquiring too closely into why language is man's unique product, and what this implies about man's nature. Rational concepts do not extend knowledge, but in their linguistic expression, they promote the retention, organization, and communication of knowledge. They organize phenomenal relations, although they stop short of noumenal being. With their help, man achieves control over his environment and thus satisfies his needs. Reason is the medium whereby the bodily organism can pursue long-range ends, through actions of considerable duration and complication.

Underlying this pragmatic conception of reason and its concepts is the *metaphysics of the will.* For, will embodies itself in the bodily needs and desires of the highly developed human organism, to which reason is subservient. Will determines human action to spring from *motives* or causal reasons specified by knowledge. In man, the motives of action are specified not only by perceptual knowledge but also by reason. Along with the other knowing powers, *reason is the tool of will,* in its effort to satisfy its desires. Concepts are the means used by will to reach its more ambitious practical ends, as expressed in bodily needs and desires.

Schopenhauer's critique of reason and the concept is of special interest, because of its transitional nature. It stands midway between Kant's critique of the ideas of reason, and the view of intelligence taken by philosophy-of-life and pragmatism. It serves as a reminder of the epistemological background against which "reason" and "the concept" were treated, during the century after Kant. Schopenhauer heightened the contrast between understanding and reason, to the disadvantage of the latter power. His opposition to Hegel, who made reason the cornerstone of his dialectic, led him to overstress the purely formal and practical function of reason. It is a *reason cut off from direct co-operation with sensibility and essentially subordinated to will and bodily needs,* that becomes the target of Nietzsche's and

Bergson's criticism. And it is the concept, regarded as a merely formal tool and a product of total abstraction or dropping-out of certain perceptual characteristics, which these thinkers compare unfavorably with the life of perception, immediacy, and concrete reality. Schopenhauer's manner of posing the problem of reason and the concept has been very influential, even where his special metaphysics of the will has been criticized.

## 4. FROM PHENOMENON TO NOUMENON: THE DEFENSE OF METAPHYSICS

The crux of Schopenhauer's philosophy is the transition from appearances to the thing-in-itself, together with the identification of the thing-in-itself with cosmic will. Schopenhauer threads his way carefully through the previous idealistic solutions to the problems raised by Kant. He refuses to accept the Kantian distinction between theoretical and practical reason, as a way of contacting the noumenal order. Reason is by nature practical, so that Schopenhauer's strictures on rational concepts apply also to their use *as practical postulates,* in the attempt to validate a belief in noumenal realities. Metaphysics must abandon the terrain of reason and its concepts entirely, if it expects to achieve a solid reconstruction. Fichte's appeal to the practical ego suffers from overreliance upon reason, as well as from the added handicap of deriving everything from a single, formal, first principle. Schopenhauer's own description of reason, as an empty and derivative power, runs counter to the Fichtean deduction. A genuine solution of the problem of metaphysics cannot rest on the basis of moral faith, practical reason, or rational intuition. There is another path to metaphysical certitude which has been overlooked by all the post-Kantian idealists.

Schopenhauer questions neither the reality of the noumenal being nor the derivation of the world from the noumenal being. But the noumenon cannot be known as existing entirely beyond the range of experience, in the sense that we would have to leave the empirical data behind, in order to reach it. The world of appearances somehow "manifests" its noumenal source, and thus provides us with a clue for reaching it. But the clue is furnished neither by the exigencies of practical life nor by the dialectical conflicts of reason. Taken by themselves, the *exigencies of practical reason* have no ontological significance. Their frustration might render life senseless and futile, but Kant offers no proof of the underlying supposition that the ultimate ground of existence and action *is* rational and orderly. This is precisely the point at issue between Schopenhauer and Kant, so that the former will not concede the basic presumption of noumenal rationality and the practical beliefs that flow from it. Yet Schopenhauer is also reluctant to find the implications of noumenal being in Hegel's account of the *dialectical conflicts of reason.* The dialectic of rational concepts has a purely formal significance and reveals nothing about noumenal being. Despite his many ironical references to Schelling and the Romantics, Schopenhauer comes closer to them than to Kantian rationalism and Hegelian dialecticism. He looks for some immediate ground of metaphysical reflection, some nonrational intuition that can serve as the priming point for a study of the noumenal being.

He finds this point of departure in *wonder,* which Aristotle had already signalized as the state of soul from which metaphysics and all philosophy spring. Schopenhauer gives what would today be called an "existentialist" exegesis of wonder. It is a peculiarly human response, since only man can establish a reflective distance between himself and the whole world of phenomena, such that he may inquire about its meaning as a totality. But the special nature of philosophical wonderment is lost upon reason, which is ordained essentially to practical ends. Philosophical doctrines like Spinoza's pantheism also blunt its edge, for there is no room for wonder in a world constituted by one, divine substance. Moreover, man would never be roused to pose questions about his existence and the nature of being, were our life a painless and immortal one. But, in fact, human existence is an affair of suffering, evil, and death. These traits supply "the itching-point of metaphysics,"[12] the stimulant to wonder about the principle behind the universal misery of things. A tragic sense of life convinces us of the possible *non*existence of the actual order, and metaphysics is just this knowledge that the phenomenal world is neither the only reality nor the absolute reality. Man is an *animal metaphysicum,* precisely because he is moved by an imaginative melancholy, that

---

[12] *The World as Will and Idea,* Supplements, XVII (Haldane-Kemp, II, 375); the entire supplementary Chapter XVII ("On Man's Need of Metaphysics," *loc. cit.,* 359–95) deserves a careful reading. In the estimation of É. Bréhier, in " 'L'unique pensée' de Schopenhauer," *Revue de Métaphysique et de Morale,* XLV (1938), 487–500, the themes of wonder, suffering, and contingency comprise the central message of Schopenhauer's philosophy, which thereby affects a "conversion" of the modern mind's attention toward some neglected aspects of finite being.

can be lulled neither by pantheistic optimism nor by naturalistic efforts to make this world absolute.

Naturalism and positivism try to convert the phenomenal order into the noumenal, by dispensing entirely with metaphysics. But this program can never succeed, due to the intrinsic insufficiency of physical explanations. The physical sciences are compelled eventually to posit an endless series of causes and a number of inscrutable forces. At this point, they either cease to explain or are transformed covertly into some metaphysical conception of natural events. The great bulwark *of* metaphysics is the very distinction between noumenon and phenomenon which Kant drew as a safeguard *against* any metaphysical speculation. Kant was justified in ruling out knowledge of that which cannot possibly be given in experience, but he had no right to regard this as the proper object of metaphysics. Schopenhauer challenges Kant's uncritical acceptance of the rationalistic description of metaphysics, as a discipline that would have to be founded, in a purely a priori way, upon formal principles drawn in no way from experience. Such a description would rule out rationalistic metaphysics in principle but it would not affect other conceptions of metaphysics. Schopenhauer himself proposes a more empirical view of *metaphysics, as the science of experience in general or as a whole.*[13] Just as the metaphysical problem is generated by such empirical facts as death, finiteness, and suffering, so the constructive metaphysical solution is based on both the material and the formal traits of experience. This means, however, that metaphysics is a purely *immanent* discipline, and must renounce all pretensions to go beyond experience.

Nevertheless, it does not follow that metaphysics is merely what Kant called a "transcendental science," i.e., a study of the limits of our knowledge, which cannot get beyond the phenomenal objects. Although it never cuts its phenomenal moorings, it does succeed in understanding the meaning of the phenomenal world as a whole. Without going *beyond* experience, metaphysics finds more *in* experience than the mere appearances. It passes from the husk to the kernel of being, from the phenomenal manifestation to the *noumenal principle,* which the phenomenon manifests and which is, nevertheless, not the same as the phenomenon. Yet metaphysics never grasps

---

[13] Variations on this definition are supplied in *The World as Will and Idea,* Supplements, XVII (Haldane-Kemp, II, 364, 379, 386–87).

the noumenal kernal of being *in itself,* as an extramundane reality, but only insofar as it is *implicated in* phenomenal modes. "In this sense, then, metaphysics goes beyond the phenomenon, i.e., nature, to that which is concealed in or behind it, always regarding it, however, merely as that which manifests itself in the phenomenon, not as independent of all phenomenal appearance."[14] Schopenhauer admits that the noumenal principle remains wholly unknowable in itself, since the forms of experience are impotent to reveal its intrinsic nature. An actual, positive (*wirkliche, positive*) solution of the problem of the thing-in-itself is beyond our power. But we can learn something about its connections without experience and something, in a relative and conditioned way, about its nature.

Schopenhauer compares the whole of experience to a giant cryptograph, whose message is unscrambled only by metaphysics.[15] Just as we know that we have broken a code, when the proposed key produces a meaningful series of words and sentences, so we know that a metaphysical explanation is successful, when it establishes meaningful connections everywhere among the appearances. Schopenhauer recommends his account of the thing-in-itself, because it *brings connectedness* into our experience, as we would expect the ultimate sufficient reason of the phenomenal world to do. It synthesizes the most heterogeneous and conflicting phenomena, casting illumination equally upon all portions of experience. Whatever his professional dislike of Hegel, Schopenhauer gladly avails himself of the Hegelian criteria of coherence, comprehensiveness, and reconciliation, as guaranteeing the truth of his own metaphysical explanation.

Man carries the final answer to the riddle of the universe within his own breast, since he carries noumenal reality within himself and indeed *is* that reality. Following Kant's procedure in solving the third antinomy, Schopenhauer bids us regard man, not only in his phenomenal nature, but also insofar as he shares in the nature of the thing-in-itself. If *reflection* can reveal man in his freedom, rather than in his physical necessitation, then it provides the bridge for passing over into noumenal terrain. Instead of limiting this insight to man's nature, however, Schopenhauer extends it to all things. *All* empirical objects can be viewed noumenally as well as phenomenally, and what self-consciousness discloses about man's noumenal nature has universal import. For, man differs from other phenomenal

---

[14] *Loc. cit.* (Haldane-Kemp, II, 389).
[15] *The World as Will and Idea,* Supplements, XVII (Haldane-Kemp, II, 388–91).

objects not in kind but only in degree. Moreover, the *principle of individuation* is constituted by the forms of *space* and *time*. Since these forms do not apply to the noumenal being as such, there is not a plurality of noumenal entities or things-in-themselves. There is but *one single thing-in-itself*, so that the noumenal findings of man's intuitive reflection apply in principle to the noumenal reality of all things. If *will* and *freedom* are revealed as the noumenal core of man, then they also comprise the noumenal core of the entire world.

The Kantian approach to the world is like that of an artist, who is constantly making sketches of the exterior of a castle, without ever viewing its interior. Schopenhauer suggests that one doorway, leading inward, is provided by the concrete feeling of *my-own-body* (another theme appropriated by later existentialists).[16] My body agrees with other objects of experience, in that it is a presentation for a knowing subject. But there is something distinctive and inalienable about this one body: it is apprehended not only as a *phenomenal object* but also as a center of *my voluntary movements*. What remains in the reality of my body, over and above its being an object of perception, is its noumenal nature as a *striving expression and objectification of will*. Hence both the self and my own body manifest themselves as having the noumenal nature of will and freedom. At least in the self and its own body, there is seen the co-presence of *causality* and *will*. Causality is the "outside aspect," and will is the "inside aspect," revealed in reflection upon the self and in the feeling of my-own-body. Schopenhauer suggests that the inference may now be extended to include all objects whatsoever of perception. This generalization cannot be demonstrated strictly, since we do not have intuitive access, by way of either reflection or the feeling of my-own-body, to the other things in the world. But the "miracle" of its coherence and truth should dazzle our minds. Just as causal determinism is present in mental life (where the region of will and freedom is strongest), so we may surmise that will is present in the realm of bodily things (where causality holds strong sway). Thus the doctrine of cosmic will recommends itself as the grand metaphysical truth, in virtue of its ability to draw together the extremes of existence and experience.

---

[16] Cf. *ibid.*, II, 18–20 (Haldane-Kemp, I, 129–41). The universal correlation between phenomenal causality and noumenal will is set forth in *On the Will in Nature* (Hillebrand translation, in the same volume as *On the Fourfold Root of the Principle of Sufficient Reason*, 317–21).

A single exception to Kant's thesis of the unknowability of the thing-in-itself is therefore demanded by our unique knowledge of our noumenal reality, as a striving agent or will. This awareness does not involve the forms of space and causality, since the noumenal will is not located in a particular place or subjected to any causal determinism. Hence the doctrine of noumenal will rests upon a *metaphysical intuition,* conveying the *sui generis* evidence of reflection and the feeling of my-own-body. Yet although our metaphysical knowledge of the will is distinctive, direct, and from the inside, it is not perfectly immediate and exhaustive. If it were, then we would have a perfectly comprehensive understanding of the nature of the thing-in-itself, apprehended in its own reality and beyond all limits of experience. Schopenhauer rejects this claim of absolute idealism, on the ground that, in fact, we do not know the will as a totality and complete unity but only in its particular acts, viz., in the acts of the body. Hence our noumenal knowledge is not free from the *form of time.* The thing-in-itself is known through reflection, which is the inner sense or the form of time — a qualification that leaves its mark upon the extent of our metaphysical knowledge. "Accordingly, in this inner knowledge the thing-in-itself has indeed in great measure thrown off its veil, but still does not yet appear quite naked."[17] The possibility is acknowledged that, beyond all the veils of mental forms, the thing-in-itself might have qualities and modes of existence which would persist, even though the aspect of time-bound will were to be removed. Schopenhauer claims only a limited victory over Kant's epistemological rejection of all theoretical knowledge of noumenal reality.

It is questionable, however, whether Schopenhauer achieves even a limited victory over the Kantian bar upon speculative metaphysics. By placing our grasp of will beyond the forms of space and causality, he succeeds in narrowing down the obstacles against knowing the thing-in-itself. But the retention of the form of time means, on Kantian grounds, that the barrier against noumenal knowledge remains, in principle, just as high and firm as ever. The sole presence of the form of time *attenuates,* but does *not radically transform,* the

---

[17] *The World as Will and Idea,* Supplements, XVIII (Haldane-Kemp, II, 407). Supplementary Chapter XVIII ("On the Possibility of Knowing the Thing In Itself," *loc. cit.,* 399–410) is a major source of Schopenhauer's doctrine on the possibility of metaphysics.

phenomenal character of our self-knowledge. The least phenomenal sort of knowledge, based on the experience of a striving will, is in no way identical with the first degree of noumenal truth. Insofar as it is *knowledge,* it still remains completely phenomenal, as far as Kant is concerned. It is still qualified by the subsumption of empirical data under a form of sensibility, and the outcome of such a synthesis is phenomenal, rather than noumenal. From the Kantian perspective, this is a repetition of the problem of self-knowledge, in which only the empirical, phenomenal self is known by means of time or inner sense.

What Schopenhauer fails to do is to show that his "way from within" for grasping the self as thing-in-itself, freedom, and will, is a piece of *knowledge,* rather than what Kant would call *belief* or moral faith. Even though he makes no appeal to the exigencies of practical reason, Schopenhauer's alleged metaphysical intuition rests upon grounds that Kant would classify on the side of belief rather than knowledge: awareness of the exercise of freedom and striving, the feeling of possessing and moving one's own body, and the appeal to wonderment and inexpugnable melancholy. No basis is provided for an *intellectual* intuition, whether of a Hegelian or a nonidealistic sort. In making his extrapolation of will beyond consciousness and one's own body to the entire world, Schopenhauer is supported only by the "miracle" of the coherence and comprehensiveness of such a hypothesis. The idealists, whom he criticized, were achieving similar miracles of explanation, on the basis of radically different hypotheses about the noumenal nature of things. There is something arbitrary about all the post-Kantian attempts to soften Kant's doctrine on the unknowable thing-in-itself and the inaccessible transcendental unity of apperception.

### 5. COSMIC WILL AND METAPHYSICAL PESSIMISM

Will or the thing-in-itself is actively present in all beings of nature, as well as in man. This view should not lead to egoism, however, since will is not a Romantic expansion of the individual ego into nature. The world may now be regarded in another light: it is will as well as presentation, noumenon as well as phenomenon. After the contribution of mind to perceptual objects is subtracted, there remains a noumenal residue in all things. There are not several noumenal wills, since will escapes the conditions of individuation, imposed by the forms of space and time.[18] The noumenal reality of will is *a single whole,* omnipresent in nature. It is called "will" rather than "force," because we gather its nature from our own intimate experience of striving.

The attribution of the single, cosmic will to all things is made more plausible by Schopenhauer's remark that, taken universally in its own nature, the thing-in-itself is not a *knowing* subject. This requires that a qualification be placed upon the identification between the knowing and the willing subject, as proposed in his doctoral dissertation. Such identification can refer only to the special conditions found in man and other perceiving subjects, where the will creates and employs cognitive powers as its instruments, at these particular levels of phenomenal being. But Schopenhauer saw that, if will is to be erected into an omnipresent, noumenal principle, the Kantian equivalence between will and practical reason must be replaced by a doctrine of *will as nonrational and even irrational.* If intelligence is regarded as derivative and phenomenal, then its absence from bodily things is no argument against the presence, there, of will. Will becomes a metaphysical principle for Schopenhauer, only in the degree that its noumenal nature is liberated from any intrinsic cognitive and rational aspect. Precisely because will is the ultimate ground for every type of sufficient reason, its own nature cannot be proportionate to any cognitive power.

As such, will is a blind, cosmic force, incessantly striving to embody itself in various ways within the world of space and time. All the grades of being, in the space-time network of causes, are manifestations of will. *Nature* is the vast phenomenal field for the multiform activities and projects of will. Schopenhauer subtitled his book *On the Will in Nature:* "An account of the corroborations received by the author's philosophy, since its first appearance, from the empirical sciences." He scanned eagerly the latest findings in astronomy, anatomy, physiology, linguistics, and even animal magnetism, for evidence that empirical scientists were groping toward conclusions bearing out his own conception of the universe. The unknown natural forces, at which the scientists point uncomprehendingly, find their systematic

---

[18] Considered in itself, the will is one (in the sense of lying beyond the principle of individuation), whereas its manifestations in the world are many (since they come under the forms of space and time or the conditions of individuation). Cf. *The World as Will and Idea,* II, 23 (Haldane-Kemp, I, 145–46).

explanation in the doctrine on cosmic will. The operation of will is displayed

> not only [in] the voluntary actions of animals, but the organic mechanism, nay even the shape and quality of their living body, the vegetation of plants and finally, even in inorganic nature, crystallization, and in general every primary force which manifests itself in physical and chemical phenomena, not excepting gravity.[19]

Schopenhauer did not argue, merely, that there is an appetitive tendency of some sort in every natural thing: his point was that the inner nature of all natural forces is a single, irrational power or will. It extends from astronomical movements to biological urges and man's purposive actions. But only metaphysics can formally grasp the sameness of the underlying force.

The cosmic dynamism is essentially a *will-to-live*. This is its proper name, since what the will does *will*, is its visible expression in the phenomenal world, and this is life in its totality. The will-to-live is incarnated at different levels of phenomenal being, and thus constitutes the scale of nature. Each stage in this scale contains a new manifestation of will, organized in a new normative pattern by a *Platonic idea* or grade of the objectification of will.[20] Each specific level of natural being results from a distinctive objectification of will, according to an archetypal idea or essential way of organizing the phenomenal conditions. What the empirical sciences study as *natural laws* are, in fact, the consequences of the various levels of correlation between the empirical elements and their "Platonic ideas" or regulative norms.

The "Platonic ideas" hold a somewhat ambiguous position in the Schopenhauerian scheme of things. They are ways of looking at will, according to its various degrees of objectification. They are posited as a way of explaining the presence of constant, widespread natural laws and species, without having recourse to intelligent planning on the part of will. The hypothesis of "Platonic ideas" is Schopenhauer's ground for maintaining the paradox that blind cunning of will (rather than the enlightened cunning of Hegelian reason) can give

---

[19] *On the Will in Nature* (Hillebrand, 217); cf. *The World as Will and Idea*, Supplements, XXIII (Haldane-Kemp, III, 32–47).

[20] On the "Platonic idea," see *ibid.*, II, 25, 26; III, 30–31 (Haldane-Kemp, I, 168–69, 174–75, 219–21). Schopenhauer recommends his conception of the will as providing a synthesis of Kant (the will as *thing-in-itself*) and Plato (the objectification of will at a definite grade as *idea*).

birth to an organized world, in which the empirical sciences discover laws, gradations, and essential forms. No explanation is offered, however, of how *ideal* patterns could be inherently resident in *irrational* will, or why there are intelligibly organized grades in the objectification of an essentially blind force. Schopenhauer wishes to avail himself of the Hegelian and Schellingian explanations for the hierarchy in nature, without having to establish his right to appropriate rational patterns within his metaphysics of will. The more the theory of "Platonic ideas" succeeds in explaining the organized gradations in nature, the more it renders implausible his reluctance to admit that the creative principle of the universe is both powerful and intelligent and provident.

The "Platonic ideas" serve not only to justify scientific laws but also to provide the metaphysical groundwork of Schopenhauer's *pessimism*. The several levels of embodiment of will are engaged in *incessant warfare,* the higher being forced to fight for the privilege of providing the will with a distinctive appearance in the world.[21] The strife among ideas, as described by Schopenhauer, moves from the realm of possibility into the world of actuality. In Leibnizian fashion, the ideas do battle with each other for the right to impress their competing patterns upon the available matter, space, and time of the world. By "higher" and "lower" ideas are meant more and less adequate expressions of the will-to-live. The higher ideas must first overcome and assimilate the lower forces, if they are to emerge in being. The human organism, for instance, must battle to organize the physical and chemical forces under its own specific law. The body is subject to the necessities of food and sleep; it renews and repairs itself; but finally, the grip of the higher form is lost and death ensues. The lower ideas then reclaim their own nature, and mock at the presumed importance of the individual man. Nothing is so precious, and nothing so inevitably doomed, as the individual higher organism.

Whereas the principle of sufficient reason enables Leibniz to give the strife among ideas an *optimistic* outcome, this principle does not

---

21 *Ibid.,* II, 27 (Haldane-Kemp, I, 188–95). O. Schuster, "Die Wurzeln des Pessimismus bei Schopenhauer," *Archiv für Geschichte der Philosophie,* XXVI (1912), 66–82, stresses the personal sources of Schopenhauer's pessimism, whereas R. A. Tsanoff, *The Nature of Evil* (New York, Macmillan, 1931), 262–307, maintains a healthy balance between personal and systematic reasons for his pessimism. Tsanoff also traces the influence of Schopenhauer upon Eduard von Hartmann and the "German Slough of Despond," in the latter part of the nineteenth century (*ibid.,* 308–63).

apply to Schopenhauer's noumenal will. Hence Schopenhauer uses the strife of ideas for a *pessimistic* purpose. To avoid hypostasizing the ideas, engaged in mortal combat, he attributes their conflict ultimately to the will itself. Cosmic conflicts among grades of being are only an objective transcription of the *will's own internal hostilities.* It is a force essentially at variance with itself. Because it is a will-to-live, it must give phenomenal expression to its conflicting impulses. Hence temporal existence is *essentially* marked by aggression, pain, and death. The moments of happiness are accidental, negative, and fugitive, since they only signify a breathing space, before will again takes up the struggle with itself, on another plane. Pain and ennui are of life's positive essence, for they are the truest mirroring of insatiable will. "The basis of all willing is need, deficiency, and thus pain."[22] The will's thirst for phenomenal realization can never be quenched: it becomes surfeited with what it has achieved, destroys its products, and moves restlessly onward to new conflicts.

Despite the likeness with Hegel's doctrine on "unhappy consciousness," Schopenhauer intends this account of things to stand in striking contrast with Hegel's emphasis upon rational synthesis and reconciliation. The conflict does not lead to any assured triumph of higher values. There is no rational principle of ultimate synthesis, since reason is a *by-product,* rather than the *motive force,* of the vital process. Man is worse off, and not better off, for having understanding and reason. These powers are required by the greater sensitivity and keener desires of the human body, but they only visit upon man greater conflicts and pains. As Schopenhauer sardonically puts it, reason gives man the great privilege of anticipating future pains, brooding over imminent evils, and meditating upon inescapable death. Man's rationality is a doleful privilege, for (as Hobbes also remarked) it only enables him to outdo the other animals in deceit, cruelty, and other ill deeds.

The human body and all its organs are will-become-visible. Teeth are hunger incarnate, the genitals are desire incarnate, and the hand embodies the myriad other cravings of will. Understanding and reason themselves are products of the brain, tools fashioned for itself by blind will. They give vision to the will, but only for the sake of satisfying its wants, arousing new desires, and giving it a sorrowful consciousness of its own unhappy nature. There is no freedom in

<hr>

[22] *The World as Will and Idea,* IV, 57 (Haldane-Kemp, I, 402).

our particular actions, since they are regulated by the *universal determinism* of phenomenal events.[23] We do have choice, in the sense that intelligence opens up a wide range of purposes and prolongs the battle among various motives. Eventually, however, the strongest motive must prevail, providing a sufficient reason from which the action must flow, as a necessary consequence. Unlike Leibniz' appeal to moral necessity, Schopenhauer makes no effort to soften the determinism of human actions, granted that our choices are regulated solely by the principle of the sufficient reason of acting or the strongest motive. Only the will itself escapes the reign of the principle of sufficient reason, and hence it alone is inherently free. Somehow, this *noumenal freedom* is brought within the sphere of human consciousness. Man is at least privileged to see that cosmic will is alone free. Yet in this very reflection, the phenomenal world is brought into contradiction with itself, since man views with revulsion the conflicting and restless nature of will. A denial of the will-to-live is sometimes the fruit of human insight into the will's nature and freedom.

The universal egoism not only drives individuals of all species to do battle with each other, but also infects *human social relations*. Schopenhauer accepts the Hobbesian description of the state of nature as a war of all against all, but he remarks that it lacks a rigorous metaphysical foundation in a doctrine of cosmic will. Will asserts itself as fully as possible in every individual, first of all in the affirmation of its own bodily integrity and then in aggressive claims over other men and things. Because the *same will* underlies all phenomena and is embodied somehow as a whole in every being, an individual is led to *desire everything for itself*. This egoistic claim generates a desire to thwart and destroy the similar claims of other individuals or, at the very least, to exercise sufficient force to control the actions of others. The satisfaction of one's individual desires is taken as the standard of good and evil, leading to endless aggression and self-justification. Schopenhauer recognizes that even his doctrine on "the world as my own presentation" can be put to egoistic ends. The individual can regard other men as being only ideas in his world, and can organize these ideas exclusively around his own

---

[23] Compare *The Two Fundamental Problems of Ethics, I: On the Freedom of the Human Will* (*Sämmtliche Werke*, edited by Deussen and Hübscher, III, 473–572); *The Basis of Morality*, II, viii (Bullock translation, 115–21); *The World as Will and Idea*, Supplements, XXV (Haldane-Kemp, III, 66–69).

plans for self-satisfaction. Thus social life provides no escape from the bottomless cravings and conflicts that pour forth from the power of will.

From this account, it is clear that Schopenhauer's pessimism is a *metaphysical* doctrine, even more than it is a reflection of his character and temperament. There is a highly selective use of concrete instances to illustrate a theoretical position, rather than a balanced weighing of the empirical evidence in its various aspects. As a metaphysical principle of interpretation of human experience, this pessimism is no stronger than the underlying argument in favor of a blind, noumenal will. Schopenhauer is still confronted with his own statement that the forms of experience, including that of time, give absolutely no insight into the nature of noumenal being as such. The experience of self-striving gives no theoretical ground for attributing irrational will to the thing-in-itself, since it remains a phenomenal experience. Schopenhauer himself admits the possibility that the *temporal view* of the thing-in-itself (as irrational will) might be removed, without disturbing the *intrinsic nature* of the thing-in-itself.[24] This means that there is no cogent ground, in the evidence he presents, for regarding the noumenal principle in itself as having only blind will or as not having intelligence-and-will.

This narrows down the discussion to the question of how the thing-in-itself manifests itself, in and through phenomenal experience. Here, some historical considerations come into play concerning the import of self-consciousness, which forms the common point of departure for Kant and his successors. Kant himself held that we become aware of will as being one with practical reason, whereas Hegel made self-consciousness terminate in an intuition of dialectical speculative reason, which encloses practical reason and will within itself. Kant's solution was rejected by Schopenhauer, as soon as he criticized practical reason, denied the plurality of noumenal selves, and attributed the same noumenal reality to all bodies in nature. Hegel's solution was equally inacceptable, since Schopenhauer wanted to limit reason and the concept to empty, formal principles, and to have a conflict of ideas, without dialectical resolution. Hence he turned to the affective side of man's nature for a metaphysical intuition and found, not surprisingly, that will and the emotions are predominant in this perspective. By giving *exclusive ontological*

[24] *Ibid.*, Supplements, XVIII (Haldane-Kemp, II, 408).

*weight* to the conative, striving aspects of human experience, Schopenhauer reached the distinctive standpoint of an irrationalistic, voluntaristic, and pessimistic metaphysics. Nevertheless, he remained closer to the tragic and antithetic aspect of Hegel's thought than he was ready to acknowledge. It was not the essential structure of being or even of integral human experience, but his own *systematic narrowing* of the evidence, that led Schopenhauer to view the essential nature of things as that of blind and tragic will.

## 6.  RELEASE THROUGH ESTHETIC CONTEMPLATION

The miserable condition of human existence is sufficient reason why men should often seek to flee this life through *suicide*. In his essay *On Suicide,* Schopenhauer toys with suicide as a remedy.[25] He quotes the Stoics and Hume in its favor, brands the opposition of Christian moralists baseless, and states the case for those, for whom life's sufferings outweigh the terrors of death. But he also advances two considerations that tell decisively against suicide, from his own standpoint. (1) If one approaches suicide in the somewhat quizzical spirit of wanting to find out what happens to human existence and knowledge after death, suicide entails the serious disadvantage of annihilating the individual inquirer himself. At death, the phenomenal individual is dissolved; all that remains unscathed is the single noumenal will, which is beyond all individual modes of being. If there is any human "immortality," it consists in acknowledging the truth of the proposition that only the cosmic will is everlasting. (2) On the other hand, if one is driven by the burdens of existence to seek the termination of human misery, then suicide is not the proper method to use. For, the death of the individual affects the will in no way, and leaves it in full possession of the field of experience. Hence suicide fails to get at the root cause of the evils and sufferings of life. Indeed, suicide is a particularly strong affirmation of the will, rather than its radical negation. The suicide prizes the will-to-live so highly, that he destroys the individual obstacle to its fruition. He removes the frustrating conditions and, simultaneously, pays tribute to omnivorous will in all its power.

The mistake of self-murder is to attack particular circumstances,

---

[25] The essay "On Suicide" is translated in *Selected Essays of Arthur Schopenhauer* (Bax translation, 257–62); cf. *The World as Will and Idea,* IV, 69 (Haldane-Kemp, I, 514–18).

rather than the very will-to-live itself. There are two major routes by which men have attempted a negation of the will in its own nature: *art* and *morality*. Schopenhauer's analysis of esthetic attempts at release from the pressures of existence rests upon a given fact and an assumed principle. The *fact* is that artists and others are capable of esthetic contemplation; the *principle* is that such contemplation is directed properly toward the "Platonic ideas," as they figure in Schopenhauer's philosophy. No proof of this first principle is furnished. A detailed account is given, however, of the *consequences* of this proposed relationship between esthetic contemplation and the Schopenhauerian ideal patterns.

Since the archetypal ideas are aspects of will itself, they transcend both the conditions of space and time and the domain of the principle of sufficient reason. Hence they cannot be known by the cognitive subject, *qua* a phenomenal or space-time individual, or by means of the principle of sufficient reason. But the fact is that men do enjoy esthetic contemplation of such ideas. This fact is explainable only through a sudden transformation of the knowing subject and of his type of knowledge. The knower ceases to be a phenomenal individual and becomes *a pure subject of knowledge*. He abandons reason and its principles, approaches the object through *intuition* (which seems to be, in this context, a conflation of sensibility, understanding, and imagination), and loses himself in quiet contemplation of the ideal nature. Being freed from the burden of sufficient reason and the practical ordination of reason, the contemplator is under no compulsion to refer his esthetic knowledge back to the bodily needs and the service of the will. His absorption in the contemplated object is so complete, that (at least for the nonce) he is forgetful of his pragmatic concerns, his individuality, and the power of will itself. His consciousness and the ideal constitution of the thing interpenetrate and achieve a perfect union. The subject is drawn out of his individual confines, to become a *"pure, will-less painless, timeless subject of knowledge,"*[26] while the object is correlatively revealed

---

[26] *Ibid.*, III, 34 (Haldane-Kemp, I, 231); cf. *ibid.*, III, 38; Supplements, XXX (Haldane-Kemp, I, 253–57; III, 126–32). W. McK. Salter, "Schopenhauer's Contact with Pragmatism," *The Philosophical Review*, XIX (1910), 137–53, maintains that, although Schopenhauer anticipated American pragmatism in regarding the cognitive powers as instruments of will for practical aims, he diverged from them in his doctrine on the pure subject of knowledge, in which he made room for a purely speculative sort of knowledge.

in the fullness of its ideal nature. The "Platonic idea" consists precisely in this fusion between the pure knower and the fully perceived object.

Whatever its emotional resonances, art is primarily an affair of *knowledge*. It takes its rise in contemplation of the ideas, and has as its end the communication of this insight to others, through the various sensuous mediums. Schopenhauer makes a happy combination of Kant's notion of the beautiful with the Romantic view of genius.[27] The *beauty* of a natural or artificial thing consists in the distinctness with which it embodies its ideal form. The apprehension of beauty is disinterested, in the sense that it involves a perception of the object, apart from regulation by the principle of sufficient reason or ordination to the will. This will-less knowledge is proper to *genius,* for genius is nothing other than the objective disposition of the mind to forget itself and feed wholly upon the ideal character of the object. Genius supposes sufficient power of *imagination* to extend our intuitive gaze from particular objects of experience to nearly the totality of actual and possible objects. Strengthened by the force of genius, the esthetic mind performs a kind of nonabstractive, nonrational generalization, in order to construct the totality from a few given parts and to discern the ideal intention in the midst of the always imperfect, phenomenal modes. All men are endowed with some measure of genius, for otherwise they could never engage in esthetic contemplation or produce works of art. The power of genius is specially strong in creative artists, for they can deliberately retain their contemplative attitude long enough to communicate the vision to others, through works of art.

Schopenhauer finds it difficult to bring this description into line with his systematic position. He attributes the power of genius to a certain *surplus energy* given by the will, a gratuitous upsurge, over and above the knowledge needed to serve the individual embodiment of will and its bodily needs. Will endows a man with an added vigor of mind, sufficient to enable him to concentrate exclusively upon the *what* or ideal essence of the object, without adverting to its usefulness to himself and his life-drive. The individual shares momentarily in the blessedness and impersonal vision of "that *one* eye of the world which looks out from all knowing creatures."[28] But this

---

[27] On genius and beauty, see *The World as Will and Idea*, III, 36–37, 29; Supplements, XXXI, XXXIII (Haldane-Kemp, I, 240–52, 260–61; III, 138–66, 173–75).

[28] *Ibid.*, III, 38 (Haldane-Kemp, I, 256). In this description, Schopenhauer comes

participation in what Emerson would call the transparent eyeball of the universe, cannot be maintained as a permanent attitude. For, the very ideas that arouse esthetic contemplation remain objectifications of will, even though the pure subject isolates them for their own sake. Since there is only a *concentration* on the ideal factor, without any deliberate and total *negation* of will, esthetic pleasure is *fleeting,* and the mind is soon brought back to practical concerns. Esthetic contemplation does not insure a permanent liberation from slavery to the will: it is not the ultimate instrument of release sought by men.

Schopenhauer's view of art is a supple one, enabling him to make many penetrating observations about the several arts, especially music. But as a component in a metaphysical and moral doctrine, it is not wholly consistent with the rest of his system. One basic deficiency is the failure to justify the identification of the *essential forms,* apprehended in esthetic contemplation, with his own "Platonic ideas." Again, there is an inexplicable about-face concerning *knowledge.* Whereas previously, its essential nature was held to be practical and will-serving, another convenient exception is now made, in order to exploit the disinterested attitude of esthetic appreciation. In an esthetic context, Schopenhauer argues as though only the presence of reason and the principle of sufficient reason makes knowledge practical. But his general metaphysical doctrine is that sufficient reason governs all the knowing powers, that will produces them all — including the constellation of sensibility, understanding, and imagination, which comprises esthetic intuition — and that it directs them *all* to the completely practical end of serving the bodily needs. No explanation is given of how the esthetic observer can escape from the radical form of time, in order to become a *timeless* subject of knowledge.[29] Furthermore, the attribution of the surplus energy of genius or the contemplative outlook to *will,* makes will the source of the disinterested attitude. Either this violates the essence of will, as a self-seeking power, or else it is an implicit admission that the previous account did not take full account of the various aspects

---

dangerously close to exemplifying his own satirical description of the pure knowing subject as "a winged cherub without a body." *Ibid.,* II, 18 (Haldane-Kemp, I, 129).

[29] In his essay "On the Metaphysics of the Beautiful and On Aesthetics," Schopenhauer bluntly calls esthetic contemplation "an unnatural and abnormal activity" (*Selected Essays of Arthur Schopenhauer,* Bax translation, 279), without showing how such activity is compatible with his metaphysics of the will and the world.

and reaches of the will's nature. The evidence, uncovered by Schopenhauer's esthetic investigations, is at odds with his foundation of pessimism in a metaphysics of the will. For instance, he admits that, in esthetic contemplation of sublime objects (which could threaten the safety of the beholder), a *deliberate act of will* is required, to cut loose the perceiver from preoccupation with his own welfare. Will displays itself here as something other than a sheer surge of the egoistic impulse to live.

Finally, the object of esthetic contemplation is the "Platonic idea," which in turn is an objectification of will. If the esthetic situation of union between mind and object is not an illusory one, then the esthetic isolation of the ideal factor does not positively deny the nature of the idea, as a level of will itself. If union of the subject with a *manifestation of will* can produce even temporary relief from the evils of life, then the latter need not be due essentially to will and need not require a total negation of will, as the condition of their removal. Schopenhauer's pure, will-less fraction of the world's one eye is a systematic fancy, which he is driven to posit only because of the contradiction between his pessimistic view of cosmic will and the undeniable fact that esthetic contemplation does bring intense pleasure to the beholder. But the beholder may remain this particular individual, fully aware of his practical concerns and the requirements of rationality, and still share in the joy that comes from viewing the beautiful object. Except on the basis of the metaphysics of will, the esthetic condition of absorption in the object can occur within the ordinary limits of the individual knowing and willing subject.

## 7. MORAL LIBERATION THROUGH SYMPATHY
### AND ASCETIC DENIAL

*Morality* is the second great means employed by men to overcome the evils of worldly existence. In his moral doctrine, Schopenhauer seeks to profit by both the success and the failure of esthetic release. Its success is due to the fact that it removes the individuality of the beholder, and unites him with the ideal actuality beneath the phenomena. Its failure lies in its transient character, which results from the unnegated presence of the will in the beholder. With the aid of Indian philosophy (or what he takes to be Indian philosophy), Schopenhauer now offers a reconstruction of ethics that will advance beyond esthetic experience, and secure man's permanent liberation from the sway of will. This program is developed in two stages, based on an analysis of the functions of *sympathy* and *ascetic denial* or *renunciation* in moral life.

The doctrine on sympathy is an answer to one of the most distressing consequences of the will-to-live: its encouragement of unrestrained egoism. Schopenhauer saw no point in counseling men *as individuals* against self-seeking, since it is precisely their individuality that makes them grasping and blind to altruistic standards. As long as men retain their full hold on individual existence, the only procedure is to establish a sufficiently powerful preventative against the appalling consequences of wrongdoing, i.e., against one man's violation of the sphere of another's assertion of will. The *state* has no moral and divine purpose, as Hegel pretended, but results from an appeal to enlightened egoism. Hobbes was right in teaching that the state rests on an agreement to renounce the pleasure of inflicting suffering on others, and that its task is the external one of preventing, by force, the violation of bodily integrity, property, and contract. Nevertheless, the moral sense of wrong and right is an interior awareness of the individual will, and does not derive from the state.

In the common-sense estimate, the good man is an altruist. He feels sympathetically close to other men, makes less of a distinction between himself and others than does the egoist, and tries to share and alleviate the suffering of his fellows. Schopenhauer offers a philosophical exegesis of this commonplace opinion. The causal determinism of will, at the rational level, is expressed in *motives*. Motives are concerned with securing *woe* or *weal*, which are therefore the determinants of human action. Since we cannot will our own woe, there are three possible routes of action open to us. We may will our own weal (egoism), another's woe (malice), or another's weal (sympathy or compassion).[30]

*Egoism* and *malice* are based upon a vehement will-to-live, and are regulated solely by phenomenal knowledge. Their outlook expresses a limitless hunger for aggrandizement and a contempt for others, who are regarded as mere objects within one's perceptual and valuational world. The egoist and the malicious man fail to penetrate to the point where the difference between *mine* and *thine* is erased. Only the mind with an intuitive grasp of the ideas sees that individuation

---

30 *The Basis of Morality*, III, v (Bullock, 165–75).

is due to space and time, which are only mental forms. These forms determine the appearance of the world to the knowing subject but they do not affect the unique noumenal reality, underlying all the appearances. An enlightened mind perceives that the hard-and-fast distinctions among individuals are illusions, part of what the Indian sages call *Maya* or the illusory web of individuals-in-nature. Once this knowledge of the true meaning of individuality is gained, the mind can embrace the self-identical nature beneath the appearances, liberate itself from egoistic and malicious motives, and endow its actions with the moral value of *altruism* or *sympathy*. Only actions prompted by the latter incentive are truly moral ones.

There are two provisions of morality at this level: "Do harm to no one; but rather help all people, as far as lies in your power."[31] The first is the negative precept of *justice;* the second is the positive precept of *love.* The just man refrains from doing wrong or asserting himself, to the point of injuring another. He refuses to work harm to another, because he begins to see that the distance is not so great between himself and the other person. Once he becomes fully aware of the basic identity of will in all men, he is led to place the interests of others on the same plane as his own. For, he now realizes that only the shadow of the phenomenon separates the victim from the inflicter of an evil, that suffering is the only positive thing in the world, and that the same cosmic will bears the travail of all things. From this wisdom, there blooms genuine *virtue,* which is the positive love that sacrifices itself for fellow men and bears their load sympathetically along with them. The virtuous man does not pretend that the pain of another is his own, but he compassionately suffers with the other and in the other.

Moral actions flow from *sympathy,* which is the only nonegoistic, and hence moral, spring of conduct.[32] It is the root of justice and love, and hence is the source of all moral virtues. In order to demonstrate that love is the same as sympathy or compassion, Schopenhauer recalls his pessimistic view that, in a world animated by the will-to-live, happiness is only a negative condition and temporary surcease of pain. Happiness does away with desire and hence with pleasure, leading once more to the prevalent conditions of want, ennui, and suffering. As a positive attitude, love is excited, not by happiness,

---

[31] *Loc. cit.* (Bullock, 175).

[32] Sympathy is discussed in *The Basis of Morality,* III, vii–viii (Bullock, 198–236); *The World as Will and Idea,* IV, 66–67 (Haldane-Kemp, I, 484–85).

but by what is positive and abiding in our temporal existence: suffering and misery. Therefore, *love* expresses itself properly in *participation in sufferings* (*Leiden*), i.e., in "sym-pathy" (*Mit-leid*) or "com-passionate" bearing of the evils of life. Only actions prompted by sympathy are morally worthy, for the sympathetic soul sees its own deeper self in another, and goes out to join it. It learns the wisdom of the universal Vedic formula: "*This* thou art, *this* thou art!"[33] The virtuous, loving man is guided by a vision of *eternal justice*, in which there is no time lag or phenomenal separation between guilt and misery, crime and punishment, the giving and the taking of pain. In his eyes, even universal suffering is justified, since it is the essential expression of the will-to-live, which is the common substance of us all. This will is present in its entirety in each individual, and hence each individual rightly should bear the full suffering of existence. Schopenhauer insists that this sympathetic love must reach out to all beings, especially the brute animals, for whom he shows special tenderness.

Knowledge of what lies behind the phenomenal veil is reconciling. It gives the virtuous man an inner contentment, a closeness to all creatures — what Albert Schweitzer termed a "respect for life as such." Yet man's ultimate salvation does not lie here, for it is also a disquieting knowledge. It delivers one from the bonds of egoism but not from the torments of life. He who has taken the misery of the universe upon himself, and recognized it as the faithful mirroring of the will-to-live, will eventually ask himself why he should continue to support this evil-bearing will. He will recoil with abhorrence from the universal suffering and, at that moment, will freely *deny the will-to-live.*[34] In this act of *ascetic denial* or *renunciation,* Schopenhauer finds the one case in which the noumenal freedom of will as such breaks into the phenomenal sphere of causal determinism. But it does so, only to enter into contradiction with itself, to deny its own nisus. In this self-abnegation of will lies our only sure deliverance from the evils and sufferings of the phenomenal world. The ascetic denial of life is true holiness, which transcends virtue and sympathy.

Schopenhauer adds that *bare knowledge* about the phenomenal nature of individuals and the universality of suffering is not enough to lead most people to forego the world, both as mental presentation

---

[33] Cf. *ibid.,* IV, 63, 66 (Haldane-Kemp, I, 459, 483; italics mine).
[34] *Ibid.,* IV, 54, 55, 68 (Haldane-Kemp, I, 367, 388–89, 489–91).

and as will. The saving resignation is achieved ordinarily through *great personal suffering,* as instanced by the innocent Gretchen, in Goethe's *Faust.* Suffering does not necessarily generate renunciation but it always bears the seeds of holiness and the call to deny the cosmic will. This denial is never perfectly achieved in this life. For, as long as the body remains, there is a visible expression of will and a constant solicitation to renew its force. Hence the ascetic life, as well as the life of virtue, is filled with temptations and relapses.

Is our deliverance founded in *nothingness?* Schopenhauer gives a cautious answer to this important question. Philosophy must reply in the affirmative: we find our salvation in nothingness. But just as the good is only relative to one's will-project, so the naught is relative to the positive thing being denied. What is denied by ascetic renunciation, is the world *as* will and presentation. It is precisely the nothingness-of-*this*-reality, which is to be embraced. Philosophy can say no more, since it can bring only this aspect to universal, communicable form. But Schopenhauer recommends the study of the lives of the saints — Christian, and especially Hindu and Buddhist — in order to gain an intimation of a further depth of experience that *may be positive,* and that certainly *is incommunicable.* It may well be that what philosophy represents as a nothingness, is only *a relative way of viewing the supreme reality.*[35] Beyond the standpoint of the will and its object, there may well lie a positive, unconditioned well of being, from which the saints drink and bid us likewise drink. But such testimony is inalienably personal and beyond philosophical analysis.

In the closing paragraphs of *The World as Will and Presentation,* Schopenhauer tussles with two major problems, raised by his

---

[35] "A reversed point of view, if it were possible for us, would reverse the signs and show the *real-for-us* as nothing, and *that nothing* [the relative nothing which is denial of will and deliverance from the world] as the real. But as long as we ourselves are the will-to-live, this last — nothing as the real — can only be known and signified by us negatively. . . . If the will were simply and absolutely the thing-in-itself, this nothing would also be *absolute,* instead of which it expressly presents itself to us as only *relative." The World as Will and Idea,* IV, 71; Supplements, XVIII (Haldane-Kemp, I, 529–30; II, 408; translation modified and first set of italics added). The possibility of an absolute actuality behind the relative nothingness of a denial of life hinges upon the other possibility, that the thing-in-itself may have a hidden reservoir of being, which remains even after the will-aspect of the noumenal principal is abrogated. in J. Maritain's essay, "The Natural Mystical Experience and the Void," *Ransoming* Some aspects of the general problem of the experience of the naught are brought out *the Time* (translated by H. L. Binsse, New York, Scribner, 1941), 255–89.

doctrine.[36] The first concerns his relation to *Christianity*, and stems from his claim to have revealed for the first time, apart from mythical form, the truth that *holiness* always consists in the *denial of life*. He interprets the Christian doctrines of original sin and salvation to mean, respectively, the original evil of a world expressive of the will-to-live and the deliverance wrought by a denial of the will, the world, and life. This exegesis does violence, however, to the constant tradition of Christianity. In Scripture, the term *world* is employed in several senses, not all of them signifying something evil and to be shunned. The world is created by an intelligent and good God, who declares that it is indeed good; Christ comes as the Saviour of the world, with the mission of wresting created things from an evil power, not itself the supreme will; all things visible and invisible are destined to be brought under the headship of Christ. Again, *salvation* is referred to as a rebirth, an attainment of the fullness of the life which Christ came to give, rather than as a denial of life as such. What must be renounced is not life but the sinful deeds and attachments, that block man's sharing in eternal life. The example of a St. Francis of Assisi shows that Christian denial of sin and self-centeredness leads to a positive reaffirmation of oneself and visible nature, regarded now as manifestations of God's glory and love for us. This exegetical problem assumes historical importance in modern philosophy, from the fact that Nietzsche accepted Schopenhauer's account as an authentic description of the Christian view of holiness and asceticism, and hence as support for Nietzsche's own thesis that Christianity is an antivital, antihumanistic movement.

The second great issue concerns the consistency of the act of renunciation with the rest of Schopenhauer's system. If the theory of complete phenomenal determinism were adhered to strictly, there would be no possibility of *noumenal* freedom manifesting itself in the *phenomenon* of human renunciation of the will-to-live. Any entrance of will into the phenomenal order would be subject to the determinism governing all phenomenal actions. To avoid this consequence, Schopenhauer makes a final exception, in favor of a type of intuitive knowledge of ideas that overcomes the principle of sufficient reason and quiets, rather than motivates, the will. He

---

[36] For Schopenhauer's interpretation of Christian asceticism and grace, cf. *The World as Will and Idea*, IV, 68, 70; Supplements, XLVIII–XLIX (Haldane-Kemp, I, 490–514, 522–28; III, 420–67).

confesses that this is not a *natural* sort of knowledge, and that the ensuing act of renunciation is not a natural act. The intuition and renunciation belong to the *kingdom of grace or freedom,* rather than to the natural zone studied in philosophy. This explanation does more credit to Schopenhauer's respect for certain facts than to the adequacy of his theory of sufficient reason and cosmic will. Man's nay-saying acts are a strong indication of his freedom, but no stronger than his affirmation of life and his scale of vital values. Both his negative and affirmative choices can spring freely from natural, rational knowledge about the end for which his will is made. Moral freedom requires an exception to Schopenhauer's principles but not to our ordinary manner of coming to decisions, with the aid of rational inquiry and practical judgment.

Schopenhauer's final hesitation about whether or not we owe our peace of soul to nothingness is significant. His reluctance on this issue accords with his earlier refusal to limit the nature of the thing-in-itself to will, as he has described it. He is obscurely aware that there is something unsatisfactory about defining will in terms of want and desire, since this may not be its most basic aspect. If desire is only one of the particular relations of the will to its object, there is no need to organize life pessimistically around restless desire. Schopenhauer divines a discrepancy between the way in which will displays itself in human experience and the way in which the supreme noumenal principle may possess it. He leaves open the possibility that renunciation and the experience of the naught may be only the obverse side of an act involving the positive adherence of the human will to the supreme reality, considered precisely in its transcendent or noumenal being. But his theory of knowledge and metaphysics of will deprive him of any philosophical means of exploring this possibility. He can only point to the lives of the saints, where it seems to be embodied in actual fact. This is a hint which Bergson will attempt to develop into a study of the religious and mystical resources of human freedom.

## SUMMARY OF CHAPTER 15

In his study of the fourfold root of sufficient reason, Schopenhauer showed that every object of knowledge must have some principle of sufficient reason and hence must be rationally determined. But since he accepted the Kantian equation between objects of knowledge and phenomena, he added that sufficient reason and the reign of rationality do not apply to the world as a whole or to its noumenal basis. This was the logical principle behind his irrationalistic and pessimistic metaphysics. The world may be regarded either phenomenally as a presentation of my mind or noumenally as will. From the former standpoint, the raw materials of sensation are transformed into structured objects of knowledge, through the application of the forms of space, time, and causality. Schopenhauer removed general concepts entirely from the understanding and located them in reason; he then pointed out the empty and derivative character of all rational concepts and knowledge. But he sought to revive metaphysics, by regarding it as a deepening of experience, rather than an escape from experience. A metaphysical intuition reveals that the noumenal principle behind the world of appearances is a blind, irrational will-to-live. It produces and uses as its tools all the grades of being in nature, including human intelligence. Will manifests itself according to certain hierarchical patterns or "Platonic ideas." The various levels of being are constantly at war with each other, and will is forever destroying its offspring. Schopenhauer examined three routes by which men have sought relief from the egoism and hatred generated by the cosmic will-to-live: suicide, art, and morality. The first solution is futile, since it destroys the phenomenal individual but not the will itself. Art provides temporary surcease, through self-forgetfulness in contemplation of the "Platonic ideas." But only in the moral attitudes of sympathy and renunciation did Schopenhauer discover a permanent victory over egoistic will. Participation in the sufferings of others and, above all, an ascetic denial of the will-to-live were his sovereign remedies for the insatiable demands of cosmic will. He suggested problematically, that this denial may lead to a positive union with the noumenal reality, beyond the aspect of pain-bearing will.

## BIBLIOGRAPHICAL NOTE

1. *Sources.* The only complete, critical edition of Schopenhauer's *Sämmtliche Werke* was edited by P. Deussen and A. Hübscher (16 vols., Munich, Piper, 1911–1942). Translations: *On the Fourfold Root of the Principle of Sufficient Reason, and On the Will in Nature,* translated by K. Hillebrand (revised ed., London, Bell, 1907); *The World as Will and Idea,* translated by R. B. Haldane and J. Kemp (fifth ed., 3 vols., London, Kegan Paul, Trench, Trübner, 1906); *The Basis of Morality,* translated by A. B. Bullock (London, Swann, Sonnenschein, 1903); *Selected Essays,* translated by E. B. Bax (London, Bell, 1891; selected from *Parerga and Paralipomena*).

2. *Studies.* V. J. McGill, *Schopenhauer, Pessimist and Pagan* (New York, Brentano, 1931), studies the man behind the philosophy. H. Zimmern, *Schopenhauer: His Life and Philosophy* (revised ed., London, Allen and Unwin, 1932), provides a brief introduction. Both for exposition and for Christian and Thomistic evaluations, F. Copleston, S.J., *Arthur Schopenhauer, Philosopher of Pessimism* (London, Burns, Oates, 1946), is outstanding; from the same standpoint, see U. A. Padovani, *Arturo*

*Schopenhauer: L'ambiente, la vita, le opere* (Milan, Vita e Pensiero, 1934), and Chapter X in P. Siwek, S.J., *The Philosophy of Evil* (New York, Ronald, 1951), 145–98. Siwek analyzes the pessimism of both Schopenhauer and Eduard von Hartmann, who continued many Schopenhauerian themes; cf. von Hartmann's main book, *Philosophy of the Unconscious,* translated by W. C. Coupland (1-vol. ed., New York, Harcourt, Brace, 1923). For a comparative study of three great German doctrines on esthetics, consult I. Knox, *Aesthetic Theories of Kant, Hegel and Schopenhauer* (New York, Columbia University Press, 1936).

3. *Further Publications.* There is a new translation of *The World as Will and Representation,* done by E. F. Payne (2 vols., Indian Hills, Colo., Falcon's Wing Press, 1958). K. Kolenda had made the first English version of Schopenhauer's prize essay, the *Essay on the Freedom of the Will* (New York, Liberal Arts Press, 1960), which defends a transcendental freedom of *esse* rather than of operation.

# Chapter 16. COMTE

## I. LIFE AND WRITINGS

AUGUSTE COMTE was born at Montpellier in 1798, of Catholic and royalist parents, whose religious and political views he soon discarded. He attended the Polytechnical School in Paris for two years (1814–1816), but was dismissed, along with his classmates, for rebellion against an unpopular instructor. After leaving school, he worked as a mathematics tutor and served as secretary to the French utopian socialist, Saint-Simon, from 1817 to 1824. From this latter association, Comte learned a good deal about modern industrial society, the power of bankers and experts, the workings of political laws, and the task of philosophy to draw out of the revolutionary movements in France some stable social order. But the thoughts that darted nervously through Saint-Simon's mind were lacking in systematic method and order. This general framework was supplied by Comte himself, about 1822, when he discovered his law of the three states of the mind: the theological, the metaphysical, and the positive. When Saint-Simon proposed to incorporate one of Comte's pamphlets as the third part of a publication of his own, without mentioning Comte's name on the title page, the latter quickly severed the connection. In 1826, Comte began a series of public lectures on the positivist philosophy but had an attack of insanity, after the third lecture. This attack, induced by overwork and by an unfortunate marriage, incapacitated him for over a year. Once, he had to be rescued from the Seine river, after a suicide attempt. But although he suffered several relapses in later years, Comte recovered sufficiently to resume his lectures in January, 1829. His *Course of Positive Philosophy* was issued in six volumes (1830–1842), on the basis of his division of the sciences. For some years, he supported himself by serving as a tutor and examiner for students of the Polytechnical School. In his *Discourse on the Positive Spirit* (1844), he summarized the main lines of his philosophy in concise and popular form, stressing the importance of his new science of sociology.

Comte's meeting with Madame Clotilde de Vaux, in 1844, was the turning point in what he himself called "my two lives." Clotilde was beautiful but in delicate health, and was further encumbered by a worthless husband, who had disappeared in order to avoid punishment for embezzling funds. Comte declared his love for her in 1845, but the lady responded only with a disinterested friendship, and died the following year. Although his critics later declared that Comte's gradual accentuation of the religion of humanity was due to mental unbalance, ensuing upon this loss, it is evident that the cultivation of feeling and religion was inherent even in his earlier views. But he did come to pattern the love of humanity after his own love and reverence for the departed Clotilde. His encounter with her showed him the need for satisfying the affective side of human nature within a positivist philosophy, by supplying the individual with a disinterested object of love: humanity itself.

The impact of the "unparalleled year" (1845–1846) was soon manifested in Comte's writings. His *Discourse on the Positivist Outlook* (1848) emphasized the culmination of positivist development, not merely in sociology, but also in a practical worship of humanity. A complete listing of the feast days in the new thirteen-month year, commemorating great men and events in human history, was contained in the *Positivist Calendar* (1849). A *Positivist Catechism* was also provided in 1852, so that the faithful could have a conspectus of the history of humanity and a guide toward its future development. The most complete statement of this final phase in Comte's thought was the four-volume *System of Positive Polity* (1851–1854), which synthesized the speculative and practical, the scientific and religious, aspects of Comte's mind. For some years, he had ceased to occupy himself with anything other than the details of his new religion of humanity. In 1844, John Stuart Mill and two friends had provided a year's funds for Comte but had not renewed their contributions, when he showed no signs of attempting to support himself. Thereafter, the pontiff of humanity lived mainly on a "positivist subsidy," which was contributed by loyal followers in France and abroad. He progressively isolated himself through the practice of "cerebral hygiene," which consisted in refraining from consulting any nonpositivist intellectual developments, lest they pollute his vision of positivist truth. At the time of his death (1857), Comte was engaged in writing the

*Subjective Synthesis* (Vol. I, 1856), whose purpose was to achieve the perfect unity of all the sciences, by referring them to the satisfaction of normal human needs.

## 2. POSITIVISM AND THE LAW OF THE THREE STATES

In his correspondence, Auguste Comte confessed that, by the age of 13 or 14, he had lost all belief in God and a supernatural order. There was no great interior struggle connected with his loss of faith. Rather, he gave up his convictions about God, in much the same way in which he surrendered all attachment to the old order of political life in France. In this respect, Comte embodied one typical nineteenth-century attitude: acceptance of atheism as an inevitable position, dictated primarily by *cultural,* rather than strictly philosophical, considerations. Since belief in God and the supernatural economy of grace seemed to him to be an integral part of the monarchial regime in France, Comte felt that it was doomed to perish along with its political and social supports. He declared himself to be, not so much an active opponent of theism, as a clear-sighted herald of its increasing desuetude and inevitable disappearance from the social scene.

But like Marx and Nietzsche — whom he resembled in accepting the cultural verdict as philosophically decisive — Comte was not satisfied with bearing passive witness to the gradual loss of faith in God. He recognized that the vacuum had to be filled with an equally imperious faith in this world of ours. Hence he replaced the *Credo in unum Deum* with a new confession: *"All is relative — here is the only absolute principle."*[1] This *absolutization of the relative,* i.e., of the method of the positive sciences and the realm of phenomenal facts, is the central dogma of the entire positivist philosophy. It is the first article of the positivist faith, suffusing all of Comte's special arguments and particular evaluations. It bears a circular relation with his total system, since the latter is intended to be both an expansion of the original principle and a vast proof, *modo ambulando,* of its adequacy in explaining all the data. Like other primary convictions, it can be defended or criticized only with great difficulty, in its original, bald statement. Within the context of the positivist system, however, its validity can be tested in various ways.

[1] *System of Positive Polity,* Preface to the General Appendix (fourth edition, 4 vols., Paris, Cres, 1912; IV, ii). Because of the dispute among English-speaking positivists concerning the existing English translations of Comte, all translations here are made directly from the French.

As Comte stated the issue confronting modern man, the true alternative is either to return to a thoroughgoing theistic and supernatural basis for intellectual and moral life or to reconstruct society around a positivist faith in humanity alone. The latter road was the one followed by Comte, but he did not want his choice to be regarded as a sterile and merely negative protest against belief in God, after the manner of the freethinking Encyclopaedists of the previous century. The only way in which he could combine *antitheism* with a *constructive* program was by grounding his opposition to God upon a *natural* and *historical law*. According to such a law, belief in God belongs properly to an early phase of mental development, and is now entered upon its final decline. To eliminate the lingering traces of this belief and to reorganize society upon a purely humanistic foundation, is a form of enlightened co-operation with an inevitable tendency of our era. Thus the natural and historical law of the three states is an indispensable bulwark for Comte's principle that all is relative.

Stated in the simplest terms, this law maintains that

> by the very nature of the human mind, every branch of our knowledge is necessarily obliged to pass successively in its course through three different theoretical states: the theological or fictitious state; the metaphysical or abstract state; finally, the scientific or positive state. . . . In other words, the human mind, by its nature, employs successively in each of its investigations three methods of philosophizing, the character of which is essentially different and even radically opposed: first, the theological method, then the metaphysical method, and finally the positive method.[2]

The *law of the three states* (*états*) concerns, first, the inherent structure and operative law of the human mind and, second, the methods and modes of scientific knowledge which depend upon the mind's operation. It is a dynamic tendency, determined by the mind's very nature, and hence it imposes a *necessary* pattern upon our mental development. Comte calls it a great, fundamental law, one which determines with invariable necessity the march of our scientific and philosophical progress, as well as our material and institutional growth. He describes the three states and their mutual relations in such a way that his own positivism is presented as the culmination of all the

---

[2] *Ibid.*, General Appendix, III (IV, 77); *Course of Positive Philosophy*, Lecture 1 (reprint edition, 6 vols., Paris, Schleicher, 1908; I, 2). For an introductory sketch of Comte's thought, cf. E. H. Ziegelmeyer, S.J., "Auguste Comte and Positivism," *The Modern Schoolman*, XX (1942–1943), 6–17.

methodological and doctrinal advances of human intellectual history. His positivist plan for reorganizing society is thus given the weight of an ineluctable, natural law, the only truly creative social principle in the industrial age.

## COMTE'S POSITIVIST PROGRAM

1. Law of the three states of the human mind.
    a) Theological state (fetishism, polytheism, monotheism; period of divine right of kings and militarism).
    b) Metaphysical state (criticism of the old regime and transition to the new order).
    c) Positivist state (real, useful, precise, certain, organic, relative, and sympathetic knowledge; period of industrialism and peace, social order and progress).

2. Hierarchical division of the basic sciences.

| Simplicity | Mathematics | Complexity |
| Generality | Astronomy | Particularity |
| Independence | Physics | Dependence |
| | Chemistry | |
| | Biology | |
| ↓ | Sociology | ↓ |

Mathematics

Inorganic physics { Celestial physics: Astronomy / Terrestrial physics { Physics proper / Chemistry

Organic physics { Physiological physics: Biology / Social physics: Sociology

(Morality or Social psychology)

3. Two fundamental methods of knowledge.
    a) Objective method: from the world to man (unity of method and homogeneity of doctrine in the positive sciences).
    b) Subjective method: from man to the world (organic synthesis or total systematization of knowledge and sentiment, through the religion of humanity).

Comte defines *philosophy,* very broadly, as the general system of human conceptions. Each of the three basic frames of mind constitutes a philosophy of a sort, since each leads to a systematic view of man and the world. The theological attitude is the initial but merely provisional interpretation of phenomena; the metaphysical attitude is essentially critical and transitional; the positivist view is alone definitive for the human mind.[3]

The *theological* mentality is ruled by the "empathetic fallacy": it reads the subjective conditions of human experience into the nature of the external world. It erects human life and volition into a general principle of interpretation for all reality, imagining that all things are moved by supernal powers of life and will. The development of the theological outlook occurs in three phases: fetishism, polytheism, and monotheism. Among primitive minds, the principle of life is attributed to all objects, so that each is moved internally by an affective power, similar to our own vital principle. In the animistic universe of *fetishism,* totems and the worship of stars are common ways of expressing respect for, and fear of, material things. Later on, the theological mind withdraws the supernal, animating powers from the immediate phenomena and locates them in fictitious entities, the gods, which always remain themselves invisible and yet dominant over all visible events. This is the *polytheistic* phase of the theological state of mind. It encourages an aggressive militarism, slavery, centralized authority, and the fusion of spiritual and temporal power. The Greco-Roman world is the best example of a civilization organized along polytheistic lines. Comte regards polytheism as the typical condition of the theological mind. Eventually, however, the many gods are consolidated into one supreme God, and *monotheism* is born. But monotheism, which had its supreme, social expression in medieval Catholicism, already represents both a decline of the full vigor of the theological mentality and a preparation for a new intellectual regime. By gathering together all cosmic power in the one God, monotheism permits nature to be studied in itself, as a regulated system, and thus opens the way for the metaphysical interpretation.

There is a wide area of agreement between the theological and *metaphysical* viewpoints. Both are in search of efficient causes, final purposes, substantial essences, and other absolute principles of knowledge. But the metaphysical mind converts the *supernatural* entities of theology into *natural* forces and causes, which are supposed to lie behind natural phenomena and serve as their productive source.

---

[3] For a general description of these outlooks, cf. *Course of Positive Philosophy,* Lecture I (I, 2–3); *Discourse on the Positive Spirit,* Part I (all page references are to the second volume of the Le Verrier edition; pp. 2–49). More detailed accounts of the three states of mind are provided in Vols. V–VI of *Course of Positive Philosophy,* and Vol. III of *System of Positive Polity.*

These forces of nature are merely personified abstractions, which tend to distract the sciences from their proper type of explanation. Comte lists the ether, chemical affinities, and vital entelechies as instances of metaphysical abstractions to which scientists have fallen victim. The distinctive feature of the metaphysical attitude is its gradual rejection of all supernatural claims and even of belief in God. It is the representative modern standpoint, having Protestantism, the Enlightenment, and the French Revolution as its progenitors. This critical spirit has undermined the medieval socioreligious synthesis, without being able to construct a stable, organic order of its own. By a necessary and inevitable law of the mind, this critical position is bound to give way to the definitive state of positivism.

Comte apologizes for designating his own doctrine as *positivistic,* since this is a vague and shifting term. Nevertheless, he singles out five common traits (real, useful, precise, certain, and organic), which help to determine its connotation, and adds two special notes of his own (relative and sympathetic).[4] The character of *reality* attaches to the positivistic view, in virtue of the fundamental rule that "every proposition which is not strictly reducible to the simple enunciation of a fact, either particular or general, is incapable of furnishing any real and intelligible meaning."[5] Since he stipulates that the *phenomenal facts* or "reality" can have no connection with causes, ends, and essences, Comte is able to regard the latter as chimerical and irrelevant for the positivistic intelligence. This limitation of the mind to phenomenal facts, as summarized in general empirical laws, is reenforced by the utilitarian aim of positivist inquiry. Although he allows, with Bacon, that we must seek after light-bearing experiments or theoretical truths for their own sake, Comte also holds that *use* or the betterment of natural conditions for man is the ultimate measure of scientific thinking and hence also of positivist philosophy. Appeal is made, therefore, to the uselessness of metaphysical questions about causes and essences, thus banishing them from a scientifically orientated philosophy.

The properties of precision and certainty of knowledge are often confused, especially by the Cartesian mathematical mind, but Comte

[4] *Discourse on the Positive Spirit,* I (Le Verrier, 92-102); *System of Positive Polity,* Preliminary Discourse (I, 57-58).

[5] *Discourse on the Positive Spirit,* I (Le Verrier, 31). R. W. Sellars, "Positivism in Contemporary Philosophic Thought," *American Sociological Review,* IV (1939), 26-42, shows how logical positivism is an outgrowth of Comte's too facile dismissal of epistemological and metaphysical issues.

declares that they must be carefully distinguished. *Precision* is obtained through submission of facts to mathematical analysis. But this technique must respect the degrees of complexity of different types of facts, so that precision is a matter of *degree,* and cannot be attained everywhere with the same success. *Certitude,* however, applies *equally* to all positive truths, i.e., to all propositions founded upon reliable facts. Positivism tends to promote the logical harmony and unity of all minds through the equal certitude of its method and conclusions, instead of dividing men through the method of Cartesian doubt and vain metaphysical investigations. Finally, positivism is not a set of unrelated and negative propositions, but a constructive, *organic* and logically coherent system of factual truths.

Comte regards the *relative* nature of positive knowledge as a distinctive and decisive trait of his philosophy. For, it recognizes that the thinker is conditioned by phenomena in the external world, by his own individual condition, and by the social evolution of the human mind. Hence there must be a shift away from the theologicometaphysical emphasis upon *the universe and its absolute causes,* to a more modest, positivistic study of *"our" world and its relative laws.* Philosophy must give up the pretense of viewing the absolute totality of things, since only the phenomena constituting our little world can be known by us, thus probably omitting many kinds of things, belonging to the rest of the universe. Furthermore, it is merely contentious and futile to seek after causes and essences, regarded as natural entities regulating natural phenomena. The proper objects of positive philosophy are the phenomenal facts, relative to our world. But the positivist mind seeks *general facts* or *laws,* and not merely the *particular* facts of experience. The history of the sciences enables us to formulate, inductively, the fundamental scientific and positivist principle that all phenomena whatsoever are constantly subject to rigorously invariable laws, which constitute an immutable order of nature. These laws of nature state the invariable relations of similitude and succession among observed phenomena, the *constancy-in-variety* which enables facts to be related to general notions.

Facts are explained in positivist fashion, only when they are linked and assimilated by means of such laws. These natural laws enable us, eventually, to dispense with direct observation and to substitute *deduction,* or *rational prevision,* for induction. Knowledge is cast in scientifically satisfactory form, only when we can "deduce from the smallest possible number of immediate data, the greatest possible number of results."[6] Against the purely a priori view of scientific laws, Comte stresses their empirical origin in observed facts. But against a complete empiricism, he defends the proper activity of the mind in abstracting the constant factor among particular facts, in generalizing the notion of a law, and in making predictions about future events. Once the general law is discovered, it can be used to foretell the course of phenomena, modify the sequence of nature, and thus improve man's lot in the world. Comte compresses the quintessence of his position on scientific knowledge into the maxim: *science, d'où prévoyance; prévoyance, d'où action:* knowledge leads to foresight, and foresight to action.[7] In his later period, Comte added a seventh differential note to his explanation of the positivist spirit: its *sympathetic* character or universal love for humanity. The positivist synthesis is fully realized, only when all scientific knowledge is related affectively to the human subject, and when our practical plans are prompted formally by the love for humanity and the duty of constantly improving it.

In a methodological perspective, there is a basic incompatibility between the theologicometaphysical approach and the positivist one. The former method *begins with man,* and interprets the world in the light of a purported intuition of the human self. This encourages belief in a background of supernatural or natural entities, especially God and Nature, which are credited with considerably more power than their human analogues possess. In order to avoid these fictions, positivistic reasoning *begins with the world,* and studies human nature in terms of nonhuman phenomena and laws. It proceeds on the premise that "the laws of the world dominate those of man, and are not modified by them."[8] Consequently, positivism repudiates *introspection,* in favor of a position that comes close to what would today be called biological and social *behaviorism.* Man does contain a special order of psychic facts but they cannot be grasped through any intuition or interior observation. Human nature can be studied only in its *overt* operations and products, especially as exhibited in societal behavior and institutions. The individual is real only within the human collectivity, so that the study of *social man,* his works and history, must replace the private or introspective method. And social

---

[6] *Course of Positive Philosophy,* Lecture 3 (I, 72).
[7] *Ibid.,* Lecture 2 (I, 35).
[8] *Ibid.,* Lecture 40 (III, 210). On the diverse starting points in the world and man, cf. *loc. cit.* (III, 141–42).

man, in turn, must be viewed within the setting of natural laws established by the other positive sciences, especially biology.

Any attempt to comment upon Comte's atheistic relativism encounters at once an insurmountable obstacle. In explaining the first two notes of positivism — its reality and utility — Comte observes that it shares these along with common sense. He does more than announce the solidarity between his philosophy and unsophisticated good sense. Far more than Descartes (whom he praises for appreciating the value of *le bon sens*), Comte employs the *appeal to good sense* as a shield against any fundamental, critical discussion of his basic premise. Vulgar wisdom is the original source of first principles, which therefore do not belong in the domain of science.[9] They are the spontaneous foundations of knowledge, and are strictly beyond criticism. Comte belabors the modern rationalistic metaphysicians, for instituting idle and dangerous researches into first principles. He is right in warning against any pretended *demonstration* of first principles, but he also uses the authority of common sense illegitimately, to excuse himself from giving any sort of *justification* for his principle of universal relativity. He fails to recognize the need for a philosophical technique, compatible with a basic realism, for examining our knowledge of first principles, bringing it to the status of scientific apprehension, and thus indirectly justifying our primary grounds of certitude. By placing completely beyond the pale of philosophical discussion his own thesis that all is relative, Comte leaves it in the condition of a subjective preference and mood. He fails to show that it *does*, in fact, belong to the realm of first principles and *does* constitute part of the public wisdom of human good sense. These are questions that may legitimately be asked about any supposed first principle in philosophy.

Comte believes that at least the law of the three states can be demonstrated, after one has worked his way through the major portion of the positivist synthesis, and has come at last to the vantage point of sociology.[10] His first two demonstrations are *historical* and *logical*. He points, first, to his interpretation of the history of the sciences and, second, to his description of the logical content of the three frames of mind. Since these "demonstrations" are patently circular, he is obliged to add a *psychological* proof, based on the intellectual, moral, and social motives for the successive adoption

9 *Discourse on the Positive Spirit*, I, III (Le Verrier, 102, 106, 221).
10 *Course of Positive Philosophy*, Lecture 1 (I, 4–8).

of the three states of mind. From the *intellectual* standpoint, the primitive mind is compelled to begin at the theological level, since it cannot make the requisite observations, without some sort of guiding hypothesis. The view that the world is peopled by spiritual forces, like unto ourselves, comes spontaneously to mind and provides a theoretical basis for observation. In the practical *moral* order, this theological hypothesis supplies the primitive mind with the needed courage to face the unknown dangers of the world; in a *social* context, it gives a common principle of belief for organizing men into stable groups. Gradually, however, the discrepancy between the original theological supposition and observed facts becomes so pronounced, that the metaphysical or critical attitude sets in. Finally, the need for obtaining a new organic way of life, based on purely relative and naturalistic grounds, leads men to adopt the positivistic standpoint. The seeds of positivism are implanted even in the primitive mind, which (as Adam Smith noted) never devises a god of weight and which soon perceives that our mental operations are subject to natural laws. But full acceptance of the positivist position had to await the development of the various special sciences and the appearance of sociology. Men are now on the verge of abandoning all traces of the earlier outlooks, and devoting themselves to an exclusively positivistic approach to nature and social life.

These observations suggest plausible reasons why men might possibly have followed some such pattern as Comte outlines. But the full import of his law of the three states is that it expresses the *necessary structure* of the human mind and hence the presiding principle of human evolution, from which strict deductive demonstrations can be made. Comte's triple schema does not acquire its rigorous character, as a necessary law of our nature, from an inductive study of the facts of mental development. Rather, Comte's entire inductive interpretation of human mental evolution already *presupposes* the unshakable truth of the law of the three states. As a fundamental premise of all positivist investigations, this law is another deliverance of Comtean good sense. Although he seeks to furnish a demonstration for the law, it remains just as much a stipulated principle and intuitive starting point as is the conviction that all is relative. His attacks upon the loose appeal of the French Eclectic School to an unexamined "intuition of common sense," do not prevent Comte himself from turning to the same obliging source for the groundwork of his system. Furthermore, despite his phenomenalism, the law of the three states *performs every philosophical function that would belong to a causal and essential law*. In his search after philosophical *prévoyance* or foresight, he avails himself of all the systematic advantages of an essential, causal principle, without accepting any of the metaphysical grounds and consequences of such a principle.

The particular arguments advanced in support of the law of the three states reveal some deficiencies, which weaken one's confidence in the basic principle of explanation itself. A case in point is the question of *finality*. Comte rejects finality, on the three following astronomical grounds: (1) the movement of the stars is not the best conceivable one, and hence ours is not the best possible universe; (2) the earth moves, showing that the universe is not ordained to the earth and man; (3) a cosmic environment suitable for life on the earth is the necessary consequence, through purely mechanical laws, of the characteristic circumstances of our solar system.[11] Therefore, he advocates the transformation of the notion of finality into that of the *conditions of existence* (viz., the correlation between the structure-and-function of the organism and the environment). These arguments suppose that the principle of finality is the same as the Leibnizian principle of the best possible world, and that it rests upon an anthropocentric view of the universe. Yet neither the fact that this is not a perfect world nor that our earth is a subordinate part of a larger system, bears directly upon the question of the necessity of an end or final cause, as an explanation of action. Comte's astronomical objections do tell against an unrestrained optimism and a loose appeal to relations of external finality, but they do not come to grips with the metaphysical analysis of action, end, and intelligence. In practice, Comte is ready enough to accept internal adaptation of parts to the whole, and external adaptation of organism to environment, just as long as no inference is made therefrom to a transcendent, intelligent cause. The ultimate reason for his failure to consider the metaphysical arguments in favor of final cause is his use of the Newtonian-Laplacean system of mechanical laws (which formally prescinds from real, physical motion and efficient causation, and hence also from the philosophical basis for final cause) as *a philosophical substitute for a causal explanation*. Since, by definition, the mechanical system of classical modern physics

---

[11] *Ibid.*, Lecture 19 (II, 16–18).

provides a completely immanent explanation, its noncausal conception of natural laws serves Comte's antitheistic purposes and hence recommends itself on philosophical grounds. Once the substitution of mechanical law for real causation is made in philosophy, finality can be explained only in ways that are vulnerable to Comte's appeal to the imperfection of the world. The real point at issue, however, is whether such a substitution adequately explains the actual changes we encounter in the world.

The main argument lodged against both efficient cause and substantial essence is that the search for such principles is useless and contentious. Because cause and essence are not useful *within the line of scientific observation and control,* he concludes that they have *no* valid use or meaning, i.e., no foundation in the observable facts of our experience. When he is not engaged in this special polemic, however, Comte is obliged to recognize that *usefulness* has a very wide range of meaning. It cannot be used in a univocal way, both because of the considerable lapse of time that often occurs between pure scientific speculation and practical application, and also because of the differences between concepts that are useful in physics and those that are useful in sociology. Hence the argument rests ultimately on the *phenomenalistic* supposition that the human mind is limited by nature to the field of appearances, which have no intrinsic connection with causes or substantial essences. The Comtean equation between "reality" and the noncausal, nonsubstantial order of "phenomenal facts" is as crucial for his system as it is for Hume's philosophy, upon which it is based. But Comte neither gives a direct justification for this equivalence nor makes a thorough critical review of the various modern conceptions of the nature of phenomenal facts, especially the Kantian theory of science. Although his pages are rich in scientific and social analyses, they are almost devoid of precise and informed discussion of the history of philosophy. By "the metaphysicians," he usually means Condillac and other representatives of the French Enlightenment. Illustrating cause and essence in terms of already obsolete scientific hypotheses or of minor schools of metaphysics, he has no difficulty in exposing the hopeless inadequacy of these principles for explaining the world of our experience. But he leaves fundamentally unanalyzed the major modern theories about the nature of "appearances," "objects of experience," and "observable facts," not to mention the several realistic defenses of the philosophical meaning of "cause" and "substantial essence."

This historical parochialism has a retroactive effect upon the law of the three states itself. As Comte describes the content of the theological and metaphysical outlooks, they have only the narrowest *historical applicability*. An attempt to fit his descriptions to historically ascertainable, philosophical positions shows that, apart from a fifty-year span in French intellectual history (c. 1780–1830), they are overwhelmed by the number of historical exceptions, drawn from every period of human inquiry. To account for the philosophical monotheism of Thomas Aquinas, for instance, which is neither opposed to religious revelation (like Comte's "Deistic metaphysics") nor based upon an amalgamated polytheism (like Comte's "theological monotheism"), requires a dialectical ingenuity that empties Comte's law of all determinate significance. The law of the three states describes how the human mind *would* operate, if his phenomenal relativism held good for the real world. Yet a study of human intellectual history shows that the law does not explain systematically the manner in which men actually *do* think.

Finally, the reasons advanced against *introspection* are worth examining.[12] (1) The main logical objection is that, whereas in every other case of cognition there is a real distinction between the observed and the observing organs, introspective study of intellectual phenomena would require that the same organ be both the observed and the observer. Comte was deeply influenced by the materialism of Cabanis and the physiological investigations of Gall. He agreed with them that men and animals share their cognitive powers in common. Hence his argument proves that genuine introspection cannot be performed by means of a *corporeal* organ. However, it does not face the pertinent question of whether reflection is the proper operation of a completely *incorporeal* or immaterial cognitive power. Once again, Comte's limited historical horizon led him to formulate the issue in a very restricted way. For, by the method of interior observation, he meant the standpoint of the contemporary French Eclectic School of Cousin and Jouffroy, whose empirical weaknesses and cloudy metaphysics he easily exposed. (2) It is only against the attempt of this school to translate German idealism into psychological terms, that the following argument has telling force: interior observation supposes that the mind is withdrawn from all intellectual labors, as well as from sense perception — but then a mental void is produced, in

---

12 *Ibid.*, Lectures 1, 45 (I, 19–20; III, 407–08).

which there are no intellectual phenomena to observe. Apart from some versions of absolute idealism, there are no philosophical positions which make introspection depend upon an evacuation of the particular activities of the intellect. In a realistic context, the intellectual power knows itself reflectively *in and through these operations*. (3) Comte's final criticism — that introspection is possible only in the case of mature, sane, human beings — was really a healthy plea for the development of techniques to study animal and child psychology, as well as the nature of pathological and insane minds. He rightly protested against an exclusive use of the introspective method in philosophy, but he then converted this protest into an equally one-sided reliance on the physiological and sociological approaches to mental life.

## 3. THE HIERARCHICAL CLASSIFICATION OF THE BASIC SCIENCES

The *classification of the sciences* assumes greater importance for Bacon and Comte than for most other modern philosophers. Comte establishes the closest bond between his theory of classification and his law of the three states, calling the former the *indispensable complement* of the latter. The various sciences attain to full positivity at different speeds and according to a definite order, which only can be determined through a theory of classification. Although Bacon saw the cardinal importance of this question, his own answer suffered from being based on the different mental powers. Since all our mental powers are engaged in the scientific enterprise, the main principle of division among the sciences must be an *objective* one. Comte criticizes all previous attempts at classification, because they lacked the indispensable guidance of the law of the three states, the ideal of humanity, and the objective developments of modern biology and Comte's own sociology.

Comte admits that every division of the sciences is unavoidably *artificial*. All positive sciences have the same general subject matter (phenomenal facts) and the same method (the positive search for laws rather than causes, for relative rather than absolute principles). But the artificiality should be kept at a minimum, and all arbitrariness should be eliminated. Biology sets a good example, with its own classification of natural species of living things. It bases its kinds upon objectively given differences, a natural order of species, and a logical chain of structures. Comte seeks to base his division of the sciences upon a similar natural and logical order, as well as to incorporate the factor of chronological development. His goal is to construct an *encyclopedic ladder,* a unique rational succession of steps regulating the passage of the sciences through the theological and metaphysical states, and gauging their order of arrival at a completely positive status.

Biology also provides Comte with a clue about how to respect the real differences among the phenomena studied by different sciences. For, biological species are differentiated according to their increasing complexity of structure and function. Hence Comte employs as his fundamental principle of classification the *inverse ratio between simplicity and complexity.*[13] There is an objective order of *decreasing* simplicity, generality, and independence of facts, to which corresponds an order of *increasing* complexity, particularity, and dependence. This inverse proportion is also correlated with the distance of phenomena from the sphere of *human interests:* those that are more remote from human concerns are also simpler and more general; those that are closer to human values are more complex and particular. With the aid of these criteria, Comte is assured that his classification is definitive and objective. It expresses the invariable, necessary order among the sciences, in respect to their attainment of the goal of positive knowledge.

No attempt is made to order all the sciences. A distinction must first be made between the abstract and the concrete sciences, the theoretical and the practical, the general and the particular. Comte's classification concerns directly only the *abstract, theoretical,* and *general* sciences. Yet since these sciences are regulative of the others, the encyclopedic ladder indirectly affects every branch of scientific knowledge. With this reservation, then, he listed the *six fundamental sciences* in the following order: mathematics, astronomy, physics, chemistry, biology, and sociology.[14] In his later writings, Comte added morality as a seventh basic discipline, but it proved to be (for him) a kind of social psychology of motives and desires. Comte's order is both a *logical* and a *chronological* one, at least with respect to the main procedures and principles. Thus mathematics is logically

---

[13] *Course of Positive Philosophy,* Lecture 2 (I, 47–48); *Discourse on the Positive Spirit,* III (Le Verrier, 241).
[14] For their systematic derivation, see *Course of Positive Philosophy,* Lecture 2 (I, 48–53).

first, because of the simplicity of its object, and also historically first in attaining the condition of a positive science.

Mathematics and sociology are at opposite poles in the classification, just as they are related historically as the oldest and the newest sciences. *Mathematics* is the most independent, simple, and general science, whereas *sociology* (a term coined by Comte) is the most dependent, complex, and particular. Mathematics is least confined to the study of peculiarly human phenomena, whereas sociology is completely preoccupied with them. The nature of scientific thinking is best revealed in mathematics, which gives a clear example of the tendency toward supplanting induction by deduction, and toward achieving a priori prediction through necessary laws. Nevertheless, Comte maintains that mathematical notions ultimately have an *empirical* origin in the primitive, simple phenomena, given through observation of the material world. Furthermore, although the quantitative analysis of phenomena instills exactness into scientific studies, it cannot be the *sole* procedure for the positive sciences. Especially as investigation moves into the biological and sociological domains, where the phenomena grow increasingly complex, there is need for devising other techniques.

Comte distinguishes between method and procedure: there is but *one* general scientific *method* (the positive study of observed facts, as formulated in general laws) and yet *several* distinct *procedures* or techniques.[15] As phenomena increase in complexity, more procedures are devised by scientific intelligence for coping with the data. Observation is perfected by astronomy, experiment by physics, rational nomenclature by chemistry, comparison and classification by biology, and the historical approach by sociology. The use of hypothesis to supplement the limitations of immediate observation is brought out clearly by both astronomy and physics. The technique of induction, which includes observation, experiment, and comparison of structures and functions, is the co-operative achievement of the several natural sciences, and is brought to perfection in biology. Finally, the very complexity of sociological data is compensated for, by the fact that all the procedures perfected by the other sciences are at the disposal of sociology. There is a *natural convergence of all scientific techniques upon the positive study of man*. Although it is difficult to bring sociological findings to the state of mathematical

---

[15] *Ibid.*, Lecture 2 (I, 59–60).

precision, the multiplicity of other scientific means and the pliability of human phenomena permit sociology to attain the required certitude and achieve the maximum of practical control over the data.

Granted the universal import of mathematics in its various degrees of applicability, the other five basic sciences may be treated as so many types of physics, in the broad sense of the study of existent phenomena. The primary divisions are inorganic and organic physics. *Inorganic physics* is further subdivided into celestial physics (astronomy) and terrestrial physics (physics, in the restricted sense, and chemistry). *Organic physics* consists of physiological physics (biology) and social physics (sociology).

Comte's attempt to make this classification necessary and definitive did not encourage the growth of such an overlapping field as organic chemistry, the content of which he wished to distribute between inorganic chemistry and physiology. He found it particularly difficult to differentiate, according to his principles, between the parts of terrestrial physics: physics proper and chemistry. His explanation that physics proper deals only with superficial, transitory changes in matter, and chemistry with deep, permanent changes, would require considerable revision in view of the past half century's advance in nuclear physics. Although he held that the characteristics of life are fundamentally physical, Comte refused to reduce the *organism* completely to its inorganic constituents and laws.[16] The organism is profoundly differentiated through its special functional and structural organization of physical and chemical laws for new purposes. The organism also marks the borderline beyond which mathematical techniques are restricted to general features. The complexity of organic phenomena hinders the isolation and numerical fixity of facts, required for an exhaustive mathematical analysis. But the recent development of a mathematical logic of organic systems and the widespread, refined sociological use of statistical analysis would also force Comte to modify some of his statements about organic physics. Finally, Comte's rigid classification of sciences rests upon the pre-Darwinian view of rigidly fixed natural species.

Logic and psychology are notable by their absence from the main division of sciences. Comte did not approve of a separate and purely formal science of the principles and practice of *logic*. He reduced the

---

[16] Cf. *ibid.*, Lecture 40 (III, 141–255), on the nature of the organism and the distinctive position of biology.

principles of logic to those of the positive scientific method, especially as employed in mathematics. Practical logic is the same as scientific method in use: it should not be separated from a study of the actual procedures followed in the different basic sciences. One of Comte's last writings was a positivist logic, in which he sought to disengage the foundations of scientific thinking. As for *psychology,* he deliberately parceled its subject matter out among biology and sociology, in line with his rejection of introspection. In answer to the pretensions of the Cousin-Jouffroy Eclectic School that the self is completely independent of the organism, Comte assigned the study of the human individual to biology or "phrenological physiology," stating that the "self" is only a complex synthesis or "tone" of bodily feelings and sensations. And to this school's claim that analysis of the self is a pathway to the absolute, Comte replied that the general study of human nature belongs only to sociology, which knows no higher mode of being than humanity itself. The eclectic-idealistic appeal to the self made Comte suspicious about *every nonbiological approach to man the individual, and about every nonsociological approach to the distinctive principle in human nature.* His position was dictated too closely by the immediate situation in French philosophy and, in any case, anteceded the rapid development of empirical psychology, later on in the nineteenth century.

The connection between the law of the three states and the classification of the sciences may now be consolidated. Because the objects of mathematics and astronomy are relatively simple and remote from man, these sciences were the first to attain the positive state. The other sciences followed according to their position in the hierarchy, the last being sociology. Although he recognized traces of *sociology* in the works of several predecessors, Comte regarded himself as the definitive founder of it, as a positive science.[17] He

---

[17] On the historical antecedents of social physics or sociology and Comte's own conception of this science, see *Course of Positive Philosophy,* Lectures 47–48 (IV, 118–247). Along with the article cited in note 5 above, consult the two following contributions to a symposium on the centenary of the coining of the term "sociology": McQ. De Grange, "Comte's Sociologies," and G. A. Lundberg, "Contemporary Positivism in Sociology," in *American Sociological Review,* IV (1939), 17–26, 42–55. Both these sociologists agree with Comte that sociology studies the cumulative results of the social exercise of the intellectual and active or affective powers of man. Inner or psychological phenomena are examined sociologically, insofar as they become embodied in social behavior and its consequences. Comte generalizes from this methodological limitation, however, and regards the individual person as an abstraction from the social collectivity or humanity.

attached extraordinary significance to the long historical delay of its appearance, since this prevented the full number of the basic sciences from being rounded out and the viewpoint of positive science, as a whole, from being clearly defined. Until the advent of sociology, the struggle between the theologicometaphysical mentality and the positivist mentality could not be resolved. For the theologicometaphysical outlook held the attraction of a *general* explanation of reality, whereas the sciences suffered from overspecialization; conversely, the positive sciences exerted influence through the *reality* of their content, whereas the theological and metaphysical doctrines were bound up with empty mental fictions. Comte aimed at combining *universality of form* and *reality of content* in a single science, sociology, which would automatically constitute the scientific attitude into a genuinely positive philosophy.

From this explanation, it follows that there was no universal and real *philosophy,* until the foundation of Comte's positivism. Philosophy is the generalized theory of the positive sciences. The problem of overspecialization, which plagued the scientific tradition in the past, is now easily settled through "the perfecting of the division of work itself. It suffices, in effect, to make of the study of scientific generalities one more great specialty," viz., philosophy itself.[18] Philosophers are to constitute a new class of savants, whose specialty is the structure and spirit of the scientific enterprise as a whole. But can the *total systematization* of knowledge be achieved through philosophy, regarded as the highest generalization of the other sciences? To this crucial question, Comte is forced to answer by making a distinction between the objective and the subjective methods of knowledge. The *objective method* makes the effort to provide an exact representation of the objective world. This is the method used by the several positive sciences. Comte admits that, in this direction, complete systematic unity cannot be obtained. For the very heterogeneity of phenomenal facts which prevents the complete reduction of any one of the basic sciences to another, also prevents the reduction of all scientific laws to one summary law, such as that of gravity. Comte labels such a reductive effort chimerical and utopian. The objective synthesis can, indeed, achieve a perfect *unity of method,* but it can attain only to a relatively loose *homogeneity of doctrine.*[19] The thoroughly positive

18 *Course of Positive Philosophy,* Lecture 1 (I, 16).
19 *Loc. cit.* (I, 28–30).

character of the method assures its perfect unity. But the content or doctrine is no more than homogeneous, i.e., concerned with factual laws, stating the relative order among several distinct and irreducible types of observable facts.

An "objective philosophical synthesis" is a contradiction in terms, since the objective method cannot bring scientific content to the degree of unity required for a philosophical synthesis. Hence it is only through a *subjective method* that philosophy can attain perfect logical coherence and the organic unity of a practical plan.[20] This synthesis is based upon the idea of *humanity*, taken as the central measure of all thought and action. Comte now makes an about-face on the methodological question. Whereas in the objective or purely specula- tive order, inquiry must proceed from the world to man, in the subjective or practical order it must proceed from man to the world. Since human reality and its needs (rather than the phenomenal world and its laws) provide the unifying principle, the synthesis of philosophical knowledge is subjective, rather than objective. But, in this case, the subject is not the psychological individual but *social* or *collective man*. Complete unity of doctrine is won only by viewing all knowledge in reference to its proper practical end: the normal satisfaction of human social needs.

This distinction between the objective and the subjective methods is not an inconsistency on Comte's part, but it does reveal the profound inadequacy of his attempt to make philosophy a generalized theory of the positive sciences.[21] Comte discovered that, taken in this way, philosophy has no formal object that is not already dictated in

[20] On the objective and subjective methods, cf. *Discourse on the Positive Spirit*, I (Le Verrier, 57–60); *System of Positive Polity*, Fundamental Introduction (I, 443–53). The union of the objective and subjective methods constitutes what Comte calls "the true human logic . . . the new religious logic" (*ibid.*, I, 448, 452). Humanity replaces God and Nature as the synthesizing principle in philosophy. The new logic combines mind and feeling, analysis and synthesis, respect for detail and for totality. On the predominance of feeling and the heart in the subjective synthesis, cf. M. S. Harris, "The Aesthetic Theory of Auguste Comte," *The Philosophical Review*, XXXVI (1927), 225–36.

[21] This point is forcibly brought out by E. Gilson, in his chapter on "The Sociologism of A. Comte," *The Unity of Philosophical Experience*, 248–70. Comte's philosophy is a "sociologism," insofar as it absolutizes the method of the positive sciences (especially as it culminates in the sociological approach to man), and then seeks to construct a philosophy around the ideal of humanity, as the social organism. On Comte's attempt to obtain the total philosophical method from a study of the procedures and history of the positive sciences, see P. Ducassé's *Méthode et intuition chez Auguste Comte*, especially Part Three, on "The Comtean Intuition" (453–572).

advance by the basic positive sciences. Reflection upon their method
and content is not sufficient to provide philosophy with a distinctive
approach to things which, as Comte himself saw, should combine
generality and reality of doctrine. His "one more speciality" is
precisely that, and no more. Hence he turned from an objective to
a subjective foundation of philosophy. This move was fatal to the
sciences, since they were now to be regulated by the needs and
sentiments of the positivistic humanist. The fact that the subjective
criterion was to be social humanity, rather than the biological
individual, did not remove the subjective and nonscientific basis of
the new principle of synthesis. And as far as philosophy was concerned, Comte was then obliged to make of humanity an absolute
principle and a final cause. Although his philosophical effort rested
on the rejection of God, he could not develop a philosophical
synthesis without instituting at least an *immanent absolute* and an
*immanent finality*. These, he qualified as being absolute only "for
us." But this qualification only underlines his predicament, since it
shows that the subjective criterion of social humanity does not
escape the limitations placed by Kant upon moral faith. Humanity,
as a substitute for the ideas of God and the world, has no more
than a regulative use in the speculative order. And when it is transferred to the practical or subjective order, it cannot function as a
principle of scientific or philosophical knowledge. Hence the Comtean
subjective synthesis provides neither the ultimate integration of the
positive sciences nor the philosophical wisdom that is also knowledge.
It leads to an extreme, quasi-religious emphasis upon society and
humanity, which is compensation for Comte's failure to discover the
distinctive object of philosophy and the existence of God, who is at
once immanent in, and transcendent of, His creation.

#### 4. SOCIAL ORDER AND PROGRESS

In the watchword: *Order and Progress,* Comte concentrated his
claim that only his philosophy could terminate the social anarchy
produced by the French Revolution, which he termed "the Great,
Final Crisis" of Western history.[22] The basic cause of this social
anarchy was the *simultaneous presence* of the three philosophical
states of mind. The theological mind advocated retrograde policies
and stressed the virtues of social order; the metaphysical mind stood

---

[22] *Discourse on the Positive Spirit,* II (Le Verrier, 114).

for progress but could only criticize and destroy the institutions of the past; the positivist mind was still too much concerned with scientific specializations to provide the overarching constructive guidance, pointing beyond the crisis. Only with the dual founding of sociology and the positive philosophy, was there supplied a sound basis for combining both order and progress in a new organization of society, according to universally valid principles.

Sociology alone provides the crowning inductive proof of the general scientific conviction that all phenomena are regulated by natural laws, since this science conquers the last frontier of observable phenomena: social facts. Social laws are of two sorts, static and dynamic. *Social statics* deals with the conditions of coexistence and organization in societies, whereas *social dynamics* studies their succession and historical growth.[23] Comte singled out Aristotle, Montesquieu, and Condorcet as his major forebears in this area. Aristotle's main contributions were to social statics, since he analyzed the various types of societies and governments; Montesquieu pioneered the study of social dynamics, through his stress on social developments and the natural agents of social change; Condorcet's great achievement was a brilliant statement on the idea of progress. But these sources did not have the advantage of Comte's own law of the three states or the more recent phases of scientific development. Furthermore, the two French thinkers lacked a proper understanding of the idea of social order, as worked out by medieval social Catholicism. Comte based his social philosophy upon a synthesis of the medieval notion of social order with the modern notion of social progress, both of which are transformed in the light of his law of the three states and the idea of humanity.

The first question to be resolved by the new positivist social philosophy is the apparent opposition between *natural laws* and human *social planning*. Comte states the case as strongly as possible for the reign of law in social affairs. "There are laws just as determined for the development of the human species as for the fall of a stone."[24] Nevertheless, the Comtean view of natural law, as a *constancy-in-variety* or a *modifiable fatality,* does not exclude the possibility of development, within certain limits. Although natural

---

[23] Together, social statics and social dynamics constitute the content of sociology. These two divisions are developed, at length, in: *Course of Positive Philosophy,* Lectures 50–51 (IV, 283–387); *System of Positive Polity,* Vols. II–III.

[24] *Letter to Valat* (September 8, 1824); quoted in L. Lévy-Bruhl, *La philosophie d'Auguste Comte* (fifth edition, Paris, Alcan, s.d.), 270.

laws are invariable in their principal dispositions, they are variable or modifiable in their secondary dispositions. The extent to which changes can be instituted, within the natural order, depends upon the complexity of the facts, i.e., their relative proximity to man. The more that human interests are involved, the more pliable are the facts. Social phenomena, being the most complex or man-centered facts in the natural economy, are also the most pliable under the efforts of the human will. Hence Comte qualifies the quotation given above, with the further remark that the development of humanity follows "a law just as necessary as, although more modifiable than, that of gravitation."[25] Thus the general principle of the *modifiability of natural laws* tells in favor of human social planning and concerted effort.

The second major problem concerns the proper balance between invariability and modifiability of social phenomena, which is the same as the problem of order and progress. Comte gave an acute analysis of the idea of progress. His position differed from many later nineteenth-century accounts, since its biological basis was in the *fixity of species*. In the pre-Darwinian controversy between Cuvier and Lamarck, he followed Cuvier's view about fixed natural species rather than Lamarck's anticipation of the transformism of species. The former position supported Comte's own doctrine on the necessary, hierarchical classification of the basic sciences, a doctrine which was patterned after the biological classification of fixed species. Within the limits set by the species, however, Comte admitted the possibility of considerable change. *Evolution within* the species was allowed by him, but not *transformation of* species.

This biological position determines the sociological relationship between order and progress. Social order concerns the structural, static aspect of society and the conditions of existence; social progress concerns the functional, dynamic aspect of society and the laws of movement. Order by itself alone would lead to social decay, whereas progress alone would result in a permanent state of anarchy. Order must be joined with progress, for *progress* is the fulfillment of the *dynamic tendencies of order itself*, in respect to complex phenomena. Yet man is not infinitely perfectible, as Condorcet supposed, since the limits of the species must be maintained in terms of structural

---

25 *System of Positive Polity*, General Appendix, III (IV, 95). The law of the modifiability of phenomena states that "the variations of universal order are always confined to the intensity of the phenomena, without ever affecting their succession, any more than their nature." *Ibid.*, Social Dynamics, I (III, 71–72).

order. "The general meaning of progression, individual and collective, can never change. For, progress always remains the simple development of order,"[26] and operates within the fixed boundaries set by this order. We can change the intensity and the speed with which a society passes through the various stages of its order, but we cannot change the nature of this social structure itself. Similarly, we can bring our knowledge through the theological and metaphysical states of a science very rapidly, and cultivate its positive condition very intensely, but we cannot alter or remove the law of the three states itself. And, on the principle that "ideas govern and overthrow the world, or, in other terms, that the entire social mechanism rests ultimately upon opinions,"[27] the modifications in the speed and intensity of our knowledge will have a profound effect upon the historical progress of social institutions themselves. The proper *order of reform* is: ideas, morals, and institutions. Comte criticized the early socialists for planning social progress without regard for the limits of human nature, and the early communists for placing the reform of working conditions and institutions before the more fundamental renovation of ideas and morals.

Comte's reason for refusing to grant that progress can transform human nature and its necessary phases is significant for the light it throws on the *rationalistic* side of positivism. In the social sphere, the primary laws or invariable dispositions are the three states of the human mind, along with their moral and political consequences. This order must remain inviolable, amid all progressive improvements of humanity, for otherwise two disastrous consequences would follow: mankind would never move forward surely toward the goal of complete positivity, and the philosophical law of the three states would be destroyed. Within the relative limits of the Comtean world, his threefold intellectual schema must obtain with unconditioned necessity. Comte is just as certain that the march of mankind is toward *la pleine positivité,* as Hegel is certain that world history points toward the full actualization of *Geist.*[28] Neither thinker can entertain the possibility of tampering with the teleology of history, for otherwise he

---

[26] *Loc. cit.* (III, 72).

[27] *Course of Positive Philosophy,* Lecture 1 (I, 26). Although both Comte and Marx bring out the interplay between human outlooks and the material conditions of existence, Comte lays more emphasis upon the initiative and dynamism of our ideas.

[28] For comparative studies, cf. É. Meyerson, *De l'explication dans les sciences,* 453–68, and F. A. Hayek, "Comte and Hegel," *Measure,* II (1951), 324–41.

would be left without a meaning for progress or a foundation for scientific knowledge. It is this search for an unshakable basis of knowledge and an irrefutable philosophy of history, that leads both Comte and Hegel to endow their basic laws of human evolution with *rational necessity.* Both philosophers interpret human progress or development as the oscillatory growth of a rational, necessary order, for this assumption is needed to construct a strictly demonstrative philosophy of history. In such a context, history becomes a "sacred science," since it traces the growth of an absolute — whether infinite spirit or humanity — and supplies the norms of conduct. Both absolute idealism and positivism locate the goal of history in the realization of an absolute, organic totality. Hence methodologically, they agree upon a rationalistic, organic totality as the mark of scientific explanation.

Comte praises both Aristotle and Christianity for seeing that the primary units of society must themselves be social in nature. Men join together in political society, in conformity with a *natural social instinct,* rather than through a Hobbesian or Rousseauvian social contract. Their motives for social union may be benevolent ones, moreover, and not purely egoistic. The political community is founded on the division of labor and the co-ordination of results for a general purpose. Government represents *l'esprit d'ensemble,* the spirit of the whole social order, and its task is to discipline our ideas and actions, so that the good of society as a whole can be achieved. Both the specialization of functions and the collective pressure of government are needed to develop our social capacities, within the limits of a given set of intellectual and material conditions.

The quality of a political society will depend upon the *goal* it sets for itself. Arguing deductively from his theory of the three states of the mind, Comte maintains that two main choices are open to men in political society: to organize their forces for the coercion of other men or to work for the control of nature and the betterment of humanity. The former alternative leads to the *military* civilization of the theological mind, whereas the latter leads to the peaceful, *industrial* civilization of positivism.[29] There is a natural antagonism between the theological outlook and modern industrialism, since the latter admits both the presence of natural, social laws and the need to improve, deliberately, upon the imperfect economy of nature

---

[29] *Discourse on the Positive Spirit,* I (Le Verrier, 70–75); *Course of Positive Philosophy,* Lecture 56 (VI, 78–80).

—principles that are incompatible with theological animism and optimism. The industrialization of modern society is visible proof that the theological mind is being superseded, and that traditionalism in politics is futile.

Positivism rejects both the divine right of kings (the basis of theological politics) and the sovereign rights of the people (the basis of the transitional period of the French Revolution and metaphysical politics). Comte deals severely with the *Revolutionary ideals,* once they have cleared away the old regime. Equality is meaningless, before the glaring differences of capacity, opportunity, and social power, unless it be understood that men are equal as servitors and members of humanity. Freedom of thought can be exercised validly only upon matters of doubt or indifference. There may be legitimate differences of opinion concerning the results of social policies, but Comte will not tolerate them concerning the fundamental principles of political life. He is no friend of democracy and the common intelligence, except where the defense of his principles, through an appeal to "good sense," is at stake. Most men should surrender the right of free scrutiny of principles, so that the few *experts* in positive polity may exercise their just authority. Political principles are to be held on faith by most men, although their faith is not based on revealed truths but on truths demonstrable by the learned (even though the intellectual elite need not actually demonstrate their truth, on every occasion). As for the "rights of man" in general, Comte advocates a shift of emphasis *from rights to duties.*[30] The former will pass away in positivist society but will be compensated for by *individual just guarantees,* resulting from our common obligation to improve humanity.

Although Comte's social and political observations are often penetrating, they suffer from the usual systematic defects attending his various philosophical generalizations. The *empirical basis* upon which they rest — the social and political movement in France, from the 1780's to the 1840's — is not broad enough to sustain an entire philosophy of historical change. Attempts to apply his principles outside this limited area require so many modifications, that the principles themselves cease to signify any definite position. The relation between theological monotheism, the divine right of kings and militarism, for instance, cannot be fitted to the evidence of

---

[30] "No one possesses any other right than that of always doing his duty." *System of Positive Polity,* General Conclusion of the Preliminary Discourse (I, 361).

medieval political theory or the early modern controversies about divine right. Similarly, the connection established between industrialism, peacefulness, and the benevolent rule of experts, is a hopeful prophecy that still awaits factual fulfillment, in this war-torn era of full industrialization.[31] A good test of the law of the three states is also provided by the antithesis which Comte sets up between the theological belief in divine providence and the goodness of creation, and the industrial revolution's recognition of natural social laws and natural imperfections. Comte mistakes the Christian view that the world God created is good, for Leibniz' doctrine that God could not but create the best possible world. There is no incompatibility between the ontological goodness of the created world and the presence of imperfections and wants, which human endeavor can remedy in some measure. Furthermore, the theistic mind is not scandalized at the operation of natural laws, in the field of human relations. Divine providence is not thereby excluded, except on the circular assumption that nature is a self-sufficient phenomenal totality, entirely removed from God's wisdom and power. With respect to human society and history, providence achieves its purpose in and through the workings of bodily natures, as well as through man's rational participation in the rule of divine wisdom. Since this latter sharing is the most proper meaning of natural law, the presence of this law is the chief natural means for the providential ordination of men and the disciplining of human freedom.

## 5. THE RELIGION OF HUMANITY

Comte's religious doctrine is not (as John Stuart Mill claimed) an odd excrescence on the surface of positivism, but an integral part of his philosophy, indeed, its crowning moment. It is a natural extension of his speculation about social order and progress, as is evident from his solution of the problem of modern social anarchy. Here, he borrowed from the writings of Joseph De Maistre, Louis De Bonald, and other French traditionalists, concerning the social institutions of medieval Catholicism. Comte admired these institutions and tried to divorce them from their doctrinal basis, writing to John Stuart Mill that positivists are the true heirs of the Middle Ages in social matters.

---

[31] H. B. Acton, "Comte's Positivism and the Science of Society," *Philosophy*, XXVI (1951), 291–310, shows that Comte's confidence in industrial society is based on his own theory, rather than on factual evidence.

Especially important is the medieval distinction between the spiritual and temporal powers, which Comte translates into modern terms, as a distinction between the *positivist experts* or priests of science and the *rulers* or heads of government.[32] The former are to have complete control over general education and public opinion, with a consultative voice in actual government. The rulers are to be supreme in matters of government and material force, but they may offer only practical suggestions concerning the aims of education. In an industrial society, it is appropriate to draw the rulers, not from the military caste, but from the *positivist patriciate* or managerial class: the bankers, employers, and other executives. *Workers* in industry are to be freely associated rather than drafted, and are to be directed by capable managers. Anarchy will be eliminated, and domestic peace secured, through universal *positivist education,* which cultivates the spirit of the whole, reminds the wealthy of their stewardship and social responsibilities, and defends the dignity of the workers. Owners and workers alike are to be instilled with the ideal of serving humanity as such. All duties are given a social reference, and all functions (especially those performed by positivist philosophers and proletarians, who have a natural affinity with each other in both Comte's and Marx's social thought) are regarded as contributions to public service.

Comte admits that this way of overcoming modern social anarchy would be purely utopian, were it not based on the path of progress which men must follow. The goal of social progress is to achieve the *sublime inversion* of our humanity (i.e., our intelligence and sociability) over our animality, of altruism over egoism.[33] Intellectually, this inversion or sublimation is carried out in function of the positivist *subjective synthesis,* which erects human welfare into the supreme criterion of the sciences. On the plane of human sentiments, appetites, and moral impulses, this inversion is the work of the positivist *religion of humanity,* which brings the subjective synthesis to completion, in the practical order. There is a moral and religious duty to make *altruism* or regard for others prevail over the desire for selfish satisfaction. For, sociology shows that humanity alone is real, and that the individual is only an abstraction.[34] Hence Comte has a naturalistic source of obligation, in the necessary predominance of the social viewpoint in the sciences and of social amelioration in practical life.

The primacy of the idea of humanity is best assured by making it the proper object of religious worship. Although he rejects the theological outlook, Comte wants to transfer religious values to the service of antitheistic humanism. For him, *religion* means, essentially, the love and service of the *Great Being, humanity.*[35] Humanity is not an unqualified absolute-in-itself, but positivist religion makes it an absolute-for-us. Whereas sociology teaches that the individual lives in and through humanity, religion adds that he should also live *for* humanity. *Vivre pour autrui,* live for others — this is the motto of the new religion of humanity. Duty and happiness coincide perfectly in the cultivation of benevolent feelings and the subordination of selfish impulses to the welfare of other men, or rather, of humanity as such. As Pascal observed, humanity is like a single man on the march, a massive organism, in which the succeeding generations influence each other and thus constitute history, through their solidarity and continuity. The individual must strive to merit incorporation in this collective organism, by devoting his thoughts and actions to its betterment, with all the fervor and self-sacrifice of religious devotion. Each man's hold on reality depends upon the degree to which he is joined to the "immense and eternal social unity" of the Great Being, humanity.

The positivist version of *immortality* hinges upon this theory of incorporation into humanity as such.[36] Comte excluded the ordinary,

---

34 *Ibid.,* General Conclusion to the Preliminary Discourse (I, 329–30); *Discourse on the Positive Spirit,* II (Le Verrier, 191).

35 The subtitle of *System of Positive Polity* is "Treatise of Sociology, instituting the Religion of Humanity." The General Conclusion to the Preliminary Discourse, in this work, outlines the religion of humanity (I, 321–99); the first chapter of the second volume of the same work presents the "General Theory of Religion, or Positive Theory of Human Unity" (II, 7–137). A popular sketch of Comte's theory of religion is given in the *Positivist Catechism,* which contains "thirteen systematic conversations between a woman and a priest of humanity." On the title page of *System of Positive Polity* appear two mottoes: "Order and Progress" (the objective rule) and "Live for Others" (the subjective rule).

36 Cf. *ibid.,* Social Statics, I (II, 60–62), and The Human Future, I (IV, 34–36). In this life, we have an existence of our own, yet one that is essentially ordained to incorporation into, and assimilation to, the life of the great organism, humanity. We become its actual organs only after death, when we slough off our individual-egoistic being and let the altruistic love of humanity constitute our entire nature.

religious conception of an *objective* immortality or survival of the soul, both because it supposes an immaterial principle in man and because he thought it drains man's attention away from social tasks on earth. Instead, he suggested a distinction between two modes of our existence: objective and subjective. As *objectively* existent in our temporal, bodily individuality, we are either servants of humanity (if we deliberately promote its ends) or else parasites upon it (if we are mainly self-seeking and anarchical). The most we can do, under the conditions of our objective existence, is to make our altruistic impulses predominate over the others, thus rendering ourselves worthy of eventual union with humanity. Actual incorporation into the nature of humanity comes only after our purification by death. Then, we begin our *subjective* existence. Although our actions have perished with our biological existence, the results of these actions persist in the historical influence of past generations of humanity upon the contemporary one. The only genuine immortality is this subjective one, of living on through our inspiring example and the social forces we helped to produce. Eventually, however, the human species will die out, and with it will be extinguished our only sort of immortality.

Comte's doctrine of subjective, *social* immortality continues the tradition of the Enlightenment on the survival of fame in men's memories, but he gives it a definitely social stress. He makes no allowance for *personal* immortality, for he does not inquire into the grounds, in individual human beings, why they alone are capable of joining in a dynamic society and of generating a history. He consistently fights shy of any nonbiological study of man as an individual existent, and for this reason he never attains a proper conception of the human person. Since he fails to recognize, in the individual man, a *distinctive unity of nature and action* that is neither purely biological nor purely sociological, Comte has no philosophical ground for maintaining that there can be personal survival.

Indeed, he has social reasons for actively opposing personal immortality. As Comte uses the term, "person" signifies the biological individuality, and hence is a synonym for whatever is egoistic and antisocial in human life. Just as his view of the human person provides him with no basis for personal survival, so it supplies no foundation for the union of men in society. There is no *personal* basis for *social* existence, because of Comte's identification of the human person with the purely biological individual. It is in spite of their biological individuality that men are social beings. Incorporation into humanity, the grand social organism, is completed only after death, because it is only then that the subsistent existence of the biological individual ceases and is replaced by the subsumed existence of an organ of humanity. Comte becomes involved in what Whitehead has called the "fallacy of misplaced concreteness," when he declares that man the individual is only an abstraction, and that only humanity or social man is real. He falls into this fallacy, because of his attempt to transform philosophy into the total generalization of the positive sciences. When man is no longer approached philosophically, as an existing rational individual, the concrete principle of human unity is dissipated. The positivist philosopher is left with the biological and sociological reports on man, with which it is impossible to achieve a unified and logically coherent philosophical synthesis. Comte is torn between regarding man as a biological individual and as a sociological component in the collectivity. When man is viewed biologically, his subsistent, distinct being is acknowledged — but in such a way that egoism and antisocial traits prevail. When he is viewed sociologically, his complete dependence upon the social organism is brought out — but then his individual integrity is invaded. In order to evade this philosophical impasse, brought about by giving absolute philosophical significance to the positive scientific approaches to man, Comte has recourse to his subjective method. In the subjective synthesis, only humanity as such enjoys a full hold upon reality, as compensation for the previous stress upon man's biological individuality. Like Hegel's organic totality of spirit, Comte's organic social whole is alone fully actual and concrete. If the concreteness is misplaced, this is not the result of an accidental choice. It is Comte's systematic fate, when he tries to account for man's nature and destiny by means of a philosophical standpoint which is only the generalization of the positive scientific method. By systematically disaggregating the human person, Comte formulates the problem of the individual and society in an insoluble way and gives us temporary immortality, without personality.

A good deal of Comte's "second career" was spent in devising the organization of the *religion of humanity*, a task which he pursued with gusto, down to the slightest details. Thomas Huxley referred to the bizarre results of this pontifical legislation as a sort of Catholicism without Christianity, whereas Comte himself (quite humorlessly) stated his aim to be the replacement of "the Catholicism of Rome by that of Paris."[37] In attempting to appropriate much of the institutional structure of Catholicism, apart entirely from its doctrinal soul, he only succeeded in constructing a grotesque parody, in which many basic human aspirations are mingled with fantastical features. Comte himself served as the high priest of humanity, during his own lifetime. The positive scientists or synthetic minds constitute a sacerdotal corps — the *priests of humanity* or experts in human wisdom. Their duty is to counsel, consecrate, and rule, through the merit of the heart and with the able, moral assistance of women. The positivist priesthood is the supreme embodiment of spiritual power, and exercises complete power over the minds of believers. It makes certain that science, art, and morality are devoted to the study and love of humanity, which is substituted for the love of God. Along with humanity, the Great Being, veneration is due to the earth, the Great Fetish, and to space, the Great Milieu. This is the positivist substitute for the Christian Trinity.

The public cult of humanity (which Comte sometimes addresses, in personal terms, as "she" or our "goddess") is to be organized into two types of religious festivals: the *static festivals* of social order and moral solidarity, and the *dynamic* ones of progress and historical continuity. The static festivals are celebrations of the abstract principles of positive society. New Year's day is dedicated, the world over, to humanity in general; the first days of succeeding months are set aside for festivals in honor of the main domestic relations: connubial, parental, filial, and fraternal. The dynamic feasts are more concrete, celebrating especially the three stages of our theological past (fetishism, polytheism, and monotheism) and the positivist future of godless humanity. Comte issued a *positivist calendar,* in commemoration of the great men who have furthered the progress of humanity. The Christian saints are supplemented by philosophers, scientists, political and military leaders, poets, and the founders of the non-Christian religions.[38] The Catholic sacramental

---

[37] *Ibid.,* The Human Future, V (IV, 463). For a critical account of Comte's neo-fetishistic myth of humanity, cf. J. Delvolvé, "Auguste Comte et la religion," *Revue d'Histoire de la Philosophie et d'Histoire Générale de la Civilisation,* V (1937), 343–68. In "La ligue universelle des religions d'après Auguste Comte," *Revue de Philosophie,* N.S., III (1932), 225–49, C. Eyselé recounts Comte's futile efforts to unite Positivists and Catholics in a temporary league against anarchy, during the interim before positivistic humanity is completely triumphant.

[38] In the positivist calendar, there are 13 months, with 28 days each. The names of the months, together with the types of the individuals commemorated during each

system is expanded into the nine positivist *social sacraments,* covering all phases of human existence, from birth to the posthumous canonization or public incorporation into the Great Being.

Comte admits the need for *private prayer,* as well as public cult. He patterns the interior life of prayer upon his own relationship with Clotilde de Vaux, especially after her death.[39] Our private cult should be directed toward exemplary women, whether living or dead, in whom we may discern the best features of humanity. The prayer of commemoration and effusion should occupy us thrice daily, as a major source of inspiration for serving humanity in a wholehearted way. In harmony with his view that human history consists in the solidarity and continuity of men of all ages, Comte declares that there are more dead than living men in humanity. Hence, there is a special place in religious exercises for *commemoration of the dead.* Not only the luminaries included in the positivist calendar, but all those adjudged worthy of incorporation in humanity, should be kept in mind. In this way, their subjective immortality is also kept fresh.

Comte makes this final summary of his philosophy:

> Love as the principle, order as the basis, and progress as the goal. Such is . . . the fundamental character of the definitive regime which positivism proceeds to inaugurate, in systematizing our entire existence, personal and social, through an unalterable combination of sentiment, reason and activity. Beyond any other previous possibility, this final systematization fulfills the various essential conditions, both with respect to the special scope of the different parts of our nature, and with respect to their general connection. . . . Today, there are only two camps: the one is retrograde and anarchical, where God confusedly presides; the other is organic and progressive, being systematically devoted to Humanity.[40]

---

month, are as follows: (1) Moses: the initial theocracy; (2) Homer: ancient poetry; (3) Aristotle: ancient philosophy; (4) Archimedes: ancient science; (5) Caesar: military civilization; (6) St. Paul: Catholicism; (7) Charlemagne: feudal civilization; (8) Dante: modern epic poetry; (9) Gutenberg: modern industry; (10) Shakespeare: modern drama; (11) Descartes: modern philosophy; (12) Frederick: modern politics; (13) Bichat: modern science. Thus, Comte dated one of his Prefaces: Paris, 23 Aristotle, Sixty-Third Year of the Great Revolution (i.e., March 20, 1851). For a list of the Positivist Great Books, cf. *System of Positive Polity,* IV, 557–61.

[39] For her influence on the religion of humanity, read Comte's astonishing Dedication of *System of Positive Polity,* together with samples of Mme. de Vaux's writings (I, i–xl). Also, E. Gilson, *Choir of Muses* (New York, Sheed and Ward, 1953), Chapter V.

[40] *Ibid.,* General Conclusion of the Preliminary Discourse (I, 321, 398).

From this passage can be gathered the sense in which Comte's theory of religion is not an appendage, but the very climax of his system. Comte attempted the impossible task of achieving a philosophical synthesis, with the sole aid of the method of the positive sciences. He discovered that, even when philosophy is regarded as the highest generalization of the sciences, it fails to secure the general explanation and systematic synthesis which are characteristic of philosophical knowledge. Hence he turned from the objective method to the subjective method, in order to achieve the requisite synthesis. In making this shift, however, he was obliged to subordinate scientific findings to the subjective demands of feeling and the heart. The result was disastrous for both the positive sciences and philosophy. The former were asked to yield more rigorously universal and necessary laws than they could provide, and were then submitted to the regimen of humanistic, social sentiment. The latter was transformed into the religion of humanity, in order to acquire the concreteness of being, which the sciences lacked.

John Stuart Mill tried unsuccessfully to divorce Comte's early positivism from his full-blown subjective synthesis of humanist religion, declaring the latter to be an alien growth on the system. But, in fact, Comte saw that there could be no philosophical system, based on the positive method, unless a subjective and practical synthesis were developed. The later religious doctrine is in organic continuity with the rest of Comte's philosophy, since it completes the movement begun with his youthful rejection of God and his absolutization of the scientific method and the zone of phenomenal, relative facts. For complete logical coherence and systematic unity, at the totally immanent level of positivism, humanity must somehow become the object of worship by its own members. Mill says that "the *fons errorum* in M. Comte's later speculation is this inordinate demand for 'unity' and 'systematization.' "[41] But this inordinate demand is at the heart of positivism, as a philosophical method and doctrine. It is operative throughout Comte's entire philosophy, endowing it with its characteristic blend of absolutism and relativism, rationalist necessity and empiricist variability. To obtain this blend, however, the objective content of scientific research must be subordinated to the exigencies of the subjective synthesis of positivist morality and religion. The outcome is neither scientific nor philosophical knowledge, but an enthusiastic myth and cult of humanity.

---

[41] John Stuart Mill, *Auguste Comte and Positivism* (London, Trübner, 1865), 141.

## SUMMARY OF CHAPTER 16

Comte's atheism was a characteristic nineteenth-century variety, for three reasons: it was based on a cultural analysis of the widespread loss of faith; it filled the void, caused by the denial of God, by absolutizing something relative; it justified itself by means of an inevitable historical law. The Comtean law of the three states declares that the mind passes necessarily through three phases: the theological, the metaphysical, and the positivist attitudes. After first interpreting the world in terms of animating forces and deities (the theological state), man then views nature as a regulated system of general forces (the metaphysical state). Finally, the mind confines itself to a sober, positivistic study of experienced facts, stated as laws. The positivistic state of knowledge has seven outstanding traits: it is real, useful, precise, certain, organic, relative, and sympathetic. It confines itself to a study of the general facts or laws of our relative, phenomenal world, with no regard for noumenal entities. Its method is nonintrospective and nonteleological. Comte prided himself upon the completeness and logical necessity of his sixfold division of the fundamental sciences, made according to a decreasing order of simplicity, generality, and independence of facts, and an increasing order of complexity, particularity, and dependence. Comte's own science of sociology served not only as the capstone of the basic sciences but also as the indispensable condition for an authentic, positivist philosophy. Through the subjective synthesis, based upon the idea of humanity, philosophy can secure complete coherence and unity. Comte's social reforms combined factors of order and progress, structure and dynamism, in conformity with the demands of an industrial, fully positivist age. He sought to consolidate all the gains made in science, philosophy, and social reform, through his religion of humanity. He laid down quite detailed instructions about the organization of humanistic religion and its objects of worship and prayer.

## BIBLIOGRAPHICAL NOTE

1. *Sources.* There is no collected edition of Comte, but various reprints continue to be issued. There are also two useful manual editions: *Oeuvres choisie d'Auguste Comte,* edited by H. Gouhier (Paris, Aubier, 1943) — contains: Lectures 1 and 2 of *Course of Positive Philosophy,* the *Personal Preface* to the *Course, Discourse on the Positive Spirit, The Founder of the Positivist Society to Whoever Desires to Join It; Cours de positive philosophie (première et deuxième leçons), et Discours sur l'esprit positive,* edited by C. Le Verrier (2 vols., Paris, Garnier, s.d.). Both editions contain valuable Introductions. Gouhier provides a useful bibliography; Le Verrier annotates his edition heavily with parallel passages from Comte's other writings. Among the English translations are: *The Positive Philosophy of Auguste Comte,* freely translated and condensed by H. Martineau (2 vols., London, Bohn, 1853), a loose rendition which orthodox positivists repudiated; *A Discourse on the Positive Spirit,* translated by E. S. Beesly

(London, Reeves, 1903); *A General View of Positivism,* translated by J. H. Bridges (London, Trübner, 1865); *System of Positive Polity,* translated by J. H. Bridges, F. Harrison, E. S. Beesly, R. Congreve, and H. D. Hutton (4 vols., London, Longmans, Green, 1875–1877); *The Catechism of Positive Religion,* translated by R. Congreve (London, Reeves and Turner, 1858).

2. *Studies.* F. J. Gould, *Auguste Comte* (London, Watts, 1920), is a brief biography. The personality and intellectual development of Comte are expertly delineated in H. Gouhier's two studies: *La vie d'Auguste Comte* (Paris, Éditions de la Nouvelle Revue Française, 1931), and *La jeunesse d'Auguste Comte et la formation du positivisme* (3 vols., Paris, Vrin, 1933–1941); the latter work gives the best account of the relations between Comte and his early master, Saint-Simon. The only thorough philosophical treatment in English continues to be L. Lévy-Bruhl's *The Philosophy of Auguste Comte,* translated by K. de Blaumont-Klein (New York, Putnam, 1903); F. S. Marvin, *Comte: The Founder of Sociology* (London, Chapman, 1936), stresses his contributions to social science. The intuitive basis for the basic premises of positivism is explored by P. Ducassé, *Méthode et intuition chez Auguste Comte* (Paris, Alcan, 1939). For a Christian evaluation, see H. De Lubac, S.J., *The Drama of Atheist Humanism,* translated by E. M. Riley (New York, Sheed and Ward, 1950), Part II, "Auguste Comte and Christianity," 77–159. See also, E. Caird, *The Social Philosophy and Religion of Comte* (New York, Macmillan, 1885). Comte's relations with our country are described by R. L. Hawkins, *Auguste Comte and the United States (1816–1853)* (Cambridge, Mass., Harvard University Press, 1936). For a recent exposition of logical positivism, see R. von Mises, *Positivism: A Study in Human Understanding,* translated by J. Bernstein and R. G. Newton (Cambridge, Mass., Harvard University Press, 1951). The most important French philosopher between Rousseau and Comte was Maine de Biran. On his doctrine, see V. Delbos, *Maine de Biran et son oeuvre philosophique* (Paris, Vrin, 1931); R. Vancourt, *La théorie de la connaissance chez Maine de Biran* (second ed., revised and augmented, Paris, Aubier, 1944); H. Gouhier, *Les conversions de Maine de Biran* (Paris, Vrin, 1947); G. Funke, *Maine de Biran: Philosophisches und politisches Denken zwischen Ancien Régime und Bürgerkönigtum in Frankreich* (Bonn, Bouvier, 1947). For a brief introductory account, cf. G. Boas, "Maine de Biran," *The Philosophical Review,* XXXIV (1925), 477–90. A lively sketch of Biran's personality and thought is drawn by Aldous Huxley, *Themes and Variations* (London, Chatto and Windus, 1950), "Variations on a Philosopher," 1–152. Comte's educational theory and influence are exhaustively studied in P. Arbousse-Bastide's *La doctrine de l'education universelle dans la philosophie d'Auguste Comte* (2 vols., Paris, Presses Universitaires, 1957). A comparison between Biran and Hume is made in P. P. Hallie's *Maine de Biran, Reformer of Empiricism* (Cambridge, Harvard University Press, 1959).

# Chapter 17. JOHN STUART MILL

## I. LIFE AND WRITINGS

THE fact that John Stuart Mill (born in London, 1806) was the eldest son of the British sensationalist and utilitarian thinker, James Mill, was of decisive importance. For, the father had definite ideas about children's education, which he put into practice with his own family. At about the age of three, John Stuart began to learn Greek and was soon able to read the Greek historians, orators, and dramatists. He began Latin at eight years and, at twelve, was introduced to Aristotelian and Hobbesian logic. In his *Autobiography,* Mill praised this educational regimen in most respects, since the emphasis was laid upon developing his own powers of analysis and reflection. After returning from a year's stay in France (1820–1821), Mill did some readings in Roman law and in a French digest of the legal philosophy of the founder of utilitarianism, Jeremy Bentham. For several years, he regarded the principle of utility or the greatest happiness as a complete doctrine and even as a religious creed. Mill was educated as an agnostic, since his father deliberately left out any training in religious principles. Hence he accepted the associationist psychology of Hartley and James Mill, the utilitarianism of Bentham, and the economic teaching of Ricardo, with religious firmness. About 1826, however, he underwent a severe intellectual and moral crisis. He became convinced that, even if all the social and political aims of his father's circle were realized, he would still be lacking in complete happiness. Thereafter, although he never abandoned the basic empiricism of his background, Mill sought to become something more than a mere reasoning machine. Through a reading of Wordsworth, Coleridge, and Carlyle, he began to cultivate the feelings, a sense of beauty, and a recognition of historical values.

In 1823, Mill had given up the study of law, in favor of a permanent position with the East India Company, where his father held a high post. Mill remained at India House for a generation, becoming chief of the office in 1856, and retiring with an ample pension in 1858, upon the company's dissolution. This employment provided him with sufficient leisure to engage in intellectual research and political activities. His aim was both to continue the tradition of Ricardo in economics and to provide an adequate logical treatise, upon which to found a program of social reform. He became acquainted with the writings of Saint-Simon and Comte; during the French Revolution of 1830, he had an enthusiastic meeting, in Paris, with Lafayette and the revolutionaries. Upon his return to England, Mill advanced the cause of the British "Philosophical Radicals," by his frequent contributions to the *London and Westminster Review*. Politically, however, the Radicals made but little headway, although they contributed to the passage of the Reform Bill of 1832. Mill decided to concentrate upon the philosophical problems which had to be resolved as a condition of social reform. His logical studies were stalled by the question of induction, but the publication of Whewell's historical account of induction enabled him to overcome this hurdle. In 1843, he finally issued *A System of Logic*. In the latter portion of this treatise, Mill's views on the logic of the social sciences were considerably influenced by Comte's writings. Mill and Comte carried on an extensive correspondence (1841-1846), and Mill even contributed to Comte's financial support, for one year. After the success of his *Logic*, Mill was able to publish an earlier work, *Essays on Some Unsettled Questions of Political Economy* (1844), and to bring to completion his *Principles of Political Economy* (1848), the principal statement of Philosophical Radicalism.

Mill's marriage to Mrs. Harriet Taylor took place in 1851, after her first husband's death. Mill had met her and established a friendship in 1830. He always paid the highest tribute to her intellectual and moral qualities; doubtless, she influenced him in respect to women's suffrage and social reform. After her death at Avignon (1858), Mill spent one half of each year in that French town, in order to be near her grave. His last years were crowded with literary and political activity. *On Liberty* (1859) and *Considerations on Representative Government* (1861) outlined his political liberalism, whereas his essay on *Utilitarianism* (1863) provided the classical defense of this ethical standpoint. He served as a member of Parliament (1865-1868). In 1865, there appeared his two polemical writings: *An Examination of Sir William Hamilton's Philosophy* and *Auguste Comte and Positivism*. In the former work, he criticized the leading representative of the intuitionist school in psychology and metaphysics, whereas in the latter he passed some severe judgments on Comte's views of religion. Mill died in 1873, and in the same year his *Autobiography* was released. The following year, his daughter-in-law published his *Three Essays on Religion*, thus revealing Mill's mind upon a subject about which he was singularly reticent during his lifetime.

## 2. PSYCHOLOGICAL ANALYSIS OF CONSCIOUSNESS

The full sweep of Mill's thought is best viewed in the light of its major purpose: *moral and political reform*.[1] This end can be accomplished successfully, only if our efforts are guided by sound principles, based upon the method of the natural sciences. In one word, moral and political action depend upon the logic of the sciences and the latter has its roots in psychology. Hence for Mill, the *proper order* in philosophical inquiry comprises three closely related steps: a psychological study of consciousness, a logical study of scientific method, and an ethical study of individual and social conduct. At the close of the main investigation, it may also be asked whether God exists, and whether religion can be fitted into the scientific world view.

Although he agreed with Comte about the empirical basis of knowledge, the exclusive competence of the scientific method, and the practical orientation of philosophy, Mill took a different position concerning the classification of the sciences. He strenuously criticized Comte for failing to give autonomy to a unified science of *psychology*. In reply to Comte's objections against the method of interior observation, Mill said curtly: "Whatever we are directly aware of, we can directly observe,"[2] either through immediate acquaintance or (as is usual in prolonged studies) with the help of memory. By comparison with the English associationists (Hartley and James Mill), Comte had taken a step backward, in regard to mental science. Comte's biological bias was useful in explaining the general influence of external and bodily circumstances upon human character,

---

[1] This orientation is emphasized in R. Cadiou's general study, "La philosophie de J. Stuart Mill," *Revue Philosophique de la France et de l'Étranger*, CXXXIX (1949), 48–59.

[2] *Auguste Comte and Positivism*, I (London, Trübner, 1865), 64.

but it could not account for the particular differences among individuals and societies. A direct study of the facts of consciousness and the laws of association is required, if a basis is to be provided for social planning.

Mill sought to determine the proper method and principles of psychology, in conjunction with his criticism of Sir William Hamilton's philosophy, which was a compromise between Scottish realism and Kantian criticism. Mill and Hamilton agreed that the analysis of consciousness is the equivalent of metaphysics, since all that we can learn about real things is given through such analysis. Nevertheless, Mill pointed out a twofold difference between Hamilton's *introspective* method and the *psychological* one advocated by himself.[3] First, Hamilton claimed that consciousness gives immediate insight into the reality of the *non-ego* or objective world, as well as into the mind itself, whereas Mill restricted the immediate testimony of consciousness to *mental phenomena*. Second, Hamilton based his major inferences upon certain necessary principles and *irreducible laws* of thought, apprehended through introspective intuition, whereas Mill made a *psychological reduction* of these principles and laws to their mental elements. Mill staked his psychology and, with it, his entire philosophy upon the belief that the only direct objects of consciousness are mental phenomena, and that all principles of thought have an empirical origin.

The task of mental science or the theory of mind is to interpret consciousness. All that we can know about the mind or anything else is supplied either by the objects directly revealed in consciousness or by those which can be inferred from the original facts. This distinction between *immediate* and *inferred* knowledge is plainly required, since otherwise there would be no foundation for the mind's movement toward new facts. The objects of intuition or immediate data of consciousness are indubitably *certain,* supplying us with the model for all knowledge and certitude. We are satisfied, if inferred results approximate to the certainty enjoyed by immediate sensations. To be convinced that there really are icebergs in the Arctic, means to be sure that, "if I were in the Arctic seas I should see" icebergs.[4] In this explanation, Mill anticipated the prag-

---

[3] On these two methods, see *An Examination of Sir William Hamilton's Philosophy,* IX (London, Longmans, Green, 1865), 145–48.

[4] *Ibid.,* IX (*John Stuart Mill's Philosophy of Scientific Method,* edited by E. Nagel, 362). There is no uniformity among the various original editions of Mill's books.

matist emphasis upon truth as a set of practical directions, leading to actual perception. The pragmatists, however, would not accept his ready trust in immediate intuitions. Whereas Mill was satisfied with his father's view that to have a feeling and to be conscious of it are equivalent, the pragmatists would inquire whether such consciousness constitutes a piece of knowledge, in any verifiable sense.

Mill's critical guns were trained in another direction. Philosophical disputes may arise concerning the precise scope of immediate knowledge, but such differences of opinion cannot be settled by a further appeal to intuition. This is where the introspective and psychological methods in mental science part company. Unlike Comte, Mill admitted the validity of introspection for grasping the present facts of consciousness. But this method can show only that certain beliefs are actually *present* in consciousness, not that they are *original* data of intuition.[5] Only the psychological or genetic account of the origin of ideas and principles can discriminate between original and acquired beliefs. Hamilton appealed to the *necessity* with which we assent to certain principles, as proof of their immediacy and indubitable force. But, as Hume demonstrated, this necessity of thought or inconceivability of the opposite can be explained as the consequence of *habitual association* among ideas, especially when the original connection through association is forgotten. Mill instanced belief in the impossibility of an inhabited Antipodes, as a case of merely subjective inconceivability, which was eventually broken down in the face of further experience. It was easier for Mill to dispose of convictions at the secondary level of the problem of the Antipodes, however, than to apply the argument from association to strictly primary principles, the necessity of which is based upon direct evidence, grasped at first acquaintance.

Mill's own positive views rest upon a *psychologizing* of both metaphysics and logic. He defines *metaphysics* as "that portion of mental philosophy which attempts to determine what part of the furniture

---

Hence wherever possible, Mill's *Examination* and *A System of Logic* (tenth edition, two vols., London, Longmans, Green, 1879) are cited, by page, according to Nagel's edition (referred to, hereafter, as *Scientific Method*). Citations by chapter or section, however, refer to the original editions only. Where page reference is made to the original editions, the passage is not found in *Scientific Method*. Nagel's policy of modernizing the text of Mill is followed throughout.

[5] *An Examination of Sir William Hamilton's Philosophy*, IX, 145–48; on the Antipodes, cf. *loc. cit.*, 150.

of the mind belongs to it originally, and what part is constructed out of materials furnished to it from without."[6] According to this definition, then, metaphysics is directed toward *mental phenomena,* and is identical with the genetic analysis of complex beliefs into their original components. Although the external world is not denied, the modes of being studied in this type of metaphysics are of a mental nature, and are defined in function of sensations, thoughts, and feelings. As for *logic,* Mill does distinguish formally between it and psychology, between the question of the validity of beliefs and the question of their mental origin. But he makes *logical validity* depend upon *psychological origin,* in such a way that the genesis of mental connections determines the question of truth of propositions. The process of getting at the original elements of consciousness is equated with that of ascertaining the only "trustworthy answer . . . the genuine testimony of consciousness."[7] Mill's psychologism climaxes the empiricist tendency to determine the nature of reality and the warranted character of propositions mainly through a description of the contents of consciousness and the growth of complex ideas and judgments. The consequences of this approach can be seen clearly in his treatment of three major problems: the existence of an external world, the nature of matter, and the nature of mind — all of which are posed, in Humean fashion, as problems primarily about our belief in such objects.

Mill denies that *belief in an external world* must be accepted as an original deliverance of consciousness.[8] He compares the external reference of sensation to the perception of distance: analysis shows that both may be *acquired,* rather than *primitive,* convictions. An object is actually being sensed during only a small portion of my experience. For the most part, it figures in my consciousness as something that could be perceived, were I to submit to the proper conditions. If I were to enter the room and focus my eyes upon the desk, I would obtain a visual impression of a white paper, which I left lying there. The paper is regarded as a "permanent substratum" or center of reference for the permanent possibilities of sensations of a certain sort. The contrast between my fleeting actual perceptions and the permanent possibilities of sensations could lead

---

[6] *A System of Logic,* Introduction, 4 (*Scientific Method,* 10).

[7] *An Examination of Sir William Hamilton's Philosophy,* IX, 147.

[8] This problem is discussed in *ibid.,* X–XI (*Scientific Method,* 364–87).

me habitually to make reference beyond my consciousness to a supposed outside world.

Despite its general import, this argument is circumscribed by the details of Mill's controversy with Hamilton. Whereas the latter regards belief in an external world as immediate, intuitive, and therefore indubitable, Mill concentrates upon showing how it might be explained as mediate or derived. His explanation does not intend to establish how the belief *actually* arises but only how it *might* possibly arise, on associative principles. But he argues as though the possibility of explaining external reference through association *excludes* any other account, and as though such a description settles the question of the *validity* of the conviction in an external world. Granted the operation of an associative mechanism in the formation of the complex belief in the external world, the problem of whether there is any core of immediately given evidence for the existence of material things, and whether this core of data can legitimately be called in doubt, remains an untouched issue. Like his predecessor Hume, Mill is lacking an existential criterion for ascertaining either the actual existence of the world or the actual origin of our belief in it, since his theory of knowledge makes mental states the primary objects of sensation. Admittedly, he must remain content with suggesting how the belief might have arisen, without reaching any conclusion about its actual origin or the actuality of its object.

Within a phenomenalistic context, *matter* is defined as "a 'permanent possibility' of sensation," and a *body* as "a group of simultaneous possibilities of sensation."[9] The material thing is supposed as the permanent substratum and cause of our actual sensations, insofar as they fall into definite groups. Apart from reference to our sensations and the possibility of sensations, the notion of a material thing is a purely negative one. A material thing can be known only *qua* possibility of sensations, never *qua* exercising its own act of being. Mill claims that his account provides the equivalent for every item in the realistic conviction about the material world. But he has difficulty with the *existential judgment*. He knows that this judgment asserts the real existence of actual facts, as having their being independently of our conceptions of them. Mill's explanation is that our concepts refer back to the series of our *sensations*, which are

---

[9] *Ibid.*, XI and Appendix to Chapters XI–XII (*Scientific Method*, 371, 383). Cf. *ibid.*, XIII, 346–53, on the inadequacies of Hamilton's theory that, in the existential judgment about actual material things, at least one term in the comparison must be a concept.

the only real facts, beyond the conceptual order, to which our minds can reach. But this does not account for the perceptual judgment of existence, insofar as it affirms the act of existing of material things, precisely as being distinct from the existence of sense perceptions about these things.

A phenomenalistic theory of the ego is constructed along similar lines. Just as sensations are referred objectively to matter, so they are referred subjectively to mind, considered as a permanent possibility of mental states. *Mind* is "nothing but a series of our sensations (to which must now be added our internal feelings), as they actually occur, with the addition of infinite possibilities of feeling."[10] Although this definition runs parallel to that of matter or body, there are some notable differences between external objects and the self. The former are small, definite parts of the series of sensations, whereas the latter embraces both these definite groupings and the indefinite fringe of sensation. Furthermore, bodies are limited to possibilities of sensations alone, but the mind or self includes the possibilities of feelings and volitions, in addition to sensations. Because of their objective reference, bodies are public possibilities, in which several minds may share; but the mind constitutes an essentially private series of feelings.

The permanence of the mind is that of a *series of feelings* or a *thread of conscious states,* not that of a substance. In following Hume's phenomenalistic interpretation of mind (which he equates with the self), Mill also falls heir to his special difficulties. Mill admits that the facts of *expectation* and *memory* cannot be explained adequately, by means of the laws of association. Expectations may be understood in terms of memory but, taken together, these two operations are irreconcilable with the notion of mind as a series of feelings. For, although memories and expectations are present states of consciousness, they involve belief in more than their own present existence. They suppose that "I myself" have had, or will have, certain sensations and feelings, in which no one else can share, and that the entire collection of past, present, and future states belongs to "the self-same series of states."[11]

These considerations lead Mill to frame the problem of the self in the form of an alternative. Either the self is distinct from any

---

[10] *An Examination of Sir William Hamilton's Philosophy,* XII, 206. For the phenomenalistic conception of mind, cf. *loc. cit.,* 204–13.

[11] *Ibid.,* XII, 212. Cf. *ibid.,* Appendix to Chapters XI–XII (*Scientific Method,* 387–92), on memory and expectation.

series of feelings and their possibilities or else the series is, para-doxically, one that can be aware of itself as a series. The former view would lead to the doctrine of a *substantial self,* and would sub-vert the phenomenalistic assumption that knowledge is confined to phenomenal states. Instead of considering such a fundamental revision, Mill prefers to accept the paradox of a *self-aware series of conscious states,* declaring that philosophy is here confronted with an ultimate but inexplicable fact. He confesses, however, that his definition of mind is basically insufficient. For, the common tie or link between the members of the series of feelings and conscious states is not itself a feeling or conscious state, but is the unknown condition, in virtue of which all these acts and states are called "mine." What makes this unifying principle an "unknown" factor is precisely Mill's original limitation of knowledge to mental states. Instead of accepting this circular process, subsequent philosophers have sought to reopen the problem of the self. Among these later explanations are: the British idealistic doctrine of an absolute self, permeating all the particular moments in the mental series; William James' reduction of the self completely to the ongoing stream of consciousness; Bergson's attack upon the view that the self is a thread for a series of states; the effort of Thomistic metaphysics to distinguish between the experi-mental studies on mental states and personality and the properly metaphysical account of the human personal substance.

Mill was sensitive to the charge that his position led to *solipsism.*[12] He replied that there is no impossibility in conceiving of other minds as series of feelings or threads of consciousness, each having its private mode of experiencing sensations and feelings. I note that my body is the one connected with the totality of my conscious states. But within my field of experience are other bodies, shaped like mine and giving rise to patterns of conduct, similar to those I originate under like circumstances. In my own consciousness, there is a threefold series: my body, my sensations and feelings, and my conduct. I can observe the first and third members of this series (the body and the conduct) in other cases, and can legitimately interpolate the second factor (sensations and feelings in a private stream of consciousness).

This argument is subject to two major drawbacks. First, since Mill (following Hume) fails to clarify the meaning of *"my* own

---

12 *An Examination of Sir William Hamilton's Philosophy,* XII, 207–12.

body" and *"my* consciousness," he leaves in at least an equal state of obscurity the significance of other bodies, having *their* own consciousness and selfhood. Second, Mill himself asks whether inductive inference can extend beyond one's individual consciousness, without some special justification. He replies in the affirmative, since there is verification of the hypothesis of other selves. Other bodies conduct themselves as one would expect them to do, if they were guided by minds, experiencing feelings similar to one's own. But this supposes that Mill's principles permit him to speak legitimately about *other bodies*. He refers to "those phenomena of my own consciousness which, from their resemblance to my body, I call other human bodies."[13] The otherness of these bodies is that of phenomena within one's own consciousness, at least as far as strict knowledge is concerned. Since Mill admits that he can demonstrate the existence of no extramental bodies — whether his own or those of other minds — a necessary premise for his proof of genuinely other minds is lacking. He cannot interpolate the other self, since he cannot know the other body and the other line of conduct, *as* being other than his own mental phenomena. If his escape from solipsism rests solely upon proof of *belief* in his own and other bodies, rather than upon evidence of their *existence,* then an inductive inference cannot extend beyond one's own mental states. Mill clearly sees, however, that in this instance the proof should extend to the actual existence of other minds, and not merely to the origin of our belief in their existence. The inconclusiveness of his reply to the charge of solipsism affects both the scope of his general theory of induction and the foundation of his views on the social relations among men. Practically, he expresses no doubt about the existence of the public world and other selves, but he does not provide a sufficient basis in his theory of knowledge for such existents.

### 3. PRINCIPLES OF SCIENTIFIC METHOD

Mill states explicitly the relation obtaining between his *psychology* and *logic*. The latter

> is not a Science distinct from, and coordinate with, Psychology. So far as it is a science at all, it is a part, or branch, of Psychology; differing from it, on the one hand as a part differs from the whole, and on the other, as an Art differs from a Science. Its theoretic grounds are

---

[13] *Ibid.,* Appendix to Chapters XI–XII (*Scientific Method,* 388, n. 6).

wholly borrowed from Psychology, and include as much of that science as is required to justify the rules of the art.[14]

The province of psychology is thought as thought, considered in its universal and necessary laws. Apart from the laws of association, there are scarcely any such laws of thought. Logic deals with the validity of thought and hence with the special marks distinguishing correct from incorrect thinking. Mill calls the formal logic of the syllogism a "smaller logic," which enjoys a legitimate place within the "larger logic" of the empiricist ascertainment of truth. In its broadest acceptation, logic is a philosophy of *evidence,* an explanation of the use of reasoning for the discovery of truth. The logic of the *scientific method* predominates, since the discovery of truth is best exemplified in the actual procedures of the positive sciences. When engaged in an attack upon purely deductive systems, Mill explains logic mainly as a branch of psychology; but when engaged in explaining scientific procedures, he stresses the distinctive aspect of logic, as the philosophy of evidence.

Mill allows that the three *first principles* of identity, contradiction, and excluded middle are formal rules of consistency, holding true for all phenomena.[15] They enjoy at least a *de facto* necessity, as the laws of phenomenal existence and of our thinking, which is confined to phenomenal existence. We cannot discover whether they apply to the "absolute existence" of things, in their own nature. But, Mill avers, if there are any inherent necessities of thought, these principles are such. He is very cautious in dealing with them, claiming only that his laws of association could account for the feeling of necessity associated with these principles. He is quite reluctant to concede to Hamilton that these first principles are a priori truths, belonging to the mind's innate structure and capable of sustaining deductions about noumenal entities. For, he agrees with Locke that they are not employed as principles of deduction by the sciences, and he argues that the Kantian noumena must remain strictly unknowable. But although Mill accepts these first principles as generalizations from

---

14 *Ibid.,* XX, 388–89.

15 *An Examination of Sir William Hamilton's Philosophy,* XXI, 417–21. A realistic approach to first principles cannot accept either pole of the disjunction between phenomenal existence (Mill) and noumenal or absolute existence (Hamilton), as the locus for these principles. Both the disjunction itself and the accepted formulation of the "fundamental laws of thought" must be viewed in the light of a critical evaluation of Hume and Kant.

experience, his phenomenalistic notion of experience does not permit him to concede that they are anything more than factually indispensable, formal rules of reasoning and phenomenal existence. Similarly, his psychological approach to the question of their necessity is unsuited for distinguishing between subjectively necessitated apprehension and apprehension of the necessities of being.

The *dictum de omni et nullo* (whatever can be affirmed or denied of a class, can also be affirmed or denied of everything in that class) is criticized by Mill, on the grounds that the class is nothing more than the particular objects contained in it. He follows Hume's general position that a *universal* signifies an isolated set of particular attributes, within the complex idea of a concrete thing, to which set a general name has been attached by association. And like Hume, Mill intends to set off his stand from medieval extreme realism, Hobbes' complete nominalism, and Locke's theory of abstract ideas. Reasoning is not based upon a distinctive order of Lockean abstract ideas, and yet it is something more than a purely formal, Hobbesian manipulation of language. As for the Scholastic theories of the universal, Mill is conversant only with extreme realism. " 'Universals' were regarded as a peculiar kind of substances having an objective existence distinct from the individual objects classed under them."[16] It is in reaction against what he calls the "scholastic dogma" that knowledge refers only to permanent, general substances, of a higher sort than concrete particulars, that Mill develops his notion of the class as a group of particulars, joined with a general name. His description of medieval extreme realism influenced John Dewey's historical views about the Aristotelian-Scholastic "spectator-theory of knowledge." Neither writer takes adequate account of the aim of moderate realism to found universal concepts abstractively upon individual existents, and to accord to the latter alone the dignity of exercising the act of existing.

In dealing with the *syllogism*, Mill seeks to avoid two extreme positions: that it is the mind's proper instrument of discovery and proof of new truths, and that it is merely a *petitio principii*, quite worthless for reasoning.[17] He distinguishes between a reasoning which

---

[16] *A System of Logic*, II, ii, 2 (*Scientific Method*, 113). On the *dictum de omni et nullo*, cf. loc. cit. (*Scientific Method*, 112–16).

[17] *Ibid.*, II, iii (*Scientific Method*, 120–35); Mill entitles this chapter: "Of the Functions and Logical Value of the Syllogism." R. P. Anschutz, in "The Logic of J. S. Mill," *Mind*, N.S., LVIII (1949), 277–305, maintains that a realistic strain in Mill's

develops new speculative truths and a reasoning which provides shorthand notes, for practical use. The syllogism is useless in the first type of reasoning, but it fills a notable role in respect to practical needs of the mind. It is not an inventive process for acquiring new knowledge, since we do not draw our inferences *from* the major premise. Still, the syllogism is valuable, insofar as we may sometimes make our inferences *in accord with* what the major premise states, in summary form. When a particular inference can validly be made from one concrete instance to another, it can be applied to an infinite number of particular instances, and hence can be summarily stated in a general theorem. The major premise in the syllogism is precisely a *memorandum* for the mind, a shorthand way of stating that a particular inference can be used in all other cases of the same kind. Syllogistic form also checks our reasoning, in cases where doubt has arisen, even though it cannot ascertain new truths of fact.

Mill has formulated a famous objection to the syllogism, considered as a *speculative* means for gaining *new* truths. The typical syllogism runs thus: All men are mortal; Socrates is a man; therefore Socrates is mortal. Now, Mill remarks, unless the conclusion about the mortality of Socrates were already presupposed in the major premise, the latter would itself be doubtful and could not certify the conclusion. For, from a general principle, no particulars can be inferred, except those which the principle already assumes as known. Hence in the speculative order, the syllogism does beg the point to be proved. No genuine speculative progress can be made through its ministration.

The operative phrase in Mill's criticism is that the general principle assumes the particulars *as known*. He rejects the reply that the major premise contains the truth of the conclusion implicitly but not explicitly, by defining implicit knowledge to mean "that you asserted it unconsciously, that you did not know you were asserting it."[18] He returns to his conception of a *general truth*, which is "but an aggregate of particular truths, a comprehensive expression by which an indefinite number of individual facts are affirmed or denied at once. . . . Generals are but collections of particulars, definite

conception of scientific method and social reform leads him to retain some elements of Aristotelian logic. His basic standpoint, however, is that of a phenomenalistic realism, which contrasts ideas with "facts" and "events," taken in the Humean sense,

18 *A System of Logic*, II, iii, 2 (*Scientific Method*, 123).

in kind but indefinite in number."[19] If the major premise must be a general truth, in the sense of a *collective proposition aggregating particular facts,* then the conclusion is already announced and the syllogism is redundant. But Mill does not consider another way of framing a general truth: through abstraction of the essential nature or property from experienced instances, and through intellectual determination of the content of that nature or property, in its own structure. This determination of meaning need not have in view this or that particular embodiment; hence a genuine inference can subsequently be made to the concrete subject, possessing the nature or property in question. Such an abstractive approach explains how general truths are "definite in kind," without taking either "the high priori road" of an extreme realism of subsistent essences or the associationist highway, which fails to elucidate the ground in being for the conviction that several particulars are *similar* instances, belonging *in a class.*

Mill marshaled his positive logical doctrine around the theory of *induction,* which he defined as "the operation of discovering and proving general propositions. . . . Induction is the process by which we conclude that what is true of certain individuals of a class is true of the whole class. . . . We feel warranted in concluding that what we found true in those instances holds in all similar ones, past, present, and future, however numerous they may be."[20] Mill had a more exalted notion of the power of inductive inference than is common among scientists today, since he accepted the Laplacean mechanical system as the ideal for scientific explanation. According to this view, the entire state of the universe at any subsequent moment is determined by its state at the present moment, so that sufficient inductive knowledge of the present agencies and laws of nature could provide an exact, predictive knowledge of the subsequent state of natural events. Mill's problem was to accommodate the determinism of natural laws and the classes of particulars within his theory of mind and knowledge.

His two major accomplishments in logic are: his formulation of the *method of induction* and his explanation of the *uniformity of nature* or law of *causality.* These are cognate questions, since scientific

---

[19] *Ibid.,* II, iii, 3 (*Scientific Method,* 124); *ibid.,* III, i, 2 (tenth edition, Vol. I, p. 328).

[20] *A System of Logic,* III, i, 2 (tenth edition, Vol. I, pp. 328–33); *ibid.,* II, iii, 3 (*Scientific Method,* 124).

induction supposes that cause and effect can be reduced to the relation of invariable antecedent and consequent events, in the phenomenal series. The aim of induction is to isolate the antecedent and consequent phenomena, which constitute an invariable, unconditional succession. Mill's inductive theory is free from Bacon's preoccupation with a search for the forms, which underlie sensible appearances; it is also more strictly formulated and carefully developed than Comte's general approbation of induction from experience. He lists *five types of induction* in the sciences: the methods of agreement, difference, joint method of agreement and difference, residues, and concomitant variations.[21] Each method is stated in a canon and is illustrated in schematic form.

1) Canon for the method of *agreement: "If two or more instances of the phenomenon under investigation have only one circumstance in common, the circumstance in which alone all the instances agree is the cause (or effect) of the given phenomenon."* If the antecedent circumstances are grouped as ABC and ADE, and the consequents as *abc* and *ade,* then in both latter instances, *a* is the effect of *A* alone. (2) Canon for the method of *difference: "If an instance in which the phenomenon under investigation occurs, and an instance in which it does not occur have every circumstance in common save one, that one occurring only in the former, the circumstance in which alone the two instances differ is the effect, or the cause, or an indispensable part of the cause, of the phenomenon."* Thus, in one instance, the antecedents are ABC, and the consequents are *abc;* in the other instance, the antecedents are BC, and the consequents are *bc;* hence the antecedent or cause of *a* is *A.* (3) Canon for the joint method of *agreement and difference* or the indirect method of difference: *"If two or more instances in which the phenomenon occurs have only one circumstance in common, while two or more instances in which it does not occur have nothing in common save the absence of that circumstance, the circumstance in which alone the two sets of instances differ is the effect, or the cause, or an indispensable part of the cause, of the phenomenon."* Here, the antecedents ABC and ADE are first

---

21 On the canons of induction, cf. *ibid.,* III, viii (*Scientific Method,* 211–33); the five-fold formulation of the canons is given in *Scientific Method,* 214, 215–16, 221, 223, 227. R. Jackson, "Mill's Joint Method," *Mind,* N.S., XLVI (1937), 417–36, and XLVII (1938), 1–17, reduces the joint method of agreement and difference to the method of difference. H. W. Schneider, in "Mill's Methods and Formal Logic," *Studies in the History of Ideas,* III, 407–26, places Mill's induction within the broader context of the deductive logic of demonstration.

correlated with the consequents *abc* and *ade;* then a comparison is made between the two antecedent groups BC and DE and the two consequent groups *bc* and *de;* thus indirectly, the exclusive causal connection between *A* and *a* is brought out.

4) Canon for the method of *residues:* "*Subduct from any phenomenon such part as is known by previous inductions to be the effect of certain antecedents, and the residue of the phenomenon is the effect of the remaining antecedents.*" To determine the cause of *c* in the succession from ABC to *abc,* A and B are eliminated, as being the causes already ascertained for *a* and *b; C* remains as the cause of *c*. (5) Canon for the method of *concomitant variations:* "*Whatever phenomenon varies in any manner whenever another phenomenon varies in some particular manner is either a cause or an effect of that phenomenon, or is connected with it through some fact of causation.*" If some modification in antecedent *A* is always followed by a change in consequent *a,* consequents *b* and *c* remaining the same, there is some causal relation between *A* and *a;* the same conclusion follows if every modification in *a* is preceded by one in *A*.

Subsequent logicians have accepted Mill's formulations as standard statements. But they have noted that these canons are of no specific help in making inductive *discoveries,* but only in *checking* discoveries made by other means, especially by mathematical constructions. What Mill said about the syllogism, applies accurately to his doctrine on inductive methods: it does not lead to new truths but it does provide a test of validity and a means of stilling doubt. But the seventeenth-century, Galilean-Cartesian ideal of a genuinely inventive, scientific logic was achieved neither by rationalists nor by empiricists, during the two following centuries. Mill himself recognized the virtual impossibility of isolating all the antecedents of a given event, so that the ideal relation of ABC to *abc* might be set up. The main question for scientific inquirers, working within the framework of his view of nature, is the manner in which this relation can be at least approximated, when the process of verification is begun. From the philosophical standpoint, the crucial issue continues to be the Humean notion of causality, which pervades the entire explanation.

Mill adduced the principle of the *uniformity of the course of nature,* to justify inference from one observed connection to all similar cases.[22] This principle asserts that all phenomena take place according to

---

[22] See *A System of Logic,* III, iii–iv, xxi (*Scientific Method,* 181–90, 287–91).

general laws, which state the regularity of sequences. In turn, the principle of uniformity is regarded by Mill as being nothing more than an inductive generalization from observed uniformities of lesser degree. It was pointed out to him that this involves a case of circular reasoning, since the principle which grounds *every* instance of induction is itself supposed to be dependent upon *valid, particular* inductions. Mill's reply to this objection took the form of a comparison between the principle of uniformity and the major in a syllogism. This principle may be regarded as the ultimate major premise, into which all inductive reasoning may be thrown. Hence it is a mere compendious memorandum about particular inferences, a necessary condition of inductive proof but not a contributing factor to such proof. But this comparison falters before the fact that the uniformity of nature is used as a ground or *reductive principle, in the line of inductive inference itself,* regardless of whether or not it can be cast into the form of a syllogistic major premise.

Mill saw this flaw in his defense, and sought to remedy it through a distinction between *scientific* and *unscientific* inductions. The uniformity-principle is presupposed by all rigorous, scientific inductions, but itself presupposes a whole series of previous, unscientific inductions. The common-sense mind makes spontaneous generalizations about the broad uniformities of life: food nourishes, and water quenches the thirst. These primitive convictions suggest the more general view that all phenomena within our range are subject to causal laws, and hence that there is uniformity of sequence throughout nature. Since the prescientific inductions cannot depend upon the general principle to which they give rise, Mill assigns them to the class of inductions through *simple enumeration.*[23] Far from following Bacon's rejection of simple enumeration, Mill calls it not only a valid process but also the only basic kind of induction open to man. The principle of the uniformity of nature is founded solely upon induction by simple enumeration, and is proved by this method alone. All that scientific methods of induction do is to make the common-sense procedure more precise and comprehensive.

Mill's reduction of the ground of scientific induction to simple enumeration is most instructive. For, it is a tacit admission that the problem of induction is radically insoluble, in purely logical terms,

---

[23] *Ibid.,* III, xxi, 2 (*Scientific Method,* 289–90); *An Examination of Sir William Hamilton's Philosophy,* XXVII, 537, n.

within the context of his phenomenalistic view of scientific method. Mill has no logical grounds for showing: (a) how *simple enumerations* can be regarded as *generalizations* about uniformities and *unconditional* causal laws in nature; (b) how *particular* uniformities can "suggest and give evidence of the *general* uniformity" of nature.[24] In order to make these inferences, he is obliged to appeal to common-sense or infrascientific experience. It is to his credit to have realized (in opposition to the Kantian tendency to depreciate common sense, in the speculative order) that there is a serious problem involved in the relation between science and common sense, precisely in regard to speculative, scientific truth. It is in this direction that realism is able to establish the distinctive foundation of metaphysics and of the principle of uniformity. But at this juncture, Mill's *psychologism* reasserts itself and prevents him from providing any realistic, metaphysical foundation for induction. Since his metaphysics is a department of psychology, and since logic derives its foundation also from psychology, Mill's appeal to the common-sense operation of simple enumeration is really a reduction of the logic of induction to the psychology of association and belief. The problem of the uniformity of nature is not settled by him in function of a logic of evidence but in function of an associationistic psychology of belief. Just as Hume explained general terms and causal beliefs through an appeal to habitual bonds, established by the mind, so Mill explains inductive generalizations through the customary associations built up by repeated, simple enumerations. The customary repetition generates a feeling of necessity and a conviction about the general uniformity of events.

This account is in conformity with Mill's theory of knowledge, and shares the limitations of the latter. It tells nothing about events in nature or their regulative principle, since phenomenalism is not strictly concerned about them. Rather, Mill's doctrine on induction confines itself to an explanation of the subjective state of belief in the uniformity of nature, as befits its Humean epistemological foundation. Even in this area, however, it does not reckon sufficiently with the common-sense conviction about the difference between having *uniform beliefs* about natural sequences and having a *belief in the uniformity* of natural sequences. Over and above any subjective feeling of being necessitated, there is an irreducible core of ontological, causal reference in the common-sense judgment about the uniform character of natural

---

[24] *A System of Logic, loc. cit. (Scientific Method,* 289).

process. Consequently, the examples Mill furnishes of spontaneous generalizations at the infrascientific level (e.g., "food nourishes"), are not simple enumerations of instances but indeterminate, causal affirmations about real process and its principles. This suggests that the common-sense mind intends to assert something about the nature or dynamic principle resident in actual things in a class, and that an adequate theory of the ground of induction must take account of the bearing of such reference upon the meaning of the ordinary conviction about the uniformity of nature.

For Mill, *causality* spells invariability of succession among antecedent and consequent phenomena.[25] He contrasts this conception of the "physical" cause with the "efficient" cause (proposed by Reid and the Scottish school), which is supposed to belong to the essential, noumenal constitution of things and actually to produce its effect. In Mill's system, the physical or phenomenal cause *precedes,* but does not actually *produce,* the effect. Hence, he admits no distinction between the antecedent conditions and the true physical cause, since the latter is nothing more than the sum of the antecedent conditions, no one of which has any specially intimate, phenomenal relation with the effect. Since the human mind can know nothing about the production of the being of the effect, Mill concludes, consistently, that there is no phenomenal basis for differentiating between causes and conditions. He adds that the cause must be not only the *invariable,* but also the *unconditional,* antecedent of the series.[26] This latter note enables him to answer Reid's objection (leveled against Hume) that, if causality consists in invariable succession, men would take the invariable sequence of night and day to mean that night is the cause of day. Mill replies that the antecedence of night to day is an accidental or conditional one, since the coming of day depends upon the presence of the sun and the absence of any opaque barrier between the sun and the earth. Experience teaches us that some sequences are conditional and others unconditional (such as the sequence of sun and daylight) : only an unconditional, invariable antecedent is a cause.

An *unconditional* antecedent not only does precede its effect but always will do so, under the present constitution of things and the

25 *Ibid.,* III, v (*Scientific Method,* 191–203); *An Examination of Sir William Hamilton's Philosophy,* XVI, 295, 305–07.

26 "We may define, therefore, the cause of a phenomenon to be the antecedent, or the concurrence of antecedents, on which it is invariably and *unconditionally* consequent." *A System of Logic,* III, v, 6 (*Scientific Method,* 200).

prevailing set of natural laws. On a purely logical basis, Mill does not try to explain the unconditional character of the physical cause, or the sense in which "experience teaches" us about the constitution of things. Because of his phenomenalistic epistemology, the explanation must come from his psychological account of the formation of necessary connections in our mind. That is why he says that causal uniformity need not pervade all of nature but only the phenomena with which induction deals, i.e., only the fixed order of succession among our sensations. Since Mill is limited historically by the alternative between phenomena and noumena, he cannot look for the ground of induction and causal judgments in the tendencies of real natures, but only in the associational laws that weave firm beliefs out of the phenomenal materials. But the *specifying principle,* whereby the original flow of atomistic sensations is differentiated into *various sorts* of uniformities and sequences, upon which the associational connections are built, remains as much of a mystery as the "efficient noumenal causes" of the Scottish school. Mill grants that induction requires not only causal uniformities but also parallel cases or natural *kinds* of facts. These kinds are real, natural groups, not mere conventional headings. No reason can be given for these initial fixed groupings of sensations, however, without discarding the dualism of phenomena and noumena.

Within the wider framework of induction, Mill finds a legitimate role for deduction, hypothesis, and verification. The principles of *deduction* themselves have an a posteriori origin, in experience. Mathematics rests upon the principles of number and space or extension, from which only numerical and spatial properties can be ascertained. Mathematical construction is assigned a much narrower function in Mill's scientific methodology than it actually fulfills in scientific investigation. In the study of nature, the inductive isolation of separate lines of causal succession must be supplemented by a deductive attempt to calculate the course of the various causal agencies, taken in conjunction. There are two methods for studying causes in conjunction: the mechanical and the chemical.[27] The *mechanical* method employs the principle of the *composition of causes:* the joint effect of several causes is the same as the sum of the separate effects. The *chemical* method is required for cases where the separate causes cease to operate in the complex effect, and where unforeseen

[27] *Ibid.,* III, vi (*Scientific Method,* 204–08).

results occur. Not only in chemical compositions but also in *vital* and *social* phenomena, the heterogeneity between the joint effect and the sum of the separate effects is very pronounced. Nevertheless, the principle of the composition of causes is the general rule, in some measure, for all phenomena in our experience. Hence some kind of deduction is possible, even at the biological and social levels, provided that the deductions are regarded as hypothetical, until they have been verified by empirical means.

### 4. THE LOGIC OF THE MORAL SCIENCES

The last part of Mill's *System of Logic* is entitled: "On the Logic of the Moral Sciences." The goal of his philosophy is the practical reform of men and institutions. The chief obstacle recognized by Mill is belief in *fixed,* social principles, given in an a priori or intuitive way. Principles of this sort would tend to support resistance to social change, and to suppress the critical examination of institutions and standards. This is the ulterior reason for his consistent reduction of metaphysical and logical questions to his own associationist psychology. The latter encourages the *genetic* analysis of all beliefs, with emphasis upon *change* and empirically founded connections.

Mill's "moral sciences" are what would today be called the humane studies (*Geisteswissenschaften*), but with the notable exception of the normative disciplines of ethics, prudential policy, and esthetics. Comte was right in wanting to apply the scientific method to man's thoughts, feelings, and actions. Since these phenomena exhibit observable uniformities of succession, they can be explained in terms of causal laws. Hence there can be a genuine *science of human nature.*[28] Within this broad discipline, Mill distinguishes between the study of individual human nature and the social sciences.

*Psychology* studies mental states, in order to determine the abstract and universal laws of human nature. But it is also important to consider man in a more concrete way, and in respect to laws of lesser generality. This perspective is to be developed by what Mill calls *ethology,* the science of the formation of human character. Ethology would stand midway between general psychology and mere empirical acquaintance with men. It would work out the corollaries of psychology into a body of intermediate laws, governing

---

[28] On a science of human nature, psychology, and ethology, cf. *ibid.,* VI, iii–v (*Scientific Method,* 309–24).

the growth of different types of characters. Its method would be the deductive one of making hypothetical predictions about the tendencies of given sets of circumstances to modify the general mental forces shaping character, and then of making experimental observations, in order to verify the hypotheses. Although Mill never actually elaborated upon his sketch of ethology or characterology, he required at least the possibility of this science as a theoretical link between his associationist psychology and the social sciences.

The *social sciences* (including history, economics, sociology, and political science) treat of man in the social state. Mill describes two erroneous approaches to social man, and then outlines the procedure which conforms with his own scientific method.[29] The first erroneous method is the "chemical" or purely *experimental* one, which is exemplified by practical politicians and by Baconian empiricists like Macaulay, the British historian. This view pretends that men brought together in society are *completely transformed,* like chemical elements, into a new type of substance, and that the laws of individual human nature no longer apply. If this were so, the social sciences would be purely experimental, lacking any deductive foundation in a general theory of human nature. This would divorce social questions from Mill's theory of knowledge and psychology, making his entire theory of scientific method sterile. The second misleading approach is the abstract or *geometrical* method of Bentham and James Mill. It has the advantage over the first type of social investigation, in that it allows for deductive inferences from a general theory of human nature, but its mistake is to support the wrong type of deduction. If social movements resulted from *one force alone,* the geometrical method would be the most appropriate in the social field. But in point of fact, social tendencies result from a combination of many real and conflicting lines of force. Consequently, the *mechanical* method of the resolution of forces or combination of causes is the model for social research.

By elimination, then, Mill arrives at the *physical* or *concrete deductive* method as the organon of the *social sciences.* It is deductive, rather than wholly experimental or "chemical"; yet it is concerned with a mechanical conjunction of many causes, and not with a single "geometrical" force, such as Bentham's self-interest. The basic premise of this approach may be stated as follows:

---

[29] *A System of Logic,* VI, vii–x (*Scientific Method,* 324–52).

However complex the [social] phenomena, all their sequences and co-existences result from the laws of the separate elements. The effect produced, in social phenomena, by any complex set of circumstances amounts precisely to the sum of the effects of the circumstances taken singly, and the complexity does not arise from the number of the laws themselves, which is not remarkably great, but from the extraordinary number and variety of the data or elements — of the agents which, in obedience to that small number of laws, co-operate toward the effect.[30]

Mill is confident that his associationist psychology and projected ethology can determine the *separate* laws regulating human thoughts, feelings, and actions. But he agrees with Comte that human social phenomena are the most complex of all. In plotting out the *conjunctive* course of these laws in the social order, the deductions can state only broad *tendencies,* not determinate facts. Furthermore, the deductions are of a *hypothetical* nature, and require verification through experimental studies of social facts. Under the heading of the "inverse deductive, or historical, method," Mill incorporates the techniques suggested by Comte for constructing a social statics and a social dynamics. Mill thinks that social progress signifies not only change but also a general improvement or "tendency toward a better and happier state,"[31] determined ultimately by the constant increment in our speculative knowledge.

## 5. UTILITARIAN ETHICS AND LIBERALISM

The moral sciences, whether of individual or social human nature, are full-fledged sciences, in that they deal with matters of fact, through propositions in the indicative mood. But ethics does not come under the moral sciences, since it treats of duties, rules, and precepts, rather than facts, and does so by means of statements in the imperative mood. Mill regards ethics, prudential policy, and esthetics as arts, rather than as sciences. He distinguishes sharply between the *sciences* or *factual* analyses of things as they *are,* and the *arts* or *normative* accounts of how things *ought to be.* An art proposes an end to be attained; the corresponding science declares, in a *theorem,* what combination of circumstances and actions will achieve this end; if these means fall within human power, the art then declares the proposed end not only desirable but also practicable, and thus converts the theorem of science into a *rule* or precept of conduct. Whereas

---

[30] *Ibid.,* VI, ix, 1 (*Scientific Method,* 332).
[31] *Ibid.,* VI, x, 3 (*Scientific Method,* 344).

science determines the relation of means to ends, it is the exclusive privilege of the arts to set the ends of human action. "Every art has one first principle or general major premise not borrowed from science, that which enunciates the object aimed at and affirms it to be a desirable object."[32] This first principle specifies what ought to be the object of approbation and the precedence among the goals sought in the normative fields. A science, as such, cannot say that certain ends ought to be pursued: this is the task of *teleology* or the doctrine on ends, which constitute the first principles of conduct. The contrast between the factual and normative disciplines was strongly emphasized by Mill, who thereby was influential in establishing the position of logical positivism, that ethics is not a strict science but only an affective expression of our desires.

Bentham had given utilitarianism its watchword: "the greatest happiness of the greatest number" (a phrase also found in the moralist, Francis Hutcheson, and the scientist-philosopher, Joseph Priestley).[33] In his essay on *Utilitarianism,* Mill came to the defense of Bentham and James Mill, whose ethical philosophy had been criticized by Kantians and intuitionists. Mill defined the principle of *utility* or the *greatest happiness* principle in these words:

> Actions are right in proportion as they tend to promote happiness, wrong as they tend to produce the reverse of happiness. By happiness is intended pleasure, and the absence of pain; by unhappiness, pain, and the privation of pleasure. . . . That standard is not the agent's own greatest happiness, but the greatest amount of happiness altogether.[34]

Pleasure and freedom from pain are alone desirable as ends in themselves, all other things being sought either as means to happiness or as ingredient parts of it. Mill usually took "pleasure" and "happiness" as synonymous, but he went beyond Bentham in main-

---

[32] *A System of Logic,* VI, xii, 6 (*Scientific Method,* 355). Cf. this entire twelfth chapter (*Scientific Method,* 352–58), for the distinction between the sciences and arts. Mill foreshadows the refusal of B. Russell and A. J. Ayer, the British logical empiricist, to allow any scientific character to ethical statements.

[33] J. Bentham, *An Introduction to the Principles of Morals and Legislation,* I, 13, n. 1 (in W. Harrison's edition of Bentham's *A Fragment on Government* and *An Introduction to the Principles of Morals and Legislation* [Oxford, Blackwell, 1948], 128–29). Harrison's Introduction to his edition provides an excellent account of Bentham's philosophy and its antecedents.

[34] *Utilitarianism,* II (Plamenatz edition, 169, 173). Read M. A. Rooney, S.J., "Mill: Utilitarianism," *The Great Books: A Christian Appraisal,* edited by Harold C. Gardiner, S.J. (New York, Devin-Adair, 1953), IV, 179–85.

taining that pleasures differ not only in *quantity* but also in *quality*. Hence it is not possible to make what Bentham called a "felicific or hedonic calculus," giving quantitative weight alone to all the pleasurable circumstances of an action. There are really different *kinds* of pleasure, some being more valuable and desirable than others. Which of two kinds of pleasure is the more desirable, can be discovered by consulting the preference of men who have experienced both, and hence who are competent to judge them, entirely apart from the question of moral consequences.

Mill counted heavily upon a natural sense of dignity in us all, or at least in the majority of men, to establish that there is a marked preference for those pleasures and grades of existence which satisfy our *higher* faculties—our capacities for speculative truth, noble sentiment, and fellow-feeling.[35] Although he rightly invoked the practice of experienced men, he admitted no other tribunal for deciding upon the hierarchy of values and pleasures than their witness. The supposition is that the majority of those *experienced* in different pleasures are also *competent to judge* their respective worth. This need not follow, however, unless there is previous agreement, within the social group, about the several grades of existence and about how our faculties are to be ranked in the scale of higher and lower perfection, i.e., unless a common view of human nature and its place in the cosmos prevails among the individuals consulted. Since sharply conflicting theories about man are also prevalent in social life, Mill's appeal to experienced judges is not sufficient by itself to settle the proper gradation of pleasures and values. This raises the question of the relation between art and science, in respect to ethical values and ends.

Mill agrees with the a priori and intuitional theories of ethics that the moral character of individual acts is not open to *direct perception*. Although in the sciences, particular truths can be discovered without derivation from explicit first principles, principles are prerequisites for all normative judgments. The morality of an action is not directly perceived but is judged in accordance with a previously accepted end or standard of conduct. The a priori and intuitional theories are wrong, however, in making the first principle of morality itself a self-evident truth. For Mill, the *first moral principle* is neither self-evident, nor an a priori form, nor in any way derived from

---

[35] *Loc. cit.* (Plamenatz, 170–73).

the sciences. What its origin is *not*, is more forcefully stated than what its positive origin actually is. Because the sciences cannot determine ends, they cannot provide the standard of morality. Hence the latter cannot be given any strict *proof*. Neither Bentham nor Mill professes to be able to prove the principle of utility directly, although they deny that the end is arbitrarily or blindly specified.[36] Their position is that, *de facto*, men do ordain their actions toward a certain end: the purpose of moral philosophy is not to give proof of the rightness of this end but merely to point descriptively toward it. That end is expressed in the greatest happiness principle, and some considerations can be advanced to win the intellect's assent to this principle. Although these considerations do not pretend to be a proof, they do bring out the rational grounds of adherence to this principle, and thus supply the equivalent of a proof.

One of these decisive points is an appeal to *honesty*. In practice, men do govern their choices by the standard of promoting the general happiness of mankind. Even philosophical opponents of utilitarianism are obliged to make tacit appeal to the greatest happiness principle, in determining moral issues. The inevitable character of this principle recommends it as the working guide for moral life.

> The only proof that a sound is audible, is that people hear it: and so of the other sources of our experience. In like manner, I apprehend the sole evidence it is possible to produce that anything is desirable, is that people do actually desire it. If the end which the utilitarian doctrine proposes to itself were not, in theory and in practice, acknowledged to be an end, nothing could ever convince any person that it was so. No reason can be given why the general happiness is desirable, except that each person, so far as he believes it to be attainable, desires his own happiness. This, however, being a fact, we have not only all the proof which the case admits of, but all which it is possible to require, that happiness is a good: that each person's happiness is a good to that person, and the general happiness, therefore, a good to the aggregate of all persons.[37]

The first conclusion is, then, that happiness is *one* of the actual ends of conduct and *one* criterion of morality.

The above-quoted passage has been severely criticized by later ethicians, but not always with historical justice.[38] They accuse Mill

---

[36] Bentham, *An Introduction to the Principles of Morals and Legislation*, I, 11–12 (Harrison, 128); Mill, *Utilitarianism*, I (Plamenatz, 166–67).

[37] *Utilitarianism*, IV (Plamenatz, 198).

[38] Among standard British criticism, cf. H. Sidgwick, *The Methods of Ethics*, III. xiii,

of confusing factual with normative truth, when he argues from the fact that happiness *is desired*, to the conclusion that it is *desirable* or *ought to be desired*. But Mill is not ignorant of this distinction and is not attempting to make a strict proof of any sort, precisely because it is a question about a normative principle. His appeal to what men actually desire is only meant to show that there is nothing impossible or alien to actual conduct, in the suggestion that men seek happiness as an end. Critics also point out that, whereas the audible means merely that which can be heard, the desirable (in the context of an inquiry into the foundation of morality) means that which is worthy of being desired or ought to be desired by one seeking moral perfection. Mill's point, however, is that no philosophy should propose as desirable an end which no man has ever actually desired.

Where Mill is truly vulnerable to criticism is not in reporting that pleasurable good is an end sought by men, but in claiming that the psychological description of what men do desire is the *sole evidence* that can be produced of what they should desire. This is a consequence of his schism between science and "art." Mill's "teleology" is merely an extension of the technique of psychological description into the normative field. There is no provision for a moral philosophy, which would constitute a practical science of human conduct and its ultimate end. The basic reason for this failure to establish a *practical ethical science* is to be sought in Mill's reduction of metaphysics to a phase of psychology. This reduction enables him to extend his associationist assumptions into the domains of logic and the "moral sciences," but at the same time it deprives him of any distinctively metaphysical analysis of the modes of being, the structure of human nature, and the relation of man's powers to the total order of being. Hence there is no speculative basis available for determining the proper end of man. Mill leaves each of the "arts" somehow to propose its own end, without benefit of any metaphysical account of the ordination of human nature and the powers of man to the various goods and ends. His teleology is saved from arbitrariness, only in the sense that it is based upon a description of the psycho-

5 (seventh edition, London, Macmillan, 1907), 387–88; F. H. Bradley, *Ethical Studies* (second revised edition, Oxford, Clarendon, 1927), 112–26; G. E. Moore, *Principia Ethica*, III, 39–44 (reprint edition, Cambridge, University Press, 1951), 64–74. For recent historical reappraisals of Mill's meaning, cf. E. W. Hall, "The 'Proof' of Utility in Bentham and Mill," *Ethics*, LX (1949–1950), 1–18; R. H. Popkin, "A Note on the 'Proof' of Utility in J. S. Mill," *ibid.*, LXI (1950–1951), 66–67.

logical facts of moral life. But the assumption that this description can provide the only source of evidence concerning moral choice is itself an arbitrary limitation of moral inquiry. The positing of an ethical end remains a brute, unclarified fact, in this report, whereas in actual ethical attitudes, it comes as an intelligent response to the place of man in the universe.

The second stage in the Millsian defense of utilitarianism consists in showing that men desire *nothing else than happiness,* and that the latter is therefore the *sole* criterion and foundation of morality. As it stands, this proposition seems to run in the face of common experience, and Mill readily grants that objects other than happiness are sought, both as means and as ends in themselves. He contends, however, that virtue or any other good is sought for its own sake, only because it had previously become associated in our mind with some pleasurable experience. Any means to happiness can become so closely associated with the primary end that, at last, it becomes for us a major ingredient in happiness and hence an end desirable in itself. Mill's third and final step is to give a naturalistic account of *moral obligation.* Whereas Bentham had stressed the external sanctions of morality (physical, political, moral or social, and religious fear of punishment), Mill gives the primacy to the internal sanction of duty. Its source is the wholly subjective one of *sympathy* or fellow-feeling, which Hume had noted as a basic constituent of our moral nature. Although the "desire to be in unity with our fellow creatures" is originally a weaker feeling than our selfish desires, it can be built up, through education and social organization, into a very powerful inclination to be in harmony with the aims of others.[39] The force of association develops the social feeling into a massive web of desires, inclining us to have regard for other men. "In this way people grow up unable to conceive as possible to them a state of total disregard of other people's interests."[40] Should one violate this standard of

---

[39] *Utilitarianism,* III (Plamenatz, 194).

[40] *Loc. cit.* P. Zinkernagel, "Revaluation of J. S. Mill's Ethical Proof," *Theoria,* XVIII (1952), 70–77, shows that, for Mill, the individual "ought" to seek the general happiness, because it is a means to his private happiness. This underlines Mill's conflict with Kant, since the latter would regard an "ought" based on the means-end relationship as a technical rule or *non*moral imperative. Mill's ultimate recourse is made to the psychological fact that our impulses — both self-regarding and other-regarding ones — do build up an associative feeling of obligation toward the social good, whatever the motive of our social actions. The psychological basis of Mill's notion of obligation is brought out clearly by G. Nakhnikian, "Value and Obligation in Mill," *Ethics,* LXII (1951–1952), 33–40.

duty, there is an internal feeling of pain and of going against the right course. The ultimate sanction of morality, the binding force of moral law, consists in this moral feeling, which is expressed in the voice of conscience.

There is a vague, unspecified sense in which (as Aristotle observes) every man desires happiness, and takes it as his ultimate end. But the basic moral problem arises only when men ask about where their *real* interests lie, and about what constitutes their *genuine* happiness. Such questions imply that the ultimate *subjective* end (happiness or actual attainment of the human good) cannot provide an adequate working criterion of morality. It must be correlated with the problem of the kinds and order among natural goods, and the kinds and order among the human powers and operations placing the agent in possession of his ultimate *objective* end. Mill's utilitarian eudaemonism concentrates upon what is "psychologically true," without rectifying the description of actual states by the standard of a speculative theory of human nature and its capacities for perfection. He finds that happiness includes: many ingredients and many kinds of pleasure, satisfaction of lower and higher faculties, access to lower and higher levels of existence or moral synthesis. These distinctions have only a conventional meaning, however, unless they are grounded in a metaphysical doctrine on the kinds of perfections or goods in being, and in a scientific ethical inquiry into the ordination of human powers to the unqualified good of man's nature, taken as an integral whole.

Because Mill does not take account of the reference of human actions to their ultimate objective good, he is also unable to provide a principle of distinction between the *feeling* and the *ground* of moral obligation. Hence he has not removed Kant's objection (*à propos* of Hume's ethical system) that the concomitant feeling of moral obligation does not constitute the basis itself of obligation. Even when joined with the greatest happiness standard, the feeling of obligation does not provide a sufficient guide for ordering our several levels of obligation, where the question of conflicting obligations arises. Hence Mill systematically narrows down the scope of obligation, in accordance with his principle that psychological necessitation should be the measure of moral necessity. He centers moral obligation in the complexus of duties owed in justice to *other men,* since he regards the social pressures upon our natural sympathy as supplying the most plausible source of a feeling of compulsion to perform certain actions. In actual moral life, however, the field of moral obligation is more extensive than this social-compulsion theory would allow.

Although Mill rejects free choice, he makes room within causal determinism for a certain feeling of responsibility for self-improvement. No political force can legitimately deprive men of their freedom of thought, taste, character development, and assembly. This carves out a zone for *social freedom,* which it is the purpose of the state to protect. In his essay *On Liberty,* Mill states as the fundamental proposition of his *political liberalism*

> that the sole end for which mankind are warranted, individually or collectively, in interfering with the liberty of action of any of their number is self-protection. That the only purpose for which power can be rightfully exercised over any member of a civilized community, against his will, is to prevent harm to others. His own good, either physical or moral, is not a sufficient warrant. . . . The only freedom which deserves the name is that of pursuing our own good in our own way, so long as we do not attempt to deprive others of theirs, or impede their efforts to obtain it.[41]

Harm may be caused to others, however, not only by actions but also by inaction. Hence, the individual may rightfully be required by public power to give evidence in court, defend his country, participate in other co-operative works necessary for the interests of society, and even perform some private acts of aid to individuals.

Nevertheless, there is a wide sphere where Mill does not think that individual liberty is at stake at all, and where the utilitarian standard of maximum happiness is best promoted by barring interference by government.[42] The government should not interfere: where the task probably can be done better by the individuals concerned (the whole economic field of business and industry); where it could be done better by the government and yet would aid individual self-

---

[41] *On Liberty,* I (London, Parker, 1859), 12. Mill admits that some limits should be placed upon discussion, if it tends to incite action harmful to others. "No one pretends that actions should be as free as opinions. On the contrary, even opinions lose their immunity, when the circumstances in which they are expressed are such as to constitute their expression a positive instigation to some mischievous act." *Ibid.,* III, 100. For suggestions about how Mill's doctrine on free inquiry can be adapted to a totalitarian age, in which there is no longer any faith in automatic progress through inductive and fragmentary steps, cf. R. C. Binkley, "Mill's Liberty Today," *Foreign Affairs,* XVI (1938), 563–73.

[42] *On Liberty,* V, 196–99.

development, if it were performed by the citizens themselves, as individuals or local groups (trial by jury, regional institutions, philanthropy); where there is danger of adding unnecessarily to governmental powers (control of utilities, schools, insurance and stock companies). These are particular areas, however, where a century of social development has shown that social freedom *is* often at stake, to the point where some governmental control is required, both in the interests of the individual and for the promotion of the common good. Mill had a weak sense of the distinctive nature of the common social good, largely because he thought that a scientific treatment of social and political matters had to rely upon his "physical, deductive" method of a mechanical composition of particular causes or individual goods.

The problems of democracy occupy Mill both in his discussion of liberty and in his essay on *Representative Government*. Since direct participation of the whole people is not practicable in modern countries, a *representative democracy* is the best form of government, at least for advanced peoples. It gives individuals the fullest opportunity for self-activity, leading to a growth in intelligence, virtue, and social responsibility. But there is something misleading about the phrases "self-government" and "government by the people." For "the 'people' who exercise the power, are not always the same people with those over whom it is exercised; and the 'self-government' spoken of, is not the government of each by himself, but of each by all the rest. The will of the people, moreover, practically means, the will of the most numerous or the most active *part* of the people."[43] In practice, Rousseau's distinction between the general will of society and the will of all the people does little to tame the effective will of the majority, in which Locke had placed so much trust. Mill proposes such practical, political devices as proportional representation for all minorities and maintenance of a permanent legislative commission of experts, as means of guarding against the main danger to democratic government: the tyranny of the majority and the power of irresponsible public opinion. But the risk is worth it, since in a representative democracy, there is a better chance of developing individual resourcefulness.

---

[43] *Ibid.*, I, 12. On the advantages and pitfalls of representative democracy, cf. *Considerations on Representative Government*, III, VI–VII (London, Parker, 1861), 45–69, 108–54.

## 6. GOD AND RELIGION

Despite his upbringing and philosophical heritage, Mill was never militantly antitheistic. He described his position with accuracy as a *rational skepticism,* which accepts neither positive religious belief nor the two varieties of atheism (complete agnosticism and antitheism). His stand was much closer to Hume than to Comte, regarding the *present* state of evidence, since he admitted some probable evidence, and not more, in favor of theism. But in respect to the *future,* he shared Comte's belief that the religion of humanity will gradually prevail and ought to supplant theism, although Mill found Comte's later development of a humanistic religion fantastic and quite repugnant.

Mill's attitude toward God and religion is best expressed in his *Three Essays on Religion.* He placed no weight on the arguments for God's existence based upon the general consent of mankind and the idea of a most perfect being. He criticized the *argument from efficient causality* severely, without inquiring whether any other meaning of cause and effect than his own phenomenalistic one has any validity. According to his view of causality, only phenomenal events (not permanent substrates) require causes, and the assigned causes are, in turn, caused by other antecedent events. Hence the causal argument can never reach an unconditionally first cause and, in any case, leaves the permanent substratum of matter and force completely uncaused.[44] This is the indisputable consequence of regarding cause and effect as a temporal series of antecedent and consequent phenomenal events. But it does not join issue with the metaphysical argument, based upon an essentially ordered series of efficient causes, contributing to the being of things.

Mill agrees with Hume and Kant that the *argument from design* is the only persuasive proof of God's existence.[45] Its value lies in its a posteriori character and its appeal to the evidence of nature. Paley's comparison of the universe to a watch is not a strict induction but a loose analogy, the weakness of which is that, whereas we have direct experience of watchmakers, we have no such experience of the supposed divine mechanic. But a genuinely inductive argument can be drawn from analysis of a complicated structure like the eye,

---

[44] *Three Essays on Religion,* "Theism," I (second edition, London, Longmans, Green, 1874), 142–54.

[45] *Loc. cit.,* 167–75.

the parts of which are mutually heterogeneous, until related to the act of seeing. Since the act of vision is physically subsequent to the conjunction of these parts, the cause of the entire structure must be an agent with the idea of the act of vision. Consequently, there exists a maker, having intelligence and will. The proof is based upon the method of agreement, which is the weakest inductive method, but this particular argument is regarded by Mill as being one of the strongest in its class. He concludes that there is an inductive probability, but no more, for an intelligent maker of the world. Mill does not think that the Darwinian explanation of the origin of the eye and other structures, in terms of the survival of the fittest, has a sufficient weight of probability behind it (at least in his own day).

Mill allowed that a God might have infinite knowledge, but not that all His attributes would be infinite. The presence of evil, imperfections, and countertendencies to order in the universe, prevented Mill from acknowledging the infinite power of God. He thought it would be morally more stimulating to conceive of a *finite God*. Mill anticipated William James and E. S. Brightman by maintaining that belief in a finite God or finite aspect of God enables us to cultivate "the feeling of helping God — of requiting the good he has given us by a voluntary co-operation which he, not being omnipotent, really needs, and by which a somewhat nearer approach may be made to the fulfillment of his purposes."[46] Actually, however, Mill advanced this notion of a finite God as a transitional concept, helping to prepare the way for universal acceptance of the positivistic *religion of humanity*. His sole criterion in natural theology is the utility principle. The happiness of mankind in general depends upon a purely moral and unselfish devotion to the welfare of others, an ideal that can be sustained without appeal to a transcendent God. The worship of humanity will eventually take the place of worship of God, and there will be no more need for belief in immortality, once men agree to work unselfishly to make this world a better place to live in.

Just as Mill admits no distinctive metaphysics or ethical science, so he has no speculatively organized, natural theology. He merges the questions of *truth* and *appropriate feeling* in religious matters, after the manner of Hume and Comte. Hence he does not discover any

---

[46] *Three Essays on Religion*, "Theism," V, 256. Cf. S. Saenger, "Mill's Theodizee," *Archiv für Geschichte der Philosophie*, XIII (1900), 401–29.

difficulty in the notion that God could have one infinite attribute, along with several finite ones, since it is emotionally satisfying (at least for Mill) to consider Him in this way and thus square the ideal of divinity with that of humanity. Similarly, no speculative effort is made to justify the assumption that our universe is incompatible with an omnipotent God, or that matter and force are uncaused. Indeed, when Mill is no longer occupied with refuting the argument from efficient cause, he reverts to his original phenomenalistic interpretation of matter, as the expectation of sensations. This can be seen from his remarks about *immortality,* which he regards as being at least intrinsically possible (although no positive evidence can be adduced in its favor). There is no contradiction in the notion of some sort of survival of a series of thoughts and feelings, since the brain itself is merely a set of actual or inferred human sensations, another suggestion which William James adopted from Mill. And "all matter apart from the feelings of sentient beings has but an hypothetical and unsubstantial existence: it is a mere assumption to account for our sensations. . . . [Mind] is in a philosophical point of view the only reality of which we have any evidence; and no analogy can be recognized or comparison made between it and other realities because there are no other known realities to compare it with."[47] With this reaffirmation of radical phenomenalism, the full circuit of Mill's philosophical investigation is completed. Mind and its sensations are his starting point, his measure of reality, and finally the barrier against developing ethics and natural theology into strict sciences. Through a systematic necessity, Mill's philosophy of religion is focused upon humanity as the sole reality having a psychological guarantee, and whose interests must therefore be regarded as absolute and self-validating.

# SUMMARY OF CHAPTER 17

Mill prolonged the empiricist tradition of taking our own thoughts and feelings as the only immediate objects of consciousness, and of reducing complex beliefs to their simple elements. He confined metaphysics to genetic comparison between complex beliefs and the original components of consciousness. Consequently, he gave a purely psychological description of body and mind, in terms of the permanent possibilities of sensations and feelings. Mill's treatment of the syllogism and the principles of scientific method also had a psychological orientation. His five canons

---

[47] *Three Essays On Religion,* "Theism," III, 202, 203.

of induction were more rigorously formulated than Bacon's similar directions. Their philosophical import, however, was bound up with his doctrine on causality and the uniformity of nature. He traced the logic of scientific induction back to the conditions of belief determining unscientific induction, thus grounding the principle of the uniformity of the course of nature in associations built up through simple enumerations. In the field of moral sciences, Mill envisaged ethology as the concrete study of human character and types. The social sciences were to be organized in accord with a concrete deductive method of calculating social trends, through the confluence of many individual lines of force. Because of a rigid contrast between factual sciences and normative arts, Mill regarded ethics as an art, rather than as a science. His defense of ethical utilitarianism revolved around a psychological description of the search for happiness and the feeling of obligation toward others. Politically, his utilitarian concern for the greatest happiness of all found expression in liberalism. Mill sought primarily to insure individual freedom, within the framework of a representative form of government. His rational skepticism in religion led him to admit some probable present-day evidence in favor of a finite God. Yet his own hopes for the future coincided with Comte's general vision of the religion of humanity. Mankind will eventually replace God as the proper object of worship, and thereby will assure its own greatest happiness in a purely immanent way.

## BIBLIOGRAPHICAL NOTE

1. *Sources.* There is no collected edition of Mill's writings. Two recent reprint editions are specially valuable for philosophy students: E. Nagel's edition of *John Stuart Mill's Philosophy of Scientific Method* (New York, Hafner, 1950) — contains the essential sections of: *A System of Logic* and *An Examination of Sir William Hamilton's Philosophy;* J. Plamenatz's edition of *Mill's "Utilitarianism," reprinted with a Study of the English Utilitarians* (Oxford, Blackwell, 1949). Both volumes have distinguished introductory essays. The complete edition of Mill's *Autobiography* was edited from the manuscript, with a Preface by J. J. Coss (New York, Columbia University Press, 1924). The Mill-Taylor correspondence was edited by F. A. Hayek, *John Stuart Mill and Harriet Taylor: Their Friendship and Subsequent Marriage* (Chicago, University of Chicago Press, 1951). The Mill-Comte correspondence was edited by L. Lévy-Bruhl, *Lettres inédites de John Stuart Mill à Auguste Comte, publiées avec les réponses de Comte* (Paris, Alcan, 1899).

2. *Studies.* For Mill's philosophical background, see L. Stephen, *The English Utilitarians* (3 vols., London, Duckworth, 1900), which devotes a volume each to: Bentham, James Mill, and John Stuart Mill; also cf. É. Halévy, *The Growth of Philosophic Radicalism,* translated by M. Morris (London, Faber, 1934). On Bentham in particular, see D. Baumgardt, *Bentham and the Ethics of Today* (Princeton, Princeton University Press, 1952). The best general introduction to Mill is R. P. Anschutz, *The*

*Philosophy of J. S. Mill* (Oxford, Clarendon Press, 1953), but A. Bain's *John Stuart Mill* (London, Longmans, Green, 1882) is still useful as a sympathetic account by a man who knew Mill intimately. Another well-informed introduction is S. Saenger, *John Stuart Mill, Sein Leben und Lebenswerk* (Stuttgart, Frommann, 1901). W. L. Courtney, *The Metaphysics of John Stuart Mill* (London, Kegan Paul, 1879), analyzes Mill's views on substance, cause, mind, and matter; J. McCosh brings the doctrine of Scottish realism to bear upon Mill in *An Examination of Mr. J. S. Mill's Philosophy* (second ed., New York, Scribner, 1890). The best studies on Millsian logic are: R. Jackson, *An Examination of the Deductive Logic of John Stuart Mill* (London, Oxford University Press, H. Milford, 1941), showing how Mill defended the syllogism up to a point and taught that deduction is serviceable, even though it is merely a verbal transformation; O. A. Kubitz, *The Development of John Stuart Mill's System of Logic* (Urbana, Ill., University of Illinois Press, 1932), on the adaptation of the theory of logic to social and economic reasoning; A. Castell, *Mill's Logic of the Moral Sciences: A Study of the Impact of Newtonism on Early Nineteenth-Century Social Thought* (Chicago, University of Chicago dissertation, 1936). J. Veitch's *Hamilton* (Edinburgh, Blackwood, 1882) is useful, since so much of Mill's thought is determined by reference to Hamilton's philosophy. The entire first volume of W. G. Ward's *Essays on the Philosophy of Theism* (2 vols., London, Kegan Paul, Trench, 1884) is reserved for a circumstantial criticism of Mill's basic metaphysical, psychological, and moral positions. For later developments in nineteenth-century British philosophy, see R. Metz, *A Hundred Years of British Philosophy* (New York, Macmillan, 1938), and J. Passmore, *A Hundred Years of Philosophy* (New York, Macmillan, 1957), which begins with Mill as the culmination of classical British empiricism. The renewed interest in Mill is exemplified by Michael Packe's full-length biography: *The Life of John Stuart Mill* (New York, Macmillan, 1954), and by Karl Britton's thorough introduction from an analytical standpoint: *John Stuart Mill* (Baltimore, Penguin Books, 1953). *Prefaces to Liberty,* edited by B. Wishy (Boston, Beacon Press, 1959), gathers together some letters and articles of Mill dealing with practical issues of civil liberty, together with his major essay *On Liberty.*

# Chapter 18. NIETZSCHE

## I. LIFE AND WRITINGS

FRIEDRICH WILHELM NIETZSCHE (1844–1900) was the son of the Lutheran pastor in the little town of Röcken, in Prussian Saxony. After his father's accidental death in 1849, Nietzsche moved with his mother and sister, Elizabeth, to Naumburg, where he attended the *gymnasium*. His home life was dominated by these two women (together with his grandmother and two maiden aunts), who maintained strict discipline and a religious atmosphere. His years at the famous school of Pforta (1858–1864) gave him a solid grounding in German literature and the Greek and Latin classics. There, he became friendly with Paul Deussen (later, a famous Orientalist), with whom he matriculated at the University of Bonn. After a futile attempt to join in the student activities of dueling and beer-drinking, Nietzsche broke with the student association, which he was unable to reform. He concentrated upon philological studies under Friedrich Ritschl and removed to the University of Leipzig (1865), when Ritschl accepted a post there. At Leipzig, he discovered Schopenhauer's philosophy, enjoyed Schumann's music, and joined with Erwin Rohde (noted, later on, for his study of the Greek conception of *psyche*) in admiring the Greek genius. By this time, Nietzsche had lost his Christian faith entirely and refused to attend the Easter communion service with his family. After a brief stint with the Prussian cavalry (1867), during which he suffered a severe fall, he returned to his studies at Leipzig and published some brilliant philological papers. On the strength of these publications and the recommendation of Ritschl, Nietzsche was given the chair of classical philology at the Swiss University of Basel, in 1869.

Nietzsche taught at Basel for ten years, with the exception of a short time in the Prussian medical corps, during the Franco-Prussian war. He contracted dysentery and diphtheria from the soldiers under his care, was released from service, and returned to his teaching post before he was fully recovered. Thereafter, Nietzsche was constantly troubled by headaches and indigestion. But at Basel, he made friendships with the great historian of the Renaissance, Jacob Burckhardt, with the church historian, Franz Overbeck, and above all with Richard and Cosima Wagner, whose villa became a second home to him. Under the spell of Wagner's music and with the hope that the Greek genius might be revived in his own day, Nietzsche wrote *The Birth of Tragedy From the Spirit of Music* (1872), in which he delineated his humanistic ideal as a synthesis of Dionysus and Apollo, turbulent energy and calm measure. This poetic essay was not what was expected from a sober classical philologist; Rohde had to spring to his friend's defense in reply to a stinging criticism, written from an academic and historical standpoint, by Wilamowitz-Moellendorf. Next, Nietzsche launched out against the philistinism of post-1870 Germany, in his *Untimely Considerations* (1873–1876), the four parts of which deal, respectively, with: David Strauss as a typical "culture-philistine," the use and disadvantage of history for life, Schopenhauer as an educator, and Wagner as the embodiment of Greek values. But already, he was moving away from Wagner, whom he came to suspect of surrendering to the reigning forces of chauvinistic Prussianism, anti-Semitism, and a sentimental Christianity. Nietzsche grew ever more bitter over his disillusionment in Wagner, and began an open attack upon the musician's philosophical principles. The fruits of this polemic were contained in three works: *Human-all-too-human, The Dawn,* and *The Gay Science,* which appeared in rapid succession, between 1878 and 1882 (Book V of *The Gay Science* issued in 1887). In these writings, the notion of Christian morality as a life-denying tendency also began to take shape.

Nietzsche's ill-health forced him to resign, with a small pension, from the University of Basel (1879). The next decade of his life was marked by an endless search for health at Swiss and Italian watering places, by a steady stream of literary production, by increasing loneliness and alienation from old friends, and by the final abyss of madness. His main doctrines on the will to power, the superman, the aristocratic moral idea, and the eternal recurrence of the same situation, were given aphoristic expression in *Thus Spoke Zarathustra* (1883–1885), which he regarded as his greatest achievement. In order to clarify its basic themes, however, Nietzsche explained his ethical position more forthrightly, in *Beyond Good and Evil* (1886) and

*Toward a Genealogy of Morals* (1887). As the shadows of insanity began to close in upon him, his anti-Wagnerian and anti-Christian preoccupations reached a high pitch. *The Wagner Case, The Twilight of the Idols,* and *Nietzsche contra Wagner* illustrated his first obsession, whereas *The Anti-Christ* and his autobiography, *Ecce Homo,* reflected Nietzsche's distorted conviction of having a mission against Christianity. As his mental control dissolved (January, 1889), he began sending incoherent notes signed "Dionysus" or "The Crucified." From 1889 until his death in 1900, Nietzsche lived in asylums and at home, without ever recovering full use of his mind.

## 2. CRITIQUE OF NINETEENTH-CENTURY CULTURE

In his autobiographical essay, *Ecce Homo,* Nietzsche spoke of himself variously as a warrior, a philosopher with a hammer, and one who sets off a charge of dynamite under the existing order. His proper role was that of a *moralist* or critic of the reigning beliefs and institutions, somewhat after the manner of Voltaire and Kierkegaard. He was the bad conscience or Socratic gadfly of his age. His keen psychological insight into human motives enabled him to detect a basic rottenness, beneath the façade of nineteenth-century optimism. His appraisals of his times were deliberately one-sided and exaggerated, for they overlooked many sound strains in contemporary life. But they did succeed in laying bare certain contradictions and tendencies toward dissolution which have become explicit in our own war-pocked, totalitarian day. However perfervid and mixed with metaphysical myth were his cultural observations, they also contained shrewd diagnoses, still relevant for understanding ourselves as the heirs of the nineteenth century.

Nietzsche's "untimely considerations" on cultural life had as their immediate target the bustling, confident Germany of the Bismarckian era, but their wider scope included the whole of European civilization. His basic message was that Europe is infected by a decadence of spirit, which cannot be healed by material prosperity and technological progress alone. This inner disintegration is symbolized at the personal level by superficially educated people, the culture-philistines, and at the social level by the nation-state. In neither individual nor social life is there to be found genuine *culture,* i.e., the unity of artistic style, which should shine forth in every expression of the life of a people.[1]

---

[1] The problem of culture is the main preoccupation of the four essays in Nietzsche's

Culture is a close-knit feeling for life, a system of experiences which should stimulate our energies to their peak performance and govern all our valuations. In actual fact, however, modern Europe is woefully lacking in these requisite qualities.

People today have no *unity of outlook.* They are satisfied with making an eclectic sampling of facts from the most widely different cultural periods, but they do not bother to digest and synthesize these facts or to apply them in their own lives. There is a mistaken notion that mere historical erudition and scientific knowledge constitute general culture, whereas in fact they are only partial constituents of a cultured mind. Between the Renaissance man of deep culture and the wandering encyclopedias of the nineteenth century, there is the wide chasm that separates synthesis from mere aggregation of information. The specialization of the sciences has accelerated the disintegration of minds, since it has broken down the living connections between the various fields of knowledge. Educational institutions have followed the trend toward specialization, leaving for the journalists the most important task of providing people with whatever common viewpoints obtain today. But journalistic materials provide only a thin gruel of short-range history and platitudinous philosophy, what Americans would call Sunday Supplement literature.

The most tragic, and yet constantly ignored, cultural fact today is that *Western man has lost dignity,* even before himself. The tendency in modern history has been toward a loss of faith, first in things divine and now in things human. Nietzsche did not deplore the loss of religious faith but he did resent the hypocrisy of those who thought that faith in man could be retained in unchanged form, even after a living, Christian faith had grown cold. He pointed out that conventional Christianity had lost its dogmatic basis and had become nothing more than pious humanitarianism, recoiling from suffering and seeking respectability and comfort as prime ends of life. The height of modern thoughtlessness was reached in the attempts of men like David Strauss and Herbert Spencer to reject Christian dogma, and yet combine Christian ethics with scientific evolutionism. In Nietzsche's estimation, *evolutionism* had proved that change is universal, that all species are in flux, and that there is no essential difference between man and the other animals. In plain language,

---

*Untimely Considerations.* K. Löwith's centenary commemoration, "Friedrich Nietzsche (1844–1900)," *Church History,* XIII (1944), 3–21, brings out Nietzsche's significance for contemporary philosophy and religious thought.

this means that empirical science recognizes no rational ground for treating man with special respect. The lesson is clear. Either man has no higher destiny than the brute, and should be treated accordingly, or else a radical attempt must be made to establish humanism upon a new basis, beholden neither to Christianity nor to its secular echo in conventional morality. Nietzsche proposed to follow the latter alternative of a humanistic reconstruction.

Unfortunately, any such radical program would have to reckon not only with philistine individuals but also with hostile social forces, especially *the state*. Nietzsche felt stifled by the commercialism, mechanization, and hollow busyness of the modern economy. Any nobler impulses were soon ground out by the impersonal regimentation of industry, as well as by the fast pace and ruthlessness of money-making operations. Nietzsche was just as emphatic as Marx about the subordination of the concrete state to commercial interests and the bourgeois spirit. He warned against the growing idolatry of the state, encouraged as it was by jingoistic nationalism and conservative Hegelianism. " 'On earth there is nothing greater than I: the ordering finger of God am I' — thus roars the monster."[2] The nation-state was being surrounded with false glamour, just at the moment when economic life and improvements in communication favored a united Europe. Nietzsche also predicted that when nationalism joins forces with racism, the result will be emotionally overpowering at first, although eventually it must prove itself quite barren. Nietzsche satirized the mendacious race swindle and especially deplored anti-Semitism (although he wrote some harsh words against the Jews).

From the cultural standpoint, Nietzsche draws up a severe indictment against the Moloch of the state. Its main effect is *anticultural*, since it levels down talents and encourages conformism among its citizens. It supports education, only to the extent of providing itself with trained civil servants and skilled technicians of industry and war. Like those of Hegel, Nietzsche's views on *war* tend to fluctuate. Sometimes, he celebrates the invigorating effect of wars, which he imagines will break the power of money and restore some rude but indispensable virtues. At other times, he recognizes the tremendous

[2] *Thus Spoke Zarathustra*, W. Kaufmann translation in *The Portable Nietzsche*, 161. On Nietzsche's theory of the state, cf. J. Binder, "Nietzsches Staatsauffassung," *Logos*, XIV (1925), 269–96.

cultural waste of wars, the sacrifice of the choicest manhood, and the corrupting effect of victory as well as defeat. He is pessimistic about *democracy* and *socialism,* regarding them as instruments of cultural mediocrity and mass regimentation.[3] This is not an unmixed evil for Nietzsche, however, since he does not think that the masses can ever share in the higher reaches of culture open to great men. The state is indirectly justified, insofar as the outstanding geniuses must have a foundation in a well-disciplined herd of ordinary laboring people. But the state usually overreaches itself, and imposes its standard upon the gifted few. To the extent that political norms tend to become absolute and binding upon all, Nietzsche is the enemy of the state.

The crisis of European humanism is brought to a head by the teachings of Darwin, but Nietzsche does not look to the empirical sciences for a positive solution. Scientific progress can improve man, only on the plane of his animal nature and material interests. But history tells us about another kind of progress, open to man. For, it pays tribute to *outstanding individuals* — warriors, statesmen, saints, artists, and philosophers — who have raised themselves above the crowd and transcended the limits of average human nature. This suggests that the evolutionary drive of nature is not toward the *general elevation* of the species (as the biologists assume) but toward the production of distinctive specimens or *geniuses.* There is solid historical background for thinking that our nature can be improved upon: man is an *as-yet-unfixed animal.* Culture is nothing else than the means for keeping human nature fluid and progressive, so that the great men may break through to a higher mode of existence (what Nietzsche will call, later on, the level of the superman). The main cultural justification for educational programs, scientific technology, and the state is that they may encourage this process of self-transcendence, at least by satisfying the material needs of men and by refraining from applying mass standards to those choice spirits who can attain the superior life. The Nietzschean answer to the problem of human dignity is framed in *aristocratic* terms: respect

---

[3] In "Nietzsche and Democracy," *The Philosophical Review,* XXI (1912), 32–50, A. K. Rogers gave a balanced account of a question, which has since been aggravated by the use to which some portions of Nietzsche's political and racial views were put by the German Nazis. Rogers noted that Nietzsche had some ground for opposing mediocrity, but that he drew the unsupported inference that the only cure lay in a doctrine of permanent grades of rank among men and moralities.

is due, not to average human beings as such, but to the potentialities in man for surpassing the given level and attaining new heights of culture.

Significantly, this aristocratic ideal was based upon an appeal to *history*. Nietzsche was proud of his "Germanic" sense of history. At the same time, he saw in the desire to learn about past cultures, rather than to create one's own, the very root of the cultural illness of modern Europe. Hence, in his essay *Of the Use and Disadvantage of History for Life,* he undertook to distinguish between various attitudes toward history and to determine an approach that will promote the growth of cultural life. He did not accept the integral, Hegelian principle that history is the necessary, rational development of the absolute idea. The contingent, voluntaristic, and individual aspects of history seemed philosophically more relevant to Nietzsche. He ridiculed the right-wing Hegelians of his day, for canonizing history and preaching conformity to the existing order. "The man who has once learned to crook the knee and bow the head before the power of history, nods 'yes' at last, like a Chinese doll, to every power, whether it be a government or a public opinion or a numerical majority."[4] Uncontrolled historicism makes us hesitant graybeards and despairing late-comers on the scene, instead of hopeful first-comers to the tasks of life.

Nietzsche sought to strike a balance between three factors in our cultural existence: the historical, the unhistorical, and the super-historical.[5] First of all, the human personality must nourish itself upon a judicious use of the *historical,* in the ordinary sense of the word. There are three types of history writing: monumental, antiquarian, and critical. *Monumental* history looks to the past for noble examples, which will convince us that great deeds are still possible for present-day man, because they once existed. It inspires us to perform heroic acts in the present age. But there is also a place for *antiquarian* history, which looks fondly to the past for its own sake. The latter approach prizes the old and traditional as such, as something worthy of reverence and capable of rendering present existence meaningful. *Critical* history is a necessary corrective of the first two types. It points out the many differences between past situations and the present (differences which monumental history glides

---

[4] *The Use and Abuse of History,* 8 (Collins translation, Liberal Arts Press reprint, 59). This essay is the second part of Nietzsche's *Untimely Considerations.*

[5] Cf. *ibid.,* 2–3 (Collins, 20–29).

over), and it passes severe judgment upon the unworthy and miserable features of the past (which antiquarian history fails to mention). A synthesis between these three attitudes toward history would provide an antidote for the cultural disease of historicism.

Yet, even a well-integrated historical outlook needs to be modified by what Nietzsche called the unhistorical and superhistorical sides of our nature. The cow munching away contentedly in the field is a purely unhistorical thing, for it lives only in and for the fleeting present. Now man cannot, and should not, completely blot out the past and future from his present considerations. But action does occur only in an actual present, making it necessary to narrow down one's horizon to the immediate situation, for purposes of effective operation. By the *unhistorical* principle, Nietzsche meant this power of strategically forgetting most things, in order to do one. Historical meditations cannot be permitted to destroy the spontaneous feeling for present, urgent, "unhistorical" action, the decisive insertion of vital purpose into a concrete here-and-now. Nevertheless, the purpose of action cannot be derived solely from one's unhistorical engagement in present conditions. Guidance is required from some *superhistorical* principle, "which turns the eyes from the process of becoming to that which gives existence an eternal and stable character — to art and religion."[6] Action in the unhistorical present derives its significance and orientation from a marriage between the super-historical and the historical factors, the former supplying the permanent aims and the latter the confidence that these aims can, indeed, be realized in time.

The *crisis* of the nineteenth century may now be stated in its essential proportions. Culture means the improvement and transcendence of human nature over its existing conditions. This process of *self-overcoming* depends upon action in the present, but action illuminated by historical and superhistorical wisdom. Modern historical science, however, transforms living men into mere memories of the past, and deprives them of a vigorous will to live and advance in the present. Furthermore, the superhistorical guidance that previously came from the Christian evangel is now lacking, due to the widespread loss of dogmatic faith. Modern biological science turns our minds exclusively toward the sea of evolutionary becoming, where no eternal values persist. Thus historical and biological sciences

---

[6] *Ibid.*, 10 (Collins, 76).

have stripped cultural action of its historical and superhistorical foundations, just at a time when religious faith has also gone into its final decline. This generates a fatal antagonism between knowledge and life, technique and culture. Complete paralysis of our cultural activities is the predictable outcome, unless a radical cure is found.

Nietzsche's reconstructive efforts begin at this point, since he proposes to effect a *new synthesis between the historical and the superhistorical*. History must be imbued once more with superhistorical significance, and the superhistorical principle must be given a temporal locus. The starting point of this cultural renovation is neither a knowledge of the past nor a supernatural revelation but *insight into one's own nature*. The message of the Delphic oracle — "Know thyself!" — is still the first word of philosophical wisdom. The creative individual must first organize the chaos within himself, and thus bring himself back to an awareness of his true needs and abilities. Knowledge of the highest potentialities of one's present existence is the superhistorical key for interpreting history. The Nietzschean conception of a philosophical interpretation of history approaches the condition of an artistic fashioning of materials. History must be viewed as a conversation among the great men peopling what Schopenhauer called the republic of geniuses. Only he who becomes aware of the supreme possibilities open to the creative will can seize upon the vital meaning of history.

Although Nietzsche constantly appeals to historical examples, his use of the empirical materials is completely governed by his philosophical conceptions. He relies chiefly upon the projection of his vivid imagination, giving us psychological *aperçus* of what might have gone on in men's hearts. For him, history must become *"a pure work of art,"*[7] and must be employed as a practical *instrument of persuasion*. Its role is the moral one of riveting attention upon the great exemplars of humanity, as interpreted by Nietzsche's personal estimate of the needs of his own soul and of his cultural age. Historical events are completely plastic in his hands, so that he is not controlled

---

[7] *The Use and Abuse of History*, 7 (Collins, 49; cf. 46 ff.; italics added). This conception of historical truth, as being measured by esthetic adequacy and the aims of life, is closely bound up with Nietzsche's general view that the function of language is primarily expressive and evocative, and only secondarily imitative and communicative. Cf. R. Hazelton, "Nietzsche's Contribution to the Theory of Language," *The Philosophical Review*, LII (1943), 47–60.

by the limitations of the data confronting the ordinary historian. In his desire to achieve a philosophical victory in the present, by pointing out how the past ought to have been, he carries to an extreme the pragmatic theory of history as a tool for promoting contemporary cultural purposes.

His famous comparison between the *Dionysian* and *Apollinian* attitudes (a comparison already suggested by Schelling) is an instance of his use of the past for the creation of universal symbols, relevant to the present age.[8] Dionysus was the Greek god of music, Apollo the god of the plastic arts. The rites of Dionysus or Bacchus were celebrated with wild frenzy and deep intoxication. They expressed the exhilirating power of life, but they led to excesses of sensuality, cruelty, and disintegration of the personality. Only the controlling influence of Apollo kept people from dissipating their strength entirely and losing their self-identity. Nietzsche concludes that the cultural ideal in every period is the combination of Dionysian and Apollinian elements. Through the former, one may share in the vital stream of existence, and feel the creative impulse surge up in oneself. But an Apollinian self-restraint and serenity of spirit are equally indispensable qualities of the cultured man, since they impose order upon the forces of life and insure the integrity of the individual self. Hence Nietzsche bids us worship at the shrines of both deities. Creative geniuses of our day should join an ecstatic, "musical" assent to life in its creative dynamism, with a measured, "plastic-visual" appreciation of rational law and individual form.

In his later writings, Nietzsche expressed both these facets of personality under the single rubric of the *Dionysian man.* The latter represents the ideal of virtue or controlled power, which appeared briefly in the Renaissance age and which Machiavelli partly described. By comparison with this Dionysian man, the contemporary European is a wretchedly underdeveloped creature. Nietzsche used the myth of the Dionysian man both as a hammer against the existing order and as an inspiration for the creative personalities who are to shape the future culture. And lest we mistake the real line of battle,

---

[8] For this comparison, see *The Birth of Tragedy From the Spirit of Music,* 1–4, 16, 21 (F. Golffing translation, 19–36, 96–102, 124–131). On the continued relevance of Wilamowitz-Moellendorf's criticism of this book, cf. J. H. Groth, "Wilamowitz-Moellendorf on Nietzsche's *Birth of Tragedy*," *Journal of the History of Ideas,* XI (1950), 179–90.

he concluded his autobiography with an unequivocal statement of the chief antagonists: *"Dionysus versus the Crucified."*[9] Beneath his criticisms of particular institutions in the nineteenth century, Nietzsche felt that the major conflict of the modern age would be between theistic, Christian religion and atheistic, Dionysian humanism.

Once the alternative is clearly posed in this way, however, certain difficulties develop in Nietzsche's cultural analysis. *Three problems* become specially urgent for him. First, he cannot keep his argument on a purely cultural and historical plane, granted the opposition between atheism and theism. For this issue is *metaphysical* as well as cultural, raising the question of how to correlate these two approaches to the contemporary crisis. Second, if there is to be a head-on collision between Christian and Dionysian man, then Nietzsche will find it in his interest to make *Christianity* responsible for the existing order of things, especially for man's debilitated moral condition today. Last, Nietzsche must square his repudiation of God and any transcendent order of being with his own cultural requirement that man's true historical reality should include a distinctive superhistorical factor. Now the latter is the principle of eternity, which usually rests upon a dualism between time and eternity. Hence, Nietzsche's final problem will be to devise a *myth of the eternal,* sufficiently powerful to persuade us that our desire for eternity can be fulfilled adequately within our temporal and changing world. Since the superhistorical principle is not to flow from God's providence, Nietzsche must enlist all the resources of art and will, to produce a totally immanent substitute for eternity. A *voluntaristic metaphysics of becoming* is his answer to the malady of European culture. Around these three problems, he organizes his entire philosophy.

### 3. THE REJECTION OF GOD AND ABSOLUTE TRUTH

Nietzsche liked Schopenhauer's frank denial of God and his systematic effort to construct an antitheistic world view. Schopenhauer's honesty contrasted favorably with the hypocrisy of those who paid lip service to God but were practical atheists in their daily lives. As for himself, Nietzsche admitted that he was an *atheist,* as a matter of course and *by instinct.* He identified the instinct

---

[9] These are the concluding words in Nietzsche's autobiography, *Ecce Homo* (Fadiman translation, Modern Library Edition of *The Philosophy of Nietzsche,* 145; modified; cf. Kaufmann, *The Portable Nietzsche,* 459).

in question as the feeling of *hubris* or rebellious pride, which overcame him whenever he was told that one must accept God and must not call His existence into question.[10] Nietzsche understood this necessity of acknowledging God's existence, to mean a call to blind, conventional submission, rather than a recognition of the cogent, speculative evidence of His existence and of the consequent moral obligation upon one's freedom. Hence his reaction took the form of steeling his mind against any objective consideration of the evidence for God's existence. If convention forbids one to think of God as nonexistent, then the unconventional man must forbid himself to think seriously of God as existent! Like Comte, Nietzsche based his whole philosophy upon this instinctive rejection of the reality of God.

Despite the fact that his atheism is *emotionally* underived from anything prior to this instinctive closing of his mind, it is derived *philosophically* from a definite metaphysical premise. This basis may be identified, by attending to Nietzsche's frequent remarks about "a great year of becoming . . . [when] the soul which, having being, dives into becoming."[11] He praised Hegel for explaining the nature of the world as a ceaseless development. But he rejected the Hegelian question: a development *of* what and *toward* what? Nietzsche proposed to substitute *sovereign becoming* for Hegel's sovereign reason. His metaphysical option or (as he himself called it) "preference" was to take the description of finite reality-in-process as a definitive and ultimate account, beyond which philosophical investigation is forbidden to move. He converted the *description* of the world as the region of constant becoming, into a *demonstration* that this world is self-sufficient and in no need of causal explanation. The ultimacy of becoming, as a character or descriptive fact of the world, was converted into an ontological ultimacy, belonging to an autonomous dynamic principle. Hence Nietzsche did not examine the causal

---

[10] *The Genealogy of Morals*, III, 9 (Golffing translation, 248).

[11] *Thus Spoke Zarathustra*, III, 12, 13 (Kaufmann, 320, 332). The two leading American students of Nietzsche (Morgan and Kaufmann) differ sharply over whether Nietzsche is an atheist and whether his views on God are determined by metaphysical considerations. Nevertheless, both of them furnish sufficient texts to show the basis of his metaphysical monism of becoming, from which a transcendent God is excluded, in principle. Cf. G. A. Morgan, Jr., *What Nietzsche Means*, 36–38, 254–59, 267–68; W. A. Kaufmann, *Nietzsche: Philosopher, Psychologist, Antichrist*, 76–81, 209–11, 288. An excellent account of Nietzsche's inchoative metaphysics is presented by J. B. Lotz, S.J., "Entwurf einer Ontologie bei Friedrich Nietzsche," *Scholastik*, XX–XXIV (1949), 1–29.

proof of God's existence, and find it wanting. Instead, he absolutized the process of becoming itself, and then concluded that philosophy need not seek beyond it for a transcendent principle. Becoming is there for Hegel and the evolutionists, but Nietzsche added that it is sovereignly and sufficiently there, so that causal analyses are superfluous.

This elimination of the question of the causal conditions of becoming is a metaphysically arbitrary decision. It is the constitutive source of Nietzsche's *fieristic monism*, i.e., his view that everything real is engaged in becoming or change, and that this world of becoming constitutes a self-enclosed unity. There is a restricted sense in which Nietzsche is a convinced pluralist: he insists upon the manyness of the states of becoming and the changing operations in the universe and in man. But these distinctions are all drawn within the context of the unique sea of becoming, and there is nothing real that does not fall within this single, cosmic process. His metaphysical monism of becoming holds a logical priority over the psychological and moral arguments advanced in its favor. The latter contain many brilliant and sensitive observations, but they are philosophically decisive only on condition that one already accepts Nietzsche's metaphysical description of the real world. And this description rests upon the will-act of decreeing that the real is coextensive with the process of becoming and, consequently, that all valid explanations are *immanent* to this world of change, and in no way transcend it.

If our experience bears no implications beyond the sphere of becoming, then philosophy does not deal with *God* but only with the *idea of God*. Hence Nietzsche consistently reduces the theological problem to a psychological one. He deems it a sufficient analysis, when he offers an explanation of how belief in the idea of God arose, what this idea signifies, and what the consequences are of a denial of theistic belief. This *psychologizing of the problem of God* is in the tradition of Voltaire, Hume, and Feuerbach, although for Nietzsche it is an unavoidable metaphysical consequence of so defining the real that a transcendent, immutable God could not figure as a real principle in any inquiry. Nietzsche pictures the idea of God as arising, sometimes from the fear of ancestors, and sometimes as a compensation for the miserable conditions of earthly life. In the latter instance, men project their desires for perfection into another region, attribute total power over the conditions of existence to a transcendent entity, and end by fearing the very product of their imagination. Believers fail to reflect upon the contradiction of supposing that God is omnipotent and benevolent toward men, and nevertheless that He allows men to live in suffering and ignorance of the truth. By setting up a contrast between the *here* and the *hereafter,* the idea of God drains human energies away from earthly tasks. "The concept 'God' was invented as the counter-concept to life, all bound together in one horrible unit."[12] Hence Nietzsche repudiates the idea of God as being antivital and inimical to human culture.

He extends this bitter line of attack to include the notion of *absolute truth.*[13] The veneration paid by both philosophers and scientists to disinterested, objective truth, is the final place of refuge for theism. Nietzsche usually links together "Platonic metaphysics," the Christian notion of God, and the ideal of an absolute truth, as containing variations on a common theme. They agree in sponsoring belief in a "beyond," a "really real" world, which stands in noticeable contrast with the here-and-now "apparent" world, emptying the latter of all significance and value for men. There is supposed to be a transcendent realm of absolute truth, eternal values, and perfect being, which provides a standard for our knowledge and conduct. But this leads to a flight from the real world of becoming. Hence a philosophy of pure becoming must eliminate the absolute truth, along with the idea of God. Nietzsche allows that there are *particular truths,* but they are all *perspectival* or relative to the situation and interests of some finite observer. These finite truths have pragmatic value but do not permit us to conclude that somewhere there is the absolute truth, to which our minds must unconditionally conform.

In this polemic, Nietzsche made a remarkable anticipation of the views of John Dewey and other American naturalists who also

---

[12] *Ecce Homo* (Fadiman, 143–144). See *The Genealogy of Morals,* II, 19–22 (Golffing translation, 221–27); *Twilight of the Idols,* in Kaufmann's *The Portable Nietzsche,* 490. A systematic analysis of Nietzsche's arguments against God is made by H. Pfeil, "Nietzsches Gründe gegen Gott," *Philosophisches Jahrbuch,* LIII (1940), 45–61, 198–209. Pfeil regards Nietzsche's biologicopostulatory atheism as the methodological counterpart of Kant's ethicopostulatory theism. Nietzsche offers three sorts of arguments: historical (belief in God has a nonrational, affective origin), metaphysical (the world is a self-sufficient whole of becoming), and dysteleological (the world is full of evil, suffering, and antipurposive factors). These objections rest upon the postulated description of the world as a plenum of becoming, animated only by the will-to-power and the values it creates.

[13] *The Genealogy of Morals,* III, 24 (Golffing, 286–89); cf. *The Antichrist* in entirety, in Kaufmann's *The Portable Nietzsche,* 568–656.

charged that the ideas of God and an absolute truth are hostile to culture and mark a failure of nerve. There is no denying that the idea of God does serve some people as an anodyne and excuse for escaping from their social responsibilities. Furthermore, truth is often reified in a mechanical way, as though it were a subsistent thing and not a perfection of the intellect, in its vital conformity with being. But Nietzsche passed from what occurs by way of corruption, in *some* cases, to the unqualified verdict that belief in God and an absolute measure of truth must *always* and *necessarily* lead to these consequences. This is a clear instance where the psychological approach cannot produce a philosophically necessary conclusion, except by begging the point to be proved. *If* all humanly relevant reality were comprised within the immanence of temporal becoming, meditation upon God and absolute truth would necessarily deflect men from the real to the imaginary. This conditional proposition is not established in fact, however, by describing what would follow upon its unconditioned truth.

Actually, Nietzsche had in mind the portrayal of the Christian idea of God and a "metaphysical world" of truth, as given by Schopenhauer and the Romantic writers. The Romantics talked poetically about annihilating the finite, once one is clothed in the splendor of the infinite and absolute; Schopenhauer bent Christianity to his own purpose, by declaring that the Christian God requires a life-denying attitude on the part of believers. Nietzsche welcomed these descriptions, uncritically, as proof that no one who wishes to "remain true to the earth" can tolerate the idea of God. He did not measure these sources against the full sweep of the Christian tradition concerning God's love for the world and loving presence in the world, as well as man's obligation to seek the fullness of life and to restore all things in Christ. Belief in a transcendent, perfect God is incompatible with Nietzsche's own metaphysics, but the issue is whether this metaphysics is the sole basis for appreciating temporal and finite values. The Nietzschean and Christian views of the cosmos are *counter*-valuations: they are not related as a prizing and a despising of the world. Their conflict is over whether or not the components of our experience are creatures, bearing witness to their creator, not about whether or not there is any significance and value in the world of becoming.

Nietzsche personifies his antitheistic standpoint in the character of *Zarathustra*, whose message is *the death of God*. Zarathustra comes down from his mountain retreat, to share the fruits of his meditations with the sons of men. In dithyrambic periods, he preaches thus:

I beseech you, my brothers, *remain faithful to the earth,* and do not believe those who speak to you of otherworldly hopes! Poison-mixers are they, whether they know it or not. . . . Once the sin against God was the greatest sin; but God died, and these sinners died with him. To sin against the earth is now the most dreadful thing, and to esteem the entrails of the unknowable higher than the meaning of the earth.[14]

By "the death of God" is meant the desuetude of all practical belief in the idea of God. Nietzsche points to the discrepancy between profession of such belief and the actual interests of European men of our age. Their real gods are power politics, riches, sensual pleasure, and war. But his message is not that they should foreswear these false idols, and return to the worship of the true God. To have urged that, he would have had to abandon his own definition of the idea of God, in favor of the reality of God Himself. But within the Nietzschean perspective, there is only the idea of God — and it is irretrievably dead, once men cease to give it credence, in their own hearts.

The real significance of loss of faith in God is *cultural nihilism* and the *downfall of all values.* Nietzsche's aim is not to deplore this predicament but to intensify it, to the point where his own Promethean solution will alone seem viable to bold spirits. The "death of God" is only conceivable on condition that all values, including the highest, are creations of man. Man is confronted with no objective norms of belief and conduct. In a world whose heart is constant flux, nothing permanent is already given to man. The cosmos as such is a chaos of becoming, but man can *will* to make it intelligible, to construct concepts, and thus to endow experience with meaning and value. Human history made a fateful mistake, when it erected the idea of God into the supreme value. In modern times, there has been a secret recession from this idea but, as yet, no open repudiation. Zarathustra bids men turn away openly from belief in a transcendent God, and forge for themselves a completely immanent, voluntaristic system of values and goals.

Nietzsche's conception of an atheistic world of human values is best understood as an *experiment of thought and imagination,* carried

[14] *Thus Spoke Zarathustra,* Prologue, 3 (Kaufmann, 125). Hegel had also spoken about "the death of God," in terms of the negative moment in his dialectic.

on within the framework of Kantian and Schopenhauerian epistemology. Let us suppose, he asks us in effect, that there is no noumenal
source — neither Kant's thing-in-itself nor Schopenhauer's cosmic will
— for the matter of sensation. Then the latter may be regarded as a
true sampling of the original flux of the cosmos. Since it is a chaotic
and completely unorganized becoming, it does not contain any
permanent, essential structures. The latter must be provided by the
decision and project of the human subject (to use language that also
fits Jean-Paul Sartre's atheistic humanism). Hence all meanings are
purely human in provenance, immanent in content, and evolutionary
in tendency. The incompatibility which Nietzsche sees between a
world of becoming and a permanent, essential principle of intelligibility in finite things is inevitable, only on condition that the fact of
becoming be interpreted in this modified Kantian way, as the *flow
of the matter of sensation, cut off from any intelligible foundation.*
Similarly, there is an essential antagonism between belief in God and
respect for the finite world, only when the latter is construed as a
field of appearances, composed solely of the surging cosmic matter
of sensation and the formal structures provided by human decision.
By postulatory definition, such a matter-form composition would
bear no reference beyond itself. Nietzsche would require us to be
loyal, not toward the earthly situation of common human experience,
but toward the experimental construct which would result, if "appearances" alone were real, and were constituted entirely by the human
resolution to tame the flux of sensations and inject meanings therein.
This hypothesis does mark the death of the idea of God, if by that
phrase is meant the final despair of nineteenth-century philosophy
over fitting the living God into the Kantian machinery of the matter
of sensation, the forms of human subjectivity, and the intelligible ideals.

## 4. REVALUATION OF MORAL VALUES

The average reaction to Nietzsche's proposal that men should set
up their own standards, without reference to God or any permanent
norms, is to brand it as immoral. Nietzsche took note of this
spontaneous judgment and gloried in the title of "the first im-
moralist."[15] He set out to show that the conventional morality is far

---

[15] *Ecce Homo* (Fadiman, 135). Cf. *Beyond Good and Evil*, 226 (M. Cowan translation, 152–53), where Nietzsche says that "we immoralists" are nevertheless "men
of duty," responsive to a higher set of values. Cf. A. Stern, "Nietzsche et le

from noble, either in origin or purpose, and that cultural advances depend upon the acceptance of many views currently being labeled immoral. In the godless age which we are now entering, there must be a critique of all accepted patterns of conduct and a radical *revaluation of all values*. The atheistic mind must wipe the slate clean with a sponge, and then compose afresh its own tables of the law.

The first step in this revolutionary program is to expose the real sources of the moral convictions, which still dominate European life. Once the ideal of God is undermined, the whole structure of Christian ethical values can also be overturned. Nietzsche has nothing but scorn for the philosophical attempts — from Kant to Spencer — to offer a laicized version of Christian ethical principles, retaining the *moral law* apart from its dogmatic setting. An absolute moral law stands and falls with the idea of God. For failure to see this, Kant is guilty of propounding a moral doctrine that is dangerous to life. The Kantian doctrine on the categorical imperative and impersonal duty sacrifices individual existence to an abstract absolute, a lingering image of the transcendent. In general, every ethical theory which supports an unconditional and universal moral law, represents an abstract and denaturalized standpoint. Nietzsche's revaluation is intended to renaturalize the moral problem, and render it concrete, by showing that moralities are *many* and that moral concepts are *evolutionary* products of our *egoistic* drives.

That there cannot be an absolute, permanent, moral standard is, for Nietzsche, merely a corollary of his monism of sheer becoming. If there are no essential structures already present in things, there are no objective bases already present for moral norms and relations. Moral ideals, like all other concepts, are born from human efforts to stabilize the stream of becoming, which is intrinsically homogeneous and undifferentiated. Man tries to introduce moral distinctions into the *chaotic flow of emotions and desires,* which comprise the practical analogue to the matter of sensation. Just as truths are many and relative to the knower, so moral standards are many and perspectival or relative to individual and group interests. Nietzsche proposes to write the natural history of the growth of the various moralities, which men have produced.

This *natural history of morals* is, in fact, a search after psychological origins of moral attitudes.[16] Nietzsche holds that psychology is the path to a resolution of the fundamental problems of morality, just as it is his pathway in dealing with God and absolute truth. When he speaks of giving a *historical* account of the formation of morals, he means a *psychological* description of some states of mind that may have contributed toward our moral convictions. His history of morals is an essay in "soul-divining," and not an empirical survey of the relevant materials. Now, Nietzsche states explicitly that a discussion of the *origins* of moral beliefs is different from a critical evaluation of their *validity*. But, in practice, he overrules this distinction and thus commits the "genetic fallacy" of deciding the worth of a moral principle in function of a psychological guess about its genesis. He prepares the mind for his own overthrow of moral values, by always discovering an unsavory origin for the targets of his criticism. His definition of the historical sense as "the instinct for 'divining' the interrelations of these value estimates" at the basis of moral conduct[17] is an index that his genetic descriptions are equivalent to placements of the moral concepts in a definite scale of values. The Nietzschean historical method is a genetic way of stating his own *valuation* of the beliefs under analysis, and hence bears a circular relation to his general metaphysical position.

## NIETZSCHE'S ANALYSIS OF MORALITIES

1. Premoral basis of morality in utility and power.
2. Historical types of moral attitudes.
   a) Early historical times
      1) Master morality (good versus worthless).
      2) Slave morality (evil versus good).
   b) European civilization based upon flock morality and the Christian ascetic ideal.
3. Extramoral aims of the select forerunners of the superman: individual "styles" of morality and cultivation of the "hard virtues," beyond good and evil.

Nietzsche distinguishes three eras in the growth of morals: the premoral, the moral, and the extramoral.[18] The *premoral* period covers the whole of human prehistory, which is by far the longest in duration. During this time, men develop the "morality of mores" or

---

[16] *Beyond Good and Evil,* 23, 186–87, 224 (Cowan, 27–28, 89–92, 148–51).
[17] *Ibid.,* 224 (Cowan, 148).
[18] *Ibid.,* 32 (Cowan, 39–40).

customs, which precedes any thought of an absolute, universal moral law. Premoral man is a creature bent upon acquiring habitual responses and patterns of conduct, so that a stable and predictable core of human character may be formed, distinguishing man from other animals. The major consideration is survival and consolidation of the species. Actions are evaluated solely in terms of their useful or harmful *consequences,* rather than in terms of their origin or motive. Premoral conduct is unalloyed utilitarianism, the standard of utility being the survival of the primitive communities. Each social group finds that survival is fostered by laying down tables of laws, expressive of the conditions of existence required for community life. In the concrete, there are many codes of conduct, corresponding to the different requirements for existence. Over several generations of adhering to these prescriptions for survival, men build up a set of *habits of conformity,* which become the accepted mores of the society. Like Mill and Bergson, Nietzsche traces moral obligation to these powerful social customs. The binding force of moral commands comes, not from the content of the mores, but from their venerable character, from the sacredness which they acquire after ages of successful guidance of community life.

At least during earlier historical times, the various types of morality are reducible to two main kinds: master morality and slave morality.[19] This follows the division of classes into the nobles and the masses, each having its own set of interests to protect and promote. Nietzsche would agree with Marx that, at bottom, all moralities are caste or class moralities. What sets off the *moral* from the premoral age, is its emphasis upon conscious *motivations* (and not merely upon practical consequences), as the source of the worth of actions. But the motives are viewed differently, according to one's position in society. The aristocrats naturally accord themselves the right to lay down values for their society. They are spontaneous creators of the moral distinctions constituting *master morality.* The pivotal contrast is between the good or noble and the bad or worthless (*schlecht*). The masters pattern the traits of the good man after themselves. An equation is set up between the good, the noble in birth, the powerful, the beautiful-and-healthy in body, and the beloved by the gods. Nietzsche instanced the Greek ruling class and the splendid Aryan, blond beasts

---

[19] *Beyond Good and Evil,* 199, 202, 260 (Cowan, 105–07, 111–13, 203–08); *The Genealogy of Morals,* I, 1–17 (Golffing, 158–88).

of prey, as exemplars of master morality. He hastened to add that the Aryan masters bear no resemblance to the Germans of our day, but his enthusiasm for blond barbarians was infectious in German racist circles. By way of contrast, the bad or worthless are the plebeian masses, who enjoy no pride of birth or social position, and who are unshapely in appearance, as well as in spirit. Whatever serves to maintain the masters in power is denominated good, whereas anything that threatens their interests is bad.

Quite the contrary standards prevail from the standpoint of the masses. The vulgar are essentially reactive, in contrast with the spontaneous activity of the noble-minded. Hence the slave mind needs the presence of aristocrats and their norms, in order to have an object for their envy and counterprinciples. *Slave morality* is the creation of the base passion of resentment (*ressentiment*). Since the masses are not in the seat of power, they can express their aggressive instincts and desire for revenge only in a suppressed way, as resentment. Hence the accusation of evil (*böse*) is primary with them, whereas the affirmation of the good was primary with the aristocrats. What the masters regarded as good is now branded as evil, from the perspective of resentful underlings. Aristocratic power and the splendors of this world are morally condemned: the paradox of the beatitudes is affirmed in their stead. The truly good and blessed of God are the weak, the hungry, the poor in spirit, the outcasts of this life. Slave morality finds its perfect expression in the counsels and precepts of the Christian life.

Nietzsche holds that master morality represents the *ascending* line in man's development, whereas slave morality represents the *descending* line. The former enhances the higher values of life and hence is healthy; the latter destroys them and so is decadent. More recent European history has witnessed the gradual triumph of decadent values and slave morality. A leveling process has been going on, striking at the heart of a stratified arrangement of society and a hierarchical view of the types of morality. The standards of the many have been made obligatory for everyone in the community. Nietzsche interprets this movement as meaning the triumph of *flock* morality over *individual* morality. The pressure of the herd — expressed in the "thou shalt" of moral commands — is overwhelming, in an antivitalistic direction. It is almost impossible for the exceptional individual to defy accepted moral standards and erect his own ethical values. Genius is subordinated to safe mediocrity, within the modern state.

Thus, the free creations of the aristocratic spirits of our age are suppressed, and the upward movement of life is thwarted.

Flock morality prevails today, largely through the agency of Christianity, humanitarian democracy, and socialism. The two latter movements are secularized offspring of Christianity. Today, they are bending Christianity to their own ends, but they are also living off the capital of this religion. The victory of decadent, flock morality is due mainly to the standards contained in the *Christian "ascetic ideal,"* which Nietzsche regards as the chief enemy of his own humanistic conception of the Dionysian man and individual or "stylized" morality.[20] Nietzsche's peculiar notion of the Christian ascetic ideal must be grasped, if one is to understand his violent reactions against Christianity.

Although he paid his respects to Jesus as a human person, Nietzsche made passionate denunciations of St. Paul and Christianity. He linked Judaism and Christianity together, as the main forces which achieved "the slave revolt in morals." By vindicating the moral value of sympathy, self-denial, and altruism, Judaeo-Christianity spread the standards of slave morality to all classes in society. It undermined the eugenic soundness of the race, by lending moral and religious sanction to the care of the sick, the weak, and the poor. This ascetic ideal despises all earthly and human values. Christian faith is "a continuous suicide of the reason. . . . The Christian faith is a sacrifice, sacrifice of all freedom, all pride, all self-assurance of the mind; at the same time it is servitude, self-mockery and self-mutilation."[21] It is little wonder that, holding this distorted conception of the Christian faith and its consequences for the self, Nietzsche should feel revolted at it. He associated it with the reduction of matter, self, and pain to illusion, a standpoint which he also attributed to the Oriental philosophies. Insofar as the contemporary mood of nihilism expressed a feeling of tiredness and nausea concerning man, he traced it to the effect of the Christian teaching on man's destiny and duty.

As a countermeasure, Nietzsche praised the "hard" virtues needed

[20] Cf. *ibid.,* III, 1–28 (Golffing, 231–99); *Ecce Homo* (Fadiman, 140–45); "A Critical Backward Glance" prefixed to *The Birth of Tragedy* [Golffing, 9–10]). Throughout these passages, Nietzsche is concerned with Schopenhauer's denial of the will-to-live and Wagner's *Parsifal*-imagery, two sources which provided him with a distorted conception of the Christian attitude toward life and humanistic values.

[21] *Beyond Good and Evil,* 46 (Cowan, 55).

for the "dangerous" life. The warrior qualities of self-discipline, endurance, harshness, and suspicion are needed for reaching the *extramoral* zone, which lies beyond conventional good and evil. Nietzsche also required of his new moral exemplar a keen intelligence, utter honesty, and a generosity that gives, not out of pity but out of a superabundance of power. The goal is not *uniformity of morals for all men* but a *gradation of rank among types of morality.*[22] The masses cannot partake in the strength and independence of the few, but this only means that the standards of the flock should not be imposed upon the geniuses among us. That a new morality can be produced, is only an inference from the fact that the moralities of the past also owed their origin to human efforts.

Nietzsche sees man as constantly engaged in a process of *sublimation* or *spiritualization* of basic impulses.[23] The concepts of duty and guilt, which figure so prominently in slave morality, are spiritualized expressions of the debtor-creditor relationship, generalized as a bond between man and God. Conscience is due to the repression and inward focusing of our aggressive instincts, once men have entered into peaceful civil relations in the state. Aristocratic and plebeian standards depend upon the different interests at stake. Thus the noblest virtues of accepted flock morality have resulted from the sublimation of egoism and cruelty. Now, if all moral concepts are evolutionary products of this sublimating activity, Nietzsche hopes that superior forms of moral existence can still emerge from the reservoir of the unconscious. At least, a few gifted individuals must be allowed to develop their own style of conduct, without concern for the common meaning of good and evil.

Nietzsche the moralist is a disconcerting mixture of shrewdness and fantasy. He looks upon human conduct with the *double vision* of a sensitive observer and a promoter of the apocalypse of the coming superman. His observations on contemporary life make salutary and chastening reading, since he exposes the dangers of a purely conventional and conformist attitude toward moral standards. His scalpel uncovers the mediocrity and corruption of many phases of modern life. But at all times, his psychological insight is controlled by his underlying metaphysical aims, which lead him to overlook whole

---

[22] *Ibid.,* 219, 228 (Cowan, 143–44, 154–56); *The Antichrist* (Kaufmann, 618–20, 643–47).

[23] *Beyond Good and Evil,* 188–89 (Cowan, 93–96); *The Genealogy of Morals,* II, 6–7 (Golffing, 197–202).

areas of evidence and to establish some false connections and mythological genealogies. In his eagerness to justify his doctrine of the superman as self-legislator of moral values, he erects surmises of what *might* have occurred, in the development of moral conscience, into a dialectical pattern of what *did* occur. Opposing views of morality are disposed of, simply by being ranked in a rigid hierarchy of vital values, and by being saddled with all the objectionable features found in present-day society. Natural history of this sort may provide a moving esthetic experience, based upon a powerful illusion and a strong polemical drive, but it cannot sustain itself before a sober resolve to submit to the controlling influence of empirical evidence, comprehensively gathered.

That there has been development in our understanding of moral principles is in accord with both God's providential governance and the role of reason in moral life. Despite what Schopenhauer taught Nietzsche, reason is not merely the servant of egoistic impulses: it is also their critic and the tireless pathfinder of further aspects and applications of the basic moral relations. The fact that there has been *some* development of moral consciousness does not permit one to conclude, however, that man has evolved from a condition in which there were *no* moral principles whatsoever. Nietzsche's notion of premorality is partly a *deduction* from his monism of undifferentiated becoming, and partly a product of his method of *prescinding* from factors that do not further his schema of moralities. For instance, he treats the creditor-debtor bond as though nothing more than self-interest were primitively involved. This enables him to draw duty and guilt out of a purely egoistic, amoral situation, and to suggest that an adequate morality of the superman can also be built on this foundation. But his analysis rests on the assumption that no element of justice is involved in the relations between the original parties to business transactions. This assumption is an instance of Nietzsche's soul-divining, rather than a deliverance gained through a patient anthropological study of early man. Similarly, the genesis of conscience is traced to the repressive effects of social life, simply by isolating the aggressive instincts and supposing that early man is completely extroverted. A quite different set of conclusions could be reached, by isolating the other-regarding impulses and stressing the intensely meditative side of the primitive mentality.[24]

[24] For Nietzsche's treatment of guilt, justice, and conscience, see *ibid.*, II, 1–6, 8 (Golffing, 189–97, 202–03). A judicious estimate of his theories is made by G.

The Nietzschean treatment of the *Christian influence* upon morality is equally one-sided and arbitrary. Present-day Christianity is presented as though it contained no internal powers of reform and regeneration. Modern Christian opposition to mere conventional acceptance of moral standards and to the bourgeois spirit of mediocrity and conformism is left unmentioned, although this is perhaps a commentary upon the quality of the Christian lives known to Nietzsche. In dealing with what he regards as the primitive message of Christian faith, he relies mainly upon Pascal, Schopenhauer, Wagner, and Dostoevski for his conception. They provide him with an abstraction, called *"the* Christian ascetic ideal," which he never compares with the integral Christian teaching. He pays no attention to the centuries of discussion by Christian thinkers concerning the proper relations between nature and grace, since it suits his thesis to regard faith as totally inimical to human dignity and freedom. And although Christian moralists have a good deal to say about the rightful search after self-perfection, Nietzsche simplifies the issue by framing it in terms of the Schopenhauerian contrast between egoistic and altruistic motives. When Nietzsche charges Christianity with being an antivitalistic force, he is uncritically accepting Schopenhauer's double claim that the Christian love of neighbor is identical with his own view of altruism, and that Christianity is antiegoistic in the same sense in which his denial of the will-to-live is antiegoistic. But the antithesis between *egoism* and *altruism,* as Schopenhauer states it, fails to do justice to the delicate problem of the relation between *self-perfection* and *the needs of others,* as analyzed by the Christian moral tradition. Hence Nietzsche's proof of the egoistic source of all morality and the antagonism of Christianity to the dignity of man, is theoretically oversimplified and historically unfounded.

He fails to accord Christianity the benefit of the capital distinction between the intrinsic, *ontological worth* of the body, the senses, and the passions, and their *moral integration* with the whole person. What Christian thought maintains on the former score is ignored, whereas what it has to say on the latter issue is interpreted as an ontological depreciation of the body. This leads to a *double-standard treatment:* Nietzsche accords himself the right to sublimate and transfigure pain and bodily urges, whereas the Christian concern with

---

Thibon, "Frédéric Nietzsche, analyste de la causalité matérielle en psychologie et en morale," *Revue Thomiste,* XL (1935), 3–36.

the same problem is presented as a suppression and defaming of the body. Nietzschean man recognizes the positive value of overcoming and disciplining oneself, whereas Christian man is never permitted to have the same insight.

## 5. THE WILL TO POWER: SUPERMAN AND
### ETERNAL RECURRENCE

The revaluation of values supposes a standard for ranking the various moralities. Nietzsche relies upon the criterion of *life* to distinguish between ascending and descending, healthy and decadent, moral standpoints. To go beyond good and evil and to reach the extramoral attitude, is to accept as good only that which enhances life, and to regard with hostility any antivital attitudes. This raises the question of the nature of life. Nietzsche's answer is that "life simply *is* will to power."[25] Hence anything that increases the *will-to-power* is valuable, according to the higher morality. Nietzsche's final task is to set forth the nature of the will-to-power, as the integrating principle for his cultural, metaphysical, and moral doctrines.

Its meaning may be specified by contrast with some other positions, upon which Nietzsche is partially dependent. He agrees with Schopenhauer that will constitutes the essential nature of the real, although the will is no longer a noumenal backdrop for Nietzsche, but is only the dynamic aspect of the "appearances." But Schopenhauer's will is led eventually to turn against itself, in an ascetic or life-denying act. Since this is patently antivitalistic, Nietzsche requires his cosmic will always to affirm itself. *Moral good* is found only in a constant affirmation of the will and an increase in its power. The Darwinian struggle of the fittest for survival bears some resemblance to the theory of an effective will-to-power. But although Nietzsche admits the high moral value of struggle, he regards survival as a tame corollary of the struggle itself. The drive of life is directed mainly toward the discharge of power, with bare existence entailed as a mere off-product. Similarly, Spencer's definition of evolution as an adaptation of the organism to external circumstances is quite secondary to the aggressive impulse of the inward forces in the organism. Nietzsche also keeps utility and pleasure in subordinate positions, as

---

[25] *Beyond Good and Evil*, 259 (Cowan, 203); cf. *ibid.*, 36 (Cowan, 43–45). The main collection of texts on this theme is *The Will to Power* (*Gesammelte Schriften, Musarionausgabe*, XVIII–XIX).

criteria of valuable action, since they express only partial aspects of the will-to-power.

This force has its metaphysical basis in the cosmic becoming itself, which produces all the forms of life. The first resonance of will in the specifically human sphere is felt in the unconscious life of the impulses and desires. But will also manifests itself in the senses and thinking: knowledge and reason are its tools for gaining foresight and control. Nietzsche thinks that the dynamic aspects of psychic life are of the same stuff as the cosmic becoming, and that therefore the universal force is a will to the increase of power. In man, it takes the form of an *overcoming of oneself*.[26] This is expressed in the synthesis between Dionysian power and Apollinian measure or constraint of intelligence. *Spirit* (*Geist*) is nothing other than the will, operating as a feeling of growth or increase in power. He who cultivates his abilities to the full and enjoys a well-rounded existence, in accord with his own individual pattern, is living the spiritual existence of a person responsive to the will-to-power.

Nietzsche does not identify his own moral position entirely with the master morality of the past. For, the aristocrats of past times were themselves a conservative caste, resistant to further change and insistent upon equality within the caste itself. But on the main point of *self-legislation of values*, they supply Nietzsche with a model for his own higher morality. How did the aristocrats gain sufficient confidence to lay down tables of laws for society as a whole? By reason of the "pathos of distance," i.e., their consciousness of superiority to the masses and their conviction that the impulse of life must continuously break through old molds.[27] Similarly, the free spirits of our own day need to have their will-to-power strengthened by an ideal that will elevate them above the masses and enflame them to advance the impulse of life one spiral higher. Nietzsche's conception of the *superman* is intended to perform this office. In the myth of the superman, he finds that combination of the historical and the superhistorical, which will move exceptional men to heroic deeds. His doctrine on the superman is essentially an invitation to develop one's personality beyond its present limits, and thus to shape the future in the direction of life and the will-to-power.

---

[26] On self-overcoming, cf. *Thus Spoke Zarathustra*, 12 (Kaufmann, 225–28); *Beyond Good and Evil*, II, 257 (Cowan, 200–01). On the relation between "mind" and the will-to-power, see *ibid.*, 230 (Cowan, 159–60).

[27] *Ibid.*, 257 (Cowan, 200); *The Genealogy of Morals*, I, 2 (Golffing, 150).

When Zarathustra comes down from the mountain, he announces not only the "death of God" but also the truth that man is a self-surpassing animal, an overman or (in Nietzsche's own sense of the word) a Superman.

> Man is a rope, tied between beast and overman — a rope over an abyss. . . . What is great in man is that he is a bridge and not an end: what can be loved in man is that he is an *overture* and a *going under.* I love those who do not know how to live, except by going under, for they are those who cross over. . . . Behold, I teach you the overman. The overman is the meaning of the earth. Let your will say: the overman shall be the meaning of the earth![28]

At the present stage of its evolution, the will-to-power aims at over-coming the mediocrity and self-satisfaction of man, through the strength of a human *fiat.* But this is a dangerous undertaking, since it involves experimenting with oneself, abandoning familiar landmarks of settled beliefs, and perhaps perishing in the effort to establish a new realm of moral values for oneself. Hence the good news of the coming of the superman is not met with enthusiasm by most people. They would rather be "last men," i.e., secure but mediocre possessors of the present level of existence, than "over-goers," en route to a new grade of life. Only a rare human being of Goethe's stature will welcome this sublime vocation, which requires perfect control over a plenitude of power.

Those who do not respond to the call of preparing for the advent of the superman, are surely lacking in sufficient will-to-power. Hence they are naturally ordained to a lower rank of dynamic perfection and to a subordinate moral station. Nietzsche does not want to eliminate flock morality but only to restrict it to the masses. Indeed, he insists upon a *difference* in moral standards for the crowd and the exceptional individuals. The former are inherently incapable of sharing in the supreme form of life, created by the moral geniuses. Hence the masses are to be governed by flock morality, while the outstanding man is to be allowed the freedom to create his own moral norms. Free spirits need the masses, as a material foundation and as a foil for their own soaring aspirations. The gifted few are justified in using the many as instruments in their own efforts to intensify their will-to-power. They are to be firm, but also nobleminded and generous, with the herd of common people.

The forerunners of the superman are those individuals who, like

---

[28] *Thus Spoke Zarathustra*, Prologue, 3–4 (Kaufmann, 125, 126–27).

Zarathustra, have the honesty and fortitude to acknowledge that the universe has no intrinsic meaning or purpose. There is only the senseless flood of becoming — except for the meanings and values laid down by man. *"But the real philosophers are commanders and legislators.* They say, 'It *shall* be thus!' They determine the 'whither' and the 'to what end' of mankind. . . . Their 'knowing' is *creating.* Their creating is legislative. Their will to truth is — *will to power."*[29] That is why Zarathustra calls upon daring individuals to resolve for themselves that superman *shall be* the meaning of the earth.

Nietzsche himself saw a weakness in this voluntaristic theory of truth. To proclaim that knowing is creating, is also to open the floodgates to every sort of subjective whim and escapist wish. Nietzsche could not remedy this situation by appeal to any objective standard in being, since he recognized none. But he did what he could, within his framework, to discourage easy dreams about what it means to aspire to the rank of the superman. For, he described the superman as one who wills to accept the doctrine of the *eternal recurrence of the same state of affairs.*[30] He calculated that this belief in a cyclical return of all the events of the past would frighten away those who are not genuinely fortified with the will-to-power, in the supreme degree. He found traces of this doctrine among the Greek and Indian thinkers. The theory of metempsychosis (rebirth of the soul), the notion of the great cosmic year, and the cyclical view of history, rested upon the image of nature as a *closed circle,* constantly repeating itself at every level. Nietzsche also appealed to the scientific con-

---

[29] *Beyond Good and Evil,* 211 (Cowan, 135). Nietzsche argues that the Kantian synthesis between autonomy and universality is impossible, so that one who seeks moral autonomy must abandon Kant's universal, formal rule of rationality and embrace Nietzsche's own extramoral standpoint (*The Genealogy of Morals,* II, 2 [Golffing, 191]). The Nietzschean superman has overthrown one half of the Kantian moral standpoint, and has taken advantage of Kant's own failure to integrate his doctrine on moral autonomy with a metaphysics of finite being and appetitive tendency. Still, Nietzsche's philosophical values-legislator is not supposed to be an irresponsible egoist but is bound by loyalty to the new aristocratic order of rank. G. W. Cunningham, in "Nietzsche on the Philosopher," *The Philosophical Review,* LIV (1945), 55–72, remarks, however, that Nietzsche hesitates upon the crucial issue of whether there is an ascertainable philosophical standard of moral value, and whether precise indications of its content are available.

[30] *The Will to Power,* 1053–67 (*Gesammelte Werke, Musarionausgabe,* XIX, 366–74); *Thus Spoke Zarathustra,* III, 30 (Kaufmann, 327–33, 340–43). Nietzsche's arguments in support of an eternal return of the same are analyzed by O. Becker, "Nietzsches Beweise für seine Lehre von der ewigen Wiederkunft," *Blätter für deutsche Philosophie,* IX (1935–1936), 368–87.

siderations of his day. If energy is finite and has a finite number of centers of force or dynamic quanta, acting in finite space but in infinite time, then the particular configurations in the temporal process must endlessly be repeated. Cosmic becoming is like a phonograph, senselessly playing the same tune over and over again. But Nietzsche specified that heroic individuals must deliberately accept this situation, place the whole meaning of their lives in it, and find therein their true joy of existence. It is this will to make an eternal recurrence one's chosen significance for the cosmos, which makes the doctrine the crucible for testing the authentic will-to-power and the coming of the superman.

The thought of an eternal recurrence shook Nietzsche's soul to the depths. He referred to it in terms of both horror and exultation. It is terrible to hold that the course of events comes around again and again, and that the whole periodic process is without purpose or culmination. This doctrine provided Nietzsche with his own variety of "asceticism," since it purges the will of any yearning for automatic, evolutionary progress and of any lingering, Christian desire for a meaningful climax of history. At the same time, eternal recurrence is the only joyful wisdom to be found in a godless world. Love functions in Nietzsche's system only as *amor fati:* love of one's fate, reconciliation to the endless cycle of things, just as they are.[31] The doctrine of the eternal recurrence is also Nietzsche's way of satisfying the condition that the superhistorical principle of action should belong to the order of eternal being. In willing that the meaning of the cosmos be nothing other than the great ring of becoming itself, one thereby *absolutizes time. Eternity* is given in the joyful moment when one wills the eternal recurrence, since an absolutized time is the same as eternity. And this belief also satisfies the search after stable *being.* For, when the will-to-power impresses an eternal round of becoming upon life, as its ultimate meaning, the human mind approaches as closely as it can to being.

Because he must accommodate eternity and being within the immanence of his monism of becoming, Nietzsche relies upon powerful illusions or life-enhancing myths, which state his desiderata in the imperative mood, but do not show that they are well grounded in experience. Despite the function of his theory of an eternal recurrence,

---

[31] *Ecce Homo (Philosophy,* 49). Bizet's *Carmen* is an artistic illustration of what Nietzsche means by the attitude of *amor fati.*

as weeding out would-be forerunners of the superman and as testing the strength of one's will-to-power, it is nonetheless an arbitrarily assigned meaning for the cosmos as a whole. It may satisfy Nietzsche's personal sense of the plenitude of power, but this is no recommendation for any other personal perspective, unless an essential structure is to be readmitted for the special case of the human mind. The doctrine of the eternal recurrence is an *axiological fiction,* useful for quickening Nietzsche's private feeling of being purged and of growing in vital strength. Yet the intrinsic meaninglessness of life prevents him from establishing it as a valid criterion for estimating the standpoints of other men. It cannot fulfill the function of a standard of values for others, unless Nietzsche supposes that human history has developed a special set of habits, requiring outstanding men to assent to his own interpretation. Since this is clearly not the case, eternal recurrence remains only a private reading of the universe.

A similar situation surrounds the cardinal doctrine of the will-to-power. Nietzsche regards the axiological aspect of this doctrine as being more important than the epistemological. This may be so, once one grants its soundness. But the basic question is whether it need be accepted at all. Whenever Nietzsche speaks about the will-to-power in general terms, he lapses back into a Schopenhauerian description. The will-to-power is the heart of every active force; it is the world seen from within; it is the essence of the world. How, then, is it known by us? Nietzsche repudiates Schopenhauer's "pure, will-less, painless, timeless knower" as a piece of mythology, since every perspective on reality is specified by a temporal act of will.[32] He himself proceeds by *extrapolating* the dynamic tendencies of our psychic life into the rest of the cosmos, without offering any careful justification of this projection. The tendency toward power is, indeed, an important component in the human personality; it is also a fact that man's will exercises some efficient, causal control over his cognitive powers. But from these data, it cannot be concluded that *all* cosmic energies constitute a single, voluntaristic movement of becoming and power-seeking, sufficient unto itself. All things are

---

[32] *The Genealogy of Morals,* III, 12 (Golffing, 255). Despite this criticism, Nietzsche avails himself of a Schopenhauerian (but phenomenalistic) intuition to establish that "the world seen from within, the world designated and defined according to its 'intelligible character' — this world would be will to power, and nothing else" (*Beyond Good and Evil,* 36 [Cowan, 45]). To reach this viewpoint, however, Nietzsche is forced to absolutize the biological categories and the human feeling of power.

moved by an appetite for their own perfection. Yet whether this inclination is one, universal, cosmic will and whether it springs from itself alone, with no transcendent implications, are speculative issues that cannot be settled in terms of a life-promoting myth. For, the nature and grades of life cannot be determined, apart from a prior settlement of the question of being and becoming. Indeed, the *grades of life* remain fundamentally unclarified in Nietzsche's thought. They bear some resemblance to Schopenhauer's grades in the manifestation of will. But since he cannot appeal to Schopenhauer's "Platonic ideas," without seeming to reinstate an absolute region of truth, Nietzsche refers to these grades of life as the degrees of "tonality" or "quantity of power" contained in various attitudes toward man and the cosmos. Yet these also remain Nietzsche's private evaluations, and do not provide a measure for other men to accept.

Nietzsche's metaphysical commitments led him to miss the full significance of each of the three "superhistorical" goals he admitted for human action: a supernature, eternity, and stable being. First, he had a deep thirst for *transcending the natural limits of our powers*. But since he knew no way of reconciling the transcendent life of God with finite reality, he confined our movement of transcendence to further immanent participation in the cosmic stuff of will and becoming. And because his higher mode of existence depended solely upon the will, and allowed nothing to God's initiative, he confounded it with the special works of genius. This forced him to rule out the possibility of a universal sharing, by all men, in the supreme form of life. The perfections of antitheistic, Dionysian humanism are only for the few supermen, since there is no direct relationship of love between every human person and God. Nietzsche's cultural exclusivism is scandalized by the Christian invitation to all men, to drink of the waters of eternal life. He mistook this for a trend toward leveling all men downward, whereas it is a call to all to move upward, even though the great men of cultural history are but few. In the second place, Nietzsche strained after a *contact with the eternal in time*. Yet his rejection of the Incarnation, as the intersection of time and eternity, left him with nothing more than a distant substitute for eternity. No matter how everlasting the temporal process of recurrence may be, it remains fundamentally distinct in kind from the eternal *now*. The reduction of eternity to its temporal image, in a closed circle of becoming, is fatal to history as a meaningful process and a progress of some sort. To say that the lack of direction is history's direction, and the lack of meaning its meaning, is to make the passionate strength of paradox the standard of philosophical truth. If speculative knowing is creating, then every man is condemned to construct his private world, which remains his alone, no matter how poetically and paradoxically he may express the dream.

Finally, Nietzsche restores *being to the process of becoming,* only in the sense that becoming itself is rendered absolute and accorded the value-status of the purely actual being, without enjoying the latter's ontological status. Although Nietzsche maintained that his aim was to effect as close a rapprochement as possible between cosmic becoming and stable being, his actual practice was to endow the Great Year of Becoming with the values of the purely actual being, God. He did this, in the desperate hope of transferring to his cosmic myth the entire scale of human responses to God. The consequence was a nebulous conflation, in which both God and the cosmos were robbed of their proper and inalienable manner of being. Nietzsche need not have tried to inject the attributes of God into the process of becoming, in order to give the latter the weight of being. He might have viewed becoming itself as a way toward existent being. To do so, however, would entail recognition that the world consists of *finite beings,* undergoing becoming, and not merely of an amorphous sea of becoming, into which human meanings are injected. This would lead to the properly metaphysical problem of explaining that sort of being which cannot be rendered absolute or entirely self-founded in its participated act of existing. Nietzsche closed the case concerning the nature of becoming, before it was ever opened to metaphysical inspection.

# SUMMARY OF CHAPTER 18

Nietzsche's severity as a critic of nineteenth-century culture was matched by his conviction that Europe was involved in a mortal crisis. The two favored sciences of biology and history were sapping the cultural foundations of life. Evolutionary biology was proving man's purely animal origin and the changing nature of all reality; history was turning men's attention away from present problems to reveries about the past. The joint impact of these two tendencies was to destroy belief in eternal values and the worth-whileness of serious engagement in the present-day situation. Moreover, this destruction occurred simultaneously with the "death of God," i.e., with the loss of effective belief in God as the transcendent and eternal guarantor of our values. Culture, as the self-surpassing activity of man, would soon be obliterated, unless men took stock of this crisis and moved ahead to the new atheistic humanism. God, the ideal of absolute truth, and every other vestige of a transcendent order, must be rejected. Moral judgments must be completely revised and values revalued. Nietzsche gave a genealogy of morals, which traced presently respected standards to an origin in the class struggle for power between masters and slaves. He regarded Christian values as the bitter fruit of resentment and the slave revolt against the nobler sort of men. His own positive proposal rested on an aristocratic division between the great masses of ordinary men, who are properly governed by a mediocre flock morality, and the few geniuses who can legislate their own values and develop individual "styles" of morality. A combination of Dionysian urge and Apollinian restraint should be the aim of the higher individuals, who are forerunners of the superman. Since man remains an as-yet-unfixed animal, he can surpass himself in the direction of the superman or supreme manifestation of the will-to-power. As a test of one's strength of mind, Nietzsche stipulated that one must will the eternal recurrence of the same state of affairs to be the totally immanent meaning of the earth, to which all one's loyalty must be given. This defiant will to absolutize the cycle of cosmic events is the nearest approach which Nietzsche's atheistic Titanism permitted toward being and eternity.

## BIBLIOGRAPHICAL NOTE

1. *Sources.* Nietzsche-scholarship has been hindered more than helped by the directing hand of his sister, Elizabeth Förster-Nietzsche. Her anti-Semitic and nationalist views interfered with the integral publication of her brother's philosophical remains. Although defective in many ways, the two following editions constitute the working basis for studies in Nietzsche: *Gesammelte Werke, Grossoktav Ausgabe* (second ed., 19 vols., Leipzig, Kroner, 1901–1913), with R. Oehler's *Nietzsche-Register* added, as Vol. XX, in 1926; *Gesammelte Werke, Musarionausgabe* (23 vols., Munich, Musarion, 1920–1929), Vols. XXII–XXIII being an expanded edition of Oehler's subject-index. Under the general editorship of C. A. Emge, a genuinely critical edition is now underway: *Nietzsches Werke und Briefe, Historisch-kritische Gesamtausgabe* (Munich, Beck, 1933 ff.), with four volumes of *juvenilia* and two volumes of letters issued to date. Translations: under the general editorship of O. Levy, *The Complete Works of Friedrich Nietzsche* (18 vols., New York, Macmillan, 1909–1913); the most convenient collection is the Modern Library Giant, *The Philosophy of Nietzsche* (New York, The Modern Library) — contains: *Thus Spake Zarathustra, Beyond Good and Evil, The Genealogy of Morals, Ecce Homo,* and *The Birth of Tragedy.* There is a separate edition of *The Use and Abuse of History,* translated by Adrian Collins (New York, Liberal Arts Press, 1949).

2. *Studies.* The best psychologico-biographical study is *Nietzsche: The Story of a Human Philosopher,* by H. A. Reyburn, in collaboration with H. E. Hinderks and J. G. Taylor (London, Macmillan, 1948). Since it

consists mainly of excerpts from the translations edited by Levy, W. H. Wright's *What Nietzsche Taught* (New York, Huebsch, 1915), provides a convenient survey, although the existing English translations of Nietzsche are inadequate. There are two excellent and complementary studies of his total philosophy: G. A. Morgan, Jr., *What Nietzsche Means* (Cambridge, Mass., Harvard University Press, 1941), a warm but well-informed defense by a convinced follower; W. A. Kaufmann, *Nietzsche: Philosopher, Psychologist, Antichrist* (Princeton, Princeton University Press, 1950), a more detached and critical account, which nevertheless exculpates Nietzsche from the common charges of anti-Semitism and "blond-beast" racism. F. Copleston, S.J., *Friedrich Nietzsche: Philosopher of Culture* (London, Burns, Oates, 1942), measures him by a Christian and Scholastic standard; W. Brock, *Nietzsches Idee der Kultur* (Bonn, Cohen, 1930), clarifies his basic notion of culture; G. Siegmund, *Nietzsche der "Atheist" und "Antichrist"* (fourth ed., Paderborn, Schöningh, 1946), studies his attitude toward religion and the springs of his anti-Christian stand. Nietzsche's views on nature and the natural sciences have been minutely studied by A. Mittasch, *Friedrich Nietzsche als Naturphilosoph* (Stuttgart, Kröner, 1952). A leading existentialist philosopher, Karl Jaspers, has made an existential interpretation, *Nietzsche: Einführung in das Verständnis seines Philosophierens* (Berlin, W. de Gruyter, 1936). The cultural and intellectual movement in mid-nineteenth-century Germany is expertly described in K. Löwith's *Von Hegel bis Nietzsche* (Zurich, Europa Verlag, 1941). The subsequent course of German thought may be followed in W. Brock, *An Introduction to Contemporary German Philosophy* (Cambridge, University Press, 1935), which stresses the background influence of Nietzsche, Kierkegaard, and Dilthey; see, also, W. T. Jones, *Contemporary Thought of Germany* (2 vols., London, Williams and Norgate, 1930–1931). For further developments of the eternal-return theme, see M. Eliade, *The Myth of the Eternal Return* (New York, Pantheon, 1955). F. A. Lea's, *The Tragic Philosopher: A Study of Friedrich Nietzsche* (New York, Philosophical Library, 1957) examines his views on romanticism, nihilism, and values.

3. *Further Publications.* A fresh impetus has been given to Nietzsche studies by the issuing of an accurate and manageable edition of his *Werke*, edited by K. Schlechta (Munich, Hanser, 1954–1957). *The Portable Nietzsche* (New York, Viking, 1954) contains fresh translations by W. Kaufmann of *Thus Spoke Zarathustra, Twilight of the Idols, The Antichrist, Nietzsche contra Wagner,* and many letters, notes, and sections of other works. There are two other translations of complete works of Nietzsche: *The Birth of Tragedy and The Genealogy of Morals,* translated by F. Golffing (New York, Doubleday Anchor, 1956) and *Beyond Good and Evil,* translated by M. Cowan (Chicago, Regnery, 1955). K. F. Leidecker has made a selection of Nietzsche's *Unpublished Letters* (New York, Philosophical Library, 1959).

# Chapter 19. BERGSON

## I. LIFE AND WRITINGS

AT THE Lycée Condorcet, where Henri-Louis Bergson (born in Paris, 1859) took his secondary training, he distinguished himself in rhetoric and mathematics. His mathematics instructor was disappointed when Bergson elected to follow the course in letters, instead of in sciences, at the Higher Normal School, which he entered in 1878. There, he held the post of student librarian and buried himself in philosophical and scientific books. His philosophy teachers were Ollé-Laprune and Boutroux, who introduced him to the French spiritualist tradition (especially Maine de Biran and Felix Ravaisson) and the positivist school. After his graduation, he taught for two years (1881-1883) at the *lycée* in Angers and then for five years at the Lycée Blaise Pascal in Clermont-Ferrand (1883-1888). While at the latter post, Bergson acquired his decisive philosophical conviction that time, as treated by the natural sciences and the positivist philosophy of a Herbert Spencer, does not endure and hence is not the real time of our inner experience. He embodied this intuition in his doctoral dissertation, the famous *Essay on the Immediate Data of Consciousness* (1889), which attracted widespread attention and won him a call to teach in Paris. For the next decade, he taught at the Collège Rollin, the Lycée Henri IV, and the Higher Normal School. During this period, he published *Matter and Memory* (1896), applying his original findings about the experience of inner duration to the psychological questions of perception and memory, matter and spirit.

Finally, in 1900, Bergson was given a chair of philosophy at the Collège de France. His success as a public lecturer was unparalleled. Members of the fashionable world vied with earnest students for the privilege of hearing this delicately framed, but intense, man proclaim the end of the reign of positivism and the right of the mind to reconstruct a metaphysics of freedom and spirituality, within the zone of experience itself. Bergson's little essay on *Laughter* (1900) investigated the meaning of the comic, as a permanent phase of human life. His early studies of duration culminated in *Creative Evolution* (1907), in which man's internal apprehension of time was integrated with the vital impetus behind all cosmic developments. At the height of his popularity, Bergson was invited to give a series of lectures (1912–1913) at Columbia University, on spirituality and freedom. The following year, however, ill-health forced him to transfer his active duties at the Collège de France to his disciple, Eduard Le Roy. At the end of World War I, he issued a collection of essays and lectures entitled *Spiritual Energy* (1919). In 1921, Bergson resigned his chair at the Collège, and retired from active academic life. But he did agree to serve as the first president of the Commission for Intellectual Cooperation, in the League of Nations, an office which he filled from 1921 until 1925. His philosophical and literary genius was given international recognition, when he was awarded the 1928 Nobel prize for literature.

Despite painful physical afflictions, Bergson worked away steadily at the moral and religious aspects of his philosophy. The results of his researches were finally embodied in *The Two Sources of Morality and Religion* (1932). Still restricting himself to what an examination of experience permits one to affirm, he distinguished between a morality of conformity and a morality of free aspiration, as well as between religion in its socio-organizational side and its mystical aspects. His last publication was a collection of papers, written earlier, on questions of method and metaphysics: *Thought and the Movent* (1934). Bergson's closing years were overshadowed by sorrow. When occupied France was under the Vichy government, during World War II, he renounced all honors that would seem to support this regime, and refused exemption from the laws against the Jews. A short while before his death, he stood in line and registered as a Jew. Although he had come to see that dynamic religion culminates in Catholicism and the Catholic mystics, Bergson never actually entered the Catholic Church, lest this action be construed as an abandonment of the suffering members of his race. His request was fulfilled, however, that a Catholic priest should say prayers at his grave. He died on January 4, 1941.

## 2. INTUITION AS THE METHOD OF A METAPHYSICS
## OF REAL DURATION

In a memorable address delivered before the Philosophical Congress at Bologna in 1911, Bergson declared that a true philosopher says only one thing in his lifetime, because he enjoys but one point of contact with the real.[1] Certainly, Bergson is a striking illustration of his own maxim, for he concentrated his entire philosophy upon an elucidation of the nature of duration. This is the primary intuition — the point of departure and abiding soul — of all his speculations. It led him, first, into the field of psychology and, then, into a general interpretation of the material and moral worlds, in terms of an intuited duration. At the same time, he reflected deeply upon the proper method for studying durational reality. In following the course of his thoughts, we may begin with his doctrine on intuition, as the philosophical method of investigation. This will be followed by a study of the findings of this method in the domains of psychology, cosmology, morality, and religion.

It was through a sudden illumination of mind that Bergson first stumbled upon the significance of *real duration (la durée réelle)*.[2] At first, the negative import of his discovery seemed most striking. For he saw clearly that the time with which scientists deal, does *not* endure and is only a substitute for real time and duration. The scientific elimination of real duration is due to the method of *spatializing time,* i.e., of conceiving the temporal flux in terms of space. It is natural for the scientific intelligence to morsel or cut up the trajectory of time into a series of "punctiform" instants and intervals, which may then be represented spatially by means of mathematical points and lines. The supposition is that points and lines can be superimposed perfectly upon the real course of duration and

---

[1] *The Creative Mind,* IV, "Philosophical Intuition" (Andison translation, 126–132), which offers some valuable suggestions for the historical approach in philosophy. A brief introduction to Bergson's thought is provided by S. E. Dollard, S.J., "A Summary of Bergsonism," *The Modern Schoolman,* XX (1942–1943), 27–36.

[2] For the genesis of Bergson's conception of duration, cf. *The Creative Mind,* I, "Introduction (Part I), Growth of Truth — Retrograde Movement of the True" (Andison, 9–32). A. C. Moulyn, "The Functions of Point and Line in Time Measuring Operations," *Philosophy of Science,* XIX (1952), 141–55, agrees with Bergson that the use of point and line as measurements extends only to objective or spatialized time, and does not apply to subjective, "lived" time or real duration.

time. For all practical purposes, Bergson admitted, this superposition is possible. In everyday life and scientific calculations, we can deal successfully with the time-factor, by representing it as so many spatial positions in a certain direction. But practical handling is not the same as *true apprehension* of the inner nature of time. The spatialized time of positive science is composed of parts (points and lines), that are themselves immobile. Now from a combination of these *abstract, discrete immobilities,* it is impossible to reconstruct the *concrete, continuous, mobile* character of real duration. Hence there is a serious discrepancy between the mathematical time-factor, used in physics, and the enduring whole which we experience as our real, temporal duration.

Bergson did not conclude that scientific time is radically false but only that it is not the same as the real time studied in philosophy. This led him to make a critical review of the historical relation between *science* and *philosophy,* especially during the modern era.[3] Greek science and philosophy tended to agree that time is unessential to things, and that becoming is a degradation of essential natures. The Greeks looked for some privileged case of motion, in which the intelligible essence would shine forth in its eternal being. A *scientific* revolution was effected by Galileo, for whom all the moments of time are indifferent or of the same rank. Modern classical physics calculates time in terms of simultaneous positions, spread out in space, according to correlated intervals. Its view of time is a "cinematographical" one, substituting a series of static "movie shots" or positional halts for the real flow of continuous time. In other words, it evacuates whatever is original, durational, and causal in temporal reality, accepting only the spatial substitutes for time.

This procedure is perfectly legitimate in scientific affairs, given the aim of modern science to control nature. For, it is in function of matter, mathematical solids, and spatial order that such control is achieved. But the error of modern *philosophy* has been to accept this scientific standpoint as an adequate *speculative* report on temporal reality, and to employ the cinematographical method to resolve properly philosophical issues. Descartes made the first compromise, when he accepted mechanism as a complete metaphysical doctrine on the material world (rather than as a convenient, practical method of handling things), and then sought to rescue man's freedom in

---

[3] This survey is made in *Creative Evolution,* IV (Mitchell translation, 331-91).

such a world. This led him to propose an extreme dualism of mind and body, giving rise to the equally artificial solutions of Spinoza and Leibniz. The efforts of classical rationalism were vitiated by the mistake of treating *rules* of scientific method as metaphysical *laws*, governing real things. Their error could have been discovered, simply by making a comparison between time as lived or experienced by us, and time as it must be described according to the reigning scientific method.

Bergson reserved his keenest criticism for Mill, Spencer, and Kant, the philosophers who had shaped his own mind, and who still enjoyed widespread acceptance in his philosophical world. He located the prime error of Mill and the empiricist school in the "physico-morphic fallacy," i.e., the tendency to interpret human nature solely in terms of the physicist's view of the material world.[4] Hume's and Mill's laws of association are the counterparts of the law of gravity: hence they yield nothing more than a *physics of the mind,* telling us about its nature only insofar as it conforms with matter and thinks about matter. Application of the scientific method of analysis to man is valuable for showing how he adapts himself to physical conditions, for practical purposes. But the limitations of the scientific method are also carried over into the psychological field, so that Mill's associationist psychology fails to explain our inner life, in its own proper character as experienced duration. His "psychological intuition" gives only a spatialized account of inner duration, allowing the real, temporal self to slip through the net. No harm would have been caused, if Mill had pretended to be nothing more than an experimental psychologist, trying to determine how far the methods of positive science can be applied to man. But he gave metaphysical weight to his findings and hence undermined the enduring self. What he forgot, however, was that his methods were not adapted to a discovery of the human self, in its distinctive mode of existing as an enduring reality.

Just as Mill advocated interior observation and yet failed to reach the interior life of man, so Spencer advocated evolution and yet failed to grasp the principle of change in nature. The evolutionary flow *in the material world* is just as unamenable to the spatializing

---

[4] On this fallacy, in its general use, consult W. Cerf, "The Physicomorphic Conception of Man," *Journal of Philosophy,* XLVIII (1951), 345–56; see, also, H. Haus-heer, "Bergson's Critique of Scientific Psychology," *The Philosophical Review,* XXXVI (1927), 450–61.

and immobilizing techniques of mathematical physics as is *psychic* duration. Spencer's approach was to halt the evolutionary process at the present, static instant, break the given world analytically into parts, and then reconstruct the present forms of life mechanically, out of the fragments. Bergson compared this method to the action of a child who cuts up a picture and then thinks that he is producing the whole pattern afresh, when he fits the pieces together in jigsaw fashion. But "it is not by dividing the evolved that we shall reach the principle of that which evolves. . . . It is within the evolutionary movement that we place ourselves, in order to follow it to its present results, instead of recomposing these results artificially with fragments of themselves."[5] The act by which we enter into the durational movement of cosmic life is the same intuitive act by which we enter into ourselves as enduring entities. Hence the philosophical method of studying both consciousness and the material world, in function of duration, is a distinctive *metaphysical intuition,* which is irreducible to physical analysis into elementary parts and laws. Bergson offers a serious challenge to the modern assumption that the analytic or elementaristic method is fully competent to resolve all philosophical issues.

The greatest modern enemy of any claim to metaphysical intuition was Kant. As Bergson viewed him, Kant was uncritical on two counts: in accepting the conventional claims in favor of a *univocal scientific method,* and in accepting the *rationalistic description* of what metaphysical knowledge ought to be. The contention that only the method of mathematical physics gives strict knowledge, rests on the supposition that experience is all of one sort. This would follow, only on condition that experience is constituted by pouring a material content into pregiven intellectual molds. This would give a purely relative or phenomenal knowledge of the sensible world, with the consequence that metaphysics would have to be regarded as a flight from time and the senses to a realm of eternal essences or things-in-themselves. On this basis, Kant denied the possibility of metaphysics. For, either the mind operates with a sensuous intuition and is confined to the realm of time and phenomena, or else it leaves all human intuition behind and so gains only an empty and unverified set of noumenal concepts. Bergson refused to accept this dilemma, since the first part of it supposes that the scientific method *does*

---

[5] *Creative Evolution,* IV (Mitchell, 386, 390–91).

give us an intuition of temporal reality. But there is a difference between scientific and real time. Hence the proper task of metaphysics is *not to abandon the temporal and empirical plane but to penetrate it intuitively and discover its real structure,* which is hidden from the scientific method of quantitative analysis and from the Kantian inner form of sensibility or physicalist time. In metaphysics,

> we should not have to get outside of time (we are already outside of it!); we should not have to free ourselves of change (we are already only too free of it!); on the contrary, what we should have to do is to grasp change and duration in their original mobility.[6]

Metaphysics has no need to flee from the senses and appeal to some new "transcendent" powers: it has only to learn how to use our ordinary faculties in a nonutilitarian, nonspatializing way. The problem of metaphysics is not to transcend the real intuition of time but rather to seize in an original way upon this intuition, which does not fall within the competence of the scientific method. Thus Bergson proposed to rehabilitate metaphysics by challenging the philosophical validity of Kant's conception of time, as well as what he called the "Platonizing" tendency of Kant's conception of what metaphysics ought to be.

The upshot of this historical criticism is a clarification, in Bergson's own mind, of the long-confused relationship between science and philosophy (especially metaphysics, the main part of philosophy). Two positive advantages accrue from the refusal to allow that positive science can provide the method and content for philosophy. First, it *frees science* itself from the Kantian mechanism of forms of sensibility, thus allowing to science a knowledge that is not purely relative and phenomenal. For, although positive science does not capture the nature of time, it is based upon sensuous perception of the real, spatial properties of matter, which is not a mere appearance. Second, there is a long frontier shared in common by science and philosophy, once their methods and standpoints are clearly distinguished. Both are concerned with the world experienced through consciousness and the senses. There are many questions where *mutual checking* and *verification* are possible, between the two approaches. Indeed, Bergson admits that his view of metaphysics is suggested by modern science, and is a prolongation of certain scientific discoveries. The success of the evolutionary hypothesis in the biological sciences plays a con-

---

[6] *The Creative Mind,* V. "The Perception of Change" (Andison, 167).

trolling role in his own description of philosophy, as the study of duration and becoming.

Both science and philosophy have a common root in the cognitive activities of the mind or spirit (*l'esprit*). They differ, however, both in their object and in their method.[7] The *object* of science is *inert matter* or the spatial aspects of nature; the object of philosophy or metaphysics is *real duration,* as displayed both in consciousness and in the material world. Different attitudes of mind are generated by the search after these diverse objects of knowledge. The scientific mind is interested in reducing things to their quantitative correlates, so that measurement and control may be facilitated; the metaphysical mind is concerned, above all, with penetrating sympathetically into the real nature of duration, simply in order to gain speculative knowledge thereof. There is a consequent difference in the *methods* of science and metaphysics, science relying upon *analysis* and *practical intelligence,* metaphysics relying upon *intuition.*

Bergson defends the value of the scientific approach to the world, because man is first of all *homo faber,* a toolmaker, before he can become *homo sapiens,* a philosopher. *Practical intelligence* attains to a limited truth, when it treats things in function of mathematical regularities and spatial stabilities. Man is born to fabricate matter and to serve his own practical interests, through quantitative control of nature. Error creeps in, only when the report of practical common sense, science, and technology is accepted as complete and philosophically decisive. In that case, the novelty and duration of temporal process are positively ruled out from the world, rendering the more valuable part of human experience unintelligible. Bergson does not regard *intuition* as an esoteric power, granted only to the few. At least the capacity for an intuition of duration is present in every man, although he must exert himself to actuate this power within himself. Metaphysical intuition requires a deliberate detachment of mental attention from practical concerns and an attachment of it to the realm of duration, as worth knowing for its own sake. The difficulty arises from the need to make a transition from the practical to the speculative way of using the mind: there is a moral problem at the bottom of many refusals to accept the metaphysical report on the real.

Bergson gives several concrete illustrations of the difference between

---

[7] This comparison is worked out in: *The Creative Mind,* II, IV, and Note 20 (Andison, 42–52, 144–49, 305); *Creative Evolution,* III (Mitchell, 196–210).

the analytico-scientific method and that of metaphysical intuition. The contrast is one between *going around* an object and *entering directly into* it, between what William James called "knowledge about" and "knowledge of acquaintance" (to which corresponds Maritain's distinction between perinoetic and dianoetic knowledge). It is the difference between reading impersonally about the adventures of a hero in a novel, and allowing oneself to share the hero's feelings, "live the scenes with him." The point is also brought out, by contrasting one's observation of another person's movement of his arm and the experience of moving one's own arm.

> We call intuition here the *sympathy* by which one is transported into the interior of an object in order to coincide with what there is unique and consequently inexpressible in it. Analysis, on the contrary, is the operation which reduces the object to elements already known, that is, common to that object and to others. Analyzing then consists in expressing a thing in terms of what is not it.[8]

Thus science translates its data into mathematical symbols, whereas metaphysics is defined by Bergson as *"the science which claims to dispense with symbols."*[9] It studies things directly in their interior reality, rather than in their mathematical substitutes.

By "symbols," however, Bergson means, not only mathematical signs and spatial images, but also all *concepts* of the *intelligence*. He attempts to restrict the terms "intelligence" and "intellect" to the mental power of manipulating matter for practical purposes. Taken in this way, intellect is the characteristic power employed by practical common sense and the positive sciences, and shares in their essential limitations. Like Schopenhauer's "reason," Bergsonian intelligence produces concepts for the purely practical purpose of supplementing the deficiencies of our sense perception of matter and filling in the gaps between perceptions, so that the spatial world can be treated as a controllable unity. Concepts yield only a spatial, mensurational, and utilitarian sort of knowledge, at the antipodes to the durational knowledge sought by metaphysics. Hence, at least in principle, Berg-

---

[8] *The Creative Mind*, VI, "Introduction to Metaphysics" (Andison, 190). Bergson's "Introduction to Metaphysics" (Andison, 187–237) is an authentic condensation of his own views on method and metaphysics. On the central problem of a distinctively intellectual intuition in metaphysics, with special reference to Kant and Bergson, cf. R. Jolivet, "L'intuition intellectuelle et le problème de la métaphysique," *Archives de Philosophie*, XI (1934), 109–219.

[9] *The Creative Mind*, VI (Andison, 191).

sonian metaphysics seeks to dispense with concepts and to rely, for its basic insights, upon intuitions alone.

In practice, however, Bergson found that this restriction of intellect and concepts to one aspect of their scope, is arbitrary and impossible to maintain. At least indirectly, he was often forced to concede the presence of *other functions of intelligence* than those which subserve the ends of positive science and human practical needs. He even admitted that

> concepts are indispensable to it [metaphysics], for all the other sciences ordinarily work with concepts, and metaphysics cannot get along without the other sciences. But it is strictly itself only when it goes beyond the concept, or at least when it frees itself of the inflexible and ready-made concepts and creates others very different from those we usually handle, I mean flexible, mobile, almost fluid representations, always ready to mould themselves on the fleeting forms of intuition.[10]

From this passage, it follows not only that concepts are needed by metaphysics in the *mediate* sense that it co-operates with other sciences (in which concepts are used), but also that concepts of an *appropriate* sort are immediately required in metaphysics itself. The experience of the intuition of duration remains inexpressible, until it is brought to the state of communicable knowledge, through the concept and judgment. Bergson is aware that not all our concepts can perform this office, but from this it only follows that conceptual adjustments must be made at each level of inquiry. Furthermore, he realizes that the basic metaphysical intuition affirms something existent, which transcends the conceptual order, insofar as the latter terminates in the order of essences. Bergson advises that special vigilance be exercised, lest we reduce the existential reality of duration to an essential structure, such as is ordinarily signified by concepts at the physical level. He does not firmly recognize, however, that the existential reality can be expressed *intellectually* in the act of *judgment* of existence, even though it does not fall directly within the scope of conceptual apprehension. Hence he cannot avail himself of the judgment of existence, in order to achieve a conceptual expression of the act of existing of real things.

The above text does reveal Bergson's concern for having some sort of conceptual way of grasping duration. But he has not liber-

---

[10] *Loc. cit.* (Andison, 198). Cf. F. Grégoire, "La collaboration de l'intuition et de l'intelligence," *Revue Internationale de Philosophie*, III (1949), 392–406.

ated himself from the same Platonizing tendency deplored in Descartes and Kant, since he poses the problem as that of *reproducing* in concepts, the very flow of durational reality. He wants to transfer to the conceptual order the very same mode of being as is found in the real order, so that the concept will not distort the real. But this rests on the general assumption that knowledge consists in a confrontation of like by like, rather than in an assimilation of the unlike, through an intentional union. In cognition, the mind becomes *intentionally united* with the thing known, but the natural mode of being of the thing known remains *other* than the natural being of its concept. Bergson's difficulty arises from regarding all concepts as constructural frameworks, and then imagining how such scaffoldings can be given a direct likeness to their real referents. The only way in which this can be done (as the novelist, Proust, showed), is by reducing concepts and judgments to the condition of vague and floating images, but then metaphysics is transformed into art.

Bergson determines the *object of metaphysics* in conformity with the nature of the primary intuition, since the metaphysical method is intuitive. Now, whatever one may think about the reality of the external world, we certainly do have an intuition of our inner life — this is his bedrock certitude. Hence, he defines *intuition,* in terms of its object, as "the direct vision of the mind by the mind . . . the attention that the mind gives to itself, over and above, while it is fixed upon matter, its object."[11] The consequence of this definition is that metaphysics itself must be regarded as *"a science of the mind . . .* principally the *intimate knowledge of the mind by the mind."*[12] Bergson never revokes this basic view about metaphysics, since philosophy is distinguished from the positive sciences mainly through the intuition of inner duration or the temporal life of the mind. Yet he does not want to end in metaphysical idealism. Hence he also holds the realistic thesis that human experience includes a direct perception of material things, in their "absolute" or non-phenomenal nature. Thus, even the geometrizing intellect and the quantitative sciences report upon a real aspect of matter. But in order to reach the temporal center of the material world, it must be seen in its durational process. This can be done only through an extension

---

[11] *The Creative Mind,* II, "Introduction (Part II). Stating the Problems" (Andison, 35, 92).

[12] *Loc. cit.,* and Note 26 (Andison, 92, 306; italics added).

of the original intuition of internal duration. Hence, without denying that metaphysics is *primarily* a science of the mind or psychic duration, Bergson adds that *secondarily* it is also a science of whatever is durationally essential and living in material nature.

A final problem is the relation between *metaphysics* and *existence*. Bergson declared that "an existence can be given only in an experience,"[13] whether that of interior intuition or of exterior perception. This raises the metaphysical question of whether the existence given in experience is a perfection confined, by its nature, to duration and the temporal mode of reality. Bergson was reluctant to admit any supratemporal existence, since he feared that this would make metaphysics revert to the Greek search after subsisting eternal essences. Hence he subordinated existence to duration and made metaphysics a study of the real *sub ratione durationis,* rather than *sub ratione entis et esse.* He did this, out of faithfulness to the actual starting point of human cognition in real being, known under the conditions of matter and temporal change (through external perception and inner intuition). Thus Bergson fell short of the metaphysical separative judgment, which states that, although being and existence are *given to us* under conditions of matter and temporal change, they are not confined, *in their own perfection,* to these conditions. Yet certain consequences of his doctrine point in the direction of this separative act. For Bergson, experience is *not* confined to sense perception, since its major metaphysical constituent is inner intuition. Furthermore, duration is *not* confined to the material world, since it is also the energizing principle of psychic life. But he knew of no way in which he might add that existence can be known *not* to be confined as such to temporal duration, without thereby leading to a metaphysical evacuation of existential reality, as given through intuition.

Hence Bergsonian metaphysics gravitates toward becoming rather than being, toward duration rather than existence, precisely from a failure to resolve the question of the analogical predication of existence and essence, as well as of experience and duration. Because being, in its essential and existential principles, was never disengaged analogically from the concrete conditions under which it is given in human experience, Bergson never fully liberated metaphysics from the danger of *psychologism.* This was his legacy from Mill and the French spiritualist philosophers, Maine de Biran and Felix Ravaisson.

---

[13] *The Creative Mind,* II (Andison, 57).

The two latter masters opened his eyes to the riches of man's interior life, but they did not enable him to rise above the alternative of choosing either Greek essentialism or psychologism as the standpoint of metaphysics.

## 3. THREE METAPHYSICAL PROBLEMS

Examination of the data of consciousness enables Bergson to deal with three major metaphysical problems: the nature of change and time, the reality of freedom, and the relation between matter and spirit. The first of these issues has the widest metaphysical import. It is approached by Bergson, however, in the same way as the latter two questions: through an introspective study of our awareness of internal duration.

1. *Change and Time.* By an act of *mental ascesis* or conversion of attention in an inward direction, we can remove the petrified layers of the physicalist conception of the mind. From the latter standpoint, Mill had pictured our inner life as a series of discrete states, strung along together as so many beads upon a string.[14] The string itself was called the self. But Mill never explained how such a combination of beads and string could even approximate to our intimate awareness of the unity and temporal flow of personal life. This failure to find the *real self* shows that scientific techniques are unsuited to investigate this domain of reality, which is open only to metaphysical means. The method of analysis breaks up the original stream of psychic life into a series of halts or states (spatialized time), whereas the method of intuition grasps our inner existence in its own nature as change and temporal duration. The philosopher must make a deliberate shift from scientific analysis to metaphysical intuition, in order to comprehend the nature of change and time, as revealed in our own interior life.

Bergson sums up, in two propositions, the findings of intuition concerning *change.*

> *We shall think of all change, all movement, as being absolutely indivisible. . . . There are changes, but there are underneath the change no things which change: change has no need of a support. There are movements, but there is no inert or invariable object which moves: movement does not imply a mobile.*[15]

[14] This image is recurrent in Bergson's treatments of the problem of the self. Cf. *The Creative Mind,* II, VI (Andison, 83, 203–04, 218–20); *Creative Evolution,* I (Mitchell, 3–4).

[15] *The Creative Mind,* V (Andison, 167–68, 173); cf. *Matter and Memory,* IV

His first point is that the continuity or uninterrupted character of the change experienced in the flow of psychic life cannot be translated adequately into any series of snapshot views, run along together rapidly after the manner of a movie sequence. We should not think of inner duration as being constructed out of a clever patchwork of still pictures, for this reduces the distinctive nature of vital and immanent operations to a mechanical, spatialized process. It may be *useful* to make this reduction, but pragmatism has not proved its case that the useful and the *true* are one. One dynamic phase of mental life grows out of another, and carries along with it the tendencies of what went before. The second proposition is a consequence of the effort to avoid spatialized imagery, in dealing with mental processes. It is only a habit of our visual sense that prompts us to look for a solid support of psychic operations, as though they could be likened to a river standing in need of a bed, entirely distinct from the river and immobile in respect to it. What we intuit within ourselves is a self-contained and indivisible flow of actions, bearing their own substantiality along with them. They are not like beads sliding rapidly down a string or like Galileo's polished balls of metal, which require a channel, down which to roll into the conscious present. The physicomorphic interpretation of inner change belies the actual testimony of reflective consciousness.

In his discussion of *time,* Bergson modifies somewhat his position on the absolute *indivisibility* of change.[16] He identifies real duration with time, perceived as indivisible. Yet he admits that there is a qualitative multiplicity and hence some kind of succession in the temporal flux. But time is not constituted by a succession of discrete, quantitative parts. Hence the indivisibility of change and time means the impossibility of analyzing their real trajectory into a series of points and lines, which would be the equivalent of a spatial simultaneity of quantitative parts. Bergson is more forthright in declaring what the temporal succession is *not,* than in determining its positive

---

(Paul and Palmer translation, 246–61). In later years, Bergson protested that he had not intended to deny substance, in Heraclitean fashion, but only to rectify the imagery surrounding it, so that one may correctly represent the persistence of existences; cf. *The Creative Mind,* Note 23 (Andison, 305). The further questions remain of whether substance primarily means persistence of existence, and whether it can be represented properly by *any* images.

16 *Ibid.,* V (Andison, 176–80). In *Time and Free Will,* Conclusion (Pogson translation, 226), duration is defined as "a qualitative multiplicity, with no likeness to number."

nature in a general, metaphysical way. He is primarily interested in time as an inner experience or "lived time." As befits a careful student of Greek philosophy, he stresses the contribution of the soul to this real time. The concretely experienced, temporal present is constituted by the active orientation of one's attention. Present duration means the span included within the ongoing attention of consciousness. This *act of attending* keeps the past alive, and is creative of the range of the future. The real foundation for temporal distinctions is the *interpenetration* and unbroken, rather than discrete, succession of our psychic states, as they coalesce with and grow out of one another. Real time is constituted by the relation between one's act of attention and the concrete flow of inner, vital actions. When this stream of inner experience is perceived to be an indivisible and continuous flow, real duration or time is being intuited.

Bergson uses the famous metaphor of a *rolling snowball,* to convey the unbroken growth and self-accumulating process of the duration of the self.[17] Our temporal experience moves along under its own impetus, gathering particular states to itself, preserving them in a single whole, and moving forward with the ever increasing weight of the past. The enduring self is nothing distinct from this rolling snowball but is precisely the forward-going movement, inclusive of all its past accretions, its present consistency, and its hurtling march toward the future. Like all images, however, this one breaks down at critical places. For, the comparison is likely to encourage the core-and-layers notion of inner life, which Bergson seeks to exorcise. Although the metaphor is stimulating, it cannot settle the metaphysical issue about *how* temporal becoming is undivided or *whether* it is a self-substantializing process. Bergson rightly wants to arouse our mind to make an active search for the nature of change and time, but these questions cannot be settled solely by piling one image upon another.

A discerning evaluation of Bergson's theory of change was made by his onetime student and Thomistic critic, Jacques Maritain.[18] The latter pointed out the discrepancy between Bergson's original experi-

---

[17] *Creative Evolution,* I (Mitchell, 2); in *The Creative Mind,* III (Andison, 112, 13), Bergson uses the image of a gradually expanding rubber balloon. In reading Bergson, it is important to observe his deliberate use of metaphor and to note the limitations of this method in metaphysics.
[18] Read J. Maritain, *Bergsonian Philosophy and Thomism,* Chapter XVI, "The Metaphysics of Bergson" (303–24).

ence of change and his conceptual formulation and generalization of the given intuition. This marks the distance between a psychological description and a metaphysical explanation of change. Bergson's metaphysical propositions about change both deny more, and affirm more, than is warranted by the experiences upon which they are founded. The psychological description denies that the movement of inner life is actually *divided,* whereas the metaphysical proposition denies that it is in any way *divisible.* The most that can be gained from the experience itself is assurance that psychic change is not composed of discrete, quantitative parts. We have a conviction that the several phases of our inner experience constitute an uninterrupted passage, an actually undivided transit. But Bergson's own remark about the qualitative interpenetration and unbroken succession of these phases indicates that real change is not incompatible with some sort of potential parts. Furthermore, Bergson's metaphysical propositions affirm more than his intuition of psychic change actually warrants. Our experience of inner duration reveals a continuity and coalescence of mental acts, which cannot be assimilated to the beads-on-a-string image. But it does not support the metaphysical contention that these mental processes are *self-substantializing.* Although the core-and-layers notion of the relation between substance and its modifications is discredited, the psychological experience does not dictate that the becoming itself must be regarded as substantial. Mental changes can be satisfactorily treated by the psychologists, without having recourse to the hypothesis of an "inert or invariable object" underlying them. But this does not settle any metaphysical issues concerning the proper relation between substance and accidents or between the changing thing and change.

In short, Bergson's fear of being imprecise in metaphysics led him to reduce the general problem of change to an introspective study of psychic changes and, then, to derive from particular psychological descriptions some general metaphysical conclusions, which the purely psychological approach to internal experiences does not warrant. This was the price paid for equating the object of metaphysics with duration, considered mainly as a psychological experience.

2. *Human Freedom.* The greatest enemy of the libertarian outlook is the theory of spatialized time. For there is a *real simultaneity* among the points in a spatial trajectory or among the parts in an extended span. It is only for methodological reasons that points not yet covered by a time-path are said to be nonexistent. Conceiving

human temporal activity in this way, one naturally regards time as the unfurling of a fan or the unrolling of a film.[19] The entire future is already there in basic pattern, precontained like the potential energy in a wound-up spring. This spatial view of our temporal decisions encouraged the Spinozistic conception of human freedom, as being an acquiescence in the unwinding of the divinely necessitated causal series. It also led to Leibniz' way of imagining the realm of possible choices as already pre-existing and exercising efficient causality upon our will. Remove the confusion between real time and the mechanistic substitute for time, Bergson suggests, and the rationalistic difficulties about our freedom are swept away as so many mirages, due to the physicalistic approach to man.

Bergson grounds his positive account of freedom upon his own theory of duration. For him, freedom does not consist in rational domination over the act of choice but in *spontaneity* or the forward surge of duration. From this standpoint, duration is the *continuous life of a memory,* prolonging the past into the present.[20] Hence concrete consciousness contains no moment without a memory, no present existence without a fringe of the past around it. There is no necessary determination by the past, if for no other reason than that the past is not a separate agent but the memorial aspect of present, dynamic duration. The act of enduring is always original and unforeseeable, since it is constantly appropriating a *new* moment of the past. Spatialized time is inert, homogeneous, and necessitated; lived duration is causally efficacious, qualitatively heterogeneous, and free. "The free act takes place in time which is flowing and not in time which has already flown. Freedom is therefore a fact, and among the facts which we observe there is none clearer,"[21] provided only that we make the effort to observe our real duration and not its spatial surrogate. Bergson refuses to define freedom, however, on the ground that

---

[19] Cf. *The Creative Mind*, I, III (Andison, 20–21, 109–10, 122). Bergson's attack upon possibility was provoked by a view of the possibles that can be expressed in such imagery.

[20] *Ibid.*, VI (Andison, 211). E. P. Cronan, S.S., "Bergson and Free Will," *The New Scholasticism*, XI (1937), 1–57, collects all the relevant texts on freedom and shows that Bergson cannot avoid identifying freedom with pure spontaneity and vital determinism, as long as he rules out any rooting of freedom in reason and any intellectual influence upon the act of choice (on the ground that the intellect is a spatializing faculty, whereas duration and choice are qualitative). See also, S. Cantin, "Henri Bergson et le problème de la liberté," *Laval Théologique et Philosophique*, I (1945), 71–102.

[21] *Time and Free Will*, III (Pogson, 221).

definition requires analysis into parts already constituted in being, and hence already subject to essential determinism.

Bergson deftly removes an empiricist objection to freedom which Hume and Mill had based upon the ability to predict human actions.[22] He distinguishes between two kinds of prediction in human affairs: *probable forecast* and infallible foresight. The ordinary claim to prediction merely maintains that a certain action is consistent or inconsistent with what we know about a man's character, from his past actions. What we declare to be "out of character" for a man is nevertheless within his power to perform, so that probable forecasting does not impugn freedom of action. But the strict determinist contends that, if all the antecedents of an action were perfectly known, we would have *infallibly true foresight* of the act itself. To this, Bergson counters with a distinction between two ways of assimilating the antecedents of an act: dynamically and statically. *Dynamically,* the observer may try to identify himself completely with the agent in question — but then he must bring himself to the very moment in which the act is to be performed. He must appropriate *all* its concrete conditions and principles, which are no longer mere antecedents of the final act but its constituents. Foresight is thereby removed entirely. There is nothing left to *foresee* but only to *do* and, since the observer is now indistinguishable from the agent, the ultimate decision can be known only in the act of self-determination. Hence the choice can be known dynamically, only as the act of a self-determining or free agent.

*Statically,* the observer may attempt to describe, from the outside, the psychic states of the agent. To do this exhaustively, however, he would have to describe not only the individual states of mind but also their relative intensity. The intensity is qualitative, but it can be described only in quantitative terms of being more or less important. Important for what? This question can be answered only by comparing a given state with the entire course of the agent's life, including the final act which, by hypothesis, has not yet occurred. Only by begging the question of being able to know this final act, can the exhaustive knowledge of the antecedents be gained. Hence dynamically, the scientific determinists confuse making a decision with foreseeing a decision to be made; statically, they must beg

---

[22] *Loc. cit.* (Pogson, 183–98).

the question of the possibility of foresight, in order to acquire adequate knowledge for infallible prediction.

3. *Matter, Memory, and Spirit.* In earlier modern philosophy, the mind-body problem had led up the blind alleys of parallelism and epiphenomenalism. Bergson proposed a new way of treating the question: in terms of a metaphysico-psychological study of memory and perception. His solution depended on the establishment of three relationships: between matter and perception, between perception and memory, and between memory and spirit. Roughly speaking, these comparisons led him to espouse a monism of duration or consciousness, within which a dualistic distinction between the extremes of matter and spirit can be drawn.

Bergson suggests that *pure perception,* unmixed with memory, is the same as *matter.* Usually, matter and perception are distinguished as the divisible and the indivisible, but what is really divisible is not matter itself but the spatial relations, constructed in matter by practical intelligence. Matter as such exists precisely as it is perceived. Since it is perceived as an image, it is nothing more than an aggregate of images. It is an equilibrium of the parts of consciousness among themselves, a static limit toward which duration tends. There are no hidden parts or powers of matter, since its reality is nothing more than it appears to be. Matter and perception are homogeneous, being related not as distinct object and subject but as whole and part. Perception is that portion of the totality of matter or images which concerns our needs and bodily actions, and hence upon which we have some immediate hold. Pure perception is a coincidence between subject and object, spirit and matter. Starting from this common ground, one may work either *downward* into the further ranges of *matter* (where simultaneity, necessity, and spatial relations prevail) or *upward* into the more distinctive region of *spirit* (where progress, freedom, and time are found). Thus perception is "mind without memory," and material nature — as Ravaisson put it — is sheer oblivion or "a slumber of the mind."[23]

---

[23] *Matter and Memory,* IV (Paul-Palmer, 297); *The Creative Mind,* IX, "The Life and Work of Ravaisson" (Andison, 283). On perception and matter, cf. *Matter and Memory,* IV, and Summary and Conclusion (Paul-Palmer, 259–66, 291–97, 300–09). Bergson's conception of matter should be compared with Schelling's remark about material nature as petrified intelligence, and with Hegel's reference to it as unconscious thought. In "La genèse idéale de la matière chez Bergson," *Revue de Métaphysique et*

## BERGSON ON THE DIVERSE DIRECTIONS OF REAL DURATION

Spirit and Freedom

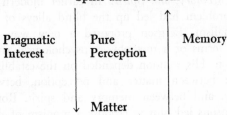

| Pragmatic | Pure | Memory |
| Interest | Perception | |

↓ Matter

Pure perception, however, is an abstraction, which needs to be restored to the twofold context of memory and the practical drives of the body. There never actually occurs a perception so wholly engrossed in the present, that it does not also involve a duration or prolongation of the past. The transition upward from matter or pure perception to spirit is made in function of the operations of memory. Bergson accentuates the difference between *memory* and the *brain,* since the former is associated with spirit, and the latter with matter. *"Memory is something other than a function of the brain, and there is not merely a difference of degree, but of kind, between perception and recollection."*[24] The brain is an instrument of action but not of representation. It does not receive and store up the sensory images but regulates their effective use for the ends of the body. The brain selects those recollections which will promote action in the present and the satisfaction of bodily needs. But the function of recollecting is intrinsically independent of the cerebral mechanism and of pure perception. Empirical studies of brain lesions and various sorts of aphasia show that brain injuries result in a weakening of the general, pragmatic vitality of memory, rather than in a point-by-point obliteration of particular memories. Hence the brain and body coincide with only that small portion of memory and spiritual life which is geared to our motor habits, for practical purposes.

These considerations enable Bergson to avoid what he dubs "the psychophysiological paralogism," i.e., the attempt to argue from the undeniable *fact* of some kind of union between mind and body

*de Morale,* LVII (1952), 325–48, M. Capek likens Bergson's doctrine to the view of Leibniz that a body is mind insofar as it is concentrated upon the present moment or as lacking memory and thought.

24 *Ibid.,* Summary and Conclusion (Paul-Palmer, 315).

to the special *hypothesis* of parallelism, upon which materialism itself ultimately rests.[25] The fact of the union is evident from the study of both pure perception (which is mind in its lowest function, and yet also a part of matter) and concrete consciousness (in which spirit or pure memory intersects with matter or pure perception). But it does not follow from the fact of some sort of union, that matter and spirit must be correlated by way of a complete one-to-one correspondence of all the acts of both series. Spirit is co-ordinated with matter, only in that narrow region where memory seeks a point of insertion into the present for useful ends, for what Bergson calls the pragmatic *attention to life*. On its own plane of reality, spirit displays itself as free activity and duration.

Since the body does not produce the recollections of spirit but only converts them into practical projects, Bergson also holds that the *immortality* of the human spirit is highly probable, and that the burden of proof rests with those who deny it. If "experience proves that only a minute part of conscious life is conditioned by the brain, it will follow that the suppression of the brain will probably leave conscious life subsisting."[26] This is all the certitude that can be derived from a study of interior consciousness. Both in this special instance and in the general question of change, Bergson leaves unclarified the metaphysical meaning of "subsistence," and the peculiar sense in which it applies to the human spirit.

In order to explain the unity-in-distinction of matter and spirit, as testified by our consciousness, Bergson makes a compromise between monism and dualism. He establishes the unity of matter and spirit by giving a *monistic* interpretation of pure perception, which is described both as consciousness or duration, at a minimal level of activity, and as a pragmatic slice of matter. Similarly, matter is viewed, monistically, as a sphere of sluggish images, sleeping spirit, or solidified consciousness. Bergson is able to make this meaning

---

[25] H. Bergson, "Le paralogisme psycho-physiologique," *Revue de Métaphysique et de Morale*, XII (1904), 895–908; cf. *Matter and Memory*, Introduction (Paul-Palmer, xv–xvi).

[26] *The Creative Mind*, II (Andison, 53). In *The Two Sources of Morality and Religion*, III, Bergson is mainly interested in the relation between immortality and the participation of mystics in the eternal life of the divine nature. "Can the after-life, which is apparently assured to our soul by the simple fact that, even here below, a great part of this activity is independent of the body, be identified with that of the life into which, even here below, certain privileged souls insert themselves?" (Audra and Brereton translation, 252–53.)

seem plausible by identifying matter with the *perceptual conditions* for grasping matter. He reduces matter to one set of its relations, and hence he does not escape the objections brought against Berkeley on this score. He supposes that the mind becomes its object in a *physical,* rather than an intentional, way and that, therefore, our images of material things are the same in kind as their objects, at least at some point of intersection. If Bergson also draws distinctions between matter and spirit, he does so, only within the context of the monism of consciousness or duration. His *dualism* describes the differences between the lower and the higher reaches of consciousness and durational reality. Perception and memory, matter and spirit, are polar opposites within the embracing realm of duration. They are the minimal and maximal extremes of operation, toward which individual consciousness can be orientated.

In this way, Bergson hopes to resolve the problem of the one and the many, as exemplified in man. But his compromise between monism and dualism postpones, rather than achieves, a firm solution. He alternates between a *psychological* monism (the oneness of the stream of duration or consciousness) and a *functional* dualism (the diversity of directions in which consciousness can move).[27] The consequence is not a coherent doctrine on the analogical unity and multiplicity of experience, but a rapid oscillation between images conveying the unity of personal life and images suggesting its many phases. Basically, the difficulty comes from Bergson's failure to develop a theory of the analogical predication of "duration," which fulfills the function supplied by "being" in other systems. To work out this doctrine, however, he would have to determine whether or not duration applies to God's nature and whether God or human consciousness is the primary analogate in the predication. But these issues are left unsettled, even in his formal treatment of creative evolution.

## 4. CREATIVE EVOLUTION

Bergson's alternation between psychological monism and functional dualism is precisely what he needs to avoid the charge of *solipsism.*[28] The passage from the primary object of intuition (inner psychic

---

[27] Cf. N. C. Barr, "The Dualism of Bergson," *The Philosophical Review*, XXII (1913), 639–52.

[28] This problem is dealt with, somewhat obliquely, in *The Creative Mind*, V, VI (Andison, 158, 217–21).

duration) to its secondary object (duration as the principle of the material universe) supposes that durational reality is the same, wherever found. The problem of the transition will then resolve itself into a description of how individual consciousness can move, by sympathetic expansion, from the inner to the outer realm. Both Plotinus and Maine de Biran come to Bergson's aid in this connection, the former to stress the *dynamic connectedness* of all things, and the latter to underline the role of *will* in intuition (a point also stressed by Schopenhauer and Nietzsche). The duration present in us is in contact with a whole series of continuous durations, analogously present in all other things. We are joined, by a bond of sympathy, with the rest of the universe. It is only necessary to dilate the act of will, at the center of the intuition of one's own duration. Through this expansion of the will, the individual can transcend his private consciousness, in the direction of other consciousnesses and the rest of the material world.

Viewed cosmologically, concrete duration is the *élan vital,* the *vital impetus,* animating all enduring things.[29] Bergson presents his theory of the vital impetus as an alternative to both the *mechanism* of Spencer and the *finalism* of Leibniz. Both mechanistic and finalistic explanations of life err, in modeling the principle of vital change upon a spatial pattern. Spencer attributes evolutionary development to outside, mechanical forces and accidental modifications, whereas Leibniz traces all changes to the tug of a predetermined future. Both thinkers reduce vital organization to a manufacturing operation, an assembling of materials into a spatial entity. Only when the evolutionary process is comprehended intuitively and nonspatially, can it be seen in its proper temporal reality. The onward rush of the vital impetus is the march of the past into and beyond the present. The past is not an effete slipping away but an efficacious *advancing-forward* of duration, to fill the present and press forward to a novel future. Contrary to Spencer, the development of living things depends primarily upon the internal impetus, rather than upon an external shock, indispensable though the latter may be. And contrary to Leibniz, development leads to original, free forms of life, and not to results read off from an ideal blueprint.

The *élan* may be studied either in its own nature or as it manifests

---

[29] Cf. *Creative Evolution,* I (Mitchell, 92–102), with special reference to how the impetus displays itself in "the infinite complexity of the organ and the supreme simplicity of the function" (*ibid.,* 94), in the case of the eye and vision.

itself under material conditions. Bergson believes that he can state its essential nature, since the movement of life tends toward reflective consciousness, in human experience. Convinced that life is basically psychological in nature and conscious (or supraconscious) in origin, he appeals to our own free actions for evidence. Since our freedom is primarily an urge toward self-realization, Bergson defines the vital impetus itself as *"a need of creation."*[30] It is a *finite* force, however, one that operates against obstacles. When we lift our arm voluntarily, we experience some vestige of the pure affirmation of life and movement. But, left to itself, the arm will fall and come to rest, so that our actual pursuit of creative purposes depends upon counteracting the inertial power of matter. Hence most of Bergson's discussion of the life-urge considers it in reference to the material context.

From this latter perspective, his theory of creative evolution revolves around a fundamental, cosmological dualism between *life* and *matter* (corresponding to the earlier psychological dualism between memory and perception, spirit and matter). The gushing flow of duration or life is somehow subject to arrest. Its movement can be congealed, and the congealed parts constitute matter. In the universe at large, matter embraces: the points of arrest of movement, the tendency toward the degradation of cosmic energy, the process of descent toward quiescence and necessity. Contrariwise, concrete duration or life is a countermovement against the fixity of material obstacles, a storing-up of energy, an ascent to the zone of free movement and creation. Matter unmakes itself; life makes itself, in a contrary direction. This inverse relationship between life and matter enables Bergson to define the vital movement as *"a reality which is making itself in a reality which is unmaking itself. . . . All our analyses show us, in life, an effort to re-mount the incline that matter descends."*[31] If the downward plunge of matter cannot wholly be stopped, at least it can be retarded by counterefforts at creation of vital forms. *Creative evolution* is this ceaseless movement of life to reverse the process of matter, and to establish the values of freedom and consciousness.

Bergson's cosmological theory of matter perpetuates the ambiguity

[30] *Ibid.*, III (Mitchell, 265; italics added). On the meaning of evolutionary "creation," cf. *loc. cit.* (Mitchell, 265–86).
[31] *Creative Evolution*, III (Mitchell, 261, 259). On life and matter, see *ibid.*, II, III (Mitchell, 103–04, 249–64).

found in his psychological approach to it.[32] Matter is both a factor within the movement of life itself and a counterforce operating against the interests of life. Life creates matter at those points where it interrupts its own vital flow, and yet these interruptions themselves are due to the hindering presence of matter. Otherwise expressed, matter *is* a congealment of life's process, and yet is the *cause* of the congealment of this movement. It is both a passive drag upon life and an agency working contrary to life. This ambiguity shows that Bergson gives both a wider and a narrower meaning to life. In the *broader* or monistic sense, life is synonymous with all degrees of duration and consciousness, including their lower limits, where they assume the form of matter. But life can also refer precisely to that aspect of duration which is a positive movement toward freedom, spiritual consciousness, and the activity of memory. In this *restricted* or dualistic sense, life stands in opposition to matter, since the latter signifies a frozen state of consciousness, quantitative determinism, and pure perception. Bergson's cosmological treatment of creative evolution cannot be divorced from his psychological principles of interpretation of matter and spirit, where the compromise between the monistic and dualistic views of duration was first proposed.

The course of the vital impetus in the material world may be represented by

> a shell, which suddenly bursts into fragments, which fragments, being themselves shells, burst in their turn into fragments destined to burst again, and so on for a time incommensurably long. . . . When a shell bursts, the particular way it breaks is explained both by the explosive force of the powder it contains and by the resistance of the metal. So of the way life breaks into individuals and species. It depends, we think, on two series of causes: the resistance life meets from inert matter, and the explosive force — due to an unstable balance of tendencies — which life bears within itself.[33]

Evolution is *divergent*, since life tends to be *dissociative* as well as cumulative. In defense of the dissociative or explosive character of life, Bergson appeals again to our experience of psychic duration. Just

---

[32] This difficulty is urged by G. N. Dolson, "The Philosophy of Henri Bergson," *The Philosophical Review*, XIX (1910), 579–96; XX (1911) 46–58; cf. A. W. Moore, "Bergson and Pragmatism," *ibid.*, XXI (1912), 397–414.

[33] *Creative Evolution*, II (Mitchell, 103). On the divergent evolutionary tendencies of accumulation and dissociation, cf. *loc. cit.* (Mitchell, 104–07).

as our personal life is a unity, formed by the interpenetration of many qualitative acts, so life in general is originally an actual unity, containing a potential multiplicity of forms. Life sends its current through matter, which tends to split up and individualize the vital movement. Although matter seeks thereby to dissipate the force of the vital impetus, the latter adapts itself to the individuating conditions of matter, and thus actuates the various forms of life implicit within itself. The various biological species and individuals comprise the history of life's struggle with matter, and the positive achievements of life's constant fragmentation. In turning the conditions of matter to good account, the Bergsonian vital impetus displays a cunning and patience reminiscent of Hegel's reason and Schopenhauer's will, considered as cosmic forces.

The two common functions of all living things are accumulation and dissociation. The *cumulative* operation gradually catches up usable energy from the material universe, so that this energy may be released suddenly, in furtherance of creative evolution. *Dissociation* or *bifurcation* is the way in which energy is canalized and expended along several lines, through explosive actions on the part of the life principle. Both functions are *contingent,* in the actual forms they assume in evolutionary history. Life could have started on earth otherwise than with the simple, protoplasmic masses that actually appeared, and could have dispensed entirely with organisms. The flood of vital energies does spread out in many directions. Divergent evolution is more realistic than Spencer's strictly necessary process and unilinear progress. It takes account of the blind alleys, retrogressions, arrests, accidental mutations, disorders and novel emergences, constituting the actual biological record. The mainstream of life bifurcates again and again, in its constant quest for more adequately organized vehicles. Each species behaves as though the movement of life terminates with itself. But in fact, life is an immense wave, using and passing over all species and individuals, engulfing them all in its common career.

The first great split in the evolutionary flood gives rise to the *plants* and *animals*.[34] Although they possess several properties in common, these two kingdoms are distinguished by their contrasting ways of emphasizing these common traits. Vegetable forms of life

---

[34] On the several evolutionary bifurcations, see *Creative Evolution,* II (Mitchell, 111–42); special attention is paid to the contrast between instinct and intelligence (*loc. cit.,* 142–59).

tend to be fixed and insensible, whereas animals are characterized by their tendency toward mobility and consciousness. Mind seems to have fallen asleep and become torpid in the plants; but in animal organisms it develops nervous systems, conscious activities, and locomotion. At the animal level, the major achievement is the development of the sensorimotor system. Here, the bifurcation of the vital impetus leads along two main paths: the arthropods and the vertebrates. The line of arthropods culminates in the *hymenoptera* (a specialized order of insects, including ants, bees, and wasps), while *man* is the supreme form of vertebrate life. Instinct is most highly developed in the hymenoptera, intelligence in man. Thus Bergson regards *vegetative torpor, instinct, and intelligence* as the three most general results of creative evolution. Vegetative, instinctive, and intelligent forms of life are not three successive stages of the same tendency. Rather, they are divergent directions taken by the dissociative, vital impetus, and hence they differ *in kind* and not merely in degree. They represent three fundamentally different splits or creative experiments at overcoming the inertness of matter.

Being finite, nature's *élan* must choose, eventually, between two higher ways of acting on the material world, for the satisfaction of practical needs. It can either produce organized instruments, which are natural parts or appendages of the organism, or else give the organism the power to shape for itself tools, made out of unorganized materials. *Instinct* is the ability to use *organized,* natural instruments, which are the specialized parts of the body; *intelligence* is the ability to construct artificial instruments out of *unorganized* materials. These are divergent, but equally fitting, ways of resolving the problem of practical needs. Each power has its advantages and drawbacks. Instinct has its instruments at hand for instant and sure use, enabling it to perform, with perfect facility, operations of the greatest intricacy. But its instruments are highly specialized and invariable, so that instinct remains fixed and unprogressive. It satisfies immediate needs quite promptly but it does not open out new perspectives for conscious effort. Intelligence has the initial disadvantage of not having appendages to satisfy its immediate needs, and hence of being under pressure to manufacture its own tools. Moreover, instruments are produced only at great cost, and without any guarantee of smooth, successful functioning. On the other hand, intelligence is limited to no set groove but can make indefinite progress, both in improving its instruments and in putting them to new uses. The very perfection of instinct *closes off* the circle of conscious life, in ants and bees, too easily and completely. In man, however, every need satisfied by intelligence creates a new one, thus keeping his conscious activity *constantly open,* free, and creative.

From an evolutionary standpoint, then, Bergson reaffirms his conviction that *intelligence* is *"the faculty of manufacturing artificial objects, especially tools to make tools, and of indefinitely varying the manufacture. . . .* Postulate action, and the very form of the intellect can be deduced from it."[35] Given the exigency of the human organism to satisfy its needs, through producing its own tools and acting on the environment, it follows that the intellect is ordained *to think matter,* in utilitarian terms, and to have the unorganized solid as its proper object. This confirms the methodological doctrine that the intellect can grasp only the discontinuous, immobile, spatial world of practical constructs, and not the living world of change. Concepts, words, and the structure of the positive sciences are so many expressions of the intellect as toolmaker, and hence they share in its intrinsic limitations. Intellect can gain knowledge only of the static or block universe, and does so through a laborious process of learning and symbolizing. This stands in marked contrast with instinct, which goes straight to the heart of life, through a divining sympathy or sure feeling for the vital. Taken by itself, however, instinct apprehends life only in its *individual* forms and *practical* aspects. The main problem facing the vital urge is to overcome the limitations of both intelligence and instinct, and to synthesize their positive qualities.

This synthesis occurs, very imperfectly indeed, in *man.* For, in concrete cases, intelligence is never found alone but always with a fringe of feeling, a vague nebulosity of instinct. In man, instinct has been transformed into *intuition,* which, within the evolutionary setting, may now be defined as "instinct that has become disinterested, self-conscious, capable of reflecting upon its object and of enlarging itself indefinitely."[36] What produces this transformation of instinct into intuition, so that instinct may transcend its bias toward the individual and utilitarian features, and thus gain speculative knowledge of life in general? Bergson replies that the requisite push comes

---

[35] *Creative Evolution,* II (Mitchell, 146–61). Bergson's view of intellect as a pragmatic, spatializing power is explained in detail (*loc. cit.,* 160–74). For a Thomistic criticism of this theory, cf. F. Sheen, *God and Intelligence in Modern Philosophy* (New York, Longmans, Green, 1925), 105–40.

[36] *Creative Evolution,* II (Mitchell, 186).

from intelligence, which converts instinct into a disinterested and general power of knowing life. The *current of life* or *durational existence* is known by intuition, the *current of matter* and its practical extensions by intelligence. In human experience, the two currents make a confluence, and the two types of cognitive power re-enforce each other. With an added impulse received from intellect, human intuition can expand itself far enough to secure reflective understanding of the *élan vital,* as the universal principle of cosmic duration and change. Philosophical knowledge is constituted in this way. It must be kept distinct from, and yet co-ordinated with, spatial relations. Together, philosophy and science enable man to acquire a comprehensive grasp of reality as life and matter.

In view of this synthesis in man, Bergson admits that his evolutionism supports a certain *finalism,* although not the Leibnizian teleology of ideal predeterminism.[37] There is an authentic sense in which man is the end of evolution. Granted that life is radically the same as intuitive consciousness, then the whole surge of evolution aims at bringing life into reflective possession of itself. This transpires only in man, even though intelligence is much too preponderant in the species to insure that everyone will gain the vision and prize it above all else. Human nature is a mechanism, created to triumph over all mechanisms, by providing an intuition of life in its own durational reality. Life is like an *immense wave,* which spreads out in all directions. The ripples are stopped everywhere along the edge by material obstacles, and are converted into oscillations: in human awareness and freedom alone, does the vital movement break through the wall of matter and progress indefinitely. Thus the life-process finds its proper term in man's intuitive consciousness.

Bergson even hints at a humanistic interpretation of the vital impetus in itself, as an evolutionary process of self-realization. *"It is as if a vague and formless being, whom we may call, as we will,* man *or* superman, *had sought to realize himself, and had succeeded only by abandoning a part of himself on the way."*[38] In this light, the plants and animals appear as our good traveling companions, upon

---

[37] *Ibid.,* III (Mitchell, 278–82).

[38] *Loc. cit.* (Mitchell, 281). Bergson also surmised that the general meaning of life can be gathered from "certain forms of maternal love, so striking and in most animals so touching, observable in the solicitude of the plant for its seed. This love, in which some have seen the great mystery of life, may possibly deliver us life's secret." *Creative Evolution,* II (Mitchell, 135). This served as a guiding principle in *The Two Sources of Morality and Religion.*

which consciousness has loaded its encumbrances, as upon experiments that have failed in part. Man alone can place himself at the center of the vital intuition and, with the aid of evolutionary philosophy, can regard intellect in the proper light, as a practical tool. In this way, freedom can be saved from modeling itself upon conceptual and spatial principles of determinism.

Two aspects of Bergson's theory of creative evolution may be evaluated here: his doctrine on intellect and his causal interpretation of evolutionary process.

1. Bergson shows a high appreciation of the *vital* and *immanent* character of knowledge, its irreducibility to a mechanical interaction. He gives preference to intuition over intellect, precisely because he thinks that the former expresses life from within. Furthermore, he realizes that there is something imperfect about the human intellect, insofar as it must ratiocinate or calculate and not see truth in a sheer vision. But instead of making a distinction between the single intellectual *power* and its several *habits* and *operations,* he assigns the intuitive and ratiocinative operations to entirely different powers. This would certainly be necessary, if by intuition were meant solely the immediate sensory apprehension of the object. But the distinction between instinct and intuition makes it clear that Bergson is concerned mainly with a suprasensuous intuitive operation. The spatial image of intuition and intellect as moving in "opposite directions" is misleading, since it precludes the possibility of relating them as different habits and acts of the same intellectual power. Furthermore, Bergson makes a surprising and unique use of the deductive approach, in the crucial question of the nature and object of the intellect. He does not define the intellectual power itself, as manifested integrally in its various operations and their common object. Rather, he defines a *deductive construct,* based upon the premise that practical action upon extended objects must be guided by a *separate* cognitive power. Since this is precisely the point at issue, his definition of the intellect as a toolmaking power prejudges the question. From the fact that the intellectual power gives a practical ordination to some of its operations, it does not follow that the nature of the intellect is exhausted by this practical reference and can be defined exclusively in its terms. Like Schopenhauer and Nietzsche, Bergson shows that the intellect takes cognizance of the good for man: and like them, he draws the unwarranted conclusion that the intellect's essential function is confined to the operation of practical intelligence.

Bergson vigorously denied, in later essays, that intuition is the same as instinct or sense perception. His account in *Creative Evolution* had left open this interpretation, since there he spoke about instinct "becoming" intuition or being elevated to intuition. Yet he also contrasted instinct and intuition, in terms of the pragmatic versus the disinterested, the particularized versus the universalized, cognitive power. Significantly, he was obliged to appeal to the intellect, in order to account for this difference. But if *intellect* provides the decisive "push," which transforms instinct into intuition, then there is a hidden reserve of disinterestedness in intellect that runs contrary to his express doctrine. This suggests that the Bergsonian definition of intellect is an *accidental,* rather than an *essential,* one. Other aspects of the intellectual power must be invoked, in order to raise instinct to the level of a supersensuous intuition. Hence there is no ground for defining intellect essentially as a fabricator of matter. Once more, the spatial image of a fringe of feeling or intuition surrounding intelligence is deceptive, in the degree that it suggests a difference in kind between the "center" and the "fringe."

2. Bergson remains close to the nineteenth-century interpretations of evolution, in ascribing *causal efficacy* to the process. The scientific trend in the present century has been to treat evolutionary explanations as descriptive rather than causal, or at least to avoid attributing unique and all-sufficient causal power to evolutionary agencies. Bergson shares the outlook of Nietzsche and Spencer, concerning the causal character of evolution. He makes it clear, however, that it is upon philosophical, rather than scientific, grounds that he maintains this view. His doctrine that the vital impetus is an efficient principle, rests upon a double basis: will and God. If the vital impetus is grasped primarily as inner duration, then it is apprehended as effort and *will.* Because of his basically psychological approach to duration, Bergson is ready to read into nature as a whole the constituent principles of conscious life, including will as a causal factor. Like Schopenhauer and Nietzsche, Bergson simply expands his analysis of will, as an efficient principle in the orientation of conscious life, into a cosmic doctrine on life as a single, causal agent. None of these thinkers explain the nature and limitations of the "analogy," which makes this projection possible.

Bergson seeks added support from his conception of *God.* God's creative activity can be visualized as:

a center from which worlds shoot out like rockets in a fire-works display — provided, however, that I do not present this center as a *thing*, but as a continuity of shooting out. God thus defined has nothing of the already made; He is unceasing life, action, freedom.[39]

Like Leibniz' remark about the continuous fulgurations of divinity, this metaphor conveys something of the tremendous dynamism and creative power of God's will. It gives a hint of the infinite life and generosity of the divine source of the world. But the passage also raises the question of whether God Himself is engaged in becoming, and whether He has durational movement. In *Creative Evolution*, Bergson does not clarify this issue. Because it is left unsettled, the fundamental speculative problem of the nature of the *predication* of duration, life, and existence is also left unsolved. At the starting point of Bergson's philosophical inquiry is the intuition that *to exist* means *to change,* and that *to be free* means *to make oneself incessantly.* Duration manifests itself in this way, when it is approached through human introspection. But since Bergson holds that God is the transcending source of the vital impetus and not identical with it, there remains the outstanding question of how to apply the perfections of existence and freedom both to our consciousness (which is a moment *within* the vital movement) and to the transcendent *principle* of the movement. The method of intuition cannot resolve this issue, and Bergson declares his preference for treating of God *ex professo* only in connection with moral and religious life. In that case, however, there is no solid, speculative ground for regarding the vital impetus as a causal agency, sharing in the causal power of God.

## 5. MORALITY AND RELIGION

Bergson's search after the "two sources" of morality and religion is a continuation of his evolutionary inquiry into the bifurcations of life, this time within human consciousness itself. In the moral and religious spheres, there is a radical split between motives of *pressure* and motives of *aspiration* (corresponding to the general biological contrast between the cumulative and dissociative functions). When our actions are governed by herd instinct, social conventions, and impersonal laws, they are being done from motives of pressure. But when we act as distinctive individuals, moved by the personal appeal

---

[39] *Creative Evolution*, III (Mitchell, 262). Cf. J. A. Baisnée, S.S., "Bergson's Approach to God," *The New Scholasticism*, X (1936), 116–44, on whether Bergson established God's transcendence any better in *The Two Sources* than in *Creative Evolution*.

of a human individual, we are following motives of aspiration. In the first instance, we do what we are bidden to do by impersonal forces; in the second instance, we act out of a yearning to be like some personal exemplar. The principle of pressure leads to a *closed* morality and a *static* religion; the principle of aspiration leads to an *open* morality and a *dynamic* religion.[40]

Bergson admits a place for the utilitarian account of *moral obligation* but restricts its scope to the closed kind of morality. He sides with Mill, against Kant, in looking for the source of obligation from below, rather than from above. It is a product of *social instinct* and not of reason. Our natural constitution is such as to contract habits: we are social animals, because we are habit-forming ones. Just as the individual ant is bound to his anthill by a social force, so habits operate, with all the force of a natural instinct, to bind human individuals to the social organism. Social habits exert a tremendous pressure and thus generate the necessitating force of obligation. All that intellect can do is to make our conduct more consistent with itself, but it cannot provide the foundation of moral obligation. The latter is based on the social demand of our habits, the nonrational formula of which is: *"You must because you must."*[41] The function of intellect is only to recognize the need for this binding force in society, and to keep particular actions in line with social pressures.

Societies are fixed islands in the sea of human flux-and-flow. They are required, in order to overcome anarchy and place human enterprises upon a stable basis. But if our conduct is molded solely by social exigencies, we are likely to develop the closed state of soul. *Closed morality* is that in which individual and society are merged as one, under general laws, for the sake of self-preservation. Obligation functions as a cumulative or conservative force to protect the common interests. Necessary as social organization is, however, it runs the risk of promoting a morality in which custom and convention are the supreme considerations. Closed morality is apt to stereotype our actions, kill initiative, and substitute the letter of the law for the spirit.

Fortunately, men are able to respond to other calls than the pressure of self-preservation and social conformity. Whereas closed morality is based upon an infraintellectual social instinct, there is also a

[40] For the general contrast, cf. *The Two Sources of Morality and Religion*, I, III (Audra-Brereton, 26–30, 41–43, 55–57, 75–76, 198–205).

[41] *Ibid.*, I (Audra-Brereton, 15; italics mine). The theory of obligation as social cohesion is set forth in the first chapter (*loc. cit.*, 1–24, 29, 73–75).

supraintellectual emotion that can be quickened into an open sort of morality. This higher emotion is the desire to emulate great men. *Open morality* flourishes, when we are inspired by the heroic deeds of noble men.[42] These moral leaders are like Nietzsche's supermen, at least insofar as they have won a victory over social conventions and have struck out on their own. Their effect upon us is a dissociative one, since they single us out, as individuals, and make us aware of our personal responsibility and choice. Bergson calls them the *geniuses of the will,* since they move us by appeal to our will and personal freedom, rather than by application of social sanctions. These exemplars awaken in our imagination a creative aspiration to follow a similar path of heroic action.

The contrast between the closed and open types of morality is best expressed in the antitheses set forth in the Sermon on the Mount: "Ye have heard that it was said. . . . But I say unto you. . . ." The great moral leaders of humanity lead us forward, by the impulse of love, to yearn to perform actions of sacrifice and devotion to all men. The effect of their teaching is to break down the parochialism and conformism of closed societies, so that all men may join together in the open society or divine city. Like Leibniz and Berkeley, however, Bergson maintains that the moral union of humanity on an open basis must be founded upon a religious union of men in God.

Yet this latter union is not directly fostered by static religion. Bergson defines *static religion* as *"a defensive reaction of nature against what might be depressing for the individual, and dissolvent for society, in the exercise of intelligence."*[43] Man alone has some form of religion, since he alone enjoys intelligence. But as Hobbes and Schopenhauer observed, the possession of intelligence is a questionable privilege. For it enables men to realize that they are going to die, that their projects may well fail, and that they are fully able to break with social codes and follow selfish ways. If men were to meditate constantly upon ineluctable death, upon the margin of the unexpected (and hence of failure) between plan and product, and upon the temptations of selfish action, they would soon fall into despair and withdraw their energies from the social enterprise. Hence, in the interests of society and the cumulative side of life, nature has fitted us with a counterpoise to the corrosive effect of critical intelligence. This counterbalance

---

[42] *The Two Sources of Morality and Religion,* I (Audra-Brereton, 26–27, 49–51, 90).
[43] *Ibid.,* II (Audra-Brereton, 194); on static religion, cf. *loc. cit.* (Audra-Brereton, 92–197).

is the *myth-making power of imagination*, which operates through the intellect itself. Static religion is based upon the myths which the human psyche weaves, as a defense reaction. These myths encourage men with stories about an afterlife and about the aid that can be expected from benign supernal powers. The claims of society are also re-enforced by a system of taboos, totems, and social worship, the effect of which is to add religious sanction to social commands. Bergson agrees with Comte that static religion performs an invaluable service to society, by securing confidence and order on a wide scale. Without the stability of organized religion in all ages, social life could not flourish and gains could not be consolidated.

Static religion does make good the deficiency in our spontaneous attachment to the vital principle. But it does so only by resorting to myths which, although powerful enough to discipline social action, are nevertheless *myths*, which critical intelligence will continue to reject. There is need for a deeper and more realistic attachment to the vital impetus. Our adherence to life is deepened by *dynamic religion*, which expands the fringe of intuition that is always surrounding intelligence. Bergson identifies dynamic religion with *mysticism*, and adds that true mysticism is a rare achievement. But those privileged souls who do rise to an intuitive union with the vital impetus (whether it be with the transcendent cause of life or the immanent principle itself), can inspire ordinary men to desire a similar union. Thus the dynamic type of religion arouses our aspiration to participate in the creative effort, manifested by life. "This effort is of God, if it is not God himself. The great mystic is to be conceived as an individual being, capable of transcending the limitations imposed on the species by its material nature, thus continuing and extending the divine action."[44] Through his offices, the purpose of the *élan* is finally achieved: to produce cocreators with itself, beings capable of free response and indefinite spiritual progress. In this sense, Bergson refers to the universe as *"a machine for the making of gods."*[45]

After reviewing Buddhism, Neo-Platonism, and other mystical movements, Bergson concluded that complete mysticism is found only in the great *Christian mystics,* such as St. Paul, St. Catherine of Siena, and St. Teresa of Ávila. He admired their robust healthiness of soul, their unselfish ardor, and, withal, their firm grasp upon practical contingencies. Their profound union with God gave them

[44] *The Two Sources of Morality and Religion*, III (Audra-Brereton, 209).
[45] *Ibid.*, IV (Audra-Brereton, 306; italics added).

an untroubled serenity of outlook and a sure simplicity of judgment. Moreover, it is a mark of authentic mysticism that contemplation overflows into action and love of men. Here is to be found the religious basis for open morality itself. Altruism and humanitarianism are insufficient motives for heroic, self-sacrificing conduct. There must also be a religious sense of co-operating with God, in His creative work. The love which consumes the mystical soul "is no longer simply the love of man for God, it is the love of God for all men. Through God, in the strength of God, he loves all mankind with a divine love."[46] Bergson adds that it is not chimerical to look for a renaissance of dynamic religion in our mechanistic civilization. Indeed (like Comte, once more), he discerns a definite affinity between *mysticism* and *machines*. The latter provide a groundwork of material security and leisure, thus permitting souls to cultivate their intuition and advance on the way of active mysticism. The modern frenzy of luxury and self-indulgence may be expected to generate the "counterfrenzy" of dedicating oneself to the love of God and men. This is Bergson's final dichotomy, and it remains a testimony to the optimistic way in which he viewed the movement of life.

There are both resemblances and differences between Bergson and Nietzsche, in the ethicoreligious field. Bergson's dichotomy between closed and open moralities recalls Nietzsche's contrast between slave and master moralities. Both thinkers regard the enhancement of life as the touchstone of the higher type of moral existence. But in Bergson, the chasm is not so profound between the two moralities: every man has a spark of the aspirational attitude within himself, so that he may heed the call of moral geniuses and share, at least imaginatively, in their sublime vocation. In Nietzsche, however, the gap is fixed and unbridgeable between the two orders, and the higher uses the lower for its own ends. Again, both Bergson and Nietzsche agree that the life-force is best associated with the "supermen," toward whom the entire evolutionary process strains. The wave of life is carrying men onward to a new humanism, or rather a *superhumanism,* in which the present limitations of the species will be definitely transcended. Yet Nietzsche looks forward to an atheistic situation, in which the conditions of earthly existence will be taken as absolute, whereas Bergson sees the term of the vital impetus in joyful love of God on the part of the *adjutores Dei,* the religious

---

[46] *Ibid.,* III (Audra-Brereton, 222). On the ideal purpose of Christian mysticism, cf. *loc. cit.* (Audra-Brereton, 216–23).

sharers in the creative work that stems from the transcendent absolute.[47] Finally, Nietzsche's doctrine of the eternal recurrence serves to eternalize the temporal process itself, and to deny any other sort of eternity. On this score, Bergson's metaphysical method of intuition fails to keep pace with his religious insights. Speculatively, he does not establish the precise relations between time and eternity, for this is part of his unsolved problem of the predication of duration and life to God's nature. Yet in one place, he describes the "attention to life" in such a way that it could be applied to that simultaneous and perfect possession of all vital reality, in which the eternal present or *now* of God consists. There are also latent resources in Bergson's rapprochement between the human spirit and memory, which might be placed upon a more rigorous metaphysical foundation, with the aid of the Augustinian and Thomistic doctrines on mind, memory, and God's eternity.

One brief criticism is suggested by Maritain's epigram that the Bergsonian ethics "preserves, I dare say, all of morals except morality itself."[48] Bergson described, as it were, the under and top coverings of morality, rather than its essential core. His theory of closed morality dissects the psychological and sociological co-ordinates of the moral act, whereas his description of open morality calls attention to some of the higher, personal phases of the moral life. But the structure of morality, as a properly *human perfection,* eludes his analysis, which is attuned only to the evolutionary description of functions. Closed morality has an *infra*intellectual basis; open morality has a *supra*intellectual foundation; but there is no provision for human morality, precisely as a perfection stemming from the practical intellect and will. This is a direct consequence of Bergson's previous restriction of intellect to a geometrizing, toolmaking power. In such a view,

---

[47] "But above all we shall have greater strength, for we shall feel we are participating, creators of ourselves, in the great work of creation which is the origin of all things and which goes on before our eyes. . . . Humbled heretofore in an attitude of obedience, slaves of certain vaguely-felt natural necessities, we shall once more stand erect, masters associated with a greater Master." *The Creative Mind,* III (Andison, 123–24). That is why Bergson remarked to Father Sertillanges, during their last conversation, that "for me, the saint is the true superman, of whom Nietzsche showed but the counterfeit." A.-D. Sertillanges, O.P., *Avec Henri Bergson,* 23; the translation is by J. M. Oesterreicher, *Walls Are Crumbling* (New York, Devin-Adair, 1952), 38–39. The first chapter of Oesterreicher's book analyzes Bergson's personal attitude toward religion. For a comparison between Nietzsche and Bergson, read F. Copleston, S.J., *Friedrich Nietzsche, Philosopher of Culture,* 205–13.

[48] J. Maritain, *Bergsonian Philosophy and Thomism,* 332; Chapter XVII, "The Bergsonian Philosophy of Morality and Religion" (325–45) evaluates Bergson's final phase. The quotation is made with the permission of Charles Scribner's Sons.

intellect is a principle of calculating and making but not of *doing,* in the sense of providing practical knowledge for human moral acts. There is no foundation in Bergson's system for a practico-moral aspect of intellect or for rational will, since intellect can have no speculative knowledge of the good and the end for man. According to Bergson, the infra- and supra-intellectual emotions project their impulses upon the intermediary plane of intellect. Intellect remains their artisan servant, so that Bergsonian morality is either below or above the level of rational, practical judgment and free choice. Consequently, his conception of freedom is confined to a spontaneous welling up of life and memory, since it cannot appeal to the dominating judgment of the morally practical intellect.

Similarly, Bergson's theory of religion casts revealing illumination upon subsidiary, social functions of religion and upon its highest manifestation, in mysticism. But it leaves untouched both the speculative roots of religion and the natural moral virtue of religion. Metaphysical and methodological commitments prevent Bergson from surveying the *middle ranges* of religious life. Between the evolutionary *divergent* motives of pressure and inspiration stand the *convergent* religious principles of rational recognition of God and free adherence of one's whole person to Him, as is His due. God, not social instinct, is the ultimate basis of moral and religious obligation. Both for the ordinary religious person and the Christian mystic, moreover, it is by no means a matter of indifference whether religious union is with God or with some earthly principle, no matter how dynamic and powerful. The vital impetus itself must be transcended, where it is a question of religious adherence to the one, true God. Bergson's biological metaphysics is marvelously sensitive to the fact that spirit is life. But it provides no precise exegesis for the Christian religious conviction that life belongs above all, and first of all, to *the living God,* in whom is no change or shadow of alteration.

## SUMMARY OF CHAPTER 19

Bergson's philosophy pivoted around the contrast between real, lived time or duration and the time of physical science and positivist philosophy. Physical time is a spatialized substitute for real time. It employs discrete, static points and lines to describe a time that has been morseled, by scientific intelligence, into instants and intervals. But the real time of our experience is a continuous flow of inner growth, which cannot be captured by spatializing symbols. The cinematographical method of positive science is valid for practical purposes but philosophy must depend upon the living intuition of duration. Being distinct from science, philosophy can use the intuition of duration to develop a metaphysics, within the limits of experience. Bergson contrasted the utilitarian concepts of practical, scientific intelligence with the metaphysical intuition, advising that metaphysics should either dispense entirely with concepts or at least elaborate distinctive ones, in order to express its own unique, speculative data. From a close study of the internal experience of duration, Bergson was convinced of the reality of human freedom, regarded as a spontaneous gushing-forth of the temporal stream. He also distinguished sharply between mind and body, memory and perception, even though his limitation of metaphysics to psychological experience forced him to include all these factors within the field of duration or consciousness itself. The independence of the upper reaches of memory or spirit, in respect to the organism, suggested to Bergson that the spiritual principle in man is properly immortal. His theory of creative evolution extended the dynamism of duration to the universe at large. He depicted the vital impetus as striving forever to overcome the inertia and divisiveness of matter. The drama of evolution centers mainly around the two divergent paths it takes in the hymenoptera and man, where instinct and intelligence, respectively, predominate. In man, however, a partial synthesis of these two powers is achieved, insofar as intelligence elevates instinct to the level of intuition. The dualistic theme reappeared in Bergson's discussion of the two sources of morality and religion. Without repudiating either the closed morality of pressure or the static religion of social myth and discipline, he staked man's future on the morality of free aspiration and on a dynamic religious mysticism. In the mystical union with God, the religious soul also forms a community of love with his fellow men.

## BIBLIOGRAPHICAL NOTE

1. *Sources.* In lieu of a collected edition, the Presses Universitaires of Paris continues to keep the books of Bergson in print. Translations: *Time and Free Will: An Essay on the Immediate Data of Consciousness,* translated by F. L. Pogson (New York, Macmillan, 1910; the English subtitle corresponds to Bergson's own title for his doctoral dissertation); *Matter and Memory,* translated by N. M. Paul and W. S. Palmer (New York, Macmillan, 1911); *Laughter: An Essay on the Meaning of the Comic,* translated by C. Brereton and F. Rothwell (New York, Macmillan, 1911); *Creative Evolution,* translated by A Mitchell (New York, Holt, 1911); *Dreams,* translated by E. E. Slosson (New York, Huebsch, 1914); *Mind-energy,* translated by H. W. Carr (New York, Holt, 1935); *The Two Sources of Morality and Religion,* translated by R. A. Audra and C. Brereton (New York, Holt, 1935); *The Creative Mind,* translated by M. L. Andison (New York, Philosophical Library, 1945; a translation of *Thought and the Movent*). A convenient anthology, drawn from these translations, is edited by H. A. Larrabee, *Selections from Bergson* (New York, Appleton-Century-Crofts, 1949).

2. *Studies.* There are a number of reliable introductions: H. W. Carr, *Henri Bergson: The Philosophy of Change* (London, Jack, 1911); A. D. Lindsay, *The Philosophy of Bergson* (London, Dent, 1911); G. W. Cunningham, *A Study in the Philosophy of Bergson* (New York, Longmans, Green, 1916). Bergson himself specially commended the following works: E. Le Roy's *The New Philosophy of Henri Bergson,* translated by V. Benson (New York, Holt, 1913); J. Chevalier's *Henri Bergson,* translated by L. A. Clare (New York, Macmillan, 1928); V. Jankélévitch's *Bergson* (Paris, Alcan, 1931). L. Husson, *L'intellectualisme de Bergson: Genèse et développement de la notion bergsonienne d'intuition* (Paris, Presses Universitaires, 1947), challenges the usual description of Bergson as an anti-intellectualist, and offers a historical explanation of the contrast between intuition and intelligence, as being due primarily to Bergson's followers. L. Adolphe investigates Bergson's characteristic way of developing his thought by means of images: *La dialectique des images chez Bergson* (Paris, Presses Universitaires, 1951); see also L. Adolphe's examination of Bergson's religious doctrine: *La philosophie religieuse de Bergson* (Paris, Presses Universitaires, 1946), and the comparative study made by J. M. Moore, *Theories of Religious Experience, with special reference to James, Otto and Bergson* (New York, Round Table, 1938). Bergson's difficult notion of creation has been studied comparatively by N. P. Stallknecht, *Studies in the Philosophy of Creation, with especial reference to Bergson and Whitehead* (Princeton, Princeton University Press, 1934). There is a rich variety of Scholastic criticism of Bergson. The fundamental work was done by J. Maritain: *Bergsonian Philosophy and Thomism,* translated by M. L. and J. G. Andison (New York, Philosophical Library, 1955); *De Bergson à Thomas d'Aquin* (New York, Maison Française, 1944). Other Scholastic evaluations have been made by R. Jolivet, *Essai sur le bergsonisme* (second ed., Lyon and Paris, Vitte, 1931), by J. de Tonquédec, S.J., *Sur la philosophie bergsonienne* (Paris, Beauchesne, 1935), and by J. J. Kelley, *Bergson's Mysticism* (Fribourg i. S., St. Paul's Press, 1954). In his *Avec Henri Bergson* (Paris, Gallimard, 1941), A.-D. Sertillanges, O.P., gives a sympathetic report on some final conversations with Bergson, concerning religious problems. The French philosophical movement in the latter part of the nineteenth century is outlined by J. A. Gunn, *Modern French Philosophy: A Study of the Development since Comte* (New York, Dodd, Mead, 1922), and by I. Benrubi, *Contemporary Thought of France,* translated by E. B. Dicker (London, Williams and Norgate, 1926).

3. *Further Publications.* There is now a handy one-volume centenary collection of Bergson's *Oeuvres,* edited by A. Robinet (Paris, Presses Universitaires, 1959), and a collection of his scattered *Écrits et paroles,* edited by R.-M. Mossé-Bastide (3 vols., Paris, Presses Universitaires, 1957-1959). Wade Baskin has made two translations from Bergson: *The World of Dreams* (New York, Philosophical Library, 1958), and *The Philosophy of Poetry* (New York, Philosophical Library, 1959). New studies include: I. W. Alexander, *Bergson, Philosopher of Reflection* (New York, Hillary House, 1957), and H. Pflug's *Henri Bergson* (Berlin, W. De Gruyter, 1959).

# INDEX

Absolute, the, 553, 557 f, 561, 566 f,
568 f, 573 ff, 578 f, 583, 584 ff, 595 f,
607, 609 ff, 624, 626, 632 f, 652 ff,
655 ff, 703, 722
Abstraction, 190, 205, 294 f, 338 f, 341,
370 ff, 381 f, 471 f, 547 f, 632 f, 638,
667, 674, 751
Altruism, 686 f, 729 f, 798
Analogy, 23, 39 f, 170, 219, 221 f, 249,
393 f, 410, 442 f, 509, 567, 830
Aquinas, see Thomas Aquinas, St.
Aristotle, 14 f, 57 f, 75 f, 282, 627, 631,
638 f, 676, 723, 726
Art, 580 ff, 652 f, 689 ff, 782 f
Association, laws of, 416 ff, 419, 446 ff,
742, 744, 748, 757, 813
Atheism, 670, 703, 769, 784 ff, 844 f

Bacon, Francis, division of the sciences,
60 ff; form, 68 ff; Great Instauration,
59 ff; idols, 53 ff; induction, 58, 66 ff;
method, 53; philosophy of nature, 63 ff;
simple natures, 68; tables of induction,
71 f
Beauty, 538, 582 f, 690
Bentham, Jeremy, 738, 759, 761 ff, 765
Bergson, change, 821 f, 823 f, 840; and
Comte, 844; concept, 817 ff; and Descartes, 812 f; duration, 811 f, 819 f, 825,
830, 831, 840, 845; evolution, 813 f;
and Galileo, 812; and Hegel, 827 n,
834; and Hume, 826; intelligence,
816 ff, 835 ff, 838 f, 842, 845 f; intuition, 814, 816 f, 819, 831, 836 f, 838 f;
and Kant, 814 f, 841; and Leibniz, 825,
827 n, 831, 840; matter, 827 f, 829 f,
832 f, 837; and Mill, 813, 820 f, 826,
841; mysticism, 843 f; and Nietzsche,
839, 844 f; psychologism, 820 f; and
Schelling, 827 n; and Schopenhauer,
673 ff, 698, 817, 834, 839; and Spinoza,
825; vital impetus, 831 ff, 835, 837,
844, 846
Berkeley, abstraction, 370 ff, 381 f; critique
of matter, 379 ff; egocentric predicament,
376 f; existence, 368, 374 ff; general
ideas, 372 ff; God's existence, 392 f; and

Hume, 385 f, 389 f; on illusionism,
383 f; and Kant, 397 n; and Locke,
330 f, 332, 369 f, 371 ff, 375, 391;
mind, 388 ff; natural law, 398 f; New
Principle, 368 f, 374 ff, 387, 393; and
Newton, 96, 397 ff; notion, 390; other
finite minds, 394 f; qualities, 380 f;
reality, 384 f; sensible thing, 374 ff
Biran, Maine de, 427 n, 820, 831
Body, see Mind-body, Individuation
Boehme, Jacob, 572, 584, 657
Brightman, E. S., 770
Bruno, 34 ff

Cajetan, 393
Category, 213, 255, 483 ff, 491 f, 497,
504 f, 554 ff, 558 f, 617, 635 f, 641,
672 f
Cause, 28, 36 f, 64, 69 f, 78 f, 89 ff, 105 f,
111, 116, 162, 165, 169, 171 f, 220 ff,
225 f, 236, 266, 291 ff, 333 ff, 349 f,
398 f, 418, 421 ff, 424 ff, 438 f, 444 f,
461, 500 f, 507 f, 586, 664, 671 f, 679,
706, 712 f, 751 f, 756 f; see also Finality
Certainty, see Knowledge
Charron, 42 ff
Christianity, 15 f, 33, 43 ff, 193 f, 307,
352, 533 f, 568 f, 603, 610, 653 ff, 657,
696 f, 726, 728, 732 ff, 777 f, 781, 784,
787 f, 794 f, 798 f, 805, 843 f, 846
City of God, 294, 307, 401
Clarke, Samuel, 441 f, 444 f
Comte, altruism, 729 f; and Bacon, 707,
715; and Descartes, 710; division of
sciences, 715 ff; and Hegel, 725 f, 732;
and Hume, 713; introspection, 714 f;
and Kant, 722; law of three states,
704, 710 ff, 714, 722; and Leibniz,
728; and Mill, 728; positivism, 707 ff;
religion of humanity, 729 ff; social man,
709 f, 719, 721 f, 729 ff; sociology, 716 f,
719 f, 723 ff
Condorcet, 723
Contingency, 264 ff, 289, 641 f
Contract, social, see Social contract
Crusius, Christian, 456, 459
Cusanus (Nicholas of Cusa), 33 f, 37 f

Da Vinci, Leonardo, 14, 81 *n*

Deism, 135, 246, 352

Descartes, clarity and distinctness, 149 f, 163 f, 168; classes of ideas, 164 f; Cogito, 160 ff; distinctions, 180 f; doubt, 155 ff, 191; error, 166 f; eternal truths, 173 f; evil genius, 159 f; existence of God, 164 ff; external world, 181 f; and Hobbes, 110, 148; immortality, 183; innatism, 144, 189 f; *mathesis universalis,* 145 ff; metaphysics, 176 ff; method, 143 ff, 176; mind-body, 178 f, 181, 184 ff, 188 f; morality, 191 ff; passion, 192 f; principles, 141 f, 161 f; qualities, 176 f; the self and the man, 185 ff; simple natures, 150 ff; and Spinoza, 147; and Stoic wisdom, 46; substance and affections, 178 ff; unity of sciences, 141 f, 147

Determinism, 112, 120, 220 ff, 234 f, 302 f, 440 f, 497, 589 f, 652, 669, 686, 767, 826 f; *see also* Freedom

Dewey, John, 117, 323, 749, 787 f

Dialectic, 552 f, 557, 619 ff, 625 ff, 636 f

Doubt, 77, 155 ff, 191, 205, 345

Du Vair, Guillaume, 45

Dynamism, 268, 277 f, 285 f

Eclecticism, 714, 719

Edwards, Jonathan, 120, 401

Egoism, 524 f, 564, 681, 686 f, 727, 729, 797, 798

Elementarism, 316, 343, 410, 416, 814

Emerson, R. W., 691

Empiricism, 8, 56 f, 65 f, 176, 183, 313, 316, 323, 326, 383, 412, 418, 436 *n,* 458 f, 471 f, 497 f, 576, 624 f

Erasmus, 15 f

Error, 208 ff

Evil, *see* Good and evil

Evolution, 270 f, 488, 576, 586, 724, 770, 777 f, 779, 781 f, 791 f, 799, 813 f, 832 ff, 839

Existence, 22 f, 147, 151 f, 155, 162, 168 f, 226 ff, 262, 272 ff, 275, 288 f, 299, 346, 348 ff, 369, 374 ff, 383, 415, 422, 425 f, 431 ff, 434 f, 442, 461 f, 503 ff, 511, 587, 593 f, 596 f, 638 ff, 744 f, 747, 806, 818, 820, 840

Experience, 14, 104, 115, 323, 409 f, 429 f, 458 f, 477, 484, 490, 505, 615 f, 677

Faculty theory, 232, 391 f, 838

Feuerbach, Ludwig, 616 f

Fichte, the absolute, 557 f, 561, 566 ff, 568 f; and Hegel, 561, 564; idealism versus dogmatism, 546 ff; intuition, 550 ff, 553; and Kant, 501, 534, 546, 549 ff, 566; method, 546, 552 f; nationalism, 565 f; obstacle or check, 559 f; positing, 554 ff, 560 f; practical antinomy, 561 f; principle of right, 563; rational faith, 567 f; systemism, 548 f, 558; theory of science, 554 ff

Ficino, 17 ff

Finality, 53, 64, 77, 82, 111, 172 f, 211, 222 f, 242 f, 294, 536, 538 ff, 577 ff, 712 f, 722, 725 f, 760 f, 764 f, 831, 837; *see also* Cause

Finite thing, 40, 166, 179, 212, 219, 225 ff, 229 f, 281 ff, 305, 374 ff, 388, 426

Freedom, 25, 29, 41, 84 f, 112, 120, 130 ff, 167, 222, 234 f, 246 f, 274 ff, 300 ff, 354 f, 357, 439 ff, 497, 499 ff, 526 ff, 531, 561 f, 566, 567, 576, 585, 588 ff, 640, 643, 647 f, 652, 678 ff, 685 f, 697 f, 767 f, 824 f; civil liberties, 130 ff; *see also* Determinism

Galileo, mathematicism, 81 f; method, 76 ff; qualities, 83

Genius, 583, 690, 779, 794 f, 842

Gilson, E., 5, 7 f

God, 24 f, 36 ff, 40 ff, 44, 84, 94 ff, 106, 134, 153, 163 f, 179, 182 f, 193 f, 205 ff, 212 ff, 232, 241 ff, 244 f, 259 ff, 262, 265, 273 ff, 290 ff, 300 f, 303 ff, 322, 353 f, 386 f, 395, 398 ff, 400 f, 478, 494, 497, 499 f, 511, 518, 526 ff, 529 ff, 536, 540, 551, 566 f, 583 ff, 588 ff, 594 ff, 653 ff, 656, 703, 706, 722, 734 f, 786 f, 805 f, 830, 839 f, 842, 844 ff; attributes, 172, 217 ff; *causa sui,* 171 f, 221; "death of God," 788 f, 801; and error, 167 f; existence, 62, 94 f, 164 ff, 215 f, 288 ff, 349 f, 392 f, 441, 502 ff, 530, 532 f, 574, 608 f, 769 f, 785 f; geometer, 81 f, 92, 261; idea of, 208 f; image of, 26, 299 f; *see also* Pantheism

Goethe, 540, 560, 577, 696

Good and evil, 118, 123, 167, 202, 240 f, 303 ff, 353, 447, 450, 590 ff, 645, 686, 793 f

Hamilton, W., 741 f, 744

Harmony, 259 ff, 271, 289 ff

Hegel, actuality, 609, 615, 622 f, 625, 631, 638 ff, 647 ff; and Aristotle, 611; being, 637 f; concept, 553; 621 ff, 629 f, 632 ff, 640 f, 655 ff; concrete universal, 616 f, 624 f, 626, 629 f, 631 f, 640; dialectic, 619 ff, 625 ff, 636 f, 643, 652; ethical life, 646 ff; and Fichte, 553 f, 556 f, 606 ff, 620, 640; history, 650 ff; and Kant, 496, 603 ff, 608, 619 f, 631 f, 635, 645 f; life, 610 ff, 621 f, 627, 629; and Locke, 624 f, 644; logic, 605 f, 621 f, 634 ff, 652, 656 f; and Newton, 640; reason, 604 ff, 608, 615, 624, 635 f, 641, 648 f, 651 f; and Schelling, 574, 579, 584, 587, 592, 607 f, 610, 620, 640, 656 f; and Spinoza, 226, 228, 610, 622, 627, 652; spirit, 609 ff, 615, 618, 622 f, 625 f, 628, 634, 635, 642 f, 650 ff, 655 ff; the state, 646 ff; systemism, 612 f, 630 f; theory of right, 644 f; unhappy consciousness, 618; war, 649 f

Heine, Heinrich, 648

Historicism, 3 f

History, 29, 61, 595 f, 634, 650 ff, 714, 725 f, 780 ff

History of philosophy, 3 ff

Hobbes, and Bacon, 62; cause, 111 f, 115 f; change, 110; civil liberties, 130 ff; commonwealth, 126 ff; and Descartes, 112; determinism, 112, 120; and Galileo, 110 f; knowledge, 112 ff; and Machiavelli, 28; materialistic mechanism, 110; method, 106 ff; nature of philosophy, 103 ff; nominalism, 104 f; passions, 118; qualities, 114; religion, 134 f; social atomism, 121, 132; social contract, 125 ff; sovereignty, 127, 129 f, 132 f; state of nature, 122 ff

Hume, and Bacon, 73; and Berkeley, 390, 393, 399, 407, 411, 418, 434; cause, 418, 421 ff, 424 ff, 756 f; and Descartes, 163, 407; external world, 434 ff; God's existence, 441 ff; habit and custom, 427 ff; and Hobbes, 112, 116; and Hutcheson, 448 f; imagination, 413 ff; impressions and ideas, 410 ff; and Kant, 755; laws of association, 416 ff, 419, 446 ff; and Leibniz, 294, 299; and Locke, 332, 335, 342, 350, 424 f, 432; logical basis, 414; loosening of ideas, 423; moral sense, 450 f; and Newton, 408 ff, 416 f; passions, 446 ff; phenom-

enalism, 408 f; philosophical religion, 444 ff; relation, 418 ff; self or mind, 436 ff; skepticism, 406 ff; sympathy, 448, 450 f

Hutcheson, F., 448 ff, 761

Huxley, T. H., 732

Hylemorphism, 36 f, 177 f, 464

Idea, 54, 104, 112, 149 f, 163, 164 ff, 189 f, 204 ff, 210, 229 f, 232, 259 f, 294 ff, 298 f, 315 ff, 321 f, 323 ff, 326 f, 328 ff, 333, 337 ff, 344 ff, 369 ff, 375 f, 383, 384 ff, 388, 410 ff, 423, 624, 631, 640, 647, 683 ff

Idealism, 8, 488, 511, 540, 546 ff, 568, 576, 583 f, 596, 613 ff, 636 f, 680, 714 f

Illusionism, 383 f

Imagination, 106, 114 f, 158, 190, 208 f, 226 ff, 240, 243, 286, 335, 375 f, 384 f, 413 ff, 427 f, 435 f, 485 f, 537, 558 f, 581, 583, 689 f, 843

Immortality, 18 ff, 41 f, 183, 193, 247 ff, 300, 307, 439, 532, 566, 730 f, 771, 829

Imperatives, 29 f, 523 ff, 562

Individuation, 230, 335, 339, 679, 693 f

Innatism, 144, 164 f, 189 f, 205, 294 ff, 318 ff

Intellect, *see* Understanding or intellect

Intuition, 148 f, 161, 244, 345, 348 f, 390, 465 f, 477 ff, 482, 495 f, 550 ff, 553, 574 f, 581, 604, 608, 652 f, 673, 680 f, 689 f, 741 f, 762, 814, 816 f, 819, 831, 836 f, 838 f

Irrationalism, 590, 656, 666, 673, 682, 687 f

James, William, 315, 376, 436 n, 634, 746, 770, 817

Jansenism, 46

Johnson, Samuel, 395, 397 n

Kant, antinomy, 496 ff; autonomy, 526 ff; and Bacon, 510; the beautiful and sublime, 538 f; and Berkeley, 383; categorical imperative, 523 ff; categories, 483 ff, 491 f, 497, 504 f; critical problem, 467 f; existence, 461 f, 504 ff; and Fichte, 540; freedom, 497, 499 ff, 526 ff, 531, 539; and Galileo, 469 f; God, 494, 497, 499 ff, 502 f, 526 ff, 529 ff, 532 f, 540; and Hegel, 649; holiness, 518, 528, 532; and Hume, 410, 451, 483, 501, 540; ideas of reason, 494 ff; intuition, 465 f, 477 ff, 482, 495 f, 550 ff; judgment,

461 f, 471 ff, 487 ff, 535 ff; and Leibniz, 268, 289, 299, 458 f, 463 f, 466, 484; matter of sensation, 480 f, 490, 549; metaphysics, 460 ff, 465 ff, 470 f, 474, 479, 490 ff, 509 ff; method of physics, 459 f, 465 f, 469 f; and Mill, 766; moral faith, 463 n, 500, 530 f, 540; and Newton, 459 ff, 463 f; noumenon, 492; objectivity, 467 f, 469, 477, 484, 486, 489 f; obligation, 516 f, 519 ff, 526, 529, 531, 533, 645 f; paralogisms, 494 ff; possibility, 491 n, 500, 504 f; reverence, 522; and Schelling, 586; space and time, 463 f, 478 f, 481 ff, 495 f; unity of apperception, 484, 489 f, 550 f

Kierkegaard, 596

Knowledge, 81 f, 180, 215, 232, 294 ff, 344 ff, 420 ff, 440 f, 471 f, 474, 484, 490, 665, 671 ff, 681, 689 ff, 697 f, 708 f, 741 f; certainty, 82, 163 f, 204, 422, 616, 636, 708; degrees of perception, 202 f, 243 f, 281 ff; mechanistic view, 113 f; and power, 67, 108 f; theory of, 314, 317, 463; truth, 117, 163, 173 f, 204 f, 257 f, 266 f, 468 ff, 615, 630, 636, 787 f; see also Intuition, Sense perception, Separative judgment

Lambert, J. H., 464
Language, 56, 117, 337 f, 674
Law, 123, 125, 129, 132 f, 353 f, 356, 398 f, 516 f, 526 ff, 708 f, 723 f
Leibniz, action and passion, 291 ff; and Bacon, 258 f; cause, 266; combinatory method, 256 ff; compossibility, 279; contingency, 264 ff, 289; and Descartes, 151, 173, 175, 187 f, 255 f, 259, 273 ff, 285; dynamism, 268, 277 f, 285 f; entelechy, 281 ff; essence and existence, 216 f, 264 f, 271 ff, 274 ff; and Galileo, 261; harmony, 259 ff, 271, 289 ff; and Hobbes, 268; innatism, 295 f; and Locke, 279 f, 295 f, 298, 319 f; mind-body, 293 f; monad, 277 ff, 289 f; moral necessity, 265, 274 ff, 301 f; and Newton, 287; optimism, 305 ff; perception, 278 ff, 281 ff, 297 f; plenitude, 261 f, 272 f; and Spinoza, 273 f, 276 f, 285, 293, 300, 303; substance, 267 f; sufficient reason, 263 f, 269, 302 f; theodicy, 303 ff; universal science, 255 ff
Lipsius, Justus, 44 f
Locke, cause, 333 ff, 349 f; and Descartes,

316 f, 318, 321, 322, 325, 330, 336 f, 344 f, 347 ff; essence, 340 f; experience, 323; freedom, 354 f; good and evil, 353; and Hobbes, 324 f, 338, 356, 359 f; idea, 315 ff; innatism, 318 ff; knowledge, 344 ff; knowledge of existence, 348 ff; method, 314 f; mode, 326 f; and Newton, 330; phenomenalism, 342 ff; property, 357 f, 360, 362 f; quality, 328 ff; state of nature, 356 f, 360 f; substance, 326 f, 331 f, 336 f, 351; universals, 338 ff

Logic, 605 f, 621 f, 634 ff, 718 f, 743, 747 ff; deductive, 58, 152 f; of discovery, 76 f, 148, 753; inductive, 58, 66 ff, 88, 751 ff

Machiavelli, 26 ff
Malebranche, 163, 169, 233, 293, 316 f, 379, 390, 394 n, 398 f, 400
Maréchal, J., 5 f
Maritain, J., 817, 823 f, 845
Marx, Karl, 358, 647, 703, 778, 793
Materialism, 110, 378 f, 385, 714
Mathematics, 14, 64 f, 76 ff, 81 f, 87 ff, 94, 145 ff, 155, 175 f, 220 ff, 256 ff, 261, 270, 273, 340, 342, 345 f, 396 f, 420 f, 441 f, 459 f, 469 f, 473, 667 ff, 716 f, 757
Metaphysics, 64, 70, 142 f, 155, 160, 175 ff, 201, 259 ff, 409, 422 f, 433 ff, 460 ff, 465 ff, 470 f, 474, 479, 490 ff, 509 ff, 530 f, 550 f, 575, 603 ff, 675 ff, 704 ff, 742 f, 764, 784, 814 f, 819 f
Method, 53, 66 ff, 71 f, 76 ff, 88 ff, 106 ff, 143 ff, 176, 201 ff, 211 f, 255 ff, 314 f, 459 f, 466, 476 f, 619 ff, 709, 717 f, 720 ff, 757 f, 814 f; starting point, 153, 205 f, 233 f, 584 f, 613 f, 636 ff
Microcosm, 24 ff, 279, 671 n
Mill, and Bacon, 752, 754; cause, 751 f, 753; and Comte, 735, 740, 742, 752, 758, 760, 769 f; and Hamilton, 748; and Hobbes, 749; and Hume, 742 ff, 746 f, 749, 753, 755, 756, 769 f; induction, 751 ff; and Kant, 769; liberalism, 767 f; and Locke, 748 f, 768; matter, 744 f; mind, 745 ff, 771; obligation, 765 ff; principle of utility, 761 ff; psychology, 740 f, 742 f, 747 f, 755, 758 f, 764, 771; on syllogism, 749 ff; uniformity of nature, 753 ff
Mind-body, 95, 178 f, 181, 184 ff, 188 f, 229 ff, 235 f, 281 ff, 284, 293 f, 336,

579, 827 ff

Mode, 40, 179, 212 ff, 224 ff, 229, 326 f, 331, 385, 418

Monad, 41, 277 ff, 289 f

Monism, 213 ff, 561, 567, 569, 656, 786, 829 f

Montaigne, 42 f

Montesquieu, 723

Moral sense, **450 f, 515**

Naturalism, 22, 445, 533 f, 677, 765, 787 f

Nature, 39, 62, 75, 81 f, 85, 94, 174 f, 185, 193, 223 f, 227, 241, 392 f, 416, 498 f, 508, 526, 528 n, 536 f, 575 ff, 582 f, 640 ff, 682 f, 694, 706 f, 709, 753 ff, 827 n; philosophy of, 23, 39, 63 f, 142 f, 175 ff, 347 f, 397 ff, 459 f, 577 ff, 640; *see also* State of Nature

Neo-Platonism, 17 f, 20 f, 190, 260, 290, 401

Newton, and Descartes, 92; and Galileo, 85, 91; and Hume, 431; hypotheses, 93 f; laws of motion, 90; method, 87 ff; rules of reasoning, 91 ff

Nicholas of Cusa, *see* Cusanus

Nietzsche, and Bergson, 793; and Comte, 703, 785; culture, 776 ff, 781 f; Dionysian man, 783 f, 795, 800, 805; eternity, 781, 784, 802 ff, 805; genesis of moralities, 791 ff; and Hegel, 778, 780, 785 f; history, 780 ff; and Kant, 790, 802 n; and Machiavelli, 33, 783; and Schelling, 783; and Schopenhauer, 673 ff, 697, 784, 788, 790, 797 f, 799, 804 f; superman, 779, 800 ff; will-to-power, 799 ff, 803 f

Nominalism, 104 f, 338, 749

Optimism, 265, 272 f, 305 ff, 684

Panpsychism, 37, 229 f, 279

Pantheism, 36, 38 f, 96, 187, 206 f, 214, 573 n, 575, 584 ff, 609, 656; *see also* **God**

Paracelsus, 25 f

Participation, 20 f, 23, 401, 569, 654 n, 655, 805 f

Pascal, 194, 730, 798

Passion, 115, 118, 124, 192 f, 235 ff, 239, 292 ff, 438, 446 ff, 651 f

Perry, R. B., 376 f

Person, *see* Self

Pessimism, 684 ff, 698

Petrarca, 14 f

Phenomenalism, 109, 268, 316 f, 342, 343, 389 f, 408 f, 437, 480 ff, 492, 505 f, 713, 744 f, 755 f, 757, 771

Philosophy, 61 f, 103 ff, 317, 408, 584, 612 f, 618, 631, 634, 655, 705, 720 ff, 735, 812 f, 815 f

Physicalism, 85, 408 f, 496, 813, 815

Pico della Mirandola, 24 f

Plato, 55 f, 58, 274 n, 619, 634

Plotinus, 831

Pomponazzi, 17 f, 19 ff

Positivism, 8, 488, 511, 677, 703 ff, 707 ff, 725 f

Principles, first, 109 f, 141 f, 161 f, 262 ff, 318 ff, 620, 626, 638 f, 710, 741, 748 f, 762 f

Probability, 76, 115 f, 156 f, 258, 318, 346, 422 f, 441, 443

Property, 129, 357 f, 360, 362 f, 450, 644

Proust, Marcel, 819

Qualities, primary and secondary, 83 f, 92 f, 110 f, 114, 176 f, 286, 328 ff, 348, 380 f

Rationalism, 8, 35, 57, 65 f, 145, 168, 205, 220, 249, 343, 422, 429 f, 458 f, 466 f, 471 f, 497 f, 505 n, 507, 533 f, 621 f, 665, 725 f, 813

Ravaisson, F., 820

Realism, 5, 114, 156 ff, 297, 321, 343, 350 f, 373 f, 377 f, 391 f, 429 ff, 449, 468 f, 471 f, 479 f, 485 f, 507, 511, 546 ff, 583 f, 596, 615, 633, 714 f, 744, 746, 749, 751, 764, 766, 818 f; mathematical, 75; *see also* Thomas Aquinas, St.

Reason, 35 f, 105, 115, 124 f, 243 f, 425, 429 f, 433, 435, 449, 459, 476, 493 f, 497 f, 516 f, 539, 594, 604 ff, 608, 615, 617, 624, 635 f, 651 f, 667, 673 ff, 682; *see also* Sufficient reason

Relation, 279, 292 f, 339 f, 344, 347, 372 f, 400 f, 418 ff, 624, 630

Religion, 33, 134 f, 245 f, 444 ff, 533 f, 567 ff, 594 f, 652 ff, 729 ff, 735, 770 f, 842 ff, 846

Romanticism, 577, 580 n, 583, 620, 621 f

Rousseau, 515, 520 f, 768

Schelling, the absolute, 583, 584 ff; absolute identity, 583 f, 588; art, 580 ff; dogmatism and criticism, 572 ff; essence and existence, 593 f; and Fichte, 571 ff, 575 f, 579 f, 583; freedom, 588 ff; good and evil, 590 ff; ground of existence, 572, 574 *n*, 579 *n*, 586 ff, 595 ff; and Hegel, 612; intuition, 574 f, 581; and Kant, 573 f, 577, 583, 594; and Leibniz, 584, 590 f; nature, 575 ff; potencies, 579; and Spinoza, 572 ff, 575 f, 584, 588 f, 590

Schopenhauer, abstract concepts, 667, 672 ff; and Fichte, 675; and Hegel, 674, 676, 678, 683 ff, 687 f, 693; and Hobbes, 685 f, 693; and Kant, 524, 664 ff, 670 ff, 675 ff, 680 f, 687; and Leibniz, 664 f, 684; metaphysics, 675 ff; pessimism, 684 ff; Platonic idea, 683 ff, 689 ff; reason, 675 f; renunciation, 695 ff; and Schelling, 583, 676; and Spinoza, 676; sufficient reason, 664 ff, 684 f; suicide, 688 f; sympathy, 693 ff; will, 668, 670, 672, 674, 679 f, 681 ff, 690 ff, 695 ff; wonder, 676 f; world, 665 f, 669 f, 675 ff, 681 f, 697

Science, 13 f, 174 f, 255 ff, 269, 342 f, 397 f, 408 ff, 416 f, 459 f, 466, 486 f, 510, 536, 554 ff, 612 f, 640, 655, 669, 677, 682 f, 705, 715 ff, 751, 777 ff, 812, 814 ff; as art, 67; method, 87 ff; Newtonian rules of reasoning, 91 ff

Self, 162 f, 166, 168, 185 ff, 299 f, 336 f, 348 f, 389 ff, 400 f, 407, 436 ff, 481, 484, 495 f, 525, 587, 611, 719, 731 f, 745 ff, 821, 823; image of God, 26, 299 f

Sense perception, 35 f, 43, 55, 77 f, 113 f, 156 ff, 159 *n*, 167, 176 f, 181 ff, 189 f, 214 *n*, 234, 296 ff, 323 ff, 346, 350 f, 375 f, 384 f, 400, 407, 410 ff, 433, 434 f, 458 f, 464, 471, 478, 511, 616 f, 671 f

Separative judgment, 22 f, 159 *n*, 632 f, 820

Simple natures, 68, 150 ff, 256, 259

Skepticism (Pyrrhonism), 42 ff, 111, 158, 186 f, 207, 368, 378 f, 396 f, 406 ff, 458

Social contract, 125 ff, 360, 564, 726

Solipsism, 267 f, 392 ff, 746 f, 830 f

Soul, 23, 95, 229 f, 282 f, 298, 494 f

Space and time, 95 f, 227 f, 286 f, 463 f, 478 f, 481 ff, 495 f, 500 f, 667 f, 671 f, 680 f, 687, 811 f, 815, 822 f

Spencer, H., 799, 813 f, 831, 834, 839

Spinoza, affects, 235 ff; and Bruno, 223; cause, 200 ff, 225 f, 236; *conatus*, 237 f, 239 ff, 242 f; degrees of perception, 202 ff; 243 f; and Descartes, 151,

153, 175, 187, 201, 206 f, 231, 235; divine attributes, 217 ff; error, 208 ff; existence, 226 ff, 248; on faculty theory, 232; freedom, 222, 246 f; God, 212 ff; good and evil, 241; and Hobbes, 237, 242; idea of God, 208 ff; love of God, 244 f; method, 201 ff; mind-body, 229 ff; mode, 224 ff; parallelism, 233; rules of definition, 212 f; true idea, 204 f

State, 28, 31 f, 126 ff, 360, 564 f, 646 ff, 693, 726 f, 767 f, 778 f

State of nature, 122 ff, 356 f, 360 f, 686

Stoicism, 21 f, 44 ff, 191, 193, 241, 533, 688

Suarez, 165, 173

Substance, 35, 38, 40 f, 68, 82 f, 110, 162 f, 178 ff, 185 ff, 231 f, 263, 267 f, 277 f, 281 ff, 285, 291 f, 295, 326 f, 331 ff, 336 f, 340 ff, 351, 418, 437 ff, 495, 610 f, 707 f, 713, 821 *n*, 824

Sufficient reason, 263 f, 269, 292 f, 461 f, 585 f, 664 ff, 684 f

Sympathy, 448, 450 f, 519 f, 693 ff, 765 f, 831

Theodicy, 587

Thomas Aquinas, St., 5 ff, 15, 19 f, 22 ff, 153, 161 *n*, 167, 171, 177 f, 214 *n*, 270, 273 *n*, 479 f, 485 f, 502 f, 638 f, 714; *see also* Realism

Time, *see* Space and time

Truth, *see* Knowledge

Unconscious, the, 280

Understanding or intellect, 36, 43, 55, 75, 115, 149, 167, 177, 219, 231, 241 ff, 295 f, 323 ff, 341 f, 390 f, 400, 464 f, 476, 493, 603 ff, 623, 667, 671 ff, 816 ff, 835 ff, 838 f, 842 f

Universals, 104 f, 338 ff, 371 ff, 417, 610 f, 616 f, 623 ff, 749 ff

Utility, 451, 519 f, 707, 761 ff, 799 f

Virtue, 15, 21, 192 f, 241, 246, 450, 521, 532 f, 795 f; *virtù*, **30 f**

Will, 119 f, 129, 167, 221 f, 234, 238, 301 f, 303 f, 353 ff, 390 f, 440, 517 ff, 522, 526 ff, 529 f, 551, 567 f, 643, 644, 668, 670, 672, 674, 681 ff, 690 ff, 695 ff, 784, 799 ff, 804 f, 831, 839

Wisdom, 45 f, 117, 140, 193 f, 202, 710

Wolff, Christian, 458 f, 460 ff, 490, 494 *n*, 503 f, 664 ff